THE BRITISH YEAR BOOK OF INTERNATIONAL LAW

THE BRITISH YEAR BOOK OF INTERNATIONAL LAW

2005

SEVENTY-SIXTH YEAR OF ISSUE

OXFORD
AT THE CLARENDON PRESS
2006

OXFORD
UNIVERSITY PRESS

Great Clarendon Street, Oxford OX2 6DP

Oxford University Press is a department of the University of Oxford.
It furthers the University's objective of excellence in research, scholarship,
and education by publishing worldwide in

Oxford New York

Auckland Cape Town Dar es Salaam Hong Kong Karachi
Kuala Lumpur Madrid Melbourne Mexico City Nairobi
New Delhi Shanghai Taipei Toronto

With offices in

Argentina Austria Brazil Chile Czech Republic France Greece
Guatemala Hungary Italy Japan Poland Portugal Singapore
South Korea Switzerland Thailand Turkey Ukraine Vietnam

Oxford is a registered trade mark of Oxford University Press
in the UK and in certain other countries

Published in the United States
by Oxford University Press Inc., New York

First published 2006

British Library Cataloguing in Publication Data
Data available

Library of Congress Cataloging in Publication Data
Data available

Typeset by Newgen Imaging Systems (P) Ltd., Chennai, India
Printed in Great Britain
on acid-free paper by
Biddles Ltd., King's Lynn

ISBN 0–19–920276–1 978–0–19–920276–8

1 3 5 7 9 10 8 6 4 2

Editorial Communications should be addressed as follows:

Articles and Notes:

PROFESSOR JAMES CRAWFORD
Lauterpacht Research Centre for International Law,
5 Cranmer Road, Cambridge, CB3 9BL.
JRC1000@hermes.cam.ac.uk

Books for Review:

PROFESSOR J. G. MERRILLS
University of Sheffield Faculty of Law,
Crookesmoor Building, Conduit Road,
Sheffield, S10 1FL.
J.G.Merrills@Sheffield.ac.uk

The British Year Book of International Law is indexed in *Current Law Index*, published by Information Access Company, and in *Legal Journals Index*, published by Legal Information Resources Limited.

CONTENTS

LIST OF ABBREVIATIONS

AAMGS	ABN AMRO Mellon Global Securities
ACOPS	Advisory Committee on Protection of the Sea
ACP	African, Caribbean and Pacific Group of States
AEMs	Area Effects Munitions
ANP	Anti-Narcotics Police (Iran)
APA	Army Prosecution Authority
ASCOBANS	Agreement on the Conservation of Small Cetaceans of the Baltic and North Seas
ASEAN	Association of Southeast Asian Nations
ATCSA	Anti-Terrorism, Crime and Security Act 2001
AU	African Union
BAT	British Antarctic Territory
BIOT	British Indian Ocean Territory
BLHIR	Business Leaders' Initiative on Human Rights
BNOTS	British Non-autonomous Overseas Territories
BOTS	British Overseas Territories
BTWC	Biological and Toxin Weapons Convention
CCW	Convention on Certain Conventional Weapons
CEA	Captured Enemy Ammunition
CEDAW	Convention for the Elimination of All Forms of Discrimination Against Women
CFE	Treaty on Conventional Armed Forces in Europe
CFP	Common Fisheries Policy
CKGR	Central Kalahari Game Reserve
CPA	Coalition Provisional Authority
CPS	Crown Prosecution Service
CSAT	Commonwealth Secretariat Arbitral Tribunal
CSCE	Conference on Security and Co-operation in Europe
DAC	Departmental Advisory Committee on Arbitration Law
DDR	disarmament, demobilization and reintegration
DEFRA	Department for the Environment, Food and Rural Affairs
DFID	Department for International Development
DFT	Department for Transport
DPKO	Department for Peacekeeping Operations
DPRK	Democratic People's Republic of Korea
DRC	Democratic Republic of Congo
DSB	Dispute Settlement Body
DSU	Dispute Settlement Understanding
DTI	Department of Trade and Industry
DVT	deep vein thrombosis
ECHR	European Convention on Human Rights
ECJ	Court of Justice of the European Communities
ECOWAS	Economic Community of West African States

ECtHR	European Court of Human Rights
EEZ	Exclusive Economic Zone
ELA	export licence application
EPA	Economic Partnership Agreement
ERBS	Extended Range Bomblet Shell
EU	European Union
EUFOR	European Union Force in Bosnia and Herzegovina
FAC	Foreign Affairs Select Committee
FCO	Foreign and Commonwealth Office
FLEG	Forest Law Enforcement and Governance
FRY	Federal Republic of Yugoslavia
GATT	General Agreement on Tariffs and Trade
GMO	Genetically Modified Organism
HC	House of Commons
HIPC	Heavily Indebted Poor Countries
HL	House of Lords
HMG	Her Majesty's Government
HP	Humanitarian Protection
HRA	Human Rights Act 1998
IAATO	International Association of Antarctica Tour Operators
IACHR	Inter-American Court of Human Rights
IAEA	International Atomic Energy Agency
IAMB	International Advisory and Monitoring Board (for Iraq)
IACHR	Inter-American Court of Human Rights
ICAO	International Civil Aviation Organisation
ICC	International Criminal Court
ICCPR	International Covenant on Civil and Political Rights
ICJ	International Court of Justice
ICRC	International Commission of the Red Cross
ICSID	International Convention for the Settlement of Investment Disputes
ICTR	International Criminal Tribunal for Rwanda
ICTY	International Criminal Tribunal for the Former Yugoslavia
IFPS	Integrated Flight Plans Systems
ILA	International Law Association
ILC	International Law Commission
ILO	International Labour Organisation
ILOAT	International Labour Organisation Administrative Tribunal
IMO	International Maritime Organisation
IMF	International Monetary Fund
INC	Interim National Constitution
IND	Immigration and Nationality Directorate
IRSS	Institute for Resource and Security Studies
Ir-USCT	Iran-United States Claims Tribunal
ISAF	International Security Assistance Force
ISS	Institute for Security Studies

IST	Iraq Special Tribunal
ITLOS	International Treaty on the Law of the Sea
ITWF	International Transport Workers Federation
IUU	illegal, unreported and unregulated (fishing)
JCHR	Joint Committee on Human Rights
JNCC	Joint Nature Conservation Committee
KRT	Khmer Rouge Tribunal
LHDA	Lesotho Highlands Development Authority
LOAC	Law of Armed Conflict
MARPOL	Marine Pollution Convention
MCA	Maritime and Coastguard Agency
MDP	Ministry of Defence Police
MEP	Member of the European Parliament
MEPC	Maritime Environment Protection Committee
MLRS	Multiple Launch Rocket System
MNF	Multi-National Force
MNF-I	Multi-National Force in Iraq
MOD	Ministry of Defence
MOU	Memorandum of Understanding
MP	Member of Parliament
MSC	Mauritius Shipping Corporation
NA	National Archives
NAFTA	North Atlantic Free Trade Agreement
NATO	North Atlantic Treaty Organisation
NBK	National Bank of Kazakhstan
NEPAD	New Partnership for Africa's Development
NGO	non-governmental organization
NIAA	Nationality, Immigration and Asylum Act 2002
NNWS	non-nuclear weapons states
NPT	Nuclear Non-Proliferation Treaty
NSA	National Security Agency
NSG	Nuclear Suppliers Group
OAU	Organization of African Unity (now the AU, see above)
OECD	Organisation for European Co-operation and Development
OPCW	Organisation for the Prohibition of Chemical Weapons
OSCE	Organisation for Security and Co-operation in Europe
OSPAR	Convention for the Protection of the Marine Environment
PCA	Permanent Court of Arbitration
PCIJ	Permanent Court of International Justice
PDT	pre-deployment training
POW	prisoner of war
PSI	Proliferation Security Initiative
PSO	peace support operation
RAF	Royal Air Force
RIA	Regulatory Impact Assessment
RMP	Royal Military Police

RN	Royal Navy
SAARC	South Asian Association for Regional Co-operation
SALW	small arms and light weapons
SBA	Sovereign Base Area
SC	Security Council
SDT	special and differential treatment
SEA	Strategic Environmental Assessment
SGSSI	South Georgia and the South Sandwich Islands
SIA	State Immunity Act 1978
SIAC	Special Immigration Appeals Commission
SOFA	Agreement regarding the Status of Forces of the parties to the North Atlantic Treaty
SPA	Stand-by Agreement (Iraq)
SPDC	State Peace and Development Council
STOL	Short Take-Off and Landing surveillance aircraft
TEU	Treaty on European Union
TNC	transnational corporation
TP	*Travaux Préparatoires*
UDHR	Universal Declaration of Human Rights
UK	United Kingdom
UKBAP	United Kingdom Biodiversity Action Plan
UN	United Nations
UNAMSIL	United Nations Mission in Sierra Leone
UNAT	United Nations Administrative Tribunal
UNCAT	United Nations Convention Against Torture
UNCITRAL	United Nations Commission on International Trade Law
UNCLOS	United Nations Convention on the Law of the Sea
UNCRC	United Nations Convention on the Rights of the Child
UNDC	United Nations Disarmament Commission
UNDDA	United Nations Department for Disarmament
UNDP	United Nations Development Programme
UNECE	United Nations Economic Commission for Europe
UNFCCC	United Nations Framework Convention on Climate Change
UNGA	United Nations General Assembly
UNHCHR	United Nations High Commissioner for Human Rights
UNHCR	United Nations High Commissioner for Refugees
UNICEF	United Nations Children's Fund
UNMIK	United Nations Interim Administration Mission in Kosovo
UNMOVIC	United Nations Monitoring, Verification and Inspection Commission
UNOCHA	United Nations Office for the Co-ordination of Humanitarian Affairs
UNPOA	United Nations Programme of Action
UNSCR	United Nations Security Resolution
UNTS	United Nations Treaty Series

US	United States
VCCR	Vienna Convention on Consular Relations
VCDR	Vienna Convention on Diplomatic Relations
VCLT	Vienna Convention on the Law of Treaties
WHO	World Health Organization
WMD	Weapons of Mass Destruction
WTO	World Trade Organization
ZANU-PF	Zimbabwe African National Union Patriotic Front

The Law and Procedure of the International Court of Justice 1960–1989

SUPPLEMENT, 2005: PARTS ONE AND TWO

By Hugh Thirlway*

* Principal Legal Secretary, International Court of Justice; Visiting Professor of International Law, University of Bristol.

PART TWO

Division B: Sources of Law

Introduction

The present series of articles on the work of the ICJ was intended as a sequel to the series written by Sir Gerald Fitzmaurice, and published in this *Year Book* between 1950 and 1963. The object was, adopting as basis the structure conceived by Sir Gerald,[1] to survey the jurisprudence of the Court from the date at which Sir Gerald had left off, and to continue up to the date at which the re-examination of the subjects covered in that structure would be completed. As a result of the greatly increased workload and judicial productivity of the Court in recent years, it has taken much longer to reach that point than was expected. A problem already foreseen at the time of publication of the first article in the new series, in 1989, has therefore become much more acute than was then contemplated.

The articles published in successive editions of the *Year Book* were not devised to deal with what were, at the time, the most recent decisions of the Court, on whatever subject; each article was devoted to examination of the Court's treatment of a specific group of subjects, covering the whole period since Fitzmaurice last dealt with those subjects, with a view to building up a complete survey of all the questions of international law dealt with by the Court over the period of publication as a whole. In this structure, there was no place for mention of jurisprudential developments in relation to a particular topic occurring after the publication of the article dealing with that topic. This was not then seen as a serious difficulty: the original intention was stated as follows: 'In principle, although the series will take some years to complete, no attempt will be made to deal with decisions after 1989; as it is, the author fears the fate of Tristram Shandy, who found that he could not write his account of his life fast enough to keep up with his living of it!'[2]

It soon became apparent, however, that the restriction imposed by the 1989 cut-off date was artificial and unrealistic, and each article therefore referred to the law as stated by the Court beyond 1989 and up to the date of publication. The result is that the series constitutes a survey of the Court's pronouncements in virtually the whole field of international law, as defined by Sir Gerald's original structure, but it is made up of a series of snapshots of the state of the Court's case-law on a given group of matters, all taken at different dates. The reader looking for guidance on, for example, the Court's attitude to procedural questions, the subject of the most recent articles, may well find those articles helpful; but if he is interested in, for example, the Court's attitude to equity, all

[1] As Sir Gerald acknowledges in the Preface to the Collected Edition of his articles, the structure and system of approach was originally devised by Sir Eric Beckett: Sir G Fitzmaurice, *The Law and Procedure of the International Court of Justice* (1986) vol I, xxix.

[2] (1989) 60 BYIL 5, quoting Sterne, *Tristram Shandy*, vol 4, ch 13.

that is offered is the study published in 1989 of the case-law as it stood then.

This was less of a problem for Sir Gerald, even when his articles were published as a compilation shortly before his death in 1982, because he had been able, at least to some extent, to return to specific categories and bring them up to date. Thus, for example, 'General Principles and Sources of Law, 1951–1954' appeared in the 1953 volume of the *Year Book*; and 'General Principles and Sources of International Law, 1954–1959' appeared in the 1959 volume. The increased amount of material to be covered resulting from the Court's increased activity has made this solution impossible up to the present. Nor is it feasible even now: an attempt to start afresh, and re-survey *seriatim* the whole body of subjects for the period from the date of publication of the relevant article up to the present would require a whole fresh series, which would entail rewriting much of the original texts, and would in turn be at least partially out of date by the time it was completed.

In the hope of preserving for the series as a whole such usefulness as it may have, a somewhat different approach has been adopted. This article and the one that should (*Deo volente*) follow it will indeed cover the whole ground, and attempt to bring each section up to date; but the form adopted will be in the nature rather of a supplement. The intention is that the researcher interested in a topic covered by an early article in the series should be able to read that article, and then turn to the supplement, which will at least draw attention to pertinent developments in later decisions of the Court; these may however frequently be treated more shortly than they would have been had they already occurred when the original article was written. The intended result is that the series as a whole will state the law as found by the Court up to the end of July 2005.

For convenience of cross-reference, the successive section and chapter headings of the complete series will be reproduced below; if on a given subject there has in fact been no new jurisprudence, the heading alone will be retained, in square brackets. A few new sections have been added: the titles of these are underscored.

The original series of articles, while devoted essentially to study of the decisions of the Court (and, to some extent, separate and dissenting opinions), took account so far as possible of the views of other scholars, in particular in commentaries on those decisions. The extensiveness of the field covered by the series as a whole, and the immense amount of legal writing that has been published over the years since 1989, has made it almost impossible, in this supplementary series, to do more than note in passing certain writings which seem particularly relevant, or have forced themselves on the author's attention. What has been attempted is a survey, as complete as possible, of the Court's jurisprudence, not of the doctrinal writings it has generated.

PART ONE

The original article on which this supplement is based appeared in (1989) 60 BYIL 1–157.

1. General Principles and Sources of Law

Division A: General Principles

Chapter I: Good Faith and Related Principles[3]

Fundamentum autem iustitiae est fides, id est dictorum conventorumque constantia et veritas.

Cicero, *De officiis*, i.23

1. The principle of good faith

(1) Good faith lato sensu*: creation of a* 'servandum'

Since the publication of the 1989 article, circumstances have not arisen in which it has been appropriate for a party before the Court to rely on an alleged obligation accepted by unilateral act, that is to say a unilateral act of the kind to which legal effects were attributed in the *Nuclear Tests* cases. On the contrary, the Court observed in its judgment on preliminary objections in the case concerning the *Land and Maritime Boundary between Cameroon and Nigeria* that both 'the principle of good faith and the rule *pacta sunt servanda* . . . relate only to the fulfilment of existing obligations'.[4] This is the confirmation of the observation made by the Court ten years earlier in the *Border and Transborder Armed Actions* case that the principle of good faith 'is not in itself a source of obligation where none would otherwise exist'.[5] What is more, it appears to come near to abandoning the concept of unilateral acts creating a *servandum* (to use the expression employed in the previous article), and therefore to restrict the concept of good faith to good faith *stricto sensu*. Nigeria was relying on what it saw as a *pactum* as a result of the conduct of Cameroon in settling border disputes with Nigeria over a considerable period of years solely by bilateral means; while this conduct necessarily had a two-sided element to it, Nigeria could not point to an agreement between the two States to settle disputes solely by this means.[6] The essentially unilateral nature of the conduct relied on was emphasized by Nigeria's coupling its argument in

[3] The question of good faith in the interpretation of treaties will be examined in a later article, in Part II, Division A, Chapter I, Section 1.

[4] [1998] ICJ Rep 304, para 59. Judge Koroma recognized this dictum as valid in general, but considered that 'perhaps the Court could have taken a less abstract position in applying the principle to this case'; ibid para 386.

[5] [1988] ICJ Rep 105, para 94; see the previous article in (1989) 60 BYIL 8, 20–1.

[6] See [1998] ICJ Rep 303, para 56.

this respect with the assertion that Cameroon was estopped from invoking the Court's jurisdiction.[7]

(2) Good faith stricto sensu

(a) Negotiations and good faith

An unusual invocation of good faith was made by Libya in the *Territorial Dispute* with Chad. A key element in the case was a Treaty concluded in 1955 between France (to which Chad was successor) and the newly independent Libya. Libya contended that:

> . . . at the time of the Treaty's conclusion, it lacked the experience to engage in difficult negotiations with a Power enjoying the benefit of long international experience. On this ground, Libya has suggested that there was an attempt by the French negotiators to take advantage of Libya's lack of knowledge of the relevant facts, that Libya was consequently placed at a disadvantage in relation to the provision concerning the boundaries, and that the Court should take this into account when interpreting the Treaty; it has not however taken this argument so far as to suggest it as a ground for invalidity of the Treaty itself.[8]

Libya had argued—and as a general point it is a good one—that a higher standard of good faith than normal is required when a sophisticated European State is engaged in negotiation with a newly independent State.[9] The Court did not specifically respond to this contention, merely recalling the customary rules of interpretation of treaties reflected in Article 31 of the 1969 Vienna Convention.[10] It is in fact difficult to see what it was being asked to do: if Gallic guile had amounted to fraud invalidating Libya's consent, then Libya could claim not to be bound by the Treaty (cf Article 49 of the Vienna Convention); but if Libya consented to the Treaty, then it consented to it as correctly interpreted, and that interpretation would result from the application of the normal customary rules. If it had been suggested that certain provisions of the Treaty had been obtained by France by, for example, the deliberate supply to Libya of misleading information as to the position of a pre-existing boundary, then possibly fraud could be invoked *pro rata* as it were to set aside part of the Treaty.[11] This however would not be a matter of interpretation. At most, the Treaty might have been regarded as having been proposed by France, the dominant partner in the negotiations, so as to justify interpretation *contra preferentem*.[12]

[7] While the existence of an estoppel requires (*inter alia*) reliance by one party on a statement or implied statement by the other, the obligation so created remains one-sided. See further, Section 2 below.

[8] [1994] ICJ Rep 20, para 36. Libya's argument was in fact wider than this summary might suggest: it embraced alleged French lack of good faith in the negotiation of the various pre-independence treaties referred to in the 1955 Treaty (see Libyan Counter-Memorial, paras 7.09–7.19). The Court evidently thought this argument too flimsy to be worth refuting.

[9] Libyan Counter-Memorial, para 7.20. For the inadequacy of ministries in some new States to cope with international relations, cf P Sands, 'Project on International Courts and Tribunals' 'Zero Issue' [1998] *International Law Forum* 21–3.

[10] ibid 21, para 41.

[11] In view of the nature and effect of the Treaty as determined by the Court, any such *dépeçage* would probably have been impossible—the Treaty would have to stand or fall as a whole.

[12] As was in fact argued by Libya: Counter-Memorial, para 7.31. A key document—Annex 1 to the Treaty—was in fact apparently drawn up by France and communicated to Libya late in the

The principle of such interpretation will be examined further in a later article under the heading of treaty interpretation.

An issue that arose in more than one way at the preliminary objection stage of the case concerning the *Land and Maritime Boundary between Cameroon and Nigeria* was whether there had been appropriate negotiations between the parties before Cameroon seised the Court on the basis of the parties' optional-clause declarations; and if not, whether this made the claims, or any of them, inadmissible. In the context of that part of the dispute that related to maritime delimitation, the Court rejected the view that, as it was expressed in the dissenting opinion of Judge *ad hoc* Ajibola, 'the process of negotiation and attempt to reach an agreement in good faith must precede any reference to third-party adjudication'.[13]

The two States were both parties to the United Nations Convention on the Law of the Sea; and the Court noted that Articles 74 and 83 of the Convention each provide for delimitation of (respectively) the exclusive economic zone and the continental shelf to be effected by agreement (paragraph 1), and 'if no agreement can be reached within a reasonable period of time', recourse can be had to third-party settlement procedures, as provided for in Part XV of the Convention. The Court noted that:

> ... in this case, it has not been seised on the basis of Article 36, paragraph 1, of the Statute, and, in pursuance of it, in accordance with Part XV of the United Nations Convention on the Law of the Sea relating to the settlement of disputes arising between the parties to the Convention with respect to its interpretation or application. It has been seised on the basis of declarations made under Article 36, paragraph 2, of the Statute, which declarations do not contain any condition relating to prior negotiations to be conducted within a reasonable time period.[14]

On this basis, the Court rejected Nigeria's contention that the application could be dismissed as inadmissible for lack of prior negotiation.

The ruling implies, *a contrario*, that if proceedings had been brought on the basis of the Convention procedure, there would have been an obligation to endeavour to reach agreement by negotiation, even though the Convention does not say as much. At an earlier stage of its judgment the Court had rejected a similar interpretation of Article 33 of the Charter, which enumerates together negotiation and judicial settlement as means for the peaceful settlement of disputes.[15] This was in response to the wider point argued by Nigeria, that for any dispute whatever, 'the exhaustion of diplomatic negotiations constitutes a precondition for a matter to be referred to the Court'.[16] The Court noted the practice

negotiations (Libyan Counter-Memorial, para 7.28). The idea of interpretation 'against' the deceitful party as a form of sanction seems to have derived from Cot, 'La bonne foi dans la conclusion du traité' [1968] *Revue belge de droit international* 143, quoted in Libyan Counter-Memorial, para 7.04.

[13] [1998] ICJ Rep 415. [14] ibid 321–2, para 109.

[15] ibid 302–3, para 56, citing *Aegean Sea Continental Shelf* [1978] ICJ Rep 12, para 29.

[16] [1998] ICJ Rep 303. In the subsequent case concerning *Fisheries Jurisdiction* between Spain and Canada, Judge Oda observed: 'It is arguable whether a "legal" dispute may be submitted unilaterally to the Court only after diplomatic negotiations between the disputing parties have been exhausted, or at least initiated', but found it unnecessary to go into the question: ibid 484, para 20.

of including a precondition to this effect in compromissory clauses of treaties, in a special agreement, or in optional-clause declarations, but that the declarations of the parties before it contained no such condition.[17]

The decision in the *Cameroon/Nigeria* case implies that it is no breach of good faith for a State to seise the Court of a dispute with another State without first affording that State an opportunity to settle it by negotiation.[18] This affords an interesting contrast with the provisions of the International Law Commission's (ILC's) Articles on State Responsibility concerning resort to countermeasures. In accordance with Article 52, paragraph 1: 'Before taking countermeasures, an injured State shall . . . call on the responsible State . . . to fulfil its obligations . . . and offer to negotiate with that State.' Admittedly, recourse to judicial settlement is much less injurious to relations between the two States, and to international order in general, than is resort to countermeasures. Yet countermeasures and judicial settlement are seen by the ILC as to some extent two parallel alternatives: as the Commission observes, the purpose of Article 52 is 'to establish reasonable procedural conditions for the taking of countermeasures in a context where compulsory third party settlement of disputes may not be available, immediately or at all'.[19]

Judge Higgins in her separate opinion suggested a different approach to the problem: for her, the question was not whether, for reasons of good faith or other, a claim submitted without prior negotiation was inadmissible, but whether in the absence of negotiations there could be said to be a 'dispute' capable of being submitted to the Court;[20] this was also the view of Judge Kooijmans.[21] The majority decision did not however reject this view of the matter; the problem was that the issue had not been formulated by the parties in those terms, and the division of views between Judge Higgins and her colleagues was whether or not the Court could go into it *proprio motu*.[22]

(b) Abuse of rights

In the case of the *Land and Maritime Boundary between Cameroon and Nigeria* Cameroon had employed the 'lightning-strike' technique first noted in the case of *Right of Passage over Indian Territory*: the deposit of an optional-clause declaration and immediate commencement of

[17] If it had been a sufficiently consistent practice for (almost) all States to include such a provision in (almost) all such instruments, it might have been argued that this showed the existence of a customary rule; or, contrariwise, that the fact that an explicit clause was found necessary showed that there was *no* such customary rule. See further, Part 2, Chapter III, Section 3 below. The Court did not however have to enquire into this problem.

[18] In the *LaGrand* case, only Judge Oda took the point that, in the absence of negotiation or even notification, there was no 'dispute' between the parties at the time of filing of the Application: [2001] ICJ Rep 527–8, para 6.

[19] Commentary to Art 52, set out in J Crawford, *The International Law Commission's Articles on State Responsibility* (2002) 297.

[20] [1998] ICJ Rep 346–9.

[21] ibid 356–9.

[22] See the Court's view, ibid 321, para 107.

proceedings against another State having deposited earlier such a declaration, before the respondent State is even aware that its opponent has filed a declaration. Among the arguments advanced by Nigeria against following the *Right of Passage* precedent upholding jurisdiction on this basis, was the contention that 'international law, especially as it relates to good faith, has evolved since' that decision,[23] and that Cameroon's conduct 'infringes upon the principle of good faith'.[24]

The Court recognized that 'the principle of good faith is a well-established principle of international law';[25] however it recalled its dictum in its 1988 judgment in the *Border and Transborder Armed Actions case* that good faith 'is not in itself a source of obligation where none would otherwise exist'.[26] It held that 'Cameroon was not bound [in law] to inform Nigeria of its intention to bring proceedings before the Court'; consequently: 'In the absence of any such obligations and of any infringement of Nigeria's corresponding rights, Nigeria may not justifiably rely upon the principle of good faith . . .'.[27]

Nigeria had however argued that even if Cameroon had the right to commence proceedings immediately after filing a declaration, 'considerations of good faith and of equity require that the right be not exercised without other States affected having an opportunity to consider their position in the knowledge of Cameroon's action, or after the lapse of a reasonable time in which they might be expected to acquire knowledge of it.'[28] The question is thus not whether Nigeria had a right to be given timely notice of Cameroon's intentions, but whether Cameroon, in exercising its right to commence proceedings, had committed an abuse of right. To say, as the Court does, that good faith can only come into play if a right has been infringed is to rob the idea of good faith of all content: if a claim can be made for infringement of a right, there is no need to invoke good faith at all. The Court's interpretation of the 1988 dictum, as to good faith not being a source of obligation, is, it is suggested, too sweeping.

It is worth recalling the context in which that dictum was given.[29] Honduras was claiming that Nicaragua was bound to refrain from commencing any dispute-settlement procedures so long as the Contadora process (of negotiation) had not been concluded. The Court observed that such an obligation could not be constructed out of thin air simply on the basis of good faith. It did not go on to consider the point whether Nicaragua, in exercising its right under the Pact of Bogotá to commence proceedings, might have acted in abuse of that right, because it found that the negotiation process had not in fact been concluded.

[23] [1998] ICJ Rep 290, para 24. [24] ibid 296, para 36. [25] ibid para 38.
[26] [1988] ICJ Rep 105, para 94, quoted in [1998] ICJ Rep 297, para 39. [27] ibid para 39.
[28] Nigerian Preliminary Objections, para 1.17.
[29] [1988] ICJ Rep 105–6, para 94, discussed in (1989) 60 BYIL 20–1.

(c) Abuse of process[30]

In the case of *Certain Phosphate Lands in Nauru* it was shown that Nauru had been somewhat inconsistent, around the time of independence, on the question whether it would regard the three States composing the Administering Authority as liable to rehabilitate the phosphate lands worked out during their administration. Australia therefore argued, as one of its preliminary objections, that Nauru had 'failed to act consistently and in good faith' in this respect and that the Court should therefore, as a matter of judicial propriety, decline to hear Nauru's claims. The Court rejected the objection as such, on the basis that it was one going to the merits, but also found specifically that Nauru's conduct did 'not amount to an abuse of process'.[31] By implication, this suggests that circumstances could arise in which a claim could be rejected *in limine* as an abuse of process; but the Court did not of course spell out the nature of such circumstances.

Only Judge Oda would have upheld the objection. For him: 'The fact that Nauru kept silent for more than fifteen years [1968 to 1983] on the subject of the alleged claim [for rehabilitation] makes it inappropriate for the Court to entertain it and, if only on grounds of judicial propriety, the Court should therefore find that the application is inadmissible.'[32]

The difference between Judge Oda and his colleagues was thus essentially whether any lack of frankness by Nauru was a ground for a finding of inadmissibility, since the majority of the Court did not exclude the possibility that, on the merits, the question of good faith might be relevant or even decisive.[33] The case does not however afford any material for assessing the effect of such lack of good faith.

A similar contention as to delay implying lack of good faith was made in the *LaGrand* case. Germany had claimed (*inter alia*) that the United States had failed to comply with the Court's Order indicating as a provisional measure that LaGrand should not be executed *pendente lite*. The United States pointed out that not only did Germany fail to express concern or protest at the alleged failure of the United States to comply with the Vienna Convention on Consular Relations in the case of the LaGrand brothers for some six and a half years, but it also only filed its application and request for provisional measures some twenty-seven hours before the scheduled execution of LaGrand.[34] Germany conceded that 'delay on the part of a claimant State may render an application inadmissible', but maintained that international law lays down no specific time limit: and there was some dispute as to when Germany became aware of the relevant facts. The Court's handling of the question is less

[30] Subsection (c) did not appear in the original article. For a reference to good faith in presentation of submissions to an arbitral body, see the Award of 14 February 1985 in the case of *Délimitation de la frontière maritime Guinée/Guinée-Bissau*, 29, para 46.

[31] [1992] ICJ Rep 255, para 38; and ibid 268, para 72 (1)(e).

[32] ibid 324, para 28.

[33] The case was later settled by agreement, and the proceedings withdrawn: see Order of 13 September 1993 [1993] ICJ Rep 322.

[34] [2001] ICJ Rep 486, para. 53.

than satisfying. While recognizing 'that Germany may be criticized for the manner in which these proceedings were filed and for their timing', it declined to declare them inadmissible; this was not however on the ground, for example, that the delay was insufficiently serious. It referred to the fact that it had made an Order indicating provisional measures, and had done so 'notwithstanding its awareness of the consequences of Germany's filing at such a late date', and concluded: 'In view of these considerations, the Court considers that Germany is now entitled to challenge the alleged failure of the United States to comply with the Order. Accordingly, the Court finds that Germany's third submission is admissible.'[35] This seems to imply that if Germany's remissness was a ground for inadmissibility, this should have been noted by the Court and given effect to at the time of the indication of provisional measures; and that since that had not occurred, no further effect could be given to considerations of delay or laches on the part of Germany. Such an approach hardly seems consistent with the nature of provisional measures proceedings, as regulated by Articles 73 to 78 of the 1978 Rules of Court; and until the cases of *Legality of the Use of Force* in 1999,[36] it was unknown for the Court to throw out a case at the provisional measures stage, however shaky the case might appear as regards jurisdiction or admissibility.[37]

In the case of *Application of the Genocide Convention*, at the provisional measures stage, the manner in which Bosnia and Herzegovina presented its case put Yugoslavia in difficulties, and might perhaps have been considered an abuse of right. The Court however chose to deal with the matter as one of 'orderly progress of the procedure' and 'the principle of equality of the parties'.[38]

In the case of the *Maritime Delimitation and Territorial Questions between Qatar and Bahrain* an allegation of lack of good faith was advanced in relation to a decision taken by the British Government in 1939. A dispute had arisen over the ownership of the Hawar Islands; the two States had agreed that the matter should be determined by decision of the British Government, and that Government ruled in favour of Bahrain. Before the Court, Qatar argued (*inter alia*) that 'the British officials responsible for the Hawar Islands question were biased and prejudged

[35] ibid 487, para 57.

[36] See the Orders of 2 June 1999 in the *Yugoslavia v Spain* and *Yugoslavia v United States* cases: [1999-II] ICJ Rep 761, 916.

[37] It is perhaps no more than a coincidence that the Order of 3 March 1999 indicating provisional measures in *LaGrand*, prepared under immense pressure of time, does not contain the standard clause in such Orders to the effect that 'the decision given in the present proceedings in no way prejudges the question of the jurisdiction of the Court to deal with the merits of the case, or any question relating to the admissibility of the Application, or relating to the merits themselves ...' (*Nuclear Tests* [1973] ICJ Rep 105, para 33; similar texts are to be found in subsequent provisional measures orders). The Order in the *LaGrand* case, by contrast, states merely that 'measures indicated by the Court for a stay of execution would necessarily be provisional in nature and would not in any way prejudge findings the Court might make *on the merits*', with no reference to jurisdiction or admissibility: [1999-I] ICJ Rep 15, para 27, emphasis added.

[38] [1993] ICJ Rep 336–7, para 21.

the matter', that the procedure followed violated the rule of *nemo judex in re sua*, and that the parties were not given an equal and fair opportunity to present their arguments.[39] The claim of bias was based on the admitted fact that 'the competent British officials proceeded on the premise that Bahrain possessed prima facie title to the islands and that the burden of proving the opposite lay on the Ruler of Qatar',[40] who did not succeed in doing so. However, the Court found that Qatar was well aware of this, and accepted to proceed on that basis. It also found, as an independent point, that the British decision was not an international arbitral award.[41] This raises the question whether an arbitrator could have approached the matter before him in the same way as did the British officials; could it be argued that, if he was already *prima facie* satisfied of the validity of the claim of one side, he could not then act in good faith as an arbitrator?[42]

(d) Other claims based on good faith[43]

Despite the 1988 finding in the *Border and Transborder Armed Actions* case that good faith 'is not in itself a source of obligation where none would otherwise exist',[44] re-stated, as noted above, in the case concerning the *Land and Maritime Boundary between Cameroon and Nigeria*,[45] parties have occasionally appealed to good faith as a sort of *tabula in naufragio* alongside claims based on more traditional and established grounds.

Reference was frequently made in the case of the *Gabčíkovo/Nagymaros Project* to considerations of good faith, but ultimately little or nothing was built in the judgment on such considerations alone.

One of the boldest arguments was advanced in the dissenting opinion of Judge Fleischhauer (and was not endorsed by the Court). The point was whether Czechoslovakia, in 'proceeding' to Variant C (a system of hydroelectric works other than those provided for in the 1977 Treaty with Hungary) was already acting unlawfully. For the Court, so long as Czechoslovakia 'confined itself to the execution, on its own territory, of the works which were necessary to the implementation of Variant C',[46] no breach of the Treaty had taken place; the Treaty was only breached when, in pursuance of Variant C, Czechoslovakia diverted the waters of the Danube into a bypass canal.[47] The Court observed (though in the context of a different part of its judgment) that the principle of good faith did no more than 'oblige[ ] the Parties to apply [the Treaty] in a reasonable way and in such a manner that its purposes can be realized'.

For Judge Fleischhauer, on the other hand, Czechoslovakia had by then already violated the obligation to perform the Treaty 'in good faith'. In his view: 'Good faith in performing a treaty does not only concern the

[39] [2001] ICJ Rep 83, para 138. [40] ibid 84, para 141. [41] ibid 77, para 114.

[42] This would be consistent with the recognized requirement that a judge or arbitrator come fresh to the matter brought before him, without having been concerned in it in any way previously: cf ICJ Statute, Art 17, para 2.

[43] Subsection (d) was not included in the 1989 article.

[44] [1988] ICJ Rep 105, para 94; commented on in (1989) 60 BYIL 8, 21ff.

[45] [1998] ICJ Rep 297, para 39. [46] [1997] ICJ Rep 54, para 79. [47] ibid 66, para 108.

manner in which the treaty is applied and implemented by the parties to it: good faith performance means also that the parties must not defeat the object and purpose of the treaty.' Judge Fleischhauer invoked Article 18 of the Vienna Convention, concerning the obligation, during the period between signature and ratification of a treaty,[48] not to defeat its object and purpose, stated by the ILC as 'an obligation of good faith', and suggested: '*A fortiori* does that obligation apply to a treaty after its entry into force.'[49]

This was a view already advanced by Waldock in his draft articles on the Law of Treaties for the ILC.[50] Judge Fleischhauer might also have cited, in support of his view, the decision in the case of *Military and Paramilitary Activities in and against Nicaragua*, where the Court apparently upheld, to some extent,[51] a claim of Nicaragua based on similar considerations. This view is not however consistent with the decision in the *ICAO Appeal* case; and the writer has suggested in an earlier article that the finding in the *Nicaragua* decision may only be applicable, at most, to treaties of friendship.[52]

It is not clear from Judge Fleischhauer's opinion whether in his view Czechoslovakia's action, prior to the diversion of the Danube, in 'proceeding' to Variant C was a breach of the Treaty, or a breach of a requirement of general (customary) law; he uses the careful formula that Czechoslovakia 'was not free to engage in this way of proceeding'.[53] Breach of the obligation imposed by Article 18 of the Vienna Convention on the Law of Treaties (VCLT) is clearly not a breach of the relevant treaty, since that treaty has not yet come into force.[54] At the same time, the obligation would not exist if the treaty had not been signed, or, in the case of the post-ratification obligation postulated by Judge Fleischhauer, had not come into force, so that the obligation is, at least, treaty-dependent. When a claim is made that a party has failed to implement a treaty provision 'in good faith', it is hardly possible to distinguish between a breach of that provision and a breach of the aspect of the principle *pacta sunt servanda* that requires good faith. That principle says, in effect, that compliance with a treaty obligation in a manner inconsistent with good faith is not compliance at all, so that an action lies for breach of the treaty, rather than of the backing principle. Is it possible to reason similarly that action which does not in itself contravene any provision of the treaty, but which can be regarded as 'calculated to deprive [the] treaty of its object and purpose' constitutes non-compliance with the treaty? The difficulty

48 For simplicity, reference is only made to the case of signature of a treaty (Art 18, para 1); the same argument applies where a State has indicated by other means a willingness to be bound (Art 18, para 2).

49 Cited at [1997] ICJ Rep 206.

50 Third Report on the Law of Treaties (1964) *ILC Yearbook* 1964, 7, quoted in (1992) 63 BYIL 50.

51 See the discussion in a previous article: (1992) 63 BYIL 48–54, and in particular the doubt expressed by Judge Oda, in his opinion, as to whether the Court had in fact accepted Nicaragua's claim (ibid 52).

52 (1992) 63 BYIL 53, citing [1972] ICJ Rep 58, para 20.

53 [1997] ICJ Rep 205.

54 As was stated by the Court in the *Nicaragua* case: [1986] ICJ Rep 135, para 270.

is that it may often be the case that it is not possible to point to a specific provision which is, in this indirect manner, not being complied with; hence the appeal to the 'object and purpose' test.

In the *Gabčíkovo* case, the majority of the Court regarded it as relevant that until Czechoslovakia diverted the waters of the Danube, it had only carried out works on its own territory (which were thus *prima facie* legal), and which 'could have been abandoned if an agreement had been reached between the parties and [which] did not therefore predetermine the final decision to be taken'.[55] Reasoning on an *a contrario* basis, one may perhaps conclude that any action by a party to a treaty may be regarded as a failure to comply with it in good faith, even if the action is otherwise lawful and does not contravene any specific provision of a treaty, if as a result of that action *a breach of the provisions of the treaty is thereby predetermined, ie rendered inevitable*. This view reconciles the points of view of the majority and Judge Fleischhauer, in the sense that the difference between them is limited to a question of fact. On this basis, there is no need to postulate an independent duty not to defeat the object and purpose of a treaty; it suffices to treat compliance 'in good faith' as excluding any anticipatory breach.[56] The initial submissions of Iran in its Application in the *Oil Platforms* case included a claim that the United States by its 'patently hostile and threatening attitude' to Iran had breached 'the object and purpose of the Treaty of Amity [between them], including Articles I and X(1), and international law'. In the Memorial and subsequent pleadings, the reference to breach of the 'object and purpose' disappeared,[57] and was therefore not examined by the Court.

(e) Bad faith will not be presumed[58]

The Permanent Court of International Justice had already declined to base part of a decision on the assumption that one of the parties might fail to comply with it in good faith.[59] A similar approach was adopted by the Court in the case of the *Land and Maritime Boundary between Cameroon and Nigeria*. As a result of the Court's determination of the land boundary, each of the parties was obliged to withdraw its administration and military or police forces from areas which had been found to be under the sovereignty of the other party.[60] Cameroon however also asked the Court

55 [1997] ICJ Rep 54, para 79.

56 A parallel problem is presented by the traditional controversy whether the passage by a State of legislation incompatible with its international obligations constitutes an internationally wrongful act, or whether such act only occurs when the legislation is to the detriment of another State. The ILC took the view that the answer depended on the nature of the obligation and of the legislation: see J Crawford, *The International Law Commission's Articles on State Responsibility* (2002) 130, para 12, and the decision in *LaGrand* there cited ([2001] ICJ Rep 497, paras 90–91).

57 See [2003] ICJ Rep 169–70, paras 18–19.

58 Subsection (e) was not included in the 1989 article.

59 See *Free Zones of Upper Savoy and the District of Gex* PCIJ Series A, No 24, 12, and Series A/B, No 46, 167: 'an abuse [of the rights recognized in the decision] cannot be presumed by the Court'.

60 The Court noted the precedents in this sense set by the *Temple of Preah Vihear* case, [1962] ICJ Rep 37, and the agreement concluded between Libya and Chad following the decision in the *Territorial Dispute* case [1994] ICJ Rep 6: see [2002] ICJ Rep 451, para 313.

to require from Nigeria guarantees of non-repetition, as contemplated by Article 30(b) of the ILC's Articles on State Responsibility. The Court, however, declined to uphold this claim:

> ... the Judgment delivered today specifies in definitive and mandatory terms the land and maritime boundary between the two States. With all uncertainty dispelled in this regard, the Court cannot envisage a situation where either Party, after withdrawing its military and police forces and administration from the other's territory, would fail to respect the territorial sovereignty of that Party.[61]

Such action would constitute a breach of the undertaking, in Article 94, paragraph 1 of the Charter, to comply with the Court's decision—a duty of compliance that must be read as involving compliance in good faith.[62] Furthermore, in the specific case, Nigeria had referred to the possibility that Cameroon's sovereignty might be recognized over areas under Nigerian administration, and had added that, 'in respect of the establishment of the municipality of Bakassi, ... there is nothing irreversible in the relevant arrangements made by Nigeria'.[63] The implication is that Nigeria was undertaking in advance to dismantle its administration if the area was awarded to Cameroon, an undertaking that should be performed in good faith.

In contrast, however, the Court in the case concerning *Legal Consequences of the Construction of a Wall in the Occupied Palestinian Territory* was ready to envisage the possibility that the wall constructed by Israel, avowedly as a temporary security measure, might become permanent, so as to limit the territory available for Palestinian self-determination.

> Whilst the Court notes the assurance given by Israel that the construction of the wall does not amount to annexation and that the wall is of a temporary nature ... it nevertheless cannot remain indifferent to certain fears expressed to it that the route of the wall will prejudge the future frontier between Israel and Palestine, and the fear that Israel may integrate the settlements and their means of access. The Court considers that the construction of the wall and its associated régime create a 'fait accompli' on the ground that could well become permanent, in which case, and notwithstanding the formal characterization of the wall by Israel, it would be tantamount to *de facto* annexation.[64]

Since the Court gives other reasons why the construction of the wall is unlawful, it is not clear to what extent this paragraph afforded a basis for the finding in the operative part of the advisory opinion that 'Israel ... is under an obligation to cease forthwith the works of construction of the wall ... [and] to dismantle forthwith the structure therein situated'. Had the paragraph cited been the only basis for this conclusion, it would be a remarkable example of the Court being prepared to condemn a State, not

[61] [2002] ICJ Rep 452, para 318.

[62] This is not, of course, to say that the parties, *by agreement*, might act otherwise than in compliance with a judgment of the Court, which does not of itself creates rules of *jus cogens*: see the discussion in the earlier article, (1989) 60 BYIL 103–5.

[63] ibid 451, para 312.

[64] [2004] ICJ Rep 184.

for what it had done, but for what it might do in the future—what 'could well' happen, in the Court's phrase. This would be a complete contradiction of the principle referred to above that bad faith, in the form of disregard of a decision of the Court, will not be presumed.

In the *Fisheries Jurisdiction* case between Spain and Canada, Canada had attached a reservation to its optional-clause declaration excluding from jurisdiction measures of conservation and fisheries management in an area which was generally admitted to be part of the high seas. The Court was divided on the question whether—assuming that the reservation was being applied, or could be applied, to prevent the Court from determining the legality of action to be classified, at least *prima facie*, as contrary to international law—that aspect had any incidence on the validity, effectiveness or interpretation of the reservation. Judge Vereshchetin, who dissented from the majority view that the reservation was valid and excluded jurisdiction over the actions complained of by Spain, argued that 'the Court should proceed from the presumption that the intent [of Canada] was to remain within the orbit of international law', and went on to say: 'The Court cannot impute to a State bad faith, an intent by way of a reservation to cover a violation of international law.'[65]

It is difficult to pin down precisely the role attributed by Judge Vereshchetin to the concept of good faith. The idea seems allied to that of abuse of process: a faculty which is given to be employed for a lawful purpose may not be employed for an unlawful one, or so as to defeat the object for which the faculty was given. Yet an examination of the various reservations in fact made by States to their optional-clause declarations[66] leaves no room for doubt that reservations are often made in order to prevent the submission to the Court of matters in respect of which the reserving State is less than confident that its position would be upheld in law. The exceptional character of the Canadian reservation was that it was made quite openly with this in view, and was unusually specific in the definition of matters excluded.[67] There was no diversion of the faculty of making reservations from its proper scheme of operation.

Judge *ad hoc* Torres Bernárdez, in the same case, invoked good faith in another way. He observes that a State is free to choose whether or not to become a party to the Charter and the Statute, but that if it does, this entails the acquisition of both rights and obligations. He continues: 'It is therefore contrary to the most elementary legal principles, including that of good faith, subsequently to invoke those rights while ignoring the

[65] [1998] ICJ Rep 580, para 20.

[66] See the texts in ch IV of the successive *ICJ Yearbooks*.

[67] Yet Judge Torres Bernárdez (see below) equated the Canadian action with that of a State committing 'an *abuse of rights* by depositing a declaration that is misleading in scope and wording, while reserving the right, when the time comes, to invoke interpretations that are at variance with the Statute, with the United Nations Charter or with general international law': [1998] ICJ Rep 635, para 138 (emphasis in original).

[68] ibid 634, para 135.

obligations assumed.'[68] This is, of course, a general legal maxim already discussed in a previous article, and referred to briefly in Section 4(1) below.

2. *Estoppel, preclusion, and acquiescence*

> 'When you've once said a thing, that fixes it, and you must take the consequences.' (the Red Queen)
>
> Lewis Carroll, *Through the Looking Glass*

[(1) *The nature of the concepts*]

(2) *The cases*

A case before the Court in which silence was relied on as having the legal effects of acquiescence or estoppel was the case of *Passage through the Great Belt* between Finland and Denmark. However, the case was settled by agreement and withdrawn, so that the Court did not have to rule on these issues; for that reason, only a brief outline of the relevant contentions is appropriate.[69]

Denmark had for years been contemplating the construction of a bridge over the Great Belt, and at various stages notified foreign missions in Copenhagen of the proposals, stating that the construction would not interfere with free passage through the Belt as an international strait. In 1988–89 a final version of the project was established, involving a vertical clearance of 65 metres, which was insufficient to allow the passage of drill rigs of a type regularly constructed in Finnish shipyards which then passed through the Great Belt. Finland brought proceedings before the Court on the grounds of a projected interference with its right of free passage. Denmark asserted (*inter alia*) that Finland had on various occasions failed to react to the Danish plans for the bridge, and that such 'silences' constituted acquiescence in the project.

Finland advanced a number of reasons for rejecting this contention, based on the facts of the case, but also added a consideration of law of a more general nature:

> Finland would in any event question whether Denmark is entitled to rely on tacit consent in the form of acquiescence as a basis for unilateral action by way of derogation from the generally recognised right of free passage for international shipping through straits . . . [I]n such circumstances, what is needed is the express agreement of the user States, that is to say, the States which have traditionally, and as of right, utilised the strait for the free passage of vessels constructed in their shipyards.[70]

[69] The pleadings in the case have been published in the Court's *Pleadings, Oral Arguments, Documents* series; and the case had already been studied at length by M Koskenniemi (counsel in the case), 'L'affaire du passage par le Grand-Belt' (1992) 38 *Annuaire français* 905, and is also analysed by I Sinclair, 'Estoppel and acquiescence' in V Lowe and M Fitzmaurice (eds) *Fifty Years of the International Court of Justice (Jennings Festschrift)* (1996) 113–15.

[70] Memorial of Finland, para 555, *Passage through the Great Belt, Pleadings, Oral Arguments, Documents*, 381–2. In support of this view, Finland cited a Joint Anglo-French Report of 1963 on a proposal for a bridge across the Straits of Dover.

This contention raises the interesting question whether it is correct that anything that can be done by express agreement can also result from an implicit agreement in the form of acquiescence, or from an estoppel. The fact that other States also enjoyed rights of passage would seem to be irrelevant: if Denmark had concluded a bilateral agreement in due form whereby Finland waived any objection to the 65-metre-high bridge, this would be opposable to Finland whatever the attitude of the other interested States.[71] Accordingly if Finland had acquiesced informally, but in such a manner as to be bound in law, in the Danish proposals, is there any reason, deriving from the particular nature of the rights involved, why Finland should not equally be bound? The response that the Court might have given on this point must however remain a matter of speculation.

The requirements of estoppel, as defined initially in the English common law, and taken over into international law, are now well established in the Court's jurisprudence. Shortly after the publication of the earlier article in this series in which those requirements were discussed,[72] the expression 'equitable estoppel' (perhaps something of a tautology)[73] was used by Nicaragua as an argument in favour of the admission of its application to intervene in the case of the *Land, Island and Maritime Frontier* between El Salvador and Honduras. This particular argument was, on the basis of the facts of the case, given very short shrift by the Chamber dealing with the case, which however took the opportunity to restate the 'essential elements required by estoppel', namely 'a statement or representation made by one party to another and reliance upon it by that other party to his detriment or to the advantage of the party making it'.[74] Nevertheless, parties still endeavour to rely on estoppel in circumstances in which nothing can be shown beyond a certain inconsistency of conduct, which is without legal effects.

In the *Territorial Dispute* between Chad and Libya, the key question was whether a 1955 Franco–Libyan Treaty had or had not determined all the frontiers between the territories of the two States, including the boundary with Chad (as successor State to France). The Court held that, on a proper interpretation of the Treaty, it had done so. Judge Ajibola was however prepared to base the decision also, or alternatively, on a finding of estoppel. After citing the relevant jurisprudence, his conclusion was that: 'All these legal, judicial as well as arbitral references fortify my view, based on the principle of estoppel, that the silence or acquiescence of Libya from the date of signing the 1955 Treaty to the

[71] On the facts, it appears that only Finland would be affected by the height clearance limitation, since it was the only State engaged in constructing the oil rigs whose passage would be prevented. The other States interested might nevertheless have objected, in order to preserve their rights for the future, so that Denmark could only safely proceed with the agreement, or absence of objection, of all of them.

[72] (1989) 60 BYIL 36ff.

[73] In some jurisdictions, a distinction is made between 'promissory estoppel' and 'equitable estoppel', otherwise 'estoppel by representation of fact': see eg 28 American Jurisprudence 2d Estoppel and Waiver, §28.

[74] [1990] ICJ Rep 118, para 63.

present time, without any protest whatsoever, clearly militates against its claim.'[75]

The judgment of the Court does not employ any argument of this kind; whether the majority regarded it as superfluous or as unsound does not appear. It may however be observed first that Judge Ajibola relies principally on the fact that Libya never invoked the invalidity of the Treaty (though he does also refer to the possibility of protest that 'the treaty had failed to create the expected boundary'); but that was not the point in dispute. The question was the correct interpretation of the Treaty. Secondly, and more material for our purposes, it is not at all clear in what way Chad suffered detriment, or Libya advantage, from the fact that Libya acted as though the Treaty was valid and satisfactory while (supposedly) believing the opposite. Such a detriment would be required by the recognized conditions of estoppel.

In the same year (1994), something resembling an estoppel, though not called by that name, was resorted to in the judgment on jurisdiction in the case concerning *Maritime Delimitation and Territorial Questions between Qatar and Bahrain*. Jurisdiction was asserted by Qatar on the basis of the Minutes of tripartite meetings (between the parties and Saudi Arabia), which, it was claimed, constituted or recorded an agreement by the parties to the unilateral submission by either of them of their dispute to the International Court. It was objected by Bahrain that its Foreign Minister, who signed the Minutes, did not consider that he was signing an instrument that would have the effect of 'committing Bahrain to a legally binding agreement', and constitutionally would not have been permitted to sign an international agreement taking effect at the time of signature.[76] The Court summarily rejected this contention, on the basis that, having signed a text 'recording commitments accepted by [his] Government, some of which were to be given immediate application', the Minister was 'not in a position subsequently to say that he intended to subscribe only' to an instrument of lesser significance.[77]

This wording is strongly suggestive of an estoppel; but it is difficult to bring the facts within the classic definition. The statement impliedly made by Bahrain to Qatar was, according to the Court's view, to the effect that it agreed to the unilateral submission of the dispute to the Court. This statement did not, in the contention of Bahrain, correspond to the true factual position; but even if that was so, this would not prevent Bahrain from being bound, since the essence of an estoppel is that it renders true, for the purposes of the relations between the parties, what may not have been, or certainly was not, true. But there remains the element of prejudice: in what respect did Qatar act (or refrain from acting) to its detriment, or to the benefit of Bahrain, on the faith of the apparent undertaking in favour of unilateral submission of the dispute to the Court? Could the filing by Qatar of the Application in the case constitute

[75] [1994] ICJ Rep 81, para 110. [76] [1994] ICJ Rep 121, para 26. [77] ibid 122, para 27.

such an action? Such an action would not be at all to the benefit of Bahrain—quite the contrary. The only detriment that Qatar could point to would apparently be the trouble and cost incurred in the preparation and submission of the Application—something comparatively trivial in international terms.

This may in fact be why the Court chose not to invoke the concept of estoppel; but if so, a further question arises. Can conduct that does not, according to the recognized conditions, amount to an estoppel be given the same effect as though it did comply with such conditions? If there is in international law a simple principle *allegans contraria non est audiendus*, then what purpose is served by the restrictive requirements of estoppel? It may be true that acquiescence and estoppel are twins; and Judge Ajibola in the *Frontier Dispute* case referred to them throughout his opinion as though they were interchangeable. It should however be recalled that acquiescence signifies actual consent, consent that can be proved, while estoppel (in relation to the state of mind of the person or State concerned) relates to a consent that never existed but appeared to exist, and led to consequences of detriment/advantage.

In the case concerning the *Land and Maritime Frontier between Cameroon and Nigeria* Nigeria drew attention to the fact that 'for a period of at least 24 years prior to the filing of the Application the parties have in their regular dealings accepted a duty to settle all boundary questions through the existing bilateral machinery'.[78] On that basis, it regarded Cameroon's action in depositing an optional-clause declaration and immediately filing an application as something of a stab in the back. One of the ways in which it expressed this sentiment was in claiming that the conduct of the parties had resulted in a legal commitment of Cameroon to using the bilateral machinery; the Court found that this could not be deduced from the history of the matter.[79]

Nigeria's second approach was to claim that 'by its conduct Cameroon is estopped from turning to the Court'.[80] The Court took the opportunity to restate its jurisprudence as to the requirements for an estoppel:

> An estoppel would only arise if by its acts or declarations Cameroon had consistently made it fully clear that it had agreed to settle the boundary dispute submitted to the Court by bilateral avenues alone. It would further be necessary that, by relying on such an attitude, Nigeria had changed position to its own detriment or had suffered some prejudice (*North Sea Continental Shelf, Judgment, I.C.J. Reports 1969*, p. 26, para. 30; *Land, Island and Maritime Frontier Dispute (El Salvador/Honduras), Application to Intervene, Judgment, I.C.J. Reports 1990*, p. 118, para. 63).[81]

The test of 'detriment' is correctly stated, but the reference to suffering prejudice is an addition, the sense of which is not entirely clear. Furthermore, some doubt may be felt about the definition in the first

78 Nigerian Second Preliminary Objection, quoted in [1998] ICJ Rep 300, para 48.

79 See [1998] ICJ Rep 303, para 56.

80 ibid 301, para 48.

81 ibid 303, para 57.

sentence. If Cameroon *had agreed* to settle the boundary dispute in the way alleged, then there would have been no need for an estoppel (and thus for proof of a detriment); Nigeria could simply have relied on the agreement and on the evidence for it to be found in Cameroon's conduct. The point about an estoppel, and the aspect that distinguishes it from a presumption, is that, as explained by Fitzmaurice, an estoppel 'recognizes the possibility that the consent (or other fact) was non-existent—in fact virtually takes it for granted that that was so':[82] 'Estoppel elevates a sort of legal fiction to the status of fact for the purposes of the relations between the parties.'[83] An estoppel against Cameroon would be based, not on the fact that it had agreed, and made clear that it had agreed, to a particular course, but on the fact that it had behaved in a manner from which it could have been (and was) concluded by the other party that it had agreed.

The conduct of Cameroon relied on by Nigeria failed to meet the criterion of 'detriment'. Nigerian counsel had foreseen the difficulty, and endeavoured to show the existence of prejudice:

> In the circumstances Nigeria has suffered prejudice as a consequence of the conduct of Cameroon and thus, in particular:
>
> (1) Nigeria has lost the opportunity to have a system of bilateral contacts which was flexible and based upon mutual negotiation and agreement. As the Court will appreciate, the result of acquiring the status of a Party to proceedings is a serious limitation upon the normal discretion of a State in matters of foreign policy.
>
> (2) As a result of the lodging of the Application the bilateral machinery has ceased to function and a valuable procedure for resolving disputes and for containing border problems of various kinds has been lost.
>
> (3) Nigeria was placed in a position in which it was dealing with Cameroon in relation to matters which were to figure in the Application without having knowledge, or means of knowledge, that Cameroon had a hidden and collateral agenda.[84]

The Court did not however consider that Nigeria had shown that it had 'changed position to its detriment or that it has sustained prejudice'; the alleged prejudice was defined as follows: 'in that it could otherwise have sought a solution to the border problems existing between the two States by having recourse to other procedures, but was precluded from doing so by reliance on the positions allegedly taken by Cameroon.'[85] This is clear: the prejudice alleged was based on Nigeria's reliance on the implicit statement attributed to Cameroon. However, the Court continued: 'Finally, the Court has not been persuaded that Nigeria has been prejudiced as a result of Cameroon's having instituted proceedings before the Court instead of pursuing negotiations which, moreover, were deadlocked when

[82] (1989) 60 BYIL 45–6; the words are those of the present writer, but the distinction had been made by Fitzmaurice.

[83] ibid 38.

[84] Nigerian Preliminary Objections, para 2.33.

[85] ibid 304, para 57.

the Application was filed.'[86] Here the strict conditions of estoppel seem to have been lost sight of. The detriment suffered, for the purposes of estoppel, is suffered as a result of the action taken by (or inaction of) the State to which the relevant declaration is addressed, in reliance on that statement, not as a result of some action taken by the declaring State by which it goes back on what its declaration suggested.[87] If Nigeria had refrained from bringing the dispute before the Court on reliance on an implicit declaration by Cameroon that it would settle it by bilateral means, the test of 'detriment' or 'prejudice' would have been satisfied. By the time Cameroon filed its application, there should, in order to found an estoppel, already have been detriment or prejudice suffered by Nigeria in reliance on the implicit declaration of Cameroon.

A similar attempt was made in a jurisdictional context by Pakistan against India in the case of the *Aerial Incident of 10 August 1999* to invoke estoppel. India's acceptance of jurisdiction under the optional clause contained a reservation excluding disputes with other Members of the Commonwealth. In 1972 the two parties had signed the so-called 'Simla Accord', in which they declared themselves 'resolved to settle their differences by peaceful means through bilateral negotiations or any other peaceful means mutually agreed upon between them'.[88]

Pakistan argued that:

> As the compulsory procedure for settlement under Article 36(2) constitutes a 'peaceful means agreed upon between them', a unilateral 'reservation' cannot be invoked by India to defeat this peaceful means of settlement in the case of Pakistan, whatever may be its effect against other commonwealth members. Article I para. (ii) of the Simla Accord creates an estoppel against the Government of India from invoking this 'reservation' against the Government of Pakistan.[89]

The Court would have none of this; it regarded the provision of the Simla Accord as 'an obligation, generally, on the two States to settle their differences by peaceful means, to be mutually agreed by them. The said provision in no way modifies the specific rules governing recourse to any such means, including judicial settlement. Thus the Court cannot interpret that obligation as precluding India from relying, in the present case, on the Commonwealth reservation contained in its declaration.'[90] The Court therefore found it unnecessary to deal with the estoppel argument:[91] its decision was a matter of interpretation of the Simla Accord, and of its

[86] Nigerian Preliminary Objections, para 58.

[87] Though this was the interpretation advanced in one of the earliest appearances of estoppel in argument before the Court: see C de Visscher in *European Commission of the Danube*, PCIJ Series C, No 13-IV, 181–2.

[88] Quoted at [2000] ICJ Rep 22, para 22.

[89] Pakistan Memorial, Section E; see also CR 2000/1, E Lauterpacht, para 13; and the counter-argument of India, CR 2000/2, Rao, para 13.

[90] [2000] ICJ Rep 31, para 45.

[91] Judge *ad hoc* Pirzada, in a dissenting opinion, referred to estoppel as a general principle of international law, and considered that 'the conduct of India is covered by the doctrine of estoppel' ([2000] ICJ Rep 78, para 26); but he does not explain either the 'detriment' point or how an estoppel could sever the reservation from the acceptance.

relationship to the optional-clause declaration. 'Peaceful means mutually agreed upon' between the parties meant such means as might be so agreed, *on the terms and conditions thereof*: if the declaration was such a means, the reference to it could not transform it by stripping it of its reservation. The only additional query one might consider is the intertemporal aspect. The Commonwealth reservation had been in India's successive optional-clause declarations since independence.[92] If however the reservation had been added after the Simla Accord, so as to reduce the scope of India's commitment *vis à vis* Pakistan, might estoppel have been invoked? The answer must probably be in the negative, for lack of any alteration of position by Pakistan, to its detriment, on the basis of the Simla Accord.[93]

In contrast, an aspect of the judgment on the merits in the *Cameroon/Nigeria* case gives ground for reflection on the extent to which conduct may produce a binding commitment. The question was whether the boundary between the two States in Lake Chad had or had not been delimited by a series of international instruments concluded during the colonial and mandates period.[94] Nigeria drew attention to certain matters of detail which in its view showed that the frontier had not been 'delimited' by those instruments, since a number of questions remained to be settled. One of the points that the Court took in rejecting this contention was as follows: 'Moreover, the Court cannot fail to observe that Nigeria was consulted during the negotiations for its independence, and again during the plebiscites that were to determine the future of the populations of the Northern and Southern Cameroons . . . At no time did it suggest, either so far as the Lake Chad area was concerned, or elsewhere, that the frontiers there remained to be delimited.'[95] Was this then a sort of estoppel by silence? If so, there is no trace of a reliance by some other international entity, and in particular Cameroon, on that silence with a consequent prejudicial change of position. If the Nigerian position is treated as an acquiescence rather than creative of estoppel,[96] there remains the question of the quasi-contractual nature of the relations thus created:[97] was Cameroon in a position in 1960–61, at the time of Nigerian independence and the plebiscite, to note and rely on a *qualifiziertes Stillschweigen* on the part of Nigeria?[98] And was there any duty (and if so,

[92] See [2000] ICJ Rep 31, para 43.

[93] A point made by Dr Rao for India (n 89 above, para 22). The question of detriment is discussed at (1989) 60 BYIL 44.

[94] The Milner–Simon Declaration of 1919, the League of Nations Mandate for the Cameroons, the Thomson–Marchand Declaration of 1929–30, and the Henderson–Fleuriau Exchange of Notes of 1931: see [2002] ICJ Rep 338–41.

[95] [2002] ICJ Rep 341–2, para 52.

[96] On the distinction between these concepts, see the previous article, [1989] BYIL 45–7.

[97] cf JP Müller and T Cottier, 'Acquiescence' in R Bernhardt (ed), *Encyclopedia of Public International Law*, vol 1, 15. A stronger case for acquiescence might have been made in the case of *Certain Phosphate Lands in Nauru* (see the view of Judge Oda quoted in n 144 below), but the merits of the case were not examined, as a result of the amicable settlement concluded by the parties.

[98] In another section of the judgment, the Court attaches importance to the fact that Nigeria voted in the General Assembly in favour of the resolution approving the result of the plebiscite, in order to

owed to whom?) on Nigeria to raise the matter at the time of independence or the plebiscite? As the Court observed in the *Temple of Preah Vihear* case, the circumstances must be such as to call for some reaction, the principle being that '*qui tacet consentire videtur*' not merely '*si loqui potuisset*' but also '*si loqui debuisset*'.[99] In the *Cameroon/Nigeria* judgment, the point is only thrown in as a makeweight, but even on that level it is not entirely satisfactory.

[(3) Analysis of estoppel]

[(4) Relationship between estoppel, preclusion, and acquiescence]

[(5) Estoppel in relation to treaty commitments]

3. *The role of equity in international law*

> With righteousness shall he judge the world; and the people with equity.
>
> Psalm 98, v 10

(1) Equity and ex aequo et bono[100]

It is still the case that paragraph 2 of Article 36 of the Statute of the ICJ has never yet been invoked in order to request the Court to decide *ex aequo et bono*;[101] and that there is general agreement that the application of equity, being distinct in nature from *ex aequo et bono*, is open to the Court without such a request.

However, the development in the law of maritime delimitation of the concepts of equity and equitable principles, with the consequent unpredictability of the Court's finding in favour of any particular delimitation line, has led Judge Oda to argue that 'there are in fact no rules of law for effecting a maritime delimitation in the presence of overlapping *titles* (not overlapping claims)'[102] and to deduce from this that:

> ... if the Court is requested by the parties to decide on a maritime delimitation in accordance with Article 36, paragraph 1, of the Statute, it will not be expected to apply rules of international law but will simply 'decide a case *ex aequo et bono*'.
>
> In other words, the presentation of a case of maritime delimitation by agreement between the States in dispute in accordance with Article 36, paragraph 1,

show that it 'acknowledged' the frontier line relating to the Bakassi Peninsula, coupled with the fact that 'there was nothing which might have led Nigeria to believe that the plebiscite ... did not include Bakassi', so that Bakassi was thereby attributed to Cameroon: [2002] ICJ Rep 410, paras 213, 214.

99 [1962] ICJ Rep 23. 100 (1989) 60 BYIL 50–1.

101 In the Judgment of the Chamber in the *Land, Island and Maritime Frontier Dispute* it was observed that a reference in the Special Agreement to Art 38, para 1, and provision therein for a decision taking account of 'the rules of international law', 'obviously excludes the possibility of any decision *ex aequo et bono*': [1992] ICJ Rep 390–1, para 47.

102 For an examination of Judge Oda's distinction between overlapping titles and overlapping claims, see [1993] BYIL 49–50.

means by implication that the parties are requesting the Court 'to decide a case *ex aequo et bono*' in accordance with Article 38, paragraph 2 of the Statute.[103]

It may however be doubted whether Judge Oda's conclusion follows from his premisses. The inexistence of rules of law on a given question raises the spectre of a finding of *non liquet*; and it will be recalled that the inclusion of 'general principles of law' among the sources to be drawn upon by the Court was directed to excluding such a finding. If there is neither treaty-law nor custom to regulate maritime delimitation in the circumstances contemplated, no authorization by the parties is required for the Court to appeal to such general principles; and if their attitude is regarded as relevant, it might be expected that they would prefer the Court to refer to such principles, however amorphous, rather than to set sail on the uncharted (or undelimited) seas of *ex aequo et bono*.[104]

(2) Equity as part of the law

In the previous article mention was made of the appeal to equity *infra legem* made by the Chamber dealing with the *Frontier Dispute* between Mali and Burkina Faso, in order to find, in the context of a land frontier question, 'an equitable solution derived from the applicable law'. The article continued: 'What that solution was will be noted elsewhere.' This however remained an unfulfilled promise, the question having been overlooked during the preparation of later articles. It may now be re-examined, in particular in view of some comments made by Judge Weeramantry in the *Kasikili/Sedudu Island* case.

One would not expect equity to play any role in the judicial determination of a land frontier: unlike a continental shelf boundary, a land frontier is simply the product of historical processes—agreement, occupation or *uti possidetis*—that produce a defined result as a matter of law, no matter how inequitable that result may seem from some points of view.[105] As the Chamber in the *Frontier Dispute* case observed: 'Especially in the African

[103] *Maritime Delimitation in the Area between Greenland and Jan Mayen* [1993] ICJ Rep 113, paras 85–6. Judge Oda also drew attention to the difficulty of finding the existence of a joint 'request' of this kind in a case brought by application, rather than by special agreement. For a similar view that invocation of a legal rule effecting a *renvoi* to equity is equivalent to seeking a decision *ex aequo et bono*, see G Abi-Saab, 'Les sources du droit international: Essai de déconstruction' in *Le droit international dans un monde en mutation (Mélanges Jiménez de Aréchaga)* 35.

[104] Note the suggestion of Sir Robert Jennings, quoted in the earlier article in this series, that a decision *ex aequo et bono* could be made, and perhaps would be better made, by someone without legal skill and training, but with expertise of another kind: (1989) 60 BYIL, 50–1.

[105] This indeed is the nature of the *uti possidetis*, and the 'maintenance of the territorial status quo' deliberately maintained in, eg, the 1964 Declaration of the Organization of African Unity. Note also, as to the 'absolute' quality of an existing frontier, the decision of the Chamber in the *Land, Island and Maritime Frontier Dispute* to the effect that, if the Chamber was satisfied that the frontier resulting from *uti possidetis* was beyond what a party was claiming, the *ne ultra petita* rule did not prevent a finding that the boundary was in that position: [1992] ICJ Rep 437, para 126. Also the finding by Judge *ad hoc* Torres Bernárdez that the island of Meanguera belonged to El Salvador and Meanguerita to Honduras, despite the shared view of the parties that sovereignty over both islands belonged to a single State, one or other of the parties: ibid 680.

context, the obvious deficiencies of many frontiers inherited from colonization, from the ethnic, geographical or administrative standpoint, cannot support an assertion that the modification of these frontiers is necessary or justifiable on the ground of considerations of equity.'[106]

How then did the Chamber apply equity? It was faced with the problem that the French administrative regulations which, through application of the *uti possidetis* principle, dictated the position of the land boundary, had treated a particular pool (the pool of Soum) as a 'frontier pool', which had to be divided between the two French administrative divisions; but there was no evidence of such a division ever having been effected. The conclusion of the Chamber was that 'it must recognize that Soum is a frontier pool; and that, in the absence of any precise indication in the texts of the position of the frontier line, the line should divide the pool of Soum in an equitable manner', which *in casu* meant an equal division of the area of the pool.[107]

The Chamber did not, as it is suggested it might have done, treat the matter as one of the intention of the French administrators of the two regions. It noted that those administrators had agreed that the pool was to be divided as a frontier pool; in the absence of any evidence to the contrary, a presumption might be applied that the division was, or was to be, on an equitable basis. This would not involve any 'application' of equity by the Chamber itself, whether *praeter legem* or *infra legem*: it would be merely a matter of interpretation of a text.[108] What would be, in the circumstances, an equitable division of the pool would have been to be assessed by the French administrators; the Chamber would, in the absence of evidence, have to determine what conclusion the administrators might be presumed to have arrived at, or to be likely to arrive at once they considered the matter;[109] but this would not be the same thing as a determination by the Chamber of what the Chamber thought would be equitable (even though the outcome would in all probability be the same).

It is also relevant that the terms of reference of the Chamber, as defined by the Special Agreement of 16 September 1983, were to reply to the question: 'What is the line of the frontier between the Republic of the Upper Volta and the Republic of Mali in the disputed area [as defined in the Agreement]?' A reply to that question could theoretically be that, in a given portion of the area, there *was* no frontier line, because none had ever been defined. This is one of the ways in which the judicial establishment of a territorial frontier differs from the establishment of a maritime delimitation; the maritime line, being essentially a function of geographical

[106] [1986] ICJ Rep 633, para 149. [107] ibid para 150.

[108] The relevant document was not in any sense an international treaty, but merely an agreement reached by two French colonial administrators during the period of colonization.

[109] cf the explanation given by the Chamber in the *Land, Island and Maritime Frontier Dispute* of its use, failing other evidence, of 'the suitability of certain topographical features to provide an identifiable and convenient boundary', that these characteristics would have been likely to be 'a factor also with those who made the provincial boundaries prior to 1821': [1992] ICJ Rep 390, para 46.

circumstances, is bound to be theoretically complete,[110] even though some or all of it may at any given time be undetermined.[111]

The Chamber appears to have approached the matter on the very reasonable basis that the parties wanted a definite and complete line, and had impliedly authorized the Chamber to create one where none had previously existed. The Chamber, without spelling the matter out, took that authorization to be an authorization to draw the line, to the extent that it did not yet exist,[112] on a basis of fairness, ie of equity. Understood in this way, the decision does not import into the domain of land boundaries a species of equity *infra legem*, which would be inconsistent with the nature of the law in that domain.

In the case concerning the *Land, Island and Maritime Frontier Dispute*, the Chamber dealing with the case quoted from the decision in the *Frontier Dispute*, in connection with a similar problem. The boundary had, in this case also, to be settled on the basis of the *uti possidetis*, and in that context the Chamber recalled that the previous Chamber had 'emphasized that even equity *infra legem*, a recognized concept of international law, could not be resorted to in order to modify an established frontier inherited from colonization, whatever its deficiencies.'[113] In respect of part of one of the sections of frontier to be determined, the Chamber noted that 'neither side has offered any evidence whatever as to the line of the *uti possidetis juris* in this region',[114] and found that 'the line of the *uti possidetis juris* in this area is impossible to determine'.[115] There had been negotiations as long ago as 1861/1869, at which a line had been agreed *ad referendum*, but no confirmation by international treaty had ever followed. The Chamber was however able to note: 'There is nothing in the records of the 1861 and 1869 negotiations to suggest that there was any fundamental disagreement between the Parties on that line; acceptance of it however was linked to the different question whether the river Negro-Quiagara did or did not form the provincial boundary.[116] That question is resolved by the present Judgment . . . '.[117] The Chamber

[110] cf the discussion in an earlier article of the question of whether 'an objectively correct delimitation' of sea areas exists for every specific case: (1993) 64 BYIL 43–54.

[111] cf *North Sea Continental Shelf* [1969] ICJ Rep 32, para 46, citing *Monastery of Saint Naoum* (1924) PCIJ Series B, No 9, 10.

[112] An intriguing question is whether the fixing by the Court of a territorial boundary that did not previously exist involves an acquisition of territory by one or both parties: in this sense H Post, 'Adjudication as a method of acquisition of territory?' in V Lowe and M Fitzmaurice (eds), *Fifty Years of the International Court of Justice (Jennings Festschrift)* (1996) 248. This issue may however be better dealt with in the context of acquisition of territory, in a later article.

[113] [1992] ICJ Rep 396, para 58, citing [1986] ICJ Rep 633, para 149; cf also separate opinion of Judge *ad hoc* Torres Bernárdez, ibid 634, para 9. In the *Kasikili/Sedudu Island* case, Judge Weeramantry was prepared to rely on equity *infra legem* where there was no 'established frontier in the sense of a settled boundary' but the Court was settling the boundary in accordance with a treaty: [1999-II] ICJ Rep 1189–90; the Court did not however adopt this approach.

[114] [1992] ICJ Rep 513, para 261. [115] ibid 262.

[116] This was because the line was to run from an identified point to a point which, if the river was the provincial boundary, would be on that river, but otherwise would not.

[117] [1992] ICJ Rep 515, para 263.

therefore held that, following the example of the *Frontier Dispute* decision, 'it can in this case resort to the line proposed in the 1869 negotiations'; as a 'corollary' of its decision concerning the River Negro-Quiagara, 'the Chamber has no doubt that it is equitable . . . to allow the 1869 agreement to take effect on this specific point'. This was, in the Chamber's view, 'a reasonable and fair solution [une solution raisonnable et équitable] in all the circumstances'.[118]

Once again, it would theoretically have been possible for the Chamber to arrive at a sort of factual *non liquet*,[119] to the effect that in the absence of any evidence on the point it was impossible to determine where the *uti possidetis* line had been drawn.[120] In their special agreement, the parties had however specifically requested the Chamber 'to delimit the boundary line in the [specified] zones or sections',[121] so that the Chamber was entitled to suppose that they had conferred upon it the power and the obligation to do so, even in the absence of evidence of the *uti possidetis* line.

In these circumstances the idea of appealing to equity for purposes of determination of a land frontier looks less daring than might be supposed. The justification for the particular line was not a generalized sense of fairness or 'equitableness': the underlying reasoning was that if the parties in 1869 had known and agreed that the provincial boundary at the time of independence was the River Negro-Quiagara (as the Chamber found it was), they would have agreed the line resulting from the negotiations. If they had at the time concluded a binding but conditional agreement that *if* the river was the boundary, then the further line should be as it emerged from the negotiations, that agreement, after having remained in limbo for 120 years, would have been brought into force by the Chamber's ruling on the provincial boundary.[122] Thus the only use of equity was to overcome the informal and *ad referendum* nature of the 1869 line.[123]

Such an application of equity in effect transfers from the Court to the parties to the task of determining what is equitable, or what they believe

[118] [1992] ICJ Rep 514–15, para 263. For an examination of the question whether the concept of 'reasonableness' can be identified in international law in parallel with that of 'equitableness', see O Corten, 'Motif légitime et lien de causalité suffisant: un modele d'interprétation rationnel du "raisonnable"' (1998) 44 *Annuaire français* 185.

[119] See further the discussion of the concept of *non liquet*, Chapter II, Section 1 below.

[120] The Chamber noted at the outset of its judgment that the frontiers based on *uti possidetis* that come before international tribunals for decision 'are almost invariably the ones in respect of which *uti possidetis juris* speaks for once with an uncertain voice': [1992] ICJ Rep 386, para 41.

[121] Reproduced in [1992] ICJ Rep 357.

[122] In another sector of the land boundary, the Chamber took account of an agreement concluded, *ad referendum* on the side of El Salvador, in 1934; in that context it made no reference to equity, but noted that El Salvador did not ratify the agreement, but did not denounce it either; and that it defined a line that produced a clear and unambiguous boundary: [1992] ICJ Rep 422, paras 100–101.

[123] This is therefore perhaps the nearest approach in the Court's case-law to a corrective use of equity, in a situation where a strict application of the law as international agreements would have worked injustice, or at least frustrated the wishes of both States. On the corrective function, see Section (3) below.

to be equitable; it recalls the decision in the *Continental Shelf (Tunisia/Libya)* case to delimit the shelf by reference to (*inter alia*) the line dividing the actual oil concessions granted by each party, on the basis that 'the Court must take into account whatever indicia are available of the [delimitation] line or lines which the Parties themselves may have considered equitable or acted upon as such . . . '.[124]

In his dissenting opinion in the *Kasikili/Sedudu Island* case, Judge Weeramantry cited the decision in the *Frontier Dispute* case (but not the *El Salvador/Honduras* case), and applied the idea of equity to justify a finding that there was, or should be, a joint international regime between the two States (Botswana and Namibia) in the interests of environmental considerations.

> In the present case, there is no established frontier in the sense of a settled boundary. Rather, the Court is in the process of settling that boundary in accordance with the 1890 Treaty. In settling that boundary in accordance with the law, it is entitled to take equitable considerations into account so long as it does not depart from the terms of the Treaty. The equitable consideration of preserving this valuable natural resource in accordance with governing principles of environmental law does not in any way militate against the basic adherence to the terms of that Treaty which lies at the root of my conclusions.[125]

Taken out of context, the first two sentences appear contradictory; but Judge Weeramantry had earlier explained the difference, to his mind, between a boundary treaty and a treaty defining the extent of spheres of influence—which was how he saw the 1890 Treaty in question. The application of such a treaty in his view gave the Court 'greater scope for the application of equitable principles'.[126]

In practical terms, where Judge Weeramantry differed from the majority was inasmuch as the majority considered that the role of the Court was merely to establish whether, under the correct interpretation of the 1890 Treaty, the boundary between the two States passed north or south of the disputed island, not to find or direct joint exploitation for environmental reasons. The judgment did not specifically refute or respond to Judge Weeramantry's arguments, but Judge Kooijmans, in a separate opinion, expressed what would appear to be the majority view: that considerations concerning the equitable and reasonable use of shared resources:

> . . . have no place in determining the boundary between the Parties. The Court cannot relocate or shift the boundary on such grounds if according to the terms of the Treaty it must be taken to be the thalweg of the northern channel. While reflecting the rules and principles of international law, referred to in the Special Agreement, these considerations can merely focus on the undertakings of the Parties entered into in the context of their efforts to settle the dispute peacefully

[124] [1982] ICJ Rep 84, para 118; discussed under the heading of 'subjective equity' in the context of maritime delimitation in (1994) 65 BYIL 20–3.

[125] [1999-II] ICJ Rep 1189–90, para 106.

[126] ibid 1187, para 98.

and on their present and future relations. As the Court has observed: 'It is not a matter of finding simply an equitable solution, but an equitable solution derived from the applicable law' (*Fisheries Jurisdiction, I.C.J. Reports 1974*, p. 33, para. 78; p. 202, para. 69).[127]

It is submitted that Judge Kooijmans' view represents the correct approach, even in the case of a treaty settling the extent of spheres of influence. The intention of the parties in such case might theoretically have been that the precise line of the boundary should be determined in the light of various considerations, including some that might have been defined as 'equitable'. But in the first place, the Treaty did define the boundary, as following the 'main channel' of the river, and the only problem was to determine which of the two channels was meant: thus there is no room for equitable considerations.[128] Secondly, even if recourse to equity had been contemplated when the Treaty was concluded in 1890, the intertemporal principle requires research into the meaning of 'equity' or 'equitable considerations' at that time,[129] which would hardly have included the concern for the preservation of the environment which has been forced upon policy-makers in the twentieth and twenty-first centuries.

The use made of equity in the field of land frontier delimitation has thus been confined to exceptional cases; and it has been closely related to the wishes, or the presumed intentions, of the States concerned. There is no warrant in the jurisprudence for an equity of 'the Chancellor's foot',[130] or of the unfettered appreciation by the judge of the fairness of possible solutions. In the present writer's submission, this is as it should be.

An interesting example of non-application of equity where, on the basis of earlier decisions, appeal to equity might have been expected—a sort of 'incident of the dog in the night-time'[131]—is afforded by the treatment of bridges crossing a river forming an international boundary, in the recent case of the *Frontier Dispute* between Benin and Niger. The Chamber had established the course of the boundary in the River Niger, which was spanned by two bridges, some 300 metres long, constructed and maintained by the parties on an equal basis. Niger contended that the

[127] [1999-II] ICJ Rep 1189–90, 1148, para 24.

[128] Judge Fleischhauer, in a dissenting opinion, was able to invoke considerations of good faith to reject an interpretation of the 1890 Treaty that would deprive Namibia of 'an equitable share' in the only navigational use of the river ([1999-II] ICJ Rep 1204), but his argument was based on the relevance to the interpretation of the Treaty of what he saw as an error of fact at the time of its conclusion, and will be considered further under the heading of interpretation of treaties.

[129] See Chapter II, Section 3 below.

[130] Selden complained that equity varied with the conscience of each Lord Chancellor, and that this was as absurd as making the measurement known as a foot vary with each Chancellor's foot (*Table Talk*, 31b). In 1818 the then Lord Chancellor, Lord Eldon, observed that 'nothing would inflict on me greater pain, in quitting this place, than the recollection that I had done anything to justify the reproach that the equity of this place varies like the Chancellor's foot': *Gee v Pritchard* (1818) 2 Swans 402, 414.

[131] See A Conan Doyle, 'Silver Blaze' in *Memoirs of Sherlock Holmes* (1894).

boundary was therefore in the middle of the bridges. While recognizing that the structure of the bridges was the joint property of the parties, and that this solution might thus have been adopted on a basis of equity,[132] the Chamber ruled that the matter was governed by the principle that a boundary divides two areas of State sovereignty, extending *usque ad coelum et ad inferum*, so that the boundary on each bridge was vertically above the boundary in the river itself.[133]

The role of equity in recent cases involving maritime delimitation will be examined further at a later stage, in the context of the law of the sea. The development of this aspect is however perhaps summed up by the observation made by the Court in the case of the *Land and Maritime Boundary between Cameroon and Nigeria* quoted in the next section.

(3) Equity as corrective or constitutive of law[134]

In matters of maritime delimitation, it has now become established that, at least for a court or tribunal asked to indicate or effect a delimitation, the appropriate course is to establish the position of an equidistance line between the relevant coasts, and then to consider whether, and if so how, to adjust it on an 'equitable' basis. This may be expressed as taking account of 'equitable circumstances' or as a means to 'achieve an equitable result'. In the case of the *Land and Maritime Boundary between Cameroon and Nigeria* the Court stressed that 'delimiting with a concern to achieving an equitable result, as required by current international law, is not the same as delimiting in equity. The Court's jurisprudence shows that, in disputes relating to maritime delimitation, equity is not a method of delimitation, but solely an aim that should be borne in mind in effecting the delimitation.'[135]

In an earlier article, the question was examined whether this process is to be classified as an example of the 'corrective' function of equity (the view expressed by Judge Gros in the *Continental Shelf (Tunisia/Libya)* case), or rather, as urged by Judge Jiménez de Aréchaga in the same case, that: 'Equity is here nothing other than taking into account of a complex of historical and geographical circumstances, the consideration of which does not diminish justice but, on the contrary, enriches it.'[136] Subsequent decisions of the Court in the field have not explicitly contributed to this debate; but it has become increasingly difficult to see the process of

[132] cf the dictum in the case of the *Frontier Dispute (Burkina Faso/Mali)* that while equity does not necessarily imply equality, 'where there are no special circumstances, the latter is generally the best expression of the former': [1986] ICJ Rep 633, para 150.

[133] [2005] ICJ Rep para 124. *Sed quaere* whether this applies to a man-made structure spanning the boundary, where the question might be referred initially to the stated or implied intention of the parties, deduced (eg) from the agreement for equal contribution to construction and maintenance costs.

[134] See (1989) 60 BYIL 56.

[135] [2002] ICJ Rep 443, para 294.

[136] [1982] ICJ Rep 106, para 24; quoted in (1989) 60 BYIL 57–8. For the situation as at 1989, see also P Weil, *The Law of Maritime Delimitation—Reflections* (1989) particularly 159–77.

taking an equidistance line as starting point and then adapting it to the circumstances as anything other than, as suggested by Jiménez de Aréchaga, an application of the law to the facts, despite the frequent use of the label 'equitable' to refer either to the circumstances to be consulted or the result to be achieved.

That same label is now to be found in the United Nations Convention on the Law of the Sea, in Articles 74 and 83 concerning delimitation of the Exclusive Economic Zone and of the continental shelf; each of these provisions requires delimitation to be 'effected by agreement in accordance with international law... in order to achieve an equitable solution'. In the case concerning the *Land and Maritime Boundary between Cameroon and Nigeria* the Court had for the first time to apply Articles 74 and 83 as treaty-law; the process followed was, exactly as in previous cases, the establishment of an equidistance line, followed by consideration whether there were circumstances requiring adjustment of that line in order to achieve the 'equitable solution' required by the Convention. If equity was applied, then it was applied as part of the applicable treaty-law; or at least was invoked by the provisions of treaty-law, by a sort of *renvoi*. In these circumstances it becomes unrealistic in the extreme to insist on seeing the matter in terms of a corrective function of equity,[137] as something apart from 'law' and intervening only when 'law' leads to injustice.

Equity in the truly corrective sense must be something that is only required in unusual cases, where the law is inadequate to ensure justice. In the particular context of maritime delimitation, this would imply that strict application of the equidistance line would be the 'normal' solution, adjustment only being necessary in exceptional circumstances.[138] In the *Cameroon/Nigeria* case, the Court did eventually conclude in favour of an equidistance line; but the sequence of reasoning that led it to that conclusion followed the classic pattern of a *provisional* adoption of an equidistance line,[139] coupled from the outset with an assumption that there might well be circumstances requiring its modification in order to reach the 'equitable solution' envisaged by the United Nations Convention.[140]

[137] Tanaka ('Reflections on Maritime Delimitation in the *Cameroon/Nigeria* case' (2004) 53 ICLQ 376) refers to it as 'the corrective-equity approach', but it appears he means merely that the operation is a two-stage one.

[138] It is of course true that delimitations which are submitted for judicial settlement may well be *ex definitione* cases of exceptional circumstances, and that they are not therefore truly representative of the general practice of inter-State delimitation. It is suggested however that this does not invalidate the point here being made.

[139] The Court in the *Cameroon/Nigeria* case quoted with approval from the case of *Maritime Delimitation in the Area between Greenland and Jan Mayen*, and from the case of *Maritime Delimitation and Territorial Questions between Qatar and Bahrain*, each of which referred to the 'provisional' drawing of an equidistance line: [2002] ICJ Rep 441, 442, para 289, quoting [1993] ICJ Rep 61, para 51 and [2001] ICJ Rep 111, para 230.

[140] cf [2002] ICJ Rep 440, para 285.

[(4) Why equity?]

4. Application of certain general legal maxims[141]

(1) The possession of rights involves the performance of the corresponding obligations[142]

As was noted in the 1989 article, an elaboration of this doctrine outside the field of treaty-law 'would probably be of little practical impact';[143] the reason is that, while in a treaty the relationship between a specific right conferred and a specific obligation incurred derives directly from the treaty, customary law rights and obligations are in principle universal, so that it is difficult to identify a right as attached to a particular obligation such as to condition its exercise. Thus the maxim reduces to a question of status: any entity that is a subject of international law *ipso facto* has the rights, and is bound by the obligations, of customary international law. This was well brought out by Judge Higgins in her separate opinion in the *Wall* case, in which Palestine had been admitted to participate, without thereby being recognized as a 'State'. Judge Higgins disagreed with the Court's finding that self-defence could not be invoked by Israel against a threat emanating from the Occupied Palestinian Territory: 'Palestine cannot be sufficiently an international entity to be invited to these proceedings, but not sufficiently an international entity for the prohibition of armed attack on others to be applicable.'[144]

At the least, the most evident application of the maxim is in the treaty-law context. It is self-evident that a State which has not, by acceding to a treaty, become bound by its obligations, cannot rely on the rights conferred by the treaty; the Court did however spell this out in the *North Sea Continental Shelf* case, in response to the argument that Germany had by conduct accepted the delimitation provisions of the 1958 Geneva Convention.[145] As between parties to a bilateral treaty, the maxim is embodied in the *exceptio non adimpleti contractus*, where the 'consideration' (to use a common-law term)[146] for the obligation of each party is the performance by the other of its treaty obligation. Two recent cases

[141] (1989) 60 BYIL 62–76. [142] ibid 62–3. [143] ibid 63

[144] *Legal Consequences of the Construction of a Wall in the Occupied Palestinian Territory* [2004] ICJ Rep 215, para 34. Note also the argument of Judge Oda in *Certain Phosphate Lands in Nauru* that Nauru, by failing to rehabilitate the phosphate lands it had itself worked, had 'disqualified itself from pursuing any allegation of Australian responsibility for the rehabilitation of lands which Australia worked during the Trusteeship period', as a matter of 'good faith': [1992] ICJ Rep 324, para 29.

[145] [1969] ICJ Rep 25–6, para 28; see the writer's comments in (1989) 60 BYIL 74. Note also that the idea of mutually related rights and obligations is also reflected, *a contrario*, in the rule of the Vienna Convention that if a non-party State would not incur obligations, but only enjoy rights, under the treaty—a *pactum in favorem tertii*—acceptance of the treaty provision may be presumed: see Vienna Convention on the Law of Treaties, Art 36 (1).

[146] For its relevance in the context of treaty-law, see (1992) 63 BYIL 16.

have however involved an examination of the application of this or a parallel doctrine to the case of a multilateral convention, *in casu* the Vienna Convention on Consular Relations. In each case the United States, which had been accused of failing to ensure that foreign nationals enjoyed the rights, guaranteed by the Convention, of contact with their consulate when arrested and charged with criminal offences, relied *inter alia* on the defence that the practice of the applicant State was no more in conformity with the Convention than that attributed to the United States.

In the *LaGrand* case, this argument took the form of an objection that 'Germany's submissions are inadmissible on the ground that Germany seeks to have a standard applied to the United States that is different from its own practice.'[147] This could be read as an argument as to the interpretation of the Convention: that Germany had showed, by the way in which it purportedly complied with the Convention, that it interpreted the Convention's requirements as less exigent than alleged in its claim against the United States.[148] This would however raise the question of what was the correct interpretation of the text: if the more rigorous standards that Germany sought to impose on the United States flowed from a correct interpretation of the Convention, a less rigorous application by Germany itself could, at most, raise considerations of estoppel. Furthermore, there are difficulties in applying the concept of estoppel to questions of international law (as distinct from questions of fact); these were adverted to in the 1989 article in this series.[149]

During the oral proceedings, counsel for the United States denied that it was invoking a defence of *tu quoque*: however, in addition to the question of interpretation, the United States argued that 'basic principles of administration of justice and equality of the parties require that both litigants in these proceedings be accountable to the same rules of international law. It would be against such principles of international law to apply against the United States alleged rules that Germany appears not to accept for itself.'[150] The emphasis is thus placed on applicable rules of law, rather than the specific obligations deriving from those rules; but the resemblance of this contention to the principle identified by Fitzmaurice, and stated above, will be apparent.

The Court disposed of the matter on the basis that 'the evidence adduced by the United States does not justify the conclusion that Germany's own practice fails to conform to the standards it demands from the United States',[151] and thus left the question of principle unresolved. However in the subsequent case of *Avena and other Mexican Nationals*, the United States argued the inadmissibility of the claim

[147] [2001] ICJ Rep 488, para 61.

[148] The United States Counter-Memorial in fact presents the matter solely as one of interpretation of the Convention shown by 'State practice including Germany's own practice' (Heading to Part V, Chapter III).

[149] (1989) 60 BYIL 38–43.

[150] CR 2000/28, para 3.48 (Mr Mathias), quoted in [2001] ICJ Rep 488, para 61.

[151] [2001] ICJ Rep 489, para 63.

presented by Mexico on the same basis as it had contended for in the *LaGrand* case. The Court on this occasion found it unnecessary to examine the substance of the allegation that Mexico's practice as regards consular notification also fell short of the standards of the Convention; it disposed of the matter by pointing out the inappropriateness of applying the *exceptio non adimpleti contractus* to a multilateral convention of the legislative kind:

> The Court would recall that it is in any event essential to have in mind the nature of the Vienna Convention. It lays down certain standards to be observed by all States parties, with a view to the 'unimpeded conduct of consular relations', which, as the Court observed in 1979, is important in present-day international law 'in promoting the development of friendly relations among nations, and ensuring protection and assistance for aliens resident in the territories of other States' (*United States Diplomatic and Consular Staff in Tehran (United States of America* v. *Iran), Order of 15 December 1979, I.C.J. Reports 1979*, pp. 19–20, para. 40). Even if it were shown, therefore, that Mexico's practice as regards the application of Article 36 was not beyond reproach, this would not constitute a ground of objection to the admissibility of Mexico's claim.[152]

This finding is somewhat elliptical. It is surely not the *importance* of consular relations that renders the United States objection inappropriate, but the fact that those relations constitute a general regime for the benefit of all. It may not be too much to say that the relevance of the nature of the Convention is that, as the Court observed of the Genocide Convention in the *Reservations* case: 'In such a convention the contracting States do not have any interests of their own; they merely have, one and all, a common interest, namely the accomplishment of those high purposes which are the *raison d'être* of the convention.'[153] Certainly each State has, as an 'interest of its own', a desire that its own nationals shall enjoy the fullest consular protection in the territories of the other contracting States, but this is achieved, not so much by a network of bilateral acceptances as by adhering to a universal regime. If it were accepted that a failure by Mexico to ensure, with sufficient consistency, consular protection for US nationals constituted an excuse for negligent performance by the US authorities of the obligations of the Convention, it would be difficult not to conclude that such failure could constitute a ground for the United States deliberately to *refuse* such protection to Mexican nationals. This would undermine the universal regime of the Convention, in which performance by each State of its obligations is not simply the consideration, the *contrepartie*, for its entitlement to assert the obligations resting on other contracting States.

Appeal was made to this principle, that the possession of rights involves the performance of the corresponding obligations, by Judge *ad hoc* Torres Bernárdez in his dissenting opinion in the *Fisheries Jurisdiction* case

[152] [2004] ICJ Rep 38, para 47. [153] [1951] ICJ Rep 23.

between Spain and Canada, in order to deduce the invalidity of the reservation made by Canada to its optional-clause declaration.

The question was whether, in proceedings instituted by Spain arising out of the arrest by Canada of a Spanish fishing vessel, Canada could invoke a reservation attached to its optional-clause declaration excluding 'disputes arising out of or concerning conservation and management measures taken by Canada' in an area allegedly forming part of the high seas. Judge Torres Bernárdez starts from the premise that if States wish to become parties to the Charter and the Statute of the Court (or to deposit an optional-clause declaration), 'This entails both rights and obligations for them', and continues with the indisputable premise that 'It is therefore contrary to the most elementary principles, including that of good faith, subsequently to invoke those rights while ignoring the obligations assumed.'[154] From this he concludes that the reservation attached by Canada to its optional clause, which he regards as intended to enable Canada to violate international law, and as such 'contrary to the Statute', can be disregarded by the Court.

It is however very difficult to see how the principle cited applies to the facts of the case. The 'right' invoked by Canada is presumably the right to deposit a declaration, or possibly the right to attach reservations to such a declaration. But what is the obligation that Canada is ignoring? The obligation at the centre of the case on the merits, the alleged obligation not to exercise fisheries jurisdiction in the area referred to in the declaration, is not an obligation attaching in any way to the right. It is on the other hand somewhat artificial to say that the right to deposit a declaration with reservations entails an obligation not to attach any reservation that is contrary to the Statute. If the reservation is invalid on that ground, that is all that needs to be said. If an act is invalid or legally ineffective, Ockham's razor shears away the idea of an obligation not to perform that act. For this reason, Judge Torres Bernárdez's argument on this point is unconvincing.

(2) Pacta tertiis nec nocent nec prosunt[155]

This principle is so well established that there has been no need for the Court to declare it, though it has sometime been alluded to in argument.[156] In the field of State succession to treaties, the question of succession amounts to determining whether the alleged successor State is a third State, or to be equated with the original party: if there has been no succession, then the treaty neither binds nor benefits the new State, in

[154] [1998] ICJ Rep 634, para 135. [155] (1989) 60 BYIL 63.

[156] eg, in the case of the *Land and Maritime Boundary between Cameroon and Nigeria* Equatorial Guinea, as intervening State, drew attention to a 2000 Treaty between itself and Nigeria delimiting a maritime boundary, and 'recognize[d] that the Treaty cannot be binding on Cameroon (*res inter alios acta*)' but also 'contend[ed] that, equally, Cameroon cannot seek to benefit from it': [2002] ICJ Rep 440, para 284.

application of the basic principle.[157] However in the *Gabčíkovo/Nagymaros Project* case, the Court reserved the question of succession, namely whether Slovakia was a successor State in respect of the 1977 Treaty between Czechoslovakia and Hungary, until a late stage of its judgment. The question was dealt with in the context of the determination of the legal consequences of its findings on the legality of the acts of each of the parties to the Treaty; yet not only did the Special Agreement recite that the Slovak Republic was 'the sole successor State' of Czechoslovakia 'in respect of rights and obligations relating to' the Project, but also it is not apparent what legal interest Slovakia could have in a decision of the Court on the performance of a treaty to which it was not a party.[158]

In the previous article on this subject,[159] note was taken of the Court's handling of the problem of the possible impact of its judgment in a case on third parties, particularly in respect of delimitation of land or maritime boundaries, and specifically the argument in the judgment in the *Frontier Dispute* case between Burkina Faso and Mali that assimilated the Court's decision to an agreement between the parties to the case, so that the *pacta tertiis* rule would protect third States.[160] This is a problem that has continued to arise, in particular in the field of maritime delimitation.

In the case of the *Land and Maritime Boundary between Cameroon and Nigeria*, the maritime boundary had to be drawn in an area where Equatorial Guinea (which had intervened in the case as a non-party) and São Tomé and Príncipe would also have entitlements. The Court was also asked to draw a boundary between the sovereignties of the parties in Lake Chad, which involved consideration of the possible rights of Chad.

In the course of the proceedings, the first issue of this kind to arise was the relevance of the interests of a third State in the delimitation in Lake Chad. Nigeria submitted a preliminary objection contending that the Court should not determine the boundary in Lake Chad 'to the extent that the boundary constitutes or is constituted by the tripoint in the Lake',[161] that is to say the point of convergence of the Cameroon/Chad boundary (already delimited by agreement), the Chad/Nigeria boundary (undetermined) and the Cameroon/Nigeria boundary (to be determined). Nigeria contended that the legal interests of Chad would be affected by the determination of the tripoint.

157 Note however the apparent distinction, between survival of the treaty and survival of the rights and obligations under the treaty, drawn by the ILC and commented on in the *Gabčíkovo/Nagymaros Project* case: [1997] ICJ Rep 72, para 123.

158 In this, the Court appears to have been following the logic of the Hungarian submissions, which invited the Court to make various findings as to the conduct of the parties to the Treaty, and then to declare 'that the legal consequences of these findings and of the evidence and argument presented to the Court are . . . that the Treaty . . . has never been in force between the Republic of Hungary and the Slovak Republic . . . ': [1997] ICJ Rep 15, para 13. The pleadings in the case are unfortunately not available in printed form or online.

159 (1989) 60 BYIL 63–71.

160 [1986] ICJ Rep 577–8, para 46; [1989] BYIL 64.

161 Quoted in [1998] ICJ Rep 309, para 74.

The Court handled the matter as one of propriety of exercise of jurisdiction, citing the decision in the case of *Monetary Gold Removed from Rome in 1943*,[162] rather than as a question of the permissible extent of a delimitation, on the lines of the *Frontier Dispute (Burkina Faso/Mali)* case for a territorial delimitation, or the case concerning the *Continental Shelf (Libya/Malta)*. It noted that the Cameroon/Chad boundary was not disputed by Cameroon or Nigeria, and deduced that:

> Any redefinition of the point where the frontier between Cameroon and Nigeria meets the Chad-Cameroon frontier could in the circumstances only lead to a moving of the tripoint along the line of the frontier in the Lake between Chad and Cameroon. Thus the legal interests of Chad as a third State not party to the case do not constitute the very subject-matter of the judgment to be rendered on the merits of Cameroon's Application; and therefore the absence of Chad does not prevent the Court from proceeding to a specification of the border between Cameroon and Nigeria in the Lake.[163]

The same result might have been attained by following the *Frontier Dispute (Burkina Faso/Mali)* decision; the Court however chose to distinguish that decision on the ground that in that case 'the relevant part of the boundary of Niger at that time was not delimited'.[164] In the *Frontier Dispute* the Chamber drew a distinction, as regards the problem of third States' interests, between cases of territorial frontier delimitations and cases of delimitation of maritime boundaries.[165] Into which category does the delimitation of a lake boundary fall? Applying the criteria indicated in the *Frontier Dispute* decision, it would seem that a lake boundary should be treated in the same way as a land boundary, since there is no legal relationship between the boundary between one pair of States, and the boundary between a different pair (even if there is one common partner), nor does the one boundary have a legal impact on the other. Territorial boundaries result essentially from agreement or from historic events (occupation in particular), while the limits of sovereign rights over submarine areas are a function of the geography of the region, translated into terms of the 'equitable'. As the *Frontier Dispute* Chamber explained: 'It follows that a court dealing with a request for the delimitation of a continental shelf must decline, even if so authorized by the disputant parties, to rule upon rights relating to areas in which third States may have such claims as may contradict the legal considerations—especially in regard to equitable principles—which would have formed the basis of the decision.'[166] A court dealing with a territorial dispute, including (it

[162] [1954] ICJ Rep 32.

[163] [1998] ICJ Rep 312, para 79. Judge Parra-Aranguren dissented on this point, because he considered that the Court could not, at the preliminary objection stage of the proceedings, determine whether or not the interest of Chad would be 'affected' by a possible, unknown, alteration of the position of the tripoint: ibid 351–2.

[164] ibid 313, para 81.

[165] [1986] ICJ Rep 578, para 47, discussed in the earlier article at (1990) 61 BYIL 65–6.

[166] [1986] ICJ Rep 578, para 47.

seems) one involving a lake boundary, is under no such obligation of restraint.

The decision on the lake boundary invoked the precedent of the decision in the *Territorial Dispute* between Libya and Chad, in which the boundary line found by the Court terminated at each end where it met the frontier of a third State, Niger to the west and Sudan to the east. In that case, the Court made no specific reference whatever to the validity of the endpoints *vis-à-vis* the neighbouring States. It should however perhaps be noted that in that case the Court did not have to consider the question of the extent of the line at a preliminary objection stage, but at the merits stage, when it had satisfied itself as to the position of the line on the basis of international instruments to which Libya and Chad were successors. In the *Cameroon/Nigeria* case, it had to deal with the question without knowing either where the line as a whole would prove to be, or what were the legal considerations on which it would be based. The Court treated the Cameroon/Chad boundary as an established legality simply on the basis of its recognition by all three States.

The maritime delimitation between Cameroon and Nigeria has already been discussed in the previous article in the context of an examination of intervention under Article 62 of the Statute of the Court.[167] The case however merits examination here, even at the risk of some repetition.

Two States not parties to the proceedings had claims over maritime areas in the region: Equatorial Guinea and São Tomé and Príncipe. As regards São Tomé and Príncipe, the Court had before it no evidence as to what its rights in the area might be, nor even as to what its claims were; it might be a simple matter to establish the extent of those claims from public documents, but would the Court be entitled to take 'judicial notice' thereof?[168] Equatorial Guinea had intervened (as a non-party), and asserted that the 'equitable line' claimed by Cameroon 'falls within the maritime area claimed by Equatorial Guinea'.[169] On the law, it contended that tribunals are bound to refrain from 'making an award which in any way presumes territory to belong to a State before the Court when it is *claimed* by a third State not party to the case before the Court',[170] the only exception being 'where the third-State claim is not known to the Court, or is so patently absurd or ill-founded as to be disregarded.'[171]

[167] (2004) 75 BYIL 48–53, 60–1.

[168] The distinction between a judge's personal knowledge, and the knowledge he derives in the exercise of his functions, is at least as old as Aquinas: 'judicare pertinet ad judicem, secundum quod fungitur publica potestae; et ideo informari debet in judicando non secundum id, quod ipse novit tamquam privata persona: sed secundum id, quod sibi innotescit tamquam personae publicae . . . ': thus in principle, on questions of fact, the judge may only take account of matters proved in evidence. Personal knowledge may at most put the judge on notice of possible defects in the evidence before him, which he may investigate: *Summa theologica*, II-II, 63.1.

[169] Written Statement of Equatorial Guinea, I.B.

[170] ibid 17–18, para 42 (emphasis added).

[171] ibid 18, para 44. It may be difficult to determine the limits of this exception, but probably the Court could, when in doubt, opt to refrain from deciding anything prejudicial to the third-State claim.

The Court treated the interests of the two third States, Equatorial Guinea and São Tomé and Príncipe, in the maritime areas off the coasts of the four States in essentially the same way as it had treated the interests of Italy in the case of the *Continental Shelf (Libya/Malta)*, but with one striking difference. The Court held that 'it [could] not rule on Cameroon's claims in so far as they might affect rights of Equatorial Guinea and Sao Tome and Principe'.[172] It based this approach on the finding that 'in the case of maritime delimitations where the maritime areas of several States are involved, the protection afforded by Article 59 of the Statute may not always be sufficient', and that in the particular case Article 59 'may not sufficiently protect' the third States 'from the effects—even if only indirect—of a judgment affecting their legal rights'.[173] In the *Libya/Malta* case, however, it indicated that: 'The limits within which the Court, in order to preserve the rights of third States, will confine its decision in the present case, may thus be defined by the *claims* of Italy.'[174]

The language used in the *Cameroon/Nigeria* case skates over the problem rather than resolving it. The whole difficulty of the situation is that, as the Court itself stated, it cannot 'decide upon legal rights of third States not parties to these proceedings'; but how therefore can the Court ascertain, and use as a basis for its reasoning, the fact that 'the maritime areas *of* several States [ie areas over which those States enjoy sovereign rights] are involved'? All that it knows is that third States *claim* certain areas: in the *Libya/Malta* case the Court was careful to indicate that it was limiting the scope of its decision 'to a geographical area in which no such *claims* exist'.[175] The Court in 2002 made the dilemma more acute for itself by trying to protect the third States from the effects of a judgment 'affecting their legal rights', without knowing what these rights might be, and therefore how they might be affected.

Even where the decision is limited to areas unclaimed by third States, there remains a difficulty, and in the *Libya/Malta* case the Court tackled this difficulty head-on:

> It has been questioned whether it is right that a third State—in this case, Italy—should be enabled, by virtue of its claims, to restrict the scope of a judgment requested of the Court by Malta and Libya; and it may also be argued that this approach would have prevented the Court from giving any judgment at all if Italy had advanced more ambitious claims.[176]

The Court's response to this was to emphasize two special features of the case before it: first, that neither party had suggested that Italy's claims

[172] [2002] ICJ Rep 421, para 238. The Court however added a rather mysterious qualification: 'Nonetheless, the mere presence of those two States, whose rights might be affected by the decision of the Court, does not in itself preclude the Court from having jurisdiction over a maritime delimitation between the Parties to the case before it, namely Cameroon and Nigeria, although it must remain mindful, as always in situations of this kind, of the limitations on its jurisdiction that such presence imposes.'

[173] ibid.

[174] [1985] ICJ Rep 26, para 22.

[175] ibid 25, para 21.

[176] ibid 28, para 23.

were unreasonable; and secondly that, by opposing Italy's attempt to intervene in the case to defend its interests, the parties had accepted in advance 'the probability of the Court's judgment being restricted in scope as a consequence of the Italian claims'.[177] Neither circumstance was present in the *Cameroon/Nigeria* case.[178]

It is also strange to find the Court doubting the efficacity of Article 59 of the Statute. That Article applies to a decision of the Court a well-established and necessary principle of law, *pacta tertiis nec nocent nec prosunt*. Particularly in the case of a court which derives its jurisdiction from consent, and in a legal system in which, as the Permanent Court observed, recourse to judicial settlement is no more than a substitute for direct settlement,[179] it is clear that two States cannot obtain from the Court a decision which gives them rights against a third State that they could not have conferred on themselves by agreement between them. How then did the Court consider that its decision in the *Cameroon/Nigeria* case could 'affect [the] legal rights' of Equatorial Guinea and of São Tomé and Príncipe?

[(3) Approbation and reprobation]

[(4) States will be presumed to use the most appropriate means of creating rights and obligations]

Chapter II: International Rights and Obligations

1. The completeness of the law and the nature of legal rights: International law as constitutive or regulatory of such rights

(1) Lacunae *in the law and the question of* non-liquet

> The law is the true embodiment/Of everything that's excellent:/It has no kind of fault nor flaw . . .
>
> WS Gilbert, *Patience*

Since the publication of the earlier article dealing (*inter alia*) with the question,[180] attention has once again been focused on the problem of *non liquet* as a result of a finding by the Court, in its advisory opinion on the *Legality of the Threat or Use of Nuclear Weapons*, a finding which has been regarded by some Members of the Court and by some commentators as a *non liquet*. Before examining that decision, some instances may be noted of apparent *lacunae* in the law to be applied in other cases, and how these have been handled.

[177] ibid.

[178] Cameroon did raise the argument mentioned in the *Libya/Malta* case of the effect of unreasonable claims by the third State: see [2002] ICJ Rep 420, para 235 *in fine*.

[179] PCIJ Series A, No 22, 13.

[180] (1989) 60 BYIL 77–84. The fullest treatment in English of the concept of *non liquet* is still that of GG Fitzmaurice, 'The problem of *non liquet*: Prologomena to a restatement' in *Mélanges offerts à*

(a) *Lacunae* in a treaty

In principle, insofar as the relations between the parties to a treaty are not governed by the treaty, either because that was their avowed intention or because the point was overlooked in the drafting, customary law operates as the default solution to regulate those relations, so that normally no question of *non liquet* arises. In practice, however, situations may arise in which this solution is less evident.[181]

In the case of the *Arbitral Award of 31 July 1989*, the parties had agreed to submit two questions to arbitration, but the second was only to be determined by the arbitrators 'in the event of a negative answer to the first question'.[182] An affirmative answer to the first question would, it was contemplated, result in a complete maritime delimitation in the disputed area. The Court noted that 'No agreement had been reached between the Parties as to what should happen in the event of an affirmative answer leading only to a partial delimitation, and as to what might be the task of the Tribunal in such case.' The Tribunal's solution was to apply a rule of strict construction to the Arbitration Agreement; it held in effect that it was *only* in the event of an entirely negative answer to the first question that it was empowered to answer the second.[183] The Court approved this approach: as it pointed out, the parties could, had they wished, have used 'some such expression as that the Tribunal should answer the second question "taking into account" the reply given to the first, but they did not'.[184] However the solution adopted by the Tribunal could in itself be regarded as the application of the customary rule *extra compromissum arbiter nihil facere potest*, and it was the existence of this rule that enabled a *non liquet* to be avoided.

A more complicated problem arose in the case of the *Gabčíkovo/Nagymaros Project* between Hungary and Slovakia. The parties had concluded a

Charles Rousseau (1974) 89. For a full-length study however, see U Fastenrath, *Lücken im Völkerrecht* (1991) esp 272ff. See also J Salmon, 'Quelques observations sur les lacunes du droit international public'[1967] *Revue Belge de droit international* 440, and 'Le droit international à l'épreuve au tournant du XXIème siècle' [2002] *Bancaja Euromediterranean Courses of International Law* 82.

[181] For an early example of the view that insufficiency of a treaty provision may require a *non liquet*, see the dissenting opinion of Judge Huber in the case of the *Rights of Minorities in Upper Silesia*. He took the view that 'the contentions of the two Parties in regard to the interpretation of' certain disputed articles of a treaty 'are neither supported by nor in opposition to the provisions of' those texts (PCIJ Series A, No 15, 54–5), and that therefore 'a *non liquet* is indicated' (ibid 54). In the same case, the majority judgment noted that a particular treaty (not the treaty to which Judge Huber was referring), for the protection of minorities, 'does not specifically state what persons belong to a minority', but refused to infer 'that there exists a gap (*lacune*) which must necessarily be filled by subsequent stipulations'. The question was whether a claim to treatment as a member of a linguistic minority in accordance with the treaty provisions had to be based on the facts of the individual case (objective principle), or merely upon the declaration of the interested person as to his own view of his status (subjective principle). The Court upheld the objective view, essentially in application to the treaty of the principle of effectiveness: see ibid 32–3.

[182] Arbitration Agreement, Art 2(2), quoted in [1991] ICJ Rep 58, para 14.

[183] Just to complicate matters further, the President of the Tribunal, while voting for this solution, appended a declaration to the Award advancing the view that a partially negative reply to the first question conferred a partial competence to answer the second; how he reconciled this with his vote on the Award is unclear.

[184] [1991] ICJ Rep 70, para 51.

Treaty in 1977 providing for the carrying out of this hydro-electric project; as the Court found, they had each of them committed breaches of the Treaty, and its implementation in the form originally envisaged had become impossible, in particular because Czechoslovakia's breach of the Treaty had been constituted by the putting into operation of a variant of the original project, without the consent of Hungary.[185] The Court could have found that the effect of the mutual breaches was to put an end to the Treaty, and left the law of State responsibility to clear up the resulting legal confusion. In fact however, it found that the Treaty, though battered almost beyond recognition, was still in existence,[186] so that the parties remained bound to execute it. It is hardly surprising that the Treaty had made no provision for the eventuality of breaches of the kind that had been perpetrated: so that it might be objected that there was no 'law of the Treaty' which could be applied. This could be regarded *pro rata*, as far as treaty-law was concerned, as a sort of *non liquet*.[187]

The Court's solution was to require that: 'the factual situation as it has developed since 1989 shall be placed within the context of the preserved *and developing* treaty relationship, in order to achieve its object and purpose in so far as that is feasible. For it is only then that the irregular state of affairs which exists as a result of the failure of both Parties to comply with their treaty obligations can be remedied.'[188] As a result, 'the Parties are under a legal obligation . . . to consider, within the context of the 1977 Treaty, in what way the multiple objectives of the Treaty can best be served, keeping in mind that all of them should be fulfilled.'[189]

Despite the reference to the treaty relationship as 'developing', which implies a process occurring of itself, without the need for an input from the parties, this may be read as a directive to the parties to go away and write a new treaty to fulfil the purposes of the old. This aspect will be re-examined at a later stage (in the context of the Court's jurisprudence on the operation and termination of treaties); for the present, what is striking is that the Court was not prepared, in this specific and complex case, to say either that where the treaty is silent, general international law intervenes,[190] or that the result of such a *lacuna* in treaty law must be a *non liquet*.

[185] [1998] ICJ Rep 54, para 78.

[186] ibid 76, para 132.

[187] Fitzmaurice, in his 1974 article (n 180 above), appears to have contemplated the possibility that a tribunal might be empowered to decide an issue solely on the basis of a particular treaty, and might find that the treaty did not make any provision for that issue. In that case, he suggested, the tribunal could not give a decision, but this would not be a *non liquet* because 'the negative result springs from the request or action of the parties, rather than from the attitude of the tribunal itself . . . ': ibid 95.

[188] [1998] ICJ Rep 54, para 133 (emphasis added).

[189] ibid 77, para 139.

[190] cf the comments of Fitzmaurice on Lauterpacht's view, in the *Frontier Land* case, that provisions in a treaty instrument should be held 'void and inapplicable on account of uncertainty and unresolved discrepancy': [1959] ICJ Rep 231. As Fitzmaurice observes, this was not to be equated with a *non liquet*: 'a finding that a treaty must be regarded as void is a legal finding, and no *non liquet* is involved': *Collected Edition*, vol II, 838.

(b) *Lacunae* in general (customary) law

In the case concerning *Maritime Delimitation and Territorial Questions between Bahrain and Qatar*,[191] the Court was enabled to avoid a *non liquet* by (in effect) rejecting the claims of both sides. The problem was the status and relevance for maritime delimitation of a low-tide elevation called Fasht ad-Dibal. Because of the closeness to each other of the coasts of the two parties, the low-tide elevation lay within the 12-mile territorial sea limit of both States. This in itself was not a problem: the Court indicated that in such case 'both States in principle are entitled to use its low-water line for measuring the breadth of their territorial sea', and that in consequence the competing rights of the two States 'would by necessity seem to neutralize each other'.[192] The difficulty was that Bahrain contended that any *effectivités* showing a superior title to Fasht ad-Dibal as territory would override this general rule, and claimed Fasht ad-Dibal as its territory on the basis of its 'display of sovereign authority'.[193] The Court considered that 'Whether this claim by Bahrain is well-founded depends upon the answer to the question whether low-tide elevations are territory and can be appropriated in conformity with the rules and principles of territorial acquisition.'[194] It continued: 'International treaty law is silent on the question whether low-tide elevations can be considered to be "territory". Nor is the Court aware of a uniform and widespread State practice which might have given rise to a customary rule which unequivocally permits or excludes appropriation of low-tide elevations.'[195] The conundrum seemed insoluble, unless by the application of the *SS Lotus* rule, discussed below, that everything that is not forbidden in international law is permitted, so that the purported appropriation of Fasht ad-Dibal by Bahrain would be recognized as valid, despite the lack of State practice in relation to low-tide elevations.

In brief, the Court resolved the matter by deciding that whatever the position 'in principle' (see the quotation above), it could be deduced from the established difference in treatment of islands and low-tide elevations in international law that neither party could use as a baseline a low-tide elevation within the 'zone of overlapping claims'. This was a decision derived from the customary law of the sea (despite the Court's general statement as to the lack of such rules), and enabled the Court to leave unsettled the problem whether such an elevation is 'territory' capable of acquisition—a matter of the law governing land territory.

Turning now to the case concerning the *Legality of the Threat or Use of Nuclear Weapons*, the passage that has been seen as a *non liquet* is paragraph 2(E) of the operative clause of the advisory opinion. After first indicating that 'the threat or use of nuclear weapons would generally be

[191] The applicable law was not treaty-law, ie the United Nations Convention on the Law of the Sea, as Qatar was not a party to that Convention; but the parties to the case agreed, and the Court accepted, that 'most of the provisions of the 1982 Convention which are relevant for the present case reflect customary law': [2001] ICJ Rep 91, para 167.

[192] [2001] ICJ Rep 101, para 202.

[193] ibid para 203.

[194] ibid para 204.

[195] ibid 101–2, para 205.

contrary to the rules of international law applicable in armed conflict, and in particular the principles and rules of humanitarian law', the Court went on to state that it could not 'conclude definitively whether the threat or use of nuclear weapons would be lawful or unlawful in an extreme circumstance of self-defence, in which the very survival of the State would be at stake'.[196] Commentators—and indeed the Members of the Court—are divided on whether or not this is in fact a finding of *non liquet* in the proper sense of the term.

In itself, the term means no more than that 'it is not clear', so that it is not possible to give a decision;[197] but the traditionally accepted interpretation is that the expression applies to the situation in which this impossibility results from the absence or insufficiency of legal rules applicable to the matter in dispute. On this interpretation, it would not cover a case in which the judge found that there was a clear rule of law, but lacked factual evidence to show whether or not that rule applied to the case in hand. Thus the French *Code civil* has from the outset prohibited judges from refusing to decide a case 'on the pretext that the law is silent, obscure or insufficient',[198] and this is generally cited as an example of a prohibition of a *non liquet*. The Code has however nothing to say about situations where the law is clear, but the facts are obscure or even indeterminable.[199]

It may be noted at the outset that the fact that the Court was engaged in giving an advisory opinion, not giving judgment in a contentious case, somewhat alters the parameters of the problem. It was observed in the earlier article that it is necessary to distinguish the absence of a rule on a specific point in a given field of law from the existence of a rule of law that there is no right of action in that respect conferred by the law in that

[196] [1996-I] ICJ Rep 266, para 105(2)(E).

[197] An alternative definition that has been advanced is that 'There is a *non liquet* when a Court declines to render justice' (P-M Dupuy, 'Between the Individual and the State: International Law at a Crossroads?' in L Boisson de Chazournes and P Sands (eds), *International Law, the International Court of Justice and Nuclear Weapons* (1999) 451). This definition however seems to lack what is generally regarded as the key element: refusal to decide on the ground that there is no clear law on the point. Dupuy appears to reach the surprising conclusion that para 105(2)(i) of the advisory opinion is not a *non liquet* because the opinion *as a whole* has introduced some clarification in the law. See also ibid 458, 459. Another view is that of Salmon, that 'Le champ d'application du *non liquet* est plus vaste que celui des lacunes, car on entend par "non liquet" l'impossibilité pour le juge compétent en l'espèce de statuter sur le fond d'une affaire—par ailleurs recevable—non seulement à cause d'une insuffisance d'information sur les faits ou faute de base suffisante relative au droit en vigueur entre les parties pour prendre une décision, mais encore parce que ce qui lui est demandé semble dépasser sa fonction judiciaire': 'Le droit international a l'épreuve au tournant du XXIème siècle' [2002] *Bancaja Euromediterranean Courses of International Law* 82.

[198] *Code civil*, art 4: 'Le juge qui refusera de juger, sous prétexte du silence, de l'obscurité ou de l'insuffisance de la loi, pourra être poursuivi comme coupable de déni de justice'. cf also the ILC Model Rules on Arbitral Procedure, Art 11; the Washington Convention on the Settlement of Investment Disputes between States and Nationals of Other States, Art 42(2).

[199] D Bodansky has expressed this distinction as that between an 'ontological *non liquet*', the lack of any rule in the applicable legal system, and an 'epistemological *non liquet*' where 'the law [lacks] sufficiently rich rules of reasoning to permit a court to answer every question': '*Non liquet* and the incompleteness of international law', in Boisson de Chazournes and Sands (eds) (n 197 above) 154–5.

field.[200] As was there noted, the Court in the *Barcelona Traction* case decided that in the circumstances of the case Belgium had no right of action in international law; it did not decline to answer the question whether such a right existed on the ground that there was no legal rule on the point. On the basis of the principle that *onus probandi incumbit actori*, in a contentious case that Court can simply find that the applicant has not proved his case, and dismiss the claim.[201] This is not however a course of action open to the Court in replying to a request for advisory opinion.[202] There are no parties on whom rests a burden of proving their contentions: States taking part in the proceedings do no more than 'furnish information'. The Court has, if necessary unaided,[203] to say what the law is on the question submitted to it.[204] On the other hand, the Court is not under an obligation to give an advisory opinion, as it is obliged (in principle) to give judgment in a contentious case: the power of the Court to decline to give an opinion is well established.[205]

Before pursuing the theoretical debate, let us consider what the Court actually found in the *Nuclear Weapons* case. At an early stage of its Opinion, the Court seems to indicate the possibility of a *non liquet*, when it defines its task as being 'to engage in its normal judicial function of ascertaining the existence *or otherwise* of legal principles and rules governing the threat or use of nuclear weapons',[206] but this may not be of great significance.

The basis in the reasoning of the Opinion for the decision in paragraph 105(2)(E), quoted above, is to be found in paragraphs 94 to 97 of the text. In summary the Court there found that (1) it could not determine the validity or otherwise of the view that limited use of 'clean' nuclear weapons under certain circumstances would be lawful;[207] (2) it could not

[200] (1989) 60 BYIL 82.

[201] There are however two difficulties here. First, if the plaintiff has failed to show the existence of a *legal rule* justifying his claim, there may be a question whether, in view of the principle *jura novit curia*, the Court may dismiss the claim on that basis. The point will be reverted to below. Secondly, as Bodansky (n 199 above, 160–1) observes, at least in municipal systems, there may be contentious proceedings in which a judge cannot fall back on a default solution of dismissing the claim: eg interpleader proceedings.

[202] It is of course recognized that the Court has the discretion to refuse to give an advisory opinion, but this discretion is probably only possible on limited grounds, which do not apparently include the silence or obscurity of the law. On the discretion to refuse an opinion, see a previous article in this series: (2000) 71 BYIL 119–42.

[203] There is no reason why, in a particular advisory case, it should not occur that neither the requesting body nor any State chose to respond to an invitation to 'supply information' under Art 66 of the Statute.

[204] This distinction between *non liquet* in a contentious case and in an advisory case is recognized by Judge Vereshchetin in his separate opinion in the case: [1996-I] ICJ Rep 279.

[205] Kohen argues that once the Court has decided to give an opinion on the basis that the question submitted is a legal question, it is no longer free to decline to give an opinion on the ground of insufficiency of the law: 'L'avis consultatif de la CIJ sur la Licéité de la menace ou de l'emploi d'armes nucléaires' [1997] EJIL 349, 360. Contra, Weil, '"*The Court cannot conclude definitely* . . . ": Non Liquet *revisited*' [1997] *Columbia Journal of Transnational Law* 117: "The duty to answer a request for an advisory opinion, however, does not imply the duty to resolve the question referred to it.'

[206] [1996-I] ICJ Rep 237, para 18 (emphasis added).

[207] [1996-I] ICJ Rep 262, para 94.

determine the validity or otherwise of the view that 'recourse to nuclear weapons would be illegal in any circumstances owing to their inherent and total incompatibility with the law applicable in armed conflict';[208] (3) it 'cannot lose sight of the fundamental right of every State to survival, and thus its right to resort to self-defence ... when its survival is at stake'.[209] In the next paragraph of its reasoning the Court then (apparently) sums up, in the same terms as in the operative part (paragraph 105(2)(E)).

The articulation of these three propositions is unclear. The finding in paragraph 105(2)(E) of the operative clause is limited to the question of self-defence and State survival. In particular, does this imply that limited use of 'clean' weapons is lawful only where the survival of the State is at stake; and contrariwise that, even in a case of defence of State survival, limited use of 'clean' weapons is all that is lawful? The question is material, since a distinction that the Court does appear to make is between the lack of information making it impossible to deal with point (1), on the one hand, and the apparent insufficiency of the law which seems to be the basis of its conclusion on point (2), in the second part of clause 105(2)(E). Judge Higgins, in her dissenting opinion, considered that the Court, in making the disputed finding, had not 'restricted itself to the inadequacy of facts and argument concerning the so-called "clean" and "precise" weapons'.[210] On this basis, she took the view that 'it cannot be doubted that the formula chosen [by the Court] is a *non liquet*'.[211]

Judge Koroma, also dissenting, considered that '[The] finding of *non liquet* is wholly unfounded in the present case', because 'The *corpus juris* on the matter is not only considerable but sufficiently clear and precise for the Court to have made a definitive finding'.[212] President Bedjaoui's position appears to favour a *non liquet*, but he declined to permit the conclusion to be drawn that there was therefore no rule on the matter limiting States' freedom of action. He gave his casting vote in favour of the adoption of paragraph 105(2)(E); in the declaration he annexed to the Opinion he stated that 'the Court could obviously not go beyond what the law says. It could not say what the law does not say'; yet he laid great emphasis on the fact that in his view 'the Court's inability to go beyond [the] statement [in that paragraph] of the situation can in no way be

[208] ibid para 95.

[209] ibid 263, para 96. For a highly critical examination of the concept of 'State survival', see M Cohen, 'The notion of "State survival" in international law' in Boisson de Chazournes and Sands (n 197 above). cf also the observation in the PCA Award in the *Russian Indemnity* case that 'the obligation for a State to execute treaties may be weakened if the very existence of the State is endangered, if observation of the international duty is ... self-destructive' UNRIAA, vol XI, 443.

[210] [1996-I] ICJ Rep 590, para 30; cf the advisory opinion ibid 262, para 94.

[211] ibid. The fact that the Court relied (apparently) *both* on a lack of factual material and on the limitations of the law leads Bodansky to the opposite conclusion, that 'the Court's opinion on this point need not be interpreted as a *non liquet*': '*Non liquet* and the incompleteness of international law', n 187 above.

[212] [1996-I] ICJ Rep 558.

interpreted to mean that it is leaving the door ajar to recognition of the legality of the threat or use of nuclear weapons.'[213]

Of the other judges who voted in favour of paragraph 105(2)(E), Judge Vereshchetin held that there was no *non liquet* essentially because that concept was inapplicable in advisory proceedings.[214] Judge Shahabuddeen made his position on the point quite explicit: he referred to the distinction, mentioned above, between a finding that the law contains no rule forbidding particular action, or no rule authorizing a particular legal claim (as in the *Barcelona Traction* case) and a finding that there is a gap in the applicable law: 'If, as it is said, international law has nothing to say on the subject of the legality of the use of nuclear weapons, this necessarily means that international law does not include a rule prohibiting such use. On the received view of the "*Lotus*" decision, absent such a prohibitory rule, States have a right to use nuclear weapons.'[215] If paragraph 105(2)(E) were to be understood as implying a *non liquet*, then Judge Shahabuddeen would 'respectfully differ from the position taken by the Court'.[216]

The question of lawfulness of a finding of *non liquet*, is thus bound up with the question of the completeness of international law. Setting aside for the moment the philosophical argument that law is of its nature complete, it is clear that in international law there is a higher probability than in municipal law that there may be, or may appear to be, no established rule on a given point. For the most part international law grows out of practice establishing custom: if there has hitherto been no practice in a particular field, is there any law? This problem may arise particularly as a result of scientific and technological development (eg use of outer space and satellites, exploitation of the continental shelf).[217] For this purpose, 'no practice' means 'no significant practice'; there may in fact have been a lot of practice, but completely inconsistent, or (more probably) the rival practices of two different groups of States—as was the case of the possession of nuclear weapons.[218]

President Bedjaoui insisted that there was a possible middle way, that there was not simply a stark choice between holding that the use of nuclear weapons was prohibited (for which there was insufficient support in customary law) or holding that, in the absence of a legal prohibition the use of nuclear weapons was lawful (an undesirable conclusion, but one which seemed inexorably to follow from the absence of prohibitory rule). He distinguished the decision in the *S.S. Lotus* case inasmuch

213 [1996-I] ICJ Rep 270, paras 10, 11. 214 ibid 279–80. 215 ibid 389–90.

216 ibid 389.

217 For Fastenrath, this would be an instance of a 'law-free area' (*rechtsfreie Raum*), since it is a domain which is entirely unregulated by law: *Lücken im Völkerrecht* 213.

218 Thus the distinction made by JHW Verzijl, *International Law in Historical Perspective* (1968) Section V.I., while useful for discussion purposes, does not seem to be fundamental. See V Vereshchetin, 'Is "deceptive clarity" better than "apparent indecision" in an advisory opinion?' in E Yakpo and T Boumedra (eds), *Liber Amicorum Mohammed Bedjaoui* (1999) 533.

as: 'Whereas the Permanent Court gave the green light of authorization, having found in international law no reason for giving the red light of prohibition, the present Court does not feel able to give a signal either way.'[219] Pursuing the metaphor, the Court was presumably showing an amber light, indicating 'proceed with caution', advice which the commentator would do well to heed!

President Bedjaoui identifies the existence of 'a very advanced process of change in the relevant international law or, in other words, of a current trend towards the replacement of one rule of international law by another, where the first is already defunct and its successor does not yet exist'.[220] This is, of course, a not uncommon situation where the law is developing: for example, the transition from the rule authorizing a territorial sea of no more than three miles, to one authorizing an extent of twelve miles. The question must be whether, until a new rule exists, the existing rule can be regarded as 'defunct'. During the period prior to general acceptance of the twelve-mile limit, the rule that there was a maximum extent of territorial sea continued to exist; it was difficult to say whether a particular claim (of six miles, say) was or was not justifiable, but no one would have suggested either that every claim to territorial sea, no matter how extensive, had to be accepted, or that no claim to any territorial sea whatever could be treated as valid.

The transformation in the law relating to the use of nuclear weapons which, in the view of President Bedjaoui, was in progress, was more radical. When first developed, nuclear weapons were not subject to any rule of law specifically directed to their use.[221] Subsequently, it was suggested, their use would become outlawed; ie at this point international law would show a red light, in President Bedjaoui's image. President Bedjaoui did not consider that that stage had yet been reached in view of the division of views and of practice between States. Had the light been at amber ever since the invention of nuclear weapons: or had an initial green light—an absence of prohibition equivalent to an authorization—given place to an amber light? President Bedjaoui's reference to a previous rule having become 'defunct' suggests the latter interpretation.

The major difficulty with President Bedjaoui's analysis is however to discern the practical implications of an 'amber light'. Nuclear weapons are not as yet prohibited as *malum in se*: so much is clear. But it must then follow that the use of such a weapon (in appropriate circumstances, and without breach of humanitarian law) cannot be regarded as unlawful. President Bedjaoui appears to be confusing what is *permitted* by a system with what is *encouraged*: it will be generally agreed that the use of nuclear weapons is not to be encouraged, but this is not the same thing as saying

[219] [1996-I] ICJ Rep 271, para 14. [220] ibid 272, para 16.

[221] This is not of course to say that their use was not regulated, like that of all weapons, by the *ius in bello*.

that it is not legally authorized. Encouragement can only be the work of a political system, not a legal one;[222] the latter works in terms of black and white, without intermediate greys.

To sum up, the Court has indicated in the *Nuclear Weapons* case that, at least in advisory proceedings it may be unable to give a complete and precise answer to the question posed, whether or not this situation is properly characterized as a *non liquet*, for one or other of two reasons. In the first place, it may simply lack the factual information to give an answer; and a conditional reply (on the lines of 'If such and such is so, then the legal consequence is . . . ') cannot be regarded as a satisfactory discharge of the Court's functions. Secondly, however, the Court may find that, on the subject of the question that has been posed, international law gives not merely no clear answer, but no answer at all; and the problem cannot be solved by rejecting a claim, as in a contentious case, on the ground that its legal basis has not been proved. The Court has thus found itself obliged, by the force of circumstance, to reject the theory that international law is a complete system, without *lacunae*; but it remains true that such *lacunae* are very infrequently to be met with.

[(2) International law as constitutive or regulatory of States' rights]

2. *International legal obligations* erga omnes *and the* actio popularis[223]

The concepts—for they are two different concepts—of the obligation *erga omnes* and the right *erga omnes* have attracted increasing attention since the publication of the comments in the first article in this series. In part this is due to the attention paid to those concepts, and the controversies surrounding them, in the International Law Commission, in the context of its work on State Responsibility (or International Responsibility).[224] The present article is however primarily concerned with the dicta of the International Court in this connection;[225] the wider realms of theory are only pertinent to the extent that such dicta may indicate that the Court was espousing, or inspired by, a particular academic approach, or that it was rejecting such an approach.

[222] A legal provision, eg governing permitted hours for the sale of alcohol, may be introduced to discourage a particular practice, ie excessive drinking; but the law *as law* neither encourages or discourages.

[223] This was the subsection-title used in the first article in this series: (1989) 60 BYIL 92–102. However, while the Court used the expression *actio popularis* in the *South West Africa* judgment ([1966] ICJ Rep 47, para 88), there is some doubt as to whether it is appropriate to the relationship existing in cases of obligations *erga omnes*: see S Villalpando, *L'émergence de la communauté internationale dans la responsabilité des États* (2005) 279.

[224] See in particular Art 48 of the Articles on International Responsibility and the commentary thereon. For reasons there explained, the Commission, while following the jurisprudence of *Barcelona Traction*, avoided using the term '*erga omnes*'.

[225] Judge Weeramantry, in his dissenting opinion in the *East Timor* case, suggested that the Court had been 'confronted with *erga omnes* obligations' not only in *Barcelona Traction* but also in the following cases: *Northern Cameroons*; *South West Africa (Preliminary Objections)*; *South West Africa, Second Phase*; *Nuclear Tests (Australia v France)* and *(New Zealand v France)*; *United States*

The whole subject has been bedevilled for many years by an unfortunate looseness of terminology. In the first place, there has been a tendency to lump together the category of rules of *jus cogens* and that of rules prescribing obligations, or enshrining rights, *erga omnes*;[226] this problem will be discussed further in Section 3 below. However, there is a temptation to use the label '*erga omnes*' to apply to rights and to obligations indiscriminately,[227] so that the right *erga omnes* and the obligation *erga omnes* are assumed to be partnered, in the same sense that a *legal* obligation corresponds to the existence of *legal* right. This is however both to neglect the precise meaning of the Latin term ('towards all') and the nature of the rights and obligations involved. If a right exists *erga omnes*, then the beneficiary of the right can invoke it against all other States (or subjects of international law). The corresponding obligation weighs on all States, but is owed solely to the beneficiary of the right, not to the other States having the obligation. An obligation *erga omnes* similarly is owed to all other States, and can be invoked by any one or more of them; the corresponding right thus inheres in all those States, but can be invoked solely against the State on which the obligation rests. In each of the two relationships there is a plurality of entities on the one side, and a single entity on the other;[228] and the essential point is that the corollary of a right *erga omnes* is not, or not necessarily,[229] an obligation *erga omnes*, and the corollary of an obligation *erga omnes* is not necessarily a right *erga omnes*.[230]

Diplomatic and Consular Staff in Tehran; and *Border and Transborder Armed Actions (Nicaragua v Honduras)*. The present writer is not wholly in agreement with this analysis; but in any event, in none of those cases did the decision contain any useful observations on the subject of *erga omnes* obligations or rights—nor did Judge Weeramantry argue otherwise.

226 For a particularly striking example, see G Gaja, 'Do States have a duty to ensure compliance with obligations *erga omnes* by other States?' in M Ragazzi (ed) *International Responsibility Today: Essays in Memory of Oscar Schachter* (2005) who cheerfully cites, in support of 'a duty which concerns cessation of serious breaches of a category of *erga omnes* obligations', Articles 40 and 41 of the ILC Articles on State Responsibility, which relate to 'peremptory norms', ie *jus cogens*.

227 Or even to 'findings' of the Court itself, which do not as such operate *erga* any party: see separate opinion of Judge Koroma in *Legal Consequences of the Construction of a Wall in the Occupied Palestinian Territory* [2004] ICJ Rep 2205–6.

228 This of course does not mean that more than one State jointly may be under an obligation *erga omnes*; the point is that the *omnes* always appear on one side only of the equation. Joint entitlement of more than one State to the same right *erga omnes* is less likely, but theoretically conceivable.

229 There is no reason why *in fact* one or more, or even all known, rights *erga omnes* should not correspond to obligations *erga omnes*: the point is that this is not a consequence of the nature of the rights, but would or could develop as a matter of customary law. For the difficulties involved in such a process, see M Byers, *Custom, Power and the Power of Rules* (1999) 197–9.

230 The point is very clearly put by Villalpando: 'L'on remarquera d'emblée que les droits *erga omnes* ne constituent pas la situation juridique active correspondant aux obligations *erga omnes*: une obligation envers la communauté internationale dans son ensemble implique un droit de tous les autres États, c'est-à-dire un droit *omnium*, mais non pas nécessairement un droit de chacun de ces derniers *envers* tous les autres, *erga omnes*': *L'émergence de la communauté internationale dans la responsibilite des États* (2005) 100. The status of an obligation *erga omnes* never implies automatically the existence of a right *erga omnes*: if such correlation exists in some cases (or even in all) it is due to considerations related to the nature of the subject-matter of the right/obligation. The convenient expression 'rights *omnium*' was employed in the Fourth Report by Arangio Ruiz on State Responsiblity, para 133; it also appears in the index to M Ragazzi, *The Concept of International Obligations* Erga Omnes (1996) but curiously enough not in the text.

This distinction has unfortunately not always been clearly recognized in the decisions of the Court that have referred to rights or obligations *erga omnes*. The problem was first raised in the *East Timor* case. It was there recognized that the right of self-determination of peoples is a right *erga omnes*; this signifies that the people of East Timor, for example, were entitled to insist that their right of self-determination be respected, not only by Indonesia which, being in occupation of the territory of East Timor, was the State able to implement the right, but also by any other State which interfered with or blocked the exercise of the right. On this basis it was argued that Australia, by entering into a treaty with Indonesia dividing up the continental shelf alleged to appertain to East Timor, was infringing the right of the people of that territory to self-determination. Had that people had capacity to appear before the Court to assert its right, the Court could well have upheld the claim against Australia (subject to the jurisdictional problem mentioned below). The proceedings were in fact brought by Portugal,[231] which was not the entity entitled to exercise the right of self-determination as regards the territory of East Timor. Only, therefore, if the obligation of Australia (among others) to respect the right of self-determination was an obligation *erga omnes* could Portugal validly require Australia to respect it; and this, as we have seen, does not follow from the mere fact that the right itself was generally admitted to be a right *erga omnes*.

The decision of the Court in fact turned on a jurisdictional question: it held that it could not decide the dispute between Portugal and Australia without passing on the legality of the conduct of Indonesia, which was not before the Court.[232] On the basis therefore of the principle laid down in the *Monetary Gold* case,[233] the Court found that it could not exercise jurisdiction. Portugal, however, endeavoured to turn the flank of the *Monetary Gold* principle by relying on the *erga omnes* character of the right asserted: 'It maintains, in effect, that the rights which Australia allegedly breached were rights *erga omnes* and that accordingly Portugal could require it, individually, to respect them regardless of whether or not another State had conducted itself in a similar manner.'[234] After conceding that 'Portugal's assertion that the right of peoples to self-determination . . . has an *erga omnes* character, is irreproachable', the Court held that this made no difference to the application of the *Monetary Gold* principle:

However, the Court considers that the *erga omnes* character of a norm and the rule of consent to jurisdiction are two different things. Whatever the nature of

[231] One basis advanced for this was Portugal's status as Administering Power of the Territory under a United Nations Trusteeship, prior to the invasion of the territory by Indonesia; this argument is not here material, and in fact was rejected on the ground that that status did not imply 'an obligation on third States to treat exclusively with Portugal as regards the continental shelf of East Timor' ([1995] ICJ Rep 104, para 32).

[232] This aspect of the case has been treated in a previous article: (1998) 69 BYIL 50–2.

[233] [1954] ICJ Rep 32, discussed in (1998) 69 BYIL 37–9.

[234] [1995] ICJ Rep 102, para 29.

the obligations invoked, the Court could not rule on the lawfulness of the conduct of a State when its judgment would imply an evaluation of the lawfulness of the conduct of another State which is not a party to the case. Where this is so, the Court cannot act, even if the right in question is a right *erga omnes*.[235]

While this is clearly a perfectly proper disposal of the case, it is a pity that the Court did not take the opportunity to point out that Portugal's argument was a *non sequitur*. The fact that the people of East Timor could assert their right to self-determination both against Indonesia and Australia (and any other State) did not authorize Portugal to assert that right against another State. This it could only do if the obligation to respect the right of self-determination was an obligation *erga omnes*; but, as we have seen, while this could be the case if the law could be shown to have developed in that sense, it does not follow from the *erga omnes* nature of the right. In this connection, the Court's reference to 'the *erga omnes* character of a norm' is unfortunate: the term is inapplicable to a norm,[236] since it only has meaning in relation to either a right or an obligation, to indicate in which direction the *erga* is pointing, as it were; and to use it to characterize a norm could imply that both the right to enforce the norm and the obligation to comply with it are necessarily *erga omnes*.

Similarly, Judge Weeramantry in his dissenting opinion referred to 'the *erga omnes* concept'.[237] After agreeing that the right of self-determination was a right *erga omnes* he invoked the *Barcelona Traction* case as the recognition of *erga omnes* obligations:

In [the *Barcelona Traction*] case, the Court was spelling out that, where a State has an obligation towards all other States, each of those States has a legal interest in its observance. If, therefore, Australia has an obligation *erga omnes* towards all States to respect the right of self-determination, Portugal (as the administering Power of East Timor) and East Timor would have a legal interest in the observance of that duty.[238]

This is of course correct as far as it goes;[239] but it remains to be shown that Australia did in fact have such an obligation, and not merely the admitted obligation, owed to the people of East Timor (and them only) to respect the *erga omnes* right of self-determination.

[235] ibid.

[236] H Thierry, 'L'évolution du droit international' (1990-III) 232 *RCADI* 49, uses the term *erga omnes* to describe the quality of rules of general international law of being applicable to all subjects of the international order; a usage rightly criticized, as leading to confusion, by G Buzzini, 'La "généralité" du droit international: réflexions sur la polysémie d'un concept' (2004) 108 *Revue générale* 392.

[237] [1995] ICJ Rep 213–16. The phrase is rendered in the French translation of the opinion as 'la notion de l'opposabilité *erga omnes*'.

[238] [1995] ICJ Rep 214.

[239] Though it is curious that Judge Weeramantry relies on Portugal's special status, since if the obligation towards it is *erga omnes*, that status is irrelevant. To avoid confusion, it may be added that the obligation to respect the right of self-determination is *erga omnes* in a looser sense, inasmuch it is owed to all peoples enjoying that right; but this of course is not the meaning of the concept as expressed in the *Barcelona Traction* case.

However, Judge Weeramantry continues: 'All the prior cases before this Court raised the question of *duties* owed *erga omnes*. That aspect is present in this case as well, for every State has an *erga omnes* duty to recognize self-determination, and to that extent, if Portugal's claim is correct, Australia is in breach of that general *erga omnes* duty towards East Timor.'[240] Since one looks in vain for any justification of the assertion of the existence of the *erga omnes* duty, it is difficult to escape the conclusion that, for Judge Weeramantry, the *erga omnes* character of the duty derives from the *erga omnes* character of the right. Indeed he himself explained his reasoning as being to adopt 'the Court's pronouncement on the *erga omnes* character of East Timor's right, and [to] follow that principle through to what I have indicated to be its logical and legal conclusion.'[241] For the reasons explained, this process of reasoning is logically unsound.

In its judgment on preliminary objections in the case concerning *Application of the Genocide Convention*, the Court referred to its 1951 advisory opinion on *Reservations to the Genocide Convention*. The question at issue was whether proceedings were properly brought against Yugoslavia for alleged breach of the Genocide Convention in respect of a conflict of a domestic nature, to which Yugoslavia was not a party, in the territory of Bosnia and Herzegovina, a territory over which Yugoslavia had no jurisdiction; Yugoslavia claimed that there was no international dispute falling within the jurisdictional clause of the Convention. In this context the Court quoted the conclusions in the 1951 opinion that 'the principles underlying the Convention are principles which are recognized by civilized nations as binding on States without any conventional obligation', and as to 'the universal character both of the condemnation of genocide and of the co-operation required "in order to liberate mankind from such an odious scourge" (Preamble to the Convention)'.[242] From this the Court deduced that: 'It follows that the rights and obligations enshrined by the Convention are rights and obligations *erga omnes*. The Court notes that the obligation each State has to prevent and punish the crime of genocide is not territorially limited by the Convention.'[243]

How this conclusion follows from the 1951 dictum is not clear. The first observation quoted does no more than state that the principles underlying the Genocide Convention are matters of general customary law, and therefore binding on all States whether or not they are parties to the Convention: it has nothing to say as to the possible status of those principles as generating rules of *jus cogens* or rights or obligations *erga omnes*. The point of the reference to the 'universal character' of the

240 [1995] ICJ Rep 215. The last phrase is puzzling: if the duty was *erga omnes*, then by definition it was not owed solely to East Timor; and the whole point of the invocation by Portugal of the *erga omnes* doctrine was to establish the existence of a duty owed to Portugal.

241 [1995] ICJ Rep 216.

242 [1951] ICJ Rep 23, quoted in [1996-II] ICJ Rep 616, para 31.

243 ibid.

condemnation of genocide and the co-operation required is as basis for the conclusion that the intention was that 'as many States as possible should participate' in the Convention.[244]

It will also be observed that there seems to be here an assumption that rights and obligations *erga omnes* can be paired, in exactly the way in which it was suggested above that they cannot—or not on any *a priori* basis.

There is also no apparent logical link between the observation that the obligation of a State to prevent and punish genocide is not territorially limited, and the preceding sentence to the effect that that obligation is *erga omnes*. The question before the Court was whether Yugoslavia was bound to punish genocide committed outside its territory. This question is quite independent of the question whether Yugoslavia was under an obligation, owed to all States and enforceable by any of them, to prevent and punish genocide. Even if an obligation is *erga omnes*, it is still necessary to ask what precisely the obligation entails; its character as *erga omnes* does not answer that question.

It is difficult to avoid the conclusion that the statement in question (that the obligation to prevent and punish genocide is an obligation *erga omnes*) was an obiter dictum, included simply to emphasize the importance of that obligation, and of the need to enforce it.

The advisory opinion of the Court on the *Legal Consequences of the Construction of a Wall in the Occupied Palestinian Territory* also dealt with obligations *erga omnes*, but cannot be said to have clarified the matter. The Court indicated that it would consider 'the legal consequences of the internationally wrongful acts flowing from Israel's construction of the wall as regards other States', and observed that 'the obligations violated by Israel include certain obligations *erga omnes*'.[245] These were specified as 'the obligation to respect the right of the Palestinian people to self-determination', and in this connection the Court recalled what it had already said in *East Timor* as to the *erga omnes* character of the *right* of self-determination; and 'certain of [the] obligations [of Israel] under international humanitarian law'.[246] In so stating, the Court clearly makes the same logical leap as was made by Judge Weeramantry in the *East Timor* case, and which the Court in that case had refrained from taking. The obligation generated by the right of self-determination is an obligation weighing upon all States to respect that right; it in no sense follows that the obligation itself is *erga omnes* in the sense that is owed to any other entity than the Palestinian people.

In the context of the advisory opinion, it is also not at first sight apparent how the possible *erga omnes* character of the obligations of Israel would be relevant: no State was seeking before the Court to enforce that obligation as owed to itself. Leaving aside an argument based on interpretation of the Fourth Geneva Convention, and applicable only to

[244] [1951] ICJ Rep 24. [245] [2005] ICJ Rep 199, paras 154–5. [246] ibid para 155.

obligations under that Convention,[247] what the Court did deduce from the violations of what it regarded as *erga omnes* obligations was, first that 'all States are under an obligation not to recognize the illegal situation resulting from the construction of the wall', secondly, that they are 'under an obligation not to render aid or assistance in maintaining the situation created by such construction'. Thirdly, 'It is also for all States, while respecting the United Nations Charter and international law, to see to it that any impediment, resulting from the construction of the wall, to the exercise by the Palestinian people of its right to self-determination is brought to an end'.[248] Do these conclusions follow? As was pointed out by Judge Higgins: 'That an illegal situation is not to be recognized or assisted by third parties is self-evident, requiring no invocation of the uncertain concept of *erga omnes*.'

As to the third consequence stated, it is not evident what is the intended meaning of 'it is for all States' to do away with impediments to the right of self-determination: does this mean that it is only States that can take appropriate action, or that States are under an obligation to take such action? The (authoritative) French text has 'il appartient' (not, for example, 'il incombe') 'par ailleurs à tous les États de veiller . . . ', which suggests that what is involved is a faculty or an option; on the other hand the inclusion of the word 'all' suggests an obligation; and it seems that this is what the Court meant to convey. Yet only the first two consequences are reflected in the operative clause, in a paragraph (paragraph 163(3)D) which then goes on to the point arising under the Fourth Geneva Convention, without restating the obligation to ensure the ending of impediments to the exercise of the right of self-determination.[249]

Judge Kooijmans seems to have read the text in this sense: he voted against paragraph 163(3)(D), and stated in his separate opinion in the case: 'I have considerable difficulty in understanding why a violation of an obligation *erga omnes* by one State should necessarily lead to an obligation for third States.'[250] His argument seems in terms to apply to the alleged obligations of non-recognition and not to give aid or assistance; but it would apply *a fortiori* to the obligation to put an end to impediments to self-determination. The logic of the Court's argument in this respect seems to be: (1) the Palestinian people have a right *erga omnes* to self-determination, ie all States must respect that right; therefore (2) the obligation of all States to respect that right is an obligation *erga omnes*,

[247] This question will not be further examined here: it raises matters of interpretation of the Convention, but it also demonstrates the wisdom of the ILC in avoiding the term *erga omnes* because, *inter alia*, 'it has sometimes been confused with obligations owed to all the parties to a treaty': Commentary to Art 48, para (9).

[248] [2005] ICJ Rep 200, para 159, citing the *Namibia* advisory opinion ([1971] ICJ Rep 53, para 115) and *Haya de la Torre* [1951] ICJ Rep 82.

[249] There is however a further paragraph (163(3)E) calling on the UN to 'consider what further action is required to bring to an end the illegal situation resulting from the construction of the wall'; but this falls short of declaring an obligation of States towards that end.

[250] [2005] ICJ Rep 231, para 40.

ie any State may invoke the right of the Palestinian people and assert it against any other State; therefore (3) all States are under an obligation to assert that right, at least against Israel, and possibly against any other State. The first proposition is universally accepted; the transition to the second is logically unsound; and the transition from the second to the third involves converting a right, or a faculty, into an obligation.

In the case of *Military and Paramilitary Activities in and against Nicaragua* the Court considered that 'there is an obligation on the United States Government, in the terms of Article 1 of the Geneva Conventions, to "respect" the Conventions and even "to ensure respect" for them "in all circumstances"'. The existence of the 'multilateral treaty reservation' to the United States' acceptance of jurisdiction however (as the Court found) debarred it from adjudicating on any alleged violations by the United States' of multilateral conventions. The Court therefore continued, 'since such an obligation does not derive only from the Conventions themselves, but from the general principles of humanitarian law to which the Conventions merely give specific expression'.[251] This finding has been seen by some commentators as a recognition that 'Article 1(1) is an obligation *erga omnes*',[252] but in fact all that the Court erected on this foundation, in the context of proceedings brought by Nicaragua, was an obligation of the United States 'not to encourage persons or groups engaged in the conflict in Nicaragua to act in violation of' the provisions of the Conventions.[253] There was thus no question of a State other than Nicaragua being found entitled, let alone obligated, to enforce against the United States the customary-law obligations paralleling those of the Conventions.

3. Jus cogens *and* jus dispositivum

[(1) Jus cogens *and reservations to multilateral conventions]*

[(2) Jus cogens *and the decision of a court]*

(3) Jus cogens *and 'intransgressible' rules*[254]

In its advisory opinion in the case concerning *Legality of the Threat or Use of Nuclear Weapons* the Court enunciated what is apparently a novel category of legal principles and rules. Referring to the fundamental rules of international humanitarian law, the Court stated that these rules 'are to be observed by all States whether or not they have ratified the

[251] [1986] ICJ Rep 114, para 220.

[252] V Gowlland-Debbas, 'Judicial Insights into Fundamental Values and Interests of the International Community' in AS Muller *et al* (eds), *The International Court of Justice* (1997) 358. G Abi-Saab, writing before the *Nicaragua* decision, was only prepared to suggest that 'each State party has a direct legal right or interest (some would go so far as saying it has a legal obligation) in the safeguard of these superior common interests': 'The specificities of humanitarian law', in C Swinarski (ed), *Studies and essays on international humanitarian law and Red Cross principles, in honour of Jean Pictet* (1984) 220.

[253] [1986] ICJ Rep 114, para 220.

[254] This subsection was not included in the original article ((1989) 60 BYIL 102).

conventions that contain them, because they constitute intransgressible principles of international customary law'.[255]

The expression 'intransgressible principles' is impressively weighty; but what does it mean? As a matter of semantics, 'intransgressible' should mean 'that is incapable of being transgressed', and to 'transgress' a principle or rule should mean to act inconsistently with what that principle or rule requires. It may be said of physical laws that they are intransgressible: the law of gravity cannot be transgressed, because any disregard of it automatically gives rise to its operation, in the form of (for example) a precipitate descent to the ground. This is paralleled in legal rules, in the sense that law is about consequences: a legal rule lays down that if a certain act is performed, or a certain omission committed, defined consequences follow, in particular international responsibility. This however is true of all legal rules; yet the Court's dictum seems to suggest that some rules are intransgressible and others not, or at least that some rules are more intransgressible than others.

The intransgressibility of the fundamental rules of humanitarian law is given as the reason why those rules 'are to be observed by all States whether or not they have ratified the conventions that contain them'. This is however the definition of any general customary rule derived from, or paralleled by, a provision in a treaty.[256] Either all such rules are 'intransgressible', however trivial they may be, or the designation 'intransgressible' adds nothing to the definition of an international principle or rule.

It is tempting to equate the 'intransgressibility' of a rule with the concept of *jus cogens*, though logically these are distinct: a rule of *jus cogens* cannot be evaded by the conclusion of a treaty or, more fundamentally, by the consent of its beneficiary,[257] but that does not make it incapable of being transgressed. In the *Oil Platforms* case, the United States denied that the Court had jurisdiction to deal with the customary law questions of the use of force and self-defence, because its jurisdiction was confined to the scope of a 1955 Treaty. The United States also invoked a provision of the Treaty whereby it was not to preclude the adoption of measures 'necessary to protect its essential security interests', and claimed that its actions were such measures. As the Court noted, however, the United States 'does not contend that the Treaty exempts it, as between the parties, from the obligations of international law on the use of force . . . '.[258]

[255] [1996-I] ICJ Rep 257, para 79. The equivalent in the authoritative French text of 'are to be observed by all States' is 's'imposent . . . à tous les États', which is rather stronger.

[256] cf the statement in the case of *Reservations to the Genocide Convention* quoted above (n 228 and accompanying text), where it was not apparently thought necessary to employ such a term as 'intransgressible', in order to reach the same conclusion.

[257] It has been contended that, since a norm of *jus cogens* overrides (as a superior norm) the principle of, eg, State immunity, States must be regarded as having implicitly waived any entitlement to immunity where it would conflict with the application of a rule of *jus cogens*, in particular in the field of human rights (Theory of Normative Hierarchy). See LM Caplan, 'State Immunity, Human Rights, and *Jus Cogens*: a critique of the Normative Hierarchy Theory' (2003) 97 AJIL 741, esp 765ff.

[258] [2003] ICJ Rep 181, para 39.

Such a contention would have been unsustainable, in view of the recognized status as *jus cogens* of the principle forbidding recourse to force; yet the United States could (and as the Court found, did) 'transgress' that principle.

However, in the *Nuclear Weapons* case, the Court, having found that the fundamental rules of humanitarian law 'constitute intransgressible principles of customary law', went on to decline to pronounce on, and thus to leave open, the question whether 'these principles and rules of humanitarian law are part of *jus cogens*'.[259] It follows from this restraint that the Court did not consider that it had already resolved the point by declaring the principles and rules 'intransgressible'.

In the case concerning *Legal Consequences of the Construction of a Wall in the Occupied Palestinian Territory* the Court noted that Israel was not a party to the Fourth Hague Convention of 1907, to which the 'Hague Regulations' were annexed; however it took the view that 'the provisions of the Hague Regulations have become part of customary law', and noted that this was 'in fact recognized by all the participants in the proceedings before the Court'.[260] For the purposes of the Court's reasoning at this stage, whether or not the provisions of the Regulations were 'intransgressible' did not arise.

However, later in the opinion, the Court observed that:

> . . . the obligations violated by Israel include certain obligations *erga omnes*. As the Court indicated in the *Barcelona Traction* case, such obligations are by their very nature 'the concern of all States' and, 'In view of the importance of the rights involved, all States can be held to have a legal interest in their protection.' (*Barcelona Traction, Light and Power Company, Limited, Second Phase, Judgment, I.C.J. Reports 1970*, p. 32, para. 33). The obligations *erga omnes* violated by Israel are the obligation to respect the right of the Palestinian people to self-determination, and certain of its obligations under international humanitarian law.[261]

On the question of what obligations of humanitarian law were to be regarded as *erga omnes*, the Court said:

> With regard to international humanitarian law, the Court recalls that in its Advisory Opinion on the *Legality of the Threat or Use of Nuclear Weapons*, it stated that 'a great many rules of humanitarian law applicable in armed conflict are so fundamental to the respect of the human person and "elementary considerations of humanity" . . . ', that they are 'to be observed by all States whether or not they have ratified the conventions that contain them, because they constitute intransgressible principles of international customary law' (*I.C.J. Reports 1996 (I)*, p. 257, para. 79). In the Court's view, these rules incorporate obligations which are essentially of an *erga omnes* character.[262]

[259] [1996-I] ICJ Rep 258, para 83. As P Weil has wittily observed, 'Une fois de plus, il s'avère qu'à l'instar de l'arme nucléaire le *jus cogens* est une arme de dissuasion qui ne vaut que si l'on ne s'en sert pas': 'L'avis consultatif sur la licéité de la menace ou de l'emploi d'armes nucléaires: deux lectures possibles' in *Liber Amicorum Mohammed Bedjaoui* (1999) 551.

[260] [2004] ICJ Rep 172, para 89. [261] ibid 199, para 155. [262] ibid para 157.

'Intransgressibility' of a rule has thus become linked with the quality of giving rise to *erga omnes* obligations,[263] and may in fact have been intended (at least in the *Wall* case) as a synonym for that quality. Nothing in the reasoning of the *Nuclear Weapons* advisory opinion paved the way for this conclusion, which is simply plucked from the air.[264] As a matter of economy of legal terminology, there seems no need to apply the new 'intransgressible' label to the concept of obligations *erga omnes*.

It is difficult to avoid the conclusion that to refer to an 'intransgressible' rule or principle is to use a high-sounding but empty phrase: what Jeremy Bentham called 'nonsense upon stilts'.[265] It is related to the well-meant but confused attempts to conceive a class of super-rules, of the kind of which Prosper Weil warned us twenty-two years ago,[266] which can be *jus cogens*, and can give rise to rights or obligations *erga omnes*, or both, at the whim of the person employing the concept. How such a rule can be said to have any basis in customary law, as developed through the usual process of practice and *opinio juris*, remains a mystery.[267]

[(4) Universality and uniformity of the rules of international law]

[(5) The limits of reaction to unlawful conduct]

Chapter III: Relationships Between Legal Orders

1. The relationship between international and national law

(1) Supremacy of international law

In the case concerning *Maritime Delimitation and Territorial Questions between Qatar and Bahrain* the jurisdiction of the Court was asserted on the basis of the Minutes of tripartite meetings (between the Parties and Saudi Arabia), which, it was claimed, constituted or recorded an agreement by the Parties to the unilateral submission by either of them of their dispute to the International Court. It was objected by Bahrain that its Foreign Minister, who signed the Minutes, did not consider that he was signing an instrument that would have the effect of 'committing Bahrain to a legally binding agreement'. Furthermore, he stated 'that, according to the Constitution of Bahrain, "treaties 'concerning the territory of the State' can come into effect only after their positive enactment

[263] These concepts are linked together in the field of environmental law in a work cited with approval by Judge Weeramantry in his dissenting opinion in the *WHO* case: *Legality of the Use of Nuclear Weapons by a State in Armed Conflict* [1996-I] ICJ Rep 140.

[264] It also leads to a confusion of thought between obligations *erga omnes* and rights *erga omnes*: see Section 2 above.

[265] 'Natural rights is simple nonsense: natural and imprescriptible rights, rhetorical nonsense—nonsense upon stilts': J Bentham, 'Anarchical fallacies' in J Bowring (ed), *Works* (1843) vol 2.

[266] P Weil, 'Towards Relative Normativity in International Law?' (1983) 77 AJIL 413.

[267] See the trenchant analysis of the question by M Byers, *Custom, Power and the Power of Rules* (1999) 187–8.

as a law". The Minister indicate[d] that he would therefore not have been permitted to sign an international agreement taking effect at the time of signature'.[268] The Court summarily rejected this contention on the basis that, having signed a text 'recording commitments accepted by [his] Government, some of which were to be given immediate application', the Minister was 'not in a position subsequently to say that he intended to subscribe only' to an instrument of lesser significance.[269]

The principle that international law prevails over municipal law was thus not raised directly, since the argument of Bahrain was not that its Constitution must prevail over its international-law commitments but simply that the existence of a constitutional limitation on the Minister's powers was of evidential value in assessing what his intentions were in signing the Minutes. Nevertheless the primacy principle is in point inasmuch as once it was established, in the Court's view, that the Minister had committed his country to a dispute-settlement agreement, the fact that that agreement would not come into effect for internal purposes in Bahrain unless and until an appropriate law was enacted was irrelevant to the internationally binding effect of the agreement.

In the case concerning *Application of the Genocide Convention* Yugoslavia raised an objection to the admissibility of the Application of Bosnia and Herzegovina, *inter alia* on the ground that 'as Mr Alija Izetbegović was not serving as President of the Republic—but only as President of the Presidency—at the time at which he granted an authorization to initiate proceedings, that authorization was granted in violation of certain rules of domestic law of fundamental significance... Mr Izetbegović was not even acting legally at that time as President of the Presidency'.[270] The Court found it unnecessary to go into these questions of domestic law. It drew attention to the rule expressed in Article 7, paragraph 2(a) of the VCLT that every Head of State is presumed to be able to act on behalf of the State in its international relations. The difficulty however remained that, according to the Yugoslavian objection, Mr Izetbegović was not the Head of State. The Court's reply to this was that at the relevant time he had been recognized as such, 'in particular by the United Nations', and was subsequently to be so recognized 'in many international bodies', and 'several international agreements... bear his signature'.[271]

The Court did not draw a parallel with Article 46 of the VCLT, whereby the purported consent of a State to a treaty may be invalidated if it was 'expressed in violation of a provision of its internal law regarding competence to conclude treaties', provided the violation was 'manifest and concerned a rule of its internal law of fundamental importance'. The institution of proceedings before the Court may be regarded as a manifestation of consent by the State concerned, particularly since it entails acceptance of the future decision of the Court; and a consent

[268] [1994] ICJ Rep 121, para 26.
[269] ibid 122, para 27.
[270] [1996] ICJ Rep 621–2, para 44.
[271] ibid 622.

conveyed by someone who has no capacity to represent the State is surely no consent at all. However, the purpose of the rule reflected in Article 46 is to protect the State whose consent is alleged to have been given;[272] and that consent can presumably be given by way of novation *ex post facto*, as is in effect recognized by Article 8 of the VCLT.

This application of the rule of primacy of international law over domestic law is still striking inasmuch as in theory it allows a 'recognition' by the United Nations to prevail over internal constitutional provisions of a State.[273]

A further example of the requirements of international law prevailing over municipal law is afforded by the case concerning the *Difference relating to Immunity from Legal Process of a Special Rapporteur of the Commission on Human Rights*. Proceedings had been brought in Malaysia against such a rapporteur (Mr Cumaraswamy), and the courts of Malaysia held that they had jurisdiction to hear the case on the merits, including making, in the same proceedings, a determination of whether he was entitled to any immunity.[274] The courts thus did not deal with the immunity question *in limine litis* as a preliminary issue. The Court held that it was 'a generally recognized principle of procedural law' that such a question be treated in this way, 'and Malaysia was under an obligation to respect it'.[275] It must be assumed that the decision of the Malaysian courts was correct according to Malaysian internal law, but it conflicted with a general principle, presumably one taken up into international law and applicable under Article 38, paragraph 1(c), of the Statute.

In the *LaGrand* case, the United States recognized that it was under an obligation, by virtue of Article 36 of the Vienna Convention on Consular Relations (VCCR), to provide foreign nationals arrested in the United States with certain rights of notification and access to their respective consuls. The LaGrand brothers had not been given these rights; and when they raised the matter on appeal, the United States courts ruled against them on the basis of the so-called 'procedural default' rule.[276] This is a rule of US domestic law, whereby in certain circumstances failure to raise an issue at the first opportunity will operate as a bar to raising it on appeal. The United States did not suggest that this internal rule exempted it from its international obligations.

[272] This is clear from the wording of the Article: 'A State *may not invoke* the fact that *its consent* to be bound by a treaty . . . '.

[273] And what is, for this purpose, 'the United Nations'? Recognition by a resolution of the General Assembly is one thing; treatment by the Secretariat of a person as a Head of State, possibly for reasons of practical and political convenience, is another.

[274] [1999-I] ICJ Rep 72, para 17.

[275] ibid 88, para 63.

[276] For a convenient definition of the rule, see *Avena and Other Mexican Nationals* [2004] ICJ Rep 56, para 111.

Examining the 'procedural default' rule, the Court emphasized 'that a distinction must be drawn between the rule as such and its specific application in the present case', and found that 'In itself, the rule does not violate Article 36 of the Vienna Convention'.[277] In the specific case, the Court considered that the application of the rule had constituted a breach by the United States of its obligations. When it came to the question of remedies, the Court observed that:

> . . . it can determine the existence of a violation of an international obligation. If necessary, it can also hold that a domestic law has been the cause of this violation. In the present case the Court has made its findings of violations of the obligations under Article 36 of the Vienna Convention when it dealt with the first and the second submission of Germany. But it has not found that a United States law, whether substantive or procedural in character, is inherently inconsistent with the obligations undertaken by the United States in the Vienna Convention. In the present case the violation of Article 36, paragraph 2, was caused by the circumstances in which the procedural default rule was applied, and not by the rule as such.[278]

Consistently with this approach, the Court did not consider that the United States could be required to change its domestic law on 'procedural default', but simply to ensure that in future cases involving rights under the Vienna Convention, 'the United States should allow review and reconsideration of the conviction and sentence', the 'choice of means' being left to the United States.[279]

This was a measured and judicious application of the rule that the international obligations of the United States prevailed over its internal legal rules, without requiring those rules in themselves to be rescinded.

The finding in the *LaGrand* case was followed in the case of *Avena and Other Mexican Nationals*, which again involved breaches by the United States of the obligation under Article 36 of the Vienna Convention. In that case, Mexico asked the Court to annul the convictions and sentences of all the Mexican nationals the subject of its claims, but the Court declined to do so. That case also raised the problem whether the Mexican nationals in question had not enjoyed the right to due process enshrined in the US Constitution. The Court pointed out that, in this context, US law was irrelevant: 'The rights guaranteed under the Vienna Convention are treaty rights which the United States has undertaken to comply with in relation to the individual concerned, irrespective of due process rights under United States constitutional law.'[280]

[277] cf the question whether it is the adoption or the implementation of internal legislation which is inconsistent with an international obligation that constitutes a breach of that obligation: see the ILC Commentary on the draft Articles on State Responsibility, Art 12, para (12).

[278] [2001] ICJ Rep 513, para 125.

[279] ibid 514, para 125.

[280] [2004] ICJ Rep 65, para 138.

[(2) Reference by international law to national law: specific systems or 'municipal law' in general?]

(3) Renvoi *to pre-existing law*

In the original article on this subject,[281] critical attention was paid to the dicta in the *Frontier Dispute (Burkina Faso/Mali)* case concerning reference, for the purpose of applying the principle of *uti possidetis*, to the pre-independence colonial law in force in the territories concerned. The Chamber in that case repudiated the idea that there was in such case 'a sort of *continuum juris*, a legal link between [colonial] law and international law', insisting that 'international law does not effect any renvoi to the law established by the colonising State'. For the Chamber, colonial law is merely a 'factual element', as evidence indicative of what was the 'colonial heritage'.[282]

The Chamber formed to deal with the case of the *Frontier Dispute* between Benin and Niger adopted this line of argument as its own:[283] consistently therewith, it referred to determination of the boundary 'in accordance with the *uti possidetis* principle, by reference to the *physical situation* to which French colonial law was applied, as that situation existed at the date of independence'.[284] For reasons explained in the earlier article, the present writer does not find this attempt to deny any effect of French colonial law, *as law*, at all convincing. However, in one respect the approach of the *Benin/Niger* Chamber seems to be less rigid than that of the *Burkina Faso/Mali* Chamber. The earlier Chamber insisted that, because of the absence of any *renvoi* or *continuum juris*, it was not required to interpret a French Order (administrative/legislative act) 'in the light of the particular rules of the legal system from which the Order derives its force as a regulation, i.e., French colonial law'.[285] The *Benin/Niger* Chamber however observed that 'the *uti possidetis juris* principle requires not only that reliance be placed on existing legal titles, but also that account be taken of the manner in which those titles were interpreted and applied by the competent public authorities of the colonial Power, in particular in the exercise of their law-making power'.[286] Similarly, when Benin contended that a letter, from the French Governor *ad interim* of Niger to the Governor of Dahomey, produced in evidence 'led to some sort of informal intercolonial understanding which bound Niger at the critical date', the Chamber observed that 'such a legal concept did not exist in French colonial law or "*droit d'outre mer*" [and] thus cannot provide Benin with title'.[287]

(4) Municipal law as a source of analogy

An area in which analogies from municipal law exercise an unobtrusive influence is that of the Court's own procedure. The creation of the Court

[281] (1989) 60 BYIL 125–7. [282] [1986] ICJ Rep 568, para 30.
[283] [2005] ICJ Rep, para 28; see also ibid para 46. [284] ibid para 25 (emphasis added).
[285] [1986] ICJ Rep 590, para 69. [286] [2005] ICJ Rep, para 140. [287] ibid para 67.

as a 'court', and the role attributed to it by its Statute, necessarily imply that its procedure be governed by what is regarded as appropriate to a court in national legal systems.[288]

A recent example of this may be found in the Orders recording discontinuance of proceedings in the cases of the *Vienna Convention on Consular Relations* (the 'Breard' case) and the two *Lockerbie* cases. In the first of these cases, Paraguay indicated that it 'wished to discontinue the proceedings with prejudice', and the United States concurred in this.[289] In the *Lockerbie* cases, the parties notified the Court jointly that they had 'agreed to discontinue with prejudice' the proceedings instituted by Libya, and the Court placed on record the discontinuance 'with prejudice'.[290] The significance of the expression 'with prejudice' has already been examined in an earlier article;[291] in the present context, what is of interest is that the term had not been used previously in the Court's procedure, and is not a term of art in the field of international judicial or arbitral procedure. It is taken, apparently, from the usage of US courts; and as such represents a use of municipal law by way of analogy to express a procedural concept in international judicial law.

The underlying idea is not new to international law; the distinction between what, in other procedural systems, is called *désistement d'instance* and *désistement d'action* lay at the root of the dispute in the *Barcelona Traction* case over the effect of the discontinuance of Belgium's first action.[292] The Court could either have ignored the qualification 'without prejudice' and simply treated the discontinuance in accordance with its own rules; or could have indicated what it understood by the expression, in terms of its own procedure, and made it clear that the right of action was extinguished along with the proceedings.[293] Instead it seems to have considered the phrase an example of 'what oft was thought, but ne'er so well expressed',[294] and taken it over into the terminology of international law.

2. *The doctrine of intertemporal law*

(1) *The principle stated and applied*

A particular problem of intertemporal law arises when it is necessary to examine the present-day status of a regime which was created at a period when the requirements and the possibilities of international law were other than they now are. Such a problem faced the Chamber dealing with the case of the *Land, Island and Maritime Frontier Dispute* between

[288] For an early example of this being indicated explicitly, see the PCIJ case of *Rights of Minorities in Upper Silesia*, in which the Court observed that 'The word *débouter* (dismiss) in the Polish Government's main submission must be taken as possessing the meaning ordinarily attaching to it in French law; . . . ': PCIJ Series A, No 15, 20.

[289] *Order of 10 November 1998* [1998] ICJ Rep 427.

[290] *Orders of 10 September 2003* [2003] ICJ Rep 150, 153.

[291] (2003) 74 BYIL 109–11.

[292] [1964] ICJ Rep 6; see (2003) 74 BYIL 103–7.

[293] Whether this would have been a wise course is another matter: see the criticism in the previous article referred to in n 291 above.

[294] Alexander Pope, *An Essay on Criticism* (1711) line 298.

El Salvador and Honduras, with the intervention of Nicaragua. The three States each have coastlines bordering on the Gulf of Fonseca, and the Chamber was asked to declare the 'legal status of the maritime spaces' within and without the Gulf. A decision of the Central American Court of Justice in 1917[295] had declared that the Gulf was an historic bay with the characteristics of a closed sea. That Court had found that 'the practice of all three coastal States had established and mutually recognized a 1 marine league (3 nautical miles) littoral maritime belt off their respective mainland coasts and islands, in which belt they each exercised an exclusive jurisdiction and sovereignty, though with rights of innocent passage conceded on a mutual basis'.[296] At the time, the maximum permitted breadth of the territorial sea had of course been three miles: but what was the effect of subsequent developments in the law of the sea? Could each of the three States now claim such a belt of twelve miles (which would have caused practical problems in view of the limited size of the Gulf), or would such enlarged territorial seas attach automatically?

The 1917 judgment had however gone on to characterize the waters of the Gulf *outside* the three-mile belts as 'territorial waters'. The Chamber took note of a shift in legal terminology in this respect, finding that the term 'territorial waters' had at the time not infrequently been used 'to denote what would now be called "internal" or "national" waters'.[297] As the Chamber noted: 'To have recognized exclusive 'maritime belts' along the littoral *inside* those 'territorial waters', the property of the three States in common, was no doubt an anomaly in terms of the modern law of the sea; but it was in accord with what had emerged from the actual practice of the coastal States in the Gulf of Fonseca at that time . . . At any rate, the 3-mile maritime belts were firmly established by practice.'[298]

The Chamber's eventual finding was that the waters of the Gulf were held in sovereignty jointly by the three States, but excluding the belt 'as at present established, extending 3 miles (1 marine league) from the littoral of each of the three States, such belt being under the exclusive sovereignty of the coastal State . . . '.[299]

A further complication was the impact of these findings on the status of the waters *outside* the Gulf; the Chamber found that since the Gulf was an historic bay, the closing line of the bay was to be treated as a baseline for the determination of the territorial sea, continental shelf and exclusive economic zone of each of the three States.[300] The result was that each State had a quasi-territorial sea within the Gulf and a true territorial sea outside it.

[295] The precise status and authority of this decision was disputed: it had been taken in a bilateral case between El Salvador and Nicaragua, without the participation of Honduras.

[296] [1992] ICJ Rep 590, para 389. [297] ibid 592, para 392. [298] ibid (original emphasis).

[299] ibid 616, para 432(1).

[300] Which of course raised the problem of how the interests of Honduras, whose territory was at the back of the bay, were to be assured; but that question is not here relevant.

The case has been discussed here under the heading of intertemporal law, since the Chamber seems to have viewed it in that light, as appears from the reference to the inconsistency of the arrangements within the Gulf with 'the modern law of the sea', cited above. It should not however be overlooked that neither the 'ancient' nor the modern law of the sea prevented the establishment by agreement of a special regime of this kind; the interests of third States, or of the international community in general, were only in play so far as the question of access to the waters of the bay was concerned: and in that respect it was the established concept of the historic bay, common to ancient and modern law, that operated.[301]

In the *Territorial Dispute* case between Libya and Chad, one of the questions debated between the parties was the status and effect of various international agreements of the nineteenth and early twentieth centuries which, according to one view, had established defined boundaries in the area in dispute at the present day; the rival view was that these had (for example) done no more than define spheres of influence between the Powers interested in African territories. The interpretation of these agreements would therefore have had to be made against the background of international law as it stood at the time, not in the light of modern international law. The Court however ruled that the effect of a 1955 Franco–Libyan Treaty was to establish complete frontiers by reference to the lines defined in the earlier instruments, as a matter of the intention of the parties to that Treaty, quite independently of the effect attributable to those instruments by the law in force at the time of their conclusion; and no reference to the intertemporal law question was therefore needed in the judgment.

Judge Shahabuddeen however, in his separate opinion, did draw attention to the fact that the so-called international community of the period:

> . . . bore little resemblance to the world as it then stood, and even less to the world as it stands today. The record of the Court speaks of those days; it is not easy to recover the various standpoints of the period. Both Parties, however, correctly accepted that the legal manners of the times were not on trial. Thus, if it were necessary to examine some of the issues bequeathed by the past to the present, it is possible that it is the law as it was then which would still govern.[302]

If this dictum is compared with the Court's earlier statement in the *Western Sahara* case,[303] it is striking that, for Judge Shahabuddeen, the application of the law in force at the time of the instrument is no more than an approach which might have been adopted, not a course required by the intertemporal principle. There is even some suggestion in the judge's choice of language, that nineteenth-century law might be set

301 The special character of the Gulf was that it was an historic bay the coasts of which were, exceptionally, not under the sovereignty of a single State; see the observations of the Chamber on this, [1992] ICJ Rep 593, para 393.

302 [1994] ICJ Rep 44.

303 [1975] ICJ Rep 38–9, para 79; discussed in this series in (1989) 60 BYIL 132.

aside as unsatisfactory in the light of modern ideas, an approach clearly rejected by the Court in the *Western Sahara* case.

The *Western Sahara* ruling was followed in the case of the *Land and Maritime Boundary between Cameroon and Nigeria*, where the question was again one of the application of nineteenth-century international law, and in particular the legal significance of a 'treaty of protection' concluded by a colonizing Power with the indigenous authorities. Citing the *Western Sahara* reference to acquisition of *terra nullius*, the Court observed that: 'Even if this mode of acquisition does not reflect current international law, the principle of intertemporal law requires that the legal consequences of the treaties concluded at that time in the Niger delta be given effect today, in the present dispute.'[304]

It is of course established by Article 64 of the Vienna Convention on the Law of Treaties that the emergence of a new *peremptory* norm of general international law causes any existing treaty in conflict with it to terminate; but this does not mean that the interpretation of the Treaty, for purposes of its application while it *was* in force, is affected by the subsequent peremptory norm. In the *Frontier Dispute* case, Judge Sette Camara was inclined to regard the League of Nations prohibition of secret treaties as having the effect of rendering previous secret treaties invalid *ex tunc*,[305] but this was for the purpose of interpreting, not those treaties, but the 1955 Treaty which referred to them as 'in force'.

On the other hand, it is evident that legal rules laid down in past judicial decisions may no longer be applicable when the same, or an analogous, question comes up for decision today. It is axiomatic that the law, other than the law uniquely defined by a treaty for the parties to it, can and does change and develop.[306] In the case of the *Legality of the Threat or Use of Nuclear Weapons*, President Bedjaoui rejected any application of the principle of State freedom of action, laid down in the *SS Lotus* case, in particular because 'the face of contemporary international society is markedly altered'.[307] Similarly in the preliminary objection stage of the *Land and Maritime Boundary between Cameroon and Nigeria* case, Nigeria attempted (though without success) to convince the Court that the precedent of the 1957 decision in the *Right of Passage* case[308] should not be followed, *inter alia* because 'international law, especially as it relates to good faith, has evolved since'.[309]

(2) Application to future acts

In the advisory opinion on the *Legality of the Threat or Use of Nuclear Weapons* the Court was prepared to find that the customary and conventional rules of humanitarian law applicable in time of war existing prior

[304] [2002] ICJ Rep 405, para 205. [305] [1994] ICJ Rep 98.

[306] And a treaty-regime may develop by agreed amendments, even adopted implicitly; or, it seems, of its own motion: cf the decision in the *Gabčíkovo/Nagymaros Project* case quoted above (nn 188, 189 and accompanying text) and below (n 318 and accompanying text).

[307] [1996-I] ICJ Rep 270, para 13. [308] [1957] ICJ Rep 147.

[309] [1998] ICJ Rep 290, para 24.

to the invention of nuclear weapons applied to those weapons also, despite the 'qualitative as well as quantitative' difference between those weapons and conventional arms. It stated that the intrinsically humanitarian character of those principles and rules 'applies to all forms of warfare and to all kinds of weapons, those of the past, those of the present and those of the future'.[310] This is a rhetorical way of emphasizing the generality of those rules and principles: the Court was not asked to what they would apply in the future, nor could it have replied to such a question. This may be contrasted with the specific determination in a conventional text that it shall apply to future members of a defined class: for example, the Third Committee of the League of Nations Assembly found it appropriate to explain, when reporting on the drafting of Article 35 of the Permanent Court of International Justice (PCIJ) Statute, that the reference to 'Members of the League' included future as well as present Members.[311]

(3) *Problems of ascertaining the applicable law*

Note the observations of Judge Shahabuddeen in the *Frontier Dispute* case, quoted above, as to the difficulty of 'recover[ing] the various standpoints of the period', namely the second half of the nineteenth century.[312]

(4) *Intertemporal* renvoi

This was the term used in the first of this series of articles to refer to the situation in which, in an instrument of a conventional nature, there exists an 'intention to subject the legal relations created to such law as might from time to time thereafter become effective',[313] the clearest example of such a construction being the interpretation given by the Court in the *Aegean Sea Continental Shelf* case to the Greek reservation under the 1928 General Act.[314] The term does not seem to have obtained wider acceptance (though some writers in French have used the term 'conflit mobile'), but it will be retained here for working purposes.[315]

In the case concerning the *Gabčíkovo/Nagymaros Project*, the time-scale relevant to an intertemporal question was more limited, since the treaty at the centre of the dispute, between Hungary and Czechoslovakia, dated from 1977. Hungary claimed that it was 'entitled to terminate the 1977 Treaty because new requirements of international law for the protection of the environment precluded performance of the Treaty'.[316]

310 [1996-I] ICJ Rep 259, para 86.

311 Hudson, *The Permanent Court of International Justice* 1920–1942 (1943) 189, para 183.

312 n 302 above and accompanying text.

313 (1989) 60 BYIL 135.

314 [1978] ICJ Rep 33, para 78.

315 In the ILC it was argued by Jiménez de Aréchaga that the process is not an application of an intertemporal rule at all, but merely the application of the intention of the parties to an instrument: *Yearbook of the ILC* (1964-I) 34, para 10. See further on the place of the matter in the work of the Commission on the law of treaties, R Higgins, 'Some observations on the inter-temporal rule in international law' in J Macarczyk (ed), *Theory of international law at the threshold of the 21st century: essays in honour of Krzysztof Skubiszewski* (1996) 178–9.

316 [1997] ICJ Rep 67, para 111.

What the Treaty required in the way of performance was of course defined by the Treaty itself at the time it was concluded; and therefore the fact that performance would entail breach of newly emerged rules of customary law would in principle not exempt a party from such performance unless the new rules were matters of *jus cogens*, and neither party contended that such was the case.[317] However, the Court noted that the Treaty contained provisions (Articles 15, 19, and 20) that did not contain 'specific obligations of performance', but required the parties, 'in carrying out their obligations' under the Treaty 'to ensure that the quality of water in the Danube is not impaired and that nature is protected', to 'take new environmental norms into consideration'. The Court concluded that 'the Treaty is not static, and is open to adapt to emerging norms of international law'.[318]

This is thus an example (though in terms suggestive of a soft-law obligation) of what was called in the previous article in this series 'intertemporal *renvoi*'. If a treaty itself provides that its provisions, or certain of its provisions, are to follow the development of general law, and be interpreted and applied on the basis of that law, then the strict application of the intertemporal principle is ousted.[319]

However, the writer found it appropriate in a previous article to criticize, as much too sweeping, the assertion in the advisory opinion in the *Namibia* case that 'an international instrument has to be interpreted and applied within the framework of the entire legal system prevailing at the time of the interpretation'.[320] In the *Gabčíkovo/Nagymaros* case, Hungary had relied on this dictum, and Judge Bedjaoui found the question sufficiently important to warrant discussion in his separate opinion. He pointed out that in 1971 the Court itself had emphasized '*the primary necessity* of interpreting an instrument in accordance with the intentions of the parties at the time of its conclusion',[321] and that 'The intentions of the parties are presumed to have been influenced by *the law in force at the time the Treaty was concluded*, the law which they were supposed to know, and not by future law, as yet unknown'.[322] He concluded that 'the essential basis for the interpretation of a treaty remains the "*fixed reference*" [*renvoi fixe*] to contemporary international law at the time of its conclusion', and that 'The "*mobile reference*" [*renvoi mobile*] to the law which will subsequently have developed can be recommended only in exceptional cases of the sort we shall be looking at'. Judge Bedjaoui's distinction corresponds to that made in the previous article in this series, though his terminology is different.[323] However he adds (*inter alia*) a distinction

[317] [1997] ICJ Rep 67, para 112. [318] ibid.

[319] T Georgopoulos, 'Le droit intertemporel et les dispositions conventionnelles évolutives'(2004) 108 *Revue générale* 123. [320] [1971] ICJ Rep 31, para 53; discussed in (1989) 60 BYIL 137.

[321] ibid 31, quoted (with added emphasis) by Judge Bedjaoui at [1997] ICJ Rep 121, para 7(i).

[322] [1997] ICJ Rep 121, para 7(ii).

[323] The present writer preferred to reserve the term *renvoi* for the reference by the treaty to the developing law, since the case of the treaty requiring interpretation by the law of the time of its

between cases in which a 'concept', identified as the 'object of the treaty', had evolved—which, in his view was so in the *Namibia* case—and cases in which the applicable law had evolved, to which he would apply the normal intertemporal law principle.[324]

As Judge Bedjaoui sapiently points out, in the interpretation of treaties the principle of intertemporal law is entailed in that of respect for the intention of the parties, which is presumed to be that the current, and known, law shall apply. A related question is whether the same reasoning applies to matters of fact; while matters of fact are what they are, and are not subject to interpretation, a reference in a treaty to a factual matter must, in principle, speak from the time of conclusion of the treaty. In the case of *Kasikili/Sedudu Island*, the relevant Treaty (of 1890) provided that the boundary between British and German spheres of influence should descend 'the centre of the main channel' of a river. However, the disputed island split the river into two channels, north and south, and the question was which of the two was to be treated as the 'main channel' for purposes of the Treaty. If as a result of changes in the flow and topography of the river, what was the main channel in 1890 had become the lesser channel in 2004, and vice versa, the boundary would, on normal principles of treaty interpretation, continue to follow the 1890 'main channel'.[325] In its judgment the Court did not expressly state this as its point of departure, probably because it found that 'on the basis of the information supplied by both Parties concerning the hydrological situation of Kasikili/Sedudu Island . . . there are compelling reasons for assuming that this situation has seen no radical change over the last hundred years'.[326] Reference to the factual position in 1890 is however implied in the following dictum: 'In order to illuminate the meaning of words agreed upon in 1890, there is nothing that prevents the Court from taking into account the present-day state of scientific knowledge, as reflected in the documentary material submitted to it by the Parties . . . '.[327]

In support of this finding, the Court cited the Arbitral Award of 21 October 1974 in the *Laguna del Desierto* case (*Chile/Argentina*).[328] In that arbitration, the Tribunal was called upon to determine a boundary by 'interpreting and applying' an earlier arbitral award, made in 1902 (Articles I and II of the Compromis of 2 August 1991).[329] It was argued by Argentina that the line claimed by Chile in 1991–94 would give it

conclusion is automatic, and not the result of a deliberate provision contained or implied in the treaty. This usage seemed closer to the use of the term *renvoi* in private international law.

[324] [1997] ICJ Rep 122–3, paras 9–11.

[325] cf the argument of Honduras as to the application of the doctrine of 'avulsion' in the case concerning the *Land, Island and Maritime Frontier Dispute*, and the proceedings in revision of the judgment in that case: what mattered was the course of the river at the date of operation of the *uti possidetis* principle. [1992] ICJ Rep 546–7, para 310.

[326] [1999-II] ICJ Rep 1065, para 31.

[327] [1999-II] ICJ Rep 1060, para 20.

[328] French translation in (1996) 100 *Revue générale* 520; see also *International Law Reports* (ILR), vol 113.

[329] (1996) 100 *Revue générale* 521.

more territory than it had claimed in 1902, and that this would infringe the principle *ne ultra petita*. The 1996 Tribunal found that in 1902 Chile had claimed on the basis that the boundary was 'the natural and effective line of the continental water-parting', but since the region in question was unexplored, the actual position of the natural water-parting was not determined until 1941.

The Tribunal emphasized that its findings were based on the geographical information available to the parties at the time of the 1902 arbitration:

Ces conclusions se fondent également sur les connaissances géographiques des Parties en 1902. Il y avait alors des zones de frontière non explorées et d'autres qui n'étaient pas suffisamment connues, ce qui n'est pas le cas aujourd'hui. Le Chili soutint que ni l'inexactitude des cartes ni le manque de connaissance d'une région ne pouvaient servir d'excuse à la non application du critère invariable de démarcation qui était, selon lui, la ligne de partage continentale des eaux. Il affirma qu'à l'égard des régions inexplorées, le même principe devait être également appliqué, même si son résultat était aléatoire, et qu'il était prêt à accepter ses conséquences. Par conséquent, la conclusion de ce Tribunal selon laquelle le Chili se réclamait dans toutes les hypothèses de la ligne de partage continentale des eaux naturelle et effective a été établie en prenant en compte les connaissances géographiques de 1902, c'est-à-dire qu'elle a strictement respecté le principe de contemporaneité.[330]

The Court in its 1999 judgment however referred to a later passage, paragraph 157, which reads:

Le Tribunal ne peut pas accueillir non plus l'argument du Chili selon lequel l'application de la Sentence de 1902 équivaudrait, à la lumière des connaissances géographiques acquises ultérieurement, à sa révision à travers l'appréciation rétroactive de faits nouveaux... La Sentence de 1902 définit, dans le secteur concerné par cet arbitrage, une ligne frontière qui suit un accident de la nature et qui, en tant que tel, est indépendante d'une connaissance certaine des lieux mais repose sur leur seule configuration réelle. Le terrain demeure. Dès lors, la ligne de partage locale des eaux entre la borne 62 et le mont Fitz Roy qui existait en 1902 est la même que celle qui peut être tracée à la date du présent arbitrage. Cette sentence ne révise donc pas mais applique fidèlement ce qui a été décidé dans la Sentence de 1902.[331]

The decision thus emphasizes the distinction between what the parties intended, to be judged by the state of their knowledge at the time (1902), and the physical facts, in respect of which present-day scientific information may be consulted.

The 'present-day state of scientific knowledge' referred to in the *Kasikili/Sedudu Island* judgment had thus *prima facie* to be scientific

[330] Award, para 97, loc cit, 567.

[331] ibid 592. For the further problems arising from a Chilean request for revision, linked with the question of the effect of glacier movement on the water-parting line, see the commentary by Garciá Jiménez in (1997) 13 *Anuario de derecho internacional* 131.

knowledge as to *what was the position in 1890*. However, if it could be shown that in 1890 each of the parties believed, on reasonable grounds, that (say) the south channel was the main channel, then that was the channel agreed on for the boundary; and for modern scientific methods to demonstrate that in 1890 it had been the north channel that was the main channel would not justify an interpretation contrary to the parties' intentions. The term 'main channel' meant what the parties agreed it should mean,[332] and if a hydrographer had told them, on seeing the treaty, that from a scientific standpoint their identification of the 'main channel' was mistaken, this would have changed nothing. What is important is the intention of the parties, at the time of conclusion of the instrument.[333]

A clearer case was that of the *Land and Maritime Boundary between Cameroon and Nigeria*, where a 1931 Exchange of Notes referred to 'the mouth of the Ebeji [river]'; the Court observed that: 'In order to interpret this expression, the Court must seek to ascertain the intention of the parties at the time.'[334]

It must be conceded that the definition of a 'main' channel, or of the 'mouth' of a river (which may split into several channels), leaves room for some subjectivity, whereas other geographical features may be determinable with certainty. Thus in the case of the *Temple of Preah Vihear*,[335] the 1904 boundary treaty between France and Siam provided for a line following the watershed between two specified river basins, and for a delimitation following the treaty by Mixed Commissions.[336] The Court referred to the indication of the line of the watershed as 'an obvious and convenient way of defining a frontier line *objectively*'.[337] The decision in the case turned on the effect to be given to a subsequent map indicating the boundary which, it was agreed, showed a line not in fact corresponding to the watershed. The question was thus not whether, when concluding the treaty, the parties had agreed to treat a particular line as the 'watershed' even if as a matter of geography it was not; they had agreed to fix the boundary at the 'watershed' in (presumably) the correct geographical definition, but the makers of the map had gone astray, despite that fact that (it seems) the watershed was unambiguously definable.[338] Yet if it could have been shown that both of the parties, in referring to

332 '[T]he Court observes that by introducing the term "main channel" into the draft treaty, the contracting parties must be assumed to have intended that a precise meaning be given to it.' (ibid para 27): but 'precise' here must mean 'specific', not necessarily 'scientifically accurate'.

333 In the *Fisheries Jurisdiction* case between Spain and Canada, the Court emphasized that an optional-clause declaration was to be interpreted 'having due regard to the intention of the State concerned at the time when it accepted the jurisdiction of the Court': [1998] ICJ Rep 454, para 49.

334 [2002] ICJ Rep 346, para 59.

335 The decision on the merits in this case was not dealt with in Sir Gerald Fitzmaurice's articles, as by that time he had become a Member of the Court (and indeed there are stylistic reasons for believing that much of it was drafted by him).

336 See the text of the relevant articles in [1962] ICJ Rep 16.

337 [1962] ICJ Rep 35 (emphasis added).

338 According to one party, 'the geographical configuration of the place is such as to make it obvious to anyone who has been there that the watershed must lie along the line of the escarpment' on

the 'watershed', had had in mind a particular line which was not the true (ie geographic) watershed, then that line would have been the boundary that they agreed to establish.

In his dissenting opinion in the case of the *Request for an Examination of the Situation* presented by New Zealand in 1995, Judge Weeramantry quoted with approval an observation by New Zealand counsel in the original proceedings in 1974, that 'an inter-temporal rule applies to fact as well as to law'.[339] That observation had been made in response to the argument that it was inconsistent for New Zealand to object to nuclear tests in 1974, when it had not done so in relation to more dangerous forms of testing in the 1950s: the response in effect was: 'If we'd known then what we know now, we would have objected'. In 1995 the Court rejected New Zealand's attempt to re-open the 1974 proceedings in order to restrain France from carrying out underground nuclear tests, essentially on the ground that the 1974 proceedings had only related to atmospheric tests, which France was then carrying out. Judge Weeramantry disagreed, *inter alia* on the basis of his application of an intertemporal rule concerning facts. It is true that *if* New Zealand had been aware that the underground tests, with which France was in 1974 proposing to replace its programme of atmospheric tests, would also cause injury to New Zealand, it would in all probability have presented in 1974 a request that France be enjoined from that kind of testing also.

The 1974 observation by New Zealand counsel constituted a reasonable response to an imputation of inconsistency of conduct; and had that been the issue in 1995, then the same argument would have been pertinent. The question before the Court was however not 'Why did New Zealand not object to underground tests in 1974?', but rather 'Given that the 1974 proceedings related solely to atmospheric tests, can *those same proceedings* now be re-opened, directed against underground tests?' Judge Weeramantry's appeal to an intertemporal principle as to facts is therefore beside the point. If the Court had been asked in 1995 whether underground tests should be restrained as injurious to other States, it should certainly have taken into account the scientific knowledge of 1995; and this would equally be so if it had been asked whether such tests had been injurious, as a matter of fact, in 1974.[340] But that was not the issue; and no intertemporal rule as to facts needed to be invoked.

As is shown by, for example, the case of *Certain Property* between Liechtenstein and Germany, intertemporal questions may arise in the application of jurisdictional instruments, such as optional-clause declarations

which the Court commented that this was 'a fact which, if true, must have been no less evident in 1908': [1962] ICJ Rep 26.

339 [1995] ICJ Rep 340, quoting *ICJ Pleadings, Nuclear Tests*, Vol. II, 255.

340 A different question would be whether such tests had been unlawful in 1974; and to this the normal intertemporal rule of law would apply. If States did not in 1974 protest against underground tests carried out by their neighbours, because they did not know how harmful these might be, then there was no customary rule of law forbidding such tests.

excluding disputes arising, or concerning facts, prior to or after a specified date. These however are better dealt with under the heading of interpretation of treaties, below.[341]

[3. The relationship between sources of law]

[(1) The nature of the rules governing the relationship between sources]

[(2) Rights and obligations with a double foundation: overlap of treaty and customary law]

PART TWO

The original article on which this supplement is based appeared in (1990) 61 BYIL 1–133.

Division B: Sources of Law

The question of the sources of international law evokes learned debate and bafflement among scholars of each successive generation, a process that shows no sign of abating;[342] but the Court continues to resolve, without evident difficulty, the matters submitted to it in the light of Article 38, paragraph 1, of its Statute, whatever the theoretical insufficiencies of that text. Nevertheless, judicial decisions since the publication of the first article in this series contain a certain amount of further material of interest to the study of the sources of international law.

Chapter I: Miscellaneous Minor Sources or Pseudo-Sources

1. Considerations of humanity

The earlier article on this question contained a discussion[343] whether the references to 'considerations of humanity' in the Court's case-law were to be understood as identifying such considerations as a separate source of law; or whether the law in this field was to be regarded as customary in nature, or as deriving from 'general principles of law'. The conclusion

[341] However, as the Court observed in the *Anglo-Iranian Oil Co* case, an optional-clause declaration is not a treaty text, and therefore not necessarily subject to the same rules of interpretation: [1952] ICJ Rep 106. On this question, see M Fitzmaurice, 'The Optional Clause system and the law of treaties: issues of interpretation in recent jurisprudence of the International Court of Justice', (1999) 20 *Australian Yearbook of International Law* 127–59.

[342] See eg G Buzzini, 'La théorie des sources face au droit international général' (2002) 3 *Revue générale* 581; J Kammerhofer, 'Uncertainty in the Formal Sources of International Law: Customary Law and some of its Problems' [2004] EJIL 523.

[343] (1990) 61 BYIL 6–12.

reached was that some of the Court's dicta pointed one way, and some another.

The advisory opinion on the *Legality of the Threat or Use of Nuclear Weapons* is clearer on this issue. The Court began its examination of 'the principles and rules of international humanitarian law' by noting that 'A large number of customary rules have [sic] been developed by the practice of States and are an integral part of the international law relevant to the question posed' by the Assembly.[344] It referred to codification by international convention, and new specific prohibitions effected by multilateral treaty. It then enumerated what it termed 'the cardinal principles contained in the texts'; only thereafter did the Court quote the phrase 'elementary considerations of humanity' from the *Corfu Channel* decision.[345] It did so in order to suggest that it was because 'a great many rules of humanitarian law applicable in armed conflict are so fundamental to the respect of the human person', and to those considerations, that 'the Hague and Geneva Conventions have enjoyed a broad accession'.[346]

The Court therefore did not base any rules or principles of international law upon humanitarian considerations alone: it found that they were solidly based in custom and in conventional law. This is clear also from the dissenting opinion of Judge Shahabuddeen. He argued that the celebrated 'de Martens clause' in the Preamble to the 1899 Hague Convention was normative in itself, and not merely as a declaration of existing customary law. He quoted Fitzmaurice's 1950 views, discussed in a previous article in this series,[347] emphasizing Fitzmaurice's reference to considerations of humanity as giving rise 'in themselves' to obligations of a legal character,[348] as well as the *Corfu Channel* dictum and the *Krupp* case before the Nuremberg Tribunal. He concluded that the de Martens clause 'provided its own self-sufficient and conclusive authority for the proposition that there were already in existence principles of international law under which considerations of humanity could themselves exert legal force to govern military conduct in cases in which no relevant rule was provided by conventional law'.[349] Judge Shahabuddeen was careful to distinguish between an enquiry into the views of States as 'indicating the state of the public conscience', and an enquiry to determine the existence or otherwise of an *opinio juris*,[350] since for him the source of the legal obligations in question was not customary law.

344 [1996-I] ICJ Rep 256, paras 74–75.

345 [1949] ICJ Rep 22, quoted in [1996-I] ICJ Rep 257, para 79.

346 [1996-I] ICJ Rep 257, para 79.

347 GG Fitzmaurice in (1950) 27 BYIL 17, reproduced in *Collected Edition*, vol I, 17; discussed in (1990) 61 BYIL 6–7.

348 But not Fitzmaurice's later, more cautious, views expressed in his 1965 paper 'Judicial Innovation—its Uses and Perils' (*Cambridge Essays in Honour of Lord McNair*), noted in the earlier article in this series (loc cit).

349 [1996-I] ICJ Rep 408.

350 ibid 409–10.

In this respect he drew attention to differences in the wording of the original (1899) text and the text included in the 1977 Geneva Protocols. The earlier text referred to 'the principles of the law of nations, as they result from the usages established among civilized peoples, from the laws of humanity, and the dictates of the public conscience'.[351]

> . . . in its 1977 formulation, the relevant phrase now reads, 'derived from established custom, from the principles of humanity and from the dictates of public conscience'. Since 'established custom' alone would suffice to identify a rule of customary international law, a cumulative reading is not probable. It should follow that 'the principles of international law' (the new wording) could also be sufficiently derived 'from the principles of humanity and from the dictates of public conscience'; as mentioned above, those 'principles of international law' could be regarded as including principles of international law already derived 'from the principles of humanity and from the dictates of public conscience.

Judge Shahabuddeen did not comment on the question of the application of Article 38 of the Statute, which does not empower the Court to employ considerations of humanity, as such, as a source; it may be that he envisaged their inclusion as an aspect of the general principles of law under paragraph 1(c). This was explicitly the position of Judge Weeramantry in his dissenting opinion.[352]

Be that as it may, the Court clearly did not follow Judge Shahabuddeen in this respect. However, it chose also to consider the question whether the principles and rules of humanitarian law that had come into existence before nuclear weapons were invented applied also to those weapons, in particular since 'there is a qualitative as well as quantitative difference between nuclear weapons and all conventional arms'.[353] A conclusion that those principles and rules did not so apply, it declared, 'would be incompatible with the intrinsically humanitarian character of the legal principles in question which permeates the entire law of armed conflict and applies to all forms of warfare and to all kinds of weapons, those of the past, those of the present, and those of the future'.[354]

So far as conventional prohibitions are concerned, strictly speaking the question is one of interpretation of the relevant texts: were they intended to cover not merely the weapons existing at the time, but also 'those of the future'? The Court reasoned on the basis that they were so intended,[355] and found it unnecessary to go into the detail of such interpretations. As to customary law, there is no difficulty in considering that the rules and principles were from the outset sufficiently broad in scope to embrace the use of novel weapons.[356] The conclusion is that the reference to the

[351] This is the text quoted in Judge Shahabuddeen's opinion at [1996-I] ICJ Rep 405 as being that of 1899, but it is in fact from the 1907 Hague Convention, and differs in a few details from the 1899 text: see T Meron, 'The Martens Clause: Principles of Humanity and Dictates of Public Conscience' (2000) 94 AJIL 79.

[352] [1996-I] ICJ Rep 259, 493–4.

[353] ibid 86.

[354] ibid.

[355] See Chapter III, Section 2(2) above.

[356] It may be significant that the Court regarded as relevant the fact that no State before it had argued that the established rules did *not* apply to nuclear weapons—indeed it quoted the statements

'intrinsically humanitarian character of the legal principles in question' does not add, and was not intended to add, anything as regards the bases of humanitarian law in the sources of international law.[357]

In its opinion on *Legal Consequences of the Construction of a Wall on the Occupied Palestinian Territory*, the Court adopted a similar classical approach to the question of sources: 'The Court will now determine the rules and principles of international law which are relevant in assessing the legality of the measures taken by Israel. Such rules and principles can be found in the United Nations Charter and certain other treaties, in customary international law and in the relevant resolutions adopted pursuant to the Charter by the General Assembly and the Security Council.'[358] The inclusion of General Assembly and Security Council resolutions is justified by recourse to them later in the opinion, but they are not advanced as a source of international law in themselves. In any event, it is clear that the Court saw no need, or considered it incorrect, to refer to 'considerations of humanity' in general as justifying its findings concerning the obligations of Israel.

2. *Legal interests, legitimate interests, economic interests*

In the case concerning the *Land, Island and Maritime Boundary* between El Salvador and Honduras, the basic principle for determination of the land boundary was that of *uti possidetis*, a principle of customary law.[359] El Salvador however put forward in addition 'a body of arguments referred to either as "arguments of a human nature" or as arguments based on "*effectivités*" '.[360] Under these headings, El Salvador drew attention to 'demographic pressures in El Salvador creating a need for territory, as compared with the relatively sparsely populated Honduras; and . . . the superior natural resources (e.g., water for agriculture and hydroelectric power) said to be enjoyed by Honduras'.[361]

The Chamber seised of the case did not accept the arguments of El Salvador under either of these two heads; first because, for purposes of the *uti possidetis juris*, 'the question is not whether the colonial province needed wide boundaries, but where those boundaries actually were'; and secondly because, following the *Continental Shelf (Tunisia/Libya)* decision, economic considerations could not be relevant for the determination of a land frontier any more than they were for delimitation of the continental shelf.[362]

of several States to the opposite effect: [1996-I] ICJ Rep 259–60, para 86. This could be a finding indicative of the existence of *opinio juris*.

357 Meron concludes that the Martens clause, in its accepted interpretation, may be a statement of the obvious, but 'does serve a humanitarian purpose and is therefore not redundant'; yet he goes on: 'Except in extreme cases, its references to the principles of humanity and dictates of public conscience cannot, alone, delegitimize weapons and methods of war . . . ': op cit (n 351 above) 88.

358 [2004] ICJ Rep 171, para 86.

359 See further Chapter III, Section 4 below.

360 [1992] ICJ Rep 395, para 57.

361 ibid 396, para 58.

362 ibid.

Neither El Salvador nor the Chamber dealt with the question as a matter of sources of law; but El Salvador did put forward as justification for advancing these arguments a provision in the General Treaty of Peace between the parties, whereby the Joint Frontier Commission thereby established was to take account of *inter alia* 'evidence and arguments of a legal, historical, human or any other kind, brought before it by the Parties and admitted under international law'.[363] Apart from the fact that, as the Chamber noted, this article, being addressed to the Joint Frontier Commission and not to the Chamber, was 'not drafted as an applicable law clause',[364] the final phrase shows that the text did not justify invocation of what may loosely be called economic interests, either as an independent source of law, or as referred to in a treaty instrument and on that basis part of conventional law.

In maritime delimitation cases, any relevance that economic interests may have lies behind the veil of 'equitable considerations', so that even where such aspects have been allowed to influence a delimitation, it is unclear what is the formal source of the relevant rules of law. This is particularly so when the only role of such considerations is to meet concern that 'the applicable of equitable criteria . . . should unexpectedly be revealed as radically inequitable, as likely to entail catastrophic repercussions for the livelihood and economic well-being of the countries concerned'.[365] Whether there is any difference in substance between the taking into account of such aspects in the determination of a delimitation line, on the one hand, and the process of checking, *ex post facto*, the line for equitableness by reference to these aspects, may be doubtful.[366]

In the case concerning the *Land and Maritime Boundary between Cameroon and Nigeria* Nigeria contended that 'State practice with regard to oil concessions is a decisive factor in the establishment of maritime boundaries', and the Court addressed 'the question of the significance of oil concessions for maritime delimitation'.[367] After examining the jurisprudence,[368] the Court concluded that 'oil concessions and oil wells are not in themselves to be considered as relevant circumstances justifying the adjustment or shifting of the provisional delimitation line'.[369] It was not, in fact, the oil interests of the parties, let alone their respective economic positions, that were of possible relevance, but rather the pattern of oil concessions as revealing or implying either an implied agreement, or a recognition of what would be 'equitable'.[370]

363 Quoted at ibid para 57.

364 ibid 391, para 48.

365 *Gulf of Maine* [1984] ICJ Rep 342, para 237.

366 cf eg Poso Serrano, '¿Hacia una solución "económicamente equitativa"? Reflexiones sobre la evolución de la jurisprudencia internacional en materia de delimitación marina' (1997) 13 *Anuario de derecho internacional* 465.

367 [2002] ICJ Rep 447, paras 303–304.

368 The *Tunisia/Libya* case, the *Gulf of Maine* case, the *Continental Shelf (Libya/Malta)* case, and the arbitration on *St Pierre and Miquelon*.

369 [2002] ICJ Rep 447–8, para 304.

370 On this, see in particular the *Tunisia/Libya* case, and the present writer's comments at (1994) 65 BYIL 20–3.

[(1) The distinction between rights and interests: the Barcelona Traction *case]*

[(2) Interests as the inspiration of a practice producing a customary right: the Fisheries Jurisdiction *cases]*

[(3) Interests underlying the establishment of prescriptive or historic rights: the Tunisia/Libya *case]*

[(4) Economic and other interests as 'relevant circumstances' for purposes of an equitable delimitation of maritime spaces]

[(5) The special case of intervention under Article 62 *of the Statute]*

Chapter II: Treaties and Conventions in Force

Fasolt: 'Was du bist, bist du nur durch Verträge;
bedungen ist wohl bedacht deine Macht'.

Wagner, *Rheingold*, Sc 2

1. Source of law or source of obligation?

In the previous article on this subject,[371] it was suggested that the wording of the judgment in the *Gulf of Maine* case indicated a tendency to play down the importance, as law, of the provisions of treaties (particularly treaties other than multilateral conventions), an approach possibly paralleling Fitzmaurice's dismissal of treaties as sources of obligation rather than sources of law. One of the issues before the Chamber in that case, the handling of which suggested this underlying approach, was the problem of the 'single maritime boundary', dividing both the continental shelf and the exclusive economic zone (EEZ). In that case the two States were parties to the 1958 Geneva Convention on the Continental Shelf, which would govern any delimitation between them that was confined to the shelf; the Chamber found it possible to set the Convention entirely aside for the purposes of the single delimitation line.

It did so however on the basis that the parties had jointly requested the Chamber to draw a single line. In the case of *Maritime Delimitation in the Area between Greenland and Jan Mayen*, on the other hand, one party requested a single line for continental shelf and fishery zones, and the other requested two lines, separate in essence but coinciding in geographical location. The Court found that the 1958 Geneva Convention was applicable to the delimitation of the shelf;[372] but it found also that the delimitation article of the Convention could not 'be interpreted and applied without reference to customary law on the subject, or wholly

[371] (1990) 61 BYIL 21–5. [372] [1993] ICJ Rep 58, para 45.

independently of the fact that a fishery zone is also in question . . .'[373] As far as the fishery zone was concerned, the parties had indicated that they saw no objection to the boundary being determined by the law applicable to the boundary of the EEZ.[374] The outcome was that the Court drew two identical delimitation lines which constituted, in the view of the Court, 'a proper application both of the law applicable to the continental shelf and of that applicable to the fishery zones'.[375]

The observation quoted above is suggestive in a number of ways. First, a treaty has to be 'interpreted and applied' on the basis of customary law rules of interpretation; but it is not evident that such interpretation and application has necessarily to take into account customary law 'on the subject' governed by the treaty. The whole purpose of the treaty may have been to diverge, as between the parties, from the customary law on the subject. Secondly, one may ask what the Court meant by saying that 'a fishery zone is also in question'. If the request made to the Court had been solely for a delimitation of the continental shelf, would the outcome be different because there was also a dispute, not before the Court, about the delimitation of the fishery zones? Or did the Court merely mean that the fishery zone was also in question in the case before it? In either case, it is not apparent why the Geneva Convention should not be applied, *quoad* the shelf, according to its terms.

The identical delimitation lines were justified by an argument that may be simply expressed as follows: the Convention (for the shelf areas) and customary law (for the EEZ, applied by consent to the fishery zones) say the same thing, or rather require application of the same criteria; and that application, fortunately, led to identical lines. But for this it would have been sufficient to take the Convention as a starting point, as something that had to be applied to the delimitation of the shelf, and to consider whether customary law led to the same conclusion for the fishery zones. It was not so much a matter of interpreting and applying the convention taking into account customary law, but of taking account of the convention in ascertaining the customary law.

To a lesser extent than in the *Gulf of Maine* case, the language of the decision in the *Jan Mayen* case suggests a certain down-grading of the status of a convention, even a multilateral convention, in relation to customary law, as though, indeed, such a convention might be no more than a source of obligation, not of law.[376]

[373] ibid para 46. [374] ibid 59, para 47. [375] ibid 79, para 90.

[376] Subsequent cases involving maritime boundaries will be dealt with in a subsequent article, under the heading of 'Law of the Sea'. They involved different relationships between custom and treaty: in *Maritime Delimitation and Territorial Questions between Qatar and Bahrain*, neither State was a party to the 1958 and 1982 Conventions, so that customary law governed. In the case of the *Land and Maritime Boundary between Cameroon and Nigeria*, the applicable law was stated to be solely that of the 1982 Convention, to which both States were parties, even though that Convention makes no express provision for single-line delimitation, and as the Court had observed in the *Qatar/Bahrain* case, 'the concept of a single maritime boundary does not stem from multilateral treaty law but from State practice': [2001] ICJ Rep 93, para 173.

2. *Interaction of customary law and treaty law*[377]

The circumstances in which the Court, in the case concerning *Military and Paramilitary Activities in and against Nicaragua*, had to try to apply customary law independently of the multilateral treaties in force between the parties, and relevant to the matters in hand, were always unlikely to recur, and have not in fact recurred before the Court.

Two more recent cases have however raised questions of interest as regards the inter-relation of treaty and customary law, though in the first of these, that of *Maritime Delimitation in the Area between Greenland and Jan Mayen*, the matter is not referred to in the judgment, and may have been overlooked by all concerned. Both parties to the case, Denmark and Norway, were parties to the 1958 Geneva Convention on the Continental Shelf, and neither was a party to the 1982 United Nations Convention on the Law of the Sea (though both had signed that Convention), which, furthermore, was not yet in force.[378] The 1958 Geneva Convention provides in Article 1 that 'For the purpose of these articles, the term "continental shelf" is used as referring (*a*) to the seabed and subsoil of the submarine areas adjacent to the coast but outside the area of the territorial sea, to a depth of 200 metres or, beyond that limit, to where the depth of the superjacent waters admits of exploitation of the natural resources of the said areas . . .'

In the *North Sea Continental Shelf* case, the Court found that the doctrine that the coastal State has 'an original natural and exclusive' right to the continental shelf off its shores was part of customary law, and reflected in Article 2 of the Geneva Convention,[379] and also that Articles 1 to 3 of the Convention were, at the time the Convention was concluded 'regarded as reflecting, or as crystallizing, received or at least emergent rules of customary international law relative to the continental shelf, amongst them the question of the seaward extent of the shelf . . .'[380] Thus, in 1958, the extent seawards of the continental shelf, as a concept, was identical in customary law and in the law of the Convention. The customary law on the point could of course develop; but in principle those States which had become parties to the Convention had agreed on a conventional definition which could only be varied by agreement between them, and—again in principle—would not be affected by subsequent developments in customary law.

The definition of the seaward extent of the continental shelf in the 1982 UN Convention, so far as relevant to the geographical circumstances of the *Greenland/Jan Mayen* case, was simply 200 nautical miles from the baselines of the territorial sea.[381] Neither of the relevant coasts enjoyed a physical shelf extending beyond 200 miles; and the distance

[377] This section was originally entitled ' "Applicability" of Law derived from a Treaty Source: "the *Nicaragua* v. *United States of America* case"'.

[378] [1993] ICJ Rep 52, para 31; 59, para 48.

[379] [1969] ICJ Rep 33, para 47.

[380] ibid 39, para 63.

[381] UNCLOS, Art 76, para 1.

between them was about 250 nautical miles; the depth of the sea between the two coasts was for the most part 'rather less than 2000 metres'.[382] Thus if the areas of 'continental shelf' appertaining to the parties were to be determined according to the criterion of the 1958 Geneva Convention, there would be no need for a delimitation, since the shelf of neither coast would extend far enough offshore to encounter the shelf of the other.

The parties in their pleadings seem to have taken it as axiomatic that they were entitled at customary law to continental shelves of the extent defined by the 1982 Convention (and it is probably true to say that customary law did at the time, even before the Convention had come into force, justify a claim to a minimum 200-mile shelf, though the detailed Convention provisions for determining the limit of a more extensive physical shelf could not be regarded as reflecting custom). Nor does it appear to have worried them that they were making such a claim while at the same time recognizing that they were bound by the 1958 Geneva Convention.[383] The Court held that the 1958 Convention 'governs the continental shelf delimitation to be effected', but passed over in silence the question whether that Convention also governed the definition of what it was that was to be delimited. It did however indicate that 'in the present case, delimitation is required between opposite coasts which are insufficiently far apart for both to enjoy the full 200-mile extension of continental shelf and other rights over maritime spaces recognized by international law . . .'.[384] Thus what it effected was a delimitation avowedly according to the 1958 Geneva Convention (Article 6) of continental shelf, but continental shelf as defined by 1993 customary law. At no point did it explain this apparent inconsistency.

In his separate opinion, Judge Shahabuddeen observed that 'account must be taken of the fact that Article 76 of the 1982 Convention has introduced a new definition of the outer limit of the continental shelf. There is little dispute that this replaces the different definition set out in Article 1 of the 1958 Convention (*Tunisia/Libya, I.C.J. Reports 1982*, pp. 114–115, paras. 52–53, Judge Jiménez de Aréchaga, separate opinion). But exactly how this has come about is less clear.[385] Judge Jiménez de Aréchaga, in the passage referred to, was however discussing the impact of the 1982 Convention definition on customary law; he expressed no view on the position as between States parties to the 1958 Convention. Judge Shahabudeen had no difficulty in accepting the same approach as regards customary law; but in relation to the 1958 Convention, he could only quote Reuter to the effect that 'a later custom . . . prevails over an earlier treaty'.[386] But is this so, as a general rule? The fact that, as generally recognized, certain exceptional norms of customary law prevail over pre-existing treaty provisions (and indeed

[382] [1993] ICJ Rep 44, para 11. [383] ibid 57, para 44. [384] ibid 66, para 64.
[385] ibid 134. [386] *Introduction to the Law of Treaties* (1989) 107–8, para 216.

render them void) as being *jus cogens*, suggests *a contrario* that the normal principle is that treaty provisions continue to prevail and bind the parties whether or not the customary law on the same matter has moved on in the meantime.

Clearly the existence of the conventional bond created by the 1958 Convention could not prevent Denmark and Norway from becoming entitled under customary law to a full 200-mile continental shelf. It was established in the case of the *Military and Paramilitary Activities in and against Nicaragua* that the same subject-matter can be governed simultaneously, as regards a particular State or States, by a treaty regime and by customary law, even when the dispositions of the two regimes are near identical.[387] One possible view of the situation in the *Jan Mayen* case would therefore be that the physical shelf off the coast of the two States was governed, as far out as the 200-metre depth line (or the exploitation limit contemplated by the 1958 Convention, whatever that might be), by the terms of the 1958 Convention, and beyond that limit by customary law. On that basis, the delimitation provisions of Article 6 the 1958 Convention would have no application between the two States, since, as already noted, their 'Convention-shelves' were at no point contiguous. The delimitation of the 'custom-shelves' would of course be governed by customary law. There is of course a certain awkwardness in contemplating two different meanings of the expression 'continental shelf' in international law; Judge Shahabuddeen took the view that 'the same facts cannot at one and the same time be subject to two contradictory rules'.[388]

From a different angle, the *Oil Platforms* case is also of interest as regards the relationship between treaty obligations between two States and the background of customary law equally binding upon them. Under Article XX, paragraph 1(d) of a 1955 Treaty of Amity, that Treaty was not to 'preclude the application of measures . . . necessary to fulfil the obligations of a High Contracting Party . . . necessary to protect its essential security interests'. The United States claimed that the attacks by its forces on Iranian oil platforms were such measures; it had also contended, in particular in communications to the Security Council, that they were justified as an exercise of the inherent right of self-defence. The Court's jurisdiction was derived from the compromissory clause (Article XXI, paragraph 2) of the 1955 Treaty, and the United States contended that the Court need not (and should not) address the issue of self-defence.

> [The United States] does not however contend that the Treaty exempts it, as between the parties, from the obligations of international law on the use of force, but simply that where a party justifies certain action on the basis of Article XX, paragraph 1(*d*), that action has to be tested solely against the criteria of that Article, and the jurisdiction conferred on the Court by Article XXI, paragraph 2, of the Treaty goes no further than that.[389]

[387] [1984] ICJ Rep 424, para 73.
[388] [1993] ICJ Rep 134.
[389] [2003] ICJ Rep 181, para 39.

The Court rejected this contention, as a matter of interpretation of the Treaty. However it also argued as follows:

Moreover, under the general rules of treaty interpretation, as reflected in the 1969 Vienna Convention on the Law of Treaties, interpretation must take into account 'any relevant rules of international law applicable in the relations between the parties' (Article 31, paragraph 3*(c)*). The Court cannot accept that Article XX, paragraph 1*(d)*, of the 1955 Treaty was intended to operate wholly independently of the relevant rules of international law on the use of force, so as to be capable of being successfully invoked, even in the limited context of a claim for breach of the Treaty, in relation to an unlawful use of force. The application of the relevant rules of international law relating to this question thus forms an integral part of the task of interpretation entrusted to the Court by Article XXI, paragraph 2, of the 1955 Treaty.[390]

The problem posed was in a sense the mirror-image of that which arose in the *Military and Paramilitary Activities* case. In that case, the Court was unable to apply the conventional law which it knew existed between the parties, and had to apply the general customary law on the same subject even though in the actual relations between the parties that customary law had been overlaid, or ousted, by the conventional law. In the *Oil Platforms* case, the Court was only empowered to judge whether or not the United States actions constituted breaches of the Treaty; it could not declare them a breach of customary law on the use of force, however flagrant a breach they might appear to be.[391] The passage quoted is one of the hinges of the process by which the Court nevertheless managed to assess and reject the United States plea that its use of force was in self-defence.

Does this mean, then, that whenever the Court has jurisdiction under a treaty to say whether or not a breach of the treaty has been committed, it may determine also (or alternatively) whether that action is also a breach of customary international law?[392] Such an interpretation would go against the whole system of international judicial jurisdiction, based as it is on consent, and with its limits defined by the limits of such consent.[393]

390 ibid 182, para 41. cf the decision in the *Greenland/Jan Mayen* case, discussed above, that the Geneva Convention on the Continental Shelf could not be interpreted and applied 'without reference to the customary law on the subject'([1993] ICJ Rep 58, para 46). Judge Higgins dissented from this part of the *Oil Platforms* judgment, in particular from the Court's reading of the Vienna Convention, Art 31, para 3 as 'incorporating the totality of the substantive international law ... on the use of force': ibid 237, para 46.

391 The operative clause of the judgment declared that the US actions could not be justified under Art XX, para 2(d) 'as interpreted in the light of international law on the use of force' (ibid 218, para 125(1)), but the inclusion of reference to general international law at all in the operative clause was objected to by, in particular, Judge Kooijmans, ibid 256–7, paras 33–35. Judge Simma on the other hand thought that the Court did not go far enough in its handling of the question of the use of force: ibid 326–8, paras 5–6.

392 Judge Kooijmans in his separate opinion observed that 'One can only wonder what the effect [of this part of the judgment] will be on States which are parties to comparable treaties with a compromissory clause': ibid 257, para 35.

393 cf the controversy as to the sources of law available to dispute settlement bodies in the WTO system, and the indication in the Dispute Settlement Understanding, Art 3.2 whereby the dispute settlement is to clarify the provisions of the WTO Agreements 'in accordance with customary rules

The matter is not one of interpretation of the Vienna Convention, since that Convention was not in force between the parties, and the Court explicitly refers to application of 'the general rules of treaty interpretation, as reflected' in that Convention. It is however presented as a matter of interpretation of the 1955 bilateral Treaty. The Court's argument concentrates on Article XX, paragraph 1(d), but its jurisdiction is regulated by Article XXI, paragraph 2, and thus extends solely to 'any dispute... as to the interpretation or application of the present Treaty...'. The Court found unacceptable the idea that Article XX, paragraph 2(d), could be 'successfully invoked... in relation to an unlawful use of force'; but this, it is suggested, is to confuse the legality (under general law) of an action and the susceptibility of that action to judgment by the Court—two things which the Court had very carefully distinguished in the *Fisheries Jurisdiction* case between Spain and Canada. In that case, the argument of Spain, in simple terms, was that the measures of maritime conservation that Canada had, by a reservation to its optional-clause declaration, excluded from the jurisdiction of the Court, could only be *legal* measures, since otherwise Canada would be giving itself licence to break the law. The Court declared that: 'There is a fundamental distinction between the acceptance by a State of the Court's jurisdiction and compatibility of particular acts with international law. The former requires consent. The latter question can only be reached when the Court deals with the merits, after having established its jurisdiction and having heard full legal argument by both parties.'[394]

Although in the *Oil Platforms* case the jurisdictional issue was being dealt with along with the merits, the principle must remain the same. If the 1955 Treaty had been specific, for example by referring to measures of security 'whether or not compatible with general international law', the Court would have had no justification for enquiring into such compatibility; but it would still have been able to say whether or not the measures were compatible *with the Treaty*. The Court however argues that, in the absence of such specification, Article XX is to be interpreted as saying that if security measures are not compatible with general international law, then they are not protected by the Treaty. One may ask why this should be so. If such measures were unlawful, then the other party would in any event have such remedies available as the general law of State responsibility affords (including, in the case of the use of force, self-defence). The Treaty was not a treaty of judicial or arbitral settlement: its object was not to enable the Court to settle all future disputes, or a wide range of future disputes, between the parties; it merely contained a compromissory clause to resolve disputes over the interpretation or application of its terms.

of interpretation of public international law': see M García-Rubio, *On the Application of Customary Rules of State Responsibility by the WTO Dispute Settlement Organs* (2001) 67ff; D Palmeter and PC Mavroidis, 'The WTO Legal System: Sources of Law' (1998) 92 AJIL 398; R Higgins, 'The ICJ, the ECJ and the Integrity of International Law' (2003) (52) ICLQ 16.

[394] [1998] ICJ Rep 456, para 55.

Judge Buergenthal put the point effectively in his separate opinion:

The problem with the Court's reliance on this provision of the Vienna Convention is that, while the rule is sound and undisputed in principle as far as treaty interpretation is concerned, it cannot have the effect of allowing the Court to take account, as it does here, of those 'relevant rules of international law applicable between the parties', which the parties to the dispute have not submitted to the Court's jurisdiction under the dispute resolution clause of the 1955 Treaty. That is, the principles of customary international law and whatever other treaties the parties to a dispute before the Court may have concluded do not by virtue of Article 31, paragraph 3*(c)*, become subject to the Court's jurisdiction. This is so whether or not they might be relevant in the abstract to the interpretation of a treaty with regard to which the Court has jurisdiction.[395]

How then does customary law intervene in the interpretation of a treaty, in the form of 'relevant rules of international law applicable in the relations between the parties'? The answer must be, insofar as the parties must be deemed to have had in contemplation international law as it stood at the time of conclusion of the treaty[396] when deciding what to put in, what to leave out, and how to express their intentions.[397] This is a matter to be considered further under the heading of interpretation of treaties. Certainly in 1955 the parties would have been aware of the prohibition on the use of force, and the exception in favour of self-defence; but they were not setting out to add a private conventional prohibition or definition to that afforded by customary law, nor to ensure that the lawfulness of a particular use of force could be judged by the Court.

3. *Status or regime-creating instruments*

In its judgment in the *Territorial Dispute* between Libya and Chad, the Court found that the boundary in the disputed area had been determined[398] by a Franco–Libyan Treaty of 1955, Article 11 of which had provided that 'The present Treaty is concluded for a period of 20 years', and that it could be terminated by either party twenty years after its entry into force. Neither party had taken any action to terminate the treaty. The Court held that: 'These provisions notwithstanding, the Treaty must, in the view of the Court, be taken to have determined a permanent frontier.' After noting that nothing in the Treaty pointed to an intention to create a provisional or temporary boundary, the Court continued:

The establishment of this boundary is a fact which, from the outset, has had a legal life of its own, independently of the fate of the 1955 Treaty. Once agreed,

[395] [2003] ICJ Rep 279, para 22.

[396] Or, exceptionally, international law as it might subsequently develop: see the remarks on 'intertemporal renvoi' in a previous article in this series: (1989) 60 BYIL 135–43, and Chapter III, Section 2(4) above.

[397] cf A Aust, *Modern Treaty Law and Practice* (2000) 195.

[398] Judge Shahabuddeen, while agreeing with the Court's conclusion, expressed doubts insofar as, in his opinion, the Court had based itself on the principle of stability of boundaries. He pointed out that that principle only comes into play once it is established that there was an agreement to fix a

the boundary stands, for any other approach would vitiate the fundamental principle of the stability of boundaries, the importance of which has been repeatedly emphasized by the Court (*Temple of Preah Vihear, I.C.J. Reports 1962*, p. 34; *Aegean Sea Continental Shelf, I.C.J. Reports 1978*, p. 36).

A boundary established by treaty thus achieves a permanence which the treaty itself does not necessarily enjoy. The treaty can cease to be in force without in any way affecting the continuance of the boundary. In this instance the Parties have not exercised their option to terminate the Treaty, but whether or not the option is exercised, the boundary remains. This is not to say that two States may not by mutual agreement vary the border between them; such a result can of course be achieved by mutual consent, but when a boundary has been the subject of agreement, the continued existence of that boundary is not dependent upon the continuing life of the treaty under which the boundary is agreed.[399]

Judge Sette Camara, in his dissenting opinion, agreed that the 1955 Treaty had lapsed in 1975, but doubted whether it could be taken for granted that its provisions were such as to benefit from 'the exception to the *tabula rasa* rule reserved for dispositive and territorial treaties'.[400]

The passage in the *Aegean Shelf* judgment to which the Court refers[401] concerns a slightly different aspect of the permanence of boundaries, namely 'the rule excluding boundary agreements from fundamental change of circumstances',[402] ie the rule that excludes the possibility of terminating such agreements on the grounds of fundamental change of circumstances. The finding in the *Territorial Dispute* case suggests that it is not so much that the rule does not apply to boundary agreements, but rather that the termination of an agreement that has fixed an international boundary, whether on the basis of fundamental change of circumstances or for other reasons, leaves the boundary unaffected.[403]

Since the publication of the earlier article commenting on these questions,[404] the Court has not had to deal directly with any other question of survival of obligations created by treaty having the nature of an international regime, of which the League of Nations mandates, discussed in the earlier article, were, it seems, a primary example. In the case of the *Gabčíkovo/Nagymaros Project*, however, it had to touch on an allied point, involving the concept of a territorial regime created by treaty.

boundary; it does not help in determining whether such agreement was ever made or whether an agreement alleged to have that nature in fact had it: [1994] ICJ Rep 45, criticizing ibid 23–4, paras 47–48.

399 [1994] ICJ Rep 37, paras 72–73.

400 ibid 98; see also ibid 102.

401 The discussion in the *Temple* case related rather to the interpretation of a boundary treaty, on the basis that 'In general, when two countries establish a frontier between them, one of the primary objects is to achieve stability and finality': [1962] ICJ Rep 34. This was also a matter of discussion in the *Territorial Dispute* case, but is not of direct relevance here.

402 [1978] ICJ Rep 35–6, para 85.

403 As does also a succession of States: cf Vienna Convention on the Succession of States in respect of Treaties, Art 12, and *Gabčíkovo/Nagymaros Project* [1997] ICJ Rep 71–3, paras 123–124.

404 (1990) 61 BYIL 27–31.

The question was the entitlement of Slovakia, as one of the successor States of the former Czechoslovakia, to invoke the 1977 Treaty with Hungary setting up the Project. Slovakia claimed such entitlement, as a matter of customary law,[405] reflected, according to Slovakia, in Articles 34 and 12 of the Vienna Convention on Succession of States in respect of Treaties. The Court found it unnecessary to deal with Article 34, but upheld Slovakia's claim on the basis of Article 12, paragraph 2, on the basis that the Treaty had created a 'territorial regime', as referred to in the title to that article, involving the interests of third States, users of the Danube river for navigation.[406] However, Article 2, paragraph 2, of the Convention provided that a succession of States should not affect obligations and rights 'established by the treaty', rather than the application of the treaty itself, or obligations and rights deriving from the status of parties to the treaty. The Court observed that:

> Article 12, in providing only, without reference to the treaty itself, that rights and obligations of a territorial character established by a treaty are unaffected by a succession of States, appears to lend support to the position of Hungary rather than of Slovakia.[407] However the Court concludes that this formulation was devised [by the ILC] rather to take account of the fact that, in many cases, treaties which had established boundaries or territorial regimes were no longer in force... Those that remained in force would nonetheless bind a successor State.[408]

The Court does not expressly approve the reasoning of the ILC, but it does nevertheless by implication recognize the existence of rights and obligations created by a treaty, in favour of non-parties,[409] that survive the disappearance of the treaty as a treaty. This concept of an independent regime seems however to be limited to cases involving territory (including boundaries).

[405] In the *Territorial Dispute* between Libya and Chad, Chad was relying, as successor State to France, on a Franco–Libyan Treaty of 1955 (see above). The Court noted that Libya did not 'question Chad's right to invoke against Libya any such provisions thereof as relate to the frontiers of Chad': [1994] ICJ Rep 20, para 36.

[406] [1997] ICJ Rep 71–2, para 123. It has been powerfully argued that Art 12 was strictly not applicable, since it 'relates essentially to what are not uncommonly referred to as servitudes' and not to a dam in a river: J Klabbers, 'Cat on a Hot Tin Roof: the World Court, State Succession and the *Gabčíkovo/Nagymaros* case' (1998) 11 *Leiden Journal of International Law* 353.

[407] Hungary had argued for a distinction between rights and obligations under the 1977 Treaty, on the one hand, and the Treaty itself, on the other: [1997] ICJ Rep 69, para 118.

[408] [1997] ICJ Rep 72, para 123, citing *Official Records of the United Nations Conference on Succession of States in respect of Treaties*, vol III, doc A/CONF.80/16/Add.2, 26–37.

[409] It seems doubtful whether an independent regime created by treaty can involve *obligations* imposed on non-parties that will survive the treaty. The obligation would have to be accepted at the outset (Vienna Convention on the Law of Treaties, Art 35); and the terms of the acceptance might govern the question of continued existence of the obligation independently of the treaty as a treaty; cf the reference in VCLT, Art 37(2) in connection with modification of rights of third parties, to the original intentions of those concerned.

Chapter III: Custom

Custom, that unwritten law,
By which the people keep even kings in awe.

D'Avenant, *Circe* (1677), Act 2, Sc 3

1. The relationship of 'general international law' and customary law

The use by the Court, remarked on in the earlier article in this series,[410] of the expression 'general international law', without a clear indication whether reference is being made to customary law, to general principles of law, or to some other kind of law, does not appear to have continued into recent years.[411] A recent commentary[412] on the concept of 'general international law' listed, as examples of the usage in decisions of the Court, nothing subsequent to the *Elettronica Sicula* case in 1989, where it was used to refer to the 'minimum international standard' for treatment of foreigners (ie a matter of customary law) in contradistinction to the obligations in that domain imposed by a particular treaty.[413] Similarly, individual Members of the Court have continued to employ the expression in their separate or dissenting opinions, fortunately in contexts in which it is clear that the reference is to customary law other than local or special custom.[414] There seems no indication that the term has continued to acquire in the Court's jurisprudence any special meaning other than this one, and it may thus be regarded as harmless.[415]

2. The elements constitutive of custom

[(1) Introduction]

(2) The opinio juris sive necessitatis

The Court has continued to espouse the classical two-element theory of custom, requiring the existence both of State practice and of the *opinio juris* for the establishment of a rule of customary international law.

[410] (1990) 61 BYIL 31–40.

[411] Though parties in their pleadings have been known to use it: see eg the Order in the case of the *Arrest Warrant of 11 April 2000*, quoting Belgium as using the term 'droit international général' and the Congo as using 'droit international commun', translated in each case as 'general international law': [2000] ICJ Rep 184, para 5 and 189, para 24.

[412] G Buzzini, 'La "généralité" du droit international général: réflexions sur la polysémie d'un concept' (2004) 108 *Revue générale* 382, citing the *North Sea Continental Shelf, Gulf of Maine* and *Elettronica Sicula (ELSI)* cases.

[413] [1989] ICJ Rep 66, para 111.

[414] See for instance *Questions of Interpretation and Application of the 1971 Montreal Convention arising from the Aerial Incident at Lockerbie*, in which a number of judges distinguished 'general international law' from the treaty-law deriving from the Convention: [1992] ICJ Rep, 18, 19, 24, 38, 39, 47, and 82.

[415] Some writers use 'general *principles* of international law' with a wider meaning; eg I Brownlie, *Principles of Public International Law* (2003) 18. Note also the usage introduced in the 9th edn of *Oppenheim* by the editors, Sir Robert Jennings and Sir Arthur Watts: 'That part of international law that is binding on all states, as is by far the greater part of customary law, may be called *universal*

In particular was this the case of an alleged customary rule forbidding the use or threat of use of nuclear weapons, asserted by numerous States in the proceedings on the request for an advisory opinion on the *Legality of the Threat or Use of Nuclear Weapons*. In its opinion, the Court began its examination of the customary law on the subject by citing with approval the statement in the case of the *Continental Shelf (Libya/Malta)* that the substance of customary law must be 'looked for primarily in the actual practice and *opinio juris* of States'.[416] It made no direct comment on the sufficiency of the practice cited, but rejected the contention on the basis that it was 'unable to find that there is such an *opinio juris* as was relied on'.[417] However, *opinio juris* does not exist in a vacuum: it is made manifest in acts of practice. The alleged existence of a customary rule may be disproved either by showing that there is insufficient consistent practice to justify deducing the existence of *opinio juris*, or by showing that the practice suggests a view of the law other than that advanced as *opinio juris*. There may be a fine line dividing these hypotheses, but they remain conceptually separate.

The practice alleged by the opponents of nuclear weapons was 'a consistent practice of non-utilization of nuclear weapons by States since 1945' which they saw as 'the expression of an *opinio juris* on the part of those who possess such weapons'.[418] Against this, the nuclear States 'invoked the doctrine and practice of deterrence', arguing that 'if nuclear weapons have not been used since 1945, it is not on account of an existing or nascent custom but merely because circumstances that might justify their use have fortunately not arisen'.[419] These States relied essentially on the absence of any prohibitory rule;[420] they did not go so far as to suggest that the practice showed an *opinio juris* suggesting the existence of a rule of international law *authorizing* the possession—and by implication, the use—of nuclear weapons,[421] nor did the Court conclude in such terms. It stated that it did not 'intend to pronounce here upon the practice known as the "policy of deterrence"', but it did take note of the existence of that practice as a relevant fact implying the lack of *opinio juris* in favour of a prohibitory rule.

Having noted the practice of deterrence, the Court continued: 'Furthermore, the Members of the international community are profoundly

international law, in contradistinction to *particular* international law which is binding on two or a few states only. *General* international law is that which is binding upon a great many States ... such as provisions of certain treaties which are widely, but not universally, binding ... ': ibid vol 1, 4. (original emphasis); cf also M Akehurst, *Modern Introduction to International Law* (7th edn, P Malanczuk) 2. So far as the present writer has been able to establish, neither the Court nor its Members have so far employed this distinction.

416 [1985] ICJ Rep 29, para 27, quoted in [1996-I] ICJ Rep 253, para 64.

417 [1996-I] ICJ Rep 254, para 67. 418 ibid 253–4, para 65. 419 ibid 254, para 66.

420 See eg US Written Statement, Section III B; Written Statement of France <http://www.icj-cij.org/icjwww/icases/iunan/iunan_ipleadings/iunan_ipleadings_199506_WriStats_19_France.pdf>, 23.

421 Except on the basis of the inherent right of self-defence, regarded as extending to the use, in certain limited circumstances, of nuclear weapons. cf UK Written Statement, para 3.36; Written Statement of France (n 420 above) 28.

divided on the matter of whether non-recourse to nuclear weapons over the past fifty years constitutes the expression of an *opinio juris*. Under these circumstances the Court does not consider itself able to find that there is such an *opinio juris*.'[422] Rather curiously, the Court here does not raise and answer the question: Does the practice show the existence of *opinio juris*?, but rather the question: Do the members of the international community think that there is an *opinio juris*? This is to raise the psychological element in custom from one level to another; more significantly, it suggests a divorce of *opinio juris* from practice, in the sense that the views of States which do not possess nuclear weapons become relevant, if not as *opinio juris*, then as *opinio* as to the existence thereof, a sort of *opinio opinionis juris*. Whatever the merits of this approach, it is inconsistent with an examination of the significance of *inaction* on the part of the nuclear States. The Court seems reluctant to uphold the simple contention that a negative practice, the non-use of nuclear weapons, does not support *opinio juris*, because it is far from being manifestly attributable to a belief in the unlawfulness of such use; it constitutes what has been termed an 'ambiguous omission'.[423]

A similar shift in the understanding of the *opinio juris* is to be found in the Court's examination, discussed below, of the significance in this domain of General Assembly resolutions proclaiming, expressly or by implication, the unlawfulness of the threat or use of nuclear weapons.

[(a) Nature of the *opinio juris*]

[(b) Application of *opinio juris* by the Court]

[(c) Whose *opinio juris*?]

[(i) The relevance of the views of the parties]

[(ii) Opinio juris *of States not before the Court]*

(d) <u>*Opinio juris* and argument from analogy</u>[424]

In the case concerning the *Arrest Warrant of 11 April 2000*, the Court concluded that a Foreign Minister enjoyed the same immunities and inviolability as are traditionally recognized for diplomatic agents.[425] It was however powerfully argued by Judge *ad hoc* van den Wyngaert that, in so deciding, the Court had failed to base its conclusion on any State practice showing an *opinio juris* to that effect.[426] She pointed out that 'a "negative practice" of States, consisting in their abstaining from instituting criminal proceedings, cannot, in itself be seen as evidence of an *opinio juris*. Abstinence [*sic*: abstention?] may be explained by many other

[422] [1996-I] ICJ Rep 254, para 67.

[423] See ILA, Report of the Committee on the Formation of (General) Customary Law (2000) 36–7, Section 17(iv)(a).

[424] Subsection (d) was not included in the earlier article on this subject.

[425] [2002] ICJ Rep 22, para 54. [426] ibid 143ff, paras 11ff.

reasons . . . '.[427] She also rejected the use of analogy to justify assimilating Foreign Ministers to Heads of State, observing that 'the two cannot be assimilated for the only reason that their functions may be compared'.[428]

We are not here concerned with whether Judge van den Wyngaert or the Court was correct in their respective assessments of the existence or otherwise of relevant State practice to show *opinio juris*. The interesting question is whether, assuming that there was *no* practice specifically relating to Foreign Ministers, the Court's approach would have been justified. There was certainly a customary rule that Heads of State and diplomatic agents enjoyed immunity; thus States had been acting and continued to act on the basis that such immunity had to be granted, as required by law. Could it be said that, because Foreign Ministers needed similar immunities, or would find such immunities appropriate for the discharge of their functions, the *opinio juris* could extend to their treatment? The logic involved would resemble that applied in the interpretation of a treaty, and the use of implied terms: if a question arises which is not specifically covered by the text of a treaty, it might still be supposed that, if the parties to a treaty had considered the point when drafting their treaty, they would have regarded it as covered by some provision that was included; that provision can then be interpreted in that sense. Similarly, in relation to *opinio juris*, there must be at least a possibility that a new situation would bear such an essential similarity with a recognized one that no one would suggest that it fell outside the established rule. The alternative would be to suppose that a rule conferring immunities on an ambassador could not cover the case of a minister plenipotentiary unless and until there had been practice showing *opinio juris* directly recognizing such extension. The matter is thus perhaps not one directly of argument from analogy (rejected by Judge van den Wyngaert *in casu*), but of *interpretation* of the *opinio juris* to ascertain whether that *opinio* can be treated as impliedly extending to the new situation.

(3) State practice

(a) The nature of the required practice to establish a rule of customary law

The practice supportive of the existence of a rule of customary law must be State practice, that is to say the practice of organs of the State, though the test is not the same as that for establishing the responsibility of a State. Whatever the precise relationship may be between practice and *opinio juris*, the practice must show, or at least be consistent with, the consciousness of the State as an entity that its acts are regulated by an existing legal rule.

In the case concerning the *Arrest Warrant of 11 April 2002*, the Court had to enquire into the existence in customary law of any exception to

[427] ibid 145, citing the *SS Lotus* case. [428] ibid 146.

'the rule according immunity from criminal prosecution and inviolability to incumbent Ministers for Foreign Affairs'. For this purpose it examined both national legislation and a 'few decisions of national higher courts, such as the House of Lords or the French Court of Cassation'.[429] This enquiry was made specifically in the context of an examination of State practice, ie decisions of municipal courts were referred to insofar as they might have contributed on that basis to the creation of customary rules.

Generally reference to municipal court decisions might more appropriately be on the basis that they might constitute evidence of an already existing rule of law. However, the question before the Court related to exceptions to a rule of immunity from prosecution, and such immunity would take the practical form of exercise by a court of jurisdiction over the person claiming immunity. In this case, therefore, it was entirely appropriate to ask whether it could be shown that municipal courts had claimed such jurisdiction: to do so would constitute practice which might be creative of a customary rule.

In the case concerning the *Legality of the Threat or Use of Nuclear Weapons* the Court was invited, as noted above, to deduce the existence of a customary rule from 'negative practice', in the sense of the non-use of nuclear weapons since 1945. There is no reason why refraining from such action should not be counted as practice, particularly against a background of, for example, previous action giving rise to protest by other States. However, even in the case of 'normal' active practice, there is always a problem in establishing its motivation,[430] and showing that it was inspired by the consciousness of complying with a binding rule—ie *opinio juris*. If it is not always easy to show why a given act was done, it is still more difficult to show why a given act was not done. As was pointed out by three judges in the case of the *Arrest Warrant of 11 April 2000*,[431] the fact that no State claims, by internal legislation, to be entitled to exercise a particular jurisdiction does not show that to do so would be unlawful, since States may well choose not to do what they are perfectly entitled to do.

For this reason, the task of the Court would have been simpler had it addressed its attention, not to the fact of non-use of nuclear weapons

[429] [2002] ICJ Rep 24, para 58. See also the joint separate opinion of Judges Higgins, Kooijmans and Buergenthal, ibid 68ff. The authors refer to their point of departure as 'the sources of international law identified in Article 38, paragraph 1 *(c)*, of the Statute of the Court' (ibid 68, para 19): query whether the limitation to subparagraph *(c)* is an oversight?

[430] As Judge Shahabuddeen observed, 'bare proof of acts or omissions allegedly constituting State practice does not remove the need to interpret such acts or omissions. The fact that States may feel that realities leave them no choice but to do what they do does not suffice to exclude what they do from being classified as part of State practice, providing, however, that what they do is done in the belief that they were acting out of a sense of legal obligation': dissenting opinion, *Legality of the Threat or Use of Nuclear Weapons* [1996-I] ICJ Rep 424.

[431] Joint separate opinion of Judges Higgins, Kooijmans and Buergenthal [2000] ICJ Rep 76, para 45.

since 1945, but to the retention of a nuclear armoury by a number of States over the same period, ie the 'practice of deterrence', upon which, it stated, it did not intend to pronounce.[432] Taking the two together, the picture is surely clear: the nuclear States refrained from using their weapons perhaps for a multitude of reasons; yet they retained them. Had they been convinced of the existence of a rule forbidding threat or use of such weapons in all circumstances, there would have been no point in retaining them, except on the assumption that they were, in certain circumstances, ready to defy international law.

A more effective use of 'negative *opinio juris*' appears in the Court's treatment (examined further below) of the significance of General Assembly resolutions concerning nuclear disarmament. Referring to the seminal resolution 1653 (XVI) of 24 November 1961, the Court noted that it 'proceeded to qualify the legal nature of nuclear weapons, determine their effects, and apply general rules of customary international law to nuclear weapons in particular'. The Court deduced that: '[the] application by the General Assembly of general rules of customary law to the particular case of nuclear weapons indicates that, in its view, there was no specific rule of customary law which prohibited the use of nuclear weapons; if such a rule had existed, the General Assembly could simply have referred to it and would not have needed to undertake such an exercise of legal qualification.'[433]

(b) Practice of or within an international organization

[(i) Action in relation to the operation of the organization]

(ii) General Assembly resolutions and general customary law

> Some therefore cried one thing, and some another; and the assembly was confused.
>
> Acts of the Apostles, Chapter 17, verse 32

Resolutions of the General Assembly were much examined and discussed in the proceedings leading to the advisory opinion on *Legality of the Threat or Use of Nuclear Weapons*, for reasons that will be evident. The significance of such resolutions in relation to customary law was examined by the Court, in the light of the contentions of the anti-nuclear States summarized as follows in the opinion:

> ... the important series of General Assembly resolutions, beginning with resolution 1653 (XVI) of 24 November 1961, that deal with nuclear weapons and that affirm, with consistent regularity, the illegality of nuclear weapons, signify the existence of a rule of international customary law which prohibits recourse to those weapons ...
>
> States which consider that the use of nuclear weapons is illegal indicated that those resolutions did not claim to create any new rules, but were confined to a confirmation of customary law relating to the prohibition of means or methods

[432] [1996-I] ICJ Rep 254, para 67. [433] ibid 255, para 72.

of warfare which, by their use, overstepped the bounds of what is permissible in the conduct of hostilities. In their view, the resolutions in question did no more than apply to nuclear weapons the existing rules of international law applicable in armed conflict; they were no more than the 'envelope' or *instrumentum* containing certain pre-existing customary rules of international law. For those States it is accordingly of little importance that the *instrumentum* should have occasioned negative votes, which cannot have the effect of obliterating those customary rules which have been confirmed by treaty law.[434]

These States did not therefore go so far as to contend that the resolutions in question constituted in themselves more than a material source of law—a convenient statement of law whose formal source is to be found elsewhere, namely in practice plus *opinio juris* adding up to international custom.

The Court however began its discussion of this question with the words: 'The Court notes that General Assembly resolutions, even if they are not binding, may sometimes have normative value.'[435] What is meant in this context by 'normative value' is obscure.[436] The expression would in general be understood as meaning that a specified action had the effect in itself of creating a norm, a rule of law;[437] yet this was not a view advanced in the proceedings.[438] Nor in fact did the Court take such a view; it continued:

[The resolutions] can, in certain circumstances, provide evidence important for establishing the existence of a rule or the emergence of an *opinio juris*. To establish whether this is true of a given General Assembly resolution, it is necessary to look at its content and the conditions of its adoption; it is also necessary to see whether an *opinio juris* exists as to its normative character. Or a series of resolutions may show the gradual evolution of the *opinio juris* required for the establishment of a new rule.[439]

The reference to '*opinio juris* as to [the rule's] normative character' might be understood as no more than a reflection of the generally accepted

[434] [1996-I] ICJ Rep 254, paras 68–69.

[435] ibid para 70.

[436] Abi-Saab suggests that resolutions 'peuvent constituer une forme ou un procédé de production normative sur le plan international', but in the context of an analysis whereby a reference to sources 'n'est pas dans le sense du fondement ultime de l'obligation, mais plutôt dans celui de procédure de production normative' ('Les sources du droit international: Essai de déconstruction' in *Le droit international dans un monde en mutation: Mélanges Jiménez de Aréchaga* (1994) 38). This is however surely a glissade between the concepts of formal and material source, and a misuse (akin to that of the Court) of the term 'normative'.

[437] cf this passage in the judgment in the *Gabčíkovo/Nagymaros Project* case: 'La presente partie [de l'arrêt] est plus normative que déclaratoire, parce qu'elle définit les droits et obligations des Parties': [1998] ICJ Rep 76, para 131. The English text has 'prescriptive' for '*normative*'. See also P Weil, 'L'avis consultatif sur la *Licéité de la menace ou de l'emploi des armes nucléaires*: deux lectures possibles', in E Yakpo and T Boumedra (eds), *Liber Amicorum Mohammed Bedjaoui* (1999) 550.

[438] The Committee of the ILA on the Formation of (General) Customary Law took the view that 'Resolutions adopted unanimously, and which evince a clear intention on the part of their supporters to lay down a rule of international law, are capable *very exceptionally*, of creating general customary law by the mere fact of their adoption' (2000, Report 61, Section 32, emphasis added). It is important not to lose sight of the fact that the law so 'created' is still *customary law*, and the adjective 'normative' is therefore no more appropriate in this context.

[439] [1996-I] ICJ Rep 254–5, para 70.

principle that, to constitute custom, practice must be accompanied by the conviction that that practice is required by a binding rule. But the Court is not, apparently, holding that resolutions themselves constitute practice:[440] it is doing no more than saying that they may be evidence that a customary norm exists.[441] Thus, consistently with the passage quoted above, the Court seems to attach importance to the views of States, in the abstract, as it were, as to their collective view of the law on a given matter—as already observed, a sort of *opinio opinionis juris*.

The Court did however consider, in relation to the resolutions relied on, the 'content' of these texts and 'the conditions of [their] adoption'. It noted that 'several of the resolutions under consideration in the present case have been adopted with substantial numbers of negative votes and abstentions; thus, although those resolutions are a clear sign of deep concern regarding the problem of nuclear weapons, they still fall short of establishing the existence of an *opinio juris* on the illegality of the use of such weapons.'[442] Here the emphasis has shifted to an '*opinio juris* on the illegality' of nuclear weapons, rather than an *opinio* on the existence of an *opinio juris* on such illegality.

If the existence of a substantial number of negative votes is relevant, is it also relevant to consider the motives of those voting? This raises the question of the category of States whose interests are 'specially affected', examined below. Furthermore, if the negative votes are significant, so also must be the affirmative votes; but the question of the effects of an Assembly resolution and that of the significance of the voting can become entangled in a sort of vicious circle: as the representative of Russia reminded the Court: 'Many States prefer rather to vote in favour of these resolutions or abstain from voting, than to vote against them, having precisely in mind that, according to the Charter, they do not create any legal norm and do not imply the recognition of any rules as such, but are only of recommendatory nature.'[443]

It is, however, not a question of rejecting verbal statements as contributing to State practice on the basis that 'talk is cheap', so that only effective action would count as State practice, a view refuted in, for example, the 2000 Final Report of the International Law Association (ILA) Committee on the Formation of Customary International Law.[444] The point is that, for each individual State participating in the voting, its vote is not directed to a particular dispute or situation affecting it, but is merely a general announcement of what it might contend if such a dispute or situation arose. Furthermore, if it were an established principle that voting for a purportedly declaratory resolution constituted acceptance of the rule therein stated, then to vote in this way would have an immediate impact on the legal position of the voting State; but so long as there exists

[440] Judge Ranjeva would have gone as far as this: separate opinion [1996-I] 297.
[441] In this sense Weil (n 437 above) 550–1. [442] [1996-I] ICJ Rep 255, para 71.
[443] CR 95/29, 48. [444] At 14–15.

no such principle, the vote by each State is legally insignificant because it is known (and intended) to be insignificant.[445] It is that aspect that is well brought out by the argument of the Russian representative quoted above.

In the case concerning the *Legal Consequences of the Construction of a Wall in the Occupied Palestinian Territory*, the Court began its examination of the applicable rules and principles of international law by observing that: 'Such rules and principles can be found in the United Nations Charter and certain other treaties, in customary international law and in the relevant resolutions adopted pursuant to the Charter by the General Assembly and the Security Council.'[446] As regards the prohibition of the use of force, it cited General Assembly resolution 2625 (XXV), but also recalled its finding in the *Military and Paramilitary Activities* case that 'the principles as to the use of force incorporated in the Charter reflect customary international law'.[447] On the disputed question whether the Fourth Geneva Convention, to which Israel is a party, is applicable in the Occupied Territories, the Court took note of General Assembly and Security Council resolutions stating as much. Israel's argument to the contrary was however based on a particular interpretation of Article 2, paragraph 2, of the Convention; whatever the relevance of the resolutions to such a question, they were not relied on as a source of law in themselves, or as constituting, or as evidence of, customary law.

(c) Divergent practice

[(i) Does divergent practice negative or merely qualify an alleged rule?]

[(ii) Recognition of the rule of law but assertion of an exception]

(iii) Whose practice? The concept of States 'specially affected'[448]

In the *North Sea Continental Shelf* case, the Court considered the conditions for a conventional rule to become a general customary rule, and its findings are generally understood to apply to the development of such a rule independently of treaty. It observed that 'a very widespread and representative participation in the convention'—or in State practice—'might suffice of itself, provided it included that of States whose interests were specially affected'.[449] It gave no further indication of in what way the interests of particular States might be 'specially affected'; obviously the interests of coastal States would be specially, if not solely, affected by the Convention on the Continental Shelf, but it seems unlikely that this is what the Court had in mind.[450]

The question was raised in argument in the case of *Legality of the Threat or Use of Nuclear Weapons*, though the Court in its advisory opinion did

[445] cf the present writer's *International Customary Law and Codification* (1972) 66–7.

[446] [2005] ICJ Rep, para 86. [447] [1986] ICJ Rep 98–101, paras 187–190.

[448] Subsection (iii) did not appear in the original (1989) article.

[449] [1969] ICJ Rep 42, para 73.

[450] Even though the Court, in considering how 'widespread and representative' participation in the Convention was, left out of account States 'which, by reason for instance of being land-locked States, would have no interest in becoming parties to it': ibid.

not touch upon it. If an international convention had been drawn up providing simply that the possession, use or threat of nuclear weapons was unlawful, it seems clear that, on the basis of the *North Sea* dictum, such a convention would not generate a general customary rule if the nuclear States declined to become parties, however many other States acceded to it. That the interests of the nuclear States would be 'specially affected' by such a convention seems undeniable. The international conventions concerning disarmament that were cited were however drawn in more moderate and *nuancé* terms, so that the nuclear States were able to become parties to them without compromising their position as to the lawfulness of their retention of nuclear arms.

The question remains however of other instances of practice, particularly the negative vote of the nuclear States and their allies on resolutions purporting to declare nuclear weapons illegal. Would the absence of affirmative votes by these States, as States whose interests were 'specially affected', hamper or prevent development of a customary rule on the basis of the resolutions? Or were their negative votes to be discounted on the ground that they were merely protecting their interests?[451]

This is not to say that the interests of non-nuclear States would *not* be affected, since such States might in theory be the target of such a weapon, or suffer incidental harm such as fallout as a result of its use. Judge Weeramantry in his dissenting opinion observed that 'If the nuclear States are the States most affected, their contrary view is an important factor to be taken into account . . . ';[452] but he drew attention to the potential for injury to non-nuclear States, and concluded with the 'balanced view' that 'no one group of nations—nuclear or non-nuclear—can say that its interests are most specially affected'.[453] While this is true in the sense that nuclear weapons can cause injury to all States, it remains true that the adoption by the international community of a ban on the possession and use of all nuclear weapons would impinge particularly, first on those States who have, 'with vast effort and expense' as Judge Schwebel recalled,[454] constructed and maintained a nuclear armoury, and secondly on those States (including the nuclear States) who have based substantial aspects of their foreign policy on the retention of nuclear weapons and the 'policy of deterrence'. How then is the *North Sea* finding to be interpreted? It was, as noted above, addressed primarily to the case of conclusion of a convention leading to creation of a customary rule. What might 'affect' to a special degree the 'interests' of certain States was the regulation of a particular matter by a newly-adopted rule. Just as it was not the continental shelf itself, but the legal regulation of it, that could affect certain States specially, so—it may be argued—it is not nuclear weapons in themselves that may 'affect' the interests of

[451] As is suggested by, eg, R Clark, 'Treaty and Custom' in L Boisson de Chazournes and P Sands (eds), *International Law, the International Court of Justice and Nuclear Weapons* (1999) 178.

[452] [1996-I] ICJ Rep 535. [453] ibid 535–6. [454] ibid 312.

certain States in particular, but the regulation, indeed the prohibition, of those weapons.

This interpretation of the *North Sea* dictum is advanced as the most consistent with the judgment in that case, but it cannot be said that the question is free from doubt—and Judge Weeramantry's interpretation is of course directed to the extremely desirable end of nuclear disarmament.

3. The influence of treaties on custom

(1) Individual treaties as elements of State practice

One field of law in which one might have expected individual bilateral treaties to be significant as elements of State practice is that of maritime delimitation, since maritime boundaries are to be determined by agreement, against a background of principles and rules (of *jus dispositivum* not of *jus cogens*) of customary law. An accumulation of delimitation agreements applying the equidistance method would point to the growth of a customary-law rule favouring, to put it no higher, that method. This indeed was the approach of the Court in the *North Sea Continental Shelf* case.[455]

In the more recent cases of maritime delimitation, however, one looks in vain in the judgment for a similar discussion of State practice; this appears to have been replaced by an enumeration of previous jurisprudence, of the Court itself or of arbitral tribunals, on matters of maritime delimitation. The phenomenon is discussed further in Chapter V, Section 3 below.

In the advisory opinion on the *Legality of the Threat or Use of Nuclear Weapons*, the attention of the Court had been drawn to a number of treaties 'dealing exclusively with acquisition, manufacture, possession, deployment and testing of nuclear weapons, without specifically addressing their threat or use'. The Court considered that these treaties 'point to an increasing concern in the international community with these weapons', but concluded that 'these treaties could . . . be seen as foreshadowing a future general prohibition of the use of such weapons, but they do not constitute such a prohibition by themselves'.[456] Even if the individual treaties had contained agreed absolute prohibitions of the possession or use of such weapons, the problem would still have remained whether their existence did not rather point to a recognized need for conventional prohibition in the absence of any customary one. The Final Report of the Committee of the International Law Association on Formation of Customary (General) International Law concluded that: 'There is no

[455] See [1969] ICJ Rep 43–5, para 75–80.

[456] [1996-I] ICJ Rep 253, para 62. This passage was hailed by Weil as a welcome reversal of the trend to confuse *lex lata* and *lex ferenda*: 'L'avis consultatif sur la *Licéité de la Menace ou de l'Emploi des Armes Nucléaires*: deux lectures possibles' in E Yakpo and T Boumedra (eds), *Liber Amicorum Mohammed Bedjaoui* (1999) 549–50.

presumption that a succession of similar treaty provisions gives rise to a new customary rule with the same content.'[457]

(2) The contribution of multilateral conventions to customary law

(a) Treaties codifying or reflecting custom

An international convention which has frequently been referred to in disputes to which it is not, as such, applicable is the Vienna Convention on the Law of Treaties (VCLT). Even where the parties to a dispute are also parties to the Convention, the limitation in Article 2 of the Convention, confining its applicability to treaties concluded subsequently to the acquisition of the status of party to the Convention, has meant that in the majority of cases in which the provisions of the Convention have been invoked, it has been on the basis that the Convention represented, or at least crystallized, customary law. This was a process which was commented on in the earlier article in this series on the subject;[458] but it has increased in frequency subsequently.

In the case of the *Gabčíkovo/Nagymaros Project*, the Court referred to the fact that 'it has several times had occasion to hold that some of the rules laid down in [the Vienna] Convention might be considered as a codification of existing customary law'.[459] As regards the case before it, the Court observed that the Convention had, in Articles 60 and 62, defined 'in a limitative manner' the conditions in which a treaty may lawfully be denounced or suspended.[460] As a matter of intertemporal law, this must mean that the Convention stated all the conditions required in customary law at the time of adoption of the Convention; the Court did not consider whether customary law subsequent to the Convention might have evolved so as to enlarge those conditions. Such an enquiry would, on this particular point, probably have proved fruitless, but it is interesting that the Court saw no need even to contemplate the possibility; The adoption of a law-making convention need not result in 'freezing' customary law on the subject-matter of the convention; but it will probably take substantial practice not in conformity with a rule stated in such a convention to bring about any development.

(b) The 'crystallization' of a customary law rule

When in the *Gabčíkovo/Nagymaros* case the Court turned to Articles 65 to 67 of the VCLT, concerning the procedures for termination, withdrawal and suspension of treaties, it employed a more cautious formula

[457] Report, 47, Section 25. For an example of a series of consistent treaties which has been thought to produce a customary rule to the same effect, see I Brownlie, *Principles of Public International Law* (2003) 627–8 (the nationality of the population of a territory that undergoes a change of sovereignty follows that change).

[458] (1990) 61 BYIL 88–9, 90.

[459] [1997] ICJ Rep 38, para 46. This finding is qualified by the words 'in many respects', which presumably means that the Court is not to be taken as saying that every detail of the Articles mentioned corresponds to customary law; its finding is limited to the provisions relevant to the case before it.

[460] ibid para 47; see also ibid 62–3, para 100.

than it had for Articles 60 to 62: 'Both Parties agree that Articles 65 to 67 of the Vienna Convention on the Law of Treaties, *if not codifying customary law*, at least generally reflect customary international law and contain procedural principles which are based on an obligation to act in good faith.'[461] The term 'codifying' is sometimes ambiguous; what seems to be meant is that the Convention did not simply state customary law as it stood at the time of adoption of the Convention. This is borne out by the *travaux préparatoires*, which suggest that the International Law Commission was concerned to lay down an orderly procedure for the future, rather than to state the existing requirements of customary law on the matter. Whether these articles had an immediate crystallizing effect, or gave rise to a subsequent custom, is not stated—nor indeed did it need to be for the purposes of the Court's decision.[462]

(c) Growth of a customary rule subsequently to a convention

An example of the process recognized by the Court in the *North Sea* case, whereby a norm begins life as a treaty norm, binding only on the parties to a treaty, but customary law aligns itself on it subsequently, was referred to in the advisory opinion on the *Legal Consequences of the Construction of a Wall in the Occupied Palestinian Territory*. The question was whether Israel was bound by the international humanitarian law expressed in the Fourth Hague Convention of 1907, and in particular the annexed Regulations. The Court observed that:

> ...in the words of the Convention, those Regulations were prepared 'to revise the general laws and customs of war' existing at that time. Since then, however, the International Military Tribunal of Nuremberg has found that the 'rules laid down in the Convention were recognised by all civilised nations, and were regarded as being declaratory of the laws and customs of war' (Judgment of the International Military Tribunal of Nuremberg, 30 September and 1 October 1946, p. 65). The Court itself reached the same conclusion when examining the rights and duties of belligerents in their conduct of military operations (*Legality of the Threat or Use of Nuclear Weapons, Advisory Opinion, I.C.J. Reports 1996 (I)*, p. 256, para. 75). The Court considers that the provisions of the Hague Regulations have become part of customary law, as is in fact recognized by all the participants in the proceedings before the Court.[463]

It will be noted that the Court cites no State practice, but only judicial decisions in support of its assertion that the content of the Regulations has become customary law.[464] It might not have been so easy to find practice to the appropriate effect. In the first place, there is the problem adverted to by the Appeals Chamber of the International Criminal

[461] [1997] ICJ Rep 66, para 109. For the relevance of the agreement of the parties, see the discussion of special custom in Section 4 below.

[462] The European Court of Justice has held that the Vienna Convention, Art 65 did not in 1991 form part of customary law: Case C-162/96 *Racke* [1998] ECR I-3655.

[463] [2004] ICJ 172, para 89.

[464] For a discussion of this trend in the Court's decisions, see Chapter V, Section 3 below.

Tribunal for the Former Yugoslavia (ICTY) in the *Tadic* case, that 'When attempting to ascertain State practice with a view to establishing the existence of a customary rule or a general principle, it is difficult, if not impossible, to pinpoint the actual behaviour of the troops in the field for the purpose of establishing whether they in fact comply with, or disregard, certain standards of behaviour.'[465] Secondly, it would for the most part be a matter of States refraining from certain acts or practices in warfare, and it is notoriously difficult to assign an *opinio juris* to an abstention. One reason for such abstention might in the circumstances be a desire not to expose one's own forces to the same action, rather than a sense of conforming to an international rule, and it will be recalled that in the *North Sea* case the Court dismissed from consideration as possible State practice conduct clearly inspired by a motive other than *opinio juris* (*in casu* compliance with existing treaty obligations).[466]

[(d) The significance of conventions: voting, participation, and the 'package deal']

4. General, special, and bilateral customary law[467]

An example of a regime that can perhaps be regarded as one of special (or local) customary law, but which was not discussed by the Court in those terms, is the situation in the Gulf of Fonseca, examined by the Chamber formed to deal with the *Land, Island and Maritime Frontier Dispute*.[468] The general rule of customary law has been, as the Chamber found, that 'All gulfs and bays enclosed by the land of more than one littoral State, however narrow their entrance, are non-territorial'.[469] The recognized exception to this was bays having the character of a 'closed sea'; and the Central American Court of Justice in 1917 had found that the Gulf of Fonseca was such a bay, a view endorsed by the Chamber. The relations between the three coastal States were therefore regulated on this basis.

However, the status of the bay as a closed sea also had an impact, and a particular impact, on other maritime States, since the rights of the coastal States were enforceable against such States. It is suggested that a special, local or particular custom normally regulates *only* the rights and obligations *inter se* of the States who have accepted it, in accordance with the dictum in the *Asylum* case;[470] and that the relations between those States and States outside the circle of the special custom are regulated by general customary law. The concept of a 'closed sea' is, on this basis, a

465 *Prosecutor v Tadic* IT-94-1-AR72, 35 ILM 63.

466 [1969] ICJ Rep 43–4, para 76;

467 Previously examined in (1990) 61 BYIL 102ff.

468 I am indebted to Maurice Mendelson for this insight: see 'The ICJ and Sources of International Law' in V Lowe and GG Fitzmaurice (eds), *Fifty Years of the International Court of Justice (Jennings Festschrift)* (1996) 71–2.

469 E Lauterpacht (ed), *Oppenheim's International Law* (8th edn), quoted at [1992] ICJ Rep 593, para 394.

470 [1950] ICJ Rep 276.

concept of general international law, even though the exact relationship between the States bordering the sea may be regulated by rules peculiar to them, and arising out of their practice. This latter regulation may be seen as a matter of special custom; the situation of the Gulf of Fonseca is thus governed by a hybrid system embracing both general and special customary law, depending on the identity of the States involved in any given controversy.

The situation, and the decision, in the case of the *Legality of the Threat or Use of Nuclear Weapons* raises the interesting question whether a developing rule of general customary law, which remains a matter of *lex lata* for lack of generality of the practice and *opinio juris* required to establish it, may yet rank as a rule of special customary law for those States which do accept it. As the information submitted to the Court showed, the States of the world were divided essentially into two camps: the States possessing nuclear weapons, who considered that such possession, and their possible use in certain limited circumstances, was lawful; and those who considered that such use would be unlawful 'in any circumstance', in the terms of the question put to the Court. Numerically, the anti-nuclear States were in the majority, though they included numerous States who, by reason of their size and economic status, would not in the foreseeable future be able to develop nuclear weapons even if they wished to.[471] Faced with the fact that 'the members of the international community are profoundly divided' on the issue, the Court 'does not consider itself able to find that there is . . . an *opinio juris*' as to the legality of the use of such weapons.[472]

The Court, naturally enough, treated the question as one of general international law; thus it did not put to itself the question: '*For whom* might the threat or use of nuclear weapons be lawful or unlawful?' Its conclusion, that at least as a matter of general customary law, there is no rule forbidding the use of such weapons signifies that those States that possess them are not acting unlawfully, and may (subject to stringent conditions) perhaps use them. But if there is no such principle of general international law, it would follow that there is also no prohibition on States which are at present non-nuclear obtaining such weapons, and using them, subject to the same stringent conditions. Such a conclusion however sits ill with the vehemence with which those States have asserted the unlawfulness of the use (and as a corollary, of the possession) of nuclear weapons. Clearly *vis-à-vis* other nuclear States, the State that has recently acquired that status cannot be held to a rule forbidding nuclear weapons; but in the relations between that State and the other non-nuclear States, who until recently shared its *opinio* as to the unlawfulness of those weapons, is there no prohibitory rule? No rule of special or local customary law could ever come into existence if the abstention, or even

[471] On the relevance to *opinio juris* of the ability of a State to act in the relevant field, see Section 2(c)(ii) above.

[472] [1996-I] ICJ Rep 254, para 67.

opposition, of States outside the circle of those whose practice and *opinio* instituted it, could block its creation.

The point may however be no more than a rhetorical one. Inconsistency is not in itself a breach of law; and as the Court observed in 1986: 'The mere fact that States declare their recognition of certain rules is not sufficient for the Court to consider these as part of customary international law, and as applicable as such to those States.'[473]

As to the possible existence of a rule of special international law, binding only the current non-nuclear States *inter se* (but continuing to bind any such States that acquire nuclear weapons), the present writer has previously argued as follows:

> It might be suggested that if two States . . . have a shared *opinio juris* as to the existence and content of a particular rule, then that rule must exist at least as a rule of special or bilateral customary law. This would however only be correct if the rule in question were one appropriate to apply solely in the restricted context of relations between [those] States, and were regarded as such by them. A belief that a rule exists as a rule of general international law cannot . . . be treated as *opinio juris* directed to a rule of special or bilateral custom.[474]

It is difficult to think of any rule less suited to application on a special-custom basis than a rule forbidding (or for that matter, authorizing) the use of nuclear weapons.

For this reason, the situation as regards nuclear weapons does not merely involve an absence of rules as between the nuclear States, on the one hand, and the nuclear-opposing States on the other.[475] This might well have been the situation in the case of the developing law as to the maximum extent of the territorial sea; between, let us say, six-mile States and twelve-mile States, where it would have been inappropriate, to say the least, for a twelve-mile State to object to the extension to twelve miles of the territorial sea of another State that had previously been content with three or six miles. These would thus be two separate groups employing two distinct rules of *special* customary law;[476] and the relations between members of the one group and members of the other would have to be treated as *pro tanto* unregulated.[477]

The question of practice (and possible *opinio juris*) as between only some of the States of the world was also present in the case of the *Arrest Warrant of 11 April 2000*. Belgium was able to point to some State practice in

[473] *Military and Paramilitary Activities in and against Nicaragua* [1986] ICJ Rep 97, para 184.

[474] (1990) 61 BYIL 51.

[475] An example of what Ulrich Fastenrath refers to as *Spaltungslücken*, *lacunae* in the law resulting from the division of States into two groups applying, as between themselves, two distinct rules or sets of rules: see *Lücken im Völkerrecht* (1991) 232–4.

[476] Not local customary law, unless the States holding a particular view happened also all to appertain to a particular region: see the present writer's *International Customary Law and Codification* (1991) 137–8.

[477] Though, as already emphasized (see Chapter II, Section 1(1) above), the concept of a territorial sea, with all its modalities, would remain as part of general law, as would (probably) the possibility of extension to the smallest distance currently claimed by States.

support of its contention that the immunities of a Foreign Minister could not prevail so as to protect him from prosecution for war crimes or crimes against humanity; but the Court did not consider it sufficient to found a general rule of customary law in that sense.[478] This involves a different hypothesis from that examined above; for while it would be desirable that such a rule should exist, if at all, as a rule of general law, it is by no means unthinkable that it could be recognized and acted on by certain States, between themselves, and not by others, as a rule of special customary law. However, there was nothing to indicate that those States who could be regarded as supporting such a rule through their practice were in fact conscious of composing such a group; and since in any event Belgium could not show that the Congo could be regarded as a member of such a group, the Court did not have to consider the question.

[(1) Bilateral custom: the Right of Passage *case]*

[(2) Relationship between general custom and special custom]

[5. Customary law and the 'persistent objector']

[6. Jus cogens *and customary international law]*[479]

Chapter IV: General Principles of Law Recognized by Civilized Nations

Nothing is as useless as a general maxim.

Karl von Clausewitz

1.–2. Introduction: Nature and derivation of general principles of law

It is worth recalling at the outset that general principles of law are treated in Article 38, paragraph 1(c), of the Statute, as a distinct source of law, and a source to be resorted to as a last resort, when other sources fail. Thus what may be referred to in argument, or even in a decision of the Court, as a 'general principle of law' may prove on examination to be a principle established in customary law, or even a principle enshrined in a treaty regime, and deriving its force from the maxim *pacta sunt servanda*. In these circumstances, Article 38(1)(c) has no application. There is always a temptation, where practice and *opinio juris* to establish the existence of a customary rule are insufficient, to fall back on the argument that the principle contended for is a 'general principle of law'; but it was not in this sense that the 1920 Committee of Jurists contemplated the suppletive function of general principles. It is when there is no rule *either*

[478] [2002] ICJ Rep 24, para 58.

[479] See Chapter II, Section 3 above.

way on a given point, leading logically to a *non liquet*,[480] rather than when the rule intended to be relied upon cannot be established (thus, in effect, showing the existence of an opposite or negative rule), that general principles may come into their own.

It remains the case that the Court has never yet founded an essential part of its decision on a principle identified as one of the 'general principles of law',[481] and applied in the absence of any rule of treaty-law or customary law.[482] However the case of *Certain Phosphate Lands in Nauru* raised some issues that might have called for such an approach, and the case therefore merits some attention here.

Nauru had brought proceedings against Australia as one of the three States constituting together the Trustee, under a United Nations trusteeship agreement, of the territory prior to independence (the others being Great Britain and New Zealand). Nauru's claims arose out of the trusteeship, not as a matter peculiar to its relations with Australia individually. Independently of the merits of the claim, a first question that would inevitably arise was whether proceedings could properly be brought against only one of the three States constituting the Administering Authority; and if this was so, a further question whether Australia would be liable (jointly or otherwise) for reparation of the whole of the damage alleged, or only for an appropriate part (presumably one-third). The case was settled amicably[483] after the Court had found in favour of jurisdiction,[484] so no judgment on the merits was ever delivered; however, for the purposes of determining whether it should exercise jurisdiction, the Court had to look at some aspects of these questions.

Australia in its preliminary objections relied on the principle laid down in the case of the *Monetary Gold Removed from Rome in 1943* to assert that the Court could not decide the case without thereby ruling on the legal position of the other co-Trustee States, whose interests would form 'the very subject-matter of the decision', in the words of the hallowed formula.[485] However, the Court understood its objection as also going to 'the nature of the responsibility', ie whether it was 'such that a claim may only be brought against the three States jointly, and not against one of them individually'. The Court reserved for the merits the question of

[480] See the discussion in Section Chapter II, Section 1(1) above. cf the dissenting opinion of Judge Schwebel in *Legality of the Threat or Use of Nuclear Weapons* [1996-I] ICJ Rep 323.

[481] Mendelson ('The International Court of Justice and the Sources of International Law', in V Lowe and M Fitzmaurice (eds), *Fifty Years of the International Court of Justice (Jennings Festschrift)* (1996)) makes the interesting suggestion that the Court has been able to avoid recourse to general principles by devices of 'judicial reasoning' (analogy, implied terms, teleological approach, etc). According to one view these might in themselves be regarded as general principles for the purposes of Art 38(1)(c).

[482] On one issue in the case concerning the *Difference Relating to Immunity from Legal Process of a Special Rapporteur of the Commission on Human Rights* the Court applied a 'general principle of procedural law' which, it held, had not been respected by the Malaysian courts, and thus by Malaysia: see Chapter III, Section 1(1) above.

[483] See *Order of 13 September 1993* [1993] ICJ Rep 322.

[484] [1992] ICJ Rep 240.

[485] [1954] ICJ Rep 32.

'joint and several liability', ie whether 'any one of the three [States] would be liable to make full reparation for damage flowing from any breach of the obligations of the Administering Authority'; it held however that that question was 'independent of the question whether Australia can be sued alone'.[486] On the latter point, it rejected Australia's objection.

What is not made clear in the decision is the legal basis for this finding, in terms of sources. It does not purport to be based on an interpretation of the Trusteeship Agreement; and since no claim of this kind had previously been asserted before the Court (or elsewhere), it is difficult to see how it could be based on a customary rule.[487] The reasoning of the Court is limited to the following:

> The Court does not consider that any reason has been shown why a claim brought against only one of the three States should be declared inadmissible *in limine litis* merely because that claim raises questions of the administration of the Territory, which was shared with two other States. It cannot be denied that Australia had obligations under the Trusteeship Agreement, in its capacity as one of the three States forming the Administering Authority, and there is nothing in the character of that Agreement which debars the Court from considering a claim of the breach of those obligations by Australia.[488]

As in the *Barcelona Traction* case, the Court dealt with an absence of rule underlying the claim, not as a case for a *non liquet*, but as a reason for dismissing the claim (the 'claim', for this purpose, being the Australian assertion that it could only be sued jointly with its partners). However, in that case, the matter was one of customary law, which, as State practice showed, *did* recognize claims by the national States or corporations for injury to the corporation, but *did not* recognize claims by individual shareholders.[489] In the *Nauru* case, there was no State practice to show the existence of any rule at all. Judge Shahabuddeen, in his separate opinion in effect appealed to general principles of law (though he did not use that term): 'If domestic analogies are to be considered, the most likely area lies within the broad principles of the law of trust in English law and cognate institutions in other systems.'[490] He quoted *Halsbury* to show that trustees are jointly and severally liable to a person who is entitled to sue in respect of a breach of trust.

3. *The process of analogy or 'transfer' of municipal principle*[491]

In the earlier article on this point, attention was drawn to the limits of the significance of the presence of a particular rule in many (or all)

486 [1992] ICJ Rep 258, para 48.

487 So far as case-law is concerned—insofar as this is an independent source—this too had, it was accepted, nothing to say on the matter: cf Pellet in CR 91/21, 63–4, cited by Judge Shahabuddeen in his separate opinion [1992] ICJ Rep 283.

488 ibid 258–9, para 48.

489 Though this has been regarded as questionable: see the first article in this series (1989) 60 BYIL 59, text and footnote 198.

490 [1992] ICJ Rep 285.

491 In the original article, this section title referred specifically to the *South West Africa* cases: (1990) 61 BYIL 117.

systems of municipal law for the purpose of establishing the existence of a 'general principle of law' of the kind contemplated by Article 38(1)*(c)* of the Statute. Reference was there made to the argument of the Applicants in the *South West Africa* cases that the presence in municipal systems of a norm of non-discrimination on racial grounds signified the existence of a general principle of law, that is to say of international law, which South Africa was violating by its apartheid policies. The present writer urged the need, when transferring a rule or principle from the municipal sphere to the international level, to respect the pattern of relationships; so that the international equivalent of a municipal of non-discrimination would be norm forbidding between subjects of international law, ie States, not a norm forbidding States from discriminating between individuals.[492]

A strictly correct application of this process is to be found in the separate opinion of Judge Fleischhauer in the case concerning *Legality of the Threat or Use of Nuclear Weapons*. In favour of the Court's finding that recourse to nuclear weapons might be justified in 'an extreme situation of individual or collective self-defence'; this result, he argued, could be reached:

> . . . if, in the absence of a conventional or a customary rule for the conciliation of the conflicting legal principles and rules, it is accepted that the third category of law which the Court has to apply by virtue of Article 38 of its Statute, that is, the general principles of law recognized in all legal systems, contains a principle to the effect that no legal system is entitled to demand the self-abandonment, the suicide, of one of its subjects.[493]

On the other hand, a confusion similar to that occurring in the *South West Africa* case is, it is suggested, betrayed by an argument advanced by Mexico in the case of *Avena and Other Mexican Nationals* (but which the Court did not find it necessary to deal with). Mexico claimed, and the United States conceded, that a number of Mexican nationals charged in the United States with serious crimes had not been notified of their right to consular assistance, contrary to the obligations of the United States under the Vienna Convention on Consular Relations. Mexico was arguing in favour of an alleged 'exclusionary rule' whereby: 'As an aspect of *restitutio in integrum*, Mexico is entitled to an order that in any subsequent criminal proceedings against the nationals, statements and confessions obtained prior to notification to the national of his right to consular assistance be excluded.'[494] The rule was said to exist 'in both common law

[492] It should be made clear that we are not arguing that there is, or was, no such norm, but simply that it would not exist as a general principle of law simply because municipal systems contained such a rule.

[493] [1996-I] ICJ Rep 308–9. For a borderline case, in which municipal systems, it is said, unite in condemning an act which is *also* an act on the international plane, namely secession, see the dissenting opinion of Judge Kreča in *Application of the Genocide Convention* [1996-II] ICJ Rep 754, para 89.

[494] [2004] ICJ Rep 61, para 126.

and civil law jurisdictions', and was presented as having the status of a general principle of law under Article 38(1)*(c)*.[495]

If however there is a general principle of law on the lines of the 'exclusionary rule', it is a principle that applies in criminal proceedings; but on the international level legal proceedings between States are strictly 'civil' claims, and adversarial.[496] It is therefore impossible to transfer the rule by analogy to inter-State relations, any more than the alleged norm of non-discrimination could be so transferred.[497]

A more difficult question is whether argument by analogy permits the assertion that there exists a general principle of law requiring respect for, and protection of the environment. Judge Weeramantry, in his opinion in the *Gabčíkovo/Nagymaros Project* case, was clear that Article 38(1)*(c)* had 'opened the door to the entry of such principles into modern international law'.[498] He observed that 'when a duty such as the duty to protect the environment is so well accepted that all citizens act upon it, that duty is part of the legal system in question'. In this case, there is perhaps no difficulty in transposing by analogy such a duty to the international sphere, and imposing it upon States; more doubt may be felt as to the factual premise, that there is a widely observed duty at national level.[499] The Court in the same case in effect found that there does exist at international level a duty to protect the environment, but did not specify whether it was customary in nature or otherwise based.[500]

4. *General principles in the hierarchy of sources*[501]

In the case concerning the *Gabčíkovo/Nagymaros Project*, Slovakia invoked, in defence of its actions in putting into operation a variant of the works contemplated by the Project Treaty, and as a general principle of law, 'the principle of approximate application' of treaties, basing itself on a view expressed by Judge Sir Hersch Lauterpacht in a separate opinion

[495] [2004] ICJ Rep 61, paras 126–127. The Court declined to examine this submission, on the basis that 'this question is one which has to be examined under the concrete circumstances of each case by the United States courts concerned in their process of review and reconsideration', the process mandated by the Court as a remedy for the breaches of the Convention: ibid para 127.

[496] For an example of a procedural rule applied by municipal courts which could without difficulty be applied by international courts, cf the rule as to exclusion of unlawfully obtained evidence; see M Reisman and L Freedman, 'The Plaintiff's Dilemma: Illegally Obtained Evidence and Admissibility in International Adjudication' (1982) 76 AJIL 737, and the present writer's response, 'Dilemma or Chimaera: Admissibility of Illegally Obtained Evidence in International Adjudication' (1984) 78 AJIL 622.

[497] This is not to say that some parallel rule might not exist in the law applicable by international criminal tribunals, such as the Yugoslavia and Rwanda Tribunals, and the International Criminal Court; that question will not be gone into here.

[498] [1997] ICJ Rep 109–10.

[499] More questionable is Judge Weeramantry's similar approach to the question of protection of future generations, in his dissenting opinion in the case of *Legality of the Threat or Use of Nuclear Weapons*: [1996-I] ICJ Rep 455.

[500] ibid 67–8, paras 112–113.

[501] In the original article this section title referred specifically to the *Right of Passage* case: (1990) 61 BYIL 120.

in 1956.[502] This principle would require that, when a legal instrument cannot be applied literally, it must be applied in a way approximating most closely to its original object. The Court found it unnecessary to determine whether there is such a principle, 'because, even if such a principle existed, it could by definition only be employed within the limits of the treaty in question', and the action of Slovakia did not 'meet that cardinal condition'.[503] It did not therefore discuss whether the principle could be regarded as a general principle of law for the purposes of Article 38, paragraph 1*(c)* of the Statute; but it would seem that the principle, if it existed, would be one of the interpretation or application of treaties, ie of the law of treaties. That law is however primarily customary in nature (though of course codified to a considerable extent by the 1969 Vienna Convention).[504]

[5. *Eclipse of general principle by conflicting principle of international law: the* North Sea Continental Shelf *cases*]

[6. *The significance of the expression 'civilized nations': Philosophy of Judge Ammoun*]

[7. Renvoi *to municipal law distinguished from application of general principles: the* Barcelona Traction *case*]

8. *General principles in procedural law*[505]

Mention has already been made of the general principle that a question of immunities must be dealt with by municipal courts as a preliminary matter *in limine litis*, asserted by the Court in the case concerning *Difference Relating to Immunity from Legal Process of a Special Rapporteur of the Commission on Human Rights*.[506] A similar contention was advanced by Mexico in the *Avena* case, concerning the alleged 'exclusionary rule' in criminal proceedings, discussed in Section 3 above. Note also that Judge Weeramantry, in his 1997 dissenting opinion in the case of *Application of the Genocide Convention*, referred the definition of a 'counter-claim', for the purposes of the Rules of Court, to (*inter alia*) 'such general principles as we can gather from scrutinizing counter-claims as they are understood in legal systems across the world'.[507]

[502] *Admissibility of the Hearing of Petitioners by the Committee on South West Africa* [1956] ICJ Rep 46, quoted in [1997] ICJ Rep 53, para 75.

[503] ibid, para 76. The reasoning is not entirely clear, but the Court seems to be saying that the Czechoslovakian action would not have been the closest approximation to the primary object of the Treaty, so that it is unnecessary to decide whether, if it had been, it would have been legitimated by the alleged principle.

[504] Note also the contention of Slovakia that there is a 'general principle of international law' requiring mitigation of damage, also not considered by the Court: [1997] ICJ Rep 55, paras 80–81.

[505] In the original article this section title contained a reference to the Maltese intervention in *Continental Shelf (Tunisia/Libya)*: (1990) 61 BYIL 126.

[506] See Part One, Chapter III, Section 1(1) above.

[507] [1997] ICJ Rep 288.

Chapter V: Subsidiary Sources: Judicial Decisions

1. Decisions of municipal courts

In the case concerning the *Arrest Warrant of 11 April 2000*, the Court was concerned to establish whether the immunities of a Foreign Minister can protect him when he is accused of war crimes or crimes against humanity. In this connection, it referred to 'those few decisions of national higher courts, such as the House of Lords or the French Court of Cassation' which were relevant to the matter.[508] However this reference is made in the context of the Court's examination of 'State practice', pointing to the existence or otherwise of a rule in 'customary international law'.[509] This approach emphasizes the essentially 'subsidiary' nature of judicial decisions, whether of international tribunals or municipal courts, as 'means for the determination of rules of law', in the terms of Article 38, paragraph 1 *(d)*, of the Statute. It was pointed out in the earlier article, in connection with decisions of the Court itself, that to suppose that such decisions are a formal source of law in themselves leads to a logical contradiction.[510] As regards the question of sources therefore, any assistance which might be afforded by municipal decisions would be as a *material* source of law, in the classic definition, the *formal* source being, in the *Arrest Warrant* case, custom. As was observed in the previous article,[511] a decision of a municipal court may be seen, alternatively or in addition, as an act of State practice contributing to the formation of a rule of customary law; and it is this aspect which seems to be emphasized by the passage quoted.[512]

It may be added that for a municipal court decision to be invoked as a subsidiary source of international law, that decision must have been taken, if not on the basis of the direct application of international law, at least on the basis of conformity of municipal law with international law on the point.

2. Arbitral decisions

Similar considerations apply to arbitral decisions. If such a decision is given to determine an international dispute on a question which in itself is purely a matter of municipal law, or if it is avowedly made *ex aequo et bono* (or on terms similarly defined so as not to require strict conformity with

508 The Court does not specify the decisions it had in mind, but clearly they were primarily the *Pinochet* case before the House of Lords and the *Qaddafi* case before the *Cour de cassation*, and the *Bouterse* case in the Supreme Court of the Netherlands. The joint separate opinion of Judges Higgins, Kooijmans and Buergenthal mentions also Australian, Austrian, and Bavarian court decisions: [2002] ICJ Rep 69–70, paras 22–23.

509 [2002] ICJ Rep 24, para 58. 510 (1990) 61 BYIL 133. 511 ibid.

512 President Guillaume in his separate opinion treats the municipal case-law along with French and German legislation under the heading of State practice: [2002] ICJ Rep 40–2, para 12. Similarly, the joint separate opinion of Judges Higgins, Kooijmans and Buergenthal cited in n 508 above.

international law: 'justice and equity', for example), then it is normally of no assistance in establishing rules of international law. Nevertheless, there are numerous international arbitral decisions that have contributed to the development of law; and in recent years the Court has been readier than in the past to mention these specifically in its reasoning.

In the case of *Territorial Questions and Maritime Delimitation between Qatar and Bahrain*, the question of the nature of an arbitral decision came under examination in a rather different light. In 1939, when both Qatar and Bahrain were under British protectorate, the British Government made a decision that islands known as the Hawar Islands belonged to Bahrain. This decision was relied on before the Court by Bahrain; and the first question considered by the Court in that respect was 'whether the 1939 British decision must be deemed to constitute an arbitral award'.[513] Citing the 1899 and 1907 Hague Conventions, and the PCIJ decision on the Treaty of Lausanne,[514] it observed that 'the word arbitration, for purposes of public international law, usually refers to "the settlement of differences between States by judges of their own choice, and on the basis of respect for law" '.[515] The Court decided that the 1939 decision was not an arbitral award on the ground that 'no agreement existed between the Parties to submit their case to an arbitral tribunal made up of judges chosen by them, who would rule either on the basis of the law or *ex aequo et bono*'.[516] Thus for purposes of defining an arbitral award *as a basis of title*, the Court added to the cited definition the possibility that the award might have been taken *ex aequo et bono*, rather than 'on the basis of respect for law'.[517] This does not affect the point that an arbitral award as a material source of law must have been made with 'respect for [international] law'.

3. Decisions of the Court itself

It is generally accepted that the Court's own decisions, in accordance with Article 38, paragraph 1*(d)*, of the Statute are not themselves anything more than subsidiary sources of law, ie are not creative of law; nor do they constitute 'State practice' for the purposes of the development of customary law.[518] A possible exception to this principle may be decisions

513 [2001] ICJ Rep 76, para 113.

514 PCIJ Series B, No 12, 26.

515 [2001] ICJ Rep 76, para 113.

516 ibid 77, para 114.

517 Judge Kooijmans, who agreed with the Court's finding on this point, gave in his separate opinion a definition corresponding broadly to the Hague Convention's definition cited by the Court, but omitting the aspect of 'respect for law'; he did not however refer expressly to *ex aequo et bono* [2001] ICJ Rep 237, para 45. Judge *ad hoc* Torres Bernárdez considered that one of the reasons why the 1939 decision was not an arbitral award was the absence of 'respect for international law as the basis of the arbitral decision, except to the extent that a non-existent *compromis* would have provided otherwise':ibid 363, para 299. The argument is somewhat compressed, but the sense is that if the 1939 decision had been made on the basis of *ex aequo et bono*, this would not have prevented its being legally an 'arbitral award' provided that this basis had been agreed by the parties.

518 In this sense, M Shahabuddeen, *Precedent in the World Court* (1996) 71–2.

on matters of the Court's own procedure; though such decisions may perhaps also be regarded as interpretations of the Statute and Rules, and thus matters of treaty interpretation.[519] The new practice of issuing Practice Directions, defining established interpretations of the Rules, points in this direction.

In connection with the jurisprudence of the Court on maritime delimitation, it was observed in the earlier article,[520] following Prosper Weil,[521] that the tendency of the Court to follow and apply earlier decisions rather than to investigate the practice of States supposedly creative of custom had led to a situation in which it might be said that maritime delimitation law was judge-made law rather than customary law. In this particular field of law, this has continued to be the case. The judgment on *Maritime Delimitation in the Area between Jan Mayen and Greenland* contains a revealing observation. The Court was seeking to ascertain 'the law applicable to the delimitation of [a] fishery zone'; it made no mention of any agreed delimitations that might have shown or constituted State practice, but observed that 'there appears to be no decision of an international tribunal that has been concerned only with a fishery zone'.[522] At a later stage of the decision, the Court considered that 'it is in accord with precedents' to begin the delimitation process by drawing a median line;[523] the Court then remarked that 'the Court must consider, *on the basis of the sources listed in Article 38 of the Statute of the Court*, the law applicable to the fishery zone';[524] however there is again no mention of agreed delimitations, but the Court continues: 'Of the international decisions concerned with dual purpose boundaries, that in the *Gulf of Maine* case . . . is here material.'[525]

Similarly in the case of *Territorial Questions and Maritime Delimitation between Qatar and Bahrain*, the Court noted that 'the concept of a single maritime boundary does not stem from multilateral treaty law but from State practice'.[526] When it came to deal with the maritime boundary beyond the territorial seas of the parties, there was no mention of any State practice in the form of agreed delimitations, but an enumeration of previous decisions of the Court.[527] On the other hand, it referred to the equitable principles/relevant circumstances rule as being developed 'in case-law and State practice'.[528]

Outside the domain of maritime delimitation, there are signs of a trend in a similar direction toward, if not a practice of *stare decisis*, at least a preference for the citation, in support of findings as to customary law, of previous decisions rather than 'raw' State practice; in many cases the

[519] Shahabuddeen (n 518 above 72, and see also 18) attributes a greater possible weight as precedent to decisions on procedural matters, apparently on a basis of procedural customary law.

[520] (1990) 61 BYIL 58. [521] P Weil, *Perspectives du droit de la délimitation maritime* (1988) 12.

[522] [1993] ICJ Rep 59, para 47. [523] ibid 61, para 51.

[524] ibid para 52 (emphasis added). [525] ibid. [526] [2001] ICJ Rep 93, para 173.

[527] *Gulf of Maine, Continental Shelf (Libya/Malta), Delimitation in the Area between Greenland and Jan Mayen* [2001] ICJ Rep 110–11, paras 225–229. [528] ibid 111, para 231.

jurisprudence is easier to handle. The decision in the case of *Certain Property (Liechtenstein v Germany)* appears even to extend this approach to questions of treaty interpretation (which is, of course, a field primarily governed, if not by the Vienna Convention where applicable, by customary law, to a considerable extent codified by that Convention). The case raised problems of the proper interpretation of a treaty conferring jurisdiction, and the classic approach would be via the text, the object and purpose, the practice of the parties, etc. What the Court did however was to equate the treaty in question with a number of similar treaties—containing similar, but not identical, wording—that had come before the Court (or the PCIJ) in previous cases, and to apply the reasoning of the decisions in those cases to the interpretation of the treaty before the Court.[529]

A distinction of course needs to be made between the canons and techniques of interpretation used by the Court itself, on the one hand, and the interpretation of a specific instrument, on the other. In the first case in particular, much of the customary 'practice' may be that of the Court itself, and can legitimately be referred to. Thus the Court in the *Fisheries Jurisdiction* case between Spain and Canada justifiably invoked previous decisions when considering the proper approach to the interpretation of the Canadian reservation to its optional-clause reservation.[530]

This is not to say that, in the *Certain Property* case, the Court's decision was incorrect; but it was founded on unavowed and perhaps dubious judicial techniques. To some extent it was the parties themselves that decoyed the Court along this primrose path: the Court began its examination of the matter by noting that: 'As recalled by the Parties . . . this Court and the Permanent Court of International Justice have dealt with a *comparable issue* in a number of cases.'[531] It is however not a matter of whether the 'issue' is 'comparable'; it is a matter of ascertainment of the intention of the parties to the treaty which the Court is called upon to apply, and no other. In an earlier article attention was drawn to the dangers of supposing that identical wording in two treaties, between different parties, necessarily carried identical meaning;[532] and these must be multiplied when what is being compared is not two identical texts, but similar conclusions drawn by the Court from the interpretation of different texts.[533]

529 Judge Kooijmans, in his dissenting opinion, considered this a useful analysis, but emphasized that 'the various Court decisions are focused on the specific case in hand and, therefore, do not reflect a transparent general policy' [2005] ICJ Rep, para 21. Note also the curious observation in the *Fisheries Jurisdiction* case (Spain/Canada) that 'The scope of the Canadian reservation' which the Court had to interpret 'appears even broader than that of the reservation which Greece attached to its accession to the General Act of 1928 . . . which the Court was called upon to interpret in the case concerning the *Aegean Sea Continental Shelf* . . . ' [1998] ICJ Rep 458. No conclusion seems however to be drawn from this circumstance.

530 [1998] ICJ Rep 447–9, paras 29–32; also ibid 454, para 47; criticized by Judge Ranjeva (dissenting), ibid 554–7, paras 6–12.

531 [2005] ICJ Rep, para 40.

532 (1991) 62 BYIL 68–9.

533 In some circumstances it might be possible to deduce the existence of a custom from the inclusion of identical or quasi-identical texts in treaties made between various parties at various times;

4. Decisions of other international tribunals

A problem which has not yet arisen before the International Court of Justice is that of the weight to be attached to findings of, for example, the International Tribunal for the Law of the Sea (ITLOS), the International Criminal Tribunal for the former Yugoslavia (ICTY), and the International Criminal Tribunal for Rwanda (ICTR); the same question may arise in the future in relation to the decisions of the International Criminal Court. As regards the Hamburg Tribunal, its jurisdiction clearly overlaps with that of the Hague Court, so that its decisions might well be cited before the Court, and would be entitled to at least as much weight as those of arbitral tribunals.

An overlap between the jurisdiction of the Court and that of the international criminal tribunals, leading to the Court being asked to deal with a point already considered by one of the tribunals, might seem less likely. The reverse situation has, it appears, already arisen. In the *M/V Saiga (No 2)* case, the ITLOS referred to the Court's findings on the 'state of necessity' in the *Gabčíkovo/Nagymaros Project* case,[534] and in the Order indicating provisional measures in the *Southern Bluefin Tuna* case, the Tribunal invoked the Court's rulings on the definition of a 'dispute'.[535] However, in the *Tadic* case, the ICTY differed from, and criticized the Court's findings in the case of *Military and Paramilitary Activities in and against Nicaragua*, on the question of the responsibility of a State for the acts of military or paramilitary groups other than organs of the State.[536] This raises the question of how the Court would deal with the same legal issue if it were to arise in a new case: should it follow its own earlier decision? What weight, if any, should it attach to the ICTY decision? To pursue these questions would be beyond the scope of the present work.

Chapter V–A: Legal Writing (Doctrine)[537]

The practice of the Court is not to quote the views of scholars in its decisions, but this is not to say that it is not influenced by them. States in their pleadings, and counsel in addressing the Court, frequently cite *doctrine*, even though the opinion of a scholar is not itself a true formal source of law, but a statement of what the scholar believes to be the law, based on one of the recognized formal sources.[538]

but even then, repeated inclusion of a particular provision may also imply that that provision is necessary because there is *no* parallel customary rule: see the previous article (1990) 61 BYIL 86. The ILA Committee on the Formation of Customary Law concluded that 'There is no presumption that a succession of similar treaty provisions gives rise to a new customary rule with the same content': Report, Section 25.

[534] *M/V Saiga (No 2), St Vincent and the Grenadines v Guinea* Judgment of 1 July 1999, paras 133–134.

[535] ITLOS, *Order indicating provisional measures*, 27 August 1999, para 44.

[536] *Prosecutor v Dusko Tadic* IT-94-1-A, Judgment of 15 July 1999, paras 115ff.

[537] This chapter was not included in the original article in (1990) 61 BYIL.

[538] Abi-Saab suggests that this is to underestimate the influence of *doctrine*: in particular, he suggests that 'dans la mesure où la frontière entre la *lex lata* et la *lex ferenda* n'est pas toujours précise, la

The advisory opinion in the case of the *Legal Consequences of the Construction of a Wall in the Occupied Palestinian Territory* gives an interesting example of preference of one sort of *doctrine* over another. The question was the interpretation of Article 1 of the Fourth Geneva Convention, providing that 'The High Contracting Parties undertake to respect *and to ensure respect for* the present Convention in all circumstances' (emphasis added). The Court, following in this the Commentary on the Convention published by the International Committee of the Red Cross (ICRC), found that: 'It follows from that provision that every State party to that Convention, whether or not it is a party to a specific conflict, is under an obligation to ensure that the requirements of the instruments in question are complied with.'[539] However, Judge Kooijmans, who disagreed with this finding, pointed out in his separate opinion that the ICRC Commentary had no authoritative status.[540] Furthermore, he drew attention to a study by a respected scholar based on the *travaux préparatoires* of the Convention, in which it was stated that the learned author had not found 'in the records of the Diplomatic Conference even the slightest awareness on the part of government delegates that one might ever wish to read into the phrase "to ensure respect" any undertaking by a contracting State other than an obligation to ensure respect for the Conventions by its people "in all circumstances" '.[541]

For the interpretation of a treaty text of this kind, the *travaux préparatoires* are, admittedly, only a supplementary means of interpretation. Yet where legal writers—the author of the ICRC Commentary on the one hand and the scholar cited by Judge Kooijmans on the other—advance completely different views as to the effect of a provision in a convention, one might expect that the view based explicitly on *travaux préparatoires* might be preferred, or at least rejected only after careful consideration.

doctrine peut favoriser ou faciliter, en proportion de la force persuasive de ses arguments, le passage des solutions qu'elle préconise de l'une à l'autre catégorie dans la perception de la communauté internationale': 'Les sources du droit international: un essai de déconstruction' in M Rama-Montalto (ed), *International Law in an Evolving World (Liber Amicorum Jiménez de Aréchaga)* (1994) 34; but *doctrine* surely cannot take the role of practice in the transition to *lex lata*.

[539] [2004] ICJ Rep 199–200, para 158. The advisory opinion does not refer to the ICRC Commentary, but Judge Higgins in her separate opinion cites it in support of the Court's interpretation, even though she rejected the Court's assimilation of the position to an *erga omnes* obligation: ibid 217, para 39.

[540] The status of the ICRC in relation to the Geneva Conventions is *sui generis*, and cannot simply be assimilated to that of, eg, the UN High Commissioner for Refugees. Aust (*Modern Treaty Law and Practice*, 191) treats the UNHCR's *Handbook on Procedures and Criteria for Determining Refugee Status* as part of the 'context' of the Refugee Convention for purposes of interpretation, on the basis of VCLT, Art 31(2)(b), an approach approved by Lord Slynn of Hadley in *R v Secretary of State for the Home Department, ex p Adan* (2000); but this analysis cannot, it is suggested, be transposed *simpliciter* to the case of the ICRC.

[541] F Kalshoven, 'The Undertaking to Respect and Ensure Respect in all Circumstances: From Tiny Seed to Ripening Fruit' in *Yearbook of International Humanitarian Law* (1999) vol 2, 3–61; quoted in [2004] ICJ Rep 233, para 47.

GHOSTS OF COLONIALISM IN THE EUROPEAN CONVENTION ON HUMAN RIGHTS*

By Louise Moor** and AW Brian Simpson***

I. The Interrelationship Between Articles 1 and 63(56) of the Convention

At a technical level this article offers an analysis of the interaction between Articles 1 and 63 of the European Convention, and Article 4 of the First Protocol. At a more general level we wish to raise for discussion a neglected issue: what can be done in the twenty-first century about the fact that the European Convention still embodies anomalous relics of the world of European colonialism? For Article 63 was the colonial clause, though this title did not feature in the text of the Convention. It has subsequently been renumbered and renamed more innocently 'Territorial Application'.[1] A related Article 4, another colonial clause, was included in the First Protocol; it too has been renamed.[2] This tinkering reflects, no doubt, a recognition that the world of the European colonial empires, now something of an embarrassment, has passed away. But these two articles, a product of that world, remain, and scant attention has been given to the implications of this for the interpretation of a Convention which, it is now settled, is to be interpreted as a living instrument. We shall conclude by considering these implications. We shall primarily be concerned with the application of the two articles to the United Kingdom and its overseas dependencies. It was, as we shall see, almost wholly as a result of pressure from the United Kingdom that the original Convention permitted the voluntary extension of the Convention, either at the time of ratification or later, to 'all or any of the territories for whose international relations' the contracting state was responsible, and the First Protocol permitted, more generously, such extension to be accompanied with reservations. The option to extend entailed an option not to extend; a power to extend protection could be used to deny it.

* We are grateful to Sonia Boutillon, Undine von Diemar, Theodora Christou, Rolf Einar Fife, Changez Khan, Laura Harlow, Jana Krenova, Nuala Mole, Andrew Thompson, Grace Tonner, and Kristien Vandervoorden for valuable assistance. We are also indebted, as ever, to the remarkable service provided by the Library of the University of Michigan Law School.

** BA, LLB 2001, Auckland; LLM 2004, Michigan; currently Refugee/Amuesty International Officer, International Secretariat.

*** Professor of Law, University of Michigan Law School.

[1] The heading was changed by the 11th Protocol. The text of 56 (4) is a revised version of 63 (4).

[2] Articles derivative of Article 4 feature in the 4th, 6th, 7th, 12th, and 13th Protocols; in the 4th Protocol the expression 'territories for the international relations of which it is responsible . . . .' is used. In the 6th and later Protocols the word territory is unqualified. We do not discuss the territorial clauses in later Protocols.

The concept of jurisdiction came to be used to define the scope of Convention protection, and there is now a considerable jurisprudence concerning its extraterritorial reach.[3] This is largely related to the words 'within their jurisdiction' in Article 1: 'The High Contracting Parties shall secure to everyone within their jurisdiction the rights and freedoms defined in Section 1 of this Convention.' Briefly the drafting history is as follows. The draft produced by the European Movement had as Article 1: 'Every State party to this Convention shall guarantee *to all persons within its territory* the following rights: . . . .' (emphasis added).

The Committee on Legal and Administrative Questions of the Consultative Assembly proposed as Article 2: 'In this Convention, the Member States shall undertake to ensure *to all persons residing within their territories* . . . .' (emphasis added) and listed the rights.[4] A majority proposed that the rights should be guaranteed not only to 'persons residing within its metropolitan territory but also to all persons residing within its overseas territories or in its colonial possessions'.[5] In the Assembly this was not questioned, and the draft was adopted.[6]

The Ministers appointed a Committee of Experts. They adopted the notion of jurisdiction, rather than that of residence, as critical: 'The High Contracting Parties undertake to guarantee *to all persons within their jurisdiction*[7] the rights listed in Article 3 below'[8] (emphasis added). In February the draft was slightly modified: 'The High Contracting Parties undertake to accord[9] *to any person within their jurisdiction* the rights listed . . .'[10] (emphasis added). This was explained:

> It seemed to the Committee that the term 'residing' might be considered too restrictive. It was felt that there were good grounds for extending the benefit of the Convention to all persons in the territories of the signatory States, even those who could not be considered as residing there in the legal sense of the word. This word, moreover, has not the same meaning in all national laws. The Committee therefore replaced the term 'residing' by the words 'within their jurisdiction' which are also contained in Article 2 of the Draft Covenant of the United Nations Commission.[11]

The reach of the Convention was to be primarily territorially based, but the *Travaux Préparatoires* do not contain any discussion of precisely what was meant by 'within their jurisdiction', over and above the passage quoted.[12]

[3] See n 18 below.

[4] *Travaux Préparatoires* (hereinafter *TP*) I 296–7, *TP* I 228–9.

[5] *TP* I 224.

[6] *TP* II 132–3, 276–7. See R Lawson, 'Life After Bankovic: On the Extraterritorial Application of the European Convention on Human Rights' in F Coomans and MT Kamminga (eds), *Extraterritorial Application of Human Rights Treaties* (2004) 88–90.

[7] ' . . . s'engagent à garantir à toute personne relevant de leur jurisdiction . . . .' And see *TP* III 26–7. The French is translated as 'within their jurisdiction', even though the word '*relevant*' does not have the locational overtones of 'within'.

[8] *TP* III 222–3.

[9] ' . . . *s'engagent à reconnaitre . . . à toute personne relevant de leur jurisdiction* . . . ' The change from 'guarantee' to 'accord' is explained.

[10] *TP* III 236–7.

[11] *TP* III 260–1.

[12] The expression 'persons within their jurisdiction' also featured in draft Art 8, which mandates an effective remedy for violations, which eventually became Art 13. Draft Art 9 somewhat

It is now established that this Article is to be taken as imposing, in general, a territorial limitation to protection. Persons 'within the jurisdiction' under Article 1 normally have to be within the territory over which the Contracting Party exercises jurisdiction, that is legislative, judicial, and administrative powers. This localization of responsibility will mean that the violation must normally occur within the relevant territory (and there may, of course, be difficulties in attributing a location to such violation) and the victim must be physically present within the territory over which the Contracting Party exercises sovereignty when the violation takes effect (again a highly problematic notion). Properly analysed, jurisdiction under Article 1 of the Convention is always *ratione personae*; the purported victim must be the right sort of person—one 'within the jurisdiction'. But in international law jurisdiction is typically conferred by territorial sovereignty.[13] As it is put in *Banković and others v Belgium and others*: 'As to the "ordinary meaning" of the relevant term in Article 1 of the Convention, the Court is satisfied that, from the standpoint of public international law, the jurisdictional competence of a State is primarily territorial.'[14] There is an oddity in the adoption of the principle stated, for it is, quite explicitly, concerned with placing limitations on the *competence* of states, whereas the issue in relation to the European Convention is not one of restricting competence but of attributing *responsibility*. The jurisprudence has never really addressed the question of why a principle of international law evolved to set bounds to state power should be used to limit responsibility under the Convention. There is nothing in the *Travaux Préparatoires* to indicate that the matter was ever considered. In Convention jurisprudence, one might think, the emphasis should not be placed on a doctrine which imposes limitations on responsibility, but, as the Preamble puts it, on 'the maintenance and further realization of human rights and fundamental freedoms'.[15] Indeed, the emphasis on *location* which is entailed by the existing jurisprudence of Article 1 seems questionable at least; if human

inconsistently used the concept of 'secured rights and freedoms within its territory'. This article was designed to ensure that the rules adopted by State parties to secure the protection of the rights and freedoms should be in accordance with the principles of law recognized by civilized nations. See *TP* III 240–1.

[13] FA Mann, 'The Doctrine of Jurisdiction in International Law' (1964) I *Academie de Droit International. Recueil des Cours* 10ff; FA Mann, 'The Doctrine of Jurisdiction in International Law, Twenty Years Later' (1984) III *Recueil des Cours* 19ff; 'Jurisdiction of states' R Bernhardt (ed), *Encyclopedia of Public International Law* (1997) vol 3, 55–9; and 'Extraterritorial Effects of Administrative, Judicial and Legislative Acts' in R Bernhardt (ed), *Encyclopedia of Public International Law* (1995) vol 2, 337–43; R Jennings and A Watts (eds), *Oppenheim's International Law* (9th edn, 1992) vol 1, para 137; PM Dupuy, *Droit International Public* (4th edn, 1998) 61; I Brownlie, *Principles of International Law* (6th edn, 2003) ch 15 and material cited on 297 n 1; P Capps, M Evans, and S Konstadinidis (eds), *Asserting Jurisdiction. International and European Legal Perspectives* (2003) chs 1 (F Berman); 8 (C Greenwood); 11 (D McGoldrick); R Higgins, *Problems and Process. International Law and How We Use It* (1994) ch 4 and esp 73–7, Coomans and Kamminga (n 6 above) *passim*.

[14] No 52207/99. Decision as to Admissibility para 59 [2001] 11 BHRC 435.

[15] The decision in *Loizidou v Turkey* (*Merits*) (1997) 23 EHRR 513 in effect distinguished between competence under general international law and responsibility under the Convention.

rights protection is to be furthered the fundamental issue is one of attributing responsibility, to which conceptions as to the location of violations are only peripherally relevant. The Human Rights Committee, interpreting the expression 'individuals subject to its jurisdiction', has indeed said that this does not refer to 'the place where the violation occurred, but rather to the relationship between the individual and the State in relation to a violation of any of the rights ... wherever they occurred'.[16]

There is some authority for the view, expressed in the same case, that the violation must occur in 'the legal space' (*espace juridique*) of the Convention or of the contracting states, another conception related to location, and one which emphasizes the regional character of Convention protection. One idea is that Convention rights are collectively guaranteed within the legal space of the Convention, where there can be no areas which lie outside the protective system, though there may be controversy as to which particular state is answerable for a particular violation; outside this legal space of the Convention there may be responsibility attributable to a particular state for violations within its particular legal space, created by the exercise of authority and control. It is unclear where such an analysis leads, given the fact that the procedures of accountability under the Convention are not designed to impose any form of collective responsibility, but only the responsibility of a respondent state. It is true that the idea of a collective responsibility does underlie the Statute of the Council of Europe, and it was expressed in the Convention through the establishment of institutions of the collectivity—the Committee of Ministers, the Court, and the Commission. But it was not expressed through the mechanisms whereby complaints of violations can be made.[17] The introduction of this category of legal space, with its Gallic title, has not, it seems to us, provided a useful analytical tool with which to elucidate problems of the territorial reach of the Convention.

Jurisdictional competence, and consequential responsibility, may, according to the jurisprudence, be extraterritorial.[18] But as the Court put it in *Banković*: 'Article 1 of the Convention must be considered to reflect this ordinary and essentially territorial notion of jurisdiction, *other*

[16] *López Burgos v Uruguay* HRC 29 July 1981, Communication No 52/1979, UN Doc CCPR/C/OP/1.

[17] The concept of legal space is elaborated by E Decaux in 'Le Territoire des Droits de L'Homme', *Liber Amicorum Marc-André Eissen* (1995) 65. For discussion see R Wilde, 'The Legal Space' or '*Espace Juridique*' of the European Convention on Human Rights: Is It Relevant to Extraterritorial State Action?' [2005] EHRLR 115, Coomans and Kamminga (eds) (n 6 above) esp at 70–1 (McGoldrick), 113–14 (Lawson), 137–8 (O'Boyle), 169–73 (Cerna), 179–80 (Cassel).

[18] The earliest decision of the Commission conceding this possibility is *X v Federal Republic of Germany* App No 1611/62 (1965) 8 EYHR 158–69. This was approved in *Hess v UK* App No 623/73 (1975) 18 EYHR 147 DR 2/72; *Cyprus v Turkey* (1975) DR 2/125; *X and Y v Switzerland* (1977) DR 9/57; *W v Ireland* (1983) 32 190. Other relevant later cases, in addition to *Banković*, include *Soering v UK* Series No A/161, [1989] 11 EHRR 439; *Cyprus v Turkey* [1997] 27 EHRR 244; *X v UK* App No 7547/76 of 15 December 77; *Ilaşçu v Moldova and Russia* [2005] 40 EHRR 1030; *Issa v Turkey* App No 31831/96, 16 November 2004.

bases of jurisdiction being exceptional and requiring special justification in the particular circumstances of each case . . . '[19] (emphasis added).

To summarize,[20] responsibility may be engaged because the complainant is, *ratione personae*, within the jurisdiction though, at the relevant time, outside the boundaries of the relevant territory. Or it may be engaged because the effects of actions taken are capable of impinging upon that person when outside those boundaries. Or it may be engaged because the violations of the person's rights take place on territory which, though not part of what we will loosely call the territory of the contracting state, is under its *de facto* authority or control. To date the exceptions have been established on a case-by-case basis, without the benefit of a doctrine providing a coherent foundation for them. If such a coherence is to be developed in the future it may come to be based upon the idea that the extent of the duty of a contracting state to secure the protection of the human rights should not be limited by its legal competence under general international law, but also be coterminous with its *de facto* ability to secure that protection. This idea underlies the decision in *Ilaşçu v Moldova and Russia* (2005).[21]

Article 1 is not, however, the only Article directly relevant to the reach of the Convention. There was, in the original text, Article 63(1):[22] 'Any State may at the time of its ratification or at any time thereafter declare by notification addressed to the Secretary General of the Council of Europe that the present Convention shall extend to all or any of the territories for whose international relations it is responsible', and in 63(2): 'The Convention shall extend to the territory or territories named in the notification as from the thirtieth day after the receipt of this notification.' Article 63(4) provided for the optional extension of the right of individual petition[23] at any time to one or more of the territories to which the Convention itself had been extended.

The related jurisprudence is much less rich than for Article 1,[24] and relevant scholarly writing is sparse.[25] The same may be said for Article 63(3),

[19] *Banković* (n 14 above) para 61.

[20] There is a comprehensive discussion in the judgment of Rix LJ and Forbes J in *Al Skeini and others v Secretary of State for Defence* [2004] EWHC 2911, [2004] All ER 197. See also Coomans and Kamminga (n 6 above) at 83ff. (Lawson) and 125ff. (O'Boyle) and the valuable discussion by R Wilde, 'Legal "Black Hole"? Extraterritorial State Action and International Treaty Law and Political Rights' (2005) 26 *Michigan Journal of International Law* 739.

[21] See n 18 above.

[22] Renumbered as 56 since the 11th Protocol; hereafter we shall use the original number except when referring to changes made since 1950.

[23] Then optional under Art 25.

[24] Thus the fine collection of essays in Coomans and Kamminga (n 6 above) does not even mention Art 56. The jurisprudence is discussed below 166–84.

[25] See, however, by way of exception, Decaux (n 17 above), and C Tomuschat, 'Turkey's Declaration Under Article 25 of the European Convention on Human Rights' in M Novak, D Steurer, and H Tretter (eds), *Progress in the Spirit of Human Rights, Festchrift für Felix Ermacora* (1988) 119–39, cited in *Loizidou v Turkey (Preliminary objections)* 20 EHRR 99 in the individual dissenting opinion of Judge Gölcüklü. For admissibility see Series A/310, 46; the reasoning is indicated by the statement that the acts complained of 'were carried out by Turkish military forces stationed in the north part of Cyprus or by forces acting under their authority'. See also the Court's opinion, 23, para 58.

which provided that: 'The provisions of this Convention shall be applied in such territories with due regard, however, to local requirements.'[26] This is also true of the system of optional extension under the broadly drafted Article 4 of the First Protocol:

> Any High Contracting Party may at the time of signature or ratification or at any time thereafter communicate to the Secretary General of the Council of Europe *a declaration stating the extent to which it undertakes* [*une déclaration indiquant la mesure dans lequelle elle s'engage*] that the provisions of the present Protocol shall apply to such of the territories for the international relations of which it is responsible as are named therein. [emphasis added]
>
> Any High Contracting Party which has communicated a declaration by virtue of the preceding paragraph may from time to time communicate a further declaration modifying the terms [*une nouvelle déclaration modifiant les termes*] of any former declaration or terminating the application of the provisions of this Protocol in respect of any territory.
>
> A declaration made in accordance with this article shall be deemed to have been made in accordance with paragraph 1 of Article 63 of the Convention.

And, most importantly, very little attention has been paid in the literature to the problematic relationship between Article 1 and the system of optional extension under Article 63, and, for the First Protocol, Article 4.

II. The Three Possible Interpretations

An adequate jurisprudence as to the reach of the Convention needs to address the relationship between Article 1 and the system of optional extension. The jurisdictional provisions need to be considered together. We start with the text. There are, on the face of things, three radically different possible analyses of the relationship between Articles 1 and 63 (and Article 4 of the First Protocol).

According to the first of these, Article 63 (and Article 4 of the First Protocol) are *facilitative*. They provide the option of extending the protection required by Article 1 to the population of territories none of whom could otherwise be protected, since none would be 'within the jurisdiction' under the governing Article 1.[27] The effect of a declaration

[26] This provision was not, as we shall see, a product of pressure from the UK, but from Belgium.

[27] This interpretation features in one case, *Bui Van Thanh v UK* (1990) App No 16137/90 (Admissibility) DR 65/336. It was rejected in *Cyprus v Turkey* (n 18 above). With some diffidence we think that Decaux (n 17 above) argues at 67 that in certain situations the Court, or earlier the Commission, has to address the interrelationship between Arts 1 and 63(56); this agrees with our argument. He goes on, however, to argue that the Court must determine whether one article is to be disregarded completely (*un phénomène d'éclipse*) or whether in such cases both articles are to be applied as operating in a complementary manner (*un jeu de substitution*) so that, for example, the jurisdiction referred to in Art 1 may be acquired, or not acquired, under Art 56(63). The interpretation of the relevant passage in Decaux is complicated by the existence in French legal theory related to the conflict of laws of a doctrine of *substitution ou transposition* (see B Audit, *Droit International Privé* (3rd edn, 2000) paras 312–316) and Decaux may be drawing an analogy which we do not understand with this doctrine.

of extension is, presumably, to bring them 'within the jurisdiction' so far as the Convention is concerned.

A second possible interpretation would treat these provisions primarily as *limiting or restricting* the scope of protection required under Article 1. They create an exception to it, which may be waived by a Contracting Party through making an affirmative declaration of extension. A class of territories whose population, as being 'within the jurisdiction', would be protected under Article 1, had the Convention not included these provisions, will not be protected unless there has been such a declaration. Failure to make such a declaration has, somewhat oddly, the effect of operating as a reservation to Article 1.[28] The Contracting Party has a free choice of whether or not to make itself answerable for violations of Convention rights which are located (however this is understood) in this class of territories. It comprises territories for whose international relations the Contracting Party is responsible, but it is problematic what other characteristics such territories must possess for their inhabitants to be excluded from protection under Article 1 in the absence of extension. Must they, for example, be in some sense 'colonies', or 'non-European', or what? Obviously not all territories for whose international relations the party is responsible are covered, since that would include the home or metropolitan territory, and parts of it, and make nonsense of the Convention.[29] An entertaining if practically insignificant illustration of the complexities is provided by Rockall, an uninhabited wave-swept rock in the Atlantic, which the United Kingdom purported to annex on 18 September 1955 under a Royal Warrant. Later, by the Island of Rockall Act 1972, it was: 'incorporated into that part of the United Kingdom known as Scotland in the District of Harris in the County of Inverness'. Did the Convention apply to it from 1955 or from 1972? If only from 1972 could it have been extended in 1955?[30] As we shall see a number of European states include distinct territories with their own special legal regimes.

A third possible interpretation would treat the provisions as having two functions, as both *permitting* extension to one class of territories which would not otherwise be covered, as in the first interpretation, and as *limiting* the scope of protection required under Article 1 in the case of another class of territories, as in the second interpretation, in the absence of affirmative extension. Both classes of territory must be territories for

[28] But not one operating under Art 64 (now 57).

[29] eg Scotland, or the Isles of Scilly. See also n 2 above for later Protocols.

[30] In 1997 Greenpeace activists landed and claimed to have established an independent republic of Waveland. They and other eccentrics have lived there for short periods. The story and information on disputes over the adjacent fishing areas and continental shelf, in which Ireland, Denmark and Iceland are interested, can be followed in (1980) 51 BYIL 440, (1982) 53 BYIL 432, (1987) 58 BYIL 585, (1989) 60 BYIL 666–7, (1994) 65 BYIL 637, and (1996) 67 BYIL 797–9. The Irish folk singers, the Wolfe Tones, have a spirited and bawdy ballad on the subject, and a Mayor of Dublin (1995–96), Sean Loftus, by deed poll assumed the name Sean Dublin Bay-*Rockall* Loftus to signal his concern. Rockall is indeed closer to Donegal than to Inverness; see his letter in the *Donegal Democrat*, 1 September 2005.

whose international relations the Contracting Party was responsible, but what other characteristics each class must possess appears problematic, the text of the Convention providing no guidance.

As discussed below, a version of the second interpretation, or possibly of the third, together with a view as to what these other characteristics should be, was put forward by the United Kingdom in support of the inclusion of a colonial clause in the Convention during the negotiations, and in other international negotiations.[31] But the distinction between the second and third interpretation was never discussed, for those involved in the negotiations never, so far as can be told from the *Travaux Préparatoires*, appreciated that the text which they had produced could be interpreted in the three different ways we have here set out.

In the negotiations of the Convention and its First Protocol there was, no doubt, a loose understanding that Article 1 was intended to provide for home or metropolitan territory and Article 63 to provide for overseas or dependent territories. Various different expressions were used to mark the difference. Thus reference was made to 'colonial territories' (*territoires coloniaux*),[32] 'metropolitan territory'[33] (*territoire métropolitain*), 'non-metropolitan' (*non métropolitain*),[34] 'overseas territories' (*territoires d'outre mer*),[35] 'certain overseas territories' (*certaines territoires d'outre mer*),[36] 'colonial possessions' (*ses possessions coloniales*),[37] non-European (*non européens*)[38] countries, 'territories under their jurisdiction' (*des territories placé sous leur jurisdiction*),[39] 'overseas territories for whose international relations they are responsible' (*territoires d'outre mer dont ils assurent les relations internationales*),[40] and 'territories for which it has international responsibility' (*dont ils assurent les relations internationales*).[41] Some of these expressions had a reasonably clear meaning in the domestic law of particular states, others did not. Nowhere is there any attempt made to define or elaborate the terms which were bandied about. We shall later consider whether state practice or the jurisprudence sheds any light on the matter.

How would our three interpretations have related to UK 'dependencies'—this term is used to include all territories not forming part of the United Kingdom over which legal authority of some kind was exercised—when the Convention and its First Protocol were negotiated? To investigate the possibilities we need to attend to the complexities of a world which has largely vanished, because it was in such a world that the Convention was negotiated. If we leave out the self-governing dominions, there were then[42] six categories

[31] See below 139. [32] *TP* VII 20–3, 154–5. [33] *TP* I 224–5, *TP* III 238–9.
[34] *TP* VI 128–9. [35] *TP* I 224–5, III 276–7, IV 38–9, 54–5, V 106–7, 166–7.
[36] *TP* III 276–7, IV 294–5. [37] *TP* I 224–5. [38] *TP* VI 128–9.
[39] *TP* VI 28–9, 42–3. [40] *TP* VII 262–3.
[41] *TP* IV 180–1, 292–3, V 100–1, 142–3, 166–7. M Wood, 'TITRE V, Article 63' in L-E Pettiti, E Decaux, and PH Imbert (eds), *La Convention Européene des Droits de L'Homme* (1995) 915ff, commenting on Art 63, contrasts metropolitan territories with *des territoires distinct ou sous leur dépendance*; again the terminology is unclear.
[42] The classic work on the Byzantine complexities of the constitutional law of British dependencies is K Roberts-Wray's, *Commonwealth and Colonial Law* (1966). The author had been Legal Adviser to the British Colonial Office (1945–60). A new category, that of associated state, was invented

of dependent territories conventionally recognized in UK law—colonies, some of which were categorized as Crown Colonies,[43] 'British Islands', which were not part of the United Kingdom but were not classified as colonies,[44] protectorates,[45] protected states,[46] trust territories,[47] and territories under *condominium*.[48] In the case of all such dependencies except *condominia* the United Kingdom was normally solely responsible for international relations.[49] The complexities of UK constitutional law in relation to the various categories was extreme and, to a considerable degree, obscure; in some instances it was, for example, not settled what the status of a particular territory was, nor what consequences followed from this.[50]

in 1967 but was short-lived; see M Broderick, 'Associated Statehood: a New Form of Decolonization' (17) ICLQ 368, and J Crawford, *The Creation of States in International Law* (2006) esp 492, 610, 623 n 82, 625–32, 751. There were six such states in the Caribbean under the West Indies Act 1967, and five have since become independent, leaving Anguilla, divided from one of them, as today a British Overseas Territory (BOT). No case relating to associated states ever arose under the European Convention. See generally M Igarashi, *Associated Statehood in International Law* (2002).

43 A Crown Colony was one in which the Crown power to legislate by Order in Council had not been lost by the irrevocable grant of representative institutions, but the concept is not clear and Roberts-Wray (n 42 above) thought it better avoided; see 44–5.

44 The Channel Islands and the Isle of Man were not then categorized as Crown Dependencies, Roberts-Wray (n 42 above) 29–32, 35–8, 672–7.

45 Briefly, a protectorate was in UK law a territory under British protection which was not a protected state and which did not form part of the dominions of the Crown, not having been acquired by conquest, cession, or settlement. Put simply a protectorate was not British territory. However, the UK exercised, so far as UK law was concerned, unlimited jurisdiction in protectorates. See Crawford (n 42 above) esp 294, who distinguishes colonial protectorates, typically African, from international protectorates, eg in the case of the UK perhaps the British Solomon Islands and the Maldives; this distinction was not, however, current when the European Convention was under negotiation. See, however, Crawford, 301.

46 In 1949 under the British Protectorates, Protected States and Protected Persons Order SI 1949/140 those listed were Brunei, the Malay states (Johore, Negri Sembilan, Pahang, Perak, Kedah, Perlis, Kelantan, Selangor, Trengganu), the Maldive Islands, the Persian Gulf states (Kuwait, Bahrain, Qatar), the Trucial Sheikdoms of Oman (Abu Dhabi, Ajman, Dubai, Kalba, Ras el Khaimah, Sharjah, Umm el Quawain), and the Kingdom of Tonga. This was for the purposes of the British Nationality Act 1948; see Roberts-Wray (n 42 above) 89, noting changes to the Sheikdoms in 1952 and 1961, and at 715–17 on the Malay states. Zanzibar, though there listed as a protectorate, was probably a protected state (see Roberts-Wray, 768, *contra* Crawford (n 42 above) 297, 299). For discussion of controversy over the Gulf states see Crawford, 291–2 and literature there cited. See also relevant material in the UK National Archives (NA) FO 371/189834 which points out that although Brunei was a protected state it was commonly treated as if it was a colony or protectorate, because the Sultan was obliged by the agreement in force to follow the advice of the British High Commissioner except in matters relating to the Muslim religion or the customs of the Malays. Crawford, at 297–8, argues that the effect of this arrangement, which dated from 1906, was to alter the status of Brunei to that of an international protectorate. See generally *Oppenheim's International Law* (9th edn, 1992) vol I, 266–74 dealing with 'states under protection', a category including both protected states and protectorates.

47 Trust territories were administered under the trusteeship system of the UN, Art 76 of the Charter. At the time of the negotiation of the Convention, South West Africa was still administered under the earlier system of mandates established under the League of Nations.

48 For the Canton and Enderbury Islands *condominium* with the US, see Roberts-Wray (n 42 above) 21–2, 53, 58, 89.

49 Even this was not wholly true, since some such territories, such as Southern Rhodesia, did conduct their own international relations, the power to do so on behalf of the UK being in theory entrusted to them. Later this became the position over the Central African and West Indies Federations.

50 Thus Crawford (n 42 above) 283–6 emphasizes the variety of dependent statuses and the fact that 'the legal incidents of a given relation are to be determined not by any inference from the label attached to it ("protectorate", "suzerain", "vassal", etc.) but from an examination of the constituent documents and the circumstances of the case'. What follows should be read in the light of this *caveat*.

Under the first interpretation, the metropolitan or home territory (however defined), together with colonies, protectorates, and trust territories would plainly automatically have been within the scope of the protection of the Convention under Article 1, without any need for extension. Colonies were within the dominions of the Crown, and the United Kingdom obviously exercised jurisdiction over them. In the case of protectorates and trust territories, the territories did not form part of the dominions of the Crown, but the United Kingdom exercised complete jurisdiction over them so far as UK constitutional law was concerned. It would also be quite implausible to argue that the population of such territories would not rank as 'within the jurisdiction' in international law, so they would have been covered. In practice, both protectorates and trust territories were normally administered in the same general way as colonies. Indeed some British dependencies administered as a single unit comprised mixtures of territories. This had been the case with the Gold Coast before independence and was the situation, for example, in the Gambia in 1950.[51]

Under this first interpretation, the position of territories under *condominium* would be more problematic. In 1950 there were effectively two[52] such territories, the Canton and Enderbury Islands, under *condominium* with the United States since 1939, and the New Hebrides, under *condominium* with France since 1906.[53] It would be uncertain whether the inhabitants, insofar as there were any, would be automatically protected as 'within the jurisdiction', and in the case of the Canton and Enderbury Islands the United States could not, of course, have become a party to the Convention. If the population of *condominia* were not automatically protected under Article 1 then, conceivably, if implausibly, under the first interpretation, protection might be voluntarily extended to them on the basis that the United Kingdom was, with the other power, jointly responsible for their foreign relations.[54]

What about protected states? Back in 1950 there were many dependencies which probably fell into this category, for example: the Sultanate of Brunei[55] and the Kingdom of Tonga,[56] the Persian Gulf states and the Trucial sheikdoms. For their international relations and defence the United Kingdom was certainly responsible. Protected states had their own rulers—in the case of Brunei the Sultan in Council, in the case of Tonga the Monarch, under a constitutional monarchy, and in the case of the Persian Gulf states their Sheiks or other rulers. They did not form

[51] Roberts-Wray (n 42 above) 785–6, 798. cf Kenya 762.

[52] The Anglo-Egyptian Sudan was in 1950 *in limbo*, Egypt having repudiated the agreement establishing the *condominium*. Talks were under way on possible independence. See AWB Simpson, *Human Rights and the End of Empire* (2001) (hereinafter *HREE*) 839 n 96.

[53] Roberts-Wray (n 42 above) 21–2, 53–4, 59, 901.

[54] *Hess v UK* (n 18 above) is the only Convention case remotely relevant.

[55] Roberts-Wray (n 42 above) 691–3; the status of protected state derived from a treaty of 1888. Arguably, however, a protectorate; see n 46 above.

[56] Roberts-Wray (n 42 above) 895, 909–13; the status derives from a treaty of 1879 or one of 1900, where, just to confuse us, Tonga was called a protectorate. The UK was entitled to exercise a degree of jurisdiction over internal affairs

part of the dominions of the Crown, and in UK constitutional law they were certainly not colonies. They were foreign countries, and probably under the territorial principle of general international law the United Kingdom did not possess jurisdiction over them. However, in protected states the United Kingdom might under treaty arrangements, or agreements not constituting treaties, exercise a limited jurisdiction over some of their inhabitants, typically over British subjects, as in the case of Brunei since 1906. In Tonga such jurisdiction was somewhat more extensive. The extent varied; there was no uniformity.[57] Furthermore the local ruler might in practice follow British advice over political issues, or even be obliged to do so.[58] And the conceptual boundary between protected states and protectorates (which were also in legal theory foreign countries) was not clearly defined, so that there could be uncertainty as to which territories counted as protected states, and which as protectorates. To complicate things still further territories which were categorized as protected states could, for some purposes, be treated as protectorates; thus it was the practice to provide the United Nations with information about Brunei under Article 73 (e) of the Charter, as being a 'non-self-governing' territory, but not information about Tonga. In protectorates the United Kingdom exercised plenary jurisdiction, normally under the Foreign Jurisdiction Act 1890. Under the first interpretation, however elaborated, the population of protected states would not, in general at least, be within the scope of the Convention under Article 1, and the function of Article 63 would, under this first interpretation, have been to permit the extension of the Convention to them. If the issue of whether the population of a protected state was 'within the jurisdiction' had ever arisen it might have been treated as dependent on the particular relationship in question, rather than under some general rule. It never did.

Under the second interpretation, the population of the United Kingdom's metropolitan or home territory (however defined), and of most UK dependencies—colonies, protectorates, and trust territories, and perhaps British Islands—would automatically have been within the scope of the protection of the Convention under Article 1, but the effect of Article 63 would be to except such dependencies from protection in the absence of an affirmative declaration of extension. So whether human rights obtained in dependencies was up to the colonial power.

According to the third interpretation, the Convention would again automatically apply to the United Kingdom's metropolitan or home territory, however defined, but the system of extension both *enabled* the United Kingdom to extend protection to protected states, and perhaps to

[57] Roberts-Wray (n 42 above) 89–90, pointing out that the arrangements with the Persian Gulf states resembled the system of capitulations under the Ottoman Empire. In some there was a resident British 'Political Officer'.

[58] NA FO 371/189834; this was the position in Brunei under Art 4(1) of the Agreement of 29 September 1959, with exceptions for matters relating to the Muslim religion or the customs of the Malays.

condominia, but also to *exclude* other dependencies, for example Crown Colonies, from a protection which they would otherwise have enjoyed under Article 1 (their populations being 'within the jurisdiction') by not making a declaration. It had a choice as to both options. Of course the United Kingdom, as responsible for the international relations of all its dependencies, whatever their status, could under general treaty law accede to international conventions on their behalf, but only to the extent to which the convention in question permitted this.[59]

It is idle to look in the *Travaux Préparatoires* or in the National Archives for any discussion of these three possible interpretations. Nor is there to be found in the *Travaux* any analysis of the diverse nature of UK dependencies, or analyses of what was meant by 'within the jurisdiction'. Much less is there any discussion of the fact that other negotiating powers, which also had overseas dependencies, categorized them in their domestic constitutional law in their own way, which did not correspond to the complicated and somewhat disorderly system used in UK law.

III. Colonialism and the Drafting History of Article 63

Under ordinary principles it is legitimate to use the *Travaux Préparatories* as an aid to the interpretation of the Convention, and the *Travaux* do contain material relevant to the purposes underlying the text of Articles 63 and 4 of the First Protocol.[60]

Four of the states involved in the negotiations, in addition to the United Kingdom, were colonial powers; their relationship with their dependencies was diverse. This diversity forms an important part of the background to the drafting history, and helps to explain why the Convention articles assumed the form they did. Consequently we shall give a very brief account of it.

The colonial powers were France, the Netherlands, Belgium, and Denmark. Of the other original members of the Council of Europe, Norway also exercised governmental control over three overseas territories which were not conceived to be in any sense colonies. They were the archipelago of Svalbard in the Arctic, which has a settled population of around 3,000 persons of Norwegian, Russian, and Ukrainian ethnicity, and was at this time, and still is, administered by a Governor appointed by and responsible to the Polar Department of the Norwegian Minister

[59] The Convention does not regulate the *location* of territories in relation to which declarations of extension may be made, and gives no guidance as to the position over territories under *condominium*.

[60] For discussion see *HREE* (n 52 above) *passim*, and earlier G Marston, 'The United Kingdom's Part in the Preparation of the European Convention on Human Rights, 1950' (1993) 42 ICLQ 796, and K Vasak, 'The European Convention on Human Rights Beyond the Frontiers of Europe' (1963) 12 ICLQ 1206, an article whose existence was missed in *HREE*.

of Justice.[61] Norway also had sovereignty over Bouvet Island in the Antarctic, which had and still has no regular inhabitants and is essentially a nature reserve, and its other territories in Antarctica, Peter I's Island and Queen Maud Land, are subject to the Antarctic Treaty, under which territorial claims are held in abeyance. It also has sovereignty over Jan Mayen Island in the Arctic, where there is a weather station but no settled population.[62] Svalbard, and Jan Mayen Island are distinct parts of the Kingdom of Norway, subject to legal regimes which differentiate them from Norway proper. Bouvet Island is not part of the Kingdom of Norway, but under current Norwegian legislation, dating from 27 February 1930, is an overseas dependency. Italy, though it lost its colonial empire during the Second World War, became responsible for the administration of Somalia as a Trust Territory under the United Nations from 1950 until 1960, but cannot be viewed as a colonial power during the negotiations.

As we have seen, the United Kingdom's dependencies fell into a number of ill-defined categories. Some were in Europe, and close to home these included the Channel Islands and the Isle of Man, which had a special status; they are today known as Crown Dependencies. These 'British Islands', as they used to be categorized, were never considered to be colonies. Further away there was Gibraltar, certainly in Western Europe, a Crown Colony,[63] and further still Cyprus,[64] also a Crown Colony. There was little uniformity in the arrangements whereby metropolitan control was exercised over dependencies,[65] or indeed over anything else. In particular there were very considerable differences in the degree of local autonomy they enjoyed. Protected states might enjoy a relatively high degree of autonomy. Other dependencies, such as Crown colonies, protectorates, and trust territories, varied very considerably in their degree of progress towards domestic self-government under some form

[61] Norwegian sovereignty was recognized by the Svalbard Treaty of 1920. Since then there have been changes. A local Svalbard Council with limited advisory functions was established in 1971, and became the Svalbard Council in 1981. Since 2002 the capital, Longyearbyen, has become a municipality with an elected council which has limited functions. Information derived from Norwegian Ministry of Justice and Police website. Svalbard includes certain remote islands, such as Bear Island.

[62] There has been a Convention case, *Boten v Norway* (Case 50/1994/497/579) relating to an issue arising on Jan Mayen; the Court noted briefly that it was part of Norway and no issue arose as to the geographical scope of the Convention. Under normal treaty law the Convention currently applies to all parts of the Kingdom, whether overseas or not, but not to an overseas dependency such as Bouvet Island, in relation to which no declaration of extension has ever been made. On Bouvet Island see (1986) 57 BYIL 337–42 (G Marston).

[63] Roberts-Wray (n 42 above) 681–2. See Crawford (n 42 above) 337–8, 637–8, 646–7 for the development of the conception of colonial enclaves to which arguably special principles apply; this conception had not been elaborated in the early 1950s.

[64] Roberts-Wray (n 42 above) 678–80; Cyprus became independent in 1960.

[65] Not all dependencies were the concern of the Colonial Office. The Home Office was responsible for the Channel Islands and the Isle of Man. Brunei, Southern Rhodesia, and the Maldive Islands were the concern of the Commonwealth Relations Office. Aden and the Aden Protectorate were a Colonial Office responsibility, the Persian Gulf states and the Trucial sheikdoms that of the Foreign Office.

of representative government. Some were more and some less advanced politically. But in 1950 all, either on their own or as part of some larger entity, possessed local governmental institutions—typically a Governor or equivalent officer appointed by the Crown, an Executive Council, and a Legislative Council. Legislative Councils could to a greater or lesser degree be democratically based, though the franchise might be very restricted. But the ramshackle nature of the British colonial empire makes all generalization perilous.[66] Thus Cyprus had no Legislative Council at all, the legislative power being vested in the Governor.

Some overseas dependencies had no settled population; such territories were administered, insofar as they were administered at all, as dependencies of territories to which it was administratively convenient to attach them. Thus until 1962 South Georgia, the South Orkneys, the South Shetlands, and the South Sandwich Islands, together with parts of the Antarctic Continent itself, were administered as dependencies of the Falkland Islands. Other territories, which had settled but tiny populations, such as Tristan da Cunha, were also administered as dependencies of other territories, in this case St Helena. Local governmental institutions there were rudimentary.[67] The attachment of such dependencies could depend solely on customary practice, or might be formalized.[68] Other territories with tiny populations, such as Pitcairn Island—in the 1950s the population was around 150—were distinct colonies, and not dependencies. Indeed Pitcairn had three uninhabited dependencies of its own, Henderson, Ducie, and Oeno islands.[69]

The underlying philosophy of British colonialism was that territories should be governed by local governmental institutions, under loose supervision from London; there was always a local administration to which, in practice, government was largely devolved. With some exceptions:[70] 'The fundamental aim is to guide the colonial territories to responsible self-government within the Commonwealth . . . '.[71] Centralization of governmental power in London was something which was progressively to be diminished. This is not the plan for certain anomalous dependencies which have evolved in more recent times.[72]

As for other 'colonial' powers, each had its own relationship with its dependencies. For the Netherlands this resembled that of the United Kingdom, as was to be reflected in the negotiation of the European

[66] See generally *HREE* (n 52 above) 280–3.

[67] Roberts-Wray (n 42 above) 805–7.

[68] Thus Letters Patent of 21 July 1908 and 28 March 1917 made South Georgia, and the South Orkneys dependencies of the Falklands.

[69] Roberts-Wray (n 42 above) 906. The population is now around 50. Obscurity could surround the name, the location and the very existence of some fragments of empire. On Thompson Island, never located, see Marston (n 62 above) 343, and generally H Stommel, *Lost Islands: The Story of Islands that have Vanished from Nautical Charts* (1984).

[70] Some, it was thought, would be retained as 'fortress colonies', whilst some were thought too tiny or isolated ever to become independent, though they might achieve independence as part of some larger entity.

[71] Colonial Office, *Colonial Office Handbook 1948* (1948).

[72] See Section VI below.

Convention.[73] The Netherlands had lost its empire in South-East Asia. In 1950 there remained Dutch New Guinea, given up in 1962, Surinam (formerly Dutch Guiana), and the six islands of the Dutch Antilles. There was increasing local autonomy—thus Surinam and the Antilles became autonomous in domestic affairs in 1954, remaining linked to the Netherlands under a form of federalism. The Netherlands retained responsibility for international relations; there was in all probability a policy of consultation with the local government but we do not have any detailed information on this. Surinam became independent in 1975.

The philosophy underlying both Belgian and French colonialism was very different. Belgium's dependencies comprised the Belgian Congo and the Trust Territory of Ruanda-Urundi, administered as a single entity. Under a Colonial Charter of 1908 the Belgian Congo was declared to be part of Belgium's national territory. There was a Governor-General and an appointed consultative Government Council, also provincial governors and consultative bodies, so that administration was localized. Political control was centralized to a degree quite at odds with British colonial practice. Legislative power was exercised by the Belgian Parliament, or by Royal Decrees issued on the advice of a central Colonial Council, whose members were appointed. Policy was in the hands of the Minister of the Belgian Congo and Ruanda-Urundi. At the time when the European Convention was being negotiated there was no plan for developing any degree of autonomy.[74] In the late 1950s policy changed radically, with schemes to develop local autonomy in the hope that the territories would remain linked to Belgium. These plans failed, and the territories were promised independence from June 1960; they descended into anarchy.[75]

The relationship between France and its overseas dependencies was again very different.[76] There were then four categories. The first, comprising Algeria and the old colonies[77] were organized as departments, and administered as parts of metropolitan France. Hence the responsible minister was the Minister of the Interior. The second comprised what were known as the 'overseas territories', *territoires d'outre-mer*. They were mainly African, but included some territories in India, over which control was being lost in 1950,[78] and some in the Atlantic and Pacific. The third comprised associated territories, originally under mandates, but in 1950 trust territories. There was a Minister of the Overseas Territories responsible for these two categories of territory. The fourth category comprised associated states, comprising Indo-China, the responsibility of the Foreign Minister. They broadly corresponded to the

[73] See n 90 below and statement of Dr DU Stikker, *TP* V 118–19.

[74] SC Easton, *The Twilight of European Colonialism: A Political Analysis* (1961) ch 16; *HREE* (n 52 above) 288.

[75] Easton (n 74 above) 469–80.

[76] ibid ch 11; *HREE* (n 52 above) 288; J Aldrich and J Connell, *The Last Colonies* (1998) 3, 24–9 describes the present position.

[77] Those predating the French Revolution.

[78] Under Indian control from 1954 and ceded to India in 1956.

United Kingdom's protected states. Under the Constitution of the Fourth Republic the first and second types of territory formed part of the French Republic, defined as 'indivisible, secular, democratic and social'. The other two categories formed part of the French Union.[79] This had a Consultative Assembly in Paris, and, on paper only, other institutions. The aspiration was evolution of a single French Union which would, it was hoped, embrace all France's dependencies and form a greater France. Legislative power was centralized in the French Parliament in Paris; persons from the overseas dependencies participated to a limited degree by sending representatives to the National Assembly in Paris.[80] The system changed under the *Loi-Cadre* of 1956, which made possible developments not unlike those which came about under British colonialism, with individual territories enjoying an increasing level of domestic autonomy.[81]

Denmark in 1950 had one overseas territory which was not in Danish law part of Denmark—this was Greenland; it became part of Denmark in 1953.[82] The Faroe Islands were 'a self-governing community within the Kingdom of Denmark', enjoying a high degree of domestic autonomy under legislation of 1948.[83] Greenland was to become largely autonomous under legislation of 1978; both send representatives to the Danish Parliament.[84] The Danish government handled international affairs.

IV. Territorial Extension: Colonial Clauses

UK practice, at the time of the negotiation of the European Convention, was to proceed on the basis that the default rule was that a treaty entered into by the United Kingdom applied to all territories for whose international relations it was responsible, rather than merely to territory over which it exercised sovereignty.[85] What the general rule of customary

[79] This existed, conceptually at least, from 1946 to 1958.

[80] For a fuller account see *HREE* (n 52 above) 280–8.

[81] Easton (n 74 above) 320–6.

[82] F Harhoff, *Rigsfœllesskabet* (1993), English summary at 601 ff. Under the Constitution of 5 June 1953 the Danish Realm was one entity comprising several equated parts, continental Denmark, including Jutland and the islands of Funen and Zealand, Bornholm and miscellaneous islets, the Faroe Islands, and Greenland.

[83] R Lapidoth, *Autonomy. Flexible Solutions to Ethnic Conflicts* (1997) 112–15, 143–52, 250 n 79, listing the extensive literature, also F Murray, *The EU and Member States. The Special Relationship under Community Law* (2004) 61–9. There is a local legislature, the Løgting, and a government headed by a Prime Minister. Denmark is represented on the islands by a High Commissioner, and remains formally responsible for foreign affairs, though there is consultation and Faroese influence—eg the current Danish claim to the right to exploit the area adjacent to Rockall arose at the instance of the Faroese government.

[84] A plebiscite in Greenland over possible independence has been sought. The theory of the relationship between metropolitan Denmark and the home rule regions is, apparently, disputed.

[85] A memorandum by DH Anderson of the Foreign Office UN Department of 1966, takes this view; see NA CO 936/966, DO 181/142, and FO 371/89834. Anderson argued in favour of a different default rule—a treaty would apply to all territories under sole UK territorial sovereignty; this

international law was in 1950 was not free from controversy. The default rule which came to be adopted by Article 29 of the Vienna Convention on the Law of Treaties (1969), was different: that the application of a treaty extends to 'the entire territory' of each party. A deliberate decision was made to use this expression rather than the earlier favoured Foreign Office expression 'all the territory or territories for which the parties are internationally responsible' so as not to stir up controversy over colonial clauses.[86] But this rule only applies when the treaty itself does not expressly or by implication indicate that the treaty is to have a more limited or wider application. Furthermore, although there seems to be a general consensus that the 'entire territory' of a state includes overseas dependencies over which there exists territorial sovereignty, it is not entirely clear that it includes all or even any protected states.[87] The distinction between protected states and protectorates, though well established in UK legal theory, was relatively undeveloped in general international law before the publication of J Crawford's monograph, *The Creation of States in International Law*, in 1979.[88]

One way of defining or limiting the territorial application of a treaty is to include a territorial application clause. British negotiators, at the behest of the Colonial Office, regularly insisted that any human rights convention should include a special form of such a clause, known as a colonial clause. The argument for such colonial clauses was presented as a response to two developments. One was the growing tendency for multilateral treaties to contain provisions which impinged on domestic affairs. The other was the changing relationship between the United Kingdom and its overseas dependencies, under which the latter were, as a general rule, progressively acquiring a greater degree of domestic autonomy. Such clauses were included in a wide range of multilateral treaties before and after the Second World War.[89] So far as Article 63(1)

was supported by Vincent Evans, the Foreign Office Legal Adviser. The Vienna Convention of 1969 adopts this default rule. See IM Sinclair, *The Vienna Convention on the Law of Treaties* (1973) 56–62.

[86] See generally *Oppenheim's International Law* (n 13 above) para 621, 1250–2, TO Elias, *The Modern Law of Treaties* (1974) 49–54, Sinclair, (n 85 above) 56–62, A Watts, *The International Law Commission 1949–1998* (1999) vol II, 672 ff, A Aust, *Modern Treaty Law and Practice* (2000) 162 ff. For thinking in the Foreign Office not long before the Vienna Convention, see NA FO 371/178380 IOC (64) 136.

[87] *Oppenheim's International Law* (n 13 above), 1251 n 3, noting the practice of the Secretary-General of the UN in relation to treaties for which the UN is the depositary. The issue is no longer of practical importance. See below 186.

[88] An enlarged second edition was published in 2006.

[89] Some post-war treaties contained a provision applying the treaty to all non-metropolitan territories, eg Art 10 of the Articles of Association of the International Bank for Reconstruction and Development (1945, TS21/1946, Cmnd 6885). Others, eg the Genocide Convention (1948), Art 12, and the Refugee Convention (1951), Art 10, have colonial clauses similar to Art 63(1). Other treaties contained no territorial clause, eg the Convention on the Privileges and Immunities of the Specialised Agencies of the United Nations (1947, TS69/1959, Cmnd 855); accession by the UK on 16 August 1949 made the Convention applicable to the UK's dependencies. The same is true of the Charter of the UN. NA CO 936/232 has a list of multilateral treaties from 1945 to 1955

and (2) is concerned the pressure for inclusion came from the United Kingdom, though with support from the Netherlands.[90] It was made clear in the European Convention negotiations that, in the absence of an acceptable colonial clause, the United Kingdom would not sign. France, Belgium, and Denmark did not press for the inclusion of such a clause.

Article 63(3) does not deal with territorial application, but rather with the manner in which human rights are to be protected. It has an entirely different history, originating in a Belgian proposal. It was opposed in principle by the United Kingdom. Colonial Office policy adopted the 'equality principle': a human rights convention should not include provisions based on the notion that human rights protection in colonial territories should differ in substance from protection at home.[91] In this there was a considerable element of hypocrisy, the reality being that the Colonial Office was consistently opposed to effective human rights protection in the colonies.[92] The United Kingdom only accepted the Belgian proposal in the final text by way of compromise.[93]

Colonial clauses could take various forms.[94] The essential requirement which British negotiators sought was an unqualified option as to whether or not to extend *after* signature or accession to its overseas dependencies. The corollary of this was that in the absence of such extension the Covenant would not apply to them. There would have been no reason for pressure to include a colonial clause unless it was assumed by British negotiators that otherwise the Covenant or Convention would automatically apply to overseas dependencies, except perhaps protected states. This assumption is only compatible with the second or third interpretations. But the position of protected states was never explicitly considered in the negotiations.

Article 63(1) and (2) satisfied the United Kingdom's requirement. Article 63(4) provided a further option in relation to the extension of the right of individual petition which had been made optional under the original Article 25.[95] The Colonial Office was adamantly opposed to such a right and wanted this option in order never to exercise it.[96] Acceptance of the jurisdiction of the Court was also made optional by Article 46, but there was no special colonial clause relating to this option in the original

indicating which contained provisions for compulsory colonial application, which had contracting-in provisions (ie Arts similar to 63(1) and (2)), and which had no colonial applications article at all. See also YL Laing, 'Colonial and Federal Clauses in U.N. Multilateral Instruments' (1951) 45 AJIL 108.

90 *TP* V 118–19, the Netherlands representative, Dr Du Stikker (Netherlands Foreign Minister), explained that the Netherlands' relationship with its dependencies resembled that of the UK. Belgium was prepared to accept the UK's colonial clause in a spirit of compromise only. For texts see *TP* V 106–7. Earlier Denmark and Sweden expressed willingness to support the form of clause insisted on by the UK but only on the ground that otherwise the UK would not accede. See *TP* IV 270–1.

91 *TP* III 211–12, 267–8; *HREE* (n 52 above) at 340–2, 374, 489, 491–3, 695.

92 For discussion see ibid *passim*, esp 294–7, 317–22, 490–504, 525–6.

93 See statement by Ernest Davies, *TP* V 118–19. See text to n 144 below.

94 For fuller accounts see *HREE* (n 52 above) 288–91, 476–7, 694, 697–8, 712, 721, 733, 739, 816, 829–31, 838. See H Blix and TH Emerson (eds), *The Treaty Makers' Handbook* (1973) 156ff for examples.

95 This is no longer the case under Art 34 as amended.

96 *HREE* (n 52 above) 299, 407–10, 489–98, 500–4, 512–13, 723–30 and *passim*.

text of the Convention.[97] Just before the Convention was signed this was noticed, but in order to avoid controversy nothing was then done about it.[98]

Especially in relation to conventions of a humanitarian nature insistence upon the inclusion of a colonial applications clause gave rise to acrimonious controversy, particularly in the United Nations. Anti-colonialists argued that their real function was to enable colonial powers to withhold humanitarian protection, and other benefits, from their unfortunate colonial subjects. British negotiators never argued that human rights protection was inappropriate in UK dependencies, and politically it was out of the question for them to have done so. Instead, they relied on a constitutional convention, mandating consultation with the local government, and extension only with consent. The importance attached to such conventions was a peculiar feature of British constitutionalism. And this convention, it was argued, was desirable as enhancing the degree of local autonomy; indeed respect for such autonomy represented a step towards the ending of colonialism.

Given the constitutional convention, if a treaty did not contain a suitable clause, the United Kingdom would, it was argued, be unable to ratify until all dependencies to whom the Convention would apply under the default rule of treaty law had been consulted, and all had given consent. And if a single dependency did object, the United Kingdom, it was argued, would never be able to sign or ratify at all.[99] This argument, it will be noted, assumes that in the absence of such a clause, or at least a territorial extension provision of some kind, a treaty, once ratified, would automatically apply to all or most of the overseas dependencies of the United Kingdom, as under the second or third interpretation.[100] At no point did British negotiators ever argue that colonial application clauses were needed to enable extension to protected states, on the assumption that in the absence of extension they would not be covered under international treaty law, as under the first and third interpretation. The position of such states was simply never mentioned.

Colonial clauses were defended by JES Fawcett:[101]

> The argument that the protection of human rights, the suppression of the traffic in women, and the establishment of freedom of information in overseas territories cannot conceivably be denied, and that they ought to be enforced as soon as

[97] Under the current Art 56(4), states which have made a declaration of extension under Art 56(1) may at any time make a declaration in relation to one or more territories accepting the right of individual, group, or NGO application to the Court.

[98] *TP* VII 20–3. The point was eventually dealt with in an amended Art 56(4) under the 11th Protocol.

[99] This feature of the argument seems absurd; it assumes that if, eg, Pitcairn Island held out, the UK would be unable to ratify a Human Rights Covenant. Unless the treaty mandated application the problem could surely have been addressed by a declaration accompanying ratification.

[100] Depending on what the default rule of international law was.

[101] 'Treaty Relations of British Overseas Territories' (1949) 26 BYIL 86–107. Fawcett, a Fellow of All Souls College, Oxford, was an assistant legal adviser in the Foreign Office. He resigned from

possible in these territories above all is, at first sight, attractive, but it rests on misconception. It assumes that the United Kingdom will use the clause [ie a Colonial Clause] to delay or even prevent the application to its overseas territories of treaties seeking to make these principles effective, but the opposite is the case. As soon as consultation has taken place and the government of each territory has made its own decision to participate, the United Kingdom puts in train the process of accession on behalf of that territory.[102]

Fawcett's argument, published when he was the Foreign Office assistant legal adviser based in Washington, does not, however, address the fact that in the absence of local consent the treaty would not be extended; thus there never was an extension to the Aden Protectorate,[103] to Hong Kong,[104] to Southern Rhodesia (now Zimbabwe),[105] or to Pitcairn Island. Nor was there extension to two *condominia*, the New Hebrides[106] and the Canton and Enderbury Islands.[107] So far as protected states were concerned[108] there were extensions only to Brunei (1967) and Tonga (1953). Nor does it address the fact that in the case of some territories, for example Hong Kong and Cyprus, the local consent was in reality simply the consent of a British official, the Governor, since in such territories government then had no democratic basis. And as we shall see there are today overseas dependencies of the United Kingdom to which there has never been a notification of extension.[109] Furthermore the colonial clause in the First Protocol made possible extreme delay, nearly thirty years, in extending the Protocol, which was conceived to be an integral part of the original Convention. Nor did Fawcett address the argument that if local autonomy generated a decision to oppose human rights protection it was not obviously deserving of respect.

In 1950 the Foreign Office circulated a memorandum in the United Nations justifying its policy.[110] This provides an authoritative statement

the Foreign Office on 30 September 1950. In 1962 he replaced Sir Humphrey Waldock on the European Commission; see below 158.

[102] At 107.

[103] This became the Protectorate of South Arabia; at the time when Roberts-Wray was writing (see 733–8a) it comprised 23 entities; earlier there had been around 25. Whether these Sheikdoms and Sultanates were protected states is discussed by Roberts-Wray (n 42 above) 50; his conclusion is against this. In 1959 some of the component entities became the Federation of South Arabia. In the 1950s air control by bombing was still in use in parts of Arabia; see *HREE* (n 52 above) 74–5.

[104] Hong Kong, including the territory leased by China in 1898, was a Crown Colony; see Roberts-Wray (n 42 above) 696–8.

[105] A colony, but treated at the time of the European negotiations as self governing. See Roberts-Wray (n 42 above) 749.

[106] ibid 903–6. Probably under UK law a protectorate, though treated for some purposes as a protected state. It became independent as Vanuatu in 1980.

[107] Roberts-Wray (n 42 above) 59. Probably under UK law a colony. Generally see *HREE* (n 52 above) 839–40.

[108] There is one NA file, FO 371/185221, recording an attempt in 1966 by the British Resident in Bahrain to construct a declaration of rights which the rulers might have been prepared to accept, but this attempt came to nothing. See *HREE* (n 52 above) 872 n 218.

[109] See text following n 201 below.

[110] Annex A to Foreign Office Circular 0119 of 17 October 1950, copy in NA FO 371/88657. See also FO 371/88658.

of the object and purpose of clauses of the type under consideration, and, therefore, on the purpose of Article 63(1) and (2). The more important passages read:

1. A Colonial Application Article in an international convention or agreement is an Article permitting the power responsible for the international relations of colonies, protectorates or other territories to apply that agreement individually or separately to these territories. The general purpose of such a procedure is to enable each of the territorial Governments to decide for itself whether to accede to the agreement in question and, in the case of an affirmative decision, to enable any necessary legislative changes, required to adapt local law to the terms of the agreement, to be made before accession is formally made on its behalf.

...

3. .... it is frequently necessary to enact legislation to give effect locally to obligations embodied in an international agreement ... it would be undesirable for the metropolitan Government to force such legislation on them. It is, therefore, the constitutional practice of the United Kingdom, as part of the general United Kingdom policy of developing self-government in the territories for which it is responsible, not to accede to international agreements on behalf of colonies or other dependent territories without consulting and securing the agreement of their respective governments.

This memorandum conceded that the United Kingdom could usually[111] impose required legislation.[112] It went on to argue that the fact that other colonial powers did not press for such clauses might be explained by differences in the relations between such powers and their dependencies. In the absence of such a clause a dissent from a single dependency would prevent UK accession completely.

That the United Kingdom's position verged on the disingenuous was well known in the Foreign Office, and a minute of 29 November 1950 by Alan Dudley,[113] after setting out the standard arguments, continued, with reference to the United Nations Covenant:

Important but not public reasons for wishing for a Colonial Applications Clause ... seem to be

(1) that a number of colonies cannot be expected to accept the Covenant [ie the UN Covenant] without reservations;
(2) that furthermore a reservations article in the Covenant is insufficient to enable colonial governments to reject the enforcement clauses;
(3) that colonial governments are particularly afraid of the right of petition.

The facts which underlie this second group of reasons are undoubtedly known to or suspected by a number of the critics of the Colonial Applications Clause and

111 The point was that in the case of protected states the UK might not possess the legal power to impose its will.

112 There were various mechanisms, including legislation by the Imperial Parliament, whereby the UK government could impose its will. At this time the Foreign Office took the line that legislation required to implement a treaty should be enacted before ratification.

113 He was head of the UN Economic and Social Department in the Foreign Office.

they do not believe that we want to apply the Human Rights Covenant ... to our colonies. There is enough truth in their arguments to make them uncomfortable to deal with.[114]

The nervousness over a right of individual petition exercisable in dependencies was principally addressed not by the system of voluntary extension of the Convention under Article 63, but by Article 25, under which it was always optional.

In the course of the negotiation of the European Convention the experts considered the applicability of the Convention to overseas territories during their first session.[115] At this stage the provisions which would eventually emerge as part of the First Protocol, including a right to participate in democratic government, were still being considered as part of the Convention itself.[116] This generated an embarrassing problem for colonial powers; there was no way in which such a right could apply to all dependencies. The Belgian expert, M E de la Vallee Poussin, submitted an amendment: 'The rules given above shall be applied within the overseas territories, in conformity with local needs and the standard of civilization of the native population, which may not yet have been able to reach the conditions necessary for the practice of democratic freedom.'[117] The experts responded with a new Article 7(d): 'In the overseas territories (*les territoires d'outre-mer*) the provisions of this Convention shall be applicable with due regard, however, to local necessities.'[118] Their thinking was explained:

Under paragraph (d) the signatory States are permitted to give due regard to special conditions which may exist in certain overseas territories. It is felt that the state of civilization of certain overseas territories does not permit the application of fundamental rights under the same conditions as for European territories. The States concerned have, however, to perform the task of bringing civilization to their overseas territories, a task of which the aim is precisely that of making the human rights applicable to these territories.[119]

This Belgian proposal became Article 63(3). It was drafted on the assumption that the Convention would automatically apply to overseas dependencies, as this explanation makes clear.

The UK proposal was quite different, and relied on a system of voluntary extension.[120] Unless there was a colonial clause permitting this the United Kingdom would be bound to oppose the adoption of the text. The papers included the text of a model colonial clause.[121] It was, except in some minor ways, the same as that of Article 63(1) and (2). There would, of course, have been no point in British insistence unless it was assumed that in the absence of such a clause the Convention would apply

114 NA FO 371/88658/US1005/31.
115 2–8 February 1950.
116 *HREE* (n 52 above) 750–3.
117 *TP* III 210–11, Doc A 803.
118 *TP* III 238–9.
119 ibid 266–7.
120 Working paper reproduced ibid 156–69 from UN Doc A 770, dated 4 January 1950.
121 *TP* III 210–11, Doc A 805. The statement that its authorship was unknown is an error.

to overseas dependencies (apart perhaps from protected states). Under pressure from the United Kingdom the draft produced by the experts included, as Article 42, a colonial clause:

This Convention shall only apply to *territories of the High Contracting Parties possessing jurisdiction within the fields covered by the present Convention* when the consent of the appropriate authorities of these territories has been obtained. The High Contracting Parties responsible for these territories shall, if necessary take steps to obtain this consent.[122]

The Report explained: 'This article contains the so-called colonial clause. It was introduced in order to make provisions for the autonomous powers enjoyed by certain overseas territories, in this matter.'[123] This draft text, which did not follow the UK model, appears to rest on a misunderstanding of the United Kingdom's position. This was not justified by the existence of *legally* autonomous powers (whatever that might mean) in its overseas dependencies, nor on the governments of dependencies possessing, to the exclusion of the home government, jurisdiction. Its justification was a conventional practice of consultation and extension only with local consent.[124] The experts, however, had drafted the provision so as to produce a text which was coherent with Article 1, and in doing so had wrongly assumed that provision had to be made to cater for local autonomous powers or local exclusive jurisdiction.

The experts were also concerned with explicit protection of democratic rights, which eventually featured in Article 3.[125] These rights were then expressly limited to the metropolitan territory (*territoire métropolitain*); they were not to apply to some undefined category of non-metropolitan territories at all.[126] The report does not provide any justification for this. The explanation is, however, obvious, and would have been embarrassing to state: colonial government was commonly not democratic. In response mainly to opposition to their inclusion in the Convention itself from the United Kingdom the Committee of Ministers decided in November 1950 to attempt to make provision for the right to education, to property, and to democratic participation in a protocol. This enabled the denial of democratic participation to be accommodated in the First Protocol by the inclusion, as Article 4, of a colonial clause. Cosmetically this was a better solution; the right to democratic participation could now be stated without limitation to metropolitan territories, and the denial of the right in dependencies could be discreetly achieved by failure to extend.[127] The United Kingdom, alone among the negotiating states, had indeed opposed including anything at all on the protection of democratic institutions.[128]

122 *TP* III 246–7 (emphasis added).

123 ibid 276–7. Cet article contient la clause dite coloniale. Il a été introduit pour tenir compte de l'autonomie réservée en la matière á certaines territoires d'outre mer.

124 *HREE* (n 52 above) 690–1.

125 These were covered by draft Art 3.

126 *TP* III 238–9.

127 *HREE* (n 52 above) 750–3.

128 ibid 705.

The experts met again from 6 to 10 March 1950, and the United Kingdom submitted various changes.[129] In the course of convoluted negotiations, not fully documented, the experts addressed the question of the overseas reach of the Convention, and produced two alternative texts, labelled Variants A and B. Variant B, in its Article 3, explicitly limits democratic rights to metropolitan territories, and includes the following in 7(b): 'The provisions of this Convention shall be applied in the overseas territories with due regard, however, to local requirements.'[130] Both versions contain, as Article 52(48):

This Convention shall only apply to territories of the High Contracting Parties possessing jurisdiction within the fields covered by the present Convention when the consent of the appropriate authorities of these territories has been obtained. The High Contracting Parties responsible for these territories shall, if necessary, take steps to obtain this consent.[131]

The final Report of the Experts, referring to this colonial clause,[132] explains that: 'This article was introduced to make provision for the political autonomy accorded to certain overseas territories.'[133] The text is internally coherent; it is to apply automatically to territories within the jurisdiction of the signatory state, but where on matters covered by the Convention the signatory state lacks jurisdiction, because an overseas dependency possesses it, there must be consent by the overseas territory. There was no provision for a declaration of extension. Thus the Convention as a whole was to be based on the idea that responsibility should follow jurisdiction, and this might rest with the overseas dependency rather than with the parent state.[134] If this was intended to satisfy the United Kingdom negotiators it was unlikely to do so, since it continued to reflect a misunderstanding of the British position. The home government did have jurisdiction over its colonial empire, whether or not it chose to exercise it.

Drafting now passed to a Conference of Senior Officials.[135] The United Kingdom submitted a colonial clause which was, with minor changes, to feature in the final text.[136] The UK lawyers made no attempt, by appropriate drafting, to achieve coherence with the primary rule based on jurisdiction. It provided for the voluntary extension of the Convention to overseas dependencies 'for which it has international responsibility', a category which on its face plainly included colonies, protectorates, and trust territories whose inhabitants were 'within the jurisdiction' under Article 1, since the United Kingdom possessed legislative, judicial, and administrative power over them. The only type of

[129] Text at *TP* III 280ff. [130] ibid 322–5. [131] ibid 334–5.

[132] Reproduced above as 52(48) but now through renumbering Art 47(51).

[133] *TP* IV 46–7.

[134] The texts annexed to the Report as Variants A and A2 contain the provision on democratic rights with the limitation to metropolitan territories and the provision quoted above as 7(d). Variants B and B2 do not include these provisions.

[135] See *TP* IV 100ff. for their deliberations. [136] eg 'ratification' replaced 'accession'.

British overseas dependency for which the United Kingdom had international responsibility but most or all of whose inhabitants were, arguably, not 'within the jurisdiction' were those of protected states. Sense could only be made of the text if the colonial clause was read as providing an exception to Article 1, as in the second possible interpretation, or as providing an exception so far as some territories are concerned and as conferring a power to extend in the case of other territories, as in the third interpretation.[137] But the text was not drafted so as to spell this out.[138] Had an attempt been made to do this it would have been necessary to specify what sort of territories were to be subject to the optional system, and which not, a very difficult task given the diversity amongst them. Since there was no mention of the special position of protected states, it is impossible to say whether it was intended to be interpreted in accordance with the third interpretation.

The Senior Officials presented to the Committee of Ministers a text containing two alternatives, both now called colonial clauses.[139] One, numbered 59(A), simply reproduced the United Kingdom's text.[140] The other, numbered 59(B), read:

(1) The provisions of this Convention shall be applied in the overseas territories with due regard, however, to local requirements.
(2) This Convention shall only apply to territories of the High Contracting Parties possessing jurisdiction within the fields covered by the present Convention when the consent of the appropriate authorities of these territories has been obtained.
(3) The High Contracting Parties responsible for these territories shall, if necessary, take steps to obtain this consent.[141]

These texts reflect radically conflicting notions of the reach of the Convention. Under 59(A) there is a category of territories to which the Convention does not apply under Article 1 unless there is an optional notification of extension. They are 'territories for whose international relations the High Contracting Party is responsible'; they do not have to be 'overseas', nor are they defined by reference to their autonomous jurisdiction. They presumably include protected states. So 59(A) created an exception to Article 1, except perhaps in the case of protected states. Under 59(B) the Convention applies to what are called 'overseas territories'; there is no system of optional extension by declaration. But there must be consent when jurisdiction in relation to matters covered by the Convention rested with the overseas dependency's government. And the protection undertaken in overseas territories was to be limited by local requirements.[142]

[137] See above text following n 30.
[138] eg by building the system of extension into Art 1 by way of exception.
[139] *TP* IV 270–1. [140] ibid 292–5. [141] ibid 294–5.
[142] The provision as to democratic rights with its limitation to metropolitan territories was no longer included in the draft of the Convention.

The report of the Senior Officials says nothing about the relationship between Article 1 and the two versions of Article 59. Perhaps the problem was simply not appreciated. So far as relevant it reads:

Art. 59(A) and (B). Article 59(A) contains the so called colonial clause proposed by the United Kingdom delegate, whilst Article 59(B) is a reproduction of the colonial clause proposed by the Committee of Experts.

The United Kingdom delegate declared that for constitutional reasons his Government could not accept Alternative B.

Against this the Italian delegate insisted that Alternative B be accepted. In particular, he pointed out that, with regard to any Convention for the protection of Human Rights, the benefits of this Convention should extend as far as possible to all the inhabitants of overseas territories; this was the aim of Alternative B.

The UK delegate considered that this was also the aim of Alternative A.[143] The report added that the Danish and Swedish delegates, whilst reserving the position of their governments, favoured 59(A) since it was essential to secure UK adherence. The Netherlands delegate said he was not opposed to 59(B) but could not accept paragraph 3. No reason was recorded; we surmise that the Netherlands did not wish to accept an obligation to bring pressure to bear on the governments of its overseas territories in matters in which they were autonomous. The Belgian and French delegates favoured 59(B) in principle, but reserved the position of their governments. The Norwegian delegate said he could accept 59(A) or 59(B), but reserved the position of his government.

The report and draft Convention was then submitted to the Consultative Assembly's Committee on Legal and Administrative questions, which favoured what it called the more liberal solution in Alternative 59(B); it hoped the Ministers would find a way of overcoming the constitutional objections (ie the British objections) which had been raised.[144]

At the meeting of the Committee of Ministers on 7 August 1950, the British representative, Ernest Davies, argued successfully for the inclusion in the draft Convention of the colonial clause submitted by the United Kingdom. He explained that:

They were not constitutionally able to accept international commitments on behalf of many of the British Colonies without first consulting and obtaining the agreement of the Colonial Governments. Therefore they preferred a text which would permit the United Kingdom to ratify the agreement at once and to deposit subsequent ratifications on behalf of the Colonies when their agreement had been obtained. If the text of the Convention made its provisions apply automatically to the Colonies, then the United Kingdom could not ratify until it had consulted all the Colonial Governments which would be affected, and, if any of them rejected the Convention, the United Kingdom would be prevented from ratifying at all.

[143] *TP* IV 270–1. [144] *TP* V 38–9.

He was stating the established Foreign Office view as circulated. By way of compromise he was also prepared to accept the Belgian 'local requirements' qualification from 59(B).

The Belgian Foreign Minister, Paul von Zeeland, reciprocated, being prepared to accept the United Kingdom's preferred text, but only in a spirit of compromise.[145] Belgium never positively advocated a system of voluntary extension. The reason is obvious enough. The Belgian African territories were, constitutionally, part of Belgium, and it would be assumed that they would be covered by the Convention automatically. For its part, the United Kingdom did not favour the inclusion of such a provision, because of the Colonial Office's 'equality principle'.[146] Thus at the Ministerial meeting on 7 August, Denmark had suggested that the Convention should not be applied at all except to metropolitan territories; the United Kingdom would have none of this.[147]

The rationale for the Belgian proposal was, as we have seen, the supposedly low state of civilization in at least some non-European territories. In November 1950 an unnamed Belgian official in charge of colonial matters explained to a British Embassy official that:

> The Belgian authorities fully appreciated the constitutional reasons which led His Majesty's Government in the United Kingdom to desire the inclusion of [colonial applications clauses]. Constitutional considerations applied with far less force in the Belgian case. The principal reason why the Belgian Government favoured the inclusion of Colonial Applications clauses[148] was for the sake of honesty, since international agreements which made good sense with reference to metropolitan territories might be quite inapplicable to colonial territories. The Belgian official then quoted the imaginary case of an international agreement laying down that everyone should be provided with a gas mask. The provision of gas masks was reasonable and might even be necessary in Belgium. But to issue them to pygmies in the remoter forests of the Congo would be difficult and ridiculous. To subscribe to such an agreement would thus savour of dishonesty unless the agreement included a Colonial Application clause.[149]

The Foreign Office did not persuade opponents of colonial clauses in the United Nations to change their position.[150] Although the Ministers

145 See ibid 118–19. The Article adopted was then numbered 62A, and emerged from the deliberations of a sub-committee, which had presented the Ministers with three alternative drafts, 62A, 62B, and 62C (see *TP* V 100–1). As adopted by the Ministers it was now numbered 62, and eventually 63. It embodied in 63(3) the provision put forward by Belgium.

146 See n 91 above and *HREE* (n 52 above) 340–2, 374, 489, 491–3, 695.

147 *TP* V 120–45.

148 He must have had in mind a clause along the lines of Art 63(3).

149 NA FO 371/88657/US 1005/20, letter of 11 November 1950.

150 The UK made another attempt in 1962 in relation to the draft Convention on Consent to Marriage, Minimum Age for Marriage and Registration of Marriages, the British delegate repeating the standard arguments; see E Lauterpacht, *The Contemporary Practice of the United Kingdom in the Field of International Law 1962, I* (1962) 236–42, also *Oppenheim's International Law* (n 13 above) para 621, 1251 n 5. The internal and later history of the matter can be followed in NA FO 371/178380, 72905, 88657, 66658, 88659, FO 372/6721, CAB 13/693, FO 371/101422 (dealing with Anglo-American talks on the subject), CO 936/767. The International Covenant on Civil and

had accepted the UK proposal, the submission of the draft Convention to the Consultative Assembly provided an opportunity for raising standard objections to colonial clauses. The clause was criticized by M Lannung (Denmark),[151] and by M Persico (Italy), who pointed out that it was of a permissive nature. Extension ought to be mandatory.[152] It was also criticized by M Silvandre (France).[153] Léopold Sédar Senghor (France), the distinguished African man of letters and prominent anti-colonialist from Senegal—he was to become its first President—tabled an amendment deleting it entirely, and this was carried by a majority.[154] This only made sense if one assumed that a Convention without such a clause would apply automatically to overseas dependencies, in accordance with the second and third possible interpretations which we have set out.[155]

Senghor alone put his finger on the problematic nature of the relationship between Article 1 and the then 62:

> Je fera d'abord remarquer que cet article 63 est en contradiction avec le principle général de la Déclaration des Droits de l'Homme, et, en particulier, avec l'article 14, qui condamne toute discrimination, et avec l'article premier, qui dispose que 'les Hautes Parties Contractrantes reconnaissent à toute personne relevant de leur juridiction les droits et libertés fondamentales des pays définis au titre I de la présente convention.[156]

If extension was required, this was in contradiction to Article 1. This was the more plausible since Article 1 was not drafted so as to explicitly provide that it was subject to an exception provided by Article 63. A coherent text would, of course, have contained a single article setting out the substance of both Article 1 and Article 63.

The Ministers met again on 3 November, after officials had met to tidy up the text, and, principally in response to the view adopted by the United Kingdom, decided not to accept the decision of the Consultative Assembly, so that the Convention as signed included the text of this article as it had been adopted by the Ministers on 7 August.[157] The United Kingdom would not have been prepared to sign unless the Convention contained an acceptable clause, which appeared in the final text as

Political Rights (ICCPR) does not contain such a clause; on ratification in 1976 the UK made a declaration, whose validity in international law is problematic, listing 17 dependent territories to which ratification was to apply. There is a comprehensive study of the territorial application of treaties in FCO 53/82 (December 1967).

[151] *TP* V 240–1. For the text of 62, see ibid 166–9; it included the provision which became 63(4). The complete text as submitted to the Consultative Assembly is at ibid 146–71.

[152] ibid 260–1. [153] ibid 280–1.

[154] *TP* VI 172–5, 182–3. See Vasak (n 60 above) 1207, noting opposition to the colonial clause in the Assembly of the Union Française in 1954. [155] Above 127–8.

[156] *TP* VI 174–5.

[157] *TP* VII 262–3, indicating that opposition to the removal of the colonial clause was not limited to the UK; the reference is probably to the Netherlands.

Article 63(1), (2) and (4). The Ministers also decided to postpone consideration of the rights which ended up in the First Protocol, one of which was, at this stage, expressly still limited in the draft to metropolitan territories.

Senghor's motion had been to delete the colonial clause completely, including the Belgian provision, which was plainly objectionable for the same reasons. But the decision of the Ministers left the Belgian proposal untouched, and it became Article 63(3). The consequence was that Article 63 both provided for the system of optional extension and for the watering down of the protection of human rights in an undefined class of territories having some kind of dependent status.[158]

It must be conjectural, but at the time of signature there may well have been a general understanding that Article 1 dealt with metropolitan territories and Article 63 with colonial territories. But the text of the two articles does not explicitly distinguish between, or even mention, either 'metropolitan' or 'colonial' or 'overseas' territories. Furthermore the territories for whose international relations a High Contracting Party was responsible include its own metropolitan territory, as well as its overseas dependencies, and what is loosely viewed as the metropolitan territory of a state can well comprise distinct territories, for example autonomous or semi-autonomous regions, or the component provinces or cantons of a federation. The use of the notion of responsibility for international relations, which was the work of Foreign Office lawyers, represented of course an attempt to provide a simple formula to cover overseas dependencies of various types without being long-winded.

The colonial clause which was adopted in the First Protocol, Article 4, differs from that which features in the Convention itself in providing not simply for declarations of extension, but for declarations 'stating *the extent to which* it undertakes that the provisions of the present Protocol shall apply to such of the territories for the international relations of which it is responsible as are named therein' (emphasis added). Such declarations could later be modified or terminated. The language used made it unnecessary to include anything similar to the Belgian provision, since it permitted the Protocol to be treated like a dish of *hors d'oeuvres*, items to be selected freely and even returned to the dish if they proved unpalatable. A consequence of the inclusion of this widely drawn text was that it became unnecessary to specify, embarrassingly, as had been done in earlier drafts, that democratic rights only applied to metropolitan territories. The original proposal by the United Kingdom did not use the concept of 'extent'[159] and the experts, who met in June

[158] The hybrid quality of Art 63 is noted by Wood in a commentary on Art 63; see n 41 above, arguing that the function of the Article is both the adaptation of the Convention to the degree of autonomy enjoyed by dependent territories and its adaptation to socio-cultural differences between metropolitan and non-metropolitan territories.

[159] *TP* VII 234–43.

1951, produced a text which provided that: 'Any High Contracting Party which is not in a position to extend the application of one or more of the foregoing articles to one or more of the territories ... may make a declaration to this effect.'[160] What this permitted was reservations, and the article appears at first sight to be at odds with the restriction on reservations in Article 64 (now 57), whose language it echoes by using the concept of 'extent' (*mesure*). But it is perhaps best viewed as giving a wider latitude over reservations, but one related only to the First Protocol. But in July 1951 the form of drafting which was to appear in the final text was adopted by the experts and in due course by the Ministers.[161] Such conflict as arose with the Consultative Assembly related mainly to form, and there was no opposition to the inclusion of a colonial clause, which was perceptively described by one speaker as 'the Article which allows the High Contracting Parties to exclude certain territories from the provisions of the Protocol'.[162] A curiosity arising from the absence of any provision limiting the applicability of the Convention to European territories, however defined, together with the fact that membership of the Council of Europe was a precondition to accession to the Convention,[163] was that the inhabitants of non-European territories might lose the protection they had previously enjoyed as a consequence of extension once the dependency became independent. There was no discussion in the course of the negotiations as to what was to happen when independence was achieved.[164] The British response, after some vacillation, was to incorporate bills of rights, usually based on the European Convention, in independence constitutions, or even before, but only if this was agreed.[165]

In the case of Malawi (Nyasaland) a declaration was made in 1964 to the Secretary General of the United Nations that the new state considered itself bound by pre-independence multilateral treaties on a basis of reciprocity until any declaration to the contrary. The idea no doubt was that Malawi succeeded to the existing obligations of former Nyasaland. The independence constitution of Malawi, unusually, did not incorporate human rights protection. In 1968 Dr Banda, who had taken to detaining his political opponents without trial, as he had been detained by the British, informed the Council of Europe that it no longer considered itself bound by the Convention.[166]

160 *TP* VII 306. 161 *TP* VII 320–1, 330–1, 340–1. 162 ibid 124–5.

163 Art 66.

164 For discussion see Vasak (n 60 above) 1214–24, and for UK practice see *HREE* (n 52 above) 844–73.

165 ibid 844–73.

166 (1968) 11 *European Yearbook of Human Rights* (hereinafter EYHR) 36. For doubts on the post-independence applicability of the Convention, see M-A Eissen, 'Malawi and the European Convention on Human Rights' (1967) 42 BYIL 191 and the same author's 'The Independence of Malta and the European Convention on Human Rights' in (1965) 40 BYIL 401–10. Malawi became independent in July 1964.

V. UK Practice over Declarations of Extension since the Negotiations[167]

The United Kingdom made its first declaration of extension of the Convention in 1953.[168] A list was submitted of forty-two territories; this included colonies,[169] protectorates, one federation,[170] trust territories (for example Nyasaland and Tanganyika), and protected states (Tonga and Zanzibar). Some named territories were administrative units; for example the named Gold Coast comprised two colonies (Gold Coast and Ashanti), a protectorate (Northern Territories), and a trust territory (Togoland). There was no specific reference to dependencies; presumably the intention was to include them. British officials were somewhat casual in the provision of formal notifications to Strasbourg, most notably over notices of derogation.[171]

The first list included Cyprus and Gibraltar, both located in Europe, and the Channel Islands (comprising the Bailiwicks of Jersey and Guernsey),[172] together with the Isle of Man, again all located in Europe. So the assumption was that the Convention permitted the denial of human rights protection even to inhabitants of parts of Europe. The only occasion on which this extraordinary power has in any way been questioned in Strasbourg jurisprudence was in the case of *Drozd and Janousek v France and Spain*.[173] In the Belgian Parliament, back in November 1953, Senator Henri Rolin expressed surprise that the United Kingdom had, by including them in the list, treated Jersey, Guernsey, Cyprus, and Gibraltar as colonies.[174]

So far as the Channel Islands and the Isle of Man, now 'Crown Dependencies', are concerned there had been some uncertainty as to whether treaties entered into by the United Kingdom automatically applied to them. However, in 1950 the Foreign Office issued a declaration:

> ... any treaty or international agreement to which His Majesty's Government in the United Kingdom may become a party after the date of the present despatch will not be considered as applying to the Channel Islands or the Isle of Man by reason only of the fact that it applies to the United Kingdom of Great

[167] Information may be obtained from the Council of Europe's website, but this is not in all cases reliable. Many declarations have been published in EYHR.

[168] (1955–57) I EYHR 46.

[169] Including North Borneo and Sarawak, now Sabah.

[170] The Federation of Malaya.

[171] *HREE* (n 52 above) 877–81, 1008, 1056–65.

[172] Alderney, and Sark are in Guernsey, as are Herm and Jethou; there are numerous other miscellaneous rocks and the like.

[173] Series A/240, Application No 21/199, Judgment of 26 June 1992 (Judgment, Merits 26 June 1992) (1992) 14 EHRR 745. See text to n 327 below.

[174] See the report of the debate in the Belgian Senate for 12 November 53 (n 291 below) 54. Senator Henri Rolin (1891–1973), a distinguished international lawyer, was a Professor of Law at the University of Brussels. A Senator from 1932 to 1968 he was, from 1947 to 1949, President of the Senate. He represented Belgium at the San Francisco Conference in 1945 and later on the General Assembly. He was involved in the European Federal Movement, and very active in the Consultative Assembly of the Council of Europe, chairing its Legal and Administrative Committee in 1951. See

Britain and Northern Ireland, and any signature, ratification acceptance or accession on behalf of the United Kingdom will not extend to the islands unless they have been expressly included. For the purposes of any treaty ... the Channel Islands and the Isle of Man will, unless the contrary is expressly stated in each case, be included among the territories for whose international relations His Majesty's Government are responsible.[175]

In 1961 the Home Office informed the Lieutenant Governor of Guernsey that the declaration of 1950 'did not change and could not have changed the rule of international law under which the signature, ratification or accession to an international agreement is presumed to be in respect not only of the State itself but of all the territories for whose international relations it is responsible'.[176] This presumption could, of course, be rebutted either by a declaration, or by the terms of the treaty, as the lawyers assumed was the case over the European Convention. The use of a declaration in 1950 provoked a discussion in the Foreign Office of the possibility of using declarations, which did not have to be negotiated, to perform in the future the function of a colonial clause, and thereby avoid acrimonious disputes. The lawyers, somewhat unconvincingly, said that such a declaration, made on signature or ratification, would not enable a treaty to be applied to colonies after initial ratification or signature.[177]

There were omissions: the Anglo-Egyptian Sudan,[178] the Aden Protectorate,[179] Brunei,[180] Hong Kong,[181] the Maldive Islands,[182] Malta,[183] the Persian Gulf states, Pitcairn, Southern Rhodesia,[184] the Trucial and Oman Sheikdoms,[185] and the *condominium* territories of the New Hebrides[186] and Canton and Enderbury Islands.[187] Some of the

eg *TP* I 184–5, 238–9, 250–1, 254–7. He became a judge of the European Court of Human Rights in 1959 and from 1968 was its President.

175 Circular No 0018, 16 October 1950, reproduced in F de L Bois, *A Constitutional History of Jersey* (1970) 269. It appears from material in NA FO 372/6966 that the declaration of 1950 was a response to problems over the extension of ILO Convention 87 to the Channel Islands, and not to problems over the European Convention. See also R Plender, 'The Channel Islands' Position in International Law' (June 1999) *Jersey Law Review* 136.

176 Plender ibid 4, who incorrectly supposes there was a change of policy; the default rule, whatever it was, remained unchanged.

177 NA FO 371/88658/US 1005/21. The proposal came from non-lawyers, LA Scopes and AA Dudley; the assistant legal adviser involved was JL Simpson. The possibility of a declaration which itself provided for later declarations of extension was not considered. On the use of declarations, see also FO 371/17830, memorandum of 1964, Aust (n 86 above) 165–9. See also n 150 above on the ICCPR.

178 See n 52 above.

179 Arguably comprising a number of protected states.

180 A protected state.

181 A Crown Colony to which the Convention was never extended; see n 190 below.

182 A protected state.

183 On the then constitutional status of Malta, see Roberts-Wray (n 42 above) 683–5.

184 Which became part of the Central African Federation on the following day; the Convention was never extended to the Federation, which was dissolved in 1963. Southern Rhodesia, now Zimbabwe, was by convention treated as if it was a dominion; see Roberts-Wray (n 42 above) 749 for its status as a 'self-governing colony'.

185 Often included in the category the Persian Gulf states.

186 With France, which did not ratify the Convention until 1974.

187 With the US.

Caribbean islands were not specifically named, but Antigua, Dominica, Montserrat, St Christopher and Nevis, and the Virgin Islands, were included within the Leeward Islands,[188] and Grenada, St Lucia and Tobago within the Windward Islands. The Cayman and Turks and Caicos Islands were included under Jamaica, since they were then treated as part of Jamaica.[189] In the case of eleven of the excluded territories, the Anglo-Egyptian Sudan, the Aden Protectorate, Hong Kong,[190] the Maldives, Malta, the Persian Gulf states, Pitcairn Island,[191] Southern Rhodesia, the Trucial Oman sheikdoms and the *condominium* territories with France and the United States the Convention was never extended. Nor was it ever extended to the short-lived Federations of Central Africa[192] and the West Indies.[193] Brunei was included in 1967.[194] As the colonial empire was dismantled further lists were submitted from time to time.[195] Thus one submitted in 1964 removed, in some cases belatedly, fifteen territories which had achieved independence.[196] The revised list submitted as covering the period 3 April 1984 to 1 May 2004 named twelve territories, and, as in the case of earlier lists, made no specific reference to dependencies.[197] A note by the Secretariat published in the Council of Europe's website, which is not entirely reliable, is dated 1 April 2004 and provides another list. It is the first specifically to mention dependencies, but only those of St Helena.[198] The practice of specifically mentioning these dependencies departed from earlier practice.

[188] At this time a federation, dissolved in 1956. See Roberts-Wray (n 42 above) 839–40.

[189] Vasak (n 60 above) 1210 is not quite correct.

[190] On the failure to extend to Hong Kong, see *HREE* (n 52 above) 6, 837–8, NA CO 936/156, FCO 40/392, 456.

[191] In the case of *R v Seven Named Accused* in the Pitcairn Supreme Court (Judgment of 19 April, [2004] PNSC 1) the Court, at para 161, stated that it was accepted by the Crown that 'UK Human Rights Legislation, where applicable, and the European Convention on Human Rights and Fundamental Freedoms' is 'relevant to Pitcairn'. The language is presumably used so as not to draw attention to the failure to extend. The ICCPR does apply. An appeal to the Privy Council was heard in July 2006, but at the time of writing no judgment has been delivered.

[192] 1953–63. There were incompatible laws in Southern Rhodesia which the local government was not prepared to amend. The Convention was extended to Nyasaland (now Malawi) and to Northern Rhodesia (now Zambia).

[193] Established in 1957 and dissolved in 1962.

[194] Declaration 12 September 1967, (1967) 10 EYHR 47–8. On the delay, see *HREE* (n 52 above) 839. On 3 April 1984 a letter informed Strasbourg that since 31 December 1983 the UK was no longer responsible for its external affairs.

[195] eg a revised list submitted in 1964 noted that the Gold Coast had become independent in 1957, (1957) 1 EYHR 32. See also (1966) 9 EYHR 22–3, (1967) 10 EYHR 46, (1969) 12 EYHR 74 (1969) removing Aden, Mauritius and Swaziland, the former somewhat belatedly.

[196] Cyprus, Gold Coast, Jamaica, Kenya, Federation of Malaya, Federation of Nigeria, North Borneo, Sarawak, Singapore, Somaliland, Tanganyika, Trinidad and Tobago, Uganda, and Zanzibar.

[197] Anguilla, Bermuda, British Virgin Islands, Cayman Islands, Falkland Islands, Gibraltar, Guernsey, Isle of Man, Jersey, Montserrat, St Helena, and Turks and Caicos Islands.

[198] Tristan da Cunha and Ascension, Nightingale, Inaccessible, and Gough Islands. The last three have no settled population but on Gough Island's resident mice, currently attacking albatross chicks, see *HREE* (n 52 above) 278, based on an account by a visiting scientist who told one of the authors that they attacked him in his sleeping bag. There is a US airbase on Ascension. There is a small resident civilian population; some members were born on the Island.

In relation to territories which have been reconstituted since the 1950s, which are discussed later in this article, it does not include either the British Antarctic Territory (hereinafter BAT) or the British Indian Ocean Territory (hereinafter BIOT), though it names the Sovereign Base Areas of Akrotiri and Dhekelia in Cyprus (hereinafter SBAs), in relation to which a declaration of extension was communicated on 1 April 2004, and South Georgia and the South Sandwich Islands (SGSSI).[199] The position over the last of these territories is a little obscure. The first explicit extension, we are informed by the Strasbourg Secretariat, was on 14 January 1991. But the territory does not appear in a list in the *Yearbook* for 1991.[200] Though not named in the current list an entry in the *Yearbook* for 1986 appears to assume that the Convention is in force there.[201] If a formal declaration of extension, naming the territory, is essential, there remain, astonishingly, British dependencies—the BAT, the BIOT, and certainly Pitcairn Island, to which the Convention still does not apply some fifty years after it came into force.

As for the First Protocol, consultation began in November 1952 and the replies indicated that many colonial governments were likely to oppose the extension of the whole protocol, or would only be agreeable if there were reservations. The Channel Islands and the Isle of Man were agreeable to extension, but no action was then taken.[202] One reason for continued inaction was reluctance to draw attention, through reservations, to the embarrassing state of affairs in some colonial territories. No decision was taken; the matter was deliberately allowed to become dormant.[203] The matter was considered again in 1967, when there was further consultation; again no action was taken. By December 1970 all remaining overseas dependencies which had been consulted were agreeable to extension;[204] those consulted do not appear to have included, however, the SBAs in Cyprus (1960), or the BAT (1962), the BIOT

[199] See text to nn 253ff below. The position over the ICCPR (n 150 above) differs from that under the ECHR; it has not been accepted for Anguilla, the BAT, the BIOT, or the SBAs, but it has been for Pitcairn, to which the ECHR does not apply. It was also accepted for Hong Kong. It was accepted for the Falkland Islands Dependencies and presumably applies to SGSSI. See generally D Harris and S Joseph (eds), *The International Covenant on Civil and Political Rights and United Kingdom Law* (1995) ch 2 (McGoldrick and Parker) 74–5. On ratification in 1976 it was accepted for 17 territories, of which 12 remain as BOTs. Insofar as this list excludes certain BOTS, its validity is uncertain. Anguilla and SGSSI did not exist as distinct territories in 1976.

[200] (1991) 34 EYHR 19.

[201] (1986) 29 EYHR 6. This may be a mistake or it may have been assumed that the earlier extension to the Falkland Islands of 3 April 1984, which did not explicitly name dependencies, still applied. In 1991 the UK in ratifying the 6th Protocol declared that it did so on behalf of SGSSI and the dependencies of St Helena.

[202] See *Wiggins v UK* (1978) and *Gillow v UK* (1986) (n 284 below), discussed below 172–4.

[203] *HREE* (n 52 above) 842–4, based on NA CO 936/291 and 292. There is also a historical account in NA FCO 41/604 and 478. The failure to act in 1967 was an oversight.

[204] There were thought to be problems over Art 3 in Ascension Island, where the Governor of St Helena was the legislature, and in Tristan da Cunha, for which, although there was an Island Council with power to issue by-laws, ordinances were made by the Governor without consultation. There were minor problems over Art 2.

(1965),[205] the Isle of Man, or Pitcairn, to which the Convention itself had never been explicitly extended. Further delay was then agreed; legislation on immigration control was pending, and an application by a number of East African Asians to the Commission was also pending.[206] Then, on 22 February 1988, after over thirty years' delay, it was extended to ten dependencies.[207] There remained significant omissions: Hong Kong, the Falkland Islands, and the Isle of Man, as well as Pitcairn and the BAT, the BIOT, the SBAs, and the SGSSI. All this is the more lamentable in view of the fact that the First Protocol was intended to form an integral part of the original Convention. So for prolonged periods of time the populations of UK dependencies have been denied Convention protection, and for some few this remains the position.[208]

Under Articles 25 and 46 of the Convention, the optional clauses, parties had a free choice over the right of individual petition and the jurisdiction of the Court; UK practice has always been to link the two options. Far and away the most important option was over individual petition, and, as might be expected, the British Colonial Office was adamantly hostile to accepting such a right.[209] For the United Kingdom itself the optional clauses were first accepted in January 1966, but only for a period of three years, the Convention expressly permitting acceptance for a term.[210] The notification bizarrely excluded responsibility for anything done or occurring even in the United Kingdom in relation to its overseas dependencies.[211] Arguably in substance this constituted an invalid reservation. This was renewed in 1969 for another three years,[212] but in 1972, and again in 1974, only for two years.[213] In 1976,[214] and again in 1981,[215] and 1986, the renewal was for five years and in the end, once the Eleventh Protocol entered into force in 1998, the optional provisions went, except for dependent territories covered by Article 56.[216]

The extension of the optional clauses to the overseas dependencies began in 1967, when they were accepted for two years for sixteen territories;[217] the notice added that they had also been accepted at the request

[205] For their anomalous status, see text following n 241 below.

[206] See nn 229 and 284 below.

[207] Guernsey and Jersey, Anguilla, the British Virgin Islands, the Cayman Islands, Gibraltar, Montserrat, St Helena and its dependencies, and the Turks and Caicos Islands; there were some reservations, mainly to preserve the practice of corporal punishment. See (1988) 31 EYHR 6–7.

[208] *Quark Fishing Ltd v Secretary of State for Foreign and Commonwealth Affairs* [2004] EWCA Civ 527, 29 April 2004, [2005] UKHL 57, 13 October 2005. An application has been submitted to the ECtHR, on which see n 382 below.

[209] *HREE* (n 52 above) 408–10, 493–8, 500–1, 512–13, 723–6.

[210] Arts 25(2), 46(2). See (1966) 9 EYHR 8.

[211] ibid, 16. The validity of this was never tested at Strasbourg.

[212] (1969) 12 EYHR 24–6.

[213] (1972) 15 EYHR 4–7, (1974) 17 EYHR 12–16.

[214] (1974) 19 EYHR 6–9.

[215] (1981) 24 EYHR 22–5.

[216] Under Art 34 as amended. Under the current Art 56(4) there is still an option as to extension of the right of individual petition to a territory to which the Convention has been extended under Art 56(1).

[217] (1967) 10 EYHR 12–15. They were Guernsey, Bermuda, British Honduras, British Solomon Islands, British Virgin Islands, Cayman Islands, Falkland Islands, Fiji, Gilbert and Ellice Islands,

of the governments of the territories, to five other territories.[218] Near to home Jersey was missed out; apparently acceptance dated from 1976.[219] Further away Mauritius, for example, was not included, probably because it was soon to become independent. Dominica was also missing. The Isle of Man was included in 1967 but does not appear in the renewals listed in 1969,[220] though this may simply have been an error. Acceptance of the optional clauses was renewed in 1972 for two years and again for two years in 1974, expiring in 1976.[221] In 1976 renewal, which covered seven territories,[222] was for five years to 1981.[223] There were significant omissions, in particular Jersey, and the Isle of Man, as well as the BAT, the BIOT, the SGSSI, and the SBAs. The exclusion of the Isle of Man from the renewal of 1976 was a response to annoyance over the proceedings, commenced in 1972, in *Tyrer v UK* challenging the use of corporal punishment.[224] The incomplete application of the Convention is well illustrated by a list published in the *Yearbook* for 1988.[225] The Convention was at that time extended to twelve territories, and there were still omissions. For eight of these the right of individual petition and acceptance of the court had been extended since 1967. Anguilla had not joined this list until 1981. The Isle of Man and Jersey had been included again. Information from the Council of Europe's website indicates that as of 9 February 2005 the right of individual petition has been accepted for eight territories for a five-year period only;[226] in the case of Jersey, the Isle of Man, and the SBAs the acceptance is now permanent. The odd men out are the Cayman Islands, the British Virgin Islands, the BAT, and the BIOT.

The ability to extend the optional provisions, and in particular the right of individual petition, for limited periods, could be used in attempts to influence the Commission or Court to defer to governments which were displeased with their rulings. That this possibility did not pass unnoticed can be documented in the case of the United Kingdom in two papers circulated by the Home Office in 1972 and 1973, the first to the Cabinet[227] and the second to the Defence and Overseas Policy

Gibraltar, Isle of Man, Montserrat, St Helena, St Vincent, the Seychelles, and the Turks and Caicos Islands.

[218] Brunei, Dominica, Grenada, Tonga, and St Lucia. The inconsistent form perhaps arose because two different officials were involved.

[219] Jersey is not included in the list for 1976 in (1976) 19 EYHR 6, 14, but this seems to be a mistake. See (1981) 24 EYHR 22–5, (1988) 31 EYHR 24–5.

[220] (1969) 12 EYHR 24, 32.

[221] (1972) 15 EYHR 46, (1974) 17 EYHR 12–18; the list at this renewal misses Jersey, perhaps in error.

[222] Listed as Guernsey, Bermuda, Falkland Islands, Gibraltar, St Helena, Tuvalu and St Lucia.

[223] (1976) 19 EYHR 8, 31 (1981) 24 EYHR 24–5.

[224] Series A No 26, 2 EHRR 1.

[225] (1988) 31 EYHR 18. The territories were now Anguilla, Bermuda, British Virgin Islands, Cayman Islands, Falkland Islands, Gibraltar, Guernsey, Isle of Man, Jersey, Montserrat, St Helena, and Turks and Caicos Islands. cf (1989) 32 EYHR 12, (1990) 33 EYHR 19, (1991) 34 EYHR 19, and (1992) 35 EYHR 20.

[226] Anguilla, Bermuda, Falklands, Gibraltar, Guernsey, Montserrat, St Helena and dependencies, and SGSSI.

[227] CAB 129/161 CP (72) 12. There was no Cabinet decision.

Committee of the Cabinet.[228] By this time the Home Office had become much involved in resisting applications in relation to immigration policy,[229] to prisoners' rights,[230] and to alleged misconduct by the security forces in Northern Ireland. [231] Acceptance of the right of individual petition had been renewed in January 1969 for three years, and was due for renewal in January 1972. The Lord Chancellor wanted to renew for three years,[232] the Attorney-General preferred two, which the Foreign Office recommended and this was accepted.[233] It was the Commission, not the Court, which then excited criticism, particularly because it had indicated that in the *East African Asians* case it might find a violation of Article 3, which was thought by Home Office officials to be 'entirely perverse'. The Home Office then submitted a paper saying that it was 'the chief (although not the only) sufferer at the hands of the Commission', and while it had not opposed renewal, suggested that there might have to be refusal to extend in two years' time: 'Unless there is a marked change of heart by the Commission, or unless the tendency of the Commission towards developing a new jurisprudence by extending the meaning of the Convention is corrected by decisions of the European Court, continued acceptance of these optional articles by the United Kingdom is likely to bring us neither benefit nor credit.' The following year another memorandum was submitted to the Defence and Overseas Policy Committee.[234] This complained that: 'The Commission's broad and expansive approach to questions of construction makes it difficult to predict where the Convention will bite next.' After conceding that refusal to renew would lead to an outcry from 'the human rights lobby' and would damage Britain's international reputation, renewal for a mere two years would signal concern. Informal contacts with the Secretariat indicated that there might be other governments also concerned; they should be approached: 'The objective should be, in the long term, to bring about a more conservative approach by members of the Commission to questions

[228] CAB 148/131 DOP (73) 71. See also on what follows, FCO 41/950.

[229] Between 1967 and 1970 a number of East African persons of Asian ethnicity sought protection in the UK against the discriminatory policies adopted by Kenya and Uganda; litigation raised the question of whether the Commonwealth Immigrants Act 1968, s 1 violated the Convention. For an account by Lord Lester, their leading counsel, see 'Thirty Years On: the East African Case Revisited' [2002] *Public Law* 52. See also (1970) 13 EYHR 928 and NA FCO 41/345, 346, 950, 951, 1105, 1106, FCO 52/11, HO 344/198. For the report of the Commission, see 78-A DR 5 (1994).

[230] This gave rise to the decisions in *Golder v UK* Series A/18, (1975) 1 EHRR 524, which went against the UK. There had been many more applications by prisoners, and there are many papers available in NA.

[231] *Republic of Ireland v UK* Series A/25, (1978) 1 EHRR 15, 225. There are many papers in NA.

[232] Two files from the Lord Chancellor's Department on objections to accepting the optional clauses, NA LCO 2/8167 and 8168, covering this issue from 1964 to 1974, have been lost.

[233] Memorandum by Vincent Evans of 18 January 1972 in NA FCO 41/950. There were also memoranda by Sir Thomas Brimelow and Lord Bridges which we have not located; these argued that it would be premature not to renew until the pending cases had been concluded and the system given a fair trial.

[234] CAB 148/131 DOP (73) 71, also PREM 15/1504. By now the *Handyside* case (1 EHRR 737) was pending.

of interpretation ....' This could, perhaps, be brought about by more suitable appointments to membership of the Commission.[235] What steps were actually taken is not documented. But in 1972 the Danish international lawyer Max Sørensen did not stand for re-election as President of the Commission, and the former Foreign Office lawyer, James Fawcett, was elected President; what lobbying went on behind the scenes cannot be established. The general dissatisfaction, which was no doubt aired in discussions with the Commission which took place over the *East African Asians* case, and the *Golder* case, in 1972 [236] provides the background to the unsuccessful efforts made by Sir Gerald Fitzmaurice, former Legal Adviser to the Foreign Office,[237] to persuade the Court in the cases of *Golder v UK* (1975)[238] and *Tyrer v UK* (1978),[239] to adopt a more restrained attitude to interpretation. It failed.

Under the provisions of the Eleventh Protocol, which abolished the Commission, acceptance of the jurisdiction of the Court ceased to be optional, and under Article 34 the right of individual petition is no longer optional except in relation to territories to which the Convention has been extended under what is now Article 56.[240] The amended Convention does not explicitly provide for this option to be exercised only for a term, but we are informed by the Secretariat that the United Kingdom has continued to follow its earlier practice; thus the right of individual petition was extended to the SGSSI for five years from 14 January 2001. So far as the First Protocol is concerned Article 4, taken literally, permits parties to do more or less anything they want, and there is no jurisprudence on the meaning of 'extent'.

VI. New and Anomalous Forms of Overseas Dependency

Since the Convention came into force the United Kingdom had established a number of distinct new overseas dependent territories, the existence of which we have already mentioned. These were not the result of the acquisition of new territory, but were created by making rearrangements to existing territories.[241] Difficult questions arise as to the applicability of the Convention and its First Protocol to these new entities.

[235] There was also a suggestion for an amendment which would enable a respondent government to challenge a decision on admissibility in the Court, before the Commission started to engage in its protracted and, it was thought, damaging fact-finding activities.

[236] Documented in (1972) 15 EYHR 38.

[237] 1953–60, Judge of the International Court of Justice (ICJ) 1960–73, Judge of the European Court of Human Rights (ECtHR) 1974–80. For discussion of Fitzmaurice's views on interpretation, see R Jennings, 'Gerald Gray Fitzmaurice' (1984) 55 BYIL 1, 36–43.

[238] Series A/18, 1 EHRR 525, 737.

[239] Series A/26, 2 EHRR 1.

[240] Art 56(4).

[241] In 1999 a government White Paper, *Partnership for Progress and Prosperity. Britain and the Overseas Territories* (Cm 4264, hereinafter *PPP*) was published which gave an account of the various territories and their governmental systems, called 'profiles', in its Appendix I. This misses out the SBAs, though the territory is included in the list of BOTs at para 1.5 and mentioned elsewhere

When Cyprus became independent in 1960 sovereignty was retained over two bases and surrounding land. The Cyprus Act, having provided that the Republic of Cyprus would comprise the whole island, went on to provide that 'nothing in the foregoing section shall affect Her Majesty's sovereignty and jurisdiction over [the air bases of Akrotiri and Dhekhelia]'.[242] At this time the European Convention, but not its First Protocol or the optional clauses, had been extended to Cyprus. There was never an explicit denunciation of the Convention with regard to the SBAs, though in 1964 Strasbourg was informed that since 1960 the United Kingdom was no longer responsible for the international relations of Cyprus, a statement which obviously could not apply to the SBAs for whose international relations the United Kingdom clearly remained responsible. Arguably the European Convention continued to apply there. As being the remnant of the Crown colony of Cyprus, which was annexed on 5 November 1914, the status of the territory is, arguably, that of a colony.[243] However, a ministerial statement of 22 February 1982 explained that it was not the intention to set up and administer 'colonies' on the Island of Cyprus.[244] There is an Administrator on the spot, with power to make laws for the 'peace, order and good government' of the territory; he is always a serving military officer. There is no Governor, and there is no Legislative nor Executive Council, nor democratic institutions, though there is an Advisory Board. The Crown retains its constituent and legislative powers under the prerogative, and the territory is of course subject to the legislative power of the UK Parliament. The Secretary of State has a power to disallow any laws made by the Administrator. There are courts with an ultimate appeal to the Privy Council.[245] The territory, which has a considerable but largely transient population of service personnel and their families, is in practice run by the Ministry of Defence in London, with service personnel in the territory subject to military law. There are also resident Greek Cypriots and access for those not living there, and a transient population of tourists.[246] There is no policy under which the territory is in the fullness of time to become an independent country within the Commonwealth. If the bases became redundant for strategic purposes sovereignty would be relinquished in favour of the Government of the Republic of Cyprus, and undertakings have been given to this effect. As late as June 2000 it was the United Kingdom's position that it would be 'inappropriate' to extend

in the document. See also UN Doc CCPR/C/UKOT/99/5, the UK Report of 2000 to the Human Rights Committee.

242 Cyprus Act 1960, s 2(1)(a). Also SI 1960/1368, 1369, SI 1966/1415, SI 1960 III, 4213 (Royal Instructions).

243 This is the view taken in Lord Mackay of Clashfern (ed), *Halsbury's Laws of England* (4th edn, 2003 reissue) vol VI, para 862 (hereinafter *Halsbury*).

244 HC Debs vol 16, col 137–8 (20 January 1982).

245 The judges hold office at Her Majesty's pleasure. See *Halsbury* (n 243 above) vol VI, para 849.

246 There is information on the official website managed by the Ministry of Defence.

the Convention,[247] but this was done on 1 May 2004 on a permanent basis.[248] For over forty years its writ, arguably at least, did not run there.

The BAT was created in 1962 and comprises the South Orkneys, the South Shetlands, Graham Land and the adjoining mainland; the territory lies south of latitude 60° S and is bounded by longitudes 20° W and 80° W.[249] It was established in response to the Antarctic Treaty 1958.[250] Its population is wholly transient, but permanent bases have been established. Before 1962 these territories were dependencies of the Falkland Islands; there were conflicting claims to some parts, but these are currently suspended. There was a High Commissioner, appointed by the Crown, who may appoint a deputy. He has legislative powers under the usual formula, subject to disallowance; he also has executive powers. There is no legislative or executive council, and no democratic institutions. There is no policy under which the territory may, at some uncertain date in the future, become a self-governing state within, or if the inhabitants so choose, outside the Commonwealth, nor could there be. In practice the Governor of the Falkland Islands administered the territory until 1989, when the practice developed of a Foreign and Commonwealth Office Official, resident in London, being appointed. The BAT has a Supreme Court and Court of Appeal; this has the same personnel and the same location as the courts of the Falkland Islands. There are a number of scientific stations, and individuals actually present there act as magistrates.[251] Arguably it ranks as a Crown Colony. The European Convention (but not the right of individual petition) was extended to the Falkland Islands in 1953, and the right of individual petition and acceptance of the court in 1967 initially for two years; this was later renewed. No formal action has been taken by the United Kingdom to terminate its application to the territory on or after its separation from the Falklands.[252] It has, however, never been included in one of the lists submitted by the United Kingdom. Although its population is transient there is no reason in principle why the rights protected under the Convention and its First Protocol should not be secured there, though the absence of lawyers might cause a slight problem under Article 6, and elections there for a local legislature, as distinct from postal voting in UK elections, would make no sense.

The SGSSI were, before 1985, dependencies of the Falkland Islands, and were separated from other Antarctic territories when the BAT was

247 HC Debs vol 352, col 38 W, noted (2000) 71 BYIL 379.

248 Council of Europe website.

249 The boundaries are defined in the British Antarctic Territory Order in Council 1962, SI 1962/400, SI 1962 I, 1039 (Royal Instructions). See now SI 1989/842, s 2. See generally *Halsbury* (n 243 above) vol 6, para 853. For a 'profile' see *PPP* (n 241 above) 648, and for history Roberts-Wray (n 42 above) 867–8.

250 (TS No 97 1961, Cmnd 1535). See E Lauterpacht, *The Contemporary Practice of the U.K. in the Field of International Law* (1963) vol I, 35–7.

251 The judges hold office at Her Majesty's pleasure. See *Halsbury* (n 243 above) vol VI, para 849.

252 The boundaries of the BAT defined by coordinates differ somewhat from those of the territory when it was a dependency of the Falklands, settled by Letters Patent in 1917.

established in 1962.[253] They have only a transient population. There is a Commissioner, who is in practice the Governor of the Falkland Islands, with a power to legislate by ordinance for peace, order, and good governance;[254] an Annex to the Statutory Instrument lists reserved subjects on which there must be prior consent from the Secretary of State. The Commissioner is under the control in defence and security matters of the officer commanding British forces in the South Atlantic. The First Secretary in the Falkland Islands administration performs similar functions for the territory. There is no legislative or executive council, and there are no democratic institutions. There is a power to establish courts or to confer jurisdiction on courts in other territories; in effect this means that the courts of the Falkland Islands do duty for the SGSSI.[255] Thus the Senior Magistrate from the Falklands presides over the magistrates' court, and there is a court of summary jurisdiction. The Crown can legislate for the territory by Order in Council and it is subject to the legislative power of the UK Parliament. The ultimate Court of Appeal is the Privy Council in London. Its status is the same as that of the BAT. When the territory was a dependency of the Falkland Islands the European Convention presumably applied there. In the Council of Europe's website the territory is currently included in a list of territories to which the Convention applies; the Convention was explicitly extended in 1986 and the right of individual petition for five years. This has been renewed for a further period of five years from 14 January 2001. The First Protocol has not formally been extended.

The BIOT was formed in 1965[256] by separating the islands of the Chagos Archipelago from the dependencies of Mauritius, which was then a Crown Colony, and certain other islands[257] from the dependencies of the Seychelles, at that time also a Crown Colony. Mauritius became independent in 1968 and the Seychelles in 1976; the islands separated from the Seychelles were restored when it became independent. The reason was to enable the United States to establish a military base; in due course it was constructed on Diego Garcia.[258] Some of the Chagos Islands, including Diego Garcia, had a long-settled population, comprising persons of African ethnicity, descendants of freed slaves; they were

[253] See *Halsbury* (n 243 above) vol VI, para 861, SI 1985/449. See *PPP* (n 241 above) 68 for a 'profile' and *R (Quark Fishing Ltd v Secretary of State for Foreign and Commonwealth Affairs* [2004] EWCA Civ 527, 29 April 2004, [2005] UKHL 57; See n 382 below.

[254] He must consult the Executive Council of the Falklands when exercising any function which might affect those islands.

[255] Also SI 1989/2339.

[256] See *Halsbury* (n 243 above) vol VI, para 854, SI 1965/1920, amended 1968/11, revoked by the British Indian Ocean Territory Order 1976, SI 1976/893 and Royal Instructions of 8 November 1965 (SI 1965 III, 6440) and SI 1981 III, 6524 and SI 1983/1888, and generally *Halsbury* (above) vol VI, para 854.

[257] The Farquhar Islands, those of the Aldabra group, and the Island of Desroches.

[258] The agreement with the US over the base was settled by an exchange of notes in 1966, 1972, and 1976, published in the UK Treaty Series as No 15 (1967) Cmnd 3231, No 126 (1972) Cmnd 516, and No 19 (1976) Cm 6413. See Crawford (n 42 above) 337 n 30.

known as the Ilois.[259] To satisfy the wishes of the US military, between about 1967 and 1973 this population was unlawfully expelled from the islands.[260] The invention of the BIOT was thus directly related to the violation of the human rights of its indigenous inhabitants; it was invented with a view to violating those rights. This expulsion has given rise to litigation in the UK courts,[261] and an application to Strasbourg under the European Convention is currently pending. The base was established under an agreement with the United Kingdom, and the population of the territory is now transient, comprising military personnel, civilian contractors and their employees, scientists, some visiting yachtsmen and fishermen, and a tiny number of British officials. There is a Commissioner appointed by the Crown by instructions issued by the Secretary of State, who enjoys legislative powers; in practice this office is held by an official of the Foreign and Commonwealth Office located in London. This is also the case with the Administrator. There is a system of courts, the judges being non-resident, though there is a locally resident magistrate and a few police officers. There is an ultimate appeal to the Privy Council.[262] The courts in the United Kingdom have exercised jurisdiction over the BIOT in a number of recently litigated cases.[263] There are no democratic institutions whatsoever and there is no policy under which the BIOT could in the fullness of time become a self-governing state either within or without the Commonwealth. An undertaking has been given to return the territory to Mauritius, which claims it, if it ever ceases to be needed for defence purposes.[264] No consultation ever took place with the Chagossians. Currently there are no plans to allow them to return.[265] The European Convention, but not the right of

[259] The expression, which just means 'the islanders' acquired offensive overtones in Mauritius, and they now prefer to be called the Chagossians or Chagos Islanders.

[260] *PPP* (n 241 above) 50 glosses over the expulsion, which involved around 2,000 persons. There were also migrant workers who were evacuated.

[261] See in particular *R v Secretary of State for Foreign and Commonwealth Affairs, ex p Bancoult* [2001] QB 1067, No 2; *Chagos Islanders v Attorney-General* [2003] EWHC 2222, decision of Ousely J, leave to appeal refused. Litigation brought in the UK by one Michel Vencatassen, in 1975, led to a settlement which provided some compensation for some Chagossians. See now *R (ex p Bancoult) v Secretary of State for Foreign and Commonwealth Affairs* [2006] EWHC 1038 (Admin) CO/4093/2004 of 11 May 2006 where it was held in judicial review proceedings that an Order in Council which had the effect of making it a criminal offence for a Chagossian to be present in the BIOT without a permit (which would never be granted) was irrational and therefore without legal effect. The UK government's appeal against this decision is pending.

[262] Judges hold office at pleasure and can be dismissed by the Commissioner.

[263] Most importantly *R v Secretary of State for Foreign and Commonwealth Affairs, ex p Bancoult* (n 261 above). This held that the Immigration Ordinance expelling the local inhabitants was unlawful. An attempt by the UK government to render this nugatory by an Order in Council has recently been held to have been invalid; see n 261 above.

[264] *PPP* (n 241 above) 51. The US base is not held under a lease with a fixed determination. Under the agreement of 1966, which relates to the entire Chagos archipelago, review is possible up to 2016, and unless a decision is taken to terminate, the arrangement will continue for a further 20 years.

[265] The UK is, or at least was, apparently agreeable but the US government is not; see HL Deb vol 464, col 1020, 8 January 2003. Under the 1966 UK-US agreement, consultation is required if persons not explicitly identified in the agreement are admitted to the BIOT. In April 2006 a short visit was permitted.

individual petition, was extended to both Mauritius and the Seychelles in 1953,[266] and after they became independent Strasbourg was informed that the United Kingdom was no longer responsible for their international relations.[267] As in the case of the SBAs, this statement could not apply to the territories comprised in the BIOT, and there was never any denunciation of the Convention in relation to the BIOT. But, as in the case of the BAT, but not in that of the SGSSI or SBAs, there has never been an explicit declaration of extension to the BIOT as such.

The SBAs, the BAT, the SGSSI, and the BIOT are all today, since the British Overseas Territories Act 2002, officially called British Overseas Territories (BOTs); the SBAs and the BIOT today fall into the category of colonial enclaves, to be handed back to Cyprus and Mauritius if they become redundant for military purposes. In terms of traditional categories they are Crown Colonies, originally acquired respectively by conquest or cession, or annexation (SBAs),[268] by annexation or discovery (BAT and SGSSI),[269] and by cession (BIOT).[270] But they do not conform to the old model of a colony or to the current model of a BOT. In an *amicus* brief submitted by the United Kingdom Government in 1997 to the Supreme Court of the United States an account was given of the normal governmental structure of dependent territories: 'The Constitutions of the Dependent Territories are set out in United Kingdom legislation. The Constitutions of the Dependent Territories contain, among other matters, provision with regard to the office of Governor, the Executive and the Legislature.'[271] This brief listed the BAT, the BIOT, the SBAs, and the SGSSI as dependent territories in a footnote, but nothing in the passage quoted, and virtually nothing in the rest of the brief, has any application to them. Again in the Government White Paper of 1999, *Partnership for Progress and Prosperity*, the Government set out its commitment to 'A new partnership—the new way forward' which was to be:

> . . . based on four fundamental principles:
> self-determination;
> mutual obligations and responsibilities;
> freedom for the territories to run their own affairs to the greatest degree possible;
> a firm commitment from the UK to help the territories develop economically and to assist them in emergencies.[272]

Only the fourth principle could possibly be applied to the four territories under discussion, and indeed much else in the paper—for example the

[266] Both were included in lists submitted in 1964 and 1966.

[267] The letter relating to Mauritius was submitted in 1969, that relating to the Seychelles in 1979.

[268] Roberts-Wray (n 42 above) 678; the island was under British administration before it was annexed in 1914; annexation was recognized by the Treaty of Lausanne (1923).

[269] Roberts-Wray (n 42 above) 867. Although there is a long history of occupation of particular sites, it would be implausible to call them settled territories.

[270] Roberts-Wray (n 42 above) 727–31.

[271] (1997) 68 BYIL 548.

[272] para 1.19.

emphasis on the importance of consultation to establish the wish of the local inhabitants to remain associated with Britain—has never been applied to them.[273] Nobody asked the Chagossians what their wishes were before they were expelled; they were simply and cruelly made to leave, and their pet dogs, for good measure, were gassed or burnt alive by way of example. And nobody asks the Greek Cypriots living in the SBAs what their wishes are, a process which would be objected to by Cyprus if attempted. The idea of asking the temporary inhabitants of the other territories is absurd.

So nothing whatever is gained by lumping these four territories into a class of BOTs as if they were in like case with, for example, the British Virgin Islands, which have a resident population of around 20,000 persons, a ministerial system of Government with an Executive Council, presided over by the Governor, a Legislative Council of thirteen elected members, and a large degree of local autonomy.[274] Although old categories, and the modern blanket category of BOT have their uses, it seems more realistic to treat these territories as falling into a new category of their own. Gerald L Neuman has used the term 'anomalous zones' to characterize certain overseas territories of the United States, which are, like the four British territories, neither fish nor fowl.[275] We need, for analytical purposes, some similar conception to mark the difference between them and regular colonies or overseas dependencies. The basic characteristics of the four territories are that they have neither a settled population, in one case because of illegal expulsion, nor even rudimentary democratic institutions. Furthermore their administrations, for it is misleading to call them governments, enjoy only a trivial measure of autonomy. They are not on a high road to independence, nor is their future affected in the least by the wishes of their inhabitants. They are better called British non-autonomous overseas territories (BNOTs), or given some similar title to mark their peculiar status.[276] *En passant* one other territory, currently classified as a dependency of another BOT, St Helena, falls naturally into the same category; this is Ascension Island, which had no indigenous population. The island is primarily used as the home of a US military base under agreements of 1941 and 1956. The Governor of St Helena has executive and legislative authority; there is a resident Administrator appointed by him. Since 2002 there has been an elected Island Council with consultative and advisory functions.

[273] See para 2.6 and *passim*.

[274] *PPP* (n 241 above) 52.

[275] He deals with territories which have permanent populations, not with those without, such as Wake Island. See GL Neuman, 'Constitutionalism and Individual Rights in the Territories' in CD Burnett and B Marshall (eds), *Foreign in a Domestic Sense. Puerto Rico, American Expansion and the Constitution* (2001) 182.

[276] Tristan da Cunha is also a dependency of St Helena, but it enjoys rudimentary democratic institutions (see *PPP* (n 241 above) 67).

VII. The Practice of Other Members of the Council of Europe

The Netherlands and Denmark, among the other original negotiating parties, are the only states which have made declarations of extension under Article 63(1). The Netherlands did so in 1953 in relation to Surinam and the Netherlands Antilles.[277] Denmark also made a declaration in the same year with regard to Greenland both in relation to the Convention and to its First Protocol, and accepted the right of individual petition for Greenland.[278]

France did not ratify the Convention until May 1974, and its instrument of ratification was stated to apply 'to the whole territory of the Republic, having due regard, where the overseas territories (*les territoires d'outre-mer*) are concerned, to local requirements, as mentioned in Article 63'. This applied to the First Protocol as well.

Belgium ratified the Convention and its First Protocol on 14 June 1955,[279] making the following declaration: 'En déposant cet instrument .. . le Représentant a.i[280] de Belgique a déclaré qu'au cas où son Gouvernment ferait dans l'avenir, en vertu de l'article 63 de la Convention, une déclaration étendant l'application de la Convention à un territoire dont la Belgique assure les relations internationales, le Gouvernment Belge pourrait faire accompagner cette déclaration de réserves imposées par les nécessités locales.'[281] This declaration, which could only refer to Belgium's African territories, clearly assumes that in the absence of a declaration of extension the Covenant and First Protocol would not apply.

Belgium, as we have seen, never supported the system of voluntary extension, but in the end went along with it by way of compromise. The thinking behind this declaration must have been that since the Convention now embodied such a system, its effect was to exclude the African territories from protection unless such a declaration was made, a view compatible with the second or third possible interpretations. Belgium never did make any declaration of extension.

The only other party to the Convention which has ever made a declaration of extension is West Germany, which on ratifying in 1952 declared

[277] (1955–7) 1 EYHR 44–6, with a reservation to Art 6(3), withdrawn in 1980; see (1980) 23 EYHR 8. A further declaration was made in 1986 explaining that Aruba had acquired internal autonomy within the Kingdom of the Netherlands and no longer formed part of the Netherlands Antilles, without this affecting the application of international treaties. A note by the Secretariat on the website notes that the Convention no longer applies to Surinam since it became independent on 25 November 1975.

[278] (1955–7) 1 EYHR 45.

[279] Under the then Belgian Constitution, Art 167, §3 the King concludes treaties, but, under a dualist system: 'Ces traits n'ont d'effet qu'après avoir reçu l'assentiment des Chambres'. This assent was given by a law of 13 May 1955. For the '*Exposé des Motifs*' presented by Paul van Zeeland, Minister of Foreign Affairs, see *Documents parlementaires Sénat* Session 1952–53, III, 161–320 and *Séance du 6 Mai* 1953, *Annales parlementaires Sénat*, 25 mars–17 juillet 1953, 1192.

[280] *Ad interim.*

[281] (1955–7) 1 EYHR 51.

that: 'The territory to which the Convention shall apply extends also to Western Berlin.' This declaration covered the period 3 September 1953 to 3 October 1990.[282] Western Berlin was not part of the Federal Republic, and was at this time still under occupation, though permitted by the Western powers a considerable degree of autonomy. Under an exchange of notes, the Federal Republic was, from 1952, permitted to extend international agreements to it, 'provided that this is not precluded by the nature of the agreements concerned'.[283] Italy, though as we have seen responsible for the administration of Somalia from 1950 to 1960, never made such a declaration. The reason may have been the fact that there was UN supervision.

VIII. The Jurisprudence

There have been only twelve cases which appear to be relevant to the subject matter of this article, though none of these cases provides a fully elaborated view of the relationship between Article 1 of the Convention and the system of voluntary extension provided for by Article 63 and Article 4 of the First Protocol.[284] In part, the explanation for this somewhat disappointing phenomenon lies in the way in which the complaints came up for decision, which did not call for elaboration. Four of the twelve cases came only before the Commission, and only one has come before the Grand Chamber.

The first of these cases was *X and others v Belgium* (1961),[285] which came only before the Commission. An application was brought by three Belgian nationals and a company, in which two of the applicants appear to have been shareholders, to seek redress for loss of property suffered as a consequence of the collapse of the Belgian administration in the Congo and Ruanda-Urundi, and the granting of independence, which took

[282] Information from Council of Europe website. The Federal Republic of Germany was established in 1949, and became an independent sovereign state in 1955.

[283] US Department of State, *Documents on Germany 1944–1985* 436–8. See ID Henry and MC Wood, *The Legal Status of Berlin* (1987) 195–206, 211–13. Crawford (n 42 above) 459–66. The ICCPR was also declared by the Federal Republic in 1973 to apply to West Berlin.

[284] *X and Others v Belgium* (App No 1065/61) (Admissibility) (1961) 4 EYHR 260–71, *Cyprus v Turkey* (1975) DR 2/125, *Wiggins v UK* (1978) (Admissibility) DR 13/40, *Tyrer v UK* (Judgment, Merits) (1978) 2 EHRR 1, *Gillow v UK* Series A/109, (1986) 11 EHRR 335, *Loizidou v Turkey* (Preliminary objections) (1995) 20 EHRR 99, *Drozd and Janosek v France and Spain* (Judgment, Merits) Series A/240, (1992) 14 EHRR (1992) 745, *Mathews v UK* (App No 24833/94) (Judgment Merits) 18 February 1999, (1999) 28 EHRR 361, *Bui Van Thanh and others v UK* (App No 16137/90) (Admissibility) DR 65/336, *Yonghong v Portugal* (1999) Judgment of 25 November 1999 Series No IX 385, *Ilaşçu and others v Moldova and Russia* (App No 48787/99) (Admissibility decision of 4 July 2001) (Merits) (2005) 40 EHRR 1030 (both Grand Chamber), *Affaire Py v France* (App No 66289/01) 11 January 2005. The *East African Asians Case (Application of East African Asians v UK)* (Admissibility) 10 October 1970, did not raise any issue over Art 63; jurisdiction over the 31 applications which were treated as a test case depended either on their possession of UK passports or on their presence in the UK. There was no dispute over the competence of the Commission to entertain the applications.

[285] (App No 1065/61) (Admissibility) (1961) 4 EYHR 260–71.

effect on 1 July 1960. In addition they claimed nominal damages on the ground that they had been excluded from voting in the metropolitan provincial and parliamentary elections of 1960; in consequence they could play no part politically in problems of Belgian policy towards the Congo.[286] Their application was based on Articles 1 and 3 of the First Protocol. The application came before the Commission, at this time chaired by Sir Humphrey Waldock, on the issue of admissibility, and was never communicated to the Belgian Government.[287] The Belgian member was Mrs G Janssen-Pevtschen, a Belgian judge from Brussels.

The Secretariat drew the applicants' attention[288] to the statement made by the Belgian representative when depositing the instrument of ratification and to the fact that Belgium had never made any declarations of extension under Article 63 or Article 4.[289] The applicants pointed out that: 'until 1st July 1960 the Belgian Congo formed an integral part of the national territory; that therefore the Convention, including the declaration made by Belgium in virtue of Article 25, was in force in the Colony equally with the metropolitan area without need for recourse to the notifications provided for in paragraphs 1 and 4 of Article 63 of the Convention and Article 4 of the Protocol'. The opinion of the Commission, that the application was inadmissible under Article 27(2), was set out in the formal French style then in use at Strasbourg. One reason given addressed the merits, and does not here concern us.[290] The other was that the application did not fall within the competence of the Commission *ratione loci*. The justification for this was complex, and it is clear that the Commission, possibly through the Belgian member, or possibly through the Secretariat, undertook its own research, in effect constructing the respondent's possible arguments even though the case had not been communicated. Reference was made to the fact that between 1953 and 1955 the Belgian Government and Parliament had considered the whole question of extension. The starting point was a Report and *projet de loi*[291] presented by Senator Henri Rolin[292] on behalf of the Senate's Foreign Affairs Committee. This recommended that Belgium should, for its metropolitan territory, ratify the Convention and accept the optional clauses, and extend the Convention to the Congo, but

[286] They also made a claim for an award of nominal damages for insult. For an account of the background see G Mwakikagile, *Africa After Independence* (Huntingdon, 2001).

[287] Communication from HE Judge Koen Lenaerts.

[288] The modern practice is for the Secretariat to write a letter drawing attention to 'certain shortcomings' in an application.

[289] See n 281 above.

[290] It was that the complaint as to the denial of the right to participate in metropolitan elections was not a violation of Art 3 of the 1st Protocol, for Belgium was not bound to give all persons a right to vote in elections, and might legitimately exclude, eg, overseas residents. This was supported by reference to the decision of the Commission on 4 January 1960 in App No 530/59; see (1960) 3 EYHR 184–97, esp 190–1.

[291] For Rolin's report and discussion in the Senate see *Séance du 12 Novembre 1953, Annales Parlementaires Sénat* Session ord 1953–54, 1–33, p 19ff, p 34ff, p 76ff. The account we give is fuller than that which appears in the report in EYHR. It is possible that Rolin was consulted over Belgian ratification, but we have no evidence for this.

[292] See n 174 above.

not to the trust territory of Ruanda-Urundi. The recommendation not to extend to the trust territory was based on the undesirability of having two systems of international control, one by the United Nations, the other by the Council of Europe, for the same territory. The Report argued that extension of the First Protocol and the right of individual petition to the Congo would be premature. Rolin had, in the Consultative Assembly, supported the system of voluntary extension, but hoped it would be employed in the most liberal fashion. But he thought it important to distinguish between:

> ... civil rights whose enjoyment ought to be capable of recognition without any distinction for the benefit of the totality of the individuals within the jurisdiction of our States, and the political rights in question [ie the rights eventually protected by Article 3 of the Protocol]. These would have to be, no doubt, the object of widely differing conditions of application, according to the degree of evolution of the different territories ...[293]

Extending the Convention to the Congo was opposed by the Government: 'Notre territoires d'outre-mer n'est pas la Métropole. Le civilisation africaine, en dépit des progrés gigantesques qu'elle a réalisés depuis plus d'une demi-siècle, n'est pas encore la civilisation du vieil Occident'.[294] The Senate voted to adopt an amended *projet de loi* which did not approve the extension, and which provided that the declaration provided for by Article 63 would come into effect only after having received the approval of both Chambers.[295] The Chamber of Representatives accepted this on 28 April 1955.[296] Throughout it was never doubted that in the absence of extensions the Convention and the First Protocol would not apply; the assumption was also that there would, eventually, be extension. The Commission's argument based on the historical material and on the declaration which had accompanied ratification, was that Belgium's understanding was that in the absence of a declaration under Article 63 neither the Convention nor the First Protocol applied to the Congo, and this was certainly correct. This treated the intention of the Contracting Party, however established, as controlling.

The Commission still had to address the argument that the Congo was an integral part of Belgium, and that it did not therefore count as a territory 'for whose international relations it is responsible' within the meaning of Article 63. The Commission argued that the language used in so-called colonial clauses, or reservations,[297] had in contemporary

[293] *TP* VI 122–35, speech during the 2nd Session of the Assembly, 7–8 August 1950.

[294] Speech of M le vicomte du Bus de Warnaffe, Minister of Justice, 39.

[295] *Projet de loi transmis par le Sénat No 26, 19 Novembre 1953, Document Parlementaires Chambre de Représentants* Session 1953–54 II, 24–200. The point of this was to rule out the possibility of the King extending the Convention and 1st Protocol under his executive power.

[296] The resolution became Art 4 of the Law of 13 May 1955, published in *Moniteur Belge*, 19 August 1955, 5028. The Chamber's Committee on Foreign Affairs, chaired by M Huysmans, agreed with the Senate.

[297] A conceivable analysis of a colonial clause is that it permits what in effect amounts to a reservation relating to territorial application.

practice 'undergone a rapid and distinct change parallel with the change in the legal position (*régime juridique*) of the territories concerned'. The expression 'territories for whose international relations [a contracting state] is responsible' had replaced other more restrictive terms formerly employed in such clauses, such as 'colonies' (*colonies*) or 'non-metropolitan areas' (*territoires non métropolitaines*). This change 'represents an effort to facilitate, although without rendering compulsory, the application of the more important international treaties to territories the status of which is as varied as it is changeable but without assigning a final degree of importance to any one such status'. It then went on to say, in view of the purpose underlying this change, in practice it was manifest (*clair*) that the Belgian Congo fell into this category, and it was therefore superfluous to inquire whether or not the Belgian Congo was, until 1 July 1960, an integral part of Belgium.[298] This reasoning in effect adopts the elephant theory. Everyone knows an elephant when they meet one; they come in all shapes and sizes, and there is neither need nor value in producing definitions. In effect it was obvious that the Congo was the sort of territory for which an extension was required if ever there was one. This approach was the more plausible since the territory in question was, in common sense, a clear example of an overseas colonial territory.

The second of the twelve cases, *Bui Van Thanh and others v UK* (1990) was again a decision of the Commission on admissibility.[299] A number of Vietnamese persons, detained in Hong Kong pending their removal to Vietnam, complained of violations of Articles 3, 5, 8, and 13 of the Convention. They had claimed refugee status, but their claims had been rejected, and they had exhausted domestic remedies. It was clear, and conceded, that no declaration of extension of the Convention had ever been made to Hong Kong. Their argument was that the responsibility of the United Kingdom was nevertheless engaged because the actions of which they complained, although those of the authorities in Hong Kong, were based on decisions taken by the UK government, and simply implemented the policies adopted by that government.

After conceding that, under Article 1, the concept of jurisdiction was not limited to the territory of a High Contracting Party,[300] the Commission continued:

> However the Convention system also provides the State with the option of extending the Convention to territories for whose international relations it is responsible by lodging a declaration ... with the result that matters relating to such territories fall within the jurisdiction of the High Contracting Party within the meaning of Article 1 of the Convention. It is an essential part of the scheme of Article 63 that a declaration extending the Convention to such a territory be made before the Convention applies either to acts of the dependent Government or of policies formulated by the Government of a Contracting Party in the

[298] It was also neither here nor there that some of the events complained of took place in any case after 1 July 1960.

[299] App No 16137/90 European Commission on Human Rights, DR 65, 330.

[300] The Commission cited 'Nos. 6780/74 and 6950/75, *Cyprus v. Turkey*' (1975) DR 2/2.

exercise of its responsibilities in relation to such territory. Accordingly, in the present case, even if the Commission were to accept that the acts of the Hong Kong authorities were based on United Kingdom policy, it must find that it has no competence to examine the application . . .[301]

The decision does not seriously address the problems surrounding the location of violations—in territorial terms did the violation occur in the United Kingdom or in Hong Kong? Or both? It also adopts an interpretation which tends to limit protection, so that an extension is required even where the authorities in a dependency are in effect acting as the agents of the metropolitan government.

The third case, *Yonghong v Portugal* (1999), a more recent decision, this time of the Court, went even further. The applicant was held in custody in Macao under an international warrant issued by the People's Republic of China on charges of fraud. The Governor of Macao, in response to a request for extradition, authorized extradition proceedings, and the courts in Macao authorized his extradition. The applicant alleged that his extradition would entail a violation of Article 1 of the Sixth Protocol and of Articles 3 and 6 of the Convention. The possible relevance of the Protocol arose because the charges could attract the death penalty, though the Chinese Foreign Minister had given an assurance that it would not be imposed. There had never been a declaration of extension to Macao of either the Convention or of the Sixth Protocol.[302]

The status of Macao at this time was that of a Chinese territory under Portuguese administration pending its return to Chinese administration. Under the Salazar regime Portugal, in Portuguese legal theory, had no colonies; Macao was an overseas province of Portugal. In 1976 it became a special territory with a high degree of autonomy, and in 1987, as a result of negotiations with the Chinese government, which had always taken the view that Portuguese presence in Macao was illegitimate, an agreement was reached under which it was acknowledged that Macao was part of China, but was to be under Portuguese administration until 1999.[303] Under Portuguese domestic law Macao was deemed to be a 'juristic person of domestic public law'. The Portuguese Constitution applied until 20 December 1999, and Portuguese legislation applied there so long as it was published in the local *Official Gazette*. The territory

[301] According to this analysis, the effect of a declaration of extension would have been to bring the applicants 'within the jurisdiction' of the UK, presumably because they would otherwise not be within UK jurisdiction. This adopts the first of the three possible interpretations which we have set out, and does not treat Art 63 as creating an exception to Art 1. Though it might have made some sense if Hong Kong had been a protected state, it makes none at all in the case of a Crown Colony, whose inhabitants are plainly within UK jurisdiction. *Cyprus v Turkey* (n 332 below) is to the contrary.

[302] The 6th Protocol has in Art 5 a provision for extension similar to Art 4 of the 1st Protocol, but drops the requirement that the territories must be ones for whose international relations the party is responsible.

[303] The basis for this was Art 292 of the Portuguese Constitution and the agreement between China and Portugal of 13 April 1987, available at <http://www.impresa.macau.gov.mo/bo/i/88/23/dc/en/>. For an account see Aldrich and Connell (n 76 above) 197–200.

was administered by a Governor, who was responsible to the President of the Portuguese Republic. Adopting the reasoning set out in *Bui Van Thanh v UK* the Court held the complaints were inadmissible. Article 1 must be read in the light of Article 56, which enabled states:

> . . . to bring issues relating to such territories within the ambit of the Convention. An essential feature of the system established by Article 56 is that the Convention cannot apply to acts of the authorities of such territories, nor to the policies implemented by the Government of the Contracting Party concerned in the exercise of their responsibilities for those territories, unless a declaration extending the ambit of the Convention has been made.

The Court then went on to deal with the argument that Portugal's responsibility was engaged when the Governor, under discretionary powers, allowed extradition proceedings to continue, pointing out that the actual decision to extradite was taken by courts in Macao, whose decisions were not open to review by courts in Portugal.

The Court did not address the question whether Macao was at this time a territory for whose international relations Portugal was responsible, so that the Convention was capable of extension to it; if it was not, and this was the position under the agreement,[304] the outcome was that a territory under the administrative control of Portugal neither enjoyed, nor could possibly enjoy, human rights protection under the Convention.[305] So Macao was a black hole so far as Convention protection was concerned.

There is no indication that the Commission or Court in any of these three cases paid any attention to the *Travaux Préparatoires*, or to the reason why Article 63(1) and (2), and Article 4 of the First Protocol, were included: to permit consultation with the local and, if not *de jure*, at least by convention autonomous government of the territory, and this as a step on the road towards decolonization. And the point of such consultation was to extend human rights protection if the local government was agreeable. No information was provided as to what, if any, consultations had taken place. Nor was there any emphasis laid on the fact that the territories concerned were non-European. Nor, further, was there any reference to the notion that the Convention should be interpreted in furtherance of the protection of human rights. The effect of the first decision was that in territory declared by Belgian law to be part of Belgium, human rights were not protected. In the cases of Hong Kong and Macao the United Kingdom had had nearly half a century to extend the Convention to the territory, and Portugal over thirty years, though it may well be that the failure to extend was a response to difficulties in relations with the

[304] This is made explicit in para VIII of Annex I to the Agreement, in which the policies of the People's Republic of China in relation to Macao are elaborated. Before 1987 it might have been a subject of dispute whether China or Portugal was responsible for Macao's international relations.

[305] The language of Art 5 of the 6th and later Protocols, allows extension to territory or territories without specifying that they have to be territories for whose international relations the party is responsible.

Chinese People's Republic, though we have no evidence for this. Nothing had been done, as if to prove that the function of colonial clauses was, as critics such as Senghor had urged, that of denying protection to colonial subjects. The International Covenant on Civil and Political Rights, but not its Optional Protocol, applied to Hong Kong from 1976, when the United Kingdom ratified, and in 1991 this was incorporated into Hong Kong's domestic law by the Bill of Rights Ordinance.[306]

The fourth case is the strange *Gillow v UK* (1986),[307] another decision of the Court, which directly, though in a most unsatisfactory manner, addressed, or perhaps one should say failed to address, the interpretation of the colonial clause of the First Protocol, Article 4. The applicants, a husband and wife, complained of violations of a number of Convention rights and of Article 1 of the First Protocol. Their complaint related to residential property, 'Whiteknights', in Guernsey which they had bought, and in which at one time they had resided. In response to a housing shortage in Guernsey the government of the island promoted legislation under which, subject to exceptions, licences from a Housing Authority were required for the occupation of property. The Guernsey Housing Authority refused them a permit to live in the house, which had been since 1960 let to tenants, when in 1978 they wished to return there. After unsuccessful litigation in the Guernsey courts, they had sold the house in 1980, allegedly at below its true value. The Commission found that there had been a violation of Article 8 of the Convention, and of Article 1 of the First Protocol. The case was referred by the Commission to the Court, and before the Court the United Kingdom conceded the violation of Article 8. But it resisted the claim based on the First Protocol on the merits.

After the oral argument had been concluded the agent for the United Kingdom informed the Court by letter, with apologies, that no declaration of extension of the First Protocol to the Bailiwick of Guernsey had ever been made. The failure to extend the Protocol was probably the result of an oversight.[308] The Home Office had informed the Foreign Office in 1952 that the Channels Islands and the Isle of Man were agreeable to extension, but the Foreign Office failed to do anything about this; initially the matter was shelved because of the cases brought by Greece over Cyprus. The merger of the Foreign Office with the Commonwealth Office led to an oversight. In the 1970s the *East African Asians* case again led to deliberate delay. There was a failure of communication between the two departments.[309] An undated memorandum in the Home

[306] Hong Kong Bill of Rights Ordinance 1991. See R Wacks (ed), *Human Rights in Hong Kong* (1992) esp ch 2.

[307] Series A/109 (Commission Report annexed at 30) 11 EHRR 335. Under the 'thirty years' rule there are no papers in the NA.

[308] See n 203 above, citing *HREE* (n 52 above) 842–4, based on NA CO 936/291 and 292. There is also a historical account in FCO 41/604 and 786. In the case of *Wiggins v UK* (1978) (n 284 above), nobody apparently noticed that there had been no extension of the Protocol to Guernsey.

[309] NA FCO 41/604.

Office file on the *Tyrer* case,[310] which provides information on the extension of the Convention, wrongly states that the First Protocol had been extended to Jersey, Guernsey, and the Isle of Man. We guess that this memorandum, or the papers relating to the earlier *Wiggins* case, which would feature in the 'previous papers', consulted under normal civil service practice, misled the United Kingdom's agent. But this is conjectural. The reason for inaction back in 1952 was probably connected with lack of enthusiasm for the extension of the First Protocol in the Colonial Office. Why the United Kingdom did not, at least for the purpose of the case, concede that the Protocol applied, failure to notify Strasbourg being simply an error, is obscure.

The Delegate for the Commission, Mr Gaukur Jörundsson, suggested that the United Kingdom must be considered as having recognized the competence of the Commission '*ad hoc*'. He suggested that the Court, in view of the United Kingdom's admission of the violation of Article 8, might not find it necessary to consider the alleged violation of the First Protocol. He added: 'In the event that the Court considered it appropriate to give a ruling on the complaint, the Delegate "would be ready to make detailed submissions on the complex problems raised by the Government's letter".' This gave the Court an opportunity to consider whether in the case of a European territory a declaration of extension was needed at all. But without hearing the submissions offered by Mr Jörundsson the Court ruled that it was entitled to examine the matter *ex officio*, and since, according to the records of the Council of Europe, no declaration of extension had ever been made, it had no jurisdiction to entertain the complaint. So it was that by deliberate decision the argument that the Convention and its First Protocol applied even in the absence of declarations of extension under Article 63(1) or under Article 4 of the First Protocol, was never considered.[311]

Under these four decisions, Contracting Parties have an absolute discretion to withhold the protection of the Convention and its First Protocol, and this for as long as they like, from the territories 'for whose international relations they are responsible'. The scope of this discretion is not restricted in any way by the apparent purpose underlying this provision of the Convention. Such territories may even be within Europe. There is no indication in the cases as to what, if any, further characteristics the governing arrangements for the dependent territory must have—for example some degree of local autonomy. Nor do these decisions attend to the Preamble's reference to 'the maintenance and further realization of human rights and fundamental freedoms' and to reaffirmation

[310] NA HO 284/11.

[311] The *Gillow* case was relied upon in *R (Quark Fishing Ltd) v Secretary of State for Foreign and Commonwealth Affairs* [2004] EWCA Civ 557 and [2005] UKHL 57 in relation to failure to extend the 1st Protocol to the SGSSI. M Wood, in L-E Pettiti, E Decaux, and PH Imbert (eds), *La Convention Européene des Droits de L'Homme* (1995) 915ff, cites the case as authority for the view that the requirement of extension under Art 63 is not limited to non-European territories.

of the parties' 'profound belief in those fundamental freedoms which are the foundation of justice and peace in the world' or to the provision of Article 3 of the Statute of the Council of Europe, which requires member states, without any qualification, to 'accept the principles of the rule of law and of the enjoyment by all persons within its jurisdiction of human rights and fundamental freedoms'. The decisions which we have discussed do seem to be, at the least, not very satisfactory.

Our fifth, sixth, and seventh cases[312] have made contributions to the interpretation of Article 63(3) of the Convention, but without addressing the relationship between this provision and Article 1. The first was *Wiggins v UK*, an admissibility decision by the Commission. The background was the same as in the *Gillow* case. The applicant challenged the refusal by the Housing Authority to grant him the licence he wanted on the ground that there had been violations of Articles 8 and 14 of the Convention, and of Article 1 of the First Protocol, which, it was wrongly assumed, had been extended to Guernsey by declaration under Article 63. The Commission, in holding that the application was manifestly unfounded stated, *en passant*, that ... 'in regard to Art. 63 of the Convention, and in particular as to the local requirements mentioned in Article 63(3), the Commission does not consider it necessary to make any separate findings in this case other than to say that it does not find any significant social or cultural differences between Guernsey and the United Kingdom which could be relevant to the application of the Articles invoked in the present case'.

The next case in this category, our sixth case, was *Tyrer v UK* (1978), which also concerned a Crown Dependency or British Island.[313] The issue was whether the application of judicial corporal punishment by birching in the Isle of Man violated the rights of the applicant. The Court, by a majority, ruled that there had been a violation of Article 3 of the Convention.[314] The Convention had been extended to the Isle of Man in 1953, and in 1967 the United Kingdom had made a declaration recognizing for a number of territories, including the Isle of Man, the compulsory jurisdiction of the Court and the right of individual petition for a period of five years. There had been subsequent renewals including one on 21 April 1972. It was argued that the use of corporal punishment in the island could be justified under Article 63(3); there was considerable popular support for the practice.[315] The Court rejected this argument,

[312] For citations see n 284 above. In *Piermont v France* (1995), discussed below the Commission simply applied the principle formulated in the *Tyrer* case and this was accepted by the Court.

[313] 2 EHRR 1. There is a file, NA HO 284/11.

[314] The Commission, also by a majority, had taken the same view.

[315] At this date birching was still employed in Guernsey; it was legally permissible in Jersey but had passed out of use. It was used or legally possible in Belize, Bermuda, the Falkland Islands, Gibraltar, the Gilbert and Ellice Islands, Montserrat, St Helena, the Seychelles, the Turks and Caicos Islands, the British Virgin Islands, in some of the West Indies, and probably in Brunei. See memorandum by DA Gordon-Smith in NA HO 284/11. When the 1st Protocol was eventually extended, there were reservations to preserve the flagellant tradition in Anguilla, the Virgin Islands,

and in doing so commented that 'the system established by Article 63 was primarily designed to meet the fact that, when the Convention was drafted, there were still certain colonial territories whose state of civilization did not, it was thought, permit the full application of the Convention'. As a member of the European family of nations the Isle of Man was not the kind of territory for which Article 63(3) was designed, and in any case Article 63(3) could never be used to permit violations of Article 3, which was not even derogable in time of war or public emergency. It was simply assumed that an extension was required.[316]

Our seventh case, which also addresses Article 63(3) (by now Article 56(3)), is *Py v France* (2005).[317] The applicant was a French University research worker, who was appointed to the University of the Pacific, located in Noumea in New Caledonia, where he was under his appointment bound to reside. In 1998 an agreement was signed which prescribed, during a transitional period, the political organization of New Caledonia and the mechanisms whereby it was to be emancipated. Under an Organic Law of March 1999, passed in order to make provision for the implementation of this agreement, ten years' continuous residence in New Caledonia was required before a person could be placed on the special electoral register for elections of members of the New Caledonian Congress and the provincial assemblies. M Py could not satisfy this requirement and was not placed on the register. He complained of a violation of his rights under Article 3 of the First Protocol, and also of discrimination, based on national origin—he was born in France—in violation of Article 14.

When France ratified the Convention and the First Protocol in 1974 it had declared that they applied to the whole territory of the Republic, having regard, in matters concerning the overseas territories, to the local requirements (*nécessités locales*) to which Article 63 of the Convention made reference.[318] The French Government argued, *inter alia*,[319] that the inclusion of the condition of residence, which ensured that only those with a firmly established connection to New Caledonia were entitled to vote, was an essential element in measures designed to end violent conflict in the process of decolonization. It was also argued on the basis of material in the *Travaux Préparatoires*, wrongly, that the purpose of Article 63(3) was to take account of the autonomy retained in the matter so far as certain overseas territories were concerned; autonomy was relevant to the purpose of Article 63(1) and (2), not (3).[320] The Court decided that there had been no violation of Article 3. In part this

the Cayman Islands, Montserrat, St Helena and its dependencies, and the Turks and Caicos Islands. See *HREE* (n 52 above) 844. For the outcome of the *Tyrer* case see (1978) 49 BYIL 310 n 1.

[316] The Court noted the UK declaration of 1950, and also noted that the UK Parliament could legislate for the island, though it was not the practice to do so against the wishes of the island's government.

[317] App No 66289/01, Judgment of 11 January 2005.

[318] See text following n 278 above.

[319] We do not discuss these other arguments.

[320] para 26.

conclusion was based on the concept of the margin of appreciation, and the contention that the restriction had a legitimate purpose, and was proportionate. But the Court also relied on Article 63(3), and ruled that the history of New Caledonia and the Organic Law of 1999 could be viewed as 'local requirements' (*nécessités locales*) which permitted the restrictions imposed on the applicant's right to vote. It satisfied the test laid down in *Tyrer v UK*, there being *la preuve décisive et manifest d'une nécessité*.

The Court did not address the fact that Article 63(3), read literally, appears only to apply the 'local requirements' qualification to territories to which there has been a declaration of extension under Article 63(1). Possibly the Court took the view that the declaration made by France on ratification did count as such a declaration, but this is not explicitly stated.

In some of these cases it would have been possible to argue (though with what success one cannot say) that an extension was unnecessary to engage the responsibility of the respondent government. For example in *Gillow v UK* it could have been argued that the Bailiwick of Guernsey was not one of those non-European territories for which, in the view of the Court in *Tyrer v UK*, Article 63 was designed. But as we have seen, no opportunity was given for such an argument to be advanced.[321] Again in the *Tyrer* case itself the Court simply assumed that in the absence of a declaration of extension under Article 63(1) the Convention would not have applied.[322] The same assumption was made in the *Wiggins* case by the Commission. But the relationship between Articles 1 and 63 was not addressed, and the possibility that such a declaration was not needed in the case of a European territory was never argued. There would have been no reason for the applicant's counsel in the *Tyrer* case to put forward such an argument, since there had been an extension, and the applicability of the Convention was not contested. The United Kingdom had conceded admissibility of the application with regard to Article 3. And in the *Wiggins* case it had been assumed that there had been an extension.

Matthews v UK,[323] the eighth of our twelve cases, does not explicitly address the interpretation of Article 63, or of Article 4 of the First Protocol, but again clearly assumed that in the absence of a declaration of extension, the First Protocol did not apply in Gibraltar—like the Isle of Man a European territory. No argument to the contrary was presented, and as in *Tyrer*, there would have been no point in presenting such an argument.[324] This was also the situation in another case, one

[321] Text following n 307 above. [322] paras 13, 23.

[323] 28 EHRR (1999) 361, Judgment of 18 February 1999. For comment see (1999) 70 BYIL 381–4.

[324] The Gibraltar Electoral Registration Officer had refused to register the applicant as a voter in the European Elections. This, it was alleged, violated Art 3 of the 1st Protocol, extended to Gibraltar on 25 February 1988. The Treaty Establishing the European Community (1976) applied to Gibraltar.

which, had the facts been slightly different, would have provided an ideal opportunity for the Court to have developed a principled analysis of the relationship between the two articles. This was the well-known Gibraltar case, *McCann, Farrell and Savage v UK*,[325] which arose out of the fatal shooting of three members of the Provisional IRA in Gibraltar by soldiers of the Special Air Service, a British military formation employed on anti-terrorist operations, and based in the United Kingdom. But the Convention had been extended to Gibraltar, together with the right of individual petition, and acceptance of the jurisdiction of the Court. Hence no issue arose over the competence of the Commission or Court to entertain the case.[326] So the relationship between the two articles was never raised. But suppose there had been no extension? The question would then have arisen as to whether the United Kingdom was so directly involved in the operation as to be responsible under Article 1. But on the facts it would have been pointless for counsel in the case to have argued the point.

The case law we have discussed necessarily assumes the possibility of black holes in the protection of human rights, and this even within Europe. *Drozd and Janousek v France and Spain*,[327] the ninth of our cases, raised this possibility in a most curious way, by adopting reasoning under which form appears to have triumphed over substance. As we have seen, the jurisprudence has adopted the position that such black holes may exist through the choice of parties to the Convention, who may decide not to extend protection to their overseas dependencies, and indeed in the *Yonghong* case protection could not have been extended. *Drozd and Janousek* goes further in relying upon formalistic reasoning to say that there can even be European territories to which it is impossible to extend the Convention. But some members of the Court expressed misgivings, and there was a powerful dissenting opinion by Dr Jochen Frowein in the report of the Commission.

The applicants had been convicted in Andorra, and sentenced to imprisonment. Since Andorra had no prison, such persons could serve

Under it the Council of the European Communities was required to lay down appropriate arrangements for elections to the European Parliament, which it did in 1976. These were set out in an Act Concerning the Election of the Representatives of the European Parliament by Direct Universal Suffrage of 20 September 1976. This was signed by the Foreign Ministers of the member states, and the provisions of the Act made no provision for elections in Gibraltar. So the basis of the complaint was that Gibraltar was within the European Community, yet the UK had, in 1976, participated in a decision which excluded residents in Gibraltar from participating in elections to the European Parliament, which exercised significant functions in the legislative process of the European Community, capable of directly affecting the applicant. For discussion see K Muller, 'Problems of European Union Citizenship Rights at the Periphery' (1999) 45 *Australian Journal of Politics and History* 35.

325 App No 18984/91, 21 EHRR (1996) 97 Judgment of 27 September 1995. The Commission's Report is in A/324.

326 The Report of the Commission is reproduced in the opinion of the Court; no reasons were given for declaring the case admissible on 3 September 1993.

327 Series A/240, 14 EHRR (1992) 745, Judgment of 26 June 1992. See text to n 17 above for the notion that there can be no black holes within the legal space of the Convention to which the collective guarantee of the Convention applies.

their sentences either in a Spanish or a French prison, at their choice, and the applicants had chosen France. They complained, *inter alia*, of violations of Article 6 of the Convention in that they had not had a fair trial in Andorra. The case is of importance for the purposes of this article only in relation to this complaint. The international status of Andorra was at this time anomalous.[328] It had, as rulers, two Co-Princes, the President of France in his personal capacity, and the Bishop of Urgel, who is appointed by His Holiness the Pope. The Co-Princes enjoyed legislative, executive, and judicial powers, which were by custom exercised jointly. These powers were normally exercised on their behalf by two Permanent Delegates, one being the French Prefect of the *Département des Pyrénées Orientales*, and the other being the Vicar General of the Diocese of Urgel. Andorra possessed its own system of courts, partially staffed by Spanish and French judges.

Andorra's relationship with both France and Spain did not, as the Court put it, 'fit into the pattern of relations between sovereign States. They have never taken the form of international agreements ... such relations take a number of forms: unilateral French acts, such as the establishment of French schools; administrative arrangements, such as those dealing with social security, telephone networks and customs regimes'.[329] Relations with Spain were similar. Andorra did not then belong to any international organizations, nor did it have diplomatic relations with other states. International relations were the joint concern of the two Co-Princes, not of Spain or France.[330] Andorra had, however, acceded to two international agreements, and at the time of the case it was envisaged that Andorra, though not yet a state, would in due course become one. Although the term is not used in the judgment of the European Court of Human Rights, the status of Andorra was at this time similar to that of a protectorate, but, as a feudal relic, did not really fit into any general category.[331] Neither France nor Spain had purported to extend the Convention to Andorra.

Spain argued that only a declaration of extension would make Spain responsible for a violation of Article 6. Not only had no such declaration been made, but there was a legal obstacle to making such a declaration, since the conduct of international relations was the joint responsibility of the Co-Princes. So Andorra was a territory for whose international relations neither Spain, nor France, nor Spain and France jointly, was

[328] For discussion see J Duursma, *Fragmentation and the International Relations of Micro-states* (1996) 331–3 and Crawford, n 42 above. This anomalous status no longer exists; Andorra is, eg, a member of the UN.

[329] paras 68 and 69. See Duursma (n 328 above) 369 noting that France had often claimed that the French Co-Prince had exclusive power over Andorra's international affairs.

[330] para 67.

[331] Crawford (n 42 above) 43 n 27, 76 n 182, 197 n 2, citing his article 'The International Legal Status of the Valleys of Andorra' (1977) 55 *Revue de Droit International, de Sciences Diplomatiques et Politiques* 259; he points out that Andorra was not under the protection of the co-Princes, who were joint sovereigns. See *Oppenheim's International Law* (n 13 above) para 83, esp 272 n 2.

responsible. France similarly contended that the President of France acted as Co-Prince in his personal capacity only, and France had in consequence no power to enter into commitments on behalf of Andorra. The Commission accepted this argument, adding that Andorra did not form part of France or Spain, so that the Convention did not apply automatically to it (ie under Article 1). The Court took the same view, that it did not have jurisdiction *ratione loci*, accepting this reasoning. It also drew attention to the fact that Andorra was not a member of the Council of Europe, so that it had never itself ratified the Convention. Furthermore Andorra was not a territory common to Spain and France, nor was it a Franco-Spanish *condominium*. So the Convention did not, and could not, apply on Andorran territory.

The Court went on to consider whether the applicants were within the jurisdiction of France or Spain through the extraterritorial reach of the Convention: 'The term "jurisdiction" is not limited to the national territory of the High Contracting Parties; their responsibility can be involved because of acts of their authorities producing effects outside their own territory.'[332] The applicant's claim was based on the fact that French and Spanish judges sat as members of Andorran courts, and by the claim that French courts exercised supervisory powers over Andorran courts.[333] The Commission by a majority, and the Court, on this point unanimously, ruled against the applicants, basically on two grounds. One was that: 'Whilst it is true that judges from France and Spain sit as members of Andorran courts, they do not do so in their capacity as French or Spanish judges.' The other was that neither France nor Spain exercised control or supervision over Andorran courts.

In the Commission there was a powerful dissenting opinion by Dr Jochen Frowein, who was joined by Messrs Soyer, Vanderberghe, and Rozakis.[334] The dissent was based upon an analysis of the practice of the relationship between France, Spain, and Andorra: 'The relevant question in establishing whether a state is responsible under the Convention is whether that state has exercised jurisdiction within the meaning of Article 1 of the Convention, and it seems clear that both states exercise jurisdiction in many fields in Andorra, notably in the field of justice.' Later in the opinion they added: 'We take the view that France and Spain are jointly responsible for guaranteeing the compatibility with the Convention of proceedings before the *Tribunal de Corts* ... Since Andorra is not regarded as a State with independent authority, but as an entity under the suzerainty of the Co-Princes, it is not possible to attribute the decisions complained of to any other subject of public

[332] para 91. The court cited *X v Federal Republic of Germany*, (1965) 8 EYHR,158, *Hess v UK* DR 2/72, *Cyprus v Turkey* (1975) DR 2/125, *X and Y v Switzerland* (1977) DR 9/57, *W v UK* (1983) DR 32/190.

[333] This was curiously treated as raising an issue of jurisdiction *ratione personae*; the 'person' normally envisioned is the applicant, but here it refers to French or Spanish officials.

[334] At 61 ff.

international law.'[335] And although the ruling that the Court lacked jurisdiction was unanimous, there was a dissenting opinion related to another complaint based on Article 5.[336] This expressed considerable unease, without adopting the reasoning of Dr Frowein. Andorra was not a state in international law and had in any event not acceded: 'Nor has France or Spain, who have ratified the Convention, declared it to be applicable to Andorra under Art. 56, and indeed a declaration under that Article could not have been made with respect to Andorra, as Andorra is not strictly speaking a territory for whose international relations France or Spain is responsible.' But the result, these judges thought, was unsatisfactory:

> Can one accept that because the Convention has been ratified by France and Spain, human rights must be respected on both sides of the Pyrenees, but not in a small piece of land in the Pyrenees, despite the responsibilities these two countries exercise there, and despite the fact that this little territory would thus not be subject to the rules of international human rights law. It seems difficult to accept that there is a watertight partition between the entity of Andorra and the States to which the Co-Princes belong, when in so many respects (enforcement of sentences being a further example) these States participate in its administration.

Eventually Andorra joined the Council of Europe and became a party to the Convention, which it signed in November 1994, and ratified in January 1996.

This leaves us with a group of just three cases which, if only to a very limited extent, have attempted to develop doctrine on the relationship between Article 1 of the Convention and Article 63. Of these our tenth case is the decision of the Commission in *Cyprus v Turkey* (1975),[337] in which an application was made seeking to establish Turkish responsibility for alleged violations of Convention rights in northern Cyprus. Turkey had ratified the Convention and its First Protocol, but had never purported to extend the Convention or Protocol to northern Cyprus. Nor could it have done so, since in international law it was not, and is not, responsible for the international relations of northern Cyprus. Its contention was in any event that northern Cyprus was an independent republic for whose activities it was in no way responsible; Turkey had never purported to annex northern Cyprus. The Commission took the view that the expression 'within their jurisdiction' (*relevant de leur jurisdiction*):

> ... is not ... equivalent to or limited to the national territory of the High Contracting Party concerned. It is clear from the language, in particular of the French text, and the object of the Article, and from the purpose of the Convention as a whole, that the High Contracting Parties are bound to secure the said rights and freedoms to all persons under their actual authority and responsibility, whether that authority is exercised within their own territory or abroad.

335 At 63–4.
336 By Judges Pettiti, Valticos, and Lopes Rocha, approved also by Judges Walsh and Speilman.
337 DR 2/125, App Nos 6780/74 and 6950/75.

The Commission then went on to try to explain, given this view, what the function of Article 63 was:

> The Commission does not find that Art. 63 ... can be interpreted as limiting the scope of 'jurisdiction' in Art. 1 to such metropolitan territories. The purpose of Art. 63 is not only the territorial extension of the Convention but its adaptation to the measure of self-government attained in particular non-metropolitan territories and to the cultural and social differences in such territories; Art. 63(3) confirms this interpretation. This does not mean that the territories to which Art. 63 applies are not within the 'jurisdiction' within the meaning of Art.1.

It is not easy to understand from this when or why an extension is necessary; perhaps the Commission meant that it was only in the case of a dependency which both enjoyed a degree of autonomy and was culturally different that one was required. But this was not actually said. The reality may be that, given its view on Article 1, the Court was unable to provide a satisfactory explanation of the function of Article 63. Conceivably the idea was that the effect of a declaration under Article 63 was not to bring the territory 'within the jurisdiction' under Article 1, but merely to trigger the application of the 'local requirements' provision in Article 63(3), but this is speculative. The fundamental reason for the Court's difficulty was that, given its view of the scope of Article 1, Article 63 with its system of voluntary extension becomes an anachronism. Nor did the Commission address the possibility, as under our third interpretation, that Article 63(1) made possible the extension of the Convention to protected states whose inhabitants could not be said to be 'within the jurisdiction' in the absence of a declaration.

Our eleventh case, the second in this group, is *Loizidou v Turkey* (Preliminary Objections) (1995).[338] Of central importance on the issue of the extraterritorial reach of the Convention under Article 1, it is also relevant to the relationship between Articles 1 and 63. It addresses the matter directly, though only in one short passage. Mrs Loizidou, who owned property in northern Cyprus, claimed that Turkish military forces there had denied her access to her property. During a protest march there she was arrested and detained by the Turkish Cypriot police force. She alleged violations of Articles 3, 5, and 8 of the Convention and of Article 1 of the First Protocol.

Objection was taken to the admissibility of the application before the Commission, which noted that 'the acts complained of "were carried out by Turkish military forces stationed in the northern part of Cyprus or by forces acting under their authority"'.[339] The Court, by a majority,[340]

[338] Series A/310, App No 15318/89, 20 EHHR 99, 23 March 1995.

[339] Quoted at para 46. See Crawford (n 42 above) 81–2, 146–7.

[340] There was a joint dissenting opinion by Mr Gölcüklü and Mr Pettiti; on the Art 1 issue or jurisdiction they thought it was premature to reach a decision before there had been a full enquiry on the merits. They did not disagree with the view that jurisdiction might be extraterritorial. They also took the view that at this stage in the case the Turkish declarations under Arts 25 and 46 should

decided that the acts complained of were capable of engaging the responsibility of Turkey under Article 1 because 'the responsibility of a Contracting Party may arise when as a consequence of military action—whether lawful or unlawful—it exercises effective control over an area outside its national territory'.[341] The Court also held that territorial limits attached to Turkey's declarations accepting the right of individual petition and the jurisdiction of the Court, which sought to confine the operation of the optional clauses to Turkey's national territory, were invalid.[342] It further took the view that where a state which had accepted the right of individual petition incurred extraterritorial responsibility through the acquisition of control over other territory, there existed no requirement that this right be further extended to the territories in question. Article 63(4) had no relevance to such a situation.[343]

The Court, like the Commission in *Cyprus v Turkey*,[344] now felt obliged to explain what, given its view on Article 1, the function of Article 63 was. It did not engage in any elaborate analysis but did, *en passant* as it were, express a general view of its function, here contrasting it with Article 25: 'Article 63 concerns a decision by a Contracting Party to assume full responsibility under the Convention for all acts of public authorities in respect of a territory for whose international relations it is responsible. Article 25, on the other hand, concerns the acceptance by the Contracting Party of the competence by the Commission to examine complaints relating to the acts of its own officials acting under its direct authority.'[345] Two points need to be noticed. The first is the use of the word 'all'; the implication is that there still might be responsibility for particular acts under Article 1, for example acts specifically authorized, even without a declaration.[346] The second is that although the point is not developed the implication of this passage must be that where responsibility is being imputed to a state for the acts of its own officials Article 63 is not relevant, and Article 1 governs the situation (just as it does when extraterritorial effect is given to the Convention through the exercise of authority and control by agents of the respondent state). It is not easy to reconcile this with the decision in *Yonghong v Portugal*, though the Court there emphasized that the gravamen of the complaint related to the acts of courts in Macao, which were not under the control of the Portuguese government.

Ilaşçu v Moldova and Russia, our twelfth case, raised the curious question whether a party could, when ratifying the Convention, validly declare that a part of its metropolitan territory over which it did not

not have been severed. A separate opinion by Mr Gölcüklü took the view that the territorial limits attached to the Turkish declarations were valid, applying, at least by analogy, Art 63.

341 paras 62–64. 342 paras 65–89. 343 para 87. 344 (1975) DR 2/125.

345 para 88.

346 Thus in British colonial practice decisions formally taken by a Colonial Governor might be authorized by a Cabinet or ministerial decision if they were of political significance, and Governors could be instructed accordingly. See for examples *HREE* (n 52 above) 899–900, 904–5, 916–17.

at the time possess *de facto* control could be excluded from being within its jurisdiction under Article 1, so as to be outside the reach of the Convention.[347] There the Moldovan Government, on ratifying the Convention on 12 September 1997, declared that it was unable to guarantee compliance with the Convention in that part of its territory under the *de facto* control of the self-proclaimed Transdniestria Republic until the conflict in the region was resolved. Moldova had ratified the Convention with regard to its whole territory, but its instrument of ratification was accompanied by several declarations and reservations. The Court ruled that this particular declaration did not rank as a legitimate reservation under Article 57 (formerly Article 64) for reasons which do not concern us here. But it also rejected the argument that Articles 56 and 57 of the Convention should be read together, and Article 56 interpreted broadly so as to permit territorial limits to be attached to a ratification, at least when the territory in question was not under the contracting parties' control. The Court rejected this, relying on two arguments. One was that under the earlier jurisprudence of the Court it had not been possible to attach territorial restrictions to acceptance of the optional right of individual petition under Article 25. It went on: 'It considers, secondly, that neither the spirit nor the terms of Article 56, which provides for extending the Convention's application to territories other than the metropolitan territories of the High Contracting Parties, could permit of a negative interpretation in the sense of restricting the scope of the term "jurisdiction" within the meaning of Article 1 to only part of the territory.' It will be seen that this decision assumes, but does not elaborate, a conception of a non-metropolitan territory to which alone the system of territorial voluntary extension or non-extension of Article 56 applies. The case also followed *Loizidou* in treating the Russian Federation as responsible under the Convention for violations occurring in Transdniestria.[348]

Conclusions

The jurisprudence, meagre as it is, wholly fails to address the way in which the world in which Article 56 operates today has changed since the 1950s, and this notwithstanding the fact that the conception of the Convention as a living instrument, to be interpreted in the light of present-day conditions, is now so embedded in the jurisprudence that it would be otiose to cite authority for it.

[347] App No 48787/99, Admissibility, 4 July 2001, Merits (2005) 40 EHRR 1030, both Grand Chamber. See Crawford (n 42 above) 83 n 208.

[348] The cases of *Öcalan v Turkey* (App No 46221/99, 14 December 2000), and *Issa v Turkey* (App No 31821/96, 30 May 2000) further illustrate the doctrine under which a party may become responsible for violations occurring outside its national territory, but do not address the relationship between Arts 1 and 56, so we do not discuss these cases. Nor do we discuss the decision of the English House

Thus one function of the colonial clause, insisted upon by Belgium, was said to be 'the standard of civilization of the native population' of some territories which, so it was said, made it inappropriate to extend the full protection of the Convention to them; the implication was that this standard was low. The underlying rationale of Article 4 of the First Protocol, insofar as can be inferred from the *Travaux Préparatoires*, was that the rights included in the Protocol, especially the right to participate in democratic government, could hardly be guaranteed to the inhabitants of territories in which there were, under colonialism, no elections at all, or elections in which most of the population did not participate. One has only to set this out to make the point that this function of the colonial clause should have no place in the world of today. If there are today good reasons for tailoring the application of the Convention to special necessities in dependencies, whether in Europe or elsewhere, or to particular regions, the matter can surely be handled through the doctrines of the margin of appreciation and proportionality—neither of which existed when the text of the Convention was negotiated.

Again the other function served by the colonial clause, that insisted upon by the major colonial power of the period, the United Kingdom, was to enable the colonial power to respect and further the autonomy enjoyed in varying degrees by overseas dependencies which were on their way to becoming independent self-governing states, and whose association with the mother country, if it continued, was to become wholly voluntary. At the time when the Convention was negotiated what may loosely be called 'colonies' were not the only territories under the sovereignty of Contracting Parties which enjoyed a measure of autonomy.[349] For example the Faroe Islands, part of the Kingdom of Denmark, enjoyed a high degree of autonomy in domestic affairs under legislation of 1948.[350] Today there are numerous other European territories which are in a similar position, such as the Åland Islands (Finland), Ceuta, Melilla, and the Canary Islands (Spain),[351] the Azores and Madeira (Portugal),[352] Greenland and the Faroes (Denmark).[353] If we have regard to substance, rather than form, such autonomous or semi-autonomous regions are in much the same position as the United Kingdom's Crown Dependencies, or such of the BOTs as enjoy domestic autonomy—for example the Cayman Islands, or Bermuda.[354] The case of the Åland Islands is particularly instructive. Finland is responsible for its

of Lords in *R v Secretary of State for Foreign and Commonwealth Affairs, ex p Quark Fishing Ltd* [2005] UKHL 57, but note that the House's view of Strasbourg law is at odds with the position adopted in this article, which was not available to Counsel involved in the case.

349 See generally Lapidoth (n 83 above).

350 Aldrich and Connell (n 76 above) 46–8, Lapidoth (n 83 above) 112–15 and n 79 on 250.

351 Aldrich and Connell (n 76 above) 220–8.

352 ibid 48–50.

353 Lapidoth (n 83 above) 143–51.

354 The complete list would include Anguilla, Bermuda, the British Virgin Islands, the Cayman Islands, the Falklands, Gibraltar, Montserrat, possibly Pitcairn, St Helena and perhaps its Dependencies, and the Turks and Caicos Islands. For this see *PPP* (n 241 above) 44–70

international relations, but must consult with the Islands' government over negotiations, and treaties do not enter into force in relation to the Islands without the consent of the government there. So as a matter of Finnish law, rather than mere convention, the relationship between Finland and the Islands corresponds to the conventional British colonial relationship which was thought, back in the 1950s, to justify insistence on colonial clauses.[355] The legal regime of the European Union has been tailored to the existence of such territories where this has been thought desirable, but without drawing a rigid line between territories which in the past ranked as colonies and those which did not.[356] There are special arrangements both for the British, French, Dutch, and Danish overseas territories and countries (OTCs), which are not part of the European Union but have links with member states, and for the outermost regions, which are part of the European Union, and comprise certain French overseas departments, the *départements d'outre-mer* (DOMs), the Canary Islands, the Azores, and Madeira.

The European Convention made no special provision for such autonomous or semi-autonomous territories over and above the colonial clause. The unfortunate result was that the United Kingdom was able to treat its European territories—the Channel Islands, the Isle of Man, Gibraltar, and Cyprus—which were and, with one exception, Cyprus, still are under its sovereignty, as falling under the arrangements established by Article 63(1) and (2) and Article 4 of the First Protocol. One consequence of this well illustrates the deplorable use to which the system of extension was put: to enable full and effective human rights protection to be withheld from them. As we have seen, such protection was indeed withheld for prolonged periods, as, for example, in the case of the Isle of Man, the Channel Islands, and Gibraltar. And, under Article 4, the metropolitan government can modify from time to time the extent of human rights protection provided, as is still the situation.

It seems extremely unlikely that there would be any support today within the Council of Europe for amending the Convention so as to introduce a new territorial applications clause, providing for voluntary extension (or failure to extend) to the numerous autonomous or semi-autonomous European regions. This being so, it seems wholly anomalous that there still exists a system of voluntary extension which, under existing jurisprudence, only applies to an arbitrary selection of autonomous or semi-autonomous territories: those once colonized by European powers, for example the Falklands, or which, as in the case of the Crown Dependencies, have been treated as if they had once been colonized, which they had not been. Why should the position of such territories be

[355] L Hannikainem and F Hern (eds), *Autonomy and Demilitarization in International Law: the Åland Islands in a Changing Europe* (1999) 90–1, 174–7, Lapidoth (n 83 above) 69–77 and notes at 235–6. Crawford (n 42 above) 108–12.

[356] F Murray, *The EU Member State Territories. The Special Relationship under Community Law* (2004).

any different under Convention law from that of the Azores, or the Åland Islands?[357] And if there is today no good reason then the system of voluntary extension, with its option of non-extension, should no longer have any place in Convention law.

On the assumption that the colonial clause, whatever name we give it, and the whole system of voluntary and partial extension is now anachronistic we now make some suggestions as to how the situation could possibly be remedied; we do not presume to offer the correct solution, but merely to suggest some possibilities.

The simplest solution, technically, if not politically, would be a new Protocol amending both the Convention and its First Protocol.[358] Article 56(3) no longer has any legitimate function, and it is difficult to see any objection to removing Article 56 from the text entirely. The only function actually served by retaining the system of optional extension under Article 56(1) and (2) of the Convention and Article 4 of the First Protocol is to provide parties with an argument for escaping the responsibilities they would have under Article 1, in the absence of these Articles. Reliance on such an argument has become all the more anomalous since the modern Strasbourg Court's jurisprudence of Article 1 gives a Contracting Party no option of evading accountability for failure to provide protection for the inhabitants of territory under its *de facto* control, as, for example, in the case of Turkey in relation to northern Cyprus and even parts of Iraq, and the Russian Federation in relation to Transdniestria.

There would, in theory at least, be a problem in that under the third possible interpretation of the existing Article it enables the benefit of the Convention to be extended, in the case of protected states, to persons who would not otherwise be 'within the jurisdiction' under Article 1. In the case of the United Kingdom this would today have no practical significance, since there are no longer any British protected states, and the same is the case for other members of the Council of Europe.[359] Indeed protected states have vanished everywhere.[360] There might also be thought to be a problem if Article 4 of the First Protocol was simply deleted, for Article 3 mandates the recognition of a right to participate in elections for the legislature. In some of the BNOTs, for example the BAT, it would hardly be practicable to hold elections for a local legislature. In the case of *Matthews v UK*[361] where the applicant, resident in Gibraltar, had been denied the right to participate in elections to the

[357] Aldrich and Connell (n 76 above) set out the problems of defining what counts as one of the last colonies (see 2–9) and give a valuable account of their diversity (9–15) but the authors do not discuss the relevance of their analysis to the scope of the European Convention.

[358] We do not in this article discuss the later Protocols, though our arguments would seem to apply to them as well.

[359] For the present status of European micro-states (Andorra, Liechtenstein, Monaco, San Marino, and the Vatican) see Duursma (n 328 above) *passim*.

[360] *Oppenheim's International Law* (9th edn) (n 13 above) paras 82 and 83.

[361] App No 24833/94, Judgment of 18 February 1999. See Muller (n 324 above).

European Parliament, the Court found that on the facts there had been a violation of Article 3; whatever may be said for or against the decision the Court referred explicitly to the relevance of the margin of appreciation under which limitations on the franchise, if appropriate, may be legitimate. Where such territories are in fact simply administered by the home government it would not require much ingenuity to satisfy Article 3 by, for example, a system of postal or proxy voting in metropolitan elections for citizens temporarily resident.[362] There is no reason why Article 1 should not apply in such territories, and if Article 2 was capable of application in that the territory had some children to educate, there is no reason why it should not apply to ensure access to education was provided, not necessarily in the territory itself. In the case of the BIOT, where the indigenous population, which included numerous children, was unlawfully expelled, and the current population comprises officials, US service personnel, civilian contractors, and visiting scientists, the application of the First Protocol would certainly raise issues which would need to be addressed. For British citizen transients Article 3 might best be satisfied by existing arrangements for postal or proxy voting, but if the Chagos Islanders were, in the future, to be allowed to return, as surely they ought to be, there seems to be no reason not to enable them to participate in the democratic process; it would be a question of whether this should be done through establishing a local legislature, and giving the territory to which they returned a degree of autonomy which it does not presently possess, or merely by giving them representation through the United Kingdom Parliament.[363]

In the absence of radical amendment by a new protocol, the existing texts have to be interpreted in accordance with the principles which have been established in the constantly evolving jurisprudence of the Court. The small number of cases is not, as we have seen, particularly helpful on the interaction between Articles 1, 63 (previously 56), and 4; some are merely admissibility decisions by the Commission, and none have provided a comprehensive analysis. Although the relationship between Article 1 and the provisions for extension was never explored in the course of the negotiations, the *Travaux Préparatoires* do make it quite clear what the purpose of Article 63(3) was, and the development of the doctrines of the margin of appreciation and of proportionality provides an obvious justification for regarding it as simply obsolete. Any reliance today on its original rationale, the supposed low state of civilization in certain overseas dependencies, would be offensive.

362 Under the British Overseas Territory Act (2002) BOT citizens have been given full British citizenship, but there is an exception under s 3(2) for those whose citizenship depends merely upon their connection with the SBAs in Cyprus, so that they do not benefit from this. There are special provisions for the Chagos which go some way to offset the consequences of their expulsion. British citizens can, of course, vote in UK elections.

363 A possible solution might be to reorganize the boundaries of the BIOT, and perhaps treat some parts of the archipelago as a distinct territory; there are two other habitable atolls, Peros Banhos and Salomon, at a considerable distance from Diego Garcia. Any development of a local autonomy which

As for the provisions for voluntary extension, the original rationale, quite plain from the *Travaux Préparatoires*—respect for and furtherance of autonomy—can certainly have no application to the BNOTs—the BAT, the SBAs, the SGSSI, and the BIOT—which have been created since the original negotiations. The Convention surely already applies under Article 1. Voluntary extension presupposes the possibility of consulting with a local governmental institution possessing some significant degree of autonomy. Ascension Island would seem to be in substantially the same position. If the reality of the matter is that such a body does not exist, or exists only in symbolic form, logic dictates that such a provision is rendered irrelevant. If a state's central government can, without consultation or approval or consent by any local democratic institution, extend or not extend the Convention to a territory, then to deny that such a territory is 'within the jurisdiction' under Article 1 is untenable if the interpretation of the Convention is related to its object and purpose.[364]

So far as the BNOTs are concerned, much the same result could be achieved in a different way through the doctrine suggested, but not elaborated, in the *Loizidou* case,[365] according to which the function of extension was explained: 'Article 63 concerns a decision by a Contracting Party to assume full responsibility under the Convention for all acts of public authorities in respect of a territory for whose international relations it is responsible. Article 25, on the other hand, concerns the acceptance by the Contracting Party of the competence of the Commission to examine complaints relating to the acts of its own officials acting under its direct authority.' The distinction here being made involves, to put it simply, drawing a line between actions of the public authorities in the dependency, and actions of the home government. Where officials in the dependency are directly controlled by the contracting state's central government there would appear to be no case for arguing that extension is required. Indeed such an analysis would have been possible on the facts of *Bui Van Thanh and others v UK*[366] and in *Yonghong v Portugal*[367] had the Commission and the Court approached the matter with a view to furthering the object and purpose of the Convention.

Such an interpretation would, at least in theory, certainly make more difficult the development of black holes in human rights protection located in a dependency of a European power. The risks involved are not fanciful; there are, for example, foreign bases administered by a state which is not and cannot become a party to the European Convention on

might lead to independence would encounter difficulties with Mauritius, given the undertakings given, and the fact that the BIOT can be viewed as a colonial enclave. Mauritius, which was at the time of independence compensated for the loss of the islands, currently claims the BIOT.

[364] The same may be said, eg, in relation to the normally uninhabited Bouvet Island, albeit an implausible location for human rights violations, though strange and nasty things do happen in outlandish places. For examples, see AWB Simpson, *Cannibalism and the Common Law. A Victorian Yachting Tragedy* (1994) *passim*.

[365] *Loizidou v Turkey* (Preliminary objections) 20 EHRR 99, at para 88. See 181–2 above.

[366] Above at 169. [367] Above at 170.

Ascension Island, Diego Garcia, and in Greenland, to give but three illustrations. We do not suggest that there have been violations of human rights in such bases by the United States (though in the Chagos Islands, we would argue, there have been by the United Kingdom), nor are such violations necessary to our argument. The point merely is that if territories are under the territorial sovereignty of parties to the European Convention such parties should surely be accountable, at least *prima facie*, for what goes on there, whether or not it happens within the foreign base, and should not be able simply to rely on a territorial clause and the lack of voluntary extension as providing any kind of unqualified exemption. It would, of course, be up to the Court, were any complaint to be brought before it, to follow the approach it took in the *Ilaşçu* case to Moldova's responsibilities in relation to those parts of its territory controlled by the Russian Federation in order to establish whether or not the relevant party to the Convention could be held responsible for activities which took place on a base under the control of another state. In January 2003 a British Government spokesman, in response to a question in Parliament, explicitly denied that any Taliban suspects were held on Diego Garcia, and said that for this to be the case United Kingdom permission would be required, the reference being to a provision of a 1976 agreement requiring prior consultation before access was given to a person not covered by the specific provisions on access.[368] This reply was at least consistent with there being United Kingdom responsibility, though the answer was not addressed to the issue.

There may of course be other situations in which a party is not in *de facto* control of the locality where the violations of the Convention have occurred. This has been the situation in northern Cyprus, and was the situation which arose in *Ilaşçu and others v Moldova and Russia*.[369] Moldova was not in effective control of Transdniestria, part of its national territory, where there existed a separatist movement in conflict with the legitimate Moldovan government. This movement, it was claimed, was being actively supported by the Russian Federation. The Court nevertheless held that this territory was still within Moldova's jurisdiction under Article 1 of the Convention, and this notwithstanding a declaration which had accompanied Moldova's ratification.[370] The Court took the position that Moldova's positive obligations still obtained even in relation to areas where it could not be held responsible for positive acts of violation: 'These obligations remain even where the exercise of the State's authority is limited in part of its territory, so that it has a duty to take all appropriate measures which it is still within its power to take.'[371] This doctrinal approach enables the Court to adapt its

[368] (2003) 74 BYIL 857–8, HL Deb vol 642, col 1019, 8 January 2003. See para 4 of the agreement (n 258 above), which could be read as requiring both parties to agree.

[369] See n 347 above. [370] See text to n 347 above.

[371] Merits, paras 313–352. This conclusion was reached by 11 votes to 6.

conception of accountability so that whether the party with territorial sovereignty will incur responsibility will necessarily turn on the particular facts and legalities of each case. And if Moldova's responsibility was incurred in relation to Transdniestria even when outside its *de facto* control the responsibility of the United Kingdom must, *a fortiori*, surely be engaged in relation to BNOTs.

In the *Ilaşçu case* the Court was also concerned with the responsibility of the Russian Federation, and, in the admissibility decision, adopted the principle, derived from *Loizidou v Turkey*[372] under which 'regard being had to the object and purpose of the Convention, the responsibility of a Contracting Party may also arise when as a consequence of military action—whether lawful or unlawful—it exercises effective control of an area outside its national territory.[373] This principle was adopted and elaborated by the Court in the hearing on the merits,[374] and on the facts the Court ruled that the responsibility of the Russian Federation was engaged, the territory falling within Russian jurisdiction under Article 1.[375] The statement of the principle in the case was wide; responsibility was incurred because the regime in the territory was 'set up ... with the support of the Russian Federation, vested with organs of power and of its own administration, remains under the effective authority, or at the very least under the decisive influence, of the Russian Federation'.[376] If Turkey can be held responsible for violations in northern Cyprus on the basis of its *de facto* control, and the Russian Federation, similarly, for violations in Transdniestria, it is difficult to see why the United Kingdom should not be responsible under Article 1 for violations in the BNOTs. The difference is that its exercise of control is lawful, but why should this be critical? It is very odd to deny responsibility predicated on 'jurisdiction' on the ground that the jurisdiction has arisen in accordance with international law.

So far as dependencies within Europe are concerned, the practice and the limited jurisprudence has, without the issue ever having been argued or fully considered, allowed the Convention and its First Protocol to be interpreted so as to permit Contracting Parties to deny the full protection of the Convention even to such European territories as the Isle of Man and the Channel Islands. There is, we suggest, a powerful counter-argument, which has never been presented to the Court, that the assumption that extension is required is incorrect. It is that the colonial clause should be interpreted as a whole, and in the light of Article 1, so that only territories to which it was appropriate, because of their low standard of civilization, to apply Article 56(3), were intended to be covered by the system of voluntary extension. The text of Article 56(3) supports this, since it provides that: 'The provisions of this Convention shall be applied

[372] 20 EHRR 99 (Preliminary objections).

[373] Admissibility decision, 21. The Court was unable at this stage to decide whether the Russian Federation was in control.

[374] paras 314–321

[375] paras 377–394.

[376] para 392.

in such territories with due regard however, to local requirements' (emphasis added). The territories in question must be those referred to in Article 56(1) or (2), to which the Convention was not to apply without extension. This would surely rule out European territories. And, if there are now no such territories, either within Europe or elsewhere, the logic of this argument would lead to the more radical conclusion that the whole system of voluntary extension has been overtaken by events and has no place in the dynamic Convention law of the twenty-first century.

Such a conclusion would indeed be in line with official statements on UK policy in relation to its overseas dependencies. In a White Paper presented to Parliament in 1999 by the Secretary of State for Foreign and Commonwealth Affairs, *Partnership for Progress and Prosperity. Britain and the Overseas Territories*,[377] it was stated that:

> We regard the establishment and maintenance of high standards of observance of human rights as an important aspect of our partnership with the Overseas Territories. Our objective is that those territories which choose to remain British should abide by the same basic standards of human rights, openness and good government that British people expect of their Government. This means that Overseas Territory legislation should comply with the same international obligations to which Britain is subject, such as the European Convention on Human Rights and the UN International Covenant on Civil and Political Rights. The Overseas Territories have a well-deserved reputation for their respect for and observance of human rights, but changes are still necessary in some territories to ensure consistency.[378]

A somewhat different and again radical approach to the interpretation of the Convention which might usefully be applied to Articles 56 and 4 is suggested by the case of *Piermont v France* (1995).[379] There the Court was faced with a problem over the interpretation of Article 16: 'Nothing in Articles 10, 11, and 14 shall be regarded as preventing the High Contracting Parties from imposing restrictions on the political activity of aliens.' This provision, though not so regarded back in the 1950s, now seems somewhat anomalous, and in 1977 the Parliamentary Assembly of the Council of Europe recommended, *inter alia*, that the Committee of Ministers should instruct experts 'to make proposals for the amendment of the European Convention ... in such a way as to exclude restrictions at present authorised by Article 16 with respect to political activity on the exercise by aliens of the freedoms guaranteed by Article 10 (freedom of expression) and Article 11 (freedom of association)'. No such amendment has yet taken place. Mrs Dorothée Piermont, a German national, was a member of the European Parliament. She visited two French Overseas Territories, New Caledonia and French Polynesia, with a view

377 Cm 4264, March 1999, para 4.1. The Foreign Secretary at the time was the late Robin Cook.

378 Specific reference was made to three human rights issues: judicial corporal punishment, the criminalization of homosexual acts between consenting adults, and capital punishment, then still possible in Bermuda, to which the 6th Protocol had not been extended. cf a note of a ministerial statement in (2000) 71 BYIL 437.

379 Series A/314, (1995) 20 EHRR 301.

to conducting political activities there. The basic issue in the case, so far as Article 16 was concerned, was whether it was legitimate in principle for measures officially taken against her in French Polynesia, which restricted her freedom of expression, to be justified under Article 16, on the ground that she was an alien under applicable French law. The Commission, emphasizing the fact that the Convention was to be interpreted as a living instrument, and must be interpreted in the light of the evolution since it was drafted of the European Community and European Union, ruled that Mrs Piermont, as a member of the European Parliament, could not be treated as an alien (*étrangère*) within the meaning of Article 16.[380] The Commission did not go so far as to rule that Article 16 could no longer apply in general because of developments since its text was adopted. The Court held by five votes to four that there had been breaches of Article 10 in both New Caledonia and French Polynesia and that 'it considers that Mrs. Piermont's possession of the nationality of a member State of the European Union and, in addition to that, her status as a member of the European Parliament do not allow Article 16 of the Convention to be raised against her, especially as the people of the Overseas Territories take part in the European Parliament elections'.[381] Again the decision does not mean that Article 16 is deprived of all function.

The *Piermont* case is, of course, directly relevant only to Article 16, but the approach adopted in the case might well prove fruitful in relation to the relics of colonialism which still disfigure the text and jurisprudence of the Convention

The United Kingdom's negotiators, supported only by the Netherlands, relied throughout on a philosophy of devolution of responsibility to colonial territories, encouraging them to be progressively governed by local institutions. This justified the supposed necessity to consult with dependencies before binding them to any international obligations. They never argued that a need to restrict protection justified colonial clauses. It could be that the colonial clause was appropriate at a time when the nature of the relationship between colonial powers and their dependencies was both too complex and too fluid for a uniform rule to be viable or politically acceptable. An option of extension was the best that could then be agreed. Understood in this way, the colonial clause was essentially an interim provision.

The question that now needs to be asked is how such a provision should be interpreted in the twenty-first century, when the colonial world, at least in the form it took in the 1950s, no longer exists. Dependencies of European powers, such as the BOTs, still exist, but if they choose to remain in a dependent relationship with a European state

380 See the report of the Commission, App Nos 15773/89 and 15774/89 of 20 January 1994, paras 57–69. For the 'living instrument' doctrine, reliance was there placed on *Marckx v Belgium* (1979) Series A/31, para 41 and *Airey v Ireland* (1979) Series A/32, para 26.

381 para 64.

and therefore cannot themselves be directly accountable under the Convention their parent state surely ought to be. What is required today is an approach to the interpretation of the Convention which is directed to ensuring that for the future the power of states, or their dependencies, insofar as they exercise autonomous powers, either *de facto* or *de jure*, to deny full human rights protection, and create, as it were, black holes in the world of human rights is reduced, ideally, to vanishing point. The modern case law on Article 1, in particular the decisions in *Loizidou* and *Ilaşçu*, has been directed towards this end. This case law sits uneasily with earlier decisions which have enabled parties to rely upon an anachronistic system of voluntary extension to evade responsibility for violations of human rights although they have enjoyed both *de facto* and *de jure* power to prevent such violations. It would be possible today for the Court to approach the interpretation of the provisions relating to extension in the same spirit as underlies the *Loizidou* and *Ilaşçu* cases, which would both conform to the basic principle embodied in Article 31 of the Vienna Convention on the Law of Treaties, and implement the doctrine, now firmly rooted in the jurisprudence, that the Convention is a living instrument which must be interpreted in the light of present-day conditions.[382]

[382] When this article was in page proof we learned that the Strasbourg Court (Fourth Section), on 19 September 2006, had declared inadmissible an application by Quark Fishing Limited against the UK (Application No 15305/06). It was not communicated to the UK Government. The ground was that the First Protocol had never been extended to SGSSI under Article 56. The brief Opinion does not contain any extensive discussion of the range of arguments presented in this article at 183–93 above, and in particular does not address the argument based on intent. It takes the view that the Court has no power to 'rewrite' the Convention; in this article we do not argue that it should.

THE INHERENT POWERS OF INTERNATIONAL COURTS AND TRIBUNALS

By Chester Brown*

Introduction

From time to time, questions of procedure arise in international judicial proceedings for which the constitutive instrument and the rules of the relevant international court or tribunal provide no clear answer. Such a situation arose recently in the preliminary objections phase of the *Legality of Use of Force* cases brought by Serbia and Montenegro against certain NATO member states before the International Court of Justice ('ICJ').[1] The issue was whether the ICJ had a power to remove cases from its List prior to deciding on its jurisdiction 'whenever it sees that this is necessary from the viewpoint of the proper administration of justice'.[2] The ICJ held that: 'Although the Rules of Court do not provide for such a procedure, there is no doubt that in certain circumstances the Court may of its own motion put an end to proceedings in a case.'[3] This issue had arisen in previous cases. While the ICJ had not made an express ruling on this question, it had in fact exercised this power. As it explained: 'Prior to the adoption of Article 38, paragraph 5, of the Rules of Court, in a number of cases in which the application disclosed no subsisting title of jurisdiction, but merely an invitation to the State named as respondent to accept jurisdiction for the purposes of the case, the Court removed the cases from the List by order.'[4]

* BA (Hons) (Melb), LLB (Hons) (Melb), BCL (Oxon), PhD (Cantab); Associate, International Law and International Arbitration Group, Clifford Chance LLP, London; Part-time Lecturer in Public International Law, Queen Mary College, University of London. The author is grateful to Daniel Bethlehem QC, Catherine Brown, Dr Alexander Orakhelashvili, Audley Sheppard, and Dr Christian Tams for their comments on an earlier draft, and to Dr Lorand Bartels and Professor Ole Spiermann for discussions and the provision of materials. The views expressed in this article are solely those of the author.

1 *Legality of Use of Force (Serbia and Montenegro v Belgium) (Preliminary Objections)* (2005) 44 ILM 299; see C Brown, 'Access to International Justice in the *Legality of Use of Force* Cases' (2005) 64 *Cambridge Law Journal* 267.

2 (2005) 44 ILM 299, 312.

3 ibid.

4 ibid. For examples of cases where this occurred, see eg *Treatment in Hungary of the Aircraft and Crew of USA (US v Hungary)* [1954] ICJ Rep 99; *Treatment in Hungary of the Aircraft and Crew of USA (US v USSR)* [1954] ICJ Rep 103; *Aerial Incident of 10 March 1953 (US v Czechoslovakia)* [1956] ICJ Rep 6; *Aerial Incident of 7 October 1952 (US v USSR)* [1956] ICJ Rep 9; *Antarctica (UK v Argentina)* [1956] ICJ Rep 12; *Antarctica (UK v Chile)* [1956] ICJ Rep 15; *Aerial Incident of 4 September 1954 (US v USSR)* [1958] ICJ Rep 158; *Aerial Incident of 7 November 1954 (US v USSR)* [1959] ICJ Rep 276. The need for the ICJ to remove such cases from its list has now been circumvented by ICJ Rules, art 38(5), pursuant to which an application is not entered in the list until the respondent state has agreed to the ICJ's jurisdiction: eg *Certain Criminal Proceedings in France (Republic of the Congo v France)* (ICJ, Order of 17 June 2003), available at

In other cases, the ICJ had received requests from respondent states to remove cases from the list on the grounds that it was 'manifestly not competent in the case'.[5] Such a request was granted in the provisional measures phase of two of the *Legality of Use of Force* cases, where the ICJ had held that:

> ... the Court manifestly lacks jurisdiction to entertain Yugoslavia's Application ... it cannot therefore indicate any provisional measure whatsoever in order to protect the rights invoked therein; and ... within a system of consensual jurisdiction, to maintain on the General List a case upon which it appears certain that the Court will not be able to adjudicate on the merits would most assuredly not contribute to the sound administration of justice.[6]

In the preliminary objections phase of the *Legality of Use of Force* cases, the ICJ ultimately held that it did not have a general power to remove cases from its List, but that its power to do so was restricted to these two situations; namely, where proceedings are instituted and no title of jurisdiction is relied on, and where the ICJ 'manifestly lacks jurisdiction'.[7] In her separate opinion, however, Judge Higgins begged to differ. Referring to the previous practice of the ICJ in removing cases from its List, she observed that:

> These were actions by the Court in the exercise of its inherent powers. The precedents on removal from the List cited by the Court—where from the outset no subsisting title of jurisdiction has been disclosed, or where the Court manifestly lacked jurisdiction—do not constitute two exclusive categories within which the Court has to fall if it wishes to exercise its inherent powers in the absence of discontinuance. There is nothing in the case law that so suggests. Indeed, it is hard to know what might be the legal source of a right to remove cases from the List provided only that this would be limited to those two examples.[8]

Judge Kooijmans expressed a similar view in his separate opinion: 'The fact that the Rules only speak of removing a case from the List by unilateral action of the applicant (Article 89) or joint action by the parties (Article 90) cannot deprive the Court of its inherent power, as master of its own procedure, to strike *proprio motu* a case from the List ... This

<www.icj-cij.org> (last visited 19 August 2005); S Yee, '*Forum Prorogatum* Returns to the International Court of Justice' (2003) 16 *Leiden Journal of International Law* 701, 707–10; H Thirlway, 'The Law and Procedure of the International Court of Justice 1960–1989: Part Nine' (1998) 69 BYIL 1, 10–11; H Thirlway, 'Procedural Law and the International Court of Justice' in V Lowe and M Fitzmaurice (eds), *Fifty Years of the International Court of Justice* (1996) 389, 394–5.

[5] For examples of cases where such a request was not granted, see eg *Nuclear Tests (Australia v France)* [1973] ICJ Rep 99, 100; *Nuclear Tests (Australia v France)* [1974] ICJ Rep 253, 257; *Aegean Sea (Greece v Turkey)* [1976] ICJ Rep 3, 5, see also 31, 32 (Sep Op Judge Tarazi); *Military and Paramilitary Activities (Nicaragua v US)* [1984] ICJ Rep 169, 178; see also 190, 204 (Diss Op Judge Schwebel).

[6] *Legality of Use of Force (Yugoslavia v Spain)* [1999] ICJ Rep 761, 773–4; *Legality of Use of Force (Yugoslavia v US)* [1999] ICJ Rep 916, 925–6.

[7] (2005) 44 ILM 299, 312.

[8] ibid, 341, 342 (Sep Op Judge Higgins).

power is not related to the intention of the parties but to the judicial task of the Court.'[9]

The disagreement between the majority of the ICJ and Judges Higgins and Kooijmans raises a question concerning the scope of the inherent powers of international courts and tribunals; these bodies can be understood as those dispute settlement fora created by international agreement.[10] Although many international courts have exercised such powers, they have only rarely sought to provide any justification for their authority to do so. And while the existence of inherent powers has doctrinal support,[11] there have been few attempts to consider fully the source, nature, and scope of inherent powers of international courts.[12] This is the task undertaken by the present article. This inquiry is important in the light of the prevalent uncertainty concerning their existence, and what the limitations are on their use. It is also timely in the light of the recent proliferation of international courts and tribunals, which has seen the creation of many new international dispute settlement fora in the last

[9] ibid, 345, 349 (Sep Op Judge Kooijmans).

[10] For other possible definitions of 'international court' or 'international tribunal', see C Romano, 'The Proliferation of International Judicial Bodies: The Pieces of the Puzzle' (1999) 31 *New York University Journal of International Law and Politics* 709, 713–14; C Tomuschat, 'International Courts and Tribunals with Regionally Restricted and/or Specialised Jurisdiction' in Max-Planck Institut für ausländisches öffentliches Recht und Völkerrecht, *Judicial Settlement of International Disputes—International Court of Justice, Other Courts and Tribunals, Arbitration and Conciliation: An International Symposium* (1974) 285, 299–312.

[11] See especially P Gaeta, 'The Inherent Powers of International Courts and Tribunals' in L Chand Vohrar *et al* (eds), *Man's Inhumanity to Man: Essays on International Law in Honour of Antonio Cassese* (2003) 353; see also A Orakhelashvili, 'Judicial Competence and Judicial Remedies in the *Avena* Case' (2005) 18 *Leiden Journal of International Law* 31; F Weiss, 'Inherent Powers of National and International Courts' in F Ortino and E-U Petersmann (eds), *The WTO Dispute Settlement System 1995–2003* (2004) 177; A Orakhelashvili, 'The Concept of International Judicial Jurisdiction: A Reappraisal' (2003) 3 *Law and Practice of International Courts and Tribunals* 501, 534–49; H Ascensio, 'La notion de juridiction internationale en question' in Société Française pour le Droit International, *Colloque de Lille: La juridictionnalisation du droit international* (2003) 163, 192–5; P Kovacs, 'Developpement et limites de la jurisprudence en droit international' in Société Française pour le Droit International, *Colloque de Lille: La juridictionnalisation du droit international* (2003) 269, 290–5, 327–30; A Orakhelashvili, 'Questions of International Judicial Jurisdiction in the *LaGrand* Case' (2002) 15 *Leiden Journal of International Law* 105, 107–8; M Buteau and G Oosthuizen, 'When the Statutes and Rules are Silent: The Inherent Powers of the Tribunal' in Richard May *et al* (eds), *Essays on ICTY Procedure and Evidence in Honour of Gabrielle Kirk McDonald* (2001) 65; JA Carrillo-Salcedo, 'The Inherent Powers of the International Criminal Tribunal for the Former Yugoslavia to Issue "*Subpoena Duces Tecum*" to a Sovereign State' in R-J Dupuy (ed), *Mélanges en l'honneur de Nicolas Valticos: Droit et Justice* (1999) 269, 274; H Thirlway, 'The Law and Procedure of the International Court of Justice 1960–1989: Part Ten' (1999) 70 BYIL 1, 2–5; Thirlway, 'The Law and Procedure of the International Court of Justice 1960–1989: Part Nine' (n 4 above), 18–19, 41, 43–4, 65; D Sarooshi, 'The Powers of the United Nations International Criminal Tribunals' (1998) 2 *Max Planck Yearbook of United Nations Law* 141, 144, 150–4; S Rosenne, *The Law and Practice of the International Court 1920–1996* (1997) 600–3; Sir E Lauterpacht, '"Partial" Judgments and the Inherent Jurisdiction of the International Court of Justice' in V Lowe and M Fitzmaurice (eds), *Fifty Years of the International Court of Justice* (1996) 465; A Arnull, 'Does the Court of Justice Have Inherent Jurisdiction?' (1990) 27 *Common Market Law Review* 683, 700–7; Sir G Fitzmaurice, *The Law and Procedure of the International Court of Justice* (1986) 451–7, 533–43, 770–1; H Briggs, 'The Incidental Jurisdiction of the International Court of Justice as Compulsory Jurisdiction' in Fvd Heydte *et al* (eds), *Völkerrecht und Rechtliches Weltbild: Festschrift für Alfred Verdross* (1960) 87, 91–5.

[12] An exception is Gaeta (n 11 above).

fifteen years.[13] Proliferation has had several effects on the international legal order, such as the emergence of inconsistent jurisprudence,[14] and the creation of overlapping jurisdictions among international courts.[15] Another noteworthy development in international adjudication since the advent of proliferation is an increase in the cross-fertilization of procedures and procedural powers from one international court to another; not only among the more established international courts, but also the newer fora for the adjudication of international disputes. As the statutes and rules of procedure of international courts are rarely drafted in identical terms, one way that such powers may be exercised is, in the absence of any agreement of the parties, by reliance on inherent powers. Furthermore, as the challenges posed by the emergence of competing jurisdictions among international courts are likely to persist given the absence of any hierarchy of international courts, international dispute settlement bodies will be required to devise procedures to deal with these situations; their competence to do so may similarly be found in their exercise of inherent powers.

This article commences with a general introduction to the sources of law relevant to international procedure (Part I). It then turns to a consideration of inherent powers as they are exercised by domestic courts, and examines the validity of some objections to the extension of this doctrine to international dispute settlement proceedings (Part II). It then provides several illustrative examples of the exercise of inherent powers by international courts (Part III). In order to determine the scope of inherent powers, it is important to have an understanding of their source, and four possible sources are considered, before the conclusion is reached that the proper source of inherent powers lies in the necessity for international courts to fulfil their judicial functions (Part IV). In the light of this conclusion, these functions are then subjected to an examination in order to determine the scope of inherent powers. It is suggested that while international courts have many functions, those which most frequently justify the exercise of inherent powers are the settlement of international disputes and the proper administration of international justice (Part V). Finally, the limitations on the exercise of inherent powers are identified (Part VI). The significance of this examination is the establishment of a sound juridical basis for the exercise of inherent powers by international courts, while identifying clear limitations to the scope of such powers; this analysis, it is suggested, can be used by international courts faced with procedural issues for which their constitutive instruments and rules make no provision.

[13] See eg Y Shany, *The Competing Jurisdictions of International Courts and Tribunals* (2003) 1–17; C Brown, 'The Proliferation of International Courts and Tribunals: Finding Your Way Through the Maze' (2002) 3 *Melbourne Journal of International Law* 453; P Sands, R Mackenzie, and Y Shany (eds), *Manual on International Courts and Tribunals* (1999).

[14] See eg J Charney, 'The Impact on the International Legal System of the Growth of International Courts and Tribunals' (1999) 31 *New York University Journal of International Law and Politics* 697; J Charney, 'Is International Law Threatened by Multiple International Tribunals?' (1998) 271 *Recueil des Cours* 101.

[15] See especially Shany (n 13 above); V Lowe, 'Overlapping Jurisdiction in International Tribunals' (1999) 20 *Australian Yearbook of International Law* 191.

I. Sources of Law Relating to Procedure in International Adjudication

As inherent powers are usually asserted in the context of the procedural law applicable before international courts, it is apposite to begin with a general inquiry into the sources of those norms. In the past, writers have expressed uncertainty about those sources. As Professor Thirlway wrote in 1996: 'The law governing international judicial procedure has not been a subject of wide general interest ... there is no fully developed general theory of international procedural law, defining its sources, for example.'[16] Earlier, the same author had expressed the view that although the identification of the sources of international law—and the sources of the procedural powers of international tribunals—was 'a matter on which there is still room for controversy', one might nonetheless begin with Article 38 of the ICJ Statute.[17] This, of course, provides in part that:

(1) The Court, whose function is to decide in accordance with international law such disputes as are submitted to it, shall apply:
  (a) international conventions, whether general or particular, establishing rules expressly recognised by the contesting states;
  (b) international custom, as evidence of a general practice accepted as law;
  (c) the general principles of law recognised by civilised nations;
  (d) subject to the provisions of Article 59, judicial decisions and the teachings of the most highly qualified publicists of the various nations, as subsidiary means for the determination of rules of law.[18]

Formally, the list of sources contained in Article 38(1) only applies to the ICJ, but it is widely regarded by writers as having general application.[19] In addition, it has been accepted by other international tribunals.[20]

[16] Thirlway, 'Procedural Law and the International Court of Justice' (n 4 above) 389; see also H Thirlway, 'Procedure of International Courts and Tribunals' in R Bernhardt (ed), *Encyclopedia of Public International Law* (1992) vol III, 1128. However, the subject of international procedure has come a long way since it was described as 'the Antarctica of international law': AH Feller, *The Mexican Claims Commissions: 1923–34* (1935) vii.

[17] H Thirlway, 'Dilemma or Chimera? Admissibility of Illegally Obtained Evidence in International Adjudication' (1984) 78 AJIL 622, 623.

[18] Statute of the International Court of Justice, opened for signature 26 June 1945, 3 Bevans 1153, Art 38(1) (entered into force 24 October 1945) ('ICJ Statute').

[19] eg M Shaw, *International Law* (5th edn, 2003) 66–7; I Brownlie, *Principles of Public International Law* (6th edn, 2003) 4–5; C Schreuer, *The ICSID Convention: A Commentary* (2001) 609–18; L Bartels, 'Applicable Law in WTO Dispute Settlement Proceedings' (2001) 35 *Journal of World Trade Law* 499, 501–2, 504; D Palmeter and P Mavroidis, *Dispute Settlement in the World Trade Organisation* (2nd edn, 2004) 49–50; Sir R Jennings, *Collected Writings of Sir Robert Jennings* (1998) vol I, 6; H Mosler, 'General Principles of Law' in R Bernhardt (ed), *Encyclopedia of Public International Law* (1992) vol II, 511, 515; M Virally, 'The Sources of International Law' in M Sørensen (ed), *Manual of Public International Law* (1968) 116, 121–2; JL Brierly, *The Law of Nations* (6th edn, 1963) 56; JL Simpson and H Fox, *International Arbitration* (1959) 130–1; G Scelle, 'Draft on Arbitral Procedure Adopted by the Commission at its Fifth Session' [1958] *Yearbook of the International Law Commission*, vol II, 1, 8, UN Doc A/CN.4/113; 'Report of the Commission to the General Assembly' [1958] *Yearbook of the International Law Commission*, vol II, 78, 84, art 10, UN Doc A/3859; UN Secretary-General, *Survey of International Law in Relation to the Work of Codification of the International Law Commission* (1948) 22, UN Doc A/CN.4/1/Rev.1; E Dumbauld, *Interim Measures of Protection in International Controversies* (1932) 177; Sir J Fischer Williams, *Chapters on Current International Law and the League of Nations* (1929) 20–1.

[20] See eg references to ICJ Statute, Art 38 in *Methanex Corp v US* (*Final Award*) para 3 (NAFTA, 9 August 2005); *Klöckner v Cameroon* (*Annulment*) (1985) 114 ILR 243, 270; *Amco v*

A question might be raised as to whether Article 38 of the ICJ Statute stipulates the sources of the substantive rules of international law—meaning its primary and secondary rules—or whether the sources indicated in that list also serve as the sources of procedural norms. However, as international law makes 'no sharp distinction' between substantive law and procedural law,[21] it is suggested that there is no reason why they may not also serve as sources of the procedural rules of international law.[22] It is apparent that some of the sources are more important than others; the obvious starting point is the constitutive instruments and rules of procedure of international courts.

A. Constitutive instruments and rules of procedure

International courts are the product of the express will of states as expressed in an international agreement, and, as such, their jurisdiction is based on the consent of the parties.[23] Likewise, consent is a source of the procedural powers of such bodies, as manifested in the form of the constitutive instrument of an international court, or a *compromis*. These instruments usually provide for certain procedural rules, and also confer certain powers on international courts. A well-known power is, for example, the competence of each international court to determine the extent of its own jurisdiction.[24] Other powers which are often expressly conferred by constitutive instruments include the power to grant provisional

Indonesia (Award) 89 ILR 405, 495 (1984); UN Secretary-General (n 19 above) 22; *Reponsabilité de l'Allemagne à raison des dommages causés dans les colonies portugaises du Sud de l'Afrique* 8 TAM 409, 413 (1928); see also *Mihaly International Corp v Sri Lanka* (2001) 17 *ICSID Review–FILJ* 142, 158; and the Report of the Executive Directors of the World Bank, who essentially deemed the term 'international law' in the ICSID Convention, Art 42 to refer to the sources of law enumerated by the ICJ Statute, Art 38(1): 'Report of the Executive Directors on the Convention', reprinted in ICSID, *ICSID Convention, Regulations and Rules* (2003) 37, para 40.

[21] Rosenne, *Law and Practice* (n 11 above) 1063, 1065.

[22] ibid 1065; see also Thirlway, 'Dilemma or Chimera?' (n 17 above) 623; Thirlway, 'Procedural Law and the International Court of Justice' (n 4 above) 389–90.

[23] Brownlie (n 19 above) 680–1; Rosenne, *Law and Practice* (n 11 above) 563–73; Thirlway, 'The Law and Procedure of the International Court of Justice 1960–1989: Part Nine' (n 4 above) 4, 21; Fitzmaurice, *Law and Procedure* (n 11 above) 492–5; Sir H Lauterpacht, *The Development of International Law by the International Court* (1958) 91–5; eg *East Timor (Portugal v Australia)* [1995] ICJ Rep 90, 101; *Continental Shelf (Revision and Interpretation) (Tunisia v Libya)* [1985] ICJ Rep 192, 216; *Corfu Channel (UK v Albania)* [1948] ICJ Rep 15, 27; *Interpretation of Peace Treaties* [1950] ICJ Rep 65, 71; *Eastern Carelia*, PCIJ Rep Series B No 5 (1923) 27.

[24] See eg ICJ Statute, Art 36(6); United Nations Convention on the Law of the Sea, opened for signature 10 December 1982, 21 ILM 1261, Art 288(4) (entered into force 16 November 1994) ('UNCLOS'); Convention on the Settlement of Investment Disputes between States and Nationals of Other States, opened for signature 18 March 1965, 575 UNTS 159, Art 41(1) (entered into force 14 October 1966) ('ICSID Convention'); Convention for the Pacific Settlement of International Disputes, opened for signature 29 July 1899, 1 Bevans 230, Art 48 (entered into force 4 September 1900) ('1899 Convention'); Convention for the Pacific Settlement of International Disputes, opened for signature 18 October 1907, 1 Bevans 577, Art 73 (entered into force 26 January 1910) ('1907 Convention'); Convention for the Protection of Human Rights and Fundamental Freedoms, opened for signature 4 November 1950, 213 UNTS 221, Art 32(2) (entered into force 3 September 1953) ('European Convention').

measures;[25] the power to permit the intervention of third parties;[26] the power to give an interpretation of judgments and awards;[27] and the power to revise judgments and awards.[28]

While the constitutive instruments set out the framework of the procedure applicable before each international court and tribunal, they do not always make detailed provision for the procedural powers of the international court it establishes. In drafting the PCIJ Statute in 1920,[29] for instance, the Advisory Committee of Jurists did not make any concerted effort to establish the procedure to be applied by the Permanent Court of International Justice ('PCIJ'), but decided that most questions of procedure should be left to the PCIJ itself.[30] The Advisory Committee of Jurists decided to include Article 30 in the PCIJ Statute, which conferred on the PCIJ the power to frame rules of procedure.[31] The Committee also confirmed the PCIJ's power to fill in *lacunae* in the PCIJ Statute and Rules of Court by adding provisions to its Rules.[32]

Likewise, many statutes of most other international courts confer on those bodies an express power to frame rules of procedure. The ICJ has retained this power in Article 30 of the ICJ Statute,[33] and other international courts also have this power.[34] In addition, most international courts have an express power to make procedural orders for the conduct

[25] eg ICJ Statute, Art 41; UNCLOS, Art 290; ICSID Convention, Art 47; American Convention on Human Rights, opened for signature 22 November 1969, 1144 UNTS 123, Art 63(2) (entered into force 18 July 1978) ('American Convention'); Treaty Establishing the European Community (2002) *Official Journal* C 325, Art 243 (entered into force) ('EC Treaty'); ECJ Statute, Art 36.

[26] ICJ Statute, Arts 62–63; ITLOS Statute, in UNCLOS, Annex VI, Arts 31–32; European Convention, Art 36; ECJ Statute, Art 37; Understanding on Rules and Procedures Governing the Settlement of Disputes, opened for signature 15 April 1994, 1869 UNTS 401, 33 ILM 1226, Art 10(2) (entered into force 1 January 1995) ('DSU').

[27] ICJ Statute, Art 60; ITLOS Statute, Art 33(3); ICSID Convention, Art 50; American Convention, Art 67; ECJ Statute, Art 40.

[28] ICJ Statute, Art 61; ICSID Convention, Art 51; 1899 Convention, Art 55; 1907 Convention, Art 83; ECJ Statute, Art 41.

[29] Statute of the Permanent Court of International Justice, PCIJ Rep, Series D No 1 (1926) 7 ('PCIJ Statute').

[30] PCIJ/Advisory Committee of Jurists, *Procès-Verbaux of the Proceedings of the Advisory Committee of Jurists, July 16th–July 24th 1920* (1920) 247–8; A Sánchez de Bustamante y Sirvén, *La Cour Permanente de Justice Internationale* (trans P Goulé, 1925) 214–15; see also O Spiermann, '"Who Attempts Too Much Does Nothing Well": The 1920 Advisory Committee of Jurists and the Statute of the Permanent Court of International Justice' (2002) 73 BYIL 187, 219, 237–8.

[31] PCIJ Statute, Art 30.

[32] PCIJ/Advisory Committee of Jurists (n 30 above) 647; M Hudson, *The Permanent Court of International Justice 1920–1942: A Treatise* (1943) 180.

[33] ICJ Statute, Art 30.

[34] See eg 1899 Convention, Art 49; 1907 Convention, Art 74. See also the International Tribunal for the Law of the Sea ('ITLOS'): ITLOS Statute, Art 16; the European Court of Human Rights ('ECtHR'): European Convention, Art 26(d); the Inter-American Court of Human Rights ('IACHR'): American Convention, Art 60, and IACHR Statute, Art 25; the Court of Justice of the European Communities ('ECJ'): EC Treaty, Art 245; panels of the World Trade Organization ('WTO'): DSU, Art 17(9); the International Criminal Tribunal for the former Yugoslavia ('ICTY'): ICTY Statute, Art 15; and the International Criminal Tribunal for Rwanda ('ICTR'): ICTR Statute, Art 14.

of the proceedings.[35] International courts have exercised these powers to expand their procedural powers appreciably.

While the power to make rules of procedure is usually expressly conferred on international courts, these rules generally do not need to be ratified by the states parties to the constitutive instrument.[36] Accordingly, while the rules of procedure might be regarded as a source of procedural law ultimately derived from the consent of states expressed in an international convention, the states parties to those instruments have in reality little control over their provisions, and it is the members of the international courts who determine their content. The provisions contained in the rules of procedure thus represent a source of law which is only indirectly derived from the consent of states, and may be said to reflect the international court's conception of the rules and powers needed to fulfil its functions. This is not to say, however, that states cannot affect the content of the rules of procedure in individual cases before certain international courts: under the ICJ Rules and the ITLOS Rules, the parties to a dispute may jointly propose modifications to the rules,[37] and in the case of tribunals constituted under the ICSID Convention, parties may agree to vary the arbitration rules.[38] In addition, in arbitrations conducted before *ad hoc* tribunals, tribunals frequently ask the parties to comment on the rules of procedure. This gives the parties some degree of control over the rules, although it appears that such modifications are only very rarely made.[39]

These sources—the constitutive instruments and the rules of procedure of international courts—provide the usual point of departure for a discussion of the powers of international courts. Yet such instruments do not necessarily make exhaustive provision for the procedural law or the procedural powers of such courts. Constitutive instruments, and even rules of procedure, often contain *lacunae*, such as gaps or ambiguities. The following section considers the approach of international courts faced with such situations.

B. *Powers of international courts faced with* lacunae

Several types of *lacuna* might be identified in international constitutive instruments. A first type may be found where an issue has deliberately

[35] See eg ICJ Statute, Art 48; ITLOS Statute, Art 27; DSU, App 3, para 11; ICSID Convention, Art 44; 1899 Convention, Art 49; 1907 Convention, Art 74; on the ICJ's power, see esp Rosenne, *Law and Practice* (n 11 above) 602–3.

[36] cf Rome Statute of the International Criminal Court, opened for signature 17 July 1998, UN Doc A/Conf183/9, Art 51 (entered into force 1 July 2002), which provides that the ICC's Rules and amendments to the Rules must be adopted by a two-thirds majority of the Assembly of States Parties; and cf also the ICSID Arbitration Rules, which were adopted by the ICSID Administrative Council, and apply in the absence of agreement to the contrary: ICSID Convention, Art 44.

[37] ICJ Rules, Art 101; ITLOS Rules, Art 48.

[38] ICSID Convention, Art 44.

[39] In the case of the ITLOS Rules, this provision was invoked in *Conservation and Sustainable Exploitation of Swordfish Stocks (Chile/EC)* (*Order of 20 December 2000*) (2001) 40 ILM 475.

not been addressed by the drafters of the instrument. As Edward Gordon observed: 'With the hope of reaching some accord, or gaining acceptance for some treaty rather than having none at all, drafters sometimes compromise by omitting all reference to a disputed subject.'[40] Thus, those framing the instrument might purposely refrain from addressing certain questions. In other cases, the drafters might leave further details to be completed by the court or tribunal itself, such as the decision of the Advisory Committee of Jurists to grant the power to the PCIJ to draft its rules of procedure. Second, even if the negotiators of the constitutive instruments of international courts seek to establish a comprehensive set of procedural rules, and manage to reach complete agreement on the powers to be accorded to the court, such drafters can never completely envisage the circumstances that might arise in the future.[41] Third, constitutive instruments may contain ambiguities. These might be inadvertent; or, ambiguous language may be intentionally included as an alternative to omitting any reference to a matter on which the negotiating parties have not been able to reach agreement. Examples of such ambiguity can be found where the parties incorporate terms and practices which are unclear, and where there is more than one authentic language version of a constitutive instrument.[42] Faced with *lacunae* in their constitutive instruments over procedure and remedies, a review of international jurisprudence demonstrates that international courts have resorted to other sources of law, such as customary international law, general principles of law, and the subsidiary sources of international law, so long as these do not contradict their constitutive instrument.[43]

It may appear somewhat incongruous to suggest that customary international law can represent a source of procedural law. Customary international law is usually thought to be generated by the practice of states and their expressions of *opinio juris*,[44] and not the practice of international courts and tribunals. Yet writers have nonetheless emphasized the relevance of custom.[45] The role of custom is also evidenced by references to

[40] E Gordon, 'The World Court and the Interpretation of Constitutive Treaties' (1965) 59 AJIL 794, 804–5; Sir H Lauterpacht, 'Restrictive Interpretation and the Principle of Effectiveness in the Interpretation of Treaties' (1949) 26 BYIL 48, 53; see eg *Constitution of the Maritime Safety Committee of the IMCO* [1960] ICJ Rep 150, 165–71; *Conditions of Admission* [1947–48] ICJ Rep 57, 94, 98–9 (Diss Op Judge Zoričić).

[41] Gordon (n 40 above) 803. This is a common problem with constitutive treaties, although the drafters of such treaties generally hope to frame an instrument which will be able to be adapted, in the words of Sir Percy Spender, to 'the unknown, the unforeseen, and, indeed, the unforeseeable': *Certain Expenses* [1962] ICJ Rep 151, 182, 185 (Sep Op Sir Percy Spender).

[42] Gordon (n 40 above) 810–13; eg *LaGrand (Germany v US)* (2001) 40 ILM 1069, 1092–3.

[43] eg Mosler (n 19 above) 515; B Cheng, *General Principles of Law as Applied by International Courts and Tribunals* (1987) 19, 22, 257–386; Thirlway, 'Dilemma or Chimera?' (n 17 above) 623–4; D Sandifer, *Evidence before International Tribunals* (revised edn, 1975) 44.

[44] Brownlie (n 19 above) 6–10; ILA, *Report of the Committee on the Formation of Customary (General) International Law* (London Conference, 2000); *North Sea Continental Shelf (Germany v Denmark) (Germany v Netherlands)* [1969] ICJ Rep 3, 43–4; *Military and Paramilitary Activities (Nicaragua v US)* [1986] ICJ Rep 14, 108–9.

[45] See esp Thirlway, 'Dilemma or Chimera?' (n 17 above) 623; Rosenne, *Law and Practice* (n 11 above) 1070.

the practice of international courts in international jurisprudence. For instance, in *Factory at Chorzów*, the PCIJ held that the obligation to make full reparation for an internationally wrongful act was 'established by international practice and in particular by the decisions of arbitral tribunals'.[46] In *US—Shirts and Blouses*, the WTO Appellate Body referred to the practice of 'various international tribunals, including the International Court of Justice' on the rule on the allocation of the burden of proof.[47] In a further example, the permanent Court of Arbitration ('PCA') tribunal in *MOX Plant* referred to 'international judicial practice' on the general requirements for the granting of provisional measures.[48]

The application of 'general principles of law' by international courts as a source of judicial procedure is well established.[49] This concept was originally intended to refer exclusively to general principles applicable in domestic legal orders, although general principles of international relations have also been applied by international courts.[50] There is a somewhat blurred distinction between a rule deriving from the 'customary practice' of international tribunals, and a rule constituting a 'general principle of law' under Article 38(1)(c) of the ICJ Statute.[51] The overlap in these categories is evident from Professor Cheng's inclusion in his work on general principles of law of rules such as that relating to *audi alteram partem*, the rule on the allocation of the burden of proof, and *res judicata*,[52] while these might equally be said to have been developed as customary rules of practice.[53] There is also much overlap concerning the use of judicial decisions as a subsidiary source of international law; as noted above, international courts frequently refer to international judicial practice as a source of procedural rules.[54]

In addition to these sources of procedural norms, international courts have also relied on a more controversial source of law relating to procedure; that is, the exercise of powers that are not conferred on them by their

[46] *Factory at Chorzów (Germany v Poland)* PCIJ Rep, Series A No 17 (1928) 47.

[47] DSR 1997-I, 323, 335 (ABR).

[48] *MOX Plant (Ireland v UK) (Procedural Order No 3)*, 42 ILM 1187, 1197 (PCA, 24 June 2003). For further examples, see eg *Nottebohm (Liechtenstein v Guatemala)* [1953] ICJ Rep 111, 119; and *Interhandel (Switzerland v US)* [1957] ICJ Rep 105, 117, 118 (Sep Op Sir Hersch Lauterpacht).

[49] Cheng (n 43 above) 299–386; G Schwarzenberger, *International Law as Applied by International Courts and Tribunals* (1986) vol IV, 584–5; see also Thirlway, 'Dilemma or Chimera?' (n 17 above) 624.

[50] See eg the discussion of the proposals of Baron Descamps, Lord Phillimore, and Elihu Root in the Advisory Committee of Jurists, referred to in Cheng (n 43 above) 11–17. See also esp Sir H Lauterpacht, *Private Law Sources and Analogies of International Law* (1927) 71, who states that general principles of law are 'for most practical purposes identical with general principles of private law'; cf D Anzilotti, *Cours de Droit International* (French trans G Gidel, 3rd edn, 1929) vol I, 117, who argues that this provision refers primarily to 'les principes généraux de l'ordre juridique international, et, en second lieu, les principes universellement admis dans les législations des peuples civilisés'. On the application of general principles of international relations, see Mosler (n 19 above) 511–12, 513, 522–4. For a consideration of the Advisory Committee of Jurists' debate on the sources of international law, see esp Spiermann (n 30 above) 212–18.

[51] Thirlway, 'Dilemma or Chimera?' (n 17 above) 624.

[52] Cheng (n 43 above) 290–8, 302–35, 336–72.

[53] eg for the suggestion that *res judicata* might be treated as a rule of customary international law, see Shany (n 13 above) 245.

[54] See above nn 45–48 and accompanying text.

constitutive instruments, and which might be regarded, in this sense, as 'extra-statutory'. These powers are inherent powers.

II. Inherent Powers in International Adjudication

A. *The concept of 'inherent powers'*

The adjective 'inherent' is used to describe something which 'exist[s] in something as a permanent attribute or quality; forming an element, esp. a characteristic or essential element of something; belonging to the intrinsic nature of that which is spoken of'.[55] An 'inherent power' might thus be said to be one that derives from an office, position, or status;[56] an inherent power of a court might, then, derive 'from its nature as a court of law'.[57] As a source of judicial power, 'inherent powers' appear to have their origin in the practice of English courts. English courts have invoked their inherent jurisdiction to exercise certain procedural powers 'from early times', as observed by Lord Blackburn in *Metropolitan Bank v Pooley*: 'from early times (I rather think, though I have not looked at it enough to say, from the earliest times) the court had inherently in its power the right to see that its process was not abused by a proceeding without reasonable grounds, so as to be vexatious and harassing—the court had a right to protect itself against such an abuse'.[58] In another frequently cited dictum, Lord Morris of Borth-y-Gest has held that: 'There can be no doubt that a court which is endowed with a particular jurisdiction has powers which are necessary to enable it to act effectively within such jurisdiction. I would regard them as powers which are inherent in its jurisdiction. A court must enjoy such powers in order to enforce its rules of practice and to suppress any abuses of its process and to defeat any attempted thwarting of its process.'[59]

The exercise of inherent powers has, however, not been limited to English courts. The courts of other common law jurisdictions, including Australian, Canadian, Singaporean, New Zealand, and US courts, have also claimed 'inherent powers' in myriad instances. These courts have variously invoked inherent powers to make rules of court and practice directions,[60]

55 *Oxford English Dictionary* (1933 edn) vol V, 293.

56 *Black's Law Dictionary* (abridged 7th edn, 2000) 953.

57 IH Jacob, 'The Inherent Jurisdiction of the Court' (1970) 23 *Current Legal Problems* 23, 24; on the inherent powers of domestic courts generally, see also R Pushaw, 'The Inherent Powers of the Federal Courts and the Structural Constitution' (2001) 86 *Iowa Law Review* 735; JA Jolowicz, 'Practice Directions and the Civil Procedure Rules' (2000) 59 *Cambridge Law Journal* 53; MS Dockray, 'The Inherent Jurisdiction to Regulate Civil Proceedings' (1997) 113 LQR 120; J Pinsler, 'The Inherent Powers of the Court' (1997) *Singapore Journal of Legal Studies* 1; K Mason, 'The Inherent Jurisdiction of the Court' (1983) 57 *Australian Law Journal* 449.

58 (1885) 10 App Cas 210, 220–1 (Lord Blackburn); see also Anthony May (Gen ed), *Civil Procedure* (2002) vol 2, 1539–40; Pushaw (n 57 above) 800–6; Jacob (n 57 above) 25–7.

59 *Connelly v DPP* [1964] AC 1254, 1301.

60 Jolowicz (n 57 above); Jacob (n 57 above) 33–7; eg *Thomas v Arn* 474 US 140, 146–7 (1985); *Connelly v DPP* (n 59 above), 1347; *Practice Direction (Trials in Middlesex)* [1958] 1 WLR 1291.

to prevent abuse of the court's process,[61] to remand cases involving pendent claims,[62] to stay proceedings,[63] to correct any injustice caused by an earlier order, such as where an individual is subjected to procedural unfairness,[64] and to allow the admission of evidence.[65] In other cases, courts have relied on inherent powers to exercise control over persons before them; such persons may be infants,[66] attorneys or other officers of the court,[67] applicants in judicial review proceedings who are seeking review of their detention,[68] or persons who are in contempt of court.[69] In addition, domestic superior courts have exercised inherent powers in order to exercise control over inferior courts and tribunals.[70] While the use of inherent powers is certainly more prevalent in common law countries, the exercise by courts of jurisdictional powers which are not expressly provided for in legislation or statutory rules is not unknown in civil law countries.[71]

Despite the widespread exercise of inherent powers by domestic courts, there appears to be no consensus on the source of these powers.[72] Two views can be discerned in the literature and case law. On one view, only 'superior' courts can exercise inherent powers; this theory was advanced by Sir Jack Jacob, who wrote that:

> ... the essential character of a superior court is that it should be invested with a power to maintain its authority and to prevent its process being obstructed and abused. Such a power is intrinsic in a superior court; it is its very life-blood, its very essence, its immanent attribute. Without such a power, the court would have form but lack substance. The jurisdiction which is inherent in a superior court of law is that which enables it to fulfil itself as a court of law. The juridical basis of this jurisdiction is therefore the authority of the judiciary to uphold,

[61] *Connelly v DPP* (n 59 above), 1301; *R v Forbes, ex p Bevan* (1972) 127 CLR 1, 7–8; *Taylor v Taylor* (1979) 143 CLR 1, 6; *Re Regina and Unnamed Person* (1985) 20 CRR 188, 190–1; *Emilia Shipping Inc v State Enterprise for Pulp and Paper Industries* [1991] 2 MLJ 379.

[62] *Carnegie-Mellon University v Cohill* 484 US 343, 357 (1988).

[63] *R v Duval* [1995] 3 NZLR 202, 205; *Spiliada Maritime Corp v Cansulex* [1987] AC 460, 476.

[64] *R v Bow Street Metropolitan Stipendiary Magistrate, ex p Pinochet Ugarte (No 2)* [2000] 1 AC 119, 132.

[65] *R v Moke and Lawrence* [1996] 1 NZLR 263, 266–7.

[66] Jacob (n 57 above) 46; *Re P (Infants)* [1967] 1 WLR 818, 824.

[67] Jacob (n 57 above) 46–8; *Chambers v NASCO, Inc* 501 US 32, 43–51 (1991); *Weaver v Law Society of New South Wales* (1979) 142 CLR 201, 207; *Myers v Elman* (1939) 4 All ER 484, 508; *Beal's Case* [1698] 12 Mod Rep 251.

[68] *R (Sezek) v Secretary of State for the Home Department* [2001] Times LR 399, 400; *Civil Procedure* (n 58 above), 1535–6.

[69] *Connelly v DPP* (n 59 above), 1301; *R v Forbes, ex p Bevan* (n 61 above), 7; *Young v US* 481 US 787, 793 (1987); *Re Regina and Unnamed Person* (n 61 above), 190–1.

[70] Jacob (n 57 above) 48–9; *R v Parke* [1903] 2 KB 432, 443–4.

[71] eg French procedural law derives not only from statutory instruments, but also from general principles of law and constitutional principles relating to fundamental rights: S Guinchard *et al*, *Droit processuel: Droit Commun et droit comparé du procès* (2nd edn, 2003) 53–8, 286–96; the jurisdiction of administrative law courts in Germany is not prescribed by statute: W Ebke and M Finkin (eds), *Introduction to German Law* (1996) 101–2; N Foster and S Sute, *German Legal Systems and Laws* (3rd edn, 2002) 267–91; in Norway, custom represents a source of procedure: A Bratholm and J Hov, *Sivil Retergang* (1973) 10–11; and in Sweden, judicial decisions may be a source of procedural law: R Bader Ginsburg and A Bruzehus, *Civil Procedure in Sweden* (1965) 39–40. Generally, on the existence of inherent powers in civil law countries, see further Jacob (n 57 above) 23; Arnull (n 11 above) 701; cf Gaeta (n 11 above) 365.

[72] Dockray (n 57 above) 120.

to protect and to fulfil the judicial function of administering justice according to law in a regular, orderly and effective manner.[73]

The view that only 'superior' courts possess inherent powers appears to be based on the origin of such bodies as exercising an 'unlimited jurisdiction' in the fulfilment of the Sovereign's judicial power. According to this view, the powers of the English High Court, together with those of the superior courts in other common law countries, are derived from the Sovereign.[74] In order to fulfil their functions, judges on such courts were able to rely on the existence of powers which were 'extra-statutory', in the sense that none of these courts was originally created by statute, but by the exercise of royal prerogative.[75] This 'inherent jurisdiction' of superior courts survived the eventual statutory creation of those courts, which occurred in England with the passing of the Supreme Court of Judicature Acts in 1873 and 1875.[76] In contrast, the jurisdiction of inferior courts is considered to be limited to that conferred on them by their founding statutes.

According to another view, all courts—whether superior or inferior—endowed with a particular jurisdiction have those powers which are necessary to enable them to act effectively. Those espousing this view regard courts as having inherent powers, to use the words of Lord Morris, 'in order to enforce [their] rules of practice and to suppress any abuses of [their] process'.[77] This asserted functional justification would appear to be supported by Sir Jack Jacob, but only in the case of superior courts. Although it is unnecessary for present purposes completely to resolve the conceptual debate between these competing positions, it is noteworthy that the latter view appears more accurately to reflect the reality; many inferior courts have asserted inherent powers,[78] and those superior courts that assert inherent powers do not justify their exercise of such powers on the basis of their status as 'superior courts'.

Before turning to the practice of international courts concerning inherent powers, it should be observed that certain theoretical objections have been made to the exercise of inherent powers by international courts. These objections are based on the fundamental differences that exist between the functions of national courts and international courts. Admittedly, there are dangers in importing concepts from domestic legal

[73] Jacob (n 57 above) 27–8.

[74] W Blackstone, *Commentaries on the Laws of England* (first published 1765, S Katz (ed), 1979) vol I, 257; Pushaw (n 57 above) 800.

[75] Blackstone (n 74 above) vol I, 257; Pushaw (n 57 above) 800–6.

[76] Supreme Court of Judicature Act 1873 (Eng) 36–7 Vic c 66, s 16; Supreme Court of Judicature Act 1875 (Eng) 38–9 Vic c 77.

[77] *Connelly v DPP* (n 59 above), 1301.

[78] eg Pushaw (n 57 above) 822, 850–67; C Plant (ed), *Blackstone's Civil Practice* (2003) 4; J Kovacevich, 'The Inherent Power of the District Court' [1989] *New Zealand Law Journal* 184, 185–6; *Langley v North West Water Authority* [1991] 1 WLR 697, 709; *Chambers v NASCO, Inc* 501 US 32, 43–51 (1991); *R v Saville* [1981] 1 QB 12, 17–18; *Jackson v Sterling Industries Ltd* paras 47, 53–54 (unreported, Federal Court of Australia, 15 October 1986); *R v Moke and Lawrence* (n 65 above).

systems into international law, where those concepts might not be relevant. Sir Hersch Lauterpacht warned of these dangers in 1927, when he criticized:

> ... the tendency on the part of many writers to resort to notions peculiar to their own municipal law or to some other system of private law regardless of the fact that conceptions of that kind cannot, owing to their technical character or the altogether special reason of their creation, claim that degree of cogency which is conditioned by the actual universality of a legal rule, from the point of view either of juridical logic or of legal justice, and which alone may serve as a basis of analogy.[79]

These words of caution have been repeated by Professor Thirlway with specific reference to the argument that the ICJ can exercise inherent powers in the context of the power to grant binding provisional measures. He referred to: 'the dangers of attributing to an international tribunal such as the Court inherent powers traced on the basis of municipal analogies. It needs to be recalled once more that the essence of jurisdiction is consent: if the Statute expresses the consent of States to a limited power to indicate provisional measures, it is self-contradictory to argue that, by creating a *court*, they implicitly consented to a wider power.'[80] Mindful of these warnings, the validity of the objections to the exercise of inherent powers by international courts is examined in the following section.

B. Arguments against the exercise of inherent powers by international courts

1. The existence of inherent powers depends on unlimited compulsory jurisdiction

The first objection to the exercise of inherent powers by international courts relates to the absence of unlimited compulsory jurisdiction in international dispute settlement. In contrast to the national courts which exercise inherent powers, international courts do not have unlimited compulsory jurisdiction derived from a sovereign prerogative. As Dr Orakhelashvili explains: 'National courts are established by the law and possess *ipso facto* compulsory jurisdiction within the ambit of their subject-matter competence. International tribunals, on the other hand, are established by international agreements and their jurisdiction is based on the consent of States.'[81] In the light of these differences, the objection might be made that international courts cannot exercise inherent powers.

This can, however, be rejected. National courts which assert the existence of inherent powers only rarely justify such powers by reference to

[79] Lauterpacht, *Private Law Sources and Analogies* (n 50 above) 84–5.

[80] Thirlway, 'The Law and Procedure of the International Court of Justice 1960–1989: Part Nine' (n 4 above) 21 (emphasis in original); see also Rosenne, *Law and Practice* (n 11 above) 528–9.

[81] Orakhelashvili, 'The Concept of International Judicial Jurisdiction' (n 11 above) 504–5.

unlimited jurisdictional powers derived from a Sovereign. Rather, they generally state that these powers are necessary for the fulfilment of their functions and the administration of justice.[82] In addition, not only superior courts have exercised powers other than those conferred on them, but statutory courts—being courts with limited jurisdiction—have also done so.[83] Furthermore, the fact that judges on international courts are not acting in pursuance of a sovereign grant of unlimited jurisdiction need not deprive them of powers needed to ensure the fulfilment of their functions. Once the states parties to the dispute have consented to the creation of the international court and the referral of the dispute to that body, it is then up to that body to decide how it is to fulfil its functions; in this sense, the method of creation of a particular jurisdiction does not necessarily explain the legal effects of that jurisdiction.[84]

2. International courts can only exercise expressly conferred powers

The second objection that can be made to the exercise of inherent powers by international courts is related to the first; this objection is that the international instruments that establish international courts are constitutive of their powers; and accordingly, such courts can only exercise those powers which are expressly conferred by the consent of states. This objection is exemplified in the following statement by Professor Thirlway:

> When jurisdiction is referred to, it must always be asked, 'jurisdiction to do what?'. Jurisdiction or competence is not, in the sense in which those terms are used in relation to a dispute, a general property vested in the court or tribunal contemplated: it is the power, conferred by the consent of the parties, to make a determination on specified disputed issues which will be binding on the parties because that is what they have consented to.[85]

The view that the statutes of international courts are constitutive of their powers reflects the 'doctrine of attribution', as it is known in the context of the law of international organizations, and according to which institutions can only work on the basis of powers specifically attributed to them.[86] The *locus classicus* of this doctrine can be found in an advisory opinion of the PCIJ, *Jurisdiction of the European Commission of the Danube*: 'As the European Commission is not a state, but an international institution with a special purpose, it only has the functions bestowed upon it by the Definitive Statute with a view to the fulfilment of that

[82] eg *R v Moke and Lawrence* (n 65 above), 266–7; *Connelly v DPP* (n 59 above), 1301.

[83] See n 78 above.

[84] See esp Orakhelashvili, 'The Concept of International Judicial Jurisdiction' (n 11 above) 505, who argues that the distinction between national courts and international courts is, in a practical sense, 'merely descriptive rather than prescriptive. It clarifies only the different ways in which national and international jurisdictions came into being. But it is unable to explain the nature of a jurisdiction as such, in particular its legal effects'.

[85] Thirlway, 'The Law and Procedure of the International Court of Justice: 1960–1989: Part Nine' (n 4 above) 6.

[86] J Klabbers, *An Introduction to International Institutional Law* (2001) 64.

purpose, but it has power to exercise these functions to their full extent, in so far as the Statute does not impose restrictions upon it.'[87] In the early twentieth century, this doctrine accorded with the prevailing positivist mode of thinking in international law.[88] It also received judicial support in the famous dictum of the PCIJ in *SS Lotus*, where it said that restrictions on the independence of states were not to be presumed.[89] In accordance with this dictum, the powers of international organizations are to be interpreted restrictively.[90]

The argument that the powers of international courts are strictly limited to those that are expressly conferred upon them is reflected in the Opinion of the German Commissioner, Herr Kiesselbach, in the *Sabotage Claims* before the US-German Mixed Claims Commission.[91] There, he argued that the power in question in that case, being the power to reopen a decision, was not a power inherent in the Mixed Claims Commission 'but a power inherent in the sovereignty *of a State* to establish such right and to authorise a court to do so under the conditions and modalities the sovereign thinks fit. *Without such authorisation no court neither in the United States nor anywhere else has a right to reopen.* And no international court can claim such right but by the authority from those powers which called it into life.'[92] Commissioner Kiesselbach showed great resistance to the concept of inherent powers generally: 'To show that a court has a certain power means ... the obligation to show that such power was transferred to it ... such transfer could be made either by act creating the courts, transferring thereby a specific right to a court as such or by a special act of legislation.'[93]

More recently, the argument that the powers of an institution established by an international treaty were limited to those expressly conferred upon it was put by Advocate-General Warner in a case before the ECJ concerning the European Commission's power to order provisional measures: 'A body that is created by a legal instrument does not have "inherent" powers. It has only the powers that are conferred on it by that instrument, either expressly or by necessary implication.'[94]

This objection can likewise be rejected for two reasons. First, it has been observed that the constitutive instruments of international courts

[87] *Jurisdiction of the European Commission of the Danube between Galatz and Braila*, PCIJ Rep Series B No 14 (1927) 64.

[88] Klabbers (n 86 above) 64.

[89] PCIJ Rep Series A No 10 (1927) 18–19.

[90] See eg Klabbers (n 86 above) 78–80; G Schwarzenberger, *International Law as Applied by International Courts and Tribunals* (1976) vol III, 52: 'If parties to an agreement establishing an international institution intend to grant any particular powers to the institution, they may be expected to define these powers in articulate language. If they fail to do so, the presumption must be in favour of the freedom of member states' (references omitted); H Kelsen, *The Law of the United Nations* (1950) 329–30.

[91] *Lehigh Valley Railroad Company (US) v Germany* 8 RIAA 160 (US-German MCC, 1933) ('*Sabotage Claims*').

[92] 8 RIAA 160, 170 (US-German MCC, 1933) (Op Comm Kiesselbach) (emphasis in original).

[93] ibid (Op Comm Kiesselbach).

[94] Case No 792/79R *Camera Care Ltd v Commission* [1980] ECRI-119, 135 (Op A-G Warner).

often contain *lacunae*; some constitutive instruments may make provision for a given situation, while others are silent. As Professor Crawford has argued, just because the constitutive instrument of one international court contains an express power where another does not, this 'should not be used to justify, *a contrario*, a failure to develop necessary or desirable rules of general international law'.[95] Second, the view that international courts can only exercise those powers which are expressly conferred on them is not borne out by substantial judicial and arbitral practice, including the decisions ultimately reached in the *Sabotage Claims* and the *Camera Care* case referred to above. It is to examples of the practice of international courts and tribunals that this article now turns.

III. Inherent Powers in the Practice of International Courts

Inherent powers have been asserted in the case law of many international courts. The ICJ discussed the nature of its inherent powers most extensively in *Nuclear Tests*, in which it held that:

> ... it should be emphasised that the Court possesses an inherent jurisdiction enabling it to take such action as may be required, on the one hand, to ensure that the exercise of its jurisdiction over the merits, if and when established, shall not be frustrated, and on the other, to provide for the orderly settlement of all matters in dispute, to ensure the observance of the 'inherent limitations on the exercise of the judicial function' of the Court, and to 'maintain its judicial character' ... Such inherent jurisdiction, on the basis of which the Court is fully empowered to make whatever findings may be necessary for the purposes just indicated, derives from the mere existence of the Court as a judicial organ established by the consent of states, and is conferred upon it in order that its basic judicial functions may be safeguarded.[96]

Here, the ICJ was arguably continuing the theme which was considered by Sir Gerald Fitzmaurice in his separate opinion in *Northern Cameroons*.[97] There, he observed that the substantive jurisdiction of an international court, being its jurisdiction to hear and determine the merits, was distinct from its incidental or inherent jurisdiction over procedural issues:

> But also, there is the Court's *preliminary* or 'incidental' jurisdiction (eg to decree interim measures of protection, admit counterclaims or third party interventions, etc) which it can exercise even in advance of any determination of its basic jurisdiction as to the ultimate merits; even though the latter is challenged; and even though it may ultimately turn out that the Court lacks jurisdiction as to the ultimate merits. Although much (though not all) of this incidental jurisdiction is

[95] J Crawford, 'International Law as an Open System' in J Crawford, *International Law as an Open System: Selected Essays* (2002) 17, 35.

[96] *Nuclear Tests (Australia v France)* [1974] ICJ Rep 253, 259–60 (references omitted); see also *Nuclear Tests (New Zealand v France)* [1974] ICJ Rep 457, 463 (references omitted).

[97] *Northern Cameroons (Cameroons v UK)* [1963] ICJ Rep 15.

specifically provided for in the Court's Statute, or in Rules of Court which the Statute empowers the Court to make, it is really an inherent jurisdiction, the power to exercise which is a necessary condition of the Court—or any court of law—being able to function at all.[98]

In pursuance of their 'inherent jurisdiction', international courts have on many occasions exercised powers not expressly conferred on them. In addition, international courts have exercised powers which are expressly conferred on them, but have noted that in doing so, they are exercising inherent powers, lending weight to the suggestion of Sir Gerald Fitzmaurice in the *Northern Cameroons* case that such provisions really do no more than declare the existence of powers which international courts already possess.[99] In this sense, the constitutive instruments and rules may be regarded as *declaratory* of an international court's powers, rather than *constitutive*.

Perhaps the most well-known example of an inherent power is the *compétence de la compétence*, or the power of international courts to determine the extent of their own jurisdiction. International tribunals have from the earliest days of modern international arbitration found that they have this power. For instance, the two American-appointed commissioners in the *Betsey* case, an arbitration under Article VII of the Jay Treaty of 1794,[100] filed separate opinions in which they defended the power of the right of the majority of the Commission to determine its jurisdiction, even though that power was not expressly provided for in the Jay Treaty.[101] Commissioner Gore observed that: 'A power to decide whether a Claim preferred to this board is within its Jurisdiction, appears to me inherent in its very Constitution, and indispensably necessary to the discharge of any of its duties.'[102] The *Betsey* case does not represent clear authority for the existence of the power, as the question of jurisdiction

[98] [1963] ICJ Rep 15, 97, 103 (Sep Op Sir Gerald Fitzmaurice) (references omitted). For a criticism of this view, see Thirlway, 'The Law and Procedure of the International Court of Justice 1960–1989: Part Nine' (n 4 above) 41–2.

[99] See eg Gaeta (n 11 above) 356; Orakhelashvili, 'The Concept of International Judicial Jurisdiction' (n 11 above) 538–49; see also discussion in Thirlway, 'The Law and Procedure of the International Court of Justice 1960–1989: Part Ten' (n 11 above) 2–5; Thirlway, 'The Law and Procedure of the International Court of Justice 1960–1989: Part Nine' (n 4 above) 18–19, 65; Fitzmaurice, *Law and Procedure* (n 11 above) 451–7; Rosenne, *Law and Practice* (n 11 above) 600, 846–52; Lauterpacht, '"Partial" Judgments' (n 11 above) 477; I Shihata, *The Power of the International Court to Determine Its Own Jurisdiction* (1965) 47–56; Simpson and Fox (n 19 above) 68–72; Scelle, 'Draft on Arbitral Procedure' (n 19 above) 8; G Scelle, 'Arbitral Procedure' [1950] *Yearbook of the International Law Commission*, vol II, 114, 136, UN Doc A/CN.4/18; K Carlston, *Process of International Arbitration* (1946) 74–81; J Ralston, *Supplement to 1926 Revised Edition of The Law and Procedure of International Tribunals* (1936) 29; J Ralston, *The Law and Procedure of International Tribunals* (revised edn, 1926) 44–8.

[100] Treaty of Amity, Commerce and Navigation, signed 19 November 1794 (GB-US), 12 Bevans 13 (entered into force 28 October 1795) ('Jay Treaty').

[101] See eg the account in J Bassett Moore, *History and Digest of the International Arbitrations to which the United States has been a Party* (1898) (hereinafter referred to as 'Moore') vol III, 2277–91 (Op Comm Gore), 2291–303 (Op Comm Pinkney).

[102] Moore (n 101 above), vol III, 2278, 2278.

was ultimately referred to the respective governments. According to the account of John Bassett Moore, Lord Chancellor Loughborough replied that 'the doubt respecting the authority of the commissioners to settle their own jurisdiction, was absurd; and that they must necessarily decide upon cases being within, or without, their competency'.[103]

In 1872, the *Alabama Arbitrations*, conducted under the Treaty of Washington,[104] also provided some support for the existence of this power. In the course of the Commission's work, a dispute arose as to whether the Commission had the power to determine claims for indirect loss.[105] This caused a stalemate, and eventually, the United States and Great Britain agreed to permit the arbitrators to decide the question, albeit on the understanding that 'any expression on the subject would not be binding upon either of the two governments unless assented to by both'.[106] While the parties ultimately accepted the Commission's decision, the Commission's award does not provide unequivocal authority for the *compétence de la compétence*.[107] Nevertheless, the principle found its way into the Institut de Droit International's 1875 'Projet de réglement pour la procédure arbitrale internationale',[108] and the drafters of the 1899 Convention conferred the power on arbitral tribunals constituted under its auspices.[109]

Subsequent arbitral awards and judicial decisions provided clearer authority for the existence of the power. In *Rio Grande Irrigation and Land Company*, for instance, the arbitral tribunal held that 'there is inherent in this and in every legal Tribunal a power, and indeed a duty, to entertain, and, in proper cases, to raise for themselves, preliminary points going to their jurisdiction to entertain the claim. Such a power is inseparable from and indispensable to the proper conduct of business ... In our opinion, this power can only be taken away by a provision framed for that express purpose'.[110]

In its advisory opinion in *Interpretation of the Greco-Turkish Agreement*, the PCIJ considered the *compétence de la compétence* to be inherent in any body possessing jurisdictional powers: 'it is clear—having regard amongst other things to the principle that, as a general rule, any body possessing jurisdictional powers has the right in the first place itself to determine the extent of its jurisdiction—that questions affecting the extent of the jurisdiction of the Mixed Commission must be settled by the Commission itself without action by any other body being

[103] Moore (n 101 above), vol I, 327; see also Cheng (n 43 above) 276; Fitzmaurice, *Law and Procedure* (n 11 above) 454.

[104] Treaty of Washington, signed 8 May 1871, (GB-US), 61 British Foreign and State Papers 40, 12 Bevans 170 (entered into force 17 June 1871).

[105] Moore (n 101 above), vol I, 624–46; Shihata (n 99 above) 17.

[106] Moore (n 101 above), vol I, 644.

[107] Shihata (n 99 above) 18–19; see also the doubts raised in M Shahabuddeen, *Precedent in the World Court* (1996) 36; cf Sir G Fitzmaurice, 'The Law and Procedure of the International Court of Justice, 1951–4: Questions of Jurisdiction, Competence and Procedure' (1958) 34 BYIL 1, 26.

[108] Institut de Droit International, 'Projet de réglement pour la procédure arbitrale internationale' (1877) 1 *Annuaire de l'Institut de Droit International* 126, art 14.

[109] 1899 Convention, Art 48.

[110] 6 RIAA 131, 135–6 (UK-US, 1923).

necessary'.[111] The ICJ confirmed the inherent nature of the power in *Nottebohm*, where it stated that 'an international tribunal has the right to decide as to its own jurisdiction and has the power to interpret for this purpose the instruments which govern that jurisdiction'.[112] The ICJ further held that although the ICJ Statute provided in Article 36(6) for this power, it possessed the power as an inherent power; this was because Article 36(6) of the Statute merely adopted 'a rule consistently accepted by general international law in the matter of international arbitration'.[113] It held that: 'Since the *Alabama* case, it has been generally recognised, following the earlier precedents, that, in the absence of any agreement to the contrary, an international tribunal has the right to decide as to its own jurisdiction and has the power to interpret for this purpose the instruments which govern that jurisdiction.'[114] The ICJ explained that the Rapporteur to the 1899 Convention had 'emphasised the necessity of this principle, presented by him as being "of the very essence of the arbitral function and one of the inherent requirements for the exercise of this function"'.[115] The ICJ concluded that: 'The judicial character of the Court and the rule of general international law referred to above are sufficient to establish that the court is competent to adjudicate on its own jurisdiction in the present case.'[116] In another case, the ICJ has held that other international tribunals also have this power; in *Arbitral Award of 31 July 1989*, the ICJ held that 'Article 4, paragraph 2, of the Arbitration Agreement *confirmed* that the Tribunal had power to determine its own jurisdiction.'[117] And most recently, in *Legality of Use of Force*, the ICJ described its *compétence de la compétence* as being '*reflected* in Article 36, paragraph 6 of the Statute',[118] rather than being '*conferred*' by that provision.

The *compétence de la compétence* has been recognized in the jurisprudence of many other international courts. In *US—Anti-Dumping Act of 1916*, the WTO Appellate Body referred to the 'widely accepted rule that an international tribunal is entitled to consider the issue of its own jurisdiction on its own initiative, and to satisfy itself that it has jurisdiction in any case that comes before it'.[119] The WTO Appellate Body reaffirmed its

[111] *Interpretation of the Greco-Turkish Agreement* PCIJ Rep, Series B No 16 (1928) 20.

[112] [1953] ICJ Rep 111, 119–20; on this point, see also *Norwegian Loans (France v Norway)* [1957] ICJ Rep 9, 34, 44 (Sep Op Sir Hersch Lauterpacht).

[113] [1953] ICJ Rep 111, 119.

[114] ibid; cf the doubt expressed at nn 104–107 above and accompanying text concerning whether the *Alabama Arbitrations* actually provide clear authority for this proposition.

[115] [1953] ICJ Rep 111, 119.

[116] ibid, 120.

[117] *Arbitral Award of 31 July 1989 (Guinea-Bissau v Senegal)* [1991] ICJ Rep 53, 69 (emphasis added); Thirlway, 'The Law and Procedure of the International Court of Justice 1960–1989: Part Nine' (n 4 above) 19.

[118] (2005) 44 ILM 299, 312, para 34 (emphasis added).

[119] *US—Anti-Dumping Act of 1916* WT/DS136/AB/R, para 54, n 30 (ABR); see also *Mexico—Corn Syrup (Article 21(5))*, WT/DS132/ABR/RW, paras 35–37 (ABR); J Pauwelyn, *Conflict of Norms in Public International Law* (2003) 448–9; J Pauwelyn, 'The Role of Public International Law in the WTO: How Far Can We Go?' (2001) 95 AJIL 535, 555–6.

right to exercise this power in *Mexico—Taxes on Soft Drinks*.[120] The IACHR confirmed its power to determine its own jurisdiction in *Ivcher Bronstein* and *Constitutional Court*, where it held that: 'The Inter-American Court, as with any court or tribunal, has the inherent authority to determine the scope of its own competence.'[121] It has also been confirmed in jurisprudence of the Iran-United States Claims Tribunal ('Ir-USCT'),[122] an ICSID tribunal,[123] the ICTY,[124] and in the separate opinion of a judge of the ITLOS.[125]

International courts have also exercised many other procedural powers as inherent powers. One such power is the power to frame rules of procedure and to make procedural orders. Although most international courts have the express power to frame such rules, the power to make rules of procedure and procedural orders can be regarded as a necessary incident of their judicial functions, so long as they are not inconsistent with the court's constitutive instrument. As Shabtai Rosenne suggests, 'the Court possesses inherent jurisdiction to control all aspects of the proceedings themselves'.[126] This has been expressly recognized by Judge Shahabuddeen of the ICTR Appeals Chamber, who held in the *Kanyabashi* case that 'a judicial body, whether civil or criminal', possessed 'the inherent competence ... to regulate its own procedure in the event of silence in the written rules, so as to assure the exercise of such jurisdiction as it has, and to fulfil itself, properly and effectively, as a court of law. Without that residual competence, no court can function completely'.[127] Similarly, the NAFTA tribunal in *United Parcel Services of America, Inc v Canada* observed that Article 15(1) of the UNCITRAL Rules, which confers the power on the tribunal to 'conduct the arbitration in such a manner as it considers appropriate', was 'essential to the very process of dispute settlement by way of arbitration and might be thought to be inherent even if not expressly stated'.[128]

120 *Mexico—Taxes on Soft Drinks* WT/DS308/AB/R, para 45 (ABR).

121 *Ivcher Bronstein v Peru* Series C No 54 paras 31–33 (IACHR, 24 September 1999); *Constitutional Court* Series C No 55, paras 31–33 (IACHR, 24 September 1999); Gaeta (n 11 above) 356.

122 *Marks & Umann v Iran* 8 Ir-USCTR 290, 296–7 (1985).

123 *Klöckner v Cameroon (Annulment)*, 114 ILR 243, 251–2 (1985).

124 *Prosecutor v Dusko Tadic* (1996) 35 ILM 32, 40.

125 *M/V Saiga (No 2)* 120 ILR 143, 239, 241 (Sep Op Judge Nelson) (ITLOS, 1999).

126 Rosenne, *Law and Practice* (n 11 above) 602; see also Sir A Watts, 'New Practice Directions of the International Court of Justice' (2002) 1 *Law and Practice of International Courts and Tribunals* 247, 255; Sir A Watts, 'Burden of Proof, and Evidence before the ICJ' in F Weiss (ed), *Improving WTO Dispute Settlement Procedures: Issues and Lessons from the Practice of Other International Courts and Tribunals* (2000) 289, 289; Scelle, 'Draft on Arbitral Procedure' (n 19 above) 8–9, art 13; M Hudson, *International Tribunals: Past and Future* (1944) 86; Ralston, *The Law and Procedure of International Tribunals* (n 99 above) 197; Institut de Droit International (n 108 above) art 15(1), (2), (4).

127 *Kanyabashi v Prosecutor (Decision on the Defence Motion for Interlocutory Appeal)*, (ICTR App Ch, 3 June 1999) 17 (Diss Op Judge Shahabuddeen) (references omitted); Gaeta (n 11 above) 358.

128 *United Parcel Services of America, Inc v Canada* (*Amici Curiae*) para 38 (NAFTA, 17 October 2001).

Many examples can be found where international tribunals have supplemented the powers conferred by their statutes by devising procedures or including provisions in the rules of procedure. These include the power to rule on counterclaims;[129] the power to reformulate the submissions of the applicants;[130] the exercise of 'judicial economy', in refraining to rule on certain claims if it is not necessary to do so to resolve the issues in dispute;[131] the creation of a special procedure as a means of maintaining jurisdiction over a dispute;[132] the power to make site visits;[133] the power to order the preparation of an independent expert report;[134] the power to issue practice directions, as several international courts have done in recent years, including the ICJ, the ICTY, the ICTR, the ECHR and the ECJ;[135] and the power to hear preliminary objections regarding the court's jurisdiction and admissibility separately from the merits. The PCIJ's dictum in *Mavrommatis Palestine Concessions* on this last question aptly describes the powers of international courts to make decisions over procedural issues that are not expressly provided for:

Neither the Statute nor the Rules of Court contain any rule regarding the procedure to be followed in the event of an objection being taken *in limine litis*

[129] PCIJ Rules (1922), art 40; see also the current ICJ Rules (2001), art 80; S Rosenne, *Procedure in the International Court* (1983) 171–2; CW Jenks, *The Prospects of International Adjudication* (1964) 135–6; C de Visscher, *Aspects Récent du Droit Procédural de la Cour Internationale de Justice* (1966) 113–16.

[130] eg *Nuclear Tests (Australia v France)* [1974] ICJ Rep 253, 271–2; where the ICJ reformulated the relief sought by Australia as the cessation of French atmospheric nuclear testing, rather than a declaration that such testing was unlawful: see eg Thirlway, 'The Law and Procedure of the International Court of Justice 1960–1989: Part Nine' (n 11 above) 18–19. The ICJ's decision to dismiss the Applications is very controversial: see eg *Nuclear Tests* [1974] ICJ Rep 253, 312 (Joint Diss Op Judges Onyeama, Dillard, Jimenez de Aréchaga and Sir Humphrey Waldock); FA Mann, 'The Consequences of an International Wrong in International and National Law' (1976–7) 48 BYIL 1, 10–11. The IACHR has also asserted this power: see *Enforceability of the Right to Reply or Correction*, Series A No 7, para 12 (IACHR, 1986), reprinted in (1986) 7 *Human Rights Law Journal* 238; see also *The Right to Information on Consular Assistance in the Framework of the Guarantees of Due Process of Law* Series A No 16, para 42 (IACHR, 2000), reprinted in (2000) 21 *Human Rights Law Journal* 24.

[131] *Mexico—Taxes on Soft Drinks* WT/DS308/AB/R, para 45 (ABR).

[132] *Request for an Examination (New Zealand v France)* [1995] ICJ Rep 288; see 317, 320 (Diss Op Judge Weeramantry); see also Gaeta (n 11 above) 365, n 31, 367, n 34.

[133] *Diversion of Water from the Meuse (Netherlands v Belgium)* PCIJ Rep Series A/B No 70, (1937) 9, where the PCIJ arguably exercised an inherent power to visit the site; see now ICJ Rules, art 66; see also the site visits undertaken in *Palena* 38 ILR 10, 17, 27–8, 55–8 (Arg-Chile, 1966); *Beagle Channel* 52 ILR 93, 115–16 (Arg-Chile, 1977); *Dispute Concerning the Course of the Frontier between Boundary Post 62 and Mount Fitzroy* 113 ILR 1, 25–6 (Arg-Chile, 1994); UN Compensation Commission, 'Report and Recommendations made by the Panel of Commissioners Concerning the Fifth Instalment of "F4" Claims', paras 87–89, UN Doc S/AC.26/2005/10 (30 June 2005).

[134] See eg *Lighthouses Arbitration* 12 RIAA 155, 228–9, 245, 256–7 (Gr-Fr 1956); see also *Benvenuti and Bonfant SRL v Congo* 67 ILR 345, 358, 376 (1980); *SOABI v Senegal* (Award), 2 ICSID Rep 190, 265–6 (1988); *LETCO v Liberia* 89 ILR 313, 318 (1986); *AMT v Zaïre* (1997) 36 ILM 1531, 1554. See also the comments of Judge Anzilotti, PCIJ Series D No 2, 3rd Add, 247 (1936); and G White, *The Use of Experts by International Tribunals* (1965) 41–2, 73–82.

[135] See eg P Couvreur, 'L'organisation et les moyens des juridictions internationales face au contentieux international' in Société Française pour le Droit International, *Colloque de Lille: La juridictionnalisation du droit international* (2003) 467, 506; ICJ Practice Directions of 31 October 2001, 4 April 2002: (2002) 41 ILM 998, and 30 July 2004 (12 in total); ICTY Practice Directions of 9 July 1998, 18 December 1998 (revised on 4 May 2001, and on 24 January 2002), 7 April 1999, 1 October

to the Court's jurisdiction. The Court therefore is at liberty to adopt the principle which it considers best calculated to ensure the administration of justice, most suited to procedure before an international tribunal and most in conformity with the fundamental principles of international law.[136]

Relatedly, international tribunals have held that they are masters of their procedure even in instances where the parties prefer the adoption of another method of handling the case. In *Larsen/Hawaiian Kingdom* the parties concluded a revised *compromis*, in which they requested the PCA tribunal to verify 'the continued existence of Hawaiian Statehood' in an interlocutory award. The PCA tribunal refused to accede to this request, holding that: 'It is not open to the parties by way of an Amendment to the Special Agreement to seek to redefine the essential issues, so as to convert them into "interim" or "interlocutory" issues. In accordance with Article 32 of the UNCITRAL Rules, and with the general principles of arbitral procedure, it is for the Tribunal to determine which issues need to be dealt with and in what order.'[137]

Other procedural powers exercised by international courts in the course of judicial proceedings have been asserted as inherent powers, such as the power to grant provisional measures. The ICJ has not made a judicial pronouncement on this question, although it has certainly been put in argument before the Court.[138] Individual judges have, however, stated that the power to grant provisional measures, which is conferred by Article 41 of the ICJ Statute, exists as an inherent power.[139] Other

1999 (revised on 7 March 2002, on 21 February 2005, and again on 16 September 2005), 12 July 2000, 19 January 2001 (revised on 5 March 2002, and on 16 September 2005), 20 July 2001, 7 March 2002, 6 May 2004, and 14 November 2005 (10 in total); ICTR Practice Directions of 16 September 2002 and 4 July 2005 (4 in total); ECHR Practice Directions of 5 March 2003 and 1 November 2003 (3 in total), based on ECHR Rules, Rule 32; and eg ECJ Practice Directions of 15 October 2004: [2004] OJ L361/15. See further Watts, 'New Practice Directions of the International Court of Justice' (n 126 above) 248; S Rosenne, 'International Court of Justice: Practice Directions on Judges Ad Hoc; Agents; Counsel and Advocates; and Submission of New Documents' (2002) 1 *Law and Practice of International Courts and Tribunals* 223, 223; Judge R Higgins, 'Respecting Sovereign States and Running a Tight Courtroom' (2001) 50 ICLQ 121, 124; and also, more generally, S Rosenne, 'Controlling Interlocutory Aspects of Proceedings in the International Court of Justice' (2000) 94 AJIL 307.

[136] *Mavrommatis Palestine Concessions (Greece v UK)* PCIJ Rep Series A No 2 (1924) 1, 16. The PCIJ later adopted a provision in its Rules to regulate preliminary objections: PCIJ Rules, art 26 (1926); D Prager, 'The 2001 Amendments to the Rules of Procedure of the International Court of Justice' (2002) 1 *Law and Practice of International Courts and Tribunals* 155, 158–9; *Aerial Incident of 3 July 1988 (Iran v US)* [1989] ICJ Rep 132, 145, 146–9 (Sep Op Judge Shahabuddeen). This practice has been followed by WTO panels: see eg *Guatemala—Cement II*, DSR 2000-XI, 5295, 5638 (PR).

[137] 119 ILR 566, 579–80 (2001).

[138] See esp *Legal Status of the South-Eastern Territory of Greenland* PCIJ Series C No 69 (1932) 32; *Legal Status of the South-Eastern Territory of Greenland (Norway v Denmark)* PCIJ Rep Series A/B No 48, (1932) 281; *Aegean Sea (Greece v Turkey)* [1980] ICJ Pleadings 88, 99, 100–4; J Sztucki, *Interim Measures in the Hague Court* (1983) 62.

[139] See eg *Northern Cameroons* [1963] ICJ Rep 15, 97, 103 (Sep Op Sir Gerald Fitzmaurice); see also *Nuclear Tests (Australia v France)* [1973] ICJ Rep 99, 108, 109 (Declaration of Judge Nagendra Singh); *Nuclear Tests (New Zealand v France)* [1973] ICJ Rep 135, 145 (Declaration of Judge Nagendra Singh); *Lockerbie (Libya v UK)* [1992] ICJ Rep 3, 50, 70 (Diss Op Judge Weeramantry); *Lockerbie (Libya v UK)* [1992] ICJ Rep 3, 78, 88–90 (Diss Op Judge Ajibola); *Lockerbie (Libya v US)* [1992] ICJ Rep 114, 160, 180–1 (Diss Op Judge Weeramantry); *Lockerbie (Libya v US)* [1992]

international courts and tribunals have also given judicial support for this proposition. One notable example is provided in the jurisprudence of the Iran-United States Claims Tribunal. The Ir-USCT has the power, under Article 26 of its Rules of Procedure, to grant provisional measures. In *E-Systems, Inc v Iran*, however, it held that it also has 'an inherent power ... to conserve the respective rights of the parties and to ensure that this Tribunal's jurisdiction and authority are made fully effective'.[140] Another recent example can be found in the practice of the IACHR, which has referred to the existence of an inherent power to grant provisional measures. In the *Velásquez Rodríguez* case it relied on: 'Articles 63(2), 33 and 62(3) of the American Convention on Human Rights, Articles 1 and 2 of the Statute of the Court and Article 23 of the Rules of Procedure and its character as a judicial body and the powers which derive therefrom.'[141] Further, the ECJ held in *Camera Care*, referred to above,[142] that a non-judicial body, the European Commission, had the power to grant interim relief, even though the EC Treaty and the relevant EC Regulation did not expressly confer such a power on the Commission.[143] In addition to these examples, instances can be found in early international judicial practice where international courts have granted provisional measures even though they lacked an express power to do so.[144]

Many international courts have recognized that they also possess inherent powers which relate to the post-adjudication phase, such as the powers of rectification, interpretation, and revision. With regard to the power of rectification, the ICJ has held that: 'The Court does of course have the power to correct, in one of its judgments, any mistakes which might be described as "erreurs matérielles".'[145] The Court of Arbitration

ICJ Rep 114, 183, 193–5 (Diss Op Judge Ajibola); *Application of the Genocide Convention (Bosnia and Herzegovina v Yugoslavia)* [1993] ICJ Rep 325, 370, 379 (Sep Op Judge Weeramantry); *Application of the Genocide Convention (Bosnia and Herzegovina v Yugoslavia)* [1993] ICJ Rep 325, 390, 397 (Sep Op Judge Ajibola).

[140] *E-Systems, Inc v Iran* 2 Ir-USCTR 51, 57 (1983); *Rockwell International Systems, Inc v Iran* 2 Ir-USCTR 310, 311 (1983); *Ford Aerospace and Communications Corporation v Air Force of Iran* 6 Ir-USCTR 104, 108–9 (1984); C Brower and J Brueschke, *The Iran-United States Claims Tribunal* (1998) 217.

[141] *Velásquez Rodríguez* (1989) 28 ILM 291, 302; J Pasqualucci, *The Practice and Procedure of the Inter-American Court of Human Rights* (2003) 298–300; Judge T Buergenthal, 'Interim Measures in the Inter-American Court of Human Rights' in R Bernhardt (ed), *Interim Measures Indicated by International Courts* (1994) 69, 83–4.

[142] See n 94 above and accompanying text.

[143] [1980] ECR-I 119, 131.

[144] eg *Honduras/Nicaragua (Treaty of Corinto signed 20 January 1902)* [1902] *US Foreign Relations* 881, also in Martens, *Nouveau Recueil Général* (2nd series) vol 31, 241; see P Guggenheim, 'Les mesures conservatoires dans la procédure arbitrale et judiciaire' (1932) 40 *Recueil des cours* 645, 660–2; Dumbauld (n 19 above) 93–6; *Gramophone Co Ltd v Deutsche Grammophon AG* 1 TAM 857, 859 (Ang-Ger MAT, 1922); *Trail Smelter* 3 RIAA 1911, 1934–7 (US-Can, 1938); *Veerman v Germany* 25 ILR 522, 523 (1957); see also *Scheidt v Germany* 25 ILR 555 (1957); VS Mani, *International Adjudication: Procedural Aspects* (1980) 289; A Cocâtre-Zilgien, 'Les mesures conservatoires décidées par le juge ou par l'arbitre international' (1966) 70 *Revue Générale du Droit International Public* 5, 24–5; Sztucki (n 138 above) 63.

[145] *Continental Shelf (Revision and Interpretation) (Tunisia v Libya)* [1985] ICJ Rep 192, 198.

in *Delimitation of the Continental Shelf between the UK and the French Republic* (Interpretation) also found that it had the power to correct errors:

The power of a court to rectify such a discrepancy, where in the interests of good administration of justice it is necessary to correct a material error that appears on the face of its decision, is considered by the Court of Arbitration to be generally accepted.... The power of the Court to rectify the resulting error remains ... its inherent power to rectify a material error found to exist in its decision.[146]

As for the power of interpretation, some early arbitral practice can be cited to support the existence of the power as an inherent power. One example is the *Portendick* case, where the King of Prussia, who was acting as arbitrator, clarified aspects of his award by stating how he had understood his terms of reference.[147] The United Nations Administrative Tribunal ('UNAT') has also exercised the power in the absence of a provision in its Statute.[148] The ECHR has described its power to interpret its judgments, contained in its Rules of Court, as part of its 'inherent jurisdiction'. In *Ringeisen (Interpretation)*, the ECHR stated that: 'In considering the request, the Court is exercising inherent jurisdiction ... Rule 53 is limited to recognising this inherent jurisdiction and to settling the way in which it is to be exercised.'[149] A further example can be found in an award rendered by an ICC arbitral tribunal, which agreed that it had the power of interpretation, holding that: 'This power is based on the arbitral clause itself.'[150]

International courts and tribunals have also made judicial pronouncements supporting the inherent nature of the power of revision, being the power to revise a judgment or award in the light of newly discovered evidence which would have had a decisive effect on the judgment. The US-Mexican Claims Commission agreed to revise some awards to take account of newly discovered evidence, although its practice is relatively inconsistent.[151] Several other early arbitral tribunals rejected the argument that they had an inherent power to revise awards.[152] In the *Sabotage*

[146] 54 ILR 139, 174 (UK-France, 1978); see also *Heathrow Airport User Charges* 102 ILR 564, 571, 579 (US-UK, 1993).

[147] A Lapradelle and N Politis (eds), *Recueil des arbitrages internationaux* (1932) vol I, 512, 530–1 (UK-Fr, 1843); see further M Reisman, *Nullity and Revision* (1971) 193; JC Witenberg, *L'Organisation Judiciaire: La Procédure et la Sentence Internationales* (1937) 365.

[148] *Crawford* (1958) 1 UNAT 331, 335.

[149] *Ringeisen (Interpretation)* Series A, No 16, 8 (ECHR, 1972). The power of interpretation is now contained in Rule 79 of the ECHR Rules of Court. See also *Ringeisen (Interpretation)*, Series A, No 16, 10 (Sep Op Judge Verdross), 12 (Sep Op Judge Zeika); approved in *Allenet de Ribemont v France* ECHR Rep 1996-III, 903, 910; see also 912 (Sep Op Judge Pettiti).

[150] *Case No 6233* (1992), in J-J Arnaldez, Y Derains, and D Hascher, *Collection of ICC Arbitral Awards 1991–1995* (1997) 332, 334.

[151] *George Moore*, Moore (n 101 above), vol II, 1357, 1357 (US-Mex CC, 1871); *Shreck*, Moore (n 101 above), vol II, 1357, 1358 (US-Mex CC); *Green*, Moore (n 101 above), vol II, 1358 (US-Mex CC); cf *Weil* and *La Abra Silver Mining Co*, Moore (n 101 above), vol II, 1324, 1329 (US-Mex CC, 1876); see further Sandifer (n 43 above) 414–16.

[152] *US-Spain Arbitration*, Moore (n 101 above), vol III, 2190, 2192 (US-Spain, 1881); *Lazare*, Moore (n 101 above), vol II, 1749, 1793, 1801 (US-Haiti, 1886).

Claims, the US-German Mixed Claims Commission held that it had a power to revise its decisions in the light of the discovery of new facts, but only those where the new facts indicated that the decision had been induced by fraud.[153] It held that: 'No tribunal worthy its name or of any respect may allow its decision to stand if such allegations are well-founded. Every tribunal has inherent power to reopen and to revise a decision induced by fraud. If it may correct its own errors and mistakes, *a fortiori* it may, while it still has jurisdiction of a cause, correct errors into which it has been led by fraud and collusion.'[154] The arbitral tribunal in the *Trail Smelter* case took a more expansive view of its powers, holding that the convention under which it was constituted '[did] not deny it the power to grant a revision', apparently for any new facts, not just those suggesting fraud.[155]

The ICJ has also suggested that it considers international courts to have an inherent power of revision.[156] In *Effect of Awards of Compensation*, in which it considered the powers of the UNAT, the ICJ essentially recognized that despite the finality of its judgments, the UNAT had an inherent power of revision:

> The rule contained in Article 10, paragraph 2 [stating that judgments of the UNAT shall be final and without appeal], cannot however be considered as excluding the Tribunal from itself revising a judgment in special circumstances when new facts of decisive importance have been discovered; and the Tribunal has already exercised this power. Such a strictly limited revision by the Tribunal itself cannot be considered an 'appeal' within the meaning of that Article and would conform with rules generally provided in statutes or laws issued for courts of justice, such as article 61 of the Statute of the International Court of Justice.[157]

Another international tribunal which has considered this question is the Ir-USCT.[158] In *Ram International Industries, Inc v Air Force of Iran* the Ir-USCT thoroughly reviewed how this question has been addressed in the constitutive instruments of other international courts,[159] discussed the instances in which arbitral tribunals had exercised an inherent power of revision, and concluded that these decisions had 'been accepted as sound in legal studies and writings discussing the circumstances under which revision can be sought'.[160] It then expressed the cautious view that

[153] 8 RIAA 160 (US-Ger MCC, 1933).

[154] ibid, 190; see also A Verdross and B Simma, *Universelles Völkerrecht* (3rd edn, 1984) 898.

[155] 3 RIAA 1938, 1954 (US-Can, 1941).

[156] *Effect of Awards of Compensation* [1954] ICJ Rep 47, 51–3; see esp DW Bowett, '*Res Judicata* and the Limits of Rectification of Decisions by International Tribunals' (1996) 8 *African Journal of International and Comparative Law* 577, 590–1, n 45.

[157] [1954] ICJ Rep 47, 55.

[158] Brower and Brueschke (n 140 above) 242–60; S Baker and M Davis, *The UNCITRAL Arbitration Rules in Practice* (1992) 200–5; J van Hof, *Commentary on the UNCITRAL Arbitration Rules* (1991) 279–83; see eg *Morris v Iran* 3 Ir-USCTR 364, 365 (1983); *Dallal v Iran* 5 Ir-USCTR 74, 75 (1984); *Dames and Moore v Iran* 8 Ir-USCTR 107, 114, 117–18 (1985); *International Schools Services v Iran* 14 Ir-USCTR 65, 70–1 (1987).

[159] 29 Ir-USCTR 383, 387–9 (1993).

[160] ibid 389. The Tribunal referred to the writings of Sir E Lauterpacht, *Aspects of the Administration of International Justice* (1991) 100; Sandifer, (n 43 above) 426; Carlston (n 99 above) 57–8, 224–8, 232; Reisman (n 147 above) 208–12; and Simpson and Fox (n 19 above) 242.

'it might possibly be concluded that a tribunal ... which is to adjudicate a large group of cases for a protracted period of time would by implication, until the adjournment and dissolution of the tribunal, have the authority to revise decisions induced by fraud'.[161]

Perhaps the most unequivocal judicial pronouncement that the power to revise judgments in the light of newly discovered facts is an inherent power is that of the Inter-American Commission on Human Rights ('IACHR') in *Genie Lacayo (Judicial Review)*.[162] In this case, the IACHR had requested the 'judicial review' of an earlier judgment. The IACHR recognized that it did not have the power of revision under the American Convention, the IACHR Statute or its Rules, but held nonetheless that it deemed it 'opportune to hear the aforementioned application for revision filed by the Inter-American Commission inasmuch as it was submitted within a reasonable time and because "[t]he transparency of this Tribunal's proceedings is enhanced by clarification ... of the content and scope of its judgements".'[163] Referring to the practice of the ICJ and the ECHR, the IACHR discussed the power of revision using the language of inherent powers, holding that: 'As stipulated in the Statute of the International Court of Justice and the Rules of the European Court, pursuant to the general principles of both domestic and international procedural law, and, in accordance with the criterion of generally accepted doctrine, the decisive or unappealable character of a judgment is not incompatible with the existence of the remedy of revision in some special cases.'[164]

Yet another example of inherent powers in international judicial practice relates to the power of international courts to provide redress to injured parties. It is well established that notwithstanding the absence of an express power, international courts having jurisdiction over a dispute also have as an essential part of that jurisdiction the power to award remedies.[165] The PCIJ clarified this in the *Factory at Chorzów* case, where Poland argued that the compromissory clause giving the PCIJ jurisdiction did not confer on it the jurisdiction to decide the quantum and form of the reparation to be made.[166] The PCIJ rejected this argument, stating that reparation was 'the indispensable complement of a failure to apply a convention and there is no necessity for this to be stated in the convention itself'.[167] This attitude was consistent with prior arbitral practice. In earlier arbitrations, tribunals which had the express power to 'settle all claims' often also saw no obstacle to their making awards of damages; in some cases where the arbitral tribunal was in fact only expressly charged with the task of determining the question of

[161] 29 Ir-USCTR 383, 390 (1993).

[162] *Genie Lacayo (Judicial Review)* Series C No 45 (IACHR, 1997).

[163] ibid, para 6, referring to *El Amparo (Interpretation)*, Series C No 46, *Considering*, para 1 (IACHR, 1997).

[164] *Genie Lacayo (Judicial Review)* (n 162 above), para 9.

[165] J Crawford, *The International Law Commission's Articles on State Responsibility* (2002) 218.

[166] PCIJ Rep Series A No 9, 20–1 (1927); Crawford (n 165 above) 201.

[167] PCIJ (n 166 above), 21 (1927).

liability, the arbitrators also assumed that they had the power to award damages.[168]

The ICJ and other international tribunals have maintained the same approach. In the *Corfu Channel* case, the ICJ had jurisdiction under a *compromis* concluded between the UK and Albania to decide, first, whether Albania was responsible for damage to UK naval vessels and loss of human life, and second, whether the UK had violated the sovereignty of Albania.[169] The UK claimed monetary compensation; Albania argued that the ICJ had no power to decide the amount of damages, but only the question of responsibility. The ICJ rejected Albania's argument: 'If the Court should limit itself to saying that there is a duty to pay compensation without deciding what amount of compensation is due, the dispute would not be finally decided. An important part of it would remain unsettled ... It would not give full effect to the Resolutions but would leave open the possibility of a further dispute.'[170] This approach has been confirmed in later ICJ jurisprudence.[171] Other international tribunals have also assumed that they have the power to award reparation, often without expressly relying on the principle established in *Factory at Chorzów* and *Corfu Channel*.[172] In some cases, international courts have held that the power to award reparation also includes the power to grant mandatory or consequential orders.[173]

The foregoing section is not an exhaustive review of the exercise of inherent powers in international adjudication, but it has merely sought to illustrate their existence in several notable situations: the *compétence de la compétence*; the power to make rules of procedure and make decisions over procedural issues; the power to grant provisional measures; the post-adjudication powers of international courts; and the power to award remedies. In the light of this practice, and in order to ascertain when international courts can exercise such powers, and what the limitations are on their exercise, there is a need to arrive at a proper understanding of their source.

IV. The Source of Inherent Powers

Writers have in the past lamented the failure of international courts to clarify the source of inherent powers.[174] Sir Elihu Lauterpacht has

[168] C Gray, *Judicial Remedies in International Law* (1987) 12, 60; referring, eg, to *Van Bokkelen*, Moore (n 101 above), vol II, 1807 (US-Haiti, 1888); *Forests of Central Rhodope* 3 RIAA 1389, 1431 (Gr-Bulg, 1933).

[169] [1949] ICJ Rep 4.

[170] ibid, 26.

[171] *Fisheries Jurisdiction (Germany v Iceland)* [1974] ICJ Rep 175, 203–5; *Military and Paramilitary Activities (Nicaragua v US)* [1986] ICJ Rep 14, 142; *LaGrand (Germany v US)* (2001) 40 ILM 1069, 1082; *Avena (Mexico v US)* (2004) 43 ILM 581, 598.

[172] eg *M/V 'Saiga' (No 2)* 120 ILR 143, 199–200 (ITLOS, 1999); *Feldman v Mexico* (2003) 42 ILM 625, 665–9; but see *Amco v Indonesia (Award)* 89 ILR 405, 503–6 (1984), citing *Factory at Chorzów* PCIJ Rep Series A No 17, 47 (1928).

[173] See eg *Rainbow Warrior* 82 ILR 499, 573 (NZ-France, 1990); *Loayza Tamayo* 116 ILR 388, 440–2 (IACHR, 1998); *Assanidze v Georgia* (2004) 39 EHRR 653, 698–9; *Arrest Warrant (DRC v Belgium)* (2002) 41 ILM 536, 556–7; *Avena (Mexico v US)* (n 171 above), 624; *Enron Corporation and Ponderosa Assets v Argentina (Jurisdiction)* ICSID Case No ARB/01/3, paras 77–81 (14 January 2004).

[174] See eg Gaeta (n 11 above) 354–5, 358–61.

observed that the ICJ has 'simply assumed' the existence of an inherent jurisdiction,[175] and added that it would be to the general advantage of all if the ICJ were to identify the use and source of inherent powers in any relevant case.[176]

In its dictum in the *Nuclear Tests* case, the ICJ arguably indicated three different sources of its 'inherent jurisdiction': 'Such inherent jurisdiction, on the basis of which the Court is fully empowered to make whatever findings may be necessary for the purposes just indicated, derives from the mere existence of the Court as a judicial organ established by the consent of states, and is conferred upon it in order that its basic judicial functions may be safeguarded.'[177] Here, the ICJ states that its inherent jurisdiction derives from 'the mere existence of the Court as a judicial organ'; this suggests that any judicial organ possesses inherent powers. The ICJ then appears immediately to contradict this assertion with the statement that the inherent jurisdiction is 'conferred upon it'. This does not sit comfortably with the idea of an 'inherent power', for if a power is 'inherent', then there is no need for any conferral. Finally, the ICJ states that the inherent jurisdiction exists in order to safeguard 'its basic judicial functions'; this suggests that the inherent jurisdiction derives from the existence of expressly conferred functions and powers, and that the inherent powers exist in order to ensure that the expressly conferred powers can be performed.

The lack of clarity in the ICJ's dictum reflects the uncertainty regarding the source of inherent powers of national courts.[178] Essentially, four possible sources of inherent powers can be discerned in the jurisprudence of international courts and the writings of publicists. These are: the concept of 'general principles of law'; the doctrine of implied powers; the identity of international courts as judicial bodies; and a functional justification.[179] There is a degree of overlap between these sources, and some of the distinctions between them may seem artificial. Nevertheless, there are subtle conceptual differences, and it is important to distinguish these possible sources in order to find the most appropriate justification for the exercise of inherent powers in international adjudication. This is because it is the source of inherent powers that will provide guidance as to the limitations that exist to restrict the exercise of such powers. If the source is located in the concept of general principles of law, for instance, inherent powers might be few in number, given the relative scarcity of such principles. If inherent powers are justified by the function of international courts, on the other hand, they are likely to be more abundant, and careful limiting factors need to be identified to curb their use.

175 Lauterpacht, '"Partial" Judgments' (n 11 above) 477. 176 ibid 483.

177 [1974] ICJ Rep 253, 259–60. 178 See nn 72–78 above and accompanying text.

179 cf Gaeta (n 11 above) 354–5, who suggests that only three possible sources can be identified: general principles of law, the doctrine of implied powers, and the judicial nature of international courts.

A. Inherent powers are derived from general principles of law

The first suggestion is that the source of inherent powers of international courts can be found in 'general principles of law'. In a few cases, international tribunals have explained the inherent character of a power by pointing to the existence of a 'general principle of law' specifically providing for such a power.[180] For instance, in *Genie Lacayo (Judicial Review)*, the IACHR held that it had an inherent power to revise its judgments, noting that this finding accorded with 'the general principles of both domestic and international procedural law'.[181] In another example, the PCIJ held, in the context of its power to indicate provisional measures, that there was a general principle of law that parties must abstain from action which would prejudice the rights which are the subject of proceedings.[182] This general principle has also been referred to by the ICJ and by ICSID tribunals.[183] This approach has also been adopted by some writers who have sought to explain the source of some inherent powers, such as the *compétence de la compétence*,[184] and the power to grant provisional measures,[185] as lying in general principles of law.

This basis for the existence of inherent powers is attractive, and does provide a sound explanation for the exercise of some inherent powers by international courts. It is suggested, however, that general principles of law are unlikely to provide a basis for all cases where international courts seek to exercise an inherent power, as general principles which are widely applicable in domestic legal orders are relatively few in number, and do not always relate to the existence of procedural powers. It is difficult to substantiate as a general principle of law, for instance, that all courts have the power to make cost orders, or order the preparation of an expert report, when those procedures might not be known to all legal systems. Moreover, when international courts invoke procedural powers that are not expressly conferred on them, they have only rarely done so by reference to a general principle of law. In other words, their methodological approach is not one which is consistent with the application of general principles of law within the meaning of Article 38(1)(c) of the ICJ Statute. For these reasons, other possible sources of inherent powers should be examined.

[180] See also Gaeta (n 11 above) 359.

[181] *Genie Lacayo (Judicial Review)* Series C No 45, para 9 (IACHR, 1997).

[182] *Electricity Company of Sofia and Bulgaria (Belgium v Bulgaria)* PCIJ Rep, Series A/B No 79, 194, 199 (1939).

[183] *LaGrand (Germany v US)* (2001) 40 ILM 1069, 1093–4; *Aegean Sea (Greece v Turkey)* [1976] ICJ Rep 3, 15–16 (Sep Op President Jiménez de Aréchaga); *Victor Pey Casado and President Allende Foundation v Chile* (2001) 16 *ICSID Review—FILJ* 567, 579; *Amco v Indonesia (Provisional Measures)* 89 ILR 402, 404–5 (1983); see also the decision of a national court, the Cour d'appel de Rennes, in *Guinea v Atlantic Triton Co* 3 ICSID Reps 3, 8–9 (1984).

[184] Cheng (n 43 above) 275–8; Carlston (n 99 above) 74–5.

[185] L Collins, 'Provisional and Protective Measures in International Litigation' (1992) 234 *Recueil des cours* 9, 23–4, 214–16; Cheng (n 43 above) 267–9; Dumbauld (n 19 above) 42–81; see also F Jacobs and R Bernhardt, in Bernhardt (ed) (n 141 above) 137–9, 140.

B. *Inherent powers are implied powers*

Another possible basis for the exercise of inherent powers can be found in the doctrine of implied powers. Like express powers, implied powers are considered to be conferred by the terms of a constitutive instrument, but they are not made express; rather, they are conferred by implication. This doctrine essentially rests on the canon of treaty interpretation known as *effet utile*, according to which the terms of treaties, including the powers of international institutions, are to be interpreted so as to make them effective rather than ineffective.[186] This principle has been applied on numerous occasions by the PCIJ and the ICJ in the context of the powers of international organizations. In *Reparation for Injuries*, for example, the ICJ observed that the UN Charter did not empower the UN to bring a claim for injuries sustained by one of its employees. Nonetheless, the ICJ held that in the light of the functions of the UN, the provisions of the Charter implied that the UN had the power to bring such a claim. The ICJ stated that: 'Under international law, the Organisation must be deemed to have those powers which, though not expressly provided for in the Charter, are conferred upon it by necessary implication as being essential to the performance of its duties.'[187]

This doctrine has been employed by international courts not only to find that international organizations have powers and capacities other than those expressly conferred on them, but also in order to ensure the effective exercise of their own functions. Thus, in *Mavrommatis Palestine Concessions*, the PCIJ held that a clause conferring jurisdiction on it can be applied to disputes arising both prior and subsequent to the entry into force of the clause in question.[188] Further, in his separate opinion in *Arbitral Award of 31 July 1989*, Judge Shahabuddeen characterized the *compétence de la compétence* as being 'ultimately derived from a grant presumed by law to have been made to the tribunal by the parties, who are always competent to do so expressly'.[189] In addition, in the *LaGrand* case, the ICJ was faced with the question of whether it had the power to order provisional measures that were binding. There, the ICJ also adopted an interpretation of Article 41 of the ICJ Statute in accordance with the principle of

[186] Lauterpacht, *The Development of International Law* (n 23 above) 227–8; H Grotius, *On the Law of War and Peace* (first published 1625, 1964 edn, F Kelsey trans) 857; E de Vattel, *The Law of Nations, or, Principles of the Law of Nature, Applied to the Conduct and Affairs of Nations and Sovereigns* (first published 1758, 4th edn, 1811) 234.

[187] [1949] ICJ Rep 174, 182; cf the more restrictive view in [1949] ICJ Rep 174, 196, 198 (Diss Op Judge Hackworth): 'Powers not expressed cannot freely be implied. Implied powers flow from a grant of express powers, and are limited to those that are "necessary" to the exercise of powers expressly granted.' The majority position was confirmed in *Certain Expenses* [1962] ICJ Rep 151, 168. See also *Competence of the ILO* PCIJ Rep Series B No 2 (1922); *Competence of the ILO* PCIJ Rep Series B No 3 (1922); *Competence of the ILO* PCIJ Rep Series B No 13, 18 (1926); *Jurisdiction of the European Commission of the Danube* PCIJ Rep Series B No 14, 64–7 (1927); *Effect of Awards of Compensation* [1954] ICJ Rep 47, 56–8; *Legality of the Use by a State of Nuclear Weapons (WHO Request)* [1996] ICJ Rep 66, 78–9.

[188] PCIJ Rep Series A No 2, 35 (1924).

[189] [1991] ICJ Rep 53, 106, 109 (Sep Op Judge Shahabuddeen).

effectiveness to find that its provisional measures had mandatory force.[190] The ECHR has also adopted this approach to the question of the binding nature of its own provisional measures.[191] In addition, the source of the jurisdiction of international courts to award remedies—which has been referred to above as an inherent power[192]—might also be regarded as an application of the principle of effectiveness in treaty interpretation. As the PCIJ and the ICJ noted in *Factory at Chorzów* and *Corfu Channel* respectively, if they found that they lacked the power to award reparation, the dispute would be left unresolved;[193] they therefore adopted an interpretation of their powers which made it possible for them to fulfil their functions and ensure the settlement of the disputes.[194]

The doctrine of implied powers certainly has some appeal as a justification for the exercise of inherent powers. The ICJ's approach to the implication of powers of international organizations in *Reparation for Injuries*, where it stated the test as being whether the power was necessary for the functions of the international organization, certainly appears to accord with much international judicial practice on the exercise of inherent powers.[195] Professor Sloan has even suggested that the implied powers of international organizations can be termed 'inherent powers'.[196] Yet it is suggested that to regard inherent powers as identical with implied powers is not entirely accurate. The doctrine of implied powers has been used by international courts far more frequently in the context of the powers of international organizations.[197] In contrast, when they have claimed powers for themselves which are not expressly provided for in their constitutive instruments, international courts have in general not sought to imply powers from the express terms of their statutes. This suggests that international courts themselves find the doctrine of implied powers inappropriate.[198] In her consideration of inherent powers, Professor Gaeta even states that there is only one example of an international court exercising an 'implied power', being the judgment of

[190] (2001) 40 ILM 1069, 1093; M Mennecke and C Tams, '*LaGrand* Case (*Germany v United States of America*)' (2002) 51 ICLQ 449.

[191] *Mamatkulov and Askarov v Turkey*, paras 108–27 (ECHR, 2005); *Mamatkulov and Abdurasulovic v Turkey*, paras 106–110 (ECHR, 2003); see generally C Tams, 'Interim Orders by the European Court of Human Rights: Comments on *Mamatkulov and Abdurasulovic v Turkey*' (2003) 63 *Zeitschrift für ausländisches öffentliches Recht und Völkerrecht* 681; C Brown, 'Strasbourg Follows Suit on Provisional Measures' (2003) 62 *Cambridge Law Journal* 532.

[192] See nn 165–172 above and accompanying text.

[193] *Factory at Chorzów (Germany v Poland)* PCIJ Rep, Series A No 9, 21 (1928); *Corfu Channel (UK v Albania)* [1949] ICJ Rep 4, 26.

[194] Lauterpacht, *The Development of International Law* (n 23 above) 245–7.

[195] *Reparation for Injuries* [1949] ICJ Rep 174, 182.

[196] B Sloan, 'General Assembly Resolutions Revisited (Forty Years Later)' (1987) 58 BYIL 39, 55–6.

[197] Gaeta (n 11 above) 360, 362.

[198] eg *Nuclear Tests (Australia v France)* [1974] ICJ Rep 253, 259–60; *Continental Shelf (Revision and Interpretation) (Tunisia v Libya)* [1985] ICJ Rep 192, 198; *Request for an Examination (New Zealand v France)* [1995] ICJ Rep 288, 303–4; see also [1995] ICJ Rep 363, 369 (Diss Op Judge Koroma) (referring to 'the Court's inherent power to accommodate the particular requirements of the case').

the ICTY Trial Chamber in *Prosecutor v Blaskic* that it had an 'implied power' to issue a *subpoena duces tecum* to a state or state official for the production of government documents.[199] On appeal, the ICTY Appeals Chamber, in overturning the Trial Chamber's decision, held that it preferred to speak of 'inherent powers' rather than 'implied powers'.[200] It is not clear that this is the only instance of international courts relying on the doctrine of 'implied powers'; the instances mentioned above, where international courts have found that they are competent to award remedies, and order binding provisional measures, arguably offer further examples, as do the reports of the WTO Appellate Body on its authority, and that of WTO panels, to receive *amicus curiae* briefs.[201] Yet Professor Gaeta's point remains a valid one; while the basic methodology of implied powers might provide a solid basis for the exercise of inherent powers, it is not one that international courts often invoke.

C. Inherent powers are derived from the identity of courts as judicial bodies

In some cases, international courts have found that they have inherent powers simply because the relevant powers are usually attributed to judicial bodies.[202] For instance, in an early decision, the arbitral tribunal in *Rio Grande Irrigation and Land Company* noted that 'there is inherent in this and in every legal Tribunal a power, and indeed a duty, to entertain, and, in proper cases, to raise for themselves, preliminary points going to their jurisdiction to entertain the claim'.[203] The ICJ has also used this language in *Nuclear Tests*,[204] and also in *Effect of Awards of Compensation* in characterizing the UNAT as a judicial body and its power to make final and binding awards.[205] In referring to the provisions of the UNAT Statute, the ICJ held that 'these provisions and the terminology used are evidence of the judicial nature of the Tribunal. Such terms as "tribunal", "judgment", competence to "pass judgment on applications", are generally used with respect to judicial bodies. The above mentioned provisions ... are of an essentially judicial character and conform with rules generally laid down in statutes or laws issued from courts of justice'.[206]

The view that certain rules of procedure can be attributed to international judicial bodies on the basis of their being called 'courts' has also attracted some doctrinal support. In discussing the existence of a

[199] *Prosecutor v Blaskic* 110 ILR 608, 624–7, 630, 637–40 (ICTY, 1997); Gaeta (n 11 above) 360.

[200] *Prosecutor v Blaskic* 110 ILR 688, 698, n 27 (ICTY App Ch, 1997); Sarooshi (n 11 above) 150; Gaeta (n 11 above) 360.

[201] See eg *US—Shrimp* DSR 1998-VII, 2755, 2783–7 (ABR) (concerning the power of WTO panels to receive *amicus curiae* briefs); *US—Hot Rolled Steel* WT/DS138/AB/R, para 36–42 (ABR) (concerning the power of the WTO Appellate Body to receive *amicus curiae* briefs); see also *EC—Asbestos* WT/DS135/AB/R, paras 50–57 (ABR) (outlining procedures for the submission of *amicus curiae* briefs).

[202] Gaeta (n 11 above) 364–5.

[203] 6 RIAA 131, 135–6 (UK-US, 1923).

[204] [1974] ICJ Rep 253, 259–60.

[205] [1954] ICJ Rep 47.

[206] ibid, 52.

procedural norm which requires international tribunals to hear both parties to a dispute, Professor Thirlway has argued that:

... a principle such as *audi alteram partem* may perhaps be regarded as a general principle of law: but it may also be considered to be contained within the concept of a 'court'. If states setting up an international body classify it as a court or tribunal, then there is no need for them to spell out in its constitutive document that it is under an obligation to hear both sides before deciding; by calling it a court they are already implicitly giving it that instruction. The concept of a court is of course borrowed from municipal legal systems, in which a 'court' that was not required to hear both sides would generally be regarded as not worthy of the name.[207]

But it is suggested that the identity of international courts as judicial bodies is also less than satisfactory as a source of inherent powers, for relying on the nomenclature of a body as a source of competences is problematic. In particular, it is difficult to maintain that courts and tribunals, whether national or international, can exercise certain powers on the basis of their being called 'courts' or 'tribunals', simply because certain procedural powers, which are sought to be established as inherent powers, are the type of powers that courts usually have. To argue that a court has certain powers because it is called a 'court' is a circular argument; it is to deduce from the word 'court' the existence of certain characteristics without which the body in question could not be referred to as a 'court'.[208] Moreover, to say that a power is inherent 'in a court' is unhelpful when one does not take account of the nature or function of the court or legal system in question.[209]

D. Inherent powers are necessary to ensure the fulfilment of the functions of international courts

It is suggested that a better view of the source of the inherent powers of international courts is their need to ensure the fulfilment of their functions. The instances reviewed above where international courts have exercised inherent powers can be justified on this basis. Significantly, it accords with one of the ICJ's asserted bases for inherent powers in the *Nuclear Tests* case, where it referred to the need to safeguard its judicial functions, and it is also consistent with the dictum of the ICTY Appeals Chamber in *Blaskic*, where it held that 'the International Tribunal must possess the power to make all those judicial determinations that are necessary for the exercise of its primary jurisdiction'.[210] The WTO Appellate Body has also stated that: 'WTO panels have certain powers that are

[207] Thirlway, 'Dilemma or Chimera?' (n 17 above) 626 (references omitted).

[208] K Zemanek, in Bernhardt (ed) (n 141 above) 129; H Schiedermair, in Bernhardt (ed) (n 141 above) 142–3; cf-Thirlway, in Bernhardt (ed) (n 141 above) 137.

[209] See also I Scobbie, *Legal Reasoning and the Judicial Function in the International Court* (PhD dissertation, University of Cambridge, 1990) 67–71.

[210] *Prosecutor v Blaskic* 110 ILR 688, 704 (ICTY App Ch, 1997).

inherent in their adjudicative function.'[211] In addition, this 'functional justification' for the existence of inherent powers has found support in doctrinal writings;[212] even Professor Thirlway, who takes a restrictive view of the inherent powers of international courts, agrees that: 'The true justification for an inherent jurisdiction must be, as stated by Fitzmaurice, that "the power to exercise it ... is a necessary condition of ... any court of law ... being able to function at all".'[213] Given that the functions of international courts provide the justification for the exercise of inherent powers, those powers might be said to derive ultimately from the consent of states; for it is the states parties who, in framing the constitutive instruments of international courts, have conferred those functions upon them.[214]

The conclusion that the source of inherent powers can be found in the necessity of international courts to fulfil their functions raises the question of the extent of those functions. This is because the functions of international courts define which powers international courts may exercise as inherent powers. Equally, the extent of the functions of international courts impose certain limitations on the exercise of such powers. In his consideration of the powers necessary for the fulfilment of the functions of international courts, Professor Thirlway has argued that only the *compétence de la compétence* should be regarded as an inherent power. As for other procedural powers, such as admitting third-party intervention, and the power to grant provisional measures, he argues that other international courts 'can and do function without such powers'.[215] This, however, is putting the case too simply; the fact that some international courts have refrained from exercising certain powers does not necessarily mean that those powers do not exist. In order to examine the scope of inherent powers, an identification of the functions of international courts is crucial, and it is to this question that this article now turns.

V. Functions of International Adjudication

There is an active debate about the functions of international adjudication,[216] and two main schools of thought can be distinguished. On one view, the function of international courts is a private function; that is, that international courts are created in order to settle disputes referred to

[211] *Mexico—Taxes on Soft Drinks* WT/DS308/AB/R, para 45 (ABR).

[212] Gaeta (n 11 above) 364–8; Lauterpacht, '"Partial" Judgments' (n 11 above) 480.

[213] Thirlway, 'The Law and Procedure of the International Court of Justice 1960–1989: Part Nine' (n 4 above) 41.

[214] See also ibid 43–4.

[215] ibid 41. The only other inherent power which appears to be admitted by Professor Thirlway is 'that "to interpret the submissions of the parties" in order to "isolate the real issue in the case and to identify the object of the claim", asserted by the Court in the *Nuclear Tests* case': ibid 19.

[216] eg on the function of the ICJ, see M Sameh M Amr, *The Role of the International Court of Justice as the Principal Judicial Organ of the United Nations* (2003); Jennings, *Collected Writings* (n 19

them. In other words, their task is 'to do justice' between the litigant states, and to render a judgment or award which takes account of all relevant facts, which is limited to the *petitum* of the dispute, and which is made with final and binding force. This function can be discerned from the constitutive instruments and the jurisprudence of many international courts. For instance, arbitration under the auspices of the PCA has as its object the settlement of disputes between states by judges of their own choice, and on the basis of respect for law.[217] This private function is also reflected in Article 42(1) of the ICSID Convention, which stipulates that the function of arbitral tribunals established under that convention is to 'decide a dispute in accordance with such rules of law as may be agreed by the parties'.[218] Article 38(1) of the ICJ Statute also states the function of that body as being 'to decide in accordance with international law such disputes as are submitted to it'.[219] It is also summed up in the statement of the WTO panel in *EC—Bananas*, in considering the role of WTO dispute settlement: 'First and foremost, that system is designed to settle disputes'.[220] The PCA tribunal in *Larsen/Hawaiian Kingdom* also emphasized that 'the function of international arbitral tribunals in contentious proceedings is to determine disputes between the parties, not to make abstract rulings'.[221] In its case law, the ICJ has repeatedly confirmed that its judicial function is the resolution of questions which must be answered in accordance with law.[222]

On another view, international adjudication also has a public function, which goes beyond the settlement of the dispute. According to this view, the goal of the mere settlement of the dispute is too focused on the private aspect of disputes, and is not conducive to the positive creation of norms which can generate obedience among members of the community being regulated by that system of norms.[223] This public function encompasses several considerations, each of which may be equally important.

above) vol I, 433–93; Sir R Jennings, 'The Role of the International Court of Justice' (1997) 68 BYIL 1, 1–9; AS Muller, D Raic, and JM Thuransky (eds), *The International Court of Justice: Its Future Role after Fifty Years* (1997); Rosenne, *Law and Practice* (n 11 above) 162–78; G Abi-Saab, 'The International Court as a World Court' in V Lowe and M Fitzmaurice (eds), *Fifty Years of the International Court of Justice* (1996) 3; N Singh, *The Role and Record of the International Court of Justice* (1989); RP Anand, 'Role of International Adjudication' in L Gross (ed), *The Future of the International Court of Justice* (1976) vol I, 1.

[217] 1899 Convention, Art 15; 1907 Convention, Art 37; Jennings, 'The Role of the International Court of Justice' (n 216 above) 5.

[218] ICSID Convention, Art 42(1).

[219] ICJ Statute, Art 38(1).

[220] [1997] DSR-II 695, 711 (PR); see also *US—Shirts and Blouses* [1997] DSR-I 323, 340 (ABR).

[221] 119 ILR 566, 587 (2001).

[222] eg *LaGrand (Germany v US)* (2001) 40 ILM 1069, 1093; *Lockerbie (Libya v UK)* [1992] ICJ Rep 3, 50, 56 (Diss Op Judge Weeramantry); *Nuclear Tests (Australia v France)* [1974] ICJ Rep 253, 270–1; *Fisheries Jurisdiction (UK v Iceland)* [1974] ICJ Rep 3, 18–19; *Namibia* [1971] ICJ Rep 16, 23; *Northern Cameroons (Cameroons v UK)* [1963] ICJ Rep 15, 29–34, 38; *Haya de la Torre (Colombia/Peru)* [1951] ICJ Rep 71, 83; Lauterpacht, *The Development of International Law*, (n 23 above) 3–5; Sir H Lauterpacht, *The Function of Law in the International Community* (1933) 105–7, 127–31.

[223] In the context of domestic adjudication, see especially O Fiss, 'Against Settlement' (1983–4) 93 *Yale Law Journal* 1073, 1085–6, 1089–90.

One of these is the function of ensuring the proper administration of international justice. This is distinct from the function of settling disputes, in that it emphasizes the need for effectiveness and efficiency in judicial decision-making, and it is well established in the jurisprudence of international courts, as well as in the literature.[224] Several inherent powers have been justified on the basis of the need to ensure the proper administration of international justice, such as the power to dismiss proceedings summarily,[225] and the power to suspend proceedings.[226] The function of international courts in the administration of justice has asserted itself recently as a result of the increased workload of international courts.[227] The proliferation of international courts that has taken place over the past fifteen years has been matched by a sharp increase in the recourse by states to third-party dispute settlement procedures. This has required such bodies to take greater control of the management of disputes. Judge Higgins has noted extrajudicially that in order to cope with this increase in activity, a modernization of ICJ procedures is required concerning 'the timetable for the speedy resolution of disputes', and which would enhance the ICJ's integrity in permitting it 'the *normal* control ... of its own procedures'.[228] The recognition that an international court such as the ICJ is a 'normal' court underlines the importance of this function. One manifestation of international courts taking greater control of their procedures is the issuing of practice directions, which has been noted above.[229]

Another aspect of the administration of international justice is the prevention of any 'abuse of process' in international adjudication. The common law doctrine of 'abuse of process' is related to the concept of 'abuse of rights', a term more familiar in civilian legal systems.[230] In common law systems, the doctrine of 'abuse of process' generally operates to preclude proceedings '*if it is necessary for a court to prevent a misuse of its procedure*', or 'to avoid the risk that the administration of justice might be brought into disrepute among right-thinking people.'[231] This doctrine has been recognized in international adjudication; Professor Kolb has

[224] See eg *Mavrommatis Palestine Concessions (Greece v UK)* PCIJ Rep Series A No 2 (1924) 16; *Legality of Use of Force (Yugoslavia v Spain)* [1999] ICJ Rep 761, 773–4; [1999] ICJ Rep 916, 925–6; see also J Bassett Moore, *International Adjudications: Ancient and Modern—History and Documents* (1929) vol I, xxii, lviii–lix, and the references cited therein.

[225] *Legality of Use of Force (Yugoslavia v Spain)* (n 224 above), 773–4; *Legality of Use of Force (Yugoslavia v US)* [1999] ICJ Rep 916, 925–6.

[226] *SPP v Egypt* 3 ICSID Rep 112, 129–30 (1985); Shany (n 13 above) 263–4; *MOX Plant (Procedural Order No 3)* (2003) 42 ILM 1187, 1191; *SGS v Philippines (Jurisdiction)*, ICSID Case No ARB/02/6, para 175 (29 January 2004).

[227] Couvreur (n 135 above) 467; Higgins (n 135 above) 131–2; Sir R Jennings, 'The International Court of Justice after Fifty Years' (1995) 89 AJIL 493, 497–8.

[228] Higgins (n 135 above) 131–2 (emphasis added).

[229] See n 135 above and accompanying text.

[230] See eg M Byers, 'Abuse of Rights: An Old Principle, A New Age' (2002) 47 *McGill Law Journal* 389; see generally R Kolb, *La Bonne Foi en Droit International Public* (2000).

[231] P Barnett, *Res Judicata, Estoppel, and Foreign Judgments* (2001) 185 (emphasis in original).

noted that it has arisen in nine cases before the ICJ.[232] For instance, in *Certain Phosphate Lands in Nauru* the ICJ held, in response to an argument by Australia that Nauru had not acted in good faith, that Nauru's conduct '[did] not amount to an abuse of process'.[233] Discussion of the doctrine also arose in *Waste Management v United Mexican States*. In that case, NAFTA proceedings were originally initiated by the claimant in 1998, but these proceedings were dismissed due to a procedural defect in the claimant's Application.[234] It subsequently brought new proceedings in 2000. Apparently at the suggestion of the President of the NAFTA tribunal, Mexico argued that the new proceedings should be dismissed as an abuse of process.[235] This lay in the claimant's serial commencement of proceedings under both Chapter 11 of NAFTA and also before domestic courts and tribunals in respect of the same claim. Mexico submitted that this power could be exercised 'not as a general legal principle, but as an inherent authority of the tribunal to safeguard the process'.[236] For its part, the claimant accepted that such an inherent power might exist in extreme cases, but denied that it was applicable in that case.[237] Ultimately, the NAFTA tribunal found it was not necessary to decide whether it possessed any inherent power to dismiss a claim on the grounds of abuse of process, or what circumstances might justify the exercise of any such power, but it suggested that 'if such a power exists, it would only be for the purpose of protecting the integrity of the Tribunal's processes or dealing with genuinely vexatious claims'.[238] More recently, in *Armed Activities on the Territory of the Congo (New Application: 2002)*, Rwanda also argued that it was an 'abuse of the process of the Court for the Congo to seek to lay before the Court an Application which [was] essentially the same as the one which it filed in 1999 and then withdrew in 2001.'[239] As was the case for the NAFTA tribunal in the *Waste Management* case, the ICJ was, ultimately, not required to rule on this issue.[240]

Another manifestation of the public function of international adjudication is the role that international courts play in the clarification and the

[232] Kolb (n 230 above) 640–6.

[233] *Certain Phosphate Lands in Nauru (Nauru v Australia)* [1992] ICJ Rep 240, 255; Kolb (n 230 above) 645–6; Rosenne, *Law and Practice* (n 11 above) 1069.

[234] *Waste Management v United Mexican States* (2000) 40 ILM 56, 70.

[235] Mexico's Post Hearing Brief (Jurisdiction), paras 21–24 (19 February 2002), available at <www.naftalaw.org> (last visited 26 August 2005); *Waste Management v United Mexican States* (2002) 41 ILM 1315, 1324–5.

[236] Mexico's Post Hearing Brief (Jurisdiction), para 23 (19 February 2002), available at <www.naftalaw.org> (last visited 26 August 2005); *Waste Management v United Mexican States* (2002) 41 ILM 1315, 1324, n 53.

[237] ibid, 1324.

[238] ibid.

[239] *Armed Activities on the Territory of the Congo (New Application: 2002) (DRC v Rwanda)* CR 2005/17, para 1.6 (Martin Ngoga) (4 July 2005); see also CR 2005/17, paras 4.2–4.10 (Chris Greenwood QC) (4 July 2005), and CR 2005/19, paras 1.40–1.42 (Chris Greenwood QC) (6 July 2005).

[240] *Armed Activities on the Territory of the Congo (New Application: 2002) (DRC v Rwanda)* (Judgment of 3 February 2006) para 126.

progressive development of international law.[241] This function was recognized in the work of the Advisory Committee of Jurists that drafted the PCIJ Statute; the Sub-Committee constituted to consider the draft scheme reported that 'the Sub-Committee considered that it would be one of the Court's important tasks to contribute, through its jurisprudence, to the development of international law'.[242] Sir Hersch Lauterpacht also saw a broader role for the ICJ than the mere settlement of disputes; he argued that 'the development of international law by international tribunals is, in the long run, one of the important conditions of their continued successful functioning and of their jurisdiction'.[243] Charles de Visscher was also of this view. He stated that: 'Much more than the establishment of peace, the development of international law is the essential function of judicial settlement by a permanent and institutionalised tribunal.'[244] In exercising this function, Lauterpacht argued that international courts could exercise 'in each case a creative activity, having as its background the entirety of international law and the necessities of the international community. The distinction between the making of law by judges and by the legislature is upon analysis one of degree ... judicial activity is nothing else than legislation *in concreto*'.[245] As an example of Lauterpacht's position, he was opposed to the use of 'judicial economy' by international courts in the settlement of disputes. Lauterpacht argued that 'there are compelling considerations of international justice and of development of international law which favour a full measure of exhaustiveness of judicial pronouncements of international tribunals'.[246] He also considered that the administration of justice in a domestic legal system 'can afford to rely on purely formal and procedural grounds', but that this could not be done in interstate disputes, 'where it

[241] Lauterpacht, *The Development of International Law* (n 23 above) 5–7; see eg Judge Gilbert Guillaume, 'Speech to the Sixth Committee of the General Assembly of the United Nations' (New York, 30 October 2002), available at <www.icj-cij.org> (last visited 19 August 2005); Judge Gilbert Guillaume, 'Address to the Lauterpacht Research Centre for International Law' (Cambridge, 9 November 2001) 9, available at <http://lcil.law.cam.ac.uk/Guillaume.doc> (last visited 19 August 2005); see also *Barcelona Traction (Belgium v Spain)* [1964] ICJ Rep 6, 65, 65 (Sep Op Judge Tanaka).

[242] See esp 'Report Submitted to the Third Committee by M Hagerup on behalf of the Sub-Committee', in League of Nations/PCIJ, *Documents Concerning the Action taken by the Council of the League of Nations under Article 14 of the Covenant and the Adoption by the Assembly of the Statute of the Permanent Court* (1921) 206, 211; League of Nations, *The Records of the First Assembly—Meetings of the Committees* (1920) 534; see also Spiermann (n 30 above) 249.

[243] Lauterpacht, *The Development of International Law* (n 23 above) 6–7.

[244] C de Visscher, *Theory and Reality in Public International Law* (1968) 390.

[245] Lauterpacht, *The Function of Law* (n 222 above) 319–20; for discussion of Lauterpacht's view of the international judicial function, see esp I Scobbie, 'The Theorist as Judge: Hersch Lauterpacht's Concept of the International Judicial Function' (1997) 8 *European Journal of International Law* 264, 277–8, 284; Sir G Fitzmaurice, 'Hersch Lauterpacht and His Attitude to the Judicial Function' (1979) 50 BYIL 1, 10–11; Sir G Fitzmaurice, 'Hersch Lauterpacht—The Scholar as Judge: I' (1961) 37 BYIL 1, 14–15.

[246] Lauterpacht, *The Development of International Law* (n 23 above) 37.

is of importance that justice should not only be done but that it should also appear to have been done'.[247] Yet while Lauterpacht supported international courts explaining, clarifying, and developing international law, he did not propose that international courts should go beyond the confines of the four corners of the dispute in exercising this creative role; to do so would be to permit legislation by the 'backdoor of transforming the nature of the judicial function'.[248] The case for this function is strengthened if the international court in question is established within the context of a particular regime. It might be said, for instance, that the ICJ, as 'the principal judicial organ' of the UN, fulfils a public or constitutional role in the UN system.[249] Its role in giving advisory opinions, which have provided guidance on the powers of the UN and its different organs, bears testament to this function.[250]

Many other international courts appear to consider that they have a broader function which includes the development of the law. The ECHR has held that its functions were 'not only to decide those cases brought before it, but more generally, to elucidate, safeguard and develop the rules instituted by the Convention.'[251] The ECJ has also sought to develop EC law, as evidenced by its willingness to give judgments in cases which were moot, in order to clarify questions of law which could arise in other cases.[252] The WTO dispute settlement system also arguably fulfils a constitutional role in overseeing the implementation of the WTO Agreement and its covered agreements.[253] Under Article 3(2) of the DSU, an explicit goal of the dispute settlement system is to provide jurisprudence to help ensure the predictability and stability of the world trading system.[254] WTO panels and the Appellate Body, as the GATT panels before them, have, in accordance with this function, substantially developed WTO law in the course of settling disputes.[255] The Appellate Body indicated its acceptance of this role in *US—Gasoline*, where it made reference to ICJ jurisprudence and general principles of law as a

[247] Lauterpacht, *The Development of International Law* (n 23 above) 39.

[248] Sir H Lauterpacht, 'The Legal Aspect' in CAW Manning (ed), *Peaceful Change: An International Problem* (1937) 135, 145; Lauterpacht, *The Development of International Law* (n 23 above) 75–7.

[249] UN Charter, Art 92; see eg M Shaw, 'The Security Council and the International Court of Justice: Judicial Drift and the Judicial Function' in AS Muller, D Raic and JM Thuransky (eds), *The International Court of Justice: Its Future Role after Fifty Years* (1997) 219; Jennings, 'The Role of the International Court of Justice' (n 216 above) 1–9; N Alford, 'Fact finding by the World Court' (1958) 4 *Villanova Law Review* 37–8.

[250] ICJ Statute, art 65.

[251] *Ireland v UK*, Series A No 25, 62 (ECHR, 1978); J Collier and V Lowe, *The Settlement of Disputes in International Law: Institutions and Procedures* (1999) 13.

[252] eg Case 26/69, *Commission v France* [1970] ECR 565, 575–6; Collier and Lowe (n 251 above) 14.

[253] J Jackson, 'The Varied Policies of International Juridical Bodies: Reflections on Theory and Practice' (2004) 25 *Michigan Journal of International Law* 869, 869–70, 878; J Jackson, 'Dispute Resolution—At the Crossroads' (3rd Annual WTO Conference, British Institute of International and Comparative Law, London, 14 May 2003).

[254] DSU, Art 3(2); see eg D McRae, 'What is the Future of WTO Dispute Settlement?' (2004) 7 *Journal of International Economic Law* 3, 7–8, 14; Jackson (n 253 above).

[255] E-U Petersmann, *The GATT/WTO Dispute Settlement System* (1997) 92–134.

basis for interpreting the WTO Agreement.[256] However, the WTO Appellate Body has stated that it would not overstep the limits of what is necessary to settle the dispute. In *US—Shirts and Blouses*, it held that it: '[did] not consider that article 3.2 of the DSU is meant to encourage either panels or the Appellate Body to "make law" by clarifying existing provisions of the *WTO Agreement* outside the context of resolving a particular dispute. A panel need only address those claims which must be addressed in order to resolve the matter in issue in the dispute.'[257]

A further element of the public function of international adjudication is the consideration of interests other than those of the parties to the dispute. For instance, the ICJ has in the past demonstrated a willingness to take account of the interests of third states which have been refused permission to intervene in disputes. In *Continental Shelf (Libya/Malta)* the ICJ refused Italy's request to intervene on the basis that it had not disclosed an interest of a legal nature which might be affected by a decision in the case, but it noted that there could be no doubt that 'the Court will, in its future judgment in the case, take account, as a fact, of the existence of other states having claims in the region.'[258] In addition, the ICJ granted the status of 'non-party intervener'—a status not contemplated by the ICJ Statute—to Nicaragua in *Land, Island and Maritime Frontier Dispute* between El Salvador and Honduras.[259] It is suggested that these decisions demonstrate an awareness of a broader function which goes beyond a role of merely settling the dispute submitted by the parties, and even beyond the role of developing the law.

Many international courts also occasionally take account of broader community interests. This is evidenced in part by the increasing practice of certain international courts in accepting the submission of *amicus curiae* briefs, frequently in the absence of an express power to do so. This practice suggests an acceptance of a broader function in settling disputes in a way that takes account of the views of other stakeholders potentially affected by the decision, rather than just the parties to the dispute. Some international courts have an express power to accept such briefs; these include the ICTY, the ICTR, the ECHR, and the International Criminal Court.[260] Other international courts and tribunals have found that despite the absence of a relevant provision in their constitutive instruments, they

[256] *US—Gasoline* DSR 1996-I, 3, 15–16, 20–2 (ABR); Petersmann (n 255 above) 93.

[257] *US—Shirts and Blouses* DSR 1997-I, 323, 340 (ABR).

[258] [1984] ICJ Rep 3, 26; see eg Sir R Jennings, 'The Judiciary, International and National, and the Development of International Law' (1996) 45 ICLJ 5, 7–8; also *Land, Island and Maritime Frontier Dispute* [1990] ICJ Rep 92, 130.

[259] ibid, 135–6; [1992] ICJ Rep 351, 360; Rosenne, *Law and Practice* (n 11 above) 1542–51; Jennings, 'The Role of the International Court of Justice' (n 216 above) 8; Jennings, 'The Judiciary, International and National' (n 258 above) 7.

[260] ICTY Rules, Rule 74; ICTR Rules, Rule 74; European Convention, Art 36(2); ECHR Rules, art 44; International Criminal Court Rules, Rule 103; see esp C Chinkin and R Mackenzie, 'Intergovernmental Organisations as Friends of the Court', in L Boisson de Chazournes, C Romano and R Mackenzie (eds), *International Organisations and International Dispute Settlement* (2002) 135.

too have the power to accept *amicus* briefs. These include the WTO Appellate Body,[261] the IACHR,[262] NAFTA tribunals,[263] and, most recently, an ICSID tribunal.[264] The ICJ has also recently stated in a Practice Direction that briefs submitted by non-governmental organizations would not be considered as part of the case file, but would nonetheless be available for consultation at the Peace Palace.[265]

International courts also fulfil other functions. They can assist in lending legitimacy to the international arrangements of states, for the existence of a forum for the settlement of disputes by adjudication can make the fulfilment of international commitments less reliant on power-oriented diplomacy. At the same time, the international obligations of states can be made more acceptable to domestic constituents if an independent and impartial tribunal is created to resolve disputes.[266] International judicial bodies may also be created to fill in gaps or ambiguities in treaties which prove too intractable to be completed by negotiation. In this sense, diplomats may choose to delegate power to a dispute settlement body to settle questions which could not be resolved by agreement.[267] This may not be the case in all treaty regimes, however; Article 3(2) of the DSU makes it clear that: 'Recommendations and rulings of the DSB cannot add to or diminish the rights and obligations provided in the covered agreements.'[268] On top of these functions, individual international courts may also have certain functions specific to the regime within which they operate. The ITLOS, for instance, arguably fulfils a broader role regarding the objects and purposes of UNCLOS, as reflected in its power to grant provisional measures to prevent serious harm to the marine environment.[269] International human rights tribunals, such as the ECHR and IACHR, exist, *inter alia*, to promote the protection of human rights.[270] ICSID tribunals, for their part, are concerned with the protection of foreign investment;[271] WTO panels have the function to assist the Dispute Settlement Body (DSB) 'in discharging its responsibilities' under the DSU;[272] WTO panels and the Appellate Body also arguably have an institutional commitment to the liberalization of rules on international trade;[273] whilst international criminal tribunals have the function of determining the criminal responsibility of individuals.

[261] See n 201 above and accompanying text.

[262] See eg *Mayagna (Sumo) Awas Tingni Community v Nicaragua* Series C No 79, paras 38, 41–42, 61 (IACHR, 2001); Pasqualucci (n 141 above) 16, 74–5, 214–15.

[263] *Methanex Corporation v United States (Amici Curiae)* paras 31, 47 (NAFTA, 15 January 2001); *United Parcel Services of America, Inc v Canada (Amici Curiae)* para 73 (NAFTA, 17 October 2001).

[264] *Aguas Argentinas, SA, Suez, Sociedad General de Aguas de Barcelona, SA, and Vivendi Universal, SA v Argentina (Amicus Curiae)*, ICSID Case No ASRB/03/19, paras 9–16 (19 May 2005).

[265] ICJ Practice Direction XII, available at <www.icj-cij.org> (last visited 19 August 2005).

[266] eg M Brus, *Third Party Dispute Settlement in an Interdependent World* (1995) 102; T Franck, 'Legitimacy in the International System' (1988) 82 AJIL 705, 727.

[267] Gordon (n 40 above) 804–5.

[268] DSU, Art 3(2); see also Art 19(2).

[269] UNCLOS, Art 290(1).

[270] *Loizidou v Turkey* (1995) 20 EHRR 99, 133.

[271] See eg *Tokios Tokeles v Ukraine (Jurisdiction)* ICSID Case No ARB/02/18 (Diss Op Weil) (29 April 2004).

[272] DSU, Art 11.

[273] See eg Brown, 'The Proliferation of International Courts and Tribunals' (n 13 above) 465–7.

These aspects of the broader public function—the proper administration of international justice, the development of the law, and the consideration of public interests—are important functions of international courts, as is the private function of settling disputes, and the fulfilment of other functions specific to individual regimes. Each of these functions may, in certain circumstances, provide the justification for the exercise of certain inherent powers, if the international court deems such powers necessary for the fulfilment of its functions. This may arise in a variety of situations, and in this sense, it is not possible to compile an exhaustive list of the inherent powers of international courts. Yet the justification for the existence of inherent powers will most often be found in the functions of settling disputes and ensuring the proper administration of international justice. This is because inherent powers are mainly connected with the procedure applicable before international courts, and the fulfilment of the more immediate functions of these bodies.

VI. Limitations to the Exercise of Inherent Powers

As the justification for the exercise of inherent powers can be found in the need of international courts to fulfil their functions, and as these functions are relatively broad, there is plainly a need to identify limiting factors to curb the exercise of such powers. Otherwise, international courts might assert the existence of inherent powers as a form of *carte blanche* to do whatever they choose. In order to prevent inherent powers from being asserted where their exercise is not justified, the following section identifies appropriate limiting factors.

A. Limitations to international judicial jurisdiction

The first limitation can be found in the limitations on the judicial function. As the ICJ observed in *Northern Cameroons*, even when it finds that it has jurisdiction, 'the Court is not compelled in every case to exercise that jurisdiction'.[274] An international court might decline to exercise its jurisdiction for several reasons, such as the mootness of the issue, the absence of a third party whose rights form the subject matter of the dispute, or for reasons of judicial propriety.[275] In this sense, even though an international court might have jurisdiction over a dispute, objections may be made to its competence to hear it. This limitation to the exercise of inherent powers, then, is not due to the international court lacking *jurisdiction*, but, rather, that it 'should rule the claim to be inadmissible on

[274] [1963] ICJ Rep 15, 29; see also *Nuclear Tests (Australia v France)* [1974] ICJ Rep 253, 259; Thirlway, 'The Law and Procedure of the International Court of Justice 1960–1989: Part Nine' (n 4 above) 19; Fitzmaurice, *Law and Procedure* (n 11 above) 434.

[275] See eg Brownlie (n 19 above) 457–83; Collier and Lowe (n 251 above) 155–62, 191–8; Thirlway, 'The Law and Procedure of the International Court of Justice 1960–1989: Part Nine' (n 4 above) 34–57; Rosenne, *Law and Practice* (n 11 above) 517–28, 546–52; Fitzmaurice, *Law and Procedure*

some ground other than its ultimate merits'.[276] Further, it does not prevent the international court from exercising inherent powers prior to deciding that the claim is inadmissible. Accordingly, this limitation should properly be understood as a bar to the exercise of international judicial jurisdiction generally, rather than a limitation to the exercise of inherent powers specifically. This has been considered elsewhere, and does not need to be examined further here.[277]

B. Functions of the particular international court or tribunal

The second type of limitation arising from the function of international courts, which is more relevant, is that because the source of inherent powers lies in the need for international courts to fulfil their functions, the particular functions of each international court will determine the scope of its inherent powers.[278] An international court cannot claim to possess an inherent power if that power is not necessary for the fulfilment of its particular functions. It has been observed above that different international courts, such as, say, the ICTY and the ITLOS, may have differing specific functions in addition to the common general functions of settling disputes and ensuring the proper administration of international justice. So, as Professor Gaeta has noted, an international criminal tribunal arguably has an inherent power to punish an individual for contempt of the tribunal, but this power would not necessarily be inherent in the functions of an interstate tribunal.[279] In a further example, a body which can be petitioned by individuals might exercise an inherent power to impose fines on individuals who abuse their right to petition by lodging frivolous or vexatious claims; but this power might not be exercised by dispute settlement bodies before which only states can appear.[280]

(n 11 above) 438–40, 447–8, 555–8; G Abi-Saab, *Les exceptions préliminaires dans la procédure de la Cour internationale* (1967); I Brownlie, 'The Justiciability of Disputes and Issues in International Relations' (1967) 42 BYIL 123. On the potential application of this doctrine in the WTO dispute settlement system, see L Bartels, 'The Separation of Powers in the WTO: How to Avoid Judicial Activism' (2004) 53 ICLQ 861.

[276] Fitzmaurice, *Law and Procedure* (n 11 above) 438–9; see also H Thirlway, 'The Law and Procedure of the International Court of Justice 1960–1989: Part Eleven' (2000) 71 BYIL 71, 74–5. The concepts 'jurisdiction' and 'competence' appear to overlap in meaning; they are often (incorrectly) used interchangeably and are denoted by the same word in French: see eg Thirlway, 'The Law and Procedure of the International Court of Justice 1960–1989: Part Nine' (n 4 above) 4; Rosenne, *Law and Practice* (n 11 above) 535; Fitzmaurice, *Law and Procedure* (n 11 above) 434–5.

[277] See eg the references cited in n 275 above. It is noteworthy, however, that the application of this limitation to the exercise of international judicial jurisdiction has, on the facts of one case, been rejected by the WTO Appellate Body: *Mexico—Taxes on Soft Drinks* WT/DS308/AB/R, paras 46–57 (ABR).

[278] See also Gaeta (n 11 above) 370–1.

[279] ibid; see also Sarooshi (n 11 above) 152–4.

[280] See eg *Vollering (No 15)* paras 8–9 (ILOAT, 1999, Judgment No 1884); *Martinuzzi* para 4 (ILOAT, 2000, Judgment No 1962); referred to by Gaeta (n 11 above) 358, 371; see also Kolb (n 230 above) 637–9; see also the express provisions in the European Convention, Art 35(3); Optional Protocol to the International Covenant on Civil and Political Rights, opened for signature 16 December 1966, 999 UNTS 302, Art 3 (entered into force 23 March 1976); Convention Against Torture, opened for signature 10 December 1984, 1465 UNTS 85, Art 22(2) (entered into force 29 June 1987).

C. Limitations in the constitutive instruments of international courts

1. Where there is a clause contraire

Inherent powers might also be displaced by the express terms of a *clause contraire* in the constitutive instrument of an international court. This was recognized in *Nottebohm*, where the ICJ held that an international tribunal had an inherent power to determine the extent of its own jurisdiction 'in the absence of agreement to the contrary'.[281] Sir Hersch Lauterpacht also recognized this in his separate opinion in *Norwegian Loans*, where he held that: 'Clearly the Court cannot act otherwise than in accordance with its Statute.'[282] So, for instance, in *Pope & Talbot Inc v Canada*, the claimant requested in its application for provisional measures the enjoining of the application of a trade measure.[283] Under Article 1134 of NAFTA, however, which confers the power to order provisional measures: 'A Tribunal may not order attachment or enjoin the application of the measure alleged to constitute a breach referred to in Article 1116 or 1117.'[284] In accordance with this provision, the NAFTA tribunal correctly held that it had no power to grant such a provisional measure.[285]

In this connection, reference can also be made to the recent decisions of three ICSID tribunals in which they have held that they have the power to grant provisional measures with binding force. The statutory power of ICSID tribunals to grant provisional measures is found in Article 47 of the ICSID Convention, which stipulates in relevant part that 'the Tribunal may, if it considers that the circumstances so require, recommend any provisional measures which should be taken to preserve the respective rights of either party'.[286] The term 'recommend' was ultimately included in the final draft of the Convention in place of the verb 'prescribe', which had originally been proposed. In his authoritative commentary on the ICSID Convention, Professor Schreuer writes that: 'The Convention's legislative history shows clearly that a conscious decision was made not to grant the Tribunal the power to order binding provisional measures.'[287]

But the ICSID tribunal in *Maffezini v Spain* found that the 'semantic difference' between the word 'recommend' and the word 'order' was 'more apparent than real'. It held that it did not believe that 'the parties to the Convention meant to create a substantial difference in the effect of these two words', and that the tribunal's authority to rule on provisional

[281] [1953] ICJ Rep 111, 119; see also Gaeta (n 11 above) 370; Orakhelashvili, 'The Concept of International Judicial Jurisdiction' (n 11 above) 539; Thirlway, 'The Law and Procedure of the International Court of Justice 1960–1989: Part Ten' (n 11 above) 4.

[282] *Norwegian Loans (France v Norway)* [1957] ICJ Rep 9, 34, 45 (Sep Op Sir Hersch Lauterpacht). See also *Interhandel (Switzerland v US)* [1959] ICJ Rep 6, 85, 93 (Diss Op Judge Armand Ugon).

[283] *Pope & Talbot Inc v Canada (Interim Measures)* (NAFTA, 7 January 2000).

[284] NAFTA, Art 1134.

[285] *Pope & Talbot Inc v Canada* (n 283 above).

[286] ICSID Convention, Art 47.

[287] Schreuer (n 19 above) 758.

measures was 'no less binding than that of a final award'.[288] Later, the ICSID tribunal in *Victor Pey Casado and President Allende Foundation v Chile* followed the ruling in *Maffezini*, and in doing so, made express reference to the judgment of the ICJ in *LaGrand*.[289] Most recently, in *Tokios Tokeles v Ukraine*, an ICSID tribunal reaffirmed the proposition that provisional measures in ICSID arbitration are binding, where it simply held that: 'It is to be recalled that, according to a well-established principle laid down by the jurisprudence of ICSID tribunals, provisional measures "recommended" by an ICSID tribunal are legally compulsory; they are in effect "ordered" by the tribunal, and the parties are under a legal obligation to comply with them.'[290]

It is suggested that these decisions should be regarded as incorrect. Whilst international courts arguably possess an inherent power to grant provisional measures that have binding force, this can be displaced by the clear terms of a *clause contraire*, such as that found in Article 47 of the ICSID Convention.

2. *Where the inherent power would be inconsistent with the constitutive instrument*

A related type of limitation can be found where the constitutive instrument does not expressly exclude the exercise of a certain procedural power, but where the exercise of that power would nonetheless be inconsistent with the procedures actually provided for in the constitutive instrument or rules. Such an instance arose in the arbitration concerning *Heathrow Airport User Charges*.[291] In that case, the US argued that international tribunals had 'inherent powers to revisit certain areas of an award', and that the principle of finality did not preclude the exercise of such powers.[292] The UK, for its part, objected to the US request.[293] The Tribunal noted that it could not 'exercise any power the existence of which is inconsistent with the terms of the Parties' agreement as a result of which alone the Tribunal has any being.'[294] It noted that under Rule 22(2) of its Rules, it could re-open the proceedings *before* the award had been rendered 'on the ground that new evidence [was] forthcoming of such a nature as to constitute a decisive factor, or that there is a vital need for clarification on certain points'.[295] As it had an express power under its Rules to re-open a decision *before* the rendering of the award, the tribunal held that it was extremely doubtful that its inherent powers included 'the much wider and less qualified power to "revisit" its awards ... in circumstances such

[288] *Maffezini v Spain (Procedural Order No 2)*, 16 *ICSID Review—FILJ* 207, para 9 (1999).

[289] *Victor Pey Casado and President Allende Foundation v Chile (Provisional Measures)*, 16 *ICSID Review—FILJ* 567, 577–80, paras 17–26 (2001).

[290] *Tokios Tokeles v Ukraine (Procedural Order No 1)*, ICSID Case No ARB/02/18, para 4 (2003).

[291] 102 ILR 564 (US-UK, 1993).

[292] ibid, 570 (US-UK, 1993).

[293] ibid, 568 (US-UK, 1993).

[294] ibid, 579 (US-UK, 1993).

[295] ibid, 580 (US-UK, 1993).

as have led the *other* Tribunals, to which [the US] refers, to revise awards that they had rendered'.[296]

Another instance in which the exercise by an international court of a procedural power might be considered to be inconsistent with its constitutive instrument relates to the question of whether WTO panels have the power to grant provisional measures. This power is not conferred by the DSU, and several features of the WTO dispute settlement system suggest that it is unlikely that WTO panels can exercise this power. The first of these features can be found in the relatively short time frames provided for in the DSU. The usual time between the lodging of a request for consultations to the adoption of a panel report by the DSB is prescribed to be between six and nine months.[297] This contrasts with the position before other international tribunals, where it could take years from the date of the institution of proceedings until final judgment.[298] A second relevant feature of the DSU is the provision it makes for expedited procedures in cases of 'urgency' where perishable goods or prohibited subsidies are concerned.[299] The existence of these procedures might be thought to diminish the necessity for WTO panels to grant provisional measures. A third factor stems from the remedies regime obtaining in WTO dispute settlement. The purpose of provisional measures is the preservation of the respective rights of the parties pending the final determination of the dispute by a competent tribunal. This purpose is consistent with the principle that reparation, as the usual remedy in general international law, seeks to 're-establish the situation which would, in all probability, have existed' if the internationally wrongful act had not been committed.[300] Reparation, therefore, covers injury suffered from the date of the breach of international law. In contrast, the DSU expressly provides for a different remedial regime which can be described as a *lex specialis*.[301] Under this regime, remedies under the WTO dispute settlement system are typically forward-looking;[302] that is, the right to a remedy arises on the date of adoption of the WTO panel report, rather than the date of the alleged internationally wrongful act. In the case of a 'violation complaint', which is the most frequently invoked

[296] ibid (emphasis in original). [297] DSU, Working Procedures, [12].

[298] See eg the disputes before the ICJ in *Land and Maritime Boundary between Cameroon and Nigeria*, which was initiated in 1994, and in which judgment was rendered in 2003; and *Oil Platforms*, which was commenced in 1992 and in which judgment was delivered in 2003.

[299] DSU, Arts 4(8)–(9), 12(8), Art 17(5); Palmeter and Mavroidis (n 19 above) 144; Appellate Body, Working Procedures for Appellate Review, Rule 31.

[300] *Factory at Chorzów (Germany v Poland)* PCIJ Rep, Series A No 17, 47 (1928); J Crawford, *The International Law Commission's Articles on State Responsibility* (2002) 201–6.

[301] See eg J Crawford, 'Third Report on State Responsibility: Addendum', para 157 (15 June 2000), UN Doc A/CN.4/507/Add.1; J Crawford, 'Third Report on State Responsibility: Addendum', para 420 (4 August 2000), UN Doc A/CN.4/507/Add.4.

[302] C Carmody, 'Remedies and Conformity under the WTO Agreement' (2002) 5 *Journal of International Economic Law* 307, 315–21; P Grané, 'Remedies under WTO Law' (2001) 4 *Journal of International Economic Law* 755, 759–63; DSU, Arts 3(7); 19(1).

action in WTO dispute settlement, Article 3(7) of the DSU establishes a hierarchy of remedies; it stipulates that the first objective of the dispute settlement system is 'usually to secure the withdrawal of the measures concerned if these are found to be inconsistent with the provisions of any covered agreements'.[303] The primacy of this objective is reinforced by the recommendations that panels or the Appellate Body shall make under Article 19(1), which are 'that the Member concerned bring the measure into conformity with that agreement'.[304] Two WTO panel reports nonetheless suggest that retrospective remedies might be available in complaints under the Subsidies and Countervailing Measures Agreement, and the Antidumping Agreement.[305] However, the general non-availability of retrospective remedies in WTO dispute settlement permits the tentative suggestion to be made that WTO panels do not have an inherent power to preserve the rights of the parties during the pendency of the proceedings.

D. Relationship between the international court and the parties

A further factor which operates to restrain the exercise of inherent powers is the relationship between each particular international court and the parties, and, in particular, the degree of deference displayed by each international court to the parties. This particularly affects the exercise of powers which might be described as 'coercive'. Some international tribunals have, for instance, demonstrated a notable reluctance to order the production of evidence. This is exemplified in the practice of the ICJ, which has called on parties before it to produce documents or other evidence in only a few instances.[306] In *Corfu Channel* and *Tehran Hostages* the ICJ did not even draw any adverse inferences from the UK's and US's refusal to provide the documents.[307] In contrast, tribunals constituted under the auspices of the PCA, ICSID, and NAFTA to settle private or mixed disputes have proved more amenable to the exercise of this power.[308] A similar disparity

[303] DSU, Art 3(7).

[304] ibid, Art 19(1) (footnotes omitted). The second remedy contemplated in DSU, Art 3(7) is 'compensation', which is to be invoked 'only if the immediate withdrawal of the measure is impracticable and as a temporary measure pending withdrawal of the measure which is inconsistent with a covered agreement'. As Palmeter and Mavroidis explain: 'Compensation typically would take the form of a reduction in tariffs or other bound trade barriers, on a most favoured nation basis, implemented by the Member concerned in lieu of compliance': Palmeter and Mavroidis (n 19 above) 265. If no satisfactory compensation has been agreed within 20 days, the claimant state may request permission from the DSB to invoke the third remedy available under the DSU, being the suspension of concessions or other obligations under the covered agreements to the member concerned: DSU, Art 22(2).

[305] *Australia—Leather* DSR 2000-III, 1189 (PR); *Guatemala—Cement II*, DSR 2000-XI, 5295 (PR).

[306] For some of the few instances where the PCIJ and ICJ have exercised this power, see *Corfu Channel (UK v Albania)* [1949] ICJ Rep 4; *Ambatielos (Greece v UK)* ICJ Pleadings, 346–7, 566–7; *US Nationals in Morocco (France v US)* ICJ Pleadings, vol II, 431–4; *Tehran Hostages (US v Iran)* [1979] ICJ Rep 7, 10; *Aegean Sea Continental Shelf (Greece v Turkey)* ICJ Pleadings, 296; *Diversion of Waters from the Meuse (Netherlands v Belgium)* PCIJ Rep, Series E No 14 (1937) 153.

[307] *Corfu Channel (UK v Albania)* [1949] ICJ Rep 4, 32; *Tehran Hostages (US v Iran)* (n 306 above) 10.

[308] See eg *CSOB v Slovakia* 14 *ICSID Review—FILJ* 251, 254 (2001); *Tanzania Electric Supply Co Ltd v Independent Power Tanzania (Award)*, ICSID Case No ARB/98/8, paras 43–44 (22 June

can be seen in the practice of international courts in issuing mandatory or consequential orders. Traditionally, the ICJ and the ECHR have been reluctant to direct parties on how they should comply with a judgment,[309] although other international tribunals have not displayed the same reticence.[310] This inconsistent approach arguably reflects the different relationship between some international courts and the litigating parties. Thus, if the proposition is advanced that international courts have an inherent power to issue such orders, one must, nevertheless, take account of the deference displayed by each particular court towards the parties, as this will have an impact on the exercise of that power.

Having considered the limitations to the exercise of inherent powers by international courts, and provided several illustrative examples of the operation of these limitations, it is appropriate to return to the question that confronted the ICJ in the *Legality of Use of Force* cases; does the ICJ have a general power to remove cases from its List prior to deciding on its jurisdiction? It has been observed above that the ICJ Statute and ICJ Rules provide for no such power, although other international courts do have an express power in this regard.[311] As the exercise of inherent powers must be considered on a case-by-case basis, a brief description of the factual background to the dispute is helpful.[312] These proceedings had been commenced in 1999 by the Federal Republic of Yugoslavia (FRY), as it was then known. The asserted bases of jurisdiction originally included Article 36(2) of the ICJ Statute, and Article IX of the Genocide Convention. In the intervening period, internal political upheaval in the FRY led to its admission to the UN on 1 November 2000 and its accession to the Genocide Convention on 12 March 2001. This saw a significant alteration in the FRY's attitude to the question of the ICJ's jurisdiction. Whereas the FRY (renamed 'Serbia and Montenegro' on 4 February 2003) had previously positively asserted that the ICJ had jurisdiction, it now merely asked that the ICJ 'decide on its jurisdiction'.[313] In this situation, in the light of the FRY's admissions that it was not party to the ICJ Statute or the Genocide Convention prior to 1 November 2000

2001); *Feldman v Mexico* ICSID Case No ARB(AF)/99/1, paras 27–41 (16 December 2002); *Plama Consortium Ltd v Bulgaria* ICSID Case No ARB/03/24, para 16 (8 February 2005); *GAMI Investments, Inc v Mexico (Procedural Order No 1)*, para 7.6 (31 January 2003); see also *Bank for International Settlements* (*Procedural Order No 3*, 5 March 2002), (*Procedural Order No 5*, 3 May 2002), (*Procedural Order No 6*, 11 June 2002), (*Procedural Order No 10*, 9 March 2003), (PCA).

309 See esp *Haya de la Torre* [1951] ICJ Rep 71, 79–83; *Marckx v Belgium* Series A No 31, 25 (ECHR, 1979).

310 eg *Loayza Tamayo* 116 ILR 388, 440–2 (IACHR, 1998); *Suarez Rosero* 118 ILR 56, 90 (IACHR, 1997); 118 ILR 92, 113 (IACHR, 1999); but see also some recent decisions of the ICJ: *Arrest Warrant (DRC v Belgium)* (2002) 41 ILM 536, 540; *LaGrand (Germany v US)* (2001) 40 ILM 1069, 1103; *Avena* (2004) 43 ILM 581, 624; and the ECHR: *Assanidze v Georgia* (2004) 39 EHRR 653, 698–9; *Broniowski v Poland* (2005) 40 EHRR 495, 564; see generally Orakhelashvili, 'Judicial Competence and Judicial Remedies in the *Avena* Case' (n 11 above).

311 eg the ITLOS and other tribunals having jurisdiction under UNCLOS: see UNCLOS, Art 294; and the ECHR: European Convention, Art 35(3).

312 *Legality of Use of Force (Serbia and Montenegro v Belgium)* (2005) 44 ILM 299, 303–11; see also Brown, 'Access to International Justice' (n 1 above).

313 (2005) 44 ILM 299, 309, 311.

and 12 March 2001 respectively, and the ICJ's role in the proper administration of justice, it is suggested that the ICJ should have exercised an inherent power to dismiss the applications by summary procedure, as articulated by Judges Higgins and Kooijmans.[314]

Conclusion

This article has examined the exercise by international courts of inherent powers relating to questions of international procedure. It has suggested that the sources of law relevant to the procedure applicable in international adjudication are the relevant international court's constitutive instruments and rules of procedure, and also include customary international law, general principles of law, and judicial decisions and doctrine. With respect to their procedural powers, international courts are not restricted to those conferred by their constitutive instruments—whether express or implied—but can also exercise inherent powers. The concept of inherent powers has its origin in the practice of common law courts, whose rich jurisprudence provides many examples of the exercise of such powers. While the source of inherent powers in international adjudication has not previously been clarified, it is suggested that it lies in the need for international courts to fulfil their judicial functions. These functions are, chiefly, the settlement of international disputes by adjudication, and the proper administration of international justice, although each international court may, in addition, have different functions specific to the regime within which it operates. In this sense, it is not possible to compile an exhaustive list of the inherent powers of international courts. There are important restrictions on the ability of international courts to exercise inherent powers; these lie in the limitations to the exercise of international judicial jurisdiction; the extent of the functions of international courts; the terms of their constitutive instruments; and, also, the relationship between a particular international court and the parties before it.

The consideration of the nature, source and scope of inherent powers in international adjudication provided in this article, together with the proposition that international courts should operate as 'normal' courts,[315] can serve to assist international tribunals faced with novel procedural issues, such as those raised by proliferation and the rise in the resort to international adjudication. International courts have the ability to devise new procedures and adopt those employed by other international tribunals in similar circumstances, and it is suggested that international courts might, through the careful exercise of such powers, better manage the complex challenges being posed to the administration of international justice.

[314] (2005) 44 ILM 299, 341, 343–4 (Sep Op Judge Higgins), 345, 348–50 (Sep Op Judge Kooijmans).
[315] Higgins (n 135 above) 131–2.

A 'PUBLIC EMERGENCY THREATENING THE LIFE OF THE NATION'? THE UNITED KINGDOM'S DEROGATION FROM THE EUROPEAN CONVENTION ON HUMAN RIGHTS OF 18 DECEMBER 2001 AND THE '*A*' CASE

By Ed Bates[1]

Introduction

The House of Lords' ruling in *A and others v Secretary of State for the Home Department*[2] ranks as one of the most important judgments delivered by an English court in recent times. A large majority of the nine Law Lords sitting held that the Government's arrangements for what was essentially the executive detention of certain foreign nationals were both disproportionate and discriminatory. The judgment has already attracted much comment.[3] It has been widely applauded for emphasizing the profound change in the English legal system that has occurred towards the protection of human rights even when 'national security' reasons are put forward by the State. The main purpose of this article, however, is not to repeat such analyses: rather it is to highlight and comment upon one aspect of the case which seems to have received less attention, yet which is potentially very important from the perspective of the international law of human rights and the ability of the State to derogate from human rights instruments. This is the issue of whether the factual circumstances said to underpin the British derogation from Article 5(1)(f) of the European Convention on Human Rights and Fundamental Freedoms ('the

[1] School of Law, University of Southampton. The author would like to thank the editors and the two anonymous reviewers, plus Professor Laurence Lustgarten, for their comments on an earlier draft of this article. Opinions expressed and any errors are, of course, the responsibility of the author alone.

[2] *A and others v Secretary of State for the Home Department* [2004] UKHL 56; [2005] 2 AC 68; [2005] 2 WLR 87; [2005] 3 All ER 169; [2005] HRLR 1 (hereinafter, '*A* judgment' or '*A*').

[3] On the '*A*' judgment see: D Dwyer, 'Rights brought home?' (2005) 121 (Jul) LQR 359; A Tomkins, 'Readings of A v Secretary of State for the Home Department' (2005) *Public Law* 259; Lord (Anthony) Lester, 'The Utility of the Human Rights Act' (2005) *Public Law* 249; C Walker, 'Prisoners of "war all the time"' (2005) 1 *European Human Rights Law Review* 50; B Dickson, 'Law versus terrorism: can law win?' (2005) 1 *European Human Rights Law Review* 11; T Hickman, 'Between human rights and the rule of law: indefinite detention and the derogation model of Constitutionalism' (2005) 68(4) *Modern Law Review* 655; S Tierney, 'Determining the state of exception: what role for Parliament and the courts?' (2005) 68(4) *Modern Law Review* 668; D Dyzenhaus, 'An unfortunate outburst of Anglo-Saxon parochialism' (2005) 68(4) *Modern Law Review* 673; J Hiebert, 'Parliamentary review of terrorism measures' (2005) 68(4) *Modern Law Review* 676; Lord (Johan) Steyn, 'Laying the Foundation of Human Rights in the United Kingdom' (2005) 4 *European Human Rights Law Review* 349; and M Arden, 'Human Rights in an Age of Terrorism' (2005) 121 (Oct) LQR 604.

Convention'), served in December 2001, actually represented a 'public emergency threatening the life of the nation' for the purposes of Article 15(1)[4] of that treaty. The issue here, as it was subsequently put before the courts, was whether the United Kingdom was entitled to derogate from the Convention on the basis that the Government considered that there was a real risk that a major terrorist atrocity might take place in the United Kingdom. By eight votes to one the House of Lords, like the lower courts, accepted that a 'public emergency' for the purposes of Article 15(1) existed. However, some of the Law Lords clearly had reservations on this point, based on doubts as to what circumstances were required for Article 15(1) to apply in the first place. Lord Hoffman alone thought that there was no 'public emergency' given his understanding of the Strasbourg jurisprudence and the extreme circumstances that were required before a State could derogate from the Convention.

The central theme of this article will therefore be to examine what shall be referred to as the 'threshold of severity'[5] (or the threshold test) for reliance on Article 15(1). How severe must circumstances be before a State is entitled to derogate from the Convention in accordance with the requirement that there must be not just a serious problem for the State but a 'public emergency *threatening the life of the nation*' (emphasis added)? As we shall see, the British derogation raised a number of novel questions here. The answers were not easily found in the Strasbourg jurisprudence, which a number of the Law Lords did not refer to and Lord Hoffman himself described as not 'particularly helpful'.[6] We shall see from a detailed examination of the Strasbourg jurisprudence that this comment was justified.

Given the factual background to and the subject matter of the British derogation, a ruling on Article 15 from the House of Lords is bound to have significant precedential value for other jurisdictions.[7] Yet it will be

[4] Derogation is permitted by Article 15 of the Convention. This states:

'15(1) In time of war or other public emergency threatening the life of the nation any High Contracting Party may take measures derogating from its obligations under this Convention to the extent strictly required by the exigencies of the situation, provided that such measures are not inconsistent with its other obligations under international law.

(2) No derogation from Article 2, except in respect of deaths resulting from lawful acts of war, or from Articles 3, 4 (paragraph 1) and 7 shall be made under this provision.

(3) Any High Contracting Party availing itself of this right of derogation shall keep the Secretary General of the Council of Europe fully informed of the measures which it has taken and the reasons therefore. It shall also inform the Secretary General of the Council of Europe when such measures have ceased to operate and the provisions of the Convention are again being fully executed.'

[5] This phrase was employed by Professor Fitzpatrick, see J Fitzpatrick, 'Protection Against Abuse of the Concept of "Emergency" ' in L Henkin and J L Hargrove (eds), *Human rights: an agenda for the next century* (1994) 203, 206.

[6] '*A*' (n 2 above) para 92.

[7] See C Michaelsen, 'International Human Rights on Trial—The United Kingdom's and Australia's Legal Response to 9/11' (2003) 25 *Sydney Law Review* 275; S Joseph, 'Australian Counter-Terrorism Legislation and the International Human Rights Framework' (2004) 27(2) *UNSW Law Journal* 428. (These authors were commenting on the '*A*' litigation in the light of the Court of Appeal ruling and as a possible precedent for legal reform in Australia.)

suggested that there were errors exhibited by the majority of the House of Lords with respect to the test employed for deciding what constituted a 'public emergency' for the purposes of Article 15(1). Some of the Law Lords conveyed the unwelcome message that the threshold of severity for Article 15(1) is relatively low. It is arguable that Lord Hoffman's dissenting opinion, suggesting a restrictive approach to Article 15(1), is to be preferred, in particular for his interpretation of the Strasbourg jurisprudence as it currently stands. However, it is also argued that the '*A*' case may have highlighted the need to review the circumstances in which a State may lawfully derogate from an international human rights instrument. Clearly there is a need for the Strasbourg Court to clarify its understanding of the concept of 'public emergency' for the purposes of Article 15(1).

The structure of this article is as follows. First, the scope of the derogation will be discussed: this requires an examination of the notice of derogation itself as served to the Council of Europe on 18 December 2001 (Section I). Next, the justification for the British derogation as set out by the Government before Parliament will be analysed (Section II). We shall see that from the very outset questions were raised as regards both the motives for the derogation and whether there really existed a 'public emergency' within the terms required by Article 15(1). In the absence of a proper explanation by the Government as to the nature of the threat facing the county, the matter of the existence of a 'public emergency' and what was required by Article 15(1) was not addressed by Parliament in detail. The underlying need for a derogation passed through the Parliamentary process with little real scrutiny. Section III examines the various steps in the legal challenges to the detention of those held as a consequence of the derogation and the associated legislation, in order to see what was concluded at each juncture with respect to the threshold of severity for Article 15(1). The judgments raised some important issues concerning when a State can derogate from the Convention and in what circumstances. Section IV acknowledges that the House of Lords' ruling stands as a landmark regarding the balance to be struck between the protection of human rights and national security. However, it questions the approach taken by the Law Lords to the threshold of severity for reliance on Article 15(1). Sections V and VI are, respectively, a general commentary on derogations from international human rights law instruments with particular focus on the issue of the threshold of severity, and a detailed examination of the Strasbourg jurisprudence on Article 15(1) and the concept of 'public emergency'. The leading cases of the European Court of Human Rights on the threshold of severity are examined in detail in Section VI in order to emphasize that Article 15(1) does not entitle a State to derogate in the face of low-level terrorist violence, as seems to have been suggested by some members of the House of Lords. Finally Section VII questions the lawfulness of the British derogation from the point of view of the threshold of severity as set out in the Strasbourg jurisprudence to date. It questions whether that threshold may need to be reviewed in the light of the threat posed by the terrorism now associated with the post-September 11 era and argues for a more effective role for Parliament in the derogation process.

I. The United Kingdom's Derogation from the European Convention on Human Rights (18 December 2001)

In the wake of the events of 11 September the UK Parliament passed the Anti-Terrorism, Crime and Security Act 2001[8] (hereinafter 'ATCSA 2001' or 'the Act'). The Bill had been presented to Parliament on 12 November and entered into force just one month and two days later. It built on terrorism laws which were already 'widely regarded as the most rigorous in Europe'[9] and contained a number of controversial provisions, the most notorious of which were contained in Part 4 (under the sub-title 'Immigration and Asylum') which in effect permitted the Home Secretary to detain indefinitely without trial certain foreign nationals whom he certified as a threat to national security and whom he reasonably suspected to be international terrorists.[10] This new power of executive detention required the Government of the United Kingdom to derogate from the Convention, as well as Article 9 of the International Covenant on Civil and Political Rights ('ICCPR').[11] At the time of writing,[12] the United Kingdom remains the only member State to both the Convention and the Covenant to have cited the threat of terrorism post-September 11 as the underlying basis for the need to derogate from these instruments.

The derogation entered with respect to the Convention was made on 18 December 2001, via a declaration contained in a *Note Verbale* to the Secretary General of the Council of Europe.[13] Under the heading 'Public Emergency in the United Kingdom' the relevant part of the *Note Verbale*

[8] The Anti-Terrorism, Crime and Security Act 2001 (c 24), see (2001) 72 BYIL 479 and C Walker, *Blackstone's Guide to the Anti-Terrorism Legislation* (2002); A Tomkins, 'Legislating Against Terror: The Anti-Terrorism Crime and Security Act' (2002) *Public Law* 205 and H Fenwick, 'The Anti-Terrorism Crime and Security Act: A Proportionate Response to 11 September?' (2002) 65(5) *Modern Law Review* 724.

[9] Joint Committee on Human Rights (hereinafter 'JCHR'), *Second Report* (Anti-Terrorism, Crime and Security Bill) (2001–02) (HL 37, HC 372) para 30.

[10] ATCSA 2001, ss 21–23.

[11] ICCPR, 1966: GA res 2200A (XXI), 21 UN GAOR Supp (No 16) 52, UN Doc A/6316 (1966), 999 UNTS 171. For the text of the notice of derogation made with respect to the ICCPR (which was virtually identical to that made with respect to the Convention) see (2001) 72 BYIL 563–4. The derogation provision for the ICCPR is Art 4, the first section of which reads: '4(1). In time of *public emergency which threatens the life of the nation* and the existence of which is officially proclaimed, the States Parties to the present Covenant may take measures derogating from their obligations under the present Covenant to the extent strictly required by the exigencies of the situation . . .' (emphasis added).

[12] 31 October 2005.

[13] For full text see (2001) 44 *Yearbook of the European Convention on Human Rights* 20; see also (2001) 72 BYIL 562.

referred to the 'terrorist attacks in New York, Washington, D.C. and Pennsylvania on 11th September 2001 [which] resulted in several thousand deaths, including many British victims and others from 70 different countries'. Resolutions 1368 (2001) and 1373 (2001) of the United Nations Security Council were then cited, whereby that body 'recognised the attacks as a threat to international peace and security'. The *Note Verbale* continued: 'The threat from international terrorism is a continuing one' and recalled that in Resolution 1373 (2001), the Security Council, acting under Chapter VII of the United Nations Charter, 'required all States to take measures to prevent the commission of terrorist attacks, including by denying safe haven to those who finance, plan, support or commit terrorist attacks'. The *Note Verbale* went on:

> There exists a terrorist threat to the United Kingdom from persons suspected of involvement in international terrorism. In particular, there are foreign nationals present in the United Kingdom who are suspected of being concerned in the commission, preparation or instigation of acts of international terrorism, of being members of organisations or groups which are so concerned or of having links with members of such organisations or groups, and who *are a threat to the national security of the United Kingdom*. As a result, a public emergency, within the meaning of Article 15(1) of the Convention, exists in the United Kingdom (emphasis added).

There was no further elaboration as to the nature of the threat facing the United Kingdom.[14] However, it was explained that provision was made in ATCSA 2001, *inter alia*, 'for an extended power to arrest and detain a foreign national which will apply where it is intended to remove or deport the person from the United Kingdom but where removal or deportation is not for the time being possible, with the consequence that the detention would be unlawful under existing domestic law powers'. Reference was made to the legal process relevant to the new power of detention under ATCSA 2001 and the avenues of legal redress available to the individuals concerned.[15] The extended power of arrest and detention in ATCSA 2001 was described as 'a measure which is strictly required by the exigencies of the situation',[16] 'a temporary provision' to expire after fifteen months unless renewed by Parliament and which would be subject to annual renewal thereafter. The provision in question would be repealed at any time if 'in the Government's assessment, the public emergency no longer exists or the extended power is no longer strictly required by the exigencies of the situation'.

[14] In this respect the derogation kept up a long tradition of British derogations insofar as only minimal information was provided to the Council of Europe, see B Simpson, *Human Rights and the End of Empire* (2001) 878.

[15] Detainees had a right of appeal against their detention to the Special Immigration Appeals Commission ('SIAC') which had power to determine whether detention was appropriate to the facts of the case (ATCSA 2001, s 25). Appeals from SIAC were only available on a point of law. Detainees were free to leave the UK at any time, though this assumed that a country was willing to accept them.

[16] cf the language of Art 15(1).

The *Note Verbale* stated that derogation was made with respect to Article 5(1)(f) of the Convention. This permits the detention of a person with a view to deportation only in circumstances where 'action is being taken with a view to deportation'. The UK derogation was intended to enable continued detention of certain individuals in circumstances where this qualifying factor was not strictly present. Those individuals were foreign nationals whom the Home Secretary suspected of involvement with international terrorism, who would not be prosecuted for this (due, amongst other things, to the sensitivity of the evidence and the high standard of proof required) and who he was unable to deport for, despite the gravity of the threat to national security posed by the person concerned, the decision in *Chahal v United Kingdom*[17] established that Article 3 of the Convention[18] prevented removal or deportation of the individual concerned to a place where there was a real risk that he would suffer treatment contrary to that Article.[19] For such individuals notwithstanding a continuing intention to remove or deport the person being detained, it would not be possible to say that 'action is being taken with a view to deportation' within the meaning of Article 5(1)(f) since, as interpreted by the European Court in the *Chahal* case,[20] deportation proceedings had to be prosecuted with due diligence and it was necessary in such cases to

[17] *Chahal v UK* (n 17 above) App No 22414/93, (1997) 23 EHRR 413. See (1997) 68 BYIL 388.

[18] Art 3 of the Convention is a non-derogable right, see Art 15(2).

[19] *Chahal v UK* (n 17 above) paras 74, 79. There must be 'substantial grounds' establishing the reality of the 'real risk', paras 74, 80. The Court, delivering its ruling in 1996, stated that it was 'well aware of the immense difficulties faced by States in modern times in protecting their communities from terrorist violence' (para 79), nevertheless Art 3 prohibited torture, inhuman or degrading treatment or punishment in absolute terms, 'irrespective of the victim's conduct' (para 79) and 'however undesirable or dangerous' (para 80) the person concerned. It was not possible to balance the risk of ill-treatment against the reasons for expulsion in determining whether a State's responsibility is engaged (para 81 cf the arguments presented by the British Government summarized at para 76). The Court's judgment with respect to Art 3 was by 12 votes to 7. In their Joint Partly Dissenting Opinion Judges Golcüklü, Matscher, Sir John Freeland, Baka, Mifsud Bonnici, Gotchev, and Levits accepted the absolute character of Art 3 as regards a State's treatment of an individual within its own jurisdiction. However, as regards the extra-territorial effect of Art 3 (as with expulsion cases) they accepted that there was scope to balance the extent of the potential risk of ill-treatment with the nature of the threat to national security interests if the person concerned were to remain. It has been reported that the British Government will be seeking to persuade the Strasbourg Court to reverse the majority view in *Chahal* and adopt the stance taken by the minority on this Art 3 point. The opportunity to do so will arise now that the British Government has been given permission to act as a third-party intervener in a Dutch Art 3 'terrorist expulsion' case to be considered by the Strasbourg Court (*Ramzy v the Netherlands* App No 25424/05), see C Dyer in *The Guardian*, 3 October 2005 (<www.guardian.co.uk>—accessed 30 October 2005). The Governments of Italy, Lithuania, Portugal, and Slovakia, plus several NGOs, have also been given permission to intervene in this case, see C Dyer in *The Guardian*, 18 October 2005.

In the wake of the July 2005 bombings in London the British Prime Minister, Tony Blair, stated that 'the circumstances of our national security have self evidently changed'. He pointed out that deportations of suspected non-national terrorists would be pursued by seeking assurances from the destination country that there would be no ill-treatment, adding 'Should legal obstacles arise, we will legislate further including, if necessary, amending the Human Rights Act in respect of the interpretation of the European Convention on Human Rights', Press Statement, 5 August 2005 (quoted in JUSTICE, *Changing the Rules: the judiciary, human rights and the constitution* (2005) iv).

[20] *Chahal v UK* (n 17 above) para 112.

determine whether the duration of the deportation proceedings was excessive.[21]

Article 15(1) of the Convention refers to 'war or other public emergency threatening the life of the nation',[22] and it was evidently with reference to the second of these two heads that the derogation was made.[23] There was no reference to a *specific* terrorist threat to the United Kingdom as such in the *Note Verbale*. Its language had been one of 'a threat to ... national security' and it would appear from the document alone that the British Government assumed that this could be equated with the notion of 'public emergency threatening the life of the nation' for the purposes of derogating from the Convention. In fact, the term 'national security'[24] is found in several places in the Convention as a permissible limitation on rights and so not a basis for derogation as such.[25] Hence, interferences with the rights to respect for private and family life, to freedom of expression and to freedom of assembly and association may all be justified for the legitimate aim of 'national security',[26] and under Article 6(1) a trial may be held in secret for the same reason.[27] Article 5(1) of the Convention protecting the liberty of individuals, does not include 'national security' amongst the 'exhaustive' list of exceptions set out within it,[28] whilst in its very first case the Court indicated that the notion of preventive detention is 'repugnant to the fundamental principles of the Convention'.[29] In order to detain an individual on national security grounds alone therefore, when there is no intention of bringing criminal charges against an individual (as would justify detention under Article 5(1)(c)) or deporting him or her (Article 5(1)(f)), it will be

[21] ibid para 113.

[22] The equally authentic French text reads: 'En cas de guerre ou en cas d'autre danger public menaçant la vie de la nation ...'.

[23] ie the UK Government did not seek to rely on there being a so-called 'war against terrorism' to justify the 2001 derogation in terms of 'war'. Even if the 'war on terrorism' could be categorized as a 'war' for the purpose of Art 15(1), it would not automatically entitle a State to derogate given the need to satisfy the qualifying criteria 'threatening the life of the nation'. On the characterization of the 'war against terrorism' see C Greenwood, 'War, Terrorism and International law' (2003) 56 *Current Legal Problems* 505 and V Lowe, '"Clear and Present Danger": Responses to Terrorism' (2005) 54 ICLQ 185.

[24] On national security and public law in the UK and in other jurisdictions see L Lustgarten and I Leigh, *In From the Cold: National Security and Parliamentary Democracy* (1994).

[25] Hence it has been observed that a limitation based on 'national security' (where appropriate) may potentially be permanent, and therefore incorporated into legislation or administrative or judicial practice. By contrast, a derogation should only ever be a temporary measure, see P Vegleris, 'Valeur et Signification de la Clause "Dans une société démocratique" dans La Convention Européenne des Droits de L'Homme' (1968) 1 *Human Rights Journal* (1968) 219, 224.

[26] See Arts 8(2), 10(2), and 11(2).

[27] See Art 6(1). Protocol 4, Art 2(3) (liberty of movement and free choice of residence) also refers to 'national security' as a limitation. On the Convention and national security see I Cameron, *National security and the European Convention on Human Rights* (2000). The preparatory work to the Convention throws little light on the intended meaning of the term 'national security', see Cameron (above) 49–50. As regards the ICCPR and references to national security, see Arts 12(3), 14(1), 19(3), 21, and 22(2).

[28] cf ICCPR, Art 9 which does not have an exhaustive list of grounds for when liberty can be denied.

[29] *Lawless v Ireland (No 3)* App No 332/57 (1979–1980) 1 EHRR 15, para 14.

necessary to derogate from the Convention. However, whether a public danger based on national security considerations suffices for a derogation under Article 15(1) will depend on whether the threat in question is so severe that it leads to a situation said to be 'threatening the life of the nation', which, according to the definition provided by the Strasbourg Court means that there must be a 'threat to the organised life of the community of which the State is composed'.[30] So, it does not follow that each and every threat to 'national security' will justify a derogation. The *Note Verbale* referred only to the existence of a 'public emergency within the meaning of Article 15(1)' and did not explain why the crisis situation apparently facing the United Kingdom was severe enough to be one that was 'threatening the life of the nation'.[31] How, therefore, was the derogation factually justified? To pursue this question we need to review the passage of ATCSA 2001 before Parliament.

II. Review of the Existence of a 'Public Emergency' by Parliament

The Home Secretary, David Blunkett, first announced proposals to combat 'the threat of international terrorism' on 15 October 2001. The first draft of what was then the ATCS Bill was tabled on 12 November 2001, with the Act receiving Royal Assent one month and two days later. The *Note Verbale* referred to above, which was dated 18 December 2001, remained unchanged since a first draft of it was published on 11 November 2001, ie one day before the publication of the Bill. It then formed an attachment to an official derogation order prepared by the Government for the purpose of compliance with domestic law.[32] The order was debated in Parliament on 19 November 2001 and was approved by it two days later. The fact that the derogation notice was prepared in advance of Parliament's analysis of the proposed legislation was the subject of criticism on the basis that it hampered effective scrutiny of the decision to derogate.[33] Arguably it provides insight into how the

[30] *Lawless v Ireland (No 3)* (n 29 above) para 28.

[31] No provision of the Convention requires a derogating State to explain the nature of the threat it is facing when derogating and precisely why it satisfies the test of 'threatening the life of the nation'. Past practice indicates that States have rarely if ever seen it as their responsibility to do this. The notices of derogation served by High Contracting Parties to the Convention in previous years are available in the respective volume of the *Yearbook of the European Convention on Human Rights*.

[32] In order to derogate from the Convention it was necessary for the Government to comply with the Human Rights Act 1998, s 14 which, in anticipation of derogation, requires the creation of a 'designated derogation' order. This was made by the Secretary of State on 11 November 2001, entering into force on 13 November 2001 as The Human Rights Act 1998 (Designated Derogation) Order 2001, SI 2001/3644. For the effect of a designated derogation on the operation of the 1998 Act, see s 1(2) of the same Act. A designated derogation will lapse after 5 years (1998 Act, s 16(1)(b)), however, the Secretary of State may extend a designation order for a further period of five years at any time before it lapses (s 16(2)).

[33] Council of Europe Commissioner for Human Rights (Mr Alvaro Gil-Robles), Opinion 1/2002, (Comm DH (2002) 7, 28 August 2002) paras 3–23 (hereinafter '*CoE Commissioner Opinion*'); also

derogation issue itself was handled more generally by the executive before Parliament. In November and December 2005 there was no real explanation as to why the specific conditions for derogation under Article 15(1) ('threat to the life of the nation') were present. To this extent the Government's stance appeared to be consistent with the view apparently presented in a document to the Parliamentary Labour Party in which the Home Secretary had said that the Government's declaration of a state of emergency was a purely technical one to allow suspected terrorists to be detained.[34]

The immigration context

The Home Secretary's appearance before the Joint Committee on Human Rights ('JCHR')[35] on 14 November 2001 provided the first major occasion for the Government's case that an Article 15 emergency existed to be scrutinized. In fact, the answers provided by the Home Secretary to the JCHR give the impression that the major driving force for derogation was immigration rather than an immediate security threat to the United Kingdom as such (although the latter was clearly important too). Asked why there was a need for derogation Mr Blunkett's immediate response was that:

> ... our case rests on the fact, and we have seen it from both other Governments and from those commentating, that there is a very real consideration about those who are using the United Kingdom as a base for aiding, abetting, supporting, helping to finance organised terrorism across the world. It is in the circumstances where, on other occasions, I would be able to adjudge as Home Secretary that someone's presence was not conducive to the public good, but because I cannot remove them to a third country, I should either leave them alone or seek to detain them, that we are moving to detain them.[36]

A major reason for the derogation was because, the Home Secretary continued, 'we have people who use the United Kingdom as a base'. Although evidence was lacking to show they had committed a crime here, 'our security and intelligence services believe they are a threat here or in the rest of the world'; in these circumstances the British Government had 'an obligation to ensure we do not act as a host, as a haven, for those people who are not British nationals, who are here as guests in our country but are abusing that hospitality'.[37] It was duly noted that 'one of the accusations

JUSTICE, *Response to the JCHR Inquiry into UK Derogations from Convention Rights* (May 2002), available at <www.justice.org.uk> (accessed 30 October 2005) and British Institute of Human Rights, *Submission to Joint Committee on Human Rights Inquiry on Derogations from Convention Rights* (2002).

[34] The present writer has not seen this document himself, see, however, the comments of Mr Kevin McNamara MP before the JCHR, *Second Report* (Anti-Terrorism, Crime and Security Bill) (2001–02) (HL 37, HC 372), Minutes of Evidence, Question 9.

[35] On the work of the JCHR see D Feldman, 'Parliamentary Scrutiny of Legislation and Human Rights' [2002] *Public Law* 323.

[36] JCHR, *Second Report* (2001–02) (n 34 above) Question 3.

[37] ibid Question 4.

that has been made about the United Kingdom is that because of the way in which it has been possible for people to be hosted here whilst planning such [terrorist] attacks, we ought to protect both ourselves and the rest of the world from [suspected international terrorists] from being able to do [this]'.[38] The derogating powers of detention were therefore required to keep detained suspected international terrorists who could not be deported by virtue of the decision in the *Chahal* case (an authority which the Government would uphold despite the temptation to avoid doing so).[39]

A threat to the life of the nation?

In making the submissions just noted, the Home Secretary referred to the House of Lords' ruling in *Secretary of State for the Home Department v Rehman*[40] (delivered on 11 October 2001). The Home Secretary's point had been that 'an attack does not have to be targeted specifically against the United Kingdom or its interests to be regarded as a danger to our national security'.[41] Precisely how this was relevant to issues under Article 15(1), given its own specific language and threshold requirement, was not made clear at the time or subsequently. However, as regards the nature of the terrorist threat confronting the United Kingdom the Home Secretary made a general comparison with previous occasions when a derogation from the Convention had been made by the United Kingdom and appeared to regard the threshold requirement for Article 15(1) as self-evidently satisfied given '11 September and the threats that have been made by bin Laden and the Al-Qaeda group' against other nations, including the United Kingdom. He challenged 'anyone' to tell him 'whether there have been, or whether there are likely to be, circumstances which are greater than those we face at the moment which would justify under Article 15 the derogation from Article 5'.[42] The threat posed, he argued, exceeded that encountered at the height of IRA activity, 'because it was very clear and understood by our intelligence services that the IRA were not using chemical, biological, radiological or nuclear provisions for attack. They never threatened to do so, they did not possess those weapons to do so, nor did they indicate that they were engaged in an international terrorist action'.[43] It seems that the resort to derogation was, in the view of the Home Secretary, mitigated by its limited extent compared to alternative possibilities[44] and also by the safeguards against abuse that were proposed.

[38] JCHR, *Second Report* (2001–02) (n 34 above) Question 6. See generally Questions 3–7 and also the statement made by Mr Blunkett in the House of Commons on 19 November 2001 explaining that the UK was generally perceived to be a country that harboured terrorist extremists who posed both an internal and an external threat, HC Debates, vol 376, col 25, 19 November 2001.

[39] JCHR, *Second Report* (2001–02) (n 34 above) Question 9.

[40] *Secretary of State for the Home Department v Rehman* [2003] 1 AC 153.

[41] Oral evidence of the Home Secretary recounted in JCHR, *Second Report* (2001–02) (n 34 above) Question 3.

[42] ibid Question 9.

[43] ibid Question 22.

[44] According to Minister Beverley Hughes, the derogation was a 'more measured and proportionate approach' than that proposed by the official Opposition, which was to denounce the Convention

The JCHR subsequently reported that it had 'considered the Home Secretary's evidence carefully' and 'recognise[d] that there may be evidence of the existence of a public emergency threatening the life of the nation, although none was shown by him to this Committee'.[45] It warned that 'it is especially important for each House to decide whether they are satisfied of the existence of a public emergency threatening the life of the nation', pointing out that according to the text of the Bill as it stood no domestic court would have the power to assess whether the derogation met the standards required by Article 15(1).[46] Nonetheless, in

and then to ratify it subject to reservations under Art 3 permitting deportation of terrorists. Derogating from Art 5(1) 'preserve[d] unequivocally ... our international obligations under the ECHR, while enabling us to implement the detention measures that we feel are necessary in the event that we cannot deport a person consistent with the provisions of Article 3'. HC Debates, vol 375, col 147, 19 November 2001. See also the comments of the Home Secretary by way of oral evidence before the JCHR, *Second Report* (2001–02) (n 34 above) Question 9.

In fact, on 26 January 2003 the idea of denouncing the Convention and ratifying it again, subject to a reservation under Art 3, was put forward by the British Prime Minister, Tony Blair, as a possible course of action in an interview on BBC television ('Breakfast with Frost'). A legal opinion provided for Liberty by David Pannick QC and Shaheed Fatima argued that such a course of action would be invalid and unlawful, see D Pannick QC and S Fatima, *Legal Opinion: Denunciation of the European Convention on Human Rights* (29 January 2003), available at <www.liberty-human-rights.org.uk/issues/pdfs/pannick-opinion-art-3.pdf> (accessed 30 October 2005).

Denunciation of the Convention is permitted by Art 58; reservations by Art 57. A denunciation takes effect six months after delivery of a notice to denounce (Art 58(1)). Neither Art 58 nor Art 57 expressly exclude the possibility of a State denouncing the Convention in order to ratify it again subject to reservations, however, it is submitted that this is very likely to be because it never occurred to the drafters that such a course of action would be taken. No High Contracting Party to the Convention has ever attempted to withdraw and re-ratify with reservations. Pannick and Fatima argued that a reservation of the nature suggested by Mr Blair might be declared invalid by the Strasbourg Court on the basis that it undermined the effectiveness of the Convention and would be an abuse of good faith (see paras 14–17). To this may be added the point that it is arguable that Art 19(3) of the Vienna Convention on the Law of Treaties would apply to any attempted reservation. This stipulates that a reservation may not be made when it is 'incompatible with the object and purpose of the treaty', and it is strongly arguable that this would be so on the facts. First, the purpose of the new reservation would have been to conclude an arrangement that sought to circumvent pre-existing legal obligations under the Convention, which the Court has described as a 'constitutional instrument of European public order' (*Loizidou v Turkey* (Preliminary objections), (1995) 20 EHRR 99 para 75). Also, insofar as the new reservation would be made with respect to Art 3, this is a non-derogable right, one that 'enshrines one of the fundamental values of the democratic societies making up the Council of Europe' (*Chahal* (n 17 above) para 96) and so one in respect of which, it may be argued, no reservation is permitted. To the extent that the substance of a new reservation may conflict with a principle of customary international law, it would also be strongly arguable that it would be invalid for the reasons set out by the Human Rights Committee in *General Comment No. 24, Issues Relating to Reservations Made Upon Ratification or Accession to the Covenant or the Optional Protocols thereto, or in Relation to Declarations Under Article 41 of The Covenant*: CCPR/C/21/Rev.1/Add.6, para 8.

[45] JCHR, *Second Report* (2001–02) (n 34 above) para 30. The Committee also warned at this stage that the lack of safeguards built into the Bill, particularly in relation to detention powers, caused it to 'doubt whether the measures in the Bill can be said to be strictly required by the exigencies of the situation' (para 30). The Committee members recognized 'the dilemma from which the Home Secretary sought to free himself by recourse to derogation' but were 'not persuaded that the circumstances of the present emergency or the exigencies of the current situation meet the tests set out in Article 15 of the ECHR' (para 78). For subsequent expressions of doubt prior to conclusion of the Bill see JCHR, *Fifth Report* (Anti-Terrorsim, Crime and Security Bill: Further Report) (2001–02) (HL 51, HC 420) paras 4–6.

[46] ibid. In fact, the final text of ATCSA 2001 permitted review of the derogation issue by the Special Immigration Appeals Commission, see text accompanying nn 80–100 below.

the weeks before the 2001 Act received the Royal Assent and the derogation notice was served, only on a small number of occasions were ministers pressed to explain why the situation facing the United Kingdom satisfied the threshold requirement of Article 15(1). An opportunity came on 19 November 2001 when the derogation was the subject of debate and Minister Beverley Hughes addressed the House of Commons. She referred to 'a number of public threats made by bin Laden and his supporters against western interests', adding that there was 'evidence to show that international terrorist organisations have links with the UK and therefore constitute a threat'.[47] Mr Mark Fisher MP asked how the risk of terrorist activity actually threatened the 'life of this country'[48] in the sense of Article 15(1). Ms Hughes thought that 'the risk we face does, or could, threaten the life of the country'. An attack of 11 September proportions 'would clearly threaten the life of the nation'; but no explanation was given as to why and how this was so. Ms Hughes nevertheless added that 'Acts of terrorism outside this country can also threaten the life of the nation in threatening our economy and well-being' and she argued for the need to 'look more broadly at the question of defining whether the risk threatens the life of the nation'. The Government had 'taken the view that it does' and that, therefore, 'the first test of article 15 has been met'.[49] She explained that the Government 'believe[d] that there are people here who are involved in international terrorism' and that this was 'part of the basis for the evidence which, taken in the round ... [met] the first test of article 15—that there must be a public emergency'.[50] She regarded the question put to her by a backbench MP and doubting the genuine need for derogation as one that, in 'current circumstances', was an 'extraordinary' one to ask. By way of reply reference was made to:

> ... the events of 11 September; the two UN Security Council resolutions that pointed to the threat to international security and gave permission, as it were, for states to take measures to protect themselves; engagement in conflict in Afghanistan[51] as a close ally of the United States; the presence of suspected terrorists here; further threats by Osama bin Laden and his supporters; and their preparedness to use nuclear, chemical and biological weapons; and the material found during the conflict in Kabul.

In view of all those circumstances, 'any reasonable person would conclude that there was a state of public emergency threatening the life of the nation'. Acknowledging that there was indeed 'no specific and immediate threat to this country of which we are aware', the Minister stressed that 'this did not mean that there is not a state of public emergency in the sense outlined by the UN Security Council resolutions' and as 'endorsed' a few weeks previously by a ruling from the House of Lords.

[47] HC Debates, vol 375, col 127, 19 November 2001. [48] ibid. [49] ibid cols 127–8.
[50] ibid, col 146. [51] This had commenced in October 2001.

What did the Minister actually mean by this? The Security Council Resolutions, which were cited in the notice of derogation, had referred to the September 11th attacks as 'a threat to international peace and security',[52] and a 'serious challenge and threat to international security'.[53] They supported the idea that all States were under a mandatory duty to help prevent acts of terrorism whether the attack would be against them or another nation. The reference to a Law Lords' ruling was presumably that in the *Rehman* case, referred to earlier by the Home Secretary.

A loosely defined threat

Statements made by the Home Secretary bolster the suggestion that the Government had a generous understanding of the notion of 'threat' and the 'life of the nation' element of Article 15(1). When pressed for an explanation of why the terrorist threat put in issue the life of the nation, Mr Blunkett's response was to refer to September 11 and other terrorist attacks, pointing out how sophisticated they were and the wider effects that they had had. Their intention had been to 'disrupt ... both the economic life and activity of a nation'. There could be no doubt, Mr Blunkett said, 'that what happened on 11 September has not had a dramatic effect on the life of the United States, on its economy and on the economy of the world ... It has had that effect, and everyone knows that. It has changed the perspective'.[54] He would not say either way whether there would be an attack on the United Kingdom; but the question was 'whether ... we would find what we are proposing acceptable if a major attack took place'.[55] Norman Baker MP asked to what extent the 'essence of the life of the country ... [was] under threat', to which Mr Blunkett responded that he was 'in a cleft stick'. On the one hand, he sought to reassure in order 'to ensure that the life of the nation was not immediately disrupted by a change in people's behaviour', but, on the other hand, this was not to deny that 'a threat to the life of the nation' existed. Two months on from September 11 there was an undiminished 'threat'. The correct course was to take action 'to preclude that threat to the life of the nation ... rather

52 UN Security Council Res 1368 (2001) UN Doc S/RS/1368 (2001).

53 UN Security Council Res 1373 (2001) UN Doc S/RS/1373 (2001). This Resolution made no reference to the preservation or protection of 'human rights'. However, the Security Council has since passed a Resolution emphasizing the duty of States to combat terrorism without infringing international legal standards in the international human rights and humanitarian fields, UN Security Council Res 1456 (2003) UN Doc S/RES/1456 (2003) Preamble and para 6. For a discussion of the work of various UN bodies (the Security Council, the General Assembly, the Commission on Human Rights) on the topic of terrorism and human rights in the post-'September 11' period see H Duffy, *The 'War on Terror' and the Framework of International Law* (2005) Ch 7, esp 373–8.

54 On why 'national security' interests should not be confused with national economic interests, see Lustgarten and Leigh (n 24 above) 27–30. The list of restrictions found under Art 8(2) of the Convention includes both 'national security' and 'the economic well-being of the country', so implying that the categories are mutually exclusive.

55 HC Debates, vol 376, cols 917–18, 12 December 2001.

than taking the action after the life of the nation has demonstrably been threatened'.[56]

By this stage the JCHR had received submissions from a number of non-governmental organizations ('NGOs'). Some of these took the view that there was no 'public emergency' for the purposes of Article 15(1),[57] whilst another appeared to cautiously accept the view that there could be.[58] All the organizations criticized the proportionality of the proposed Part 4 detention scheme. At a late stage in the passage of the the Act, certain judicial safeguards were inserted and, with respect to the controversial Part 4 detention powers, provision was made for a 'sunset' clause of 10 November 2006, plus the need for annual Parliamentary approval. Royal Assent was granted on 14 December 2001. The United Kingdom's derogation took effect on 18 December 2001.[59] It was withdrawn over three years later, on 16 March 2005, following the challenges that culminated in the Law Lords' ruling,[60] by which stage a total of sixteen people had been detained under the Part 4 powers.[61]

Some comments on the derogation and the Parliamentary process

Having set out the basis for the derogation of December 2001 as set out by the Government, some general comments may be made about the derogation itself and the process by which it was put in place.

[56] HC Debates (n 55 above) col 918.

[57] On behalf of Liberty it was submitted that Art 15 did not apply as there was 'no imminent threat of the complete breakdown of civil society in the UK', moreover 'although there are threats, the nation itself is not in jeopardy'. A distinction was drawn between the proposed derogation and those relating to Northern Ireland in the 1980s and 1990s: Liberty, *Memorandum from Liberty (the National Council for Civil Liberties) on the Anti-Terrorism, Crime and Security Bill 2001* (3 December 2003). Liberty had commissioned an opinion from David Pannick QC who also cast doubt on the lawfulness of the derogation both in terms of whether the conditions required for derogation were present and as regards the proportionality of the measures proposed: see *Opinion of David Pannick QC prepared for Liberty (the National Council for Civil Liberties) on the derogation from Article 5(1) of the European Convention on Human Rights to allow for detention without trial.* See also *Memorandum from Amnesty International on the Anti-terrorism, Crime and Security Bill.* These documents are included as Appendices to JCHR, *Fifth Report* (2001–02) (n 45 above). Academic commentators subsequently queried the existence of a 'public emergency', see Tomkins. (n 8 above) 6, Fenwick (n 8 above) 743–6 and D Bonner, 'Managing Terrorism while respecting Human Rights? European Aspects of the Anti-Terrorism Crime and Security Act 2001' (2002) 8(4) *European Public Law* 497, 513–17.

[58] See *Memorandum from JUSTICE on the Anti-Terrorism, Crime and Security Bill,* also *Joint Opinion prepared for JUSTICE by David Anderson QC and Jemima Stratford on the proposed derogation from Article 5 ECHR and the Anti-Terrorism, Crime and Security Bill, Clauses 21–32.*

[59] There was no special declaration of a 'public emergency' as such, cf ICCPR, Art 4(1) which requires that States 'officially proclaim' an emergency. The ECtHR has stated that formal public notification of an emergency in Parliament suffices for the purpose of 'official' proclamation, which may be read in to Art 15(1) via the last 14 words of that provision, see *Brannigan and McBride v UK* App Nos 14553/89 and 14554/89 (1994) 17 EHRR 539, paras 72–73.

[60] See below. Although the Council of Europe was notified of the withdrawal on 16 March 2005, for the purposes of domestic law withdrawal was effected by the Human Rights Act 1998 (Amendment) Order 2005 (SI 2005/1071) which came into effect on 8 April 2005.

[61] For a useful summary of the legal position of the detainees under ATCSA 2001, see the judgment of Lady Hale in '*A*' (n 2 above) para 223.

The specific nature of the derogation and the immigration context

The derogation was unusual in nature given the factual circumstances said to underpin it. At the time of derogation there was a lack of material evidence relating to a threat to the United Kingdom, other than that demonstrated by the activity of terrorists elsewhere in the world. The threat to the United Kingdom was based on secret intelligence information. The British derogation therefore immediately stands out from other derogations to the Convention examined by the Strasbourg Court in the last twenty-five years. Those derogations[62] had been made with respect to Northern Ireland and South-East Turkey, in each case against the backdrop of an organized campaign of terrorist violence whereby Article 5(3)[63] had been derogated from so as to allow the authorities extra time to detain (and so interrogate) an individual suspected of terrorist involvement prior to his or her appearance before a judge or judicial officer. The derogations did not involve such a significant interference with the fundamental rights of the individuals concerned, as was the situation for the individuals in '*A*'.

The British derogation of 2001 seemed designed to target a predetermined group of people: suspected international terrorists who were certified as such and as a threat to national security by the Home Secretary but who could not be deported owing to European human rights law. According to the Government in December 2001, the threat only existed owing to the presence of such people. One might ask whether, from the perspective of December 2001, there would have been a 'public emergency' in the first place if the constraint rooted in Convention jurisprudence on Article 3 had not existed. During the passage of the 2001 Act David Pannick QC argued on behalf of Liberty that it was 'strongly arguable that the Secretary of State [was] not seeking to derogate from Article 5(1) because of a public emergency threatening the life of the nation, but because Article 3 prevent[ed] him removing from the United Kingdom asylum-seekers who may face persecution abroad'. It was 'very doubtful that it is a valid use of Article 15(1) to impose detriments on persons because they seek to take advantage of rights conferred by Article 3, especially when Article 15(2) prohibits any derogation from Article 3 itself because of its fundamental nature'.[64] With this in mind it is interesting to note that, initially at least, it seems that the derogation was apparently justified by the Home Secretary less on the basis of a threat to the United Kingdom as such and more by the Government's intention to prevent the country being used as a base for international terrorists.[65] Again the *Note Verbale* had referred explicitly to UN Security Council

[62] See Section VI below.

[63] Art 5(3) reads: 'Everyone arrested or detained in accordance with the provisions of paragraph 1.c of this article shall be brought promptly before a judge or other officer authorised by law to exercise judicial power and shall be entitled to trial within a reasonable time or to release pending trial. Release may be conditioned by guarantees to appear for trial'.

[64] Liberty, *Memorandum from Liberty* (n 57 above).

[65] See text accompanying n 36 above.

Resolutions requiring States not to act as 'safe haven[s]' for terrorism.[66] It was fundamental to the Law Lords' ruling, delivered three years later, that the detainees' case was viewed not from the perspective of the Government's right to control immigration but from the perspective of the right to liberty owed to everyone under Article 5 of the Convention. That ruling exposed the irrationality of using immigration control as the means of dealing with a threat to international security posed by suspected terrorists.

The Government's approach to derogation

To summarize, the derogation was made in the weeks following the events of September 11 when, for understandable reasons, there was anxiety that the United Kingdom might be the target of a similar attack. The associated legislation made its way through Parliament in just over one month, with the content and scope of the derogation having been drafted (if not served) in advance of the commencement of the legislative process and debated only one week into it. The JCHR expressed doubts both as to the existence of a public emergency and the strict need for the specific measures being taken in response. As one academic has commented 'little if any evidence of the nature of the threat was presented to Parliament and in many ways the Act was passed on trust'.[67] The European Commissioner for Human Rights was generally critical of the British Government in this regard. He argued that the 'failure to disclose any information at all [regarding the nature of the terrorist threat], where it is maintained that such information exists' was 'manifestly incompatible with the requirement of the democratic control of executive authority which is of particular importance in respect of measures limiting rights guaranteed by the Convention'.[68] The implication was that the classified nature of the information underpinning the threat to the United Kingdom left Parliament uninformed and therefore compromised as a fully effective scrutinizer of the executive in this crucial area of governance.[69]

Thus the reality of the threat specifically facing the United Kingdom was hardly clarified by the various statements and submissions made to Parliament by Government officials in late 2001. Parliament was provided with what were in effect general appeals to the increased risk of terrorist activity, a risk that was heightened owing to the presence of suspected international terrorists. It was clear from the outset that the threat, so far as it existed, was *unspecific* in nature. Ministerial statements on 15 October 2001 and 5 March 2002 accepted that 'There is no immediate intelligence pointing to a specific threat to the United Kingdom, but we remain alert, domestically as well as internationally'[70] and 'It would be wrong to say that we have evidence of a particular threat'.[71]

[66] See text accompanying n 36 above. [67] Tierney (n 3 above) 672.

[68] *CoE Commissioner Opinion* (n 33 above) para 22. [69] See ibid, paras 13–23.

[70] HC Debates, vol 372, col 925, 15 October 2001.

[71] House of Commons Select Committee on Defence, *Fourth Special Report* (The Threat from Terrorism: Government Response) (2001–02) (HC 667), Appendix, para 13.

A 'technical emergency'?

The Guardian newspaper reported that it was the Home Secretary's view that the declaration of a public emergency under Article 15 was a 'legal technicality' enabling the United Kingdom to opt out of Article 5(1)(f).[72] Overall one senses that the derogation provision of the Convention was viewed by the Government as a convenient tool to facilitate its proposed scheme of detention without trial in an immigration context. This is not to lose sight of the very serious situation confronting the United Kingdom. But it does seem that first and foremost the British Government regarded the particular measures it was taking as being required given the predicted conflict with Convention standards (Article 3), and justified above all by necessity. This consideration appeared to overtake all others and to avoid the need for any detailed governmental justification for the derogation in terms of Article 15(1) as a 'threat to the life of the nation'. On this specific point the justification for the derogation which was presented to Parliament and subsequently to the courts was the potential impact very serious terrorism could have as regards lives and infrastructure damage, but also wider vital national (and even international) interests, above all economic, that would be jeopardized were a terrorist event such as those which occurred on September 11 to occur on British soil. Hence the justifications provided by the Government seemed to suggest that Article 15(1) could be read as if that provision read 'public emergency in which the lives of people within the nation' are seriously at risk, or as if the 'public emergency' could be one which put at risk the 'life of the nation' in the more general sense (as with the reference made by Mr Blunkett to the 'dramatic effect on the life of the United States' that the terrorists' attacks had had).[73] It was never explained just how a terrorist atrocity, even on the proportions of the September 11 attacks, would actually threaten the life of the nation in the sense later described by Lord Hoffman in the House of Lords.[74]

III. The Legal Challenge to Derogation and Detention

The Special Immigration Appeals Commission

Section 20 of the 2001 Act provided that any challenge to detention under its Part 4 had to be to the Special Immigration Appeals Commission (SIAC)[75] and gave it all the powers which would otherwise be exercisable

[72] M Tempest, *The Guardian*, 19 November 2001 <www.guardian.co.uk>. See also Human Rights Watch, *Commentary on the Anti-Terrorism, Crime and Security Bill 2001*, 16 November 2001, available at <www.hrw.org/backgrounder/eca/UKleg1106.htm> (accessed 30 October 2005). See text accompanying n 13 above.

[73] See text accompanying n 54 above.

[74] See p 272 below.

[75] The Special Immigration Appeals Commission Act 1997 (c 68) created SIAC following the Strasbourg Court's ruling in *Chahal* (n 17 above). It is a legal body with the status of the High

by the High Court. On 30 July 2002 SIAC delivered a ruling ('the SIAC judgment')[76] on the legality of the detention of the nine individuals then being detained under Part 4 of ATCSA 2001, which itself required an assessment of the legality of the derogation (over which SIAC had sole jurisdiction by virtue of section 30 of the Act).[77] On these issues SIAC was entitled to consider not only material which could be made public, but also 'closed material', non-disclosable for national security reasons[78] and which it took into account in the assessment of the existence of a 'public emergency'.[79]

Assessment of the existence of a 'public emergency'

In his capacity as Chairman of SIAC, Collins J delivered the only opinion. Before addressing the issue of the existence of a public emergency, he set out the approach to be taken. It was accepted that an assessment of the existence of an emergency would require adoption of the approach set out by Lord Steyn in *R (Daly) v Secretary of State for the Home Department*,[80] adapted to the context of the case before SIAC which included, on the one hand, the importance attached by the Strasbourg Court to the right to liberty,[81] and on the other, the importance of maintaining national security[82] and the preservation of the safety of British citizens. Collins J stated: 'It seems to us to be self evident that where ... [the] risk is of destruction and mayhem on a very substantial scale, those responsible for deciding whether the risk exists and what measures are necessary to try to ensure that it is not translated into a reality must be allowed a reasonably wide margin of discretion.'[83] SIAC would not undertake a full merits review of the existence of an emergency; even though it had access to closed material it lacked 'the *specific advice and expertise* in this area of enormous importance for all the citizens of this country which was and is available to the Secretary of State' (emphasis

Court, but has special procedural rules allowing it to address deportation cases involving national security issues. SIAC's operation was amended by ATCSA 2001. For a full analysis of SIAC's functioning, see House of Commons Constitutional Affairs Committee, *Seventh Report* (The Operation of the Special Immigration Appeals Commission (SIAC) and the use of Special Advocates) (2004–05) vol I (HC 323-I). It has been argued that the procedural rules operated by SIAC fall short of the requirements of Art 6 of the Convention (the right to a fair trial), see Amnesty International, *UK: Text of Amnesty International submission to the House of Lords opposing indefinite detention* AI Index: EUR 45/027/2004 (4 October 2004) Part 5.

[76] *A and others v Secretary of State for the Home Department* (Special Immigration Appeals Commission) 30 July 2002, [2002] HRLR 45 (hereinafter 'SIAC judgment'). See M Elliott, 'Developments: United Kingdom' (2003) 1 *International Journal of Constitutional Law* 334.

[77] As regards SIAC's jurisdiction with respect to Art 15(1), see Tomkins (n 3 above) 260–1.

[78] SIAC judgment (n 76 above) para 9.

[79] ibid paras 11–21.

[80] *R (Daly) v Secretary of State for the Home Department* [2001] 2 AC 532, [2001] HRLR 49, see SIAC judgment (n 76 above) para 21.

[81] ibid para 22. Collins J stated, 'in carrying out the exercise of balancing the need for derogation against its impact on personal liberty consideration must be given to the human rights of probably thousands, including in particular the even more important right to life, which may be gravely affected if the risk materialises'.

[82] Lord Hoffman's judgment in *Rehman* (n 40 above) was cited, SIAC judgment (n 76 above) para 15.

[83] ibid para 21.

added). The 'proper function [for SIAC] in the context of this case [was] to decide whether the decision that there was ... an emergency as justified derogation was one which was reasonable on all the material or to put it another way, was one which he [the Secretary of State] was entitled to reach'.[84] Brief reference was made to the meaning of 'public emergency' as set out by the Strasbourg institutions in the judgment of *Lawless v Ireland*[85] and the European Commission of Human Rights' Report in 'the "*Greek*" case'.[86] Slightly more detailed attention was given to the relatively recent decision of the European Court in *Marshall v United Kingdom*,[87] from which SIAC concluded that 'it is clear that the [Strasbourg] court accepted that the existence of a real threat of terrorist outrages and the retention by the terrorists of an organisational capacity to kill or maim on a wide scale sufficed to establish the existence of an emergency within the meaning of Article 15(1)'.[88] SIAC apparently took the genuine threat of a major terrorist outrage as the legal threshold for reliance on Article 15(1) and so Collins J turned to an assessment of whether that test was satisfied on the facts.

Here the essence of the Government's case was that there was a public emergency in the United Kingdom because of the threat of terrorist attack based on the following grounds. The horrors of September 11 had changed everyone's appreciation of the risks posed by international terrorists and heightened the need on the part of the Government to take preventive action. There was a genuine belief that a significant body of foreign nationals in the United Kingdom might carry out atrocities which could be even worse since there was an intention to use weapons of mass destruction in such attacks. The potential impact of such an attack in terms of harm to people, to 'the economic life of the nation', and the global economy was obvious.[89] No other European nation was threatened in the same way as the United Kingdom, as, due to the stance the British Government had taken both before and after September 11, it was a prime target of Al-Qaeda, second only to the United States. This helped to answer why the United Kingdom remained the only Council of Europe State to derogate from the Convention.

Tackling the awkward issue of 'imminence'

One of the obstacles for the Government in sustaining the case of a 'public emergency' was its acknowledgement that intelligence sources knew of no specific attack that was being planned. At the time of SIAC's decision there

84 ibid para 21. See also para 22.

85 *Lawless v Ireland (No 3)* (n 29 above). (Cited in SIAC judgment (n 76 above) para 23.) Under the Human Rights Act 1998, s 2 domestic courts are required merely to take into account the case law of the Strasbourg institutions.

86 'The *Greek* case' (*Denmark, Norway, Sweden, Netherlands v Greece*) Application Nos 3321–23/67, Commission Report 12* *Yearbook of the European Convention on Human Rights* (1969—special edition).

87 *Marshall v UK* App No 41571/98, Decision of 10 July 2001, unreported.

88 SIAC judgment (n 76 above) para 23.

89 ibid para 25.

had been no terrorist attack on the United Kingdom. As the appellants pointed out, this seemed hard to square with the Strasbourg jurisprudence and other international legal standards concerning derogations from human rights instruments which state that key qualities for a derogation are that there be an 'actual' or 'imminent' emergency.[90] In response, Collins J pointed out that 'it is not the imminence of a threat which is required: it is the actuality or imminence of an emergency'.[91] He added: 'The measures which involve the need to derogate (here, the detention of suspected terrorists) are required to try to prevent the outrages which would have a disastrous effect if they occurred'. It would be 'absurd', Collins J stated, 'to require the authorities to wait until they were aware of an imminent attack before taking the necessary steps to avoid such an attack. Otherwise, those who are planning such an outrage could not be stopped until their plans had reached a stage when the outrage was about to occur. It might by then be too late to prevent it'.[92] Apparently, therefore, the sophistication of the terrorist actors, the significance of the threat and the very grave consequences which would flow from it all contributed to the existence of the public emergency in the first place.[93] SIAC concluded that: 'An emergency can exist and can certainly be imminent if there is an intention and a capacity to carry out serious terrorist violence even if nothing has yet been done and plans have not reached the stage when an attack is actually about to happen.'[94] Consequently, for SIAC, the line allowing a derogation to be made could be drawn a considerable way back from the point whereby it could be said that a public emergency, represented by a *specific* attack, was imminent. Yet it could not be drawn back so far that the threat in question was non-existent. There was a controlling requirement: SIAC stipulated that there should be 'a real risk that an attack will take place unless the necessary measures are taken to prevent it'.[95] Assessing this controlling requirement was crucial if one was to avoid the danger that resort to Article 15 would be made too lightly. However, in its assessment of the 'real risk' SIAC extended a considerable degree of deference to the executive ('a reasonably wide margin of discretion') on separation of powers grounds, which included an acknowledgement that SIAC lacked

[90] See text accompanying nn 241 and 239 below. For a summary of the Government's submission on this point as set out before the House of Lords, see Lord Bingham's judgment in '*A*', para 25.

[91] SIAC judgment (n 76 above) para 24.

[92] ibid.

[93] In an earlier part of his judgment, Collins J stated that the September 11 attacks had 'demonstrated at least three matters of considerable importance in assessing whether there exists an emergency': (i) the terrorists intended to cause absolute maximum loss of life; (ii) 'those responsible had the capacity to act with great skill, secrecy and co-ordination against the most powerful nation'; (iii) the terrorists were willing to perform suicide missions making it very hard to counteract an attack. Furthermore, Al-Qaeda was 'a loose-knit body which is linked to other terrorist organisations, some at least of which are supported by those in and funded from the United Kingdom and this makes it the more difficult to identify its members and supporters', SIAC judgment (n 76 above) para 26.

[94] ibid para 24. This view was cited with approval by Brooke LJ when '*A*' came before the Court of Appeal, see *A and others v Secretary of State for the Home Department* [2002] EWCA Civ 1502, [2004] QB 335, [2003] 2 WLR 564, [2003] 1 All ER 816, [2003] HRLR 3, para 114 (hereinafter 'Court of Appeal judgment').

[95] SIAC judgment (n 76 above) para 24.

proficiency in assessing the intelligence information before it, compared to the Secretary of State who had the advantage of expert advice.

Collins J accepted that there were acceptable reasons why only the United Kingdom, as opposed to other Council of Europe States, had needed to derogate from the Convention,[96] that there was no reason to regard the September 11 attacks as an isolated event, and that the United Kingdom was an obvious target for terrorist attack.[97] After referring to arguments raised by the appellants generally and specifically questioning the reliability of some of the intelligence in issue, on the existence of a public emergency SIAC concluded:

> 35. We have ... scrutinised all the material put before us with care. We recognise that much is at stake for those such as the appellants who are affected by the decisions of the Secretary of State but we recognise too that much is at stake for all the ordinary inhabitants of the United Kingdom. We are satisfied that what has been put before us in [the open material] ... does justify the conclusion that there does exist a public emergency threatening the life of the nation within the terms of Article 15. That the risk has been heightened since September 11, 2001, is clear, but we do not regard that description as in any way inconsistent with the existence of an emergency within the meaning of Article 15. The United Kingdom is a prime target, second only to the United States of America, and the history of events both before and after September 11, 2001, as well as on that fateful day, does show that if one attack were to take place it could well occur without warning and be on such a scale as to threaten the life of the nation.[98]

Only after this conclusion did Collins J make reference to the 'closed material' which, as he put it, 'confirm[ed] our view that the emergency is established.'[99] In other words, SIAC's assessment that there existed an Article 15(1) qualifying emergency had been made on the open material alone, 'much' of which, it acknowledged, consisted of 'reports in the media'.[100]

SIAC went on to assess whether the actual measures taken on the authority of the derogation were 'strictly required by the exigencies of the situation' as required by Article 15(1). It accepted the Government's submission that the provisions for judicial and democratic supervision contained in the 2001 Act were appropriate and sufficient. It considered the argument on behalf of the plaintiffs that less intrusive measures were available to the Government than detaining the individuals concerned. Here SIAC considered precedents of the European Court[101] and the Canadian Supreme Court,[102] concluding that its approach should not be one of second-guessing the executive as to the best ways of dealing with a given situation and that some leeway had to be given to the legislator.[103]

96 ibid para 30. 97 ibid para 29. 98 ibid para 35. 99 ibid para 36.

100 ibid para 31. The appellants questioned the veracity of some of this evidence, see ibid paras 33–34.

101 ibid para 43.

102 ibid para 44.

103 There was a marked difference of approach on this point subsequently by the House of Lords, which stated that SIAC had committed an error of law.

However, it proceeded to find that the derogation from Article 15 of the Convention was discriminatory for the purposes of Article 14 of the Convention ('on the grounds of national origin') when read with Article 5, since: 'A person who is removable cannot be detained or kept in detention simply because he lacks British nationality.'[104]

The Court of Appeal and the House of Lords—assessment of the existence of a 'public emergency'

The Government appealed what became known as the '*Belmarsh detainees*'' case to the Court of Appeal,[105] which reversed the SIAC judgment on the issue of discrimination, but upheld it as regards the existence of the emergency and the proportionality of the measures. On appeal, the House of Lords[106] upheld the existence of the public emergency but reversed the Court of Appeal's ruling, holding that the powers of extended detention under Part 4 of ATCSA 2001 were both disproportionate (not 'strictly required by the exigencies of the situation' (Article 15(1)) and discriminatory under Article 14 of the Convention. It is worth reiterating at this point that the appellate courts did not have access to the closed material that had been before SIAC; their jurisdiction was confined to assessing whether that body had erred in its approach to the law.[107]

The Court of Appeal

In terms of the threshold of severity for the application of Article 15, the Court of Appeal endorsed the statements made by SIAC and accepted that that body had made no error of law.[108] Little reference was made to the Strasbourg jurisprudence on the threshold for Article 15(1), except for Brooke LJ, who referred to several Strasbourg authorities to suggest that in at least one case, *Lawless*, the Court had been prepared to interpret the threshold issue quite broadly.[109] He accepted the reasoning of SIAC on the issue of 'imminence', and, although with 'a good deal of hesitation' concluded: 'it would be wrong to give an over-literal interpretation to the word "imminent" in the present context . . . Although the

[104] SIAC judgment (n 76 above) para 94. In December 2001 the UN Human Rights Committee, which monitors compliance with the ICCPR, had noted with 'concern' that the British Government was considering derogating from the ICCPR when it published its Concluding Observations on the UK's 4th and 5th combined report to it (CCPR/CO/73/UK;CCPR/CO/73/UKOT, 6 December 2001, para 6). The UK Government subsequently cited the SIAC judgment as justification for its position as regards the derogation, see *International Covenant on Civil and Political Rights: United Kingdom's 5th Periodic Report* (CCPR/C/UK/99/5) (CCPR/CO/UKOT/5), available at <www.dca.gov.uk/hract/ngo/bg_ccprcuk995.htm> (accessed 30 October 2005).

[105] For reference, see n 94 above.

[106] See n 2 above.

[107] ATCSA 2001, s 27.

[108] Lord Woolf CJ accepted SIAC's position on the imminence of an emergency, in particular that the UK was regarded as a 'prime target for Al-Qaeda' and that there was 'ample evidence that if a strike were to be made against the United Kingdom the results would be devastating', adding that 'quite apart from the possibility of an attack similar to that which took place on 11 September 2001 there are other possibilities', Court of Appeal judgment (n 94 above), para 33.

[109] ibid para 74.

rights of the claimants to liberty and due process are potent considerations, so, too, as SIAC observed, are the rights of very many other people which the Home Secretary judged to be threatened if the claimants remain at large, including the right to life itself'.[110]

The House of Lords

A panel of nine judges delivered the Law Lords' celebrated ruling in '*A*'[111] on 16 December 2004. One would be hard put to find another House of Lords judgment which contains as many references to international legal instruments and Parliamentary committees. By the time of the ruling, some of the nine appellants had been detained for approximately three years and, quite inexplicably, almost two years had elapsed since the Court of Appeal's judgment. The intervening period had witnessed the terrorist attacks in Madrid of March 2004,[112] and, in early 2004, the faulty intelligence assessments on the basis of which the United Kingdom took part in armed conflict in Iraq had been prominently in the news (of relevance since the threat of terrorist attack said to underpin the derogation was the product of intelligence).[113] The bombings in London did not occur until July 2005, six months after the Law Lords' ruling. The appeal was heard against the background of growing official criticism of the scheme for the appellants' detention, if not the actual existence of a 'public emergency' as such. In December 2003 the so-called Newton Committee of Privy Counsellors (established pursuant to section 122 of the 2001 Act) had undertaken an independent review: it had 'strongly recommended' that the power of detention without trial be ended 'as a matter of urgency'[114] and that a new legislative scheme be put in place to address suspected terrorists which would not require derogation from the Convention.[115] Part 4 of ATCSA 2001 was renewed in March 2004, despite hostile comment in Parliament. In a debate in the

[110] ibid para 85. Brooke LJ also referred to the threat that 'this country [might] be destroyed, together with the ideals it stands for' para 87, and stated that: 'On this appeal we are concerned not only with matters of personal liberty but with matters of life and death for possibly thousands of people.'

[111] See n 76 above. Before the Law Lords Liberty made written and oral submissions in support of the appellants, see *Submission to the House of Lords in the 'A' case (David Pannick QC)*, available at <www.liberty-human-rights.org.uk> (accessed 30 October 2005); Amnesty International also made written submissions (n 75 above).

[112] Cited by Lord Bingham ('*A*' judgment (n 2 above)) para 96 and Lord Scott, para 154 as adding credibility to the argument that there was a threat to the UK.

[113] The point was mentioned by Lord Bingham, para 94, Lord Scott, para 155, and Baroness Hale, para 226, although they did not cast doubt on the intelligence relating to a threat to the UK.

[114] Privy Counsellor Review Committee, *Anti-terrorism, Crime and Security Act 2001 Review: Report* (HC 100) (18 December 2003) (hereinafter 'the *Newton Committee Report*') para 205.

[115] ibid para 203. See generally paras 185–204. The same Committee observed that France, Italy and Germany had all been threatened but that: 'The UK is the only country to have found it necessary to derogate from the ... Convention.' This was 'puzzling', para 189. In response on behalf of the Government it was stated that it was believed that the powers of detention 'continu[ed] to be necessary to address the current threat' and that it would 'consider how this threat could be changing and what else might be done', *Counter-Terrorism Powers: Reconciling Security and Liberty in an Open Society* (Cm 6147) para 31, p 33.

House of Lords, for example, Lord Lester had agreed with the former Law Lord, Lord Browne-Wilkinson, that the Part 4 detention powers were 'not a tolerable system in a civilised society'.[116] The March 2004 renewal had witnessed only very limited discussion of the issue of the actual existence of a 'public emergency'; it seemed to be treated by the Government almost as a formality, so much so that the Home Secretary felt the need to get it 'on the record' that there was a 'risk to the life of the nation that constitutes a public emergency within article 15 of the ECHR'.[117] In July 2004 the JCHR reported that 'Derogations from human rights obligations are permitted in order to deal with emergencies [and] ... are intended to be temporary', but that 'According to the Government and the Security Service, the UK now faces a near-permanent emergency'.[118] With respect to the Part 4 powers generally, there had been considerable criticism from NGOs, from international bodies,[119] and in academic literature.[120]

Before the House of Lords the Attorney-General's case was, once again, that in late 2001 the United Kingdom might have been the target of an attack of September 11 proportions and that this was supported by intelligence.[121] Lord Bingham gave the leading speech[122] and made the

[116] HL Debates, vol 658, col 817, 4 March 2004. In its review of counter-terrorism powers, the JCHR firmly supported the 'Newton' Committee's conclusion as to reform, JCHR, *Eighteenth Report* (Review of Counter-terrorism Powers) (2003–04) (HL 158, HC 713) para 5.

[117] HC Debates, vol 418, col 299, 25 February 2004. See also the comments of Ms Beverley Hughes at HC Debates, vol 418, col 379, 25 February 2004 and the written response to the JCHR dated 6 February 2004 by the Home Secretary, JCHR, *Sixth Report* (Anti-terrorism, Crime and Security Act 2001) (HL 38, HC 381) Appendices (Response from Rt Hon David Blunkett MP, Secretary of State for Home Affairs, to the Chair).

[118] JCHR, *Eighteenth Report* (n 116 above) para 4, cf Lord Hope in '*A*', at para 122. As noted above (text accompanying n 45 above) the JCHR had indicated that it had doubts as to the existence of a 'public emergency' in October 2001 given the lack of information provided to substantiate this. In a subsequent review of the operation of ATCSA 2001, the JCHR indicated that it was reassured as to the existence of a public emergency in the light of the ruling delivered by SIAC, see JCHR, *Fifth Report* (Continuance in Force of Sections 21 to 23 of the Anti-Terrorism, Crime and Security Act 2001) (2002–03) (HL 59, HC 462) para 27. However, in this report as well as subsequent reports it continued to express criticism of the scheme of detention generally: see also *Sixth Report* (Anti-terrorism, Crime and Security Act 2001: Statutory Review and Continuance of Part 4) (2003–04) (HL Paper 38, HC 381) para 34; also *Eighteenth Report* (n 116 above).

[119] See eg *CoE Commissioner Opinion* (n 33 above). Having visited the detainees twice, the European Committee for the Prevention of Torture had also made adverse comments: *Report to the Government of the United Kingdom on the visit to the United Kingdom carried out by the European Committee for the Prevention of Torture from 17 to 21 February 2002*, CPT/Inf (2003) 18. For the Government's reply see CPT/Inf (2003)19. In December 2003 the (UN) Committee on the Elimination of Racial Discrimination had also stated that it was 'deeply concerned' about ACTSA 2001, Part 4, indicating that it potentially raised issues under the International Convention on the Elimination of Racial Discrimination, see *Concluding Observations of the Committee on the Elimination of Racial Discrimination Kingdom of Great Britain and Northern Ireland*, December 2003, (CERD/C/63/CO/11, 11 August 2003) para 17. The British derogation of 2001 was condemned by the former Director of the Netherlands Institute of Human Rights as 'a giant retrogressive step in the application of an important human rights standard at the regional level', P Baehr, 'Column—Human Rights After September 11th' (2002) 20(1) *Netherlands Quarterly of Human Rights* 3, 4, writing in his personal capacity.

[120] cf Lord (Johan) Steyn, 'Guantanamo Bay: the Legal Black Hole' (2004) 52 ICLQ 1

[121] See Lord Scott, para 154 and Lord Hoffman, para 95.

[122] See '*A*' judgment (n 2 above) paras 20–29 where the arguments presented by the appellants (paras 20 and 24) and on behalf of the Government (para 25) are summarized.

most detailed reference to the Strasbourg jurisprudence on what he termed 'the threshold test'.[123] The key legal standards set down by the Strasbourg institutions as regards the meaning of 'public emergency threatening the life of the nation' were cited,[124] as was Article 4 of the ICCPR and commentary thereon in 'The Siracusa Principles on the Limitation and Derogation Provisions in the International Covenant on Civil and Political Rights'.[125] Lord Bingham set out the appellants' arguments that the emergency was ill-founded as it was neither 'imminent' nor temporary,[126] and that its existence was questionable given that no other European nation had derogated from the Convention. Reference was made to the criticism of the derogation both within the United Kingdom and at the international level.[127] He summed up the Attorney-General's replies to the appellants,[128] which included a restatement of SIAC's position on imminence, an assertion that, as regards the issues of temporariness, no artificial temporal limit to 'an emergency of the present kind' should be imposed (and that in any case the Strasbourg Court had accepted continuing derogations for periods approaching a decade),[129] and a rejection of the viability of comparisons with other European nations. The Attorney-General had stressed that the appellate courts only had capacity to determine whether SIAC had made an error of law and emphasized the essentially political quality of the assessment of the Article 15(1) threshold test, entailing that deference had to be owed to the executive.[130]

The threshold test—a political question (for the majority)

Was there a 'public emergency threatening the life of the nation'? The House of Lords was not in a position to undertake a full merits review of this issue for the reasons pointed out by the Attorney-General. Lord Bingham was clear that SIAC had not misdirected itself.[131] Moreover, on separation of powers grounds, the issue of the existence of a 'public emergency' was one where the executive was entitled to considerable deference: the existence of a public emergency was 'a pre-eminently political judgment'[132] and 'great weight should be given to the judgment of the Home Secretary, his colleagues and Parliament on this question', this also being in accordance with the ruling in the *Rehman* case,[133] as well as the 'the unintrusive approach of the European Court to such a question'. Lord Bingham concluded 'that the appellants have shown no ground strong enough to warrant displacing the Secretary of State's decision on

[123] ibid para 16. [124] ibid paras 17 and 18. [125] ibid para 19. [126] ibid para 22.
[127] ibid paras 23–24. [128] ibid para 25.
[129] This was a reference to *Marshall v UK* (n 87 above), discussed in text accompanying n 396 below.
[130] The '*A*' judgment (n 2 above) para 25. The Attorney-General did not dispute the jurisdiction of the House of Lords to examine the derogation by reference to the legal standards set down by Art 15(1), cf the important comments made by Tomkins (n 3 above) 260–1 and Lord Scott, para 152.
[131] ibid para 27. See also Lady Hale, para 226 and Lord Rodger, para 166. [132] ibid para 29.
[133] See *Secretary of State for the Home Department v Rehman* (n 30 above), Lord Hoffmann, para 62.

this important threshold question'. This was a telling illustration of the deferential stance taken, since it appeared to place a burden on the appellants to disprove the existence of a 'public emergency', something they could hardly do.[134] The political character of the assessment of the existence of an emergency appeared critical to the opinions of the other seven Law Lords who also accepted that Article 15(1) applied.[135] As Lady Hale stated: 'Protecting the life of the nation is one of the first tasks of a Government in a world of nation States'. The courts could intervene in the face of a public emergency that was evidently a sham because: 'Unwarranted declarations of emergency [were] a familiar tool of tyranny.'[136] However, the Law Lords were 'considering the immediate aftermath of the unforgettable events of 11 September 2001' and these 'attacks ... were clearly intended to threaten the life of' the United States. It was added that 'SIAC were satisfied that the open and closed material before them justified the conclusion that there was also a public emergency threatening the life of this nation' and Lady Hale 'would not feel qualified or even inclined to disagree'.[137]

Thus the existence of a public emergency was largely a political question best left to the executive. This was in keeping with the traditional role of the courts *vis-à-vis* the other branches of Government when issues of national security had been relied on by the Government.[138] The reality was that in the absence of the closed information available to SIAC, the superior courts were in no real position to make a determination on the reality of the threat. Hence Tomkins[139] has suggested that the Law Lords were only really guessing at the existence of the public emergency and that in these circumstances they should simply have stated that they had not been presented with sufficient evidence either way.

Elements of doubt regarding the existence of a 'public emergency'

However, some of the Law Lords did engage, to some extent at least, with the threshold issue, and here the Strasbourg jurisprudence on the threshold test accounted for some difficulties of interpretation and application.[140] Lord Bingham acknowledged that he had some 'misgiving'[141]

[134] Hickman is highly critical of Lord Bingham's position on the issue of burden of proof, Hickman (n 3 above) 663.

[135] See eg Lord Hope, paras 115–116 (existence of a public emergency and whether it threatened the life of the nation was 'pre-eminently for the executive and Parliament', para 116), Lord Scott granting the Home Secretary 'the benefit of the doubt', para 154 and Lord Nicholls holding that 'All courts are acutely conscious that the Government alone is able to evaluate and decide what counter-terrosim steps are needed and what steps will suffice. Courts are not equipped to make such decisions, nor are they charged with that responsibility', para 79.

[136] ibid para 226.

[137] ibid.

[138] See B Simpson, *In the Highest Degree Odious* (1992) 418–22 and D Dyzenhaus, 'Limitations of Legality amid the Clash of Arms' (2004) 2 *International Journal of Constitutional Law* 244.

[139] Tomkins (n 3 above) 261–2.

[140] See eg Lord Hope's struggle to reconcile the UK's derogation with the requirement that a 'public emergency' should be 'imminent', paras 118–119. Also Lord Walker, para 208.

[141] ibid para 26.

as to whether Article 15(1) was applicable in the first place. He referred to the key Strasbourg cases where it had been accepted that Article 15(1) applied—*Ireland v United Kingdom*,[142] *Brannigan and McBride v United Kingdom*,[143] and *Aksoy v Turkey*[144]—noting that they were of limited use for the facts before him as in 'each case the member State had actually experienced widespread loss of life caused by an armed body dedicated to destroying the territorial integrity of the State'. By contrast, *Lawless v Ireland*[145] had concerned 'very low level IRA terrorist activity in Ireland and Northern Ireland between 1954 and 1957':[146] this was an old authority and the Strasbourg Court might have given the benefit of the doubt to the State on the facts. Nonetheless: 'If it was open to the Irish Government in *Lawless* to conclude that there was a public emergency threatening the life of the Irish nation, the British Government could scarcely be faulted for reaching that conclusion in the much more dangerous situation which arose after 11 September.'[147] The rather feeble threshold test—as Lord Bingham appeared to view it—was therefore met.

A reading of the other speeches gives the impression that, as with Lord Bingham, the decision reached on the threshold test was not without some doubt, but could be answered in favour of the Government given the political nature of the question, the fact that Strasbourg set a rather low threshold, and the compelling images of September 11.[148] Lord Walker noted that the threshold set by the European Court was 'not set ... very high',[149] whilst Lord Rodger referred to 'the (relatively modest) scale of the terrorist activities'[150] in *Lawless*. Even so, Lord Rodger acknowledged his 'hesitation'[151] on the matter of the existence of an emergency, whilst Lord Scott had 'very grave doubt whether the "public emergency" [was] one that justif[ied] the description of "threatening the life of the nation"'.[152] Lord Hoffman alone thought that there was no 'public emergency', although Lords Bingham[153] and Rodger[154] were prepared to express some sympathy with his view.

[142] *Ireland v UK* App No 5310/71 (1980) 2 EHRR 25.

[143] See n 59 above.

[144] *Aksoy v Turkey* App No 21987/93 (1997) 23 EHRR 553.

[145] See n 29 above.

[146] '*A*' judgment (n 2 above) para 17.

[147] Lord Bingham, para 29, see also paras 27 and 20.

[148] According to Lord Hope there was a threat to 'the life of the nation' within the meaning of Art 15 given 'the appalling consequences that would affect us all if [a terrorist attack] were to occur here' (para 119), he made reference to the 'massive casualties' and 'devastating effect on the functioning of the nation' (para 118) that would be associated with a September 11-type attack in the UK. Lord Rodger referred to the threat of 'devastating attacks' (para 166) that might occur. Interestingly, the issue of 'imminence' was not really discussed by any of the Law Lords with the exception of Lord Hope, who seemed to accept SIAC's approach without expressly citing it, see paras 119–120.

[149] ibid para 208.

[150] ibid para 165. Lord Rodger also made reference to the decision in *Marshall v UK* (n 87 above).

[151] Lord Rodger, para 165.

[152] Lord Scott, para 154. By contrast, Lord Hope expressed the view that there was 'ample evidence ... to show that the Government were fully justified in taking the view ... that there was an emergency threatening the life of the nation', para 118.

[153] ibid para 26.

[154] ibid para 165.

Lord Hoffman's distinct approach to the threshold test

It is important to appreciate that Lord Hoffman did not take his stand on the lack of credibility of the threat. He was willing to accept that credible evidence of Al-Qaeda plots existed against the United Kingdom of the order seen in New York and Madrid.[155] What he objected to was the suggestion that the threat of terrorism from Muslim extremists threatened the life of the British nation in the specific way required by Article 15(1).

The majority had deferred to the Executive on the basis of separation of powers considerations and so had largely avoided an assessment of what the threshold test required. Lord Hoffman looked in detail at that test and took the view that SIAC and the Attorney-General had erred in their understanding of what was required. They had 'treated a threat of serious physical damage and loss of life as necessarily involving a threat to the life of the nation'.[156] But for Lord Hoffman this did *not* accord with Article 15(1) and the Strasbourg Court's understanding of the notion of 'threat to the organised life of the community of which the State is composed' ('a rather desiccated description')[157] which had been spelt out as an abstract definition of 'public emergency threatening the life of the nation' in the case of *Lawless v Ireland*. He argued:

> The 'nation' is a social organism, living in its territory (in this case, the United Kingdom) under its own form of Government and subject to a system of laws which expresses its own political and moral values. When one speaks of a threat to the 'life' of the nation, the word life is being used in a metaphorical sense. The life of the nation is not coterminous with the lives of its people. The nation, its institutions and values, endure through generations. In many important respects, England is the same nation as it was at the time of the first Elizabeth or the Glorious Revolution. The Armada threatened to destroy the life of the nation, not by loss of life in battle, but by subjecting English institutions to the rule of Spain and the Inquisition. The same was true of the threat posed to the United Kingdom by Nazi Germany in the Second World War. This country, more than any other in the world, has an unbroken history of living for centuries under institutions and in accordance with values which show a recognisable continuity.[158]

The nation, Lord Hoffman argued, had survived physical destruction and catastrophic loss of life during the war. Whilst 'fanatical groups of terrorists' could kill and destroy: 'Terrorist violence, serious as it is, does not threaten our institutions of Government or our existence as a civil community.'[159] The threat of terrorism from Muslim extremists did not threaten the life of the British nation, whereas, by comparison with the derogations made by the United Kingdom with respect to Northern Ireland in the past, it had been 'reasonable to say that terrorism in Northern Ireland threatened the life of that part of the nation and the territorial integrity of the United Kingdom as a whole. In a community

[155] '*A*' judgment (n 2 above) para 94. [156] ibid para 95. [157] ibid para 92.
[158] ibid para 91. [159] ibid para 96 (emphasis added).

riven by sectarian passions, such a campaign of [terrorist] violence threatened the fabric of organised society'.[160]

Having concluded that there was indeed no 'public emergency threatening the life of the nation' in the sense of Article 15, Lord Hoffman did not go on to address whether the actual measures taken were proportional, ie were 'strictly required by the exigencies of the "situation"'. Nonetheless he did indicate his abhorrence of the indefinite executive detention that was central to the facts of the case with his concluding lines: 'The real threat to the life of the nation in the sense of a people living in accordance with its traditional laws and political values, comes not from terrorism but from laws such as these. That is the true measure of what terrorism may achieve.'[161]

'Strictly required by the exigencies of the situation': The courts as the traditional guardians of liberty

The '*A*' case is potentially of great importance given the stance taken by the House of Lords to the second limb of Article 15(1): ie whether the actual measures taken in accordance with the emergency were 'strictly required by the exigencies of the situation'. Here the Attorney-General had again argued that this matter of national security was predominantly a political issue and that the courts, on separation of powers grounds, should refrain from closely scrutinizing the actions of democratic, political institutions.[162] However, whereas the argument for deference based on the political nature of the issue had largely succeeded on the question of whether there existed a 'public emergency', it was rejected as regards this second limb of Article 15(1). The House of Lords undertook what Lord Rodger described as the 'duty' of the British courts in 'performing their traditional role of watching over the liberty of everyone within their jurisdiction, regardless of nationality'.[163] Here was an area where the courts 'may legitimately intervene', in their role as an essential safeguard, 'if individual rights and freedoms are to be protected in a democratic society which respects the principle that minorities, however unpopular, have the same rights as the majority'.[164]

The House of Lords upheld the appeal by eight votes to one. Lord Hoffman found for the appellants on the basis that there was no public emergency, while, by seven votes to one (Lord Walker dissenting)[165] the

[160] ibid para 93.

[161] ibid para 97. For criticism of Lord Hoffman's judgment, see Arden (n 3 above) 615–16. At a Press Conference held at 10 Downing Street on 25 July 2005, Prime Minister Tony Blair said that he doubted if Lord Hoffman's words 'would be uttered now' (ie after the London July bombings), *The Guardian*, 27 July 2005 <www.guardian.co.uk>.

[162] See Lord Bingham's judgment, para 37. Relevant legal authorities on this point included *R v Secretary of State, ex p Hosenball* [1977] 1 WLR 766 (*per* Lord Denning at 783) and *Secretary of State for the Home Department v Rehman* [2003] 1 AC 153.

[163] Lord Rodger, para 178, see also at paras 176–177. cf Lord Hope's comments noting the duty of Government in a democratic society (protection of lives and security) and the duty of the courts (to protect the rights of the individuals), para 99.

[164] Lord Hope, para 108.

[165] See para 209 for a useful summary of his views.

appellants' case on proportionality and discrimination was upheld.[166] As to proportionality,[167] the Secretary of State had not established that the special detention arrangements were 'strictly required' by the public emergency, in that he had not shown that monitoring arrangements or movement restrictions less severe than incarceration in prison, would have sufficed to meet the exigencies of the situation facing the United Kingdom in late 2001.[168] Perhaps most crucial of all, the special detention arrangements were also disproportionate in the sense that they were unnecessary to meet the Government's objectives as set out in the legislation—as they did not apply to United Kingdom nationals who were also suspected terrorists. Moreover, the arrangements permitted the detainees to leave the United Kingdom and so left them free to pursue activities threatening the United Kingdom from abroad. As Lord Bingham put it: 'the choice of an immigration measure to address a security problem had the inevitable result of failing adequately to address that problem (by allowing non-UK suspected terrorists to leave the country with impunity and leaving British suspected terrorists at large) while imposing the severe penalty of indefinite detention on persons who, even if reasonably suspected of having links with Al-Qaeda, may harbour no hostile intentions towards the United Kingdom'.[169] Furthermore, the measures were discriminatory under Article 14 of the Convention (which had not been derogated from), given the unjustifiable distinction made regarding the enjoyment of the right to liberty between suspected terrorists who were non-nationals (the detainees) as against those who were nationals (who could not be detained on similar grounds).

This account would not be complete without reference to the unusually robust statements made by some of the Law Lords in condemnation of the Part 4 detention scheme. In most cases the appellants had been detained for three years. They had been held on an indefinite basis, without charge, as foreign nationals and on the basis that they were merely suspected international terrorists. They had had little or no idea of the information on the basis of which they were detained. Such a scheme of detention was, according to Lord Nicholls, an 'anathema in any country which observes the rule of law';[170] it was 'antithetical to the instincts and traditions of the people of the United Kingdom'.[171] Such measures were 'the real threat to the life of the nation'[172] (Lord Hoffman); according to Lord Scott, 'the

[166] The House of Lords held that the Human Rights Act 1998 (Designated Derogation) Order 2001 (see n 32 above) be quashed as it was disproportionate for the purposes of Art 15(1). It also declared that ATCSA 2001, s 23 was incompatible with Arts 5 and 14 of the Convention. Given these findings, the House of Lords did not go on to consider the crucial issue of whether the certification and detention process established under Part 4 of the 2001 Act amounts, in substance and effect, to the determination of a criminal charge for the purposes of Art 6(1) of the Convention. This had been central to the Third Party Intervention submitted by Amnesty International (n 75 above).

[167] See Lord Bingham, paras 31–44.

[168] See eg the judgment of Lord Scott, para 155.

[169] Lord Bingham, para 43.

[170] ibid para 74.

[171] Lord Hoffman at para 86.

[172] ibid para 97.

stuff of nightmares, associated whether accurately or inaccurately with France before and during the Revolution, with Soviet Russia in the Stalinist era and now associated, as a result of section 23 of the 2001 Act, with the United Kingdom'.[173]

Withdrawal of the derogation (16 March 2005); but an ongoing 'public emergency' in the United Kingdom

On 14 March 2005, almost three months after the House of Lords' ruling, the provisions of ATCSA 2001 providing for extended power of arrest and detention for certain foreign nationals ceased to operate.[174] The derogation from the Convention was withdrawn with effect from 16 March 2005[175] and the Government confirmed that the relevant provisions of the Convention would be given full effect once more.

Although the new Home Secretary (Charles Clarke) stated that the detention of suspected international terrorists had served a purpose,[176] and although there was no obligation under the scheme of the Human Rights Act 1998 requiring the relevant parts of ATCSA 2001 to be changed,[177] the ruling in '*A*' prompted the Government to review the legal regime applying to the detainees. The Government stated that it would now follow a twin-track approach. A first part of this was to deport foreign nationals who could be deported with assurances against ill-treatment from the destination country. A second part was to release the detainees but to immediately make them the subject of a new statutory regime providing for 'control orders'[178] and, potentially, 'derogating control orders'.[179] The

[173] ibid para 155.

[174] The detention provisions under ATCSA 2001, s 23 were due to expire on 13 March 2005 but were repealed with effect from 14 March 2005 by section 16(2)(a) of the Prevention of Terrorism Act 2005 (c 2). The new Act passed through Parliament in just 18 days, at such a speed that the JCHR complained that it was 'impossible' for it to 'scrutinise the Bill comprehensively for human rights compatibility in time to inform debate in Parliament' (see JCHR, *Tenth Report* (Prevention of Terrorism Bill: Preliminary Report) (2004–05) (HL 68 334) para 1). On the passage of this new legislation see Hiebert (n 3 above).

[175] See <http://conventions.coe.int>.

[176] They had been 'the means of containing those foreign nationals' activities where prosecution was not possible' (HC Debates, vol 430, col 305, 26 January 2005). He insisted that 'he believe[d] that the powers have played an essential part in addressing the current public emergency, because they have been successful in containing the threat posed by those certified and detained under them'. The powers had served to help 'make the UK a far more hostile environment for international terrorists to operate in', some such individuals having been 'deterred from coming here, and others have left entirely, to avoid being certified and detained' (cols 305–6).

[177] A declaration of incompatibility does not affect the continuing operation or validity of the provision of legislation which it is relevant to (Human Rights Act 1998, s 4(6)). As a result the relevant provisions of ATCSA 2001 remained in force even after the House of Lords' ruling and provided the legal basis for the continued detention of the detainees until the new legislative arrangements of March 2005 were in place. An application (No 3455/05) was made to the ECtHR on behalf of the detainees, contending that their continued detention as of February 2005 was in breach of Arts 3, 5 (alone and with Art 14), and 13 of the Convention. At the time of writing the application has been communicated to the British Government and no decision on admissibility has been taken.

[178] Prevention of Terrorism Act 2005, s 1.

[179] ibid s 4.

former did not require derogation from the Convention whilst the latter, providing potentially for loss of liberty, did.[180] However, the Home Secretary noted on 22 February 2005 that the advice from the police and security authorities was that control orders were 'sufficient to deal with the individuals concerned and that deprivation of liberty, although valuable, [was] not "strictly required", in the language of the convention'.[181]

Thus at the time of writing no further derogation from the Convention has been entered by the United Kingdom. However, the Government has indicated that in its view the conditions for such a derogation remain present. In a statement to the House of Commons on 26 January 2005, the Home Secretary said that he was 'left in absolutely no doubt that nothing has happened recently that diminishes the threat, or calls into question the state of public emergency threatening the life of the nation'.[182] Indeed the Government's understanding of 'the threat ha[d] advanced' because 'networks consisting of foreign nationals with international links remain' and 'some British nationals are now playing a more significant role in these threats'[183]—a telling remark given what was to occur in London in July 2005. Mr Clarke referred to the terrorist 'attacks' that had occurred elsewhere in the world in the previous year—Spain (March 2004), Saudi Arabia (May and December), Indonesia (September) and Egypt (October). 'In these circumstances, my judgment is that there remains a public emergency threatening the life of the nation'.[184] In the context of the 'security situation' the Government had to strike a careful balance between 'the rights of individuals and the protection of society against threats from organisations that seek to destroy central attributes of our society, such as freedom of belief, speech and association, freedom of expression and even our central democracy'. The Home Secretary's 'principal responsibility' was 'to preserve our democracy against those who seek to destroy it through terrorist attacks', and that 'threat [was] real'.[185] The threshold test did not seem to receive any attention at all during the passage of the Prevention of Terrorism Act 2005.

[180] On 'control orders' see E Metcalfe, 'Protecting a Free Society? Control Orders and the Prevention of Terrorism Bill' (2005) 2(1) *JUSTICE Journal* 3. See also JCHR, *Ninth Report* (Prevention of Terrorism Bill: Preliminary Report) (2004–05) (HL 61, HC 389) and *Tenth Report* (Prevention of Terrorism Bill: Preliminary Report) (2004–05) (HL 68, HC 334), plus Council of Europe Commissioner for Human Rights, *Report on the visit to the United Kingdom (4–12 November 2004)* (CommDH(2005)6) 8–12.

[181] HC Debates, vol 431, col 153, 22 February 2005. The Home Secretary also stated that he envisaged that derogating control orders would only be made with respect to 'the most dangerous forms of terrorism' such as 'international terrorism of the Al-Qaeda variety' and so 'the most extreme threats that we face', JCHR, *Tenth Report* (n 180 above) Appendix, Question 14.

[182] HC Debates, vol 430, col 306, 26 January 2005. Art 15(3) of the Convention and Art 4(3) of the ICCPR require a State to serve a notice of derogation when an actual derogation is made, not when a 'public emergency' is said to exist as such.

[183] HC Debates (n 182 above) col 306.

[184] ibid col 309.

[185] Approximately one month later he stated that he was 'clear that a derogation is justified on the basis of the threat that we currently face'; it emanated from 'the threat from Al-Qaeda, its agents and its adherents, including the different groups and linkages that make up the Al-Qaeda movement in

IV. The '*A*' case before the House of Lords and the Threshold Test

It was fundamental to the Law Lords' approach that, despite the national security context, the '*A*' case was viewed as one concerning the human rights of the individual, in particular the right to liberty and not, as the Government had contended before it, one of immigration control. As Lord Hope emphasized, the issue that the derogation order was designed to address 'was not at its heart an immigration issue at all. It was an issue about the aliens' right to liberty'.[186] More generally the ruling in '*A*' stands out for the Law Lords' strong assertion of the constitutional role of the courts as the guardians of civil liberties even when national security is in issue. Broad arguments put by the Attorney-General in favour of almost complete deference to the other branches of Government based on the unelected status of the judiciary were not accepted, not only generally[187] but also in view of the fundamental nature of the right in issue before the court—indefinite detention without trial. On the general issue of separation of powers Lord Bingham accepted that the Attorney-General was of course 'entitled to insist on the proper limits of judicial authority'. But he had been wrong in his claim that judicial decision-making was to be stigmatized as 'in some way undemocratic'.[188] Such arguments were 'particularly inappropriate' given that Parliament, via the Human Rights Act 1998, had given the courts 'a very specific, wholly democratic, mandate'.[189] The courts 'were charged by Parliament with delineating the boundaries of a rights-based democracy'.[190]

The House of Lords therefore refused to defer to the executive on the 'strictly required' question. In this respect the approach may be contrasted with that of the Strasbourg Court, which is generally to grant respondent Governments a 'wide' margin of appreciation on this matter.[191] Given the

its broadest sense' (HC Debates, vol 431, col 153, 22 February 2004). Subsequently, during debates on the passage of the new legislation, Home Office Minister Hazel Blears noted that the House of Lords had upheld the existence of an Art 15 'public emergency' in its ruling of 16 December 2001, referring to the 'action that we need to take to meet the threat and to protect the security of this country and its people'. There was a need to 'strike the right balance between security and liberty, but my personal starting point is that terrorism poses a real and serious threat to the structures and people of this country', HC Debates, vol 430, col 1416, 8 February 2005.

186 Lord Hope, para 103.

187 On the underlying debate regarding the limits of deference and the constitutional role of the courts in protecting citizens from abuse of power, see Lord (Johan) Steyn, 'Deference: a Tangled Story' [2005] *Public Law* 346.

188 Lord Bingham, para 42, cf Lord Hope, paras 107–108.

189 ibid. Lord Bingham also noted the limited nature of 'declarations of incompatibility' under the Human Rights Act 1998, s 4. See also Lord Nicholls, para 80.

190 ibid quoting J Jowell, 'Judicial Deference: servility, civility or institutional capacity?' [2003] *Public Law* 592, 597.

191 See esp Lord Bingham, para 42. On the Strasbourg approach see text accompanying n 299 below. Perhaps, however, the Strasbourg Court would not have granted a 'wide' margin of appreciation on the facts of the '*A*' case given the severity of the interference with rights and the period of time involved. In *Brannigan and McBride v UK* (n 59 above) the Court stated that 'in exercising its supervision the Court must give appropriate weight to such relevant factors as the nature of the

importance of the right at stake, several of the Law Lords emphasized the duty of a national court, as distinct from an international one, to scrutinize the actions of the executive with great attention. In particular it was thought more appropriate for a domestic court to assess the relative effectiveness of competing alternative measures that might be less harmful to the rights of the individuals concerned so as to establish whether the existing measures were disproportionate. For example, Lords Scott[192] and Bingham[193] indicated that the onus was on the Secretary of State to show that monitoring arrangements and movement restrictions less severe than incarceration in prison would not suffice on the facts. Lord Rodger pointed out that the standard of review to be employed by the domestic court should not stop at merely assessing whether the Secretary of State had acted in 'good faith', as this did not eliminate the risk of the measures being disproportionate.[194] He argued that 'the considerable deference which the European Court of Human Rights shows to the views of the national authorities in such matters [as to the proportionality of measures taken] really presupposes that the national courts will police those limits'.[195] For Lord Hope, 'that the European Court will accord a large margin of appreciation to the contracting States on the question whether the measures taken to interfere with the right to liberty do not exceed those strictly required by the exigencies of the situation cannot be taken as the last word on the matter so far as the domestic courts are concerned'. For him: 'Final responsibility for determining whether they do exceed these limits must lie with the courts, if the test which article 15(1) lays down is to be applied within the domestic system with all the rigour that its wording indicates.'[196]

The ruling in '*A*' therefore sent out a message of constitutional importance: actual measures impinging on fundamental rights should be the subject of close examination by the courts, the traditional guardian of civil liberties, as to their proportionality, even if the Government maintains that those measures are necessary for national security reasons in the context of a public emergency. Lord Steyn, who did not sit in '*A*' following a challenge to his neutrality,[197] has taken the view that the judgment ranked 'with historic judgments of our courts'; it represented 'a great day for the law—for calm and reasoned judgment, analysis without varnish, and for principled democratic decision-making by our highest court'.[198] Lady Justice Arden has argued that for the United

rights affected by the derogation, the circumstances leading to, and the duration of, the emergency situation', para 43.

[192] '*A*' judgment (n 2 above) para 155. [193] ibid para 44. [194] ibid para 177.

[195] ibid para 176. See also Lord Walker's comments, para 197.

[196] Lord Hope, para 114, see also para 108 and paras 130–131. The Council of Europe Commissioner for Human Rights had been critical of the detention scheme on proportionality grounds, *CoE Commissioner Opinion* (n 33 above) paras 36–40. Lord Hope cited this *Opinion* (para 113) as did Lord Bingham (paras 23, 34, 40, 57). [197] For elaboration see Steyn (n 3 above) 350.

[198] ibid 350–1.

Kingdom the case 'marks the transition to a rights-based democracy';[199] it was 'a landmark decision that will be used as a reference point by courts all over the world for decades to come, even when the age of terrorism has passed ... a powerful statement ... of what it means to live in a society where the executive is subject to the rule of law'.[200]

The threshold of severity test before the House of Lords

Is it realistic to think that the Law Lords might have taken a strict approach to the threshold test and so held that there was no 'public emergency'? The primarily political nature of the national security issues behind the threshold test itself must be recognized: the House of Lords did not have access to the secret information justifying the threat of terrorist attack. Given such a veil of secrecy it could be said that ' "the law" had nothing to contribute'; in the 'conflict between secrecy and the rule of law secrecy [won]' on this point.[201] By contrast, the findings made as regards proportionality and discrimination were taken on the facts of the case as presented to the Law Lords and did not involve qualitative assessments of intelligence information.

Further, for the Law Lords to hold that there was no 'public emergency' would have branded the Government with a stigma in relation to Article 15(1) which public opinion might not have regarded as appropriate given the serious terrorist threat which the events of July 2005 would prove. Even if doubts had existed on the part of some Law Lords it may well have been that they were willing to grant deference on the existence of a 'public emergency', comforted by the fact that they could take a stricter approach to the second limb of Article 15(1).[202] Like the Government, on the whole the English courts too gave priority to the *need* for a derogation based on the importance of protecting people against a risk of very major harm. One can obviously sympathize with this. Furthermore, before the House of Lords at least, the issue of the existence of an emergency does not appear to have been pursued by the appellants with great vigour.[203]

Yet were the Law Lords right to defer on the Article 15(1) threshold issue quite as easily as they did?[204] If there were no 'public emergency' in the first place, no measures in derogation from the Convention would be possible, no matter how proportionate and nuanced. A number of the Law Lords acknowledged the association between a government's resort

199 Arden (n 3 above) 624. 200 ibid 622 (footnotes omitted).

201 Simpson (n 138 above) 421.

202 Lord Walker came close to making this very point, para 208 (noting that there was no need to set the threshold for the existence of an emergency very high, given the assessment of proportionality to follow). See also Lord Bingham, para 29 and Lord Hope, para 116.

203 See Lord Bingham, para 29.

204 The House of Lords seemed content that they had jurisdiction to consider the issue, however, see Tomkins (n 3 above) 260–1.

to measures based on 'national security' considerations and abuse of power by the State:[205] thus Lady Hale noted that 'unwarranted declarations of emergency are a familiar tool of tyranny'.[206] In such circumstances it might be thought that the relatively limited assessment of the actual legality of the 'public emergency' before the English courts was surprising.

The result of the majority approach on the threshold issue, it would seem, was to grant the Government an almost exclusive say as regards what is a 'public emergency' within the meaning of Article 15(1). Such an approach seemed to foreclose analysis of whether the key *legal conditions* for a derogation as required by Article 15(1) were present in the first place—was the situation of such severity that it was a threat 'to the life of the nation'? The majority of the Law Lords, like SIAC before them, accepted that this was the threshold test for reliance on for Article 15 and accordingly, that a major terrorist attack *would* threaten the life of the nation. It is true, of course, that such an attack would have awful consequences and would have ramifications for the 'life of a nation' understood in a general sense. Yet, without in any way trivializing abominations such as the terrorist attacks in recent years, there was no real articulation at any stage as to *precisely* how the life of the nation as such was threatened in the specific sense required by Article 15(1). Indeed it is striking that none of the other Law Lords addressed the specific issues that Lord Hoffman had identified as regards the threshold test.

The core legal point remains: does the threat of a major terrorist atrocity on its own suffice for reliance on Article 15(1) or is more required in accordance with the restrictive terminology of Article 15(1)—a threat to the 'life of the nation' under the *Lawless* definition? This remains very much a live issue given the possibility of further derogations with respect to the Convention. Indeed, in proposing new legislative arrangements on terrorism[207] which potentially provide for derogation from the Convention, the Government can now point to the ruling in '*A*' as one whereby the House of Lords 'confirmed that a public emergency was threatening the life of the nation'.[208] It will be submitted below that Lord Hoffman's stance on the Article 15(1) threshold test was largely a correct interpretation of the Strasbourg approach.

Moreover, there is perhaps a more serious criticism to be made of the majority ruling in '*A*'. In their brief look at the threshold test, some of the Law Lords seemed to suggest that the Strasbourg jurisprudence on Article 15(1) sets relatively low standards with respect to terrorist violence,[209] the apparent message being that a State might easily derogate from an international human rights instrument when confronted with

[205] Lord Rodger, para 177; Lord Walker, para 193 (dissenting).
[206] Lady Hale, para 226.
[207] Prevention of Terrorism Act 2005 (n 174 above).
[208] Minister Hazel Blears HC Debates, vol 430, col 1416, 8 February 2005.
[209] See text accompanying nn 146, 149, and 150 above.

low-level terrorist violence. It is submitted that to give this impression is a mistake. The finding that a State may easily derogate from a human rights instrument has the capacity to undermine the derogation clause found not only in the Convention but also in instruments such as the ICCPR. If this view were accepted, the protection afforded by international human rights instruments could be diminished significantly.

V. Derogations from International Human Rights Instruments[210]

In times of war or other exceptional crisis facing a nation, most constitutions enable the executive to take emergency action of some sort for the protection of the State as a whole and the welfare of its people.[211] In doing so the State may temporarily compromise the full enjoyment of certain fundamental rights otherwise enjoyed in 'normal' times. The rationale for a state of emergency is therefore protective in nature insofar as it exists to defend the wider interests of the State. As Nowak has put it, the emergency 'offers a State's democratically legitimated, supreme constitutional organs a basis for avoiding exceptional, irreparable damages to the general public resulting from an international or civil war, the attempt to topple the constitutional order or particularly grave natural and environmental catastrophes'.[212] Nowak points out that it is chiefly in order to accommodate this domestic constitutional law position that leading international legal instruments such as the European Convention, the American Convention on Human Rights ('ACHR')[213] and the ICCPR[214] enable a State to derogate from certain, but not all, of their commitments in times of 'public emergency'.[215] Under the ICCPR a derogation may

[210] The principal items from an extensive literature on emergency derogations are R Higgins, 'Derogations Under Human Rights Treaties' (1976–77) 48 BYIL 281; J Hartman, 'Derogation from Human Rights Treaties in Public Emergencies' (1981) 22 *Harvard International Law Journal* 1; N Questiaux, *Study of the Implications for Human Rights of Recent Developments concerning situations known as State of Siege or Emergency* (E/CN.4/Sub.2/1982/15); International Commission of Jurists, *States of Emergency: Their Impact on Human Rights* (1983); R Ergec, *Les Droits de l'homme à l'épreuve des circonstances exceptionelles: Etude sur l'article 15 de la Convention Européenne des droits de l'homme* (1987); S Chowdhury, *Rule of Law in State of Emergency: The Paris Minimum Standards of Human Rights Norms in a State of Emergency* (1989); J Oraá, *Human Rights in States of Emergency in International Law* (1992) (hereinafter '*Oraá*'); J Fitzpatrick, *Human Rights in Crisis* (1994); A-L Svensson-McCarthy, *The International Law of Human Rights and States of Exception* (1998) (hereinafter '*Svensson-McCarthy*'); D McGoldrick, 'The Interface between Public Emergency Powers and International Law' (2004) 2(2) *International Journal of Constitutional Law* 380.

[211] See M Nowak, *UN Covenant on Civil and Political Rights: CCPR Commentary* (1993) 73. For a detailed examination of the constitutional law position on emergency powers in a number of European States, see European Commission for Democracy Through Law, *Emergency Powers* (1995).

[212] Nowak (n 211 above) 73.

[213] ACHR, OAS Treaty Series No 36, 1144 UNTS 123.

[214] See n 11 above.

[215] The African Charter on Human and Peoples' Rights, OAU Doc CAB/LEG/67/3 rev 5, 21 ILM 58 (1982) has no derogation provision. The African Commission on Human and Peoples' Rights has stated that: '[67] ... limitations on the rights and freedoms enshrined in the Charter

only be made if there is 'a public emergency which threatens the life of the nation',[216] whilst the ACHR refers to the need for a 'public danger, or other emergency that threatens the independence or security of a State Party'.[217]

The origin of the derogation clause

The initial drafts of the ICCPR produced by the UN Commission on Human Rights in the late 1940s saw the first introduction of a derogation clause in a draft human rights treaty.[218] By June 1949 the UN Commission had produced what was almost the final version of Article 4 of the ICCPR.[219] This was borrowed by the drafters of the European Convention in 1950. Indeed, the draft produced by the UN Commission was inserted in the draft European Convention with little further amendment and with virtually no controversy, detailed analysis, or debate.[220]

The particular wording 'public emergency threatening the life of the nation' was chosen in order to emphasize the truly exceptional nature of the circumstances envisaged by the drafters for when derogations were permissible and the fact that the emergency in question should affect the whole nation. Derogations would not be permitted in situations of lesser importance.[221] Before the UN Commission: 'Reference was made to the history of the past epoch during which emergency powers had been invoked to suppress human rights and to set up dictatorial regimes.'[222] In 1950 such recent history had demonstrated how the enjoyment of rights could be suspended for 'reasons of State', that is not genuinely for the

cannot be justified by emergencies or special circumstances. [68] The only legitimate reasons for limitations to the rights and freedoms of the African Charter are found in Article 27(2), that is that the rights and freedoms of the African Charter "shall be exercised with due regard to the rights of others, collective security, morality and common interest". [69] The reasons for possible limitations must be found in a legitimate state interest, and the evils of limitations of rights must be strictly proportionate with and absolutely necessary for the advantages which are to be obtained. [70] Even more important, a limitation may never have as a consequence that the right itself becomes illusory.' *Media Rights Agenda and Constitutional Rights Project case* (Comm Nos 105/93, 128/94, 130/94, 152/96), 12th Annual Activity Report 1998–99, paras 67–70.

216 ICCPR, Art 4 there is no reference to 'war', for an explanation see *Oraá* (n 210 above) 12.

217 ACHR, Art 27, see *Oraá* (n 210 above) 14–16, who looks at the drafting of Art 27 and concludes that the concept of emergency under the ACHR 'does not differ from that of the other two treaties', 16. See also J Fitzpatrick, 'States of Emergency in the Inter-American Human Rights System' in D Harris and S Livingstone (eds), *The Inter-American System of Human Rights* (1998), noting that the term 'public danger' was added to accommodate exceptional measures during natural disasters, 376.

218 On the origins of the derogation clause generally see *Oraá* (n 210 above) 7–9 and 12–14 (ECHR) and *Svensson-McCarthy* (n 210 above) 200–17 (UN) and 286–90 (ECHR).

219 *Oraá*, 8.

220 For a detailed review, see the explanation provided by Mr Eustathiades in his separate Opinion attached to the European Commission of Human Rights' Report in the *Lawless* case (*Lawless v Ireland*, Commission Report (1960–61) Series B) 90–3. As to the British input in the drafting of Art 15 of the Convention, see Simpson (n 14 above) 874–7, noting that, from the British perspective at least, the significance of the derogation clause was not properly thought through.

221 *Oraá* (n 210 above) 13.

222 Doc A/2929, ch 5, para 37: extracted from M Bossuyt, *Guide to the 'Travaux Préparatoires' of the ICCPR* (1987) 83–4.

benefit of the State but as cover for severe abuse of human rights and to keep the current regime in power.[223] Against this background, the records of the UN Commission on Human Rights indicate that the drafters of the derogation clause sought 'to provide for a qualification of the kind of public emergency in which a State would be entitled to make derogations from the rights contained in the covenant [ie the ICCPR] which would not be open to abuse'.[224] The wording chosen was 'based on the view that the public emergency should be of such a magnitude as to threaten *the life of the nation as a whole*' (emphasis added),[225] these restrictive words being chosen to avoid too wide a reading of the concept of 'public emergency' for fear of the risk of abuse.[226]

Article 15(1) of the ECHR refers to 'war or *other* public emergency threatening the life of the nation' (emphasis added).[227] In one of the first cases when the Strasbourg institutions addressed this provision it was strongly argued by several members of the European Commission of Human Rights that the word 'war', when read in conjunction with 'other' (public emergency), served to indicate that the latter category of emergency had to be analogous to a warlike situation in terms of the magnitude of the emergency, representing as it did not just a threat to part of the population but the very life of the nation as a whole. In the *Lawless* case, according to the Greek member of the Commission, Mr Eustathiades, who had been a member of the Committee of Legal Experts of the Council of Europe which had contributed to the drafting of the Convention:[228] 'Generally speaking, the preparatory work on Article 15 and its background show that the word "nation" is used to make it clear that what is meant is a threat to *the existence* of the population as a whole from some particularly serious emergency far outweighing any problems of public order and safety that may arise in other circumstances' (emphasis added).[229] He reviewed the drafting of Article 15(1) and came to 'the obvious conclu" emergency of such magnitude that it threatens the existence of the nation as a whole, that is to say the whole population and not merely a part of it'.[230] Several other members of the Commission supported this view.[231] More recently, a careful review of the drafting

[223] See esp the speech of Pierre-Henri Teitgen, recognized as one of the founding fathers of the Convention, before the Consultative Assembly of the Council of Europe in September 1949 in Council of Europe (Robertson (ed)), *Collected edition of the 'travaux préparatoires' of the European Convention on Human Rights* (1975–1985) vol I, 48–50.

[224] 10 GAOR Annexes, UN Doc A/2929, part II, ch 5, para 8 (1955), cited by T Buergenthal, 'To Respect and to Ensure: State Obligations and Permissible Derogation' in L Henkin (ed), *The International Bill of Rights* (1981) Ch 3, 79.

[225] ibid.

[226] *Oraá* (n 210 above) 13.

[227] There has been no case before the Strasbourg organs when a respondent State has claimed that it has derogated from the Convention on the basis that a state of war exists.

[228] Council of Europe (Robertson (ed)) (n 223 above) vol III, 180.

[229] *Lawless v Ireland*, Commission Report (1960–61) Series B, Opinion of Mr Eustathiades, 92.

[230] ibid 91.

[231] ibid. Mr Dominedo considered that the emergency must be 'an extremely grave one and it must threaten the very life of the nation, in other words its very existence as such', 94, 98.

history of Article 4 of the ICCPR, and so by analogy Article 15(1), concludes that the discussion that took place before the drafting organs of the United Nations conveyed 'the clear impression that the concept of public emergencies was at all times linked to warlike situations or situations brought about by violence, or grave natural disasters, which make it impossible or well nigh impossible to control the functioning of a country's institutions'.[232]

In summary, as intended by the drafters, Article 15(1) set a clear limit, a 'threshold of severity', to be passed before a State could derogate at all. Through the phrase 'life of the nation' the main situation the authors had in mind was war or rebellion, situations jeopardizing the survival of the State itself. Moreover, only certain rights could be derogated from[233] and even then, as regards the derogable rights, it would only be possible to infringe them 'to the extent strictly required by the exigencies of the situation'[234] and only if 'such measures are not inconsistent with [the State's] other obligations under international law'.[235] In addition, certain technical requirements were added, including notification of the emergency to the Council of Europe's Secretary-General and the duty to transmit information as to the measures taken and the reasons for them.[236] This signalled the special distinction to be made between a derogation and the other accommodation clauses in human rights treaties, for example, those found in the second paragraphs of Articles 8 to 11 of the Convention.

Abstract Definitions of 'Public Emergency Threatening the Life of the Nation'

The drafting history of both Article 4 of the ICCPR and Article 15(1) of the European Convention thus tend to support Lord Hoffman's view of the threshold test. What counts, however, is how international human rights institutions have interpreted the concept of 'public emergency' in practice. In fact, neither Strasbourg institution has accepted the fundamental view of the threshold test that seems to have been specifically intended by the drafters. In *Lawless v Ireland*[237] by a legitimate process of interpretation the Court avoided reference to the Convention's preparatory work and adopted the language of the majority of the

Mr Süsterhenn, also in dissent, argued that war meant 'total war', and so 'other public emergencies' had to be of a similar magnitude, 92.

232 *Svensson-McCarthy* (n 210 above) 215–16 (emphasis added).

233 See Art 15(2) of the Convention, allowing for the suspension of four rights. The list of non-derogable rights is greater under both the ICCPR (Art 4(2)) and the ACHR (Art 27(2)), although both instruments protect more rights than the Convention.

234 Art 15(1) of the Convention, cf ICCPR, Art 4(1).

235 Art 15(1) of the Convention, cf ICCPR, Art 4(1) which adds the stipulation that the measures must 'not involve discrimination solely on the ground of race, colour, sex, language, religion or social origin'.

236 Art 15(3) of the Convention, cf ICCPR, Art 4(3), and Art 4(1) which requires that a 'public emergency' must be 'officially proclaimed'.

237 (n 85 above) para 28.

Commission in holding that, in the general context of Article 15, the natural and customary meaning of the words 'other public emergency threatening the life of the nation' were sufficiently clear. The words referred to

> ... an exceptional situation of crisis or emergency[238] which affects the whole population and constitutes a threat to the organised life of the community of which the State is composed.[239]

This definition will be referred to hereinafter as 'the *Lawless* definition'. In over forty years since the *Lawless* ruling of 1961 the Strasbourg Court has never departed from this definition. Nor has it ever cited the definition of a 'public emergency' employed by the European Commission of Human Rights in what has become popularly known as 'the *Greek* case'.[240] This evidently drew significantly on the *Lawless* definition: the Commission stated that for a 'public emergency' to be one that met the threshold of 'threatening the life of the nation', the following characteristics were required:

> 153 ....
>
> (1) It must be actual or imminent.
> (2) Its effects must involve the whole nation.
> (3) The continuance of the organised life of the community must be threatened.
> (4) The crisis or danger must be exceptional, in that the normal measures or restrictions, permitted by the Convention for the maintenance of public safety, health and order, are plainly inadequate.[241]

It will be appreciated that in the third criterion the words 'of which the State is composed' from the *Lawless* definition were dropped by the Commission. The fourth criterion nevertheless firmly underlines the distinction to be made between a derogation and the Convention's usual accommodation or 'clawback' clauses, such as those found in the second paragraph of Articles 8 to 11, through which certain restrictions may be placed on the full enjoyment of rights in 'normal' times.[242] It was a

[238] The (authentic) French text reads: 'une situation de crise ou de danger exceptionnel et imminent'—so adding the notion of 'imminence' to the definition.

[239] The (authentic) French text reads: 'une menace pour la vie organisée de la communauté composant l'Etat'. The majority of the European Commission of Human Rights in the *Lawless* case had formulated the following definition: 'a situation of exceptional and imminent danger or crisis affecting the general public, *as distinct from particular groups*, and constituting a threat to the organised life of the community which composes the State in question', *Lawless v Ireland*, Commission Report (n 229 above) 82 (emphasis added).

[240] 'The *Greek* case' (*Denmark, Norway, Sweden, Netherlands v Greece*) (n 276(iii) below).

[241] ibid 72 (para 153).

[242] See *Oraá* (n 210 above), 8–10; see also European Commission of Human Rights, *Case-Law Topics (No. 4): Human Rights and their Limitations* (1973). In her classic examination of derogation clauses in human rights treaties, Rosalyn Higgins draws a distinction between '"clawback" clauses and derogations clauses *stricto sensu*'. She comments, 'a "clawback" clause is one that permits, in normal circumstances, breach of an obligation for a specified number of public reasons. Derogations *stricto sensu* are those which allow suspension or breach of certain obligations in circumstances of war or public emergency', Higgins (n 210 above) 281. See also A Kiss, 'Permissible Limitations on

reflection of the Commission's view of the high threshold for Article 15 that the 'normal measures or restrictions' must be 'plainly inadequate'. Derogation is an extraordinary event that can only be resorted to in exceptional circumstances and then only temporarily; it is not a convenient tool for a State to resort to in the same way as other permissible restrictions on Convention rights that may be reasonably resorted to, possibly on a permanent basis, in 'normal times'.

In fact, as regards the specific issue of the threshold of severity the contribution of international human rights tribunals has been limited and, it may be said, rather unsophisticated.[243] It may be noted, for example, that the jurisprudence of the Inter-American system for the protection of human rights has set down some important principles of relevance to the derogation provision of that treaty, in particular on the topic of non-derogable rights.[244] However, no organ under the Inter-American system has provided a definition of 'public emergency', which is perhaps surprising given the history of the region.[245] The jurisprudence of the Inter-American Court has not focused on the issue of the threshold of severity,[246] whilst statements made by the Inter-American Commission on Human Rights have also been limited.[247]

With respect to Article 4 of the ICCPR, the Human Rights Committee has made 'no attempt ... to provide an abstract definition of or criterion for a "public emergency"'.[248] True, it has delivered two General Comments regarding Article 4, most recently in 2001; but even this did

Rights', in Henkin (ed) (n 224 above) 290–1. The Human Rights Committee has emphasized that derogation from certain human rights obligations in emergency situations are 'clearly distinct from restrictions or limitations allowed even in normal times under several provisions of the Covenant', UN Human Rights Committee, *General Comment No 29 (on Article 4 ICCPR)*, UN Doc CCPR/C/21/Rev1/Add.11 (2001) para 4.

[243] Fitzpatrick (n 5 above) 203, 206, noting that the threshold of severity 'remains underdeveloped because monitoring bodies have tended to defer to assertions of emergency conditions by Governments appearing to act in good faith, to reject out of hand emergencies declared without plausible basis' and that 'where the existence of an actual emergency condition is a close question, monitoring bodies have generally not undertaken the careful analysis that might provide precise guidance as to the scope of this principle' (footnotes omitted).

[244] Art 27(2) provides that the list of non-derogable rights includes 'the judicial guarantees essential for the protection of such rights'. In two leading Advisory Opinions, the IACHR has concluded that this category includes the remedies of *amparo* and *habeas corpus*: *Habeas Corpus in Emergency Situations (Arts. 27(2), 25(1) and 7(6) of the American Convention on Human Rights)*, Advisory Opinion OC-8/87 of 30 January 1987; and *Judicial Guarantees in States of Emergency (Arts. 27(2), 25 and 8 of the American Convention on Human Rights)*, Advisory Opinion OC-9/87 of 6 October 1987. See generally J Pasqualucci, *The Practice and Procedure of the Inter-American Court of Human Rights* (2003) 48–9; Fitzpatrick (n 217 above) 391 and *Svensson-McCarthy* (n 210 above) 242ff.

[245] See Fitzpatrick (n 217 above) 391. [246] ibid.

[247] The Inter-American Commission has stated that 'In order to consider that there is an emergency justifying suspension of rights, there must be an extremely grave situation of such a nature that there is a real threat to law and order or the security of the state, including an armed conflict, public danger, or other emergency that imperils the public order or security of a member state', Inter-American Commission on Human Rights, *Report on Terrorism and Human Rights*, OEA/Ser.L/V/II.116, Doc 5 rev 1 corr (22 October 2002) para 51.

[248] McGoldrick (n 210 above) 392. On the ICCPR and Art 4 see *Svensson-McCarthy* (n 210 above) 242ff and S Joseph, J Schultz, and M Castan, *The International Covenant on Civil and Political Rights: cases, materials and commentary* (2004) 824–7.

not set down principles as regards the threshold requirements.[249] The *Lawless* definition has strongly influenced definitions of 'public emergency threatening the life of the nation' used in the two texts on public emergencies drafted by non-governmental experts with specific reference to Article 4 of the ICCPR: the International Law Association's *Paris Minimum Standards of Human Rights Norms in a State of Emergency*[250] and the *Siracusa Principles in the Limitation and Derogation Principles of the ICCPR*.[251] The *Lawless* definition is cited almost verbatim in the former,[252] and it directly influenced the definition adopted within the latter.[253] Principles 39, 40, 41, and 54 of the *Siracusa Principles* state:

A. 'Public Emergency which Threatens the Life of the Nation'

39. A State party may take measures derogating from its obligations under the International Covenant on Civil and Political Rights pursuant to Article 4 (hereinafter called 'derogation measures') only when faced with a situation of exceptional and actual or imminent danger which threatens the life of the nation. A threat to the life of the nation is one that:

(a) affects the whole of the population and either the whole or part of the territory of the State, and
(b) threatens the physical integrity of the population, the political independence or the territorial integrity of the State or the existence or basic functioning of institutions indispensable to ensure and protect the rights recognized in the Covenant.

40. Internal conflict and unrest that do not constitute a grave and imminent threat to the life of the nation cannot justify derogations under Article 4.

41. Economic difficulties per se cannot justify derogation measures.

. . .

54. The principle of strict necessity shall be applied in an objective manner. Each measure shall be directed to an actual, clear, present, or imminent danger and may not be imposed merely because of an apprehension of potential danger.[254]

[249] See S Joseph, 'Human Rights Committee: General Comment No. 29' (2002) 2(1) *Human Rights Law Review* 81, 85.

[250] R Lillich, 'The Paris Minimum Standards of Human Rights Norms in a State of Emergency' (1985) 79 AJIL 1072. The Paris Principles were adopted by the International Law Association in 1984 after almost 8 years of drafting. See generally Chowdhury (n 210 above).

[251] The *Siracusa Principles in the Limitation and Derogation Principles of the ICCPR* (the '*Siracusa Principles*'), UN Doc E/CN.4/1985/4 (1985) Annex, published in (1985) 7 *Human Rights Quarterly* 1 (with accompanying introduction). The principles were drawn up in 1984 by a group of 31 distinguished experts in international law.

[252] Principle 1 of *The Paris Minimum Standards* reads:

1(a) The existence of a public emergency which threatens the life of the nation, and which is officially proclaimed, will justify the declaration of a state emergency.
(b) The expression 'public emergency' means an exceptional situation of crisis or public danger, actual or imminent, which affects the whole population or the whole population of the area to which the declaration applies and constitutes a threat to the organised life of the community of which the State is composed.

[253] See D O'Donnell, 'Commentary by the Rapporteur on Derogation' (1985) 7 *Human Rights Quarterly* 23–4.

[254] The author of the working paper on Principle 39 stated in her commentary that 'the peril which leads the authorities to suspend rights must be actual or closely imminent rather than speculative,

The opening words of Principle 39(b), which might be applicable to armed conflict or a major natural disaster, and the choice of words 'physical integrity' with reference to population in particular, suggest that the drafters of this Principle had in mind an overwhelming situation before derogating measures could be taken. Insofar as a 'public emergency' might stem from internal disorder, the terms of Principle 39(b) ('the existence or basic functioning of institutions indispensable to ensure and protect the rights recognized in the Covenant') indicate that what the legal experts had in mind was a situation of major public disorder, one whereby the normal functioning of the constitutional order of the State would be under significant threat or pressure as with a civil war or an attempt to overthrow the legitimate government. A broad reading of the notion of 'institutions' would include the institutions of law enforcement. Hence if internal public disorder leads to a situation so severe that the ordinary means of law enforcement are not possible then there may be a 'public emergency' of the order required by Article 4 of the ICCPR. In his commentary on Principle 39(b), the Rapporteur noted that the emphasized words were 'substituted for the concept of the organized life of the community [ie the *Lawless* definition] in order to emphasize that the ultimate purpose of derogation is to protect human rights in exceptional circumstances; it may not be used for other ends'.[255]

The high threshold set for a 'public emergency' of a level of severity entitling a State to derogate from human rights treaties is further evident from expert comments on the concept. In her working paper produced for the *Siracusa* conference, Hartman argued that 'the emergency provoking the suspension of fundamental rights must imperil the nation as a whole and its ability to function as a democratic polity';[256] 'No derogation is legitimate unless it is clearly aimed in good faith at the preservation of democratic institutions and a return to their full operation at the earliest opportunity'.[257] Elsewhere the same commentator has suggested that the

potential, latent, or lingering' (J Hartman, 'Working Paper for the Committee of Experts on the Article 4 Derogation Provision' (1985) 7 *Human Rights Quarterly* 89, 91). With respect to the notion of 'imminence' it has been argued that in order for a crisis to be covered it must 'if not actually exist, be on the verge of breaking out at any moment' (*Svensson-McCarthy* (n 210 above) 299). Thus, 'the time element should make no room for measures that are merely intended to prevent a potential danger that may only materialize in a few weeks or months' F Van Hoof, 'The Protection of Human Rights and the Impact of Emergency Situations under International Law with Special Reference to the Present Situation in Chile' ((1977) X(1–2)) *Human Rights Journal* 239.

[255] O'Donnell (n 253 above) 24. The Rapporteur noted that the change also reflected the belief that 'certain events which might be considered threats to "the organized life of the community", such as major strikes or natural disasters, normally can be responded to adequately by restrictions on freedom of movement, expression, association, and assembly which are permitted by the [regular limitation clauses of the ICCPR]. They, therefore, do not constitute true threats to the life of the nation'. It was also pointed out that 'Because not all social or public institutions are of critical importance to the life of the nation, and given that some interference or obstruction of the operation of public institutions should be expected and tolerated in democratic societies, the wording "existence of *basic* functioning of institutions *indispensable* for the protection" of fundamental rights is employed in order to emphasize that only the most serious disturbances of the public order qualify as threats to the life of the nation' (original emphasis) 24.

[256] Hartman (n 254 above) 91.

[257] ibid 92.

'life of the nation' element of Article 15 requires that: 'Some fundamental element of Statehood, such as the functioning of the judiciary or legislature or the flow of crucial supplies, must be seriously endangered.'[258] This comment has been cited with approval by Joan Fitzpatrick in her work on states of emergency and international human rights law.[259] Chowdhury has referred to Principle 39 of the *Siracusa Principles* and commented 'the public danger must be such as to imperil those institutions which are essential for the proper functioning of a democratic Government'.[260] The former UN Special Rapporteur on States of Emergency has also placed great emphasis on protection of democratic institutions and the 'protective' nature of a state of emergency, observing that 'international monitoring bodies with increasing precision and clarity have been tying the exercise of this exceptional measure to the defence of democracy, which is understood not only as a particular form of political organization that it is unlawful to attack but as a system that "lays down absolute limits for the unfailing observance of certain essential human rights"'.[261] This perspective is understandable since there has been a strong association between the declaration of a public emergency by a State and significant human rights abuse. In this regard, attention devoted to the phenomenon of states of emergency was probably at its greatest in the 1970s and early 1980s when 'the world found itself in the grip of what amounted to an institutional epidemic of States of emergency, which, like a contagious disease infecting the democratic foundations of many societies, were spreading to countries in virtually all continents'.[262] In Latin America in the 1970s, two-thirds of the countries were at one time or another under a state of emergency. Expert studies[263] revealed the almost incurable tendency on the part of authoritarian regimes to abuse the device of the 'public emergency' as a 'legalised' means of justifying human rights abuse for their own ends.[264]

Summary

Thus certain key qualities of a 'public emergency threatening the life of the nation' emerge. What is required is not 'an exceptional situation of crisis or emergency' alone, but one that is so serious that it is a threat to 'the organised life of the community of which the State is composed' (the *Lawless* definition and the *Paris Minimum Standards*) or to 'the existence or basic functioning of institutions indispensable to ensure and protect the rights recognized in [the Covenant or human rights treaty in question]' (Siracusa Principle No 39). If the very survival or existence of the State as

[258] Hartman (n 210 above) 16. [259] Fitzpatrick (n 210 above) 16.

[260] Chowdhury (n 210 above) 27.

[261] L Despouy (Special Rapporteur on the Question of Human Rights and States of Emergency), *Tenth Annual Report to the UN Commission on Human Rights* E/CN.4/Sub.2/1997/ (23 June 1997) paras 43–44, footnotes omitted. [262] ibid para 2.

[263] See esp International Commission of Jurists (n 210 above) and Questiaux (n 210 above).

[264] The situation is summarized by Despouy (n 261 above) paras 3–5.

such does not need to be immediately in issue,[265] nonetheless there is a critical threshold and it is set at a high level. There should be an imminent threat to what might be termed the 'constitutional' life of the nation in the sense that vital public institutions or functions are imperilled and the ability of the State to govern is in jeopardy. A war, or very significant internal disorder (perhaps caused by terrorism) are typical situations that *might* lead to this threshold being approached. But they will not always be sufficient—this will depend on the severity of circumstances. As regards a State threatened by terrorist violence, it would seem that what is required is a situation, or an imminent situation, of such public disorder, strife, and general breakdown in communications that it is not possible, at least for the time being, for the State *fully* to maintain 'organised life' in terms of the normal existence of the democratic constitutional order, including the normal operation of the law and its enforcement. Finally, there is near universal recognition that derogations from human rights instrument should only be of a temporary nature.[266] This corresponds with the understanding that derogation clauses echo arrangements under domestic constitutions for the suspension of constitutional guarantees in a situation of exceptional crisis and in order to preserve democracy.

Given what has just been stated, reconciling a 'public emergency' as it seems to be understood from the perspective of international human rights law with the situation confronting the UK Government in late 2001 may not be as easy as the English courts seem to have assumed. Lord Hoffman may have been incorrect if he was suggesting that the very existence of the United Kingdom would need to be in issue for Article 15(1) to apply. But he appears to have been correct to claim that the restrictive essence of the phrase 'threatening the life of the nation', as well as the *Lawless* definition, entailed that a 'public emergency' required *more* than the threat of major loss of life and destruction of property.

Does the Strasbourg jurisprudence echo the understanding of the threshold test for the declaration of a public emergency that we have just seen? Some of the Law Lords, and to some extent SIAC, seemed to take the view that the Strasbourg Court had set a low standard. But it is at least arguable that the Strasbourg jurisprudence on the threshold test, correctly understood, confirms the reading of 'public emergency' just set out.

[265] Sir J Fawcett, *The Application of the European Convention on Human Rights* (1987) 308.

[266] eg see *Paris Minimum Standards*, Principle 3(a); Human Rights Committee, *General Comment No. 29* (n 242 above) paras 1 and 2 ('The restoration of a state of normalcy where full respect for the Covenant can again be secured must be the predominant objective of a State party derogating from the Covenant' (para 1)); Chowdhury (n 210 above) 27, 45; *Oraá*, 30; The *Guidelines of the Committee of Ministers of the Council of Europe on human rights and the fight against terrorism* (adopted in 2002, hereinafter '*CoE Terrorism Guidelines*') also highlight the temporary nature of emergencies, see Guideline XV(1). Guideline XV(3) states 'The circumstances which led to the adoption of such derogations need to be reassessed on a regular basis with the purpose of lifting these derogations as soon as these circumstances no longer exist'. The International Commission of Jurists has also recently confirmed the understanding of the temporary nature of derogations, see *The International Commission of Jurists Declaration on Upholding Human Rights and the Rule of Law in Combating Terrorism* ('The Berlin Declaration' adopted 28 August 2004) para 4.

VI. The Threshold of Severity Test in the Strasbourg Jurisprudence

While there is no shortage of comment on Article 15(1) generally,[267] there has been surprisingly little analysis on the threshold test for Article 15(1).

First, it may be observed that derogation from the Convention has been an exceptional event, with a very large majority of the States never having resorted to Article 15 at any time, including States such as Italy and (West) Germany which were afflicted by serious terrorist violence in the 1970s. As of 31 October 2005, the only derogations entered under Article 15 concerned Jersey, Guerney, and the Isle of Man.[268] With the exception of a brief derogation made by Albania,[269] the only derogation activity that has occurred since 1990 has concerned just two States: Turkey[270] and the United Kingdom (with respect to Northern Ireland[271] and, of course, the British derogation of 2001, now withdrawn). No other Council of Europe State has derogated on the basis of the terrorist threat said to exist since September 11, including Spain, which was the subject of bombings in Madrid in March 2004.

A second general point to note is that, since the 1990s, the Strasbourg jurisprudence on Article 15(1) has been the subject of repeated and quite severe criticism. It has been argued that, through the use of the margin of appreciation doctrine, the Court has been too deferential to the State in its scrutiny of the existence of a 'public emergency', but especially in its examination of whether the measures taken in accordance with a derogation are 'strictly required'.[272] The Court, it is said, has not proven

[267] See D Harris, M O'Boyle, and C Warbrick, *Law of the European Convention on Human Rights* (1995) Ch 16; C Ovey and R White, *Jacobs and White: The European Convention on Human Rights* (2002) Ch 21; J Merrills and AH Robertson, *Human rights in Europe: a study of the European Convention on Human Rights* (2001) 205–12; P van Dijk and D van Hoof, *Theory and Practice of the European Convention on Human Rights* (1998) 730–47.

[268] For technical reasons these derogations remained in place after, on 19 February 2001, the UK withdrew a derogation, put in place in connection with terrorism concerning Northern Ireland, which had originally been submitted in 1988.

Despite the gravity of the situation in Chechnya, Russia has not derogated from the Convention at any time.

[269] This lasted from 10 March 1997 until 24 July 1997, for details see <http://conventions.coe.int.>.

[270] Since 1987 through the 1990s and into the early 2000s Turkey entered a series of derogations primarily relating to Art 5(3) and mainly concerning the south-eastern part of that country, which was blighted by terrorist activity. All such derogations had been revoked by the end of 2002.

[271] In 1988, soon after the case of *Brogan v UK* App No 11209/84, (1991) 13 EHRR 439, the UK entered a derogation to Art 5(3) of the Convention with respect to Northern Ireland. This was addressed by the Court in *Brannigan and McBride v UK* App Nos 14553/89 and 14554/89, Commission Report and Court judgment, Series A 258-B (1993) also (1994) 17 EHRR 378 and subsequently, from the perspective of 1998, in *Marshall v UK*, App No 41571/98, decision of 10 July 2001, unreported. The derogation was withdrawn in 2001. See generally C Campbell, '"Wars on Terror" and Vicarious Hegemons: the UK, International Law, and the Northern Ireland Conflict' (2005) 54 ICLQ 321, 334–42.

[272] O Gross and F Ní Aoláin, 'From Discretion to Scrutiny: Revisiting the Application of the Margin of Appreciation Doctrine in the Context of Article 15 of the European Convention on Human Rights' (2001) 23(1) *Human Rights Quarterly* 638–9; S Marks, 'Civil Liberties at the

to be an effective scrutinizer of whether the emergency powers drawn upon and enabled by the derogation were effective in practice or were 'strictly required' because the normal or ordinary criminal law was insufficient. It has been argued that the deference employed 'inject[s] a strong subjective element into the interpretation of the European Convention, weakening the Court's authoritative position *vis-à-vis* national Governments', which may 'in turn, undermine any hope of effective regional supervision and enforcement of rights protected by the European Convention'.[273] With respect to derogations made regarding Northern Ireland, the Court has been severely criticized for condoning prolonged or entrenched public emergencies in defiance of the principle that public emergencies must be temporary in nature.[274] It has also been argued the Court's approach has led to a gulf in standards between a European human rights approach to the 'public emergency' condition and that existing elsewhere.[275] It is against the background of such criticism that we should applaud the stance taken by the Law Lords in '*A*' as regards the second limb of Article 15 ('strictly required by the exigencies of the situation').

Thirdly, whilst the jurisprudence on most aspects of the Convention is now voluminous, the jurisprudence on Article 15 remains relatively limited.[276] With the exception of 'the *Greek* case', all Article 15 cases that

Margin: the UK Derogation and the European Court of Human Rights' (1995) 15 OJLS 85; O Gross, '"Once More Unto The Breach": The Systemic Failure Of Applying The European Convention On Human Rights To Entrenched Emergencies' (1998) 23 *Yale Journal of International Law* 437; see also Campbell (n 271 above) 342, 353.

[273] Gross and Ní Aoláin (n 272 above) 628–9.

[274] Gross (n 272 above); Marks (n 272 above).

[275] F Ní Aoláin, 'The Emergence Of Diversity: Differences In Human Rights Jurisprudence' (1995) 19 *Fordham International Law Journal* 101; see also Campbell (n 271 above) 339.

[276] The leading cases on Art 15 from the Strasbourg jurisprudence are as follows:

(i) *Greece v UK* App No 176/56 (1958) 2 *Yearbook of the European Convention on Human Rights* 176; Commission Report (1997) 18 *Human Rights Law Journal* 348; Committee of Ministers Res (59) 12. The case was not referred to the Court and was only fully reported in 1997. See esp B Simpson, *Human Rights and the End of Empire* (2001) Chs 18 and 19.

(ii) *Lawless v Ireland (No 3)* App No 332/57, Commission Report (1960–61) Series B (hereinafter '*Lawless* Commission Report'), judgment (1979–80) 1 EHRR 15 (hereinafter '*Lawless* judgment'). See esp B Doolan, *Lawless v Ireland (1957–1961): the first case before the European Court of Human Rights. An international miscarriage of justice?* (Aldershot: Ashgate, 2001). See also P O'Higgins, 'The Lawless Case' [1962] *Cambridge Law Journal* 234; R Pelloux, 'L'arrêt de la Cour européenne des droits de l'homme dans l'affaire Lawless (fond)' (1961) VI *Annuaire Français de Droit International* 251; AH Robertson, 'The first case before the European Court of Human Rights: Lawless v Ireland' (1960) 36 BYIL 343 and 'Lawless v Republic of Ireland (second phase)' (1961) 37 BYIL 536.

(iii) 'The *Greek* case' (*Denmark, Norway, Sweden, Netherlands v Greece*) App Nos 3321–23/67, Commission Report 12* *Yearbook of the European Convention on Human Rights* (1969—special edition), Committee of Ministers Res (70) DH 1, and Committee of Ministers Res (74) DH 2, 17 *Yearbook of the European Convention on Human Rights* (1974) 618. See H Coleman, 'Greece and the Council of Europe: The international legal protection of human rights by the political process' (1972) 2 *Israeli Yearbook of Human Rights* 121 and T Buergenthal, 'Proceedings against Greece under the European Convention on Human Rights' (1968) 62 AJIL 441.

have reached Strasbourg have concerned terrorist violence,[277] despite the fact that the drafters of the Convention do not seem to have had terrorism specifically in mind in 1950 when the particular choice of words 'other public emergency threatening the life of the nation' was made. Perhaps the need to adapt Article 15 to terrorist violence of the kind experienced in Europe accounts for the willingness of the Commission and the Court to approach the interpretation and application of certain aspects of Article 15 flexibly. For example, although in *Lawless* the Court referred to 'an exceptional situation of crisis or emergency *which affects the whole population*' (emphasis added), this has been interpreted by the Court so as to allow a declaration of a public emergency for a region of a State—Northern Ireland or certain provinces in south-east Turkey—on the basis that the nation's population as a whole are generally affected.[278]

A further preliminary point that may be made is how limited the Court's own jurisprudence on the threshold question is. In the great majority of the cases that have reached the Court's attention, the existence of an Article 15(1) qualifying emergency was not contested. As a result, the main focus of what follows will be on the two Strasbourg cases that have reached the Court when the threshold matter was in issue, *Lawless v Ireland* and *Marshall v United Kingdom*. Before looking at these cases in detail, however, a few words should be said about the very first applications considered by Strasbourg in which Article 15 matters were seriously in issue, for they set the tone as regards the approach to be taken at Strasbourg to the adjudication of Article 15(1) issues.

(iv) *Ireland v UK*, App No 5310/71, Commission Report Series B 23-I, judgment (1980) 2 EHRR 25. See M O'Boyle, 'Torture and Emergency Powers under the European Convention on Human Rights: Ireland v. the United Kingdom' (1997) 71 AJIL 674; D Harris, 'Decisions of the ECHR during 1978' (1978) 49 BYIL 301; J Andrews, 'The Northern Ireland Case before the Court' (1978) 3 *European Law Review* 250; D Bonner, 'Ireland v United Kingdom' (1978) 27 ICLQ 897.

(v) *Brannigan and McBride v UK* App Nos 14553/89 and 14554/89, Commission Report and Court judgment, Series A 258-B (1993) also (1994) 17 EHRR 378. See J Andrews, 'Derogation from Article 5(3) by the United Kingdom' (1994) 19 *European Law Review* 110; E Crysler, 'Brannigan and McBride v United Kingdom: A new direction on Article 15 Derogations under the ECHR?' (1994) 27 RBDI 603; Marks (n 272 above); J Merrills, 'Decisions on the European Convention on Human Rights during 1993' (1993) 64 BYIL 522; C Warbrick, 'The European Convention on Human Rights' (1994) 14 *Yearbook of European Law* 653.

(vi) *Aksoy v Turkey* App No 21987/93, Commission Report and Court judgment, Reports of Judgments and Decisions 1996-VI also (1997) 23 EHRR 553.

(vii) *Marshall v UK*, App No 41571/98, decision of 10 July 2001, unreported.

[277] On European human rights law in relation to terrorism, see C Warbrick, 'The Principles of the European Convention on Human Rights and the Response of States to Terrorism' (2002) 3 *European Human Rights Law Review* 287; and by the same author, 'The European Response to Terrorism in an Age of Human Rights' (2004) 15 *European Journal of International Law* 989; P Jean, 'The jurisprudence of the European Commission and Court of Human Rights with regard to terrorism', in R Higgins and M Flory (eds), *Terrorism and international law* (1997) 217. See also *CoE Terrorism Guidelines* (n 266 above) and Duffy (n 226 above) Ch 7.

[278] See eg *Aksoy v Turkey* (n 276(vi) above). The Court will, however, construe territorial limitations strictly, see *Sakik v Turkey* Application No 23878/94, (1998) 26 EHRR 662.

Greece v United Kingdom *and* Lawless v Ireland*: setting the Strasbourg approach to the adjudication of Article 15(1)*

Article 15 was of fundamental importance in the first application declared admissible by the Commission, *Greece v United Kingdom*.[279] This concerned the last years of British rule in Cyprus, when, to counteract an insurgent terrorist movement on the island ('EOKA'), certain exceptional legislative and administrative measures had been introduced by the colonial Government.[280] The Commission's Report of 1958 did not provide an abstract definition of 'public emergency', and so the case is of limited value in terms of our attempt to elucidate the precise requirements of the threshold test for Article 15(1). The background to the case had been one of significant acts of violence on the part of EOKA, as well as other serious tensions existing on the island. For the period when the violence and disorder was at its peak, the Commission appeared easily satisfied that Article 15(1) applied.[281] But derogating measures had been taken prior to this period and were kept in place for some time after it, when the number of terrorist incidents was relatively low. Nonetheless the Commission accepted that these phases of the situation were still covered by Article 15(1), illustrating that it would take a practical approach as regards the timing of the implementation of derogation measures. As with the *Lawless* case, which followed very shortly afterwards, there is a sense that the Commission as an institution leant favourably towards a State fighting an organized terrorist movement with the political objective of overthrowing the Government. On the question of whether the British Government had been entitled to derogate at a stage when the violence had only been rather limited, the Commission accepted that one had to consider that the relatively low number of incidents 'emanated from a fast growing and militant organisation which, according to its own statements, aimed at obtaining self-determination for Cyprus by all possible means, including force and violence'.[282]

Birth of the margin of appreciation[283]

Although the Commission's findings in *Greece v United Kingdom* are certainly open to criticism,[284] sight should not be lost of the major advance in the international law of human rights that it represented at the time, as well as the fact that the case established a cardinal principle for Strasbourg jurisprudence on Article 15(1): the notion that the Convention organs had competence[285] to address and express an objective opinion upon a

[279] *Greece v UK* (n 276(i) above).

[280] For a superb account of the facts of the case and the Commission's handling of it, see Simpson (n 14 above).

[281] *Greece v UK* (n 276(i) above) paras 131–136. See, however, the dissenting opinion of Mr Eustathiades.

[282] ibid para 132.

[283] On the evolution of the margin of appreciation doctrine in the context of Art 15 see M O'Boyle, 'The Margin of Appreciation and Derogation under Article 15' (1998) 19(1) *Human Rights Law Journal* 23.

[284] See Simpson (n 138 above) 1018–19.

[285] *Greece v UK* (n 276(i) above) para 129.

Government's appreciation as to the existence of a 'public emergency' for the purposes of Article 15(1). The stance taken by the Commission, in the late 1950s, is remarkable when one considers that in the '*A*' case the House of Lords regarded the existence of a 'public emergency' as primarily a political question. However, the Commission's Report in *Greece v United Kingdom* indicated that it would afford to a respondent State a measure of 'discretion in appreciating the threat to the life of the nation'.[286] In this way the case witnessed the origins of the famous 'margin of appreciation' doctrine in Strasbourg jurisprudence.[287] It would seem that this doctrine was at least in part a reaction to the British Government's pleading that 'the Government of the territory is in the best position to judge whether an emergency threatening the life of the nation has arisen', this being a question on which 'Governments always tend to reserve their own discretion'.[288] It was suggested to the Commission that it would be 'very, very risky if [it did not] at least ... lean favourably towards the opinion of the Government, because the Government has in its possession all the relevant information, much of which must, in the nature of things, be subject to security classifications, and the same considerations apply to the measures which have to be taken to meet the emergency'.[289]

It was in *Lawless v Ireland*[290] that the term 'margin of appreciation' first made an appearance. The Irish Government had argued that the Strasbourg organs had no competence to consider Article 15(1) matters and that their only capacity was to assess the good faith or otherwise of the respondent State under Article 18.[291] Following *Greece v United Kingdom*, the Commission rejected this viewpoint. It held that it did have competence to provide an objective assessment under Article 15(1), though in performing this task the State concerned would benefit from a 'margin of appreciation'. In oral proceedings before the Court, the extension of a margin of appreciation was justified having regard to the responsibility of the State in maintaining law and order and the fact that a well-informed State would be better placed in principle than international organs to make an assessment of a given (and potentially highly delicate) situation.[292] Although the Court did not refer to a margin of appreciation, it was noted that 'its whole approach to the matter was consistent with that of the Commission'.[293]

A 'wide' margin of appreciation

The existence of a 'public emergency' was in dispute in 'the *Greek* case'.[294] This did not reach the Court but was the subject of a Report by

[286] ibid para 136. [287] See Simpson (n 138 above) 998–1005.

[288] *Greece v UK* (n 276(i) above) para 18. [289] ibid.

[290] *Lawless v Ireland* (n 276(ii) above).

[291] See the comprehensive account provided by Robertson, 'Lawless v Republic of Ireland (second phase)' (n 276(ii) above) 542–3.

[292] ibid 543. See the statements made by Sir Humphrey Waldock (President of the Commission, 1955–1962), in Series B (1960–1961) 408.

[293] Robertson 'Lawless v Republic of Ireland (second phase)' (n 276(ii) above) 544.

[294] See n 276(iii) above.

the European Commission of Human Rights and a final decision by the Committee of Ministers. It is an important Article 15 case in which the Commission slightly elaborated upon the *Lawless* definition of a 'public emergency'.[295] The case will not be discussed in any detail here, as in practice it adds little to the debate on the threshold of severity for Article 15(1). The chief reason is that it concerned a patently undemocratic Greek Government—a military *junta* which had seized power from the legitimate Government; no doubt this was why, uniquely, the Commission placed a burden on the respondent State to show that the conditions justifying measures of derogation under Article 15(1) applied and granted only a very limited margin of appreciation.[296] After a close examination of the facts it concluded that there was in fact no 'public emergency' at the material time, the only occasion on which a Strasbourg organ has reached such a conclusion.[297]

This leads to some more general comments that may be made about the Strasbourg jurisprudence on Article 15(1). The relevant judgments have concerned respondent States—Ireland, the United Kingdom and Turkey—who, at the time of the case being heard by the Court, could be identified as, in the words of the Convention's Preamble, 'the Governments of European countries which are like-minded and have a common heritage of political traditions, ideals' and which by ratifying the Convention had: 'Reaffirm[ed] their profound belief in those fundamental freedoms which are the foundation of justice and peace in the world [and the view that these are] ... best maintained on the one hand by an effective political democracy and on the other by a common understanding and observance of the human rights upon which they depend.' It is arguable that the democratic credentials of such States largely explain why the Strasbourg Court has granted respondent States a *wide* margin of appreciation on both the Article 15(1) threshold issue and the assessment of what measures are 'strictly required'.[298] This indicates how reluctant the Strasbourg organs have been even to situate themselves in a position whereby they may seriously examine the actual existence of

[295] See text accompanying n 241 above.

[296] 'The *Greek* case' Commission Report (n 276(iii) above) para 154. Hartman (n 210 above) 29, has suggested that: 'It was probably the Commission's distrust of the motivations of the Greek military Government and revulsion against its anti-democratic character that explained the difference in the majority opinions in the *Greek* and *Lawless* cases.' See also *CoE Commissioner Opinion* (n 33 above) para 10.

[297] Although the Court has held that measures taken by a State pursuant to a derogation were disproportionate insofar as they were not 'strictly required by the exigencies of the situation', see eg *Aksoy v Turkey* (n 276(vi) above).

[298] Sir James Fawcett, President of the European Commission of Human Rights (1972–81), has explained the application of the margin of appreciation in the derogation context as follows: the Strasbourg organs do 'not, as of course, accept the judgment of the respondent Government as conclusive; but [they] rather place [themselves] in the position of citizens in a democracy who, because they have accorded to their legislature and executive the responsibility for their Government and the means of discharging it, will accept ... derogations which appear, within the limits of reasonableness and good faith, necessary to Government', Fawcett (n 311 above).

a public emergency, whilst paying greater attention to the proportionality of the measures taken in connection with it. The Court recently set out its general approach to Article 15(1) in the case of *Marshall v United Kingdom*.[299] It recalled that 'it falls to each Contracting State, with its responsibility for "the life of [its] nation", to determine whether that life is threatened by a "public emergency" and, if so, how far it is necessary to go in attempting to overcome the emergency'. On such questions the Court grants a '*wide* margin of appreciation'[300] (emphasis added) to the respondent State, because: 'By reason of their direct and continuous contact with the pressing needs of the moment, the national authorities are in principle better placed than the international judge to decide both on the presence of such an emergency and on the nature and scope of the derogations necessary to avert it.' The Court adds:

> Nonetheless, Contracting Parties do not enjoy an unlimited discretion. It is for the Court to rule whether, inter alia, the States have gone beyond the 'extent strictly required by the exigencies' of the crisis. The domestic margin of appreciation is thus accompanied by a European supervision. In exercising this supervision, the Court must give appropriate weight to such relevant factors as the nature of the rights affected by the derogation and the circumstances leading to, and the duration of, the emergency situation . . .

A reading of the actual text of Article 15(1) confirms that the phrase 'extent strictly required by the exigencies' refers back to the actual and specific 'measures derogating' from the Convention. Accordingly, the Court apparently sees its main task as being to scrutinize the proportionality of the actual measures taken in conjunction with the 'public emergency', as opposed to the very existence of the emergency itself—though here too the Court grants the State a wide margin of appreciation.[301]

299 *Marshall v UK* (n 276(vii) above) 11–12.

300 The reference to a '*wide* margin of appreciation' was first made by the Court in *Ireland v UK* (n 276(iv) above) para 207.

301 In contrast to the Strasbourg Court, the Human Rights Committee grants no margin of appreciation to the State on the question of what is 'strictly required'. In its General Comment on ICCPR Art 4, it has stated that, 'the obligation to limit any derogations to those strictly required by the exigencies of the situation reflects the principle of proportionality which is common to derogation and limitation powers. Moreover, the mere fact that a permissible derogation from a specific provision may, of itself, be justified by the exigencies of the situation does not obviate the requirement that specific measures taken pursuant to the derogation must also be shown to be required by the exigencies of the situation. In practice, this will ensure that no provision of the Covenant, however validly derogated from will be entirely inapplicable to the behaviour of a State party. When considering States parties' reports the Committee has expressed its concern over insufficient attention being paid to the principle of proportionality', UN Human Rights Committee, *General Comment No. 29 (on Article 4 ICCPR)*, UN Doc CCPR/C/21/Rev.1/Add.11 (2001) para 4.

There is no reference to the notion of margin of appreciation within the *Siracusa Principles* or the *Paris Minimum Standards*, which were drafted with reference to Art 4(1) of the ICCPR. Further, the Human Rights Committee does not employ the margin of appreciation doctrine for this same provision; see McGoldrick (n 210 above) 399–400. In fact, the Human Rights Committee's jurisprudence under the First Optional Protocol to the ICCPR indicates that when a State is relying on Art 4(1) it is not open to it merely to invoke the existence of exceptional circumstances, but must provide 'a sufficiently detailed account of the relevant facts' said to justify the 'public emergency'. The burden of proof is on the respondent Government to provide 'full and comprehensive information' to satisfy

It is arguable that when the Strasbourg institutions have granted a wide margin of appreciation to a State in the context of Article 15 and as regards the existence of a 'public emergency', they have implicitly accepted that the derogation has been made in good faith and for sound motives growing out of a culture of 'effective political democracy' and 'common understanding and observance of the human rights'. Certainly the Article 15 cases that the Court has heard have not involved what might be termed 'repressive' states of emergency whereby, for example, a military *junta* has seized power from the legitimate Government[302] or a Government that has resorted to a derogation to keep itself in power and, to achieve this, suspends democratic institutions.

More generally, it may be argued that the theoretical underpinnings of the margin of appreciation doctrine in Article 15(1) jurisprudence are a reflection of the deference owed to the national authorities by international organs on the basis that the former inevitably has greater 'institutional competence'[303] to assess the existence of a 'public emergency'.[304] As was accepted by the House of Lords, this would correspond with the inherently political nature of the assessment of the existence of a 'public emergency'. However, this does not mean that the assessment of an Article 15(1) 'public emergency' is an entirely subjective matter, for the Court has provided a general definition of that term and specifically reserved for itself the competence to assess whether Article 15(1) applies.

Lawless v Ireland*: the leading authority on the threshold test*

The leading case on the threshold of severity for Article 15 remains *Lawless*. This concerned a derogation[305] from Articles 5 and 6 of the Convention submitted by Ireland in late 1956 against the background of IRA activity between 1954 and 1957. The derogation was intended to allow detention without trial of certain suspected IRA members. Terrorists had been operating from bases in the north of the Irish Republic, crossing the border into Northern Ireland where a number of serious criminal incidents occurred, such as the bombing and destroying of police huts, bridges, railway lines, and electricity substations.[306] Such incidents were evidently not trivial, but the scale of the activity was rather limited, as is apparent from the fact that over the six-year period between 1956 and 1962 approximately half a dozen RUC members were

the Human Rights Committee that the situation described in Art 4(1) exists or existed in the country concerned. If such information is not furnished, the respondent State's derogations will not be accepted as legitimate under the terms of the ICCPR. See *Silva v Uruguay* UN Doc A/36/40, 130 para 8.2 and *De Montejo v Colombia* UN Doc A/37/40, 168, para 10.3, as discussed by McGoldrick (n 210 above) 399–401. The UK has not ratified the First Optional Protocol to the ICCPR.

302 cf 'the *Greek* case' (n 276(iii) above).

303 This term was employed by Liberty in its submissions in the '*A*' case, see Lord Bingham's judgment, para 29.

304 See esp O'Boyle (n 283 above) 26.

305 See *European Commission of Human Rights: Documents and Decisions: 1955–1956–1957*, (1959) 47–8.

306 See Doolan (n 276(ii) above) Ch 3.

killed.[307] In his study of the *Lawless* case, in which he draws extensively on unpublished material in the National Archives in Dublin, Doolan suggests that at the material time the situation in Ireland was far from being a 'public emergency threatening the life of the nation'.[308] For this reason, amongst others, Doolan has gone so far as to suggest that the *Lawless* case, the result of which was to uphold the legality of the Irish derogation in issue as well as the regime of internment it provided for, was a miscarriage of justice. He is particularly critical of the European Commission of Human Rights for its failure to undertake a fact finding visit to Ireland, for: 'It was admitted at every level within the Government, that the case was lost if such an investigatory visit occurred.' For Doolan this underlined 'how illusory, and in a sense fraudulent' the claim had been that there was an emergency which threatened the life of the nation.[309]

It was certainly true, then, as was noted by several of the Law Lords in '*A*', that the *Lawless* case concerned low-level terrorist violence.[310] However, insofar as the same Law Lords read it as supporting the conclusion that low-level terrorist violence of itself entitles a State to derogate from the Convention, it is suggested that the *Lawless* case was misunderstood. As will be demonstrated, the actual 'public emergency' which the European Court accepted the Irish State was seeking to prevent corresponded to a high threshold for Article 15(1), correlating with a restrictive view of the 'threatening the life of the nation' element of that provision. At the same time the *Lawless* case is very much relevant to the factual circumstances underpinning the British derogation as it suggests that to some extent a State may derogate from the Convention on a preventive or '*potential* emergency' basis and that the Strasbourg institutions were very deferential indeed to the State on this matter. This point appeared to go largely unnoticed by the English courts in their assessment of the Article 15(1) jurisprudence, although it was generally accepted that a derogation could be made in the face of an emergency that had not yet happened but was 'imminent'.[311]

Lawless *and 'potential' emergencies*

The *Lawless* judgment itself contains no reference to the notion of a *potential* public emergency. However, one contemporary commentator pointed out that the Commission's Report clearly supported the view that there was no actual emergency, only a potential one.[312] The

[307] These figures are derived from a 'Background document' prepared by the British Government available at the Public Record Office under file number FCO 87/268. The Public Record Office contains a number of files which indicate that the British Government kept a close eye on the progress of the *Lawless* case at Strasbourg, see eg FCO 371/146292.

[308] Doolan, (n 276(ii) above) 38.

[309] ibid 105, see also 99 and 106.

[310] See text accompanying nn 146, 149, and 150 above.

[311] See, for example, text accompanying nn 90–95 above.

[312] See esp C Morrisson, *The Developing European Law of Human Rights* (1967) 167–8.

Commission had concluded, by nine votes to five, that there was a 'public emergency' for the purposes of Article 15(1) and, by eight votes to six, that the derogating measures were 'strictly required'. When the case was pleaded before the Court, the President of the Commission, Sir Humphrey Waldock, referred to an 'important question of interpretation of Article 15' which the Court would have to resolve:

Some of the minority opinions rejected the idea of the potential or conjectural existence of an emergency as a basis for invoking Article 15. The other point of view [ie that of the majority of the Commission] is that it would perhaps frustrate the purposes of the emergency powers accorded to Governments under Article 15, to preserve a nation from a threat to its life, if the Governments had always to wait until a potential threat had turned into an actual one, with an already occurring impact upon the life of the people. Moreover, in their view, account has to be taken of the natural consequences to be expected of a situation in which a mounting series of acts of violence directed against a neighbouring Government [ie the terrorist attacks on Northern Ireland emanating from the Republic's territory] have been and are taking place. It will be the task of the court to choose between these different points of view.[313]

In a judgment that was inadequate for its brevity on Article 15(1) in particular, it is submitted that the Court adopted the latter of the alternatives put to it by Sir Humphrey Waldock. Hence, the public emergency, to the extent that it existed in Ireland in 1957 was merely 'potential', but, the Court accepted, it was on the verge of erupting into a full-blown active and existing 'public emergency threatening the life of the nation'. This places in proper context what was said in paragraph 29 of the judgment, as the Court came to the conclusion that a 'public emergency' had existed:

... despite the gravity of the situation, the Government had succeeded, by using means available under ordinary legislation, *in keeping public institutions functioning more or less normally*, but whereas the homicidal ambush on the night 3rd to 4th July 1957 in the territory of Northern Ireland near the border had brought to light, just before 12th July—a date, which, for historical reasons is particularly critical for the preservation of public peace and order—*the imminent danger to the nation caused by the continuance* of unlawful activities in Northern Ireland by the IRA and various associated groups, operating from the territory of the Republic of Ireland ... [314]

So it was accepted that Article 15(1) might apply on the basis of the '*imminent danger to the nation*'[315] existing at the time when the Irish Government made the derogation. This was a time when the level of terrorist violence was low, but when it was accepted by the Strasbourg institutions that there was a real risk of a fully-blown 'public emergency threatening the life of the nation'.

[313] *Lawless v Ireland* (1960–61) Series B, Verbatim Record of the Hearing before the Court (10 April 1961, Sir Humphrey Waldock) 412.

[314] *Lawless*, para 29 (emphasis added).

[315] ibid.

In summary, *Lawless* entitles a State to derogate when a 'public emergency' is merely potential in order to 'nip trouble in the bud' (low-level terrorist violence threatening to explode into major trouble for the ordered life of the nation). At first sight this is highly pertinent to the British derogation of 2001 the legality of which, it will be recalled, was contested on the basis that there was in existence no *actual* 'public emergency' at the material time when the derogation had been made, since there had been no attack on British soil at that juncture. However, for a potential public emergency to be acceptable under Article 15, there has to lie behind it the genuine prospect of a fully-fledged actual 'public emergency threatening the life of the nation'. But what must this encompass?

Lawless *and the 'threshold' test for Article 15(1)*

The *Lawless* case, it is submitted, sets a high threshold for Article 15(1), although to appreciate this one has to look at the affair in some detail. It set down an abstract definition of 'public emergency', but this needs to be read in the context of the case as a whole. It indicates, first, that the actual measures taken in conjunction with the derogation will only be justified if the situation is so serious that 'the ordinary law' and other non-derogating measures are unable to counteract the danger to the nation that was being faced.[316] Secondly, and more importantly, as regards the Court's test of 'threat to the organised life of the community *of which the State is composed*' (emphasis added), *Lawless* implies that the potential emergency stage would need to be the prelude to a very serious state of affairs indeed in the life of the nation. Much more than serious public disorder would be required in that the actual 'public emergency' would have to reach a stage that threatens the community organized and regulated of the basis of the democratic State. Thus, the Court referred to 'the imminent danger *to the nation*' (emphasis added) caused by the operation of the IRA. It acknowledged that 'despite the gravity of the situation' the Irish Government had succeeded 'in keeping public institutions functioning more or less normally', but that the particular events of July 1957 prompted the authorities to declare a public emergency. The implication is that it was a condition precedent for a public emergency to be validly declared that the situation must be so severe that the normal

[316] The Court's judgment set out the extent of the difficulties facing the Irish Government as it (according to the Court) struggled to cope with the situation facing it. It was noted that 'in 1957 *the application of the ordinary law had proved unable to check the growing danger which threatened the Republic of Ireland*; ... *the ordinary criminal courts, or even the special criminal courts or military courts, could not suffice to restore peace and order*; ... in particular, the amassing of the necessary evidence to convict persons involved in activities of the IRA and its splinter groups was meeting with great difficulties caused by the military, secret and terrorist character of those groups and the fear they created among the population; whereas the fact that these groups operated mainly in Northern Ireland, their activities in the Republic of Ireland being virtually limited to the preparation of armed raids across the border was an additional impediment to the gathering of sufficient evidence; ... the sealing of the border would have had extremely serious repercussions on the population as a whole, beyond the extent required by the exigencies of the emergency', *Lawless*, para 36 (emphasis added).

operation of 'public institutions' should be under threat in some way, with the continued functioning of the State being in some sort of jeopardy.[317] In his concurring judgment in the *Lawless* case, Judge Maridakis spoke in terms of the State being involved in a 'life and death struggle', adding that the terminology 'public emergency threatening the life of the nation' referred to 'a quite exceptional situation which imperils *or might imperil the normal operation of public policy established in accordance with the lawfully expressed will of the citizens*, in respect alike of the situation inside the country and of relations with foreign Powers'.[318]

It must be conceded that the Court in *Lawless* hardly engaged with the question of how the 'organised life' criterion of the public emergency test was met on the facts. It simply stated that the Irish Government had:

> ... reasonably deduced [the existence of an Article 15(1) qualifying public emergency] ... from a combination of several factors, namely: in the first place, the existence in the territory of the Republic of Ireland of a secret army engaged in unconstitutional activities and using violence to attain its purposes; secondly, the fact that this army was also operating outside the territory of the State, thus seriously jeopardising the relations of the Republic of Ireland with its neighbour; thirdly, the steady and alarming increase in terrorist activities from the autumn of 1956 and throughout the first half of 1957.[319]

These three reasons, set out in remarkably concise terms, echoed those set out in the majority opinion of the Commission in *Lawless*; it is to that opinion which we may turn for a greater appreciation of the threshold question. The first reason cited by the Court (the existence of the IRA, its effectiveness, and ambitions) corresponded with a point made at length by the majority of the Commission. This was that the sheer existence of the IRA as 'an illegal underground organisation, which repudiated the authority of the Government elected by the people and which was dedicated to achieving the ending of the partition of Ireland by the use of armed force'[320] was in itself of relevance for Article 15. Moreover that fact had to be considered against the ability of the Irish State, 'a small and not very rich country',[321] with limited policing resources, to cope with such a presence. The Commission stressed:

> The mere existence within a State of an illegal organisation which declines to recognise the legal authority of the elected Government and recruits and equips with arms an underground military force, appears to us to represent in some degree a threat to the life of a democratically organised State. We recognise that different opinions may be held as to whether the mere existence of such an organisation represents a sufficiently imminent threat to the life of the nation for

[317] A number of the dissenting Commissioners had argued that there was no 'public emergency' as the organs of the State were still functioning normally, see eg Separate Opinion of Mr Eustathiades, *Lawless* Commission Report (n 276(ii) above) 93, of Mr Süsterhenn, 95 and Mr Ermacora, 101.

[318] *Lawless*, Individual Opinion of Mr G Maridakis (emphasis added).

[319] *Lawless*, para 28.

[320] *Lawless* Commission Report, Majority Opinion (1960–61) Series B, 84 (though see generally 83–6 as regards the significance of the existence of the IRA for Art 15).

[321] ibid 85.

it to constitute by itself 'a public emergency threatening the life of the nation'. That it constitutes a substantial threat *to the principles and institutions of democracy within the State appears to us, however, to be self-evident.*[322]

As regards the third reason employed by the Court (the steady and alarming increase in terrorist activities), it may be noted that elsewhere the Court referred to the fact that the derogation was made by the Irish Government just after a homicidal ambush on the night of 3 and 4 July, just one week before the controversial date of 12 July, the anniversary of the Battle of the Boyne (1690). In terms of the timing of the derogation, the Commission majority noted that it was made in anticipation, at least in part, of the release of over a hundred IRA sympathizers from prisons which, in the circumstances, led the Government to be 'afraid' that there would be 'a large intensification of the violence'.[323]

But it is the second reason cited by the Court that is most interesting, expressing as it did the view that IRA cross-border raids into Northern Ireland were 'seriously jeopardising' Anglo-Irish relations. What exactly did this mean? The Commission majority had made much of a similar point in that they had referred to the real risk of 'serious reactions'[324] and 'serious repercussions on the part of the United Kingdom'.[325] Any Government, the Commission majority had stated, was 'bound to react most strongly'[326] to the launching of terrorist attacks from a neighbour. The same Commissioners accepted the argument that if the Irish State did not do all that it could to suppress terrorist activity this could lead to 'most serious results'.[327] What the Commission meant by this, on the one hand, was the plea by the Irish Government of a 'very real'[328] danger that terrorist activity emanating from Ireland would stoke up severe disruption amongst the sectarian communities in Northern Ireland and might lead to virtual civil war there.[329] On the other hand, the reference to 'serious *reactions*' and 'serious *repercussions*' from the British suggested more than this. Archival research into the previously confidential records of the hearings before the Commission confirms that the Irish Government had pleaded that it was necessary to intern IRA suspects as otherwise, with the terrorist activity evolving, there was a 'possibility, or perhaps the probability, of the outbreak of war between the British forces and ours'. Again internment was required, according to the Irish Government, in order to forestall 'a civil war between the citizens of Ireland or citizens of Ireland in the North [ie Northern Ireland]'.[330] It seems highly likely that

322 ibid 87 (emphasis added). 323 ibid 89 324 ibid 88. 325 ibid. 326 ibid.
327 ibid 89. 327 ibid 88. 328 ibid.
329 ibid 88–9. The Commission accepted that there was a 'serious possibility' of this (89).
330 Doolan (n 276(ii) above) 123 (the quotations are extracted from the unpublished transcript of proceedings before the European Commission, held in the National Archives in Dublin, cited by Doolan as within DJ File S.9/58/18). Doolan regards the claims made by the Irish Government as 'staggering' for their exaggeration (121). He is highly critical of the Commission for its failure to verify the Irish Government's submissions on this point either through a fact-finding mission or at the pleadings stage of proceedings (105–6, 121–4, and 142–3), leading to the conclusion that the

this is what the Commission majority were alluding to by their reference to 'serious repercussions' etc. It is true that their opinion made no specific reference to war, but a number of the dissenting Commissioners did. Their point was to stress that the suggestion that there might be war simply had no evidential basis and was far-fetched.[331]

It would seem, therefore, that it was the combined effect of the three factors (the existence of the IRA; the impact on relations with Northern Ireland and the United Kingdom; the escalation in terrorist violence up to July 1957) which allowed first the Commission and then the Court to say that the Irish Government had 'reasonably deduced' the existence of a 'public emergency'. The essential point is that it was these factors, not the low-level terrorist violence in isolation, which was the dominant factor for the Commission and the Court in leading them to accept that Article 15(1) applied. The very existence of the IRA as an illegal army refusing to acknowledge the legitimacy of the Governments on either side of the border was crucial. So too, it seems, was the acceptance of a view that, had action not been taken, things might have developed in accordance with a worst-case scenario whereby the situation would degenerate into a possible Anglo-Irish war[332] and/or potential civil war in the North or South. *This* scenario, combined with the elements already referred to, represented the potential 'public emergency *threatening to the life of the nation*' and it is easy to see why in full-blown form such a scenario would represent a *danger* to the 'organised life of the community of which the State [was] composed', if not the territorial integrity of the Irish State as such. Very clearly this correlated to the restrictive value of the 'threatening the life of the nation' element of Article 15(1), which implied that there be some sort of constitutional crisis whereby the normal unhampered functioning of the legislature, or the judiciary, or the administration was not possible, or that even the survival of the State would be threatened.[333]

investigation as a whole was 'flawed and inadequate' (130). Unsurprisingly, therefore, he is highly critical of the conclusions reached by the Commission (Ch 7) and subsequently the Court (Ch 10) on the Art 15(1) points.

[331] See the Separate Opinion of Mr Süsterhenn, *Lawless* Commission Report (n 276(ii) above) 96, also of Mr Dominedo, 100, Mme Janssen-Pevtschin, 101 and Mr Ermacora, 101–2. See also the criticism of the Court by Morrisson (n 312 above) 169.

[332] A general point of significance to be noted from *Lawless*, therefore, is that the Strasbourg organs accepted in principle that, in the words of the Commission, 'if of sufficient gravity, acts endangering the external relations of a State may constitute a threat to the life of the nation no less than acts endangering its internal order', *Lawless* Commission Report, Majority Opinion (n 320 above) 87. The 'acts' in question were the terrorist actions of the IRA in Northern Ireland, though launched from the safety of the Republic. The Commission's point evidently has a wider significance today in terms of terrorist activity launched from one State into another.

[333] This strict approach to Art 15(1) was reflected in contemporary writing on Art 15(1). In his monograph on the Convention published in 1969, Sir James Fawcett, the British member of the Commission at that time, suggested that for Art 15(1) to apply there needed to be an emergency of such gravity that 'there is such a breakdown of order or communications that organised life cannot, for the time being, be maintained'; citing the Court's judgment in *Lawless*, he implied that there would need to be a threat to the normal function of public institutions. J Fawcett, *The Application*

The value of the precedent set by the Lawless *case*

Having created a strict definition of public emergency, in practice it would seem that the Commission and Court were generous in their reading of the facts of the *Lawless* case [334] The apparent leniency toward the Irish Government and the Strasbourg institutions' willingness to uphold the legality of the derogation might be explained in several ways, although what follows is inevitably conjectural. First, there was general acceptance of the Commission majority view, as Sir Humphrey Waldock had put it, that a State should be able to take action to 'preserve a nation from a threat to its life' *before* a crisis actually erupted. Secondly, the derogation had to be viewed as a whole. In this respect it should be noted that importance was attached by the Court to the 'number of safeguards designed to prevent abuses in the operation of the system of administrative detention':[335] the Court highlighted the fact that, amongst other things, it was subject to 'constant supervision' by an informed Parliament[336] which had a power of annulment; detainees could apply to a Detention Commission which might order release, and in practice any detainee could obtain his release if he undertook to observe the law and refrain from illegal activities contrary to the security of the State, the Court noting here that 'in a democratic country such as Ireland the existence of this guarantee of release given publicly by the Government constituted a legal obligation on the Government to release all persons who gave the undertaking'. Finally, and perhaps most importantly, in terms of an approach which was apparently very favourably disposed to the Irish Government, sight should not be lost of the possible *realpolitik* considerations operating in the background to this case and which would have served to encourage the Strasbourg Court to find in favour of the Irish Government, burdened as it was with the terrorist issue. *Lawless* was one of the very first affairs to reach the Commission and the first ever decision on the merits for the Court.[337] In 1961 the finding that the

of the European Convention on Human Rights (1969) 246. An official publication produced by the Secretariat to the European Commission of Human Rights in the early 1970s discussed the *Lawless* case in detail under an examination of Art 15 of the Convention (alongside Art 17) which proceeded under the heading 'The overriding right of the State to protect its democratic institutions', European Commission of Human Rights, *Case-Law Topics* (n 242 above) 3. Writing on the subject of Art 15 in the light of the *Lawless* case a leading Strasbourg-based commentator in the 1960s noted that for Art 15(1) to apply it was not sufficient that there simply be a difficult situation for the State concerned. Rather the exceptional measure of derogation could only be invoked when the normal operation of the ordinary law under (non-derogating) Convention principles was insufficient to counteract the danger in question and only in circumstances which actually amounted to a true 'threat to the life of the nation', see J Velu, 'Le Contrôle des Organes Prevus par la Convention Européenne des Droits de l'Homme sur le But, le Motif et l'Object des Mesures d'Exception Dérogeant à Cette Convention' in H Rolin (ed), *Mélanges Offerts á Henri Rolin* (1964) 462, 472.

334 A point that was noted by contemporary critics, see Morrisson (n 312 above) 170 (arguing that the *Lawless* definition was a good definition, but that the institutions had 'force[d] the facts to fit it') and O'Higgins (n 276(ii) above) 38.

335 *Lawless* judgment (n 276(ii) above) para 37.

336 See, however, Doolan (n 276(ii) above) 39–44.

337 cf Lord Bingham's comments in '*A*' judgment (n 2 above) para 28.

Strasbourg institutions had any meaningful power of review over whether a 'public emergency' existed under Article 15(1) was a milestone for international human rights law and one achieved over very strong objections from the Irish Government.[338] The *Lawless* judgment was delivered at a time when the Convention was in its very infancy,[339] several years before the United Kingdom accepted the right of individual petition to the Commission (1966) or France would even ratify the Convention (1974).[340] The outlook for European Human Rights supervision in the early 1960s was bleak, as was evident from a speech delivered by the Court's Vice-President, Henri Rolin, in 1965, under the title: 'Has the European Court of Human Rights a future?'[341]

Given the apparent deference shown by the Strasbourg institutions, *Lawless* should therefore be treated with some caution;[342] it may well be that the Court would take a more robust approach today.[343] However, the point remains that the case, the leading authority on the threshold for Article 15(1), sets that threshold at a high level in principle. It does not necessarily support the view that terrorist violence alone suffices for Article 15(1).

Subsequent Article 15(1) judgments—the paucity of the Strasbourg jurisprudence on the threshold test

There have been a number of well-known judgments since *Lawless* when the Court has addressed Article 15(1), most notably *Ireland v United Kingdom*, *Brannigan and McBride*, and *Aksoy v Turkey*. However, in no case heard on the merits by the Court since *Lawless* has the existence of a 'public emergency' been a genuine matter of dispute between the

338 See Counter-Memorial of the Government of Ireland, in *Lawless v Ireland* (1960–61) Series B, 224–7 and Robertson (n 276(ii) above) 542–3.

339 Silvio Marcus-Helmons, a former Special Adviser to the Belgium Government in the 1960s, has reflected that the early 1960s was a time when 'it was considered to be an insult for a democratic State to be expected to defend itself before the European Court of Human Rights', S Marcus-Helmons, 'Belgium' in Blackburn and Polakiewicz (eds), *Fundamental Rights in Europe: The European Convention on Human Rights and its Member States, 1950–2000* (2001) 167, 185.

340 Professor Francis Jacobs pointed out in 1975 that one of the reasons that France waited until 1974 to ratify the Convention and other States hesitated to accept the right of individual petition was due to the 'essentially political character' of Art 15, F Jacobs, *The European Convention on Human Rights* (1975) 209.

341 H Rolin, 'Has the European Court of Human Rights a future?' (1965) 11 *Howard Law Journal* 442.

342 It has been suggested that: 'The Lawless Case could be viewed as deviant, a product of all the uncertainties that must have been engendered in the Court by its first case. The Court was bereft of precedent to guide it and probably uncertain that a ruling contrary to the Government would be followed.', T O'Donnell, 'The Margin of Appreciation Doctrine: Standards in the Jurisprudence of the European Court of Human Rights' (1982) 4 *Human Rights Quarterly* 474, 494.

343 cf the statement made by a Grand Chamber of the Strasbourg Court in 1999 (in an Art 3 case): 'the increasingly high standard being required in the area of the protection of human rights and fundamental liberties correspondingly and inevitably requires greater firmness in assessing breaches of the fundamental values of democratic societies', *Selmouni v France* App No 25803/94, Commission Report and Court Judgment, Reports of Judgments and Decisions 1999-V also (2000) 29 EHRR 403, para 101.

applicant and the respondent State. The Court's commentary on the threshold test for Article 15(1) has therefore been limited indeed and one must turn to the little-known admissibility decision in *Marshall v United Kingdom* for an indication of the Court's more recent position. The earlier cases should, however, be briefly noted.

Ireland v United Kingdom

The Court seems to have been as economical as possible with its treatment of Article 15 in its case law. Certainly it is hard to say that the judgments 'serve[d] not only to decide those cases brought before the Court but, more generally, to elucidate, safeguard and develop the rules instituted by the Convention, thereby contributing to the observance by the States of the engagements undertaken by them as Contracting Parties'.[344] That statement was made in *Ireland v United Kingdom*. Regrettably, however, little can be gleaned from that case regarding the qualifying factors for the existence of a 'public emergency threatening the life of the nation'. As is well known, it concerned events in Northern Ireland in the early 1970s when there was a situation of civil unrest on a significant scale plus, above all, a degree of violence from paramilitary terrorist organizations such that, as the Commission Report grimly described it, there had been 'nothing precisely comparable in the history of the Convention'.[345] With the normal criminal courts apparently unable to restore peace and order, internment on a significant scale was introduced in August 1971[346] (necessitating derogation from Article 5 of the Convention)[347] and there were changes to the normal operation of the courts with respect to

[344] *Ireland v UK* (n 276(iv) above) para 154.

[345] *Ireland v UK* Commission Report, Series B 23-I, 123. Colm Campbell has suggested that the level of violence occurring could be compared to post-invasion Iraq (n 271 above) 324. According to statistics cited by the British Government before the Commission in 1975 there had been 1,100 deaths, 11,500 injured, and over £140,000,000 worth of property destroyed, *Ireland v UK* Commission Report, Series B 23-I, 366.

[346] See the summary provided in *Ireland v UK* (n 276(iv) above) paras, 20–91. Internment was radically reduced and then discontinued after the introduction of 'home rule' in March 1972.

[347] In fact, the UK had entered a derogation from the Convention with respect to Northern Ireland as early as in June 1957 (see *European Commission of Human Rights: Documents and Decisions: 1955–1956–1957* (1959) 48–51), when certain individuals were interned under the Special Powers Acts 1957–1961 (although the Council of Europe was not informed of the internment itself). The derogation remained in place through the 1960s (at least it was never withdrawn) and was in fact added to in 1969 ((1969) 12 *Yearbook of the European Convention on Human Rights* 72–4) and in 1971 ((1971) 14 *Yearbook of the European Convention on Human Rights* 32). The 1971 notice stated that: 'Over recent months in Northern Ireland there has been a series of acts of terrorism, including murders, attempted murders, maimings, bombings, fireraising and acts of intimidation, and more recently violent civil disturbances. The Government of Northern Ireland has therefore found it necessary since 9 August for the protection of life and the security of property and to prevent outbreaks of public disorder, to exercise, to the extent strictly required by the exigencies of the situation, powers of detention and internment'. Copies of the relevant Regulations were sent to the Secretary-General of the Council of Europe, who was subsequently notified when the power of internment was no longer being used; see (1975) 18 *Yearbook of the European Convention on Human Rights* 18. As early as 1954, and then through the 1950s and into the 1960s, the British Government entered a series of derogations in respect of various colonial possessions under its authority, see Simpson (n 14 above) Chapter 17.

terrorist offences. Whilst the various notices of derogation submitted by the British Government suggested that the immediate need for derogation was to protect the population from terrorist violence,[348] there was evidently a wider context to the situation so far as there was a 'public emergency threatening the life of the nation'. In its pleadings the British Government emphasized that the emergency had been 'caused by the activities of the IRA . . . a clandestine organisation, with quasi military dispositions, which accepts neither the structure of Government in the Republic of Ireland nor the existence of Northern Ireland as part of the United Kingdom, and is dedicated to changing both by force'.[349] It was also stated that the emergency grew out of IRA activity as that body pursued its ambition to 'destroy the existence of Northern Ireland as part of the United Kingdom and to subvert the structure of Government in the Republic of Ireland, activities which deliberately and avowedly deny the right to life and security of person of others'.[350]

One reason why *Ireland v United Kingdom* throws little light on the threshold of severity is that from the very outset of proceedings the Irish Government did not contest the existence of an emergency as such.[351] Rather, so far as Articles 5, 6, and 15(1) were concerned,[352] it alleged that the regime of internment and associated measures introduced by the authorities in Northern Ireland were excessive. Thus detailed submissions were not made to the Strasbourg institutions on the topic of what has been referred to in this article as 'the threshold of severity'. For its part, the Commission accepted that Article 15(1) applied. Its Report indicated that, on the facts, the critical issues for the application of Article 15(1) were: first, the organized, widespread, systematic, and paramilitary nature of the hostilities, together with the fact that terrorism was based on the cleavage line of factions within the community; and, secondly, the sheer level and intensity of that violence in that normal law and order could not be maintained even with a military presence in the province.[353] It is implicit from this that the Commission considered there to be a real

[348] Simpson (n 14 above) Ch 17.

[349] *Observations of the Government of the United Kingdom on the admissibility of the application No. 5310/71 lodged by the Government of the Republic of Ireland*, paras 13 and 14. This unpublished document is available at the Public Record Office under file FCO 41/954 (Annex to WDC 7/3/7). Much of the British Government's documentation relating to *Ireland v UK* is now available at the Public Record Office under the 30-year rule (see esp files FCO 87/136–146 and FCO 87/399–406).

[350] *Observations* (n 349 above) para 20.

[351] This is evident from the Commission's Decision on Admissibility, see *Ireland v UK* Decision on Admissibility, Series B 23-I, 606.

[352] The Irish Government had also raised allegations under Arts 1, 2, 3, 5, and 14 of the Convention, see generally *Ireland v UK* Decision on Admissibility, Series B 23-I.

[353] The Commission stated that it 'was satisfied that there existed in Northern Ireland at all times material for the present case a public emergency threatening the life of the nation'. It added: 'The degree of violence, with bombing, shooting and rioting was on a scale far beyond what could be called minor civil disorder. It is clear that the violence used was in many instances planned in advance, by factions of the community organized and acting on para-military lines. To a great extent the violence was directed against the security forces which were severely hampered in their function to keep or restore the public peace.' *Ireland v UK* Commission Report, Series B 23-I, 117.

and genuine threat to the *life* of the nation of Northern Ireland; there was a need to derogate from the Convention in order to forestall the prospect of even greater division and so, eventually, a real threat to the long-term survival and prosperity of the region. The same message came from the Court's judgment. In its lengthy ruling the Court devoted a number of pages to a factual description of the 'Emergency situation and its background' and subsequently reference was made to the 'subversive role' played by the IRA and the 'particularly far-reaching and acute *danger for the territorial integrity of the United Kingdom, the institutions of the six counties* and the lives of the province's inhabitants'[354] that the terrorist violence posed. But the part of the judgment that actually addressed the law on Article 15 was exceptionally brief, the Court simply noting that: 'The existence of such an emergency [one threatening the life of the nation] is perfectly clear from the facts summarised above ... and was not questioned by anyone before either the Commission or the Court. The crisis experienced at the time by the six counties therefore comes within the ambit of Article 15'.[355]

Brannigan and McBride v United Kingdom

In 1984 the British Government withdrew the derogation made with respect to Northern Ireland,[356] but in 1988, following the Court's ruling in *Brogan v United Kingdom*,[357] it submitted a new derogation[358] specifically concerning Article 5(3)[359] and with respect to the point of law impugned by the *Brogan* case. It was this further derogation which generated the next Article 15(1) case heard by the Commission and Court, *Brannigan and McBride v United Kingdom*.[360] This focused on the tragic story of Northern Ireland in its later phase, 1988–89, although specifically the case concerned the length of time that an arrested person could be detained prior to their initial appearance before a judge under Article 5(3). In the proceedings at Strasbourg it was claimed by the British Government that in order to combat terrorism effectively it was

[354] ibid para 212 (emphasis added). [355] ibid para 205.

[356] Information Bulletin on Legal Activities within the Council of Europe and in Member States, vol 21, 2 [July, 1985].

[357] *Brogan v UK* (n 271 above) (for a description of events leading to the 1988 derogation see the commentary within the *Brannigan and McBride* judgment ((n 276(v) above) paras 30–32). On the context to the *Brogan* case and the follow up case of *Brannigan and McBride*, see J Merrills, 'Decisions on the European Convention on Human Rights During 1993' (1993) 64 BYIL 522. The British derogation of 1988 was the subject of strong academic criticism, see, eg G van Hoof, 'The Future of the European Convention on Human Rights' (1989) 7 *Netherlands Quarterly of Human Rights* 451.

[358] As regards the existence of conditions giving rise to an emergency, the derogation notice stated: 'There have been in the United Kingdom in recent years campaigns of organised terrorism connected with the affairs of Northern Ireland which have manifested themselves in activities which have included repeated murder, maiming, intimidation and violent civil disturbance and in bombing and fire raising which have resulted in death, injury and widespread destruction of property. As a result, a public emergency within the meaning of Article 15(1) of the Convention exists.' (1988) 31 *Yearbook of the European Convention on Human Rights* 15, cf (1988) 19 BYIL 470 (detailing the very similar derogation submitted with respect to the ICCPR).

[359] For the text of Art 5(3) see n 63 above. [360] *Brannigan and McBride v UK* (n 276(v) above).

necessary to extend the Article 5(3) period for Northern Ireland (for suspected terrorist offences) given, amongst other things, the difficulties of interrogating terrorists, the need to avoid disclosing certain intelligence sources in court, and to prevent the independence of the courts from being jeopardized in Northern Ireland where the judiciary was small and vulnerable to terrorist intimidation.[361] But was there still a 'public emergency threatening the life of the nation' in 1988? By way of background the Court's judgment stated:

Between 1972 and 1992, over 3,000 deaths were attributable to terrorism in Northern Ireland. In the mid 1980s, the number of deaths was significantly lower than in the early 1970s, but organised terrorism has continued to grow.

Since the commencement of the terrorist campaign there have been 35,104 people injured in Northern Ireland as a result of terrorist acts. Many of these injuries involved loss of limbs and permanent physical disability. In the same period there have been a total of 41,859 terrorist shooting or bombing incidents. Other parts of the United Kingdom have also been subjected to a considerable scale of terrorist violence.[362]

As to the existence of a 'public emergency', the Commission first noted that its review of the Article 15(1) threshold issue would be 'limited'.[363] It then cited in full the *Lawless* definition of public emergency[364] as well as that from 'the *Greek* case' before stating that it had examined whether the situation in Northern Ireland had changed significantly since the case of *Ireland v United Kingdom*. It added:

Judging by the statistics [which it had recounted earlier] on deaths, maimings, explosions and bombings presented to the Commission by the Government, it is clear that the situation in Northern Ireland remains very serious. In 1988 when the derogation was made these figures were still high and the Commission can only conclude in the present case that there was, and continues to be, a state of emergency in Northern Ireland threatening the life of the nation.[365]

This cursory 'statistical' examination undertaken by the Commission, a semi-judicial body, is hardly compelling. The fact that the Court, sitting in plenary session, adopted a similar approach was more disappointing given its status as 'the "last-resort" protector of the fundamental rights and freedoms guaranteed under the Convention'[366] and as a derogation can be said to affect 'the integrity of the Convention system of protection as a whole'.[367] In fact, before the Court neither of the applicants in *Brannigan and McBride* nor the Standing Advisory Commission on Human Rights (as a third-party intervener) contested the existence of the emergency for the purposes of Article 15(1).[368] However, Liberty (with Interights and the Committee on the Administration of Justice) as

[361] *Brannigan and McBride v UK* (n 276(v) above) para 56. [362] ibid para 12.
[363] *Brannigan and McBride* Commission Report (n 276(v) above) para 45. [364] ibid para 46.
[365] ibid para 49. [366] *Brannigan and McBride* Concurring Opinion of Judge Martens, para 4.
[367] ibid. Dissenting Opinion of Judge Makarczyk, para 1.
[368] *Brannigan and McBride v UK* (n 276 (v) above) para 44.

another third-party intervener did do so.[369] It argued that the situation of exceptional crisis that had existed in the early 1970s no longer applied and it pointed out that between 1985 and 1989 there were fewer than 400 killings (the figures for 1971–1975 had been 1,100). Liberty and its partners thus argued that while terrorism certainly disrupted normal life in Northern Ireland, it in no way threatened the life of the nation:

For instance, despite an upsurge of violence in the early months of 1992, voters in Northern Ireland were able to vote freely in the general election held on 9 April 1992. Further, setting aside any criticisms of the criminal justice process in Northern Ireland, the rule of law still runs throughout that part of the UK. Further, the economic and social life of Northern Ireland continues despite the serious situation which prevails there.[370]

Regrettably, the Court did not respond to these points,[371] nor did it respond to the applicants' point[372] that the burden rested on the respondent Government to satisfy the Court that a 'public emergency' of the order required by Article 15(1) really existed.[373] It simply stated that both the Commission and the British Government had maintained that there was an emergency[374] before 'recalling' its earlier case law in *Lawless* and *Ireland v United Kingdom* (no reference being made to 'the *Greek* case'). It affirmed that it was 'making its own assessment, in the light of all the material before it as to the extent and impact of terrorist violence[375] in Northern Ireland and elsewhere in the United Kingdom' and concluded that 'there can be no doubt that *such a public emergency* existed at the relevant time' (emphasis added).[376] The emphasized words plus the referral

369 *Third Party Intervention of Liberty, Interights and The Committee on the Administration of Justice* (August 1992) (copy on file with the author).

370 ibid 21 (para 4.3.7). Liberty also noted the withdrawal of the derogation in 1984 and submitted that the 1988 derogation could only be justified if there had been a demonstrable deterioration in the situation (judgment, para 44). The Court did not deem it necessary to compare the situation of 1984 with that of 1988 (judgment, para 47). It took the view that the decision to withdraw the derogation in 1984 was, in principle, a matter within the discretion of the British Government and had been taken on the view that the relevant legislation was compatible with the Convention (a view that proved to be mistaken, as the *Brogan* judgment, delivered in 1988, had revealed). The judgment also accepted that the derogation was linked to 'the persistence of the emergency situation' and that there was 'no indication that the derogation was other than a genuine response' to the situation confronting the British Government in 1988 (para 51).

In other words, the Court implicitly accepted that the factual conditions of a 'public emergency' may have existed all through the 1980s and that this factual situation was not changed by the withdrawal of derogation in 1984. Article 15(3) of the Convention only requires a State to notify the Council of Europe when a derogation is made, not when a 'public emergency' as such exists and no actual derogating measure is taken.

371 Nor did it respond to Liberty's argument that the margin of appreciation should be narrower the more permanent the emergency becomes, *Brannigan and McBride v UK* (n 276(v) above) para 42.

372 ibid para 44.

373 cf the approach of the Human Rights Committee, see n 301 above.

374 *Brannigan and McBride v UK* (n 276(v) above) para 46.

375 Earlier in its ruling the Court had cited relevant statistics, see the text accompanying n 362 above.

376 *Brannigan and McBride* (n 276(v) above) para 47. It has been observed that the Court's assessment in the *Brannigan* case was 'hardly different from accepting the parties' own view of the situation', see Harris *et al* (n 267 above) 493.

back to the appropriate paragraph from the *Lawless* case indicate that the Court was indeed employing the definition of public emergency derived from the 1961 case. Hence, without expressly citing the relevant passage from *Lawless*, the Court accepted that the British Government was entitled to derogate because there was a threat to the 'organised life of the community of which the State is composed' (*Lawless*). As with the previous case law, however, and despite the submissions of the intervenors, what was missing was any real explanation as to precisely how the *Lawless* threshold test was satisfied on the facts. It seems that the Commission and Court took it as read that the 'organised life of the community of which the State is composed' test was met given the undisputed high level of terrorist violence still occurring. It should be noted too that the Court stated that a wide margin of appreciation was owed to the State in assessing the existence and scale of a public emergency.[377]

The *Brannigan* ruling therefore indicated that for Article 15(1) to apply it is not necessary for there to be a near complete breakdown of public order in the community of the kind seen previously in *Ireland v United Kingdom* or the type of very high-level disruption to the life of the community suggested by Liberty and the other intervenors. Nevertheless, the level of public disorder and level of harmful activity occurring still needed to reach a critical level and intensity, and it was undoubtedly on a very significant scale in Northern Ireland in the late 1980s. As the ruling was so vague, however, questions remain as regards the threshold test. Did the Strasbourg institutions accept that the sheer level of terrorist violence alone was sufficient to merit the existence of a 'public emergency' within the meaning of Article 15(1)? Or was the wider context to the terrorist violence (designed to cause further splits in a community already deeply divided on sectarian lines and, as regards IRA violence at least, ultimately the disintegration of Northern Ireland as an entity) also a critical factor? With respect to this last point both Strasbourg institutions seemed keen to look at cumulative statistics for Northern Ireland and to make a connection between the *Brannigan* case and *Ireland v United Kingdom*. So it may be suggested that a key factor in accepting that Article 15(1) applied was that the *Brannigan* case was viewed in the context of a long-term *campaign* of terrorist violence[378] that had seen its height in the early 1970s when the threat to the life of the nation had been, according to the Court, 'perfectly clear'.[379] Evidently there was acceptance of the Government's arguments that derogation was required under Article 5(3) to fight terrorism effectively.[380]

377 *Brannigan and McBride v UK*, para 44.

378 In *Brannigan and McBride*, for example, the Court referred back generally to the crisis in Northern Ireland since the early 1970s (judgment, para 12) and also made reference to 'the persistence of the emergency *situation*' (para 51) (emphasis added).

379 See text accompanying n 355 above.

380 cf also the Court's statement in *Ireland v UK* that the 'priority' objective of the authorities should be the return of the 'proper functioning of the authorities and ... [restoration of] peace within the community', para 220.

Aksoy v Turkey

The opportunity to clarify the law on Article 15(1) as regards the threshold test and the points just mentioned was not taken up in the next public emergency case to reach the Court, *Aksoy v Turkey*.[381] This concerned acute terrorist violence in south-east Turkey instigated by the PKK terrorist organization.[382] The Commission and the Chamber maintained their apparent approach of stating as little as possible as regards the threshold issue,[383] the Chamber referring to 'The particular extent and impact of PKK terrorist activity in south-east Turkey [which had] undoubtedly created, in the region concerned, a "public emergency threatening the life of the nation"'.[384] However, as with the *Brannigan* case the Chamber allowed a wide margin of appreciation and was prepared to assess the existence of a 'public emergency' by reference to statistics relating to the death and destruction caused by terrorist violence. So the question remains: did the level of death and destruction alone suffice for the purpose of Article 15(1); or was the wider historical backdrop of strife in the respective regions of Turkey and the motives of the terrorists, in particular the separatist motives of the PKK, an equally important factor?

It is worth adding that the *Aksoy* case marked a new departure in the jurisprudence as the Court ruled that, even in the circumstances of the emergency situation created by terrorism, periods of police custody for up to fourteen days under Article 5(3) could not be justified as 'strictly

[381] *Aksoy v Turkey* (n 276(vi) above).

[382] *Aksoy* was one of several cases where the Court has held Art 15(1) to be applicable in the context of a PKK terrorist guerrilla campaign motivated by the call to establish an independent State for Kurds in south-eastern Turkey and neighbouring countries. Under the heading 'The situation in the South-East of Turkey' the Court judgment stated: 'Since approximately 1985, serious disturbances have raged in the South-East of Turkey between the security forces and the members of the PKK (Workers' Party of Kurdistan). This confrontation has so far, according to the Government, claimed the lives of 4,036 civilians and 3,884 members of the security forces', judgment, para 8. The Court then noted that at the time of its judgment (1996) 10 of the 11 provinces of south-eastern Turkey had since 1987 been subjected to emergency rule. It set out the contents of the Turkish Government's derogation notice of 1990, which referred, amongst other things, to the Government's assertion that: 'The Republic of Turkey is exposed to threats to its national security in South East Anatolia which have steadily grown in scope and intensity over the last months so as to amount to a threat to the life of the nation in the meaning of Article 15 of the Convention.' Other than this the Court provided no further comment on the details of the crisis in south-east Turkey prior to its statement that it considered that 'in the light of all the material before it ... *the particular extent and impact of PKK terrorist activity* in South-East Turkey has undoubtedly created, in the region concerned, a "public emergency threatening the life of the nation"', judgment, para 70 (emphasis added). With no elaboration the Court then cited the relevant passages from the judgments in *Lawless*, *Ireland v UK*, and *Brannigan and McBride*. The applicants did not dispute the existence of a 'public emergency' in the *Aksoy* case but submitted that the matter was for the Court to decide (para 69). In its Report the Commission, with no reference to precedent, noted that there was no dispute between the parties as to the existence of a 'public emergency'. It simply stated that: 'In view of the grave threat posed by terrorism in this region, the Commission can only conclude that there is indeed a state of emergency in South-East Turkey which threatens the life of the nation', Commission Report (n 276(vi) above) para 179.

[383] ibid.

[384] *Aksoy* judgment (n 276(vi) above) para 70. Virtually identical statements have been made in *Demir v Turkey* 1998-VI; (2001) 33 EHRR 43, para 45.

required by the exigencies of the situation' (Article 15(1)).[385] This was the first time ever that the Court, as opposed to the Commission,[386] had concluded that a violation of the Convention (here Article 5(3)) was not saved by a subsisting derogation under Article 15(1). The same conclusion was reached on very similar facts in the subsequent case of *Demir v Turkey*[387] when, significantly, the Court stated that in order to be convinced that the 'strictly required' limb of Article 15(1) had been satisfied, it was 'not sufficient [for the respondent Government] to refer in a general way to the difficulties caused by terrorism and the number of people involved in the inquiries'.[388]

By contrast, there had been no failure to meet the 'strictly required' limb of Article 15(1) in *Brannigan and McBride* when the maximum period of Article 5(3) detention had been seven days. By twenty-two votes to four the court's conclusion was that the United Kingdom's derogation satisfied the requirements of Article 15 and that the applicants (detained for a period falling just short of seven days) could not validly complain of a violation of Article 5(3).[389] The Court's acceptance that the measures taken were 'strictly required by the exigencies of the situation' was reached after it had placed considerable emphasis on the safeguards that were in place against abuse of the derogating powers in practice,[390] as well as 'the nature of the terrorist threat in Northern Ireland', 'the limited scope of the derogation',[391] and the reasons advanced in support of it.[392] No member of either the Commission or the Court denied the actual existence of a 'public emergency', but the conclusions reached as regards what was 'strictly required' on the facts were certainly controversial, as is evident from the dissents attached to the Commission's Report and the Court's judgment.[393] There was

385 *Aksoy v Turkey* (n 276(vi) above) para 65.

386 cf 'the *Greek* case' (n 276(iii) above).

387 *Demir v Turkey* (n 384 above).

388 ibid para 52.

389 By the same margin the Court held there was no violation of Art 5(5) or Art 13 of the Convention.

390 *Brannigan and McBride v UK* (n 276(v) above) paras 61–65.

391 There is a significant contrast with the facts of the '*A*' case here, which had concerned detention without trial for 3 years.

392 *Brannigan and McBride v UK* (n 276(v) above) para 66.

393 Some of the Separate Opinions raised further questions regarding Art 15 and are of some relevance to the situation in '*A*'. Judge Russo's Separate Opinion pointed out that his concurring vote had been based on his view of the situation existing when the applicants were detained. However, more generally an emergency situation could only remain valid for 'the time necessary for the Government to find a means of ensuring greater conformity with Convention obligations.' He warned that if 'the derogation were to be extended and to become almost permanent' then it would be 'incompatible with the guarantees which the Convention affords in respect of liberty of the person and which are of fundamental importance in a democratic society'. Similarly, in his dissenting judgment Judge Pettiti commented that a 'derogation cannot constitute a *carte blanche* accorded to the State for an unlimited duration, without it having to adopt the measures necessary to satisfy its obligations under the Convention'. Judge Matscher (joined by Judge Morenilla) argued that a valid derogation was akin to a temporary reservation; it led to the inapplicability of the specific provision of the Convention derogated from for the State concerned. Judge Walsh (dissenting) argued that the reference to 'nation' in Art 15(1) meant that a threat to the life of the whole of the UK was required, not merely that of the province of Northern Ireland. This view has been implicitly rejected in the Court's case law.

considerable criticism of the ruling.[394] It was argued that the employment of a *wide* margin of appreciation tended to communicate a message that potentially encouraged resort to derogation and that this was inappropriate given the relevance of the derogation clause to international human rights law generally and so for States that do not necessarily have a long tradition of democracy and the rule of law.[395]

Marshall v United Kingdom

The cases discussed under the previous section concerned applications made to Strasbourg at times when there was serious terrorist violence occurring on a significant scale. However, this was not so for *Marshall v United Kingdom*,[396] which was decided in July 2001 and remains unreported. It has received very little comment in the academic literature but is an important decision since the threshold test for Article 15(1) was central to it. It will be recalled that Collins J in SIAC regarded the *Marshall* case as supporting the proposition that the Strasbourg Court 'accept[s] that the existence of a real threat of terrorist outrages and the retention by the terrorists of an organisational capacity to kill or maim on a wide scale suffice[s] to establish the existence of an emergency within the meaning of Article 15(1)'.[397] With respect, one might question whether SIAC's reading of this case was entirely correct to the extent that it overlooked the wider 'Northern Ireland' context to the derogation.

Factual background: the Northern Ireland context

As in *Brannigan and McBride* the emergency situation in Northern Ireland was in issue, and so the continuation in force of the derogation relating to Article 5(3). The applicant claimed he had been detained in circumstances that would have been a violation of Article 5(3) but for the subsisting derogation. The key distinction was that Marshall had been detained in 1998, nearly one decade later, when the level of violence occurring in Northern Ireland was very much less acute. The Court stated that it would 'address with special vigilance the fact that almost nine years separate the prolonged administrative detention of the applicants Brannigan and McBride from that of the applicant in the case before it'. Given this and the criticism that the *Brannigan* case had previously provoked it might be thought remarkable that the Court, sitting as a Chamber of seven Judges, rejected the application at the admissibility stage of the proceedings (Article 35(3) and (4)) as 'manifestly ill-founded'. The judges might have been comforted by the fact that the derogation had been withdrawn in February 2001, shortly before the

394 See the commentaries cited in n 276(v) above.

395 See the Concurring Opinion of Judge Martens and the Dissenting Opinion of Judge Makarczyk, both arguing for a restrictive approach to Art 15(1).

396 *Marshall v UK* (n 276(vii) above).

397 SIAC judgment (n 76 above) para 23.

admissibility decision of July 2001 was delivered.[398] Nonetheless, it is respectfully submitted that the rejection of the case as 'manifestly ill-founded' was an unsatisfactory and controversial way of concluding an application which, given the paucity of the Article 15(1) jurisprudence, as well as the general importance of the issues raised, was surely ripe for consideration on the merits by the Court.[399]

The Court's decision should be seen against the statements it recounted under the heading of 'The political and security situation in Northern Ireland'. This included cumulative statistics[400] on death and personal injury for Northern Ireland over the thirty-year period up to 1999, plus a year-by-year breakdown of the same for the years 1989–99. For 1994 there had been sixty-two 'deaths (military and civilian) due to the security situation', the figure for 1995 being nine, and for the other years up to 1999 as follows: 1996: fifteen; 1997: twenty-two; 1998: fifty-five; 1999: six. As for 'persons (military and civilian) ... injured as a result of the security situation', the figures were 1994: 825; 1995: 937; 1996: 1,419; 1997: 1,237; 1998: 1,564; 1999: 550. Relatively detailed reference was also made to the Annual Reviews of the relevant legislation undertaken by JJ Rowe QC between 1993 and 1998. The Court pointed out that for 1996 'the reviewer noted that there had been a marked increase in the level of terrorist activity in the wake of the IRA's decision to end the cease-fire which it called in August 1994'.[401] The 1997 Report noted that the threat of terrorism continued to be real and rejected arguments for the normal Article 5(3)-compliant regime to be reintroduced. The 1998 Report noted that in spite of the four-year-old cease-fire:

> ... there are dissident elements who are intent upon causing injury and damage, and they have the capacity to do so. All in all there is a real threat that some terrorist activity will continue in Northern Ireland ... My conclusion is this, criminals with a terrorist or paramilitary disposition have the means to carry out attacks with explosives and firearms at any time; furthermore, some of them have maintained an organisation which has structure and influence.[402]

Before the Court the British Government placed emphasis on these Annual Reviews and argued that a 'public emergency' still existed, pointing out that 'in the seven-week period leading up to the applicant's arrest in February 1998 thirteen murders had taken place in the province', whilst there had been 'numerous bombing incidents'. Arguments were presented concerning the continuing necessity of the Article 5(3) derogation in the context of the criminal justice system in Northern Ireland

[398] It is impossible to know for sure, but possibly the submission of the application itself to Strasbourg may not have been without influence in the decision to withdraw the derogation. Certainly the timing of the withdrawal and the subsequent delivery of the decision is quite a coincidence.

[399] It has been suggested on behalf of the former European Commission of Human Rights that issues relating to Art 15(1) should, as of course, be examined on the merits and should not be disposed of at the stage of admissibility, see *Case Law Topics No. 4* (n 242 above) 12.

[400] *Marshall v UK* (n 276(vii) above) 5. [401] ibid. [402] ibid 5–6.

and the safeguards that existed against abuse. Against this the Applicant relied on the improved security situation in Northern Ireland to contest the legitimacy of the on-going 'public emergency' and as the basis for his claim that his Article 5(3) rights had been infringed. He had been detained in 1998, four years on from the decision of the main paramilitary groups to call a cease-fire and the year of the Good Friday Agreement which paved the way for a power sharing devolved assembly and, so it was submitted, reduced the prospect of a return to violence on the part of the main paramilitary groups. It was put to the Court that there had been 'a marked decline in the use of emergency powers of arrest, search and detention, less frequent recourse to extended periods of detention, the closure of army bases and the running down of the number of army personnel involved in operational duties in the province'.[403] Marshall asserted that if there had been a 'public emergency' at one time, it was effectively over by 1998 and that it was not open to the United Kingdom Government to retain a derogation by reference to possible future outbreaks of terrorist violence which could be dealt with if and when they occurred. He argued for a strict approach to be taken by the Court as regards both the existence of an emergency and the necessity of the actual measures taken pursuant to it. Finally, he asserted that the Annual Reviews of the legislation were an inadequate basis for any decision on the continued need for the derogation: 'none' of the Reviews, he asserted, 'gave prominence to the compatibility of the extended detention power with Article 5(3) of the Convention and to the continuing need for the derogation; nor [did] they address issues such as the capacity of the ordinary criminal law process to deal with the security situation'.[404]

The Court's rejection of the application in Marshall

The Court accepted the arguments of the British Government that a public emergency 'threatening the life of the nation' continued to exist in Northern Ireland. It noted that at the relevant time there had been 'an outbreak of deadly violence' and that 'the authorities continued to be confronted with *the threat of terrorist violence* notwithstanding a reduction in its incidence' (emphasis added). There had been 'no return to normality' and given the application of the margin of appreciation owing to the State, the Court was not prepared to 'controvert the authorities' assessment of the situation in the province in terms of the threats which organised violence posed for the life of the community and the search for a peaceful settlement'.[405]

The Court's reasoning—'no return to normality', continuance of 'the *threat* of terrorist violence' although reduced in practice, 'the *threats* which organised violence posed' (emphases added)—implicitly acknowledged that when Marshall was actually detained the level of violence and

[403] ibid 8–9. [404] ibid 9–10. [405] ibid 12.

public disorder confronting the authorities may not have crossed the threshold for Article 15(1). This might explain why the Court seemed to be at pains to stress that a wider perspective was necessary, hence the Court's reference to 'the political and security situation in Northern Ireland'[406] and 'the search for a peaceful settlement'. The Court once again explicitly recalled its earlier case law concerning Northern Ireland even though it was making a fresh assessment of the emergency situation as of 1998. This was more clearly seen in the context of the question of whether the measures taken by the British Government were 'strictly required by the exigencies of the situation' when the Court stated:

> The reasons which the Government gave in the *Brannigan and McBride* case against judicial control continue to be relevant and sufficient. It notes in this respect that the threat of terrorist outrage was still real and that the paramilitary groups in Northern Ireland retained the organisational capacity to kill and maim on a wide scale. The applicant contends that it would have been open to the authorities to contain the level of violence prevailing at the relevant time by means of the ordinary criminal law. He observes in this connection that violence on a similar scale in other parts of the United Kingdom [*sic*] have been addressed without recourse to the displacement of due process guarantees. The Court has examined this argument. However, it considers that the applicant's reasoning does not take sufficient account of the specific nature of the violence which has beset Northern Ireland, less so the political and historical considerations which form the backdrop to the emergency situation, considerations which the Court described at length in its Ireland v. the United Kingdom judgment . . . [407]

So, for the purpose of the Article 15(1) threshold test, in *Marshall* the Court emphasized the connection between the application before it and the Northern Ireland 'emergency situation' generally as it had already been in issue before the Strasbourg Court. In the last stages of a 'public emergency' which had previously clearly satisfied the Article 15(1) threshold, the Court refused to step in and second-guess the national authorities' determination of the 'security situation' in terms of when to *withdraw* a derogation, at a time when a political solution to the problem of Northern Ireland was beginning to emerge, but outbreaks of terrorist violence remained a possibility. It is important to note this context in order to appreciate that *Marshall* does not necessarily establish the principle suggested by SIAC, namely that *in isolation* the threat of terrorist outrages from a body with organizational capacity to commit the same suffices for the Article 15(1) threshold.

In conclusion the *Marshall* case, in particular the fact that it was dismissed as manifestly ill-founded, sends a strong message that, when there is a reasonable risk of terrorist violence recurring in the context of a political and security situation such as had been in evidence in Northern Ireland and which had previously satisfied the Article 15(1) threshold,

[406] ibid 11. [407] ibid 14.

the Court will accept a precautionary approach on the part of the respondent State as regards the removal of a derogation.[408] Nonetheless, contemporary as opposed to purely historical evidence of a threat of return to terrorist violence must still underpin the derogation. The Court places reliance on the need for safeguards against abuse of the derogating powers and a level of meaningful review of the existence of the emergency situation. But it must be acknowledged that the Court does not appear to set very strict standards.[409] More generally the decision implies that, at least in the Northern Ireland context, the Court would only reject the authorities' assessment of the situation if it was beyond dispute that there had been a return to normality. It is arguable that this dilutes the standards required by the specific language of Article 15(1) and that this approach is a recipe for encouraging entrenched emergency situations. Overall it is hard not to view the *Marshall* case as a prudential decision, with the Court content to avoid getting embroiled in the delicate constitutional affairs of Northern Ireland at a critical time. The decision is certainly difficult to reconcile with a strict approach to Article 15(1).[410]

VII. The Threshold Requirement, 'September 11', and the British Derogation

We are now in a position to draw some conclusions as to the Strasbourg jurisprudence on the threshold of severity test, before proceeding to an assessment of whether the circumstances underpinning the derogation in late 2001 might have justified resort to Article 15(1). The core question is whether a real risk of a terrorist atrocity on the scale of the September 11 attacks justifies a derogation from the Convention.

Strasbourg jurisprudence on the threshold requirement and the timing of derogations

The first comment to be made is that it is evident that in practice the Strasbourg Court has demonstrated its willingness to condone a precautionary approach favouring the needs of the democratic State and its ability to govern with strength in the face of terrorist campaigns in their

[408] cf the Separate Opinion of Judge Russo in *Brannigan and McBride v UK*. As to the temporary nature of derogations, see n 276(v) above.

[409] *Marshall v UK* (n 276(vii) above) 13–14. For comment on the past ineffectiveness of Parliamentary review of terrorism measures, see N Whitty, T Murphy, and S Livingstone, *Civil Liberties Law: The Human Rights Act Era* (London: Butterworths, 2001) 151–3.

[410] As to the wider political context to the case, Professor Brice Dickson (Chief Commissioner, Northern Ireland Human Rights Commission) suggested in 2000 that the Northern Ireland Human Rights Commission had been informed that there would be no relaxation of the 'emergency laws ... not because of security risks but because of political fallout', B Dickson, 'The Protection of Human Rights: Lessons From Northern Ireland: The Paul Sieghart Memorial Lecture' (British Institute of Human Rights, King's College, London, 6 April 2000) 9, available at <http://www.bihr.org> (accessed 30 October 2005).

nascent/potential (*Lawless*), live (*Ireland v United Kingdom*, *Brannigan and McBride*, *Aksoy*), or dying (*Marshall*) stages. It has been willing to give a large benefit of doubt to a democratic Government in the 'twilight period'[411] when derogating measures are, according to the Government, needed either to prevent a full-blown emergency developing in the first place or are still required to prevent one from returning out of a 'smouldering' situation. In the *Lawless* case the Court endorsed the view that a democratic State could declare a 'public emergency' in order to nip trouble in the bud. In the *Marshall* case, the Court indicated that, provided safeguards were in place, a democratic State was entitled to guard against possible future outbreaks of terrorist violence. *Marshall* firmly endorses the comment, made after *Brannigan and McBride*, that the Strasbourg authorities have been willing to 'accept a view of some emergencies as "campaigns" or continuing events which involves some reconsideration of the derogation power as a temporary expedient'.[412]

The Strasbourg Court therefore allows a State to derogate at moments when, viewed in isolation, the threshold of severity for an *actual* public emergency under Article 15(1) as set out in *Lawless* has not been clearly crossed. This may be at odds with the view that derogations are so exceptional that they may only be resorted to at the point of absolute necessity, ie the point of an actual emergency or when it is quite literally 'imminent',[413] and that they must be withdrawn at the earliest opportunity. Yet it might be argued that the Court's approach is pragmatic in its acknowledgement of the reality that the device of the derogation is a crude one for a democratic Government seeking in good faith to combat *a campaign* of terrorism. A strict approach might require a Government to swing back and forth from 'public emergency' situations to supposed normality in response to the ebb and flow of a terrorist campaign. In reality, when the terrorist organization retains its strength and resources, the end of its campaign cannot be tied down to a particular day. To some extent it would seem that the Court regards its flexible approach to the timing of derogations to be compensated for by the safeguards it requires at the domestic level as regards the operation of the derogating measures for individual cases. Nor should sight be lost of the relatively limited scope of the derogation in the later cases concerning Northern Ireland, which had concerned extensions to detention under Article 5(3) for up to seven days.

The Strasbourg Court's position on the timing of *when* derogations may legitimately be made and withdrawn must be distinguished from the issue of the actual threshold of severity for reliance on Article 15(1) itself. It has been argued that it is a mistake to read the *Lawless* case in particular as permitting a State to derogate in the face of low-level terrorist violence *alone*. On closer inspection that case supports the

[411] Simpson (n 14 above) 1065–6, also Ch 17.
[412] Harris *et al* (n 267 above) 493.
[413] See text accompanying n 241 above.

conclusions reached in Section V of this article. As to the later jurisprudence concerning Northern Ireland and Turkey, it must be acknowledged that this is far from clear as regards the content of the threshold test. Certainly the Court has refused to elaborate on what is covered by the notion of 'threat to the organised life of the community', as derived from the *Lawless* case. One can see how the later cases can be read as indicating that a State may derogate from the Convention in the face of major terrorism causing death and destruction, for, in concluding that Article 15(1) applied, the Court has generally relied on statistics relating deaths and personal injury and referred generally to the 'the extent and impact of terrorist violence'. However, the cases relating to Northern Ireland have always been linked back to *Ireland v United Kingdom* and the emergency 'situation' as a whole. Moreover, the Court has never expressly stated that terrorist violence alone suffices for Article 15(1), *Lawless* has never been overruled and the Court in its later case law has been careful to cite that authority. It must be observed too that the Turkish and Northern Irish case law has arisen in the context of long-term terrorist campaigns that at various times clearly did, in the words of Lord Hoffman, 'threaten institutions of government' and the respective regions' 'existence as a civil community'. In conclusion, it would seem that the Strasbourg jurisprudence maintains the high threshold to Article 15(1) found in the *Lawless* case. The occurrence of even very serious incidents of terrorist violence, if these are sporadic incidents, does not necessarily satisfy the threshold of severity for Article 15.

The threshold requirement applied to the British derogation

According to the Strasbourg jurisprudence on Article 15(1), would the attacks of September 11 (assuming these occurred within a member State to the Convention), the bombing in Madrid in March 2004, or the terrorist activity in London in July 2005 justify the declaration of a public emergency and so derogation from the Convention in their aftermath? Without trivializing these incidents in any way, according to a strict reading of the Strasbourg jurisprudence on the threshold requirement as set out in the *Lawless* case, and with the benefit of hindsight, it is hard to see that they would. For the reasons articulated by Lord Hoffman in '*A*', it cannot be said that the events were ones literally 'threatening the life of the nation' concerned, in terms of the respective nation or Government's existence. Did the atrocities represent 'a threat to the organised life of the community of which the State is composed' (*Lawless*)? They were abhorrent and no doubt represented an attack on many things western democracies stand for. But such events, and the prospect of further atrocities by the same or related organizations, would not automatically satisfy the threshold of 'organised life of the community' if what is required by this is terrorism leading to or threatening a breakdown of civil society and ordered governance for the nation concerned (this being central to the concept of 'public emergency' envisaged in the *Lawless* and *Ireland v United Kingdom* cases).

It is respectfully submitted that Lord Hoffman was correct in his view that loss of lives and destruction of property *alone* are not conditions justifying derogation from the Convention (at least when such terrorism does not pass the 'organised life of the community' threshold).[414] Nor are threats to a nation's economic interests and power, or more generally the global economy, these being issues that featured prominently in the Government's justification for derogation as set out to Parliament in late 2001.[415]

The September 11 attacks deserve special consideration given their magnitude and the targets concerned: the World Trade Center, the Pentagon, and a third site assumed to be in Washington, DC.[416] In '*A*' Lord Bingham stated in passing that the attacks were 'intended to disable *the Governmental* and commercial power of the United States'[417] (emphasis added). To the extent that this was in fact so and that the attacks represented a *threat* to Governmental stability and the continued functioning of the 'organised life' of the State, it may be that there was a 'public emergency threatening the life of the nation' as understood at Strasbourg. But this would only be justified given the flexibility provided by the *Lawless* formulation in terms of the ability of a Government to derogate on a precautionary basis, and, on the facts, while the strength of the threat to 'organised life' was being determined.[418] The derogation would need to be withdrawn at the stage when it became clear that the Governmental power of the United States was not in danger of being disabled, the authorities

[414] There is no reason to believe that the Strasbourg Court would differ from the Human Rights Committee's view that in principle a 'natural catastrophe'—an earthquake, major flood, volcanic eruption, a tidal wave—or a 'major industrial accident' *can* provide the basis for the declaration of a public emergency (see *General Comment No. 29* (n 242 above) para 5). If so one would assume that a State should be able to derogate in the light of terrorist events as serious in terms of physical destruction and loss of life, ie the events of 11 September. However, this is not necessarily the case. The Human Rights Committee has pointed out that when public emergencies are declared on the grounds of natural disaster etc the State 'must be able to justify not only that such a situation constitutes a threat to the life of the nation, but also that all . . . measures derogating from the Covenant are strictly required by the exigencies of the situation'. With respect to measures that may be taken by a State, the Committee has pointed out that 'the possibility of restricting certain Covenant rights under the terms of, for instance, freedom of movement (article 12) or freedom of assembly (article 21) is generally sufficient during such situations [ie natural disasters] and *no derogation from the provisions in question would be justified by the exigencies of the situation*' (emphasis added) para 5.

[415] See text accompanying n 54 above.

[416] Due to what is assumed to be the heroic sacrifice of some of its passengers, one aircraft crashed in the Pennsylvanian countryside, 125 miles from Washington, DC.

[417] '*A*' judgment (n 2 above) para 6.

[418] In one of the very few comments that have been made regarding whether the attacks of 11 September constituted a 'public emergency' within the meaning of, in fact, Art 4 of the ICCPR, Professor Fitzpatrick stated, rather guardedly, that they would. Her view was that '*arguably* [the attacks] created an emergency, especially while the identity of the perpetrators remained unknown and the nation was apprehensive about additional *imminent* attacks' (emphasis added). She added: 'A permanent risk of international terrorism, however, would not satisfy this threshold because of the essential temporary nature of emergencies'. J Fitzpatrick, 'Jurisdiction of Military Commissions and the Ambiguous War on Terrorism' (2002) 96 AJIL 345, 350–1.

retained full control over law and order, and, above all, when it was evident that the attacks were not part of a campaign of terrorism allowing comparisons to be drawn with the Strasbourg jurisprudence from Northern Ireland and Turkey. The *Marshall* decision indicates that the State would be given considerable leeway in judging when the threat had passed—but consistently with Article 15 a normally-functioning State successfully dealing with a situation through normal measures can hardly maintain a derogation into the indefinite future.

If this analysis is accepted then it is suggested that the United Kingdom might have legally derogated from the Convention in the uncertain times immediately after 11 September 2001 and on the basis that, in principle (and assuming intelligence verifying the point), the United Kingdom could have regarded itself as equally threatened as the United States at that stage. But, given the slender basis for the derogation just set out, and the Government's position as pleaded before the House of Lords that the purpose of the detention was to prevent a very major terrorist atrocity, would derogation two months later, on 18 December 2001, have been lawful? Could the same be said for a derogation still in place nearly three years further on, when the Law Lords delivered their ruling on 16 December 2004?

Time for an evolutive interpretation of 'threatening the life of the nation'?

Rather than attempting an answer to such questions there is a more important issue that is ripe for examination. From his analysis of '*A*' Dickson has stated that: 'What seems to emerge most clearly from the [Law Lords'] judgments taken as a whole, although none of the judges actually states this explicitly, is that the phrase "public emergency threatening the life of the nation", which is used in both Article 15 ECHR and Article 4 ICCPR, is not an altogether satisfactory one.'[419] Given the magnitude of the threat demonstrated on September 11 the question should be posed whether Article 15(1) of the Convention should allow a State to derogate in circumstances falling short of the strict threshold requirement. In principle, should a derogation be permitted when a population is confronted by a genuine risk of terrorist violence on a significant scale, even when the restrictive requirement of a 'threat to the life of the nation' or 'organised life of the community' is not obviously present?

In the words of the former Secretary-General to the Council of Europe, Walter Schwimmer, we have now entered 'an era of chaos, in which the threat and use of massive violence against civilians is considered by some as a legitimate weapon'.[420] It is apparent that it is the specific intention of

[419] Dickson (n 3 above) 20.

[420] W Schwimmer, Foreword, in W Benedek and A Yotopoulos-Marangopoulos (eds), *Anti-terrorist Measures and Human Rights* (2004).

certain fundamentalist groups to cause maximum loss of life as well as destruction of infrastructure, and that in pursuit of this ambition they regard themselves as being martyrs for their cause. Acting without warning and apparently in pursuit of religious fundamentalist ideals such terrorists seem to be unrestrained by a need to avoid public disgust (and so loss of support for their cause) in the way that persons who regard themselves as freedom fighters might have. Fundamentalist groups have proven their organizational capacity to act against high-profile targets in major capitals and have acted with 'great skill, secrecy and co-ordination',[421] taking advantage of the modern communications revolution and the ease of global travel. It has been stated that: 'Whilst the UK has faced a variety of terrorist threats in the past, a unique combination of factors—namely the global reach, capability, resilience, sophistication, ambition and lack of restraint of Al-Qaeda and associated groups from around the world—place the current threat on a scale not previously encountered.'[422] In short, the impact and harm that such terrorism might inflict in one horrendous event or in a small number of events is now potentially of a much greater order than previously experienced, not only in terms of the loss of life and property,[423] but also given the wider impact such terrorism can have on the modern State and the global economy.[424]

It is arguable that cases such as *Brannigan and McBride* and *Marshall* demonstrate that the critical issue for the Court has been to allow a Government to derogate in order to grant it more freedom of action to tackle the threat that terrorism posed to public safety in the broad sense.

[421] SIAC judgment (n 76 above) para 26.

[422] The quotation is taken from the website for MI5: <http www.mi5.gov.uk/output/Page8.html> (accessed 30 October 2005). As regards the new form of the terrorist threat see esp: House of Commons Defence Committee, *Sixth Report* (Defence and Security in the UK) (2001–2002) vol 1 (HC 518-I); Sir D Williams, 'The United Kingdom's Response to International Terrorism' (2003) 13 *Indiana International and Comparative Law Quarterly* 683; T Eicke, 'Terrorism and Human Rights' (2002) 4 *European Journal of Migration and Law* 449, 464–5; and The International Council on Human Rights Policy, *Human Rights After September 11th* (Versoix: Switzerland, 2002), available at <http://www.ichrp.org> (accessed 30 October 2005).

[423] This point was acknowledged by SIAC, see text acccompanying n 89 above.

[424] According to a Report by the House of Commons Defence Committee of 2002: 'The attacks of 11 September demonstrated some of the physical vulnerabilities of western society, but they also highlighted less tangible vulnerabilities in the way in which the shock at the attacks was transmitted rapidly throughout a globalised, interconnected system, costing billions of dollars in economic damage through direct losses, lost growth, instability to certain industries (airline, insurance). The attack also had major knock-on effects in political and social terms, as well as psychological. The psychological knock-on effects of the relatively small scale anthrax attacks at the same time, for example, were alarming. Some of the effects may pass in the short to medium term (for example, the numbers of people travelling by air has picked up in the last few months); others however, may prove longer-lasting.

... The fact that we live in an interdependent, highly connected and technology dependent, but socially and politically open, society means that we live in a more vulnerable society. This is a society in which economic, technological and political changes have left us more vulnerable to massive disruption. Throughout much of the last century, massive disruption to the economy and the infrastructures upon which we relied could only be caused by a large-scale campaign of aerial bombardment, blockade and/or special forces operations. In the 21st Century, the threat may be from small groups using technology to carry out asymmetric attacks ...' House of Commons Defence Committee, *Defence and Security in the UK* (2001–02) vol I, 37, paras 118–119.

Arguably this would be in keeping with the initial drafts of Article 15(1) which at one stage read 'In time of war or other public emergency *threatening the interests of the people* a State may take measures derogating from its obligations under this Convention to the extent strictly limited by the exigencies of the situation . . .'[425] (emphasis added). More generally, since September 11 there appears to be a heightened awareness of the State's duty to protect a population from terrorist atrocities together with a recognition that terrorism has as its objective the destruction of the very principles underpinning the existence of the Convention and the Council of Europe: the maintenance of a political democracy and the protection of human rights.[426] The Guidelines of the Committee of Ministers of the Council of Europe on Human Rights and the Fight Against Terrorism (adopted in 2002) state that 'terrorism seriously jeopardises human rights, threatens democracy, and aims notably to destabilise legitimately constituted Governments and to undermine pluralistic civil society' and refer to 'the imperative duty of States to protect their populations against possible terrorist acts'.[427] The first guideline recounts that: 'States are under the obligation to take the measures needed to protect the fundamental rights of everyone within their jurisdiction against terrorist acts, especially the right to life. This positive obligation fully justifies States' fight against terrorism in accordance with the present guidelines.'[428] The Guidelines go on to emphasize that this protective principle does not provide the State with a free hand to compromise human rights[429] and, although terrorism is a significant special feature for the Court in the application of restrictions to Convention rights,[430] the *Guidelines* provide no suggestion that the threshold for reliance on Article 15(1) should be adjusted.[431]

Under the Vienna Convention on the Law of Treaties[432] the intention of the drafters of a treaty is a subsidiary means of interpretation. Article 31(1) of the Vienna Convention requires that a treaty be interpreted according to the ordinary meaning to be given to the terms considered in their context and in the light of the object and purpose of the treaty. In this way it is submitted that Article 15(1) is capable of being interpreted

425 Council of Europe (Robertson (ed)), *Collected edition of the 'travaux préparatoires'* (n 223 above) vol III (Meeting of Committee of Experts) 280–2. The concept of threat to the 'interests of the people' is, of course, dangerously vague.

426 Eicke (n 422 above) 464.

427 *CoE Terrorism Guidelines* (n 266 above) Preamble, para (f).

428 In fact, the specific obligation on the State to protect in this way is of a relatively circumscribed nature; see *LCB v the United Kingdom* App No 23413/94 (1999) 27 EHRR 212, para 36. See also the commentary attached to the *CoE Terrorism Guidelines* (n 266 above) 20.

429 See *CoE Terrorism Guidelines*, Principles II–XIV.

430 The Court has stated that 'for the purposes of interpreting and applying the relevant provisions of the Convention, due account will be taken of the special nature of terrorist crime, the threat it poses to democratic society and the exigencies of dealing with it . . .', *Murray v UK* App No 14310/88 (1995) 19 EHRR 193, para 47.

431 The *CoE Terrorism Guidelines* add very little to what the text of Art 15(1) of the Convention already states, although they do specifically state that only 'temporary' derogations are permissible. See Principle XV, para (1).

432 UNTS vol 1155, 331.

in an evolutive way. The object and purpose of the Convention is the effective protection of human rights. The derogation clause was included in the Convention and other international human rights instruments to protect the interests of the nation as a whole in times of major crisis and public danger. The threats that seemed to be prevalent at the time of the drafting of the Convention (1949–50) were 'war' and events of a similar magnitude ('other public emergency threatening the life of the nation'). If the nature of the threat evolves or changes, arguably the efficacy of the derogation clause as a key aspect of the Convention will fall away.[433] Already the Strasbourg institutions have adopted an approach to the interpretation of Article 15(1) that provides for derogation in circumstances of a lower severity than specifically envisaged by the drafters, as the definition set out in *Lawless* demonstrates. But in 2005 it may be questioned whether this definition, put in place in 1961, remains a sufficient basis for derogation given the threat posed today by fundamentalist terrorists. Certainly in practical terms there are strong arguments for the Strasbourg Court to develop its understanding of the concept of 'public emergency threatening the life of the nation' in response to the threats prevalent in the twenty-first century.

A modified derogation threshold: dangers to guard against

Thus there are strong practical arguments for an evolved approach to the threshold test for Article 15(1) (and indeed Article 4(1) of the ICCPR), one adapted to the new form of terrorist threat and which, in principle, allows a derogation to be made in the context of the threat of significant loss of life and destruction of property caused by isolated acts of terrorism. But how does one reformulate the threshold test to address this? From the human rights perspective there are very serious dangers to guard against. How does one formulate the threshold test so as to ensure that derogations are only made in the gravest of terrorist scenarios, ie perhaps only when there is a real risk of terrorism of an order similar to that witnessed on September 11? But even this enquiry invites the next question, where does one draw the line between major and lesser terrorist atrocities? It is clear that the broader the interpretation given to the threshold test for reliance on Article 15(1), the weaker the Convention and other international human rights instruments will be as safeguards. Reframing the threshold test seems bound to revive the predicament that faced the drafters of Article 4 of the ICCPR, and so Article 15(1) of the Convention, namely the fear of abusive resort to the derogation clause, a fear which apparently led the drafters to settle on the phrase 'threatening the life of the nation' in the first place.[434]

The matter is further complicated given the likelihood that a derogation will be made on a precautionary basis owing to the *threat* posed by

[433] cf Jacobs (n 340 above) 15–20.

[434] See nn 224–226 above.

potential terrorism. This may require a more flexible understanding of the notion of when a 'public emergency' may be said to be 'imminent'.[435] It is evident that there are real practical considerations on the part of Government that will make a precautionary approach tempting, especially when it concerns measures depriving a comparatively small number of people of their rights, and given the high price to be paid for misjudging a threat, together with the need to provide public reassurance during a period of heightened tension. However, assuming that in principle a derogation can lawfully be made in such circumstances, the problems that may be associated with this position are clear. There is a danger of emasculating the system of human rights protection under instruments such as the Convention and the ICCPR. Potential emergencies of the type declared by the British Government in December 2001 could exist in dozens of States. As Lord Walker put it in '*A*', 'the uncertainty increases the gravity of the emergency, since it creates widespread anxiety and the need for comprehensive precautions'.[436] Further, the state of emergency said to be substantiated on a 'threat' of serious terrorist activity may easily become quasi-permanent[437] on the basis that the elusive potential terrorists retain the motivation and capacity to strike[438] and since, as Fitzpatrick has stated: 'Long periods without incident do not signal safety, because the enemy is known to operate "sleeper cells".'[439] This presents challenges to the understanding that, by definition, a 'public emergency' can only ever be temporary.[440] According to the JCHR in July 2004: 'Long-term derogations from human rights obligations have a corrosive effect on the culture of respect for human rights on which effective protection of all rights depends. They undermine the State's commitment to human rights and the rule of law, and diminish the State's standing in the international community.'[441] The European Court has in the past expressed an awareness of the dangers that laws designed to combat terrorism have of 'undermining or even destroying democracy on the ground of defending it'[442] and its jurisprudence has repeatedly emphasized the importance for there to be safeguards against the abuse of such laws.[443]

In short, it is evident that an adjustment to the threshold for Article 15(1), and implicitly Article 4(1) of the ICCPR, brings in its train the potential to undermine a cornerstone to these international human rights instruments. For these reasons such an adjustment, ie a widened power

435 cf the conclusions reached by SIAC, text accompanying nn 90–95 above.

436 Lord Walker, para 208.

437 See J Fitzpatrick, 'Speaking Law to Power: The War Against Terrorism and Human Rights' (2003) 14 *European Journal of International Law* 241, 251–2.

438 cf *Marshall v UK* (n 276(vii)above).

439 Fitzpatrick (n 437 above) 251.

440 See n 266 above.

441 JCHR, *Eighteenth Report* (Review of Counter-terrorism Powers) (2003–04) (HL 158, HC 713) para 5.

442 *Klass and others v Federal Republic of Germany* (1979–80) 2 EHRR 214, para 49. This case did not involve Art 15 of the Convention.

443 ibid para 50.

to derogate in the face of the threat of a major terrorist atrocity, if it is to be regarded as acceptable at all, is only permissible if accompanied by safeguards against arbitrary resort to derogation and which ensure, so far as it is possible to do so, that the derogating measures put in place are fully justified by the threat. On the facts of situations such as those relevant to the '*A*' case, for the Government to substantiate the case for an Article 15 emergency this will require it to produce compelling evidence relating to the real danger posed to the public by terrorism, plus a convincing case that the ordinary criminal law, in keeping with the Convention, is unable to address the problem identified by the Government. That is, the Government must *thoroughly* substantiate its case as to the genuine need for the derogating powers on the basis that no other 'Convention-compliant' course of action is possible. This makes the fourth criterion set out in 'the *Greek* case'—'normal measures or restrictions, permitted by the Convention for the maintenance of public safety, health and order, are *plainly inadequate*' (emphasis added)—the critical issue. But it must not be the executive alone which determines the criterion. There must be effective scrutiny of that point and the decision to derogate at the domestic level.

The need for effective domestic scrutiny

In the circumstances of an emergency said to exist on the basis of the threat of terrorism, a significant factor is a lack of accountability on the Government's part regarding the existence and extent of that threat. On this the European Commissioner for Human Rights stated as early as in August 2002 that: '*Effective domestic scrutiny* must . . . be of particular importance in respect of measures purporting to derogate from the Convention: parliamentary scrutiny and judicial review represent essential guarantees against the possibility of an arbitrary assessment by the executive and the subsequent implementation of disproportionate measures' (emphasis added).[444]

Was there 'effective domestic scrutiny' of the British derogation in late 2001? The analysis above indicates that at that time Parliament provided hardly any scrutiny at all of the existence of terrorist threat. It is true that SIAC had a very important role in assessing the legality of an emergency. It delivered a ruling on this in July 2002. However, within the context of the '*A*' litigation, SIAC's assessment was the one and only opportunity for effective review by the courts of the existence of a 'public emergency' based on an informed view of the intelligence said to underpin the threat.

SIAC viewed the open and closed material. It accepted the argument that lack of evidence as to a specific threat is not the same as a lack of a threat for the purpose of what was seen as an *existing*, not potential, 'public emergency' based on the view that it was credible that there could

[444] See *CoE Commissioner Opinion* (n 33 above) para 5. The Commissioner's comments were made in the context of his criticism of the procedures that led up to the UK's derogation.

be a very serious terrorist attack at any moment.[445] Collins J stated that conditions allowing for derogation were in place when there was 'an intention and a capacity to carry out serious terrorist violence' he also stipulated that there should be 'a real risk that an attack will take place unless the necessary measures are taken to prevent it'.[446] For convenience this will be referred to as 'the SIAC test'. Of course, the requirement of 'serious terrorist violence'[447] is a concept that is open to interpretation.[448] Again assessments as to 'capacity', 'intention', and 'real risk' will be subjective and may depend on access to closed information. Only in the light of that assessment can a secondary assessment be undertaken of whether the Government has adopted the 'necessary measures' (unless, of course, from the open evidence alone the measures are regarded as irrational, as was concluded by the House of Lords).

Having formulated the SIAC test, Collins J recognized that there were practical limitations on SIAC's ability to apply it. He acknowledged his lack of specific advice and expertise and so his compromised ability to come on his own to a meaningful conclusion on the nature of the security situation confronting the United Kingdom, even with the 'closed material' before him.[449] One should certainly not dismiss the value of judicial review, as the House of Lords powerfully demonstrated in '*A*'. But it is also important to be realistic about the courts' capacity to make their own assessment of a security situation even when given access to 'closed material'. The nature of the terrorist threat will fluctuate over time; it is bound to be one about which reasonable people will have differences of opinion. It seems that any assessment of the nature of the threat will be based on diffuse sources of information, the significance of which depends on one's grasp of a bigger overall picture, plus expert insights into the evolution of the modern terrorist threat.[450] It seems that for reasons of 'relative institutional competence'[451] these issues call for mainly political not judicial judgment.

Strengthening Parliament's role

The limited capacity of the courts to effectively apply the SIAC test in practice would be less of a cause for concern if it could be said that Parliament had been able to perform the same test and with a rigorous level of scrutiny. Yet, in terms of identifying the threat posed, the adequacy and effectiveness of the Parliamentary process at the time of the

[445] See text accompanying nn 90–95 above. [446] See text accompanying n 95 above.

[447] cf Lord Hope in '*A*' referring to terrorists with 'the capacity ... to inflict massive casualties and have a devastating effect on the functioning of the nation', '*A*' judgment (n 2 above) para 118.

[448] The same criticism could be made of the definition of 'emergency' found in The Civil Contingencies Act 2004, s 1(1): '(a) an event or situation which threatens serious damage to human welfare in a place in the United Kingdom, (b) an event or situation which threatens serious damage to the environment of a place in the United Kingdom, or (c) *war, or terrorism, which threatens serious damage to the security of the United Kingdom*' (emphasis added). The Civil Contingencies Act 2004 (c 36).

[449] See text accompanying n 84 above. cf Lord Hope's comment in '*A*', para 116.

[450] cf Lord Bingham, para 29. [451] ibid.

decision to derogate is open to real doubt.[452] As regards the on-going necessity of the Part 4 detention powers in the years that followed December 2001, this was the subject of mounting criticism by Parliamentary bodies, yet reform of the law only came following the Law Lords' ruling in late 2004. Over the entire period during which the derogation was in place no Parliamentary committee was presented with a significant amount of the intelligence information relating to the terrorist threat.[453] The JCHR never received any such evidence and it questioned the 'democratic legitimacy' of this general situation.[454] It highlighted the importance of appraising the level of the threat from the point of view of its ability to make an informed assessment of the proportionality of the measures taken in conjunction with it.[455] More generally, the European Commissioner of Human Rights observed that the role of the British Parliament in scrutinizing derogations is notably weaker than that of the equivalent institutions in many other nations in Europe.[456] He argued that 'parliamentary scrutiny of derogations depend[ed] in large measure on the access of at least some of its members to the information on which the decision to derogate [was] based'.[457] Both the JCHR[458] and the Commissioner[459] suggested that a specialist committee made up of a small number of Parliamentarians could have access to the classified information said to underpin the terrorist threat and that that body might in turn report its assessment to Parliament. There is no reason in principle why such a recommendation could not be implemented and why the body in question should not take the SIAC test identified above as a good starting point for its own analysis of the existence of a 'public emergency' (which assumes that the threshold test may be met by the threat of terrorist atrocity alone).[460] This would inform wider debate within Parliament not only as to the 'real risk' of an atrocity, but also whether the 'necessary measures are [in place] to prevent [a terrorist atrocity]'.

[452] See also *CoE Commissioner Opinion* (n 33 above) paras 13–23.

[453] The Privy Counsellor Review Committee (n 114 above) had access to a small sample of such information. But its remit was not to review the existence of a 'public emergency'.

[454] JCHR, *Eighteenth Report* (2003–04) (n 441 above) para 20.

[455] ibid.

[456] *CoE Commissioner Opinion* (n 33 above) para 11; see also British Institute of Human Rights (n 33 above) para 4.

[457] ibid para 12.

[458] JCHR, *Eighteenth Report* (2003–04) (n 441 above) see generally paras 15–23.

[459] *CoE Commissioner Opinion* (n 33 above) paras 22–3.

[460] In oral evidence taken before the JCHR following the ruling in '*A*' the Home Secretary was asked whether, in order to retain public confidence, there should be 'some element of independent scrutiny of the Government's assessment of the nature and level of the overall threat to the life of the nation'. In response he agreed that it was right that there should be 'an element of judicial review' of this matter as had been undertaken by SIAC. He also pointed to the work of the Intelligence and Security Committee (the ISC) in assessing the existence of threats and which had access to information not in the public domain. However, beyond this he was not in favour of 'some constitutional structure . . . to second guess' the nature of the security threat facing the nation. The ISC is made up of senior Parliamentarians and has cross-party membership, it does not, however, have the status of a Select Committee and is not accountable to Parliament, but to the Prime Minister who appoints members to it. See JCHR, *Tenth Report* (Prevention of Terrorism Bill: Preliminary Report), (Session 2004–05) Appendix, Questions 1–3.

Executive detention a 'necessary measure'?

A strengthened role for Parliament will be especially important when it is argued by the Government that those 'necessary measures' include the need for imprisonment by way of executive detention, that is, when the chosen policy of the Government is a security measure, involving derogation from the Convention, rather than imprisonment for criminal offences. In the immediate post-September 11 context it was in the nature of things that preventive detention would be based on intelligence assessments relating to the threat of an atrocity. At that time the urgency for security measures to be in place was also apparent for there was an obvious need to stop an atrocity happening in the first place.[461] In circumstances such as those existing in late 2001 there will be a natural tendency for a Government to seek a relatively free hand to tackle such a crisis situation. It is likely to make the claim that the other branches of Government should defer to the executive. Yet, it is during times of crisis that human rights may be most under threat and there is a greater need for vigilance and close supervision of the executive.

Such close supervision would require the legislature to be given greater insight as to the nature of the threat. Only then would it realistically be better equipped to answer the wider question of whether, instead of reliance on executive detention, it would realistically be possible for the criminal law to be used to prosecute the very people who were being detained without charge. However, given the veil of secrecy existing as regards the nature of the threat, Parliament's role as an effective scrutinizer of whether preventive detention was a 'necessary measure' compared to the criminal law was severely compromised in late 2001 as well as after, a point expressly acknowledged by the JCHR.[462] The longer the emergency measures have remained in place and the more serious the interference with fundamental rights is,[463] the greater should be the burden on the Government to justify why less drastic alternatives are not available and why they would not be effective.[464] This in itself assumes an effective dialogue between the executive and legislature.

461 For a discussion of some of the issues surrounding executive detention as a security measure, as against resort to the criminal law, see Simpson (n 138 above) 1–2.

462 JCHR, *Eighteenth Report* (Session 2003–04) (n 441 above) para 18.

463 In terms of the fundamental rights in issue in the '*A*' case, as Lady Hale put it, executive detention was 'the antithesis of the right to liberty and security of person', para 222.

464 During the passage of the Prevention of Terrorism Act 2005 (c 2), it was stated on behalf of the Government that the law would not be changed to allow intercept evidence to be admissible in court, something which might have enabled the prosecution of some of the detainees. cf the *Newton Committee Report* which had indicated that adjustments to the laws relating to evidence and surveillance might entail that no derogation from the Convention would be required (n 114 above) 9. It is understood that the UK is the only country in the world, apart from Ireland, which does not permit the use of telephone intercept evidence in court. For the Home Secretary's explanation as to why the law would not be changed in this way, see JCHR, *Tenth Report* (Session 2004–05) (n 460 above) Appendix, Question 27. More generally, on the issue of whether the ordinary criminal law (amended if necessary) could have been used to address the security problem identified by the Government, a number of proposals had been put forward by the JCHR, see JCHR, *Eighteenth Report* (Session

In the light of what has just been stated, and assuming the Strasbourg Court is prepared to read Article 15(1) so as to allow a State to derogate in anticipation of very serious terrorist violence of September 11 proportions, should it not also now take the opportunity to read in to the same Article a procedural requirement for effective domestic scrutiny of derogations by the legislature? The European Commissioner for Human Rights has hinted that this would be a welcome development.[465] Although Article 15(1) does not expressly require such a procedural dimension to it, and 'the Court has not yet had occasion to pronounce on the matter', in his view it is 'easily discerned'.[466] He pointed out that: 'The Court has repeatedly emphasised the close relationship between democracy and the rights guaranteed by the Convention, stating, for instance, that "democracy appears to be the only political model contemplated by the Convention and, accordingly, the only one compatible with it".'[467] Highlighting the importance of the separation of powers as a 'constitutive element of democratic governance', the Commissioner has argued that proper Parliamentary scrutiny of derogations was consistently found to be a feature of the constitutions of a number of European countries.[468] The mere rubber-stamping of a derogation by a Parliament was clearly problematic, as may be the case when the Parliamentary body, or its representatives, is denied access to the critical information upon which the derogation is based, as when this is said to be classified information.[469] Nonetheless the wide margin of appreciation previously granted by the Court to States in Article 15(1) cases was 'precisely because the Convention presupposes domestic controls in the form of a preventive parliamentary scrutiny and posterior judicial review'.[470]

The time is ripe for the European Court of Human Rights to follow the lead suggested by the European Commissioner of Human Rights. The Court should read in to Article 15(1) an inherent procedural safeguard: no derogation coming before the Strasbourg Court could be valid unless it was satisfied that there had been effective accountability for the executive's decision to derogate in the first place and, if the derogation remains in place, that there has been effective and informed periodic review of that derogation. A combination of *informed* judicial

2003–04) (n 441 above) paras 48–84. The same Report contained comparative information on how other European States addressed the issue of terrorism through the law.

465 See generally *CoE Commissioner Opinion* (n 33 above) paras 1–28.

466 ibid para 5. In fact, the Court has pointed to the importance of domestic accountability in its Art 15(1) case law, though it has tended to do so in the context of whether the actual measures of derogation themselves were 'strictly required'. In *Brannigan and McBride v UK* (n 276(v) above) the Court noted that there had been regular independent review of the legislation impugned (para 65). In *Marshall v UK* (n 276(vii) above) the Court rejected the submission of the applicants that the annual Parliamentary debate and executive review of the legislation in issue was a meaningless exercise (13–14). See also *Lawless v Ireland* (n 276(ii) above) para 37.

467 ibid. The quotation is extracted from *United Communist Party of Turkey v Turkey* App No 19392/92 (1998) 26 EHRR 121, para 45.

468 ibid para 11.

469 ibid para 12.

470 ibid para 10.

and on-going Parliamentary scrutiny applying the SIAC test should help to provide safeguards against the potential abuse of the power of derogation and, equally important, help to ensure that the measures taken in accordance with it remain strictly proportionate and necessary. An evolution in the Strasbourg jurisprudence in this way would emphasize that derogations from human rights treaties must remain a last resort. It would help to give real content to the view that derogations remain in principle strictly temporary measures and must be removed when they are no longer strictly necessary.

Conclusion

As we saw in Section II of this article, the derogation to the convention of 2001 was submitted by the British Government in circumstances when it was not at all clear that the threshold test for reliance on Article15(1), as understood in the Strasbourg jurisprudence to date, was met. There was little attempt on the Government's part to explain properly to Parliament how that particular test was satisfied either in late 2001 or subsequently. It was evident nonetheless that the Government's case for the existence of an emergency was based on the need to detain certain individuals extra-judicially in order to check the threat of a major terrorist atrocity of the order seen on September 11. Three years subsequently the House of Lords' ruling in '*A*' was a landmark for English law. Despite the national security context to the case, 'amidst the clash of arms the law [was *not*] silent'.[471] The House of Lords, backed by the Human Rights Act 1998, accepted that 'in times of distress, the shield of military necessity and national security must not be used to protect Governmental actions from close scrutiny and accountability'.[472] Although the House of Lords deferred to the executive on the question of the existence of a 'public emergency', it did not do so on the issue of whether the measures put in place by the Government were proportional and discriminatory. It held that the indefinite detention of foreigners was, on the facts, in violation of the Convention.

The Law Lords' ruling revealed that the Strasbourg jurisprudence on the threshold test for Article 15(1) was far from clear. The leading judgment remains the very first case that the Strasbourg Court ever decided, the *Lawless* case of 1961. This article has sought to demonstrate that some of the Law Lords misunderstood what is admittedly a very unsatisfactory legal precedent. It is submitted that the *Lawless* case, correctly understood, does not allow a State to derogate in the face of low-level

471 cf Lord Atkin (dissenting) in *Liversidge v Anderson* [1942] AC 206, 244.

472 Patel J in *Korematsu v US* 584 F Supp (1984) 1406 (ND Cal 1984) 1420 (cited by Lord Bingham, 'Personal Freedom and the Dilemma of Democracies' (2003) 52 ICLQ 841, 857–8).

terrorist violence, as suggested by some Law Lords. To be consistent with *Lawless*, a derogation can only be made in those circumstances if genuinely submitted on a precautionary basis in order to forestall a 'public emergency threatening to the life of the nation'. What this entails is the 'life of the nation' in a constitutional sense, as with Lord Hoffman's reference in the '*A*' case to an emergency that 'threaten[s] institutions of government' or a region's 'existence as a civil community'. It has been argued that this understanding of 'public emergency threatening to the life of the nation' is in keeping with general international human rights law (Section (V)) and that the later Strasbourg jurisprudence, though opaque, has remained consistent with this (Section (VI)). On that basis, it has been argued that, according to the Strasbourg case law on Article 15(1), there was only a limited and temporary legal basis for the British derogation of 2001.

Although the House of Lords has been criticized for the stance that it adopted on the threshold test, the institution that deserves the greatest reproach is the Strasbourg Court, given the lack of clarity of its jurisprudence on that test and the missed opportunities to take a more principled approach. It is arguable that there is no more important provision within the Convention than Article 15(1). In a previous case concerning a British derogation a Judge of the Strasbourg Court argued that a 'derogation made by any State affects not only the position of that State, but also the integrity of the Convention system of protection as a whole'.[473] The position taken on Article 15 of the Convention by one State, it was said, was to some extent relevant to all States as it communicated a message regarding the gravity of the circumstances that were acceptable before the human rights commitments could be derogated from. It is high time for the Strasbourg Court to deliver a better-reasoned judgment on the threshold of severity for Article 15(1), one that undertakes a rigorous examination of that concept and establishes the relevant principles with clarity.[474]

Whilst some of the Law Lords apparently misunderstood some of the key Strasbourg jurisprudence on the Article 15(1) threshold question, it is also arguable that their ultimate conclusion on that issue was correct. It has been argued above that the threshold for a 'public emergency threatening the life of the nation' needs to be adapted to the twenty-first century. The fact of fundamentalist terrorism and its gravity as demonstrated on September 11 is incontestable. The answer to the question whether events such as those seen on September 11 in principle justify derogation from the Convention is surely that, potentially at least, they must. *Potentially*—for extension of the basis for derogation is a dangerous step with the capacity to diminish very significantly the protection

[473] *Brannigan and McBride v UK* (n 276(v) above), dissenting opinion of Judge Makarczyk, para 1.

[474] L Wildhaber, 'A constitutional future for the European Court of Human Rights?' (2002) 23 *Human Rights Law Journal* 161, 164.

afforded by the Convention. Any new understanding to the threshold test for reliance on Article 15(1) must confirm and encourage the philosophy that was foremost in the minds of those who drafted the derogation clause:[475] the fear of abusive and arbitrary resort to derogation. An evolved approach to the threshold of severity should only be permissible if inherent safeguards providing for effective and informed domestic scrutiny of the derogation are read into Article 15(1).

It is suggested that the restrictive language of 'public emergency threatening the life of the nation' and the *Lawless* test, whilst remaining very important as an indicator of the ominous circumstances required for resort to Article 15(1), are secondary to the issue of whether it can be said that the specific derogating measures taken by a Government are, as Article 15(1) also stipulates, 'strictly required by the exigencies of the situation'. The measures must be fully and properly justified by reference to the extent and nature of the threat. For the scenario said to face the United Kingdom in late 2001, SIAC formulated a test whereby there should be 'an intention and capacity to carry out serious terrorist violence' as well as a 'real risk that an attack will take place *unless the necessary measures are taken to prevent it*' (emphasis added).

The SIAC test is a very valuable starting point. But what are the 'necessary measures'? It may be said abstractly that no derogating measure can be 'necessary' if the ordinary criminal law, in harmony with the human rights standards required by the Convention in 'normal' times, is able to meet the threat effectively.[476] The question therefore becomes: does the ordinary, Convention-compliant criminal law have the capacity to address the threat effectively? An accurate answer to that question requires detailed knowledge and assessment of the qualifying elements set out in the first part of the SIAC test, ie the practical nature of the threat. Here elementary principles of democracy demand that the Government must not merely assert that there is a 'public emergency', but that there must be *informed* domestic scrutiny of the extent of the threat as a starting point in assessing what are the appropriate measures needed to meet it. Parliament should perform that function first and foremost, and on a periodic basis as appropriate. The courts will have an important secondary role in assessing whether proper regard has been paid to human rights considerations. It is submitted that the Strasbourg Court should develop the threshold test in a way that ensures that there is proper domestic scrutiny of the decision to derogate from the Convention.

[475] See text accompanying nn 224–226 above.

[476] This may in turn require domestic criminal law to be amended. See the *Newton Committee Report* (n 114 above).

SOME LEGAL ASPECTS OF THE ANGLO-EGYPTIAN CONDOMINIUM OVER THE SUDAN: 1899–1954

By FAISAL ABDEL RAHMAN ALI TAHA*

INTRODUCTION

In September 1898 a military force composed of British and Egyptian troops and commanded by a British officer defeated the Mahdist armies at the battle of Omdurman. On 19 January 1899, the British Government and the Government of the Khedive of Egypt concluded an agreement 'relative to the future administration of the Sudan'.[1] The agreement was prepared under the general instructions of the British Agent and Consul-General in Egypt, then Lord Cromer. The task of drafting the agreement was entrusted by Cromer to Sir Malcolm McIlwraith, the Judicial Adviser to the Egyptian Government.[2] Until the process of dismantling the Anglo-Egyptian rule in the Sudan was put in train in the early 1950s, the 1899 Agreement formed the basic constitutional instrument of the Sudan.

Nowhere in the 1899 Agreement was the term 'condominium' used, nor the expression 'joint sovereignty'. Not surprisingly, the legal status of the Sudan under the Agreement became a perpetual source of conflict between the successive British and Egyptian governments. The Anglo-Egyptian Treaty of 1936 did not resolve the conflict. On the contrary, it provided for maintaining the *status quo*. It was stated in the Sudan provisions of the Treaty (Article 11) that the administration of the Sudan should continue to be carried out on the basis of the 1899 Agreement, and that nothing in the Article prejudiced the question of sovereignty over the Sudan.[3] As far as the Sudanese themselves were concerned, the only novelty was the agreement of the parties that the primary aim of the administration in the Sudan must be the welfare of the Sudanese.

As will be explained below, the better view is that the 1899 Agreement created an Anglo-Egyptian condominium over the Sudan. This article seeks to cast light on some of the legal issues which arose during the span of the condominium, and to examine the impact, if any, of the anomalous status of the Sudan as a condominium on its international relations.

* LLB (Khartoum), LLM, PhD (Cantab), Sometime Associate Professor of Law, University of Khartoum.

[1] British and Foreign State Papers, vol 91, 19.

[2] Cromer, *Modern Egypt* (1908) vol II, 116.

[3] UK Treaty Series No 6 (1937), Cmd 5360.

I. Condominium or Dual Administration

As was indicated above, the British and Egyptian viewpoints never coincided on the legal status of the Sudan under the 1899 Agreement. The British Government and most of the western legal writers on the subject took the view that the legal effect of the 1899 Agreement was to establish the Sudan as an Anglo-Egyptian condominium.[4]

Support for the British view could be detected in the preambular clauses of the Agreement. One clause expressed the desire of the parties 'to give effect to the claims which have accrued to her Britannic Majesty's Government by the right of conquest'. Another clause recognized the rights of the Khedive in the Sudan anterior to the Mahdist revolution. Allusion was made in this latter clause to certain provinces in the Sudan which were in rebellion against the authority of the Khedive and had been reconquered by the joint military and financial efforts of the British and Khedive Governments.

The British claim to sovereignty based on the right of conquest, coupled with the rekindled rights of the Khedive, thus established a joint Anglo-Egyptian sovereignty over the Sudan. The joint sovereignty was accorded an outward manifestation by Article II of the Agreement which provided that the British and Egyptian flags should be flown together throughout the Sudan. Malcolm McIlwraith pointed out that the presence of the flag was, *par excellence*, the sign and symbol of sovereignty. He thus regarded the flying of the British flag in the Sudan as an impairment of Egypt's rights of sovereignty there.[5]

The Explanatory Memorandum to the draft of the 1899 Agreement submitted in November 1898 by Cromer to Lord Salisbury afforded further support for the British view. Cromer strongly advised against the annexation of the Sudan by Britain or its recognition as a part of the Ottoman Dominions, in no way distinct from the rest of Egypt. To strike a compromise between these two extremes, he proposed the creation for the Sudan of a 'status hitherto unknown to the law of Europe'. The rights of the British Government accruing from the reconquest constituted, according to Cromer, the real justification for the creation of a political and administrative status in the Sudan different from that which existed in Egypt.[6] He warned that if the status of the Sudan were to be assimilated in all respects to that of Egypt, the necessary consequence would be the introduction of the capitulations to the Sudan.[7]

[4] See for instance H Lauterpacht, *Oppenheim, International Law* (8th edn, 1955) vol 1, 453. VA O'Rourke, 'The Juristic Status of Egypt and the Sudan' in (1935) 53 *Johns Hopkins University Studies in Historical and Political Science*, 9, 142.

[5] Letter to the Editor of *The Times*, 20 May 1930, Records of the Foreign Office at the Public Record Office, London (hereinafter FO) 371/14613.

[6] Explanatory Memorandum enclosed in Cromer to Salisbury, 10 November 1898, FO 78/4957.

[7] Cromer (n 2 above) 114.

On the other hand, the Egyptian Government, backed by Egyptian jurists, contended that the 1899 Agreement did not deal with the matter of sovereignty in any way and that Britain had a share in the administrative machinery of the Sudan but not in sovereignty over it, which remained vested in Egypt alone. In 1947 Egypt's Prime Minister, Nokrashi Pasha, told the Security Council: 'Ever since the 1899 Agreement was concluded, the British have sought to broaden the significance of this instrument. By constant use of the term "condominium" which appears nowhere in its text, they sought to convey the idea that they share with Egypt the sovereignty of the Sudan.'[8]

The legal status of the Sudan under the 1899 Agreement was raised in 1910 before the Mixed Tribunal of First Instance of Cairo, in *Bencini and Quistas v The Egyptian and Sudan Governments*. The action in that case was brought against the Sudan and Egyptian Governments by a firm of contractors to recover certain sums of money in respect of work done at Port Sudan. The plaintiffs had contracted with the Sudan Government only, but it was sought to make the Egyptian Government liable on the basis that the Sudan had never ceased to be an integral part of Egypt. The Egyptian Government disclaimed liability on the ground that under the terms of the 1899 Agreement the Sudan Government was an autonomous Government, absolutely distinct and separate from the Egyptian Government. The Sudan Government, on the other hand, pleaded the incompetence of the Tribunal on two grounds: first, that Article VIII of the 1899 Agreement excluded the Sudan from the jurisdiction of the Mixed Tribunals, and secondly, that the 1899 Agreement established a condominium of Britain and Egypt over the Sudan possessing legislative, administrative, and judicial powers distinct and independent from those of the Egyptian Government.

The Tribunal attached great significance to the British military and financial contribution to the campaign for the reconquest of the Sudan and found that according to the law of nations, Britain acquired title to the Sudan by conquest. Therefore the Sudan reverted to Egypt encumbered with the rights of conquest accruing to the conqueror, Britain.

The Tribunal accepted the pleas of both the Egyptian and Sudan Governments and stated that the effect of the 1899 Agreement was to establish a condominium for the benefit of the conquering states and to constitute the Sudan as 'a new state, distinct and separate from Egypt'.[9]

The emphasis which the Tribunal placed on the fact that the 1899 Agreement created an entity which was distinct and separate from either *co-dominus* should not be taken to mean that the Tribunal regarded the

[8] Security Council, Lake Success, New York: 175th Meeting, 5 August 1947, para 40. The verbatim Record of the Meetings of the Council regarding the Anglo-Egyptian dispute was published by the Sudan Government in 1947. The dispute was brought by Egypt under Arts 35 and 37 of the 1936 Treaty.

[9] For the French text of the Judgment see FO 371/14620, for the English text see (1910) 4 AJIL 745.

Sudan as sovereign. That seemed to have been the interpretation which Abdalla El Erian placed on the Tribunal's judgment when he said that it was contradictory of the Tribunal 'to maintain that a new state has arisen in the Sudan and at the same time to regard the territory of the Sudan as a territory under the sovereignty of Egypt and Great Britain'.[10]

But the Foreign Office rejected the view that the Sudan had a separate sovereign existence because its sovereignty was not embraced in the individual sovereignty of either *co-dominus*. The Foreign Office stated that when sovereignty over a given territory was shared, that should not necessarily imply that the territory itself was in any way sovereign: 'It is a separate entity from either condominium Power and independent in the sense of separate but not independent in the sense of sovereign, nor has it been suggested that the New Hebrides Islands, are in any sense sovereign'.[11]

Cromer expressed his gratification at the result of the *Bencini and Quistas* case. He regarded it as a triumphant vindication of the principles on which the 1899 Agreement was based.[12] The principles which Cromer then had in mind would no doubt include the assertion by Britain of a valid title to the Sudan on the basis of the right of conquest, and the complete separation of the administration of the Sudan from that of Egypt.

In an opinion dated 16 January 1925, the Legal Adviser to the British Foreign Office, Sir Cecil Hurst, hailed the decision in *Bencini and Quistas* as 'extremely useful'. He said that by 'emphasizing the separateness from Egypt of the political entity which the 1899 Agreement was held by the Mixed Tribunals to have brought into being, British control can be assured and Egyptian interference avoided'.[13] We shall see in particular that Britain relied in many ways on the ruling of the Mixed Tribunal in the *Bencini and Quistas* case to secure the British predominance in the Sudan through the magnification of the office of the Governor-General.

II. Articles III and IV as Vehicles for British Predominance

One of the prime objects of the 1899 Agreement was to ensure British predominance in the Sudan with a view to averting the misrule which

[10] A El Erian, *Condominium and Related Situations in International Law* (1952) 140.

[11] FO 371/22001, Bentick to Lampson, Cairo, 9 June 1938. This dispatch was drafted by Eric Beckett who was then Legal Adviser to the Foreign Office. Beckett described the Sudan and the New Hebrides as being 'in a class by themselves': FO 371/35576, Beckett to Carter, Treasury Solicitor's Department, 1 January 1943. On the Condominium of the New Hebrides see DP O'Connell, 'The Condominium of the New Hebrides' (1968–69) 43 BYIL 71.

[12] Quoted in a letter dated 9 May 1930, from Malcolm McIlwraith to the Editor of *The Times*, 10 May 1930, FO 371/14613.

[13] Enclosure 1 in Austen Chamberlain to Allenby, 22 January 1925, FO 371/10883.

had existed prior to the Mahdist revolution and to make that predominance formal and permanent.[14] British administrative and legislative predominance was catered for by Articles III and IV respectively of the Agreement. In the explanatory memorandum of the draft of the 1899 Agreement, Cromer stated that Articles III and IV were in some respects the most important provisions of the Agreement.[15]

A. Adminstrative predominance

Article III of the 1899 Agreement provided that the supreme military and civil command of the Sudan was to be vested in the Governor-General who was to be appointed by the Khedive of Egypt on the recommendation of the British Government. The holders of the post had always been British. The Egyptian Government did not have any say in their selection. The role of that Government was confined to appointing the nominee of the British Government.

That practice was in conformity with the British interpretation of Article III. In his 1925 opinion referred to above, Sir Cecil Hurst said:

> . . . the Governor-General, in whom the supreme military and civil command is to be vested, will always be an Englishman, and will always carry out whatever wishes the British Government express to him. Consequently, the convenient way to ensure British control, while preserving the façade of the condominium, will be to magnify the office and the importance of the Governor-General, who, though in form a functionary deriving his authority from both the British and the Egyptian Governments, will, in practice, always obey the instructions of His Majesty's Government.[16]

The Egyptian Government had on several occasions criticized the British monopoly of the office of Governor-General and put a different interpretation on Article III. One such occasion was the submission in 1947 of the Anglo-Egyptian dispute to the Security Council. In his presentation of the Egyptian case, Nokrashi Pasha, the Egyptian Prime Minister, claimed that though there was nothing in the 1899 Agreement to prevent the nomination of an Egyptian to the office, the Governor-General had always been British.[17] The British response to that claim was clearly stated by the British representative, Alexander Cadogan. He said: 'It is true that the Governor-General has always been a British subject. I do not think that it was ever in the minds of either party to the Condominium Agreement that the United Kingdom Government would recommend a person of any other nationality'.[18]

The British Governor-General was evidently instrumental in securing British control over the administration of the Sudan. His office and

[14] On this, see Cromer (n 2 above) 113–17, also FO 371/8957, Memorandum by Headlam-Morley on the Relation of the Sudan to Egypt, 17 January 1923.

[15] Explanatory Memorandum (n 6 above).

[16] Enclosure 1 (n 13 above).

[17] 175th Meeting, 5 August 1947, para 40.

[18] 179th Meeting, 11 August 1947, para 44.

importance were magnified to the extent of being considered as the embodiment of 'the new, separate state' which the Mixed Tribunal had recognized the Sudan to constitute under the 1899 Agreement. Thus when the Sudan Defence Force was established in 1925, it owed allegiance to the Governor-General and all commissions were issued in his name. Sir Cecil Hurst was of the view that allegiance to the Governor-General implied that he was 'the head of a political unit of the nature of a separate state'.[19] We shall also see that Sudan Government passports were drawn up in the name of the Governor-General and bore his seal.[20] Moreover, prior to the conclusion of the 1936 Treaty, the Sudan was considered by the British Government as a separate entity or a state with the Governor-General as virtually the head of the state, in whom treaty-making power was vested.[21]

Egypt never had an equal share in the administration of the Sudan. Britain took advantage of her predominant position to whittle down Egyptian influence in the actual machinery of the Government. The Chief Justice of the Islamic or *Sharia* Division of the Legal Department, the Grand *Kadi*, was the only Egyptian holding a high-level post in the Sudan Government. Following the 1924 revolution in the Sudan and the assassination of the Governor-General of the Sudan, Sir Lee Stack, in Cairo in November 1924, Egyptian troops were expelled from the Sudan and so were eighty-four Egyptian administrative officers, known locally as *Mamurs*. Amongst the junior clerical staff, only those who were engaged in adverse political activities were expelled.[22]

In 1930, during the protracted negotiations which preceded the conclusion of the 1936 Treaty, the British Government rejected the Egyptian Government's proposal for the restoration of the *status quo ante* 1924, as well as its claim for a joint and effective share in the administration of the Sudan. According to the Egyptian Government, 'a joint and effective share' meant the appointment of an Egyptian Deputy Governor-General and Egyptian officials to cooperate with the British officials in the administration of the Sudan.[23]

For his part, the Governor-General of the Sudan, then Sir John Maffey, accepted in principle the return to the Sudan of an Egyptian battalion. But he vehemently opposed the return of Egyptian personnel to share in the administration. He was of the opinion that the Egyptians could play on very dangerous strings in the Sudan. Maffey summed up his fears thus: 'A battalion is a unit. It is not an infiltration. A tooth can be pulled out. Blood poisoning is a more serious matter'.[24]

[19] Enclosure 1 (n 13 above). [20] See Section III below. [21] See Section IX below.

[22] Memorandum on the Sudan, 28 February 1932, Annex A in Foreign Office to Law Officers of the Crown, 12 April 1932, FO 371/18015.

[23] Memorandum dated 15 May 1930, by Cecil Campbell on the Course of the Negotiations in regard to the Sudan from 31 March to 8 May 1930, FO 371/14613.

[24] Memorandum by Maffey dated 4 June 1930, enclosed in Loraine to Henderson, 10 June 1930, FO 371/14615.

Maffey's successor, Sir Stewart Symes, rejected the Egyptian proposal for the appointment of an Egyptian Deputy Governor-General with a seat on the Governor-General's Council. Symes told Mustafa Al-Nahas Pasha, Egypt's Prime Minister, and the Egyptian delegation in July 1936 that it was almost unthinkable that an Egyptian arriving new to the Sudan would in the absence of the Governor-General be able to control the difficult type of administration in which practically all of the senior officials were British. He further pointed out that an Egyptian member of the Council without portfolio would not acquire the necessary experience, for members of the Council had full-time duties as heads of departments and meetings in Council did not take more than fifty hours a year.[25]

When the 1936 Treaty was eventually concluded, it provided in Article 11(2) for the appointment of candidates of British and Egyptian nationality to posts in the Sudan Government for which qualified Sudanese were not available. Ironically, the Sudan Government relied on Article 11(2) to Sudanize the only senior post in the administration held by an Egyptian, namely that of Grand *Kadi*.[26]

Under the terms of the 1936 Treaty, Egypt did not secure a seat on the Governor-General's Council. Provision was, however, made for inviting the Inspector-General of the Egyptian Irrigation Service in the Sudan to attend the Governor-General's Council when matters relating to his departmental interests were before the Council.[27]

The proposal for the appointment of an Egyptian Deputy Governor-General was revived in 1939 by King Farouk. He told the British Ambassador, Sir Miles Lampson, that the condominium could not be a 'true condominium' unless there was an Egyptian 'understudy' to the Governor-General. The Foreign Office noted that the King's proposal was a 'very bad' one and directed that the arguments so effectively used by Symes in July 1936 could do just as well for King Farouk.[28]

B. Legislative predominance

Article IV of the 1899 Agreement conferred on the Governor-General unlimited power to legislate by Proclamation. The *co-domini* did not reserve for themselves, separately or jointly, the power to review, disallow, or revoke legislation proclaimed by the Governor-General.[29] The Governor-General was only required to notify the Proclamations he issued to the British Agent and Consul-General in Egypt and to the President of the Council of the Ministers of the Khedive.

[25] Lampson to Eden, 3 August 1936, transmitting record of meeting of 29 July 1936, between Symes and Al-Nahas, FO 407/220.

[26] See Section V below.

[27] Note No 3 dated 12 August 1936, from Lampson to Mustafa Al-Nahas. For the source of the text of the Note see n 3 above.

[28] FO 371/23323, Lampson to Foreign Office, 8 May 1939, and Oliphant to Lampson, 22 June 1939, ibid.

[29] See Memorandum by Sir Maurice Amos, 15 February 1925, Enclosure 2 in Allenby to Austen Chamberlain, 11 March 1925, FO 371/10883.

In 1905, Cromer, acting on his own initiative, imposed a procedure which ran counter to the express terms of Article IV. He subjected the issue of Sudan ordinances to the prior approval of the Khedive of Egypt acting through his Council of Ministers and the British Agent and Consul-General in Egypt.[30] In effect, Cromer re-introduced the original draft Article IV which he had submitted in November 1898 to Salisbury but which had not met with the latter's approval. Cromer's rationale for draft Article IV was that the Governor-General should be under some effective control.[31]

However, the requirement of the prior approval of the Egyptian Government for Sudan legislation seemed to have been dispensed with after the establishment of the Governor-General's Council in 1910. The Governor-General's Council Ordinance 1910 provided that all laws, ordinances, and regulations to be made by the Governor-General by virtue of Article IV of the 1899 Agreement should be made by the Governor-General in Council. But the establishment of the Council did not prejudice the Governor-General's unlimited legislative competence. He retained the power to overrule the decisions of the majority of the Council.[32]

The British Agent and Consul-General in Cairo, then Eldon Gorst, laid down guidelines for the exercise by the Council of its functions. One of these was that the approval of the Agent and Consul-General should be obtained beforehand for all laws, ordinances, and regulations made by the Governor-General in Council.[33] The prior approval of the Egyptian Government was not stipulated. Gorst's guidelines clearly revoked the 1905 procedure whereby the prior approval of both *co-domini* for Sudan ordinances was required.

When stating his country's grievances against the British administration in the Sudan, Nokrashi told the Security Council, in 1947, that the Sudan Government had abandoned the practice followed up to 1912 whereby laws promulgated in the Sudan were subject to the approval of the Egyptian Government.[34] Presumably Nokrashi was complaining about the discontinuance of the procedure imposed by Cromer in 1905.

Quite often, the British administration in the Sudan spoke of a distinction between ordinary legislation concerning the internal administration of the Sudan and legislation which had effect on the constitution of the Sudan and claimed that the prior approval of both *co-domini* was required in the case of the latter type of legislation. But the distinction had never been spelt out in practice. To reinforce its position at the

[30] On this see M Daly, *Empire on the Nile: The Anglo-Egyptian Sudan 1898–1934* (1986) 44–5.

[31] Explanatory Memorandum (n 6 above).

[32] Enclosure 2 in Gorst to Grey, 28 February 1910, FO 371/891.

[33] Enclosure 3, Gorst to Wingate, 13 January 1910, ibid.

[34] 175th Meeting, 5 August 1947, para 41.

helm, the British administration arrogated to itself the right to determine the category to which a particular type of legislation should be allocated.

The alleged distinction was first put to the test when the legislation establishing the Advisory Council was drafted. That draft legislation consisted of three documents: the Advisory Council Ordinance 1943, the Advisory Council for the Northern Sudan Order 1943, and the Local Government (Province Councils) Ordinance 1943. Miles Lampson, the British Ambassador in Cairo, described the Advisory Council legislation as 'a most important step forward in the political development of the Sudan'.[35] Governor-General Huddleston also expressed the view that the Advisory Council legislation represented 'a political development of far reaching import which may well ultimately affect the constitution of the Sudan'.[36] Strangely enough, the Advisory Council legislation was submitted for the prior approval of the British Government but not that of the Egyptian Government. Lampson advised the Foreign Office to treat the Advisory Council legislation as ordinary legislation falling within the ambit of Article IV of the 1899 Agreement and therefore no special arrangement needed to be made to associate the Egyptian Government with the legislation before it was passed into law.[37]

As was expected, the Egyptian Government protested. The Egyptian Prime Minister, Mustafa Al-Nahas, criticized the Sudan Government for carrying out a vital change in the adminstration without the previous knowledge and agreement of the two Governments 'and in particular of the Egyptian Government'.[38] In his reply, Governor-General Huddleston contended that Article IV of the 1899 Agreement did not contain any provision that the steps taken to establish local self-government in the Sudan or to set up an Advisory Council should have been submitted for the prior approval of the Egyptian Government.[39]

The alleged distinction between routine legislation on internal matters and legislation affecting the constitution of the Sudan was put to the test once more in 1947–48 when the Report of the Sudan Administration Conference and the draft Executive Council and Legislative Assembly Ordinance regarding certain constitutional reforms were submitted to the *co-domini*. The draft Ordinance was considered a first step on the path to self-government. Provision was made for replacement of the Advisory Council by a Legislative Assembly and the Governor-General's Council by an Executive Council. Government legislation would be initiated by the Executive Council and passed by the Legislative Assembly before being submitted to the Governor-General for his assent. The Governor-General retained the power to veto decisions of the Executive

[35] Lampson to Eden, 10 April 1943, FO 371/35576.

[36] Huddleston to Lampson, 21 March 1943, ibid, enclosure in n 35 above.

[37] FO 371/35576 (n 35 above).

[38] Mustafa Al-Nahas to Huddleston, 1 January 1944, FO 371/41363.

[39] Huddleston to Mustafa Al-Nahas, 18 May 1944, ibid.

Council and to enact Bills which the Assembly rejected.[40] The veto was conceived as necessary in order to accord with Articles III and IV of the 1899 Agreement, and to enable the Governor-General to discharge his responsibilities under them.[41]

The Egyptian Government levelled various criticisms at the Report and the draft Ordinance. In particular, the Egyptian Government criticized the absolute power given to the Governor-General to approve or reject legislation, and proposed that the Governor-General should obtain the prior consent of the *co-domini* before approving or rejecting legislation passed by the Legislative Assembly and the Executive Council.[42] The British Government argued that the Egyptian proposal would curtail the Governor-General's executive power for the enactment of legislation concerning only the internal affairs of the Sudan. On the other hand, the British Government recognized that by virtue of the terms of the Condominium Agreement, the Governor-General could not, without the consent of the *co-domini*, promulgate legislation materially affecting the constitution or the international status of the Sudan.[43]

To overcome the Egyptian opposition to the draft Ordinance, in May 1948 the British Ambassador in Cairo, Sir Ronald Campbell, entered into negotiations with the Egyptian Minister for Foreign Affairs, Ahmed Khashaba Pasha. The negotiations failed to obtain the approval of the Egyptian Government for the draft Ordinance. Consequently the British Government authorized the Governor-General on 14 June 1948 to promulgate the ordinance without Egyptian approval.[44]

In permitting the promulgation of the Executive Council and the Legislative Assembly Ordinance without obtaining the consent of the Egyptian Government, the British Government seemed to have acted contrary to the opinion of its Attorney-General, Sir Hartley Shawcross. The Foreign Office Legal Advisers, Beckett and Fitzmaurice, requested the opinion of Shawcross on whether the Governor-General was entitled under the 1899 Agreement to introduce constitutional changes in the Sudan in spite of the objection of one of the two condominium powers.

Shawcross expressed the view that the Governor-General had no right to introduce such changes without the assent of the two *co-domini*. He was of the view that to accord to the Governor-General a power to make fundamental changes of a constitutional nature was inconsistent with the terms of the Condominium Agreement and contrary to its intention of enabling both Governments to share in the development of the Government of the Sudan.

[40] For text of the Executive Council and Legislative Assembly Ordinance, 1948 see: Documents on the Sudan 1899–1953, issued by the Egyptian Society of International Law, March 1953, 12.

[41] Howe, Khartoum to Sargent, 11 December 1947, FO 371/62949.

[42] Abdel Fattah Amr to Bevin, 25 November 1947, FO 371/63055.

[43] Lascelles to Abdel Fattah Amr, 15 January 1948, FO 371/69155.

[44] Minute by Clutton regarding Khashaba/Campbell Conversations, 2 June 1948, FO 371/69166. The Ordinance was passed on 15 June 1948 and was published in the *Sudan Gazette* on 19 June 1948.

Shawcross also stated that the effect and intention of the 1899 Agreement was to create a delegation of legislative powers from the *co-domini* to the Governor-General and therefore he had no authority without the concurrence of the *co-domini* 'to vest them in someone else, to share them or to fetter his own exercise of them'. He further stated that the proposed legislative machinery established by the draft Executive Council and Legislative Assembly Ordinance would effect a substantial delegation of powers which under the Agreement were vested in the Governor-General alone to a tripartite legislature of which he was only one part, albeit the most powerful. Shawcross concluded by saying that if the matter was eventually referred to the International Court of Justice, it was probable that the Court would find that the Egyptian interpretation of the powers of the Governor-General under Article IV of the Agreement was correct.[45]

III. Protection of Condominium Subjects Abroad

A condominium subject travelling abroad would be required to carry an identification document or passport. When abroad, a condominium subject would expect to be able to turn to a consular officer for assistance or protection. Condominium subjects were, however, not eligible for the nationality of either of the *co-domini*, and before 1948 the Sudan Government did not promulgate a nationality or citizenship law defining the persons to whom the term 'Sudanese' applied.

In August 1925 it was decided to issue a special form of passport. The passport bore the seal of the Governor-General: the holders of such passports received the same treatment as British-protected persons and did not require a British visa for the purpose of travelling to British territory. However, that did not confer on them any right of admission to British territory, or relieve them from the necessity of obtaining permission to land. The Egyptian Government was informed in May and August 1926 by the British High Commissioner of the decision to issue Sudanese passports.[46]

To get over the difficulty arising out of the absence of a nationality or citizenship law, certain rules were prescribed for determining the eligibility for Sudan Government passports. According to those rules, Sudan Government passports were issued to the following classes of persons:

(i) (a) Persons born in the Sudan being members of the indigenous tribes and races of the Sudan.

(b) Persons wherever born being issue of a lawful marriage whose fathers come under (i)(a) provided that they have not (after coming of age) by voluntary act lawfully acquired the nationality of some other state.

45 Shawcross to Beckett, March 17, 1948, FO 371/ 69157.

46 Memorandum on the Sudan (n 22 above).

(ii) Persons of Egyptian origin born and permanently established in the Sudan, together with their minor children, provided that such persons or their ancestors became permanently established in the Sudan before the Mahdia (1882).

(iii) Any persons not included in (i) or (ii) who have become permanently established in the Sudan and who
(a) were themselves born in the Sudan of a father born in the Sudan; or
(b) do not possess the nationality of any other state; and also in both cases (a) and (b) their minor children.

(iv) The wife of any person coming under (i), (ii), or (iii) unless she is the national of some other state.[47]

We shall see that when the question of nationality was debated in the Advisory Council for the Northern Sudan, it was proposed to adopt the rules of eligibility for Sudan Government passports as the basis for a citizenship ordinance.

No agreement between the *co-domini* regarding the protection of condominium subjects abroad can be traced. However, the understanding of the British Government was that holders of Sudan Government passports should not be allowed to claim protection of the British Government in Egyptian territory or of the Egyptian Government in British territory.[48] Because of the establishment of a Sudan Agency in Egypt, holders of Sudan Government passports previously had recourse to the Sudan Agent for assistance. That arrangement seemed to have worked smoothly. Indeed the Egyptian Government authorities themselves referred cases of condominium subjects requiring protection to the Sudan Agent.[49]

As for condominium subjects in foreign countries, the British Government held the view that a condominium subject should have the right to apply to the representative of whichever of the two *co-domini* he might prefer. The Legal Adviser to the Foreign Office, Cecil Hurst, stated the position as follows:

> Passports drawn up in the name of the Governor-General should be issued to Sudanese, and the British representatives abroad should be notified that if any Sudanese should apply to them for aid he is entitled to all the assistance that can be rendered. The powers enjoyed under the condominium would certainly justify this. If a Sudanese chooses to apply to an Egyptian representative for assistance when he is abroad, there is no reason that he should not do so, for the right of Egypt to help him would also be derived from the condominium.[50]

When an Egyptian Consul had been appointed in Benghazi in the late 1930s, the British Consul was advised to continue to act on behalf of the

[47] Statement by the Legal Secretary on the Problem of Sudan Nationality, the Advisory Council for the Northern Sudan, Proceedings of the Second Session, 5–10 December 1944, 48.

[48] Lampson to Halifax, 20 January 1939, FO 371/23361, transmitting letter of 5 November 1938 from Symes.

[49] ibid.

[50] Enclosure 1 (n 13 above).

condominium subjects who approached him for assistance. But if the Egyptian Consul claimed an exclusive right in this respect, he should then be told that, as equal partners in the condominium, both the British and Egyptian Governments had the right to protect condominium subjects in foreign countries.[51]

IV. Nationality of Condominium Subjects

While Article I of the 1899 Agreement partly defined the territory of the condominium, it contained no provision defining who were Sudanese. The need to introduce a nationality law in the Sudan was first posed in 1923 in correspondence between the Governor-General and the British High Commissioner in Egypt. It was agreed that the existence of a Sudanese nationality was a matter of doubt and possible controversy.[52] The first legal reference to the Sudanese as a class of persons occurred in Article 11 of the 1936 Anglo-Egyptian Treaty. In Article 11(1) the contracting Parties agreed that 'the primary aim of their administration in the Sudan must be the welfare of the Sudanese'. They further agreed in Article 11(2) to accord preference to 'qualified Sudanese' in government appointments.

The question of Sudanese nationality was taken up by the Graduates Congress shortly after its formation in 1938. On 3 April 1942, the Congress unveiled its political face and submitted to the Governor-General, on behalf of the Sudanese people, a memorandum containing twelve demands. The sixth demand was promulgation of a Sudanese nationality law. That produced no positive response because of the outright rejection by the Sudan Government of the entire memorandum on the ground that the Graduates Congress could not claim to be the mouthpiece of the whole country.[53]

In 1944 five members of the Advisory Council requested leave of the Governor-General to include in the Agenda of the Council an item on the subject of Sudanese nationality so that members might have an opportunity to express their views.[54] Because of the constitutional implications, that request seemed to have put the Sudan Government in a difficult dilemma. Acceding to the request would worry both *co-domini*, particularly Egypt which at the time had suspicions that the Sudan Government was encouraging a separatist movement in the Sudan. On the other hand, refusal to allow discussion of the matter would be a rebuff to enlightened Sudanese opinion.[55] Sir Douglas Newbold, the Sudan's Civil Secretary, summed this up in the following terms: 'Enlightened and ambitious Sudanese dislike intensely having no nationality. The

[51] Foreign Office to the British Consul, Benghazi, February 16, 1939, FO 371/23361.

[52] See Explanatory Note to the Sudanese Nationality Bill 1957, FO 371/126009.

[53] On this, see KDD Henderson, *The Making of the Modern Sudan* (1952) 540–3.

[54] Explanatory Note to the Nationality Bill (n 52 above).

[55] Henderson (n 53 above) 412.

condominium precludes their being British subjects or Egyptian subjects, nor in fact do the majority want to be either, as they consider they are passing out of "colonial" status. But they would like to have some legal identity.'[56]

When leave was granted for inclusion of the question of Sudanese nationality on the Agenda of the Advisory Council, it was conceived that the best approach was to preface a debate on the question with the submission to Council of a factual statement of the position. That, it was hoped, would serve the twofold purpose of educating councillors on the subject and correcting the Sudanese conceptions of nationality. Then after digesting the statement, councillors would be better able to express their views.[57]

The proposed statement was submitted to Council by the Legal Secretary in December 1944. The Legal Secretary stressed that the passing of a nationality law required the existence of three elements, namely a defined territory, a sovereign government exercising sovereign powers over the territory and recognized as such internationally, and a class of people owing allegiance to that government. The second requisite was lacking in the case of the Sudan Government because it exercised its authority by virtue of the 1899 Agreement and the 1936 Treaty between the British and Egyptian Governments. To overcome that obstacle, the Legal Secretary proposed the passing of a citizenship ordinance which would in many respects resemble a nationality law and achieve the same purpose. The Legal Secretary drew on the precedent of Palestine, then under British Mandate. The absence of sovereignty in the Mandatory or Governing Power had been overcome there by the enactment, in 1925, of a citizenship order rather than a nationality law.[58]

When the question of nationality was subsequently debated by the Advisory Council, the Legal Secretary emphasized from the outset that the Sudanese were not eligible for the nationality of the *co-domini*. He also strongly advised Council to approach the question of nationality as a purely practical and administrative matter and to steer clear of the political aspects of the question.[59] The outcome of the debate was that some members of the Council were in favour of passing a nationality law but the majority preferred that some law defining who were Sudanese should be passed rather than none at all.[60]

A. Proposed classification of persons into 'Sudanese' and 'Sudan Denizens'

The first draft ordinance submitted to the Advisory Council in its Seventh Session adopted as a definition of the persons to whom the term 'Sudanese' applied, the rules of eligibility for Sudan Government

[56] Henderson (n 53 above). [57] ibid.
[58] Proceedings of the Second Session (n 47 above) 48.
[59] Proceedings of the Sixth Session, 1–6 January 1947, 143. [60] ibid 145.

passports.[61] The Council made various criticisms of that draft. The main criticism was that it was too wide. For:

> ... a person who had only a recent connection with the Sudan of not much more than ten years, and was of a very different race from the majority of Sudanese such as a person of Greek race, may be given a Sudan passport if he has no nationality and is permanently established in the Sudan. It is right to give him a Sudan passport if he travels ... but why should that entitle him to be called a Sudanese when he is so very different from the real people of the Sudan that no one would think of calling him Sudanese in ordinary speech?[62]

To remedy that situation, the Legal Secretary submitted in 1948 in the Eighth Session of the Advisory Council, a draft ordinance which classified persons into 'Sudanese' and 'Sudan Denizens'. When explaining to the Foreign Office the rationale for the classification, the Civil Secretary said that the object of the Sudan Government was to define genuine Sudanese not so much for passport purposes, where they could be treated alike with non-native Sudanese, but for other purposes like the rights and duties of citizenship, such as voting and serving on Government bodies, and priority in Government employment. He pointed out that the Sudan Government was ready, through its *co-domini*, to give protection to the non-native Sudanese when travelling abroad, but that was not a reason for giving them *ipso facto* all the privileges of a native Sudanese. The new draft ordinance therefore defined as 'Sudanese' only those who were genuine Sudanese and defined as 'Sudan Denizens' those who were not genuine Sudanese.[63]

The proposed classification provoked harsh criticism from the Foreign Office. It was observed by the Foreign Office that the Sudan Government was in the process of creating a class of persons who were Sudan nationals but did not enjoy citizenship rights. Enemies of the Sudan Government would be quick to see a precedent for that in the treatment of Jews by Hitler. If political rights in the Sudan were to be confined forever to persons who were descendants of the original indigenous races, that would be an unfortunate and retrograde step, more especially in view of the fact that under the Charter of the United Nations efforts were being made to abolish all discrimination based on race, religion, language, or sex. The Sudan Government was therefore urged by the Foreign Office to reconsider the whole idea or to put up new and more cogent reasons if they decided to proceed with it.[64]

The Sudan Government heeded the advice of the Foreign Office and produced a revised draft ordinance which dropped the classification of persons as 'Sudanese' and 'Sudan Denizens'. Instead, domicile was

[61] Proceedings of the Seventh Session, 20–24 May 1947, para 7078.
[62] Proceedings of the Eighth Session, 3–10 March 1948, 82.
[63] Civil Secretary to Lascelles, 8 January 1948, FO 371/69198.
[64] Lascelles to Civil Secretary, 9 February 1948, ibid.

adopted as a basic criterion for defining the term 'Sudanese'.[65] The Foreign Office did not find the revised draft ordinance politically objectionable but noted that it was based on two principles proved by the experience of many states to be unworkable for the purposes of a nationality law, namely domicile and the absence of dual nationality. Nevertheless, the Foreign Office encouraged the Sudan Government to go ahead with its enactment: it was more important to have some ordinance defining 'Sudanese' than to wait indefinitely until a faultless one could be devised.[66]

B. *The Definition of Sudanese Ordinance 1948*[67]

Thus when the Definition of Sudanese Ordinance was eventually promulgated in 1948, the classification of persons into 'Sudanese' and 'Sudan Denizens' was dropped. Moreover, the blood qualification of being of the indigenous population of the Sudan was also abandoned for a single qualification based on the length of establishment in the Sudan by domicile. In an Explanatory Note, the Legal Secretary said that the omission of the blood qualification was because it was not exact and because many prominent 'Sudanese' could not be said to belong to the indigenous population.[68]

Under the 1948 Ordinance, a person was regarded Sudanese as of right if he had no other nationality and had been domiciled in the Sudan since 31 December 1897[69] or his ancestors in the direct male line since that date had all been so domiciled. Under Article 4 of the Ordinance the status of Sudanese could also be acquired not as of right but by a grant similar to naturalization. The grant was, however, at the discretion of the Civil Secretary and subject to the fulfilment of certain conditions.

When speaking before the Security Council in 1947, Nokrashi cited 'the attempt to create a separate Sudanese nationality' as evidence of the policy of the Sudan Government to segregate the Sudan from Egypt.[70] Although the Sudan Government tried to impress on Nokrashi that the purpose of promulgating an ordinance defining the term 'Sudanese' was purely administrative, Nokrashi remained adamant that the proposed ordinance should not be enacted without obtaining the prior approval of the Egyptian Government.[71] The Sudan Government was of the view that the Egyptian Government had no right to interfere since the ordinance was devoid of any constitutional effect but was a mere administrative act and

[65] Robertson to Lascelles, 1 April 1948, ibid.

[66] Foreign Office to Khartoum, 30 April 1948, ibid.

[67] Laws of the Sudan, vol 1, Title 1, Sub-Title 5, 149.

[68] Explanatory Note dated 1 April 1948, enclosed in Robertson to Lascelles, FO 371/69198.

[69] The date was chosen because it would include all persons permanently established before the reoccupation of the Sudan, and would exclude all persons who, though permanently established in the Sudan, had come into the Sudan after that date: Explanatory Note to the Sudanese Nationality Bill, FO 371/126009.

[70] 175th Meeting, 5 August 1947, para 43.

[71] Nokrashi to Governor-General, 14 March 1948, FO 371/69198.

therefore fell within the competence of the Governor-General. The Egyptian Government's prior approval of the ordinance was thus not sought but the Government was subsequently informed of its enactment.[72]

During the Anglo-Egyptian negotiations on constitutional reform in the Sudan in 1947–48, the Egyptian Government managed to obtain the agreement of the British Government to include the nationality of the Sudanese within the reserved matters in respect of which the Legislative Assembly should have no legislative powers.[73]

V. Interpretation of Article 11(2) of the 1936 Treaty

A. Sudanization of the post of Grand Kadi

Since the establishment of the condominium in 1899, the post of Grand *Kadi* had been held by Egyptian Islamic or *Sharia* judges. The Grand *Kadi* assumed headship of the Islamic law or *Sharia* Division of the Legal Department. In that capacity he supervised the adminstration of *Sharia* law in the Appeal, Provincial, and District courts. The last Egyptian judge to fill the post of Grand *Kadi* was Hassan Mamoun.[74]

Shortly before the expiry of the contract of Hassan Mamoun in January 1947, the Sudan Government decided to appoint the Sudanese *Mufti*, Ahmed Al-Tahir, to the post of Grand *Kadi*. The Sudan Government based its decision on the Sudanization policy and its interpretation of Article III of the 1899 Condominium Agreement, which vested in the Governor-General the supreme military and civil command of the Sudan, and Article 11(2) of the 1936 Treaty, which gave preference to qualified Sudanese in appointments to posts in the Sudan Government.[75]

Nokrashi made representations on the subject when he met the British Ambassador, Ronald Campell, on 23 December 1946. Nokrashi said that the effect of the decision on Egyptian opinion would be disastrous. The post of Grand *Kadi* was the only high post held by an Egyptian and to remove an Egyptian at that moment in favour of a Sudanese and thus sever that link with Egypt would furnish additional evidence of a British policy to separate the Sudan from Egypt. Nokrashi proposed the retention of Hassan Mamoun in office, the creation of a post of deputy Grand *Kadi* to be filled by Ahmed Al-Tahir and to replace the latter as *Mufti* of the Sudan by another Sudanese. Nokrashi offered, if necessary, to meet the expense of the new post.[76]

72 Robertson to Lascelles, 4 April 1948, ibid.

73 Executive Council and Legislative Assembly Ordinance, 1948, s 54 (n 40 above).

74 Memorandum on the History of the Appointments of Sudan Grand Kadis since the 1899 Condominium Agreement, July 1947, FO 371/62989.

75 ibid. Also Huddleston to Campbell, 25 December 1946, FO 371/53263 and Huddleston to Campbell, 31 December 1946, FO 371/62958. The Mufti is the expounder of Islamic Law, in seniority he was then second to the Grand Kadi.

76 Campbell to Bevin, 23 December 1946, FO 371/53263.

Campbell assured Nokrashi that his Government did not pursue a policy of separation and told him that the decision to appoint a Sudanese to the post of Grand *Kadi* was based on a policy agreed in Article 11 of the 1936 Treaty. Campbell warned that, as a qualified Sudanese was available for the post, failure to appoint a Sudanese would cast doubts on the policy of Sudanization as part of the programme of promoting the welfare of the Sudanese and preparing them for self-government.[77]

B. The respective interpretations of the co-domini

The Sudan Government based the decision to Sudanize the post of Grand *Kadi* on its interpretation of Article III of the 1899 Agreement and Article 11(2) of the 1936 Treaty. The Sudan Government held the view that neither in the 1899 Agreement nor in the 1936 Treaty was there any express or implied provision that the post of Grand *Kadi* should be excluded from the category of other ordinary posts in the Sudan administration, to which the Governor-General should only appoint non-Sudanese officials if a Sudanese candidate with adequate qualifications could not be found.[78]

The interpretation of the Sudan Government found strong endorsement from the British Government. Cadogan informed the Security Council in 1947 that the proposal to appoint a Sudanese as Grand *Kadi* was merely another step in the policy of implementing the pledge made in the 1936 Treaty to give preference to qualified Sudanese in appointments to posts in the Sudan administration.[79] Commenting on Nokrashi's claim that the holder of the post should always remain an Egyptian in accordance with the traditions hitherto followed, Cadogan said: 'This claim contrasts strangely with the Egyptian Prime Minister's assertion that the Egyptian and Sudanese are one and indivisible, one people and one race ... To reserve it in perpetuity for an Egyptian would not only be a defiance of the Treaty but a denial to the Sudanese, on purely racial grounds, of their natural rights.'[80]

The Egyptian Government's interpretation was that the posts referred to in Article 11(2) of the 1936 Treaty were the posts to which Egyptian or British officials might be nominated. But the post of Grand *Kadi* had never been one of the posts to which a British official could be appointed. The Egyptian Government also contended that the post of Grand *Kadi* was a religious post of special consequence and could not be considered as falling within the category of civil or military posts over which the Governor-General had supreme authority.[81]

To resolve that conflict of interpretation, on 15 March 1947 the Governor-General, Sir Hubert Huddleston, requested the Egyptian

[77] Campbell to Bevin (n 76 above). [78] Howe to Nokrashi, 10 June 1947, FO 371/69216.

[79] 179th Meeting, 11 August 1947, para 56. [80] ibid.

[81] Campbell to Foreign Office, 3 February 1947, FO 371/62958, transmitting translation of a note dated 2 February 1947, from Egyptian Prime Minister.

Government to approach the British Government with a view to considering together the interpretation of Article 11(2) of the 1936 Treaty and to communicate to him as a matter of urgency their agreed interpretation. Huddleston's successor, Sir Robert Howe, expressed to the Egyptian Government, on 10 June 1947, his full agreement with his predecessor's suggestion. Howe informed the Egyptian Government that the issues to be settled were, first, whether the Governor-General was entitled to select and appoint the Grand *Kadi*, and, secondly, whether he was bound by Article 11(2) of the 1936 Treaty in making the selection and the appointment.[82]

As the Egyptian Government took no action to secure the jointly agreed interpretation asked for by the Sudan Government, the Acting Governor-General proceeded to announce, in October 1947, the appointment of the Sudanese *Mufti* to the post of Grand *Kadi* and notified the *co-domini* accordingly. It was also announced that the appointment was made on the basis of Article 11(2) of the 1936 Treaty regarding the appointment of qualified Sudanese to high posts in the Sudan administration.[83]

In a note of protest, on 6 January 1948, the Egyptian Government considered the action of the Acting Governor-General irregular since it exceeded the powers vested in him. The Egyptian Government reiterated its earlier stance that the post of Grand *Kadi* did not fall within the ambit of Article 11(2) of the 1936 Treaty.[84] However, as a considerable interval had elapsed since the Egyptian note was communicated and a much longer period had elapsed since the Grand *Kadi* was appointed, the Foreign Office decided not to communicate any reply to the Egyptian note.[85]

VI. Consular Representation

Article X of the 1899 Agreement provided that no consuls, vice-consuls, or consular agents should be accredited or allowed to reside in the Sudan without the previous consent of the British Government. Cromer expected this provision to be challenged by those who held the view that the status of the Sudan was in no way different from that of other parts of the Ottoman Dominions. He also expected that provision to cause hardship to Europeans who were married or buried in the Sudan. He therefore advised any European who considered it essential that his marriage or burial should be attested by a consular representative of his country to remain in the territory lying north of the 22nd parallel of latitude.[86]

82 Howe to Nokrashi, 10 June 1947, FO 371/69216.

83 Press Office, Khartoum, to Sudan Agent, London, 11 October 1947, FO 371/62989.

84 Egyptian Ambassador to Foreign Secretary, 6 January 1948, FO 371/69216.

85 Campbell to Bevin, 10 February 1948, and Foreign Office to Campbell, 20 December 1948, ibid.

86 Cromer (n 2 above) 118.

We shall see that though the question of the appointment of consular representatives in the Sudan had been posed at intervals since 1906, no such officers were appointed until the termination of the condominium. In January 1953, Selwyn Lloyd, the British Minister of State for Foreign Affairs, said in an answer to a question in Parliament that there were no diplomatic or consular representatives in the Sudan. In the material prepared for the answer, it was stated that the refusal to accept consular representatives in Khartoum was because the presence of accredited representatives of foreign Powers in the Sudan might well be embarrassing to the administration.[87] Another reason often adduced to justify the reluctance to admit foreign consuls to the Sudan was that it would stir up questions regarding sovereignty over the Sudan, since approval of the appointments had to be given by the 'sovereign' of the state to which the consul was appointed.[88]

There was thus no dearth of evidence to substantiate the Egyptian allegation that the British Government had used Article X of the Condominium Agreement to isolate the Sudan from the outside world. One such allegation was put forward by Nokrashi when addressing the Security Council in 1947. He said that the British 'have done all in their power to isolate the Sudan from the outer world in general and from Egypt in particular. Not a consul, not a consular agent, is admitted from abroad'.[89] However, shortly before the condominium drew to a close, the Governor-General gave permission to unofficial agents of some countries, called Liaison Officers, to establish themselves in Khartoum.

A. Appointment of consuls proposed in 1906

The subject of consular representation in the Sudan first came up in 1906. Following the completion of the new railway line from the Red Sea to the Nile and the establishment of a new harbour at Port Sudan, there was expected to be a considerable influx of foreigners into Port Sudan and a great increase in shipping interests. It was also expected that some of the Powers would soon wish to arrange for recognition of consuls to represent their interests at Port Sudan. In fact the Italian representative in Cairo several times alluded to the idea in official conversations. Moreover, Iddings, the United States Consul-General in Cairo, approached Cromer on the subject and proposed to recommend to his Government the appointment of a consul at Port Sudan. Iddings requested to be furnished with a memorandum explaining the conditions subject to which the appointment would be recognized and the source from which the consul should receive the *exequatur*.[90] Even Cromer himself suggested to

[87] 24 and 28 January 1953, FO 371/102925.

[88] Draft Note on Consular Representation in the Sudan, FO 371/108576.

[89] 175th Meeting, 5 August 1947, para 43.

[90] Cromer to Grey, 8 March 1906, FO 369/15.

the Foreign Office the appointment of a British Consul to look after British shipping and commercial interests at Port Sudan.[91]

The memorandum asked for by Iddings was prepared by Malcolm McIlwraith and was communicated by Cromer to Iddings.[92] McIlwraith stated that the 1899 Agreement created a special status for the Sudan.[93] He pointed out that whereas Article VIII of the Agreement implicitly excluded the operation of the capitulations in the Sudan, the exclusion was more expressly indicated by the terms of Article X. McIlwraith then distinguished the appointment of consuls in the Sudan from the appointment of consuls in Egypt and other Ottoman Dominions. For the appointment of consuls in Egypt, preliminary negotiations were conducted by the power concerned with the Sublime Porte. The firman of *exequatur* was issued in Constantinople and communicated to the Egyptian Government. But for the appointment of consuls in the Sudan, application should not be made to the Sublime Porte but to the British Government. If the British Government consented, they would address the Egyptian Government on the subject and ask for their assent. As to who should issue the *exequatur*, McIlwraith suggested that the Governor-General acting in the name of both the British and Egyptian Governments was the suitable authority for granting the *exequatur*. But McIlwraith emphasized that the appointment of a United States Consul would not affect the legal position of the United States citizens in the Sudan or imply recognition by the Sudan Government, for any purposes of extra-territorial rights of foreigners, in the nature of those accorded to them by the capitulations. He therefore indicated that the application for the appointment of a United States Consul in the Sudan might state that the United States did not propose to claim any such rights for its citizens. With respect to the relations which might be established for administrative purposes between the proposed consular officer in the Sudan and the Consul-General in Cairo, McIlwraith was of the view that the Egyptian and Sudan Governments could not be expected to take official cognizance of such relations or to recognize the Consul-General or any other United States consular officer in Cairo as having any official connection with the Sudan.

When addressing the Foreign Office on the subject of the appointment of a United States Consul in the Sudan, Cromer reiterated the views expressed by McIlwraith. He placed major emphasis on the fact that the status of the Sudan was different from that of Egypt. Under the 1899 Agreement foreigners were precluded from being subject to the jurisdiction of their consuls as well as from other privileges secured to them by the capitulations in force in Egypt and other parts of the Ottoman Dominions. Cromer further conveyed to the Foreign Office his reluctance to recognize the subordination of any consular officer in the Sudan

[91] Cromer to Grey, 10 March 1906, ibid. [92] Cromer to Grey, 8 March 1906, ibid.
[93] The Memorandum was enclosed in Cromer to Grey, 8 March 1906, ibid.

to his Consul-General in Cairo. Cromer suggested that the Governor-General be authorized to issue *exequaturs* to foreign consuls on condition of prior recognition by the sending state of the 1899 Agreement.[94]

On the whole, the Foreign Office accepted Cromer's approach. But to avoid the necessity of issuing *exequaturs* by the Governor-General, the Foreign Office proposed the appointment of vice-consuls or consular agents without commission who would require no *exequatur* but only recognition by the Governor-General.[95] Cromer so informed Iddings. Though Iddings promised to communicate the suggestion to Washington, for the time being the subject of United States consular representation in the Sudan was not pursued.[96]

B. The subject re-opened in 1945

In 1945 the United States Government re-opened the question. As a result of the Second World War there were a number of American servicemen stationed in the Sudan. The United States Legation in Cairo made an informal approach to ascertain the views of the British Embassy in Cairo on the subject of United States consular representation in the Sudan. As no formal approach was made, the British Embassy proposed to take no action. However, the Embassy was in agreement with the view expressed by the Governor-General that the time was inauspicious for the appointment of a United States or any other foreign consul.[97]

According to the Governor-General, it was singularly difficult to justify special treatment of the United States because of the tiny number of its citizens resident in the Sudan and its negligible commercial interests in the country. Secondly, even in the case of larger communities like the relatively more important Greek Community, there were no sufficient commercial or other interests to keep consuls reasonably busy and they would almost inevitably become involved in political intrigue. Thirdly, because of the precariousness of the political future of the Sudan and Anglo-Egyptian relations, there was little to be said for upsetting a system which had worked well in the past in favour of a system which would introduce new practical complications. Among the many anomalies of the Sudan, the maintenance of the anomaly of having no consular representation in the Sudan need cause no undue concern.[98]

C. Appointment of liaison officers

The question of consular representation in the Sudan was also raised in 1949 by the Saudi Arabian Government, which wished to appoint a

94 Cromer to Grey, 10 March 1906, ibid.

95 Foreign Office to Cromer, 5 April 1906, Cromer to Foreign Office, 6 April 1906, and Foreign Office to Cromer, 11 April 1906, ibid.

96 Cromer to Grey, 12 April 1906, ibid.

97 Killearn to Churchill, 6 June 1945, FO 371/46034.

98 Acting Governor-General to Killearn, 24 September 1945, enclosed in Bowker to Foreign Office, 18 October 1945, ibid.

consul to Port Sudan. In March 1949 India applied to appoint a trade agent in the Sudan. The response of the Sudan Government reflected a modification of their earlier position in respect of foreign representation in the Sudan. They adopted the view that the Governor-General was competent to admit trade agents but not consuls because of the difficulty of who should issue *exequaturs*. Thus while Saudi Arabia's application was turned down, India was told to apply to the Governor-General for permission to appoint a trade agent in the Sudan.

Then in July 1949 France applied to be allowed to appoint a French representative in the Sudan. As France did not have adequate trade with the Sudan, a liaison officer was appointed in February 1950. His main function was to deal with the adminstrative matters arising out of the annual movement of pilgrims between French African territories and the Red Sea, and the currency problems arising therefrom. But the British Government expected that he would also send reports to his Government.[99] The application for the appointment of the French Liaison Officer was made direct to the Governor-General who gave his consent direct to the French Government. The Governor-General did not seek the approval of the Egyptian Government. Nor was the appointment officially approved by the British Government. The British Government was of course aware of the French application and agreed 'unofficially' to the appointment.[100]

A United States Liaison Officer was appointed in September 1952. The object of his appointment was to put the State Department more fully in the picture with regard to political developments in the Sudan.[101] The appointment of the United States Liaison Officer had been dealt with in the same way as that of the French Liaison Officer. The Egyptian Government was, however, consulted by the United States Government and when the appointment was made it was announced publicly by the United States Ambassador in Cairo.[102]

D. *The effect of the 1953 Self-Government Agreement*

Early in 1953 the Ethiopian Government wished to appoint a liaison officer in Khartoum. But on 12 February 1953 the Egyptian Government and the British Government signed the Agreement concerning self-government and self-determination for the Sudan. Article 6(a) of the Agreement provided that the Governor-General should remain directly

[99] Draft Note on Consular Representation in the Sudan, FO 371/108576. Also see material prepared for the answer to a question in Parliament, FO 371/102925.

[100] FO 371/108576, also FO 371/102925, Minute by Morris on the present position of Sudanese representation abroad and foreign representation in the Sudan and the desirability of consulting the Egyptians before making appointments, 25 June 1953.

[101] Draft Note on Consular Representation, FO 371/108576, also material prepared for answer to a question in Parliament, FO 371/102925.

[102] Minute by Morris, (n 100 above), also material prepared for answer to a question in Parliament, FO 371/102925.

responsible to the two Contracting Governments as regards external affairs. Article 12(2) of the revised Self-Government Statute provided that in the discharge of his responsibilities in respect of external affairs referred to in Article 6(a) of the Agreement, the Governor-General should be directly responsible to the two Governments.[103]

The Agreement gave rise to a difference of opinion about the procedure for the appointment of Liaison Officers in the Sudan and the desirability of consulting the *co-domini* before making any appointment. The British Ambassador in Addis Ababa, acting on the suggestion of the Foreign Office, advised the Ethiopian Government to approach the British and the Egyptian Governments on the subject. The British Embassy in Cairo argued that appointments of liaison officers were matters of external affairs which should be referred to the *co-domini*. The Sudan Government objected to this procedure, arguing that the provision in the 1953 Agreement that the Governor-General should remain responsible to the two Governments for external affairs did not introduce any change in the position. Moreover in 1949 it had been agreed that the Governor-General was competent to admit trade agents; and to start referring applications to the *co-domini* would, in the opinion of the Sudan Government, be a retrograde step.[104]

On the basis of legal opinion, the Foreign Office came to the conclusion that Article 6(a) of the 1953 Agreement and Article 12(2) of the Self-Government Statute did not mean that the Governor-General could not carry out an act in relation to external affairs without seeking the prior approval of the *co-domini*, but merely that he was responsible to both of them for what in fact he had done. If there was an established practice according to which the Governor-General was accustomed to perform certain limited functions having bearing on external affairs on his own motion, he could continue to do so; though of course he would remain responsible to the *co-domini* for his actions. Thus he could agree to the establishment of unofficial missions on the analogy of the French and United States missions without specific authority from the *co-domini*.

On the other hand, the appointment of consuls, as opposed to trade agents or liaison officers, would clearly go beyond anything the Governor-General had hitherto been accustomed to do on his own. He would, in the opinion of the Foreign Office, require the consent of the *co-domini* before he could agree to the establishment of foreign consuls in Khartoum. With specific reference to the precedent of the United States Liaison Officer, the Foreign Office saw no need to stop the Ethiopian Government from consulting the Egyptian Government about the proposed appointment of an Ethiopian Liaison Officer in Khartoum.[105]

The precedent of the United States Liaison Officer was followed in December 1953 when the Greek Government sought permission to

[103] Texts in 161 UNTS 157. [104] Minute by Morris (n 100 above).
[105] Allen to Luce, 2 July 1953, FO 371/102925.

appoint a Liaison Officer to Khartoum. The Greek Government informed the British and Egyptian Governments of the proposed appointment. Neither of them raised any objections. But the approval for the appointment was given by the Governor-General.[106]

In March 1953, the United Kingdom established a Trade Commission in the Sudan. At a press conference held in Khartoum on 25 March 1953, Selwyn Lloyd said that the establishment of the Trade Commission at that time was most appropriate, for it showed recognition of the changing relationship between the British Government and the Sudan resulting from the 1953 Self-Government Agreement, which made it no longer appropriate that purely British questions should be dealt with by the Sudan Government.[107]

The United Kingdom Trade Commission in the Sudan was staffed by Foreign Service Officers and its function was to serve trade interests and other general interests of the British Government. It was also thought that the establishment of the Trade Commission would put the British Government on a roughly equal footing with that of the Egyptian Government as regards independent representation in the Sudan, since the Egyptian Government already had a Trade Representative there.[108] However, official intimation to the Egyptian Government of the intention of the British Government to establish a Trade Commission in the Sudan was unfavourably received and was viewed with grave suspicion.[109]

The question of admitting foreign consuls to the Sudan was also mooted during the transitional period provided for by the 1953 Self-Government Agreement. The view was expressed that in the then more advanced state of the Sudan, consular representation would be of benefit to the country. It was therefore thought desirable in principle that foreign countries' representation to a self-governing Sudan should be regularized in accordance with normal international practice.[110] In the event, nothing materialized and no consular or diplomatic representatives were accredited to the Sudan until after the country attained independence in January 1956. Most of the then existing Liaison Offices and Trade Commissions were elevated to embassies.

VII. Delimitation of Condominium Territory

Article I of the 1899 Agreement provided that the word 'Sudan' meant three categories of territory lying south of the 22nd parallel of latitude.

[106] Draft Note on Consular Representation, FO 371/108576.

[107] Riches, UK Trade Commissioner, Khartoum, to Allen, 8 May 1953, FO 371/102921.

[108] Bowker to Howe, 2 March 1953, ibid. Under the 1936 treaty Egypt was allowed to appoint an economic expert for service at Khartoum: Note dated 12 August 1936, from Lampson to Mustafa Al-Nahas, for source see n 3 above.

[109] Stevenson to Foreign Office, 11 December 1952, FO 371/96965.

[110] Draft Note on Consular Representation, FO 371/108576.

The first category comprised all the territories which had never been evacuated by the Egyptian troops since 1882. That formula was adopted in order to include within the Sudan the two towns of Wadi Halfa and Suakin, neither of which had been evacuated by the Egyptian Government during the Mahdist revolution. The second category embraced territories which before the Mahdist revolution had been under the administration of the Government of the Khedive but 'were temporarily lost to Egypt and have been reconquered by Her Majesty's Government and the Egyptian Government acting in concert'. The third category referred to territories which might subsequently be reconquered by the British and the Egyptian Governments acting in concert.[111] It is not proposed to dwell here on a detailed examination of the treaty basis of the international boundaries of the condominium, but simply to ascertain the extent to which the Egyptian Government had been associated with the delimitation or demarcation of condominium territory, particularly when that involved cession of territory.

In London, on 21 March 1899, France and Britain signed a Declaration to establish their Spheres of Influence in Central Africa.[112] The Declaration defined the boundary between the Sudan and French Equatorial Africa and was subsequently amplified by the Supplementary Convention of 8 September 1919, between France and Britain. The Convention resolved the dispute regarding sovereignty over Dar Tama and Dar Masalit. Dar Masalit and parts of Dar Gimir were left in Dar Fur whereas Dar Tama, Dar Sila and the remaining parts of Dar Gimir were left to France.[113] In execution of Paragraph 4 of the London Declaration, a Boundary Commission was appointed to demarcate the boundary between the Sudan and French Equatorial Africa. The outcome of the work of the commission was embodied in the Protocol of 10 January 1924. Britain and France ratified the Protocol by the Exchange of Notes of 21 January 1924.[114]

The Egyptian Government did not participate in the negotiations which resulted in the London Declaration of 21 March 1899. Moreover, the Egyptian Government was not consulted on the terms of the Supplementary Convention of 1919 nor on the terms of the Exchange of Notes of 21 January 1924. The Sudan was, however, referred to in all those instruments as the Anglo-Egyptian Sudan. But, in the case of the 1924 Protocol and the Exchange of Notes, the Egyptian Prime Minister took exception to the fact that he had not been consulted. In reply he was informed by the British Government that the matter under discussion had been the demarcation of a boundary which was settled in principle

[111] Cromer said that this provision had been so worded as to include extensions southwards or westwards acquired by Anglo-Egyptian action, and at the same time to exclude extensions from Uganda northwards made by the English Government acting alone: Explanatory Memorandum to Condominium Agreement (n 6 above).

[112] E Hertslet, *The Map of Africa by Treaty* (1909) No 244, 796.

[113] UK Treaty Series No 6 (1921) Cmd 1239.

[114] ibid No 28 (1924) Cmnd 2221.

as long ago as 1899, at a time when the British Government was the only power enjoying the diplomatic status necessary for useful discussion of the boundaries of the valleys of the Upper Nile.[115]

The boundary between the Sudan and the Independent State of the Congo was delimited by Article II of the Agreement of 9 May 1906, between Britain and King Leopold II, Sovereign of the Independent State of the Congo. Article I of the Agreement preserved the lease to King Leopold of the tract of territory known as the Lado Enclave. Article III of the Agreement secured the interest of Egypt in maintaining some control of the waters flowing into the Nile both from the Lakes and from the affluents situated in Bahr El Ghazal. Under this Article the Government of the Independent State of the Congo undertook not to construct, or allow to be constructed, any work on or near Semliki or Isango River, which would diminish the volume of water entering Lake Albert, except in agreement with the Sudan Government.[116] Although the Sudan was referred to in the 1906 Agreement as the Anglo-Egyptian Sudan, the Egyptian Government were not consulted about its terms. A copy of the Agreement was, however, communicated to the Egyptian Prime Minister, Boutrous Ghali, who on behalf of the Council of Ministers asked Cromer to thank the British Government for the satisfactory settlement of the question.[117] On Leopold's death in 1909 the lease of the Lado Enclave was terminated. The actual transfer of the Enclave to the Sudan was effected by a *procès-verbal* concluded by an Anglo-Belgian Commission on 16 June 1910.[118] The Egyptian Government's role in the matter had been confined to the conferment by the Khedive of decorations on the Belgian delegates.[119]

Delimitation of the northern sector of the boundary between Eritrea and the Sudan began before the conclusion of the 1899 Condominium Agreement. However, allusion should be made here to Article III of the 15 April 1891 Protocol between Italy and Britain for the Demarcation of their respective spheres of influence in Eastern Africa. Pursuant to that Article the Italian Government undertook not to construct on the River Atbara for the purpose of irrigation, any work which might 'sensibly' modify its flow into the Nile.[120] The southern sector of the boundary with Eritrea up to the River Setit was delimited, demarcated, and re-demarcated by a series of agreements concluded between 1899 and 1916. Though the Sudan was referred to in some of those agreements as the Anglo-Egyptian Sudan, the Egyptian Government does not seem to have been consulted or informed.[121]

115 Memorandum on the Delimitation of Sudan Boundaries: Position of Egyptian Government, 21 September 1938, FO 371/22019.

116 Hertslet (n 112 above) No 165, 584.

117 Memorandum on the Delimitation of Sudan Boundaries (n 115 above).

118 Cheetham to Grey, transmitting dispatch from Governor-General, 16 July 1910, FO 407/174.

119 Memorandum on the Delimitation of Sudan Boundaries (n 115 above).

120 Hertslet (n 112 above) No 289, 949.

121 For analysis of these agreements, see FAR Taha, *The Sudan-Ethiopia Boundary Dispute* (1983) Ch 3, 19–35.

The need to define the boundary with Libya presented itself in the form of a dispute regarding sovereignty over the Sarra Triangle situated in the extreme north-western corner of the Sudan. In 1931 Italian troops occupied the Kufra Oasis and established themselves in the Sarra wells and Ain Doua wells on the south-western side of Jebel Oweinat. Notwithstanding the British and Italian activities in the Sarra Triangle, in 1933 and 1934 the two Governments conducted negotiations to settle the dispute.[122] The eventual conclusion of an agreement was greatly facilitated by the attitude of the Sudan Government in respect of the Triangle. The Sudan Government intimated to the British Government that the Sarra Triangle was of no value to the Sudan from the administrative or military point of view, and that no objection would be raised to the cession of the Triangle to Libya.[123]

Because of the publicity which attended the military operations in the Triangle, in January 1934 the Acting British High Commissioner in Cairo informed the Egyptian Prime Minister orally of the position. However, Egypt did not take part in the negotiations held in Rome in 1933 and 1934, but when the agreement to cede the Sarra Triangle to Libya was reached, Egypt was invited to participate in the notes exchanged in Rome with the Italian Government on 20 July 1934, recording the agreement. The wording of the notes was decided in consultation with the Egyptian Government.[124]

To facilitate the administration of their respective tribes, in 1911 the Sudan Government proposed to the Government of Uganda an interchange of territory.[125] When a general agreement on the interchange was reached, the Khedive and his Prime Minister were informed and their approval obtained.[126] The proposed interchange was sanctioned by the Order in Council of 21 April 1914, issued by the Secretary of State for the Colonies.[127] Part of the Order became the basis of the boundary between the Sudan and Kenya when, in 1926, Rudolf Province of Uganda was transferred to Kenya.[128] As the 1914 Order left four matters unsettled, the Ugandan and Sudan Governments agreed to accept the boundary described therein as provisional and subject to such modifications as the circumstances might require. The unsettled matters included the Turkana tribe grazing grounds and the delimitation of the southern boundary of the Kuku tribe.[129]

[122] For details of the dispute and the respective positions at the parties see FAR Taha, 'The Sudan-Libya Boundary' (1977) 58 *Sudan Notes and Records* 65 (hereinafter SNR).

[123] Campbell, Acting High Commissioner, Cairo, to Simon, 1 July 1933, transmitting dispatch of 19 June 1933, from Acting Governor-General of the Sudan, FO 407/217.

[124] UK Treaty Series No 21 (1934) Cmnd 4694. Also see Memorandum on the Delimitation of Sudan Boundaries (n 115 above).

[125] Kitchener to Grey, 27 October 1911, embodying his views on the details of the delimitation of the Sudan-Uganda boundary, FO 371/1115.

[126] Memorandum on the Delimitation of the Sudan Boundaries (n 115 above).

[127] *Uganda Official Gazette*, No 10, 30 May 1914, 255.

[128] See FAR Taha, 'The Sudan-Kenya Boundary' (1975) 56 SNR 37.

[129] Director of Intelligence, War Office, Cairo, to Private Secretary of Sudan's Governor-General, April 1914, and Director of Intelligence and Sudan Agent, Cairo, to the British Agency, Cairo, 6 May 1914, and also Sudan Agent to Kitchener, 22 May 1914, FO 141/648/234.

A modification of the Sudan–Uganda boundary took place in 1926. It was then agreed for administrative purposes to transfer to the Sudan a small portion of territory near Mount Langia. The modification was effected by an Order in Council of 17 September 1926. The Egyptian Prime Minister was informed of the reasons for the modification and was given a copy of the Proclamation which the Acting Governor-General of the Sudan proposed to issue.[130] But in 1928 the Sudan Government turned down a proposal to rectify the boundary between the Chua and Gulu Districts of Uganda and the Opari District of the Sudan in such a way as to include in Uganda all sections of the Acholi Tribe. As the proposed rectification would have involved the transfer to Uganda of 1,200 square miles of territory in the neighbourhood of Nimule, the Ugandan Government were informed that it could not be entertained, for the Egyptian Government would not consent to any cession of Anglo-Egyptian territory to a British colony.[131]

Negotiations for the delimitation of the Sudan–Ethiopia boundary commenced in April 1899 between Emperor Menelek II and Harrington, the British representative in Addis Ababa. The Egyptian Government was informed that as it was desired to obtain from Menelek an assurance that the waters of Lake Tsana would not fall under the control of any private company, it might be necessary to make some moderate territorial concessions in exchange for such an assurance. Moreover, the instructions sent to Harrington were communicated to the Egyptian Government.[132] The negotiations culminated in the signature, on 15 May 1902, of a Treaty between Ethiopia and Britain for the delimitation of the Sudan–Ethiopia boundary from the River Setit to the 6th parallel. Under Article III of the Treaty, Menelek agreed not to construct or allow to be constructed, any work across the Blue Nile, Lake Tsana, or the Sobat which would arrest the flow of their waters into the Nile, except in agreement with the British and Sudan Governments.[133] North of the 9th parallel the boundary delimited by the 1902 Treaty closely followed the line of the Ethiopian escarpment with a view to separating the tribes inhabiting the Sudan plains from those inhabiting the Ethiopian table-land. South of the 9th parallel the boundary parted company from the escarpment of the Ethiopian table-land. Instead, it followed the Baro, Bibor, and Akobo Rivers, constituting a salient projecting into the Sudan. In this way the boundary cut across the tribal boundaries of the areas inhabited by the Nilotic Nuer and Anuak tribes.[134]

[130] For the text of the Order see Enclosure 2 in Memorandum on the Delimitation of Sudan Boundaries (n 115 above).

[131] Sudan's Acting Governor-General to Uganda Governor, 13 May 1928 and Cairo Residency Minute (undated but of about 19 May 1928), FO 141/648/234. See also FAR Taha, 'The Sudan-Uganda Boundary' (1978) 59 SNR 1.

[132] Memorandum on the Delimitation of Sudan Boundaries (n 115 above).

[133] Hertslet (n 112 above) No 100, 431.

[134] Joint Memorandum on the Sudan-Ethiopia Frontier by the Foreign and Colonial Secretaries, 25 November 1938, FO 371/23373.

Following the Italian conquest of Abyssinia, an Anglo-Italian Agreement was concluded on 16 April 1938. This provided that negotiations would be opened, in which the Egyptian Government would be invited to participate, so far as all questions affecting Egypt or the Anglo-Egyptian Sudan were concerned, with a view to a definitive agreement on the boundaries between the Sudan, Kenya, and British Somaliland on the one side and Italian East Africa on the other.[135] On 25 March 1939, the British and Egyptian Governments jointly proposed to the Italian Government the inclusion of the whole of the Nuer grazing grounds within the Sudan and the cession of the whole Anuak to the Sudan.[136] The Italian Government rejected those proposals as being too extensive.[137] Had Italy accepted, she would have been compensated by some border territory further south.[138]

It is of interest to note that a Foreign Office memorandum summed up the position of the Egyptian Government in relation to the delimitation of the boundaries of the Sudan in the following terms:

> . . . there are cases where the Egyptian Government were associated with the determination of the frontiers of the Sudan and where they were not: cases where prior consultation with the Egyptian Government took place or where they were kept informed of negotiations; cases where they were notified subsequently and where there was no action in this respect apart from general publication.[139]

VIII. Capacity to Conclude Bilateral Agreements

Although the 1899 Agreement did not confer on the Governor-General the power to conclude bilateral agreements, the British Government unilaterally adopted the view that the Governor-General could conclude local and technical bilateral agreements with neighbouring governors of the same kind as the governor of a British colony would conclude with neighbouring territories which were generally, but not always, colonial territories too. The Egyptian Government was not consulted but did not seem to have contested the British view or the practice which was based on it.[140] On the question of whether the Governor-General should consult the *co-domini* when exercising the power to conclude bilateral agreements, Beckett, the Legal Adviser to the Foreign Office, said: 'Of course the Governor-General, in exercising this power, should not in the matter of consulting the co-domini, distinguish between one or the other.

[135] UK Treaty Series, No 31 (1938) Cmd 5726.

[136] Joint Memorandum submitted by the Egyptian and British Governments to the Italian Government, 25 March 1939, enclosed in Halifax to Pearth, 13 February 1939, FO 371/23373.

[137] Loraine to Halifax, 22 August 1939, transmitting Italian *aide-mémoire* of 10 August 1939, FO 371/23374.

[138] Joint Memorandum by the Foreign and Colonial Secretaries (n 134 above).

[139] Memorandum on the Delimitation of Sudan Boundaries (n 115 above).

[140] Summary of the controversy regarding the interpretation of the Annex to Article 11 of the Anglo-Egyptian Treaty of Alliance, 1936, regarding the right of the Sudan to attend international conferences, August 1951, FO 371/90126.

Theoretically he should consult neither or else both but, again unofficially and under the counter, there was the same never-to-be-admitted consultation of a secret nature with His Majesty's Government'.[141]

Thus, to resolve local problems, the Governor-General negotiated bilateral agreements with neighbouring colonial governors on matters of *bon voisinage*.[142] To give some examples: on 16 April 1901 delegates of the Governments of the Sudan and Eritrea signed an agreement regarding the alignment of the boundary from Sabderat to Todluc;[143] in 1902 the Egyptian and Sudan Governments reached an arrangement as to the Reciprocal Service of Process and Surrender of or Execution of Sentences against Fugitive Offenders;[144] on 12 December 1924 the Acting Governor-General of the Sudan, Wasey Sterry, and the Governor of Eritrea exchanged notes regarding the Utilization of the Waters of the Rivers Gash and Setit;[145] in February 1926 an agreement was concluded between the Governor-General of the Sudan and a representative of the King of Hejaz and Eastern Telegraph Company to work Port Sudan-Jeddah Cable;[146] and on 12 February 1935 delegates of the Governments of the Sudan and Abyssinia signed an Agreement concerning the payment of compensation for certain frontier raids and confirmation of a certain sector of the frontier between the two countries.[147]

As we shall see below, the Annex to Article 11 of the Anglo-Egyptian Treaty of 1936, did not contain any provision on the competence of the Governor-General to conclude bilateral agreements. However, in the post-Treaty era there had been a modification of the British view regarding the conclusion of bilateral agreements by the Governor-General or his delegates. Thus, because of the changed circumstances, namely the Italian annexation of Ethiopia and the relations between the Sudan and the Egyptian Governments arising out the 1936 Treaty, the British Government directed that any question concerning frontier delimitation, or even confirmation of existing frontiers, should be dealt with between the British and Egyptian Governments on the one hand and the Government of the colonial power concerned on the other.[148] That instruction was followed by concluding the Anglo-Italian Agreement of 16 April 1938, referred to in the section above.

A further post-Treaty development was the British trend to associate the Egyptian Government with the exercise by the Governor-General of the power to conclude *bon voisinage* agreements falling short of frontier

141 Quoted ibid.

142 Chancery, Cairo, to Secretariat, Khartoum, 31 August 1937, FO 371/20913. Also Lampson to Halifax, 31 May 1938, FO 371/22002.

143 Hertslet (n 112 above) No 343, 1115.

144 *Sudan Gazette*, No 37 of July 1902.

145 British and Foreign State Papers, vol 121, 798. The notes were subsequently approved by other notes exchanged in Rome on 12–15 June 1925, between the British and Italian Governments.

146 Referred to in Annex IV to the Memorandum on the Postal Status of the Sudan, enclosed in Governor-General to the British Ambassador, Cairo, 29 January 1938, FO 371/22001.

147 Text in FO 371/19182, enclosed in Sudan's Legal Secretary to the British Minister, Addis Ababa, 26 February 1935.

148 Chancery, Cairo, to Secretariat, Khartoum, 31 August 1937, FO 371/20913.

agreements. That trend was presumably explicable by reference to the British resolve to obviate any hindrance to a successful conclusion of the general negotiations with the Egyptian Government regarding the participation of the Sudan in international conferences and conventions.[149] Thus, following the decision in 1938 to resume the negotiations for the establishment of direct wireless communication between the Sudan and French Equatorial Africa, the approval of the Egyptian Government was sought. In the event, the Egyptian Government did not reply. Nonetheless, when the agreement was concluded Khartoum was directed to send a copy thereof to the President of the Egyptian Council of Ministers in the same way as Sudan ordinances were communicated.[150]

In 1946 the question arose of whether the Sudan Government could conclude bilateral air agreements. Beckett remarked that civil aviation agreements were not agreements which governors of colonies could conclude for themselves. But he admitted that to adopt the alternative view of saying that such agreements must be made by the *co-domini* would be intolerably difficult and slow. He therefore advised that the Sudan should make those agreements, but they should be done in the most informal way possible between an official representing the Governor-General and some appropriate official of the foreign government concerned.[151]

IX. Adherence to Multilateral Agreements and Representation at Conferences

A. The pre-1936 Treaty position

According to British records, up to 1924 the Sudan had never been represented separately at international conferences and there was no instance of accession of the Sudan to international instruments.[152] The British Government realized that in view of the status of the Sudan as a condominium, it was not possible to extend international conventions to the Sudan in the same manner as they were extended to the British colonies and protectorates, by actions under the colonial articles of such conventions. Similar reasoning also led to the conclusion that such conventions could not be extended to the Sudan as a colony or protectorate of Egypt.[153]

In January 1925 the Foreign Secretary, Austen Chamberlain, adopted a solution for the position of the Sudan in regard to international

[149] Civil Secretary to British Ambassador, Cairo, 14 May 1938, Lampson to Halifax, 31 May 1938, Kelly, Foreign Office, to Lampson, 24 June 1938, and Lampson to Acting Governor-General, Khartoum, 11 July 1938, FO 371/22002.

[150] Lampson to Symes, 12 January 1939, and Lampson to Foreign Office, 30 November 1939, transmitting copies of the Agreement and a reply to Khartoum, FO 371/23361.

[151] Summary of the controversy regarding the interpretation of the Annex to Article 11 of the 1936 Treaty (n 140 above).

[152] The Technical Status of the Sudan, 6 March 1924, FO 371/10057.

[153] Foreign Office to Law Officers of the Crown, 12 April 1932 (n 22 above).

agreements and conferences which rested on a principle defined by Cecil Hurst. Hurst considered that just as in the case of the Sudan Defence Force the Governor-General had been regarded as the embodiment of the condominium, so in the case of representation at international conferences and the signature and ratification of international agreements, or the accession to such agreements where that was possible, the Governor-General should be regarded as the embodiment of that 'new, separate and independent state' which the Egyptian Courts had regarded the Sudan as constituting.[154]

Chamberlain left it to the British High Commissioner in Cairo, Allenby, to decide on the manner in which the principle laid down for the representation of the Sudan in international conferences and adherence to international agreements should be made known to the Egyptian Government.[155] Allenby, however, expressed the view that it would be preferable not to make any direct notification to the Egyptian Government at that stage, but tacitly to assume the right of the Sudan Government to be represented at some particular conference and to ratify the subsequent agreement, if any, independently.[156]

The first opportunity to establish the British principle regarding the adherence of the Sudan to international agreements came about in connection with the second Opium Convention, which was adopted in February 1925 and was open for signature until 30 September 1925. The Sudan was among the 'states' which were not members of the League of Nations and were not represented at the second Opium Conference, to whom the Secretary-General of the League was authorized by the Council of the League to make the necessary communications so as to enable their competent authorities to sign or to accede to the Convention.[157] The Sudan's Legal Secretary, Wasey Sterry, had been furnished with full powers by the Governor-General to sign the Convention on behalf of the Sudan.[158]

The General Sanitary Convention of 1926 was also signed by delegates acting under full powers issued by the Governor-General, and was ratified by an instrument signed by the Governor-General. In the list of the Heads of the State in the preamble to the Convention 'the Governor-General representing the sovereign authority of the Sudan' appeared alongside the King of Great Britain and the President of the French Republic.[159]

The Egyptian Government was not apprised beforehand of the intention of the Sudan to sign, to ratify, or accede to an international agreement.

[154] Austen Chamberlain to Allenby, 22 January 1925. Hurst's Opinion dated 16 January 1925 was Enclosure 1 in Chamberlain's dispatch, FO 371/10883.

[155] ibid.

[156] Allenby to Chamberlain, 11 March 1925, ibid.

[157] Allenby to Chamberlain, 27 March 1925, and the Annexes to Enclosure 1 of the dispatch, ibid.

[158] Allenby to Foreign Office, 5 May 1925, transmitting copy of Khartoum's dispatch of 26 April 1925, FO 371/10884.

[159] Foreign Office to Law Officers of the Crown, 12 April 1932 (n 22 above).

In December 1931 the Foreign Office and the Cairo High Commission concluded that the Egyptian Government should be notified, after the event, when the Sudan had ratified or acceded to an international agreement except in cases where it was considered that such notification would be undesirable.[160] However, in the case of the Opium Convention, the Egyptian Government was informed by its representative in Geneva of the decision of the Council of the League of Nations to include the Sudan among the countries invited to sign or accede to the Convention. The Egyptian Prime Minister, Ahmed Ziwar Pasha, transmitted to Allenby, informally, three Egyptian documents raising the question of the right of the Sudan to adhere independently to international conventions and setting out Egyptian reserves in respect of the invitation addressed to the Sudan to sign or to accede to the Opium Convention. One of those documents was a draft of instructions to be sent to the Egyptian representative in Geneva to protest the action of the League of Nations on the basis of the 1899 Agreement and the Declaration of the Independence of Egypt of 28 February 1922 which provided for maintaining the *status quo* in respect of the Sudan. Allenby was, however, able to persuade Ziwar to defer sending the instructions until the receipt of a statement of the views of the British Government on the question.[161]

The ratification by the Sudan of the International Convention for the Preservation of the Fauna and Flora of 8 November 1933 marked the first instance of the Egyptian Government formally expressing to the British Government in writing its reservations regarding the participation of the Sudan in international conferences and its adherence to international conventions.[162] In response, the British Government contended that the method by which the Sudan adhered to international conventions through the Governor-General was fully consistent with the legal position as established by the Condominium Agreement, and that it should continue until some other procedure was substituted for it by agreement between the British and Egyptian Governments.[163] As we shall see, that other procedure was provided for by the Annex to Article 11 of the Anglo-Egyptian Treaty of 1936.

B. *The post-1936 Treaty position*

The adherence of the Sudan to international conventions was dealt with in the Annex to Article 11 of the 1936 Anglo-Egyptian Treaty. According to Paragraph 1 of the Annex, international conventions should become

[160] High Commissioner, Cairo, to Foreign Office, 19 December 1931, and Foreign Office to Cairo, 31 December 1931, FO 371/15426.

[161] The Egyptian documents were enclosed in Allenby to Austen Chamberlain, 14 June 1925, FO 371/10884.

[162] The Egyptian Note containing the reserves dated 13 January 1936, was enclosed in Lampson to Eden, 11 February 1936, FO 371/20099.

[163] Foreign Office to Lampson, 23 April 1936, ibid.

applicable to the Sudan by the joint action of the Governments of Great Britain and Egypt: such joint action should similarly be required if it was desired to terminate the participation of the Sudan in an international convention which already applied to it.

According to Paragraph 2, conventions to which it would be desirable that the Sudan should be a party would generally be conventions of a technical or humanitarian character; as such conventions invariably contain a provision for subsequent accession, that method would be adopted to make the convention applicable to the Sudan. Accession would be effected by a joint instrument signed on behalf of Egypt and Britain Kingdom by two persons duly authorized. The method of depositing the instruments of accession would be agreed upon in each case between the two Governments. If the convention did not contain an accession clause and it was desired to apply the convention to the Sudan, the method to effect that should be the subject of consultation and agreement between the two Governments.

Under Paragraph 3, if the Sudan was already a party to a convention and it was desired to terminate the participation of the Sudan, the necessary notice of termination would be given jointly by Britain and Egypt. Paragraph 4 stated that the participation of the Sudan in a convention and the termination of its participation could only be effected by joint action specifically taken in respect of the Sudan and would not follow merely from the fact that Britain and Egypt were both parties to the convention or had denounced it. Paragraph 5 provided that at international conferences where conventions were negotiated, the Egyptian and Britain delegates would keep in touch with a view to any action which they might agree to be desirable in the interests of the Sudan.[164]

No sooner had the 1936 Treaty been concluded than a divergence of opinion arose between the two *co-domini* on the interpretation and implementation of the Annex to Article 11, in particular regarding the representation of the Sudan at international conferences. For whereas the Annex laid down the procedure for participation of the Sudan in international conventions, it made no reference to the participation of the Sudan at international conferences. The divergence of opinion lingered on until the winding-up of the condominium. It led to each case of Sudan representation at conferences being settled on an *ad hoc* basis.

The British proposals in respect of the implementation of the Annex to Article 11 were communicated semi-officially in August 1937 to Egypt's Acting Minister for Foreign Affairs.[165] It was proposed by the British Government that in the case of international conventions containing a provision for subsequent accession, the instrument of accession should be prepared by the Sudan Government and forwarded by the

[164] For the Source of the text of the 1936 Treaty, see n 3 above.

[165] Lampson to Eden, 28 January 1938, FO 371/22001.

Governor-General to the Egyptian Minister for Foreign Affairs for signature on behalf of the Egyptian Government. The latter would then forward the instrument through the British Embassy in Cairo for communication to the British Foreign Secretary for signature on behalf of the British Government. It was further proposed, as a general rule, that when it was a foreign government which convened the conference the instrument should eventually be deposited, on behalf of the Sudan Government, by the British Government.[166] But in the case where the convention was signed at a conference convened by the League of Nations, it was suggested that it would be more convenient that the instrument when signed should be returned to the Sudan Government which would communicate it direct to the League of Nations for deposit, since the Sudan Government was already in direct communication with the League of Nations' Secretariat on routine matters.[167] Indeed, the Sudan Government itself pressed hard for maintaining the pre-Treaty practice of communicating direct with the Secretariat of the League. The Governor-General pointed out that it would be 'an intolerable encumbrance if every report, say of a drug seizure in Honolulu, had to be transmitted through His Majesty's Government and the Egyptian Government channels'.[168]

In the case of international conventions where there was no provision for subsequent accession, it was proposed by the British Government that a joint declaration should be made at the conference by the British and Egyptian delegations after prior consultation with the Sudan Government or the Governor-General's representatives at the conference. After such consultation, the convention would be signed on behalf of the Sudan Government by both the British and the Egyptian delegations. If only one delegation was present, the required declaration would be made by that delegation after consultation and with the consent of the Government not represented, and also after prior consultation with the Sudan Government.[169]

As for representation of the Sudan at international conferences, it was proposed by the British Government to distinguish between diplomatic and non-diplomatic or purely scientific conferences. At diplomatic conferences where legally binding conventions were drawn up, the Sudan could not be separately represented. It was therefore proposed that the representatives of the Sudan should be attached to the British and Egyptian delegations, if both delegations were present at the conference, or to one of them if only one was present. At non-diplomatic conferences where no legally binding conventions were drawn up but only documents embodying the conclusions of the conference, the British Government

[166] Memorandum dated 14 January 1938, to the Egyptian Government regarding the implementation of the Annex to Art 11 of the 1936 Treaty, ibid.

[167] ibid.

[168] Stewart Symes to British Ambassador, Cairo, 2 June 1938, FO 371/22002.

[169] Proposals for Implementing the Annex of Art 11 of the 1936 Treaty, FO 371/22001.

suggested that it would be more convenient for the Sudan Government to be separately represented by their experts than for those experts to be attached to British and Egyptian delegations.[170]

In a lengthy *aide-mémoire* dated March 1938, the Egyptian Government cited the 1899 Agreement and the last paragraph of Article 11 of the 1936 Treaty and contended that Sudan itself was incapable of being a party to an international convention, even if its adherence was effected by a joint instrument of the two *co-domini*. To substantiate that contention, reliance was placed on Paragraph 4 of the Annex and on certain phrases used in Paragraphs 1 and 2 respectively, namely 'shall only become applicable' and 'making the convention applicable'. The proposed distinction between diplomatic and purely scientific conferences found no favour with the Egyptian Government. It claimed that the distinction could not be justified and that there was even more reason for excluding separate representation for the Sudan in these comparatively unimportant scientific meetings than at diplomatic conferences.

On the basis of the views set out in the *aide-mémoire*, the Egyptian Government endorsed the British proposal for accession of the Sudan to the 1936 Convention for the Suppression of Illicit Traffic in Dangerous Drugs and the Protocol of Signature of the Convention. But it rejected the proposal that the Sudan Government should deposit the instrument of accession to the Convention with the Secretariat of the League of Nations. The Egyptian Government argued that as the Sudan was neither an autonomous state nor a member of the League of Nations, it had no right to communicate directly with the League even on routine matters, and in particular had no right to deposit an instrument of accession. It also responded negatively to the British proposal of separate representation of the Sudan at the International Leprosy Conference to be held in Cairo on 21 March 1938 under the auspices of the International Leprosy Society. According to the British Government, the Conference fell into the category of non-diplomatic conferences. The Egyptian Government acknowledged that the conference was not concerned with the negotiation of a convention, but merely with technical steps with a view to international action. Nevertheless, it supported following the procedure laid down in the Annex to Article 11. Accordingly, the Governor-General should communicate to the *co-domini* the observations and proposals which he thought desirable to put forward in the interests of the Sudan at the conference.[171]

The Foreign Office contested the Egyptian viewpoint on three counts. First, Paragraph 2 of the Annex to Article 11 used the words 'accession' and 'instrument of accession' because the appropriate words for a territory

[170] ibid, and the Memorandum of 14 January 1938 (n 166 above).

[171] The French text of the Egyptian *aide-mémoire* is in FO 371/22001. See also Egyptian Note of 2 December 1937 regarding representation of the Sudan at the International Leprosy Conference, enclosed in Lampson to Eden, 28 January 1938, ibid.

participating under a colonial article were 'extension' and 'notification of extension'. Secondly, it stressed the provision at the end of Paragraph 4 of the Annex that the termination of a convention in respect of the Sudan would not follow from the fact that the United Kingdom and Egypt had both denounced the convention, whereas a colonial territory could not remain bound by a convention when its metropolitan state was no longer bound. Thirdly, the Annex to Article 11 clearly envisaged that the Sudan should participate in conventions as an independent country.[172]

Given the absence of agreement or principle to be adapted, the differing views of the *co-domini* led to decisions on representation of the Sudan at international conferences being taken on an *ad hoc* basis. The differences were aggravated further when, in September 1947, the proceedings at Lake Success ended in deadlock and the Security Council adjourned *sine die* consideration of the Anglo-Egyptian dispute. By this stage the Egyptian Government had adopted a policy of non-recognition of the Condominium Agreements and of claiming that the Sudan was an integral part of Egypt.[173]

Beckett rightly noted that the line which had been taken with respect to the Sudan in international affairs had been largely empirical, depending on the state of Anglo-Egyptian relations with regard to the Sudan at the time in question.[174] Thus in March 1948, when the constitutional reforms in the Sudan were under consideration by the *co-domini*, the British Government decided to modify their policy of ignoring the Egyptian objections to separate representation of the Sudan at non-diplomatic conferences. The new policy was expressed in the following formula: 'At non-diplomatic conferences, i.e. conferences at which no treaties for signature are drawn up and at which colonies are represented by delegations separate from those of their metropolitan countries, the Sudan should be entitled to separate representation provided that her co-domini agree on this method of representation.'[175]

The new formula marked a clear reversal of the British policy, adopted since 1938, pursuant to which the Sudan was entitled to separate representation at non-diplomatic conferences without reference to the *co-domini*. It was argued in support of the new formula that a colony could not participate in a non-diplomatic conference without reference to its metropolitan country and that participation without reference to the *co-domini* would go beyond the powers of the Governor-General, which did not extend to foreign affairs.[176]

It was, however, expected that the new formula coupled with Egypt's policy of non-recognition of the Condominium Agreements would bar the representation of the Sudan at all kinds of conferences. Thus, it

[172] Bentinck to Lampson, 9 June 1938 (n 11 above).

[173] Summary of the controversy regarding the interpretation of the Annex to Art 11 of the 1936 Treaty (n 140 above).

[174] Minute dated 11 June 1948, FO 371/69245.

[175] Lascelles to Speaight, Cairo, 8 March 1948, ibid.

[176] Lascelles to Speaight 5 April 1948, ibid.

would be virtually impossible for the Sudan to be represented at diplomatic conferences because the Egyptian Government would not invoke or accept the invocation of the relevant provisions of the Annex to Article 11 for that would be tantamount to an implied admission of the continued validity of the Condominium Agreements. As for non-diplomatic conferences where the Egyptians were represented, they would always insist that the Sudan representatives should be attached to the Egyptian delegation, and the British Government would never agree.[177]

The new formula provoked strong protests from the Sudan Government. The Governor-General regarded the new formula as a very serious inroad upon the position established by a large number of precedents, thus reducing the Sudan in practice to a status lower than that of non-self governing territories. He also stated that to retreat from that position would constitute a severe blow to the material interests of the Sudan.[178] The Civil Secretary, James Robertson, was also very critical of the new formula and strongly urged its reconsideration. He said that the 1899 Agreement and the 1936 Treaty were so brief and obscure about the Sudan's position with regard to international conferences that the actual practice which had been followed under them was of very great importance in arguing their meaning. He explained that practice in the following words: 'For the past 11 years the uninterrupted practice has been to send separate Sudan representatives to non-diplomatic conferences without asking the consent of the co-domini. We see no reason why we should abandon this strong position, particularly when to do so would make it virtually impossible thereafter for the Sudan to participate in such conferences.'[179]

The new formula was short-lived. Several months later, the original formula adopted in 1938 was reinstated. The Foreign Office wrote to the Governor-General in May 1948:

> ... we do fully realize the practical importance of proper representation of the Sudan at non-diplomatic conferences which, as a result of the present Egyptian attitude on the Sudanese question, would be impossible if this representation was dependent on the consent of the Egyptian Government. We have therefore decided that, in principle, the Sudan should be separately represented at non-diplomatic conferences as heretofore, i.e. without prior agreement of both co-domini, until, or unless, one of these conferences refuses to allow the separate representation of the Sudan.[180]

The Foreign Office then struck the following note of caution: 'On occasions circumstances might arise where our support to separate representation of the Sudan might conflict with questions of wider policy regarding Egypt and the Sudan. In such a case we might have to trim our sails.'[181]

[177] Memorandum dated 2 April 1948, on the representation of the Sudan at international conferences and the application to the Sudan of international agreements, ibid.

[178] Howe to Sargent, 10 April 1948, ibid.

[179] Robertson to Speaight, 26 April 1948, ibid.

[180] Sargent to Howe, 10 May 1948, ibid.

[181] ibid.

The promulgation in June 1948 of the Executive Council and Legislative Assembly Ordinance posed the question of whether this would produce alterations in the conduct of the international relations of the Sudan. Although under the Ordinance foreign relations was a reserved subject, the Sudan Government thought that since the establishment of the Legislative Assembly progressed the Sudan towards self-government, the *co-domini* should come out in favour of the separate representation of the Sudan at conferences.[182]

Beckett seemed to have been sympathetic to this view. Though admitting that foreign relations fell outside the purview of the Legislative Assembly, he argued that it would not always be possible to draw a clear line between internal and international affairs. By achieving a measure of self-government, the Sudanese themselves might be expected soon to resent being kept out of technical conferences, and if Egypt opposed the appearance of Sudanese at appropriate conferences, it might come to realize that this would not help the Egyptian cause in the Sudan. Beckett revealed that:

> Hitherto representation of the Sudan at international conferences has taken the form of the appearance there of some impeccably English-looking officials, who almost always agreed entirely with the views of the U.K. delegation. It is not surprising, therefore that when in the period prior to 1936, we were pushing the Sudan representation at international conferences very far, other delegations considered it to be an entirely phoney affair and, apart from legal considerations were opposed to it. Now, it may well be that amongst a Sudan delegation there will be some tall, very dark looking men, and it will look different.[183]

It was eventually decided at the Foreign Office that the Anglo-Egyptian relations should not be jeopardized and the Sudan Government was advised to discourage the Sudanese from pressing for the time being the question of separate representation at conferences.[184]

The British records refer to two conferences in 1949 when the condominium arrangement was followed and the representation of the Sudan acquired the joint approval of the *co-domini*. The two conferences concerned were the International Health Office Conference held in Cairo in 1949 and the meeting of the International Civil Aviation Organization in London in the summer of the same year. Both conferences were characterized as diplomatic and the Sudan was represented by expert advisers at the disposal of the British and Egyptian delegations.[185]

It is not possible to canvass here all of the instances where the Egyptian Government objected to the separate representation of the Sudan at technical or non-diplomatic conferences. Suffice it to give some examples. The so-called 'Africa Conference' was convened by the British Colonial

[182] Summary of the controversy regarding the interpretation of the Annex to Art 11 (n 140 above).

[183] Minute dated 22 June 1948, FO 371/69245.

[184] Summary of the controversy regarding the interpretation of the Annex to Art 11 (n 140 above).

[185] ibid.

Office in September 1948 to discuss general questions of colonial administration. The conference was attended by delegates of British colonial territories in East, Central, and West Africa. The French, Belgian, and Portuguese Governments were invited to send observers. The Foreign Office agreed that the Sudan should send observers too. The Egyptian Government protested. The British Government explained that the Sudan was invited because it had common frontiers with Kenya and Uganda and therefore an interest in the business of the conference.[186]

The Egyptian Government was unimpressed by the British explanation. It was contended in the Egyptian reply that the Sudan could in no respect be considered as a non-self-governing territory within the meaning of Chapter XI of the United Nations Charter, and that it constituted an integral part of Egypt to which it was united by close bonds of language, religion, and race and with which it formed a complete geographical entity. It was further contended that the regime of the Sudan did not create for it any international legal status to permit any participation in any type of international conference or committee whether the conferences or committees were political or otherwise, and whether its representation thereon was by delegates or observers. In the event, the British Government ignored the Egyptian objection and the Sudan observers did attend the conference.[187]

The International Cotton Advisory Committee could be cited as another example. The Sudan was a separate and full member of the Committee since its inception in 1939 and had remained such, receiving the usual invitations to attend subsequent meetings. The Committee was a technical and non-diplomatic body.[188] The Egyptian Government raised no objections to the membership of the Sudan until the Committee's meeting of 1947, where the Sudan was separately represented. The Egyptian Government then declared that the 'Sudan administration' was not entitled to direct contact with international organizations. The British representative stated that the Sudan was independently represented before the war on the body to which the Committee was a successor and that the Egyptian Government could not take unilateral action in the matter.[189] The meeting supported the British view and adopted the following motion by eleven votes to one:

> The Committee notes the objections raised by Egypt to the membership of the Sudan, but agrees that the *status quo* be continued and the Sudan contribution be accepted for the present without prejudice to the final outcome of the general discussion of the issue between Egypt and the United Kingdom and its effect on the Sudan's status and its membership of the International Cotton Advisory Committee.[190]

186 ibid. 187 ibid.

188 Governor-General to Nokrashi, 22 February 1949, FO 371/69245.

189 Summary of the controversy regarding the interpretation of the Annex to Article 11 (n 140 above). 190 Quoted in Governor-General to Nokrashi (n 188 above).

Because of the Egyptian objection, the Sudan was not represented at the annual meetings of the Committee during the period 1949–53. Each year the Egyptian Government insisted on the attachment of the representative of the Sudan to the Egyptian delegation. But the Sudan Government considered that incompatible with the Sudan's status of full membership, and with the nature of the Committee whose functions were by definition advisory and whose decisions were not binding.[191]

The matter arose once more in 1953, when the Sudan Government received an invitation to be represented at the second session of the 12th Plenary Meeting of the Cotton Committee to be held in Washington, DC. The Sudan Government accordingly notified the *co-domini* that the Sudan would attend the meeting in its capacity as a full member and that it would be represented by the chairman and managing director of the Sudan Gezira Board. The Egyptian Government objected to the separate representation of the Sudan and criticized the choice of delegates. The Sudan Government, on the other hand, adduced a number of reasons in support of the separate representation of the Sudan. They argued that it was unsatisfactory for the Sudan to be represented by the *co-domini* who had conflicting interests, one as a consumer and the other as a producer of the Sudan's main product and its main competitor. It was further argued that since the whole object of the Anglo-Egyptian Agreement of February 1953 was to enable the Sudanese to advance further towards responsible government and self-determination, it would be inconsistent with that object if the Sudan should become more dependent than before as a result of the Agreement.[192]

The question of representation of the Sudan at international conferences and organizations was eventually settled during the transitional period, which began in January 1954. The newly constituted Sudanese Council of Ministers was then called upon to decide on certain matters of external relations of immediate importance. They included an invitation from the Food and Agriculture Organization to nominate a representative to the Co-ordinating Committee for Desert Locust Control, membership of the International Committee on Irrigation and Drainage, and separate associate membership of the World Health Organization.[193]

On the basis of a note dated February 1954 submitted by the Governor-General's Office, the Sudanese Council of Ministers adopted Resolution 56, which incorporated *in toto* the British point of view. The terms of the resolution were as follows:

(a) The Sudan should endeavour to seek associate membership in international diplomatic organizations like the World Health Organization which usually discuss subjects concerning the Sudan and membership

[191] William Luce, Khartoum, to Boothby, Foreign Office, 2 February 1954, transmitting a draft note it was proposed to submit to the Council of Ministers on the question of the representation of the Sudan at conferences, FO 371/108585.

[192] ibid.

[193] ibid.

of which was enjoyed by the countries which were not responsible for the administration of their external affairs. The Sudan would thus be able to attend as an independent member.

(b) In the case of international diplomatic conferences where the Sudan was not an associate member, Sudanese representatives should attend as advisers to the delegations of both the British and Egyptian Governments.

(c) If the Sudan was invited to attend international conferences of a purely technical nature or of non-diplomatic organizations (including conferences where the Sudan acquired independent membership), the Sudan would have the right to send independent representatives.

(d) If the Sudan was invited by a British or an Egyptian Department, for instance, the British Colonial Office or the Egyptian Ministry for Social Affairs, the Sudan would send independent observers.

The Council further decided that all Sudan representatives should be Sudanese but could be accompanied by expatriate advisers.[194] William Luce, the Adviser to the Governor-General on Constitutional and External Affairs, described Resolution 56 as satisfactory and noted that it accepted in full the policy proposed by the British Government.[195]

Concluding Observations

For textbook writers the Sudan and the New Hebrides Islands are the favoured historical examples of condominiums. Research into the British records of the Anglo-Egyptian condominium over the Sudan did not, however, support the view that this was a typical example of a 'successful' condominium. The faltering of the condominium of the Sudan cannot be attributed to inherent defects in the concept of condominium as such, but rather to the unfettered British administrative and legislative predominance in the Sudan, the relentless Egyptian refusal to acknowledge the existence of the condominium and the entanglement of the Sudan in the wider and delicate fabric of Anglo-Egyptian relations.

If the exercise of joint governance on the basis of equality is indeed the principal characteristic of a condominium, on this score the condominium of the Sudan was a total failure. Egypt never enjoyed an equal share in the administration of the Sudan, with the result that the government of the country was as much under the control of the British Government as was that of any colony. The successive British Governors-General were, with the backing of the Foreign Office, instrumental in this respect. Instead of

194 Luce to Boothby, 1 May 1954, ibid.

195 ibid. For historical reasons the principle enunciated by Cecil Hurst was not applied in the case of postal and telecommunications conferences. The Sudan was technically regarded as the third postal region of Egypt and consequently the signature by Egypt of postal and telecommunications conventions had been held to cover the Sudan. See Memorandum on the Postal Status of the Sudan, (n 146 above).

exercising their delegated administrative and legislative powers as agents of the two *co-domini*, they were styled by the Foreign Office as 'absolute autocrats'[196] wielding unlimited power. On more than one occasion they introduced major constitutional reforms in the Government of the Sudan and either did not involve the other *co-dominus*, Egypt, in the reforms or overlooked its objections to them. Furthermore, on the analogy of the powers of the governors of British colonies, the British Government unilaterally invested the Governor-General of the Sudan with the power to conclude bilateral agreements on matters of *bon voisinage* of the same kind as a governor of a British colony would conclude with neighbouring territories.

The history of the condominium of the Sudan recorded only two substantive matters in respect of which a real measure of equality between the two *co-domini* was observed, namely the alienation of condominium territory and the dismantling of the condominium. Thus, for instance, the consent of the Egyptian Government was sought and obtained for territorial concessions to be made to Emperor Menelek of Ethiopia in exchange for an assurance that the waters of Lake Tana would not fall into the hands of a private company. Egypt was also a party to the notes exchanged with the Italian Government in Rome in 1934 to sanction the cession of the Sarra Triangle to Libya. Moreover, the Egyptian Government was actively associated with the liquidation of the condominium under the terms of the Anglo-Egyptian Agreement of February 1953 concerning Self-government and Self-determination for the Sudan.[197]

The status of the Sudan as a condominium was at times used by the British administration in the Sudan as an excuse for not embarking on politically undesirable measures. The proposal for the promulgation of a nationality law and the accrediting of foreign consuls to the Sudan were cases in point. In the 1940s nationality was a politically charged issue in the Sudan. The promulgation of a nationality law would have identified the British administration with Sudanese political factions who were ill-disposed towards the Egyptian cause in the Sudan and who formed the majority of the membership of the Advisory Council. On the other hand, for almost half a century the status of the Sudan and the allied technical difficulty of who should issue *exequaturs* had been the standard official justification for not allowing foreign consuls in the Sudan. But it was generally believed that the underlying reason was the reluctance of the British administration in the Sudan to expose the affairs of the country to any form of international scrutiny.

Whereas for the purposes of internal administration the Sudan was run by the Foreign Office as a colony, the British Government unilaterally built up for the Sudan a position as an independent state for the

[196] This description of the Governors-General was used by Beckett: see Beckett to Carter, 1 January 1943 (n 11 above).

[197] See n 103 above.

purposes of participation in international agreements and representation at international conferences. It was claimed that there were no other practical means for arranging for the Sudan to participate or to be represented. Up to 1924 the Sudan had never been separately represented at international conferences and there was no instance of accession by the Sudan to international instruments.

The legal basis for the British action was a benevolent interpretation of the Judgment of the Egyptian Mixed Tribunal in the *Bencini and Quistas* case. It was asserted that for the purposes of representation at conferences and participation in international agreements, the Governor-General should be considered the embodiment of that new, separate, and independent state which the Egyptian Tribunal regarded the Sudan as being. Pursuant to that legal fiction of independence, the Governor-General became a virtual head of a state, albeit a state *sui generis*. Thus, acting under full powers emanating from the Governor-General, the Sudan delegates signed, ratified, and acceded to international agreements. The decade of the legal fiction of independence (1925–36) became the most productive in terms of treaty participation. Eight agreements, conventions, and protocols became applicable to the Sudan, which came to be acknowledged as a separate entity on many technical matters like sanitation, the white slave traffic, whaling, narcotic drugs, and the protection of fauna and flora.[198] The legal fiction of independence also qualified the Sudan to initiate a direct channel of communication with the League of Nations' Secretariat on routine matters. One hardly needs to add that as far as the international relations of the Sudan were concerned, the condominium was practically in abeyance during this decade.

The Annex to Article 11 of the 1936 Anglo-Egyptian Treaty put an end to the legal fiction of independence. The Annex marked the first occasion on which the *co-domini* agreed on a procedure for the participation of the Sudan in international conventions. It required joint action for the participation of the Sudan in international conventions and for the termination of the application of international conventions to the Sudan. Had the procedure set out in the Annex been implemented, it would have accorded admirably with the status of the Sudan as a condominium. But no sooner had the 1936 Treaty been concluded than a wide divergence of opinion cropped up between the *co-domini* regarding the interpretation and implementation of the Annex. While admitting that joint action was required, the British Government held the view that the Annex envisaged the Sudan participating in international agreements as a separate entity. On the other hand, the Egyptian Government contended that the Sudan was incapable of being a party to international agreements even if its adherence was effected by a joint instrument of the *co-domini*. The Egyptian Government also declined to contemplate the

[198] For a list of the instruments made applicable to the Sudan see FO 371/119630, Chancery, Khartoum to African department, Foreign Office, 15 June 1956.

British proposal that the Sudan should be represented separately at non-diplomatic conferences. The intransigent attitude of the Egyptian Government was prompted by its non-recognition of the condominium status of the Sudan and its claim that the Sudan was an integral part of metropolitan Egypt. Thus, the international relations of the Sudan were drastically curtailed during the period 1936–54. The *co-domini* agreed in principle in 1938 to the accession of the Sudan to the 1936 Convention for the Suppression of the Illicit Traffic in Dangerous Drugs, but Egypt rejected the British proposal that the Sudan Government should deposit the instrument of accession with the Secretariat of the League of Nations. Joint action was agreed upon in 1949 regarding participation in two conferences characterized as diplomatic: the conferences of the International Civil Aviation Organization and the International Health Office. In a limited number of non-diplomatic conferences, the British Government, acting unilaterally, secured separate representation for the Sudan. In 1949 the Egyptian Government rejected the British proposal to seek associate membership for the Sudan in the World Health Organization and the World Meteorological Organization.[199] In summary, for almost two decades, the discord between the *co-domini* regarding the interpretation and the implementation of the Annex to Article 11 of the 1936 Treaty denied the Sudan the benefits it would have reaped from international relations.

Whether the experience of the condominium of the Sudan casts doubt on the idea of condominium as a viable institution is debatable. No doubt the use of a condominium or some similar device may be valuable as an interim expedient pending final settlement for a disputed tract of territory. But the term 'condominium' is a recipe for disagreement, unless it is accompanied by a carefully drafted agreement negotiated between equal parties. The Anglo-Egyptian Sudan, it may be argued, worked as an institution only to the extent that the idea of a condominium was set aside.

[199] Summary of the controversy regarding the interpretation of the Annex to Art 11 (n 140 above).

THE SCIENCE OF INTERNATIONAL LAW AND THE CONCEPT OF POLITICS: THE ARGUMENTS AND LIVES OF THE INTERNATIONAL LAW PROFESSORS AT THE UNIVERSITY OF DORPAT/IUR'EV/TARTU 1855–1985

By Lauri Mälksoo*

1. Introduction

The central question of legal scholarship is a normative one: 'What is the law?' In order to answer it, legal scholars study and apply sources of law. But the question of what the law is can be approached from another perspective. We can also ask: 'What is it that lawyers do?'

We are accustomed to the fact that in legal disputes lawyers present arguments biased in favour of their clients. This is the bread and butter of practising lawyers and legal advisers. From legal scholars, however, we generally expect objectivity and neutrality, these being scientific. We expect them to write about *lex lata* 'the way it is'. The question is to what extent this is possible and realistic. What, in international law, are the criteria for 'objectively conducted' scholarship? Take for instance the famous debate between Hugo Grotius (1583–1645) and John Selden (1584–1654) about the freedom of navigation on the high seas, in which the Dutchman Grotius defended the interests of the Dutch East India Company and the Englishman Selden the position of the British Crown. Was their work scholarship or advocacy or both? To take another example, the first original work on international law in Russia was written in 1717 by Petr P Shafirov (1669–1739), *A Discourse Concerning the Just Causes of the War Between Russia and Sweden.* The title itself implied that Tsar Peter *had* just causes to go to war against Sweden (1700–21); the task was merely to present them. Peter the Great himself helped to set out the arguments in Shafirov's book.[1]

* Dr Lauri Mälksoo is Associate Professor of International and European Law at the Faculty of Law of the University of Tartu, Estonia. Many thanks to Professors Martti Koskenniemi and Benedict Kingsbury for their valuable guidance and support while carrying out this project. The inspiration and support given by these two professors has been crucial for this study. I am also indebted to history Professor Matti Klinge for his comments and to Professor James Crawford for his thorough editing and useful comments. The bulk of the study was written during my stay as Hauser Research Scholar at New York University School of Law in 2004–05. I would like to thank Rita Hauser for her generosity. Talks with Professor Joseph Weiler, Professor Mattias Kumm, Dr Simon Chesterman, Dr Piibe Jõgi, Dr Nico Krisch, and participants in NYU School of Law's colloquia have had a stimulating effect on this study. In Estonia, Professor Peeter Järvelaid, Professor Marju Luts, Kerli Valk, and Maarja Naagel have been very helpful. The responsibility for possible errors remains solely the author's.

[1] WE Butler, 'On the Origins of International Legal Science in Russia: The Role of P. P. Shafirov' (2002) 4 *Journal of the History of International Law* 1, 31. The book is also interesting in the context

The fundamental question that has troubled and fascinated scholars of international law at least since the nineteenth century is the relationship between the discipline of international law and the world of politics. Is international law a type of 'political' law? If yes, what does that mean? Can international law be, or can it be made autonomous of political influences, and if so how? Since at least John Austin (who argued that international law was only 'positive morality' and not 'law properly so called')[2] almost every significant international law scholar of the nineteenth and twentieth centuries has taken some stance on this question.

I suggest that the issue of the relationship between international law and politics is a paradigmatic one for the field of international law. The concept of paradigm has been elaborated in the writings of Thomas S Kuhn (1922–96) on the philosophy of science.[3] Kuhn argued that developed sciences were characterized by established paradigms, ie shared beliefs and consensual truths within scientific communities. Kuhn, who took the natural sciences as model sciences, did not clearly state whether the social sciences had yet achieved their own paradigms.[4] I would argue that in the discipline of international law, the emergence of paradigms has been dependent on the solutions given to the central question of its relationship to politics.

From the late nineteenth century, no school of thought has had as great an influence on theoreticians and practitioners of international law as positivism. Thanks to positivist theoreticians of the late nineteenth century, the emerging paradigm within the 'thought collective'[5] of international lawyers expressed both what the discipline was supposed to be about (the study of a body of objectively verifiable and legally binding norms) and what it was not and should not be about—namely, politics.[6] The separation of international law from politics was considered essential for both the relevance of international law to international relations and the seriousness of the academic discipline of international law.

of the present study since it laid out Russian claims over the Baltic provinces. Shafirov claimed that historically, 'the greater part of the Provinces of Livonia and Estonia were under the jurisdiction and protection of the Russian crown'. This was in his view evidenced, *inter alia*, by the fact that the 'city of Dorpat' was, 'according to the testimony of credible Russian chronicles', built in the year 1030 by a Russian grand prince Iuri and named after him. The city of Reval (Tallinn) likewise was built by a Russian grand prince 'who lived in ancient times'. Cited in Butler, 7.

[2] J Austin, *The Province of Jurisprudence Determined* (1832).

[3] TS Kuhn, *The Structure of Scientific Revolutions* (2nd edn, 1970).

[4] ibid 15. See also TS Kuhn, 'Second Thoughts on Paradigms', in Kuhn, *The Essential Tension: Selected Studies in Scientific Tradition and Change* (1977) 293–319.

[5] The notion of 'thought collective' strongly influenced Kuhn and was developed in L Fleck, *Genesis and Development of a Scientific Fact* (1979) (originally *Entstehung und Entwicklung einer wissenschaftlichen Tatsache: Einführung in die Lehre vom Denkstil und Denkkollektiv* (1935). Fleck wrote: 'Thought style of the thought collective undergoes social reinforcement that is subject to independent development for generations. It constrains the individual by determining "what can be thought in no other way".' ibid 99.

[6] See for the history of this argument, M Koskenniemi, *From Apology to Utopia: The Structure of International Legal Argument* (1989).

International politics was considered to be a field full of subjectivity, passion, discretion, irrationality, and power. The discipline of international law, in contrast, could be characterized by objectivity, rules, constraints to power, rationality, and progress. But within the discipline of international law, it remained unclear whether international law was supposed to be anti-political or only 'different from politics but still related to it'.

During the second half of the nineteenth century, two Baltic German international law professors at the University of Dorpat, August Bulmerincq and Carl Bergbohm, took up the issue of the separation of the discipline of international law from politics. They argued that the discipline of international law before them had failed to acquire its due respect, even among legal scholars, while writings in the field were too speculative, philosophical, and political. The work of Bulmerincq and Bergbohm contained a manifesto for the positivist and objective science of international law as a field separate from the subjective field of politics.

In this article, I look at the role of politics in the academic discipline of international law from the point of view of the history of the discipline. Specifically I will present a micro-history of the academic discipline of international law—a study of the arguments and lives of Bulmerincq, Bergbohm, and their successors to the chair of international law at the University of Dorpat/Iur'ev/Tartu. I will ask whether Bulmerincq and Bergbohm themselves lived up to their demand that the discipline of international law be separated from politics. What positions did their successors, Vladimir Hrabar, Ants Piip, and Abner Uustal, take on the question of international law and/versus politics? Furthermore, what became of the normative demand of Bulmerincq and Bergbohm? How did it play out historically?

The statement of the question in historical terms calls to mind the Newtonian metaphor of scholars 'standing on the shoulders of giants'.[7] The collective nature of scientific activity is undisputed.[8] Whether or not this is true of international law, in international law, too, successive generations of scholars have had to deal with questions and solutions presented by earlier generations. It is thus not surprising that since Bulmerincq, every international law professor at Dorpat/Iur'ev/Tartu has taken some position in response to his predecessor(s)—thus, *inter alia*, revealing something about his concept of politics in the discipline of international law. The scholars overtly or covertly engaged in an inter-generational debate over 'The Question'—the relationship between

[7] See RK Merton, *On the Shoulders of Giants: A Shandean Postscript*, with an afterword by Umberto Eco (1993). The book outlines the history and philosophy of Newton's famous metaphor 'if I have seen farther, it is by standing on the shoulders of giants'.

[8] But Bourdieu argues that to speak of a scientific field—a concept he developed and that will also be employed in the present article—is to break with the Mertonian idea that scientists form a unified, even homogeneous group. See P Bourdieu, *Science of Science and Reflexivity* (trans R Nice, 2004) 45. (French orig 2001.)

international law and politics. The deceased too appeared to be part of Oscar Schachter's 'invisible college of international lawyers'; they became consecutive runners in the 'torch run' (*Fackellauf*) of Norbert Elias.[9]

What do I mean by 'overtly or covertly'? To write a legal philosophical work on the very question of the relationship between international law and politics—as Bergbohm did, for example—is not the only way to engage with or be affected by the issue. Even though a legal scholar might not openly address the question in general terms, his or her way of formulating international legal arguments or practising international law may also reveal a concept of politics. No scholar can ignore the question of the relationship between international law and politics. For the discipline of international law, it remains the elephant that stands in the middle of the room.

Thus a study of the development of the concept of politics in international law scholarship should not be restricted to the arguments of scholars about the nature of international law. Often, approaches also become apparent when arguments are studied within the framework of international law or evaluated in the context of their formulation. Sometimes there is a possibility of self-delusion—ie while a scholar may think that his or her concept of politics is one thing, in the light of the practice and other arguments of this scholar, the concept may appear to be something else. As informative as the arguments themselves are the lives of the scholars, their activities beyond their scholarly work.

In fairness, I first need to indicate my own perspective on the issue. In 2002, I wrote a doctoral thesis on the international legal status of the three Baltic republics of Estonia, Latvia, and Lithuania, following the end of the Soviet occupation and restoration of their independence in 1991.[10] Subsequently, I returned to teach international law at my *alma mater*, Tartu University, Estonia. When I started to trace the history of international law scholarship in Tartu, a fact of which I had been unaware while writing my doctorate caught my attention. I learned that Tartu's international law professor during most of the Soviet era, Abner Uustal (1915–85), had argued against the position I held in my dissertation. In my dissertation, I had argued that due to the illegality of the Soviet occupation and annexation in 1940, the three Baltic republics had in effect maintained their continuity under international law until their restoration in 1991. Just about twenty years before, at a conference organized at Riga State University, Latvia, Uustal presented a paper in which he vehemently rejected the claims made by 'Baltic *emigrés*' concerning the continued legal existence of pre-World War II Estonia, Latvia, and Lithuania as subjects of international law.[11]

[9] See further N Elias, *Über den Prozess der Zivilisation* (The Civilizing Process) (1936).

[10] L Mälksoo, *Illegal Annexation and State Continuity: the Case of the Incorporation of the Baltic States by the USSR. A Study about the Tension between Normativity and Power in International Law* (2003).

[11] A Uustal, *Nesostojatelnost' 'teorii' liderov estonskih emigrantov o sustshestvovanii v nastojastshee vremja burzhuaznogo estonskogo gosudarstva, in: Burzhuaznaya pravovaja ideologia v Pribaltike v*

The methodological-philosophical question that haunted me was whether *any* stance on the contested status of the Baltic States in 1940–91 had in some sense to be 'political'. No one can say that it would not be appropriate for a lawyer to deal with the question. But it struck me that Abner Uustal's interpretation of the historical facts of 1940 and their international legal significance was diametrically opposed to my own. Simply to consider Uustal wrong and myself right would be to fail to grasp what was really going on in this disagreement. My arguments may have been 'better'—but if so, only or mainly in the sense that history turned out differently from what Uustal anticipated. It was not illogical to argue in 1984 that the 'bourgeois' Baltic republics did not exist under international law. Both Uustal and I had been doing essentially the same thing: following a chain of argumentation and evidence and coming to certain conclusions regarding the quintessential lawyer's questions 'what is the law?' and 'how is the law to be applied in a particular context'? It was just that our conclusions were diametrically opposed. I sensed that the difference between our conclusions revealed something fundamental about the discipline of international law, about the conditions and constraints under which international legal arguments are formulated.

The present article is an attempt to explore the *conditio scolari iuris inter gentes*. At the same time, it is a study about the accumulated practices and experiences of representatives of the 'invisible college of international lawyers'. With all the differences between individual members that exist, the issue of the relationship between international law and politics decisively defines the common habitus of international law scholars.[12]

2. The International Law Professors at the University of Dorpat/Iur'ev/Tartu 1855–1985

The subject of my research is the lives and work of five successive international law professors at the university of Dorpat/Iur'ev/Tartu, Estonia, in the period starting roughly with the birth of 'professional' international law scholarship and finishing with the end of the Cold War. These professors are:

August Michael von Bulmerinq (1822–90, Professor at Dorpat 1856–75)
Carl Magnus Bergbohm (1849–1927, Associate Professor at Dorpat 1877–91)
Vladimir Hrabar (1865–1956, Professor at Iur'ev 1893–1918)
Ants Piip (1884–1942, Professor at Tartu University 1920–40)
Abner Uustal (1915–85, Lecturer and Associate Professor at Tartu State University 1950–62, Professor 1963–85, ie six years before the end of Soviet rule).

period burzhuaznoi diktatury i ee retsidivy v srede sovremennoi emigratsii (Riga: Latvian State University, 1984).

[12] Pierre Bourdieu defined the notion of habitus in his 'Outline of a Theory of Practice' (1972). According to his theory, habitus signifies systems of durable transposable dispositions, ie the habitual, patterned ways of understanding, judging, and acting which arise from our particular position

In several cases, my analysis will also include parallel discussion on some of their more noteworthy colleagues, disciples, and/or opponents among international law scholars (for example, Axel Freiherr Freytagh-Loringhoven, Nikolai Maim, Jüri Uluots, Nikolai Kaasik, and Artur Taska).

Why Tartu University and this *dramatis personae*? The first reason is the centrality of Bulmerincq and Bergbohm to the 'belligerent' positivism of nineteenth-century European international law scholarship.[13] But their successors Hrabar, Piip, and Uustal—each in his own way—were no less significant as scholars and/or representatives of the international law profession. Furthermore, as holders of the same chair they constitute a certain unity, a microcosm—notwithstanding all the ruptures and discontinuities between them.

Why 1855–1985? The first of these years, 1855, roughly signifies the beginning of Bulmerincq's activity at the Faculty and the emergence of international law theses at Dorpat.[14] It also, by and large, coincides with the emergence of professional international law scholarship in Europe. The year 1985 is the year of Uustal's death—and the year which marks the beginning of the end of the USSR (and the Cold War). Since Uustal's death in 1985, an ordinary professor of international law has yet to be named at the University.

A study of international law scholars at the University of Dorpat/Iur'ev/Tartu cannot, of course, ignore one other scholar—Friedrich (aka Fyodor) Martens (1845–1909), the famous professor of international law at St Petersburg University. The international fame of Martens overshadowed that of the protagonists of this article. Inevitably, Martens was a central reference point to the internationalists in Tartu. Bulmerincq reviewed his younger colleague, Martens' textbook in the *Revue de droit international et de législation comparée*, criticizing the latter's notion of 'international administrative law' as pointless, but otherwise praising the work.[15]

Bergbohm translated Martens' textbook into German—but disagreed with him about some politically contested aspects of Russian history. Hrabar generally held the work of his distinguished colleague in high esteem but clashed with Martens after the latter arguably sacrificed 'objective international law' to Russian *raison d'état*. Piip referred to 'my famous countryman Martens' when advocating international recognition for the Republic of Estonia in 1920. And as far as Uustal is concerned, it

as members of one or several social 'fields', and from our particular trajectory in the social structure. See also P Bourdieu, *The Logic of Practice* (1990) esp 52–65 and Bourdieu, 'The Force of Law: Toward a Sociology of the Juridical Field' (1987) 38 *Hastings Law Journal* 805–53.

[13] cf M Koskenniemi, *From Apology to Utopia: The Structure of International Legal Argument* (1989) 98–119.

[14] See also N Deppisch, *Das Recht des neutralen Seehandels, geschichtlich entwickelt von der ältesten Zeit bis zum Schlusse des achtzehnten Jahrhunderts* (1855).

[15] (1883) XV *Revue de droit international et de legislation comparée* 631 (hereinafter '*Revue de droit*').

is possible that Estonian students learned more about international law from Jaan Kross's brilliant novel, *Professor Martens' Departure* (1984), than from Uustal's textbook (1984). Somehow, Martens always managed to remain the significant other.

It is to a certain extent ironic that the most famous Russian international law professor, Fyodor Martens, was non-Russian by descent. Born Friedrich Martens in Pernau (Pärnu) in the province of Livonia, his mother tongue was quite likely to have been Estonian. (However, some German sources speculate about whether he might have been Baltic German.) He was orphaned at an early age but was lucky enough to receive a good education in St Petersburg, the imperial capital. When he graduated from the Faculty of Law of St Petersburg University in 1867, the Dean suggested that Martens stay at the chair of international law: 'Then we will have *our* Martens.'[16]

'*Our* Martens' became a perfect example of the success of the imperial idea. Estonian by birth, Martens saw the imperial rather than national idea as guarantor of peace, prosperity, and individual rights. The views of Martens on the 'nationality question' illustrate this claim. Martens believed that the State must relate 'with complete respect to national elements' and be respectful of the rights and interests of citizens 'of whatever national origin they are or whatever language they speak'.[17] At the same time, he wrote: 'To see a panacea in the principle of nationality for the settlement of all international difficulties seems to us to be unfounded and the conviction that it has exclusive supremacy over all the leading ideas of our time is dangerous.'[18] He held that the stable foundation of a State was not the national idea, not 'historical legends', but 'identical cultural interests', 'identical State ideals', an 'identical understanding of political freedom', and 'identical respect for the highest values of human civilization'. He believed that the 'principle of nationality, having no historical foundation, will create nothing stable, but it is in a condition to destroy much.'[19]

Historically, the big question was whether or not imperial Russia granted to its numerous nationalities the freedoms advocated by Martens. In any case, much of this article illustrates the historical struggle between the imperial/universalist and the national idea in Russia and its successor States in the Baltics.

The idea that Estonia and the other Baltic republics have historically been a showcase of the conflict between Russia and Germany, Western and Eastern Christianity, even different civilizations, has become a kind of cliché. Thus in his much-debated book, *The Clash of Civilizations and the Remaking of World Order*, Samuel P Huntington drew a line between

[16] VV Pustogarov, 'Our Martens' trans from Russian by WE Butler (ed), *F.F. Martens. International Lawyer and Architect of Peace* (2000) 19.

[17] F Martens, *Sovremennoe mezhdunarodnoe pravo tsivilizovannyh narodov* (1883) vol I, 150.

[18] ibid 151–2. [19] ibid. English translation of Pustogarov (n 16 above) 54.

the Western Christian and the Orthodox civilizations—a border that according to him runs in part through the Russian–Estonian border.[20]

There is indeed some truth to the argument that the geopolitical constant of Estonia has been its role as borderland. Throughout the late Middle Ages, Estonia was politically and culturally contested territory among different political powers, most notably the Germans and the Russians. Generations of scholars and travellers have been struck by the view at the border crossing between Estonia and Russia in the town of Narva. On opposite banks of the Narva River lie two castles, directly opposite each other—the one on the Estonian side, the Hermann castle, was built by the Teutonic order following its conquest of Estonia in the thirteenth century. The castle on the Russian side, in Ivangorod, was erected by Tsar Ivan III during Muscovy's expansion towards the Baltic Sea in the sixteenth century. For anyone looking for symbolic proof of the clash between different political powers, it is there in Narva.

A similar mood is evoked by the Russian film director Sergey Eisenstein's celebrated drama *Alexander Nevski*. The film dramatizes a famous battle of 5 April 1242 in which the troops of the Russian prince Alexander Nevski beat the heavily armed Teutonic knights on the ice of Lake Peipsi. Lake Peipsi lies to the south-east of Narva and down its centre runs the present-day border between Estonia and Russia. To the Russian consciousness, the Russian victory in this battle stopped the expansion of the German crusaders towards the east, their *Drang nach Osten*. Eisenstein's movie was produced in 1938; it was an allegorical work in which the director suggested a troubling continuity between the Teutonic knights and the threatening *Wehrmacht*.

The birth of the University of Dorpat in 1632 was also marked by historical fights and struggles. The Swedish king, Gustavus II Adolphus (1594–1632), signed the orders for the establishment of a university in Dorpat in 1632, shortly before his death in battle. The Thirty Years' War ended with the signing of the Peace of Westphalia in 1648—the accepted starting point of the modern European State system and the *ius publicum Europaeum*. The historical context surrounding the founding of the University of Dorpat is thus significant. The War was waged over religious freedom and dominance in a Europe divided between Catholics and Protestants. The Poles had established Catholic seminars in Vilnius, Lithuania, in 1579, and in Dorpat when they ruled in Livonia in the late sixteenth century. The Swedish king, the leader of the Protestant camp, was concerned at Catholic intellectual influence in the region. The *Academia Gustaviana* was established in Dorpat as a Protestant counterweight to the Catholic seminar in Vilnius.[21]

[20] S Huntington, *The Clash of Civilizations and the Remaking of World Order* (1996) 158–62, esp 159.

[21] See G von Rauch, 'Reflexe des abendländischen Geisteslebens an der schwedischen Universität Dorpat' in G von Pistohlkors, TU Raun, Kaegbein (eds), *Die Universitäten Dorpat/Tartu, Riga und*

The University of Dorpat was closed when Tsar Peter the Great attacked Sweden in 1700. In the ensuing Nordic War (1700–21), Russia defeated Sweden and the provinces of Estonia and Livonia became part of the Russian Empire. Peter the Great regarded the conquest of the provinces of Estonia and Livonia as essential to the development of the Russian Empire, like 'breaking a window to Europe'.

The university was reopened on the orders of the relatively liberal Tsar Alexander I in 1802 as the *Kaiserliche Universität zu Dorpat*. The Faculty of Law had been one of the four original faculties in 1632, and public international law was included in the curriculum in the 1830s (quite early in the context of nineteenth-century Europe).

From the time of August Bulmerincq onwards, each successive international law professor faced a new political situation, a new crisis. Political conflicts were even revealed in the change of the name of the university (and town) in the course of history. While Bulmerincq and Bergbohm were professors, the University of Dorpat was the only university in the Russian Empire where the language of instruction was German. In the last quarter of the nineteenth century, the Baltic provinces became subjects of the politics of Russification, and in 1889 the Faculty of Law was Russified.[22] Dorpat's university council lost its right to elect professors and all lectures had to be given in Russian. In 1893, the town and university of Dorpat were renamed Iur'ev. The new official name referred to an ancient Russian chronicle which narrated how, in 1030, the Kiyevian Russ prince Iaroslav (Iuri) conducted a successful military campaign against the Estonians, conquered their castle in Tarbatu (Tartu), and forced the Estonians to pay tribute to the Russians. Iur'ev, the town's new name, was intended as a reminder of that ancient continuity of the Russian presence and as a message to the Baltic Germans: we came here before you.

The fight for domination between the Baltic Germans and the Russians in the second half of the nineteenth century was carried out against the background of the emancipation of the native peoples, the Estonians and the Latvians.[23] Since both the Estonians and the Latvians shared the Lutheran faith with the German settlers, their national identity was primarily based on linguistic nationalism, but also on social belonging. A distinct feature was their relatively low numbers—ethnic

Wilna/Vilnius 1579–1979. Beiträge zu ihrer Geschichte und ihrer Wirkung im Grenzbereich zwischen West und Ost (1987) 11.

[22] See P Järvelaid, *Istoria prepodovania juridicheskih distsiplin v Tartuskom universitete za period s osnovania universiteta (1632 g) do ego reformy (1889)* (1989). See also M Hagen, 'Hochschulunruhen und Regierungspolitik im Russischen Reich vor 1914' in von Pistohlkors, Raun, Kaegbein (eds), *Die Universitäten Dorpat/Tartu, Riga und Wilna/Vilnius 1579–1979*. (n 21 above) 54.

[23] For the origins of this movement, see M Laar, *Äratajad. Rahvuslik ärkamisaeg Eestis 19. sajandil ja selle kandjad* (2005).

Estonians made up around one million and ethnic Latvians, fewer than two million people at that time.

National emancipation finally led to the creation of the Estonian and Latvian nation States in 1918. The Republic of Estonia was proclaimed on 24 February 1918, just before the entry of the German occupation army during World War I. For six months during 1918, the University of Dorpat was known as the Baltic German *Landesuniversität*. In November 1918 when the German army retreated and the Bolsheviks tried to re-establish Russian control over Estonia, a war of secession (the Estonian War of Independence) broke out. On 2 February 1920, the Republic of Estonia concluded the Tartu peace treaty with Russia. The University of Tartu was reopened on 1 December 1919 as the Estonian national university, a university in which the language of instruction was to become primarily Estonian. Ants Piip became the professor of international law and held this post until the country was occupied and annexed by the USSR in 1940.

In the course of World War II, Estonia lost approximately a quarter of its population. Following the Soviet annexation in 1940, many Estonians, including professors of the University of Tartu, were arrested and sent to Siberian prison camps. The German occupation of 1941–44 devastated the university further; part of its historic main building was used by the German military command. When the Soviets returned in 1944, many professors managed to escape to the West. The university was named Tartu State University. Although ideologically sovietized, the language of instruction remained primarily Estonian.

Throughout its history, the University of Dorpat/Iur'ev/Tartu has been the only university providing legal education in the Baltic provinces of Estonia, Livonia, and Curonia. This remained the case so far as the Republic of Estonia after 1919 was concerned and in Soviet Estonia during the Soviet period. According to Bourdieu, the power struggles that occur within a 'field' (in this case, an academic juridical field) are its defining elements.[24] The university's dominant position in the region and its monopoly of legal education made the university a microcosm, and underlines the representative function of its professors.

3. Methodological Issues

The subject of this article is the history of the academic discipline of international law. It is thus both a history of ideas and of individuals. The hero of this study is more the international lawyer than international law. I hope to explore the passion, the pulsating life behind international legal arguments, to map positions and the social trajectories of individuals, and to highlight how pre-juridical necessities were turned into legal

[24] P Bourdieu, *The Force of Law* (1987) 816.

arguments. Consequently, this history of ideas also borders on sociology of knowledge: it asks where the knowledge and arguments of international law scholars came from, what they were conditioned by, etc.[25]

The relationship between the development of knowledge and the development of politics has for some time been treated as an important yet problematic area of the sociology of knowledge.[26] The principal method applied here may be called 'contextualizing'—putting the arguments of international lawyers in their context. In order to learn why those scholars wrote about international law the way they did, it will be necessary to link their ideas to their lives and times. The reconstruction of past lives is, however, not a goal in itself. The main goal is an understanding of the origin of their arguments. What influenced these scholars intellectually and emotionally? What were the underlying conflicts and issues of their time? In particular, what stance did they take towards the defining political conflicts of their time? In presenting the biographies of the five scholars, I will rely on previously published materials as well as on original documents in the Estonian Historical Archive and in the library archive of the University of Tartu.

The decision to consider the context of international legal arguments rather than 'pure' doctrine alone is of course influenced by those approaches to international law that refuse to restrict legal analysis to the analysis of rules. For example, W Michael Reisman has explained that policy-oriented jurisprudence:

> Has adapted, with a number of adjustments, a scheme of cultural anthropology in which any social process is described systematically in terms of those who engage in it (the participants), the subjective dimensions that animate them (their perspectives), the situations in which they interact, the resources upon which they draw, the way they manipulate those resources and the aggregate outcomes of the process of interaction, which are conceived in terms of a comprehensive set of values.[27]

However, writing a history of the discipline of international law raises a number of methodological and philosophical questions. Thomas S Kuhn wrote in 1978: 'There seems at times to be two distinct sorts of history of science . . . The still dominant form, often called the "internal approach", is concerned with the substance of science as knowledge. Its newer rival, often called the "external approach", is concerned with the activities of scientists as a social group within a larger culture. Putting the two together is perhaps the greatest challenge now faced by the

[25] See RK Merton, 'Paradigm for the Sociology of Knowledge' in *Social Theory and Social Structure* (1957), reprinted in JE Curtis and JW Petras, *The Sociology of Knowledge. A Reader* (1970) 342–72.

[26] See eg the discussion in M Scheler, *Problems of a Sociology of Knowledge* (trans MS Frings, 1980) 157–82.

[27] M Reisman, *The View from the New Haven School of International Law* (1992) excerpted in Reisman *et al*, *International Law in Contemporary Perspective* (2004) 3.

profession.'[28] Here I have chosen the 'external approach' (not restricting myself to the substance of science as knowledge) while at the same time still 'coming from the inside' (first as an international law scholar and second, as a scholar affiliated with the university of Bulmerincq and his successors).[29] Thus, my own previous preoccupation with arguments presented by Uustal may already reveal certain prejudices (Gadamerian *Vorverständnisse*) on my part.[30]

Quentin Skinner has emphasized the importance of placing historical texts in their intellectual and linguistic contexts, in order to establish the intentions of their authors when they advanced their arguments.[31] Skinner describes several basic problems that arise when old texts are interpreted. One such problem is the temptation to judge somebody in the past not on the basis of what he or she knew, but what came to be known subsequently. The question is whether the historian of ideas should be permitted to characterize certain beliefs or statements of historical agents as 'false' or erroneous.[32] Skinner advises against this, arguing that the only standard by which such statements and beliefs should be measured is some generally accepted standard of epistemic rationality. A historian is in the position of reporting what would be or would not be an appropriate belief for that particular agent to have espoused in that particular society at that particular time.[33] If, however, we come to the 'uncharitable' conclusion that the historical agent should not have thought/argued in the way he or she did, we confront a new set of questions: why was the agent irrational? 'Is he nursing some private grievance? . . . Should we be looking for a strongly emotional component in [his or her] political beliefs?'[34] The approach advocated by Skinner clearly highlights the importance of context in understanding texts and arguments.

Another question is to what extent the exegete should trust the words of the writer himself regarding his intentions. Skinner has invited us to venture a look behind the mere meaning of the words in the 'intended acts of communication':

If we wish to understand any such text, we must be able to give an account not merely of the meaning of what was said, but also what the writer in question may

[28] TS Kuhn, *The Essential Tension. Selected Studies in Scientific Tradition and Change* (1977) 110.

[29] See on the 'challenge of studying a world to which we are linked by all sorts of specific investments' in P Bourdieu, *Homo Academicus* (trans P Collier, 1988) 7ff.

[30] See Bourdieu's discussion about whether science can 'survive' the relativization of historicism in P Bourdieu, *Science of Science and Reflexivity* (2004) 2ff.

[31] Q Skinner, *Visions of Politics, Volume 1: Regarding Method* (2002).

[32] For instance, Bulmerincq called Kant's project of a *Staatenstaat* (today we would say international organization) a 'mistake' since international law had to be founded on the independence of States. A Bulmerincq, *Die Systematik des Völkerrechts* (1858) vol 1, 144. He also believed that the English language could never compete with French in the international realm. Bergbohm, on the other hand, argued that human rights can have no place in positivist international law, etc ('Human ideas have nothing to do with international law'). CM Bergbohm, *Staatsverträge und Gesetze als Quellen des Völkerrechts* (1877) 8.

[33] Skinner (n 31 above) 37–8. [34] ibid 40.

have meant by saying what was said. A study that focuses exclusively on what a writer said about some given doctrine will not only be inadequate, but may in some cases be positively misleading . . . We need, that is, to grasp not merely what people are saying but also what they are doing in saying it. To study what past thinkers have said is . . . to perform the first of two hermeneutic tasks.[35]

Skinner goes on to say that:

... to gain 'uptake' of [author's] intentions is equivalent to understanding the nature and range of the illocutionary acts that the writer may have been performing in writing in a particular way ... It is equivalent, that is, to being able to say that he or she must have meant the work as an attack on, or a defence of, as a criticism of, or as a contribution to, some particular attitude or line of argument, and so on ...Whatever an author was doing in writing what he or she wrote must be relevant to interpretation, and thus that among the interpreter's tasks must be the recovery of the author's intentions in writing what he or she wrote ... it may sometimes be appropriate to discount their own accounts of what they were doing.[36]

4. Bulmerincq: The Conservative Mind

4.1 Vita: noblesse oblige

Er war der ächte und treue Lutheraner seiner liefländischen Heimat ... ein guter deutscher Protestant, wurzelnd in protestantischer Wahrheit und Wahrhaftigkeit.[37]

August Bulmerincq was a leading figure among the first generation of international law professionals, one of the 'men of 1873'. Professor of International Law at the University of Heidelberg, when he died, in Stuttgart on 18 August 1890, many friends and colleagues had reason to look back on his fruitful life and activities with deep gratitude. The initiator of the *Institut de droit international*, Gustave Rolin-Jaequemyns (1835–1902), reminisced in Bulmerincq's obituary, published in the *Annuaire de l'institut de droit international*, about a recent procession of the members of the *Institut*, led by Bulmerincq, to the tomb of Bulmerincq's predecessor at the chair of international law at Heidelberg's Ruprecht Karl University, the recently deceased Johan Caspar Bluntschli ('*lui aussi avait eu deux patries*').[38] And now it was time to say farewell to Bulmerincq himself. Rolin-Jaequemyns remarked:

S'il fallait résumer d'un mot l'apparence exteriéure, la caractère, le talent et la science de Bulmerincq, je crois que nulle épithéte ne lui conviendrait mieux que

[35] ibid 79, 82. [36] ibid 100–10.

[37] W Hönig, *Stadtpfarrer von Heidelberg, Rede am Grabe des Herrn Geheimen Rats Dr. August von Bulmerincq: gestorben am 18. August 1890.*

[38] G Rolin-Jaequemyns, 'Notices nécrologiques—M. de Bulmerincq' in (1892–1894) *Annuaire de l'institut de droit international* 335, 336.

celle de solide. Solides étaint son port, sa démarche, sa stature, solides ses amités, solides ses connaissances. C'est sur la base solide du droit positif et des traités qu'il voulait fonder le droit international.[39]

It is not clear in retrospect whether the word 'solidity' truly meant recognition or consituted a hidden insult, implying mediocrity.

August Michael Bulmerincq was born in Riga, then the largest city of the Baltic provinces of the Russian Empire, on 31 July (12 August) 1822. His family had Scottish origins but had established itself in Lübeck centuries before, moving from this former Hanseatic capital to Riga in the seventeenth century.[40] Bulmerincq's family was one of the richest and most respected families in Riga. His father was the senior of the Great Guild (*Grosse Gilde*), whose members were the richest merchants in Riga;[41] he expected August Michael to take over the family business after finishing his studies at a *gymnasium* in Riga. But August Michael's interests lay elsewhere and in the end his father yielded to his wish to study law.

Bulmerincq studied law at the University of Dorpat from 1841 to 1845. In 1847 he became candidate of law at the same university. His father was willing to finance further studies in Heidelberg, but a few weeks after his arrival a revolution broke out and his father, a 'rigid conservative',[42] immediately called him back to the Baltics. Bulmerincq started to practise law in his home town of Riga. On 16 July 1848 he became the second notary at the Riga *Landvogteigericht* and, in 1850, secretary for the criminal law division of the Riga city council. At the same time, he continued his studies, and in 1849 in Dorpat defended his master's thesis on alternative dispute resolution, his first published book.[43]

In Riga, young Bulmerincq participated actively in the social and intellectual life of the city. As secretary of the *Literarisch-praktische Bürger-Verbindung zu Riga*, an intellectual society established for practical and charitable purposes by the city's German elite, he wrote the history of the society.[44] These were the noble and influential people of Riga who, like the Boston Brahmins, did not have to worry so much about their own material well-being and could dedicate their free time to public causes. They cared deeply about their home city and even the Baltic provinces as a whole.[45] Bulmerincq's years in Riga were also significant for his private

[39] Rolin-Jaequemyns (n 38 above) 339. [40] ibid 336.

[41] O Welding *et al*, *Deutschbaltisches biographisches Lexikon 1710–1960* (Wedemark: Verlag Harro von Hirschheydt, 1998) 129. [42] Rolin-Jaequemyns (n 38 above) 336.

[43] A Bulmerincq, *Von der Wahl und dem Verfahren des freiwilligen Schiedsgerichts*, master thesis (1849).

[44] A Bulmerincq, *Geschichte der Allerhöchst bestätigten literarisch-praktischen Bürger-Verbindung zu Riga. Bei Gelegenheit ihrer fünfzigjährigen Jubelfeier am 12. Dezember 1852* (1852).

[45] See eg Bulmerincq's 'Das alte und das neue Riga' in *Baltische Monatsschrift* 1881 468–76. See also, for the spirit of the time, A Bulmerincq, *Carl Eduard Otto. Doctor der Philosophie und Rechte und Professor emeritus der K. Universität Dorpat. Eine biographische Skizze* (1858).

life—in 1852 he married Mathilde Hernmarck, daughter of the mayor (*Oberbürgermeister*) of Riga.[46]

In 1853, Bulmerincq left Riga and settled in Dorpat where, to attain his *venia legendi* in the Faculty of Law, he presented his first study in the field of public international law, a thorough investigation of the law of asylum from a historical point of view.[47] In 1854, he became privatdocent with a secured salary (*Etats-mässiger Privat docent*) and taught commercial and maritime law from 1854 to 1856.

Bulmerincq had been introduced to the field of international law by Professor Erdmann Gustav von Bröcker (1784–1854; also born in Riga), whose speciality was the law of the Baltic provinces, but who was also appointed professor of 'positive constitutional law, international law and politics' in 1831. According to Bulmerincq, von Bröcker was a 'fatherly friend' to his students.[48] However, the field of international law was completely new to von Bröcker—a fact that in the words of Bulmerincq created 'plenty of new difficulties' for him. Von Bröcker never published anything on international law and, according to Bulmerincq, his lectures were characterized by his emphasis on its 'practical' aspects.[49]

Yet Bulmerincq did not appear in Dorpat on completely uncultivated ground. Perhaps intellectually more influential than the 'practical' von Bröcker had been the legacy of the legal historian Johann Philipp Gustav Ewers (1779–1830). Ewers, in many ways the central figure at Dorpat during the first half of the nineteenth century, was an import from the University of Göttingen, a leading European university of the Enlightenment period. Rector of the University of Dorpat from 1818 to 1830, Ewers had studied at Göttingen's Georgia Augusta in 1799–1803. Although he had primarily studied theology, he had almost certainly been in contact with or at least been influenced by the ideas of Georg Friedrich von Martens (1756–1821), the leading international law scholar of his period and one of the founders of 'modern' positivism. In Dorpat, Ewers became one of the founding fathers of the discipline of the history of Russia and, in particular, of Russian legal history.[50]

From 1826 to 1830, Ewers was Professor at the Faculty of Law, lecturing on politics, 'European international law', and 'positive State law'. In 1828, he published a brief study in which he tackled the main philosophical problem of the legal science of his time: the distinction

[46] Rolin-Jaequemyns (n 38 above) 337.

[47] A Bulmerincq, *Das Asylrecht in seiner geschichtlichen Entwickelung beurtheilt vom Standpunkte des Rechts und dessen völkerrechtliche Bedeutung für die Auslieferung flüchtiger Verbrecher. Eine Abhandlung aus dem Gebiete der universellen Rechtsgeschichte und des positiven Völkerrechts* (1853) (repr 1970).

[48] A Bulmerincq, 'Dr. Erdmann Gustav von Bröcker' in *Das Inland* No 13, 29 March 1854, 200, 211.

[49] ibid.

[50] See eg JPG Ewers, *Vom Ursprunge des Russischen Staats. Ein Versuch, die Geschichte desselben aus den Quellen zu erforschen* (1808), and *Das älteste Recht der Russen in seiner geschichtlichen Entwickelung* (1826). See further L Leppik, *Rektor Ewers* (2001) (summary in German).

between natural law and positive law.[51] His attitude towards natural law was somewhat ambiguous. On the one hand, he recognized the importance of international arrangements such as the decisions made by the Holy Alliance in Aachen in 1818. On the other hand, he held that natural law remained the common source for private law, State law, and international law. He postulated the coexistence of positive law and natural law, and contrasted natural law as philosophical law based on human reason with positive law as enacted by the legislator. International law was natural law applied to international relations.[52] Thus although Ewers followed certain ideas of Georg Friedrich von Martens and another well-known internationalist in Göttingen, Johann Stephan Pütter (1725–1807), he was no positivist.

In 1856, Bulmerincq defended his doctoral dissertation in Latin: *De natura principiorum iuris inter gentes positivi*[53] and was named extraordinary professor in public law, international law, and politics. In 1858, he published another work on public international law, the ambitious *Die Systematik des Völkerrechts* and was named ordinary professor in the above-mentioned disciplines. He continued to serve in this function in the Faculty of Law at the University of Dorpat until his retirement in 1875. In 1874, his most personal and powerful account of public international law, *Praxis, Theorie und Codification des Völkerrechts*, was published.

We do not know very much about Bulmerincq as a teacher. However, during his professorship in Dorpat, several noteworthy works in the field of public international law with an emphasis on theory and the history of international law were defended under his supervision. One of Bulmerincq's students was Witold Załeski, the son of a Polish nobleman of Grodno, who was born in Warsaw and went to *gymnasium* in Vilna.[54] Since the Third Partition of Poland, severe constraints had been placed on higher education, and more than two thousand Poles such as Załeski, living in the part annexed by Russia, received their university education in Dorpat (thus their nickname, *dorpatchiki*). Dorpat was at that time known for its relative autonomy, academic freedom, and the fact that the language of instruction was German.[55]

During his approximately twenty years of teaching in Dorpat, Bulmerincq continued to participate actively in public life. Showing a more practical side, which his father would perhaps have wished to see expressed in an even more determined fashion, Bulmerincq established

[51] JPG Ewers, *Rhapsodische Gedanken über die wissenschaftliche Bedeutung des Naturrechts* (1828).

[52] ibid.

[53] A Bulmerincq, *De natura principiorum iuris inter gentes positivi* (1856).

[54] See Estonian History Archive F 402/2/28072 and F 402/2/28073. The title of Załeski's master thesis was *Zur Geschichte und Lehre der internationalen Gemeinschaft* (1866). The title of his doctoral thesis, *Die völkerrechtliche Bedeutung der Kongresse* (1874).

[55] See further E Amburger, 'Die Bedeutung der Universität Dorpat für Osteuropa' in von Pistohlkors *et al* (eds) (n 21 above) 163–81.

in Dorpat in 1863 a magazine dedicated to economic issues, *Baltische Wochenschrift für Landwirthschaft, Gewerbfleiss und Handel Liv-, Est- und Curlands*. He remained the editor-in-chief of the magazine for the first three years and organized the first agricultural congress and the first exposition of the products of light industry in the Baltic provinces.[56]

Though Professor of International Law, Bulmerincq did not neglect the particular law of the Baltic provinces. As efforts at Russifying gained momentum, preoccupation with the German-influenced law of the Baltic provinces acquired a political meaning, and in effect became a patriotic act.[57] Bulmerincq emphasized the historical importance of the (German) particular law of the Russian Baltic sea provinces[58] and served as one of the editors of a collection of the sources of this law.[59]

As an international lawyer, Bulmerincq was known not only as a prolific writer but also as an active member of the *Institut de droit international*. When the *Institut* was established in Gent in 1873 he had been invited to attend, but the invitation did not reach him in time. In a letter sent to the *Institut* he wrote that he was glad to be accepted as member 'd'abord parce qu'il y voit une occasion de travailler en communauté avec des hommes, que depuis longtemps il a souhaité de connaitre, et ensuite parce qu'il y voit un plus large champ ouvert à ses efforts pour contribuer à fonder sur le droit le bonheur des peuples'.[60] He was subsequently considered a founding member of the *Institut*.[61]

Upon his retirement in 1875, Bulmerincq moved to Wiesbaden, Germany. During his professorship in Dorpat he had maintained close ties with Germany and spent most of his summer vacations there. There has been speculation as to whether his sudden move to Germany after his retirement can partly be explained by his unease at the tightening Russian grip in the Baltic provinces. As a retired professor in Wiesbaden, Bulmerincq continued to publish extensively, both in newspapers such as the Augsburg *Allgemeine Zeitung* and in legal periodicals. As letters to his former faculty colleagues in Dorpat demonstrate, he continued to keep in touch with Baltic developments. In 1877, Bulmerincq began an article in *Baltische Monatsschrift* with the following sentence: 'Wenn ich auch nicht mehr im Inlande für das Inland wirke, so folge ich dennoch aus der Ferne mit vollem Interesse dessen Entwickelung und erkenne durch Vergleich mit Zuständen des Auslandes Vorzüge und Mängel der Heimath nur um so mehr und unbefangener.'[62] This made it clear that one could work for

[56] 'August v. Bulmerincq', in *Brockhaus Konversations-Lexikon* (1901) vol 3, 688.

[57] M Luts, *Juhuslik ja isamaaline: F.G. von Bunge provintsiaalõigusteadus* (2001).

[58] A Bulmerincq, 'Die Rechtsbildung und das Rechtsstudium der Ostseeprovinzen Russlands' (1873) 22 *Baltische Monatsschrift* 68–78.

[59] FG von Bunge, H Hildebrand, P Schwartz, A von Bulmerincq, and L Arbosow d Ä (eds) *Liv-, Esth- und Curländisches Urkundenbuch nebst Regesten* (1889).

[60] G Rolin-Jaequemyns (1874) VI *Revue de droit* 176.

[61] ibid 150.

[62] A Bulmerincq, 'Wann wird in Liv- und Estland eine Volkszählung stattfinden?' (1877) XXV *Baltische Monatsschrift* S345. Criticizing indirectly the politics of the Russian central government that had postponed the *Volkszählung* in the Baltic provinces.

one's home country even when living outside it—as a Baltic German, *Inland* always remained *Inland*, even when he lived in Germany.

Bulmerincq acquired a second life as an international lawyer due to his involvement in the *Institut*. On the pages of the *Revue*, he adopted the role of active polemicist and figured as one of the most frequent contributors.[63] In 1881, upon the death of his colleague Johan Caspar Bluntschli, he was invited to take up the Chair of Public International Law at Heidelberg—a position he maintained until his death on 18 August 1890. As a professor in Heidelberg, Bulmerincq finally published a systematic treatment of public international law in Marquardsen's *Handbuch des öffentlichen Rechts*.[64] A treatment of disputes between States followed in another German international law series in 1889.[65]

For the *Institut*—which at that time served as the voluntary codifier of international law, a kind of predecessor of the United Nations International Law Commission—Bulmerincq served as special rapporteur on the regulation of the law of prizes in naval war[66] and the passage of troops or material of war by belligerents on the territories of neutral States during the war.[67] It was probably the professional culmination of August Bulmerincq's life when he was elected president of the *Institut* in 1887; he presided over the session in Heidelberg which accepted his report on prize courts in naval war, which recommended the creation of international and impartial rather than national prize courts. Moreover, he chaired the *Institut*'s committee on 'desired reforms' in the judicial institutions of the countries of the Orient.[68] When Bulmerincq died, nobody could say that he had left his 'life work' unfinished.

4.2 The concept of politics in Bulmerincq's work on international law

> If theory does not clearly distinguish between both fields of law and politics and their subjects, how can this be expected from practice?[69]

Characteristic of his time, Bulmerincq's conception of politics was 'positivist'. He maintained that the separation of law and politics underpinned

[63] See eg A Bulmerincq, 'Règlement international des transports par chemin de fer' (1878) X *Revue de droit* 83ff.

[64] A Bulmerincq, 'Das Völkerrecht' in Marquardsen, *Handbuch des öffentlichen Rechts* (1884) vol 1.

[65] A Bulmerincq, 'Die Staatsstreitigkeiten und ihre Entscheidung' in *Holtzendorff, Handbuch des Völkerrechts* (1889) vol 4.

[66] A Bulmerincq, *Commision des prises maritimes* (Institut de droit international) (1880). (Also published in (1878–80) X–XIII *Revue de droit*.)

[67] A Bulmerincq, 'Du passage de troupes ou de materiel de guerre des belligérants sur territoire neutre en temps de guerre' (1889) XXI *Revue de droit* 139ff.

[68] A Bulmerincq, 'Réformes désirables dans les institutions judiciaires ajourd'hui en vigueur dans les pays d'orient' (1888) XX *Revue de droit* 379–82.

[69] A Bulmerincq, *Praxis, Theorie und Codification des Völkerrechts* (1874) 96–7.

the identity of international law. As early as 1858, he demanded the separation of positivist legal material from philosophical speculation:

> Until today distinguished authors hold the view that the system of positive international law could not exist without the inclusion of the philosophical. However, this view is based on a misunderstanding of the most general nature and purposes of positive international law ... The historical direction in legal scholarship which has in other fields won over natural law, should also in positive international law bring the purely positive material to validity and here too substitute the philosophical law with the philosophy of law.[70]

In creating the system of international law, one could thus only take into account legal and not political elements: 'What is therefore in treatises of positive international law not of purely legal nature has to be expelled from our systematisation ... to every field must belong its own. It seems to us that the scholarly organisation of the State external relations has to be mainly based on two general ideas: law and wisdom.' Bulmerincq therefore held that it was necessary to distinguish from international law 'the external politics or State wisdom, the scholarly nature of which is at the time yet problematical'.[71]

Bulmerincq reiterated the same positions in his *Praxis, Theorie und Codification des Völkerrechts* (1874):

> A lot that has been counted as international law is not law at all but belongs to international relations. It is completely overlooked that international law is shaped by different principles and *not every international maxim is a legal one*. Thus, the separation of the political and legal is unclear both in historical works and in most systems or individual studies on international law.[72]

> Every law, and so also international law, has no greater enemy than the phrase, and international law has been overwhelmed by phrases. But it has emancipated itself from phrases and it will stand demanding recognition and equality with other disciplines of law—as law ... The essence of international law is law itself by which it can be distinguished from foreign policy, which may not do anything against law but for which nevertheless enough tasks remain. If theory does not clearly distinguish between both law and politics and their subjects, how can this be expected from practice?[73]

> The substance of international law is of a legal nature, as should be self-evident with a legal discipline, although often the political is mixed in with international law. But the legal and political have to be differentiated as unconditional and conditional. Law establishes and does not leave a choice; politics offers different means to a goal and leaves the choice open. What is different in principle does not suit in the same system: the legal belongs to international law, the political to external politics.[74]

70 *Die Systematik des Völkerrechts* (1858) 2, 6. Unless otherwise indicated, all translations are mine.

71 ibid 7–8. Many international lawyers continue to be sceptical about the scientific foundations of the field of international relations. See eg P Allott, *Eunomia: New Order for a New World* (2001) Foreword and *passim*.

72 Bulmerincq, *Praxis, Theorie* (n 69 above) 94–5 (emphasis in original).

73 ibid 96–7.

74 ibid 143.

Later, Bulmerincq explained his positivist separation of law and politics further in an article entitled 'La politique et le droit dans la vie des états'.[75] Here Bulmerincq conceived of law and politics, both domestically and internationally, as opposites fighting for supremacy. As an international lawyer, he adopted a hostile approach to politics as the enemy of law.

Bulmerincq recognized that although scholars had made efforts to draw a clear distinction between law and politics, there was no clear consensus on the solution to the problem. One might have desired a state of peace between law and politics, but this was impossible: they were opponents ever determined to maintain and expand their empires:[76] 'The maxim of politics is: force rules over law. The maxim of law is: law rules over force.'[77] In Bulmerincq's view, it was mistaken to base the distinction between law and politics on the notion of interest, since law served lasting interests, while politics only temporary ones.[78] The difference between politics and law consisted of the absence or presence of free will. While politics could choose the means that seemed appropriate under particular circumstances, in law only one rule could be applied correctly.[79] An enlightened humanistic civilization, the existence of which depended on the certainty of law, would not hesitate to expand the realm of law at the cost of the realm of politics. It was necessary for law, the guardian of civilization, to advance step by step just as the light conquered the shadows: 'Who does not any more believe in the final triumph of law, does not any more believe in the triumph of civilization.'[80] Law emerged with civilization while politics already existed among primitive peoples.

Finally, Bulmerincq maintained that politics left its mark on international legal practice by causing States to act in an egoistic and hypocritical manner. A case in point was England, which Bulmerincq criticized for lecturing other nations on humane practices while it demonstrated a backward egoism unforeseen in his century of 'progrés et de lumières' when its own interests were at stake.[81]

Thus Bulmerincq's concept of international law as separate from politics contained another keyword that, as we will see, enabled him to present his own politics as 'science' and as 'non-politics'. This keyword was 'civilization'[82]—a concept without which the separation of law and politics in the work of early positivists would have hardly survived. The 'men of 1873' did not always know how to define 'civilization'—but they knew it when they saw it. Through this notion, political preference could be neutralized as an objective, even scientific truth.

[75] A Bulmerincq, 'La politique et le droit dans la vie des états' (1877) IX *Revue de droit* 361–79.

[76] ibid 361. [77] ibid 362. [78] ibid. [79] ibid 363. [80] ibid 364.

[81] ibid 377; in particular, his critique of England, 374–9. See also M Koskenniemi's observation in *From Apology to Utopia* (1989) 117 that a controlling assumption for international law writing at the time of Bulmerincq was 'the inevitable march of history toward progress and enlightment'.

[82] See M Koskenniemi, *The Gentle Civilizer of Nations. The Rise and Fall of International Law 1870–1960* (2001) Ch 1.

4.3 Politics of Bulmerincq's arguments in the context of international law

4.3.1 Asylum: empowering the State over the Catholic Church and the individual in the aftermath of the 1848 Revolution

An important aspect of Bulmerincq's identity was his strong Protestant religious affinity, predominant among Baltic Germans. Bulmerincq's Lutheran faith led him to take strong positions against what he perceived as Catholic universalistic ambition.

The antagonism between the Church and State had since Bulmerincq's earliest works constituted a central theme in his scholarly discourse. His history of the institution of asylum in international law is illustrative.[83] This is both an erudite study and an interesting work from a methodological point of view. At the outset, Bulmerincq explains why he turns to history to discover whether according to international law States can offer asylum to citizens of other States.

> Recently, extradition treaties have been concluded between States but they are not sufficient since constrained with time and not binding to non-members. The general norm has yet to be established ... To observe this development and to tie to it a future development is a purpose of this work that should prove the unconditional obligation of all States to extradite fugitive criminals. But how can one best accomplish this task? The historical development has to be taken as the basis of observation.[84]

It is astonishing that Bulmerincq explains beforehand what the outcome of this reference to history will be, what history *should* demonstrate. He does not leave it open whether there exists such an unconditional obligation to extradite or not. Here, history serves a classical teleological purpose: to prove a particular claim or thesis. Bulmerincq's approach to the history of international law was generally teleological: the historical foundation of international law was supposed to raise the potential of and respect for the discipline.[85] Earlier, in his *Systematik des Völkerrechts* (1858) he had insisted that: 'In the current problems of international law, the deniers of this law may not even present the biggest problem: the main guilt falls to scholarship because it has not done what it had to do: to demonstrate positive international law historically and through that as unassailable.'[86]

Bulmerincq's view of the history and development of humankind was Hegelian:[87] he believed there was a logic, a purpose to the history of

[83] Bulmerincq, *Das Asylrecht in seiner geschichtlichen Entwickelung beurtheilt vom Standpunkte des Rechts und dessen völkerrechtliche Bedeutung für die Auslieferung flüchtiger Verbrecher* (n 47 above). [84] ibid 9.

[85] See eg Bulmerincq, *Brief an die Dorpater Juristen-Facultät anlässlich der Glückwünsche zum Doktorjubiläum*, Wiesbaden, 14. Mai 1881: 'Überhaupt aber war der Unterzeichnete bemüht die Bedeutung der publizistischen Fächer zu heben, indem er einerseits sie zu systematisieren und andererseits auf historischer Basis aufzurichten trachtete.' Estonian History Archive, F 402/3/204.

[86] Bulmerincq, *Die Systematik des Völkerrechts* (n 70 above) vol 1, 3.

[87] See GWF Hegel, *The Philosophy of History* (1956).

international law as of other human endeavours. Every human order develops towards its completion.[88] When explaining the significance of the historical right of the Church to offer asylum to individuals, Bulmerincq claimed: 'Everything that exists and will emerge has its necessary connection with the past and future of world history. So the right to asylum has been a necessary means towards the consolidation of the unitary power of the State.'[89] He added that 'the present thankfully enjoyed the fruit of the past' and 'safely strove towards its goal': 'dem Recht auf dem Wege des Rechts immerdar sein Recht werden zu lassen'.[90]

Bulmerincq's main thesis is that the right of asylum belonged to the past, to the era when the State had not yet emerged as a significant power; in filling this vacuum, the Church could exercise power and jurisdiction over individuals. By Bulmerincq's time, however, the Church had lost the battle over secular authority to the States and there was no longer any reason or justification for the institution of the right to asylum in a world dominated by States.

Bulmerincq started his historical exposé with a reference to God in a way that was still characteristic of the period when positivist arguments were intertwined with references characteristic of the natural law tradition. Initially, places of asylum were created by 'God himself' (*Gott selbst*) in times of rough unbridled power.[91] Later in the same work, Bulmerincq subordinated international law to divine law, claiming that 'international law too stands under the law that God has revealed and that people have to fulfil'.[92] This was consistent with other treatments in the contemporary international law literature.

In the light of historical development, the main problem with the institution of asylum was that an institution initially designed to protect unjustly persecuted people had been transformed into a hindrance to the pursuit of justice and the punishment of evil.[93] The right to asylum was recognized in ancient Israel and developed in ancient Greece. The State later offered the right to give asylum to the Christian Church as a privilege.[94] But the Church having received this privilege from the State did not consider it as such, but as a natural expression of its own rights. As the State did not recognize this interpretation, a conflict developed and the State took away the Church's right to provide asylum. The justifications given by the Church for its retention did not hold up to criticism.[95]

While the Protestant claim of jurisdiction was from the first limited,[96] the Catholic Church up until the reign of the Austrian monarch Maria-Theresia claimed its old rights. In short, the Church had over time expanded its concept of asylum illegitimately.[97] The Popes even claimed jurisdiction over those individuals who had violated the Church's right to asylum.[98] Only recently did the Popes recognize that the Church could

[88] Bulmerincq, *Die Systematik des Völkerrechts* (n 70 above) 3. [89] ibid 136.
[90] ibid 138. [91] ibid 7. [92] ibid 160. [93] ibid 7. [94] ibid 73. [95] ibid 75.
[96] ibid 82. [97] ibid 84. [98] ibid 94.

not offer asylum to the perpetrators of the gravest crimes.[99] 'The right to asylum in the Church was backed by capital punishment, excommunication or severe monetary penalties. But whom did this right protect? Often those who had violated the rights of others. But those upon whom injustice was inflicted, it did not protect. And what punishment did the right to give asylum inflict upon the fugitive who was a criminal?'[100] So the State that was consolidating power and authority took the right to asylum away from the Church: 'A person in danger does not need to take refuge in order to find protection in front of the altar of God, he finds the protection in normal court proceedings.'[101]

Bulmerincq claimed that the era of diplomatic asylum in international law had ended. It would have amounted to a violation of international law to grant such asylum.[102] In the worst case, if such asylum was still illegally granted, the host State was entitled to pursue the person, while showing due respect for diplomatic premises.[103] Thus the last expression of the right to asylum—diplomatic asylum—had disappeared from international law.

The culmination of Bulmerincq's argument is again presented in a historical-teleological—and paradoxically, quasi-theological—fashion:

> Through the misuses of the right of asylum the State became conscious of its authority. By establishing itself and granting protection to the unhappy ones, and punishment to the violator according to its laws, the State has broken the power of the right to asylum. The State is now itself the asylum but not the one of the deliberate asylum, but the one of the application of the existing laws. In its asylum, the law is applied and the violation of law prosecuted. It is the haven from any lack of law and any who flee to it find protection when they are seeking their rights. The State embodies goodness in law; the development of the State has led to that. But through mistakes it has had to acquire knowledge since not everything that carried the name of law was law ...[104]

The reason why there had to be a customary obligation to punish or extradite (*aut punire aut judicare*) was intrinsic to the system of nation States: 'As every State had the task to advance the cause of law, so is it the general task of all States: to guarantee to every other State legal help and to safeguard the capture and punishment of fugitives of other nations.'[105] There was no right to asylum for fugitive criminals. By committing a wrong against a member, the criminal committed a wrong against the whole.[106] Extradition had become a duty of all States that protected their existence, so that no one may doubt its necessity, its generality, and its justification in the law of nations.[107] With what right then could the institution of asylum serve as a pretext? The reasons for the right to asylum have disappeared: 'Der Verbrecher, wo er sich auch hinwende, sei seiner Strafe gewiss!'[108]

[99] ibid 103. [100] ibid 104. [101] ibid 105. [102] ibid 125–32. [103] ibid 134.
[104] ibid 137. [105] ibid 156. [106] ibid 157. [107] ibid 157–8. [108] ibid 159.

Bulmerincq's thesis may be contrasted with the position of Robert von Mohl (1799–1875), a leading German international law scholar.[109] Mohl's treatise was published in the same year as Bulmerincq's.[110] Mohl explained how the significance of the asylum question stemmed from the aftermath of the 1848 Revolution and the question of political refugees. He compared the asylum legislation in different countries, noting that Great Britain and the United States offered almost unlimited asylum and almost never extradited refugees and fugitives to other countries.[111] In contrast, most German states did not recognize the right to asylum and extradited refugees to their countries of origin.[112] Most other countries adopted a position somewhere in between.[113] Due to the lack of consensus in practice, it was no wonder that there was disagreement among scholars about whether international law allowed asylum or, conversely, imposed a duty to extradite.

Mohl's approach was subtle—while he criticized Britain's broad approach to asylum, he also observed that if a country in general failed to accept foreigners and refugees, it would make itself indirectly responsible in cases of 'irresponsible suppression'.[114] According to Mohl, one could take a cosmopolitan and egoistic view of the right to asylum (remarkably, Mohl argued that it was Britain that had taken the egoistic view).[115] However, the right to asylum was needed, since no one could be sure that he would not himself need asylum one day. The purpose was not to help hardened criminals who deserved punishment, but to offer refuge to those who were being unjustly persecuted.[116]

Reasoning not so much on the basis of history (as Bulmerincq) or treaties (which in any case contained contradictory principles), Mohl argued more or less on the grounds of a philosophy based on common sense, offering a compromise solution. A State should not grant asylum and should extradite criminals who have violated a State's criminal law code. However, there had to be a political exception doctrine for crimes committed against the State.[117] Sometimes governments were not motivated by the desire to see justice prevail but wanted to take revenge, and the courts simply acceded to the will of the State. There was a danger of sacrificing the 'inner law and humanity' to a formal duty and of humiliating 'oneself in the position of an executer of the most noble among people and the most justified friends of the fatherland'.[118] Mohl's was a liberal approach.

[109] The attempt of the rector of Dorpat University, Gustav Ewers, to acquire Mohl from Tübingen in 1825 was unsuccessful. See P Järvelaid, *Sissejuhatus kultuuripiiri teooriasse: Friedrich Georg von Bunge ja Leo Leesment* (2004) 21.

[110] R Mohl, 'Revision der völkerrechtlichen Lehre vom Asyle' *Zeitschrift für Staatswissenschaft* (1853) 461–604.

[111] ibid 476–80.

[112] ibid 486–90.

[113] About the regulation in Russia, see another Dorpat dissertation: F Witte, *Meditationes de jure criminali respectu juris internationalis institutae* (1851).

[114] Mohl (n 110 above) 527–8. [115] ibid 532–5. [116] ibid 528.

[117] ibid 548–9, 553. [118] ibid 553.

By contrast, Bulmerincq's concern seemed to be that people should not violate their country's laws in the first place. He was not alert to the need to check and balance the right of States to define crimes—if a State said that somebody was a criminal, he had to be treated as criminal by other States. A civilized State would guarantee fair treatment for all: 'The State is now itself the asylum', Bulmerincq maintained.[119] Could he have foreseen the totalitarian regimes and the mass repressions of the twentieth century committed in the name of the State?[120]

4.3.2 The emerging conflict over the status of the Baltic Sea provinces (1865)

When the young Bulmerincq wrote the obituary for von Bröcker, the professor who had introduced him to international law, he pointed out that von Bröcker had been a true admirer of the Russian Emperor's court, and had even given a speech in honour of the deceased Russian Emperor 'Alexander the Legislator' in the main hall of the university on 21 April 1827.[121] Alexander I had ruled Russia as a liberal and enlightened monarch, especially during the first part of his reign (1801–25) when he abolished serfdom in the Baltic provinces (earlier than elsewhere in the Russian Empire). Prussia and Russia had been allies in the fight against Napoleon's France, and many leading generals of the Russian army in 1812, such as Barclay de Tolly, had been Baltic Germans. The contribution and sacrifice of the Baltic German noblemen in the Russian army's fight against France is reflected in an epitaph for the fallen Baltic Germans in Tallinn's (Reval's) Lutheran Dome Church. Von Bröcker's support for the St Petersburg court was in essence support for the principle of monarchy as a guarantor of conservative politics. At that time, the German-dominated Baltic provinces enjoyed autonomy and thus constituted a Western outpost in the vast Russian Empire.

But not all Emperors turned out to be 'good'. Alexander I's successor, Tsar Nicholas I (1825–55) was a reactionary autocrat. Nicholas I's successor Alexander II (1855–81) was conservative and authoritarian. With the rise of Prussia, they started to take a much less favourable view of German autonomy in the Baltic provinces.

When Bulmerincq became professor in Dorpat in 1856, he gave the standard oath, as used by any other State official, confirming his loyalty to the Russian Emperor. The oath was read in both Russian and German: in German it was as follows:

> Ich, August Bulmerincq, gelobe und schwöre bei Gott dem Allmächtigen und seinem heiligen Evangelium, dass ich will und soll Seiner Kaiserlichen Majestät, meinem Allergnädigsten wahren und angeborenen Großen Herrn und Kaiser

[119] Bulmerincq, *Die Systematik des Völkerrechts* (n 70 above) 137.

[120] The currency of the topic in post-1848 Europe was shown by another Dorpat master's thesis on the law of aliens. See V Polevoi, *Das Heimsfallsrecht (droit d'aubaine) vom völkerrechtlichen Standpunkte* (1855).

[121] *Das Inland* 29 March 1854, 211.

Alexander Nikolajewitsch, Selbstherrscher aller Reussen, und seiner Kaiserlichen Majestät Erben des Thrones aller Reussen, Seiner Kaiserlichen Hoheit, dem Großfürsten Caräwitsch Nikolai Alexandrowitsch, treu und redlich dienen und in Allem unterwürfig sein, ohne meines Lebens, bis zum letzten Blutstropfen zu schonen ... [122]

This was a pledge of allegiance to the principle of monarchy and to the Russian Emperor.

However, monarchy was now being challenged by the principle of nationalism. Rivalry between Prussia and Russia had been growing, increasing tensions between loyalty and identity among Baltic Germans. If your Russian monarch competes or even fights with the monarch of your German brethren, who do you support? At least indirectly, Bulmerincq's position in 1871 was expressed in his jubilant speech entitled 'Kaiser und Reich',[123] published in the *Baltische Monatsschrift* on the occasion of German unification.

During Bulmerincq's professorship in Dorpat, the debate between the Russian imperial writers and the Baltic Germans had become heated. The idea of Russification of the Baltic provinces had already been taken up in the 1830s by Count SS Uvarov, minister of education (1833–49). The question whether Baltic German autonomy could be trusted was especially acute in the light of the 1848 Revolution in Germany and Austria. According to one Baltic German author, the time of Uvarov became:

... the birth hour of a specific Baltic spirit that first expressed itself in negation, partiality and harshness. Individually and instinctively, the Baltic German already felt alienated from Russia and the Russians; after the great wake-up of 1845 the move was consciously away from the East. The mental border [Grenzwall] that had to defend the West from the East became essential.[124]

After the Polish upheaval of 1863, the Russian press became particularly alert to the threat of German autonomy in the Baltic provinces.[125] Additional provocation came when, in 1864, the Livonian Lutheran Bishop, Ferdinand Walter, preached the Germanization of the Latvians and Estonians, in order to achieve 'national and confessional identity and equality with their masters'.[126] In 1862, a history professor at Dorpat, Carl Schirren (1826–1910), gave an influential series of public lectures arguing that the Baltic Germans differed fundamentally in their culture from the Russians.[127] In 1863 the leader of German Baltic autonomy,

[122] Tartu University Archive, F 402/3/204.

[123] A Bulmerincq, 'Kaiser und Reich' (1871) XX *Baltische Monatsschrift* 170–80. See also Bulmerincq's other articles in *Baltische Monatsschrift*, 'Das germanische Nationalmuseum und unsere historische Arbeit', 204–31; 'Aus der Literatur über deutsche Einheit und deutsches Reich' 191–208.

[124] W Wulffius, 'Carl Schirren' (1927) 58 *Baltische Monatsschrift* 2–21.

[125] S Isakov, *Ostzeiskij vopros v russkoi pechati 1860-kh godov* (1861).

[126] M Haltzel, *Der Abbau der deutschen ständischen Selbstverwaltung in den Ostseeprovinzen Russlands* (1977) 29.

[127] A Kärssin, *Politiker Carl Schirren und seine 'Livländische Antwort'* (1995).

Count Lieven, demanded that erroneous presentations in the Russian media be countered by reliable individuals.[128] This was the context in which Bulmerincq published his views in 1865 on the legal and historical development of the Baltic provinces.

'Rußland. Die deutschen Ostseeprovinzen' was published in Bluntschli's *Deutsches Staatswörterbuch*.[129] Note the tension in the title of the contribution—were those provinces indeed Russian or German, or both? Bulmerincq's narrative again moved between history and the law, though again his argument is essentially based on history. He begins with German colonization (Bulmerincq's own term) in the thirteenth century, citing civilizational superiority as the ultimate justification for the act of colonization:

> We leave aside the question whether since the ninth century the Estonians, Latvians and Livonians had to pay tribute to the Russians. In any case the mere duty to pay tribute could not be the basis of a closer and more efficient relationship. Therefore, the recently intensified dispute over the priority of civilization in the Baltic Sea provinces 'through the Russians or the Germans?' is superfluous since even if Russia has made civilizing attempts, in any case for the Germans as the more civilized parties there remained, and still remains, enough work to do.[130]

On the arrival of the German colonizers the native peoples were almost exclusively heathens. 'The level of the culture was low.' One could not really speak of science and art—only Latvian and Estonian folk songs and tales were testimony to some sort of cultural development. The native peoples had not yet even learned to write. As far as their material life was concerned, only shipbuilding had to a modest extent been developed.[131]

Modern authors have pointed out how the most outstanding Baltic German lawyers and historians (for example Arbusow) had, up until the early twentieth century, held that only through the arrival of the German colonizers in the thirteenth century did the Baltic lands gain access to culture and history.[132] Bulmerincq was no exception in this regard. He recounted how 'the Baltic Sea provinces historically recognized Protestantism, the predominance of the German language and German law'. Nevertheless, Bulmerincq was not a political hardliner; he recognized it as a historical problem that social stratification largely followed ethnic lines, while native Estonians and Latvians, constituting a big

[128] A von Tobien, *Die livländische Ritterschaft in ihrem Verhältnis zum Zarismus und russischen Nationalismus* (1925) vol I, 126.

[129] A Bulmerincq, 'Russland. Die deutschen Ostseeprovinzen' in JC Bluntschli and K Brater (eds), *Deutsches Staatswörterbuch* (1865) vol 9. For Bluntschli's prominent role in 19th-century international law scholarship, see B Röben, *Johann Caspar Bluntschli, Francis Lieber und das moderne Völkerrecht 1861–1881* (2003).

[130] Bulmerincq, 'Russland' (n 129 above) 2.

[131] ibid.

[132] M Garleff, 'Stereotypen im wechselseitigen deutsch-baltischen Kulturtransfer' in H Henning Hahn (ed), *Stereotyp, Identität und Geschichte: die Funktion von Geschichte in gesellschaftlichen Diskursen* (2002) 349, 352.

numerical majority in the provinces, were peasants and servants at the lower levels of society.[133]

It is also worth looking at Bulmerincq's account of the end of the independence of Old Livonia after the Russians caused its collapse in 1558 by breaking an earlier peace treaty and starting a military campaign against the country. 'Old Livonia could have continued to exist for further centuries, if the neighbouring peoples had not pushed it too hard, if the scarcity of its own military forces and the lack of inner unanimity had not defended it too badly and if the German Reich had not left it helpless, notwithstanding the repeated requests for support.'[134] There was a sense of nostalgia for the lost independence of Old Livonia in this interpretation of events. In addition, there was an expression of disappointment and sense of betrayal, so often felt by colonists and borderlands with respect to their distant 'motherlands'.

In the end, Russia failed to gain control over Old Livonia and the country was divided between Poland and Sweden in 1583:

> Thus Livonia was not only divided but had also had its political independence stolen, the divided lands and conquered towns had at the very least to be vigilant in the defence of their religion, their language, their laws, their unique institutions and possessions. Although at this hour of danger, the motherland was not ready to help and keep the German colonies through their connection and independence, nevertheless it remained a duty of the colonizers to defend their most precious assets.'[135]

In other words, the Baltic Germans were left to fight for national self-rule and autonomy on their own. Following centuries were difficult for the cause of Baltic German self-rule. In the early seventeenth century Poland started to implement its plans for the destruction of German religious and linguistic autonomy of the provinces.[136] In Bulmerincq's view, Swedish rule was also disappointing, since it was ultimately directed towards the destruction of the 'uniqueness of the country' (ie Baltic German autonomy).[137]

After Russia finally managed to wrest Estonia and Livonia from Sweden in the course of the Nordic War (1700–21), the Baltic Germans and the cities presented their conditions for subjugation (*Accord-Puncten*) to the Russian Tsar. The Baltic German nobility wanted confirmation of its earlier rights and privileges and ultimately its political, linguistic, and religious autonomy. Peter the Great accepted these conditions by an act of grace on 30 September 1710.[138] And now in 1865: 'The colonies established on the Baltic Sea have started their life with a fight, lost independence in a fight but have notwithstanding all fights preserved their Lutheran religion, their German language, their German education, their German law and their unique administration.'[139]

[133] Bulmerincq, 'Russland' (n 129 above) 5. [134] ibid 9. [135] ibid 10.
[136] ibid 10–11. [137] ibid 13. [138] ibid 15. [139] ibid 19.

Nevertheless, under Emperor Alexander II, the colonies needed to realize that a new politics and attitude were necessary. The native peoples had to be included more in the government, but at the same time, the German Baltic provinces, Estonia, Livonia, and Curonia, had to realize that there was no alternative to unification: 'Then but also only then will a new time of development break out and the work of colonization be continued in a worthy manner ... Should old Livonia stand up anew, the old Livonians have to transform into new ones, the special notions of Livonians, Estonians and Curonians must disappear before there can be a unifying meaning to the name: the Baltic Germans.'[140] But unity with whom? If the essence of the Baltic provinces was their German identity and their drive for national self-determination, what was to be done with the overwhelming majority of the population, the non-German native population, the Estonians and Latvians? If national self-determination was the guiding principle, should the native Estonians and Latvians have also somehow counted? Although Bulmerincq recognized the need for institutional reform and the wider inclusion of the native peoples, this inclusion had to be undertaken under German Baltic leadership. In Bulmerincq's view, this was dictated by the inherent cultural-historical superiority of the Germans over the native peoples—a typically colonialist argument often employed by Europeans outside Europe.[141]

The political-intellectual race for the identity of the Baltic provinces had started. After Bulmerincq published his views, the conflict escalated with the outbreak of the so-called *Broschyrenstreit*. In 1868 the Russian publicist Juri Samarin (1819–76) published a polemic declaring that it was high time to subject the Baltic provinces to the Russian language and the Orthodox religion.[142] The privileges of the Baltic Germans had to come to an end. Carl Schirren, the history professor of Dorpat, responded with a fiery reply,[143] emphatically rejecting Samarin's claims for further Russification as unfounded and illegal.[144]

Law thus became a central argument in the question regarding supremacy in and the identity of the Baltic provinces. Schirren and other Baltic German scholars, such as Georg von Bunge (1802–97) and Theodor Schiemann (1847–21), maintained that the *Accord-Puncten* of 1710 constituted an international treaty to which the principle *pacta sunt servanda* applied.[145] According to this 'Baltic constitution' theory, the

140 ibid 19.

141 cf A Anghie, *Imperialism, Sovereignty and the Making of International Law* (2005).

142 J Samarin, *Okrainy Rossii. Serija pervaja. Russkoe baltijskoe pamor'e* (1868).

143 C Schirren, *Livländische Antwort and Herrn Juri Samarin* (The Livonian Answer to Mr Juri Samarin) (1869) (repr 1971).

144 See ibid 155. For Schirren's other historical works of political relevance at that time, see also his *Qullen zur Geschichte des Untergangs livländischer Selbständigkeit. Aus dem schwedischen Reichsarchive zu Stockholm* (1861).

145 Schirren, *Livländische* (n 143 above) 157. See also I Raudma, 'Vaidlused Eestimaa rüütelkonna 29. sept. 1710 alistumisakti juriidilise iseloomu üle' (1935) 5 *Üliõpilasleht* 218–23.

Baltic provinces were in personal union with Russia and were not 'usual' provinces of the latter. Schirren concluded: 'We have not been conquered ... Therefore, the Tsar's documents give beside 'legitimate and victorious arms' an equal place to 'privileges and freedoms' of the land, so that the nature of the union becomes immediately clear—the union of power and law. On that side is power; we have the law/right.'[146]

In comparison with Schirren's, Bulmerincq's tone was softer, his politics more liberal. In his 1865 text, Bulmerincq the international lawyer did not base his central claim regarding the Baltic provinces on international law. Paradoxically it was the history (and geography) professor Schirren who, in response to the attack by Samarin, put forward that argument. Schirren failed to distinguish legal from political arguments: in his presentation, *Völkerrecht* arises together with other moral and political arguments. On the other hand, in presenting the Baltic German claim, Bulmerincq sought no help from international law; for him the argument of different levels of civilization seemed convincing enough.

4.3.3 Praxis, Theorie und Codification des Völkerrechts *(1874)*

One of the surprising characteristics of 'positivist' international law scholars, such as Bulmerincq and others of his time, was how easily they could express in a single breath demands for objectivity and scientific legalism and at the same time make utterly subjective political comments. What G Rolin-Jaequymans said of Bulmerincq's book, *Praxis, Theorie und Codification des Völkerrechts*—'un livre qui sort de la banalité'[147]—seems to hold true.

On the one hand, Bulmerincq demanded that subjectivism and 'phrases' be expelled from international law. For instance, he demanded neutrality of the universal history of international law and the expulsion of the political. Such a history had yet to be written: 'We expect equally little the glorification of one single nation as for example in Combes (*Histoire générale de la diplomatie Européenne*, Paris, 1854) or throwing dirt at others as for example in Mitchell's *Memoirs and Papers* (1850).'[148] At the same time, Bulmerincq revealed at least three clear political biases: as a German regarding the Franco-German rivalry, as a Lutheran *vis-à-vis* the Catholic Church and, thirdly, his political (conservative) disagreement with the socialist movement that envisaged an 'impossible future'. In a non-legal festive speech entitled 'Kaiser und Reich', published in 1871 in the *Baltische Monatsschrift*, Bulmerincq had already celebrated

[146] Schirren, *Livländishe* (n 143 above) 115.

[147] (1874) VI *Revue de droit* 694, 696.

[148] Bulmerincq, *Praxis, Theorie* (n 69 above) 95. In a later addendum, Bulmerincq added that it was in the nature of this work that it had to be international and not national. No nation could feel privileged in advancing the work of completing the history of international law. Qualified men from all countries had the right to participate, without jealousy and presumption. See 'Notice de M. A. Bulmerincq sur la littérature récente du droit international en Allemagne, traduite par M. Rivier et lue par lui en séance du lundi matin, 30 aout 1875' (1875) VII *Revue de droit* 99, 103–4.

the unification of Germany. This was a moving patriotic speech in which the author expressed the wish that the Germans:

> ... will live at home in an undisturbed manner, outside, in the council of peoples, let its mighty voice be heard, to the just ones for help and defence [*zum Schutz und Trutz*], to the arrogant ones for warning and punishment.[149]
>
> The strong people in the Middle Empire are ordered to serve as the guardian and guarantor [*Hüter und Wächter*] of world peace.[150]

Bulmerincq was confident that 'the German people are peace loving, their Emperor may not be a breaker of peace. He will defend his own people, not attack the others'.[151] While this was of course not formulated as a legal text, it demonstrated that even international lawyers who insisted on the separation of law and politics, were individuals with political dreams and social aspirations needing to be expressed and celebrated.

In *Praxis, Theorie und Codification des Völkerrechts*, the same work in which Bulmerincq demanded objectivity and the separation of international law from politics, he made passionate comments on the Franco-Prussian War of 1870–71 and the ensuing unification of Germany, the new Middle Empire (*Reich der Mitte*). According to Bulmerincq, it was necessary for the maintenance of peace that France give up its 'chauvinism and revanchist dreams'.[152] He was also upset that international laws of neutrality had been violated in the war between Prussia and France—when citizens of third countries 'in the greatest fashion' delivered shipments of war material to 'one of the warring parties'. It was again history that explained quite a lot about the state of international affairs. For example, in some countries (such as France, Spain, and Italy) monarchs could claim title according to the principle of legitimacy but as their dynasties were 'not grown together with the people' but 'only wanted to rule', the legitimacy they held neither safeguarded their power nor enabled them to regain it. They were not 'part of the people' and did not represent them.[153] Even Napoleon I lacked an intimate relationship (*inniges Verhältnis*) with his people.[154] The most deplorable thing about him was that he was striving towards universal monarchy—but this was also the reason why this once feared ruler was destined to fail and became a 'powerless prisoner in St. Helena'.[155]

Bulmerincq also found an opportunity to give his opinion on Germany's new constitution. Although he admitted it had found its critics among scholars of Southern Germany (such as von Mohl), he believed it was a 'reasonable compromise' implemented by a 'non-doctrinal *homme d'État*'.[156]

And yet he had more to add about the rulers of France:

> Statesmen have repeatedly tried to switch attention from unsatisfactory domestic circumstances to glorious wars and this has especially been the politics of the

[149] Bulmerincq, *Praxis, Theorie* (n 69 above) 170. [150] ibid. [151] ibid. [152] ibid 6.
[153] ibid 7. [154] ibid 11. [155] ibid 11–12. [156] ibid 13.

Bonapartes—but they were never representatives of international law ... Their victories did not increase their prestige as subjects of international law; Napoleon I was only feared, never respected and Napoleon III issued almost unnoticed demands for the creation of a universal congress. As he experienced his last failure, the one at Sedan, the world felt relieved from a nightmare and even France breathed freely, France that is now again manipulated by Bonapartism and has begun to forget Sedan. A France that would entangle itself in the Bonapartian nets of revenge could only deserve political disrespect.[157]

Bulmerincq's criticism of the policies of France did not, however, prevent him from recognizing the position of the French language as the language of international law. Bulmerincq believed that the French language was especially well-suited for international law, more so than English or German.[158] This was so for reasons inherent in the French language itself: English would never achieve this status.[159] But Bulmerincq also made it clear that preferring a certain language did not imply preferring the nation of its native speakers.[160]

Secondly, equally clear as Bulmerincq's disdain of policies of Napoleon's France was his rejection of Catholic universalism. His angry reaction to claims of Catholic universalism invoked images of age-old conspiracy theories regarding the Church's pursuit of power. He criticized ultramontanist 'disturbers of the peace' whose political propaganda was 'unpatriotic and radical'.[161] Essentially, the Church with its universalistic claims was waging a battle against the State. To fight the ultramontanists was not only a political necessity; it was an 'international legal obligation'.[162] 'The head of the religious-political International has its seat in Rome, its constitutive members [Bundesgenossen] are ... knights of legitimacy ... The religious-political International has far-reaching goals, it wants to create a Christian-Catholic world state. It is an international legal obligation to intervene against all those enemies of the State and of the States.'[163]

The antagonism which existed between the Catholic Church and the nation State was a historic phenomenon. According to Bulmerincq, the Germans and other Germanic peoples played a crucial role in ensuring the victory of the nation State:

The power position desired by the Catholic Church had been disturbed before the Reformation. The nations acquired their complete independence only when they broke completely from the Catholic Church. This was the work of the Reformation that was carried out by the Germanic peoples led by a German monk. It was of German origin and German and Swedish blood sealed it in the Thirty Years' War. The reformation was an uprising against the papacy because the latter was disrespectful towards and even tried to undermine the independence of nations and the freedom of individuals.[164] [The Swedish king] Gustavus Adolphus saved the Reformation and therefore indirectly the principle of nationality.

[157] Bulmerincq, *Praxis, Theorie* (n 69 above) 22. [158] ibid 119–20. [159] ibid 121.
[160] ibid 122. [161] ibid 18–19. [162] ibid 20. [163] ibid 21. [164] ibid 59.

Moreover, Bulmerincq claimed that the principle of individuality also originated in German thought.[165]

Bulmerincq's attack on Catholicism in his international law treatise becomes more understandable when one takes into account the position he expressed in his speech 'Kaiser und Reich'—namely, that the Lutheran Church would become the church of the German people in which the national and the Christian would be united and express everything that was 'healthy' in the German people.[166] Bulmerincq thus positioned himself clearly in the German *Kulturkampf* on the side of Bismarck against the Catholic ultramontanists, in particular the (Catholic conservative) Centre Party.[167]

But Catholic ultramontanists were not the only enemies of the State Bulmerincq fought against in 1874. An equal danger was posed by the social democratic movement which, as Bulmerincq claimed, had a lot in common with the ultramontanists. Both the ultramontanists and the socialists (*Socialpolitiker*) had been accorded the 'undeserved honour' of equal rights with legitimate political parties, instead of being considered enemies of the concept of political parties.[168]

> Although the social democrats are only represented in minor numbers in elected assemblies, they constitute a power that is more and more a danger to the State, since outside the chambers, in the circles of material work, they attract bigger and bigger crowds to their anti-State doctrines in order to manipulate the masses. While first limiting themselves to economic and societal questions, the social democrats later turned to political questions and now seek to overthrow the State through the economy and society.[169]

Social democrats and ultramontanists offered various points of comparison:

> Both hold the organs of the State in contempt and the existing laws in disrespect; both are unpatriotic, both write and talk fanatically, without piety and moderation; both see their activities in agitation and therefore organize strikes for the employees and workers, while ultramontanists organize time-wasting pilgrimages for the masses ... The difference between the two consists in the fact that the ultramontanists recognize the authority of the Church and Jesuitism while the social democrats, denying all religion and morality, seek supporters through a political economy and dialectic created by themselves and that mainly consists in negation and envisages an impossible future.[170]

Bulmerincq drew his readers' attention to the fact that the agitation of the workers had turned to the creation of a social-democratic fraternalism crossing State borders, and had created a central organ for its

[165] ibid 60. This thought was Hegelian. Hegel wrote in *The Philosphy of History* that 'the Orient knew and knows only that one is free, the Greek and Roman world that some are free; the Germanic world knows that all are free' (n 87 above) Foreword by CJ Friedrich.

[166] Bulmerincq, 'Kaiser und Reich' (n 123 above) 175.

[167] See on Bismarck's *Kulturkampf* eg in GA Craig, *Germany 1866–1945* (1978) 63ff; E Feuchtwanger, *Bismarck* (2002) 187ff.

[168] Bulmerincq, *Praxis, Theorie* (n 69 above) 23.

[169] ibid 24.

[170] ibid 24–5.

goals: 'the so-called International'. With that development, 'not only a reason but a duty to react' had emerged for international law:[171] 'The States that in bold overestimation of their conditions have offered their soil to socialists for spreading propaganda in other countries will one day recognize that they have themselves fed and raised the disturbers of their own order as well.'[172]

Note that Bulmerincq's assault on ultramontanists and social democrats completely coincided with Bismarck's policies and campaigns and that the book immediately preceded Bulmerincq's move from Dorpat to Wiesbaden, Germany. It is likely that he simply wished his political views to be known in clear terms in his new homeland. Indeed, it turned out that there was a reason why a differentiation between 'practice' and 'theory' had been made in the title of Bulmerincq's book.

In his 1874 book, Bulmerincq also asked: has international law given nations the right to secession and the creation of their own nation States? The French Revolution of 1789 initiated the international legal treatment of the 'nationality principle'. Abbé Greggoire had declared at a meeting of the National Convent in 1795 that nations were independent of each other and sovereign. On 5 March 1848, following the February revolution, Lamartine had issued a proclamation of the French government insisting that peace should be based on the recognition and respect of the independence of nations.[173] There was no doubt that the unification of Germany in 1871 found its justification in the 'nationality principle'.[174] Other such examples were Greece, Belgium, and Italy. The Italian author Manzini (1817–88) had even argued that nations rather than States were the elementary units of international law.[175] Bulmerincq argued against Manzini's view that peoples existed without the unity of their country or with no country at all (for example the Jews) and that international law demonstrated that a community of law could exist without being a community of nationalities.[176]

True, Bulmerincq 'completely supported' the opinion of Rolin-Jaequemyns, according to whom States that 'represented' the nationality principle had the right to follow their natural development and unite the same people, living in different States, into one State.[177] The nationality principle could legitimately be a factor in domestic politics, being a basis for the request of guarantees such as the use of a language. But in Bulmerincq's view, to go further would have brought about the dissolution of existing States, revolution, and war. He warned prophetically: 'Such as earlier religious wars, so in the future, wars between nationalities can be led and have already been led. Today no longer religion but nationality is the driving force but this too does not lead to peace but to struggle.'[178] This concern and the limited number of precedents made

[171] Bulmerincq, *Praxis, Theorie* (n 69 above) 26. [172] ibid 27. [173] ibid 61.
[174] ibid 63. [175] PS Manzini, *Della nazionalitá come fondamento del diritto delle genti* (1851).
[176] Bulmerincq, *Praxis, Theorie* (n 69 above) 67. [177] ibid 68. [178] ibid 69.

Bulmerincq conclude that international law could not be based on the 'nationality principle'.[179] Would he have held the same opinion if Germany had not yet been unified?

Although Bulmerincq did not explicitly use the argument of civilization in his assaults on the Bonaparte family, socialism, and Catholic ultramontanism, it is implicit. In comparison to Bismarck's Germany, Bonaparte's France represented a pre-modern type of monarchy—not 'uncivilized' but irrational, unnatural, and obscure. Ultramontanist mysticism certainly was obscure and socialist agitation constituted an assault on European 'civilization'.

4.4 Conclusion: Bulmerincq's 'positivist' approach

August Bulmerincq belonged to the first modern generation of international law professionals.[180] A more focused specialization among international lawyers had not yet taken place. Bulmerincq and his *Gründergeneration* of professional international lawyers saw themselves as activists for various good causes.[181] The development of international law was not the only challenging project at hand. Bulmerincq's writings and interests ranged from international law to different issues and aspects of public life, as far afield as agriculture. Yet although Bulmerincq had many interests, he was first and foremost an activist for 'positive' international law.

His work and character had been described as 'solid' by his contemporaries. This was appreciated by his successors at Dorpat. Carl Bergbohm recognized that, in his time, Bulmerincq had possessed 'the best knowledge of the material contained in the treaties'.[182] From the positivist point of view, this was the best possible compliment on one's craftsmanship.[183] Vladimir Hrabar, Bergbohm's successor at Dorpat (Iur'ev), maintained that although Bulmerincq's works may sometimes have been difficult to read, they were deep and rich in content and demonstrated how hardworking their author had been.[184]

[179] ibid 70.

[180] For the distinction between the 'classicists' of the 18th and 'the professionals' of the 19th century, see M Koskenniemi, *From Apology to Utopia: The Structure of International Legal Argument* (1989) 83–127.

[181] cf T Veblen, *The Theory of the Leisure Class* (1967) (first published 1899): 'The leisure class is in some degree sheltered from the stress of the industrial situation, and should, therefore, afford an exceptionally great proportion of reversions to the peaceable or savage temperament . . . There is, for instance, an appreciable proportion of the upper classes whose inclinations lead them into philanthropic work, and there is a considerable body of sentiment in the class going to support efforts to reform and amelioration', 234. See also on leisure (*skholè*) as a precondition for the 'scholastic point of view', P Bourdieu, *Pascalian Meditations* (trans R Nice, 2000) 13.

[182] C Bergbohm, 'August von Bulmerincq' in *Allgemeine Deutsche Biographie* (1903) vol 47, 348, 349.

[183] At the same time, Bulmerincq's work proves that 19th-century professionals, as opposed to some 18th-century classicists, 'do not collect facts merely to achieve full description'. See Koskenniemi, *From Apology* (n 180 above) 122.

[184] V Grabar, 'August Bulmerincq' in I Andreevski (ed), *Entsiklopeditseski slovar Brokhausa-Efrona* (1891) 910. (See reference to spellings, Hrabar and Grabar, in section 6.1 below.)

Bulmerincq's 'solidity' did not automatically imply his affiliation with political conservativism. After all, there was a Catholic and a Protestant version of conservativism in Bismarck's Germany. First of all, Bulmerincq was an admirer of Bismarck and therefore could have no sympathy for Catholic conservatives.[185] But he had strong convictions on issues that touched upon his identity. At a deep level he remained a conservative in regretting that, thanks to secularism, States were no longer seen as moral institutions and had become subject to steady political changes, without a determined goal.[186] He remained a conservative when, in his history of the Baltic provinces, he concluded that the German *Kulturträgerei* in the Eastern part of Europe, the *mission civilisatrice* that was started in the thirteenth century, had to be continued. He remained a conservative when he depicted the looming danger of the socialist movement that did nothing but wish for an 'impossible future'. He was unable to give up what was dear to him—and there was a lot that had to be defended.

Bulmerincq's international law reflected this identity, one he never tried to hide. Like many positivist lawyers, his own subjectivity never seemed to be an issue for him. In Bulmerincq's times, national identity was so self-evident for most intellectuals that no one was surprised when an international lawyer also argued as a patriot.

Almost like Dr Jekyll and Mr Hyde, there are two Bulmerincqs: the protagonist for 'positive' international law who advocates the expulsion of politics from legal discourse and the German patriot and pamphleteer for various (mostly conservative) political causes. There was less apparent contradiction here as long as items written for different purposes and audiences were printed in different forums—the legal *Revue de droit international et de législation comparée*, the cultural-political *Baltische Monatsschrift*, etc. But sometimes, as in particular in *Praxis, Theorie und Codification des Völkerrechts* (1874), the international lawyer and the political pamphleteer met, blurred, and contradicted each other. For his positivist successors, such as his disciple Carl Bergbohm, this amounted to professional failure. It was true, Bergbohm said of Bulmerincq, that he had been working during a period when the state of the general theory of international law was still weak and there was no clarity concerning sources. But Bergbohm was also compelled to conclude that Bulmerincq finally lacked 'the sharpness of definition and the energy for an uncompromising defence of a scientific system promising objective truths against subjective ideas'.[187]

But taking into account Bulmerincq's sharp intellect and wide knowledge, it is unlikely that he simply missed out something really essential

[185] A Bulmerincq, 'La politique et le droit dans la vie des états' (1877) IX *Revue de droit international et de législation comparée* 361, at 370 he criticized the fact that in the German Reichstag the collaberation of conservatives, ultramontanes, and social democrats was only explained by their common negation of liberalism.

[186] ibid 366.

[187] Bergbohm, 'August von Bulmerincq' (n 182 above) 348, 349.

or was professionally short-sighted with his inconsequential 'positivism'. Just as other 'men of 1873', he may have used the concept of 'civilization' as a neutralizing strategy. Of course, law was and had to be separate from politics—but 'civilization', a concept which dictated many answers, was not part of politics! It is impossible to establish retrospectively to what extent this strategy of neutralization was a conscious effort. The inclusion of 'subjective ideas' later criticized by Bergbohm could have been consciously continued while at the same time maintaining the separation of law from politics. If so, the price this kind of positivism paid was hypocrisy.

The immersion of an international legal text in politics can no doubt be regarded as professional failure. (This was essentially Bergbohm's judgment on Bulmerincq.) But it may be a strategy of argumentation,[188] the strategy of positivism, or even international legal discourse as a whole. The context of international legal texts indicates that such texts not only aim at presenting knowledge, they also attempt to persuade, take a stance, change the world. International law is an argumentative framework produced in the context of historical struggles. One of the ways of persuading and claiming authority in international legal argument is to emphasize 'interest in disinterestedness'. Bulmerincq realized that to claim a distinction between law and politics was essential for the authority of international law. International law was developing into a formalized, seemingly depoliticized language for addressing the world of political and social struggles. Bulmerincq's legal positivism freed from politics was politics disguised, where politics appeared officially only as the politics of others. The fight against asylum or social democracy or ultramontanist agitation, however, dictated by the 'civilization' itself, became in Bulmerincq's discourse an international legal obligation of the utmost importance.

5. Bergbohm: The Radical Mind

5.1 Der Kampf ums Recht: *Bergbohm's life*

> . . . before its suppression, [Dorpat] was a Holy Place of *Baltentum*, in association and tradition incomparably rich . . . It was a true German University with an atmosphere of *Burschen* and *Wilden, Philister, Manichäer*, and the rest of it . . . The professional atmosphere was one of vigorous, not to say pugnacious, disputation, with the whole world as the field of discussion. Professors imported from Germany often found it difficult to acclimatise themselves to the argumentative atmosphere,

[188] In a similar context, Benedict Kingsbury has interpreted Lassa Oppenheim's normative positivism as political, and as best suited to advance his moral and political values. See B Kingsbury, 'Legal Positivism as Normative Politics: International Society, Balance of Power and Lassa Oppenheim's Positive International Law' (2002) 13(2) EJIL 401–37.

> for the modern German Professor is neither so catholic nor so combative as was an earlier generation: '*die baltischen Kollegen*', one such importation once wrote, '*sind alle noch die alten Schwertbrüder*'.
>
> British author Ralph Butler, 1919[189]

Carl Bergbohm, Bulmerincq's successor at Dorpat, is nowadays principally remembered as a legal philosopher due to his influential and controversial work *Jurisprudenz und Rechtsphilosophie* (1892). As a legal theorist, Bergbohm was the most outspoken and radical representative of legal positivism before Hans Kelsen (1881–1973).[190] Like Kelsen, Bergbohm's legal theory was especially influenced by his interest in international law. Bergbohm started his academic career as an international law scholar and published both his masters and doctoral thesis on the theoretical and historical aspects of international law.

Like Bulmerincq, Bergbohm was the son of a merchant family from Riga. (Bergbohm's father was a member of the 2nd merchant's guild while, in his time, Bulmerincq's had been the head of the 1st guild.) Carl Magnus Bergbohm was born on 18 September 1849 and went to school in Riga. His father insisted on his preparing for a practical profession and sent him to Riga's *Realgymnasium* where the education emphasized the natural sciences rather than the humanities and languages. When Carl Magnus completed his *gymnasium* studies in 1867, he could not immediately take up legal studies at Dorpat due to his inadequate knowledge of Latin. Instead, he matriculated in the Department of Astronomy, in the Faculty of Physics, and mathematics. In 1869, however, Bergbohm transferred to the Faculty of Law and completed his law degree in 1874.

Tempora mutantur et nos mutamur in illis. It is difficult to imagine now how a masters thesis could earn any scholarly acclaim or attention. It seems that the words (for example 'master') are the same but that their meaning has been degraded over time. However, Bergbohm's masters thesis, *Staatsverträge und Gesetze als Quellen des Völkerrechts*,[191] drew a lot of attention in the German-speaking scholarly community.

In 1877, Bergbohm was appointed Associate Professor (*etatmässiger Dozent*) at Dorpat. In 1883 he published a German translation of the international law textbook of Friedrich von (Fyodor) Martens (1845–1909).[192] Shortly thereafter, in 1884, he defended his doctoral thesis, *Die bewaffnete Neutralität von 1780–1783*—a work which we will consider in more detail.

[189] R Butler, *The New Eastern Europe* (1919) 30–1.

[190] Writing in 1925, Julius Binder, when distinguishing Bergbohm from Kelsen, considered Bergbohm the leading positivist, and Kelsen, the leading 'neo-Kantian'. See J Binder, *Philosophie des Rechts* (1925). See also H Kelsen, 'Reine Rechtslehre. Mit einem Anhang: Das problem der Gerechtigkeit', *2. vollständig neu bearbeitete und erweiterte Auflage* (1960).

[191] (1877). The thesis was prepared in part during study trips to Berlin and Leipzig and defended at Dorpat in 1876.

[192] F Martens, *Das Völkerrecht der civilisierten Nationen* (1883). For a review, see Geffcken (1884) XVI *Revue de droit* 100–5.

In 1885, with the help of an influential recommendation from Bulmerincq, he was elected associate member of the *Institut de droit international.*[193]

In 1888, Bergbohm married Lilly Lieven, the daughter of an influential Baltic German attorney, Sigismund Lieven, and 21 years his junior. Two children were born from this marriage after the couple had moved to Germany.

The struggle between the Russian centralists and the Baltic Germans for supremacy in the Baltic provinces left an even bigger mark on Bergbohm's life than on that of his predecessor, Bulmerincq. As a result of this conflict, Bergbohm was not appointed ordinary professor in Dorpat. Indeed, his not formally becoming an *ordinarius* is a remarkable part of his story as professor.

Bergbohm's troubles started with his masters examination. Like everyone else, as part of the examination he had to demonstrate sufficient knowledge of the Russian language. However, the certificate he received on 3 February 1875 indicates that he was considered 'not capable of conducting written business in Russian'.[194]

Bulmerincq retired as Professor of International Law in 1875. In 1877, Edgar Friedrich Löning (1843–1919) of the University of Straßburg (now Strasbourg) was called to Dorpat to take Bulmerincq's chair.[195] However, in 1883 Löning, probably unable to cope with the contentious atmosphere at Dorpat, gave up the chair and moved to Rostock, Germany. This was an opportunity for Bergbohm, who had just completed his doctoral thesis.[196] In March 1884, Dorpat's law faculty elected Bergbohm Professor of State and International Law.[197] The Russian press had started a campaign against his appointment, suggesting that an ethnic Russian be appointed instead. But by a small majority, the university council consisting of ordinary and extraordinary professors approved Bergbohm's appointment.

The minister of education in St Petersburg did not follow the council's recommendation to appoint Bergbohm. Although officially the 'insufficiency of humanistic education' was quoted as the reason,[198] it was clear to everyone that the real reasons lay elsewhere. In the elections that took place at the university, Ottomar Meykow, a pro-Russian colleague of German origin at the Faculty of Law and later Rector, had hinted in his dissenting opinion that Bergbohm had in his dissertation showed disrespect towards the Russian Empress Catherine II.[199] Bergbohm's

[193] See (1885–1886) VIII *Annuaire de l'Institut de droit international* 350.

[194] See the certificate in the Estonian State Archive, F 402/2/1537.

[195] See V Hrabar, 'Edgar Friedrich Löning' in G Levitski (ed), *Biograficheski slovar professorov i prepodovatelei Imperatorskago Iur'evsago, byvshago Derptskago, Universiteta* (1902) vol I, 630–3. For a work defended in Löning's time, see O Eichelmann, *Ueber die Kriegsgefangenschaft. Eine völkerrechtliche Studie* (1878).

[196] See TF Kremer, *Die 'wissenschaftliche Rechtsphilosophie' Carl Magnus Bergbohms. Versuch einer analytisch-kritischen Rekonstruktion* (2001) 5ff.

[197] See the letter of the faculty to the university council in the Estonian History Archive, F 402/3/95, 71.

[198] See V Grabar, 'Carl Magnus Bergbohm' in Levitski (ed) (n 195 above) 639.

[199] See *Extract aus dem Journal des Conseils der Kaiserlichen Universität Dorpat, 16.03.1884*, Estonian History Archive, F 402/3/95, 90 etc.

dissertation became the object of intense scrutiny and prejudgement. Bergbohm himself commented in a letter to German colleague Friedrich Thudichum: 'I am on my side playing in this affair the role of a harmless person that has ended up on railway tracks on which two overheated locomotives are racing towards each other. I will probably find my miserable end in this!'[200]

For the rest of his Dorpat years, Bergbohm continued as an associate professor (*Dozent*) who had been elected professor but not confirmed by the Ministry. In a letter to a friend, he explained that he intended 'to hold through until the last moment ... for the best of the German cause in Livonia'.[201] But due to the politics of Russification, things looked gloomier for that cause. In a letter to Ferdinand von Martitz, Bergbohm summed up the effects of Russification on the Faculty of Law: 'For every German professor who has remained', wrote Bergbohm, the authorities had appointed a Russian 'who reads the discipline in the Russian language, competing with the German professor, while those students who were enrolled after February 1889 are obliged only to take the Russian lectures'.[202] Indeed, while Bergbohm continued as Associate Professor, a Russian scholar, I Dityatin, was appointed to a chair of International and Constitutional Law. Bulmerincq's old Chair was *de facto* split, Dityatin taking over the constitutional law courses and Bergbohm remaining responsible only for the international law part.[203] Bergbohm's time at Dorpat can be characterized as the time of the liquidation of Baltic German autonomy or self-determination by the Russian Empire.

In the notes that students took during Bergbohm's earlier lectures on constitutional law, Russia seems to be conspicuously absent. It does not come up even as a comparison with the countries of Western Europe.[204] Russia, an absolutist monarchy, was for Bergbohm worlds apart from the European constitutional monarchies and republics. By contrast, the courses of AD Gradovskii, Professor of State Law at St Petersburg University until 1889, the 'father of the Russian science of State law' and a teacher of Fyodor Martens (1845–1909), were characterized by the 'excessive idealisation of the Russian State system', including idealization of the 'unlimited autocracy'.[205]

[200] Letter to F Thudichum, Dorpat, 16/4 January 1885, University Library of Tübingen, Signature: Md 728/6. Quoted in Kremer (n 196 above) 7.

[201] Quoted in ibid 8.

[202] Letter to F von Martitz, Dorpat, 24/12 December 1890, Staatsbibliothek zu Berlin, Signatur: Slg. Darmstaedter (2 h 1900).

[203] See V Hrabar, 'Carl Magnus Bergbohm' in Levitski (ed) (n 198 above) 639.

[204] See C Bergbohm, *Theorie des Staatsrechts*, Vorlesungen an der Universität Dorpat im II. Semester 1883, nachgeschrieben von einem Studenten, Tartu University library, manuscripts department, F 55/1/140. But see AW Hupel, *Versuch die Staatsverfassung der Russischen Reiches darzustellen*, 2 Theile, Riga, 1791/1793.

[205] VV Pustogarov, *Our Martens. F.F. Martens, International Lawyer and Architect of Peace* (2000) 17 (quoting *Granat Encyclopedic Dictionary* of 1913).

In the same lectures on constitutional law, Bergbohm demonstrated his typically Baltic Lutheran point of view when he discussed the French and German 'Catholic reactionaries'.[206]

Like Bulmerincq before him, Bergbohm did not limit himself to being merely a scholar while living and working in Dorpat. There were different ways to participate in the struggle. A Baltic German daily edited by Carl Schirren, the conservative *Dorpater Tagesblatt*, and an alternative to the liberal *Baltische Monatsschrift*, was published from 1862 to 1864 and then shut down, presumably by the censor's intervention.[207] Some time later, Baltic German intellectuals launched another newspaper, the *Neue Dörptsche Zeitung*, on which Bergbohm served as editor from 1888 to 1889. However, this newspaper was also shut down by the authorities.

Bergbohm wrote to a colleague in Germany that he had 'never made a secret of the fact' that he 'felt like a Baltic German'.[208] Though in his writings and throughout his life he had been a fighter, he eventually had to give up. In early 1885 he wrote with resignation: 'I am now finished with myself—unfortunately also with the *German* university Dorpat that has grown close to my heart—and I will, the sooner the better ... wipe the dust of my homeland off my shoes and turn to my old homeland in the West.'[209]

In 1893, Bergbohm left Dorpat—now officially renamed Iur'ev—with his family and was appointed Extraordinary Professor of International Law and Church Law in Marburg. In 1895, he left Marburg, having become an ordinary professor at the University of Bonn, where he taught until his retirement on 26 October 1918. He died in Bonn on 12 November 1927.

If Bergbohm is still remembered today, it is principally because he controversially and emphatically articulated positions that are by and large out of fashion today. As late as 1970, the Viennese Alfred Verdross (1890–1980), a representative of the natural law tradition, was horrified and defensive in reaction to Bergbohm's radical positivism.[210] In particular Bergbohm's statement that even the 'meanest codified law' had to be regarded as valid by lawyers has been criticized as mentally paving the way for the post-1933 breakdown in Germany.[211] Bergbohm made legal positivism a religion and fought the remnants of natural law in legal doctrine every step of the way with the vigour of a crusader.[212]

206 See Bergbohm, *Theorie des Staatsrechts* (n 204 above) 138–43.

207 A von Tobien, *Die livländische Ritterschaft in ihrem Verhältnis zum Zarismus und russischem Nationalismus* (1925) vol I, 125.

208 Letter to F Thudichum, Dorpat, 16/4 January 1885, University Library of Tübingen, Signature Md 728/6. Quoted in Kremer (n 196 above) 196.

209 ibid.

210 See A Verdross, *Statisches und dynamisches Naturrecht* (1971).

211 But B Kastner, 'Karl Magnus Bergbohm—Werk und Wirkung' (1998) 84 *Archiv für Rechts- und Sozialphilosophie* 232–49 argues that to a certain extent, this sentence has been taken out of context. See also R Kaas, *Karl Bergbohms Kritik der Naturrechtslehre des ausgehenden 19. Jahrhunderts*, Dissertation, Kiel, 1972.

212 C Bergbohm, *Jurisprudenz und Rechtsphilosophie* (1892) 95: 'Es muß das Unkraut Naturrecht, in welcher Form und Verhüllung es auch auftreten möge, offen oder verschämt, ausgerottet werden, schonungslos, mit Stumpf und Stiel.'

Bergbohm also demonstrated a polemic and sometimes offensive style of writing that became his trademark. He asked if it was not time to put together a *Bibliotheca inutilium*—a library of all useless books.[213] He made use occasionally of the *argumentum ad hominem*—a tendency which eventually brought him trouble. In 1877, he debated on the pages of the *Baltische Monatsschrift* with an anonymous critic of legal education at Dorpat.[214] The anonymous critic complained that legal scholars had turned away from the needs of the present and practical life and preferred to study things in the past that for reasons of private interest looked more interesting to them.[215] In a lengthy and passionate response, Bergbohm did not attempt to hide his feeling that proposing arguments to such a biased and malevolent person as his opponent was a waste of time: 'Aber, das thut ja nichts. Die Jurisprudenz soll eben krank, ihre Literatur in der traurigsten Verfassung sein; die historische Schule soll eben nichts als Verirrungen zu verzeichen haben; Savigny's Ruhm soll ein erschwindelter, sein Werk von Rechtswegen der Vergessenheit anheimgeganen sein. Warum? Gründe? Car tel est notre plaisir!'[216]

His departure from Dorpat for essentially political reasons marked Bergbohm for the rest of his life. On his seventieth birthday, shortly after his retirement from the Faculty of Law at the University of Bonn, a *Festschrift* was published in his honour. The publication opened with a poem by a colleague, Ernst Zittelmann (1852–1923), which sought to capture not only the essence of Bergbohm's fate as an émigré but also reflected a sentimental attitude in German culture that was characteristic of that time:

> Der neuen Heimat froh, doch heimwehkrank
> Zum leidenvollen teuren Land der Balten.
> So hier wie dort hast Treue Du gehalten—
> Treu warst Du auch den Freunden ohne Wank
> In gut und böser Zeit. Hab' Dank, hab' Dank![217]

Our primary interest here is whether Bergbohm's faithfulness to his roots influenced his writings on international law, in particular his concept of politics. What exactly *was* contained in the famous dissertation that became a subject of scandal and controversy?

[213] Bergbohm, *Jurisprudenz* (n 212 above) 11.

[214] C Bergbohm, 'Abwehr gegen "Ein Wort über die Jurisprudenz und das juristische Studium der Gegenwart"' (1877) XXV *Baltische Monatsschrift* S 581–636.

[215] ibid 586.

[216] ibid 610. Translation: 'However, this does not matter. Legal scholarship just has to be sick, its writings in the saddest condition; the historical school can demonstrate nothing but mistakes; Savigny's fame has to be cheated, his work outdated. Why? Reasons? Car tel est notre plaisir!'

[217] E Zittelmann, *Festgabe der Bonner juristischen Fakultät für Karl Bergbohm zum 70. Geburtstag* (1919) introduction. Translation: 'Happy about the new homeland yet homesick, missing the dear suffering land of the Balts, you remained faithful both there and here, faithful you also remained to your friends in good and evil times. Be thanked, be thanked!'

5.3 *The campaign against Natural Law Doctrine*

> The weed of natural law, in whatever form and camouflage it would present itself, openly or shyly, has to be annihilated, without mercy, with root and branch.[218]

Bergbohm's *Staatsverträge und Gesetze als Quellen des Völkerrechts* (1877) was a positivist manifesto on the basis and nature of international law. Positivist law, as opposed to 'imagined law', for example natural law, had 'declared legal will' as its basis and had nothing to do with its being just or unjust.[219] Bergbohm described the emergence of the need for international law in the course of history and observed that the stronger, more intelligent, and richer a people were or felt themselves to be, the less they tended to accept the idea of universal justice and binding international law.[220] The scholarship of international law was also to be criticized since it had not concentrated on the analysis and systematization of the wealth of legal material contained in treaties. Only in specific topical cases arising in world politics—'the treatment of which can by their nature remain without the influence of daily interests and daily opinions only in rare cases'—did international law scholarship turn to such treaties.[221] However, since the 'positive-legal sources' did not cover the whole system of international law, legal scholars believed that they were entitled, in a natural law fashion, to fill the *lacunae* with doctrinal opinions.[222] Those writings were a reflection of the wishes of their writers rather than what really existed. It was illegitimate to present international law 'as it could be' as international law as it really was, instead of using the law which existed to substantiate one's favoured positions.[223]

Thus, international law was not yet free of subject matter which did not belong to it. It had to be freed, since it was never possible to capture political maxims in legal rules. Neither did moral principles—'seldom rejected yet even more seldom followed'—nor 'human ideas' which governments had started to defend in their foreign relations, belong to international law.[224] When, for instance, Bluntschli had envisaged that in the future, international law would be conceptualized as a tool for the defence of certain human rights,[225] Bergbohm responded: 'Should this really ever be entitled to become a task for international law? This law has, just as domestic law, its limits and constitutes, also for human aspirations, a certain restriction of activity.'[226]

It was according to such ideas that journalism made up its own international law—ideas that were not applied to international relations, a pseudo-international law that was not at all a law and that had not only

[218] Bergbohm, *Jurisprudenz* (n 212 above) 118.
[219] C Bergbohm, *Staatsverträge und Gesetz als Quellen des Völkerrechts* (1877) 40–1.
[220] ibid 4. [221] ibid 6. [222] ibid. [223] ibid 7. [224] ibid 8.
[225] JC Bluntschli, *Das moderne Völkerrecht der civilisirten Staaten als Rechtsbuch dargestellt* (2nd edn, 1872) 20. [226] Bergbohm *Staatsverträge* (n 219 above) 8.

to be denied but also fought by scholarship.[227] The presentation of these kinds of idealistic (and, Bergbohm added, otherwise perhaps very progressive) ideas as 'international law' had only managed to raise doubts about the existence of this law.[228] The matter was, of course, even worse when the misuse of international law was backed by unjust demands.

Real international law was based on egoism and the self-interest of States.[229] In his exposé, Bergbohm directs most of his energies towards the proof of the thesis that international law exists on a 'positive' and not just on a philosophical basis.[230] Positive international law was sometimes rejected because the lack of peace in world affairs was erroneously identified with the lack of law. But sometimes war remained the last resort when striving for law and order, while peace often masked naked injustices.[231]

Bergbohm's book also contained what became his most noteworthy contribution to the doctrine of international law, in particular the doctrine of sources: justification for the validity of international treaties on the basis of State will (*Willenstheorie; Selbstbindung der Staatswillen*).[232] He also made an important distinction between the different types of agreements between States based on the nature of will—*Vereinbarung* and *Vertrag*. Later on, Carl Binding (1841–1920) and Georg Jellinek (1851–1911)[233] built upon these same ideas when developing their theories on the binding nature of international treaties.[234]

Finally, Bergbohm argued that codification of international law, desirable as it might have been, was impossible.[235] International law, in Bergbohm's view, was simply not yet ready for this task.

Following this 1877 contemplation on the sources and nature of international law, Bergbohm returned to general theory in his 1892 book *Jurisprudenz und Rechtsphilosophie*.[236] This was planned as the first of an ambitious trilogy which, however, never materialized. Was it because the passionate reactions that the first book stirred exhausted Bergbohm so much that he had to give up the whole project?

In *Jurisprudenz und Rechtsphilosophie*, one of Bergbohm's basic assumptions was the unity of all law. He argued that arguments were no longer to be sought in a special field—for example, constitutional law or international law—but generally in a legal theory that was the basis of all legal disciplines.[237] He also argued for the removal of all remnants of natural law thinking from the science of law. He understood his task to

[227] Bergbohm *Staatsverträge* (n 219 above) 7–8. [228] ibid 9. [229] ibid 12.

[230] ibid 12ff. [231] ibid 14, 37ff. [232] ibid 19–24.

[233] G Jellinek, *System der subjektiven öffentlichen Rechte* (1892) (reprint of 2nd edn, 1963).

[234] See Bergbohm, *Staatsverträge* (n 219 above) 77–82. See also Hrabar, 'Carl Marcus Bergbohm' (n 203 above) 561 and A Piip, *Rahvusvahelise õiguse süsteem* (1927) 8. For more recent discussions on the reception and development of those ideas see eg A Cassese, 'Remarks on Scelle's Theory of "Role Splitting" (dédoublement fonctionnel) in International Law' (1990) 1 EJIL 210, 220.

[235] ibid 49–70.

[236] Bergbohm, *Jurisprudenz* (n 212 above). For its immediate reception, see the book review by Adolf Merkel in (1893) VIII AöR 608–12. [237] Bergbohm, *Jurisprudenz* (n 212 above) vii.

be as overwhelming and important as that of St George: natural law was a dragon whose heads keep growing back after being cut off: 'After a head of the hydra had been cut off, ten new ones had grown in its place.'[238] Natural law thinking was like a bed of 'weeds' (*Unkraut*) that had to be annihilated.[239]

Even after the victory of Savigny's and Puchta's historical school in the 1820s, international law in particular remained speculative and influenced by vagueness characteristic of natural law.[240] Influential writers, such as the Scottish scholar James Lorimer (1818–90), remained completely speculative in their writings.[241] Problems started with the lack or insufficient clarity of definitions and concepts. International law writers did not reveal their definitions of law, making their works illogical and incoherent.[242] The concept of right (*Recht*) was often used in a meta-juridical sense. When justice was lacking in the fate of a people, writers often spoke of a 'right', even a 'holy' right, merely to secure the attention and compassion of other nations and writers.[243] 'In fact, why indeed give up the influence that the expression of the "holy" right has had since time immemorial on the people, why give away the magic power of such high words as "eternal human rights"?'[244]

Bergbohm's attitude towards the idea of human rights was thus in striking contrast to that of his contemporary Fyodor Martens who, in his textbook of international law, emphasized the central role of the 'principle of respect for the human individual' in the development of international law.[245] Martens famously wrote: 'We are persuaded that if in a State the human individual as such is deemed to be a source of civil and political rights, then international life represents a high degree of development, order, and law. On the contrary, in a State in which the human individual enjoys no such rights, where he is without rights and oppressed, international relations can neither develop nor be established on stable grounds.'[246]

Coming back to Bergbohm's work, he further criticized the fact that even the concept of international law remained vague, since many authors—for example, when they said that Grotius was the father of international law—must have meant the *science* of international law instead.[247]

Bergbohm argued that in the field of international law, Savigny's and Puchta's historical method failed to displace other, more speculative methods—for example Johann Caspar Bluntschli's (1808–81) 'historical-philosophical' method was a regrettable compromise.[248] Bluntschli's *Rechtsbuch des modernen Völkerrechts*[249] was based 'purely' on the method

[238] ibid 113. [239] ibid 118. [240] ibid 114. [241] ibid 115, 330–1. [242] ibid 19.
[243] ibid 43. [244] ibid 210.
[245] FF Martens, *Sovremennoe mezhdunarodnoe pravo tsivilizovannych narodov* (1883) vol I, 23.
[246] ibid vol I, v. [247] Bergbohm, *Jurisprudenz* (n 212 above) 62. [248] ibid 66.
[249] 1868, 3rd edn, (1878).

of natural law. Bluntschli never gave an explanation for or defence of this method, and his writings represented an impenetrable mixture of positive law and natural law.[250]

Bergbohm the conservative legal theorist insisted:

> The point of thinking, understanding and philosophical activity is not to create a new 'is' according to previously thought principles ... This is a trivial truth but it is still violated in our day.[251]

> We have to see that the desire to reshape is the main enemy of our scholarly method and simultaneously one of the strongest motives of natural law. In fact it is much easier to express than to follow the strict commandment given to the disciples of legal science to split one's own self and separate the attacking influences of the spheres of wishing and wanting from the field of cognition. Many never learn the art. The natural desire to act disturbs the pure circles of the science, throws in thoughts of creating and making better. Who would want to make do with cognition only?[252]

From Bergbohm's point of view, legal scholars could not have been driven in their scholarly activity by the desire to bring happiness to the world (*Weltbeglückung*) and improve the human condition.[253] Only truth can make the world a happier place, and truth, for legal scholars, had to be found using positivist methods.

Bergbohm considered Grotius (1583–1645) and Kant (1724–1804) to be major representatives of natural law thinking. Both were primarily interested in how the world ought to be and therefore did not pay much attention to the definition of concepts.[254] Bergbohm defined natural law in the following fashion: 'The natural law method exists everywhere where the norm necessary for the analysis of a legal question is deduced from subjective convictions instead of the objective means of the cognition of matured law (*gewordene Recht*).'[255] In this sense, all individuals were 'natural born lawyers'[256]—a fact that should have sufficed to render natural law thinking unscientific and harmful.

'Political reasons' were central to the expansion of natural law (especially before Savigny and Puchta).[257] Natural law had a 'political mission' and actually served a good purpose.[258] Historically, natural law contained indirect criticism of the existing order. Its success and benevolent reception were thus guaranteed.[259] 'Natural law always contained more criticism of law and the politics of law than legal philosophy. Under its cover, an enormous amount of critical work was delivered ... It was an effective method in the struggle for the creation of law. Though *not* yet law itself, it was necessary to call it law.'[260] Thus, natural law doctrine possessed an enormous 'agitating power'. At the same time, it caused a 'complete ruination of the legal science as science',[261] leaving lawyers incapable of expelling subjective ideas from the exercise of their profession.[262]

250 Bergbohm, *Jurisprudenz* (n 212 above) 67. 251 ibid 80. 252 ibid 201–2.
253 ibid 203. 254 ibid 89. 255 ibid 141. 256 ibid 122. 257 ibid 204.
258 ibid 214–15. 259 ibid 204. 260 ibid 210 (emphasis in original). 261 ibid 212.
262 ibid 223.

The science of international law in particular was influenced by natural law doctrine, indeed even initiated by it. Bergbohm warned that other legal disciplines would never recognize the science of international law as an equal unless the latter freed itself from its natural law 'cover'.[263] Up to then, the science of international law had been usurped by politics.[264]

According to Bergbohm, all previous writers had essentially been negatively influenced by the speculative nature of natural law. Among authors in Germany who could be named were KT Pütter,[265] R von Mohl,[266] Heffter,[267] Gareis,[268] Bluntschli,[269] Bulmerincq,[270] and von Kaltenborn;[271] in France Gérard de Rayneval, G Bry, Funck-Brentano, and Sorel.[272] The British continued to be natural law lawyers as long as they continued to argue in favour of principles that served their interests—such as those regarding neutrality in armed conflicts at sea.[273] Even English authors such as Austin, Wheaton, Hall, Amos, and Sidgwick, who considered international law to be a kind of 'positive morality', fell squarely on natural law ground.[274] The first Russian textbook authors, Katschenovsky and Stoyanov, employed the concept of 'necessary' international law and so also did not stand on positivist ground.[275]

Bergbohm argued strongly against speculating about or predicting new laws, as this was characteristic of the non-positivist approach: 'The researchers of nature do not predict which natural laws will come one day—should lawyers have the talent and the profession to proclaim new laws in a prophetic way?'[276] Finally, he criticized the metaphysical idea of 'legal consciousness', first expressed by Savigny and Puchta, which was

[263] ibid 226. [264] ibid 228.

[265] ibid 250. See KT Pütter, *Beiträge zur Völkerrechts-Geschichte und- Wissenschaft* (1843).

[266] Bergbohm, *Jurisprudenz* (n 212 above) 278. R von Mohl, *Encyclopädie der Staatswissenschaften* (1859) (2nd edn, 1872) who at 200ff and 402ff makes a distinction between philosophical and positive law.

[267] Bergbohm, *Jurisprudenz* (n 212 above) 284. Criticizes AF Heffter, *Das europäische Völkerrecht* (1st edn, 1844) §7, s 12, (6th edn, 1873) §3, s 5 position that 'unwritten law exists by oneself'.

[268] Bergbohm, *Jurisprudenz* (n 212 above) 284. Criticizes K Gareis, *Institutionen des Völkerrechts* (1888), §9, s 29ff, for raising the law of necessity (*jus necessarium*) to the status of a source of law.

[269] Bergbohm, *Jurisprudenz* (n 212 above) 290. Criticizes Bluntschli, *Das moderne Völkerrecht als Rechtsbuch* (n 225 above) (3rd edn, 1878). In Bergbohm's opinion, Bluntschli's discussion on 'necessary' international law (at 5) and other examples proved that for Bluntschli, international law was solely a 'becoming law', a station on the way to 'world law'. It was natural law in which the author included those parts of positive law that he liked. Bluntschli did not understand the historical school's teachings correctly and criticized elements of positive law as 'unjust' (*Unrecht*) (308–9).

[270] Bergbohm, *Jurisprudenz* (n 212 above) 290. Bulmerincq, in *Völkerrecht* (Marquardsen) defined law §1, s 1 as 'becoming' (*werdende*) norms—too 'uncertain' for Bergbohm.

[271] Bergbohm, *Jurisprudenz* (n 212 above) 293. Bergbohm found that von Kaltenborn, *Kritik des Völkerrechts* (1847) was strongly influenced by natural law thinking. This was also true of his *Grundsätze des praktischen europäischen Seerechts* (1851). Bergbohm maintained, however, that by the end of his academic career, Kaltenborn had made a turn towards real positivism.

[272] Bergbohm, *Jurisprudenz* (n 212 above) 313–21. [273] ibid 335. [274] ibid 337.

[275] ibid 339. [276] ibid 433.

still deeply rooted in the minds of international lawyers such as Bluntschli and Bulmerincq.[277]

Bergbohm returned to these fundamental themes in his short monograph *Theorie des Völkerrechts*,[278] published in 1901 when he was a professor in Bonn. Bergbohm again criticized natural law doctrine, which in his words twisted '*cogito ergo sum*' into 'I think it, therefore it exists' and was based on subjectivism and speculation, ultimately obliterating 'real juridical science'.[279] Writers, the media, and public opinion were guided by patriotic instinct—with a change in the political climate opinions were reversed. 'For example, recently we were at war, and then the obligations of the neutrals were considered extensive, now that we are neutral, the rights of the belligerents are again very restricted. This is human but highly subjective, meaning not scholarly.'[280] Bergbohm argued that it was also scholarship's fault that international law was treated so poorly by the educated public and other lawyers. On the one hand, 'educated nations' had produced an enormous amount of literature on international law. At the same time, people of power and those outside scholarly circles were highly critical, saying: 'Your books don't become better; they only become more and fatter ... If one reads your treatises, one asks on every third page whether it is all honest-to-God legal scholarship or merely tricky politics.'[281]

Most lawyers in Germany continued to be sceptical about whether international law was 'really law'. One could not, for example, recognize Bluntschli's treatise on international law as 'really legal'. It may be that it 'had advanced the cause of humanity but to the cause of juridical international law it did more damage than a hundred sceptical writings'.[282] Writers on international law either idealized this law, reading more into it than it could contain, or offered 'juridical formulations of national interest'.[283] Bergbohm criticized his fellow international lawyers for failing to understand that there were major issues of international life that were of a non-legal character: 'an international earthquake cannot be fought by prohibiting its emergence, or conflagration with paragraphs'.[284] 'Poets and politicians may use legal terms as they wish ... but for scholarship, this is dangerous.'[285]

5.3 Reflections of politics in Bergbohm's history of armed neutrality

The only time Bergbohm wrote about international law in concrete and not purely abstract-theoretical terms was in his doctoral thesis *Die bewaffnete Neutralität 1780–1783. Eine Entwicklungsphase des Völkerrechts*

[277] Bergbohm, *Jurisprudenz* (n 212 above) 497.

[278] K Bergbohm, 'Theorie des Völkerrechts' *Festgabe für J. F. von Schulte von der juristischen Fakultät der Universität Bonn* (1901).

[279] ibid 7.

[280] ibid 9.

[281] ibid 11.

[282] ibid 21.

[283] ibid 25.

[284] ibid 27.

[285] ibid 30.

im Seekriege.[286] At first glance, the historical topic seems somewhat obscure, even irrelevant. Why would an international law scholar turn in 1884 to events that took place a hundred years before? However, on closer inspection we see intrigues flaming and passion sparking. We see the use of the history of international law as a metaphor and allegory.

The events described in Bergbohm's dissertation took place during the American War of Independence (1775–83), when France (since 1778) and Spain (since 1779) sided with the American colonies against Great Britain. The commerce of neutral nations suffered heavily due to the arrest of ships and goods by warring parties. However, during the war a declaration that quickly acquired legal significance was issued. On 28 February (10 March) 1780, the Russian Empress Catherine II issued a 'Declaration to the Courts of London, Versailles and Madrid' in which the claims of the neutral States were laid out. These included the demand that the warring parties not hinder neutral ships and the demand that all goods under the flags of neutral ships (including goods belonging to citizens of the warring parties) be given safe passage. An alliance of eight sea powers (Russia, Denmark, Sweden, Netherlands, Prussia, Austria, Portugal, and the Two Sicilies) emerged. France, Spain, and America soon agreed to the principles. The effect of Catherine's declaration on the law of naval war was to some extent comparable to President Truman's proclamation on the continental shelf in 1946 that gave a new direction to the law of the sea.

Only Great Britain, which was still a dominant sea power, put up any resistance to the principles. However, it too finally conceded to Catherine's initiative—with the declaration of Paris on 16 April 1856. The so-called armed neutrality proposed by the Russian Empress was thus an important landmark in the development towards the humanization of war.[287]

But was the 'epochal importance of armed neutrality' sufficient reason to turn to history? Weren't there more tangible problems at hand in Bergbohm's own times? According to Bergbohm, the other reason (beside its importance) for studying armed neutrality was the 'mysteriousness regarding its emergence'. Bergbohm's aim was to establish the historical truth.[288]

In reality, the book is not so much about armed neutrality as about honour. If armed neutrality was such a good thing, to whom does the honour for its creation belong? And if somebody has tried take credit falsely for the invention of this concept, how dishonourable is this? Two people vied for the honour of having invented the concept of armed neutrality. The memoirs of the Prussian ambassador in St Petersburg (1779–85), Count Eustach von Goertz, suggest that it was the pro-Prussian Chancellor of Russia, Panin, who skilfully 'sold' to his Empress

[286] Parallel publication—Berlin, 1884 and Dorpat, 1884. [287] ibid 215. [288] ibid 5.

the idea of the declaration regarding armed neutrality. Moreover he emerged as the winner in the court intrigue involving Grigory Potemkin, the pro-British favourite of the Empress. This interpretation is backed by the fact that Catherine II was pro-English: since armed neutrality would in practice be directed against the interests of England, she must have been subject to outside influence. It seems logical then that the influence originated from the Prussian-friendly Chancellor Panin.

But Russian historians had found in an archive a note written by Catherine II herself contradicting the view that the idea was Panin's. In the margin of a book she had read, Catherine commented: 'The idea originated in my own head.' Russian historians and international lawyers aligned to conclude that since 'the Empress herself has said so', she must have been the originator of the declaration. This was the view of the Russian historians Obolensky and Leshkov and international law scholars Katshenovsky and Martens.

Bergbohm stood decidedly by the account given by Count von Goertz. He regretted 'how fascination with a great woman on the throne of a powerful empire and a misunderstood patriotic duty stood in opposition to the truth'.[289] An objective look at facts would 'teach everybody who is not determined to find what he is looking for'. But alas, the instinct for historical authenticity which was needed for such research was not 'everybody's business'.[290]

Bergbohm wondered whether his opponents were even playing fair. Katshenovsky, for example, had attempted to prove that the Prussian ambassador had sought to *discredit* the project of armed neutrality. Bergbohm could not understand this: 'As the whole continent, the governments, the individuals and not least, the writers greeted armed neutrality with joy, where do these haters and jealous people come from, where does the mood for writing pamphlets among them come from?'[291] Moreover, Katshenovsky had attempted to prove the existence of a conflict between Catherine II and Panin: 'That is an incomprehensible mistake—if not something worse.'[292] Whatever Catherine II had said, one had to read her words as a historian would, and not engage in panegyrics.[293]

Bergbohm went on to reconstruct events to confirm his own account. During Catherine's time, there were two leading ambassadors sent to St Petersburg: the British ambassador, Sir James Harris and the Prussian Count Eustach von Goertz: 'The rest were of no importance, only business representatives sent by their governments, without individual significance.'[294] Both wanted to provide the best service for their respective motherlands. Harris hoped to push Russia into the war on its side. If only Count Panin hadn't been at court with his views about the real needs of the Russian Empire! Panin preferred stronger connections with Prussia and France over the alliance with Britain.[295] The only reason for Russia

[289] Bergbohm, *Die bewaffnete Neutralität 1780–1783* (n 286 above) 19. [290] ibid 22.
[291] ibid 24. [292] ibid 25. [293] ibid 27. [294] ibid 59. [295] ibid 112.

to have accepted the British proposals would have been the 'vanity of the Empress'.[296]

According to Bergbohm, Panin played on Catherine's anger over the arrest of some Russian ships by Spain. 'Catherine was angry with Spain—but never with England!'[297] Panin managed to get Catherine to sign the declaration, the real implications of which the Empress failed to grasp.[298] And so Catherine did—without, however, realizing the damage it would cause to England's interests.[299] Bergbohm imagined how 'Harris might have felt when he heard from Panin about the declaration ... Although it is not true, as sometimes gossiped, that he got icterus thanks to this—this he already had'.[300]

Bergbohm suggested that the driving force behind the desire to give all the credit to Catherine was 'patriotic enthusiasm'.[301] He also knew that it was going to be difficult to 'place historical truth against the "official" view of history'.[302]

But he was left with an inevitable complication: what, then, was one supposed to think of Catherine's own comment? Neither alternative—that Catherine, vain as she was, had lied to enhance her reputation or that she had simply been mistaken—would be accepted by Russian patriots. Bergbohm argued that Catherine really believed in what she wrote—and that her words had merely been misinterpreted. Panin, he believed, had put the idea into Catherine's head: Catherine thought that the idea originated in her own head because Panin wanted her to believe that the idea was her own. True, this account made the Empress look a bit silly. But at the same time, Bergbohm claimed that his account preserved rather than sullied Catherine's honour. It was better that Catherine had not understood that her declaration was directed against England than if she had consciously played a double game, first promising help to the British ambassador, and then suddenly coming out with the declaration.[303] It was more honourable for Catherine not to have understood than for her to have been hypocritical and dishonest.

Bergbohm's dissertation caused a scandal in Dorpat. Russian colleagues and students claimed that Bergbohm had insulted Catherine II and the Russian people. Bergbohm was accused of having written with an anti-Russian bias—for example when he referred to Catherine II as having been in charge of the 'barbaric Eastern Empire'.[304] Hrabar, who recounts this significant episode, reports that Bergbohm had responded to this accusation by maintaining that the expression had been taken out of the context of a sentence which otherwise referred positively to Catherine's image. But Bergbohm had also added: 'How good they did not notice my comment about Catherine's love for corps éclatant!'[305]

296 ibid 62. 297 ibid 123. 298 ibid 111, 131. 299 ibid 242. 300 ibid 134.
301 ibid 227. 302 ibid. 303 ibid 246.
304 V Hrabar, 'Karl Magnus Bergbohm 1849–1927' [1928] *Zeitschrift für Völkerrecht* 559–63.
305 ibid 562.

Bergbohm's dissertation was written at a time when the Baltic Germans were on the defensive, feeling threatened and bullied by the Russian Empire. Bergbohm seems to have specially chosen the topic as a pretext to make arguments against exaggerated Russian patriotism and Russia's choices and interests.

Another interesting aspect of the book was the portrayal of the choice Russia had to make in 1780: Prussia or England. England was often depicted as 'tyrannical', 'egomaniacal', and occasionally 'unfaithful'.[306] Writing in 1884, Bergbohm seemed to suggest: today, too, Russia should listen to von Goertz rather than Sir James. Bergbohm's nations, like their diplomatic and political agents, seemed to possess their own characters, strengths, and idiosyncrasies. The history of international law was instilled with allusions to the current problem of the balance of power between the larger European states. This parallel seems plausible since the question of the balance of power and Russia's role in it was an increasingly important issue in European diplomacy after the unification of Germany by Bismarck. True, on 18 June 1881, Austria, Germany, and Russia concluded the Alliance of Three Emperors.[307] But as the balance of power in Europe remained very volatile and every player sought to increase its power, the Russian elite remained divided as to what extent their country should be bound with Bismarck's Germany.

Bergbohm's account was later vehemently rejected by Fyodor (Friedrich) Martens.[308] Martens' own candidate work at St Petersburg University in 1867 had been on the relations between Russia and the Ottoman Empire during the reign of Catherine II. Moreover, in 1882 Martens had published a historical essay entitled 'Russia and Prussia under Catherine II'.[309] Thus, he could consider the period treated by Bergbohm 'his own' as well.

The treaty collection edited by Martens is revealing because of its mixture of legal and historical-political topics (texts of treaties accompanied by often lengthy commentaries on diplomatic history). Martens had won the Russian Emperor's trust and gained access to the imperial archives for the compilation of the collection of Russian treaties. Relying heavily on the memoirs of Harris, Martens called Bergbohm's account a 'strange legend/fairytale' (*strannaya skazka*):[310] the 'time had come to put an end to such legends' since 'on the basis of archival documents ... a satisfactory account of the plans of the Empress' could be given.[311] It was not Panin, 'cet homme de génie',[312] who was the author of the Declaration, but the Empress herself. Martens concluded that no intrigue against the

306 See eg *Die bewaffnete Neutralität* (n 286 above) 56–7, 190.

307 See V Hvostov and I Mints in V Potjomkin (ed), *Diplomaatia ajalugu. Diplomaatia Uusajal (1872–1919)* (1948) 71.

308 FF Martens, *Sobranie traktatov i konventsii zakljutshennych Rossieju s inostrannymi derzhavami* (1892) vol 10, 296ff.

309 See VV Pustogarov, *Our Martens. F.F. Martens. International Lawyer and Architect of Peace* (1882) 39.

310 Martens, *Sobranie* (n 308 above) 296.

311 ibid 297.

312 ibid 305.

British ambassador Harris had ever existed: the Declaration did not signify Catherine's hostility towards Britain but rather her contempt for the violent acts committed by the British corsairs.[313]

BE Nolde (1876–1948) later observed that Martens had demonstrated in his *Recueil* an 'exaggerated assessment of the political abilities of many Russian public figures of the nineteenth century' and reproached Martens for an 'excessive deference to our diplomatic tradition'.[314] Martens himself had fought intellectual battles involving the international legal aspects of the Russian and British expansion to Central Asia,[315] and he had no particular reason to 'prefer' Britain to Prussia (Germany). What made Martens go into lengthy and extensive explanations of the true role of Catherine II in proclaiming armed neutrality? Was it the honour of the greatest Empress of Russia?

5.4 *Conclusion*

In the title of this section, I called Bergbohm 'radical'. Bergbohm's radical positivism seems to have been based on the intuition that politics meant change, and the changes Bergbohm experienced in his life tended to be dangerous. If only people (not least the Russians at the University of Dorpat and in St Petersburg) had kept their word, honoured what had already been agreed upon! Instead, treacherous politics prevailed everywhere, often disguised beneath the rhetoric of natural law. In this sense, Bergbohm's concept of (international) law was also conditioned by his particular Baltic German situation.

Radical positivism also meant opposition to new ideas and social change, including the rejection of human rights as an element of international law taken as a vehicle for social change. Like Bulmerincq, Bergbohm's mindset was conservative: what the law had to contain, it already contained. Suggestions for change—such as the inclusion of human rights in the body of international law or the Russification of the German Baltic politics—were all politics. Natural law was politics. Bergbohm's harsh rejection of natural law and his defence of positivism therefore constituted a reaction. He took a defensive posture 'in reaction' to something 'political'—the Russification of the Baltic provinces, the immersion of the body of legal norms in politics by the school of natural law. Therefore, it was not surprising that Bergbohm developed a notion of international law which rejected politics. Ideally he would have had all politics expelled from the science of international law. Law was—or had to be—a defence, an asylum in the face of dangerous politics.

But Bergbohm was also radical in that in a certain sense he misunderstood his teacher's, Bulmerincq's, main point, exaggerating it *ad absurdum*.

313 ibid 304. 314 BE Nolde, 'FFMartens', *Russkaya mysl no 12*, December 1909, 30.

315 See FF Martens, 'Étude historique sur la politique russe dans la question d'Orient' (1877) IX *Revue de droit* 49–76 and 'La Russie et l'Angleterre dans l'Asie Centrale' (1879) XI *Revue de droit* 293ff. See also Martens, 'Le fondement du droit international (1882) XIV *Revue de droit* 244ff.

For Bulmerincq, the point that international law had to be kept separate from politics implied a certain playfulness, a certain feeling for game—a sense of 'civilization' that gentlemen shared and that was beyond debate. Unfortunately, Bergbohm took the game *ad literam*, too seriously. Neither his teacher Bulmerincq, nor any other international law scholar, matched Bergbohm's absolute demand for the separation of law from politics. Bergbohm should have repudiated his own dissertation since its reception could not live up to his own underlying objectivist presumptions!

Bergbohm became a radical 'positivist' partly because he was a poor politician by nature. He was not playful enough and his polemical and divisive way of putting things alienated people and brought him enemies. As Bergbohm's own dissertation demonstrated, politics could not be completely suppressed. It remains unclear to what extent Bergbohm himself was aware of the political implications of his dissertation. His choice of topic can be viewed in two ways—as an escape from the politicized nature of everyday life, or as a conscious allusion or metaphor. If the first were true, the fact that the dissertation turned out to be political (notwithstanding the author's intention to avoid politics), may have represented a Freudian outburst of the subconscious. Politics, repressed for the sake of scientific integrity, had found its way to the surface.

But Bergbohm's conclusions may also have been conditioned by his own inherent notions of culture and 'civilization'. It was a question of basic trust: a German nobleman's word had a different weight than the writings of Russian historians and lawyers. Bergbohm's politics had then found a way out via the history of international law. This raises the question of the place of history in international legal arguments. Outi Korhonen, referring to Ian Brownlie's leading textbook on international law, observes: 'A standard textbook of international law contains somewhere embedded in the discussion a statement that "law, at least in one sense, is history". Few would disagree, but the question is: what sense is this?'[316]

Law and history have one important trait in common: both are used as arguments to legitimize something. It has even been argued, cynically perhaps, that both law and history serve as the auxiliary sciences of politics. The French historian Marc Ferro has convincingly demonstrated how in different countries history, especially school history, is presented in the light of patriotic education and national legitimization.[317] In international legal arguments too, history often appears as ideologically driven and contested, and often reveals the scholar's politics of international law.

In his dissertation, Bergbohm had chosen a concrete problem for the application of historical legal methods. When arguing in 1877 with his anonymous opponent about the purposes of a legal education, Bergbohm had insisted that studying the history of law was not a goal in itself, but

[316] O Korhonen, *International Law Situated* (2000, 129) (1990, also 129).

[317] M Ferro, *The Use and Abuse of History, or How the Past is Taught* (1984).

was meant to be a method.[318] But a method for learning what? Bergbohm had argued that history served as a method for the cognition of *law*. In fact, Bergbohm himself saw the significance of his dissertation *Die bewaffnete Neutralität* in the historical demonstration of how law was created through State action and enforced State will.[319] At the same time, in the same book, the main focus of the argument was certainly not law. Bergbohm's turn to history only marginally contributed to a better understanding of 'positive' law.

Bulmerincq had balanced his claim of separation of international law from politics with the concept of 'civilization'. 'Civilization' constituted the conceptual valve through which politics, expelled by the separation of law and politics, could invisibly yet victoriously return. Bergbohm found a similar valve in the concept of 'struggle'. Bergbohm saw the idea of Rudolf von Ihering (1818–92) that one must struggle for one's law[320] confirmed in his study of armed neutrality. According to Bergbohm, Russia's successful insistence on the principles of armed neutrality against British interests proved that: 'The life of peoples and world history will without mercy surpass any law that is not ready to put up a fight.'[321] Bergbohm's radical positivism did not neglect the importance of power. A lawyer's object of study (law) may have been static, but this stasis was balanced by the realist dynamism of law's becoming law via struggle.

6. Hrabar: the Cosmopolitan Mind

> Many of the achievements of European civilization have been frivolously sacrificed in war by this or another warring party in order to achieve short-term gains. A lot of contemporary international law has been swept away in this global fight. But we do not need to worry about the future. In history, periods of peaceful construction follow periods of destruction. So it will be now too.
>
> Vladimir Hrabar, March 1917[322]

6.1 Life

In 1952, an old and distinguished scholar, Vladimir Emmanuilovich Hrabar, arrived with his wife Maria Passek (1893–1975)—the daughter of the pre-World War I rector of Iur'ev University—on a Moscow train at the train station in Tartu. He was welcomed by the rector of Tartu State

[318] See Bergbohm, 'Abwehr' (n 214 above) 607.
[319] Bergbohm, *Die bewaffnete Neutralität* (n 286 above) 218.
[320] R von Ihering, *Der Kampf ums Recht* (1872).
[321] Bergbohm, *Die bewaffnete Neutralität* (n 286 above) 224. 'Über ein Recht, das sich nicht zum Kampfe stellt, geht das Völkerleben, geht die Weltgeschichte rücksichtslos hinweg.'
[322] Hrabar, Foreword to Liszt (n 405 below) iv.

University, Fyodor Klement, and the then lecturer (later professor) of international law, Abner Uustal. Hrabar's personal notes reveal that he had been moved by the occasion: he had not seen Tartu since leaving the university town in 1918. Many things had changed, especially given the destruction suffered during World War II, yet the essence of the old university town had remained unchanged. Later Hrabar remarked in his memoirs: 'I am more than 87 years old. 25 of those years I have lived in Tartu. The time spent there was the happiest in my life and the most fruitful in terms of my scholarly activity. Today, I remember it with gratitude.'[323]

Hrabar was born on 10 (22) January 1865, in Vienna, in an intellectually active Carpatho-Rusin (Ruthenian) family.[324] Hrabar's father Emmanuil, a lawyer who sympathized with the revolutionary movement in the Austro-Hungarian Empire, was elected to Parliament in 1869 by the Magyar-Russian constituency in Maramures County. Because of his political activities, Vladimir's father came into conflict with the Austrian authorities and was obliged to emigrate in 1871. He moved the family first to Italy and then to Paris and they eventually found themselves in Russia in 1876. Vladimir's father later found employment as a teacher of modern languages in Egor'evsk, in the Riazan' Province, at Izmail on the Danube, and finally in 1895, a few years after the appointment of his son Vladimir at Iur'ev, where he became an aide to the vice-president of the university. It is therefore worth noting that Hrabar's family were political refugees.

In 1881, Hrabar's mother Olga and her father Adolph von Dobrianski were tried for treason in L'viv, together with several other Galician Russophiles. The chief prosecutor in their trial was Kalman Tisza, the Minister-President of Hungary. Vladimir Hrabar's mother and grandfather were acquitted due to lack of evidence, but Dobrianski was no longer allowed to live in localities with a Russian or Slavic populace.

Hrabar's family background, origin, and national identity are thus somewhat more complex than those of the other professors considered in this article. (According to a faculty legend, he was Jewish.) *Nomen est omen*: puzzles begin with his family name. William E Butler, the distinguished British specialist on Hrabar, has adopted the Russian transcription of the scholar's family name (Grabar). The same is true of Tartu University's library archives. However, since in the Russian language an 'h' beginning a non-Russian name is transformed into 'g' ('Heinrich Heine' becomes 'Geinrih Geine'), so it was the case with Hrabar. What should count in my opinion is the author's own preference, which seems to be reflected in the fact that he published all his non-Russian works (his works in French, German, and Latin) under the name Hrabar.

[323] V Grabar, 'Veerand sajandit Tartu (Derpti, Jurjevi) ülikoolis' in S Issakov (ed), *Mälestusi Tartu Ülikoolist (17.-19. sajand)* (1986) 402.

[324] See the following: WE Butler's Foreword to VE Hrabar, *The History of International Law in Russia, 1647–1917. A Bio-Bibliographical Study* (1990), xxxvff.

Hrabar spent his childhood years with his uncle in Ukraine, in the Carpathian mountains near Uzhgorod. Later on, both he and his brother Igor succeeded in winning scholarships, Vladimir at the Pavel Galagan College in Kiev and Igor at the Moscow Lycée. After Vladimir graduated in 1884, he continued his studies in the Faculty of Law at the University of Moscow, from which he graduated in 1888 with a candidate's degree. His candidate's thesis was entitled 'About the Status of Foreigners among Ancient Jews'.[325] Vladimir's brother Igor also studied law—in St Petersburg—but later became a famous artist and director of the Tretiakov Gallery in Moscow.

After graduation from Moscow's Faculty of Law, Hrabar spent a year in Paris, where he attended the lectures of the international law professor Louis Renault. After his return he worked briefly in the Moscow Commercial Court and then earned his living as a teacher. In 1893, he passed his master's examination in Moscow and became *Privat-Dozent* in the Faculty of Law. In the same year, he was appointed assistant professor at Iur'ev; in 1901, he became Extraordinary Professor of International Law. It was at Iur'ev that he published the work that earned him international recognition, *Roman Law in the History of International Legal Teachings*.[326]

During his years at Iur'ev and alongside his professorial activities, Hrabar twice served as Dean of the Faculty of Law (1907–08; 1915–16) and also served as the Director of the University Library from 1910 to 1915.

In 1918, the German occupation army forced the Russian professors out of Dorpat/Iur'ev/Tartu. Hrabar's doctoral dissertation on the science of international law in pre-Reformation England was lost in a fire during World War I at Iur'ev and only part of it could be published.[327] The Bolsheviks evacuated university personnel, including Hrabar, to Voronezh with the task of setting up a new university there.

After his relatively short stay in Voronezh (1918–19), Hrabar advised the new Soviet government in matters of foreign commerce.[328] From 1922–23 he attended the Lausanne Conference as a member of the Soviet delegation. On 23 March 1923, he was appointed part-time Professor of International Law at Moscow State University. In 1926, he was elected a member of the Ukrainian Academy of Sciences. Butler recounts how an article published in Ukrainian in 1929 accused Hrabar of being a 'known

[325] See Hrabar on himself in: G Levitski (ed), '*Biograficheski slovar professorov i prepodovatelei imperatorskago Iur'evskago, byvshago derptskago, universiteta, za sto let ego sushestvovania (1802–1902)* (1902) 640.

[326] V Grabar, *Rimskoe pravo v istorii mezhdunarodno-pravovyh uchenii. Elementy mezhdunarodnogo prava v trudah legistov XII–XIV vv* (1901).

[327] V Grabar, 'Ponyatie estestvennogo prava i mezhdunarodnogo prava v angliskoi literature XII–XVI vekov', 'Iuridicheski Vestnik', 1917, No 1.

[328] Already during World War I, Hrabar had given advice to the Russian government on the question of the historical development of Russia's legal interests in the Bosporus and the Dardanelles. See Hrabar's archive, *Obozrenye mezhdunarodnych soglashenii po voprosu o prolivah Bosfore i Dardanellah*, undated.

reactionary who had carried on Moscophile policy in Galicia',[329] a reference to Hrabar's service in the Russian military during World War I in Galicia.

Hrabar retired in 1929 for health reasons and dedicated his time to the writing of a definitive history of international law in Russia. When World War II broke out, he was again appointed a professor at Moscow State University and served as an associate at the Institute of Law of the Soviet Academy of Sciences. He died in Moscow on 26 November 1956 at the age of 91.

6.2 *Politics*

In the 1880s, Tsar Alexander III pursued a policy of assimilation in the Baltic provinces. Since almost all Baltic German scholars rejected this, Russian scholars were offered appointments at the University, including Hrabar. While Hrabar had nothing personally to do with Bergbohm's semi-forced departure from Dorpat/Iur'ev, his appointment became possible thanks to imperial policy. When Hrabar arrived, all instruction in the Faculty of Law was already being carried out in Russian, though all five chairs were still occupied by Baltic German professors.[330] No doubt having in mind recent events, Hrabar let the audience of his inaugural lecture know that he held the scholarly achievements of his predecessors, Bulmerincq and Bergbohm, in high esteem.[331] As a scholar, he chose to emphasize continuity rather than a break in the chair of international law.

Nevertheless, the political conflict between the Baltic Germans and the Russians—all this against a backdrop of strengthening Estonian national identity—was fierce. In 1890, 1,111 students from the Baltic provinces (ie Germans, Estonians, and Latvians) studied at the university; in 1901 there were only 395 students. As Hrabar recounted, 'the 600 individuals who had left were German students, who had been encouraged to leave the Russified university in protest'.[332] While most Baltic Germans boycotted the university, the number of Russian students increased from 89 in 1895 to 1,536 in 1907.[333]

One can trace the development of the German–Russian conflict in Hrabar's archive in the Tartu University library. Hrabar carefully preserved excerpts from both Russian and German newspapers that mirror the conflict over the Baltic provinces. For instance, there are contradictory newspaper accounts of the armed clash between the Baltic German militia (*Bürgerwehr*) and the mostly Estonian workers demonstrating on the Great Market Square (now the City Hall Square) on 12 December 1905,

[329] See WE Butler's Foreword to Hrabar, *The History of International Law in Russia* (n 324 above) xlv.

[330] Grabar, *Veerand sajandit* (n 323 above). 408.

[331] V Grabar, 'Voina i mezhdunarodno'e pravo' in *Uchenye zapiski imperatorskago Iur'evskago universiteta No. 4* (1893) 24–5.

[332] Grabar, *Veerand sajandit* (n 323 above) 411.

[333] ibid 412.

ie during the 1905 Revolution.[334] The archive also contains complaints published in the Baltic German newspapers about the decision of the Russian authorities to abolish the chair of private law in the Baltic Sea provinces.[335]

What was Hrabar's stance on the policy of Russification? Archival documents and Hrabar's own memoirs testify to the fact that he was one of the leaders of the liberal opposition within the university. Following the 1905 Revolution, he proposed at the University Council on 27 March 1906 to allow the teaching of elective subjects in any of the local languages, with the instructor choosing the language of instruction. The Council asked Hrabar 'to explain his proposal further' and postponed its decision. A German newspaper gossiped in 1908 that 'liberal professors want ... to elect Professor Grabar, the dean of the Faculty of Law, rector.'[336]

In his memoirs, Hrabar explained the tense and complex nationality situation among students and professors at the time:

> Due to differences in upbringing, customs, habits and means, students of different nationalities lived in a segregated fashion and seldom communicated with each other ... Especially separated were the German students who closed themselves off from the others and lived in fraternities ... Two non-German fraternities—the Russian 'Ruthenia' and the Polish 'Polonia'—had ceased their activities at the time of my arrival: unionist discipline was not in accordance with the love of liberty characteristic of Slavonic nature. Poles however wished to restore their fraternity and turned to me for advice as the then dean of the faculty of law. Every fraternity had a cup and decorative ribbon in certain colours. The Poles wished to use their national colour, raspberry red, in Polish *amarantowy*, but were certain of rejection and were afraid to request it, since in Warsaw the police hunted down the bearers of this Polish national emblem. I asked: 'Do you want this *amarantowy* so much?' 'Yes, we do but we do not even dare to dream about it', was the response. 'Write your wishes down on paper; you overestimate how informed the officials in St Petersburg are; I am certain that your wishes will be granted.' I was right: the approval arrived indeed quite soon. The students were out of their minds with joy and did not know how to thank me and Y. Passek, the Rector of the university, who had sent the application to St Petersburg with his approval. I was invited together with the Rector and Professor F. Taranovski, a former student of Warsaw University, to the festive opening of the fraternity. F. Taranosvki greeted the students in Polish. We spent several hours in the fraternity, conversing in a friendly manner and only got home at dawn.[337]

The official university policy was nevertheless quite different, especially under the reactionary Rector Budilovich. Among Hrabar's newspaper extracts there is a speech by Budilovich,[338] given in Riga at the farewell

334 Grabar archive F 38/75, Beilage zur *Nordlivländischen Zeitung*, 20 December (2 January) 1905.

335 *Nordlivländische Zeitung* 15 (28) July 1908, No 159, 'In Sachen des Katheders für ostseeprovinzielles Privatrecht'.

336 *Nordlivländische Zeitung*, 10 (23) July 1908, No 155.

337 Grabar, *Veerand sajandit* (n 323 above) 412–13.

338 See references to Budilovich in T Karjahärm, *Ida ja Lääne vahel. Eesti ja Vene suhted 1850–1917* (1998) 169.

ceremony for Archbishop Arseni and printed in an undated Baltic German newspaper (probably published in 1903):

Ten years ago traces of the Teutonic Order, of the time of knights, of the Hanseatic League were very much alive on this historic soil, only vague legends connected it with the name and legacy of Iaroslav Mudry (the Wise). Now they have been resurrected, together with the name of Iur'ev, implying not just a historical memory but also a program for the future. Ten years ago at the dome of Iaroslav Mudry there existed an institution that had nothing in common with the old foundations of Russian education and that in its spirit, its tasks and goals did not in almost any respect differ from similar institutions in Königsberg, Rostock, and Kiel. Now, however, the university has finally been liberated from the legacy of Gustavus II Adolphus and has been directed to the path that corresponds to the scholarly, State and national tasks. As the university now stands at the focal point of Russian cultural work, it had to be connected with other factors of Russian education, especially the Orthodox Church. As an external symbol for this connection, the Russian Orthodox cross has been erected on the top of the main building of the university ... The Alexander Nevski Church of the University has been inaugurated.[339]

Thus, when Germany and Russia clashed militarily in 1914, it evoked special associations in the Baltic provinces. From 2 August 1914 to 7 May 1915 Hrabar was appointed by the Russian Ministry of Foreign Affairs as a legal adviser to the headquarters (*Stavka*) of the Russian Supreme Command. He had been selected by Boris Nol'de, a high official and Russianized Baltic German international law scholar from St Petersburg.[340] The idea was to combine his linguistic and cultural knowledge of Galicia, his childhood playground, with his qualities as a specialist of international law. He was stationed with the Russian Supreme Command in Galicia, which the Russians had taken over from the military forces of Austro-Hungary. There, Hrabar was struck by how little knowledge the Russian military commanders had of the situation in Galicia and in particular by the anti-Semitism that was rife among the Russian military staff. Hrabar had repeated conflicts with Nikolai Ianushkevich, Chief of Staff for the Russian Supreme Commander in Chief, Grand Duke Nikolai Nikolaevich. Ianushkevich wanted Hrabar to denounce more vigorously German violations of the Hague Regulations on the laws of war, but Hrabar found Russian accusations exaggerated and wanted them to be balanced with an account of Russia's own atrocities. Finally Ianushkevich dismissed Hrabar after he had refused to write an indictment of German military conduct which did not also mention Russian violations. Officially, his resignation took place 'for health reasons'. Soon after his dismissal, Hrabar returned to teach in Iur'ev.

[339] Grabar archive F 38/87 (newspaper excerpts).

[340] In describing this significant episode, I rely on unpublished archival material that has been communicated to me by Peter Holquist. The episode is also briefly outlined in WE Butler's Foreword to Hrabar (n 324 above) xli and in the correspondence between Sazonov and Hrabar in the Krasnyi arkhiv 27 (1928) 15.

But the old order in Russia had already begun to crumble. In the Baltic provinces, previously inflicted attacks now produced angry counter-attacks. One of the first things the German occupation army did when it conquered Dorpat at the end of February 1918, was to take down the Orthodox cross from the top of the university main building. Lieutenant General Adams, the commander-in-chief of the German troops, issued the following order on 7 March 1918:[341]

I hereby proclaim: the university of Dorpat is a German university.

Lectures in Russian may take place only so that students will have the opportunity by the following exam period [20th March according to the German calendar] to finish their studies.

German professors are entitled to adopt measures so that the university may from now on appear as a German university.

To what extent Russian chairs and students may remain in Dorpat will be decided according to instructions issued by a representation of the German army [Ortskommandatur].

The Council of the University authorized Hrabar to write in its name to the German authorities.[342] As his first argument, Hrabar invoked the 1907 Hague Regulations, arguing that the Council was unable to see in such measures 'any legal basis, since however one would understand the legal status of Livonia and Estonia, it is beyond doubt that measures ordered to be taken at the university can be deduced neither from the rights of the Occupying Power on enemy territory nor from the text of the Peace Treaty [of Brest-Litovsk]'. Hrabar went on to point out that in the case of *occupatio bellica*, the occupying power was according to Article 43 of the 1907 Hague Regulations obliged to respect the laws of the country, as long as there were no 'insurmountable hindrances'. The norm was not, Hrabar continued, created in 1907 but reflected an old custom and was, for instance, reconfirmed by a German Proclamation of 30 August 1870 in the Franco-German war: 'As this rule was respected in Alsace-Lothringia that Germany intended to annex in 1870, it should be even more respected in the occupied Baltic provinces, since the German Chancellor has declared that Germany has no intention of annexing those provinces.' Finally, he quoted from the work of the 'well-known Berlin Professor' (in the first draft described as 'famous') Franz von Liszt, who maintained that university property in an occupied territory must be treated analogously to private property.

Secondly, Hrabar argued that the legal basis for such drastic measures could not be found in the Brest-Litovsk Peace Treaty between Germany, its allies, and 'the [Lenin's] government of Petersburg'. As this treaty had primarily accorded to Germany as the occupying power police authority in the Baltic provinces, such a fundamental reform as the reform of the university of the provinces could not be pursued, especially as 'not only Germans but also the other peoples living in the country, such as the

341 Grabar archive F 38/72. 342 ibid.

Russians, Poles, Lithuanians, Jews and in the first place, the Estonians and Latvians had an interest in it.'

Thirdly, Hrabar invoked the argument of 'higher German authority'. He referred to the words of Chancellor Bethmann-Hollweg in a speech to the Reichstag: 'I emphasise that we are not even thinking of establishing ourselves in Livonia and Estonia.' This had to be interpreted as higher law *vis-à-vis* the orders of Lieutenant-General Adams.

After these legal arguments marshalled against the German orders, 'political' arguments were listed in the second part of the Memorandum. It was noted that the majority of the students were Estonians and Latvians, most of whom were unable to follow lectures in German without further language instruction. Furthermore, pupils in high schools had received their education exclusively in the Russian language during the preceding decades and knew German 'neither practically nor theoretically'. Finally, the memorandum again highlighted that the 'reform' was extremely undesirable since the future status of Livonia and Estonia still remained open.

However, the Germans took a firm course towards the creation of a Baltic German 'independent' State, the *Baltisches Herzogtum*. On 10 May 1918, a response of a sort to the Council's Memorandum was received by Rector Alekseev. It came from the Commander-in-Chief of the German Eighth army, Count Kirchbach:[343]

> In connection with further political developments, the decision of the land council on 12.04.1918 and the response to it by the German Reich's leadership, the reopening of the University of Dorpat as a *Russian* university is no longer a matter for debate. I therefore issue the following orders:
>
> The Russian rector of the university is obliged to cease all official activity. This will be supervised by the head of the police [*Stadthauptmann*] of Dorpat.
>
> The rector is prohibited from undertaking any relations with the Russian government. [*Ein Verkehr des Rektors mit der russischen Regierung findet nicht statt.*]
>
> I insist that the rector and the Russian professors leave Livonia voluntarily and move to Russia, and look forward to the declaration of the intentions of these gentlemen [*Herrn*] in that regard.

Hrabar, together with the other Russian personnel of the university, left Dorpat on 18 July 1918 on an evacuation train that had been allowed to come from Soviet Russia. 'There was nothing to do ... I was sorry to leave the town and the university ... I had to console myself with the thought that we were to create the foundations for the first university established by the young Soviet government.'[344]

6.3 Politics in Hrabar's international law works

6.3.1 Inaugural lecture

As noted, Hrabar started his 1893 inaugural lecture at Iur'ev University with respectful remarks about Bulmerincq and Bergbohm, insisting that

[343] Grabar archive F 38/72, 22.

[344] Grabar, *Veerand sajandit* (n 323 above) 418.

he intended to follow in their footsteps 'if not in method, then in the way of posing questions'.[345] He argued that war and international law had been in conflict with each other since the latter's inception and that, in time, war would have to heed international law. Nevertheless, he noted that there were different views as to law's place in war: 'During the war of 1870, the Prussian general, Falkenstein, claimed: What can one do? In war there is one law that surpasses all others, and that is: the law of force.'[346]

Another international legal approach was that of 'military realism', led by Carl Lueder, Professor at Erlangen.[347] General Count von Moltke had suggested that everything was allowed in war that could inflict damage on the enemy and thus law had to give way to force, though not all military leaders of 'contemporary civilized nations' shared this view.[348] Hrabar pointed out that it was from amongst the Russian army that Duke Nikolai Leihtenbergski responded critically to the thoughts of Moltke in a letter sent to Professor Friedrich Martens. Unlike von Moltke, Leihtenbergski insisted that one should not inflict damage on civilians; if the army respected human life and property, passions in war would soon calm down.[349] Hrabar concluded: 'In that way, lawyers standing on the ground of "military realism", demanded the restriction of law and humanism in the name of force; military men embedded in "legal idealism", defend the law against force and from the attacks of those who were meant to defend it—lawyers.'[350] Nevertheless, Hrabar maintained that 'military realism' as understood by the German scholar Lueder, had no place in State practice. Von Moltke, Rüstow, Hartmann, and other Prussian generals together with the lawyers of the 'realist' direction, remained the only defenders of this misuse of military force.[351]

In time of war, Hrabar continued, States had sometimes attempted to justify their violations of international law with the argument of 'military necessity'. For instance, during the war of 1870, Germany decided to impose a tax of 25 francs on every French citizen. Hrabar maintained that this 'contribution' was exacted in order to turn the French people against the war and stir them to put pressure on their parliamentarians to that effect. 'But such an extortionist contribution is not permitted under the law of war of our time', wrote Hrabar.[352] Lueder, representing 'his fatherland', had admitted that the Prussian measure had violated the laws of war (*Kriegsmanier*) but still insisted that it was in accordance with military necessity (*Kriegsraison*). Hrabar noted ironically that in Lueder's view, this military necessity consisted of the fact that Germany needed victory and desired an expedient peace.[353]

Another such case in the war of 1870 had been the confiscation of cigarettes and wine by the Prussian army in France. Hrabar admitted that

[345] V Grabar, 'Voina i mezhdunarodno'e pravo' in *Uchenye zapiski imperatorskago Iur'evskago universiteta No. 4, Jur'ev* (1893) 23–4. [346] ibid 27.
[347] ibid 28. [348] ibid 29. [349] ibid. [350] ibid 30. [351] ibid.
[352] ibid 33–4. [353] ibid 34.

under international law, food could be confiscated in wartime but pointed out sarcastically that neither wine nor cigarettes were items of the first necessity, without which soldiers would not have survived. 'The Prussian soldier managed without them, but only in peacetime, while at home.'[354] Lueder had again 'in a naïve manner' justified this act with the argument of military necessity. Altogether, in Hrabar's view, Lueder had, instead of offering a straightforward and honest legal theory of force's supremacy over law in time of war, taken the position 'of a person sitting between two chairs'.[355] Ultimately one had to make a choice between war and international law.[356] 'Military realism' as represented by Moltke, idealized war and had a 'metaphysical-idealised understanding of war, created by the fantasy of Hegel'.[357]

Hrabar pointed out that some industrial complexes thrived on war: without war, 'the armament industries of Stumm and Krupp, having obtained international acclaim and significantly enriching Germany, could not have acquired their present prestige'.[358] He opposed the militarist argument that war had a natural uplifting and 'purifying' effect on a nation:

> Victory over the enemy in great measure brings along with it the decline of morality, a cessation of development. This happened in Germany after its glorious victory over France in 1871. The general decline of morality in Germany connected with the decline of science and art is recognised by the Germans themselves. Professors complain about the lack of interest in knowledge, the disappearance of ideals and the prevalence of pragmatism. At the same time, defeat sometimes brings with it the rise of nations. We remember Russia after the Crimean war and France after its defeat by Prussia.[359]

Nevertheless, one could not conclude that defeat brought renewal either, since there was no connection between success or defeat in war and the rise of a nation: 'Russia would have renewed herself even without the Eastern war, France would have embarked on new ways even without blows delivered by Germany, but no war was able to reinvigorate Turkey.'[360]

Hrabar concluded that international law had to abolish war and instead enable peaceful struggle between nations, since struggle was the 'source of all life, all movement and development'. Struggle 'could be called divine: without beginnings that live in it, nations would be threatened by death'.[361] Hrabar's final remarks were replete with both optimism and pathos: 'The science of international law is the science of peace. Its task is to strengthen peace on Earth and to eliminate war from inter-State relations. This great task gives to the science of international law a deep philosophical meaning.'[362]

Hrabar's views on military conflict and international law, as expressed in his inaugural lecture, can be interpreted as progressive and were influenced

354 Grabar, 'Voina i mezhdunarodno'e pravo' (n 345 above). 355 ibid 35. 356 ibid 36.
357 ibid 37. 358 ibid 40. 359 ibid 42. 360 ibid. 361 ibid 43.
362 ibid 45.

by pacifism. A certain anti-German streak can be traced, but this was based on reasoned principles and concrete examples, not on propagandistic nationalism. The German generals and scholars Hrabar criticized really had said things that Hrabar opposed. The humanistic spirit Hrabar expressed anticipated the Hague Peace Conferences of 1899 and 1907 and the first codifications regarding restrictions on the conduct of war.

At the same time, Hrabar's argument was moralistic and—to use Koskenniemi's dichotomy—utopian. The conduct of war had to be restricted for reasons of goodness and righteousness (philosophy) rather than for reasons stemming from legal deduction (positivism) or the State's immediate interests (realism).

6.3.2 Hrabar's critique of Fyodor Martens regarding declarations of war

In his subsequent international law works, Hrabar established himself as one of the great historians of international law of the first part of the twentieth century.[363] He also became known for his passion for intellectual honesty. When E Simson, a former student of Carl Bergbohm at Dorpat, published in St Petersburg a treatise entitled *A System of International Law*,[364] Hrabar was quick to point out the clear plagiarisms in Simson's work[365] and thus effectively ended Simson's career as an international law scholar.[366]

But the question of the intellectual honesty of international law scholars emerged even more spectacularly in the debate Hrabar held with Friedrich Martens concerning a letter the latter published in *Le Figaro*. The course of events can be traced in Hrabar's treatise *Declaration of War in Contemporary International Law*.[367]

The debate took place against the background of the Russo–Japanese War of 1904. In 1898, a part of Manchuria (Port Arthur and Daljanvan), formerly controlled by Japan, was given to Russia on what Hrabar qualified in inverted commas as a 'lease' of twenty-five years. In January 1904 negotiations between Japan and Russia foundered and on the night of 27 January 1904, the Japanese navy attacked the Russian fleet at Port Arthur.[368]

[363] V Hrabar, *Joh. Wilh. Neumayr von Ramsla. Beitrag zur Geschichte der staatswissenschaftlichen Literatur im Zeitalter des Hugo Groot* (1897); V Hrabar, 'Un traité de droit d'ambassade: "Ambaxiator brevilogus" de Bernard du Rosier' (1899) XXXI *Revue de droit*; V Hrabar, 'L'époque de Bartole (1314–1358) dans l'histoire du droit international' (1900) *Revue general de droit international public*; V Hrabar (edited and commented on by), 'De Legatis et Legationibus Tractatus Varii' in *Uchenye zapiski Imperatorsogo Iur'evskogo Universiteta No 4* (1906); V Hrabar, Martinus Navarrus (de Azpilcueta) et son traité sur la contrebande de guerre' (1911) XLIII *Revue de droit*.

[364] EK Simson, *Sistema mezhdunarodnogo prava* (1900) vol I.

[365] V Grabar, *Neudachnaia popytka natsionalizatsii mezhdunarodnogo prava* (1901).

[366] See VN Durdenevski, *Vladimir Hrabar—jurist i istorik (k 60-letiju nauchnoi dejatelnosti), 'Vestnik Moskovskogo Universiteta'* (1949) No 7.

[367] V Grabar, *Ob'avlenie voiny v sovremennom mezhdunarodnom prave* (1904).

[368] ibid 98–101.

When presenting arguments on topics such as these, Hrabar started with his general views on international law and politics. He emphasized the need for a positivist treatment of international law and criticized the tendency to label any acts that violate ideas of justice, fairness, and honesty as 'illegal': 'If a country implements the freedom of action that it is entitled to according to the law and some other country's interests are hurt, it will immediately be accused of a violation of international law. On the basis of such facts, afterwards it will be concluded that international law does not exist at all since its norms can be violated so easily, often and after all without punishment.'[369] But, Hrabar went on to state that domestic law also allowed the exploitation of some groups by others—in short, was unjust—but nobody considered criticizing it on the basis of civil or constitutional law:[370] 'The voices of judgment and accusation could even be sympathetic if only they were sincere.' This, however, was not the case: 'Usually voices of protest can only be heard among the representatives of the nation that suffered from such a "violation of law" or, at least, did not gain any advantages from it. The same act would receive a different appraisal if it brought such advantages.'[371] Hrabar once again strongly emphasized the need for positivism:

> If one recognised that any just norm is at the same time a norm of actual law, and its violation is a violation of law, then, inevitably, one must accept the situation that in international relations violations of law appear to be the rule, and respect for the law—the exception. Many imagine current international law to be this way. This can be explained by the influence of the natural law school, which does not distinguish what is from what ought to be . . . positive law, quite often unjust, from just law.[372]

Hrabar went on in particular to praise international law scholarship in Germany, where the distinction between valid law and just law had been made most rigorously. In contrast, international law scholars in France continued to write in the spirit of natural law.[373] He also maintained that making a rigorous distinction between valid law and just law was 'necessary in the interests of strengthening international law. Law will become less just—but more firm. The future task is then self-evident: one needs to strive for norms corresponding better to the requirements of justice, honesty, and humanity, on the condition that compliance with those norms is safeguarded by real guarantees.'[374] He turned to the question in international legal doctrine of declaring war, proceeding to demonstrate that together with the development of arms, those voices became dominant in international legal literature that claimed that declarations of war had become less essential and legally no longer required. There remained the problem of partiality in the literature—when, for example, Heffter

[369] Grabar, *Ob'avlenie* (n 367 above) 4.
[370] Apparently, the idea of fundamental constitutional rights was as yet alien to Hrabar.
[371] Grabar, *Ob'avlenie* (n 367 above) 4–5. [372] ibid 5. [373] ibid 6. [374] ibid.

and Bluntschli modelled their doctrinal views on the wars conducted by the Prussian King Frederick II.[375]

Finally, Hrabar came close to the issue at the heart of his writing: whether or not Japan had violated international law by attacking Russia in 1904 without a prior declaration of war. Hrabar demonstrated that the Anglo-American view which did not consider a declaration of war legally mandatory was rooted in the Japanese literature. Japan's first war after the country's acceptance by the European concert, its war against China, had been triggered without a declaration of war. Japanese international law scholars (for example Nagao Ariga) considered the Sino–Japanese war to be another instance confirming that there was no such requirement.[376]

Hrabar turned to the views expressed by Russian international law scholars. It appeared that the real impetus for Hrabar's account was not so much the confusion between 'valid' and just law in the particular case but the fact that Fyodor Martens had expressed 'inconsequent' and ultimately dishonest views. In his much-acclaimed textbook on international law, Martens had written that declarations of war had become 'useless':

> All recent wars have started without a prior declaration. Sometimes, however, States considered it necessary to inform the enemy of the beginning of hostilities. In our time, it is hardly possible to defend the necessity of a festive declaration of war or even some sort of prior diplomatic notice. Given the current development of telegraphic connections, it is always possible to know earlier what the relations between the States are, and to foresee the final break.[377]

Hrabar pointed out that the reading of this passage left no doubt that Martens embraced the Anglo-American view 'in its most extreme form'—namely, not only that such a declaration was not made mandatory by law but that it had also become superfluous.[378]

However, Hrabar went on to recount how on 8 (21) February 1904, Martens had written a letter to *Le Figaro* in which a change in his views became apparent and 'which surprised everyone so much'.[379] He added a humorous comment: he could not attribute this sudden change of mind on Martens' part to anything other than his subsequent 'reading of French authors' (who had held a minority view to the effect that diplomatic notice was required before the outbreak of hostilities).[380] Martens had claimed that 'now, just as thirty years ago, I remain convinced that a formal or festive declaration of war is in our time not required'. However, he also added that it was 'unconditionally necessary that both adversaries be convinced on the basis of positive facts that a state of war exists between them and that hostile activities are imminient. Briefly, it is absolutely necessary that both sides be informed that war is about to break out'.[381]

375 ibid 33. 376 ibid 8.

377 F Martens, *Sovremennoe mezhdunarodnoe pravo* (4th edn, 1900) vol II, 524.

378 Grabar, *Ob'avlenie* (n 367 above) 41–2. 379 ibid 42. 380 ibid.

381 F Martens, Letter to the Editor, *Le Figaro*, 8 (21) February 1904. Russian translation in *Novoe Vremya* 1904, No 10056.

A debate between the titans of Russian international law scholarship ensued. A former student of Martens and his later successor to the chair of international law, AA Pilenko, published an article 'Yasno'e obnaruzhenie namereni' ('Clear expression of intentions') in which he expressed his surprise at the change in Martens' position: 'I as a long-time disciple of Professor Martens, support the view that was taught to me by my teacher', ie that neither a formal declaration of war nor diplomatic notice was necessary.[382]

Martens responded that he considered the outbreak of hostilities without a declaration of war to be legal but not '*bona fide*' (*dobrosovestno*). He intended to include in the next edition of his textbook on international law the statement that 'civilized nations always have to remember that Asian nations attack their enemies by surprise and in a cowardly manner, with the pretext that there is no duty to declare war'.[383] Hrabar's comment on Martens' remark was laconically sarcastic: *sapienti sat*.[384]

After having carefully examined views expressed in legal writings, Hrabar turned to the examination of State practice. He pointed out that just as Napoleon did not declare war against Russia in 1812, so Russia itself did not declare war against Sweden in the war of 1808–09, and this notwithstanding the fact that hostilities came as a surprise to Sweden.[385] This war, initiated by Russia, had been highly informative because of the similarity of circumstances to those of the Russo–Japanese War. The same was true in the Russo–Turkish War (1806–12) in which Russia seized Moldavia and Walachia, and Turkey was taken by surprise. The Russo–Turkish War of 1878 was another fascinating case: Russia declared war with a diplomatic note but by the time it was received, the Russian forces had already crossed the border into Romania.[386] This episode was significant also in that it had given rise to Martens' view on the declaration of war, a view he had maintained for twenty-five years.[387] In his book, Martens had considered nonsensical the accusation that Russia started the war against Turkey without formally declaring it: most writers considered such a declaration a mere formality. Martens insisted that even during the eighteenth century outstanding lawyers demonstrated the superfluousness of a declaration of war. (Hrabar commented: 'It is difficult to say it in a more categorical form.')[388] Martens had also considered the example of the Ottoman Porte in this regard: 'The Porte should not forget that we live at the end of the 19th century when between really civilized nations different views on "international customs and rules" were established.' Note again the sarcasm: 'It would be interesting

[382] AA Pilenko, Letter to the Editor, *Novoe Vremya* 1904, No 10053
[383] F Martens, Letter to the Editor, *Novoe Vremya*, 1904, No 10058.
[384] Grabar, *Ob'avlenie* (n 367 above) 43. [385] ibid 53. [386] ibid 74–6.
[387] F Martens, *Vostochnaya voina i Brjusselskaja konferentsia 1874–1878* (1879).
[388] Grabar, *Ob'avlenie* (n 367 above) 76.

to know whether Martens considers those customs still to be in use at the beginning of the 20th century.'[389]

It was strange then, Hrabar pointed out, that as to Russia's war against Turkey Martens had claimed that a '*really* civilized nation'[390] had the right to attack another country without a proper declaration of war.[391] In his *Le Figaro* letter, Martens had even criticized Japan for not wanting to conduct a so-called *bonne guerre* 'in the sense it was led by European nations in the Middle Ages'.[392] Hrabar commented: 'This demand to return to the Middle Ages is especially strange to hear from the mouth of Professor Martens, after his historical teachings on Turkey regarding the customs of really civilized nations.'[393] Thus, Hrabar concluded that Japan had by no means violated international law by attacking Russia without diplomatic notice. He expressed surprise that not only Martens but also the Russian Ministry of Foreign Affairs had argued the opposite. 'True, the ministry may have been misled by its collaborator, Professor Martens ... but this cannot be a sufficient excuse for the ministry. Although for a theoretician it is normal and excusable not to be concerned with daily life, for a ministry, in contrast, it is impossible not to observe changes in real life ... Undoubtedly, our ministry had not heard of a number of the most recent wars ...'[394] Hrabar finally noted that Martens still owed an explanation for his sudden change of views 'both to the Russian literary public and the science of international law'.[395]

At the end of the polemic Hrabar breathed an almost audible sigh and confessed that his article had turned out 'much longer than initially planned'.[396] One can understand why. Hrabar's long and passionate involvement with Martens' fluctuating views demonstrated that, for him, the very credibility of international law and international legal arguments was at stake. Hrabar was far from questioning the intellect of Martens, but he questioned his moral judgment, accusing the latter of favouring the momentary needs of Russian foreign policy, and probably his personal career and position as the leading international lawyer in Russia, over 'positive international law'. In addition, Hrabar had also been angered by the 'civilized nations' argument, while it had been over-exploited by Martens and in the tsarist foreign policy rhetoric.[397]

This was *par excellence* a debate between an international lawyer-legal adviser and an international lawyer-legal theoretician. In the eyes of other scholars of international law, Hrabar probably came out as the

389 ibid 77.
390 The emphasis added by Martens in *Vestnik prava*, 1904, 181–4.
391 Grabar, *Ob'avlenie* (n 367 above) 111.
392 F Martens, Letter to the Editor, *Le Figaro*, 8 (21) February 1904, in Russian in *Novoe Vremja*, 3 March 1904, No 10056.
393 Grabar, *Ob'avlenie* (n 367 above) 111.
394 ibid 142.
395 ibid 145. See also 'Prof. Martens sostoit v dolgu pered naukoju mezhdunarodnogo prava' *Vestnik prava*, December 1904.
396 Grabar, *Ob'avlenie* (n 367 above) 147.
397 See also E Myles, '"Humanity", "Civilization" and the "International Community" in the Late Imperial Russian Mirror: Three Ideas "Topical for Our Days"' (2002) 4 *Journal of the History of International Law* 310–34.

moral victor in the debate with Martens, but the latter probably led a more rewarding life in terms of political recognition, representation, and glamour.

6.3.3 Hrabar's theory of the inequality of States

In his international law lectures at Iur'ev, Hrabar painted a progressivist, pro-democratic picture of the development of international law, maintaining around 1904 that the era was being lived under the banner of the ideas of the French Revolution of 1789.[398] He argued that the self-determination of nations had gained more and more ground, that the inner structure of States had begun to play an increasingly greater role, while the will of the people gained in importance (thus pointing to the republican ideal).[399] Finally, the first limits on the outbreak of war had been established in international law. Nevertheless, talking about the literature of international law, Hrabar divided it into 'Russian', 'German', 'Italian' branches, etc, according to nationality.[400]

In 1912, Hrabar published *The Principle of the Equality of States in Contemporary International Law*.[401] In this short book, he advanced the theory of inequality and legal hierarchies between States. The book was primarily inspired by the second Hague Peace Conference of 1907, or more precisely, by its failure. At this conference, the Great Powers had suggested the creation of a Permanent International Court of Arbitration and had insisted that the principle of the equality of States had to be abandoned for the undertaking to succeed. Moreover, eight of the fifteen judges of the International Prize Chamber were to be appointed by the Great Powers. Hrabar's main argument was that it was necessary to recognize not only the actual but also the legal inequality of States. He recounted how the six Great Powers had led European politics since the fall of Napoleon and how at the end of the nineteenth century, the interests of the Great Powers and small States clashed at international conferences. Hrabar argued that the behaviour of small States in preventing the creation of a permanent adjudicatory body at the 1907 Hague Conference had been tantamount to obstruction. He turned to the literature on the issue of equality and pointed out that recent treatises against the erosion of equality in international law had been written by Belgian, Swiss, and Greek scholars, ie authors who came from small States. Hrabar's own sympathy lay with the Scottish lawyer James Lorimer's argument that international law, if it wanted to be respected, had to be respectful of the power of the Great Powers and integrate it.

Hrabar went on to construct a classical apologetic argument in which he argued that the law must take State practice more into account and that legal doctrine should come closer to actual facts. International law

398 Hrabar's international law lectures, student's transcript in the university archive, 129.

399 ibid 130–1. 400 ibid 131.

401 V Grabar, *Nachalo ravenstva gosudarstv v sovremennom mezhdunarodnom prave* (1912).

had to recognize some sort of aristocratic supremacy of the Great Powers. There was no danger that this aristocracy would turn into oligarchy, since the interests of the competing Great Powers were too different. Recognizing the leading role of the Great Powers both in politics and in law would also be in the interests of 'civilized' small States, since they would be able to serve as brokers between and provide meeting places for the Great Powers, as experience with Brussels, Geneva, and The Hague already demonstrated. The formal recognition of the principle of juridical inequality was needed, since the Great Powers had to be rewarded for taking the small States on board at all in international decision-making. It was a mistake to postpone taking a political approach to law until the point was reached where the Great Powers might decide to abandon law altogether.

In any case, the Great Powers were adopting international legislation, like the London Declaration of 1909, that may have been formally binding only on its participating Great Powers but had *de facto* become generally applicable law. The small States were also in practice unable to utilize several institutions of international law—such as reprisals in the law of State responsibility. As a case in point, Hrabar described how Serbia had initially protested against the annexation of Bosnia and Herzegovina by Austria but had then been pushed by the latter to declare that it intended to give up its 'protesting and opposing attitude' and to live from then on with Austria on 'good neighbourly terms'. In that case, Hrabar asked rhetorically, could one speak of equality?

Hrabar finally took a 'positivist' position, maintaining that more 'political than legal elements' existed in the arguments of the supporters of the principle of the equality of States. As if 'law' would have so clearly been on his side and 'politics', on the other! He further argued that the talk of juridical equality was simply a kind of protest against the activities of the Great Powers: from a theoretical point of view, the equality of States was a miscarriage of the Vattelian analogy that conceptualized States in the abstract as autonomous entities, comparable to human beings under domestic law. This resulted in 'State fetishism' and in the recognition of the 'absolute value of statehood'. It was simply wrong to argue, Hrabar concluded, that the equality of States was the only possible foundation for the edifice of international law. Instead, the 1907 Hague Conference accepted three ranks between States: great, middle, and small States. In every single issue of international law and order, different powers could have different statuses, depending on their influence. But there was also a strong case for legitimacy: instead of the 'fictive equality' of nominally equal States, a 'real equality' was needed, based on how many people lived in a country. In other words, a major basis for the inequality of States was the inequality of their populations. 'Instead of the equality of States, the equality of populations' had to be taken into account. Although Hrabar had earlier pointed out that the defenders of the equality of States came mostly from small countries, it would be unfair if Russia and Great Britain were legally equal to Luxembourg or Panama.

Hrabar's theory of the inequality of States, written in 1912, sounds surprisingly modern and realistic today, and not only because Hrabar counted *eight* Great Powers (cf the G8). Hrabar's predictions and doctrinal suggestions both did and did not come true in the twentieth century. *De facto*, inequality of States was legally recognized; *de jure*, it was rejected. The United Nations Charter constitutes a *complexio oppositorum* in this sense: although it recognizes the privileged role of the UN Security Council, especially the veto right-possessing permanent members, at the same time it upholds the equality of sovereign States.

Hrabar's theory of the inequality of States, expressed in 1912, was a reaction to a crisis in international relations. Something—Sarajevo, perhaps—was already in the air. Suggestively, the French translation of Hrabar's booklet was published in 1914.[402] In the context of its time, Hrabar's argument for legal inequality was not so unusual. Some pre-World War I British and American scholars held similar views.[403] Hrabar's views were also shared and discussed by a former student of his, the Russian scholar Baron Sergey Aleksandrovich Korff (1876–1924),[404] who defended his doctoral thesis at Iur'ev in 1910.

When arguing in favour of the legal inequality of States, Hrabar's claim was not so much driven by *his* imperialism but by the imperialism of his *time*. Hrabar's goal and ideal was to make international law relevant, to bring it 'closer to the facts'. Importantly, Hrabar characterized his own viewpoint as legally more sound, while making it clear that his opponents on the issue were pursuing politics rather than legal analysis. But as an answer to his argument that supporters of the equality principle came from small States, it should be noted that Hrabar himself was a professor in the largest continental Empire. In contrast to his utopian inaugural lecture of 1893, Hrabar theorized in 1912 in a much more realist and down-to-earth manner. Here Hrabar clearly argued as a 'modern' (to use Koskenniemi's term), mixing realist arguments such as power (Great Power status should be legally recognized) with idealism (democracy matters; it is important to make international law more relevant).

6.3.4 Optimism about the future of international law in 1917

Did the Great War of 1914–18 somehow change Hrabar's views on the equality of States? In 1917, Hrabar published another edition of his meticulous Russian translation of the leading international law textbook

[402] V Hrabar, *La crise actuelle du principe de l'égalité juridique des états* (1914).

[403] See G Simpson, *Great Powers and Outlaw States. Unequal Sovereigns in the International Legal Order* (2004).

[404] SA Korff, 'Printsip ravenstva gosudarstv v sovremennom mezhdunarodnom prave' *Izvestia Ministerstva Inostrannyh Del*, 1914, 139–47. See also DB Levin, *Nauka mezhdunardodnogo prava v Rossii v kontse XIX i nachale XX v* (1982) 170ff.

by Franz von Liszt (1851–1919).[405] Hrabar's foreword is dated March 1917, ie immediately after the February revolution in Russia. He had remained faithful to his earlier idealistic view that war had simply been an expression of politics, which was not able to undermine the validity of international law. Note the impressive impartiality of his words when he invoked history in support of his view: 'Many of the achievements of European civilization have been frivolously sacrificed in war by this or another warring party in order to achieve short-term gains. A lot of contemporary international law has been swept away in this global fight. But we do not need to worry about the future. In history, periods of peaceful construction follow periods of destruction. So it will be now too.'[406] This kind of idealistic old-European spirit expressed by Hrabar and reminiscent of Stefan Zweig's *The World of Yesterday* did not survive in the discipline after World War II and the rejection of international law by disappointed émigré scholars such as Hans Morgenthau. Hrabar's words would have sounded naive: in 1945, the failures and deficiencies of 'legalistic-moralistic' (George Kennan) constructions of international law were too tangible.

Hrabar's foreword to von Liszt's textbook also departed to some extent from his earlier legal inequality argument and at the same time captured the new direction of international law and the development of Russia. He argued that the February revolution in Russia had immediately 'given a meaning' to the Great War.[407] 'The great nation no longer sought conquests and Constantinople, instead it now had a dream of remaking the old world.'[408] From the February revolution of 1917 on, Hrabar continued, the slogans of 'justice, freedom and national self-determination' were 'no longer only words'. Against the power of those ideas as represented by the new Russia, any 'physical force was powerless and had to lay down its arms'.[409] Thus, the right to self-determination had arrived in international law: according to Hrabar, its pursuit gave to new Russia a completely new legitimacy, a legitimacy that was much stronger than the one stemming from military might. Again, this was a very 'idealistic' view but it is also worth noting that it had a legitimizing function, giving—from the perspective of international law—new messianic meaning and identity to republican Russia. In the words of Pierre Bourdieu:

> In science, art, or politics, the creative power of representation never manifests itself more clearly than in periods of revolutionary crisis. Nonetheless, the will to transform the world for naming it, by producing new categories of perception and judgment, and by dictating a new vision of social divisions and distributions, can only succeed if the resulting prophecies, or creative

[405] Hrabar discovered in Liszt's work a number of substantive mistakes that he communicated to the author of the textbook and that were corrected in later editions. F von Liszt, *Mezhdunardonoe pravo v sistematicheskom izlozhenii, 4e russkoe izdanie, perevod s shestogo nemetskogo izdania pod redaktsiei i s dopolneniem prof. V. E. Grabarja* (Iur'ev: 1917).

[406] Hrabar, foreword to Liszt (n 405 above) iv. [407] ibid v. [408] ibid. [409] ibid.

evocations, are also, at least in part, well-founded pre-visions, anticipatory descriptions.[410]

With his 1917 foreword to von Liszt's textbook, Hrabar envisaged post-1917 Russia and a future world.

6.3.5 Hrabar's writings while an international lawyer in Communist Russia

The year 1917 signified a break, not only in Dorpat/Iur'ev/Tartu, but in the whole world. Europe started to be marked increasingly by ideological divisions between liberal democracy and its two challengers, Communism and Nazism/Fascism.[411]

[410] P Bourdieu, 'The Force of Law: The Logic of Practice' (1987) 38 *Hastings Law Journal* 839.

[411] There is a significant biographical side- and afterstory to Hrabar's activities as an international law professor at Iur'ev. Among the students in his international law class in 1900–01 was Alexander (Axel) August Gustav Johann Baron Freiherr von Freytagh-Loringhoven (1878–1942), a member of a family belonging to the Baltic German nobility and coming from Arensburg (Kuressaare) on the largest Estonian island Saaremaa (Ösel). (See Tartu University Archive in the Estonian History Archive in Tartu, F 402/1/27784.) In 1907, Freytagh-Loringhoven passed his masters degree examinations at Iur'ev while Hrabar was the Dean of the Faculty of Law. However, Freytagh-Loringhoven defended his masters thesis in 1910 at St Petersburg University. On 23 May 1911, Freytagh-Loringhoven was appointed Extraordinary Professor of Roman Law at Iur'ev. He defended his doctoral degree at Harkov University in 1915 and became Ordinary Professor of Roman Law at Iur'ev in 1916. At the outbreak of World War I, Freytagh-Loringhoven was the dean of the law faculty—a position from which he stepped down in November 1914, 'taking into account the situation at the faculty'. (See ibid F 402/3/1781 and F 402/3/1783) It seems likely that the immediate reasons were questions of loyalty and tensions in the background of the war between Germany and Russia. (For the anti-German sentiment cultivated in the Russian Empire at that time, see T Karjahärm, *Ida ja lääne vahel. Eesti-Vene suhted 1850–1917* (1998) 199ff.) In July 1917, Freytagh-Loringhoven requested his release from the position of Professor of Roman Law, a wish that was granted with retroactive effect in September 1917.

After the end of World War I, Freytagh-Loringhoven moved to Germany. He became a professor in Breslau (Wrocław) and was actively involved in Weimar Republic politics. He represented national conservative views and was elected as a member of the Prussian State Council and the German Reichstag. In terms of scholarship, Freytagh-Loringhoven moved from his previous field of Roman law to international law, becoming one of the most influential international law figures in Nazi Germany. (See PK Steck, *Zwischen Volk und Staat. Das Völkerrechtssubjekt in der deutschen Völkerrechtslehre (1933–1941)* ((2003) 46–53.) He was active in the German Society for Questions Regarding the League of Nations (*Deutsche Gesellschaft für Völkerbundfragen*), the editor-in-chief of the magazine *Völkerbund und Völkerrecht* (The League of Nations and International Law) and a member of the Permanent Arbitral Court in The Hague. Freytagh-Loringhoven's politics of international law was directed towards the legitimization of Germany's increasing appetite for power and the revision of the 'humiliation' of the Treaty of Versailles. (See F von Freytagh-Loringhoven, 'Der Widerruf des Kriegsschuldbekenntnisses' in (1936/1937) 3 *Völkerbund und Völkerrecht* 725–31. See also his 'Rückkehr zum europäischen Gleichgewicht?' ibid 507–13.) He argued that the League of Nations had failed but suggested that international law should not be identified with the League of Nations. (See F von Freytagh-Loringhoven, 'Rechtfertigung des Völkerrechts' (1936) 3 *Völkerbund und Völkerrecht* 161–6.) His journal defended the rights of the ethnic Germans outside Germany, eg complaining about discrimination against them and unjust treatment (*Volkstumsunrecht*) in Latvia. (See (1936) 2 *Völkerbund und Völkerrecht* 653–711.) Particularly interesting from the point of view of this article is Freytagh-Loringhoven's harsh criticism of the decision of the Council of the League of Nations to admit the USSR to the organization. In Freytagh-Loringhoven's view, the old Baltic German concept of *Ostwall* against the Russian influence merged together with the National Socialist rhetoric of the civilizational otherness of the Bolshevist regime. Freytagh-Loringhoven argued that the times when international law could

After the Communists came to power in Russia in 1917, Hrabar essentially turned to the history of international law in Russia—the final result being the publication of his *Materials on the History of International Law in Russia* in 1958. Hrabar's only theoretical article of his post-Iur'ev period was a critique of Soviet scholar Evgeni Aleksandrovich Korovin's (1892–1964) essay 'International Law of the Intermediary Period',[412] published in 1927.[413] In this critical review, Hrabar defended the unity of international law against emerging tendencies in Soviet scholarship and in particular criticized Korovin's theoretical attempt to separate the international law of socialist States from that of bourgeois States. He characterized Korovin's theories as outdated and was dismissive of the latter's attempt to create a unique Soviet approach to international law.

A question that immediately comes to mind is, how could such an article have been published in 1927, ie when 'enemies of the people' were already sought and found in Soviet Russia? The editor of the *Zeitschrift für Völkerrecht*, Max Fleischmann, noted in his brief commentary that Hrabar's article was a message from an otherwise isolated country, and this explained why Hrabar had been unable to compare Korovin's views with those of his Western counterparts.[414] One explanation was the immediate backdrop of the Rapallo Treaty, which sought to normalize relations between Germany and Soviet Russia in 1923. Stalin's purges had not yet started; the USSR was still living in the relative economic freedom of the New Economic Policy. It seems that Hrabar hoped (too optimistically)

remain neutral towards the form of government of its constituent members, States, had ended. There were conditions for that in the 19th century but not any longer in the 1930s since 'a State [had] emerged that denied all foundations of the moral, cultural and economic order, and that simultaneously declared it its highest goal, to make this negation victorious in the whole world. A State like that excluded itself from the international community, and when it was nevertheless permitted access to the international community, this symbolized the denial of any instinct for self-preservation . . . Facts that prove the magnitude of the Bolshevist danger are innumerable . . . The denial of international law stands in the beginning of the Soviet Union.' (See F von Freytagh-Loringhoven, 'Sowjetrußland und das Völkerrecht' (1936/1937) 3 *Völkerbund und Völkerrecht* 365, 367. See also his earlier account 'Sowjetrußland im Völkerbund' (1934/1935) 1 *Völkerbund und Völkerrecht* 307–12.) He concluded that 'history will one day form a judgment' of those 'who did not realize the need for unity against the Bolshevist danger, and had admitted the USSR to the international community' (ibid 370). For the arguments that international law had to be used against the Bolsheviks, see also EH Bockhoff, *Völker-Recht gegen Bolschewismus* (1937).) Freytagh-Loringhoven's viewpoint becomes more easily understandable when one thinks of his student and professorship years at Iur'ev, the tensions between the Baltic German nobility and the Russian Empire, the violence of the Russian revolutions of 1905 and 1917, and the expropriation of the Baltic German properties in 1919. In the 1930s, Freytagh-Loringhoven was on the other side of a *cordon sanitaire* from his own former professor of international law and colleague, Vladimir Hrabar. But Freytagh-Loringhoven did not seem to make much secret of the fact that, for him, international law was no more than a means of foreign policy. (Therefore, his activism and publications in the field of international law coincide with his rise in German politics.) In particular, in comparison with Freytagh-Loringhoven's writings, Hrabar's silence on questions of contemporary theory and his preoccupation with the more silent trenches of the history of international law in the 1930s start to speak volumes.

[412] E Korovin, *Mezhdunarodnoe pravo perehodnogo vremeni* (1923).

[413] V Hrabar, 'Das heutige Völkerrecht vom Standpunkte eines Sowjetjuristen' (1927) XIV *Zeitschrift für Völkerrecht* 188–214.

[414] ibid 188.

that Soviet Russia would eventually 'normalize' ideologically.[415] He was eager to play down the ideological idiosyncrasy of the Soviet concept of international law as represented by Korovin. In Hrabar's reading of Korovin, there seems to have been some wishful thinking—or hoping—that eventually everything was going to be 'normal'. In any case, in approach, language, and conclusions, Hrabar's article could not be distinguished from non-Marxist 'bourgeois' scholars' works of the same time. He did not criticize Korovin from a position of power—as another influential Soviet lawyer of that period, Yevgeni B Pashukanis (1891–1937), had done. Instead, Hrabar insisted on the unity of international law at a time of ideological divisions.

It was clear that under Stalin's reign such independent thinking was not going to be tolerated much longer. In the 1930s and 1940s, the only original Soviet works published on international law were those zealously in the service of Soviet official ideology—and Hrabar was not among their authors. This is quite a significant fact. During the Soviet period, Hrabar never published anything that would have been in complete discordance with the ideas that he had expressed before 1917. In the Soviet textbook of international law, written by a group of authors and published in 1947, the part co-authored by Hrabar—on the history of the law of nations—was a relatively neutral and, as usual, very erudite piece. It was a well-balanced ray of scholarly light in an otherwise ideologically overcharged propagandistic textbook.[416] (For example, the last chapter of the book was entitled 'The Struggle of the USSR for Peace'.) Most of the chapter written by Hrabar would also have suited any leading 'bourgeois' textbook on the history of international law, while the rest of the book could be very easily distinguished in both style and content from its Western counterparts. Hrabar continued to teach the history of international law at Moscow's Diplomatic Academy at an advanced age even after 1945, and his disciples remember him once saying with self-irony: 'If I do not get the newer material right, my younger faculty colleagues will surely correct it for you later on.'[417]

6.4 Conclusion: advancing international law as the politics of Vladimir Hrabar

Hrabar's politics of international law was international law itself—its progressive development and its justification. At a time when so many used history to legitimize their respective Empires and nation States,

[415] See eg Hrabar, 'Das heutige Völkerrecht' (n 414 above) 194–5 where Hrabar insisted that all 'abnormal' behaviour of the Soviet State belonged to the past.

[416] V Durdenevski and S Krylov (eds), *Mezhdunarodnoe pravo* (1947).

[417] Told to the author by a former student of Hrabar at the 49th annual meeting of the Russian Association of International Law in Moscow in June 2006.

Hrabar used history to legitimize international law. In Hrabar's works, international law was everywhere—in the Middle Ages, in the works of glossators and post-glossators, in post-Reformation England. It only needed to be found and brought to light. Surely no maleficent World War could endanger such a historical phenomenon as international law!

Hrabar's vision of international law was 'idealistic'. He chose to be a cosmopolitan defender of the objectivity of international law, even against the propagandistic interests of his own nation State (the Martens case). At the same time, his international law was 'realistic'. He recommended making international law more relevant and abandoning excessively rigid interpretations of the principle of the equality of States. In skilfully combining idealism and realism, Hrabar was a true representative of the 'moderns' in international law scholarship.

He was also a successful survivor. He was probably the only international law scholar in Russia who was able to continue to work in the field of international law even after the 1917 Communist October Revolution—at the same time not actively writing 'in the new way'. However, what seems most important about his survival is not simply the fact itself, but that at the same time he was able to maintain his principles. He never started to write in the 'true Communist spirit' and his wife even continued to exchange greeting cards annually with his closest friends on the name day of Tsar Nicholas II.[418] Taking into account how the Soviet State 'liquidated' its own leading international law voices (for example Pashukanis in 1937), Hrabar's survival is notable.

Since Hrabar was the only 'imported' professor among the internationalists holding the chair, he seemed to have less academic and political interest in the Baltic situation. In local ethno-political struggles, he played the role of a liberal balancer between Russia's interests and those of local ethnic groups.

Of the university's five international law professors, Hrabar probably came closest to the ideal of an independent international law professor, capable of speaking the truth to those in power. At least, that is true of Hrabar during the Tsarist period. He publicly criticized the Russian *Kronjurist* Martens for his lack of scientific integrity. In the service of the Tsarist Russian army during World War I, he took issue with the war crimes committed by the Russians as well as those committed by the German army (and was ultimately fired for this lack of partiality). In several publications he sought to rectify the injustice which his predecessor at the international law chair had suffered—while Bergbohm had been dismissed not because he was not qualified, but because his politics were 'wrong' (not for valid 'legal' reasons but for 'political' ones).[419]

[418] Interview with Liidia Uustal, April 2005.

[419] See esp Hrabar's account on Bergbohm in GV Levitski (ed), *Biograficheski slovar professorov i prepodovatelei Imperatorskogo Iur'evskogo, byvshego Derptskogo Universiteta* (1902) 633.

Never has belief in international law been greater than when Hrabar wrote in March 1917 that there were many reasons to remain optimistic about the future of international law. He believed that the significance of World War I and in particular the 1917 Russian Revolution lay in the creation of a new, better international law. But peace based on a new international law proved illusory, and 1917–18 just signified a milestone in the chain of conflicts that historians later started to call the 'European Civil War' (1914–18, 1939–45).

In Hrabar's experience, encounters with international law in State practice turned out to be frustrating. States only wanted to talk about international law when it seemed useful to them. Hrabar's carefully drafted protest against the liquidation of the Russian University at Iur'ev, based on arguments of international law, did not make much of a difference to the outcome—the Germans treated it as just another moralistic 'scrap of paper'. Nevertheless, Hrabar personified the professional belief that even when international law was gravely violated, it continued to be present. The task of the international lawyer was to speak law to those in power. When those in power had gone mad and true international law was suppressed, one had to wait patiently in one's apartment near 'Park Kultury' metro station and study the history of international law in the way that a believer in an anti-religious or otherwise intolerant society would keep reading old religious texts and waiting for the Messiah. ('But we do not need to worry about the future', 1917.)

In terms of the development of the positivist concept of international law, Hrabar brought it skilfully to a new level of sophistication. For example, he managed to neutralize a highly political question—what should be the relative power of small States *vis-à-vis* Great Powers—with the amazing argument that 'law' has to be 'close to the facts'. Yet generally, what balanced his positivist claim of separation of law from politics was cosmopolitan humanism. Most likely, Hrabar simply postulated that Great Powers were the most stable guarantors of humanity.

7. Piip (and His Circle): The Nationalist Mind

Is Estonia not too small for independence?

AJ Balfour, British Foreign Secretary to the Estonian envoy Ants Piip, 23 April 1918

'Where did the respective leaders come from? They were of course already there earlier, in our midst; they were simply not noticed. So much of everything depends on the interpretation ... Certainly some things that were now happening seemed not only violent but also artificially created. A literary language that had to correspond to all modern requirements had to be handy. The first statesmen invented

> personally word by word ... It was a modern version of what the oldest myths tell us: some king invented the language, created the concepts ... '[420]
>
> Baron Hermann Keyserling (1880–1946), Baltic German philosopher from Raikküla, Estonia

7.1 *Ants Piip: key facts*

Ants Piip was born on 16 (28) February 1884 in the Tuhalaane county in Estonia, where his parents Jaan Piigert and Ann Piip were peasants.[421] He attended the local school and the Goldingen (Kuldiga) Teachers' Seminar in neighbouring Latvia. From 1905 to 1912 he worked as a school teacher in the Maritime School of Kuressaare (on Saaremaa island). In Kuressaare, he passed the *gymnasium* exams as extern in 1908. In the same year he entered the Faculty of Law of the University of St Petersburg, where he soon specialized in public international law under Mikhail Aleksandrovich Taube (1869–1960), who was Professor of Public International Law at St Petersburg from 1903 to 1911. Piip graduated from the Faculty of Law with distinction in 1913. During his legal studies in the imperial capital, he worked as a teacher in a commercial *gymnasium*. In 1912, he studied for a while at the University of Berlin, attending in particular the classes of Franz von Liszt. Between 1913 and 1916, Piip continued as a research scholar in international law at the Faculty of Law of the University of St Petersburg. His supervisor was Taube's successor at the international law chair, Aleksandr Aleksandrovich Pilenko (1873–19??), professor from 1911 to 1917. In 1916, Piip passed his masters exam in international law and was appointed *Privat-Dozent* in the subject of international law.

During the pre-1917 period the University of St Petersburg was a hothouse of Estonian intellectuals, in particular, lawyers. Without much exaggeration it can be said that the Republic of Estonia was proclaimed in 1918 and then built up in the ensuing years by the former Estonian students of the University of St Petersburg, in particular its Faculty of Law. In the 1920s, the young Republic of Estonia had sixty-eight of these lawyers among its government members and higher State officials.[422] When the University of Tartu was opened in 1919 as the Estonian national university, a circle of three graduates or former students of the Faculty of Law of St Petersburg University—Ants Piip, Nikolai Maim, and Jüri Uluots—played a crucial role in setting up the new Estonian Faculty of Law at Tartu.[423]

420 GH Keyserling, *Das Spektrum Europas* (1928) 371–2.

421 Here and in the following: AR Cederberg (ed), *Eesti biograafiline leksikon* (1926–29), entry Piip, Hans (Ants), 380–1.

422 See R Pullat, *Lootuste linn Peterburi ja Eesti haritlaskonna kujunemine kuni 1917* (2004) 130.

423 See Nikolai Maim archive at Tartu University Library, Maim's and Piip's exchange of letters in 1919 regarding the setting up of the faculty of law at Tartu, F 88/2/17.

Between 1916 and 1918 Piip worked as a military official in the central administration of the courts and in 1917 served in the department of minority peoples of the Russian Ministry of Interior Affairs.

Piip was appointed Extraordinary Professor of International Law at the University of Tartu in 1919. In 1924, he became an ordinary professor, a position he held until 1940. Between 1932 and 1938 he also taught commercial law at the university. He was a member of the London-based International Law Association, a foreign member of the Grotius Society, and a member of the Paris-based Society of Comparative Law.

His wife Benita was almost twenty years younger than her husband, and—according to the gossip of the American tabloids during their stay in Washington, DC, in the mid-1920s—thrilled her contemporaries with her attractiveness.[424]

Piip's life was political *par excellence*. After the February Revolution of 1917, a commission of Estonian lawyers was formed in the Russian capital, now re-named Petrograd. The commission was led by Ants Piip, and its other members included Jüri Uluots and Nikolai Maim, the later core of the Estonian Faculty of Law at the University of Tartu. The commission promulgated the idea of federalism for Russia, but all attempts to draft a constitution for an autonomous Estonia and Latvia in the composition of Russia were rejected by the central authorities. Piip later related this negative experience with the central government in St Petersburg: 'I am recalling this fight in order to demonstrate that Russian democracy did everything it could in order to destroy the trust in it of small nationalities ... The gap between the Russian democracy and our own deepened further.'[425]

On 20 November 1917, Ants Piip and Jaan Tõnisson, two leading Estonian politicians, were sent by the Estonian National Council or Diet (a temporary parliament elected under Russian law) abroad, initially to Scandinavia, as the first Estonian 'diplomatic' representatives.[426] Piip wrote in 1923:

> It was thought, I remember, that we would complement each other very well—one from the right, the other from the left; one—an older representative of society, the other: prepared for this task as scholar; one—more impulsive, the other more cautious and reflective. After all, I as a 'seaman' was considered knowledgeable in the English language. Our task was to prepare the ground in Western countries for the recognition of our independence.[427]

Piip first discussed and negotiated in Petrograd with diplomatic representatives of the British and French governments, handing over a

[424] T Põder, *Kompromissikuningas*, Edasi, 20 February 1989.

[425] A Piip, 'Iseseiswuse esipäiwilt' in *Iseseiswuse tuleku päiwilt. Mälestused, Tartu: Postimees* (1923) 38, 40.

[426] See A Piip, *Tormine aasta. Ülevaade Eesti välispoliitika esiajast 1917–1918. aastal dokumentides ja mälestusis* (1934).

[427] Piip, 'Iseseiswuse' (n 425 above) 43.

memorandum on the independence plans of Estonia. 'The American envoy, Mr Francis listened to us once again but did not reply with anything except politenesses.'[428] Piip went with colleagues through Finland to Western Europe. He subsequently described the road as dangerous and adventurous, and himself as 'looking like a man from the countryside, with a big beard and Finnish winter cap.'[429] When stopped by the German military on the Åland islands, Piip eased the tension and managed to relax the German officer's vigilance by 'telling him stories about my time as a student in Berlin, student societies and drinking parties'.[430] The road to Sweden through the German-occupied Finnish islands was full of dangerous incidents but finally Piip and his companions 'were safe and reached Europe'[*sic*].[431]

After Imperial German troops had begun occupying Estonia in February 1918, the argument in favour of Estonia's independence also resonated in the West as a move against German interests. In April 1918, Piip went by ship from Norway to Great Britain, passengers along the way were fearful of the activities of German submarines.[432] The British Secretary of State for Foreign Affairs, AJ Balfour, received the Estonian delegation in London on 23 April 1918. Piip 'as lawyer' formulated the Estonian demand that Britain recognize Estonia's independence.[433] Balfour asked whether Estonia, 'a couple of million people', was not too small for independence: 'we explained that we want to be completely independent'.[434] 'The friendly audience lasted more than half an hour and left an unforgettable impression on us delegates. After all, this first official audience that official representatives of an independent people had achieved with a leader of a great power was going to be decisive for our political future.'[435] The result of the meeting with Balfour was that on 3 May 1918 Britain accorded *de facto* recognition to the independence of Estonia. France followed on 13 May 1918 and Italy on 29 May 1918.

In 1918 Piip acted substantively as the head of the 'temporary Estonian legation' in London. Every Wednesday, he would lunch with the Finnish representative Dr Holsti, Latvian representative Meierowitz, and Georgian representative Ghambashidze,[436] a meeting of all four breakaway States from the former Russian Empire.

In September 1918 Piip published in *The Contemporary Review* a polemical piece entitled 'Esthonia—a Second Belgium'. What was it that 'Esthonia' and Belgium had in common? It was not multiculturalism, but the fact that both countries had suffered from German violations of international law. The heart of the argument was directed against the Baltic Germans and Germany and made the case for Estonia's independence. Piip pointed out that although the Baltic Germans constituted 'only 2.4 per cent of the population' they had 'unexpectedly' made the attempt

[428] ibid 46. [429] ibid 50. [430] ibid 49. [431] ibid 52. [432] ibid 53.
[433] ibid 55. [434] ibid. [435] ibid. [436] ibid 59.

to speak in Estonia's name, requesting the German occupation of Estonia.[437] When the Germans finally arrived in February 1918:

> ... commenced in Esthonia the materialisation of the usual German trend of thought: the breaking of international law, the violating of the Brest-Litovsk treaty, and the trampling under foot of the laws of humanity, with the result that at present the whole of Esthonia, like the other Baltic provinces, is under the cruel and unjust domination of the Germans ... The Esthonians have nothing in common, politically, with Germany; they desire neither annexation nor personal union: they claim their right to be independent, to be free of German domination, and also to be dissociated from the anarchic policy of the Great-Russians. Esthonia strongly protests against the violation of international law ... [438]

Although the 1907 Hague Regulations provided that the occupier must respect the laws of the country 'the Germans break these rules every day ... international law, by Article 6 of the Brest-Litovsk treaty, has been violated by the Germans, who ignore all treaties and pledges, and no doubt justify their position on the principle that "Might is right" '.[439] He concluded:

> It has been stated in the *Round Table* (March, 1918) that it would be difficult to find a peasantry so well cultured as is the Esthonian peasantry. This brave little nation, even now, under the German yoke, is making a wonderful stand for its independence. For reasons that are obvious, it desires neither personal union with Prussia nor association with Russia. The Germans are hated by the Esthonians for national and social reasons, and the Russians on political grounds.[440]

This was an argument in which the political was combined with the fragmentary legal. This is not exceptional: 'what works as a professional argument depends on the circumstances ... The final arbiter of what works is nothing other than the context (academic or professional) in which one argues.'[441]

Piip's arguments worked at least in the sense that Estonia managed to establish its independence. He later recounted that 11 November 1918, the day of German defeat, was a 'day of general happiness' in London. The German occupation forces retreated from Estonia and Britain sent its navy to support Estonia against the incoming Bolshevik army. Piip wrote: 'Finally, on 12 December the British Navy reached Tallinn. At 6 o'clock I was visiting Admiral Freemantle: "The Navy is there" and the honourable admiral keeps his finger on the map on Tallinn. The joy was indescribably great: the necessary help had arrived! Help is not too late, as it was in 1343 ...'[442]

Piip spent the first half of 1919 as the Estonian envoy to the Paris Peace Conference, lobbying for the Allied *de jure* recognition of the

437 Professor [*sic*] A Piip, 'Esthonia—A Second Belgium' *The Contemporary Review*, September 1918, 2–3.

438 ibid 4.

439 ibid 4–5.

440 ibid 6.

441 M Koskenniemi, 'Letter to the Editors of the Symposium' (1999) 93 AJIL 351, 356.

442 Piip (n 437 above) 61. In 1343 Estonians rebelled against the Teutonic Order and the Danish, elected their own kings, and sent envoys to Finland for help, but the rebellion was suppressed before help arrived.

independence of Estonia. In Paris, Piip and his East European colleagues-diplomats were often seen as part of the problem rather than the solution. Nevertheless, Britain supported Estonia's independence and Piip and his colleagues laid the foundations of the British orientation of Estonian foreign policy.[443] Piip returned to Estonia on 21 September 1919 and was appointed Minister of Foreign Affairs on 9 October 1919. He met with leaders of the Russian Whites but recognized their hostility to the independence of Estonia. He later recounted how one of them watched the sunset from Tallinn's medieval castle with Piip and joked: 'How can we leave all this beauty to you?' The political situation was unstable: on 19 November 1919 the government changed and a new foreign minister was appointed.

Piip became a member of the Estonian delegation that was appointed to negotiate the peace treaty with Communist Russia. The peace conference started in Tartu on 5 December 1919. At the end of the Peace Conference Piip, together with the Russian delegate Adolf Joffe, arrived at a formulation regarding Article II of the Tartu Peace Treaty[444] which stipulates:

On the basis of the right of all peoples freely to decide their destinies, and even to separate themselves completely from the State of which they form part, a right proclaimed by the Federal Socialist Republic of Soviet Russia, Russia unreservedly recognizes the independence and autonomy of the State of Estonia, and renounces voluntarily and forever all rights of sovereignty formerly held by Russia over the Estonian people and territory of Estonia by virtue of the former legal situation, and by virtue of international treaties, which, in respect of such rights, shall henceforth lose their force.

Piip later emphasized that it was consciously drafted that the article spoke of the 'States' of Russia and Estonia, without specifying their respective forms of government.[445] On 2 February 1920, the Tartu Peace Treaty was finally signed by the Russian and Estonian delegations. The Treaty was the 'birth certificate' of the Republic of Estonia and signified the beginning of the end of the isolation of the Russian Soviet government in international politics. From the point of view of international law, it was the first international treaty that explicitly recognized the separation of a people on the basis of the right of peoples to self-determination.[446] Piip later emotionally described the solemn feelings of the Estonians at the negotiating table: 'We were sitting around the conference table and observing our distinguished chairman (Mr Poska) who, having fallen into deep thought, finally told the delegation members: "Today is the most

443 See J Poska, *Eesti iseseisvuse võitluses kõige ponevamal ajajägul.* J Poska päevaraamat rahukonverentsilt (AH Tammsaare redigeeritud) (1921).

444 A Piip, *Mälestused iseseisvuse võitluspäevilt*, II köide, Vabadussõda 1918–1920 391.

445 ibid.

446 International law treatises often quote the 1921 decision of the League of Nations in the Aaland Islands dispute as first evidence on the right of peoples to self-determination in International law. However, although the right as such was recognized in the Aaland Islands settlement, the predominantly Swedish-speaking population of the islands was not allowed to separate from Finland.

important day for Estonia in its history over the last seven hundred years because today Estonia for the first time determines with finality the fate of its people".'[447]

After the successful completion of the Tartu Peace Conference on 2 February 1920, Piip returned to Britain as Estonia's diplomatic envoy. On 6 July 1920, he read a paper on 'Esthonia and the League of Nations' before the Grotius Society.[448] He was introduced as 'Professor of International Law of the Dorpat University, and Prime Minister of the Republic of Esthonia'. The main point of the paper was to make a case, on the basis of international law, for the British *de jure* recognition of the Republic of Estonia. Quoting various British and American international law scholars, Piip argued that international law doctrine had started to support the declaratory rather than the constitutive theory of the effects of recognition. He insisted that 'continental' (French, German, Russian) doctrine held even more progressive views than the conservative British one, being even more clearly in favour of the declaratory theory of recognition. Piip was perhaps the first Estonian to claim partiality with Friedrich/Fyodor Martens: 'My famous countryman, Professor Martens, holds similar views.'[449] Piip's preference for the declaratory theory over the constitutive one was not of course a choice with merely academic implications. Its consequence was that the Republic of Estonia existed already as a subject of international law; now it only needed to be recognized *de jure* for diplomatic purposes.

After Piip first laid out the applicable international law, he turned to the facts, especially that British courts had started to recognize Estonia as a sovereign power and Estonia had concluded a peace treaty with its former motherland on 2 February 1920. Piip must have been very aware of and fully enjoying the difference in self-confidence and style between his presentations in 1918 and the conclusion in his 1920 paper: 'The question of recognition is only a matter of courtesy towards the Esthonian State, since Esthonia has accomplished de facto her struggle for independence and sovereignty, being now completely independent under the rule of a democratic duly elected Government.'[450]

The title of 'prime minister' in the Grotius Society was somewhat anticipatory. Piip became Estonia's prime minister only in October 1920 (and the government remained in office only until January 1921). In the next government, from January 1921 to November 1922, Piip was again foreign minister.

On 7 November 1923, Piip was appointed the Estonian extraordinary envoy and minister plenipotentiary in Washington. President Calvin Coolidge accepted his credentials on 31 December 1923. While

See Decision of the Council of the League of Nations on the Aaland Islands, September 1921 [1921] League of Nations Official Journal 697.

[447] Piip, Mälestused (n 444 above).

[448] A Piip, 'Esthonia and the League of Nations' in *Transactions of the Grotius Society, Volume VI, Problems of War and Peace* (1921) 35–44.

[449] ibid 38.

[450] ibid 43.

representing Estonia in the United States, Piip introduced the emerging Estonian constitutional system to a circle of interested American lawyers,[451] and was invited to attend a trip organized by the Georgetown University School of Foreign Service.[452] His major diplomatic mission as envoy was to arrange the terms of the settlement under which Estonia would repay its debt to the United States. On 23 December 1925, Piip signed with Frank Kellogg a US-Estonian friendship, commerce, and consular treaty; a few days later he returned to Estonia. During his diplomatic mission in Washington, DC, he had had time to work on his textbook of international law, the first edition of which would appear in Estonia in 1927. In 1926, he returned for a brief time to the United States, holding lectures on international law at California State University in Los Angeles.

Subsequently he served as Foreign Minister in the government of Teemant from December 1925 to July 1926. Between 1919 and 1926, Piip was freed from his duties as Professor of International Law at Tartu. He could begin his professorial work only when the second semester of 1926 started.

As a politician and professor of international law during the 1930s, Piip published texts that give insight into his political worldview. In 1932, a popular work entitled *Current World Politics and Estonia* was published. In his analysis of international affairs, Piip highlighted continuities rather than breaks between Tsarist Russia and the USSR: 'Communism has become a religion of redistribution that, it is believed, could be implemented by the State enforcement apparatus and the dictatorship of the Communist party. However, the USSR is currently giving up its messianism and missionarism and the former saviours of the world are now busy ruling the great Russian power according to a slightly changed ideology.'[453] He explained that a clash of civilizations existed between Russia and the West: 'Among the problems of Europe, the struggle between the Communist East and the individualist Western worldview must be highlighted. The conflict is old, since in Russia, for example, the peasants have never acquired individual property rights.'[454] The clash also explained the difficulties in Baltic–Russian relations: 'The main purpose of Russian politics throughout history and partly up to today has been the expansion of its power. Its imperialistic direction has destroyed or threatens to destroy the particularism and independence of some smaller and less powerful nations.'[455] The Baltic States and Russia did not:

> share cultural and economic concepts since the Baltic States are based on a Western European Christian culture and private property based on Roman law. However, Russia in contrast is the result of the Byzantine or Eastern culture

[451] A Piip, 'The Constitution of the Republic of Esthonia' (1925) IX *The Constitutional Review* 3–12.
[452] Piip's diary of 1925, entry of 9 May 1924.
[453] A Piip, *Nüüdne maailmapoliitika ja Eesti. Sissejuhatus poliitikasse II* (1932) 14.
[454] ibid 25.
[455] ibid 98.

and the notion of private property has never gained ground among the masses ... The Baltic States are the furthermost outposts of Western civilization that want to offer safe ground to the merchant who wants to go to the East, today just as in the days of the Hanseatic League.[456]

In 1933, Piip was once again foreign minister, now in the government of Jaan Tõnisson.

In 1936, Piip explained developments in Estonian politics to a European audience, especially the *coup d'état* of Konstantin Päts on 12 March 1934, which Piip supported as a 'lesser evil' in comparison with the coming to power of the Estonian pro-fascist far-right party.[457] This time the venue was no longer London but Berlin, a fact symbolic of ongoing shifts and ambitions of power in Europe. Piip both started and ended his presentation with a reference to the fact that Estonia was at a crossroads in the conflict between the Western and Eastern/Russian civilizations, belonging to the former and even having a 'historical mission as a frontier outpost of Western culture in the East'.[458] His description of constitutional changes in Estonia was not free of contradictions: on the one hand, he emphasized that Estonia had followed influential countries in Europe where the *Führerprinzip* had been established; on the other hand, he maintained that Estonia had not given up its essentially democratic form of government.[459] He was trying to represent his country as a diplomat would, downplaying his own political differences with the government of Päts. In Estonia's domestic politics, Piip was considered one of the leaders of the so-called 'democratic opposition' which was critical of Päts' rule.

Internationally, Piip's connections with émigré international lawyers who taught during the pre-1917 era at St Petersburg University are likely to have played a role in gaining Baron Boris Nolde as lead agent of the Republic of Estonia in its 1938–39 debate with the Republic of Lithuania in the *Panevezys-Saldutiskis* case at the PCIJ.[460]

In 1938, Piip was elected member of the first chamber of the new parliament, the Riigivolikogu. As a member of the Foreign Affairs Committee, he prepared for the adoption of the Neutrality Act of 20 October 1938, through which the Republic of Estonia declared itself a neutral State. In discussions with fellow parliamentarians, he argued that Estonia could declare itself neutral without violating international law, especially the 1907 Hague Conventions.[461] But again, international

[456] Piip, Nüüdne (n 455 above) 98 and 111.

[457] A Piip, *Estlands Weg zur neuen Verfassung. Vortrag, gehalten in Berlin am 25. Juni 1935 vor der 'Deutschen Gesellschaft zum Studium Osteuropas'* (1936) 24. Piip refers to the 'complicated geopolitical situation of the Republic of Estonia' which forced Päts and other 'responsible personalities' to abandon the democratic constitution in order to prevent the coming to power of the autoritarian right.

[458] ibid 27.

[459] ibid 18 and 22.

[460] *The Panevezys-Saldutiskis Railway Case* Judgment of 28 February 1939, Series A/B No 76. On Nolde, see P Holquist, 'Dilemmas of a Progressive Administrator: Baron Boris Nolde' (2006) 2 (7) *Kritika: Explorations in Russian and Eurasian History* 241–73.

[461] See H Arumäe (ed), '*Riigivolikogu Välis- ja Riigikaitsekomisjoni protokollid 1938–1940*, Akadeemia No 10 2005, 2298–9.

legal questions could hardly overshadow the main political problem: would it suffice for a small country unilaterally, ie without gaining recognition by its bigger neighbours, to declare itself neutral in the face of an approaching war?

In September 1939, Moscow presented an ultimatum to the Estonian minister Karl Selter, requesting an immediate right to establish military bases on Estonian territory, at the same time promising not to endanger Estonia's sovereignty. Selter flew back to Estonia and later returned to Moscow with a small Estonian delegation, among its members Ants Piip and Jüri Uluots. Finally, on 28 September 1939, the Estonians signed a treaty of mutual assistance with the Soviets which gave military bases to the USSR on Estonian territory. At the same time, the USSR guaranteed Estonia's sovereignty and independence, and the continued validity of the Tartu Peace Treaty was reconfirmed. According to the memoirs of a staff member of Konstantin Päts, the President of the Republic of Estonia, Piip was at first convinced that 'Stalin as a Caucasian [would] keep to the treaty'. However, later on Piip expressed himself more sceptically: 'the fate of Estonia hangs on a spider's net that is called Stalin's (Soviet) honesty'.[462]

After the government of the USSR presented its first ultimatum to Estonia in September 1939 and, as a consequence, Soviet military bases were established in Estonia, Piip's faculty colleague in Tartu, Professor Jüri Uluots, formed an Estonian government on 11 October 1939. Piip again became the foreign minister, confirming his already established reputation as 'Estonia's professional foreign minister'. The Uluots government with Piip as foreign minister lasted until 21 June 1940, the beginning of the occupation of the Republic of Estonia and the formation of the pro-Soviet government.

Estonian leaders made an effort not to 'provoke' the USSR and, occasionally in an embarrassingly conciliatory way, did not speak up about increasing violations of Estonia's 'neutrality' by the USSR. For example, Estonia failed to protest when, contrary to the terms of the Mutual Assistance Pact of 28 September 1939, the Soviets started to use their bases in Estonia for flights against Finnish cities in the Soviet-Finnish Winter War. On 2 February 1940, the twentieth anniversary of the Tartu Peace Treaty,[463] Piip gave a radio speech in which he emphasized the importance of the Treaty and expressed the conviction that Estonia and Russia would continue to demonstrate 'how the relationship between a big and small country can be based not on force and subjugation but on trust and mutual support'.[464] How much naivety was there in these words, how much mere clinging to a last hope (the 'spider's net that was Stalin's honesty'), and how much of it was disinformation and cowardice?

[462] E Tambek, *Tõus ja mõõn* (1964) Part I, 289.

[463] See also A Piip, 'The Peace Treaty of Tartu' (1940) 1 *Revue Baltique* 32–9.

[464] A Piip, *20 aastat rahu. Välisministri raadiokõne rahu allakirjutamisest Tartus 20 a eest'* Päevaleht 4.

Appeasement did not work. In the summer of 1940, when Estonia was already being occupied by the USSR, Piip was arrested by the Soviet NKVD in the field of his farmstead. Tambet writes that 'not even the fact that he had Stalin's photograph with a dedication from "batyushka" himself saved Piip from destruction'.[465] Stalin had presented his photo to Piip during the Moscow negotiations of 1939, and Piip took Stalin's photo with him when he was arrested and sent to a Gulag camp in Siberia. According to a witness, Piip even showed the photo to the camp administration, hoping it might save his life.[466] Thus, an international law professor would have had to rely on the 'argument' of a dictator's photo in order to secure his own right to life. Piip had helped to introduce the principle of self-determination: this controversial principle was loaded with politics, making its proclaimer a martyr. The Empire took back what it had once conceded in a moment of weakness, regarding Piip's political acts as high treason. In 1940–42, Piip as a leader must have felt the full weight of a sentence from the Estonian national epic *Kalevipoeg*: those on the frontline will be thrown away, those at the rear will be killed, those in the middle will come home. Piip had been on the frontline. He died in miserable conditions on 1 October 1942, as a political prisoner in the Gulag camp Nyrob in the Ural mountains.

7.2 Piip's concept of politics in international law

> If international law were nothing more than a body of morality-etiquette then the argumentation for establishing our rights vis-à-vis other peoples would diminish.[467]
>
> Ants Piip (1927)

Piip's concept of the nature of international law and the role of politics was characteristic of successful practitioners of international law but also, at least to some extent, of the 'second generation' international law scholars. The word that best captures the essence of this approach is 'pragmatism'. Earlier theoretical debates between naturalists and positivists about the nature of international law did not seem to have led to clear truths; and yet, international law was there (or at least, needed). In his first textbook of international law, Piip set out the well-known historical representatives of the natural law and positivist schools. But he did so in a non-passionate way that indicated the author's own approach: this was all history, important to know; but one did not have to be too dogmatic about it or indicate a clear choice between the schools. Piip

[465] Tambek (n 462 above) 302. We don't know exactly what Stalin had written to Piip. According to Tambek, Stalin's dedication on the photo offered to President Päts read 'To the wise president of the Estonian people Konstantin Jakovlevich Päts. J. Stalin' ibid.

[466] 'The memoirs of Tamara Kask-Skolimowska' in L Lauri (ed), *Kirjutamata memuaare VI, Tallinn Perioodika*, (1991) 176–7.

[467] A Piip, *Rahvusvahelise õiguse süsteem* (1927) 3.

simply concluded that 'the 19th century brought about such development of the science of international law that in every country representatives of unique approaches emerged'.[468]

What counted as important was that international law was there; now it was time to use it. As the quotation from Piip at the beginning of this section implies, too much digging in and pondering about the 'nature' and 'foundation' of international law might have become dangerous and counter-productive. International law served a socio-political function. If the very essence of international law was normative (in the philosophical sense of the word)—to help to support rights and claims *vis-à-vis* other nations—why undermine the discourse's authority? It was important to maintain that international law was 'real' law. International law could only function as law when lawyers did not hesitate too much about its legal nature.

That international law existed was essential for the success of Piip's politics. These favoured the reshaping of international relations according to an entirely new principle: the right of peoples to self-determination. Piip needed strong international law because self-determination and especially the statehood of small (or 'weak') States would hardly have been feasible against the background of the overwhelming strength of the Great Powers. He implicitly agreed with the main point of his predecessors at Tartu: international legal arguments could be taken seriously only when the discipline established a certain rhetorical distance from politics. However, this constituted a paradox, since the reason why international law was needed was ultimately 'political'.

Piip's main challenge as an international lawyer was the following: how to explain as objective 'international law' norms that one has oneself brought to life as historical agent? Every new State needed a certain understanding of international law and to develop its own unique approach towards international law. This is what Piip and his circle delivered. On the one hand, they translated international law into the Estonian language. On the other hand, they felt that the contribution the Estonians could make to the general discourse of international law was by explaining, promoting, and refining the principle enshrined in the 1920 Tartu Peace Treaty and which opened the door of the international community for Estonia—the right of peoples to self-determination.

7.3 The politics of national self-determination in the writings of Piip and his circle

The main task Piip set himself as an international law professor was to translate international law, its concepts, and doctrine into the Estonian language. He started to write the Estonian textbook on international law while he was still ambassador in Washington.[469] An expanded collection

[468] ibid 26. [469] Piip, *Rahvusvahelise õiguse süsteem* (n 467 above).

of lectures was published in 1929/1930,[470] and the final substantially revised edition came out in 1936.[471]

These books are best viewed in the context of the wave of international law textbooks written and published in the national languages of the newly independent States of Eastern Europe during the 1920s. For instance, the first Romanian study, written by George Plastara, a professor in Bucharest and formerly a student at the Sorbonne, was also published in 1927.[472] At the same time, Polish textbooks authored by Zygmunt Cybichowski (1879–1946), a professor in Warsaw and formerly a student in Berlin, came out.[473] The publication of those textbooks clearly accompanied the (re-)birth of the respective nation States. Textbooks in the languages of other smaller European nations with less interrupted histories had been published earlier in the eighteenth and nineteenth centuries.[474]

In the foreword to the 1927 edition, Piip explained why a textbook on international law in the Estonian language was needed. He noted that very good textbooks already existed—'like that of professor Franz von Liszt under whom I studied in Berlin'—but they did not give answers to a number of questions that were 'particularly interesting for us'.

The language of the 1927 edition is archaic and undeveloped, reminding us today of a child taking her first steps. Due to the lack of suitable Estonian words, Piip simply referred to the original concepts in another language (League of Nations as *Universal Zweckverband*, sources as *istochniki*). The language of the 1936 edition was already more self-assured; the terminology developed there is still by and large in use today in Estonia.

Piip's textbooks were solid and comprehensive compilations of the contemporary literature of international law. Quite reasonably, he had not set out to reinvent the wheel. However, given his lack of original theory, Piip remained in the shadow of his more famous contemporaries in European scholarship (Anzilotti, Huber, Strupp, Schücking, etc). He managed, in the positivist tradition, to keep law and politics apart. He published his political commentaries and analyses on international relations separately from his international law textbooks (cf his *Contemporary World Politics and Estonia*, 1932 and *International Law*, 1936.) This general policy of the separation of the legal and political was not always followed in international law textbooks published in Eastern Europe at that time.[475]

[470] A Piip, *Rahvusvaheline õigus. Konspekt loenditest kõrgemas sõjakoolis 1929/1930.a* (1930).

[471] A Piip, *Rahvusvaheline õigus* (1936).

[472] G Plastara, *Manual de drept international public* (1927) reprinted by Beck in 2004.

[473] Z Cybichowski, *Prawo miedzynarodnowe publiczne i prywatne* (1928) and *Geneza i rozwój prawa miedzynarodnowego* (1930).

[474] See eg in Denmark L Holberg, *Moralske kierne eller Introduction til Naturens og Folkerettens Kundskab* (1715) F Chr Bornemann, *Forelaesninger over den positive Folkeret*, Blandede Skrifter udg. ved Goos og Krieger (Kjobenhavn 1866–1868).

[475] Thus eg the professor of international law in Iaşi, Romania—N Daşcovici, in his textbook *Curs de drept international public* (1935), dedicated almost half of the space of the book to the analysis

Mostly, however, his work was that of reception and 'transfer of knowledge'. He did not share the theoretical preoccupations of the leading scholars among the 'moderns' about the nature of obligation in international law or what made this law relevant.[476] As indicated above, this was probably a conscious pragmatic 'political' choice, not necessarily a lack of deeper theoretical interest per se. A new small State could not be set up without legal support in international relations.

When Piip touched *terra incognita* and translated the discourse of international law into the Estonian language, he did not do so mechanically. He felt that something specific about Estonia's heritage must be added. However, even with his best efforts he could not have spoken of huge Estonian 'contributions' (except that he was the first to insist that Fyodor Martens was 'actually' Estonian). But he made great efforts to demonstrate that contrary to what Baltic Germans and many others had thought and taught, Estonia had historically not been merely an object but was still a subject of international law in its own right. He argued that in the thirteenth century, when the Germans and the Danes attacked the Estonians and finally conquered the country, Estonia had already achieved statehood.[477] He admitted that the exact structure and organization of this statehood was open to debate, but the concept of statehood was in itself developed, both militarily and diplomatically. Moreover, Estonia's form of government differed from the feudal system of Central European States—'Estonia was free'.[478]

Moreover, Piip argued that the conquest of Estonia by the Germans and the Danes in the thirteenth century did not destroy the country's independence, but only transformed it: 'The intrusion in our country is reminiscent of the conquest of England by the Normans, which, as in our case, did not destroy the country's independence. The territory of Estonia remained sovereign.'[479] In 1936, Piip added that the status of Estonia as a subject of international law changed in the thirteenth century only to the extent that 'besides the local people, intrusive new elements took part in the government of the country ... Even after the foreign intrusion, Estonians did not cease relations with other peoples, as we can see from the preparation for the 1343 rebellion, in which help was requested from Finland, Sweden and Russia ... Thus, 1561 was the final year of the Old Estonian State.'[480]

Although Piip did not deduce any direct legal consequences from the continuity of Estonia's independent statehood before 1561 and after 1918, the argument carried a significant symbolic weight. Estonia's statehood was not to be seen as a whim of history, an anomaly born out of the

of the political situation in Europe, the political background of treaties of alliance, and Romania's security policy.

[476] On 'moderns' and their doctrines, see M Koskenniemi, *From Apology to Utopia. The Structure of International Legal Argument* (Helsinki: Lakimiesliiton Kustannus, 1989) 131.

[477] Piip (n 469 above) 20. [478] ibid. [479] ibid.

[480] Piip, *Rahvusvaheline õigus* (n 471 above) 41, 43.

mutual weakening of Russia and Germany in World War I. The year 1918 was not point zero—instead, this year marked a return to an old and natural state of affairs and ideas. Centuries of other countries ruling in Estonia were bridged by the continuity of statehood.

Piip realized that the question of who the Baltic nations belonged to was linked to different perceptions of continuity. Discussing the question of prescription in international law, he referred to the negotiations held by the Russian and Swedish delegations during the Livonian War in 1575:

> At those negotiations, Moscow's representatives demanded Tallinn for Russia, relying on the imagined fact that their 'forefather Yuri Yaroslav' had built the city approximately 600 years before. The Russians relied on their chronicle ['letopiss'] which tells of the building of Iur'ev [Tartu] in 1030 but includes no mention of Tallinn. It is not known whether the Russians have consciously distorted facts or presented such an argument unknowingly. The Swedes affirmed that [the Danish king] Waldemar built the city [in 1219], but the Russians did not give up their arguments.[481]

In other contexts, however, Piip was not very dogmatic about the official positions of his country. In his textbook, Piip described how during the Tartu Peace Conference Estonia (ie Piip himself) had argued that the old Russia had ceased to exist owing to dismemberment, while the Soviets maintained that the change of form of government and the separation of some territories had not affected Russia's statehood. But he added: 'Of course our construction is not really certain.'[482] In the 1936 edition of the textbook, Piip also left the question of the international legal status of the USSR undecided, on the one hand quoting an exiled Russian author for the support of the Estonian view,[483] and on the other, pointing out that when recognizing the Soviet government, Western powers considered it the successor to the Tsarist government's legal obligations.[484]

It is noteworthy that in the 1936 edition of his textbook, Piip recognized subjugation (*debellatio*) as a means for the extinction of statehood. Thus, Transvaal and the Orange Free State were eliminated through subjugation by Britain in 1902, and Georgia through subjugation by the USSR in 1921. Piip did not consider the possible legal ramifications of the 1928 Paris Pact when he maintained that: 'In such circumstances the victorious State conquers the previously existing State's territory and destroys the former State's power over the population so completely that the invaders have no need or chance to negotiate with anybody.'[485] Note the ambiguity of this position—for example, from the point of view of the post-World War II Baltic claim of State continuity, Piip's position can be seen either as the outright recognition of the right to conquest or, alternatively, as the recognition of the right to conquest conditioned by the absence of a government-in-exile.

[481] Piip, *Rahvusvaheline õigus* (n 471 above) 205–6.
[482] Piip, *Rahvusvaheline òiguse* (n 467 above) 35.
[483] MA Zimmerman, *Vmeshatelstvo i priznanie v mezhdunarodnom prave* (1922) 219.
[484] Piip, *Rahvusvahelise õigus* (n 471 above) 92. [485] ibid 117.

Also in his presentations abroad, Piip repeated his main international legal argument—that the Republic of Estonia constituted a restoration of an ancient State on a territory that had in the periods when it lacked outright sovereignty had always enjoyed substantive autonomy.[486]

Quite similar views on the history of Estonia's statehood were presented by the professor of legal history at Tartu, Jüri Uluots (1890–1945). Uluots had studied at the same time as Piip at the Faculty of Law of St Petersburg University (1910–15). He insisted that the subjugation of the Estonians in the early thirteenth century by the Germans took place on the basis of international treaties, the originals of some of which, from 1241 and 1255, had been preserved. The claim was that in the thirteenth century the Estonians were subjects equal to the Germans under medieval international law. Moreover, the treaties concluded preserved part of the ancient Estonian laws and institutions.[487] In 1940, Uluots came back to the same ideas and concluded: 'Thus, the Estonian State is not a young or recent offspring of passing events, but rather a social-political body that reaches back from ancient times to our own days through several historical formations.'[488] Piip would not have opposed this formulation.

The third member of Piip's 'St Petersburg Circle', Tartu's professor of constitutional law, Nikolai Maim, turned in his research towards the international principle that justified Estonia's statehood, ie the right of peoples to self-determination. Maim was born on 14 (26) February 1884 in Tartu and died in January 1976 in the United States. In 1903–08 he studied law in St Petersburg but finally graduated in 1909 as *cand iur* at the Faculty of Law of the University of Moscow. He then studied for a masters degree in Iur'ev under Leo Challande: his thesis was entitled *The Solidarity Theory of Leon Diguit*. In 1915–17, Maim worked in the Russian Ministry of Interior Affairs on issues of autonomy.

Writing in American exile in 1958, Maim looked back at his intellectual development and confessed that during World War I, especially in 1917, his 'intellectual life went through a difficult crisis':

> I was used to the idea which was up to that point confirmed by my scholarly studies—that statehood offers to individuals conditions in which they can express themselves in a broader manner than is possible by the way of local ethnic existence. As a result I did not finally want to bind myself with homeland ... Since States seemed to be centres mutually competing with each other, it was natural to try to belong to the State that seemed particularly strong. So I myself was part of the big Russian State, and the idea of leaving it did not cross my mind. But the First World War brought up the principle of self-determination of peoples.[489]

486 A Piip, *Estlands Weg zur neuen Verfassung* (1936) 5.

487 See J Uluots, *Die Verträge der Esten mit den Fremden im XIII. Jahrhundert* (1937). (Estonian original in *Õigus* (1935) 2 and (1936) 2.)

488 J Uluots, 'Eesti riik ajaloolisest vaatepunktist' (1940) 2 ERK 49, 54.

489 Nikolai Maim archive at the library archive of the University of Tartu, F 88/2/2, 'Minu elulugu nagu ta mulle näis' (My Life as It Seemed to Me), Lewes, US, written during Christmas 1958, 7–8.

In Maim's account, what finally alienated him from Russia was the anarchistic and at the same time anti-individualistic agenda of the Russian Bolsheviks.

In Tartu, Maim's area of teaching was constitutional law, but in the early 1930s he became more interested in issues of public international law. In 1932, he published an interesting account of statehood and the emergence of 'global public law' in the framework of the League of Nations, *Völkerbund und Staat*.[490] Why did Maim the constitutional lawyer turn towards international law? An answer can be found in a letter that Maim wrote on 22 October 1945 as a refugee in Germany to the Dean of the Faculty of Law of Marburg University, Professor Hippel. Maim laid out his intellectual path and explained his 1932 turn towards international law with the comment that the 'international legal status of Estonia seemed to be insecure'.[491]

Maim's account was the most philosophical one among the trio Piip-Maim-Uluots, perhaps due to the fact that (except for a brief period in 1919), he was not involved in Estonian politics and thus could dedicate himself completely to scholarship. But it can also be seen as a kind of division of labour between the three. In *Völkerbund und Staat*, Maim theorized on the implications of the creation of the League of Nations for the international community in general and statehood in particular. He noted the successes of the principle of national self-determination since Manzini had formulated it in the nineteenth century. Ever since, the principle of national self-determination had radiated 'enormous vitality' and sought its materialization in the nation State.[492] Maim argued that the principle legitimized changes in the international *status quo*.[493]

Maim pointed out in particular the importance of Soviet Russia's 1920–21 peace treaties with Estonia, Lithuania, Latvia, Persia, and Poland, in which Russia recognized the right of the respective peoples to self-determination. Thus the right of peoples to self-determination had already become part of specific international law although not yet a general rule ('which would be important for its expansion').[494] While many scholars of the 1920s and 1930s were critical of the right of peoples to self-determination, Maim argued that 'nevertheless, with the idea of nationality one may emphasise rather a positive influence since it triggers creative, constructive energy and psychical powers that were previously dormant, and pushes them to cultural activity in order to produce new values. The realisation of the principle of nationality has contributed to a richer European culture, not the contrary'.[495] Maim further asked whether the recognition of the right to self-determination meant that smaller nationalities had the right to secede from a 'highly cultured

[490] N Maim, *Völkerbund und Staat. Ein Beitrag zur Ausarbeitung eines allgemeinen öffentlichen Rechts* (1932).
[491] Maim archive F 88/2.
[492] Maim *Völkerbund und Staat* (n 490 above) 266–8.
[493] ibid 264.
[494] ibid 267.
[495] ibid 269.

powerful State'? In principle, this question had to be answered in the affirmative.[496] This was a courageous statement which Maim knew he somehow had to balance: 'At the same time, one has to recognise that such a decision would be for any nationality so serious and fundamental that it must be accompanied by very significant motives.'[497] Maim maintained that all the new European nation States of the nineteenth century had emerged because political conditions had become unbearable. This was also the case with the new nation States which had emerged in Central and Eastern Europe; the backdrop was the collapse of the monarchical system in this part of the Continent, which in Tsarist Russia was due to internal political conditions.[498] Maim concluded that 'the emerging international legal order' could no longer tolerate repressive nation States in which developed nationalities were kept together by brute force.[499]

However, whoever invoked the principle of the right of peoples to self-determination had to think about the reverse side of the coin, minority rights. Maim pointed out that the necessity for the respect of minority rights was logical—since the small nations of Central and Eastern Europe had founded their States on the principle of self-determination, they had to recognize that minorities in their State possessed an essentially similar right.[500] In Maim's view, an exemplary solution was provided by the Republic of Estonia in its Cultural Autonomy Act of 12 February 1925.[501]

The right of peoples to self-determination also played a significant role in the dissertation of Nikolai Kaasik, a notable student of Ants Piip, published in Paris in 1933.[502] During the 1930s Kaasik also worked in senior positions at the foreign ministry of the Republic of Estonia, and Piip arguably saw him as his successor to the chair of international law. His work was essentially about what nowadays would be called international 'governance'. Kaasik expressed his concern that the destiny of the right of peoples to self-determination still continued to be fought over in the no-man's-land between law and politics. He pointed to the tragic fate of Armenia and Georgia, whose independence had been solemnly recognized in the early 1920s but which were then soon re-annexed by Russia without any outside intervention. Although the right of peoples to self-determination had been stipulated in the Estonian-Russian Peace Treaty of 1920, Estonia had to carry on a very tough fight in order to maintain its independence.[503] As always, the downside of the right of peoples to self-determination was the rights of the minorities. Kaasik pointed out that minorities tended to use their rights to justify their fight against the

[496] ibid 270. [497] ibid. [498] ibid 270–1. [499] ibid 271. [500] ibid 274.

[501] ibid 276.

[502] N Kaasik, *Le contrôle en droit international* (1933). Kaasik's book was reviewed by William I Hull in (1934) 28 AJIL 195–6 and Georges Scelle in (1934) 41 RGDIP 728–31. In Estonian, Kaasik published *Rahvasteliit* (The League of Nations) (1933).

[503] ibid 27.

State, often finding support from the outside from their ethnic brother's nation State.[504] Finally, Kaasik was concerned with the security of his country, criticizing the idea expressed by some of exempting Estonia, Latvia, and Lithuania from the guarantees of Article 10 of the League of Nations Pact as 'legally impossible and incorrect (pour ne pas dire davantage)'.[505] Minority rights continued to occupy Estonian international law students after World War II.[506]

By the time Piip had vanished as a political prisoner in Sarmatia and the Germans had occupied Estonia in World War II, Uluots had taken their common cause to the logical conclusion when the Germans in 1944 enabled (and encouraged) his radio broadcast in order to mobilize Estonian men to fight against the Soviets.[507] Relying again on history and the ancient chronicles, Uluots, supporting the German mobilization of Estonian men, spoke to the Estonians about the 'fortieth war' that his country was facing against the *Drang nach Westen* of its Eastern neighbour. His previous scholarly activity of counting all the historical peace treaties and military campaigns in Estonia enabled him to specify this number.

Just as Uluots did, Maim continued as a law professor in German-occupied Tartu (1941–44). In November and December 1943, Maim taught a course with a politically charged title—'The Right of Peoples to Self-Determination'.[508] However, in September 1944 the Soviet Army reconquered Estonia and Maim escaped as a refugee to Marburg, Germany. In 1950, he was able to move on from Marburg to New York.

Since we can never find out what Piip thought when his principle, the principle of national self-determination, had been crushed, it is particularly interesting to turn to Maim's recorded afterthoughts. In front of a camp of Estonian refugees in Germany, he gave a presentation on 25 September 1945, entitled 'The International Legal Status of Estonia'.[509] Maim started his presentation with a question that obviously troubled him a lot. In 1940, ie when the Soviet occupation and repressions had already started, a younger colleague[510] at the faculty had reproached

[504] Kaasik, *Rahvasteliit* (n 502 above) 116. [505] ibid 237.

[506] Karl Aun, another student of Piip in Tartu, defended in Hamburg under Rudolf von Laun his dissertation on the protection of minorities in pre-war Estonia. (K Aun, *Der völkerrechtliche Schutz nationaler Minderheiten in Estland von 1917 bis 1940* (1951.)) Aun found an explanation for the separation of the new nation States from Russia in 1917–18 in the failed politics of Pan-Slavism and Russification that had been systematically carried out by the Tsarist government. Both the 'great number of minority peoples' (in 1897 Russians made up only 44.3% of the population of the Empire) and the 'incomparably higher cultural level of the minority population vis-à-vis the Russians' made it inevitable that the politics of Russification would fail. ibid 15.

[507] On those events and a discussion of their significance for Estonia's status in international law, see L Mälksoo, 'Professor Uluots, the Estonian Government in Exile and the Continuity of the Republic of Estonia in International Law' (2000) 69 *Nordic Journal of International Law* 289.

[508] 29 November to 31 December 1943. For its text, see F 88/2/29. [509] F 88/2/11.

[510] There is no watertight proof for this claim but it is quite possible that this colleague was Artur-Tõeleid Kliimann, the young and talented professor of administrative law and legal theory. See on Kliimann, L Mälksoo, 'Von der Demokratie bis zur Diktatur: Ein verborgener Dialog zwischen Artur-Tõeleid Kliimann und Carl Schmitt' (2004) 43 *Der Staat* 57–82.

him: 'What good did these 20 years [of independence] do us? They have only made matters worse! If we had simply been a Soviet republic for the last 20 years, Estonian youth would not be suffering so much now.'

For Maim, it was really important to know whether the younger colleague had been right; whether he, Piip, and Uluots had over-estimated the power of small nations; made idealistically a terrible mistake and triggered the anger of the returning imperial Leviathan. But Maim did not think independence had been a mistake, or at least he did not say so. Instead, he explained: 'The situation of small peoples and States is characteristic of the degree of civilization of the international order. Destruction is characteristic of barbarianism ... The legal order in international relations has to rely on the right of peoples to self-determination.'[511]

Since Estonian self-determination had been taken away, Maim at least found some relief in returning to his (modified) pre-1917 position: to be part of a nation, big or small, was not the most important thing in one's life. For a free man, universalism was less constraining than particularism. In exile, Maim started to talk of the need to create a universal and all-inclusive science, the so-called 'mundology'.[512]

7.4 Conclusions

Ants Piip together with his colleagues Jüri Uluots and Nikolai Maim appear together like one 'metaprofessor'. Piip and Uluots in particular, both pre-1917 graduates of the Faculty of Law of St Petersburg University and co-founders of the Estonian Faculty of Law at Tartu University, appear together as mythmakers. Through law and legal arguments, they gave to the small Estonian nation what every nation needs: stories, myths, and legends. One such legend they had a hand in spreading was that international treaties and history proved that Estonia had been a free State since time immemorial, until the arrival of the Germans in the thirteenth century. Together with 'imported elements', independent statehood then continued until the sixteenth century. Thus, Piip and Uluots finally 'corrected' the history that had seldom before been favourable to the Estonians. As JL Austin has suggested, lawyers command a special linguistic capacity: making things true *simply by saying them*.[513]

Ants Piip has his place on the list of academic international lawyers-statesmen, together with, for example, Boutros Boutros Ghali of Egypt and Adrian Nastase of Romania. Moreover, Piip was not only a statesman—he was also a State founder. In the juridical field, there is a constant tension between those two positions, that of the professor-theoretician and that of the practitioner-statesman.[514] In the case of

[511] F 88/2/11.

[512] See N Maim, *Weltwissenschaft. Immer noch die akopalyptischen Reiter?* (1946) and *Mundology or World Science* (1966).

[513] See J Austin, *How to Do Things With Words* (1962).

[514] P Bourdieu, 'The Force of Law: Toward a Sociology of the Juridical Field' (1987) 38 *Hastings Law Journal* 821.

Piip, the international law professor definitely shaped Piip the politician—but the opposite is true as well.

Piip became who he was because of the new directions in international law and international politics in the early twentieth century. He came from a simple environment: had he been born a generation earlier, he would not necessarily have progressed further than his schoolteacher position. It would perhaps be an exaggeration to say that both Estonia as a new country and Piip as an international lawyer owed their 'emergence' to international law. But international law—and certainly the new catch-phrase of the right of peoples to self-determination—encouraged and empowered Piip and his colleagues in Tartu. It was much easier to secede from the corrupt and neglectful Russian Empire when one knew that, together with the British Navy, international law was *there*. Piip gave to international law a new subject (Estonia) and opened to Estonia a new field (international law).

Piip's historical role was to translate the idea of the right of peoples to self-determination into an international treaty, the first of its kind in international law. The fact that the right of Piip's people to self-determination was recognized in the 1920 Peace Treaty with Russia was Piip's biggest contribution to international law. Treaties can be violated and their makers can even be killed, but it is impossible to think them away—once they are signed and ratified, those treaties become part of historical reality.

Language constituted the soul of the new nations—thus, Piip and his contemporaries in Latvia, Lithuania, Hungary, Poland, Romania, and Czechoslovakia 'translated' international law into those national languages, previously non-existent in the field of international law. This was the new Europe, on the one hand, shy and insecure, on the other, courageous and nationally passionate. Everybody in the region added to global international law a shade, a national viewpoint, a complaint, a few differing interpretations, idiosyncrasies.[515] On the one hand, international law became more fragmented, on the other, more diverse. Via the international law textbooks that Piip and his colleagues wrote, new nations acquired their own distinct voices. It was an extensive learning process but it was also a process of reshaping the historical reality. This was the new international law with many more subjects than old Fyodor Martens (an Estonian who never actually considered himself an Estonian) could have envisaged.

In terms of method, Piip continued in the already established positivist tradition. His positivism was pragmatic[516]—he wanted to leave the

[515] cf also N Berman, 'Nationalism, Legal and Linguistic: The Teachings of European Jurisprudence' (1992) 24 *New York University Journal of International Law and Politics* 1515 and N Berman, 'A Perilous Ambivalence: Nationalist Desire, Legal Autonomy, and the Limits of the Interwar Framework' (1992) 33 *Harvard International Law Journal* 353.

[516] For the insight that 20th century international law was pragmatic in comparison with the philosophical 19th century, see also D Kennedy, 'International Law and the Nineteenth Century: History of an Illusion' (1997) 17 *Quinnipiac Law Review* 99, 114ff.

impression that the theoretical edifice of international law had already been erected by the previous generations. Instead of having to 'set up' the discipline of international law as a convincing and reliable construction, Piip's main attention was turned to the applications of international law. What seemed like lack of theoretical interest or pragmatism in Piip's positivism, appeared as something utterly normative and thus 'political'—small States needed a firm basis in international law; international law was supposed to be their ultimate defence against the Great Powers.

8. Intermezzo: Jaan Kross, from International Law Scholarship to Literature; Boris Meissner, from International Law to *Ostrecht*

Tartu's faculty of law experienced substantive reorganizations in its personnel, structure, and ideology when Estonia was incorporated into the USSR. Students with 'nationalist' views and/or 'bourgeois' origin had no chance of staying at the faculty. One of the outstanding students at the faculty during the late 1930s and early 1940s was Jaan Kross, who dreamed of becoming a diplomat and representing the Republic of Estonia in Paris. In 1944, Kross became involved in the Estonian resistance movement against the Nazis and was arrested by them, but nevertheless released before the Russians reconquered Estonia in September 1944.

Kross, who had studied international law under Ants Piip, had been working since the autumn of 1944 on his dissertation on the notion of international treaties. Kross writes in his recently published memoirs that by 1944, especially due to the Yalta Conference, he had started to understand that 'with respect to the Baltic States, probably on the basis of treaties between the Allies and the USSR, international law had been liquidated. The era of international law, as relative as it had been in the past, had for more immediate or distant times been substituted with an era of some sort of hyper-cryptic secret diplomacy.'[517] Kross also explains why he nevertheless intended to turn in his dissertation to the theory of international treaty law: 'I would confess: my whole interest in the notion of international treaty was in reality a game. A game, the reason of which was the lack of a better game. And the hope that by playing this game, it would be possible at least initially (and maybe even in the long run) to live my life. If my pretensions were strictly limited to academic ramifications and did not venture into politics—perhaps the Soviet power would allow me to *exist*?'[518] It did—but with reservations. In 1945, Kross was arrested in Tartu as a 'bourgeois nationalist' and sent to Siberia where he spent the next eleven years. Upon his return to Estonia in 1956, he felt no more inclination for the academic study of international law;

[517] J Kross, *Kallid kaasteelised* (2003) 169. [518] ibid.

neither would it have been possible. Instead, he became the leading Estonian fiction writer of the second half of the twentieth century. Among his novels *Professor Martens' Departure* stands out, and is perhaps the only novel that has been written about the life of an international law professor.[519] The novel is based on academic research done by Kross and in part conveys the accusations made by Hrabar and others that Martens was acting 'too pragmatically' on the question of the Japanese-Russian war of 1904–05. With much psychological insight and sensitivity, Kross makes Martens say that future times (and writers) subjectively see in the past international law scholars primarily what they want to see: 'Anyway, our afterworld will not remember in us what we were but rather what it needs itself. If by any chance it needs us. By the way, in that case it needs us in different places and times differently and paints us a different face each time and in each place. And we are so defenceless in front of this that it would be completely hopeless to care about it.'[520]

In 1998, Kross gave a series of lectures at Tartu University in which he discussed the autobiographical elements in his fiction (there were, as he himself revealed, many). One of the few novels written by him that he did not discuss in his course was *Professor Martens' Departure*.[521] Perhaps he preferred not to admit that with this book he was living out a dream that he had not been not able to realize, the dream of having become an international law professor?

Several students who had studied international law under Piip left Estonia as refugees in 1944 and became or continued as scholars in exile.[522] Two parallel Estonian cultures emerged—the one in Estonia itself that was under Soviet control and the émigré culture. We will soon see how these dynamics played out in the discipline of international law.

Several Baltic German students who had studied in Tartu during the 1930s (for example Boris Meissner, Walter Meder), became leading scholars in Western Germany of *Ostrecht*, a sub-discipline focusing on the study of the law of Eastern and Central Eastern Europe. Boris Meissner was born in 1915 in Pskov (Pleskau) in Russia and during the 1930s studied law in Tartu. In the early 1950s, in Hamburg, Meissner defended his doctorate on the legal status of the Baltic States, influentially arguing that Estonia, Latvia, and Lithuania continued to be illegally occupied by the USSR.[523] Meissner continued as a prolific

[519] J Kross, *Professor Martensi ärasõit* (1984). English translation *Professor Martens' Departure* (trans A Hollo, 1994).

[520] ibid 117.

[521] J Kross, *Omaeluloolisus ja alltekst. 1998.a Tartu Ülikooli filosoofiateaduskonna vabade kunstide professorina peetud loengud* (2003).

[522] See eg I Tammelo, *Treaty Implementation and Practical Reason: Towards a General Theory of Legal Interpretation, Studies in Legal Methods Series, No. 1* (1967); 'Relations between the International Legal Order and the Municipal Legal Orders—a "Perspectivist" View' (1967) *Australian Yearbook of International Law* 211–18.

[523] See B Meissner, *Die Sowjetunion, die baltischen Staaten und das Völkerrecht* (1956).

writer and founded the Institute for the Study of *Ostrecht* at the University of Cologne. *Ostrecht* was defined by Meissner as a sort of legal Sovietology—however, its conceptualization as a geographically-culturally special legal sub-field was not free of political implications. Soviet propaganda replied to Meissner's critical writings with *argumentum ad hominem*, pointing out that Meissner had fought in World War II against the Russians and even participated in war crimes (a claim that was never substantiated and must thus be dismissed). But it was sufficient to discredit a scholar critical of the USSR as an 'old biased Nazi'.

9. Uustal: The Communist Mind

> The time was passed when man had only the monster of his own soul to grapple with ... [now] the monster comes from outside and is called History; it no longer has anything to do with the train the adventurers used to ride; it is impersonal, uncontrollable, incalculable, incomprehensible—and it is inescapable.[524]
>
> Milan Kundera

9.1 Life

Tartu's international law professor during most of the Soviet era was Abner Uustal. Soon after Abner Uustal died in 1985, a 'wind of change' started to blow in Gorbachev's USSR. In 1991 and 1996, Uustal's widow Liidia gathered Uustal's international law papers together in order to hand them over to the library archive of the University of Tartu. One list contained Uustal's recent hand-written autobiography, which ended with the statement: 'I was and will remain a confirmed Communist.' Although Liidia Uustal had decided to give the papers and materials of her deceased husband to the archive of Tartu University, she recollects that she hesitated about the 'political correctness' of making this particular autobiography public.[525] Researchers will be thankful to her that she finally decided to do so.

Abner Uustal was born on 22 January 1915 on the Estonian island Saaremaa.[526] His father was a seaman, had sailed on British ships, and had lived for ten years in the United States. So it happened that Abner first saw his father only when he was seven years old ('the happiest day of my childhood').[527] The family was poor and at the age of 13, Abner himself started to work on the sea during the summers. On Saaremaa, Uustal graduated from the local *gymnasium* in Kuressaare in 1934.

[524] M Kundera, *The Art of the Novel* (1990) 11.

[525] Author's interview with Liidia Uustal in Tartu, April 2005.

[526] Here and in the following passages materials from the rare manuscripts department of the library of the University of Tartu, F 120/1.

[527] L Koik, 'Interview with A. Uustal' (January/February 1985) 19(1) *Sovetskoe pravo* 36, 37.

In 1936, after completing his mandatory military service in the Estonian army, he became a law student in Tartu. During his student years, he had to work in parallel with his legal studies. Nevertheless, he also found time to become a member of a student fraternity, 'Revelia'. Uustal graduated from Tartu's faculty of law *cum laude* in 1940. Thus, his first international law professor was Ants Piip (although Uustal never himself highlighted this fact, but rather pointed out that since Piip was in the government, his lectures were sporadic and 'did not cover all the material').

In August 1940, the Republic of Estonia was annexed by the USSR. During the first year of Soviet rule in Estonia (1940–41), Uustal was employed in Tallinn as the head of the transportation office at the National Commissariat of Light Industry. When Germany attacked the USSR in the summer of 1941, Uustal played a leading role in the organization of the Soviet evacuation and defence in Tallinn. He was mobilized in the Soviet army and retreated with the Soviet army in the face of the advancing German forces. On 18 August 1941, the Soviet battleship *Sibir*, on which Uustal together with many wounded Soviet soldiers was heading on the Baltic Sea towards Leningrad, was attacked near Tütarsaar island by Finnish aircraft. The ship received a direct hit by a bomb and burst into flames. More than 2,500 Soviet soldiers and evacuated personnel drowned. Uustal was among the seventy-three people who were rescued.[528] After the war, Uustal confessed that the memory of that day was the most difficult one for him in World War II. It seems quite obvious that this experience was one of the defining moments in Uustal's life. Having been one of the few who managed to be rescued from the hell on the Baltic Sea, he must have felt like 'one of the chosen'. Perhaps here was the beginning of Uustal as a Cold War warrior.

The mobilized and evacuated Estonians were taken to Siberia where they were first put to work in the labour camps. The conditions were harsh and thousands died during the winter of 1941–42. They were considered politically unreliable and, contrary to initial Soviet suggestions (why else would they have been 'mobilized'?), no military unit was created. Finally, in 1942 the Estonian Rifle Corps (*Eesti Tagavara Laskurpolk*) was formed from them. In fact, a significant number of the men went over to the side of the Germans during the first military encounters. Uustal served until the end of the war as an officer in this Estonian unit of the Red Army. He considered his happiest memory of the war to be the moment he again set foot on Estonian soil near Narva when he entered Estonia with the advancing Red Army in 1944. He remained in the army until 9 May 1945.

After the end of the war, he returned to the University of Tartu (now named Tartu State University) and taught until 1947 at the newly created department of military education. In 1947, he started to work for his

[528] ibid 37.

candidate's degree in international law and was accepted in the candidate's degree programme at Mikhail Lomonossov Moscow State University. At first, he did not have a supervisor, since there were no international law specialists left in Tartu. Then, however, the Dean of the Faculty of Law of the Mikhail Lomonossov Moscow State University and its professor of international law, Fyodor Kozhevnikov (1903–98), came to oversee the situation at the Faculty of Law in Tartu. Kozhevnikov accepted Uustal as his student for a candidate's degree in Moscow. Uustal recounted that Kozhevnikov was very busy while he was his supervisor in Moscow: 'Many of the consultations with my supervisor looked like this: I was carrying his portfolio from one university to another and during these walks the consultation took place. We left the University of Moscow and set off for Frunze Military Academy where I waited while the professor held his lecture. Then we moved on to the All-Soviet Juridical Distance-Learning Institute.'[529] Uustal defended his candidate's thesis in international law in 1950; it was entitled 'The Fight of the USSR in the UN for the Peace and Security of the Peoples'.[530]

In 1948, while studying in Moscow, Uustal had a fateful encounter in the library of the Soviet Academy of Sciences for the Institute of State and Law. Here he was introduced to the elderly Vladimir Hrabar, who was at that time checking the footnotes for his *Materials on the History of International Law in Russia*. Hrabar soon became Uustal's 'main teacher of international law',[531] a teacher of a more personal kind than most other students of international law have had. For some years Uustal lived in Hrabar's apartment near 'Park Kultury' metro station, in a small room without a window. 'This apartment became a kind of university for me.' Almost every evening, Hrabar, eager for communication and conversations, would lecture Uustal on international law, particularly on the history of the discipline. After Uustal returned to Tartu, Hrabar (who otherwise does not seem to have been proficient in Estonian) addressed his letters to him with the words 'Minu armas seltsimees' ('My dear comrade').

Having returned to Tartu in 1950, Uustal was employed at the Faculty of Law, first as a senior teacher and then, beginning in 1954, as an associate professor. He also started to work on his doctoral dissertation. Since he came from the island of Saaremaa and felt close to the sea, he was intrigued by developments at the UN Law of the Sea Conference and with the USSR as a rising sea power. Thus, he became one of the first specialists in the USSR on the international law of the sea. In 1961 at the Academy of Science of the USSR he defended his dissertation 'The Legal Regime of the Territorial Sea and Inner Waters'. It was the first dissertation in the USSR on the codification of the law of the sea. In

529 P Järvelaid, 'Jutuajamine prof. Abner Uustaliga' *Edasi* 20 January 1985, 5.

530 A Uustal, *Borba SSSR v Organizatsii Ob'edinennych Natsii za mir i bezopasnost narodov* (1950).

531 ibid.

1966, he was finally elected Ordinary Professor of International Law at the University of Tartu. During the ensuing two decades, he was also an active member of the International Law Association.

As a professor, Uustal published two books in the Estonian language, *The United Nations Organisation* (1st edition 1970, 2nd edition 1976) and, just before his death, *International Law* (1984). Moreover, he was active in what he himself called 'propaganda work' at the Marxist Leninist University. He was a frequent foreign policy commentator at Tartu's newspaper, *Edasi*. During the 1950s, his foreign policy commentaries in *Edasi* were published under the title 'To the aid of the agitator and propagandist'.[532]

In an interview given just five days before Uustal's death on 27 January 1985, he was asked several 'what is your favourite ... ?' type of questions. Among other responses, he replied that his favourite historical personality was the Bulgarian Communist Georgy Dimitrov and that he considered the Soviet foreign minister Grigory Chicherin to be the most significant diplomat of all time.[533]

9.2 *Uustal's Concept of Politics*

In 1984, ie shortly before his death, Uustal's comprehensive international law textbook was published.[534] Uustal wrote in the foreword that: 'Up to now, a systematic treatment of international law in the Estonian language has been absent. A. Piip's book was published in 1936 but to the contemporary reader this may be of interest only from the point of view of the history of international law.'[535] Uustal's textbook symbolizes a clear break with an earlier tradition in the sense that there is not the slightest attempt to separate international law from politics. Marxist analysis demonstrated that law was politics: 'Marxism revealed a lie spread in the bourgeois doctrine as if the goal of international law would be the achievement of some general wellbeing of the peoples. Marxism demonstrated that the purpose of international law of the bourgeois doctrine, as of the law generally, is to help to strengthen the interests of the ruling bourgeois class in international relations and to implement its favourite politics.'[536] Consequently, Uustal's own concept of international law was the promotion and legitimization of Soviet foreign policy:

> The main document adopted at the meeting of the representatives of the Communist Parties in Moscow in 1969 says: 'The defence of peace is inseparably linked to the fight to impose on the imperialist States the peaceful co-existence of States with different social orders. As a result of the energetic fight of

[532] See eg 'Kolooniate ja sõltuvate maade vabadusvõitlus pärast Teist maailmasõda', 6 May 1950, 'Nõukogude demokraatia ja kodanlik demokraatia' 19 February 1954.

[533] Koik (n 527 above) 37.

[534] As faculty legend has it, the book was called among students, due to its bluish covers and ideological veil, 'the blue mist'.

[535] A Uustal, *Rahvusvaheline õigus* (1984) 3.

[536] ibid 41.

the USSR and other socialist States, remarkable success has been achieved in the recognition of this principle by capitalist States ... During recent years, distorting the events of Afghanistan, the US unfortunately gave up on the deepening of the détente. Commencing a comprehensive build-up of military capabilities, extending military bases in foreign countries and intervening militarily in the domestic affairs of other peoples, they endanger international peace ... Notwithstanding the imperialist clank of arms, the USSR steadfastly pursues the politics of peace.'[537]

The first chapter also contains a quotation by the head of the Soviet Communist Party, Yuri Andropov, who by the time the book came out was already dead, starting the road to the appointment of Mr Gorbachev.

According to Uustal, the USSR could be proud of many progressive accomplishments: 'As a consequence of the fight that lasted years, the USSR achieved that contemporary international law prohibits aggressive wars, annexations and unequal treaties. As a particularly significant achievement of the Soviet diplomacy one has to count the recognition of the individual responsibility of war criminals.'[538] As every international law textbook does, Uustal's tackled the issue of the relationship between international and domestic law. Hans Kelsen argued that international law must have supremacy over domestic law, a position recognized, for example, in the constitutions of France, Italy, and Germany. But it was nevertheless to be rejected, since such a position created 'favourable conditions for imperialist Great Powers to intervene with the help of international law in the domestic affairs of other countries in the interests of their reactionary politics'.[539] But Uustal considered equally wrong another group of authors who gave priority to the norms of domestic law. For example, Germany argued after World War I that it could not extradite its nationals to foreign countries since its domestic laws prohibited this—'in practice this leads to the denial of international law.'[540] The dogmatically right solution, according to Uustal, was to differentiate between socialist and capitalist countries:

Norms of both domestic and international law based on common principles would create favourable conditions for the unwavering acceptance of obligations deriving from international law and would strengthen good neighbourly co-operation between the States. Such harmony can be observed in completeness in the countries of the socialist block (except the Chinese PR) ... Often, we see a different picture in imperialist States. There, often laws are enacted which are in complete contradiction to the generally recognised principles of international law, such as those justifying racial or sexual discrimination.[541]

Likewise on another textbook topic, States as the subjects of international law, he distinguished reactionary from socialist policies:

Views trying to transform the individual into a subject of international law, serve reactionary purposes. Under the banner of the 'protection of human rights', the

[537] ibid 6–7. [538] ibid 8. [539] ibid 14–15. [540] ibid 15. [541] ibid 16–17.

imperialist Great Powers are trying to find possibilities for intervention in the domestic affairs of other countries and for the preparation of counter-revolutionary rebellions. Very clearly this is evident in many socialist foreign countries (Hungary, Czechoslovakia, Bulgaria) . . . [542]

In these as in other cases, the basis of Uustal's argument was Soviet foreign policy positions (which would sometimes change over time). He criticized the 1950 UN General Assembly 'United for Peace' resolution for circumventing the Security Council: 'The resolution was clearly unjust because it changed the UN Charter in an improper way. But together with the strengthening of the position of democratic powers in the UN, this stipulation may also prove useful in the containment of aggressors.'[543] His list of 'reactionary schools of thought in contemporary bourgeois international law' reads like the 'who's who' of non-Soviet/Marxist international legal theory: Hans Kelsen and the normativists, Georges Scelle and the solidarists, the natural law school and 'the most reactionary approach', the sociological school in the United States, all are duly criticized and rejected.[544]

In Uustal's work there are legitimizations of Soviet policies in World War II. The Soviet-Finnish Winter War of 1939–40 was 'provoked by reactionary powers in Finland'.[545] A special chapter in his textbook was dedicated to international legal relations between the socialist countries. There are lengthy justifications for the Soviet intervention in Hungary in 1953 and Czechoslovakia in 1968, ending with the conclusion that 'the members of the Warsaw Treaty Organisation fight untiringly for peace'.[546]

Regarding human rights we are told that: 'The General Declaration of Human Rights and the [1966] Pacts are fully observed only in the USSR and other socialist States . . . In the capitalist States, most stipulations of the pacts have remained on paper.'[547] Uustal's learned teacher and 'comrade' (*seltsimees*) in Moscow, Vladimir Hrabar, would have said: *sapienti sat*.

9.3 Reflections of Cold War politics in Uustal's international legal arguments

The Cold War saw battles for supremacy on many fronts, not least ideological ones. History in particular offered inventive answers to the question of who was going to lead, the West or Soviet Russia. On this question Uustal's position was always clear and categorical, as the following examples show:

The legal protection of foreigners in Russia was by the early Middle Ages already much more developed than in the West. 'Russkaya Pravda' declared foreigners legally equal to Russians and guaranteed the inviolability of their person

[542] Uustal, *Rahvusvaheline õigus* (n 535 above) 18. [543] ibid 20. [544] ibid 20–2.
[545] ibid 73–92. [546] ibid 54–5. [547] ibid 167.

and property. Treaties that the Muscovite State later on concluded with foreign countries recognised the same principles regarding legal regime for protection of foreigners.[548]

Treaties that Russian princes concluded with the Livonian Order and German cities during the 12th–16th centuries recognised the freedom of the use of seas and rivers. In the West, the same principles prevailed only in the 19th century.[549]

All this demonstrates that international law norms known in the Kievian and Muscovite States were considerably more progressive compared to norms known in the West at the same time.[550]

Indeed, the concept of sovereignty was first developed by Russian scholars: 'In Western Europe, Jean Bodin in his work 'De la République' (1577) gives a theoretical justification for the supremacy of the king's power—sovereignty. In the Muscovite State, such teachings had been known even earlier. Their authors were the counsellors of Ivan IV (Peresvetov, Svanin, etc).'[551] Russian practice influenced the progressive development of international law decisively:

In 1709 the Russian minister Matveyev was arrested in England. Russia submitted a sharp protest against this unjust treatment. As a result of the protest, the minister was released and in order to prevent such incidents in the future, the English parliament adopted a law that recognised the immunity of diplomatic envoys.[552]

With the development of sea commerce, an attack against the usurpation of power on the seas and oceans was initiated. In that regard, too, Russia took groundbreaking positions, since it was the first that stood by the freedom of the high seas. When the English queen Elizabeth requested the closing of the White sea to the merchant ships of other countries, the Russian tsar Feodor rejected that in 1588, arguing that 'the sea is God's route' that all States may use.[553]

Likewise, Uustal praised Shafirov's 1717 treatise on the legal aspects of the Nordic War initiated by Peter's Russia:

Against the general practice of that time, a new progressive principle had been advanced that required the humane treatment of enemy prisoners who had given up resistance. The author gives examples of the atrocities committed by the Swedes ... On the basis of those works we may conclude that Russia's original international legal literature did not lag behind the Western literature of that period. With its humane positions, it set an example for Western literature and State practice for the progressive development of international law.[554]

548 A Uustal, *Rahvusvahelise õiguse ajalugu* (1965) 19. 549 ibid.

550 ibid 20. Uustal's other writings demonstrate an obsession with the idea that Russian/Soviet international law scholarship had to be 'at least equal' to its Western counterpart. For Uustal, the fact that Hrabar discovered mistakes and shortcomings in von Liszt's textbook which the latter recognized, 'demonstrated the high level of our international law scholarhip and its equality with the level of the Western science'. A Uustal, 'Rahvusvaheline õigus Tartu Ülikooli õigusteaduskonnas (1802–1918)' (1981) 6 *Nõukogude õigus* 438, 443. 551 Ustal (n 548 above) 25.

552 ibid 26. 553 ibid 27. 554 ibid 32.

According to Uustal, while progressive literature was produced in Russia, the West became influenced by the cynical teachings of Niccoló Machiavelli:

> Machiavelli's ideas were later on appropriated by the imperialist, especially fascist States.[555]
>
> From the point of view of the development of international law, one should mention the establishment of the International Law Institute in Geneva [*sic*] by a number of outstanding specialists. The idea for the creation of this international scientific organisation was given by a Russian scholar—a professor of Kharkov University, D.I. Katshenovsky, who in 1858 gave a lecture at London's legal society entitled 'On the Present State of International Jurisprudence'.[556]

Thus again, this time in particular in respect to the late nineteenth and early twentieth centuries: 'All this demonstrates that Russian science did not lag behind the bourgeois Western doctrine of international law, as some have tried to argue. In many cases it was more progressive, showing the way also to Western authors and to States . . . '[557]

The historical competition between Russian scholars and their Western counterparts was occasionally reminiscent of the 'space race' of Uustal's own time: Lieber's codification of the laws of war in the United States appeared in 1863 and Bluntschli's in Germany in 1868, but the authorship of the first private codification nevertheless belonged to the Russian Domin Petrushevitsh (1861).[558]

Uustal's negative attitude towards the United States and the 'imperialist block' went beyond mere distaste for those States—American international law scholars were also dismissed because they defended US interests. For example the proposal of Philip Jessup at the International Law Commission (ILC) to unify State practice in matters of recognition provoked 'justified counterarguments and was rejected.'[559] Jessup had proposed that the International Court of Justice (ICJ) be entitled to decide on the international legal subjectivity of the State entities that had come into existence in the course of national resistance movements. Uustal argued that the proposal was evidently made in bad faith: 'Jessup hoped of course for the numerical majority of the imperialist States at the ICJ and in the General Assembly. But this hope failed.'[560]

Uustal published several articles on his teacher Hrabar. He emphasized the importance of the message contained in Hrabar's 1901 masters thesis *Roman Law in the History of International Legal Teachings*. For Uustal, Hrabar's *History of International Law in Russia* invalidated the degrading estimation of some Western scholars that in Russia international law scholarship was historically underdeveloped: 'It was ahead of the West in the progressive treatment of many problems and institutions.'[561] In

555 Uustal, Rahvusvahelise *õiguse* (n 548 above) 33. 556 ibid 55. 557 ibid 57–8.
558 ibid 29. 559 ibid 97. 560 ibid 102.
561 A Uustal, 'Professor V. E. Grabar—progressiivne vene ja nõukogude rahvusvahelise õiguse teadlane (100. sünni-aastapäevaks)' *Tartu Riikliku Ülikooli Toimetised, vihik* 175 (1965) 14.

rejecting wars in international law and 'German juridical nihilism', Hrabar 'expressed the interests of progressive people, fought for those ideas for which progressive humankind now wages a decisive battle under the leadership of the Soviet people'.[562]

9.4 *Artur Taska's critique of Uustal*

What was Uustal's position regarding the status of Estonia, Latvia, and Lithuania from the point of view of international law? 'In June 1940 socialist revolutions took place in the bourgeois Baltic States. The entering of Estonia, Latvia and Lithuania into the composition of the USSR as Soviet republics strengthened our border on the Baltic sea.'[563] It is a crucial sentence: 'we' here meant the USSR (as opposed to 'them', the independent bourgeois republics), and the 'revolutions' in the above-mentioned republics were a means for the strengthening of 'our' border.

> The USSR supplemented the Atlantic Charter of 1941 with one important principle. Namely during the Allied conference the Soviet delegation made a declaration in which it also recognised the right of all peoples to freely choose their social order. The USSR acted on the basis of this principle with regard to the States that were liberated by the Soviet army. The USSR, liberating the peoples of Central and South-Eastern Europe, guaranteed those peoples complete freedom in their choice of form of government and social order.[564]

According to Uustal, the 1920 Soviet peace treaties with the Baltic States, Finland, and Afghanistan were early examples of the benevolent Soviet politics of peaceful coexistence with capitalist States. 'With those treaties the Soviet State tried, as much as it could, to help those formerly enslaved peoples to organise their lives independently. It handed over to them for free tsarist Russian property located on the territory of those States ...'[565] In expressing these views Uustal was simply repeating what the officially approved programme for the Soviet academic institutions envisaged. Indeed, to say anything else in a Soviet Estonian international law textbook would have been impossible. Moreover, the passages praising the progressiveness of Russia's role in the history of internatinal law were taken from the influential work of Uustal's academic supervisor in Moscow, Fyodor Kozhevnikov, *The Russian State and International Law*.[566]

Not surprisingly, Uustal's views upset Estonian émigré scholars. The exiled Estonian international law scholar Artur Taska published a review of Uustal's international law textbook in the émigré Estonian magazine *Tulimuld*. Taska was born in 1913 and graduated from Tartu's Faculty of Law in 1940, the same year as Uustal.[567] Part of the interest of Taska's

562 ibid 16. 563 Uustal (n 548 above) 74. 564 ibid 80. 565 ibid 33.

566 FI Kozhevnikov, *Russkoe gosudarstvo : mezhdunarodnoe pravo* (do XX veka) (1947 repr 2006).

567 See T Pruuli's biographical note on Taska in (1989) (2) *Looming* 244–6.

scholarly assault on Uustal was that he too had defended his doctoral dissertation on the international law of the sea—in 1952 in Kiel under Wiktor Böhmert.[568] Taska argued that throughout the nineteenth and twentieth centuries, Russia had been trying to establish a regime of *mare clausum* on the Baltic Sea. He criticized in particular a 1950 article by Molodtsov which came to the conclusion that the Baltic Sea was *mare clausum*—a theory that at the time of writing clearly favoured Soviet interests.[569] Uustal too had written an article in 1960 on the legal status of the Baltic Sea.[570]

In his criticism of Uustal, Taska pointed out the use of words such as 'revelation', 'destruction', 'gave a deadly blow', 'to camouflage the justification of violence' in Uustal's textbook and argued that those were not legal expressions but political ones,[571] 'put there according to the dictates of Soviet propaganda'.[572] Uustal's terms 'proletarian internationalism', 'brotherly help', 'intense and close cooperation', and 'mutual help' were misplaced in a work of international law: 'Neither do these concepts speak about law as science but about politics and political pursuits.'[573]

Taska was right in the sense that the language of Uustal's textbook occasionally resembled the militant outbursts of his foreign policy commentaries in Tartu's daily newspaper *Edasi* ('Forward').[574] Furthermore,

568 A Taska, *Die Grenzen des Küstenmeeres Estlands* (1974).

569 ibid 29. See also A Taska, 'Dominium Maris Baltici und die Sowjetunion' in J Poska (ed), *Pro Baltica. Mélanges dédiés à Kaarel R. Pusta. In memoriam* (1965) 203–12.

570 See Uustal archive F 120/30, 'O pravovom rezhime Baltiskogo morja' (1960)

571 A Taska, 'Rahvusvahelisest õigusest Tartu ülikoolis' (1986) 37(4) *Tulimuld* 216, 217.

572 ibid 217. 573 ibid 219.

574 See eg 27 July 1950 Reaktsiooni tööriist ('Tool of the Reaction'; about the UN); 15 December 1959, Miks takistavad imperialistlikud suurriigid Julgeolekunõukogu mittealalise liikme valimist ('Why do imperialist great powers prevent the election of a UN Security Council non-permanent Member?'); 14 December 1960, Likvideerida koloniaalsüsteem ('To liquidate the colonial system'); 1 February 1961 Piraadid ei taltu ('Pirates Won't Stop'; about the 'acts of piracy' of the US); Vabadus Patrice Lulumbale! ('Freedom to Patrice Lumumba!'); 15 February 1961, Häbiväärne agressiooniakt ('Shameful act of aggression', about an incident with a French aircraft that followed Brezhnev's plane above the Mediterranean); 8 April 1961, Rahu huvides ('In the interests of the peace'); 19 April 1961, Kuuba rahva võitlus on õiglane ('The fight of the Cuban people is just'); 17 May 1961, Imperialistide kosmosestrateegia ('The space strategy of the imperialists'); 8 September 1961, Imperialistlikel suurriikidel puudub õiguslik alus Lääne-Berliinis okupatsiooni jätkamiseks ('The imperialist great powers have no basis for the continuation of the occupation of West Berlin'); 2 March 1962 Ühendriikide monopoli tööriist ('The tool of the US monopoly'; about the OAS); 10 April 1962, Agressiivsete sõdade ideoloogia ('The ideology of the aggressive wars'); 23 May 1962, Ohtlik mäng ('Dangerous game'); 29 June 1962, Panama kanal peab kuuluma Panamale ('Panama Canal has to belong to Panama'); 10 July 1962, Ühisturu kammitsais ('In the constraints of the Common Market'; about the European Economic Community); 24 October 1962, Sulgeda sõjaõhutajate suu ('To shut the mouth *sic* of the warmongers'); 27 October 1962 Tõkestada tee fashismile! ('To Block the Road to Fascism!'; about the French referendum); 22 January 1964 Rünnak Valgele Majale ('Attack to the White House'; about the US presidential elections); 24 January 1964 Väga hea initsiatiiv ('Very good initiative'; about the proposal of Khruschev to the other States to solve the border issues in a peaceful manner); Kodumaa, 9 May 1966, Keda nad esindavad? ('Who do they represent?'; about the Estonian consuls in the US, Jaakson and Kaiv, who will be thrown into the 'trashcan of history'); Edasi, 7 October 1966, Saksa DV—rahumeelne riik ('German DR—peaceful state'); 26 January 1968, Kas jälle fashism? ('Again fascism?'); 9 October 1976 NSV Liidu ja Prantsusmaa suhted arenevad edukalt ('The relationships between the USSR

Taska criticized Uustal's (and Soviet) views regarding the termination of treaties: 'International treaties are according to the Soviet interpretation not legal acts but political literature. An international treaty does not regulate legal positions and future legal questions but fixates the political situation at the moment of the signature.'[575]

Taska was also disturbed by the fact that Uustal had, in his foreword, played down the importance of the previous Estonian textbooks by Piip (starting that they 'can be of interest to the reader only from the point of view of the history of international law'), and that he failed to mention Taska's own textbook, published in Sweden in 1977.[576]

Taska came to the following conclusion:

> The book is very far from the science of international law and to a large extent contains the purposes and goals of Soviet foreign policy. International law, as little of it as is presented, is given a class nature. This is not a law that relies on the people but serves the programme of the Communist party ... It is a pity that the Tartu University faculty of law, this old and famous institution of science, is forced to listen to the political propaganda of the USSR under the guise of international law. It is also a pity that a scholarly perspective and objectiveness are robbed from the science of international law.[577]

But he did not criticize the fact that Uustal's international legal arguments were political; he criticized the politics of Uustal's arguments. Taska's own international law textbook, published in Lund in 1977, relied primarily on positions developed and accepted in the Western, mostly German, international law literature. Nevertheless, one feature makes the book stand out—the Republic of Estonia was presented as a legal reality. Thus, the textbook talked about 'the current Eastern border of the Republic of Estonia',[578] referred to Estonian Supreme Court practice regarding international law during the 1930s,[579] and contained detailed discussions of Estonian legislation regarding international law of the same pre-World War II era.[580] Occasionally, an antiquated feeling emerged when Taska referred to conventions such as those fighting against pornography (the Paris Convention of 4 May 1910 and the Geneva Convention of 12 September 1923) to which the Republic of Estonia became party before 1939.[581] It was true that these Conventions had mandated that the member States prosecute individuals preparing and/or selling pornographic materials, but had Taska really not noticed the impact of the sexual revolution? Altogether the impression one got was that time had frozen sometime before the outbreak of the War.

Taska's own picture of Russian influence on international law in the Baltic States was very negative. He wrote that with Russia's conquest of

and France develop successfully'; in connection with Brezhnev's visit to France); 21 December 1982, Nõukogude Liit, inimõiguste kaitsja ('USSR, the defender of human rights').

[575] Taska (n 571 above) 218. For the same point, see also A Taska, 'Enesemääramisõigusest rahvusmõrvani—Nõukogude Liidu sõnad ja teod Eesti Vabariigi ja rahva suhtes' (1989) 2 *Looming* 235, 243.

[576] A Taska, *Rahvusvaheline õigus* (1977) 220–1.

[577] ibid 221. [578] ibid 27. [579] ibid 46. [580] ibid 97ff. [581] ibid 185.

the Baltic provinces in the Nordic War (1700–21) 'the Russian period or the period of darkness in the life of our people' began. 'Of the great powers, Russia with its steady enlargement towards the West and later with its intense pressure and the politics of Russification has had the most destructive impact on the people of Estonia. Notwithstanding this, State structures on the territory of Estonia preserve their substantive affiliation with Christian Western States.'[582] He maintained that Estonia had been illegally occupied by the USSR since the invasion by Soviet troops on 16 June 1940.[583]

Thus, in the early 1980s, two parallel modern international law textbooks in the Estonian language existed—one pro-independence published in Swedish exile, the other published in Soviet Estonia. In the early 1990s, when the political situation changed dramatically, Uustal's textbook became more and more neglected as 'outdated' at the university, while the students were encouraged to work with the help of Taska's book instead.

9.5 Conclusion: Uustal's politics of international law

Uustal's international law was thoroughly political. However, there is a certain difficulty with understanding Uustal's politics of international law. Is there any way for us to understand his politics today? Should his arguments be taken at their face value? In that case, a gap emerges between Uustal's texts and how his colleagues and students remember him. For example, he is remembered as having been a reasonable man on very good terms with his students. Among friends, he expressed criticism of certain Soviet policies, for example Solzhenitsyn's expulsion from the USSR.[584] He advised his students not to write about certain historical topics—since it was 'impossible to write about them properly and one should not write improperly'.[585] To some extent Uustal's textbook of international law, published in 1984, witnessed a certain doublespeak in comparison with his actual attitudes, almost as suggested in George Orwell's *1984*.

When one looks at Uustal's student fraternity photos, one wonders whether what he wrote in his late autobiography—that he was a 'confirmed Communist' and 'had felt sympathy with the USSR already during the gymnasium years'—was really true. In an autobiographical note handwritten in 1955, Uustal mentioned that the last he had heard of his brother Paul was during the war in 1944, when the brother was arrested by the Germans for not having shown up for work duty. The note implied that the Germans might have done something to his brother. Only in the autobiography written in 1985 did Uustal reveal that his brother lived 'as a worker in Canada'. On the one hand, during the Soviet period many Balts were silent about escaped and exiled relatives, in fear

582 Taska, *Rahvusvaheline õigus* (n 576 above) 34. 583 ibid 38, 80, 84.
584 Memoirs of Eimar Rahumaa, Uustal's student and assistant. 585 ibid.

of retaliation by the authorities. On the other hand, would Abner's brother have left the 'paradise of the working people' in 1944 if Abner had already during the 1930s been so enthusiastic about the USSR?

I would suggest that Uustal's politics can be explained by reference to the brutality and treacherousness of the Soviet takeover of Estonia in 1940 and the ensuing war. As we have seen, in 1940, a younger colleague had asked Nikolai Maim provocatively: 'What good did these 20 years [of independence] do us? They have only made matters worse! If we had simply been a Soviet republic for the last 20 years, Estonian youth would not be suffering so much now.' Perhaps the rebellious disappointment reflected in these sentences might echo what Uustal could have felt? Different people reacted differently to the Soviet invasion of 1940. It seems that Uustal concluded that there could not be self-determination for small peoples. International treaties failed to protect independent statehood; it was smarter to keep close to the Empire. Had not young Maim in pre-1917 St Petersburg also asked himself whether affiliating oneself with the Empire was not a less risky choice than statehood based on the ethnic nationalism of a small group? Perhaps in 1940 Uustal realized that Soviet Communism offered an identity that was protected by a Great Power and could not be endangered so easily. Perhaps he could console himself that what happened in his country in 1940 was not a victory of force over the will of a small people, but the materialization of dialectical laws of history?

Uustal was clearly the most constrained of the protagonists of this study; his room for manoeuvre was severely restricted. To what extent was it an accident that Abner was mobilized in the Soviet army and that his brother Paul ended up as a refugee in Canada? In what circumstances could the roles have been reversed? One wonders to what extent Uustal in World War II and subsequently in the Cold War chose his side, and to what extent his side chose him. In Siberia, the State offered to him and other 'mobilized' Estonian men a simple choice: you fight with us or you starve to death. Perhaps the fact that he was one of the few saved from the battleship *Sibir* and that he nevertheless could eventually return to Estonia with the victorious Soviet army deepened in him the conviction that he chose his side himself and that his choice was the right one.

Whatever the answers, Uustal remained constrained as a scholar. While studying in Moscow, he had come across the secret protocols to the Hitler–Stalin Pact in an archive. When this had come out, he was warned that he should be much more careful. Moreover, the way he transcribed in his publications names of several Western international law scholars demonstrates that he had not been able to use the original works, but rather references or translations in the Soviet/Russian literature.

Uustal's politics of international law was thus a politics of survival—both on an individual and perhaps even on a national level. Behind its inflammatory and aggressive rhetoric hid insecurity and the fact that in the USSR, the role of an individual international law scholar could only be to sing in a choir with a predetermined repertoire. In a State that officially recognized the ideological monopoly of historical materialism, the arguments of international lawyers could not do otherwise than obey this higher 'truth'. In this sense, although Taska accused Uustal of false politics, he and Uustal represented two sides of the same tragic story. Perhaps neither of the two 'inimical brothers' realized that in a way they were both victims.

In 1892, Carl Bergbohm criticized natural law doctrine for dangerously believing in 'eternal truths'.[586] Uustal's Soviet/Communist international law with its 'eternal truth' of historical materialism was a peculiar revival of natural law doctrine (also without being aware of it), an expression of a seventy-year long Soviet/Russian *Sonderweg*.

Uustal's arguments prove that international law which is identical with politics turns into its own farce. Uustal represented an extreme, since his example demonstrated the results of altogether giving up the ideal of the independence of international law from international politics. For the Soviet doctrine, law was the representation of class interests. Uustal was not dishonest when he justified and defended Soviet foreign policy in his international law works. In the USSR, that was the lawyer's task, his job. The good soldier Uustal simply did what he was supposed to do.

It would, however, be wrong to say that Soviet international law was political while Western scholarship of the same period was not. The politics and the styles were different—but, for instance, the New Haven school's concept of international law was not 'apolitical'.[587] Both Uustal's Communism and McDougal's 'policy-oriented jurisprudence'[588] were representatives of the natural law school. Perhaps a true natural law adherent hates no one more than another natural law supporter who has a different vision of natural law.[589] Nevertheless, there remains a significant difference in degree. During the Cold War, the Western science of international law enjoyed a relatively greater autonomy *vis-à-vis* politics.[590] Uustal had essentially no choice about whether to defend the 1968 Soviet intervention in Czechoslovakia or not (had he not done so, he would have lost his position and most likely faced other serious consequences). At the same time, Richard Falk and other American international law scholars

[586] C Bergbohm, *Jurisprudenz und Rechtsphilosophie* (1892) 201.

[587] For an interesting German discussion, see Wilhelm Wengler's foreword to *Modernes Völkerrecht. Form oder Mittel der Aussenpolitik. Eine Gegenüberstellung der Lehren von M.A. Kaplan und N. de B. Katzenbach—USA und G. I. Tunkin—UdSSR* (1965).

[588] David Kennedy has outlined the opposition of Yale's 'naturalist'-inclining counterpoint with the mainstream US positivism-inclined school of thought, associated with Henkin and Schachter from Columbia. See D Kennedy, *My Talk at the ASIL: What is New Thinking in International Law?*, Proceedings of the 94th Annual Meeting of the American Society of International Law, 5–8 April 2000, 104, 117.

[589] Uustal discussed the 'sociological' school (together with Kelsen's normativists, Scelle's solidarists, and Del Vecchio's natural law school) under the heading 'Reactionary Directions in Contemporary Bourgeois International Law'. See Uustal, *Rahvusvaheline õigus* (n 535 above) 20–2.

[590] See more generally about political constraints to science in the USSR, LL Lubrano and S Gross Solomon, *The Social Context of Soviet Science* (1980).

were critically attacking the American involvement in Vietnam War, *inter alia*, on the basis of international law.[591]

Taska's attack on Uustal's vocabulary of international legal discourse was also significant. Taska essentially accused Uustal of giving up the specialized language of law. Bourdieu has argued that some specialized language is an invariable condition for the existence of any disciplinary or professional field. In Western culture, legal language usually bears the marks of a rhetoric of impersonality and neutrality.[592] Koskenniemi and Kennedy have pointed out that the legal argument, notwithstanding (or because of?) law's substantive indeterminacy, is constrained by a rigorously formal language—learning to speak it is the key to legal competence.[593]

However, the fact that Uustal merged legal and political language was not an accident nor due to a lack of professionalism. It reflected his Marxist concept of law and the critique that law was *in any case* an expression of the politics of class (or State) interests. From Uustal's point of view, Western authors were hypocritical; he was honest in doing openly what others preferred to do secretly (but did *in any case*, irrespective of their preferences). Nevertheless, his rhetoric completely eliminated international law as a field even partly independent of politics. In not believing in non-political international law while continuing to argue on the basis of 'legal' concepts, Uustal made international law an instrument of Soviet propaganda. Law as a discipline was completely subjugated to the politics and interests of the Soviet State. In the 'bourgeois' Western tradition, the judicial situation operated like a neutralizing space—at least to a degree. In the Soviet tradition, as represented by Uustal, legal rhetoric (with the lack of judges, the law professor being the 'mediator') did not neutralize—it further radicalized the situation, making it clear that while a nuclear war was, of course, the last thing the government wished, it might become inevitable for reasons of defence.

Thus, it seems that Pierre Bourdieu overly universalized the Western tradition when he characterized the adoption of the neutralizing 'scholastic point of view' as the entry ticket to the recognition of the world of science.[594] In the USSR, the entry ticket was acquired via adopting the right ideology. Uustal, the simple seaman's son from Saaremaa, did not play such an elitist game of neutralization and disinterestedness as, for example, Bulmerincq had done. This was an altogether different concept of international law, a break with 'objectivist' tradition, and it must be understood as such.

591 See RA Falk (ed), *The Vietnam War and International Law* (1968).

592 See P Bourdieu, 'The Force of Law: Toward a Sociology of the Juridical Field' (1987) 38 *Hastings Law Journal* 819.

593 See M Koskenniemi, 'Letter to the Editors of the Symposium' (1999) 93 AJIL 351, 355; D Kennedy, 'Theses about International Law Discourse' (1980) 23 *German Yearbook of International Law* 353–91.

594 P Bourdieu, *Practical Reason. On the Theory of Action* (1998) (1994, Seuil) 128.

10. Concluding Observations

The works and arguments of the international law professors at the University of Dorpat/Iur'ev/Tartu 1855–1985 remind me of a palimpsest—an ancient manuscript in which the text reveals traces of several earlier texts underneath it. Instead of composing a linear history from the nineteenth century until the end of the Cold War, it would have been possible to read these texts in reverse order, 'back to front'—from Uustal to Bulmerincq.

The story from Bulmerincq (1855) to Uustal (1985) is a story of ruptures and discontinuities, beneath the great continuity of the main question of the discipline of international law, ie its relationship to politics. The development 'from Bulmerincq to Uustal' reveals an underlying logic, a dynamic from the emphasis on the autonomy of law to the instrumentalization of law as part of 'politics'. For August Bulmerincq, and especially Carl Bergbohm, law had to be independent of politics, to the point of being anti-politics. Vladimir Hrabar, especially in his 'Declaration of War in Contemporary International Law', clearly stood on the same positivist ground of separating 'positive' law and political interests. Ants Piip maintained the dominant rhetoric of the discipline—and at the same time skilfully included his politics in international legal arguments, both as policy-maker and as scholar. Finally, for Abner Uustal, international law became the same as politics. Thus both extreme positions were represented; the circle closed.

So what was the connection between law and politics in the present article? I have examined the arguments (and thus the politics) of the protagonists closely. As to social science concepts I have relied most on Pierre Bourdieu's concepts of 'habitus' and 'field'. I think they represent a reasonable and realistic compromise between the two extreme positions—the untenable notion that scientific activity and thinking are completely independent of context (objectivism) and the instrumentalist (for example Marxist) idea that scientific activity and thinking as 'superstructures' merely reflect social, material, and political conditions and interests. To understand the politics of international law, I chose to study and combine *both* the text and the context (the individual's life and time). The present study demonstrates that reality is a two-way street of the knowing and arguing subject shaped by circumstances and pulled along by the common habitus on the one hand while being to a degree autonomous and capable of influencing external reality—the field—on the other. The arguments of international law professors were not completely predetermined by the education, class, race, ethnicity, etc of the individuals concerned. For example, Hrabar's and Uustal's international law of the Soviet period was different—ie their arguments were not completely predetermined by the constraints of the political order. There was space for choice and individuality.

Bourdieu has claimed that one of the characteristics that most differentiates fields is their degree of autonomy and, closely related to this, the force and form of the entry requirements imposed on new entrants:[595] 'Given the determinant role it plays in social reproduction, the juridical field has a smaller degree of autonomy than other fields, like the artistic or literary or even the scientific fields, that also contribute to the maintenance of the symbolic order and, thereby, to that of the social order itself. External changes are more directly reflected in the juridical field and more directly decided by external forces.'[596] The present study suggests that in the academic field of international law those entry conditions were partly political. Bergbohm and Bulmerincq belonged to the upper class of the dominant ethnic group. Hrabar was imported in 1893 by Iur'ev as a Russian-speaking international law professor. Piip's rise in 1919 coincided with the rise of the programme of the 'Estonian university' and the establishment of Estonia's statehood—a process in which Piip himself was very much involved. (An Estonian newspaper article of 1921 reports rumours that Hrabar had made inquiries from Russia about whether he could continue as an international law professor in Tartu.)[597] Finally, Uustal too was chosen and promoted to a professorship from among the right and proven men—one who had proved his loyalty in fighting against the Germans in World War II. He literally exchanged his Red Army uniform for a lectureship and later professorship in international law.

Thus the academic field of international law has its idiosyncracies: its independence of politics is relatively limited, being a relatively politicized science. The pressure of political interests on international legal arguments is considerable; in some cases international law can degenerate into a science that merely serves the needs of politics.[598]

In particular, international law is characterized by the scarcity of (or even lack of) mandatory adjudicatory bodies capable of issuing binding judgments. Thus scholars being capable of saying what international law 'is', fulfil in certain circumstances a quasi-judicial function. Where there is no judge it is the professor of international law who determines (at least for a particular group, people, and time) what international law 'is'. When Piip wrote in 1927 that Estonia was a 'free State' in the thirteenth century, some perhaps imaginary Estonia of the thirteenth century *did* become a free State for the people who read and were influenced by Piip's argument. When Uustal wrote that the Soviet suppression of the Hungarian (1956) and Czechoslovakian (1968) revolutions was not only lawful but the correct thing to do, or that Estonia joined the USSR in 1940 following a socialist revolution, it legitimized and provided a certain comfort, at least to believers in the righteousness of Soviet foreign policy.

Koskenniemi suggests: 'It may be too much to say that international law is only what international lawyers do or think. But at least it is

595 P Bourdieu, *Science of Science and Reflexivity* (2004) 47.

596 ibid 850.

597 *Postimees*, 2 March 1921, No 48, 3.

598 For a discussion on 'pure science' and 'science in the service of . . .' see P Bourdieu, *Les usages sociaux de la science. Pour une sociologie clinique du champ scientifique* (1997) 14–16.

that . . .'[599] Another leading exponent of the Critical Legal Studies approach, David Kennedy, makes a similar point in suggesting that international law is the product of a 'group of people sharing professional tools and expertise, as well as a sensibility, viewpoint, and mission'.[600] In more critical terms, Hans Morgenthau wrote in 1940 that international lawyers were similar to 'sorcerers of ancient times, trying to exorcize social evils with magic formulae'.[601] This point echoes what the American social theorist Thorstein Veblen realized in 1899: 'In point of derivation, learning, as well as the priestly office, is largely an outgrowth of sympathetic magic; and this magical apparatus of form and ritual therefore finds its place with the learned class of the primitive community as a matter of course.'[602]

But by doing that, international law scholars are not 'cheating', since there appears to be a deep social need for arguments of international law. One should also not obscure an evident fact: the position of an international law professor, like that of an ancient 'sorcerer' or 'priest', is a position of power.[603] Just as ancient sorcerers had the power of giving meaning and direction to things by inventing and using their 'magic formulae', international lawyers have had a similar power by calling things into existence (making them real) by giving them names and classifications.

Because of its proximity to politics and its relative lack of autonomy, the practice of international law often fulfils a legitimizing function. A professorship of international law is a professorship in international legitimization because international legal arguments are inevitably linked to politics. In this sense, Bulmerincq, Bergbohm, and Hrabar underestimated how deeply intertwined with politics international law was (and their own arguments were). International legal arguments come from somewhere that is not international law itself but is transcendent to it. International law cannot be separated from politics; international law without politics would be both boring and useless. At the same time, declaring the separation of international law from politics is historically a playful, rich, and imaginative legal doctrine. In practice, it can also be a very smart form of politics. Positivism entails a measure of hypocrisy, but at the same time it may be the only framework that successfully enables us to make legal arguments—and consequently makes the discipline of international law possible.

Thus, modern international legal doctrine and practice are based on a paradox. On the one hand, international law cannot be separated from

[599] See M Koskenniemi, *The Gentle Civilizer of Nations. The Rise and Fall of International Law 1870–1960* (2001) 7.

[600] Kennedy, *My Talk at the ASIL* (n 588 above) 123.

[601] See HJ Morgenthau, 'Positivism, Functionalism and International Law' (1940) 34 AJIL 260–84.

[602] See T Veblen, *The Theory of the Leisure Class* (1967) 368.

[603] For the sociological insight that in terms of power, the faculty of law does comparatively well in the 'conflict of the faculties', see P Bourdieu, *Homo Academicus* (1988) 41.

politics. On the other hand, the claim of the separation of international law from politics as a certain ideal makes international law as a viable discourse possible. When Jaan Kross writes that his dissertation on international treaties was a 'game', there is perhaps more in this remark than a historical reference to playing hide-and-seek with Soviet totalitarianism. Modern positivist international law is a game whose rules were first successfully formulated and practised by, among others, August Bulmerincq. The main rule has remained that the game's official name is 'international law is separate from politics'. The one who can most successfully hide his/her politics in law wins.

As in real life, international legal arguments can appear comical but also deeply tragic in time. In the present article, there was a certain human tragedy in the fact that the world was always becoming something else. Bulmerincq did not leave Dorpat with a positive feeling about how things were developing in his homeland. Centralists forced his successor Carl Bergbohm to leave the university and go into exile. The creation of independent Estonia and Latvia in 1918 destroyed the Baltic German political dream of a unified German Baltic State. The Great Power for whom Hrabar had, in 1912, demanded special status in *The Principle of the Equality of States* (which should rather have been called 'The Principle of the Inequality of States') crumbled in 1917, a short German occupation followed, and Hrabar had to leave his dear Iur'ev—as he himself wrote nostalgically—'forever'. Piip's international law, based on the right of peoples to self-determination, was pulled down by the Soviet conquest of Estonia in 1940; Piip himself was starved to death in Siberia two years later. And the legitimizer of the Soviet order, Uustal, died in the same year as the Soviet reformer, Gorbachev, came to power and the collapse of the USSR was much more imminent than any Western 'Sovietologists' had predicted. The legitimization of political ideals through international law, it seems, had been in vain.

The tasks of ordering anarchy and explaining order are often tragic by nature. As the Franco-Czech novelist Milan Kundera observes, the social world (of which international lawyers cannot free themselves) remains fundamentally unpredictable:

> Everyone is wrong about the future. Man can only be certain about the present moment. But is that quite true either? Can he really know the present? Is he in a position to make any judgment about it? Certainly not. For how can a person with no knowledge of the future understand the meaning of the present? If we do not know what future the present is leading us toward, how can we say whether this present is good or bad, whether it deserves our concurrence, or our suspicion, or our hatred?[604]

604 M Kundera, *Ignorance* (trans from French L Asher, 2002) 143–4.

NOTE

CUSTOMARY INTERNATIONAL HUMANITARIAN LAW—AN INTERPRETATION ON BEHALF OF THE INTERNATIONAL COMMITTEE OF THE RED CROSS*

By GEORGE H ALDRICH**

Customary International Humanitarian Law, Volume 1, Rules. Edited by Jean-Marie Henckaerts and Louise Doswald-Beck, with contributions by Carolin Alvermann, Knut Dörmann, Baptiste Rolle. Cambridge, Cambridge University Press, paperback £27.99; hardback, £55.00.

Customary International Humanitarian Law, Volume 2, Practice, Parts 1 and 2. Edited by Jean-Marie Henckaerts and Louise Doswald-Beck, with contributions by Carolin Alvermann, Angela Cotroneo, Antoine Grand, Baptiste Rolle. Cambridge, Cambridge University Press, hardback, £280.00.

This monumental study has been written by two members of the legal division of the International Committee of the Red Cross (ICRC) pursuant to a resolution of the 26th International Conference of the Red Cross in 1995 requesting the ICRC to prepare a report on customary rules of international humanitarian law applicable in international and non-international armed conflict. The conclusions of this study are set forth in a single Volume of 621 pages divided into six parts containing 161 proposed rules, each accompanied by relatively brief commentary. The six parts are entitled: 1. The Principle of Distinction; 2. Specifically Protected Persons and Objects; 3. Specific Methods of Warfare; 4. Weapons; 5. Treatment of Civilians and Persons Hors de Combat; and 6. Implementation. All are topics dealt with in the Geneva Protocols I and II of 1977[1] or in the four Geneva Conventions of 1949,[2] although the part dealing with weapons is related primarily to a variety of other

** Judge, Iran-United States Claims Tribunal, The Hague.

[1] Protocol Additional to the Geneva Conventions of 12 August 1949, and Relating to the Protection of Victims of International Armed Conflicts, 12 December, 1977, 1125 UNTS 3, reprinted in 16 ILM 1391 (1977) [hereinafter Protocol I]; Protocol Additional to the Geneva Conventions of 12 August 1949, and Relating to the Protection of Victims of Non-International Armed Conflicts, opened for signature 12 December 1977, Art 1, 1125 UNTS 609 [hereinafter Protocol II].

[2] Geneva Convention for the Amelioration of the Condition of the Wounded and Sick in Armed Forces in the Field, 12 August, 1949, 6 UST 3114, 75 UNTS 31; Geneva Convention for the

international agreements, from the St Petersburg Declaration of 1868[3] to the Ottawa Convention of 1997.[4]

Volume II, which in fact fills two immense volumes totaling 4,411 pages, contains the information gathered by the authors on which their conclusions with respect to their proposed rules are based. Volume II is organized in the same manner as Volume I, in order to facilitate finding the background material relevant to each rule. This material includes treaty provisions, reports of state practice, provisions of national military manuals, legislation, and court cases, as well as a very wide range of decisions, resolutions, and opinions expressed by international organizations and tribunals and even by some NGOs and armed opposition groups.

From the study's acknowledgements of the assistance provided by the members of the national research teams, international research teams, an ICRC research team, a twelve-member steering committee, and a large number of academic and governmental experts, it is clear that during the decade in which this study was prepared, significant contributions of time and thought were made by a very wide range of knowledgeable persons. Such a broad source of information and advice was, of course, essential, not merely to facilitate the collection of information about state practice, but also to lend greater credibility to the study than would naturally accrue to conclusions by two staff members of the ICRC.

The authors' twenty-six-page Introduction explains the scope of the study, and it should be noted that the study excludes the law of naval warfare as well as much of the law covered by the Geneva Conventions of 1949. The Introduction also explains how the work was done and indicates the limited, but significant, extent to which drafts were reviewed and advice was given by the steering committee or by individual experts. That Introduction concludes with the customary, and in this case very important, statement that the authors, jointly, bear the sole responsibility for the content of the study. That statement is particularly important because the ICRC, as an institution, justifiably has substantial credibility resulting from its past and continuing efforts to assist in the codification of and compliance with international humanitarian law. That credibility should not be jeopardized by mistakenly thinking that it is responsible for the conclusions of this study. It must be recognized that helping

Amelioration of the Condition of the Wounded, Sick and Shipwrecked Members of Armed forces at Sea, 12 August, 1949, 6 UST 3217, 75 UNTS 85; Geneva Convention Relative to the Treatment of Prisoners of War, 12 August, 1949, 6 UST 3316, 75 UNTS 135; Geneva Convention Relative to the Protection of Civilian Persons in Time of War, 12 August, 1949, 6 UST 3516, 75 UNTS 287 [hereinafter Fourth Geneva Convention].

[3] Declaration Renouncing the Use, in Time of War, of Explosive Projectiles under 400 Grammes Weight, 29 November 1868 (11 December), 18 Martens Nouveau Recueil (1e sér) 474, translated and reprinted in THE LAWS OF ARMED CONFLICTS 101 (Dietrich Schindler and Jiri Toman (eds), 3rd revised edn, 1988) [hereinafter St Petersburg Declaration].

[4] Convention on the Prohibition of the Use, Stockpiling, Production and Transfer of Anti-Personnel Mines and on Their Destruction, 18 September 1997, 2056 UNTS 21, reprinted in 36 ILM 1507 (1997) [hereinafter Ottawa Convention].

states to draft and negotiate treaties and monitoring and urging compliance with them are not at all the same things as purporting to determine the content of customary international law. While the copyright to this study is held by the ICRC, its findings are solely those of Mr Henckaerts and Mrs Doswald-Beck.

I certainly do not mean to suggest by the preceding remarks that this study is not important. I believe it is a very important study, but I think its importance rests on its being used as a basis for further work and as a spur to such works, rather than on its conclusions. While I cannot agree with the comment by my old friend Dr Yves Sandoz, a member of the ICRC, in his foreword that the study represents 'the truest possible reflection of reality',[5] I share his hope that it will be read and commented on and thereby prompt renewed examination of international humanitarian law.

Given the fact that international humanitarian law—the law applicable in armed conflict, or the law of war as it used to be called—is perhaps the most completely codified part of international law, one might well ask as a preliminary question why it should be considered important to determine the customary law. In his foreword to this study,[6] the President of the ICRC, Jakob Kellenberger, states three reasons: because not all States are parties to some recent treaties, because the treaties provide only limited coverage of non-international armed conflicts, and because customary law is relevant to the interpretation of the treaty law. In my view, however, it is really only the first of those three reasons that has resulted in this expensive and extensive study. In particular, I believe that it is the failure of some very important nations to become parties to one critical treaty—Geneva Protocol I of 1977—that lends sufficient urgency to the subject to inspire this work.

By most standards, Protocol I has done reasonably well, as it now has 163 Parties, but ratifications and accessions have slowed to a crawl in recent years, and at this writing there remain twenty-nine States that have not become Parties to it. In alphabetical order, they are Afghanistan, Andorra, Azerbaijan, Bhutan, Eritrea, Fiji, Haiti, India, Indonesia, Iran, Iraq, Israel, Kiribati, Malaysia, the Marshall Islands, Morocco, Myanmar, Nepal, Pakistan, Papua New Guinea, the Philippines, Singapore, Somalia, Sri Lanka, Sudan, Thailand, Turkey, Tuvalu, and the United States of America. While some of those States may simply have overlooked the Protocol, that is certainly not the case with many of them, including the key states of India, Indonesia, Iran, Iraq, Israel, Pakistan, Turkey, and the United States of America.[7] While most of the provisions of the Protocol probably do reflect customary law, substantive and public dissent by at least some of those States to various provisions of the Protocol makes it

5 Vol I, xvii. 6 Vol I, x.

7 See <http://www.icrc.org/ihl.nsf/WebSign?ReadForm&id=470&ps=P> (last visited 3 November 2005).

impossible to suggest that the Protocol, like the 1949 Geneva Conventions, should be considered to represent as a whole a codification of customary international humanitarian law. If these missing key States had become Parties, even with reservations and understandings, it would be possible to determine which provisions of the Protocol were applicable in any conflict in which they were involved, but their failure to accept the Protocol makes such a determination impossible.

Geneva Protocol I, which along with Protocol II, resulted from prolonged negotiations in Geneva from 1974 to 1977,[8] was the only treaty since the 1907 Hague Convention (IV)[9] to codify the law governing the conduct of hostilities in international armed conflicts. While the Geneva Conventions of 1949 were built largely on the structure of a series of earlier conventions that dealt with the protections to be accorded sick or wounded soldiers, prisoners of war, and persons in occupied enemy territory, the task facing the negotiators of Protocol I was more delicate in that it involved developing completely new treaties that would bring customary law and the seventy-year-old Hague Convention (IV) treaty law up to date in the light of the experiences of the intervening two World Wars. And that task was made politically awkward by the sensitivities at that time of many nations to the slow and then still incomplete process of decolonization and to the related Arab-Israeli conflict.

With respect to non-international armed conflicts, Geneva Protocol II presented even greater difficulties to its negotiators, because it built solely on the precedent of a single Article, common Article 3 to the four Geneva Conventions of 1949, and because it was viewed by the governments of those nations that feared internal rebellions as a treaty that could hinder their repression of such rebellions. That anxious group included the governments of most newly independent States. Consequently, Protocol II emerged from the Conference in 1977 as a much more limited set of rules than many developed States and the ICRC desired. Nevertheless, if Protocol I had achieved near universal acceptance, I doubt that the ICRC would have commissioned this massive study solely to find a more detailed customary international humanitarian law for non-international armed conflicts. It is the failure of key States to become Parties to Protocol I that justified this effort.

One can sympathize with the desire of the ICRC to have a legal standard against which to measure the degree of compliance or non-compliance with international humanitarian law of non-Parties to Protocol I in the course of their involvement in international armed conflict, but one must also recognize the magnitude of the difficulty inherent in making the

[8] It should be noted for the record that this reviewer was the head of the delegation of the US to those negotiations and, with the late Judge Richard R Baxter, shared the position of Rapporteur of Committee 3 of that conference.

[9] The Hague Convention (IV) Respecting the Laws and Customs of War on Land and the Regulations annexed thereto, 18 October 1907, 36 Stat 2277, 1 Bevans 631 (entered into force Jan 26, 1910) [hereinafter Hague Convention (IV)].

necessary judgments, particularly as none of the non-Parties has, to my knowledge, made authoritative, comprehensive, and contemporary statements of its views on the matter.

This study, in its Volume II notes where relevant, official statements, such as the remarks by the Deputy Legal Advisor of the United States Department of State at a 1987 meeting in Washington, DC,[10] as well as public reports or statements by military officials or agencies of many other States that give some indication of official attitudes with respect to how hostilities have been or should be conducted. But such materials, while helpful, fall short of defining with any precision the extent of contemporary State acceptance of or objection to specific provisions of Protocol I, and they certainly cannot indicate the extent of probable State agreement with the proposed rules of customary international humanitarian law made by this study. From such material, the authors of this study could properly have proposed drafts of rules for the further consideration of States. However, the study goes too far in declaring its proposed rules to be customary law, for in doing so, its credibility crumbles.

Analysis of the proposed rules reveals that the authors have frequently sought to simplify provisions of Protocol I, presumably in a belief that a customary rule of law would likely, or even necessarily, be less complex than a treaty provision. Unfortunately, at least so far as the proposed rules reflect provisions of Protocol I, that is not true. As the Rapporteur of a Conference Committee that produced many of the articles of Protocol I considered by the study, I know that complexity was often essential to achieve a text that could be adopted in the conference by consensus or by a substantial majority. In proposing rules that are simplified versions of such articles, the authors frequently create problems they probably do not realize.

An examination of some specific rules proposed by this study is necessary to demonstrate at least some of the problems the study presents. In general, I shall limit this examination to the application of these rules to international armed conflict. Nevertheless, I note that the authors frequently posit their proposed rules as applicable also to non-international armed conflicts without much, if any, analysis of the potential political implications for States engaged in such conflicts. Such States will usually be reluctant to accept rules that appear to restrict their actions in suppressing rebellions and will always oppose anything that appears to give rebels belligerent status. I feel certain that the study will receive criticism from that quarter.

[10] Remarks of Michael J Matheson, Deputy Legal Advisor, US Dept of State, The Sixth Annual American Red Cross-Washington College of Law Conference on International Humanitarian Law: A Workshop on Customary International Law and the 1977 Protocols Additional to the 1949 Geneva Conventions, (1987) 2 *American University Journal of International Law and Policy* 426.

Distinguishing Civilian Persons and Objects from Combatants and Military Objectives

This topic is treated by the first 10 rules proposed by the study.

Rule 1: The parties to the conflict must at all times distinguish between civilians and combatants. Attacks may only be directed against combatants. Attacks must not be directed against civilians.

Compare this rule with Article 48 and the first sentence of Article 51(2) of Protocol I.

Article 48—Basic Rule

In order to ensure respect for and protection of the civilian population and civilian objects, the Parties to the conflict shall at all times distinguish between the civilian population and combatants and between civilian objects and military objectives and accordingly shall direct their operations only against military objectives.

Article 51(2)

The civilian population as such, as well as individual civilians, shall not be the object of attack. Acts or threats of violence the primary purpose of which is to spread terror among the civilian population are prohibited.

The second sentence of the proposed rule seems unnecessary and conceivably misleading, as attacks may also be directed against any military objective, as the study notes in its proposed Rule 7. While there should be no real difference between the phrase used in the rule, 'attacks directed against civilians', and the phrase used consistently in Protocol I, 'making civilians the object of attack', the latter seems somewhat clearer in its requirement that civilians not be made the target of attacks.

A related question arises in proposed Rule 6, which states: 'Civilians are protected against attack unless and for such time as they take a direct part in hostilities.' The phrase 'protected against attack' might be interpreted as meaning protected against the effects of attacks, which would not be a feasible rule. Also, I note that, while the study asserts that Rule 6 is customary law in both international and non-international armed conflicts, it should be noted that its discussion of the related Rule 5 states that 'practice is not clear as to whether members of armed opposition groups are civilians subject to Rule 6 . . .'[11]

Rules 8 and 10

Rule 8: In so far as objects are concerned, military objectives are limited to those objects which by their nature, location, purpose or use make an effective contribution to military action and whose partial or total destruction, capture or neutralisation, in the circumstances ruling at the time, offers a definite military advantage.

[11] Vol I, 19.

Rule 10: Civilian objects are protected against attack, unless and for such time as they are military objectives.

While the study in its Rule 8 correctly uses the definitions of objects that are military objectives, found in Article 52 of Protocol I, in Rule 10 it again uses the phrase 'protected against attack', which, as in Rules 6 and 7, is too open to misinterpretation. From my experience during the negotiation of the Protocols in 1974–77, I am confident that the phrase preferred by the study would not have been accepted in Geneva in 1977 for use in Protocol I.

The study also does not include in Rule 10 the reference to cases of doubt whether an object normally used only for civilian purposes is being used in ways that make it a military objective, as is done in paragraph 3 of Article 52 of Protocol I, but the issue is discussed in the commentary to Rule 10.[12] This omission from Rule 10 may be appropriate, as that provision in Protocol I may appear to promise a greater prospect of protection than it can deliver, and the need for care is sufficiently addressed in Rule 16 of this study and in Article 57 of Protocol I dealing with precautions in attack. The problem with establishing a presumption in case of doubt is that it is difficult, if not impossible, to indicate adequately the circumstances that would justify rebutting the presumption. I recall learning from veterans of the Second World War that the allied armed forces in Normandy in 1944 soon learned that German artillery spotters made good use of the bell towers of the local churches and, consequently allied tanks routinely destroyed those towers by shell fire. Obviously, it was not feasible at a distance to verify the presence in each of those towers of the enemy spotter.

Precautionary Measures

Rules 14, 15, 16, 17, 18, and 19

Rule 14: Launching an attack which may be expected to cause incidental loss of civilian life, injury to civilians, damage to civilian objects, or a combination thereof, which would be excessive in relation to the concrete and direct military advantage anticipated, is prohibited.

Rule 15: In the conduct of military operations, constant care must be taken to spare the civilian population, civilians and civilian objects. All feasible precautions must be taken to avoid, and in any event to minimise, incidental loss of civilian life, injury to civilians and damage to civilian objects.

Rule 16: Each party to the conflict must do everything feasible to verify that targets are military objectives.

[12] Vol I, 35–6.

Rule 17: Each party to the conflict must take all feasible precautions in the choices of means and methods of warfare with a view to avoiding, and in any event to minimising, incidental loss of civilian life, injury to civilians and damage to civilian objects.

Rule 18: Each party to the conflict must do everything feasible to assess whether the attack may be expected to cause incidental loss of civilian life, injury to civilians, damage to civilian objects, or a combination thereof, which would be excessive in relation to the concrete and direct military advantage anticipated.

Rule 19: Each party to the conflict must do everything feasible to cancel or suspend an attack if it becomes apparent that the target is not a military objective or that the attack may be expected to cause incidental loss of civilian life, injury to civilians, damage to civilian objects, or a combination thereof, which would be excessive in relation to the concrete and direct military advantage anticipated.

The rule of proportionality expressed by Rule 14 is found in Article 57 of Protocol I, but there it is stated to be an obligation of those who plan or decide upon an attack, as opposed to those who are ordered to carry out the attack. In general, the rules proposed by the study are phrased in broad terms, often as the obligation of a Party, whereas the text of the Protocol makes useful distinctions that reflect the realities of military command. Thus, Article 57 of Protocol I distinguishes between the responsibility of those who plan or decide upon an attack and those who carry out an attack, but Rules 14 and 16–19 are simply stated to be rules for each party to the conflict. Rules 14, 15 (the second sentence), 16, 17, and 18 can only be relevant to those who plan or decide upon an attack and should be stated as relevant to attacks, not to the much more general term, 'warfare'. Moreover, Rule 18 which is drawn from Article 57(2)(a)(i) of Protocol I would better be combined with Rule 16 and rephrased along the lines of Protocol I. Rule 19 is properly made applicable to each Party to the conflict, but it curiously replaces with a more limited rule the broader obligations of Article 57(2)(b) of the Protocol to cancel or suspend an attack if it becomes apparent that the objective is not a military one, or is subject to special protection, or that it may be expected to cause civilian losses or damage that would violate the proportionality requirement.

Rule 21: When a choice is possible between several military objectives for obtaining a similar military advantage, the objective to be selected must be that the attack on which may be expected to cause the least danger to civilian lives and to civilian objects.

Presumably the authors intended to say 'the objective to be selected must be the one the attack on which'. While this rule is one to which there should be no serious objection, it should be understood as directed to those who plan or decide upon the attack, and the circumstances it foresees are unlikely to arise except in rare circumstances.

Rule 22: The parties to the conflict must take all feasible precautions to protect the civilian population and civilian objects under their control against the effects of attacks.

Rule 23: Each party to the conflict must, to the extent feasible, avoid locating military objectives within or near densely populated areas.

These rules are drawn from Article 58 of Protocol I, which set forth the precautionary obligations of defenders against attacks. As with previous rules dealing with precautions to be taken by the attacker, I question the desirability of dividing the substance of the Protocol provision, but here there is little difference in the substance, except that Rule 23 has omitted the without prejudice reference in Article 58 to Article 49 of the Fourth Geneva Convention (protection of civilians), an important provision that limits transfers from occupied territory.

Protected Zones

In Protocol I, the situation of non-defended localities (often called 'open cities'), which had its origin in Article 25 of The Hague Regulations of 1907,[13] is spelled out in detail. In summary, such a locality is one near or in the zone where the forces of both sides are in contact and which has no defenders between it and the adverse Party and, consequently, is open for occupation by the adverse Party. Moreover, it must be notified to the adverse Party and, to be effective and avoid abuse of such notification, the following conditions that are prescribed in Protocol I must be fulfilled:

(a) All combatants, as well as mobile weapons and mobile military equipment must have been evacuated;
(b) no hostile use shall be made of fixed military installations or establishments;
(c) no act of hostility shall be committed by the authorities or by the population; and
(d) no activities in support of military operations shall be undertaken.[14]

Clearly these conditions which were essential for the acceptance of the concept of non-defended localities will normally be difficult to secure, and the adverse Party is obligated to respect such a locality only if it, in fact, meets those conditions. How does the ICRC study deal with this? Simply by its Rule 37, which is the following single sentence: 'Directing an attack against a non-defended locality is prohibited.' Even in its explanation of

[13] Regulations Respecting the Laws and Customs of War on Land, annexed to Convention Respecting the Laws and Customs of War on Land, 18 October 1907, 36 Stat 2277, 1 Bevans 631 [hereinafter Hague Regulations].

[14] Protocol I, Art 59, para 2.

this rule, the study makes no reference to the necessary conditions. Only in the relevant documents in Volume II are the conditions established by Protocol I quoted.[15] This appears to be an example of deliberate deception by the authors of the study, who should have recognized that such efforts to avoid conditions they find troubling can only increase scepticism about their conclusions on other topics.

While Rule 36 dealing with demilitarized zones at least indicates that it must be agreed upon between the Parties, Rule 35 is stated simply as follows: 'directing an attack against a zone established to shelter the wounded, the sick and civilians from the effects of hostilities is prohibited'. Only by reading the commentary and then the cited, but not quoted, provisions of the First and Fourth Geneva Conventions of 1949, will the reader learn that such zones must be established by agreement. Thus, the proposed Rule 35 is deceptive, even for international armed conflicts. How the authors can assert that such a rule is applicable also in non-international armed conflicts, in which States have shown themselves most reluctant to conclude agreements with rebels, is very difficult to understand. That difficulty is not overcome, in my opinion, by the references in Volume II to agreements between Yugoslavia and Croatia and to various instances in Vietnam, Cambodia, Cyprus, and Sri Lanka in which the ICRC unilaterally declared and administered as neutralized certain buildings or zones. While it certainly would be desirable from a humanitarian perspective if the ICRC could establish such zones in non-international armed conflict, such desirability and a few welcome instances do not make customary law. In that connection, it should be noted that a majority of States participating in the conference that produced the Geneva Protocols in 1977 insisted upon the inclusion in Protocol II on non-international armed conflicts of the following provision:

Article 3—Non-intervention

1. Nothing in this Protocol shall be invoked for the purpose of affecting the sovereignty of a State or the responsibility of the government, by all legitimate means, to maintain or re-establish law and order in the State or to defend the national unity and territorial integrity of the State.

2. Nothing in this Protocol shall be invoked as a justification for intervening, directly or indirectly, for any reason whatsoever, in the armed conflict or in the internal or external affairs of the High Contracting Party in the territory of which that conflict occurs.

Special Protection for Dams, Dykes, and Nuclear Power Stations

Article 56 of Protocol I establishes a complex and controversial special protection regime for three specified types of facilities containing dangerous

[15] Vol II, 703.

forces—floodwater in the case of dams and dykes and radioactive debris in the case of nuclear power stations. That provision prohibits only attacks of a kind that may cause the release of the dangerous forces and only in circumstances where such release may cause consequent severe losses among the civilian population. The provision applies in addition to the normal protection of civilians afforded by the rule of proportionality, and it also ceases to apply in certain circumstances, as described in its paragraph 2:

Article 56

2. The special protection against attack provided by paragraph 1 shall cease:
   (a) for a dam or a dyke only if it is used for other than its normal function and in regular, significant and direct support of military operations and if such attack is the only feasible way to terminate such support;
   (b) for a nuclear electrical generating station only if it provides electric power in regular, significant and direct support of military operations and if such attack is the only feasible way to terminate such support;
   (c) for other military objectives located at or in the vicinity of these works or installations only if they are used in regular, significant and direct support of military operations and if such attack is the only feasible way to terminate such support.

As the principal drafter of this provision, I believed—and still believe—that it should be generally acceptable, although I recognized that some States might need to make statements of understanding or reservation, with respect to it. In fact, both the United Kingdom and France made statements upon ratification of the Protocol that indicated they would take all necessary precautions to avoid severe collateral civilian losses, but that they could not grant absolute protection to those installations.[16] The United States has used the provision as part of its reasons to reject Protocol I, although I am certain that it could settle for a statement similar to those by the United Kingdom and France.

The ICRC study reduces its proposed customary rule to a simple requirement of 'particular care'.

Rule 42: Particular care must be taken if works and installations containing dangerous forces, namely dams, dykes and nuclear electrical generating stations, and other installations located at or in their vicinity are attacked, in order to avoid the release of dangerous forces and consequent severe losses among the civilian population.

This standard is reasonable and is a formulation I would have been satisfied to use in Protocol I, but it would have been unacceptable then at the conference to a group of States led by Switzerland and the Netherlands. Lest it be thought that the authors of the study were buckling in the face of the reservations of the major Powers, I note that they add in their

[16] See, Vol II, 815.

commentary to Rule 42 an absurd suggestion that Rule 42 should also apply to 'other installations, such as chemical plants and petroleum refineries'.[17]

Protection of the Natural Environment

The ICRC study proposes three rules for the protection of the environment, two of which would go far beyond the relevant provisions of Protocol I. Those provisions, Articles 35(3) and 55, required that care be taken in warfare to protect the natural environment against 'widespread, long-term and severe damage'. That phrase is similar to, but different from the language of the 1976 United Nations Convention on the Prohibition of Military or Any Other Hostile Use of Environmental Modification Techniques (the ENMOD Convention), which referred to environmental modification techniques 'having widespread, long-lasting or severe effects'.[18] By long-lasting, it meant some months or a season.

The negotiating history of Article 55 of Protocol I shows clearly that the three requirements are, as indicated by the connective 'and', cumulative and that long-term meant decades. Such a long duration seemed essential when addressing the possible collateral and unintended effects of modern warfare, rather than, as in the ENMOD Convention, deliberate efforts to modify the environment. Note also that, for the nuclear Powers, it was necessary that these provisions of Articles 35(3) and 55 of Protocol I were clearly new restrictions, so that they would be covered by their subsequent Statements of Understanding that the new rules introduced by the Protocol have no effect on and do not regulate or prohibit the use of nuclear weapons.

The authors of the ICRC study understand the meaning of Articles 35(5) and 55,[19] but they refuse to be limited by it. Recognizing that warfare is inherently bad for the environment, they propose three rules, numbered 43, 44, and 45.

Rule 43: The general principles on the conduct of hostilities apply to the natural environment:

A. No part of the natural environment may be attacked, unless it is a military objective.
B. Destruction of any part of the natural environment is prohibited, unless required by imperative military necessity.
C. Launching an attack against a military objective which may be expected to cause incidental damage to the environment which would be excessive in relation to the concrete and direct military advantage anticipated is prohibited.

[17] Vol I, 141–2.

[18] Convention on the Prohibition of Military or Any Other Hostile Use of Environmental Modification Techniques, Art I, para 1, 10 December 1976, 1108 UNTS 15, reprinted in 116 ILM 88 [hereinafter 1976 ENMOD Convention].

[19] See, Vol I, 157.

This is a wish list that is unnecessary and, to the extent that it is new, has no foundation in existing law. Part A adds nothing to the existing law, as only an object that is a military objective may be made the object of attack, Part B is new, but I think it would be unacceptable to many States because forests, fields, and other land areas, for example, frequently are unavoidably damaged or destroyed as a consequence of combat between armed forces. Such damage to or destruction of a part of the environment, whether foreseeable or not, cannot be expected to be a deciding factor for those who plan or decide on attack. Part C appears to equate the environment to civilians for purposes of proportionality, for which I know of neither a need nor a precedent in existing law.

Rule 44: Methods and means of warfare must be employed with due regard to the protection and preservation of the natural environment. In the conduct of military operations, all feasible precautions must be taken to avoid, and in any event minimise, incidental damage to the environment. Lack of scientific certainty as to the effects on the environment of certain military operations does not absolve a party to the conflict from taking such precautions.

Again, there is little, if any, precedent for this in existing law. Article 35, paragraph 3 and Article 55 of Protocol I serve as evidence of how far this proposed rule is from the maximum that could be accepted in the most recent international humanitarian law treaty. With respect to warfare at sea, the San Remo Manual does indicate that means and methods of warfare should be employed with due regard for the natural environment and that damage to it that is carried out wantonly in disregard of military necessity is prohibited.[20] That is no precedent for the proposed Rule 44 of this study.

Rule 45: The use of methods or means of warfare that are intended, or may be expected to cause widespread, long-term and severe damage to the natural environment is prohibited. Destruction of the natural environment may not be used as a weapon.

This proposed rule seems to be based on both the 1976 ENMOD Convention, and on Articles 35, paragraph 3 and 55 of Protocol I. As such, it would at least have a basis in treaty law. In the Commentary, the authors of the study refer to the United States, the United Kingdom, and France as persistent objectors to the first part of their proposed rule with respect to nuclear weapons. In that connection, I note that the authors of the study appear to believe that other provisions of Protocol I, for example, those on indiscriminate attacks or on proportionality might make the use of nuclear weapons unlawful;[21] but those provisions are also new rules created by Protocol I and, consequently, are covered by the understandings made by the nuclear Powers.

[20] *San Remo Manual on International Law Applicable to Armed Conflicts at Sea* L Doswald-Beck (ed) (1995) Rule 44.

[21] See Vol I, 155.

With respect to conventional weapons, I agree that the proposed Rule 45 may have an adequate basis to be considered customary law, but only if the very high level of damage required by Articles 35, paragraph 3 and 55 of Protocol I is kept in mind.

Specific Methods of Warfare

Part III of the ICRC study comprises a collection of disparate topics that the authors have distilled into 23 rules (numbers 46–69). Included are denial of quarter (Rules 46–48), the destruction or seizure of property (Rules 49–52), starvation of civilians and relief operations (Rules 53–56), deception (Rules 57–65) and communication with an enemy (Rules 66–69).

In general, these rules summarize briefly, but accurately, the relevant treaty provisions, whether from the 1907 Hague Regulations, the 1949 Geneva Conventions, or the 1977 Geneva Protocols. I note with regret that the authors did not include in their proposed rules the substance of Article 41, paragraph 3 of Geneva Protocol I which requires the release of prisoners of war (POWs) captured by long-distance patrols or in other unusual circumstances where it is impossible to detain them. The Commentary accompanying Rule 47[22] indicates that the authors agree that quarter may not be denied even in such unusual circumstances, so I can only assume that the desire for simplicity kept that out of the Rule. The Commentary also includes interesting references to certain ICRC archives that record conversations with representatives of some unidentified opposition groups involved in non-international armed conflicts with respect to their policies and the practical difficulties they face in detaining prisoners even briefly.[23]

Rule 53: The use of starvation of the civilian population as a method of warfare is prohibited.

Rule 54: Attacking, destroying, removing or rendering useless objects indispensable to the survival of the civilian population are prohibited.

The principle stated by Rule 53 was a new principle in 1977 when it was established by Article 54, paragraph 1, of Geneva Protocol I. Its importance is obvious. By contrast, Rule 54, which is based on paragraph 2 of that Article, appears to promise more restraint than it will generally be feasible to show. Article 54 of Protocol I established some complex, but important, new rules prohibiting the destruction or removal of certain objects considered indispensable to the survival of the civilian population

[22] Vol I, 168–9. [23] Vol I, 169 and Vol II, 976–7.

'such as foodstuffs, crops, livestock, drinking water installations and supplies and irrigation works for the specific purpose of denying them for their sustenance value to the civilian population or to the adverse Party . . . '. In addition to requiring that specific purpose, the Article, in its paragraph 3, provided that its prohibitions would not apply to such of those objects as are used by an adverse Party as sustenance solely for its armed forces and 'if not as sustenance, then in direct support of military action'. Rule 54 ignores these limitations, and, by so doing, states a simple, sweeping, and unworkable prohibition. As written, Rule 54 would have been unacceptable in 1977 to the negotiators of Protocol I and, in my judgment, it would be unacceptable to most States today. To give just one example, that rule, unlike Article 54 of Protocol I, would appear to prohibit a military unit from destroying growing crops or an orchard in order to clear a field of fire or to make an approaching enemy visible at a distance.

Rule 55: The parties to the conflict must allow and facilitate rapid and unimpeded passage of humanitarian relief for civilians in need, which is impartial in character and conducted without any adverse distinction, subject to their right of control.

Rule 56: The parties to the conflict must ensure the freedom of movement of authorized humanitarian relief personnel essential to the exercise of their functions. Only in the case of imperative military necessity may their movements be temporarily restricted.

These rules are designed to facilitate relief operations for civilians in need and, as such, are appropriate and important, but, by themselves, they provide a misleading impression that the Party in or through whose territory they operate has no rights with respect to these operations except to restrict temporarily their movements 'in case of imperative military necessity'. A careful examination of the relevant articles from Protocol I reveals that relief actions 'shall be undertaken, subject to the agreement of the Parties concerned in such relief actions'.[24] Moreover, with respect to the duty of a State to permit passage of relief personnel and supplies, that State has the right to 'prescribe the technical arrangements, including search, under which such passage is permitted' and to make such permission conditional on the distribution of assistance being made under the local supervision of a Protecting Power.[25] Also, a Party has the right to bar relief personnel from its territory if they fail to respect its security requirements.[26] A simplified rule that deletes most of the rights of the States involved in relief actions is simply deceptive.

[24] Protocol I, Art 70, para 1. [25] ibid para 3. [26] ibid Art 71, para 4.

Rules 57–65 dealing with ruses, perfidy, the misuse of flags and uniforms and other deceptive practices raise no problems, except that they avoid indicating some of the useful examples of perfidy noted in Article 37 of Protocol I. With respect to the controversial question of the use of the uniforms of an enemy, the Commentary of the ICRC study states the following safe conclusion: 'It cannot be concluded that the wearing of enemy uniforms outside combat would be improper.'[27]

Rules 66–69 dealing with communications by military commanders with an enemy and the rights and duties of 'parlementaires' are careful restatements of accepted customary law.

Weapons

Part IV of the ICRC study (Rules 70–86) reflects the determination of the ICRC to inject itself, whenever possible, into a rapidly developing field of international law in which it had little, if any, involvement prior to the conclusion of Protocol I in 1977. In that Protocol, provisions dealing specifically with weapons were limited to two: the repetition in Article 35 of the superfluous injury or unnecessary suffering standard of the St Petersburg Declaration and the new requirement in Article 36 that States have an obligation to determine whether the employment of any new weapons they acquire would be unlawful in some or all circumstances. The conference that produced Geneva Protocols I and II established an ad hoc committee for the discussion of issues relating to weapons which, in effect, served as a preparatory body to the subsequent United Nations conferences that produced the 1980 Convention on Prohibitions or Restrictions on the Use of Certain Conventional Weapons Which May be Deemed to be Excessively Injurious or to Have Indiscriminate Effects.[28]

The 1980 Conventional Weapons Convention included three Protocols: Protocol I on fragments not detectable by x-ray; Protocol II on mines, booby traps and other devices; and Protocol III on incendiary weapons. A new Protocol IV on blinding laser weapons was concluded in 1995,[29] and an amended Protocol II was concluded in 1996.[30] In addition, a Chemical Weapons Convention was concluded in 1993,[31] and the

[27] Vol I, 216.

[28] UN Doc A/CONF.95/15, Apps A–D (1980), opened for signature 10 April 1981, 1342 UNTS 137, reprinted in 19 ILM 1524 (1980) [hereinafter Conventional Weapons Convention].

[29] Additional Protocol on Blinding Laser Weapons (Protocol IV) to the Convention on Prohibitions or Restrictions on the Use of Certain Conventional Weapons Which May be Deemed to be Excessively Injurious or to Have Indiscriminate Effects, opened for signature 12 October. 1995, UN Doc CCW/CONF.I/7 (1995).

[30] See n 1 above.

[31] Protocol on Prohibitions or Restrictions on the Use of Mines, Booby-Traps and Other Devices (Protocol II) as Amended, adopted 3 May 1996, UN Doc CCW/CONF.1/14 (1996), 1342 UNTS 168, reprinted in 35 ILM 1206 [hereinafter Chemical Weapons Convention].

Ottawa Convention on Landmines was concluded in 1997.[32] While the ICRC did not have a role in the drafting and negotiation of these treaties that was as central as its role with the Geneva Conventions and Protocols, its interest in the prohibition and restriction of the use of weapons is understandable, even though its views are frequently at odds with those of many governments.

The ICRC study restates the superfluous injury or unnecessary suffering standard in its Rule 70, prohibits the use of weapons which are by nature indiscriminate in Rule 71, prohibits the use of poison or poisoned weapons in Rule 73, and chemical weapons in Rule 74. These prohibitions are so well established that these rules should not result in controversy. Wisely, the authors offer no rule dealing with nuclear weapons, deferring in that regard to the International Court of Justice, as its 1996 Advisory Opinion on that subject remains the definitive, if unsatisfactory, exposition of the law.

Rule 75 prohibits the use of riot-control agents as a method of warfare, which is consistent with the terms of the Chemical Weapons Convention. In its commentary[33] the study takes note of the fact that the United States, which is a Party to that Convention, maintains that some limited uses of riot-control agents are still permissible in warfare, as they would not constitute a method of warfare. The authors express no views on that issue.

Rule 76: The use of herbicides as a method of warfare is prohibited if they:

(a) are of a nature to be prohibited chemical weapons;
(b) are of a nature to be prohibited biological weapons;
(c) are aimed at vegetation that is not a military objective;
(d) would cause incidental loss of civilian life, injury to civilians, damage to civilian objects, or a combination thereof, which may be expected to be excessive in relation to the concrete and direct military advantage anticipated; or
(e) would cause widespread, long-term and severe damage to the natural environment.

While this rule appears to involve new restrictions by prohibiting the use of herbicides as a method of warfare, even when their use would not be prohibited as either a chemical or a biological weapon, in fact, it permits the use of non-poisonous herbicides in warfare. Instead of the words 'would cause' in points (d) and (e), it would be preferable for the authors to use the words used in Articles 51 and 57 of Protocol I, 'may be expected to cause', as foreseeability is important. The concern about

[32] See n 4 above. [33] Vol I, 264.

wartime use of herbicides stems from the widespread use of herbicides by the United States in South Vietnam to defoliate large areas so that enemy soldiers in those areas would be more visible. That use was made with the consent of the sovereign Government of the areas involved, but one of the principal herbicides used was found to cause serious health problems for persons, including United States soldiers, who were in or who went into those areas.

Rule 77: The use of bullets which expand or flatten easily in the human body is prohibited.

The 'dum dum' bullet has been prohibited for use in warfare since 1899,[34] and its use has recently been included as a crime in the Statute of the International Criminal Court.[35] Consequently, the continued appearance here of Rule 77 is no surprise. Nevertheless, a careful reading of the supporting material in Volume II[36] raises some doubt about its long-term viability, particularly in non-international armed conflicts. Certainly, domestic police forces are increasingly using ammunition that, like the dum dum bullet, expands in the body. This increased use has a double purpose, both to protect the police by incapacitating armed criminals instantly and to protect innocent bystanders from bullets that miss and ricochet or that pass through the body of the criminal. Given the almost inevitable involvement of law enforcement agencies in non-international armed conflicts and in the potential terrorist aspects of some international armed conflicts, one wonders how this inconsistency will be resolved. The Commentary to the ICRC study offers no answers.

Rules 81–83 relate to the use of landmines. More than 140 States have ratified the Ottawa Convention of 1997 which completely prohibits the use of landmines, but a number of important States[37] have made it clear that they are not yet ready to accept that prohibition, so the Ottawa Convention cannot be considered to embody customary law. Given that awkward situation, the authors have struck a credible compromise by proposing rules that require any user of landmines to take care to minimize their indiscriminate effects, to record their placement as far as possible, and, at the end of hostilities, to remove or neutralize them or 'facilitate' their removal.

[34] See The Final Act of the Peace Conference of 1899, 29 July 1899, 2 JB Scott, *The Hague Peace Conferences 1899 and 1907* (1909) 61 [hereinafter 1899 Final Act], reprinted in D Schindler and J Toman (eds), *The Law Of Armed Conflicts* (3rd revised edn, 1988) 49.

[35] Rome Statute of the International Criminal Court, 17 July 1998, at Art 8(2)(b)(xix), 2187 UNTS 3, reprinted in 1 *United Nations Diplomatic Conference Of Plenipotentiaries On The Establishment Of An International Criminal Court, Official Records*, UN Doc A/CONF.183/13 (Vol I) (2002).

[36] Vol II, 1771–86.

[37] The Commentary names China, Finland, India, South Korea, Pakistan, Russia, and the US. Vol I, 282.

Incendiary weapons presented the authors of the study with serious problems. Protocol III to the 1980 Conventional Weapons Convention was concerned exclusively with protecting civilians and civilian objects from incendiary munitions, and the authors drew from that Protocol their proposed Rule 84 requiring care in the use of incendiary weapons to prevent or, in any event, to minimize injury to civilians.[38] However, the authors were unwilling to stop there, so they also proposed the following new Rule:

Rule 85: The anti-personnel use of incendiary weapons is prohibited, unless it is not feasible to use a less harmful weapon to render a person *hors de combat*.

What, one may ask, is meant by 'less harmful'? Is it less painful? Or is it less long-lasting? The Commentary is not explicit about that, but it seems that the authors believe that incendiary weapons, particularly air-delivered napalm and ground-delivered flame throwers, cause unnecessary suffering to the affected combatants since they could have been killed or wounded by other weapons. That may well sometimes be true, but it cannot always be true. In any event, this proposed rule has no treaty precedent and can only be seen as an effort to propose a new rule of law. The only bases the authors suggest for their proposition that it is now customary law are the past comments by a number of States that indicated they believed such weapons caused unnecessary suffering and by the authors' assertion that there have been few reports of the use of napalm since 1980. To this reviewer, Rule 85 is not soundly based in the practice of States and, even as a proposal, it is flawed. Combatants do not generally have much, if any, choice of weapons; they have to use what they have at hand. Moreover, it would seem unrealistic in the extreme to ask them to decide in the midst of combat whether it is feasible to use a 'less harmful' weapon than an incendiary weapon. Either the anti-personnel use of napalm and flame throwers should be prohibited by treaty, or the legitimacy of such use should be acknowledged.

Rule 86: The use of laser weapons that are specifically designed, as their sole combat function or as one of their combat functions, to cause permanent blindness to unenhanced vision is prohibited.

Although this rule of law was adopted only in 1995, as Protocol IV to the 1980 Conventional Weapons Convention, the authors propose it as a rule of customary law. They make convincing arguments that the acceptances of it by ratification of the treaty or by public statements of

[38] Convention on Prohibitions or Restrictions on the use of Certain Conventional Weapons which May be Deemed to be Excessively Injurious or to have Indiscriminate Effects, Oct 10, 1980, Protocol on Prohibitions or Restrictions on the Use of Incendiary Weapons (Protocol III), reprinted in 19 ILM 1523, 1534 (1980).

official policy by all States that have developed the weapon justify that conclusion. If it is possible to outlaw a weapon as a matter of customary international law before such a weapon has ever been used in combat, this is the first example.

Remaining Rules

The second half of this study is relatively non-controversial, as it deals almost entirely with issues that have been resolved for some time. In fact, most of the substance of Rules 87–161 is found in the four Geneva Conventions of 1949. Part V covers the treatment of civilians in the power of a Party to the conflict and persons *hors de combat*, and Part VI deals with implementation of international humanitarian law. All of these matters are important, but they are mostly well settled. The proposed rules are carefully drafted and represent a concise statement of the relevant law. Simply reading these rules and the Commentary in Volume I would provide an excellent education in those parts of international humanitarian law.

Of all this material, I shall offer comments on only three points that relate to Protocol I. First, Rule 106 addresses the right of combatants to POW status upon capture.

Rule 106: Combatants must distinguish themselves from the civilian population while they are engaged in an attack or in a military operation preparatory to an attack. If they fail to do so, they do not have the right to prisoner-of-war status.

I admire both the clarity and brevity of this rule. Had it been negotiable in Geneva from 1974 to 1977, I would have loved to use it as paragraph 3 of Article 44 of Protocol I, for it truly states the essential rule of distinction, which is important for the protection of civilians. However, as a Rapporteur who needed a provision that could command majority support in the conference, I had to accept the reality at that time that a majority of States represented in the conference was insistent on something more. Some of those States had fresh memories of resistance efforts while they had been occupied during the Second World War, and many others had subsequently achieved their independence from colonial Powers by means that included armed conflict by liberation movements or were supporters of armed resistance groups in Palestine. Those experiences led almost all of those States to insist that such underground combatants must be entitled to POW treatment upon capture, even though they had been compelled to act clandestinely. Consequently, I was compelled to add to the provision an exception for such combatants. I made it as narrow as possible by limiting the right to POW status to those who carried their arms openly during each military engagement and during such time as they were visible to the adversary while they were deploying in preparation for launching an attack.

It will be interesting to see whether the passage of time since the 1970s will permit the States that then insisted on that exception to accept the authors' proposed Rule 106. Memories fade over time, but the continued Arab-Israeli conflict may make it difficult for many of those States to agree now to that which they rejected then.

Second, proposed Rule 117 obligates each Party to a conflict to take all feasible measures to account for persons, both civilians and military, who are missing as a result of the conflict. While the proposed rule lacks the detail of Article 33 of Protocol I, it states at least the core of that important addition to the law. Moreover, the task of tracing missing persons is one for which the ICRC has much experience and is one where it can assist the Parties.

Third, Rules 146 and 147 prohibit reprisals against persons and objects protected by the Geneva Conventions or by the Hague Convention on the Protection of Cultural Property.[39] It is true that the various treaties defining international humanitarian law consistently prohibit reprisals. Protocol I virtually closed the door on belligerent reprisals, except for reprisals against combatants, for example by resort to illegal weapons, but, in defining customary law, one must remember that reservations may be made to that Protocol, as well as to the 1949 Geneva Conventions. I know that several of my colleagues on the United States delegation to the conference that adopted Protocol I felt that the United States would want to reserve at least a limited right of reprisal in the event of attacks on our civilians, as there would not be any other way to apply real pressure for compliance with the law. In that connection, the United Kingdom has made such a reservation.[40] While the authors of this study might wish that such reservations to the prohibition of reprisals were prohibited, they must recognize that, as the treaties do not prohibit reservations, they can only be discouraged.

In conclusion, I would not want my criticisms of particular proposed rules in this monumental work to obscure the major contributions it makes to the available knowledge of the present state of international humanitarian law. Most of the authors' conclusions are clearly correct, and a great many others are reasonable proposals to be considered in the future development of the law. Their principal mistake is to claim customary law status for some simplified rules that would not have been accepted in the negotiation of Protocol I and would not be accepted today by many States. Without question, the vast collection of backup

[39] 1954 Hague Convention for the Protection of Cultural Property in the Event of Armed Conflict, 14 May 1954, 249 UNTS 240.

[40] Vol II, 3406.

material in Volume II is irreplaceable and should be in the collection of every library concerned with law and every scholar of international humanitarian law.

International humanitarian law is almost completely codified. If a few important States that have not yet become Parties to the Geneva Protocols would do so, even with reservations and statements of understanding, the apparent need to define customary international humanitarian law would dissipate. In any event, this truly monumental study should be a catalyst for further efforts to identify both feasible improvements in the body of that law and in the level of compliance with it.

CUSTOMARY INTERNATIONAL HUMANITARIAN LAW—A REJOINDER TO JUDGE ALDRICH*

By JEAN-MARIE HENCKAERTS**

Judge George Aldrich is certainly one of the most significant observers of the development of international humanitarian law in our time. His note on the study on customary international humanitarian law in this volume is therefore of great interest. As one of the co-authors of the study, I have been given an opportunity to comment on his note.

THE REASONS FOR CARRYING OUT THE STUDY

The study was first proposed by the open-ended Intergovernmental Group of Experts for the Protection of War Victims in January 1995 and formally mandated by the 26th International Conference of the Red Cross and Red Crescent in December of the same year. It is important to note that all States have a vote at the International Conferences of the Red Cross and Red Crescent, which are held, in principle, every four years. The study was therefore carried out at the request of States. The purpose was for the ICRC to assist States in the arduous and time-consuming task of collecting and assessing practice with a view to determining the content of customary international humanitarian law.

The study was commissioned against the background of the massive violations of international humanitarian law in the armed conflicts in the former Yugoslavia and Rwanda, both of which had, at the time, ratified the Additional Protocols. Then as now, 8 out of 10 armed conflicts are non-international and the regulation provided for in Additional Protocol II is insufficient. In particular, key aspects of the law on the conduct of hostilities are missing from the Protocol.

This problem is exacerbated in armed conflicts in which Additional Protocol II is not applicable because the State concerned has not ratified it, such as in Sudan, Sri Lanka, or Nepal. In the latter conflicts, common Article 3 may be the only applicable treaty provision. The ICRC's main interest, therefore, was precisely in seeing whether customary international law provides a more detailed framework for non-international armed conflicts. In fact, the ICRC preferred to be mandated to prepare a report on non-international armed conflicts only but that was unacceptable to some States at the International Conference of the Red Cross and

** Legal Adviser, Legal Division, International Committee of the Red Cross, Geneva. The views expressed here are personal and are not necessarily those of the ICRC.

Red Crescent and so the organization was asked to look at both types of armed conflict.

It is true that several important States are not party to Additional Protocol I, but in case of international armed conflicts we can rely on the vast regulation of the universally ratified Geneva Conventions, the customary principles of the Hague Regulations and the many accepted customary rules enshrined in Protocol I, such as the principles of distinction and proportionality, the prohibition of indiscriminate attacks and the obligation to take precautions in attack. The clarification of the customary status of the provisions of Additional Protocol I was therefore a less pressing need than the clarification of the customary rules applicable in non-international armed conflicts.

The Assessment of Customary International Law

The ICRC took the mandate for the study very seriously and invested a considerable amount of time and energy to conduct this exercise in a scientific manner. The resulting 161 rules are gleaned from the collected practice which can be found in Volume II. The rules were all distilled from the collected practice and drafted on that basis. In this respect the process of assessing customary international law is quite different from a study of the negotiating history of a treaty. It may be true that custom and treaty law have a natural tendency to converge to some extent as custom gets codified in treaty form and new treaty rules may become customary over time. But the two sources of international law obviously still remain distinct. Therefore, it is not necessary to have a prior treaty rule in order to have a customary rule, nor is it necessarily the case that what could not be agreed upon in a treaty may not have become customary since then.

The study is not a handbook on international humanitarian law. It provides a photograph of practice without commenting on it. So where conflicting practices exist, the study simply describes them. And where practice has not clarified an issue, the study has not sought to suggest answers. It has stayed true to its aim of assessing customary international law and, therefore, of describing practice.

The Principle of Distinction

The formulation of 'attacks directed against civilians'—rather than 'making civilians the object of attack'—was chosen following the final experts' consultations to indicate more clearly than the language of Additional Protocol I that the prohibition concerns attacks that intentionally target civilians and does not cover the incidental effects of attacks directed against military objectives. The formulation chosen is also used in the

Statute of the International Criminal Court, and the Elements of Crimes make clear that this formulation is equivalent to 'making civilians the objects of attack'.[1]

The phrase in Rules 6 and 10 that civilians and civilian objects respectively are 'protected against attack' was used since the very first drafts and did not elicit any comment from the experts consulted. This refers to protection against direct attack and does not cover incidental loss of civilian life, injury to civilians, or damage to civilian objects. This is stated in the Commentary on the interpretation of the principle of distinction:

> Several States have stressed that the rule contained in Article 52(2) of Additional Protocol I, which provides that 'attacks shall be limited strictly to military objectives', only prohibits direct attacks against civilian objects and does not deal with the question of incidental damage resulting from attacks directed against military objectives.[2] The purpose of these statements is to emphasise that an attack which affects civilian objects is not unlawful as long as it is directed against a military objective and the incidental damage to civilian objects is not excessive. This consideration is taken into account in the formulation of the current rule by the use of the words 'attacks *directed* against'. The same consideration applies *mutatis mutandis* to Rule 1.'[3]

Clarification Provided by the Commentary

This brings me to a general point on the value of the Commentary. The study catalogues rules of customary international humanitarian law. As such, only the black letter rules are identified as part of customary international law, and not the commentaries to the rules. The commentaries may, however, contain useful clarifications with respect to the application of the black letter rules and this is sometimes overlooked by commentators.

For example, the Commentary to Rule 54 on attacks against objects indispensable to civilian survival indicates that there are exceptions to this rule.[4] The rule should be examined in that light.[5] Similarly, the

[1] See the Elements of Crimes for Art 8(2)(b)(i) and (e)(i). Element 2 provides that 'the object of the attack was a civilian population as such or individual civilians not taking direct part in hostilities'.

[2] See the reservations and declarations made upon ratification of the Additional Protocols and other statements by Australia (cited in J-M Henckaerts and L Doswald-Beck (eds), *Customary International Humanitarian Law* (2005) vol II, ch 2, § 51), Canada (ibid §§ 52 and 71), France (ibid § 53), Federal Republic of Germany (ibid § 75), Italy (ibid § 54), the Netherlands (ibid § 80), New Zealand (ibid § 55), UK (ibid §§ 56 and 86) and US (ibid § 92).

[3] See J-M Henckaerts and L Doswald-Beck (eds), *Customary International Humanitarian Law* (2005) vol I, 29.

[4] ibid 192–3.

[5] Hence, the observation made by the Eritrea-Ethiopia Claims Commission that the study concludes that a broader prohibition than the one stated in Art 54(2) of Additional Protocol I has become customary law is based on a misreading of the study. See Eritrea-Ethiopia Claims Commission, Partial Award, *Western Front, Aerial Bombardment and Related Claims, Eritrea's Claims* 1, 3, 5, 9–13, 14, 21, 25, and 26, between the State of Eritrea and the Federal Democratic Republic of Eritrea, The Hague, 19 December 2005, 30, n 23. The authors of the study did not intend Rule 54 to go

commentary to Rule 56 on access for humanitarian aid discusses the requirement of consent.[6] A final example are Rules 57–65 on deception. The examples of perfidy in Article 37 of Additional Protocol I are all discussed in the Commentary to Rule 65.[7]

Protected Zones

When the formulation of Rule 35 on safety zones was discussed, we came to the conclusion that, in general, such zones need not be established by agreement in order to benefit from protection. This is because the wounded and sick are *hors de combat* and, as such, in principle protected against attack. An agreement would of course be a *sufficient* condition for a zone to benefit from protection, but it is not a *necessary* condition. This conclusion is therefore not in conflict with the fact that the Geneva Conventions provide a model agreement for hospital and safety zones. Also, the conditions provided for in the model agreement are generally comprised within other rules on the conduct of hostilities (in particular rules concerning the loss of protection for combatants *hors de combat*, loss of protection for civilians, and the definition of military objectives). It may be noted that in the consultations no expert commented on this issue.

The commentaries to these rules also provide useful indications as to their setting up. For example, the conditions for declaring a non-defended locality are part of its definition and are discussed in that context in the Commentary.

Works and Installations Containing Dangerous Forces

It is true that installations other than dams, dykes, and nuclear electrical generating stations, in particular chemical plants and petroleum refineries, may constitute important military objectives. But even so, when they are attacked all feasible precautions must be taken to avoid, and in any event to minimize, incidental loss of civilian life, injury to civilians, and damage to civilian objects. In addition, such losses, injury and damage must not be excessive in relation to the concrete and direct military advantage anticipated for the attack. It seems reasonable, therefore, to suggest that Rule 42 requiring particular care in attacking works and installations

beyond the content of Art 54(2) of Additional Protocol I, for State practice would not support such a conclusion. As a result, the study actually confirms the finding of the Commission that Art 54(2) of Additional Protocol I 'may reasonably be considered to have come to reflect customary international humanitarian law'. See Henckaerts and Doswald-Beck (n 3 above) 30.

[6] ibid 196–7. [7] ibid 224.

containing dangerous forces *should* also apply to chemical plants and petroleum refineries, whereby the dangerous forces could be chemical substances that can pollute soil and water and cause severe losses or injuries among the civilian population and damage to civilian objects.

Protection of the Environment

While the negotiating history of the Additional Protocols is certainly relevant in assessing this part of the law, it should be borne in mind that, in general, the law and practice have considerably evolved since 1977. The protection of the environment has become a major international concern, including during armed conflict. This is exemplified, for example, by the intense debate about the environmental damage caused by Iraq's action in Kuwait during the first Gulf War and, more recently, by NATO's attacks on chemical plants in Serbia.

Rules 43 and 44 recognize that, in principle, the natural environment is a civilian object and, as such, enjoys the protection enshrined in the rules on the conduct of hostilities. Rule 43 B, for example, is an application of the old Hague principle according to which the property of an adversary may not be destroyed unless required by imperative military necessity. That this principle applies to the environment is borne out by the evidence collected in Volume II and summarized in the Commentary to the rule in Volume I. This includes the advisory opinion of the International Court of Justice on the legality of nuclear weapons and the opinion of the committee established by the Office of the Prosecutor of the ICTY to review the NATO bombing campaign against the Federal Republic of Yugoslavia. It also includes a variety of State practice, including from the United States.[8] This rule prohibits unnecessary and wanton destruction but would not preclude the destruction of forests, fields, and other areas of land when required by imperative military necessity.

Rule 43 C is an application of the principle of proportionality to the natural environment and exemplifies the development in the law and practice alluded to above. Again, the sources on which this rule is based are set forth in Volume II and are summarized in the Commentary to the rule in Volume I. This includes the advisory opinion of the International Court of Justice on the legality of nuclear weapons, as well as a NATO statement concerning its bombing campaign against the Federal Republic of Yugoslavia and the opinion of the committee established by the Office of the Prosecutor of the ICTY to review the NATO bombing campaign.

[8] See eg US, *Naval Handbook* (1995) § 8.1.3; US, Department of Defense, Final Report to Congress on the Conduct of the Persian Gulf War, Appendix O, The Role of the Law of War, 10 April (1992) 31 ILM 636–7; US, Department of Defense, Report to Congress on International Policies and Procedures Regarding the Protection of the Natural and Cultural Resources During Times of War, 19 January 1993, 202–4.

Rule 44 on due regard for the environment also exemplifies the development in the law and practice since 1977. The practice on which this rule is based is contained in Volume II and is summarized in the Commentary to the rule in Volume I. The first sentence of the rule is supported, among others, by military manuals, including from the United States, and by State submissions to the International Court of Justice in the *Nuclear Weapons* case.[9] The second sentence, requiring precautionary measures in attack to spare the environment, is also supported by military manuals and other sources.[10]

Both Rules 43 and 44 are further supported by the Guidelines on the Protection of the Environment in Times of Armed Conflict which the ICRC prepared, with the assistance of a group of experts, in the wake of the first Gulf War and submitted to the UN General Assembly.[11] The UN General Assembly in turn invited all States to 'disseminate widely' the Guidelines.[12] The Guidelines are based on the consideration that, in addition to the high-threshold prohibition of widespread, long-term, and severe damage to the environment contained in Additional Protocol I, the general rules and principles on the conduct of hostilities, in particular distinction, proportionality, and precautions, also offer protection to the environment. These rules reflect this consideration and do not go beyond existing law.

Weapons

The history of the ICRC's involvement with this issue is far longer than indicated in the note and can in fact be traced back to the final paragraph of Henry Dunant's 'A Memory of Solferino'. Another important step includes, for example, the Appeal against poison gas issued by the ICRC in 1918. Later, in 1956, following expert consultations, the ICRC prepared Draft Rules for the Limitation of the Dangers Incurred by the Civilian Population in Time of War (Articles 14 and 15 of which deal with weapons) which were submitted to the XIXth International Conference of the Red Cross in New Delhi in 1957. Then, from 1971 onwards, the ICRC discussed weapons

[9] See eg Australia, *Defence Force Manual* (1994) § 545; South Korea, *Operational Law Manual* (1996) 129; US, *Naval Handbook* (1995) § 8.1.3 and the oral pleadings of or the written statements submitted to the ICJ in the *Nuclear Weapons* case by Egypt (cited in *Customary International Humanitarian Law* (n 2 above) vol II, ch 14, § 88), Iran (ibid § 93), Malaysia (ibid § 97), Qatar (ibid § 102) and Solomon Islands (ibid § 103) and the written statements submitted in the *Nuclear Weapons (WHO)* case by Costa Rica (ibid § 87), Mexico (ibid § 98) and Sri Lanka (ibid § 104).

[10] See US, *Naval Handbook* (1995) § 8.1.3 and the materials summarized in *Customary International Humanitarian Law* (n 3 above) vol I, 149–50.

[11] Revised Guidelines for Military Manuals and Instructions on the Protection of the Environment in Times of Armed Conflict, prepared by the ICRC and presented to the UN Secretary-General, annexed to Report of the Secretary-General on the United Nations Decade of International Law, UN Doc A/49/323, 19 August 1994, 49–53.

[12] UN General Assembly, Res 49/50, 9 December 1994, § 11.

issues in expert consultations.[13] On the basis of these consultations, the ICRC organized the Lucerne (1974) and Lugano (1976) expert meetings which ultimately led to the adoption in 1980 of the Convention on Certain Conventional Weapons (CCW). This involvement has continued to this day with initiatives, in particular, on anti-personnel landmines, blinding laser weapons, and explosive remnants of war which resulted in the adoption of Amended Protocol II, Protocol IV, and Protocol V to the CCW, respectively. The ICRC was also deeply involved in the negotiation of these Protocols, as well as in the negotiation of the Ottawa Convention Banning Anti-Personnel Landmines. The ICRC's contributions to the CCW meetings and those under the Ottawa Convention have been specifically encouraged and welcomed in various resolutions of the UN General Assembly and in final documents of Review Conferences of these treaties.

Concerning Rule 85 on the anti-personnel use of incendiaries, most of the considerations in the note on this rule are correct. It is true that combatants do not generally have much, if any, choice of weapons. But this is taken into account by the use of the words 'unless it is not feasible'. The conclusion that 'either anti-personnel use of napalm and flame throwers should be prohibited by treaty, or the legitimacy of such use should be acknowledged', is also addressed in the rule, ie the rule acknowledges the legitimacy of such use, subject to the general principle prohibiting means and methods of warfare which are of a nature to cause superfluous injury or unnecessary suffering (which applies to the use of any weapon). This rule is merely a specific application of that general principle. That this principle applies to incendiaries is recognized, among others, in a number of military manuals, including most recently in the 2004 UK *Manual of the Law of Armed Conflict*.[14]

Concerning Rule 77 on expanding bullets, the note remarks that the study offers no answers as to the possible conflict between the prohibition to use such bullets in armed conflict and the fact that their use by law enforcement officials outside armed conflict is not prohibited. This is a clear example of the nature of the study. It is not a handbook; it provides a description of current practice. That description can only be as good as the practice upon which it is based. It cannot provide answers to questions that have not yet been resolved in practice.

Combatants and Prisoner-of-War Status

Rule 106 only states a general principle but does not indicate the precise manner in which a combatant has to distinguish him- or herself. Clearly,

[13] See eg ICRC report on 'Weapons that may cause Unnecessary Suffering or Have Indiscriminate Effects, Report on the Work of Experts', Geneva, 1973.

[14] See eg Canada, *LOAC Manual* (1999) 5–4, § 35; New Zealand, *Military Manual* (1992) §§ 513(7) and 620(7); UK, *Military Manual* (1958) § 110 n 1; UK, Ministry of Defence, *The Manual of the Law of Armed Conflict* (Oxford University Press, 2004), § 6.12.1; US, *Field Manual* (1956) § 36 and US, *Air Force Pamphlet* (1976) § 6–6(c).

the conditions contained in Article 4 of the Third Geneva Convention—carrying arms openly and wearing a fixed distinctive sign recognizable at a distance—would be sufficient. Whether the limited exception contained in Article 44(3), second sentence, of Additional Protocol I is also customary is discussed in detail in the Commentary to Rule 106 and the Commentary is inconclusive on this point. However, it must not be forgotten that Article 44 is still binding law for all 164 States that have ratified Additional Protocol I, even though customary law may not be as clear on this point because the exception for underground combatants has not commanded the required uniformity of practice.

Conclusion

These brief comments are meant to underline what our study is—a report published at the request of States—and, importantly, what it is not—a handbook. The study bears witness to the continuing development of practice and, hence, of customary international law. It is important that the rules be examined in the light of the clarifications provided for in their commentaries.

The study has been nearly 10 years in the making and more than 150 governmental and academic experts from all corners of the world contributed to the research and consultations. We are grateful therefore that Judge Aldrich notes that most of the study's conclusions are 'clearly correct'.

REVIEWS OF BOOKS

The Impact of International Law on International Cooperation. Edited by E BENVENISTI and M HIRSCH. Cambridge: Cambridge University Press, 2004. 316pp £55.

There is a greater convergence today of the research agendas of international relations and international law, with a process of bridge-building occurring between the two disciplines. This edited book, which arose out of a conference in 2001, seeks to 'examine in what ways, if at all, international norms and institutions shape the attitude of states towards international cooperation' (5), with the presumption that 'the disciplines of IL and IR are inexorably interlinked' (1). The fourteen contributors include some of the most well-known writers on the linkages between international law and international relations.

Anne-Marie Slaughter's chapter begins the substantive part of the book. She provides a valuable summary of the main political science/international relations theories. She clarifies why these theories and approaches are important for international lawyers to understand, as she notes that these 'differing analyses will in turn suggest different political and legal strategies as to how to resolve those problems [eg armed conflict] in the service of the posited affirmative goals' (18). In applying this, she analyses, for example, soft law, power, domestic politics, and regime design, as needing to be looked at differently by an international lawyer once they have knowledge of international relations. To some extent these examples are developed in the chapter by Kenneth Abbott and Duncan Snidal, who focus on the legalization of cooperation, such as through soft law, and the chapter by Helen Miller, Peter Rosendorff, and Edward Mansfield, in their application to international trade. The final two chapters, by Petros Mavroidis and Robert Howse, examine closely the issues of trade and human rights/labour standards within international and regional trade agreements, with strong defences being provided of the international trade agreements. All these chapters demonstrate a range of issues, not least that domestic politics directly affects the agreements entered into and the legally binding nature of those agreements (including the use of 'escape clauses'), as 'international cooperation may only be feasible if it solves domestic political problems for leaders' (243). Unfortunately, there seems to be a lack of engagement in these chapters with the critiques by a range of international legal scholars about the international agreements on which these contributors rely, including, for example, that the signing or ratification of an international agreement can be deliberately used by political leaders to ensure that no compliance or effective action on the issue is taken on the domestic scene.

There is a range of contributors who consider the issue of enforcement of international law through the notion of compliance. This is a wise approach, as enforcement can too often be seen as solely about sanctions, imprisonment, or other domestic criminal law actions. Edith Brown Weiss provides a careful and coherent argument about the various compliance strategies in different areas of international law. She sees the three key strategies as being transparency (eg reporting), positive incentives (eg technical assistance) as well as coercive (eg penalties), with the former two becoming more used over time. Others who examine compliance issues are Moshe Hirsch, in terms of globalization, George Downs and Michael Jones, concerning States' incentives to comply to protect their multiple reputations, and Arie Kacowicz, in dealing with Latin American territorial arbitrations. Taking international arbitrations one step further, Eyal Benvenisti examines the important role of international arbitrators, judges, and other adjudicators in developing customary international law as a method of international cooperation. He shows that these adjudicators, and the International Court of Justice in particular, have the power and authority to create (indeed 'invent' (86)) customary international law and thereby aid efficiency and cooperation in the allocation of a range of economic and other resources.

This is an excellent collection of writers who clarify the necessities of engaging in the linkages between international law and international relations. One particularly refreshing aspect is that there is no uniform adoption of a State-based approach to the international system, as such an approach implies that the only actions that matter for international cooperation are those of States. Instead, a number of the contributors rightly acknowledge that the roles of non-State actors are a vital part of international cooperation. However, a disappointing aspect of this book is that it seems to concentrate primarily on the assistance that an understanding of international relations would give to international lawyers. There is insufficient analysis as to how an understanding of international law would benefit international relations scholars. One consequence of this limited approach is that the concepts of international law that are offered here are primarily of the (dominant) liberal positivist approach. There is a neglect of much of the considerable debate within international legal theory as to the nature of international law and the challenges this makes to understanding international relations.

This edited book is a valuable addition to the process of bridge-building occurring between the research agendas of international relations and international law. It offers a perspective from those who are able to understand both sides of the bridge and who seek to obtain a better view from that bridge. The view provided here, though, is slightly one-eyed as it tends to focus more on the need for international lawyers to look over the edges of the bridge than for international relations scholars to do so.

Robert McCorquodale

Enforcing International Law Norms against Terrorism. Edited by A Bianchi. Oxford and Portland, Oregon: Hart Publishing, 2004. xxii + 549 pp £60.

As often affirmed in doctrine, terrorism impacts on the content and scope of a number of legal categories in international law. The need to prevent terrorist attacks, respond to them and hold the perpetrators accountable raises serious questions in several fields, above all in terms of the law related to the use of force, international human rights, humanitarian law, international criminal law and the law of international organizations. This explains the development of the research project which culminated with the publication of this collection of contributions edited by Bianchi, whose foreword explains that the foundations of that project were laid in the aftermath of the September 11 attacks. In this book, a number of specialists, some of them known as leaders in the relevant fields, such as Abi-Saab, Cassese, Condorelli, Dupuy, and Reinisch, attempt to resolve the pertinent issues related to the legal framework of the legal response to terrorism by individual States and international organizations.

Several essays deal with the definition of terrorism which has proved a very puzzling doctrinal and practical issue in the last few decades. Dupuy considers a definition of terrorism as an internationally wrongful act, with requisite consequences in the law of State responsibility (4–16). Cassese points to the process of evolution of the notion of terrorism since the inter-war period up to the present times. He also examines the concept of terrorism in the context of international criminal law and whether and in which circumstances can the acts of terrorism amount to war crimes and crimes against humanity (214–24). Robert Kolb's extensive essay on the exercise of criminal jurisdiction over international terrorists is also very useful because it examines systematically a number of jurisdictional titles that can apply to the prosecution of suspected international terrorists (227–81).

A special, extensive and thought-provoking emphasis is laid on the responses to terrorism under the law of the use of force. Several contributors discuss forcible responses to terrorism in terms of the inherent right of States to self-defence. Abi-Saab considers that forcible responses to terrorism are justifiable only if they are in compliance with the requirements for the exercise of the right to self-defence, including the requirement for an armed attack (xvii–xviii). Dupuy shares the view that the claims of certain States to expand the scope of the right to self-defence so as to encompass therein forcible actions not preceded by an armed attack has no basis in international law and such claims weaken the UN collective security system (13–14). Fassbender, who also maintains that the authority of the UN Security Council must be preserved, is similarly critical of the attempts to extend the scope of the right to self-defence with a view of making it encompass the legality of a variety of actions, and especially emphasizes that 'the United States does not seem to appreciate that international law is a reciprocal system of rules, and that a freedom of action claimed by it cannot be denied to other States now or in the future' (96).

In a similar context, Ronzitti deals with the specific issues of self-defence as relevant in terms of covert operations on the territory of another State. He concludes that if the requirements of the right to self-defence are met, covert operations can be lawful (18–19). It must be added to Ronzitti's reasoning that in such cases the relevant covert operations must not only be preceded by an armed attack, but also be consistent with the principles of necessity and proportionality, that is be necessary for repelling an armed attack and be proportional to the aim pursued. These requirements have been affirmed, explicitly or otherwise, by the International Court in cases like *Nuclear Weapons*, *Oil Platforms*, and *Palestinian Wall*. The observance of these requirements would substantially restrict the legality of covert operations in practice. It is also particularly relevant that most of these judicial findings were made quite recently, after the September 11 attacks.

Parallel to the extensive examination of *jus ad bellum*, the essay of Condorelli and Naqvi focuses on the humanitarian law issues relevant to the wars against terrorism and suggests that humanitarian law standards must necessarily be observed in this process because they represent a cornerstone of modern civilization. Neglecting those standards could be a factor undermining the very foundations of that civilization (25–37).

The essay of August Reinisch deals with the action of the European Union to combat international terrorism. Special emphasis is laid upon the process of evolution of the EU policies in this field in recent years, the relationship of that policy to the operation of UN Security Council resolution 1373 (2001), and the impact of that policy on the rights and freedoms under the European Convention on Human Rights (83–102). The discussion is conveniently continued by the essay of Andrew Clapham, who deals with the process of supervision of the combating of terrorist activities in international human rights treaties, such as the procedures established under the European Convention and the International Covenant on Civil and Political Rights (283–306).

These and other contributions confirm that it is a useful addition to the literature on the legal responses to terrorist attacks. Through it readers may learn much about the issues relevant to the process of combating international terrorism. With its accumulation of insights, this book will provide a valuable source for scholars, students and practitioners interested in the ways in which and methods by which international law responds to terrorism.

ALEXANDER ORAKHELASHVILI

Protection of Property Rights Within the European Convention on Human Rights. By AR COBAN. Aldershot: Ashgate, 2004. 274 pp £55.

The genesis of this monograph lies in a PhD thesis submitted at the University of Leeds in 2002. Of course, the thesis has been modified, updated and developed into publishable form. Essentially, the book examines, as its title indicates, the provision on protection of property rights contained in Article 1 of the First Protocol (1952) to the European Convention on Human Rights. This is a provision of some considerable and growing importance in the Strasbourg jurisprudence and certainly merits scholarly treatment. A clear development of the parameters of such a fundamental right as this is an essential requisite of the rule of law in the Council of Europe. The author asserts that the protection of property rights must be placed in its theoretical context in order to clarify how far public authorities may go in interfering with such rights. This work attempts to provide such a framework.

The monograph is divided into two Parts. Part I deals with theoretical aspects of property rights; Part II examines the jurisprudence of the Strasbourg Court (and the former Commission) on the protection of property rights under Article 1 of the First Protocol. Part I contains three separate chapters; Part II comprises four separate chapters, plus an additional short concluding chapter. The book contains also the customary full bibliography and a very brief index.

In Part I, the author focuses on three main questions: What is property? Is property a human right? What are the permissible limitations on property rights? This part provides the theoretical basis for the examination of the relevant jurisprudence of the Strasbourg organs in Part II. Although property rights under the ECHR have been considered and analysed in the academic literature on several previous occasions, never before has the examination of this Convention right been located in an appropriate theoretical framework. The author explains carefully how Article 1 of the First Protocol has grown in importance since the 1980s and 1990s and attributes this to a number of political (and legal) developments: the departure from a socialist/social welfare State towards a market-oriented State in Council of Europe countries, including the privatization of public services and industries; the consequent and substantial enlargement of the quantity of property in Europe under private ownership; the resulting conflict between property rights and other fundamental rights, necessitating more regulations; more conflicts between property rights and environmental issues; and finally, the spate of technological developments resulting in the creation of new forms of property such as body parts, human genetic materials, software, etc. Within the theoretical framework, chapter 2 examines the definition of constitutionally protected property; chapter 3 explores the interesting question of whether the right to property truly is a human right; and chapter 4 investigates how far, and in what circumstances, property rights can be interfered with lawfully by public authorities and, of course, what compensation is consequently payable.

Part I as a whole is well conceived. It considers a number of fundamental theoretical issues which underpin judicial protection under the ECHR system. It gives these issues considerable and critical treatment and analysis. It presents a robust framework from which an examination of the relevant jurisprudence can take place in Part II.

In Part II, chapter 5 examines the historical background and drafting process of Article 1 of the First Protocol, including the *travaux préparatoires*, in order to discover what philosophical and political considerations precipitated the protection of property rights under the Convention system. Chapter 6 reviews the nature of the right protected by Article 1 from two perspectives: an evaluation of the relevant jurisprudence in the light of the theoretical framework proposed in Part I, together with an analysis of whether the right is negative only, or imposes also a positive obligation to protect; this chapter broaches also the complex issue of State responsibility for private actions.

Chapter 7 deals with limitations on the right; the types of permissible interference with the right by the State and their bases; and, the conditions on which such interference may be imposed, including the usual criteria such as proportionality. Chapter 8 examines the relationship between Article 1 of the First Protocol and certain other articles in the Convention, including Article 8 (right to respect for family and private life), 14 (prohibition of discrimination), 41 (just satisfaction), 6 (right to a fair trial), and 15 (derogation in time of public emergency). Chapter 9 summarizes the principal thrusts of the thesis and concludes the monograph.

The discussion and analysis in Part II shows a good familiarity with the case-law of the Strasbourg Court (and former Commission) and the relevant academic literature. The examination is detailed and critical, and novel in its linkage to a secure theoretical basis. Occasionally, comparative material (principally with municipal systems) is included, but no comparisons are made with other provisions in international law generally. This is a pity.

In sum, this book is a substantial addition to the learning on Article 1 of the First Protocol and will deservedly attract the attention of academics and practitioners alike.

SANDY GHANDHI

The European Union: An Ongoing Process of Integration. Liber Amicorum Alfred E. Kellermann. Edited by JAAP W DE ZWAAN, JAN H JANS, FRANS A NELISSEN and STEVEN BLOCKMANS. The Hague: TMC Asser Press, 2004. 371 pp £55.

This collection of essays is a tribute to the work of Alfred E Kellermann, the long-standing General Secretary of the TMC Asser Institut in The Hague. As Judge Timmermans, a contributor to the collection, puts it, the reputation of the Asser Institut is 'largely due to the unfailing efforts of Alfred Kellermann, particularly his initiatives over the years to organise international legal conferences in The Hague where, each time, he was successful in bringing together eminent specialists on European law from all over the world' (155). The collection is divided into three substantive sections: Part I deals with the institutional and constitutional aspects of the current EU structure and the anticipated changes associated with the draft Constitution; Part II deals with general principles and substantive aspects of EU/EC law; and Part III deals with legal issues associated with—and prompted by—the accession of the former Communist states of eastern Europe. In terms merely of its subject-matter, the volume is careful—rightly so—to reflect Kellermann's wide-ranging intellectual interests. Furthermore, each contribution is well-informed and offers arguments of a current and extremely sharp-edged nature. In consequence, it might well be said that the volume presents an excellent, across-the-board snapshot of issues of current European constitutional interest. Nonetheless, one is also left with the impression that the editors perhaps chose to reflect the *width* of the honorand's intellectual interests rather more than the *depth* of current scholarship in any or all of the areas falling within the remit of the volume. Considered purely as a thematic set of essays, one might therefore say that the resulting volume is sometimes rather too descriptive, instead of engaging in suitably hard-edged scrutiny. In fairness, though—given some of the relatively novel subject areas (in legal terms) that are presented for analysis—such a comment may perhaps be inevitable at the present, somewhat transitional, stage in the EU's development.

These general observations are well reflected in any discussion of Part I of the volume, although it should be stressed that most of the chapters falling within this Part take great care—in a way that is helpful—to analyse the likely impact on their subject-matter of the draft Constitution. Keon Lenaerts' exploration of the structure of the EU under the draft Constitution provides a useful and subtle overview of its subject-matter. The author suggests that the Constitution will clarify the legal powers of the EU and its institutions—an argument likely to win favour with supporters of legal transparency—although he does not address the tricky question of how the Constitution is likely to be received in the differing national constitutional structures of the EU Member States (an issue which appears to fall within the remit of Part III of this book). A somewhat more sceptical view surfaces in Judge Koopmans' essay, in which it is argued that the Constitution does not seek realistically to tackle the problems posed for the EU's institutional machinery by the accession of the former Communist states. Koopmans proposes that institutional alignments might work differently for different subject-matters—including, ambitiously, military action. This chapter may usefully be contrasted with the last chapter in Part I of the volume, namely Bruno de Witte's analysis of inter-governmental co-operation in the light of the Treaties of Amsterdam and Nice. Also within Part I, Laurence Gormley offers a detailed account of the relative powers of the different European institutions, albeit with far greater reference to legal formality as opposed to institutional practice: an omission which is surely questionable in the light of recent institutional history. Jan Wouters presents a useful, but perhaps unduly short, analysis of the role of the proposed EU Minister for Foreign Affairs (a much deeper, normatively interesting analysis, would—by contrast—have considered what it means *to be* a minister within an executive, and how the proposed EU office fits within such a constitutional structure). WT Eijsbouts embarks upon an interesting analysis of the nature of constitutionalism and its application to the EU pre- and post-enlargement. Deidre Curtin conducts a very promising—but ultimately, from the standpoint of constitutional law notions such as the separation of powers, insufficiently sophisticated—analysis of the roles of various categories of decision-maker. Ellen Vos provides a practical and very helpful discussion of the role of (EP) Parliamentary committees, but perhaps in a way that falls short of the analysis promised in the title of her chapter. Each of these contributions might be said to offer a short—but nonetheless fairly well-informed and detailed—introduction to current problems. They advance—where appropriate—context-specific solutions, without generally engaging in broader, more principled analysis. The weaker contributions in Part I of the volume are Jaap de Zwaan's entirely descriptive (and sometimes bullet-point) discussion of the role of the Commission, and Richard Lauwaars' strangely short (but, insofar as the analysis is developed, nonetheless interesting) discussion of the European Council and the presidency thereof.

Part II, as mentioned above, deals with both general principles and substantive aspects. It is hard to avoid the conclusion that it continues in similar vein to Part I, but with greater—and perhaps more random—variety in terms of its subject-matter. Localized substantive aspects thus appear to be emphasized at the expense of general principles, every chapter amounting to a brief foray into a new (presumably substantive, although the meaning of that term is not expanded upon) area. The adjective 'brief' deserves to be stressed, given that each contribution in this Part of the volume is much too short to develop a conclusive argument (one fears that this may be due to editorial imposition). Judge Timmermans conducts a scholarly and interesting—but alas *far* too short—analysis of the European Court of Justice case law concerning the infringement procedure and judicial errors (a potentially explosive area, for a whole number of reasons), before concluding with the frighteningly brief observation that 'Fortunately, these final remarks [and, by implication, all preceding remarks in the chapter] are purely of academic interest' (163). JH Jans provides a useful case note—but really *not* an essay—concerning State liability in damages. Sacha Prechal conducts a very interesting—but again bizarrely brief—analysis of the European Court of Justice's handling of fundamental rights concepts in the context of the *Defrenne* litigation ([1976] ECR 455), also taking into account the possible implications of the draft Convention. Piet Jan Slot offers an interesting—and, if expanded beyond the current eight pages, really very promising—account of the European Court of Justice's understanding of the significance of the internet in relation to vexed, but ultimately foundational, questions concerning the definition of a market (for example, do we define the relevant market geographically or virtually, subject to the over-riding prohibition against nationality discrimination?). It is rather hard to assess the comparative quality of the contributions in Part II given the undue brevity of all the essays in this Part, but it should perhaps be noted that—in contrast to the essays already discussed—Anne-Marie van den Bossche provides an almost wholly descriptive account of the EU competition provisions; that Robert Siekmann and Janwillem Soek provide an almost entirely narrative account of legal and political responses to doping in sport—albeit with occasional recognition of the deeper-level constitutional (ie separation of powers) arguments that are in fact crucial to their terrain; and that Frans Nelissen provides a descriptive account of the role of the EU in relation to maritime safety (although this is an area in which such little scholarship has appeared to date that a descriptive account is perhaps necessary before more substantive work can be done). Gerard Tanja's very brief account of the role of law firms in European legal education may very well be relevant for certain purposes, but alas the editors do not tell us why it should be relevant here.

The first essay in Part III—by Judge Tanchev—is longer and better developed. His chapter contains a useful comparative analysis of the reception of EU norms at national level, albeit accompanied by an analysis of constitutional pluralism which is perhaps something of a work-in-progress. Later chapters revert to the snapshot model mentioned above. Jeno Czuczai's chapter contains a case study relating to Hungarian accession. Nicholas Emiliou's chapter does the same, in slightly briefer form, in relation to Cyprus, as does Jiri Zemanek's chapter (in a demonstrably inadequate six pages) in relation to the Czech Republic and fundamental rights. Three chapters then follow concerning the position of Russia in relation to European-integration. Yury Matveevsky's chapter is short and wholly descriptive; Gennadi Tolstopyatenko's chapter is more analytical—and supplies helpful criteria for assessing the development of westernized notions of the rule of law within Russia—but is perhaps slightly unsophisticated in relation to the nature of European integration; and Wybe Douma's chapter offers a usefully discursive account of the EU's (foreign) relations with Russia. Finally, the role of the EU in relation to the former Republic of Yugoslavia is discussed (albeit rather more descriptively than analytically) by Steven Blockmans.

It is inevitably difficult to arrive at a conclusion concerning the overall coherence of the contents of *Festschriften*, and perhaps it is unfair to do so. What can quite properly, and strongly, be said of the collection under review is that it contains a number of dynamic contributions to on-going debates concerning the desirability and the appropriate legal architecture of an enlarged European Union. If I were to recommend to students a book which contained a series of snap-shot discussions of issues confronting politicians and lawyers who advocate the adoption of the draft Constitution—whether they are from current Member States or potential applicants—I would happily recommend the current volume. But on a deeper intellectual level, I would assert nonetheless that the editors have wrongly chosen to prioritize coverage (and hence short essays) over in-depth analysis of a smaller number of carefully selected areas. In consequence, some of the essays are question-begging or are too short and perhaps too flimsy to be of meaningful assistance to academics, practitioners or students. Nevertheless, the volume has important things to say about a very wide range of questions of current political and legal importance in the EU/EC context. For this reason, it focuses questions for further debate in a way that provides a well-meaning and generally high-quality tribute to its honorand.

NICHOLAS BAMFORTH

Issues of State Responsibility Before International Judicial Institutions. Edited by MALGOSIA FITZMAURICE and DAN SAROOSHI. Oxford: Hart, 2004. vii + 236 pp £40.

The law of State responsibility has been reinvigorated as an area of study. This is largely as a result of the work of the International Law Commission and the Articles in which their endeavours culminated. However, as the editors of this volume, which came out of a conference organized by University College London and Queen Mary, London say (vii), there is more to the law of State responsibility than the ILC Articles. As the quickest perusal of the Commentaries to those articles will make clear, international tribunals have made huge contributions to the law of State responsibility. Furthermore, the fate of the ILC Articles themselves is closely bound up to the extent to which they find favour in the jurisprudence of international courts and tribunals.

As a result, a collection of essays on State responsibility before international tribunals is most welcome. This is particularly the case as the contributing authors are something of a roll-call of international lawyers in the area. For example, the chapters dealing with the ICJ are by Judge Dame Rosalyn Higgins, alongside Professors Ian Brownlie, Malcolm Shaw, and Maurice Mendelson. The case-law of the European Court of Human Rights is canvassed by Judge Benedetto Conforti and Professor Malcolm Evans. The two other international tribunals (the Human Rights Commission and the UN Compensation Commission) are dealt with by Professor Dominic McGoldrick and Dr Olufemi Elias respectively.

Unsurprisingly, the quality of the various chapters is high, even if some, for example Conforti's, are rather short. It might be noted that other international tribunals, such as the Inter-American Court of Human Rights or WTO dispute resolution panels are not given separate consideration. To be fair, however, the large number of international tribunals that have dealt with State responsibility (which, given the cross-cutting nature of this aspect of the law, is practically all such tribunals) would have made any work that sought comprehensiveness fairly unwieldy. Within the constraints of having to make judgments as to inclusion, the selection of tribunals is very sensible.

Had the work been limited solely to appraising the approaches of these tribunals, it would have been open to the critique that by focusing on international litigation, the work only focused on the arbitrary instances upon which matters of State responsibility have come before international tribunals. However, not entirely consistently with its title, the book also contains chapters on more general matters. Professor Christopher Greenwood discusses State responsibility for the acts of domestic courts, concentrating, it must be confessed given the above comment, on the controversial *Loewen* decision of a NAFTA Tribunal. More generally, Professor Guy Goodwin-Gill takes us through good faith in State responsibility, and Professor Gerhard Loibl explains the non-compliance procedures available under various international environmental treaties that have been developed partially because of the difficulties that arise when attempting to invoke State responsibility for environmental damage. Again the essays are both useful and well written.

A personal favourite is Professor Matthew Craven's excellent chapter on Rights and Interests in State Responsibility. In the chapter, Professor Craven investigates the relationship between human rights and State responsibility in order to bring to the fore the countervailing trends of the traditional, bilateral thrust of most of the law of State responsibility, and the cosmopolitan/community-oriented focus of human rights and the parts of State responsibility that deal, for example, with *erga omnes* obligations such as Article 48 of the ILC Articles. Although sophisticated throughout, the conclusion (126–7), in which Craven canvasses the relationship between cosmopolitanism and realism that the law on State responsibility manifests, is particularly well done.

The fact that the interrelationship between human rights law and State responsibility is also canvassed, from different perspectives, by Malcolm Evans and Dominic McGoldrick does point towards one omission in the book. It would have been very helpful if the editors had provided either an introductory or concluding chapter that commented on some of the cross-cutting themes raised by the essays. Such a chapter could also perhaps have commented upon some of the more general issues raised by the increasing number of international tribunals, such as whether the unity of international law is threatened by this. The law of State responsibility, given its more general applicability across diverse areas of international law, is singularly appropriate for such an investigation. Unfortunately the editors limit themselves to a one-page preface to the work. Although, naturally, there is room for disagreement with some of the substantive claims made in the individual chapters this criticism, alongside the fact that the work is unindexed, is the only real gripe that can be made against this high-quality selection of essays, which contain much upon which to ruminate.

ROBERT CRYER

The American Tradition of International Law: Great Expectations 1789–1914. By MW JANIS. Oxford: Clarendon Press, 2004. vii + 156 pp + index £30.

> . . . the ill-repute which America has of late so liberally earned for herself by repudiation, and other disreputable practices

It is very easy, both for the popular press and within academic writings, to castigate the United States for its role in undermining international law and failing to respect its most fundamental norms. Most recently, one need only think, *inter alia*, of the United States' renunciation of the 1972 Anti-Ballistic Missile Treaty, its refusal to ratify the 1997 Kyoto Protocol on Climate Change, its failure to respect the rights of foreign nationals on death-row to consular assistance, the 2003 Iraq conflict, and, most of all, its treatment of detainees at Guantamano Bay, to come to the conclusion that here is a nation that has the capacity and self-belief not to be constrained by rules others are considered bound by. Moreover, this criticism, predominantly European in nature, has a long pedigree. The above quotation—seemingly so apt to the present situation—was, in fact, part of a piece written in the *Law Times (London)* in 1844. The situation that had so galvanized the *Law Times* into such vociferous comment was the 'monstrous sentence of death recently passed by an American tribunal of unexceptional characters, for the *crime* of aiding the escape of a female slave'.

However, outright condemnation of any nation—particularly the United States—is neither appropriate, nor particularly useful. Without in any way disputing the clear illegality of certain recent acts, what this important book (the issue as to why it is important is one I will return to) reminds us is that the United States has played a central role in the history of international law. More than that, the role of the United States in this process has arguably been fundamental. While the author ultimately leaves it to the reader to assess the significance of the contribution of US politicians, diplomats, lawyers, judges, and activists in the formation of international law, there is no question that, both intellectually and politically, the United States has a particular claim to assisting the development of the discipline into its present form.

This is a relatively short book, divided into six—largely self-contained—chapters. There must be many ways to categorize a nation's understanding of, contribution to, and domestic reliance on, international law. This is one of the more interesting. Chapter one begins with, what Janis calls, the 'English Legacy', principally focusing upon the writings of Bentham and Austin. Chapters two to six then seek to emphasize the writings and work of particular American 'actors' (chapter two: the jurists, chapter three: the lawyers and judges, chapter four: the 'utopians' (the peace societies so prevalent in the United States and, to a lesser extent, the United Kingdom), chapter five: the 'scientists' (those interested in codification), and chapter six: the 'dreamers and diplomats' (a chapter which focuses principally on the attempts to take international law forward, politically at the Hague Peace Conferences, judicially, through arbitrations and intellectually, through such organizations as what is now the International Law Association (ILA)). Whether this division into separate chapters always works is not entirely clear; my one thought was that the book may have read more coherently if, with the necessary amendments, chapters four and five had been reversed.

For those who have read M Koskenniemi's *The Gentle Civilizer of Nations: The Rise and Fall of International Law 1870–1960* (Cambridge), this book will provide an interesting follow-up. Janis notes in his preface that though he was initially concerned that, with the publication of *Gentle Civilizer*, 'my thunder had been stolen', he came to the conclusion that the books are usefully complementary. That does not prevent Janis gently rebuking Koskenniemi for 'mostly excluding the British and virtually entirely forgetting the Americans' from his book. This gentle rebuke in the preface is followed up much more strongly later in the text when Janis criticizes Koskenniemi's disregard for the Anglo-American pacifist movements; '[t]his seems so wide of the mark that one suspects that continental civil lawyers, then as now, have trouble with common law moralizing and are more comfortable drawing a black line between the "science" of law and the "emotions" of morality and religion' (112). If this tells us anything, it is that even though the United States can certainly claim a share of the history of international law, even this is not without contention.

If there are criticisms of this book, they are few. There are many—often very long—excerpts from the primary material from which he cites. This is undoubtedly a positive feature, but some are so long that in places it makes the author's narrative somewhat disjointed and difficult to follow (without rereading the previous paragraph). But possibly better that, than having a book which uses only brief, unduly curtailed, extracts, always leaving the reader wanting to know more. If there was an issue that was dealt with too briefly it was the discussion of the *Alabama Arbitration* (delivered in 1872). Rightly said to be 'probably the most influential event of nineteenth-century American international law' (135), the analysis of the dispute, the legal judgments and its consequences was all too brief (contrast that with the extensive discussion of the US Supreme Court decision in *Dred Scott v Sandford* (1857)). In particular, Janis failed to discuss, in necessary detail, the arbitral agreement and, in particular, its provisions on applicable law. His statement that the tribunal was called upon to 'decide whether Britain had violated international law when it permitted British companies to build warships for the Confederacy during the American Civil War' simplifies what was a much more heated debate over whether what the tribunal was applying was international law or actually a set of rules *specialis* agreed for that dispute alone.

A further—slight—inaccuracy is Janis's claim that the International Law Association 'quickly became what it remains [in its current form] . . . a forum more for the promotion of private than public international law' (141). This is a distortion of the current work of the ILA, in which—if anything—the balance is skewed too much in favour of public international law.

This book is ultimately important in that it adds a much needed piece in the jigsaw of the history of international law. It also reminds those who are always ready to criticize the United States that it has had a proud and distinguished history in this area, much beyond that which most are prepared to credit it with. The author's decision to finish the book at the advent of the First World War seems particularly apt; as he concludes, '[a]s Europe's armies began to kill millions, it was plain that the nineteenth century promise of international law had not been kept' (156).

D French

Corporations and Transnational Human Rights Litigation. By Sarah Joseph. Oxford: Hart Publishing, 2004. xii + 177pp £30.

Transnational human rights litigation refers broadly to civil proceedings in the courts of one State in respect of human rights violations that occurred in another State. In the seminal case of *Filartíga v Peña-Irala* (2nd Cir 1980), on the basis of the then 191-year-old Alien Tort Claims Act (ATCA), a Paraguayan family sued a Paraguayan police officer in New York for torturing and murdering a young boy in Asuncion. The enactment of subsequent companion legislation—most notably, the Torture Victim Protection Act (TVPA) and certain questionable amendments to the Foreign State Immunity Act (FSIA)—has broadened the scope of possible defendants in US transnational human rights litigation to include seven black-listed sovereign States, heads of State, officials, political parties and, more recently, transnational corporations (TNCs). This last class of litigation, against TNCs, forms the topic of Sarah Joseph's book.

The tome is refreshingly slender, which is both a result of the author's lean writing style and of the field's relative novelty. Indeed, aside from the 1987 *cause célèbre* concerning Union Carbide Corporation and the Bhopal disaster, the cases under study only date back to the mid-1990s, with the bulk arising only within the last five years. In fact, none of the salient cases has been decided on the merits yet; they have either been dismissed on procedural grounds, settled or are still ongoing. One might accordingly question the timeliness of this book and wonder whether it would not have been preferable to wait for further developments. On the other hand, it may be that there won't be any developments to discuss; transnational human rights litigation as a whole is still an emerging enterprise, one that, as Judge Higgins pointed out in the *Arrest Warrant* case, 'has not attracted the approbation of States generally' (para 48). Be that as it may, US transnational human rights litigation is not likely to go away anytime soon, though the number of cases will probably decrease as a result of the Supreme Court's 2004 decision in *Sosa v Alvarez-Machain*, which substantially narrowed the class of admissible claims under ATCA. Though Sosa was released after the publication of Dr Joseph's book, her analysis of the decision's impact on litigation involving TNCs can be found on the publisher's website www.hartpub.co.uk/updates.html.

The book comprises eight chapters. In chapter 1, transnational human rights litigation is situated in the larger context of multilateral, national, and self-regulatory efforts to hold TNCs accountable for human rights abuses. Chapters 2 and 3 focus on the US experience under ATCA, the TVPA, state tort law, and other federal jurisdictional bases. These chapters properly form the centrepiece of the study of what remains largely (though not exclusively) a US phenomenon. The discussion is balanced and the research thorough, though certain revisions would be required in the light of *Sosa*, particularly concerning the substantive requirements of ATCA (22–33). Chapter 4 examines the issues of personal jurisdiction and *forum non conveniens*, which the author presents as 'procedural obstacles'. A glass-half-full perspective might view *forum non conveniens* as an important and desirable opportunity for judicial restraint. Chapter 5 wraps up the US portion of the study by discussing the curious case of *Kasky v Nike* (SCt Cal 2002), in which an individual sued the Nike corporation under California competition laws for making false and misleading statements in the media concerning its human rights practices in South East Asia. The author acknowledges that the *Nike* case, though highly interesting for its own reasons, is not a true transnational human rights litigation case. This chapter is correspondingly misplaced.

Chapter 6 concisely examines the corporate transnational human rights litigation experience of the United Kingdom, Australia, and Canada. The absence of ATCA-style legislation in these countries has not prevented national courts from asserting jurisdiction (if only on a *prima facie* basis) over claims involving TNCs incorporated in the forum. The main question that appears to arise in such cases is not whether jurisdiction exists, but whether it ought to be declined in favour of a more convenient alternative forum. The resulting chapter is a valuable, well annotated comparative analysis of the *forum non conveniens* doctrine as developed in the United Kingdom, Australia, and Canada, particularly when read in parallel with chapter 4 on the US application of the doctrine.

Chapter 7 touches on the manner in which transnational human rights claims engage first principles of company law and corporate liability. Though generally well presented, the discussion on corporate unveiling as well as direct, joint parent-subsidiary and multinational group liability is rather undeveloped and, because of the preliminary stage of the salient cases, remains largely *a priori*. Finally, in chapter 8, after summarizing the current litigation, the author comments on the overall desirability, promises and pitfalls of transnational human rights litigation against TNCs. Dr Joseph presents a realistic and balanced assessment: while emphasizing the international community's interest in holding powerful TNCs accountable for their role in grave breaches of human rights, transnational human rights litigation is no panacea. Rather, it should properly remain one of multiple strategies—along with self, national, and multilateral regulation—aimed at promoting good corporate behaviour and social responsibility.

Very well researched and tightly written, *Corporations and Transnational Human Rights Litigation* makes a notable contribution to the burgeoning literature on transnational human rights litigation. The book will foreseeably be improved in subsequent editions as the salient cases finally go to trial.

François Larocque

The European Union and Conflict Prevention: Policy and Legal Aspects. Edited by Vincent Kronenberger and Jan Wouters. The Hague: TMC Asser Press, 2004. xxix + 614 pp £95.

As the common foreign and security policy of the European Union has become more sophisticated, has begun to equip itself with better instruments and critically to assess its past and present performance, its focus has turned increasingly to conflict prevention. Whether motivated by enlightened self-interest or by altruistic desire for a better world, foreign ministers now universally recognize that there is no point in scattering the seeds of trade preferences and financial aid if the soil where they fall is riven by corruption or conflict. Yet as aptly expressed in the quotation from Javier Solana at the outset of the Conclusion to this book,

> Of all policy objectives, the prevention of violent conflict is the most ambitious, the most demanding and the most thankless . . . Address a crisis and you will be praised. Prevention is often unseen. It requires a different level of political courage.

In their Introduction, the editors show how recent is this emphasis on conflict prevention. Unlike crisis management and post-conflict peacemaking, it is not listed among the Petersburg tasks but has developed without an explicit legal base anywhere in the Treaty on European Union. From the outset, prevention of the recurrence of conflict among Member States was an essential though implicit element in the Treaties establishing the Communities. It has since grown through successful deployment in the context of enlargement to a position where—as almost every contributor tells us—it is mainstreamed into all external policies of the Union.

Notwithstanding the initial limited definition of conflict prevention, most of the contributors take the expression in the wider sense used by the European Commission: 'actions undertaken in the short term to reduce manifest tensions and/or to prevent the outbreak or recurrence of violent conflict'. As pointed out by Simon Duke, this leads to the problem of deciding what does *not* fall under the rubric of conflict prevention. The first half (almost 300 pages) of this substantial book brings out clearly through successive chapters how pervasive conflict prevention has become throughout Union external action, but at the expense of a great deal of repetition of history, of institutional capabilities, available instruments, and analysis. There are 25 entries in the Index for 'Mainstreaming'. This is in no way a criticism of individual contributions—most of them written by officers working in the fields they describe and containing practical and realistic criticisms of current policies. Particularly interesting is the chapter by Lagendijk and Seela, which calls for a cool appraisal of Union policies which actually fuel conflict (such as weapons sales to conflict-ridden areas, insistence on protection of patent rights over medicines, encouraging privatization of water and, of course, the CAP).

In the centre of the book lie two excellent case studies of European Union conflict prevention, by Steven Blockmans on the Western Balkans and by Erik Eidem on Strategies for Sub-Saharan Africa. Blockmans shows convincingly that of all the organizations which have grappled with the problems of the Western Balkans, the Union is the only one with *all* the relevant capacities for action. This lays a heavy responsibility on it, but one which it is, now beginning to discharge successfully.

In Part Three the scope widens to describe the experience of other actors in the field—the UN, the OSCE, NATO, the Council of Europe, the G8, and the World Bank, as well as the Red Cross and non-governmental organizations. These accounts of different instruments and techniques are of great comparative interest, and they pave the way for an examination of how all those well-meaning bodies can better exchange information and early warnings, establish priorities among themselves and collaborate efficiently and effectively in areas of potential or actual conflict. The chapter by John Kriendler on NATO crisis management and conflict prevention is particularly topical in view of the effort that went into negotiation of the Berlin-plus arrangements between NATO and the Union on principles of cooperation and access to military assets.

A better structure for cooperation among international organizations emerges in the conclusions of Kronenberger and Wouters as a key to improved conflict prevention. For the Union, they also recommend more systematic early warning of likely conflicts, together with greater political readiness to act on them rapidly and prompt access to the necessary money from the EU Budget. To improve available information they argue that the EU Satellite Centre should be enlarged so as to become in effect a European CIA and that the proposed Union delegations (which are likely to go ahead in some form whatever the ultimate shape of the Constitution for the European Union) need better training. Some other suggestions are based on misplaced confidence on the early entry into force of the Constitution, or on the unlikely idea that the Member States would agree not to undertake any preventive military action without the mandate of the Security Council. But the call for better sharing of information and allocation of priorities is soundly based and realistic. It is also encouraging to read a book which balances constructive criticism of structures and policies with acknowledgement of how much has already been achieved by a European policy barely kitted out with the equipment for such an ambitious undertaking.

E Denza

From '9–11' to the Iraq War 2003: International Law in an Age of Complexity. By Dominic McGoldrick. Oxford: Hart Publishing, 2005. xv + 380 pp £18 pb.

There is no doubt that for international lawyers as for any individual the issues covered by this book are of profound importance:

> This book is a tale of two towers, two wars and two visions. The 'two towers' are those of the World Trade Centre in New York, destroyed by a terrorist attack on 11 September 2001. The 'two wars' are the War on Terrorism and the War on Iraq. The wars are linked inasmuch the War on Iraq was portrayed as part of the War on Terrorism. The 'two visions' are of the possible international legal and political order for the twenty-first century. (1)

While the author admits at the outset that he 'seeks to identify the kind of questions that need to be asked, as much as proffer answers to them' (2), the book does not develop the 'two visions' limb sufficiently to assess the impact of the destruction of the two towers and the wars against Afghanistan and Iraq on the international legal and political order. Readers are told that 'we are in an age of "Global Complexity" ' in which '9–11' is a 'tipping' or 'turning point' for such an order (7–8), but such theoretical constructs are not developed or adequately explained, at least at the outset. The author admits that 'the images of the attacks' on the World Trade Center 'were almost surreal—more cinematic than realistic' (9), but to explicitly equate the tragedy of the twin towers with the nuclear destruction of Hiroshima and Nagasaki, and to implicitly evaluate their impact as having more significance than the genocide in Rwanda of 1994, or the slaughter in the Democratic Republic of the Congo at the turn of the century, is reflective of the huge effect of emotive, symbolic acts, and our relative immunity to images of pure naked brutality. It is also reflective of a very Western view of international law and politics in which the images of the collapsing twin towers are central to our (re)thinking, while the memory of the Rwandan genocide is only re-awakened by a recent Hollywood film. Despite these serious reservations, it may be that the author is right to suggest that '9–11' is still a turning point, but is it a turning point for international law? In a sense, despite the small section on this issue (21–3), this is what the book is about.

To his credit, the author tries to tread a careful path amongst the ruins of the twin towers and the destruction wrought in Afghanistan and Iraq, to assess the impact of a single act of terrorism and the military responses to it. He considers both international and national responses taken in the 'metaphoric war' on terrorism, where we are at one and the same time both at 'war' and in a state of 'peace' (28). There is a great deal of interesting discussion, a wide range of literature from many disciplines, in addition to a considerable number of primary sources (ranging from the adoption, for instance, of Resolution 1441 in November 2002, to the Hutton Inquiry into the death of Dr David Kelly) that are brought to bear in the main chapters dealing with the wars on terrorism, Afghanistan, and Iraq. Furthermore, in addition to significant extracts from primary sources in the substantive chapters, nearly half of the book is made up of further documents in the appendices. As well as being a useful source book, the legal debates are well described, making it a good textbook for students, but the critical analysis is tentative. On the war against Iraq the conclusion is that 'the legality argument of the US and the UK based on SC Resolutions is a tenable and defensible one' but this is more than balanced later in the same paragraph: 'Unless we have an international legal system in which all states ultimately, rather than merely initially, exercise a right of auto-interpretation, then one is forced to the conclusion that the better interpretation of international law in 2003 is that the US and the UK acted illegally' (85).

Thus somehow, despite the turning point of '9–11', the principles of international law by which we judge the legality or otherwise of a use of force have survived the purely self-serving and short-term legal justification put forward by the US and the UK. Superpowers have tested international law before and will do so again', but '[u]timately it will always be in the interest of even a superpower for the system of international law to survive'. Perhaps the author ought to have explained why, though one cannot but agree with his conclusion that 'the challenge for the US is to remedy what it sees as the defects of the current system without destroying the credibility and effectiveness of the system itself' (121).

The book ends with the most illuminating chapter that considers world orders for the twenty-first century, where the debate makes up to a certain extent for the underdeveloped conceptual framework at the outset. The choice is more than between a French vision of a multipolar world and a US vision of a unipolar one (155), though this is the starting point of the discussion, and presumably the 'two visions' referred to at the outset. There is no doubt that international law has to adapt to deal with non-State actors, whether they be terrorists, mercenaries, or multinational corporations, for the threat to the security of States, especially developing ones, can arise from any of these. The norms on the use of force are not the only ones in the spotlight in the twenty-first century, but also those on democracy, free trade, self-determination (economic as well as political), and fundamental human rights. Individual and State security may be more at risk from environmental factors than from uses of force, brought home by the natural disaster of the Asian tsunami. While this book provides a stimulating look at the consequences of '9–11'—'the day the world shook' (198)—it does not provide a cure for the inadequacies of international law. It does, however, provide us with a balanced, often darkly humoured account (see, for example, the equation of international lawyers to undertakers on page 6), of many of the issues that we will have to consider in shaping its future development.

ND WHITE

The Permanent International Criminal Court: Legal and Policy Issues. Edited by DOMINIC MCGOLDRICK, PETER ROWE, and ERIC DONNELLY. Oxford: Hart Publishing, 2004. xviii + 498 pp £35pb.

Coming as it did in the aftermath of the establishment of the tribunals for the former Yugoslavia and Rwanda, the Rome Statute of the International Criminal Court finally made possible what some had advocated for over a century. The Rome Statute established the permanent institution that in future potentially would be able to deal with all crimes within its jurisdiction, whether they were on a relatively small scale, or on the massive scale witnessed in south-eastern Europe and central Africa in the early 1990s. The setting-up of the Court also fully resuscitated the study of international criminal law; a topic which had become somewhat stagnant soon after the Nuremburg and Tokyo trials but had undergone a degree of revival by the establishment of the *ad hoc* tribunals. The conclusion in 1998 of the ICC at the Rome Conference has led to a massive amount of academic commentary not only on the legal and political repercussions of that treaty but also on international criminal law in general. Books dealing with some of the issues raised by the Court and the *ad hoc* tribunals by Cassese (alone and with others), Kittichaisaree, Bentekas and Nash, McCormack and Simpson, and Schabas, to name but a few, have all appeared in recent years. The literature on the Court in the academic journals of various disciplines is now vast. If the book under review had a bibliography, which it does not, then the size of this literature would be clear. One can, however, trawl through the footnotes to get a very good idea of the size of the literature and the different perspectives that have been adopted in analysing the Court.

Bearing the above in mind, one of the questions foremost in my mind while reading this book was, what can it say that has not been said already? The short answer is, quite a lot. This is an excellent book and a welcome and valuable addition to the literature. The editors and contributors, a substantial number of whom have a connection to the Law School of the University of Liverpool, have produced a thought-provoking collection of essays which discuss some of the implications and repercussions of the establishment of the Court. While there is already detailed legal discussion of the drafting of the Statute and each of the provisions, for example in the gargantuan collection edited by Cassese, Gaeta, and Jones and published by Oxford University Press in 2002, each of the essays in this collection which deals with such issues is still to be welcomed and says something new. Equally those essays that deal with the political aspects of the negotiation of the Statute, or the subsequent attitude of some States to its conclusion, bring new insights. One of the book's virtues lies in the fact that it does not aim or pretend to be a comprehensive account of the history and legal and policy issues of the Court, but simply to look at selected issues.

After the introductory chapter by two of the editors, the book is divided into seven parts. Part I broadly deals with the origins and development of the Court. Part II examines the key issues of jurisdiction and admissibility and the relationship between the Court and the Security Council. Part III deals with the various crimes outlawed by the Statute, the issue that has already received some of the most detailed analysis. Part IV deals with the questions of liability and defences in international criminal law and the manner in which the Court's Statute approaches them. Part V deals with evidential issues and the rights of victims, the latter an issue which was the cause of much debate before the *ad hoc* tribunal for the former Yugoslavia. Part VI examines the issue of national implementation and political responses to the Court. Part VII, which is composed of one chapter, examines the legal and political significance of the International Criminal Court.

Each part of the book is composed of a different number of chapters of various lengths. While some are substantially longer than others they are, almost without exception, of a very high standard. Often collections of essays such as that under review are the product of a conference. This, however, is not the case in this instance. The absence of conference does make coherence between the chapters more difficult to attain. Contributors do not have the benefit of hearing what some of the other authors are going to say, or the angles they are going to take. The editors of this volume should be congratulated therefore, because between them the chapters do make a coherent whole, even if I did wonder, once or twice, about the wisdom of a particular chapter in a certain part of the book. Gerry Simpson's chapter entitled 'Politics, Sovereignty, Remembrance', for example, has very interesting things to say but I am not quite convinced it should be in the part of the book entitled 'The Origins and Development of the Permanent International Court' as opposed to the section entitled 'The Significance of the International Criminal Court' which broadly deals with the legal and political significance of the Court.

Professor McGoldrick's contribution to this book should not go unmentioned. Apart from co-editing it, he also co-authored one chapter and solely authored three other very broad and detailed chapters. Those chapters are not only very lengthy but also very high in terms of quality. The publishers should also be commended. Far too often books of this nature are published solely in hardback and usually at prices that are somewhat unreasonable. This book is not only published in paperback, but at a price that allows anyone interested in the subject to buy a copy for their own personal collection. It will be money well spent.

URFAN KHALIQ

Doha and Beyond: The Future of the Multilateral Trading System. Edited by MIKE MOORE. Cambridge: Cambridge University Press, 2004. xx + 177 pp + index £40.

The World Trade Organization continues to be an important area of study and analysis, both for international lawyers and those interested, more generally, in international relations and international organizations. This edited collection is just one of a number of books that have appeared in recent years that seek to reflect upon the present state of the multilateral trading system—and the WTO as its institutional face—and consider how the organization of global trade might be improved.

The essays contained in this collection are edited by Mike Moore, who was Director-General of the WTO from 1999 to 2002. The authors were members of an advisory panel that he established during his period of office to 'advise [him] on the challenges and opportunities confronting the . . . WTO' (v). The essays in this book are, however, clearly the work of each individual author and certainly do not represent any established view of the WTO secretariat, which in any event must stay neutral on such matters.

The principal momentum for the book—as can be gleaned from its title—is the significance of the commencement of a new round of negotiations, as agreed by the parties at Doha, Qatar in 2001, and the question of the extent to which the ministerial declaration agreed at Doha reflects an opportunity to tackle the various challenges the WTO continues to face. However, my principal concern with this book is that though it was published in the Spring of 2004, there is no mention of how the 'Doha' negotiations were significantly de-railed by the ministerial meeting at Cancún, Mexico in September 2003. Despite copyediting and typesetting deadlines, not to have included such a major (non-) development seems to me to be a critical weakness. Of course, the failure to incorporate such an issue is made with hindsight and, in any event, the adoption by the WTO of the 'July package' in 2004, which will hopefully put the necessary impetus back into the Doha Development Round, may make the failure at Cancún only a temporary stumble. And if the book were to have waited for developments such as the 'July package', it would never have been published at all. (As an aside, one can only speculate as to what state the negotiations may be at by the time of the publication of this volume of the *Year Book*).

The topics included cover many of the 'key' issues within the WTO. Issues such as transparency, legitimacy, the developmental aspects of trade (including the controversial subjects of differential treatment and non-reciprocity), and the dispute settlement process are all touched upon in greater of lesser depth. Other topics discussed include the effect of China's accession to the WTO and EU enlargement on the Doha negotiations. However, one needs to be aware that most of the contributors are not lawyers and their focus is therefore not specifically legal. The majority of the chapters lack the precision that one ordinarily associates with legal analysis (this includes a lack of footnoting and relevant citations). The style of the writing is likely to prove infuriatingly impressionistic for a legal readership. The various references to the *Shrimp/Turtle* case are a good example: not necessarily incorrect, just lacking detail.

As an introduction to some of the broad issues surrounding the WTO and the international system of global trade, with particular reference to the 2001 Doha Development mandate, this is an interesting, but certainly not the definitive, work. There is much to consider and ponder, though admittedly the level of analysis does vary. As I have already noted, this is clearly not a 'legal' text, as one might understand that term, and will therefore only ever be supplementary to the more recognized legal works on this topic. But as a reminder to international trade lawyers that the WTO is so much more than the minutiae of anti-dumping law, this is a welcome—if somewhat dated—collection of essays.

D FRENCH

Human Rights in Africa: From the OAU to the African Union. By Rachel Murray. Cambridge: Cambridge University Press, 2004. viii + 349 pp £50.

The African Charter on Human and Peoples's Rights, adopted by the Organization of African Unity (OAU) in 1981, has rightly attracted considerable attention from commentators. However, whilst the African Charter is arguably the OAU's best known achievement in the field of human rights, it should not be overlooked that the OAU, now replaced by the African Union (AU), has sought to build upon this enterprise and further strengthen human rights throughout the continent. This it has done by adopting additional instruments relating to the human rights of women and children and, crucially, setting up the African Court of Human and Peoples' Rights, as well as a series of other initiatives. The book under review analyses, from a human rights perspective, the work of the OAU/AU in promoting and protecting human rights in Africa. In so doing the author eschews detailed commentary on the various treaty provisions, adopting rather an expansive approach, taking account, for example, of the practice of the different African organs and relevant soft law documents.

The first chapter introduces the reader to the OAU and traces its development from its early years, when human rights was at best of marginal consequence, through its later years when it evolved a growing awareness of the significance of human rights, resulting in the adoption of the African Charter, other normative instruments, and the reinforcement of existing mechanisms. The AU, for which human rights is a core concern (as is good governance and the rule of law, as evidenced by their inclusion in the Constitutive Act), is also covered. The next chapter also has an institutional emphasis, concentrating on the role of the African Commission on Human and Peoples' Rights and its relationship with the OAU/AU. While the African Commission may have been somewhat neglected by the OAU, the author is optimistic that it will play a more prominent role under the AU.

The focus of the succeeding chapters is on thematic, and topical, problems. The rights of refugees, women, and children, on which the OAU adopted treaties, are comprehensively covered. The issues of democracy, conflict and development, which are inter-linked, are also considered. Although the OAU/AU has taken steps to promote and consolidate democracy and good governance throughout Africa, the sad fact remains that too many African States pay lip service to democratic ideals. Conflict situations continue to undermine Africa's attempts at progress and the AU has therefore been endowed with an extensive mandate to ensure peace and stability on the continent, with the support and backing of the international community. Particularly worthy of note is the AU's power to intervene in the domestic affairs of Member States in instances of genocide, war crimes, and crimes against humanity. In the context of development, issues of governance and corruption are discussed, and the role played by the New Partnership for Africa's Development (NEPAD), which places a high priority on human rights, is assessed.

Africa has not lacked initiatives for the protection of human rights. The problem is often that reality does not keep pace with the rhetoric. As the author points out in the Conclusion, what is necessary is better implementation of existing laws and practices. Given its commitment to democracy, human rights, good governance, and the rule of law, the AU has the mandate to bring about real change in Africa. But is it a case of 'old wine in new bottles'?

This is an interesting monograph by a scholar with considerable expertise in the area. The author's approach brings a fresh and informative outlook to the subject. There is also a useful bibliography. Anyone with an interest in Africa will find this book rewarding.

Gino J Naldi

Ecological Sensitivity and Global Legal Pluralism: Rethinking the Trade and Environment Conflict. By OREN PEREZ. Oxford and Portland, Oregon: Hart Publishing, 2004. 290 pp £42.

The conclusion of the Marrakesh Agreement in 1994 establishing the World Trade Organization was a major landmark in the history of international trade relations among nations. Since the WTO was established, the world has witnessed a rapid growth in international economic activity, as well as a massive increase in the volume of international trade. Accordingly, the WTO has seen an expansion of its activities in recent years and has thus become one of the most important international organizations. Nearly 150 States, developed and developing, small and big, powerful and weaker, have now become Members of this organization. The new dispute settlement system of the WTO has received over 300 trade disputes from its Members and given its rulings in more than 80 of such cases, providing for greater stability and predictability in global commercial exchanges. On the strength of such a short history, it is tempting to claim that the WTO has been a success. However, it is necessary to go deeper into the workings of this organization within the past ten years before reaching the conclusion that this is so and this book by Oren Perez seeks to do this in relation to the issues concerning the interaction between international trade and the environment. It depicts the emerging trade and environment conflict as 'a composite phenomenon—the product of multiple dilemmas, constituted by a myriad of institutional and discursive networks' and aims to grapple with them to provide a fascinating reading on the debate on the need for environmental protection when promoting international trade.

Based on a doctoral thesis submitted by the author to the London School of Economics and Political Science, the book, published in the series on International Studies in the Theory of Private Law, is a welcome addition to the literature on the WTO in general and the relationship between trade and environment in particular. It provides a thorough and competent treatment of the manner in which environmental concerns have been addressed not only within the WTO framework, but also within the wider international discourse on the subject. It has eight chapters including the introduction and conclusions. The first two provide a theoretical framework for discussion of the trade and environment conflict through a pluralistic perspective and the rest, ie Chapters Three to Seven, examine several global legal domains, ranging from the WTO to 'private' transnational regimes, such as transnational litigation, international construction law, and international financial law.

Beginning by deconstructing the trade and environment conflict through a pluralistic perspective, the author goes on to assess the trade-environment problem within a broad framework before focusing on the GATT-WTO Trade-Environment jurisprudence in Chapter Three. This perhaps is the best chapter in the book, containing a systematic and thorough analysis of the recent trend in jurisprudence within the WTO's Dispute Settlement Body (DSB). The author has provided an excellent critique of some of the leading cases dealing with the trade-environment nexus, including the *Tuna Dolphin I* and *II*, *Shrimps and Turtle* cases. In doing so, the author outlines how the GATT's 'mercantilist ethos' or 'pro-trade' bias is gradually giving way to a more balanced approach. Indeed, environmental concerns are relatively recent arrivals in the whole WTO framework but they now are having their impact on the traditional approach.

However, the author, who is sympathetic to this trend, often appears to read more into the pronouncements of the DSB in favour of environmental concerns, and expects the DSB to play a greater role than it is capable of doing within the inherent limitations imposed by the framework of the GATT-WTO law. For instance, pointing to the reports of the DSB in the *Shrimp* dispute, the author states that the environmental jurisprudence of the WTO 'reflects a bold attempt to construct a broader social vision for the WTO'

(65). It is arguable whether one can make such bold claims on the basis of the pronouncements made by the DSB in one or two cases. Nevertheless, the present reviewer finds himself in agreement with the author that '[t]he environmental reform of the WTO should be guided . . . by one key insight: the deep and persisting gap between the institutional capacity of the trade and environmental domains' (80). Accordingly, it makes good sense to state that '[t]he asymmetry between these two regulatory domains constitutes probably the most convincing argument for constructing a broader social vision to the WTO' (81).

The structure of the book is logical, the style of presentation is mature and balanced, and the analysis presented is sound. However, the book gives the impression of a rather unorthodox style of presentation at times—the language used is rather clumsy and the flow of ideas is rather disjointed on occasions. Equally, the material presented in appendices at the end of each of the chapters could very well have been put together at the end to avoid the impression of a book containing a collection of self-standing chapters. After all, it is a monograph based on a doctoral thesis.

Above all, this is an interesting, informative and extensively researched book on a topical theme which brings together different strands of thought to present a cohesive study. It can be hoped that the ideas that the author has presented for harmonizing international trade policies with environmental objectives are able to influence the future developments in this area both within and outside the WTO framework. This book can happily be recommended to anybody interested in the legal issues surrounding the interaction between international trade and the environment.

SURYA P SUBEDI

Droit des Immunités et Exigences du Procès Équitable. Edited by Isabelle Pingel. Paris: Editions Pedone, 2004. 162 pp €20.

This book reports a colloquium held on 30 April 2004 at the *Centre de Recherches Communautaires, Faculté de Droit de Paris Saint-Maur*. It is divided into two parts, which apparently mirror the two sessions of the colloquium (chaired by Anne Levade and Allain Pellet respectively). Part I concerns jurisdictional immunities and the right of access to court, while Part II deals with immunity from execution and the effectiveness of judicial decisions. Both parts eschew a discussion of general principles and focus instead—quite justifiably—on actual practice (mainly case law) on both the international and national levels. Each part also contains a 'debates' section, which makes particularly interesting reading as it records questions and rebuttals at the colloquium.

Part I discusses the jurisprudence of the European Court of Human Rights (ECtHR) (Frédéric Sudre), France (Régis de Gouttes), Switzerland (Dominique Favre), and the common law countries (Hazel Fox, author of *The Law of State Immunity*, 2002)

Sudre delivers a scathing criticism of the 'disappointing', negative response given by the ECtHR to the question of whether denial of justice could be avoided by upholding the primacy of the right of access over immunities. To him the Court appears 'seized with schizophrenia' in developing a 'contradictory jurisprudence'. That is, the Court, while affirming the principle of ensuring the compatibility of jurisdictional immunities with the right of access, has tried hard to subordinate that right to immunity. In his view, the grant of immunity constitutes a denial of justice that violates the right to an equitable process and therefore offends against the 'European public order of human rights', which ought to 'neutralise' immunity. While Sudre's analysis itself is criticized as 'sweeping' by one participant (Ronny Abraham) during the debate, Fox suggests that, in relation to the right of access, the true criterion for lifting immunity may be a proper jurisdictional connection with the forum State rather than the nature of the proceedings.

Gouttes notes a new development in French jurisprudence concerning contracts of employment. In a 2003 decision involving an industrial dispute against the Saudi Embassy, the French Court of Cassation looked beyond the contract of employment itself to the issue in dispute, ie the employee's inclusion in the French labour protection scheme.

Part II features an introduction to the Convention on Jurisdictional Immunities of States and Their Property (Gerhard Hafner, Chairman of the UN Ad Hoc Committee on Jurisdictional Immunities) followed by accounts of State practice of France (Ronny Abraham and Emmanuel Gaillard), Switzerland (Dominique Favre) and the common law countries (Hazel Fox).

The most important development on the international level with regard to immunity is the evolution of the Convention on Jurisdictional Immunities, the draft articles of which were completed by the International Law Commission (ILC) in 1991. Hafner states that, with the demise of communist regimes and the gradual convergence of State practice during the 1990s, the political conditions have turned more favourable. This led to the adoption of the Convention by the UN General Assembly in its Resolution A/RES/59/38 on 2 December 2004. Hafner points out in particular that the greatest problem in the course of the deliberations on the draft Convention concerned measures of constraint (a term used by the ILC to cover both pre-judgment attachment and execution of judgments), the main controversy centring on the definition of State property that can be subjected to measures of constraint. In the original draft, the property had to be 'specifically in use or intended for use by the State for other than government non-commercial purposes and ... in the territory of the State of the forum and [have] a connection with the claim which is the object of the proceeding or with the agency or instrumentality against which the proceeding was directed' (Article 18(1)(c)). Diverse positions were taken by various States, ranging from applying such measures to all the property of a State except what is used for governmental purposes, to confining these measures to what is allocated for the satisfaction of the claim. A consensus emerged, however, that a distinction ought to be drawn between pre-judgment and post-judgment measures. Two separate articles were finally adopted, with pre-judgment measures subject to more stringent conditions (Article 18) and the aforementioned 'specifically in use' condition now applicable (in an altered form, with the 'connection with the claim' struck out) only to post-judgment measures (Article 19).

Gaillard highlights the incompatibility between three principles, ie the effectiveness of arbitral awards, immunity from execution, and the independence of corporate State entities. He is of the opinion that respect for any two of these principles would result in disregard of the third. His analysis provides some insights into the ongoing debate on these points, especially into what is commonly referred to as the issue of 'piercing the corporate veil'. Continuing with her theme, Fox concludes that immunity from execution imposes a serious limitation on the right of access and that, in practice, the most effective method of satisfaction is by obtaining the consent to pay of the foreign State.

Paul Lagarde concludes that there is an 'irreducible contradiction' between immunity and the right to an equitable process: where there is immunity, however qualified, the right of access will be held in check; on the other hand, if the right of access is to be ensured for the individual claimant, there can be no immunity. This view, in a final analysis, seems to form the general tenor of the colloquium.

Just as rightly summarized in the introductory remarks by Isabelle Pingel (author of *Les Immunités des États en Droit International*, 1997), diverse sources and multiple beneficiaries are two striking features of immunity. The colloquium—and hence the book—discusses the issue of immunity in its most general sense, including immunities accorded by national as well as international law. And wisely so. Since the designated object of the colloquium was to examine the relationship between immunity and the right of access, it would have been impossible to achieve the main aim within the space of one day, had one tried to make fine distinctions between various types of immunities and beneficiaries. On the other hand, such a truncated treatment would entail ignoring or at least glossing over certain crucial points of differentiation, for example immunities granted under internal law to officials and governmental bodies and those afforded by international law to foreign States or to international organizations. Unavoidably, many questions are left unanswered.

However, this should not detract from the value of the project. In demonstrating the tension between immunity and the right of access, it testifies to a mission excellently accomplished. Attended by some of the most pre-eminent scholars in this field (among the participants was also Michel Cosnar, author of *La Soumission des États aux Tribunaux Internes*, 1996), the colloquium/book provides both up-to-date information and personal insights derived from years of meticulous research. Informative, authoritative, and compact, the book is an essential *vademecum* for anyone excited by the mind-boggling issue of jurisdictional immunities.

XIAODONG YANG

Provisional Measures in International Law: The International Court of Justice and the International Tribunal for the Law of the Sea. BY SHABTAI ROSENNE. Oxford: Oxford University Press, 2005. xx + 240 pp £60.

Requests for provisional measures have become more plentiful and diverse; and the binding nature of orders indicating them has become firmly established, first in the 1982 United Nations Convention on the Law of the Sea and then in the 2001 judgment of the International Court of Justice in the *LaGrand* case (the order of these events hardly being a mere coincidence). Against this background, the doyen of international dispute settlement, Shabtai Rosenne, has found time to re-examine 'in greater detail' matters relating to provisional measures (viii). Rosenne has participated, as counsel, in bringing about many of those details, and, given the learned author's first-hand knowledge of individual cases and proceedings, it does not come as a total surprise that provisional measures are seen as 'an exceptional remedy' and the conditions for ordering them 'a matter of fact and of appreciation by the organ seised of the request and . . . not given to any systematic analysis or presentation' (223). The reader will have grasped this point well before the concluding section, in which the just-quoted passage is found.

The first part of the book, Chapters 1 to 3, essentially develops a history of basic texts relating to provisional measures, the narrative being perhaps unduly complicated by the division between statutes and rules of court in separate chapters. The second part, Chapters 4 to 7, deals with main aspects of ordering provisional measures, ie jurisdiction, urgency, duration, and procedure. Essentially an area of 'judge-made law' (33, 46, and 225), focus is on decisions which, just as the basic texts, are ordered mainly chronologically. The final Chapter 8 surveying decisions is indeed a further attempt to systematize what is 'not given to systematic analysis', a delicate area being maintenance of international peace and security and the relationship between the Security Council and the International Court of Justice.

Although appearing in the broadly conceived International Courts and Tribunal Series, the book is confined to the International Court of Justice and the International Tribunal for the Law of the Sea, with an emphasis on the former. This is a perfectly legitimate choice, but hardly a choice that is dictated by the different settings of other international courts and tribunals (cf 6–7). The *LaGrand* case was foreshadowed, to some degree, by a procedural order issued by an ICSID tribunal on 28 October 1999 in *Maffezini v Spain* (cf 72), and in turn the *LaGrand* case has had effects elsewhere, such as the judgments of the European Court of Human Rights in *Mamatkulov and Askarov v Turkey* (Chamber, 6 February 2003 and Grand Chamber, 4 February 2005). The *LaGrand* case was partly based on the notion of a court of justice and 'the basic function of judicial settlement of international disputes by binding decisions'. This notion is not exactly unfamiliar to other international courts and tribunals, taken as it is from national contexts. Still, the author finds that '[t]he most that domestic experience and precedents can do is to point to the existence of the problem, and perhaps suggest the direction in which possible solutions might be found' (4). Rosenne doubts that domestic analogies may justify the view that an applicant for provisional measures should provide guarantee for damages and costs to the other party in the event that measures are granted but the case ultimately lost on the merits (132). The question was the subject of argument in the *Case concerning Passage through the Great Belt*, but the ICJ did not mention this aspect in its order (rejecting Finland's request for lack of urgency).

The fundamental question underpinning the vague wording of Article 41 of the ICJ Statute still lingers in the background, or rather in a footnote: 'What is the scope of a binding decision of an unenforceable character?' (31). Rosenne's straightforward answer is that 'non-compliance with it could give rise to a claim for reparation as an internationally wrongful act' (36). There may be subtle ways to achieve this result in specific cases, yet none comes immediately to mind. It is far from obvious that the alleged claim for reparation survives ultimate defeat on the merits. And even if the injured State prevails on the merits, would the other party's non-compliance with an order for provisional measures entail a remedy? Irreparable prejudice might have been caused to rights held by the injured State and restitution thus a more remote possibility. Compensation would require proof of extra damage caused specifically by not complying with the order.

Rosenne notes 'the increasing tendency of parties to use requests for the indication of provisional measures as an opportunity to provide an early outline of their case on the merits' (122), and he applauds the ICJ's use of orders on provisional measures to facilitate possible settlement in 'judicial dicta, not part of the *ratio* but relevant to a collateral matter' (213). Whether the ICJ actually contributed to the settlement of the *Case concerning Passage through the Great Belt*, the example pointed to by Rosenne, is another matter.

The book contains a wealth of information and practical hints as well as a host of wonderful observations of a more personal kind, for example that distribution of information through the internet and e-mail 'is not a satisfactory or reliable substitute for hard copies of important messages and texts' (163). While this particular observation may be lacking in appeal for younger generations, lawyers of all ages looking for practical guidance on provisional matters will be rewarded if consulting this piece by a master, whether concerned with the ICJ, the ITLOS or some other international forum.

OLE SPIERMANN

Great Powers and Outlaw States: Unequal Sovereigns in the International Legal Order. By GERRY SIMPSON. Cambridge: Cambridge University Press, 2004. 391 pp £65.00hb, £22.99pb.

The basic thesis of the book may be stated simply enough. It is a challenge to the orthodox view of international law as a 'horizontal' system—meaning a system of juridically equal states carpeting the entire world without gaps, and with no sovereign reigning over all. The author puts the alternative thesis that international law should be seen as a sort of 'vertical' order, which is given the somewhat peculiar label 'juridical sovereignty'. It is conceded that there is a large horizontal midriff (so to speak) of states. But some stand out proudly 'above' the crowd, while others sink ignominiously 'below' it. Those above are the great powers, to which the label 'legal hegemony' is attached. Those below are criminal or 'outlaw states'. To those whose terminology is more old-fashioned, it may be said that this book presents a case for seeing international law in terms of what Aristotle called 'distributive justice' rather than of 'commutative justice'.

Much of the argument in favour of this vertical analysis—and much of the interest of the book—is historical in character. The idea of a legally privileged position for great powers is held to have emerged in 1815 with the Vienna settlement of the French Revolutionary Wars. An effort was made, chiefly in the Hague Peace Conferences of 1899 and 1907 and also with the League of Nations, to institute a true horizontal, 'democratic' order in its stead. But this effort was, in historical terms, both anomalous and temporary. Since 1945, the vertical character of international society has re-emerged—and particularly in the outstanding cases of the Kosovo intervention of 1999 and the Afghanistan conflict of 2001. In this same period, the concept of outlaw or criminal states (a phenomenon labelled 'anti-pluralism' by the author) has emerged into the juridical mainstream, with states such as Cambodia, Afghanistan, and Libya in the starring roles.

It is likely that this analysis will appeal more strongly to persons of an international-politics, or international-relations, turn of mind than it will to lawyers. Consider first the upper tier, the great-power hegemons. Interestingly, the author places little reliance on the various ways in which legal privileges are openly and explicitly accorded to great powers—permanent seats on the UN Security Council, weighted voting in the IMF and so forth. Instead, he concentrates on two phenomena: first, the claim of major powers to a right of humanitarian intervention, on conspicuous display in Kosovo; and second, the United States' claim to a broad (and arguably over-broad) right of self-defence, manifested chiefly in Afghanistan. Some readers will object that neither of these really involves a claim to *exclusive* privileges by the major powers. In the case of Kosovo (and arguably of Iraq in 2003), what the major powers did was to step in as self-appointed enforcers of *general* community norms—without claiming to be exempt from those norms themselves. Similarly, the United States' view of self-defence may be over-broad—but there is little (if any) real evidence that the United States attempts to deny to others what it claims for itself. A ready example is the support of the United States for robust self-defence measures by Israel, which goes virtually unmentioned in the discussion.

Regarding the author's analysis of the nether region of this vertical world, there will also be serious misgivings. Here, the principal objection is that, while expressions such as 'outlaw' states or 'criminal' states have a certain appeal from the political standpoint, they are highly problematic legally. The idea of the criminality of states is woefully undeveloped in international law, to put it mildly (if, indeed, it makes any sense at all). Similarly, outlawry is only the loosest of metaphors, since there are no real instances of states undergoing a wholesale forfeiture of legal personality, as that term would imply to a lawyer.

These criticisms, it must be emphasized, would not be worth voicing unless the author's case was powerfully made—which it certainly is. The book is a strongly argued work of advocacy, with the author constantly present in the first person singular, pressing his points against potential foes and sceptics with both vigour and skill. (In fact, the text often reads like the transcript of a seminar presentation.) The case presented is likely to elicit—at least from lawyers—rather more in the way of lively debate than of hearty assent. That is not to condemn the book. On the contrary, it is to give it a warm, and merited, endorsement. This author forcefully compels his readers to think about international law in different ways from those that they are accustomed to. If he does not wholly persuade, he does invariably stimulate—and that is high praise indeed.

STEPHEN C NEFF

The International Law on Foreign Investment. By M SORNARAJAH. Cambridge: Cambridge University Press, 2004, 2nd Edition. xxv + 488 pp + bibliography + index. £70hb, £30pb.

To review a second edition of a book is not something that any journal or yearbook will do automatically. Thus, when one decides to publish such a review, there are generally very good reasons for doing so; and this is the case here. Whatever criticisms I might have of this book (and in fact there are few), *The International Law on Foreign Investment* is clearly an excellent book and the second edition remains an extremely important contribution to an area of law that continues to be much ignored academically. As Eileen Denza noted in her review of the first edition in the *Year Book*, 'this is a book which deserves to become a classic in a sensitive, important and rapidly changing area of law' ((1994) 65 BYIL 483–4). The last decade has more than proved Denza correct; as the author himself notes in the preface to the second edition, '[t]he international law on foreign investment has witnessed an explosive growth since the last edition' (xv).

The significance of this book is that international investment law is considered as a subject clearly worthy of study in its own right. As Sornarajah says, '[t]he time is now ripe for the isolation and separate development of this branch of international law' (33). Whilst one might caution against the compartmentalization of international law into relatively artificial 'sub-disciplines', the sentiment expressed that international investment law is sufficiently established to emerge as a coherent legal framework—though still arguably somewhat optimistic—is certainly not unrealistic.

However, the attempt at specialism in this area of the law has, in the past usually led to a one-sided view of investment issues: international investment law referring to nothing more than scrutiny of the domestic law of the host State. Such a view, which long overshadowed much of the discussion of this topic and clearly flowed from the many political controversies surrounding foreign investment, is fortunately gradually being replaced by a more rounded approach (again, arguably in response to the changing investment climate). In particular, this book recognizes that the activities of the investor (and, in certain instances, home State) are equally worthy of academic analysis. Though the book gives great weight to the 'traditional' topics of investment law (such as regulation of entry, standards of treatment, bilateral investment treaties (BITs), expropriation and compensation), the inclusion of a separate chapter on potential liabilities of multinational corporations and the home State is very welcome—even if much remains arguably *lex ferenda*.

There is also discussion of various attempts to negotiate standards of behaviour for multinational corporations, principally the draft code of the United Nations Commission on Transnational Corporations. Though the work that went into the draft code remains extremely valuable and it is not surprising that the book discusses this, it is arguable that greater emphasis should have been given to the OECD Guidelines for Multinational Enterprises, which are, in fact, operative. The lack of substantive analysis of the OECD Guidelines within the book is difficult to explain, and constitutes, for me, one of its principal weaknesses.

However, in the light of the amount of material that the author has had to sift in the period between the two editions, such criticism is possibly too harsh. The volume of case law, on its own, since 1994 has been substantial; many of the most important cases—though certainly not all—having arisen under Chapter XI ('investor protection') of the 1992 North American Free Trade Agreement (NAFTA). Significantly, many of these cases also raised new concerns, particularly environmental considerations, as well as reconsideration of older issues, such as the precise nature and scope of expropriation. Sornarajah notes, I think correctly, that '[a]s the same arbitrators and arbitral institutions are often involved in the settlement of other foreign investment disputes, the tendency to use decisions made under NAFTA will ensure that the trends become widespread' (355). Though this clearly relates back to the earlier point about the need for greater coherence within international investment law as a discrete legal topic, there must also be some caution. The reasoning in many of these arbitral decisions has not gone unchallenged; many commentators remain concerned that the rather isolated nature of investment arbitrations often makes balanced judgments more difficult. Though the case law arising under NAFTA will surely continue to be at the forefront of where international investment law is progressing in the current global economic climate, this is not the same as saying that such decisions are actually correct.

Moving beyond the case law, the book justifiably dwells upon recent attempts at creating a more global approach to international investment. After noting the attempt to negotiate, as well as the ultimate failure of, the draft Multilateral Agreement on Investment within the remit of the OECD (the World Bank Guidelines on Foreign Investment are also noted), the book quickly moves on to the current forum of debate, the World Trade Organization. Though the book is already out of date on this point (in its 'July package' (WTO General Council decision, 1 August 2004), the WTO decided that 'no work towards negotiations' would take place, during the Doha negotiations, on, *inter alia*, trade and investment matters), the author's discussion of the issues raised continue to remain extremely pertinent. In particular, he is keenly aware of the implications of the developmental imperative of the 2001 Doha WTO Ministerial Declaration on investment issues for an acceptable investment instrument to be created 'there must be sufficient flexibility to accommodate the interests of the developing states' (*sic*) (314). He rightly concludes that '[t]he battle-lines are clearly drawn' (ibid).

International investment law has come a long way since 1994; possibly further than in any other similar time-period. On that basis alone, this second edition is both necessary and extremely well timed. Though not all will agree with the conclusions that it reaches (unsurprising in such a contentious area of the law), even those who hold very differing views will find much to think about. The author has seemingly responded to the request in this *Year Book*'s first review to include a table of cases cited. I would now make a similar request for a table of treaties and other documents, which I think would be equally useful.

D French

Civil Society, International Courts and Compliance Bodies. Edited by Tullio Treves *et al* The Hague: TMC Asser Press, 2005. xx + 317 pp £55.

This volume, which contains the essays written by professors of international law and activists of non-governmental organizations (NGOs), examines the process of participation of NGOs in international judicial proceedings, notably the legal framework of such participation, the forms of participation and the outcomes. The analysis covers a variety of NGOs, as well as different international judicial and quasi-judicial organs, from the International Court of Justice to the World Bank Inspection Panel.

As for the International Court of Justice, the essay of Dean Zagorac (11–40) examines the possibilities of NGOs' involvement in proceedings, especially in terms of the 1950 Advisory Opinion on *International Status of South-West Africa*, in which the Court allowed international NGOs to present submissions. The Court has not taken a position on this issue since then. In *DRC v Belgium* an NGO presented to the Court a 750-page memorandum on universal jurisdiction, but as the judges had no facilities to read CD-ROMs, it was not clear if that memorandum was seen by all judges. The essay by

Eduardo Valencia-Ospina (227–32) also examines the role of NGOs before the ICJ and concludes that the practice of the Court has not clarified the matter. He quotes Judge Guillaume's statement that national governments must be independent enough to resist the pressures by NGOs which besiege them with the support of mass-media. However, Valencia-Ospina concludes that it is not clear whether Judge Guillaume's approach is shared by the entire Court, and the Court itself has not closed the gate that it opened in 1950.

With regard to other tribunals, Catharina Harby's essay on the European Court of Human Rights is interesting (41–6). She discusses the role of NGOs in taking cases to Strasbourg and also the issue of the cost of litigation. The essay of Marco Frigessi di Rattalama is on similar issues (57–66). He discusses in particular the role of NGOs in representing the victims before the Strasbourg Court and concludes that NGOs have no general authority to represent victims before this Court. Gianluca Rubagotti examines the role of NGOs in the proceedings of the UN Human Rights Committee (67–92). He examines the issue of inter-State communications to the Committee and concludes that NGOs have not dedicated resources to this mechanism, especially because of the tendency of States to tolerate some violations of the Covenant in order not to compromise the often delicate balance of international relations. This reasoning does not seem convincing, however. NGOs ought not to ignore the law-enforcing potential that can be offered by inter-State litigation before human rights tribunals. While acting in democratic societies, NGOs have to promote public awareness of the benefits this kind of litigation may offer the victims of human rights violations, as well as improve the general human rights situation in States parties to the relevant human rights treaties.

The volume contains a number of essays related to the role of NGOs in the process of international criminal justice. In this regard, the essay of Mariacarmen Colitti (107–12) should be singled out because it concerns the role of NGOs in examining cases of massive human rights atrocities. This essay focuses on the mission of the organization 'No Peace Without Justice' in Kosovo in 1998 and its report which was presented to the Rambouillet Peace Talks and the UN Commission on Human Rights. The essay of Chiara Ragni (129–42) focuses on a similar role of the same organization in East Timor. Such activities can be very useful, especially if not limited to one single place, but extended to other spots where massive human rights violations are a common occurrence, such as Iraq, Liberia, or Sudan.

There are also several essays on the role of NGOs in the protection of the environment. From these, the essay of Laurence Boisson de Chazournes on the World Bank Inspection Panel (187–204) is significant. She examines the legal framework established by the 1994 Resolution of the World Bank establishing the Inspection Panel and its 1996 and 1999 Clarifications with regard to the standing of persons who may bring the relevant situations to the attention of the Panel. Paragraph 12 of the 1992 Resolution assumes here the utmost importance because it specifies the circle of such actors. At the same time, the suggestion that the Inspection Panel is not a dispute settlement procedure, or that it is not a mechanism of challenging or asserting the international organisation's legal responsibility (199), does not seem to reflect the legal framework within which the Inspection Panel operates.

In general, this volume must be commended for its comprehensive outlook and its successful attempt to bring together the insights and experiences of a number of academics and practitioners dealing with the role of NGOs in international judicial proceedings. In this sense, it can be offered as a useful source of reference to those students, scholars, and practitioners who are interested in such problems. At the same time, it would have been better if this compilation had supported more active involvement of NGOs in such processes, not only in the sense of applying existing mechanisms, but also in terms of improving such mechanisms and using those channels which are for good or bad reasons deemed irrelevant. It should also be mentioned that every essay deals with proceedings within one specific instrument or procedure and the book thus lacks comparative or systematic insights into the problems to which it is dedicated. The development and presentation of such insights would be very important, as the victims of many human rights violations could be offered an opportunity with the help of NGOs, to advance their cause before more than one international institution.

ALEXANDER ORAKHELASHVILI

The Emergence of a European Asylum Policy. Edited by CD URBANA SOUSA and P DE BRUYCKER. Brussels: Bruylant, 2004. 344 pp €65.

This edited volume contains proceedings of the second Congress of lawyers specializing in European immigration and asylum law that took place in Lisbon in November 2002. The seventeen chapters offer a mixed bag of conference-based presentations, and commentaries by academics, as well as practitioners, from several EU Member States. Not all contributions are original; some are based on material already published elsewhere. The introductory chapter aside, most chapters discuss a specific element of the 'future' common asylum policy: Dublin II Regulation, the procedure Directive, the reception Directive, and the qualification Directive, following a critical approach. The last three chapters, however, have a clear international law focus and are dedicated to identifying some of the key principles in international refugee law and human rights law which should impact on the content and scope of the common asylum policy. Most chapters are written in English; five of them are in French.

The book contains some truly insightful contributions to the debate on the development of a common asylum policy. I will refer briefly to four of them. First is the introductory chapter by Jean-Yves Carlier focusing on the rationale for a common policy and discussing its characteristics in terms of norm creation, norm content, and norm review. This provides a clear and effective introduction to many of the later chapters. In his conclusion, Carlier also warns the Member States against too much legislative activity (as was the case with the common agricultural policy) and against the lack of a strong common objective in its own right (in terms of defining the scope *ratione personae* of protection). Second is the valuable contribution by Agnès Hurwitz, offering a clear analytical framework for understanding the Dublin Regulation based on the principle of authorization and the principle of extra-territoriality. She also develops concluding remarks on the principle of solidarity (or burden-sharing) and calls for the recognition of this principle in European refugee law by the European Court of Justice. Third is the detailed contribution by John Handoll on Directive 2003/9, on the reception conditions of asylum seekers, adopted in January 2003. This is a remarkably precise (if still lengthy) account of the background of the Directive as well as its content. It also provides insightful suggestions for further discussion, in particular around two concepts: the concept of 'risk', in that the Member States may view the adoption of generous reception conditions as a threat because it may attract more asylum seekers, and the concept of 'dignified standard'. Finally, in the last chapter of the book, Elspeth Guild skilfully discusses the effect of the jurisprudence of the European Court of Human Rights, on one hand, and of the Dublin Convention, on the other, on the development of an EU asylum policy. Her conclusion discusses the consequences of the EU adopting legislation that fails to meet the standards in the European Convention on Human Rights, in particular in terms of the 'constitutional integrity of the Union', in terms of Article 6(2) of the Treaty on European Union, and in terms of a history of respect for fundamental rights.

In sum, this is a useful read for anyone interested in this fast-moving area of law. Most of the draft legislation discussed here has since been adopted (with the exception of the Procedure Directive), yet most of the arguments and observations remain valid. This is particularly true regarding the tension between political difficulties and legal obligations in the building of a common European asylum policy which several chapters successfully manage to highlight.

HÉLÈNE LAMBERT

L'actio popularis *ou la défense de l'intérêt collectif devant des juridictions internationales*. By FRANÇOIS VOEFFRAY. Paris: Presses Universitaires de France, 2004. 403 pp €40.

This book is a systematic and comprehensive examination of the phenomenon of judicial action in the public interest in international law. The author starts with historical and comparative analysis of the concept of *actio popularis* (3–38). Then he proceeds with the development of this and related concepts in the jurisprudence of the World Court (43–106), and considers the resources available in regional and specialized international tribunals for the realization of *actio popularis* (107–219). Afterwards, the normative foundations of *actio popularis* such as peremptory norms and *erga omnes* obligations are examined (229–319). Finally, after dealing with the conceptual objections to the relevance of the concept of *actio popularis* in international law (335–55), the author concludes that *actio popularis* indisputably exists in international law (383). A good systematic analysis and accurate examination of materials is characteristic of each and every part of the book, and several aspects of the analysis developed therein deserve a closer attention and emphasis.

The book defines *actio popularis* as judicial action which can be instituted by any member of the community with a view to protect a totally or partially common interest (38). Obligations *erga omnes* are identified as a conceptual and normative basis of *actio popularis*. It is emphasized that the concept of *erga omnes* obligations accepted by the Court in *Barcelona Traction* supports the concept of *actio popularis* (78). The *Nuclear Tests* case also confirms the existence of a close link between *erga omnes* obligations and *actio popularis* (82). The Court's consideration of the *East Timor* case involved some considerations of *actio popularis*, which was one of the bases of the applicant's case; although in the Court's Judgment another basis for the applicant's action—its status as East Timor's administering power—proved more relevant. It must also be added that the Court said nothing against the concept of *actio popularis*. The *East Timor* case does not itself concern the issue of *actio popularis* and, as the author remarks, the Court was concerned with *erga omnes* rights not *erga omnes* obligations, the former being the rights opposable to all and the latter obligations in the observance of which everyone has a legal interest (86).

The author deals with the International Court's jurisprudence on the matter of *actio popularis*. The 1966 second phase judgment in *South-West Africa* is the only instance of judicial disapproval of the concept of *actio popularis*, which by itself means that there is not much evidence to prove that such public action is not permissible in international law. The author, interestingly enough, goes a step further by asserting that the second phase *South-West Africa* judgment did not prohibit *actio popularis* but merely laid down a presumption against this concept (92).

But, while following this proposition, is it necessary to speak about presumptions and the possibility of their rebuttal? Bearing in mind all relevant factors, including the circumstances of adoption of the second *South-West Africa* judgment and factors that ensured that the Court's composition would be what it was in 1966, the fact that other judgments at least implicitly approve the concept of *actio popularis*, and, most recently, the treatment of the outcome of the 1966 judgment in the commentaries of the UN International Law Commission's Articles on State responsibility, and it can be suggested that the second *South-West Africa* case was perhaps an unfortunate deviation from an established line of jurisprudence suggesting that, in the limited circumstances where the relevant substantive norms and obligations so require, States can sue without the need to prove that the case involves their individual interest.

Thus, if the relevant issues are considered in context, then the kinds of presumptions the 1966 Judgment laid down, and the entire value of that judgment, becomes less relevant. But the author's argument is nevertheless interesting and useful as an explanation of the case for those who still believe that the second *South-West Africa* judgment is a correct statement of law.

While following his understanding of the *Barcelona Traction* case as supporting the concept of *actio popularis*, the author develops the idea that this case has effected a public rectification, even if in a discrete form, of the second *South-West Africa* judgment (93). It is emphasized that *Barcelona Traction* established that the issue of suing in the public interest cannot be decided at the preliminary objections stage in the International Court's proceedings, but must be treated as part of the substance of the pertinent dispute (94). In several other places it is emphasized that the relevance of *actio popularis* is linked to the substantive nature of relevant legal relations, such as the involvement of *erga omnes* obligations and integral, or objective, obligations embodied in treaties. These legal phenomena themselves imply that *actio popularis* is available (157–8, 220, 261). In general, the concept of *actio popularis* is viewed as part of a broader development of the system of international law towards admitting a number of legal concepts regulating legal relations that go beyond individual and bilateral interest of States (235–6).

As a matter of the constant development of the international legal system, the book examines the resources available in the adjudication systems of several specialized and regional international tribunals and finds that a number of such systems contain the resources for the realization of *actio popularis*. At the same time, similar resources in the regime of nullity of treaties conflicting with peremptory norms under the 1969 Vienna Convention on the Law of Treaties are considered. A clear conclusion emerges, that the concept of nullity for contradiction with *jus cogens* itself requires that any State, at least any State party to the Vienna Convention, can invoke such nullity, whether or not it is itself a party to the relevant treaty (272).

The author affirms the conceptual link between peremptory norms and *erga omnes* obligations (243) and examines the concept of peremptory norms at some length. However, more could be said about the relevance of peremptory norms beyond the law of treaties than is discussed here (258–9), and the analysis of the relationship between peremptory norms and *erga omnes* obligations (259–60) could be developed, for instance by pointing out the precise legal basis of those *erga omnes* obligations that are not, in the author's view, based on peremptory norms. For there must be a reason why those *erga omnes* obligations that are not based on *jus cogens* possess their *erga omnes* character; a self-explanatory argument would be circular.

A major virtue of this book is that it encourages seeing the conceptual and normative links between similar phenomena in different legal frameworks and institutions. This is partly achieved by the use of the method of comparative analysis. Not only is all relevant data accounted for, but also a clear account is given of the development and evolution of rules, concepts, and institutions. The accuracy and systematic approach in clarifying concepts and definitions is also an important asset. The author uses categorical and conceptual approaches to demonstrate the essence of the relevant legal phenomena and this results in a freedom from evidence-based constraints on thought and analysis. Such an approach makes it possible properly to comprehend the legal character of the relevant phenomena and institutions; it also makes it possible to view different elements of the international legal system as parts of a single system, which facilitates making parallels between the legal phenomena resembling *actio popularis* in different fields. All this confirms that the book is not only a good analysis of law, but also a good exercise in thinking. It is only regrettable that not everybody among the English-speaking readers will be able to become familiar with it.

ALEXANDER ORAKHELASHVILI

DECISIONS OF BRITISH COURTS DURING 2005 INVOLVING QUESTIONS OF PUBLIC OR PRIVATE INTERNATIONAL LAW

A. PUBLIC INTERNATIONAL LAW[1]

*European Convention on Human Rights, article 3—*Soering *jurisprudence—threatened ill-treatment by non-State actors in receiving State—Human Rights Act 1998—Refugee Convention—whether claimant relying on ECHR, article 3 to resist expulsion in context of real risk of harm by non-State actors must prove authorities of receiving State are unwilling or unable to provide reasonable level of protection*

Case No 1. R (Bagdanavicius) v Secretary of State for the Home Department, 26 May 2005, [2005] UKHL 38, [2005] 2 AC 668, [2005] 2 WLR 1359, [2005] 4 All ER 263, 2005 WL 1185497 (HL).

The claimants, a married Lithuanian couple not qualifying as refugees within the meaning of the Refugee Convention,[2] challenged the Secretary of State's certification of their claim to remain in the UK as 'clearly unfounded',[3] arguing, on the basis of the *Soering*[4] line of jurisprudence, that it was incompatible with their right not to be subjected to inhuman or degrading treatment, as guaranteed, via the HRA, by article 3 of the ECHR. They contended that they would be at real risk of violence from the wife's brother and his associates, alleged members of the Lithuanian mafia, on account of the husband's Roma origins. (The possibility of a *Soering*-style claim in respect of harm by non-State actors had been recognized by the ECtHR in *HLR v France*[5] and was accepted by the Secretary of State.) The claimants did not show, however, that there was an unwillingness or inability on the part of the Lithuanian authorities to provide them with protection against the threatened ill-treatment; indeed, they conceded that the Lithuanian authorities would so provide. For his part, the Secretary of State conceded for the purposes of the case that the claimants would indeed face a real risk of violence of the sort they feared, despite the protection afforded by the Lithuanian authorities. The question for determination by the House of Lords was whether, in order to resist expulsion on the basis of a *Soering*-style claim under article 3, it was enough in cases such as this for the claimants to establish that they would be at real risk of serious harm from non-State actors or whether they were

[1] © Dr Roger O'Keefe, 2006.

[2] Convention relating to the Status of Refugees, Geneva, 28 July 1951, 189 UNTS 2545.

[3] See Nationality, Immigration and Asylum Act 2002, s 115.

[4] *Soering v United Kingdom* (1989) 11 EHRR 439.

[5] (1997) 26 EHRR 29.

also obliged to show that the authorities of the receiving State did not provide those within its territory with a reasonable level of protection against such harm.

The House of Lords held unanimously that, in addition to showing that they would face a real risk, if returned, of serious harm at the hands of non-State actors, the claimants were required to prove that the authorities of the receiving State were unwilling or unable to afford them a reasonable level of protection against this. Lord Brown, giving the leading judgment with which all the other Lords agreed, stated:

> 23 It is noteworthy that the risk referred to in the first sentence of para 91 [of *Soering*] is of 'being subjected to torture or to inhuman or degrading treatment or punishment' ('proscribed ill-treatment' as that is conveniently summarised in the fourth sentence); the later formulation speaks of 'a real risk of being subjected to treatment contrary to article 3'. All these expressions in terms refer to harm which, if it eventuates, would involve a violation (actual or notional) of article 3. The position surely is plain. There is no warrant whatever for reading *Soering* or any of the other cases as barring expulsion where the real risk is not of 'proscribed ill-treatment' but is merely of harm, however serious.
>
> 24 The plain fact is that the argument throughout has been bedevilled by a failure to grasp the distinction in non-state agent cases between on the one hand the risk of serious harm and on the other hand the risk of treatment contrary to article 3. In cases where the risk 'emanates from intentionally inflicted acts of the public authorities in the receiving country' (the language of *D* v. *United Kingdom* (1997) 24 EHRR 423, 447, para. 49) one can use those terms interchangeably: the intentionally inflicted acts would without more constitute the proscribed treatment. Where, however, the risk emanates from non-state bodies, that is not so: any harm inflicted by non-state agents will not constitute article 3 ill-treatment unless in addition the state has failed to provide reasonable protection. If someone is beaten up and seriously injured by a criminal gang, the member state will not be in breach of article 3 unless it has failed in its positive duty to provide reasonable protection against such criminal acts. This provides the answer to [the claimants'] reliance on the UK's obligation under article 3 being a negative obligation and thus absolute. The argument begs the vital question as to what particular risk engages the obligation. Is it the risk merely of harm or is it the risk of proscribed treatment? In my judgment it is the latter. The very identification of the issue for determination by the House in the agreed statement of facts and issues illustrates the confusion:
>
>> 'If, on removal to another country, there is a real risk that a person would suffer torture or inhuman or degrading treatment or punishment from non-state agents, will removal violate article 3 of the ECHR, or must the person concerned also show that there is in that country an insufficiency of state protection against such ill-treatment?'
>
> Non-state agents do not subject people to torture or the other proscribed forms of ill-treatment, however violently they treat them: what, however, would transform such violent treatment into article 3 ill-treatment would be the state's failure to provide reasonable protection against it.[6]

[6] [2005] 2 AC 668, 676–7.

Nor did any jurisprudence of the ECtHR suggest the contrary.[7] Rather, the case of *HLR v France* showed that the claimant 'had to succeed on two independent points to establish his article 3 claim'.[8] Since the claimants in the present case had not proved that the Lithuanian authorities were unwilling or unable to provide them with a reasonable level of protection against the harm they feared from the non-State actors in question, their appeal had to be dismissed.

Lord Brown, continuing avowedly obiter, also considered the Refugee Convention:

29 . . . A large part of the judgment below—and a good deal of the argument before your Lordships—was devoted to the relationship between the question presently for decision and the concepts of a well-founded fear of persecution and the sufficiency of state protection arising under the Refugee Convention. It is, of course, plainly established that, in cases under the Refugee Convention where the well-founded fear of persecution emanates from non-state agents, the asylum seeker must establish not merely the risk of severe ill-treatment but also that his home state was unwilling or unable to provide a reasonable level of protection from it: see *Horvath* v. *Secretary of State for the Home Department* [2001] 1 AC 489. As, however, [counsel for the claimants] was at pains to emphasise, that is a different Convention from the ECHR, providing in certain respects narrower, though in others wider, protection than the ECHR, the one founded on the principle of surrogacy, the other on more general humanitarian considerations, one (the ECHR) subject to the rulings of a supranational court, the other (the Refugee Convention) not. Moreover, not all those party to the Refugee Convention recognise even the concept of persecution by non-state agents.

30 All that said, however, it is perhaps not surprising that where, as in the United Kingdom, the concept of persecution by non-state agents *is* recognised, a broadly similar approach is adopted under both Conventions to the requirement for the person concerned to demonstrate in addition to the risk of harm a failure in the receiving state to provide a reasonable level of protection. . . . Certainly your Lordships should state for the guidance of practitioners and tribunals generally that in the great majority of cases an article 3 claim to avoid expulsion will add little if anything to an asylum claim.[9]

His Lordship finally noted, 'by the way', that Lithuania had, in the meantime, joined the EU, giving the claimants a right to seek work in the UK.[10]

The House's decision, although a sensible one, is arguably not the correct one. Its reliance on the distinction between the risk of serious ill-treatment, on the one hand, and the risk of treatment amounting to a violation of article 3, on the other, is questionable.

For a start, their Lordships' position betrays an over-determined and self-contradictory reading of the Strasbourg jurisprudence. Lord Brown never countenances the possibility that the expressions 'being subjected to torture or to inhuman or degrading treatment or punishment'

[7] [2005] 2 AC 668, 677, para 25. [8] [2005] 2 AC 668, 678, para 27.
[9] [2005] 2 AC 668, 678–9. [10] [2005] 2 AC 668, 679, para 31.

(*Soering*)[11] and 'being subjected to treatment contrary to article 3' (subsequent cases, such as *HLR*)[12] may, when applied to the threatened fate of the claimant in the receiving State, have been used by the ECtHR in what his Lordship refers to elsewhere as a 'notional' sense—in this case, to refer to ill-treatment severe enough that it would, if perpetrated by State authorities, constitute a violation of article 3. At the same time, his Lordship freely accepts that these same expressions are used notionally insofar as the receiving State is not a Contracting State to the ECHR and is thus incapable of violating the Convention—in other words, that the expressions are used to refer to ill-treatment which would, if the receiving State were a party to the ECHR, constitute a violation of article 3.

Lord Brown's reading of the Strasbourg authorities is also selective, within and as between cases. He quotes *HLR* to the effect that, in a non-State actor case, it 'must be shown that the risk is real and that the authorities of the receiving State are not able to obviate the risk by providing appropriate protection';[13] but he does not quote from the many paragraphs which show quite convincingly that the Court treated the second limb merely as an aspect of the first. Indeed, the final paragraph of *HLR* reads:

> In the light of these considerations, the Court finds that no substantial grounds have been established for believing that the applicant, if deported, would be exposed to a real risk of being subjected to inhuman or degrading treatment within the meaning of Article 3. It follows that there would be no violation of Article 3 if the order for the applicant's deportation was to be executed.[14]

His Lordship brushes off cases which do not fit his thesis. *D v United Kingdom*—where the ECtHR held that the expulsion of the claimant, who was being treated in the UK for the advanced stages of HIV/AIDS, to a State where he would receive no such treatment amounted to a violation by the UK of article 3—is raised (only after, it might be noted, his Lordship's effective dismissal of the appeal) merely to be cast aside as a curiosity:

> *D*, of course, was a case where article 3 was found to be engaged notwithstanding that the risk of harm (amounting there to the certainty of imminent death) involved no actual or notional breach of article 3 on the part of the receiving state. *D*, however, was a very exceptional case—just how exceptional has recently been made clear by the decision of this House in *N* v. *Secretary of State for the Home Department (Terrence Higgins Trust intervening)* [2005] AC 296—and the present appellants cannot and do not seek to rely upon it.[15]

Perhaps more significantly, *Ahmed v Austria* gets short shrift:

> *Ahmed* v. *Austria* 24 EHRR 278 appears to be the only [*Soering*-style case relating to non-State actors] where the court has in fact concluded (as by then

[11] (1989) 11 EHRR 439, 468, para 91.
[12] (1998) 26 EHRR 29, 29, para 1.
[13] (1998) 26 EHRR 29, 50, para 40.
[14] (1998) 26 EHRR 29, 51, para 44.
[15] [2005] 2 AC 668, 678, para 28.

Austria too had concluded) that 'the applicant's deportation to Somalia would breach article 3 of the ECHR for as long as he faces a serious risk of being subjected there to torture or inhuman or degrading treatment' (p. 292, para. 47). As, however, had already been pointed out at p. 291, para. 44 (see para. 10 above), there existed in Somalia both danger and a complete absence of state protection.[16]

By 'complete absence of state protection', his Lordship is referring to 'the [then-] current lack of State authority in Somalia'[17]—that is, to the complete absence of State authority, replaced, in the words of paragraph 44, by 'a state of civil war ... between a number of clans vying with each other for control of the country'. But surely, on Lord Brown's own reasoning, if there were no State authorities in Somalia notionally capable of 'proscribed ill-treatment' through their failure to take positive steps to protect the applicant, there could be no breach of article 3 by Austria. In other words, what the European Court must be taken to have said in *Ahmed* was that insufficiency of State protection is not an independent requirement for a successful *Soering*-style claim in a non-State actor case but goes, rather, to the reality of the risk: a real risk of serious ill-treatment by non-State actors and an absence of protection from State authorities equals a real risk of serious ill-treatment on the applicant's expulsion to the receiving State.

More fundamentally, as *Ahmed* shows, Lord Brown rejects the more obvious justification for the statement in *HLR* that claimants must show that the authorities of the receiving State are unwilling or unable to provide them with appropriate protection. Yet he never offers compelling reasons for doing so, perfunctorily dismissing it on the basis of a personal and unexplained preference:

> I should perhaps record at this point [the defendant]'s alternative submission. This, as put in para. 96(3) of the Secretary of State's printed case, is that:
>
>> 'the sufficiency of state protection is an integral part of the "real risk" test: the reality of risk is assessed by reference to the sufficiency of such protection. Where a reasonable level of protection is provided, the threshold for the engagement of article 3 will not be met.'
>
> It rather seems as if this essentially fallback submission was the main basis of the Court of Appeal's decision in the Secretary of State's favour: see [2004] 1 WLR 1207, 1230–1231, para. 55(7)-(16). For my part, however, I prefer to decide the appeal by reference to the issue earlier formulated.[18]

Symptomatic of this seemingly *a priori* dismissal of the idea of sufficiency of State protection as an issue going to the reality of the risk is his Lordship's substitution of the expression 'appropriate protection', as used in *HLR*,[19] with the phrase 'a reasonable level of protection'.[20]

[16] [2005] 2 AC 668, 677, para 25.
[17] (1997) 24 EHRR 278, 292, para 46.
[18] [2005] 2 AC 668, 674, para 13.
[19] (1998) 26 EHRR 29, 50, para 40.
[20] [2005] 2 AC 668, 678–9 paras 29 and 30. See also [2005] 2 AC 668, 677, paras 24 and 26 ('reasonable protection').

The former, the language of the ECtHR itself, is directed not towards the blameworthiness or otherwise of the conduct of the authorities in the receiving State but simply towards the adequacy of any protection they may provide to prevent the occurrence of the harm from which the claimant is at risk. Lord Brown's 'reasonable level of protection' stands in similar contrast to the expression 'insufficiency of state protection' used in the agreed statement of facts and issues in the instant case.[21]

Lord Brown ultimately pins his reasoning on Lord Hope's translation of the word 'obvier',[22] as used in the crucial sentence his Lordship takes from *HLR*,[23] to mean 'to take precautions against'. But *pace* Lords Hope and Brown, 'obvier' can and usually does mean 'to obviate' or 'to avoid' or 'to prevent'—that is, it can and usually does denote result—and not simply 'to take measures against'. Lord Brown also draws on Sedley LJ's words in *McPherson v Secretary of State for the Home Department* to assert that 'the apparent requirement [in *HLR*] that the protection is sufficient to "obviate" the risk "cannot be right"', further quoting the latter to claim that ' "[w]hat the state is expected to do is take reasonable measures to make the necessary protection available" '.[24] But Sedley LJ himself appears to confuse the *Soering*-style cases with cases where the State called upon to take positive measures to obviate a risk of serious ill-treatment by non-State actors is the respondent to the claim. In the second type of case, it may well be that 'the positive obligation to take reasonable steps to protect people against serious harm ... is not absolute' but rather must, in the words of *Osman*, 'be interpreted in a way which does not impose an impossible or disproportionate burden on the authorities'.[25] But this has no necessary bearing on *Soering*-style cases, where it is the expelling, not receiving State which is defending the claim.

In the end, if there is any principled rationale to the *Soering* jurisprudence, especially as applied in cases such as *HLR* to a risk of serious ill-treatment by non-State actors, it is simply this: that the expelling State engages in conduct, viz expulsion, which will, on the balance of probabilities ('a real risk'), result in ill-treatment to the claimant in the receiving State of a severity considered inhuman or degrading within the meaning of article 3 of the ECHR. In this sense, the expelling State can be considered to have 'subjected' the claimant to inhuman or degrading treatment, and a Contracting State's subjection of a person to this sort of treatment is prohibited by article 3. Whether or not the receiving State is itself in 'notional' breach of article 3 through its failure or unwillingness to take positive measures against this treatment is immaterial: the

[21] See [2005] 2 AC 668, 677, para 2.4. [22] [2005] 2 AC 668, 678, para 27.

[23] 'Encore faut-il démontrer que le risque existe réellement et que les autorités de l'Etat de destination ne sont pas en mesure d'y obvier par une protection appropriée.'

[24] [2005] 2 AC 668, 678, para 27, quoting [2002] INLR 139, 147, para 22.

[25] *Osman v United Kingdom* (1998) 29 EHRR 245, 305, para 116.

blameworthiness of the receiving State can make no logical difference to the blameworthiness of the expelling State, unless responsibility pursuant to *Soering* is to be characterized as some form of imputed or transferred responsibility from the receiving to the expelling State, which would be even less coherent than things are already. Rather, the inability or unwillingness of the receiving State to prevent the threatened ill-treatment must properly be considered as an issue going to the probability of that ill-treatment. In this light, in order to recover in *Soering*-style cases under article 3 in respect of threatened ill-treatment by non-State actors in the receiving State, a claimant must, as posited in *HLR*, establish that the authorities of the receiving State do not provide an appropriate—as distinct from 'reasonable'—level of protection against the harm feared, in the sense of a level of protection sufficient to prevent that harm. In other words, claimants must establish that any protection which the receiving State authorities do offer would not, on the balance of probabilities, obviate the risk. In cases such as the present one, therefore, where the receiving State is willing and able to take preventive measures but where these measures would not, on the balance of probabilities, be sufficient to prevent the ill-treatment, the claimants should succeed. But this is not what the House of Lords has ruled.

All this said, the Lords' decision ought probably not to be read as a neutral application of the Strasbourg jurisprudence, especially in the light of paragraphs 29 and 30 of the judgment. It smacks instead of a push to approximate article 3 of the ECHR to the Refugee Convention. And this push is likely to be welcomed. The UK government has shown increasing impatience with the impact of the *Soering* jurisprudence, which ranks as one of the more overtly law-making and less convincing of the European Court's confections. The government's not unreasonable line is that the Refugee Convention is the *lex specialis* on *non-refoulement*: if claimants fail to satisfy its definition of a refugee, the ECHR ought not to afford them a second bite of the cherry. Presently, of course, it does, thanks to *Soering*. But the House of Lords has clearly decided that the two regimes should, where possible, be aligned. The present case does for article 3 of the ECHR what *Horvath*[26] did for article 1A of the Refugee Convention.

Immunity of foreign head of State—State Immunity Act 1978, section 20(1)(a)—Diplomatic Privileges Act 1964—Vienna Convention on Diplomatic Relations 1961, articles 29 and 31(1)—Matrimonial Causes Act 1973, section 27—Civil Procedure Rules, rules 39.2(1), 39.2(3)(c), and 39.2(4)—Family Proceedings Rules 1991, rule 2.66(2)—whether

[26] *Horvath v Secretary of State for the Home Department* [2001] 1 AC 489, (2000) 71 BYIL 418–22.

preliminary issue of immunity of foreign head of State raised in response to application for ancillary relief under Matrimonial Causes Act, section 27 to be heard in private and made subject to secrecy orders

Case No 2. Harb v His Majesty King Fahd Bin Abdul Aziz (No 1), 26 May 2005, [2005] EWCA Civ 632, 2005 WL 1185498 (CA (Civ Div)).

The applicant issued an originating application against the respondent, His Majesty King Fahd bin Abdul Aziz of Saudi Arabia, for ancillary relief under section 27 of the Matrimonial Causes Act 1973. Pursuant to this provision, the court may order one party to a marriage (the respondent) to make payment to the other (the applicant) where it is satisfied that the former has failed to provide the latter reasonable maintenance. The applicant alleged the bare essentials for such an application, namely that she was the respondent's wife and that he had failed to provide her reasonable maintenance. In support of her application, as required by the Family Court Rules, she filed an affidavit, the contents of which were a potential source of embarrassment to the King. In reply, the respondent argued that he was immune from the jurisdiction of the court in accordance with section 20(1)(a) of the State Immunity Act 1978 (SIA).[27] For her part, the applicant accepted that the Kingdom of Saudi Arabia was a State for the purposes of Part I of the SIA and that the respondent was the sovereign and head of that State within the meaning of section 20(1)(a), both concessions being reflected in agreed recitals to the District Judge's directions order. The preliminary issue of the respondent's immunity was tried in chambers before the President of the Family Division of the High Court (Butler-Sloss P).

The President first rejected the applicant's application for the preliminary issue of state immunity to be heard in open court in accordance with the general rule laid down in rule 39.2(1) of the Civil Procedure Rules, viz that a hearing is to be in public. She relied on rule 2.66(2) of the Family Proceedings Rules 1991, which states that where an application for ancillary relief has been referred to a judge, 'the hearing or consideration shall, unless the court otherwise directs, take place in chambers', the preliminary issue of state immunity being a question arising from an application for ancillary relief. Nor did she exercise her discretion to hear the application in public, since 'it would not be appropriate for it to be heard in public, for all the reasons that most of these cases should not be heard in public', namely that it was 'a very delicate and sensitive issue', 'the only advantage for it to be heard in public [being], from the point of view of the applicant, that there would be

[27] SIA 1978, s 20(1)(a) provides:

> Subject to the provisions of this section and to any necessary modifications, the Diplomatic Privileges Act 1964 shall apply to—
> (a) a sovereign or other head of State ...
> as it applies to the head of a diplomatic mission ...

immediate press interest in it'.[28] She did not see 'why a public figure such as the King should be in a worse position than any other litigant in family ancillary relief proceedings and that this issue, which would if it were not the King be heard in private, should because it is he be heard in public'.[29] In addition, the President ordered that the tape recordings of the proceedings and/or transcripts of them not be released or disclosed to any person or published in any form whatsoever without written permission. She also gave the case the fictitious name of *Maple v Maple*, after the District Judge. In the event, the President upheld the King's claim to immunity—presumably on the straightforward basis of article 31(1) of the Vienna Convention on Diplomatic Relations 1961,[30] applicable, via the Diplomatic Privileges Act 1964, to the King by virtue of section 20(1)(a) of the SIA—and refused permission to appeal. Additionally, she ordered that the judgment not be reported or published, refused the applicant permission to obtain transcripts of the proceedings, withheld publication of the names of the parties and/or of any other information which might lead to their identification in connection with the proceedings, and prohibited publication of any documents filed in connection with the proceedings and/or any other particulars of, or information relating to, any part of the proceedings, save insofar as such publication by or on behalf of either party was for the purposes solely of the proceedings.

The applicant sought permission to appeal the President's ruling on the King's immunity, and appealed both the President's dismissal of her application for a public hearing and all bar the last of the secrecy orders. The respondent applied in turn to hold the Court of Appeal hearing in chambers, on the basis of CPR 39.2(3)(c),[31] or, in the alternative, to maintain the anonymity of the parties, in accordance with CPR 39.2(4).[32] He relied principally on article 29 of the Vienna Convention on Diplomatic Relations (VCDR),[33] arguing that the court was a limb of the receiving State and that, were it to sit in public, it would fail in the duty imposed by article 29 to prevent any attack on his dignity.

The Court of Appeal (Civil Division), Thorpe LJ giving the leading judgment, dismissed the respondent's application, granted the applicant permission to appeal the President's ruling on immunity, and allowed her appeals against both the President's dismissal of her application for a public hearing and the relevant secrecy orders.

28 Quoted at [2005] EWCA Civ 632, para 25.

29 Quoted at [2005] EWCA Civ 632, para 25.

30 Vienna, 18 April 1961, 500 UNTS 95.

31 'A hearing, or any part of it, may be in private if ... it involves confidential information (including information relating to personal financial matters) and publicity would damage that confidentiality.'

32 'The court may order that the identity of any party or witness must not be disclosed if it considers non-disclosure necessary in order to protect the interests of that party or witness.'

33 Incorporating the 'necessary modifications' referred to in SIA 1978, s 20(1)(a), the VCDR, art 29 provides: 'The person of a [head of state] shall be inviolable. He shall not be liable to any form of arrest or detention. The receiving State shall treat with due respect and shall take all appropriate steps to prevent any attack on his person, freedom or dignity'.

Thorpe LJ held that the President had misdirected herself in the exercise of her discretion to grant a private hearing. She had elided the preliminary issue of state immunity with the application under section 27 of the Matrimonial Causes Act, 'which would only be activated by the dismissal of the claim to immunity'.[34] Considerations of the delicacy and sensitivity of the issues and comparisons with ordinary litigants would 'only become apt if the plea of immunity failed and the King had to plead to or concede the originating application'.[35] No evidence was required on the immunity issue, given the recitals to the District Judge's order, with the result that the press could not have put anything into the public domain that would not already have been in the President's judgment; and, since the President had removed all mention of Saudi Arabia from the recitals to the District Judge's order, her judgment would have referred only to an unidentified 'Head of State'.[36] More generally, Thorpe LJ stated:

> In my judgment a claim to State immunity is essentially a public claim that demands open litigation. I would say the same of a claim to sovereign immunity particularly in relation to private rather than governmental acts. In relation to private acts the boundaries of immunity are not forever fixed as absolute and the issue is in my judgment one of legitimate public interest and debate.[37]

(He would nonetheless have exercised the discretion to exclude entirely the contents of the applicant's affidavit.)[38] His Lordship acknowledged that the originating summons was founded on the assertion of an existing marriage, 'but mere assertion proves nothing', and it was unnecessary for the King to rebut the assertion unless and until his claim to State immunity failed.[39] If the application for ancillary relief was to be defeated by the King's immunity from suit, 'that deprivation should be declared by open and not by secret justice'.[40] Nor did his Lordship see any grounds for imposing reporting restrictions, since the identity of the sovereign was 'relevant to any public debate of the issues raised by the plea of immunity'.[41]

Wall LJ, agreeing with Thorpe LJ, additionally held that article 29 of the VCDR did not bar a public hearing on the preliminary issue of State immunity, which—given that the applicant had alleged merely the bare facts necessary to invoke section 27 of the Matrimonial Causes Act and had accepted, for the purposes of the SIA, that Saudi Arabia was a State and that the respondent was its sovereign and head of State—was a pure point of law:[42] 'In my judgment, Article 29 is not breached either by the court hearing the issue relating to sovereign immunity

[34] [2005] EWCA Civ 632, para 27. See also [2005] EWCA Civ 632, para 36 (Wall LJ).
[35] [2005] EWCA Civ 632, para 27. See also [2005] EWCA Civ 632, para 36 (Wall LJ).
[36] [2005] EWCA Civ 632, para 27.
[37] [2005] EWCA Civ 632, para 28.
[38] [2005] EWCA Civ 632, para 28.
[39] [2005] EWCA Civ 632, para 28.
[40] [2005] EWCA Civ 632, para 28.
[41] [2005] EWCA Civ 632, para 31.
[42] [2005] EWCA Civ 632, para 39.

in open court, or by this court hearing an appeal in public against the President's decision to hear the sovereign immunity issue in private'.[43] The obligation under article 29 to prevent attacks on the respondent's person, freedom, or dignity was an issue going to his entitlement to immunity from suit on the ground that 'enforced engagement in litigation relating to his private life is an attack on his dignity': 'certainly on the facts of this case', it was not an argument which could properly protect him from publicity generated by his raising in open court the plea of head of State immunity.[44]

The Court of Appeal's judgment is essentially sound. Whichever way one looks at it, the President of the Family Division, in refusing a public hearing, conflated the preliminary procedural issue of the respondent's immunity under section 20(1)(a) of the SIA with the subsequent substantive issue of the applicant's entitlement to ancillary relief under section 27 of the Matrimonial Causes Act. One could take the view that, for the purposes of FPR rule 2.66(2), the adjudication of the plea of immunity is formally distinct from the hearing of the application for ancillary relief, so that there is no reason why the first should take place in chambers to begin with. Alternatively, one could adopt the Court of Appeal's reasoning and say that, on the facts of the instant case, nothing necessary for the determination of the plea of immunity could genuinely cause the King embarrassment, consideration of the applicant's affidavit not being required, so that the President had no reason to decline to exercise her discretion to hear this aspect of the application for ancillary relief in public. This second rationale also justifies the dismissal of the respondent's application under CPR 39.2(3)(c) for private proceedings in the Court of Appeal. As for the respondent's argument based on article 29 of the VCDR, this was simply specious. Article 29 deals with the inviolability of the person of a diplomat and, for present purposes, of a head of State; and an attack on a diplomat or head of State's person, freedom, or dignity, for the purposes of the provision, involves more concrete and immediate acts, such as manhandling, jostling, and direct verbal assault. It does not encompass every word and deed that may (if believed) reflect upon his or her reputation.

In the event, the applicant did not have the chance to pursue her appeal. The respondent died on 1 August 2005 and the Court of Appeal subsequently held that an order under section 27 of the Matrimonial Causes Act could be made only during the joint lives of the spouses. Since she no longer had a substantive claim, the applicant's appeal on sovereign immunity became academic and, although the question was an important one of public interest, it was not sufficiently important for the appeal to be permitted to continue.[45]

[43] [2005] EWCA Civ 632, para 40. [44] [2005] EWCA Civ 632, para 40.
[45] See *Harb v His Majesty King Fahd Bin Abdul Aziz (No 2)* [2006] 1 WLR 578 (CA (Civ)).

Arbitration—challenge to award by way of Arbitration Act 1996, section 68(2)(b)— Convention on the Recognition and Enforcement of Foreign Arbitral Awards 1958 (New York Convention)—UNCITRAL Model Law on International Commercial Arbitration—whether an error of law an excess of power within meaning of Arbitration Act, section 68(2)(b)

Case No 3. Lesotho Highlands Development Authority v Impregilo SpA, 30 June 2005, [2005] UKHL 43, [2006] 1 AC 221, [2005] 3 WLR 129, [2005] 3 All ER 789, 2005 WL 1505127 (HL).

In a commercial arbitration—held under the International Chamber of Commerce Rules of Conciliation and Arbitration (the 'ICC rules') with London as its seat—over a construction contract between the Lesotho Highlands Development Authority (LHDA) and Impregilo SpA, the arbitrators were alleged to have made an error of law when specifying the currency of the award, an error characterizable as either a misinterpretation of the contract or a misinterpretation of their powers under section 48(4) of the Arbitration Act 1996.[46] The contract excluded any appeal on points of law under section 69 of the Arbitration Act.[47] LHDA applied under section 68 of the Arbitration Act for an order from the High Court quashing or remitting the award on the ground of serious irregularity in the form of an excess of power causing substantial injustice within the meaning of section 68(2)(b) of the Act.[48] Morison J, in the Commercial Court, held that the arbitrators had exceeded their jurisdiction, a decision upheld by the Court of Appeal.

The House of Lords (Lord Steyn giving the leading judgment), reversing the decision of the Court of Appeal, held that a mere error of law does not constitute an excess of power under section 68(2)(b) of the Arbitration Act. The only remedy in such circumstances was an appeal on a point of law under section 69 of the Act, which the contract in the present case excluded.

In coming to his conclusion, Lord Steyn emphasized that the purpose of section 68 of the Arbitration Act 1996, which had brought about a 'radical ... alteration of [English] arbitration law', was to secure the

[46] Arbitration Act 1996, s 48(4) empowers the arbitral tribunal, unless it is otherwise agreed by the parties, to order the payment of a sum of money 'in any currency'.

[47] Arbitration Act 1996, s 69(1) provides that, unless otherwise agreed by the parties, 'a party to arbitral proceedings may (upon notice to the other parties and to the tribunal) appeal to the court on a question of law arising out of an award made in the proceedings'.

[48] Arbitration Act 1996, s 68 states in relevant part:

> (1) A party to arbitral proceedings may (upon notice to the other parties and to the tribunal) apply to the court challenging an award in the proceedings on the ground of serious irregularity affecting the tribunal, the proceedings or the award ....
>
> (2) Serious irregularity means an irregularity of one or more of the following kinds which the court considers has caused or will cause substantial injustice to the applicant—
>
> ... (b) the tribunal exceeding its powers (otherwise than by exceeding its substantive jurisdiction: see section 67)...

autonomy of arbitration by 'reduc[ing] drastically the extent of intervention of courts in the arbitral process':[49]

27 The legislative technique adopted to achieve this purpose was spelled out explicitly in the Report on the Arbitration Bill and in particular in discussion of clause 68, which became section 68 of the 1996 Act. The DAC [Departmental Advisory Committee on Arbitration Law] observed about clause 68 that it 'is really designed as a long stop, only available in extreme cases where the tribunal has gone so wrong in its conduct of the arbitration that justice calls out for it to be corrected': p. 58, para. 280. On the other hand, the DAC recommended adoption of 'the internationally accepted view that the court should be able to correct serious failure to comply with the "due process" of arbitral proceedings: cf. article 34 of the [UNCITRAL Model Law on International Commercial Arbitration]:' p. 59, para. 282. The ethos of the DAC report was that parties are entitled to a fair hearing leading to an impartial adjudication. But the idea that section 68 contemplated an adjudication which arrives at the 'right' conclusion would have been wholly out of place in these recommendations. The DAC report was the matrix of the Parliamentary debates.

[. . .]

30 The New York Convention on the Recognition and Enforcement of Foreign Arbitral Awards (1958) and article 34 of the UNCITRAL Model Law on International Commercial Arbitration were in part a provenance of section 68: see General Note to section 68 of the Arbitration Act 1996 as published in Current Law Statutes 1996, p. 23–46. Specifically, it is likely that the inspiration of the words 'the tribunal exceeding its powers (otherwise than by exceeding its substantive jurisdiction)' in section 68 are the terms of article V(1)(c) of the New York Convention and the jurisprudence on it. The context is that article V(1)(a) stipulates that the invalidity of the arbitration agreement is a ground for non-enforcement of an award: it involves the competence of the arbitrator. Article V(1)(c) relates to matters beyond the scope of the submission to arbitration. It deals with cases of excess of power or authority of the arbitrator. It is well established that article V(1)(c) must be construed narrowly and should never lead to a re-examination of the merits of the award . . . The policy underlying section 68(2)(b) as set out in the DAC report similarly points to a restrictive interpretation.[50]

His Lordship concluded:

31 . . . Section 68(2)(b) does not permit a challenge on the ground that the tribunal arrived at a wrong conclusion as a matter of law or fact. It is not apt to cover a mere error of law. This view is reinforced if one takes into account that a mistake in interpreting the contract is the paradigm of a 'question of law' which may in the circumstances specified in section 69 be appealed unless the parties have excluded that right by agreement. In cases where the right of appeal has by agreement, sanctioned by the Act, been excluded, it would be curious to allow a challenge under section 68(2)(b) to be based on a mistaken interpretation of the underlying contract. Moreover, it would be strange where there is no exclusion agreement, to allow parallel challenges under section 68(2)(b) and section 69.

[49] [2006] 1 AC 221, 234, para 26.

[50] [2006] 1 AC 221, 234–6.

32 In order to decide whether section 68(2)(b) is engaged it will be necessary to focus intensely on the particular power under an arbitration agreement, the terms of reference, or the 1996 Act which is involved, judged in all the circumstances of the case. In making this general observation it must always be borne in mind that the erroneous exercise of an available power cannot by itself amount to an excess of power. A mere error of law will not amount to an excess of power under section 68(2)(b).

33 For these reasons the Court of Appeal erred in concluding that the tribunal exceeded its powers on the currency point. If the tribunal erred in any way, it was an error within its power.[51]

Lord Steyn added by way of epilogue:

I am glad to have arrived at this conclusion. It is consistent with the legislative purpose of the 1996 Act, which is intended to promote one-stop adjudication. If the contrary view of the Court of Appeal had prevailed, it would have opened up many opportunities for challenging awards on the basis that the tribunal exceeded its powers in ruling on the currency of the award. Such decisions are an everyday occurrence in the arbitral world. If the view of the Court of Appeal had been upheld, a very serious defect in the machinery of the 1996 Act would have been revealed.[52]

That the instant case had been before courts at three levels and that enforcement of the award had been delayed for more than three years 'reinforce[d] the importance of the point'.[53]

Their Lordships' decision is welcome and Lord Steyn's judgment, as it relates to this central issue, could not be bettered. While the arbitration in question was one under the ICC rules, the Arbitration Act is equally applicable to arbitrations under the UNCITRAL rules[54] (but not to ICSID arbitrations).[55] Especially given the present proliferation of bilateral investment treaties providing for the settlement of investment disputes by mixed arbitration, the House's ruling and its endorsement of a non-interventionist approach under the Arbitration Act stand to make London a more attractive seat of arbitration, for the speed of service, even if not always, *pace* Lord Denning, for the quality of the goods.[56]

European Convention on Human Rights, article 5 (right to liberty)—Human Rights Act 1998—United Nations Security Council resolution 1546 (2004)—fourth Geneva Convention, article 78—United Nations Charter, articles 24(1), 24(2), and 103—justiciability of international

[51] [2006] 1 AC 221, 236–7. [52] [2006] 1 AC 221, 237, para 34.

[53] [2006] 1 AC 221, 237, para 34.

[54] Arbitration Rules of the United Nations Commission on International Trade Law, *Official Records of the General Assembly*, Thirty-First Session, Supplement No 17 (A/31/17), ch V, s C.

[55] Arbitration (International Investment Disputes) Act 1966, s 3(2).

[56] See *Owners of the Motor Vessel 'Atlantic Star' v Owner of the Motor Vessel 'Bona Spes'* [1973] QB 364, 382.

instrument—whether detention without trial in British-run facility in Iraq compatible with Human Rights Act

Case No 4. R (Al-Jedda) v Secretary of State for Defence, 12 August 2005, [2005] EWHC 1809 (Admin), unreported (QBD (Admin Ct) Div Ct).

The claimant, a suspected member of a terrorist group implicated in attacks against the Multinational Force (MNF) in Iraq, brought proceedings for judicial review of his preventive detention, viz detention without charge and without prospects of charge, in a British-run facility in Basra, alleging that this was contrary to his right to liberty, as guaranteed by article 5(1) of the ECHR and secured to him under English law by the Human Rights Act 1998 (HRA). The official justification for his internment was that it was necessary for imperative reasons of security in Iraq. The claimant, while denying the allegations against him, did not seek to challenge them in the present proceedings. Similarly, the Secretary of State, while not accepting the correctness of the Divisional Court's ruling in favour of the sixth claimant in *Al-Skeini*,[57] reserved his position on the extraterritorial reach of the HRA. He conceded too that if article 5(1) of the ECHR did apply to the claimant's detention in Iraq, the detention was a *prima facie* breach of the claimant's right under that article, as it did not satisfy any of the exceptions enumerated in the provision. The Secretary of State argued, however, that the effect of United Nations Security Council resolution 1546 (2004), 8 June 2004, was to override the claimant's article 5 right under the HRA, since the resolution authorized internment by the MNF 'where this [was] necessary for imperative reasons of security' in Iraq.

The Divisional Court dismissed the claim on the ground that Security Council resolution 1546 (2004), adopted under Chapter VII of the UN Charter, authorized the claimant's internment by the MNF and that, by virtue of article 103 of the Charter, this overrode the right to liberty otherwise guaranteed to him by the HRA.

Moses J, giving the judgment of the court, recognized that the right to liberty in article 5, as set out in Schedule 1 to the HRA, 'is a domestic right, conferred by the United Kingdom's statute', whose 'scope, and any limitations to its effect, depend upon a proper construction of the Act'.[58] Since the parliamentary intention behind the HRA was 'to enable victims to enforce the same rights within the United Kingdom as would be enforceable in Strasbourg',[59] 'those rights should be of the same scope and not a greater ambit'.[60] That is, they should not bear a different meaning.[61]

[57] *R (Al-Skeini) v Secretary of State for Defence* [2005] 2 WLR 1041, (2004) 75 BYIL 513–18 (QBD (Admin Ct), Div Ct).

[58] [2005] EWHC 1809 (Admin), para 36.

[59] [2005] EWHC 1809 (Admin), para 39.

[60] [2005] EWHC 1809 (Admin), para 43. See also [2005] EWHC 1809 (Admin), paras 41, 45, 47, 54, 55, 69, and 74.

[61] [2005] EWHC 1809 (Admin), paras 51, 57, 59, and 63. See also [2005] EWHC 1809 (Admin), paras 40 and 73 ('meaning and scope').

And this scope and meaning could only be determined by reference to the effect of Security Council resolution 1546 (2004) on any rights enforceable in Strasbourg.

The court was not prevented from analysing the meaning and effect of resolution 1546 (2004) by the non-justiciability of unincorporated treaties and of resolutions adopted pursuant to them. Drawing on the words of Simon Brown LJ in *R (Campaign for Nuclear Disarmament) v Prime Minister of the United Kingdom*, where his Lordship stated that the English courts were barred from considering unincorporated international instruments 'which it is unnecessary to interpret for the purposes of determining a person's rights or duties under domestic law',[62] Moses J held that the court in the instant case was 'required to construe the meaning and scope of Article 5 [of the ECHR] as a matter of English law' and that if the HRA compelled the court to examine the effect on the ECHR of 'a Security Council resolution when read with the United Nations Charter', then it had to do so.[63]

Moses J observed that the purpose of resolution 1546 (2004), adopted in anticipation of the handover of power in Iraq from the Coalition Provisional Authority to the Iraqi interim government, was 'to continue the mandate of the multinational force (MNF) and to establish the framework within which that force was to operate'.[64] He drew attention to paragraph 10 of the resolution, in which the Security Council—having 'reaffirm[ed] the authorization for the multinational force under unified command established under resolution 1511 (2003) having regard to the letters annexed to this resolution'—decided 'that the multinational force shall have the authority to take all necessary measures to contribute to the maintenance of security and stability in Iraq in accordance with the letters annexed to this resolution expressing, *inter alia*, the Iraqi request for the continued presence of the multinational force and setting out its tasks, including by preventing and deterring terrorism . . . '.[65] One of the annexed letters was from the Iraqi President and sought 'a new resolution on the Multinational Force (MNF) mandate to contribute to maintaining security in Iraq, including through the tasks and arrangements set out in the letter from the Secretary of State Colin Powell to the President of the United Nations Security Council'.[66] In turn, the annexed letter from Secretary of State Powell outlined the arrangements between the interim Iraqi government and the MNF, pursuant to which the latter stood ready 'to undertake a broad range of tasks to contribute to the maintenance of security and to ensure forces protection', including 'activities necessary to counter ongoing security threats posed by forces seeking to influence Iraq's political future through violence', such

[62] [2005] EWHC 1809 (Admin), para 71, quoting (2002) 126 ILR 727, (2002) 73 BYIL 444–52 (QBD (Admin Ct), Div Ct).

[63] [2005] EWHC 1809 (Admin), para 73.

[64] [2005] EWHC 1809 (Admin), para 77.

[65] See [2005] EWHC 1809 (Admin), paras 79–80.

[66] [2005] EWHC 1809 (Admin), para 80.

measures being expressly stated to embrace 'internment where this is necessary for imperative reasons of security in Iraq'.[67] The last was a reference to the power previously exercised by the MNF under article 87 of the fourth Geneva Convention, which permits an Occupying Power to intern persons if it 'considers it necessary, for imperative reasons of security', a power implicitly recognized in Security Council resolution 1483 (2003), 22 May 2003 and reaffirmed in Security Council resolution 1511 (2003), 16 October 2003;[68] and the terms of resolution 1546 (2004) made it clear that that resolution was to be interpreted in the context of those preceding it.[69] In short, the Powell letter 'provide[d] a clear indication of the intention that the powers previously derived from Article 78 of Geneva IV were to be continued'.[70] 'Further, the essential purpose of UNSCR 1546 was that the MNF should continue its existing efforts to maintain peace and security within Iraq, without which the Iraqi interim government would not be able to fulfil its purpose of providing democratic institutions for the people of Iraq.'[71] In this light, the Divisional Court concluded 'that by UNSCR 1546, read in the context of the earlier resolutions, the Security Council conferred on the MNF the power which that force had previously held as a belligerent occupant to intern those suspected of conduct creating a serious threat to security in Iraq'.[72]

The court rejected the claimant's contention—based on a combined reading of articles 24(2), 1(3), and 55 of the UN Charter and on an analogy with *Simms*[73]—that it was 'not to be supposed ... that the Security Council displaced one of the most fundamental rights without any expressed intention to override fundamental human rights'.[74] Article 24(2) of the Charter, in accordance with which the Security Council is bound by the Purposes and Principles of the Charter, had to be read in the light of article 24(1), conferring on the Council primary responsibility for the maintenance of international peace and security.[75] There was 'no basis for reading UNSCR 1546 in a way which preserves an equivalent right to that protected by Article 5 in the Convention', since, '[f]or the purposes of restoring and maintaining ... peace and security', the Security Council had authorized 'such detention as [was] necessary for imperative reasons of security in accordance with Article 78 of Geneva IV'.[76]

The Divisional Court also dismissed the claimant's submission that resolution 1546 (2004) did not engage article 103 of the Charter, as the latter applied to obligations imposed on Member States, whereas the former merely authorized internment by Member States contributing to

[67] [2005] EWHC 1809 (Admin), para 81, emphasis omitted.

[68] [2005] EWHC 1809 (Admin), paras 82–85.

[69] [2005] EWHC 1809 (Admin), para 82.

[70] [2005] EWHC 1809 (Admin), para 87.

[71] [2005] EWHC 1809 (Admin), para 88.

[72] [2005] EWHC 1809 (Admin), para 93.

[73] *R v Secretary of State for the Home Department, ex p Simms* [2002] AC 115.

[74] [2005] EWHC 1809 (Admin), para 97.

[75] [2005] EWHC 1809 (Admin), para 103.

[76] [2005] EWHC 1809 (Admin), para 108.

the MNF. Once it was accepted 'that those Security Council resolutions, made under Chapter VII, which impose obligations supersede other treaty commitments', there was 'no sensible line to be drawn between those resolutions and resolutions which confer authorisations'.[77] Although there was no unanimity of opinion, there was 'ample authority from leading academic commentators that resolutions which authorise can override international conventional obligations pursuant to Article 103'.[78] The court concluded therefore that resolution 1546 (2004) did engage article 103 and that actions taken in pursuance of it prevailed over other treaty obligations, such as article 5 of the ECHR.[79] Nor did the claimant's further argument that article 103 could not set aside fundamental human rights such as article 5 (which it was accepted did not enjoy the status of *jus cogens*) find any support 'in the commentaries of any respected author'.[80]

The claimant had further argued that, as his detention did not comply with the procedural obligations embodied in article 78 of the fourth Geneva Convention, it fell outside the scope of the authorization granted by Security Council resolution 1546 (2004). The court ruled that, while it was substantively lawful, the procedures applied to the claimant's detention did not strictly meet the requirements of article 78, since the periodic decision to keep him detained was taken by a single individual, rather than by an administrative board; this non-compliance, however, was 'more technical than substantial', since the decision-maker had in practice acted on each occasion on the recommendation of a board.[81] In this light, the court saw 'no reason in principle why an approach broadly similar to that under Article 5 ECHR, as exemplified in *Kolanis* v. *United Kingdom*, should not also apply in relation to Article 78, so that the detention itself may be lawful even if the detainee has been denied certain procedural rights'.[82]

The claimant, a dual UK-Iraqi national, had additionally challenged the refusal of the Secretary of State to return him to the UK. He argued that any security risk he posed in Iraq could be met by repatriating him and making him the subject in the UK of a control order under the Prevention of Terrorism Act 2005. As such, his detention in Iraq was not 'necessary for imperative reasons of security' and was therefore not authorised by Security Council resolution 1546 (2004). The Divisional Court rejected this line of reasoning. The power of internment conferred on the MNF by paragraph 10 of resolution 1546 (2004) was 'directed towards the detention of persons in Iraq, not their removal from Iraq', so that 'the exercise of powers of detention as a means of securing removal from Iraq would fall outside the scope of the authorisation and

[77] [2005] EWHC 1809 (Admin), para 110.
[78] [2005] EWHC 1809 (Admin), para 112.
[79] [2005] EWHC 1809 (Admin), para 112.
[80] [2005] EWHC 1809 (Admin), para 113.
[81] [2005] EWHC 1809 (Admin), para 140.
[82] [2005] EWHC 1809 (Admin), para 144, referring to App No 517/02, Judgment, 21 June 2005.

would involve actions inconsistent with the resolution'.[83] Moreover, the assessment made by the Secretary of State was that the claimant's detention in Iraq was necessary for imperative reasons of security, and the claimant had not sought to challenge that assessment, making it impossible for the court to conclude that this detention was not, in fact, necessary.[84]

The Divisional Court's decision on the main claim is, with the greatest respect, flatly wrong, even if its judgment is not without its redeeming features.

First, the issue in the instant case is not the 'scope' or 'meaning' of the right to liberty guaranteed by the HRA but whether the right enures in the first place. And this is a function of the HRA and the HRA alone. As the court itself acknowledges at the outset, the right to liberty set out in Schedule 1, Part I of the HRA, labelled a 'Convention right' in section 1(1)(a) of the Act, 'is a domestic right, conferred by the United Kingdom's statute', so that 'any limitations to its effect ... depend upon a proper construction of the Act'.[85] Nothing in the Act, however, provides that a right guaranteed therein—in other words, applicable as a matter of UK law—is to be disapplied by virtue of an obligation imposed on the UK as a matter of international law by the UN Charter. As provided for in section 1(2) of the HRA, the rights cited in section 1(1) and set out in Schedule 1, Part I of the Act can be deprived of effect by a designated derogation, viz a derogation by the UK from an article of the ECHR 'which is designated for the purposes of [the] Act in an order made by the Secretary of State',[86] or by a designated reservation, viz a reservation by the UK to an article of the ECHR 'which is designated for the purposes of [the] Act in an order made by the Secretary of State'.[87] But these are the only circumstances in which the domestic rights secured by the HRA are to be disapplied—and, even in these circumstances, subordinate legislative intervention by the Secretary of State is required to transform the UK's derogation from or reservation to the ECHR, applicable on the international plane, into the disapplication of a domestic right. The effect of the Divisional Court's confused reasoning is to make the HRA do precisely what the court itself, quoting Lord Hoffmann In *re McKerr*, acknowledges it not to do, namely 'transmute international law obligations into domestic ones':[88] the claimant's international-law right under article 5 of the ECHR is ineffective, courtesy of Security Council resolution 1546 (2003), *ergo* his domestic-law right under the HRA is ineffective. In doing so, moreover, the court gives direct effect to articles 42, 25, and 103 of the UN Charter, none of them incorporated.

[83] [2005] EWHC 1809 (Admin), para 149.

[84] [2005] EWHC 1809 (Admin), para 151.

[85] [2005] EWHC 1809 (Admin), para 36.

[86] HRA 1998, s 14(1)(b).

[87] HRA 1998, s 15(1)(b).

[88] [2005] EWHC 1809 (Admin), para 36, quoting [2004] 1 WLR 807, 827, para 66, (2004) 75 BYIL 411–19 (HL).

This is a case where, even though the UK may have a defence to a claim under the Convention, the Secretary of State does not have a leg to stand on under the Act. As recalled time and again by the Divisional Court, the aim of the Act was to obviate the need to go to Strasbourg (although there may still be cases where this is required). But this does not mean that a victim who would find no joy on the Ill cannot have a healthy claim by the Thames. As the court itself observed in the present case, an English court 'may well recognise a narrower arena of discretion than that which falls within the margin of appreciation recognised [by the ECtHR]'.[89] Equally, Security Council resolution 1546 (2004) may well override article 5 of the Convention to the extent of any inconsistency, but, without its transformation into domestic law in a manner which overrides a right guaranteed by the Act, a victim will retain a claim in the English courts.

As it is, it is doubtful whether paragraph 10 of resolution 1546 (2004) can be taken to override the claimant's right to liberty under article 5 of the ECHR. At most, paragraph 10 merely authorizes internment in Iraq by the MNF, and, *pace* Professor Frowein's teleological analysis cited in support by the court,[90] it is difficult to get around the text of article 103 of the UN Charter, which provides that '[i]n the event of a conflict between the *obligations* of the Members of the United Nations under the present Charter and their obligations under any other international agreement, their obligations under the present Charter shall prevail'.[91] The court's suggestion that 'no sensible line [can] be drawn' between Security Council resolutions imposing obligations and those authorizing Member States to take certain actions[92] comes as a surprise; even more so does the view that, '[w]ithout Article 103, military action taken in pursuance of a resolution which merely authorised such action would breach the prohibition in Article 2(4) of the Charter'.[93]

Nor is the Divisional Court's view that article 24(2) of the Charter—pursuant to which the Security Council must act in accordance with the Charter's Purposes and Principles—has to be read in the light of article 24(1) an answer to the claimant's submission based on articles 1(3) and 55 of the Charter, even if the conclusion drawn by the Court is correct. The reason the Council, when taking coercive measures under Chapter VII of the Charter, is permitted to act contrary to other rules of international law is to be found by construing the very first of the Charter's purposes, embodied in article 1(1), viz:

> To maintain international peace and security, and to that end: to take effective collective measures for the prevention and removal of threats to the peace, and for the suppression of acts of aggression or other breaches of the peace, and to bring about, by peaceful means, and in conformity with the principles of justice

[89] [2005] EWHC 1809 (Admin), para 41.
[90] See [2005] EWHC 1809 (Admin), para 112.
[91] Emphasis added.
[92] [2005] EWHC 1809 (Admin), para 110.
[93] [2005] EWHC 1809 (Admin), para 111.

and international law, adjustment or settlement of international disputes or situations which might lead to a breach of the peace ...

Quite simply, the phrase 'and in conformity with ... international law' refers only to the second limb of the provision ('and to bring about ... '), which itself refers to pacific settlement of disputes by the Council under Chapter VI of the Charter. *A contrario*, when taking collective measures for the prevention and removal of threats to the peace and for the suppression of acts of aggression or other breaches, viz coercive measures under Chapter VII, the Security Council is not obliged to act in conformity with international law.[94] In short, the Council is to be regarded as acting in accordance with the Purposes of the Charter in such circumstances.

In the present case, the only way out for the government, short of amending the HRA by inserting provision for action taken pursuant to Security Council authorization under Chapter VII, is for the UK to derogate from article 5 of the Convention in respect of internment in Iraq and for the Secretary of State to issue a designated derogation order under section 14(1)(b) of the Act. But, even if done on a 'without prejudice' basis, this would probably be seized on by the media and potential claimants as a concession that the Act applies to British-run detention centres in Iraq, something denied by the government in the ongoing case of *Al-Skeini*. The Secretary of State is stuck between a rock and a hard place.

Relationship between treaty and English law—justiciability—bilateral investment treaty—investment dispute—mixed arbitration—Arbitration Act 1986, section 70—whether court barred from having regard to bilateral investment treaty in challenge under section 70 of Arbitration Act 1986 to jurisdiction of arbitrators appointed to settle investment dispute

Case No 5. Republic of Ecuador v Occidental Exploration and Production Co, 9 September 2005, [2005] EWCA Civ 1116, [2006] 2 WLR 70, [2005] 2 All ER (Comm) 689, 2005 WL 2161965 (CA (Civ)).

In 1993, the United States of America and Ecuador concluded a typical bilateral investment treaty (BIT).[95] Article VI provides in the event of an investment dispute for mixed arbitration: that is, nationals and companies of one State investing in the other State enjoy the right to bring arbitral proceedings against that other State without recourse to the traditional mechanism of the diplomatic protection of the first State.

[94] See eg H Kelsen, *The Law of the United Nations. A Critical Analysis of its Fundamental Problems* (1951) 294–5.

[95] Treaty between the United States of America and the Republic of Ecuador concerning the Encouragement and Reciprocal Protection of Investment, Washington, 27 August 1993, Senate Treaty Doc 103–15 ('US-Ecuador BIT').

Paragraph 1 of article VI defines 'investment dispute' as 'a dispute between a Party and a national or company of the other Party arising out of or relating to (a) an investment agreement between that Party and such national or company; (b) an investment authorization granted by that Party's foreign investment authority to such national or company; or (c) an alleged breach of any right conferred or created by this Treaty with respect to an investment'.

Occidental, a US company, acquired the right to explore and exploit certain oil reserves in Ecuador under a contract with a State-owned Ecuadorian corporation. A dispute arose between it and the Ecuadorian tax authorities over VAT. In accordance with article VI of the US-Ecuador BIT, Occidental submitted the dispute for settlement by binding arbitration under the Arbitration Rules of the United Nations Commission on International Trade Law (the 'UNCITRAL rules').[96] The place of the arbitration, as recorded in the award, was London. Ecuador unsuccessfully contested the tribunal's jurisdiction and, on the merits, the arbitrators found for Occidental on all but one point. Ecuador applied to the High Court to have the award set aside under section 67 of the Arbitration Act 1996, in accordance with which a party to arbitral proceedings may challenge 'any award of the arbitral tribunal as to its substantive jurisdiction' or may seek 'an order declaring an award made by the tribunal on the merits to be of no effect, in whole or in part, because the tribunal did not have substantive jurisdiction'. It sought to argue that the tribunal had misinterpreted article X of the US-Ecuador BIT, which ought to have precluded Occidental's claim. The trial of a preliminary issue was ordered in respect of Occidental's prior objection that the claim was non-justiciable insofar as it required the court to interpret provisions of the US-Ecuador BIT. Aikens J, in the Queen's Bench Division, found for Ecuador.

The Court of Appeal (Mance LJ giving the judgment of the court) dismissed Occidental's appeal, holding that the court enjoyed jurisdiction to entertain Ecuador's claim under section 67 of the Arbitration Act.

Mance LJ first disposed of Occidental's submission that what the company was doing by way of its claim under article VI was enforcing the US's rights under the BIT. His Lordship took the view that where, as under article VI(1)(a), a dispute arises out of or relates to a commercial agreement between a Party and an investor, it was 'both artificial and wrong in principle to suggest that the investor is in reality pursuing a claim vested in his or its home state'.[97] As for claims under article VI(1)(c), and probably also those under article VI(1)(b), any substantive right on the investor's part would have to be found in the treaty, in which case the treaty 'would have to be regarded as conferring or creating direct rights in international law in favour of investors'.[98] Citing *Jurisdiction of*

[96] *Official Records of the General Assembly*, Thirty-first Session, Supplement No 17 (A/31/17) ch V, s C.

[97] [2006] 2 WLR 70, 83, para 17.

[98] [2006] 2 WLR 70, 83, para 18.

the Courts of Danzig and *LaGrand*, and drawing attention to human rights instruments such as the ECHR, Mance LJ considered it well established that 'treaties may in modern international law give rise to direct rights in favour of individuals', 'particularly where the treaty provides a dispute resolution mechanism capable of being operated by such individuals acting on their own behalf and without their national state's involvement or even consent'.[99] As regards the US-Ecuador BIT, the language of article VI(1) made it clear that injured nationals or companies were to have standing in respect of all three types of claim specified in subparagraphs (a), (b), and (c) respectively, which led to the conclusion, in the words of one author and in line with the views expressed in numerous international arbitral awards cited by his Lordship, that ' "the investor is bringing a cause of action based upon the vindication of its own rights rather than those of its national state" '.[100] Nor did his Lordship believe that the NAFTA case of *Loewen* was to be read as running counter to this conclusion; if it were, he respectfully disagreed with its analysis.[101]

Mance LJ then addressed the issue of non-justiciability in exhaustive detail (albeit with a certain lack of focus), dealing with both the broad doctrine of 'judicial restraint or abstention'[102] enunciated by Lord Wilberforce in *Buttes Gas and Oil Co v Hammer (No 3)*, namely that the English courts 'will not adjudicate upon the transactions of foreign sovereign states',[103] and the narrower doctrine recognized by Lord Oliver in the *Tin Council* case, that the English courts 'have not and cannot have the competence to adjudicate upon or to enforce the rights arising out of transactions entered into by independent sovereign states between themselves on the plane of international law'[104]—in short, that unincorporated treaties are non-justiciable. As regards the latter, Mance LJ stressed Lord Oliver's acknowledgement that the principle he posited '[did] not ... involve as a corollary that the court must never look at or construe a treaty',[105] highlighting the exceptions identified by his Lordship, to which he added a few more drawn from the case-law before concluding

[99] [2006] 2 WLR 70, 83, para 19, citing *Jurisdiction of the Courts of Danzig* PCIJ Series B, No 15 (1928) 17–18 and *LaGrand (Germany v United States of America)* ICJ Rep 2001, 466.

[100] [2006] 2 WLR 70, 84–5, para 20, quoting Z Douglas, 'The Hybrid Foundations of Investment Treaty Arbitration' (2003) 74 BYIL 151–289, 182 and citing *Enron Corp v Argentine Republic* ICSID Case No ARB/01/3, 14 January 2004 (unreported) para 38; *LG & E Energy Corp v Argentine Republic* ICSID Case No ARB/02/1, 30 April 2004 (unreported) para 52; *GAMI Investments Inc v Government of the United Mexican States* (2004) 44 ILM 545, para 30; *Camuzzi International SA v Argentine Republic* ICSID Case No ARB/03/2, 11 May 2005 (unreported) paras 138–145; *Camuzzi International SA v Argentine Republic* ICSID Case No ARB/03/7, 10 June 2005 (unreported) para 44; *Gas Natural SDG SA v Argentine Republic* ICSID Case No ARB/03/10, 17 June 2005 (unreported) para 34.

[101] [2006] 2 WLR 70, 87, para 22, referring to *Loewen Group Inc v United States of America* (2003) 42 ILM 811.

[102] [1982] AC 888, 932, (1982) 53 BYIL 259–68 (HL).

[103] [1982] AC 888, 931.

[104] *JH Rayner (Mincing Lane) Ltd v Department of Trade and Industry* [1990] 2 AC 418, 499–500, (1989) 60 BYIL 461–73 (HL).

[105] [2006] 2 WLR 70, 90, para 28, quoting [1990] 2 AC 418, 500–1.

that 'English courts are not ... wholly precluded from interpreting or having regard to the provisions of unincorporated treaties'.[106] They were permitted to do so 'for the purposes of determining a person's rights or duties under domestic law', in the words of Simon Brown LJ in *R (Campaign for Nuclear Disarmament) v Prime Minister of the United Kingdom*.[107] In the instant case, the court, which under the relevant English-law principles of private international law recognized the agreement to arbitrate between Ecuador and Occidental, was 'being asked to interpret [the treaty's] scope in order to give effect to the rights and duties contained in the agreement to arbitrate',[108] and, as such, was not barred from considering the US-Ecuador BIT. On the *Buttes* question, Mance LJ observed that the agreement to arbitrate gave rise to rights on the part of Ecuador and Occidental respectively, 'including the right to have disputes arbitrated within its terms and not to have disputes arbitrated which fall outside its terms',[109] and he saw 'no good reason why any arbitration held pursuant to such an agreement, or any supervisory role which the court of the place of arbitration may have in relation to any such arbitration, should be categorised as being concerned with "transactions between states"' so as to implicate *Buttes* non-justiciability.[110] Having earlier emphasized Lord Wilberforce's concern over the absence of 'judicial or manageable standards' by which to judge the issues in *Buttes*,[111] his Lordship conceded that the present questions were unlikely to be as clear-cut as those in *Kuwait Airways Corp v Iraqi Airways Co (Nos 4 and 5)*,[112] where the House of Lords distinguished *Buttes* on this point, but he was confident that they were not 'remotely comparable in difficulty of manageability or resolution or in sensitivity' to the issues in *Buttes* itself.[113] It was 'equally impossible to see' how the challenge to the arbitrators' jurisdiction 'could be said to raise any considerations relating to this country's national and international interests remotely equating to those found in the *Buttes Gas* case'.[114] Moreover, his Lordship believed that:

> ... the fact that the states party to the treaty deliberately chose to provide for a mechanism for dispute resolution which invokes consensual arbitration, with its domestic legal connotations, is a factor which should make the English court hesitate long about subjecting such arbitration proceedings to special principles of judicial restraint developed in relation to international transactions or treaties lacking any foundation or incorporation in domestic law.[115]

He noted, finally, that courts in other countries had 'exercised or assumed that it was open to them to exercise equivalent supervisory power to

[106] [2006] 2 WLR 70, 91, para 31.

[107] [2006] 2 WLR 70, 91–2, para 31, quoting (2002) 126 ILR 727, (2002) 73 BYIL 444–52 (QBD (Admin Ct), Div Ct).

[108] [2006] 2 WLR 70, 98, para 46.

[109] [2006] 2 WLR 70, 96, para 40.

[110] [2006] 2 WLR 70, 96, para 41.

[111] [2006] 2 WLR 70, 87–8, para 23, quoting [1982] AC 888, 938.

[112] [2002] AC 883, (2002) 73 BYIL 400–4 (HL).

[113] [2006] 2 WLR 70, 97, para 42.

[114] [2006] 2 WLR 70, 97, para 42.

[115] [2006] 2 WLR 70, 98, para 47.

review the jurisdiction of arbitrators appointed under investment treaties',[116] citing *Czech Republic v CME Czech Republic BV*[117] and *Canada (Attorney General) v SD Myers Inc.*[118]

On these core issues, the Court of Appeal's judgment is unimpeachable, and evidences an assured understanding on the part of Lord Mance (as he now is) of complicated questions regarding the relationship between international and English law. On the other hand, one might differ from his view, expressed *en passant*, that the agreement to arbitrate deemed by the BIT to have arisen between Ecuador and Occidental was best seen as governed by international law,[119] rather than the law of Ecuador, although his lack of dogmatism on this score is refreshing. The decision will no doubt see more mixed arbitrations challenged in the English courts, although what the Court of Appeal giveth the House of Lords taketh away with its decision on section 68(2)(b) of the Arbitration Act in *Lesotho Highlands Development Authority v Impregilo SpA.*[120] More generally, the case marks a further stage in the slow death of *Buttes* non-justiciability.

First Protocol to European Convention on Human Rights, articles 1 and 4—European Convention on Human Rights, article 56—application of First Protocol to territories for whose international relations UK is responsible—Human Rights Act 1998, sections 1, 6, and 7—territorial scope of application of Human Rights Act—meaning of 'public authority' under Human Rights Act—relationship between Convention and its protocols and Human Rights Act—South Georgia and South Sandwich Islands Order 1985—whether claim available under Human Rights Act in respect of conduct by Secretary of State for Foreign and Commonwealth Affairs pursuant to South Georgia and South Sandwich Islands Order in relation to South Georgia and South Sandwich Islands

Case No 6. R (Quark Fishing Ltd) v Secretary of State for Foreign and Commonwealth Affairs, 13 October 2005, [2005] UKHL 57, [2005] 3 WLR 837, 2005 WL 2493311 (HL).

The facts of the case have been recounted in an earlier volume.[121] The applicant claimed damages under the HRA for the deprival of a possession contrary to article 1 of the First Protocol to the ECHR.[122] The

[116] [2006] 2 WLR 70, 101, para 55. [117] (2003) 42 ILM 919. [118] [2004] 3 FCR 368.
[119] [2006] 2 WLR 70, 93, para 33. [120] [2005] 3 WLR 129, (2005) 76 BYIL 576–8 (HL).
[121] (2004) 75 BYIL 435–7.
[122] Art 1 of the First Protocol states: 'Every natural or legal person is entitled to the peaceful enjoyment of his possessions. No one shall be deprived of his possessions except in the public interest and subject to the conditions provided for by law and by the general principles of international law. The preceding provisions shall not, however, in any way impair the right of a state to enforce such laws as it deems necessary to control the use of property in accordance with the general interest or to secure the payment of taxes or other contributions or penalties.'

Secretary of State appealed the Court of Appeal's finding that he had acted on behalf of the Crown in right of the UK when acting pursuant to section 5 of the South Georgia and South Sandwich Islands Order 1985[123] to direct the Commissioner of the South Georgia and South Sandwich Islands (SGSSI) not to grant a fishing licence to the applicant's vessel. The applicant cross-appealed the Court of Appeal's ruling that no right protected by the HRA had been violated, since the UK had not extended the application of the First Protocol to SGSSI.

The House of Lords upheld the appeal and dismissed the cross-appeal. The fact that the UK had not extended the application of the First Protocol to SGSSI, in accordance with article 4 of that instrument, was fatal to the applicant's claim. The Strasbourg jurisprudence[124] made it clear that a declaration under article 4 extending the Protocol's application to an overseas territory was required before Protocol rights could arise in that territory, and it was 'not the purpose of the [HRA] to impose liability on a public authority where the complaint would not be within the jurisdiction of the European court in Strasbourg'.[125] In short, the applicant did not enjoy a Convention right, within the meaning of section 1 and for the purposes of sections 6 and 7 of the HRA, in the first place.

Lord Nicholls further took the view that, even if the UK had extended the application of the First Protocol to SGSSI, 'sections 6 and 7 of the Act are confined in their scope to Convention rights arising from obligations assumed by the United Kingdom under the Convention and its protocols other than the extended obligations assumed by the United Kingdom pursuant to a notification given by it under article 56 [of the Convention] or equivalent provisions in the protocols':[126]

The Human Rights Act is a United Kingdom statute. The Act is expressed to apply to Northern Ireland: section 22(6). It is not expressed to apply elsewhere in any relevant respect. What, then, of Convention obligations assumed by the United Kingdom in respect of its overseas territories by making a declaration under article 56? In my view the rights brought home by the Act do not include Convention rights arising from these extended obligations assumed by the United Kingdom in respect of its overseas territories. I can see no warrant for interpreting the Act as having such an extended territorial reach. If the United Kingdom notifies the Secretary General of the Council [of Europe] that the Convention shall apply to one of its overseas territories, the United Kingdom thenceforth assumes in respect of that territory a treaty obligation in respect of the rights and freedoms set out in the Convention. But such a notification does not extend the reach of sections 6 and 7 of the Act. The position is the same in respect of protocols.[127]

[123] SI 1985/450, as amended by South Georgia and South Sandwich Islands (Amendment) Order 1995, SI 1995/1621.

[124] Their Lordships cited *Gillow v United Kingdom* (1986) 11 EHRR 335, *Bui van Thanh v United Kingdom* App no 16137/90, Judgment, 12 March 1990 (unreported), and *Yonghong v Portugal* (1999) Reports of Judgments and Decisions 385.

[125] [2005] 3 WLR 837, 864, para 92 (Lord Hope). See also [2005] 3 WLR 837, 847, para 25 (Lord Bingham) and 849, para 34 (Lord Nicholls).

[126] [2005] 3 WLR 837, 849, para 35.

[127] [2005] 3 WLR 837, 850, para 36.

Lord Hoffmann similarly stated that a declaration under article 56 of the Convention or article 4 of the First Protocol had effect only in international law:[128] '[F]or the purposes of the 1998 Act, it does not matter whether the Protocol has been extended to SGSSI or not. The Act is concerned only with the Convention as it applies to the United Kingdom and not by extension to other territories'.[129] For analogous reasons, Lords Bingham, Hoffman, and Hope held that a 'public authority', within the meaning of sections 6 and 7 of the HRA, necessarily meant a UK public authority, and that the Secretary of State had acted in the instant case as a public authority not of the UK but of SGSSI.[130] Lord Hoffmann added that this construction of the HRA was not inconsistent with the Secretary of State's concession that the High Court had jurisdiction to quash his direction, as there was 'authority both ancient and modern for the High Court's exercise of jurisdiction, first by prerogative writ and then by judicial review, over all Her Majesty's territories'.[131] It did not mean that the acts impugned were acts of a UK public authority, since the jurisdiction existed whether the acts were those of a UK public authority or not.[132]

Their Lordships were right to dismiss the applicant's cross-appeal. The First Protocol, and consequently the HRA, clearly cannot give rise to rights in a territory for whose international relations the UK is responsible unless the UK has extended the Protocol's application to it in accordance with article 4 of that instrument. But in the light of the persuasive dicta of Lords Nicholls and Hoffmann, one wonders whether the question needed to be addressed. It is distinctly arguable that the Protocol's territorial scope of application is irrelevant to a claim under the HRA. The Act does not provide for the litigation in UK courts of rights enjoyed under the ECHR and its protocols as such. What the HRA does 'is to create domestic rights expressed in the same terms as those contained in the Convention' and in the First and Sixth Protocols.[133] The distinction is crucial, since it means that questions as to the scope of application of rights enjoyed under the HRA are to be answered by reference to the domestic rules of statutory construction, not by reference to the scope of application of the ECHR and its protocols. The point was emphatically

[128] [2005] 3 WLR 837, 854, para 56.

[129] [2005] 3 WLR 837, 855, para 62. Baroness Hale expressly left the question undecided: [2005] 3 WLR 837, 866, para 98.

[130] [2005] 3 WLR 837, 847, para 25 (Lord Bingham), 856, para 64 (Lord Hoffmann) and 857–60, paras 70–80 (Lord Hope). Lord Bingham left open whether the non-extension of the Protocol's application to SGSSI would have been fatal even in the event that the Secretary of State had acted on behalf of the Crown in right of the UK: [2005] 3 WLR 837, 847, para 26. Baroness Hale considered the distinction between acts in right of the UK and acts in right of SGSSI to be overly formalistic: [2005] 3 WLR 837, 852, paras 94–95. Lord Nicholls thought the question irrelevant: [2005] 3 WLR 837, 852–3, paras 45–48.

[131] [2005] 3 WLR 837, 856, para 65, citing *R (Bancoult) v Secretary of State for the Foreign and Commonwealth Office* [2001] QB 1067, (2000) 71 BYIL 433–4 (QBD (Admin Ct), Div Ct).

[132] [2005] 3 WLR 837, 856, para 65.

[133] In *re McKerr* [2004] 1 WLR 807, 826, para 63 (Lord Hoffmann), (2004) 75 BYIL 411–19 (HL).

made In *re McKerr* by Lord Hoffmann: 'The Act did not transmute international law obligations into domestic ones. It created new domestic human rights. The simple question is whether, as a matter of construction, those rights applied . . .'[134]

Turning to the instant case, it is an axiom of statutory construction that Acts of the UK Parliament, in the absence of conclusive evidence to the contrary, apply only to the UK and not to its overseas territories; and the HRA provides no evidence, let alone conclusive evidence, to the contrary. As such, even if the application of the First Protocol had been extended to SGSSI by way of article 4, an act of a public authority incompatible with the Protocol would still not give rise to an action under the HRA. The Act brought rights home, as the slogan has it. It did not re-export them to the colonies.

No doubt it could be said that the HRA's silence as to its territorial scope of application is ambiguous; that where a statute enacted to give effect to a treaty obligation incumbent upon the UK can reasonably be ascribed more than one meaning, one of them consonant with the treaty and the other or others not, the meaning consonant with the treaty is to be preferred;[135] and that a construction of the Act which excluded its application to overseas territories to which the application of the Convention and/or its protocols had been extended would leave the UK in breach of treaty. This very argument was successful before the Divisional Court, precisely in relation to the extraterritorial scope of the HRA, in *Al-Skeini*.[136] But the argument can be rebutted. To begin with, one might query whether this really is an instance of ambiguity: first, it is not a case of a word or phrase in a particular provision being capable of more than one meaning; secondly, it could be said that, in the light of Parliament's undoubted awareness of the territorial canon of construction, the absence from the HRA of any indication of its extraterritorial application points unambiguously to Parliament's intention that the Act is to apply to the UK alone. At the very least, there is scope to query which would prevail in this contest between canons of construction. Even more to the point, however, a construction of the HRA which restricts its application to the UK does not in fact place the UK in breach of its treaty obligations. This occurs when the UK violates the substantive right in question. All such a reading does is to deny the victims a remedy in the UK courts, forcing them to take their claim to Strasbourg, as they would have had to do before the coming into force of the HRA. The distinction is surely crucial.

The views of Lords Nicholls and Hoffmann have relevance beyond the immediate context of territories for whose international relations the UK

[134] [2004] 1 WLR 807, 827, para 66.

[135] *Salomon v Commissioners of Customs and Excise* [1967] 2 QB 116, 143 (Diplock LJ), (1967) 42 BYIL 291–3 (CA).

[136] *R (Al-Skeini) v Secretary of State for Defence* [2005] 2 WLR 1041, (2004) 75 BYIL 513–18 (QBD (Admin Ct), Div Ct).

is responsible. If embraced by other members of their Lordships' House, they stand to scotch all argument over the extraterritorial ambit of the HRA. Whatever the position in Strasbourg, cases like *B*[137] and *Al-Skeini* would never get off the ground in the UK courts.

It must be noted, however, that the dicta of Lord Nicholls cited above starkly contradict what his Lordship says earlier in his speech as to the respective ambits of the ECHR and HRA that 'the territorial scope of the obligations and rights created by sections 6 and 7 of the Act was intended to be co-extensive with the territorial scope of the obligations of the United Kingdom and the rights of victims under the Convention. The Act was intended to provide a domestic remedy where a remedy would have been available in Strasbourg'.[138] It is remarkable that his Lordship failed to spot the inconsistency and unfortunate that it should relate to a question of pressing importance.[139]

State immunity—immunity from measures of enforcement—property of central bank—State Immunity Act 1978, sections 13(2)(b), 13(4), and 14(4)—meaning of 'property' under State Immunity Act—ICSID award—Arbitration (International Investment Disputes) Act 1966, section 1—European Convention on Human Rights, article 6—First Protocol to European Convention on Human Rights, article 1—Human Rights Act 1998, section 3—UN Convention on Jurisdictional Immunity of States and Their Property 2004—'commercial purposes' under State Immunity Act, section 13(4)—whether assets held in name of foreign State's central bank on behalf of that State immune from enforcement of ICSID award

Case No 7. AIG Capital Partners, Inc and another v Republic of Kazakhstan, ABN AMRO Mellon Global Securities Services BV, ABN AMRO Bank NV and National Bank of Kazakhstan, 20 October 2005, [2005] EWCA 2239 (Comm), [2006] 1 All ER 284, 2005 WL 2802313 (QBD (Comm Ct), Aikens J).

Pursuant to a global custody agreement, governed by English law, between ABN AMRO Mellon Global Securities (AAMGS) and the National Bank of Kazakhstan (NBK), the central bank of the Republic of Kazakhstan, AAMGS in London held, in the name of the NBK, cash and securities forming part of the National Fund of Kazakhstan ('National Fund'). The National Fund was designed to ensure 'stable social and economic development of the country, accumulation of financial

[137] *R (B) v Secretary of State for the Foreign and Commonwealth Office* [2005] 2 WLR 618, (2004) 75 BYIL 483–9 (CA (Civ)).

[138] [2005] 3 WLR 837, 849, para 34.

[139] The passage was picked up and relied on in the Court of Appeals' subsequent judgment in *R (Al-Skeini) v Secretary of State for Defence* [2005] EWCA Civ 1609, (2005) 76 BYIL 634–40 (CA).

resources for future generations, [and] reduction of the vulnerability of the economy to the influence of unfavourable external factors'.[140] Under the terms of the global custody agreement, AAMGS acted as custodian of these assets for the NBK. As a matter of Kazakh law, which does not distinguish between legal and beneficial ownership, the National Fund was under the 'trust management' of the NBK 'for the benefit' of the government of Kazakhstan, meaning that the property of the Fund remained under the full ownership of the government of Kazakhstan but that the NBK enjoyed the right to take any action with respect to the property, for the purpose of its proper management, that could have been taken by the government. In a letter to the court, the Kazakh ambassador to the Court of St James certified that 'the assets held in custody in NBK's accounts with AAMGS ha[d] never been used for commercial purposes since they were opened in 2001, and they [were] not intended to be used for such purposes'.[141]

The claimants had obtained an award in their favour in an ICSID arbitration against the Republic of Kazakhstan held in Washington, DC pursuant to a bilateral investment treaty between the US and Kazakhstan. They registered the award in the High Court under section 1 of the Arbitration (International Investment Disputes) Act 1966, which gives effect in the UK to the Washington Convention.[142] They sought to have the award enforced as a judgment by obtaining a Third Party Debt Order and a Charging Order against the London assets of the National Fund, and had already obtained Interim Orders to this effect. They argued that the London assets of the National Fund were assets of the Republic of Kazakhstan that could and should be the subject of Final Orders. The NBK intervened and applied to discharge the Interim Orders, arguing that the London assets of the National Fund were property of the NBK and, as such, were immune from enforcement under sections 13(2)(b)[143] and 14(4) of the State Immunity Act 1978 (SIA).

Section 13(2)(b) of the SIA provides that 'the property of a State' shall not be subject to any process for the enforcement of a judgment or arbitration award, although section 13(4) makes an exception in respect of 'property which is for the time being in use or intended for use for commercial purposes'. Section 13(5) states that, for the purposes of section 13(4), the certificate of the head of a State's diplomatic mission in the UK that any property is not in use or intended for use by or on behalf of the State for commercial purposes shall be accepted as sufficient evidence of that fact until the contrary is proved. Section 14(4) provides that '[p]roperty of a State's central bank or other monetary authority shall not be regarded for the purposes of subsection (4) of

[140] [2006] 1 All ER 284, 290, para 12. [141] [2006] 1 All ER 284, 295, para 25.

[142] Convention on the Settlement of Investment Disputes between States and Nationals of Other States, Washington, DC, 18 March 1965, 575 UNTS 159.

[143] SIA 1978, s 13(2)(b) provides that, subject to s 13(4), 'the property of a State' shall not be subject to any process for the enforcement of a judgment or arbitration award.

section 13 ... as in use or intended for use for commercial purposes', adding that, where any such bank or authority is a separate entity, subsections (1) to (3) of section 13 'shall apply to it as if references to a State were references to the bank or authority'.

Aikens J, in the Commercial Court, discharged the Interim Orders. As regards the cash accounts, this was simply a function of the wording of Part 72.2(1)(a) of the Civil Procedure Rules, under which the court is empowered to make a Third Party Debt Order.[144] As for the London assets of the National Fund generally, these were immune from measures of enforcement by virtue of sections 13(2)(b) and 14(4) of the SIA. On the basis of the ordinary rules of statutory construction, the word 'property' had the same meaning in each of sections 13(2)(b), 13(4), and 14(4), and encompassed all real and personal property and any right or interest, legal, equitable, or contractual, in assets; and the phrase 'property of a State's central bank' in section 14(4) meant any asset allocated to or held in the name of the central bank—irrespective of the capacity in which or the purpose for which the central bank holds the asset—in which the central bank has some form of property interest, within the above meaning.[145] The assets in the instant case were held in the name of the NBK, the central bank of Kazakhstan, and were thus immune from enforcement by operation of section 14(4). His Lordship elaborated:

In my view the wording of section 14(4) is clear and imperative; hence the wording ' ... **The property of a State's central bank ... shall not be regarded** ...'. The words are, in their natural meaning, not capable of qualification. When they are set in their context, ... it is clear that they should not be qualified. This has the following consequences:

(1) All **'property'** of a State's central bank or other monetary authority is covered by section 14(4). The only question is whether the central bank (etc) has one of the types of interests in the property concerned, as I have described the interests above, so that the assets concerned can be described as the **'property'** of the central bank concerned.

(2) It does not matter whether the central bank is a department of the State or a separate entity. In all cases the central bank's property **'shall not be'** regarded as in use or intended for use for commercial purposes **'for the purposes of** [section 13(4)]'.

(3) Given the wording of section 14(4), then, the property of a State's central bank (or other monetary authority) must enjoy complete immunity from the enforcement process in the UK courts.

144 The cash accounts were in the name of the NBK and thus constituted a debt owed by AAMGS to the NBK, a debt over which the Republic of Kazakhstan had no contractual rights. As such, there was no 'debt due or accruing due' from the third party (AAMGS) to the judgment debtor (the Republic of Kazakhstan) within the meaning of CPR Pt 72.2(1)(a). See [2006] 1 All ER 284, 299–300, paras 30–32.

145 [2006] 1 All ER 284, 302–3, para 45. Aikens J drew support for this 'broad scope' from *Alcom Ltd v Republic of Colombia* [1984] AC 580, 602 (Lord Diplock), (1984) 55 BYIL 340–3 and *AIC Ltd v Federal Government of Nigeria* [2003] EWHC 1357, para 47 (Stanley Burnton J).

(4) If the central bank (etc) has an interest in the property concerned, but the State of the central bank has another interest in the same property, then in my view the effect of section 14(4) is that the relevant property is immune from enforcement in respect of a judgment against that State, whether the property concerned is in use or intended for use for commercial purposes or not.[146]

Further to the last point, Aikens J explained:

In the case of a central bank that is a separate entity from a department of the State, there can be no problem (in English law at least) about it having 'property' in assets. Thus in the present case it is clear that the NBK has 'property' of some form in the London Assets; **viz** a contractual right to the payment of debts in the case of the cash accounts held by AAMGS, and a beneficial interest in the securities held by AAMGS. At the same time the State could also have an interest in the same property; it may be some kind of beneficial interest, as it is agreed to be in this case. But in all cases, whatever the nature of the 'property' right of the central bank, the assets concerned are immune from the enforcement process.[147]

His Lordship considered the policy behind section 14(4) of the SIA, having noted earlier that the explanation for the provision given on behalf of the government of the day by the Parliamentary Secretary to the Law Officers was 'somewhat laconic':[148]

One can only speculate on why a separate sub-section was introduced by amendment to deal with the position of property of central banks and other monetary authorities with regard to the enforcement process in UK courts. But one can note, first, that generally speaking, when a central bank or a State's monetary authority is performing its key functions of acting as guardian and regulator of the State's monetary system, it will be exercising governmental or sovereign authority; it will not be acting for commercial purposes. Secondly, it is likely that the most obvious 'property' of a central bank, a State's reserves, will be held and used for governmental, or sovereign purposes and not for commercial purposes. It may be that it was recognised by the draftsmen of the Act that it would be difficult, if not impossible, to determine whether a particular asset of a central bank or monetary authority was, at a relevant time, being used or intended for use for sovereign purposes or for commercial purposes. The assets of a State's central bank (or monetary authority) would be an obvious target for the enforcement process in relation to judgments against the State or its central bank (etc). This might lead to unwelcome and perhaps embarrassing litigation in UK courts.[149]

'Therefore this possibility was pre-empted by the all-embracing and imperative immunity granted by section 14(4).'[150]

The claimants submitted, however, that the immunity created by an ordinary construction of section 14(4) of the SIA was incompatible with their right of access to the court guaranteed by article 6 of the ECHR and that section 3(1) of the HRA thus compelled a narrower construction.[151]

[146] [2006] 1 All ER 284, 305, para 57.
[147] [2006] 1 All ER 284, 306, para 60.
[148] [2006] 1 All ER 284, 300, para 33.
[149] [2006] 1 All ER 284, 305, para 58.
[150] [2006] 1 All ER 284, 305, para 58.
[151] HRA 1998, s 3(1) states that, '[s]o far as it is possible to do so, primary and subordinate legislation must be read and given effect in a way which is compatible with Convention rights'.

In response, Aikens J held that section 14(4) did implicate the right to fair trial secured by article 6, in accordance with which the claimants were entitled to a hearing for the determination of a civil right:

A party to an ICSID arbitration has the right, by virtue of the 1966 Act, to enforce an ICSID Award as a judgment of the English court. Execution of that judgment is an integral part of the 'trial' because it is part of the overall process of the ICSID arbitration procedure that was set up by the Washington Convention to which the UK is a party. The 1966 Act was passed to give effect to the Washington Convention in the UK and so as to assist in effective enforcement of ICSID arbitration awards in the UK.[152]

But the restriction on this right imposed by section 14(4) of the HRA was both for a legitimate end and proportionate, for four main reasons:

80 First, I regard the UN Convention on Jurisdictional Immunities of States and their Property, adopted by the General Assembly, as a most important guide on the state of international opinion on what is, and what is not, a legitimate restriction on the right of parties to enforce against State property generally. I accept that the Convention does not constitute a *jus cogens* in international law. I recognise that the Convention has not yet been adopted by any States. But its existence and adoption by the UN after the long and careful work of the International Law Commission and the UN Ad Hoc Committee on Jurisdictional Immunities of States and Their Property, powerfully demonstrates international thinking on the point. [Articles 19 and 21(1)(c) of the Convention, in accordance with which the property of the central bank or other monetary authority of a State is immune from measures of enforcement] suggests that the grant of immunity to all the property of a State's central bank is, in the eyes of the international community of States, legitimate. It must be their view that it will promote comity and good relations between States through respect of one another's sovereignty as regards a State's central bank and its property.

81 Secondly, in the existing legislation of States there is no consensus which grants only limited immunity as to enforcement procedures against the property of a State's central bank. Some States' legislation permits enforcement against a central bank's property if used for commercial purposes; other States' legislation does not.

82 Thirdly, the wording of section 14(4) provides a sensible rule which is easy to apply and thereby assists the promotion of comity and good relations between States. As I have already pointed out, the overwhelming presumption must be that a central bank's work is for sovereign purposes and that its property is used for sovereign purposes. But if there had to be a more restrictive provision than section 14(4) then there could be much scope for litigation. A party could obtain a legitimate judgment against a State. It might wish to enforce it in the UK and that State's central bank may maintain funds in the UK. Those funds would be the obvious target for enforcement. Such an attempt could lead to a dispute over whether the funds are for use or intended for use for commercial purposes, with the need for disclosure, statements and a hearing. That is not conducive to comity and good relations between States. The interpretation of section 14(4) I have adopted avoids all that.

[152] [2006] 1 All ER 284, 309, para 71.

83 Fourthly, the fact that the Claimants would not be able to enforce the ICSID award against the London Assets does not mean that the award is ineffective and a nullity. I do not know what other assets might be available for enforcement purposes. But there is no evidence before me to indicate that the Claimants would be left without a remedy worldwide.[153]

Since article 6 of the Convention was not violated, section 3 of the HRA did not compel any modification of the ordinary construction of section 14(4) of the SIA. As it was, even the reading of section 14(4) argued for by the claimants would not have helped them, since Aikens J's 'firm view' was that the London assets of the National Fund were not in use or intended for use for commercial purposes at any stage:[154]

(1) The London Assets formed part of the National Fund. That Fund was, in my opinion, created to assist in the management of the economy and government revenues of the [Republic of Kazakhstan], both in the short and long term. Management of a State's economy and revenue must constitute a sovereign activity.

(2) The National Fund had to be managed by the NBK in accordance with the law set out in the Budget Code, in particular Article 24. That demanded that the National Fund be invested: Article 24 para. 2. I accept that this required that investment had to be placed in authorised financial assets in order to secure, amongst other things, **'high profitability levels of the [National Fund] in the long term outlook at reasonable risk levels'**. I also accept the uncontroverted evidence that the Securities Accounts held by AAMGS on behalf of the NBK were actively traded at all times and that the NBK obtained from the [Republic of Kazakhstan] a commission on good results and paid a penalty for poor ones. But I cannot accept that this activity is inconsistent with the Stability and Savings Funds of the National Fund being used or intended for use for sovereign purposes. The aim of the exercise, at all times, was and is to enhance the National Fund. To do that the assets have to be put to use to obtain returns which are reinvested in the National Fund, ie. to assist the sovereign actions.

(3) [Counsel for the claimants] relies on the definition of **'commercial purposes'** set out in section 17(1) of the SIA and points to the fact that **'commercial purposes'** means transactions and activities mentioned in section 3(3) of the Act. Those include **'any transaction or activity (whether of a commercial ... financial ... or similar character) into which a State enters or in which it engages otherwise in the exercise of sovereign authority'**. He says that the trading activities of the Securities Accounts by AAMGS are clearly financial transactions and their aim is to make profits. Therefore they could not be transactions **'in the exercise of sovereign authority'** within section 3(3). So, for the purposes of 13(4), at least, the Securities Accounts of the London Assets constitute **'property in use or intended for use for commercial purposes'**. Again, I must disagree. The dealings of the Securities Accounts must, in my view, be set against the background of the purpose of the [global custody agreement]. That was established to assist in running the National Fund. The Securities Accounts contain assets which are part of the National Fund. In my view the dealings are all part of the overall exercise of sovereign authority by the Republic of Kazakhstan.

[153] [2006] 1 All ER 284, 310–11, reference omitted.

[154] [2006] 1 All ER 284, 312, para 92.

(4) Last, but not least, there is the certificate of the Ambassador. That is clear and unambiguous. I have seen no evidence to contradict it other than the fact that the Securities Accounts are traded. For the reasons I have given, the trading of those accounts does not mean they were being used or were intended for use for commercial purposes.[155]

For these reasons, his Lordship was confident that, even if he were wrong about the construction of the word 'property' in section 14(4) and were to conclude instead that the London assets of the National Fund could not be regarded as the property of the NBK but were at all times the property of the Republic of Kazakhstan, these assets would still be immune from the enforcement process of the UK courts by virtue of section 13(2)(b), since they 'were the subject of transactions that were (through the NBK and AAMGS) the exercise of sovereign authority': they were not in use or intended for use for commercial purposes within the meaning of section 13(4), which in turn derived its meaning from section 3(3).[156]

Nor did Aikens J accept the claimants' contention, based on *Stran Greek Refineries v Greece*,[157] that section 14(4) of the SIA amounted to a deprivation of a possession contrary to article 1 of Protocol 1 to the ECHR, even though the defendants accepted that an ICSID award was a 'possession' within the meaning of that provision:

The ICSID arbitration procedure, the award that resulted from it and the judgment obtained using the 1966 Act were all subject to the existing law, which included section 14(4). In other words, the 'possession' always had limitations on its utility and value from the moment it was created. The 'possession' was always going to be subject to the existing rules concerning immunity of States and the property of central banks. The case is entirely unlike the *Stran Greek Refineries* case where the Greek government passed legislation *after* the award to render it invalid and unenforceable. So I hold that Article 1 of the Protocol is not involved. But even if it is, to the extent that the Claimants have been deprived of the peaceful enjoyment of their possession by virtue of section 14(4), that is legitimate and proportionate. My reasons are the same as those set out in relation to the Article 6(1) point.[158]

Again, since article 1 of Protocol 1 was not violated, section 3 of the HRA did not oblige a different construction of section 14(4) of the SIA.

A few aspects of Aikens J's judgment, which for the most part is hard to fault, call for consideration.

First, having rightly held that the word 'property' in sections 13(2)(b), 13(4), and 14(4) of the SIA must be taken to encompass 'any right or interest, legal, equitable, or contractual in assets',[159] his Lordship posits

[155] [2006] 1 All ER 284, 312–13, para 92.

[156] [2006] 1 All ER 284, 313, para 94. SIA 1978, s 17(1) provides that the term 'commercial purposes' means 'purposes of such transactions or activities as are mentioned in section 3(3) above'.

[157] (1994) 19 EHRR 368, esp paras 61 and 62.

[158] [2006] 1 All ER 284, 311, para 87, original emphasis.

[159] [2006] 1 All ER 284, 302, para 45.

the view that where both a central bank and that central bank's State have interests in the asset in question, 'the effect of section 14(4) is that the relevant property is immune from enforcement in respect of a judgment against that State, whether the property concerned is in use or intended for use for commercial purposes or not'.[160] The problem with this statement is that it elides the property and the asset: having characterized the *interest* in the asset as the relevant property, Aikens J then uses the term 'property' to refer to the asset as such, with the consequence that the asset itself is immune from enforcement on the basis of the central bank's interest in it. This is stated explicitly by his Lordship a few paragraphs later, when he says that 'in all cases, whatever the nature of the "property" right of the central bank, the assets concerned are immune from the enforcement process'.[161] But if the relevant 'property' is the interest in the asset, not the asset as such, there appears no reason in principle why the central bank's property, viz its interest in the asset, should not be severable from the State's property, viz its particular interest in the same asset. So, for example, where the central bank has the legal interest in the asset and the State the equitable, the legal interest would be immune by virtue of section 14(4) but the equitable not, and, in this light, there would be no reason in principle why, all other things being equal, a judgment debtor could not enforce the judgment against the State's equitable interest in the event that it is in use or is intended for use for commercial purposes. In the present case, while the NBK had a contractual right to the debt represented by the cash assets and a beneficial interest in the securities held by AAMGS, it was agreed that the Republic of Kazakhstan retained at all times some form of ultimate beneficial interest in these assets, against the securities accounts of which (but not the cash[162]) the judgment ought to have been enforceable by way of sections 1 and 2(1)(a) of the Charging Orders Act 1979 in the event that they were in use or intended for use for commercial purposes—unless obstacles were posed by the law of equity, private international law, or the Civil Procedure Rules. In the final analysis, however, such an approach would not, on Aikens J's further reading, have altered the outcome, since even if the London assets of the National Fund were not to be seen as property of the NBK but were the property of Kazakhstan alone, they were not in use or intended for use for commercial purposes within the meaning of section 13(4) of the SIA, and were thus immune from enforcement by virtue of section 13(2)(b).

Whether, in the instant case, the property could truly be said not to be in use or intended for use for 'commercial purposes' within the meaning of section 13(4) would seem an easier question than that which needs to be posed under section 3(3), where the issue is whether the State has entered into a 'commercial transaction'. Section 3(3), as elaborated on by Lord

160 [2006] 1 All ER 284, 305, para 57.

161 [2006] 1 All ER 284, 306, para 60.

162 Recall CPR Pt 72.2(1)(a).

Wilberforce in *I° Congreso del Partido*,[163] turns on the almost theological distinction between the character of a transaction and its purpose or motive. The issue under section 13(4) is restricted to the latter. If this were not plain on the provision's face, section 17(1) provides that the term 'commercial purposes' means 'purposes of such transactions or activities as are mentioned in section 3(3) above'. This does not make things straightforward, by any means. But, on the facts of the present case, Aikens J probably concluded correctly, particularly given the certification to the same effect by the Kazakh ambassador, which, in accordance with section 13(5), was, until the contrary was proved, to be accepted as sufficient evidence of that fact that the London assets of the National Fund were not in use or intended for use by or on behalf of Kazakhstan for commercial purposes.

As noted by his Lordship, the blanket immunity afforded to property of a central bank by section 14(4) marks a point of difference between the SIA and the equivalent Australian, Canadian and US statutes.[164] On the other hand, it is in line with article 21(1)(c) of the more recent UN Convention on Jurisdictional Immunity of States and Their Property 2004[165] and more likely than not gives effect to an obligation under general international law, justifying Aikens J's conclusion, *à la Al-Adsani*,[166] that the restriction it imposes on the claimants' right of access to the court is for a legitimate aim and is not disproportionate.

Immunity of foreign Minister for Commerce and International Trade—special mission immunity—Convention on Special Missions 1969—customary international law—torture—Convention against Torture and Other Cruel, Inhuman or Degrading Treatment or Punishment 1984—Criminal Justice Act 1988, section 134—whether visiting foreign Minister for Commerce and International Trade immune from criminal process in respect of allegations of torture contrary to Torture Convention

Case No 8. *Re Bo Xilai*, 8 November 2005, unreported (Bow Street Magistrates' Court, Judge Workman, Senior District Judge).

A warrant was sought under section 134 of the Criminal Justice Act 1988[167]—by which the UK asserts universal jurisdiction pursuant to the

[163] [1983] 1 AC 244, (1981) 52 BYIL 314–19 (HL).

[164] See the comparison at para 41, n 54.

[165] UN Doc A/RES/59/38, Annex, 2 Dec 2004.

[166] (2002) 34 ECHR 11, esp paras 53–56.

[167] In accordance with CJA 1988, s 135(a), proceedings for an offence under s 134 shall not be begun in England and Wales except by, or with the consent of, the Attorney-General. But the Prosecution of Offences Act 1985, s 25(2)(a) provides that the requirement of the Attorney-General's consent shall not prevent the issue of a warrant for the arrest of a person for any offence. In the instant case, Judge Workman was satisfied that Mr Bo was likely to leave the UK within days and that there was, therefore, 'an urgency which could justify the issue of a warrant'.

Convention against Torture and Other Cruel, Inhuman or Degrading Treatment or Punishment[168]—for the arrest of Bo Xilai, Minister for Commerce and International Trade of the People's Republic of China, on charges of conspiracy to torture allegedly committed in the PRC since 1999. At the time of the application in the Bow Street Magistrates' Court, Mr Bo was accompanying the President of the PRC on an official visit to the UK.

The application was refused by Judge Workman, Senior District Judge, on the ground that Mr Bo was immune from the criminal jurisdiction of the UK courts. First, as Mr Bo was the serving Minister for Commerce and International Trade of the PRC, Judge Workman concluded that his functions were equivalent to those exercised by a Minister for Foreign Affairs, and, 'adopting the reasoning of the International Court of Justice in the case of *Democratic Republic of Congo* v. *Belgium*', he held that 'under the customary international law rules' Mr Bo enjoyed immunity from prosecution, 'as he would not be able to perform his functions unless he [were] able to travel freely'.[169] Secondly, since Mr Bo was part of the official delegation for the state visit to the UK of the President of the PRC, he was a member of a special mission 'and as such [had] immunity under customary international law',[170] as reflected in article 31(1) of the Convention on Special Missions 1969.[171]

Judge Workman's decision—which, not emanating from a superior court of record, has no precedential value in the English courts—points for the second time in as many years[172] to the long shadow cast by the judgment of the International Court of Justice in *Arrest Warrant of 11 April 2000 (Democratic Republic of the Congo v Belgium)*.[173] The Court's teleological and analogical reasoning in that case[174] is potentially applicable to a wide range of state officials who could be said when abroad to perform a representative function akin to that of a diplomat or head of State. There is no principled reason, however, why an English court, directly applying the customary international law of immunities as part

[168] UN Doc A/RES/39/46, Annex, 10 December 1984.

[169] Judgment, 2.

[170] Judgment, 2.

[171] New York, 8 December 1969, 1400 UNTS 231. Art 31(1) provides that '[t]he representatives of the sending State in the special mission and the members of its diplomatic staff shall enjoy immunity from the criminal jurisdiction of the receiving State'. A 'special mission' is defined in art 1(a) of the Convention as 'a temporary mission, representing the State, which is sent by one State to another State with the consent of the latter for the purpose of dealing with it on specific questions or of performing in relation to it a specific task'. In accordance with art 1(e), a 'representative of the sending State in a special mission' is 'any person on whom the sending State has conferred that capacity'.

[172] See *Judgment in the matter of the application for the issue of an arrest warrant against General Shaul Mofaz*, 12 February 2004, unreported, (2004) 75 BYIL 408–11 (Bow Street Magistrates' Court, Judge Pratt, District Judge).

[173] ICJ Rep 2002, 3.

[174] See ICJ Rep 2002, 3, paras 53–55.

of the law of England, should embrace the ICJ's reasoning in *Arrest Warrant* to grant absolute immunity *ratione personae* to 'novel' state officials. As rightly decried by Judge *ad hoc* Van den Wyngaert,[175] the methodology adopted by the Court in that case for identifying a rule of customary international law flew in the face of the requirement of State practice and *opinio juris*—of the need for 'a general practice accepted as law', in the words of article 38(1)(b) of the Court's Statute. While it would be a bold domestic court which held, *pace* the ICJ, that a Minister for Foreign Affairs does not in fact enjoy absolute personal immunity from the criminal jurisdiction of a foreign State, there is no good reason why a domestic court should adopt *Arrest Warrant*'s brand of purposive assertion when determining other points of the customary international law of personal immunity. Indeed, if customary international law forms part of the law of England, this includes the customary rules on identifying a positive rule of custom, which demand widespread and representative State practice performed in the belief that this practice comports with a rule of law, and according to which decisions of international tribunals are only subsidiary sources for the determination of international rules.[176] In this light, the substitution of the reasoning in *Arrest Warrant* for an orthodox survey of State practice and *opinio juris* is contrary to English law.

As for article 31(1) of the Convention on Special Missions, it might be queried whether this is consonant with customary international law, since it is difficult to discern a relevant body of State practice clearly differentiated from the practice relating to diplomatic, head of State and head of government immunity, on the one hand, and to State immunity, on the other.

Statutory construction—statute enacted to give effect to treaty obligation—jurisdiction to prescribe criminal laws on basis of territoriality—'objective' territoriality—jurisdiction of English and Scottish criminal courts—extraterritorial conspiracy to commit territorial offence—partly extraterritorial, partly territorial offences—European Council Framework Decision on the European arrest warrant—surrender of sentenced persons on basis of European arrest warrant—'framework offences'—Extradition Act 2003, Part 1—'conduct' within meaning of Extradition Act, section 65—whether London-based conspiracy to commit crime in Belgium conduct occurring in Belgium for purposes of Extradition Act, section 65—whether surrender for framework offence permissible under section 65(3) to (6) of Extradition Act—Extradition Act, section 2(2) and (5)—whether absence of statement

[175] ICJ Rep. 2002, 3, sep op Van den Wyngaert, para 11.
[176] Statute of the ICJ, art 38(1)(d).

required by Extradition Act, section 2(2) and (5) a bar to execution of European arrest warrant by UK judicial authorities

Case No 9. Office of the King's Prosecutor, Brussels v Cando Armas, 17 November 2005, [2005] UKHL 67, [2005] 3 WLR 1079, [2006] 1 All ER 647, 2005 WL 3066994 (HL).

The European Council Framework Decision of 13 June 2002 on the European arrest warrant and the surrender procedures between Member States[177] does away with extradition among the Member States of the European Union in respect of certain serious offences, replacing it with a straightforward transfer of suspects and convicts from the judicial authorities of one Member State to the judicial authorities of another on the basis of a 'European arrest warrant'. (Framework Decisions, taken under Title VI of the EU Treaty, are equivalent, for all intents and purposes, to multilateral treaties.) The essence of the Framework Decision on the European arrest warrant is captured in article 1(2), which provides that Member States 'shall execute any European arrest warrant on the basis of the principle of mutual recognition and in accordance with the provisions of [the] Framework Decision'. In accordance with article 2(1), a European arrest warrant 'may be issued for acts punishable by the law of the issuing Member State by a custodial sentence or a detention order for a maximum period of at least 12 months or, where a sentence has been passed or a detention order has been made, for sentences of at least four months'. Article 2(2) is the heart of the regime. It contains a list of offences which, 'if they are punishable in the issuing Member State by a custodial sentence or a detention order for a maximum period of at least three years and as they are defined by the law of the issuing Member State, shall, under the terms of this Framework Decision and without verification of the double criminality of the act, give rise to surrender pursuant to a European arrest warrant'. That is, the Member State called upon to execute a European arrest warrant (the 'executing Member State') may not condition surrender for a 'framework offence'[178] on the requirement of double criminality. In contrast, article 2(4) permits the executing Member State to impose a requirement of double criminality for all other offences for which a European arrest warrant may be issued.[179] Articles 3 and 4 enumerate grounds for non-execution of a

[177] Decision 2002/584/JHA [2002] OJ L190/1. Recital 5 of the preamble speaks of 'abolishing extradition between Member States and replacing it by a system of surrender between judicial authorities'.

[178] The widely-used term is not actually found in the Framework Decision.

[179] In effect, as regards all other acts punishable by the law of the issuing Member State by a custodial sentence or a detention order for a maximum period of at least 12 months or, where a sentence has been passed or a detention order has been made, for sentences of at least four months, Member States remain entitled to apply art 2(1) of the European Convention on Extradition, 13 December 1957, ETS No 24, which provides: 'Extradition shall be granted in respect of offences punishable under the laws of the requesting Party and of the requested Party by deprivation of liberty or under a detention order for a maximum period of at least one year or by a more severe penalty. Where a

European arrest warrant. Article 4(7)(a) allows the executing Member State to refuse execution where the warrant relates to offences which 'are regarded by the law of the executing Member State as having been committed in whole or in part in the territory of the executing Member State or in a place treated as such'.

The obligations undertaken by the UK through the Framework Decision on the European arrest warrant are reflected in Part 1 of the Extradition Act 2003, which deals with what it insists on calling 'extradition'[180] to so-called 'category 1 territories'.[181] Section 65 of the Extradition Act defines what constitutes an extradition offence for the purposes of Part 1 in relation to persons unlawfully at large after being sentenced for an offence.[182] Paragraph 2 of section 65 defines as an extradition offence conduct included within the European framework list[183] for which a custodial sentence of at least twelve months has been imposed, where, in accordance with section 65(2)(a), that conduct occurs in the category 1 territory 'and no part of it occurs in the United Kingdom'. In accordance with article 2(2) of the Framework Decision, section 65(2) embodies no requirement of double criminality. Paragraphs 3 to 6 of section 65, on the other hand, provide for a range of extradition offences which remain subject to double criminality. Section 65(3) speaks of conduct which occurs in the category 1 territory, which would constitute an offence under the law of the relevant part of the UK if it occurred in that part of the UK, and for which a custodial sentence of four months or more has been imposed.

The defendant was convicted in Brussels *in absentia* and sentenced to five years' imprisonment for directing, from his base in London, illegal immigration via Belgium into the EU. The Belgian judicial authorities issued a European arrest warrant pursuant to which the defendant was arrested in the UK and his surrender sought under Part 1 of the Extradition Act for conspiracy to commit (or acting as instigator or leader in the commission of)[184] the framework offences of trafficking in human beings, facilitation of unauthorized entry and residence, and forgery of administrative documents. Belgium was designated a category 1 territory by way of the Extradition Act 2003 (Designation of Part 1 Territories) Order 2003.[185] The District Judge held that the conduct in question did not constitute an extradition offence: part of it had occurred

conviction and prison sentence have occurred or a detention order has been made in the territory of the requesting Party, the punishment awarded must have been for a period of at least four months.'

[180] As explained by Lord Hope, the system provided for in Part 1 'is really just a system of backing of warrants': [2005] 3 WLR 1079, 1090, para 22.

[181] These are territories designated for the purposes of Part 1 of the Act by order made by the Secretary of State: Extradition Act 2003, s 1(1).

[182] Section 64 does the same—and in terms which are, *mutatis mutandis*, identical to those in s 65—in relation to persons accused of an offence or unlawfully at large after conviction of, but before sentencing for, an offence.

[183] The list is reproduced in Sch 2 to the Act.

[184] See the terms of the warrant reproduced at [2005] 3 WLR 1079, 1087, para 12.

[185] SI 2003/3333.

in the UK, ruling out reliance on section 65(2), and it did not take place exclusively in Belgium, ruling out section 65(3). The Divisional Court, allowing the King's Prosecutor's appeal, held that the conduct referred to in section 65 meant such of the conduct as amounted to a criminal offence under the law of the category 1 territory, and not necessarily the whole of the conduct, and that paragraphs 3 to 6 of section 65 were not limited to non-framework offences, with the result that the defendant's conduct constituted an extradition offence under both section 65(2) and 65(3).

The House of Lords, dismissing the defendant's appeal, held that reliance could not be placed on section 65(2) of the Extradition Act in the instant case, as part of the impugned conduct had occurred in the UK, but that the conduct amounted to an extradition offence under section 65(3), since nothing in that paragraph required the conduct to occur wholly in Belgium and nothing prevented sections 65(3) to (6) from applying to framework offences.

Lords Bingham and Hope, giving the leading judgments with the conclusions and reasoning of which the other Lords agreed, highlighted the general principles to be brought to bear on the task of construction before them. Lord Bingham, noting that Part 1 of the Extradition Act 'did not effect a simple or straightforward transposition, and it did not on the whole use the language of the Framework Decision', nonetheless took the view that 'its interpretation must be approached on the twin assumptions that Parliament did not intend [its provisions] to be inconsistent with the Framework Decision and that, while Parliament might properly provide for a greater measure of cooperation by the United Kingdom than the Decision required, it did not intend to provide for less'.[186] Lord Hope, while in broad agreement, was somewhat more circumspect:

In *R* v. *Governor of Ashford Remand Centre, Ex p Postlethwaite* [1988] AC 924, 947, Lord Bridge of Harwich said that the court should not apply the strict canons appropriate to the construction of domestic legislation to extradition treaties. In *In re Ismail* [1999] 1 AC 320, 327, Lord Steyn, noting that there was a transnational interest in bringing those accused of serious crime to justice, said:

> 'Extradition treaties, and extradition statutes, ought, therefore to be accorded a broad and generous construction so far as the texts permit it in order to facilitate extradition.'

These passages describe the approach to the issues of statutory construction that have been raised in this appeal. But the liberty of the subject is at stake here, and generosity must be balanced against the rights of the persons who are sought to be removed under these procedures. They are entitled to expect the courts to see that the procedures are adhered to according to the requirements laid down in the statute. Unfortunately this is not an easy task, as the wording of Part 1 of the 2003 Act does not in every respect match that of the Framework Decision to

[186] [2005] 3 WLR 1079, 1084, para 8.

which it seeks to give effect in domestic law. But the task has to be approached on the assumption that, where there are differences, these were regarded by Parliament as a necessary protection against an unlawful infringement of the right to liberty.[187]

Turning to specifics, Lord Bingham made light work of the first two issues:

16 I would accept the submission ... that 'the conduct' in section 65 means the conduct complained of or relied on in the warrant. Such a reading is consistent with the language and purpose of the Framework Decision, obviates the need for an undesirable inquiry into the niceties of a foreign law and is consistent, so far as that is relevant, with the earlier decision of the House in *In re Neilsen* [1984] AC 606, 614–615. I would accordingly agree with the deputy senior district judge and differ from the Divisional Court in holding that, since some of the conduct complained of or relied on in the warrant occurred in the United Kingdom, the condition in subsection (2)(a) is not satisfied and subsection (2) is accordingly inapplicable.

17 I cannot, however, accept that subsection (3) is to be read as requiring that all the conduct complained of should have occurred in the category 1 territory. The subsection does not so provide, and the qualification that no part of the conduct should have occurred in the United Kingdom, expressly stipulated in subsections (2)(a), (5)(a) and (6)(a), is not found in (3)(a). It must be inferred that that qualification was not intended. It is enough, under subsection (3)(a), if some of the conduct complained of or relied on occurred in the category 1 territory. ...[188]

Lord Hope agreed with Lord Bingham's conclusions and reasoning, before adding a few comments of his own. He prefaced his discussion as follows:

The definitions of what constitute an extradition offence for the purposes of Part 1 are based on the principle, recognised in international law, that states claim criminal jurisdiction over conduct which takes place within their territory. The judge need not concern himself with the criminal law of the requesting state when he is addressing the question whether the offence specified in the Part 1 warrant is an extradition offence. But he does have to consider where the conduct which is alleged to constitute the offence took place.[189]

His Lordship then focused on two questions he thought raised by the application of section 65(3) of the Act to the present case, namely '(1) whether the [defendant] must be within the territory of the requesting state at the time of the conduct which he is alleged to have committed, and (2) whether the conduct must have occurred exclusively within that territory'.[190] He continued:

The answers are to be found in the first place in the language which has been used by the legislature which Lord Bingham has analysed. The context in which

[187] [2005] 3 WLR 1079, 1090–1, para 24.
[188] [2005] 3 WLR 1079, 1088.
[189] [2005] 3 WLR 1079, 1092, para 30.
[190] [2005] 3 WLR 1079, 1093, para 34.

that language has been used is, of course, provided by the common law. It is provided in particular by the rules which apply when jurisdiction is claimed on the basis of territoriality. It is now well established that the physical presence of the defendant in the territory is not required so long as the effects of his actions were intentionally felt there. That rule is matched by its corollary which is that, if the effects of those actions were intentionally felt here, criminal jurisdiction can be exercised in respect of their effect irrespective of where the actions took place that gave rise to them. Section 65(2) modifies these rules in the case of framework offences where the test of double criminality is dispensed with, as it requires that no part of the conduct took place in the United Kingdom. But the test of whether conduct occurs in the category 1 territory is satisfied for the purposes of section 65(3) so long as its effects were intentionally felt there, irrespective of where the person was when he did the acts which constituted such conduct.[191]

His Lordship cited *Director of Public Prosecutions v Stonehouse*,[192] as well as the Scottish cases of *Clements v HM Advocate*[193] and *HM Advocate v Megrahi*,[194] which in turn cited *R v Doot*,[195] *Liangsiriprasert v Government of the United States of America*[196] and dicta from *R v Treacy*.[197] He concluded:

I would construe the word 'conduct' in sections 65(2)(a) and 65(3)(a) of the 2003 Act in the light of these authorities. The conduct must occur 'in' the category 1 territory if the condition which is set out in these paragraphs is to be satisfied. But a purposive meaning must be given to the word 'conduct' in this context. It would impose a wholly artificial restriction on the extradition process if it were to be taken as meaning that all the conduct which resulted in the offence must have taken place exclusively within the category 1 territory. Actings elsewhere will be sufficient to constitute conduct in that territory so long as their intended effect was to bring about harm within that territory. It would be immaterial to a request for extradition to Belgium, for example, that the actings which had a harmful effect were all in France or in Germany. The situation would be different, of course, if some part of those actings occurred in the United Kingdom. But that is because of the qualification that section 65(2)(a) has introduced, which prevents cases where some of the conduct occurs in the United Kingdom from being treated as an extradition offence under that subsection. The fact that it was thought necessary to insert this qualification is consistent with the existence of a general rule of the kind that I have described.[198]

As for whether framework offences could be dealt with under paragraphs (3) to (6) of section 65 of the Act, Lord Bingham was again in no doubt:

More fundamentally, I cannot accept that, because subsection (2)(a) is specifically directed to framework list offences, subsections (3) to (6) should be understood to exclude such offences. It is only if a case falls within subsection (2) that

[191] [2005] 3 WLR 1079, 1093–4, para 35. [192] [1978] AC 55, (1978) 49 BYIL 279–81 (HL).
[193] 1991 JC 62. [194] 2000 JC 555.
[195] [1973] AC 807, (1973) 46 BYIL 425–6 (HL) (also known as *Director of Public Prosecutions v Doot*). [196] [1991] AC 225.
[197] [1971] AC 537, (1971) 45 BYIL 393–5 (HL) (also known as *Treacy v Director of Public Prosecutions*). [198] [2005] 3 WLR 1079, 1095–6, para 40.

the double criminality requirement is dispensed with, as subsections (3)(b), (4)(c), (5)(b) and (6)(c) make clear. This reflects the thrust of the Framework Decision. But there is nothing in the section to suggest that subsections (3), (4), (5) and (6) cannot apply to framework list offences where the relevant requirement of double criminality is met. No reason of logic or justice was suggested to support such a rule, and it is plain from hypothetical examples suggested in argument that it would lead to results which neither the European Council nor Parliament could ever have intended. I am accordingly of the opinion that there is nothing in the language of subsection (3) which would preclude its application to this case.[199]

Lord Hope agreed that section 65(3) was 'not restricted to framework offences' but was 'capable of applying to any offence which satisfies the [relevant] requirements . . . , including those on the framework list'.[200]

On an unrelated note, and although it was not a question for their Lordships' determination, most of the Lords commented on a divergence between Part 1 of the Extradition Act and the Framework Decision on the European arrest warrant. 'Extradition' under Part 1 is initiated by the receipt from a category 1 territory of a 'Part 1 warrant', which in accordance with the definition contained in section 2(2) must, in the case of a sentenced person, contain a statement that 'the person in respect of whom the Part 1 warrant is issued is alleged to be unlawfully at large after conviction of an offence specified in the warrant by a court in the category 1 territory', in the words of section 2(5)(a). No such statement is required by article 8 of the Framework Decision, which sets out the form and contents of the European arrest warrant, and the warrant issued by the Belgian authorities in the instant case did not include one. The issue was whether this rendered the warrant void, as not being a Part 1 warrant as defined in section 2(2). Lord Hope stated:

It would be unduly strict in these circumstances to insist that a statement must appear in the actual words used in section 2(5) if a European arrest warrant is to qualify as a Part 1 warrant. The purpose of the requirement is to provide protection against an unlawful infringement of the right to liberty, so it is an important part of the procedure provided for by Parliament. But the court should be slow to construe those words in a way that would make it impossible to give effect to a warrant which is in the terms which the Framework Decision has laid down. The purpose of the statute is to facilitate extradition, not to put obstacles in the way of the process which serve no useful purpose but are based on technicalities.[201]

The matter had arisen in *R (Bleta) v Secretary of State for the Home Department*,[202] where Crane J held that the actual words of the Act were not required to be used; rather, the relevant authority was entitled to consider not only the request but also the documents incorporated by reference and to come to the conclusion, although only in a clear case, that the request was effectively stating that the person was unlawfully at

199 [2005] 3 WLR 1079, 1088, para 17.
200 [2005] 3 WLR 1079, 1093, para 33.
201 [2005] 3 WLR 1079, 1097, para 44.
202 [2005] 1 WLR 3194.

large after being convicted. Lord Hope was unwilling to decide the matter in the absence of full argument on point, especially since the House had not been referred to *Bleta*. But his Lordship stated:

It is sufficient for present purposes to say that it is open to the court to draw inferences from the material available to it to determine whether the requirements of the statute have been satisfied. But those against whom the system for extradition is invoked are entitled to protection against its use in circumstances which have not been provided for by Parliament. So I think that Crane J was right to indicate that, if there is a gap in the information, it ought not to be filled by mere guesswork. The fact that Part 1 of the 2003 Act does not match the requirements of the Framework Decision is confusing to the unwary, and it appears likely that it will be a source of continuing difficulty. Steps should be taken to remind the authorities in the category 1 territories that the statements referred to in section 2(2) of the Act are a necessary part of the procedure that has been laid down in Part 1 of the Act.[203]

Lord Bingham, also reserving his opinion, nonetheless indicated that he 'would for [his] part be slow to read into Part 1 of the 2003 Act a condition not found in the Framework Decision'.[204] Baroness Hale was similarly minded:

It would be most unfortunate if the judicial authorities in our European partner states, using the form of warrant prescribed by the Framework Decision, were to find that the English judicial authorities were unable to implement it. Whether the solution should be legislative, or administrative, for example by way of routine requests to include such a statement where none appears on the face of the warrant initially presented, or whether it is possible for the judiciary to find a practical solution which is true to the spirit and the requirements of the Framework Decision, while properly safeguarding the liberty of the individual, it is not at present possible to say.[205]

Lord Scott felt more strongly about the matter, and to the opposite effect. He first characterized the gist of the procedure created by the Framework Decision, as captured in article 1(2):

The principle underlying these changes is that each member state is expected to accord due respect and recognition to the judicial decisions of other member states. Any inquiry by a member state into the merits of a proposed prosecution in another member state or into the soundness of a conviction in another member state becomes, therefore, inappropriate and unwarranted. It would be inconsistent with the principle of mutual respect for and recognition of the judicial decisions in that member state.[206]

His Lordship then considered the form and content of the European arrest warrant:

55 Where extradition is sought for the purpose of executing a custodial sentence, the form in the annex to the Framework Decision does not provide for any

[203] [2005] 3 WLR 1079, 1098, para 48.
[204] [2005] 3 WLR 1079, 1089, para 18.
[205] [2005] 3 WLR 1079, 1101, para 60.
[206] [2005] 3 WLR 1079, 1099, para 52.

information to be given as to the legal effect of the sentence on the right of the person sentenced to remain at large or as to whether any supervening events have altered its effect. In the present case, for example, it appears that the appellant was sentenced following a judgment in default given in his absence. It may be the case, but cannot, in my opinion, simply be assumed, that such a sentence takes immediate effect. It may be that notice of the sentence has to be served on or given to the person sentenced before he can be described as being unlawfully at large. In other cases, similar uncertainties might arise. An individual might have been released on licence on conditions that are alleged to have been broken. Or he might have been given bail pending appeal and the conditions of bail then broken. Would he then be unlawfully at large? It appears to me that it would be quite contrary to an important principle underlying European arrest warrants for the judicial authority in the requested state to have to inquire into the question whether under the law of the requesting state the individual who had been sentenced was unlawfully at large.

56 These potential problems explain, I think, why section 2(5)(a) of the 2003 Act requires an arrest warrant issued for the purpose of executing a custodial sentence to state that the person whose extradition is sought is unlawfully at large. An arrest warrant which contains neither the section 2(3) statement nor the section 2(5) statement does not, it appears to me, comply with the requirements of the Act and, if that is right, would not constitute a warrant on which an extradition under Part 1 of the Act could be ordered.

57 The requirement that an arrest warrant must contain one or other of these statements seems to me to be a natural and desirable feature of an extradition system that does not permit the merits of the extradition request to be investigated by the judge who is asked to order the execution of the arrest warrant. At the least, the state seeking extradition can be, and under section 2 of the Act is, asked to commit itself to the propriety of the extradition. These statements are not, in my opinion, formalities. They form an important part of the new extradition procedure.

58 Since this is a case where the appellant appears to have been convicted and sentenced under a default judgment given in his absence, it is the 'unlawfully at large' statement that needed to be included in the warrant. It is nowhere expressly included. It would be possible for the deputy senior district judge to whom the case is to be remitted to inquire into the question whether under Belgian law the default judgment took effect automatically, or whether it first had to be served on the absent defendant or otherwise drawn to his attention, or whether any other procedure was necessary before it could be said that the appellant was 'unlawfully at large'. But such an inquiry would, it seems to me, be inconsistent with the principle on which the new extradition procedure is based. We have not heard argument on the issue but my present, necessarily provisional, view is that if the 'unlawfully at large' statement is included in a warrant to which subsection (5) applies the judge cannot go behind it, but that if it is not included, and cannot be unequivocally implied from what is included, the warrant is bad.[207]

His Lordship alluded to 'several other points on the content of this arrest warrant that might be raised', but left it at that.[208]

[207] [2005] 3 WLR 1079, 1100–1. [208] [2005] 3 WLR 1079, 1101, para 51.

On the main points raised by the appeal, their Lordships' is a sensible reading of section 65 of the Act. As to where the conduct the subject of the warrant occurred, what Lords Bingham and Hope say in effect is that 'the conduct', within the meaning of section 65, is a holistic concept which encompasses, in cases such as the present one, not just the inchoate offence for which the surrender is sought—here, conspiracy, although equally complicity or even, in certain cross-border contexts, attempt—but also the relevant substantive (or 'complete') offence, in this case trafficking in human beings, facilitation of unauthorized entry and residence, and forgery of administrative documents; and that if either the inchoate or substantive offence occurs in the territory of the category 1 state, 'the conduct' took place in the territory of that State. This is a common-sense and workable approach, which, as Lord Bingham observes, avoids the need to delve into technical points of foreign criminal law relating to the venue of the offence the subject of the warrant.

It is unfortunate, however, that Lord Hope elided the issue of extraterritorial inchoate offences leading to territorial substantive offences, as raised in the present case, with that of substantive offences occurring partly without and partly within a State's territory. His Lordship prefaces his discussion by noting, quite rightly, that 'many of the offences in the framework list such as trafficking in human beings are commonly committed across borders' and, not quite rightly, that the defendant 'is alleged to have engaged in conduct of that kind, so these questions must be addressed in his case'.[209] The defendant was not alleged to have trafficked in human beings but to have conspired to traffic in human beings, and, in this light, the conduct for which his surrender was sought, comprising the inchoate offence of conspiracy, occurred wholly outside Belgium. His Lordship draws from a mixed bag of authorities, one of them relating to a substantive offence which was partly territorial and partly extraterritorial,[210] and others dealing with extraterritorial conspiracies[211] or extraterritorial attempts[212] to commit a territorial offence—authorities which conflate the issues too, albeit more self-consciously.

But even when the issues are accurately characterized (and in cases where the conspiracy comes to fruition, this may just be pedantry), there are reasons beyond the pragmatic to say that, for the purposes of article 65 of the Extradition Act, an extraterritorial conspiracy to commit a substantive offence in a category 1 territory can be treated as conduct which occurs in that territory. First, it would seem that general international law permits a State to criminalize, on the basis of so-called 'objective' territoriality, an extraterritorial conspiracy to commit an offence within its territory;[213] and if the international legal concept of territoriality, for

[209] [2005] 3 WLR 1079, 1093, para 34.

[210] *Clements v HM Advocate*, 1991 JC 62.

[211] *R v Doot* [1973] AC 807.

[212] *Director of Public Prosecutions v Stonehouse* [1978] AC 55.

[213] The State in which the conspiracy takes place would enjoy concurrent jurisdiction to criminalize it on the basis of 'subjective' territoriality.

the purposes of prescriptive criminal jurisdiction, takes in 'objective' territoriality in relation to conspiracy, it stands to reason that the Framework Decision on the European arrest warrant takes in the same. Secondly, as highlighted by Lord Hope, both English and Scots law permit the prosecution of conspiracies entered into abroad to commit an offence in England and Wales and Scotland respectively, in the former case (*pace* the dictum of Lord Keith quoted by Lord Hope)[214] even when no act in furtherance of the conspiracy occurs within the territory;[215] and in the absence of unambiguous evidence to the contrary, it makes sense to construe the Extradition Act, as Lord Hope suggests, against this common-law background.

It is regrettable, nonetheless, that Lord Hope should perpetuate the terminology used in cases such as *Stonehouse* and *Treacy*, where the various Lords asserted the jurisdiction of the English criminal courts over extraterritorial conduct on the ground that the conduct gave rise or was intended to give rise to effects within England and Wales. As a matter of international law, there is a distinction to be drawn between jurisdiction on the basis of objective territoriality, mentioned above, and jurisdiction on the basis of the so-called 'effects' doctrine. The former refers to jurisdiction over offences which, while initiated outside, are consummated inside the territory (that is, offences whose constituent elements take place partly without and partly within the territory) or, in the case of inchoate offences committed extraterritorially, where the substantive offence takes place or is intended to take place within the territory, whether wholly or partly. The effects doctrine, on the other hand, refers to jurisdiction over wholly extraterritorial conduct—that is, where no constituent element of the offence or, for inchoate offences, where neither the inchoate nor substantive offence takes place or is intended to take within the territory—solely on the ground that the impugned conduct has some deleterious effect, whether intended or not, within the territory. The permissibility of the first is uncontested. The second is controversial, and was even more so when *Stonehouse* and *Treacy* were decided. In this light, in the words of Brownlie, '[i]t is to be doubted if [*Stonehouse* and *Treacy*] intended to nourish the "effects" doctrine of jurisdiction to be found in the well-known American jurisprudence on extra-territorial jurisdiction'.[216] As it is, such a characterization does not, in fact, assist Lord Hope's argument, which is directed not towards whether the courts could lawfully exercise jurisdiction over the defendant's

[214] [2005] 3 WLR 1079, 1094, para 36, quoting *Director of Public Prosecutions v Stonehouse* [1978] AC 55, 93. Delivering the judgment of the Privy Council in *Liangsiriprasert v Government of the United States of America*, Lord Griffiths expressly declined to adopt Lord Keith's dictum, which he viewed as unsupported by authority or policy: [1991] AC 225, 244–52. Although *Liangsiriprasert* came on appeal from Hong Kong, Lord Griffiths stated that '[t]he law of conspiracy in Hong Kong is the same as the common law of conspiracy in England': [1991] AC 225, 244.

[215] *Liangsiriprasert v Government of the United States of America* [1991] AC 225.

[216] (1971) 45 BYIL 395.

acts but towards whether these acts could be said to have occurred within the territory.

The seemingly arcane issue raised by the Act's required inclusion in the 'Part 1 warrant' of material not required in the European arrest warrant is actually a classic one. Article 1(2) of the Framework Decision obliges Member States to execute the European arrest warrant, the form and contents of which are specified in article 8, 'on the basis of the principle of mutual recognition and in accordance with the provisions of [the] Framework Decision'. The failure of the authorities of a Member State, for any reason other than one enumerated in articles 3 and 4, to execute a European arrest warrant satisfying the requirements of article 8 constitutes a breach of article 1(2) of the Framework Decision, which for all intents and purposes is a treaty. The requirement posited in article 2(2) and 2(5) of the Extradition Act is extraneous to article 8 of the Framework Decision: whatever Lord Scott may say about its purpose and desirability (and this is questionable), it is a unilateral requirement over and above those agreed by the parties as conditions precedent to the obligation to execute a European arrest warrant. As such, a UK authority's refusal to execute an article 8-compliant warrant on the grounds of its failure to comply with article 2(5) of the Act is a breach of treaty. Now, insofar as a statute implementing a treaty to which the UK is party is ambiguous, and a construction consonant with the treaty's obligations is possible, the English courts must prefer that construction.[217] As a consequence, as rightly stated by Lord Bingham, the interpretation of Part 1 of the Extradition Act 'must be approached on the twin assumptions that Parliament did not intend [its provisions] to be inconsistent with the Framework Decision and that, while Parliament might properly provide for a greater measure of cooperation by the United Kingdom than the Decision required, it did not intend to provide for less'.[218] But sections 2(2) and 2(5) of the Act are in no way ambiguous. A statement that 'the person in respect of whom the Part 1 warrant is issued is alleged to be unlawfully at large after conviction of an offence specified in the warrant by a court in the category 1 territory'[219] is clearly a definitional requirement: '[a] Part 1 warrant is an arrest warrant which is issued by a judicial authority of a category 1 territory and which contains . . . the statement referred to in subsection (5) . . . '.[220] And only a Part 1 warrant can trigger Part 1 of the Act. So there is simply no scope to argue that the statement in question can be dispensed with. Nor can it be willed into being in the manner suggested in *Bleta* and by Lord Hope. A statement is a statement, not an inference. It may well be a formality, but on a straightforward reading of the Act it is a necessary formality.

[217] *Salomon v Commissioners of Customs and Excise* [1967] 2 QB 116, 143 (Diplock LJ), (1967) 42 BYIL 291–3 (CA).

[218] [2005] 3 WLR 1079, 1084, para 8 (Lord Bingham).

[219] Extradition Act 2003, s 2(5)(a).

[220] Extradition Act 2003, s 2(2), chapeau and subs (b).

Admissibility of witness evidence obtained through torture abroad by authorities of foreign State—common law—European Convention on Human Rights, articles 6 and 5(4)—Convention Against Torture, article 15—interpretation of treaties—Anti-terrorism, Crime and Security Act 2001, sections 21, 23, and 25 (repealed)—Special Immigration Appeals Commission (Procedure) Rules 2003, rule 44(3)—whether witness evidence obtained through torture abroad by authorities of foreign State admissible in proceedings before Special Immigration Appeals Commission under Anti-terrorism, Crime and Security Act, section 25

Case No 10. A and others v Secretary of State for the Home Department (No 2), 8 December 2005, [2005] UKHL 71, [2005] 3 WLR 1249, [2006] 1 All ER 575, 2005 WL 3299089 (HL).

The facts of the case have been recounted in a previous volume.[221] Although Part IV of the Anti-terrorism, Crime and Security Act 2001 (ATCSA), the legislative provisions at issue before the Court of Appeal, was repealed in the wake of *A (No 1)*[222] by section 16(2)(a) of the Prevention of Terrorism Act 2005, the case proceeded on appeal to a seven-strong House of Lords, where seventeen non-governmental organizations were granted permission to intervene. In putting his case, the Secretary of State emphasized that, as a matter of policy, it was not his intention actually to rely on, or to seek to present to the Special Immigration Appeals Commission (SIAC) or to the Administrative Court, evidence which he knew or believed to have been procured through torture committed abroad by the officials of a foreign state. He accepted too, as the Court of Appeal had held, that it would not be open to a court to admit into evidence statements procured by means of torture committed by or with the connivance of UK officials. Lastly, he also conceded that material obtained through torture by third parties in the UK would be inadmissible.

The House of Lords unanimously reversed the decision of the Court of Appeal,[223] holding that, when hearing an appeal under section 25 of ATCSA by a person certified and detained under sections 21 and 23 of the Act, SIAC was not permitted to receive evidence which was or may have been procured by means of torture by foreign state officials abroad without the complicity of the UK authorities. If, in a challenge under section 25 of ATCSA, there were reasonable grounds for suspecting that material relied on by the Secretary of State had been obtained in this

[221] See *A and others v Secretary of State for the Home Department (No 2)* [2005] 1 WLR 414, (2004) 75 BYIL 468–83 (CA).

[222] *A and others v Secretary of State for the Home Department* [2005] WLR 87, (2004) 75 BYIL 518–35 (HL).

[223] As regards the Court of Appeal, Lord Rodger noted that '[u]nfortunately, outside the courts, the decision of the majority, Pill and Laws LJJ, has been subjected to sweeping criticisms which to a large extent ignore their reasoning and the very factors which led them to their conclusion': [2005] 3 WLR 1249, 1305, para 128.

way, for example if the detainee was able to point to the fact that it may have come from a country where torture was allegedly practised, it was incumbent upon SIAC to initiate the relevant inquiries; and (Lords Bingham, Nicholls and Hoffmann dissenting), where it was established by such inquiries as were practicable that, on the balance of probabilities, the evidence in question had indeed been procured through torture by foreign state officials, SIAC was obliged to exclude it.

All of their Lordships held that, in spite of the absence of authority on point, the common law forbade the admission into evidence of witness statements obtained by means of torture.[224] The lack of case-law was simply a function of the fact that torture itself had always been prohibited by the common law. Even if the executive had in the past resorted to it under warrant, no legally sanctioned torture had taken place in England since the mid-seventeenth century.[225] Further, unsworn statements made out of court had been inadmissible, as hearsay, since at least the beginning of the nineteenth century. Although the analogy was inexact, Lord Bingham thought it significant that the common law excluded confessions procured by oppression or inducement of the accused, rather than treating involuntariness as a question going to the weight to be accorded such material.[226] Nor was this just a question of the reliability of evidence of this sort:[227] Lord Bingham described the admission of such evidence as 'unreliable, unfair, offensive to ordinary standards of humanity and decency and incompatible with the principles which should animate a tribunal seeking to administer justice'.[228] Several of their Lordships believed that it was not a question of reliability at all. In Lord Hope's view, the use of such evidence 'is excluded not on grounds of its unreliability—if that was the only objection to it, it would go to its weight, not to its admissibility—but on grounds of its barbarism, its illegality and its inhumanity'.[229] The exclusionary rule existed 'to uphold the integrity of the administration of justice',[230] since, in the words of Lord Hoffmann, 'the stain attaching to such evidence [would] defile an English court'.[231] In Lord Carswell's eyes, to permit the admission of evidence obtained by torture 'would shock the conscience, abuse or degrade the proceedings and involve the state in moral defilement'.[232] For Lord Rodger's part, while he observed that

[224] Exceptions to the rule, suggested by Lords Nicholls and Brown, were where the police, having arrested a suspect on the basis of material obtained through torture abroad, face a challenge to the legality of the arrest or where the Secretary of State is compelled to defend himself against a civil claim, such as for false imprisonment: see [2005] 3 WLR 1249, 1289–90, para 72 (Lord Nicholls) and 1318, para 169 (Lord Brown) respectively. The latter explained that it was not a question of relying on the truth of the evidence in such cases; rather, the evidence went merely to the state of mind of the police or Secretary of State at the relevant time.

[225] The Lords noted that torture was not outlawed in Scotland until 1708.

[226] [2005] 3 WLR 1249, 1261, para 15.

[227] See also [2005] 3 WLR 1249, 1262, para 17 (Lord Bingham) and 1311–12, paras 147–148 (Lord Carswell).

[228] [2005] 3 WLR 1249, 1283, para 52 (Lord Bingham).

[229] [2005] 3 WLR 1249, 1300, para 112 (Lord Hope).

[230] [2005] 3 WLR 1249, 1294, para 91 (Lord Hoffmann). See also [2005] 3 WLR 1249, 1316, paras 1318, 164 and para 171 (Lord Brown).

[231] [2005] 3 WLR 1249, 1294, para 91 (Lord Hoffmann).

[232] [2005] 3 WLR 1249, 1312, para 150.

'[i]nformation obtained by torture may be unreliable', he noted that 'all too often it will be reliable and of value to the torturer and his masters'.[233] 'That is why torturers ply their trade'.[234] Eschewing the moralistic tenor of his noble and learned brethren, his Lordship stated: 'To rely on [statements procured through torture] is inconsistent with the notion of justice as administered by our courts. The Home Secretary does not defile SIAC by introducing such a statement, but he does ask it to rely on a type of statement which British courts would, ordinarily, reject on broad grounds of public policy.'[235] The common-law rule enunciated by their Lordships applied in principle as much to section 25 proceedings before SIAC, a superior court of record, as to any other judicial proceedings.[236]

Nor was the exclusionary rule simply one of evidence. Lord Bingham, with whose reasoning on point the other Lords agreed, stated: 'It trivialises the issue before the House to treat it as an argument about the law of evidence. The issue is one of constitutional principle, whether evidence obtained by torturing another human being may lawfully be admitted against a party to proceedings in a British court, irrespective of where, or by whom, or on whose authority the torture was inflicted'.[237] Since the common-law rule at issue represented a constitutional principle, their Lordships, applying the doctrine enunciated in *Simms*,[238] held that it could be displaced by nothing less than express words in primary legislation, with the consequence that rule 44(3) of the Special Immigration Appeals Commission (Procedure) Rules 2003, promulgated by the Secretary of State, did not override it. Lord Hoffmann held:

> Rule 44(3) is in my opinion far too general in its terms to justify a departure from such a fundamental principle. It plainly disapplies technical rules of evidence like the hearsay rule. But I cannot for a moment imagine that anyone in Parliament who considered the statutory power to make rules of procedure for SIAC could have thought that it was authorising a rule which allowed the use of evidence obtained by torture or that the Secretary of State who made the regulations thought he was doing so. Such a provision, touching upon the honour of our courts and our country, would have to be expressly provided in primary legislation so that it could be debated in Parliament.[239]

In this light, the appeals had to be upheld. Lord Bingham added, however, that 'it would of course be within the power of a sovereign Parliament (in breach of international law) to confer power on SIAC to receive third party torture evidence'.[240]

Their Lordships then lay down procedures to be followed by SIAC under section 25 of ATCSA. Given the severe restrictions placed on the

[233] [2005] 3 WLR 1249, 1306, para 130.

[234] [2005] 3 WLR 1249, 1306, para 130.

[235] [2005] 3 WLR 1249, 1308, para 137 (Lord Rodger).

[236] See, explicitly, [2005] 3 WLR 1249, 1290–1, para 76 (Lord Nicholls) and 1295, para 95 (Lord Hoffmann).

[237] [2005] 3 WLR 1249, 1282, para 51 (Lord Bingham).

[238] *R v Secretary of State for the Home Department, ex p Simms* [2000] 2 AC 115.

[239] [2005] 3 WLR 1249, 1295, para 96 (Lord Hoffmann). See also [2005] 3 WLR 1249, 1282, para 51 (Lord Bingham), 1300, para 113 (Lord Hope) and 1308, para 137 (Lord Rodger).

[240] [2005] 3 WLR 1249, 1282, para 51 (Lord Bingham).

material available to detainees and their counsel in such cases, the Lords held unanimously that the maintenance of the ordinary burden of proof would be inappropriate. Lord Bingham stated:

> 55 I do not for my part think that a conventional approach to the burden of proof is appropriate in a proceeding where the appellant may not know the name or identity of the author of an adverse statement relied on against him, may not see the statement or know what the statement says, may not be able to discuss the adverse evidence with the special advocate appointed (without responsibility) to represent his interests, and may have no means of knowing what witness he should call to rebut assertions of which he is unaware . . . .
>
> 56 The appellant must ordinarily, by himself or his special advocate, advance some plausible reason why evidence may have been procured by torture. This will often be done by showing that evidence has, or is likely to have, come from one of those countries widely known or believed to practise torture (although they may well be parties to the Torture Convention and will, no doubt, disavow the practice publicly). Where such a plausible reason is given, or where SIAC with its knowledge and expertise in this field knows or suspects that evidence may have come from such a country, it is for SIAC to initiate or direct such inquiry as is necessary to enable it to form a fair judgment . . . [241]

The other Lords were of the same view.[242]

When it came, however, to the test to be applied by SIAC in deciding whether or not to admit given evidence, the House split 4:3, with Lords Bingham, Nicholls, and Hoffmann dissenting from the view put as follows by Lord Hope: 'SIAC should not admit the evidence if it concludes on a balance of probabilities that it was obtained by torture. In other words, if SIAC is left in doubt as to whether the evidence was obtained in this way, it should admit it. But it must bear its doubt in mind when it is evaluating the evidence'.[243] Lord Rodger, along with Lords Carswell and Brown,[244] adopted the same position, concluding that 'SIAC should ask itself whether it is established, by means of such diligent inquiries into the sources as it is practicable to carry out, and on the balance of probabilities, that the information relied on by the Secretary of State was obtained under torture'.[245] Lord Hope elaborated on the reasoning behind his position:

> The effect of rule 44(3) of the [SIAC] Procedure Rules is that sources of all kinds may be relied upon, far removed from what a court of law would regard as the best evidence. SIAC may be required to look at information coming to the attention of the security services at third or fourth hand and from various sources, the significance of which cannot be determined except by looking at the whole picture which it presents. The circumstances in which the information was first obtained may be incapable of being detected at all or at least of being determined without a long and difficult inquiry which would not be practicable.

[241] [2005] 3 WLR 1249, 1285 (Lord Bingham).

[242] See [2005] 3 WLR 1249, 1291, para 80 (Lord Nicholls), 1301, para 116 (Lord Hope) and 1314, para 155 (Lord Carswell).

[243] [2005] 3 WLR 1249, 1301, para 118.

[244] See [2005] 3 WLR 1249, 1315, para 158 (Lord Carswell) and 1318–19, para 172 (Lord Brown).

[245] [2005] 3 WLR 1249, 1311, para 145.

So it would be unrealistic to expect SIAC to demand that each piece of information be traced back to its ultimate source and the circumstances in which it was obtained investigated so that it could be proved piece by piece, that it was not obtained under torture. The threshold cannot be put that high. Too often we have seen how the lives of innocent victims and their families are torn apart by terrorist outrages. Our revulsion against torture, and the wish which we all share to be seen to abhor it, must not be allowed to create an insuperable barrier for those who are doing their honest best to protect us. A balance must be struck between what we would like to achieve and what can actually be achieved in the real world in which we all live. Articles 5(4) and 6(1) of the European Convention, to which Lord Bingham refers ... must be balanced against the right to life that is enshrined in article 2 of the Convention.[246]

His Lordship took as 'the best guide to what is practicable'[247] article 15 of the Torture Convention,[248] according to which each State Party to the Convention must 'ensure that any statement which is established to have been made as a result of torture shall not be invoked in any proceedings, except against a person accused of torture as evidence that the statement was made':

[T]he exclusionary rule extends to any statement that 'is established' to have been made under torture. The rule does not require it to be shown that the statement was not made under torture. It does not say that the statement must be excluded if there is a suspicion of torture and the suspicion has not been rebutted. Nor does it say that it must be excluded if there is a real risk that it was obtained by torture. An evaluation of risk is appropriate if the question at issue relates to the future: see *Mamatkulov and Askarov* v. *Turkey*, 4 February 2005, para. 71. The question in that case was whether there was a real risk for the purposes of article 3 of the European Convention at the time of their extradition that the applicants would be tortured. The rule that article 15 lays down looks at what has happened in the past. It applies to a statement that is established to have been made under torture. In my opinion the test that it lays down is the test that should be applied by SIAC. It too must direct its inquiry to what has happened in the past. Is it established, by means of such diligent inquiries into the sources that it is practicable to carry out and on a balance of probabilities, that the information relied on by the Secretary of State was obtained under torture? If that is the position, article 15 requires that the information must be left out of account in the overall assessment of the question whether there were no reasonable grounds for a belief or suspicion of the kind referred to in section 21(1)(a) or (b) of the Anti-terrorism, Crime and Security Act 2001. The same rule must be followed in any other judicial process where information of this kind would otherwise be admissible.[249]

Lords Hope and Rodger drew support from the fact that the same approach had been taken by the **Hanseatisches Oberländesgericht** in Hamburg in *Re El Motassadeq*.[250]

[246] [2005] 3 WLR 1249, 1302, para 119. See also [2005] 3 WLR 1249, 1310–11, paras 144–145 (Lord Rodger).

[247] [2005] 3 WLR 1249, 1302, para 120.

[248] Convention against Torture and Other Cruel, Inhuman or Degrading Treatment or Punishment, UN Doc A/RES/39/46, Annex, 10 December 1984.

[249] [2005] 3 WLR 1249, 1302–3, para 121.

[250] 14 June 2005, NJW 2326.

In dissent on this point, Lord Bingham concluded that '[i]f SIAC is unable to conclude that there is not a real risk that the evidence has been obtained by torture, it should refuse to admit the evidence'.[251] His Lordship explained:

58 I agree, of course, that the reference in article 15 to 'any statement which is established to have been made as a result of torture' would ordinarily be taken to mean that the truth of such an allegation should be proved. That is what 'established' ordinarily means. I would also accept that in any ordinary context the truth of the allegation should be proved by the party who makes it. But the procedural regime with which the House is concerned in this case ... is very far from ordinary. A detainee may face the prospect of indefinite years of detention without charge or trial, and without knowing what is said against him or by whom.

...

59 My noble and learned friend, Lord Hope, proposes ... the following test: is it established, by means of such diligent inquiries into the sources that it is practicable to carry out and on a balance of probabilities, that the information relied on by the Secretary of State was obtained under torture? This is a test which, in the real world, can never be satisfied. The foreign torturer does not boast of his trade. The security services, as the Secretary of State has made clear, do not wish to imperil their relations with regimes where torture is practised. The special advocates have no means or resources to investigate. The detainee is in the dark. It is inconsistent with the most rudimentary notions of fairness to blindfold a man and then impose a standard which only the sighted could hope to meet. The result will be that, despite the universal abhorrence expressed for torture and its fruits, evidence procured by torture will be laid before SIAC because its source will not have been 'established'.

60 The authorities relied on by my noble and learned friends, Lord Hope of Craighead and Lord Rodger of Earlsferry, to support their conclusion are of questionable value at most ....

62 I regret that the House should lend its authority to a test which will undermine the practical efficacy of the Torture Convention and deny detainees the standard of fairness to which they are entitled under article 5(4) or 6(1) of the European Convention. The matter could not be more clearly put than by my noble and learned friend, Lord Nicholls of Birkenhead, in the closing paragraph of his opinion.[252]

In turn, Lord Nicholls stated: 'The contrary approach would place on the detainee a burden of proof which, for reasons beyond his control, he can seldom discharge. In practice that would largely nullify the principle, vigorously supported on all sides, that courts will not admit evidence procured by torture. That would be to pay lip-service to the principle. That is not good enough'.[253] Lord Hoffmann took the same view, holding that SIAC ought 'not to admit the evidence unless it is satisfied that such suspicions have been rebutted'.[254]

[251] [2005] 3 WLR 1249, 1285, para 56 (Lord Bingham). [252] [2005] 3 WLR 1249, 1286–7.
[253] [2005] 3 WLR 1249, 1291, para 80. [254] [2005] 3 WLR 1249, 1296, para 98.

All of the Lords accepted that, while no court could admit evidence obtained by means of torture by foreign state officials, the Secretary of State was entitled to rely on such evidence when certifying, arresting, searching, and detaining persons.[255] Use by a court was one thing, use 'by the executive when making operational decisions or by the police when exercising their investigatory powers, including powers of arrest', was another:[256] 'In both these instances the executive arm of the state is open to the charge that it is condoning the use of torture. So, in a sense, it is. The government is using information obtained by torture. But in cases such as these the government cannot be expected to close its eyes to this information at the price of endangering the lives of its own citizens. Moral repugnance to torture does not require this.'[257] Lord Brown put it even more forcefully:

> Generally speaking it is accepted that the executive may make use of all information it acquires: both coerced statements and whatever fruits they are found to bear. Not merely, indeed, is the executive entitled to make use of this information; to my mind it is bound to do so. It has a prime responsibility to safeguard the security of the state and would be failing in its duty if it ignores whatever it may learn or fails to follow it up. Of course it must do nothing to promote torture. It must not enlist torturers to its aid (rendition being perhaps the most extreme example of this). But nor need it sever relations even with those states whose interrogation practices are of most concern. So far as the courts are concerned, however, the position is different.[258]

Their Lordships emphasized that '[t]he executive and the judiciary have different functions and different responsibilities':[259]

> It is one thing for tainted information to be used by the executive when making operational decisions or by the police when exercising their investigatory powers, including powers of arrest. These steps do not impinge upon the liberty of individuals or, when they do, they are of an essentially short-term interim character. Often there is an urgent need for action. It is an altogether different matter for the judicial arm of the state to admit such information as evidence when adjudicating definitively upon the guilt or innocence of a person charged with a criminal offence. In the latter case repugnance to torture demands that proof of facts should be found in more acceptable sources than information extracted by torture.[260]

Lord Brown took this difference to be reflected in article 15 of the Torture Convention: 'Article 15's concern is with the use of "any statement ... made as a result of torture ... as evidence in any proceedings". It creates no bar to the use of coerced statements as a basis for executive

[255] [2005] 3 WLR 1249, 1281–2, para 47 (Lord Bingham), 1289, paras 68–69 (Lord Nicholls) and 1311, para 149 (Lord Carswell).

[256] [2005] 3 WLR 1249, 1289, para 70.

[257] [2005] 3 WLR 1249, 1289, para 69 (Lord Nicholls).

[258] [2005] 3 WLR 1249, 1316, para 161 (Lord Brown).

[259] [2005] 3 WLR 1249, 1289, para 70 (Lord Nicholls).

[260] [2005] 3 WLR 1249, 1289, para 70 (Lord Nicholls). See also [2005] 3 WLR 1249, 1294–5, para 93 (Lord Hoffmann).

action.'[261] Lords Bingham and Hoffmann acknowledged that the distinction created a mismatch, in that the Secretary of State, in certifying and detaining a person under sections 21 and 23 of ATCSA, would be entitled to base his decision on material that SIAC was barred from considering.[262] But, to Lord Bingham's eyes, this was 'not an unusual position':[263]

> It arises whenever the Secretary of State (or any other public official) relies on information which the rules of public interest immunity prevent him adducing in evidence ... It is a situation which arises where action is based on a warranted interception and there is no dispensation which permits evidence to be given. This may be seen as an anomaly, but ... it springs from the tension between practical common sense and the need to protect the individual against unfair incrimination.[264]

'The common law', his Lordship added, 'is not intolerant of anomaly'.[265]

Finally, the Lords made clear that the exclusionary rule they posited applied only to evidence obtained through torture: it did not extend to evidence obtained by means of other cruel, inhuman, or degrading treatment or punishment prohibited by article 3 of the ECHR.[266] Lord Bingham observed, however, that what was considered to constitute torture was liable to change over time.[267] Lord Hope noted that '[v]iews as to where the line is to be drawn may differ sharply from state to state',[268] adding: 'SIAC must exercise its own judgment in addressing this issue, which is ultimately one of fact. It should not be deterred from treating conduct as torture by the fact that other states do not attach the same label to it. The standard that it should apply is that which we would wish to apply in our own time to our own citizens.'[269] For his part, Lord Hoffmann was 'content for the common law to accept the definition of torture which Parliament adopted in section 134 of the Criminal Justice Act 1988, namely, the infliction of severe pain or suffering on someone by a public official in the performance or purported performance of his official duties'—which would, in his opinion, 'include the kind of treatment characterised as inhuman by the European Court of Human Rights in *Ireland* v. *United Kingdom* but would not include all treatment which that court has held to contravene article 3'.[270]

The courts of common law have a hallowed tradition of coining rules to thwart executive expediency through the robust invocation of extralegal values such as humanity, decency, integrity, civilization, and the vaunted

261 [2005] 3 WLR 1249, 1316, para 162 (Lord Brown).
262 [2005] 3 WLR 1249, 1282, para 48 (Lord Bingham) and 1294–5, para 93 (Lord Hoffmann).
263 [2005] 3 WLR 1249, 1282, para 48 (Lord Bingham).
264 [2005] 3 WLR 1249, 1282, para 48 (Lord Bingham).
265 [2005] 3 WLR 1249, 1282, para 48 (Lord Bingham).
266 [2005] 3 WLR 1249, 1284, para 53 (Lord Bingham), 1295–6, para 97 (Lord Hoffmann) and 1305, para 126 (Lord Hope).
267 [2005] 3 WLR 1249, 1284, para 53.
268 [2005] 3 WLR 1249, 1305, para 126.
269 [2005] 3 WLR 1249, 1305, para 126.
270 [2005] 3 WLR 1249, 1295–96, para 97, referring to (1978) 2 EHRR 25.

attachment to liberty of the English-speaking peoples. There is no intellectual dishonesty to such self-consciously judge-made law, and in a common-law system it is constitutionally proper. That tradition is on proud display here in the Lords' outright assertion of the existence of a common-law rule against the admissibility of evidence obtained through torture. Some of their Lordships maintained the customary pretence of declaring a 'deeply-rooted tradition': thus Lord Bingham, having earlier acknowledged the 'paucity of English judicial authority on this subject',[271] nonetheless proclaimed that the English common law has regarded the 'fruits [of torture] with abhorrence for over 500 years'.[272] More to this commentator's taste is Lord Carswell's frankness:

> Some of your Lordships have expressed the opinion that the common law as it stands would forbid the reception in evidence of any statement obtained by the use of torture ... This view may well be justified historically, but even if it requires some extension of the common law I am of the clear opinion that the principle can be accommodated. We have long ceased to give credence to the fiction that the common law consists of a number of pre-ordained rules which merely require discovery and judicial enunciation .... I am satisfied that, whether or not it has ever been affirmatively declared that the common law declines to allow the admission of evidence obtained by the use of torture, it is quite capable now of embracing such a rule. If that is any extension of the existing common law, it is a modest one, a necessary recognition of the conclusions which should be drawn from long established principles. I accordingly agree with your Lordships that such a rule should be declared to represent the common law.[273]

But whichever way the common-law rule was reached, its enunciation is a good thing for human dignity, as well as for the honour[274] and good name[275] of British justice.

When it comes to the crux of their Lordships' **ratio**, the judgment is a noble lie. To call a rule excluding evidence obtained abroad through the torture of a foreign national by a foreign state, and without the involvement of the UK executive, a constitutional principle, thereby bringing it within the doctrine enunciated in *Simms*, seems a calculated mischaracterization. Importance alone does not make a common-law rule a constitutional principle. That said, if the rule is put more broadly—as done by the Lords in the present case—as one prohibiting the use by the courts of evidence procured through torture wherever, against whomever, and by whomever committed, it can arguably be seen as one bearing more generally on the powers of an organ of State, namely the courts, and on the protection of the fundamental rights of citizens—in short, as a constitutional principle. But whether this broader characterization of the otherwise extraordinarily narrow evidentiary issue before the House was

[271] [2005] 3 WLR 1249, 1260, para 13. [272] [2005] 3 WLR 1249, 1282, para 51.
[273] [2005] 3 WLR 1249, 1312–13, para 152.
[274] See [2005] 3 WLR 1249, 1291–2, para 82 (Lord Hoffman).
[275] See [2005] 3 WLR 1249, 1319, para 174 (Lord Brown).

just a sleight of hand remains a question hanging over the judgment. Their Lordships no doubt reckoned that playing a little fast and loose in the face of such a threat to basic human dignity and judicial integrity was justified, especially given the government's ever-more freewheeling approach to the constitution. Perhaps they figured that the executive's stretching of credulity excused their own in a higher cause. Either way, the Lords' sin seems no more than venial.

Less pardonable is Lord Bingham's apparent acceptance of what appeared to be the further submission that either article 6 or article 5(4) of the ECHR—via the HRA—also compelled the recognition of a rule excluding evidence obtained by torture, since, applying a dictum of the ECtHR in *Al-Adsani*,[276] these provisions had to be read in the light of article 15 of the Torture Convention and a smorgasbord of what might be called tangentially relevant international and comparative material. In the admirably restrained words of Lord Carswell, the argument is 'not without [its] difficulties',[277] and the Secretary of State quite reasonably 'question[ed] the effect and applicability of some of the material on which the appellants rel[ied]'.[278] The basic proposition rests on a misunderstanding of what the ECtHR meant in *Al-Adsani* when it stated that the ECHR, including article 6, 'cannot be interpreted in a vacuum' but that it 'should so far as possible be interpreted in harmony with other rules of international law of which it forms part'.[279] What the Court was saying was that the notion of what is 'fair' within the meaning of article 6 must be taken to reflect what the States Parties to the Convention are permitted to do by general international law, which the Convention cannot be understood to compel them to breach. The Court did not mean that the obligations imposed on a State Party to the Convention are to be fleshed out by reference to its other conventional obligations, owed, in principle and almost always in practice, to a different group of states—let alone by reference to the Charter of the United Nations, the Rome Statute of the International Criminal Court, the Rules of Procedure and Evidence of the two *ad hoc* international criminal tribunals, articles 40 and 41 of the International Law Commission's Articles on Responsibility of States for Internationally Wrongful Acts,[280] the judgment of the International Criminal Tribunal for the former Yugoslavia in *Prosecutor v Furundžija*,[281] the advisory opinion of the International Court of Justice in *Legal Consequences of the Construction of a Wall in the Occupied Palestinian Territory*,[282] the views of the Human Rights Committee, the Committee Against Torture and sundry special rapporteurs and representatives, along with declarations, recommendations, domestic case-law, and domestic criminal codes, all of it said to reflect an 'all but universal

[276] (2002) 34 EHRR 273, 289, para 55.
[277] [2005] 3 WLR 1249, 1312, para 151.
[278] [2005] 3 WLR 1249, 1281, para 46.
[279] (2002) 34 EHRR 273, 289, para 55.
[280] Annexed to UNGA res 56/83, 12 December 2001.
[281] 121 ILR 213, 260, para 153.
[282] ICJ Rep 2004, 136.

consensus embodied in the Torture Convention'[283] that 'the *jus cogens erga omnes* nature of the prohibition on torture'[284] compels States not to permit evidence obtained by resort to this practice. Far from being supported by article 31(3)(c) of the Vienna Convention on the Law of Treaties, as alleged, such a proposition is contraindicated by the provision, which refers to 'any other relevant rules of international law applicable *in the relations between the parties*'.[285] Lord Bingham's approach, which chimes with that taken by Neuberger LJ in the Court of Appeal, would result in an obligation drawn from one treaty regime, applicable among States Parties to that treaty, hitching a ride into another, applicable among a different set of States Parties. Transposed to the domestic level, it would permit the domestic application of an unincorporated treaty provision as long as Parliament had incorporated a different provision, from some other treaty, on a common subject-matter.[286] As for Lord Bingham's dismay at the suggestion that 'an international obligation solemnly and explicitly undertaken can be overridden by a statute and a procedural rule which make no mention of torture at all',[287] his Lordship might have spared himself distress by reflecting more on the relationship between treaties and English law.

As for the majority's guidance to SIAC, it is surprising that torture and its fruits should be condemned so utterly but that material possibly procured through torture abroad should be admitted if, on the balance of probabilities, it cannot be proved to be so derived. The surprise goes double for their Lordships' unanimous dicta on the executive's use of foreign torture evidence for operational purposes. The cohabitation in the Lords' reasoning of Kantian ethics and pragmatism is a little anomalous. But, in the words of Lord Bingham, the common law is not intolerant of anomaly,[288] and common-law judges have never prized philosophical purity. The Lords are nothing if not astute, crafting judgments which allowed them to lay down in headline-grabbing terms an uncompromising common-law rule without sabotaging, for the second time in a year,[289] the government's efforts to meet the threat of terrorism. It was open to them on the law to do so. Indeed, as several of them noted, article 15 of the Torture Convention—not binding on the court, but a legitimate source of guidance on point—lends support to the view both that evidence should be admitted unless it is 'established' to have been obtained by torture and that the use of such evidence by the executive is a separate question. The second point, not in issue before the House, is also supported by constitutional considerations. While the judges are the guardians of the integrity of the judicial process, they have no mandate

283 [2005] 3 WLR 1249, 1283, para 52 (Lord Bingham).
284 [2005] 3 WLR 1249, 1275, para 34. 285 Emphasis added.
286 The point was well made in the Court of Appeal by Laws LJ at [2005] 1 WLR 414, 508, para 267.
287 [2005] 3 WLR 1249, 1282, para 51.
288 [2005] 3 WLR 1249, 1282, para 48 (Lord Bingham).
289 See *A and others v Secretary of State for the Home Department* [2005] 2 WLR 87.

to declare general restrictions on the powers of the executive. Even if the issue were justiciable, which is unlikely, the Secretary of State would not act *ultra vires* any statutory power or irrationally or contrary to principles of natural justice by taking a decision on a matter of national security on the basis of evidence procured through torture committed abroad by foreign state officials.

The practical upshot of the case will not be great. As Lord Brown remarked, there was 'a certain unreality'[290] about adjudicating upon the legality of repealed provisions. That said, the question of foreign torture evidence and rule 44(3) of the Special Immigration Appeals Commission (Procedure) Rules 2003 crops up in appeals under section 2 of the Special Immigration Appeals Commission Act 1997, as substituted by Schedule 7, paragraph 20 of the Nationality, Immigration and Asylum Act 2002; and the question of foreign torture evidence and the courts more generally arises in appeals to the Administrative Court under section 10 of the Prevention of Terrorism Act 2005 in relation to the renewal or modification by the Secretary of State of the non-derogating control orders provided for in section 2. Perhaps more to the point, the majority's ruling on the test to be applied by ATCSA and its green light to the executive's use of foreign torture evidence for operational purposes may mean murky business pretty much as usual.

Interpretation of treaties—general rule of interpretation—ordinary meaning of terms—whether onset of deep vein thrombosis caused by cramped seating on aircraft an 'accident' within meaning of article 17 of Warsaw Convention on International Carriage by Air

Case No 11. In re Deep Vein Thrombosis and Air Travel Group Litigation, 8 December 2005, [2005] UKHL 72, [2005] 3 WLR 1320, [2006] 1 All ER 786, 2005 WL 3299091 (HL).

Damages for personal injury caused by accidents on aircraft are governed in the UK, to the exclusion of the common law,[291] by article 17 of the Warsaw Convention for the Unification of Certain Rules Relating to International Carriage by Air 1929, as amended at The Hague in 1955,[292] which is scheduled to the Carriage by Air Act 1961. Article 17 provides that the carrier 'is liable for damage sustained in the event of the death or wounding of a passenger or any other bodily injury suffered by a passenger, if the accident which caused the damage so sustained took place on board the aircraft or in the course of any of the operations of embarking or disembarking'. It is unnecessary to show that the carrier was in any way at fault.

[290] [2005] 3 WLR 1249, 1317, para 167.
[291] *Sidhu v British Airways plc* [1997] AC 430, (1997) 68 BYIL 307–11 (HL).
[292] Warsaw, 12 October 1929, 137 LNTS 12, as amended The Hague, 28 September 1955, 478 UNTS 372.

Former aircraft passengers launched group litigation in the English courts in respect of deep vein thrombosis (DVT), a potentially fatal vascular condition incurred by them as an alleged result of sitting in cramped positions on long-distance flights. An order was made by the senior master directing that the preliminary issue of whether the onset of DVT could be considered an 'accident' within the meaning of article 17 of the Warsaw Convention be determined on the basis of a specimen matrix of fact. The specimen matrix stated that the cabin was configured and the flight operated in accordance with the defendant's usual standards, procedures, and practices and in line with all applicable aviation regulations, and that nothing occurred during the flight to affect adversely the performance of the aircraft or the normal cabin environment. It was accepted solely for the purpose of the preliminary issue of law that the claimants had indeed suffered symptomatic DVT caused by their respective flights.

The House of Lords held unanimously that the onset of DVT was not an 'accident' within the meaning of article 17 of the Warsaw Convention. The Convention's provisions were to be construed in accordance with the international rules of treaty interpretation, rather than domestic legal principles and case-law;[293] and, since the aim of the Convention was the 'partial harmonisation' of the laws applicable in the various Contracting States to carriage by air, the courts of the respective States should seek to adopt, where possible, a uniform interpretation of its provisions.[294] The international rules of treaty interpretation were those embodied in articles 31 and 32 of the Vienna Convention on the Law of Treaties,[295] the starting point being article 31(1), pursuant to which a treaty must be interpreted in accordance with the ordinary meaning to be given to its terms in context and in the light of the treaty's object and purpose.[296] 'The primacy of the treaty language, read in context and purposively, is therefore of critical importance.'[297] Proceeding on this basis, it was clear that, for the purposes of article 17 of the Warsaw Convention, the injury

[293] [2005] 3 WLR 1320, 1330, para 27 (Lord Steyn) and 1336, para 54 (Lord Mance), the latter citing *Stag Line Ltd v Foscolo, Mango & Co Ltd* [1932] AC 328, 350 (Lord Macmillan), *James Buchanan & Co Ltd v Babco Forwarding and Shipping (UK) Ltd* [1978] AC 141, 152 (Lord Wilberforce), (1978) 49 BYIL 274–9 (HL), *Fothergill v Monarch Airlines Ltd* [1981] AC 251, 272 (Lord Wilberforce), 282 (Lord Diplock), 285 (Lord Fraser) and 293 (Lord Scarman), (1980) 51 BYIL 316–25 (HL).

[294] [2005] 3 WLR 1320, 1322, para 1 and 1328, para 18 (Lord Scott), citing [2005] 3 WLR 1320, 1330, para 27 (Lord Steyn) and *Morris v KLM Royal Dutch Airlines* [2002] AC 628, 635, para 12 (Lord Steyn), (2002) 73 BYIL 389–400 (HL); [2005] 3 WLR 1320, 1330, para 27 and 1332, para 35 (Lord Steyn); [2005] 3 WLR 1320, 1337, para 55 (Lord Mance), citing *Morris v KLM Royal Dutch Airlines* [2002] AC 628, 633, para 5 (Lord Nicholls), 634, para 7 (Lord Mackay), 657, para 81 (Lord Hope) and 677–8, para 147 (Lord Hobhouse).

[295] Vienna, 23 May 1969, 1155 UNTS 331. Lord Mance recalled at [2005] 3 WLR 1320, 1336, para 54 that Lords Diplock and Scarman in *Fothergill v Monarch Airlines Ltd* [1981] AC 251, 282 and 290 respectively, had considered VCLT, arts 31 and 32 to be consonant with customary international law.

[296] [2005] 3 WLR 1320, 1325, para 11 (Lord Scott, not expressly citing the Vienna Convention), 1331, para 31 (Lord Steyn) and 1336, para 54 (Lord Mance), the last citing *Fothergill v Monarch Airlines Ltd* [1981] AC 251, 272 (Lord Wilberforce), 282 (Lord Diplock), 287 (Lord Fraser) and 290 (Lord Scarman).

[297] [2005] 3 WLR 1320, 1331, para 31 (Lord Steyn).

suffered by the claimant 'cannot itself be the "accident"': 'Article 17 distinguishes between the bodily injury on the one hand and the "accident" which was the cause of the bodily injury on the other. It is the cause of the injury that must constitute the "accident".'[298]

Putting it another way, 'the event or happening that has caused the damage of which complaint is made must be something external to the passenger'.[299] Moreover, the event must be unusual or unexpected:[300] 'an event or happening which is no more than the normal operation of the aircraft in normal conditions cannot constitute an article 17 accident'.[301] As stated by O'Connor J in the US case of *Air France v Saks*, a judgment 'widely followed both in the United States and in the courts of other signatory states',[302] 'when the injury indisputably results from the passenger's own internal reaction to the usual, normal, and expected operation of the aircraft, it has not been caused by an accident, and article 17 of the Warsaw Convention cannot apply'.[303] In the words of Baroness Hale: 'Once it is clear that the accident which causes the injury must be something other than the injury itself, it becomes equally clear that the suffering of an internal reaction to an ordinarily uncomfortable journey by air, during which nothing untoward other than that reaction took place, cannot fall within article 17 of the Warsaw Convention.'[304] This ruled out recovery for DVT, as allegedly caused by cramped seating conditions. '[V]iewing the matter in the simple terms of article 17 (which is the ultimate test), the situation [did] not fall within any ordinary or extended conception of "accident"'[305]—a conclusion in line with the case-law of the courts of other Contracting States.[306]

Although regard was rightly had by several of their Lordships to, in particular, the US and Australian authorities, Lord Scott interposed 'a word of caution':

> It is not the function of any court in any of the Convention countries to try to produce in language different from that used in the Convention a comprehensive formulation of the conditions which will lead to article 17 liability, or of any of those conditions. The language of the Convention itself must always be the starting point. The function of the court is to apply that language to the facts of the case in issue. In order to do so and to explain its decision, and to provide a guide to other courts that may subsequently be faced with similar facts, the court

[298] [2005] 3 WLR 1320, 1326, para 14 (Lord Scott).

[299] [2005] 3 WLR 1320, 1329, para 23 (Lord Scott). See also [2005] 3 WLR 1320, 1331, para 33 (Lord Steyn).

[300] [2005] 3 WLR 1320, 1327, paras 15 and 17 (Lord Scott) and 1330, para 30 and 1331, paras 32–33 (Lord Steyn).

[301] [2005] 3 WLR 1320, 1329, para 23 (Lord Scott).

[302] [2005] 3 WLR 1320, 1327, para 18 (Lord Scott). His Lordship added that '[b]oth the standing of the court and the reasoning of the opinion justify that reliance'.

[303] [2005] 3 WLR 1320, 1327, para 17 (Lord Scott), quoting 470 US 392 (1985), 406.

[304] [2005] 3 WLR 1320, 1334, para 49.

[305] [2005] 3 WLR 1320, 1351, para 86 (Lord Mance).

[306] *Povey v Qantas Airways Ltd and British Airways plc* [2005] HCA 33 (Australia); *McDonald v Korean Air* (2003) 171 OAC 368 (Canada); *Scherer v Pan American World Airways Inc* 387 NYS 2d 580 (1976), *Blansett v Continental Airlines Inc* 379 F 3d 177 (2004) and *Rodriques v Ansett Australia Ltd* 383 F 3d 914 (2004) (US). In addition, Lord Scott refers to a judgment of October 2001 of the Regional Court of Frankfurt am Main, Germany: [2005] 3 WLR 1320, 1328, para 19.

may well need to try to express in its own language the idea inherent in the language used in the Convention. So a judge faced with deciding whether particular facts do or do not constitute an article 17 accident will often describe in his or her own language the characteristics that an event or happening must have in order to qualify as an article 17 accident. But a judicial formulation of the characteristics of an article 17 accident should not, in my opinion, ever be treated as a substitute for the language used in the Convention. It should be treated for what it is, namely, an exposition of the reasons for the decision reached and a guide to the application of the Convention language to facts of a type similar to those of the case in question.[307]

His Lordship had in mind the decision in *Olympic Airways v Husain*,[308] in which a majority of the US Supreme Court, relying on certain statements by O'Connor J in *Air France v Saks*, held that a stewardess's refusal to move an asthmatic further away from the smoking section of the aircraft, leading to his death by severe asthmatic attack, qualified as an 'accident' for the purposes of article 17 of the Warsaw Convention. He mentioned the case explicitly towards the end of his opinion, adding:

[I]t is not necessary for your Lordships in this case to express any preference between the majority and dissenting opinions in *Husain*. I venture, however, to express my respectful disagreement with an approach to interpretation of the Convention that interprets not the language of the Convention but instead the language of the leading judgment interpreting the Convention. This approach tends, I believe, to distort the essential purpose of the judicial interpretation, namely, to consider what 'accident' in article 17 means and whether the facts of the case in hand can constitute an article 17 accident.[309]

Baroness Hale agreed with the gist of the criticism:

I would particularly like to associate myself with the observations of my noble and learned friend, Lord Scott of Foscote, on the dangers of interpreting the words of the decision of a court, which is interpreting the words of the Convention, as if the court's words were those of the Convention. If I fall over during a flight to New York, and break an arm, I suspect that we would all agree that my broken arm was caused by the accident of my fall; and we would do so irrespective of the reason for my fall ... In reaching those conclusions, we should not be agonising too much over whether my fall was an event 'external' to me. We should simply be asking whether it was an 'accident' which led to my injury.[310]

Her Ladyship added that '[her] own synonym for "accident" would be "untoward event" ', although she acknowledged that this was by the by.[311]

Their Lordships' judgment is beyond reproach. Its emphatic insistence on the ordinary meaning of the words of a treaty provision is heartily welcome, as are the telling dicta of Lord Scott and Baroness Hale. The absurd result in *Olympic Airways v Husain* shows what

307 [2005] 3 WLR 1320, 1326, para 12.
308 124 S Ct 1221 (2004).
309 [2005] 3 WLR 1320, 1329, para 22.
310 [2005] 3 WLR 1320, 1334–5, para 49.
311 [2005] 3 WLR 1320, 1335, para 49.

happens when a domestic court called on to interpret a treaty gets tied up in knots of judicial over-sophistication.

Grant of nationality—registration as British citizen—British Nationality Act 1981—refusal to register British citizenship on public policy grounds—deprivation of British citizenship on ground of acts seriously prejudicial to vital interests of UK—differential treatment among British citizens—diplomatic protection—whether Secretary of State entitled to refuse to register British citizenship on public policy grounds

Case No 12. R (Hicks) v Secretary of State for the Home Department, 13 December 2005, [2005] EWHC 2818 (Admin), 2005 WL 3464398, unreported (QBD (Admin Ct), Collins J).

The claimant, an Australian citizen detained by US authorities in Guantánamo Bay, Cuba, was scheduled to be the first alleged 'unlawful combatant' tried by the Military Commission established pursuant to the US President's Military Order of November 13, 2001—Detention, Treatment, and Trial of Certain Non-Citizens in the War Against Terrorism.[312] By chance he ascertained that he was eligible, by reason of his mother's birth in the UK, to be registered as a British citizen under section 4C of the British Nationality Act 1981 (BNA). He applied for registration, in the hope of being afforded diplomatic protection which would lead to his release to the custody of the UK authorities and repatriation to the UK, as had eventually been the case with those British citizens previously detained at Guantánamo. (In contrast, the Australian government was content for him to continue to be detained and to be tried by US Military Commission.) The Secretary of State accepted that the claimant met the conditions set out in section 4C of the British Nationality Act but that he, the Secretary of State, retained a residual discretion to refuse to register the claimant as a British citizen on public policy grounds. In the alternative, the Secretary of State was prepared to accede to the claimant's registration but argued that he could, and would, immediately deprive him of his citizenship on the basis of section 40(2)(a) of the British Nationality Act, inserted by section 4 of the Nationality, Immigration and Asylum Act 2002 (NIAA), which, in cases of dual nationality, authorizes the Secretary of State to deprive a person of British citizenship if he or she 'is satisfied that the person has done anything seriously prejudicial to the vital interests of ... the United Kingdom'. Section 4(4) of the NIAA permits recourse to the provisions of the BNA as originally enacted in order to determine what may be taken into account as justification for deprivation of citizenship; and section 40(3)(a) of the original version of the BNA provided that the citizen

[312] Federal Register, Vol 66, No 222, Friday, November 16, 2001, 57833.

in question could be deprived of British citizenship if he 'has shown himself by act or speech to be disloyal or disaffected towards Her Majesty'. The claimant denied that the Secretary of State had the power either to refuse to register him or to deprive him of citizenship on the ground of public policy. He also complained that the Secretary of State was not treating him in a manner consistent with his treatment of the other British citizens of dual nationality formerly detained at Guantánamo, none of whom had been deprived of his British citizenship despite being alleged to have acted as the claimant was alleged to have acted. The Secretary of State sought to justify this differential treatment 'on the grounds that the others all had close links with the United Kingdom, having lived here for most of their lives, whereas the claimant had no such links and was seeking to use his adventitious entitlement to registration to obtain an advantage which the country in which he had been born and brought up would not provide'.[313]

Collins J, in the Administrative Court, allowed the claim. The Secretary of State was not entitled to refuse to register the claimant as a British citizen on public policy grounds. Such a discretion had been exercised only in cases where the claimant had done something criminal in order to establish the necessary conditions to be registered as a British citizen, such as obtaining marriage by fraud,[314] the relevant consideration of public policy in such cases being that a person should not be permitted to benefit from his or her criminal conduct. This was not the case here, where the Secretary of State was relying in essence on the claimant's bad character, and '[s]ince Parliament has not set down any precondition based on good character, it would be wrong to extend public policy to close what is now regarded as an unfortunate gap'.[315] As for depriving the claimant of his citizenship immediately upon registration, this too was impermissible. Section 40(3)(a) of the BNA, and hence section 40(2) of the BNA, applied only to conduct after registration of citizenship or naturalization. Thirdly, although the point was rendered moot by his first two rulings, Collins J expressed the view that the Secretary of State 'was entitled in the exercise of his discretion to distinguish between the claimant and the other British citizens' of dual nationality, since this 'was a rational exercise of his discretion having regard to the matters referred to' by the Secretary of State.[316] In conclusion, he added:

> Once [the claimant] is a British citizen, he should be entitled to all assistance which can be given to a British citizen. There is no doubt that Her Majesty's Government has a discretion as to what assistance should be given (if any) in a given case. But in my view it would be improper to fail to give assistance which

[313] [2005] EWHC 2818 (Admin), para 35.

[314] See eg *R v Secretary of State for the Home Department, ex p Puttick* [1981] QB 767, cited at [2005] EWHC 2818 (Admin), para 28.

[315] [2005] EWHC 2818 (Admin), para 28.

[316] [2005] EWHC 2818 (Admin), para 36.

would otherwise have been given simply because the claimant was believed to be involved in terrorism and has not had any previous connection with this country. Once he is a citizen, the considerations relied on by [the Secretary of State] do not in my view apply.[317]

His Lordship recognized, however, that he had not heard argument on the point, so that what he said in this regard 'should not be taken as more than an indication of [his] views'.[318]

While Collins J's decision is sound, his closing dictum is contestable. If the Secretary of State would be permitted to treat the claimant differently from other dual nationals formerly held at Guantánamo for the purposes of deprivation of nationality, it is hard to see how Her Majesty's Government would not be permitted to treat him differently for the purposes of diplomatic protection. The answer would seem to be that Collins J is not talking of a legal obligation: his choice of the words 'should' and 'improper' make this clear enough. But if he is not referring to the law, he would do well, while sitting, to keep his counsel.

European Convention on Human Rights, article 2 (right to life)—obligation to conduct inquiry into death through State's alleged failure to take appropriate steps to safeguard lives of persons within its jurisdiction—Human Rights Act 1998—legality of invasion of Iraq—armed forces—whether government obliged to conduct inquiry into circumstances leading to invasion of Iraq

Case No 13. R (Gentle) v The Prime Minister, the Secretary of State for Defence and the Attorney-General, 20 December 2005, [2005] EWCA 3119 (Admin), 2005 WL 3700041 (QBD (Admin Ct), Collins J).

In another attempt to have the legality of the 2003 invasion of Iraq litigated in the English courts,[319] the parents of soldiers killed in that country while on active service with Her Majesty's forces sought permission to apply for judicial review of the government's refusal to conduct an inquiry into the circumstances leading to the conflict. The immediate background to the case was the much-publicized leak of official documents showing that the Attorney-General had shifted in his legal advice in the run-up to war. The applicants argued that, in accordance with the right to life guaranteed, via the HRA, by article 2 of the ECHR, a State is obliged to investigate where death has occurred as an alleged result of

[317] [2005] EWHC 2818 (Admin), para 39.

[318] [2005] EWHC 2818 (Admin), para 39.

[319] See, previously, *R (Campaign for Nuclear Disarmament) v Prime Minister of the United Kingdom* [2002] EWHC 2759 (Admin), (2002) 73 BYIL 444–52 (QBD (Admin Ct), Div Ct); *R (Manson) v Bow Street Magistrates' Court* [2003] EWHC 2720 (Admin), (2003) 74 BYIL 493–6 (QBD (Admin Ct), Div Ct); *R v Jones (Margaret)* [2005] QB 259, (2004) 75 BYIL 450–64 (CA (Crim)).

its failure to take appropriate steps to safeguard the lives of persons within its jurisdiction.[320]

Collins J, in the Administrative Court, refused permission to apply for judicial review. The applicants had failed to make out an arguable case. The fact that the legality of the invasion was irrelevant to whether there was a breach of article 2 posed 'a serious obstacle to relief'.[321] Added to this, while the identification of a specific risk to a particular individual was not a prerequisite to a successful claim under article 2, it was 'a relevant consideration to be taken into account in deciding whether or not an investigation is, in the circumstances of any particular case, required'.[322] Thirdly, his Lordship quoted the ECtHR in *Edwards v United Kingdom*,[323] cited with approval by Lord Bingham in *R (Amin) v Secretary of State for the Home Department*,[324] to hold that the 'essential purpose of such investigation is to secure the effective implementation of the domestic laws which protect the right to life and, in those cases involving State agents or bodies, to ensure their accountability for deaths occurring under their responsibility'.[325] He continued: 'In this case the circumstances in which the deaths occurred are, of course, known. The only purpose of the inquiry ... is to try to make a political point or to show that the Prime Minister has not told the truth. That, in my view, is not a proper reason for requiring an inquiry where a member of the armed forces has been killed in circumstances such as these'.[326] For these and related reasons, the claim had no real prospect of success.

Collins J's decision, although supported by a judgment not always a model of coherence, is the correct one. The applicants' submission—which elided *McCann*'s[327] requirement of an inquiry where death has occurred in unclear circumstances through the use of force by the State with *Osman*'s[328] obligation on the State to take appropriate steps to safeguard the lives of persons within its jurisdiction—was the advocate's classic invitation to the court to lose sight of the wood for the trees, and was rightly rejected. In terms of the *McCann* limb of the argument, the circumstances of the deceased's deaths were perfectly clear: one was killed in a helicopter crash, one in a motor vehicle accident, one by 'friendly' fire and three by improvised explosive devices.[329] As for the *Osman* limb, if a State's deployment of its volunteer armed forces on active service constitutes a failure to take appropriate steps to safeguard their lives, then the ECHR has effectively outlawed war—a consummation devoutly to be wished, but doubtless a surprise to Contracting

[320] Collins J was not required to consider the extraterritorial application of the ECHR, as he was satisfied that the UK's armed forces remain within its jurisdiction at all times: [2005] EWHC 3119 (Admin), para 17.

[321] [2005] EWHC 3119 (Admin), para 29.

[322] [2005] EWHC 3119 (Admin), para 26.

[323] (2002) 35 EHRR 487, 511, para 69.

[324] [2004] 1 AC 653, 666, para 22.

[325] [2005] EWHC 3119 (Admin), para 30.

[326] [2005] EWHC 3119 (Admin), para 31.

[327] *McCann v United Kingdom* (1995) 21 EHRR 97.

[328] *Osman v United Kingdom* (2000) 29 EHRR 245.

[329] [2005] EWHC 3119 (Admin), para 5.

States. The legality of the invasion of Iraq and the circumstances surrounding the Attorney-General's advice make no difference whatsoever on either score.

'Jurisdiction' within meaning of European Convention on Human Rights, article 1—extraterritorial application of ECHR—ECHR, article 2 (right to life) and article 3 (freedom from inhuman and degrading treatment)—obligation to provide independent official investigation into death and alleged severe ill-treatment of next-of-kin—extraterritorial application of Human Rights Act 1998—whether ECHR and HRA applicable to certain conduct of UK armed forces in belligerent occupation of southern Iraq

Case No 14. R (Al-Skeini) v Secretary of State for Defence, 21 December 2005, [2005] EWCA Civ 1609, 2005 WL 3464404, unreported (CA (Civ)).

The facts of the case have been recounted previously.[330] The five unsuccessful claimants before the Divisional Court appealed its ruling that the ECHR, and thus the HRA, did not apply to the situations in relation to which they brought their respective claims. For his part, the Secretary of State accepted the Divisional Court's declaration that the ECHR applied in respect of the single successful claim, but cross-appealed the ruling that the HRA applied and that he, the Secretary of State, had acted in a manner incompatible with articles 2 and 3 of the ECHR by failing to provide an independent official inquiry into the death and alleged severe ill-treatment of the deceased in a British-controlled prison in Basra, Iraq. He rested his contention as to the non-applicability of the HRA on the canon of statutory construction that, in the absence of clear indication to the contrary, an Act of the UK Parliament applies only within UK territory. The upshot, he argued, was that the sixth claimant was obliged to pursue his claim in Strasbourg, under the ECHR itself, rather than in the UK under the HRA. In response to the Secretary of State's argument regarding the HRA, the claimant relied on the Court of Appeal's finding in *R (B) v Secretary of State for Foreign and Commonwealth Affairs*[331] that the HRA was capable of extraterritorial application in certain situations and on Lord Nicholls' dictum in *R (Quark Fishing Ltd) v Secretary of State for Foreign and Commonwealth Affairs* that 'the territorial scope of the obligations and rights created by sections 6 and 7 of the Act was intended to be co-extensive with the territorial scope of the obligations of the United Kingdom and the rights of victims under the Convention'.[332] As for the merits of the six claims, the Secretary of State argued that the Divisional Court's ruling was premature.

[330] *R (Al-Skeini) v Secretary of State for Defence* [2005] 2 WLR 1041, (2004) 75 BYIL 513–18 (QBD (Admin Ct), Div Ct).

[331] [2005] 2 WLR 618, (2004) 75 BYIL 483–9 (CA (Civ)).

[332] [2005] 3 WLR 837, 849, para 34.

The Court of Appeal (Civil Division) dismissed the five appeals and the cross-appeal.

Brooke LJ, giving the leading judgment, upheld the Divisional Court's decision, albeit by a different route, that the ECHR did not apply in respect of the five unsuccessful claims. He did not believe that *Banković v Belgium*[333] ruled out the application of the Convention outside its *espace juridique*.[334] Nor did he think it prevented the Convention's application in situations where military forces—although not exercising sufficiently effective control over foreign territory in the context of military occupation as to fall within the scope of *Loizidou v Turkey*[335] and *Ilaşcu v Moldova*[336]—exercised control and authority over the victim.[337] The post-*Banković* decisions of *Issa v Turkey*[338] and *Öçalan v Turkey*[339] were taken as authority for both these propositions.[340] In the five unsuccessful cases, however, British forces exercised neither a sufficient degree of territorial control over Basra nor any control or authority over the victims.[341] (In contrast, his Lordship would have held in the sixth case that the ECHR applied from the moment the victim was arrested by British troops).[342] 'In the interests of completeness', Brooke LJ made it clear that the existence of a legal state of belligerent occupation within the meaning of article 42 of the 1907 Hague Rules did not of itself amount to effective control so as to bring the territory within the Occupying Power's jurisdiction for the purposes of article 1 of the ECHR, as had been submitted by the five unsuccessful claimants.[343] On the issue of effective control, however, Sedley LJ was '[i]n respectful disagreement' with Brooke LJ:[344]

> 196 ... I do not see why the presence or absence of adequate civil power for effective control in international law should be tested by asking whether there is sufficient control to enforce the full range of Convention rights. Nor does the ECtHR seem to have thought so in *Banković*. What seems to me more material is the fact that, as Brooke LJ explains ... , the United Kingdom was an occupying power within the meaning of Article 42 of the Hague Regulations because the Basra region was under the authority of its armed forces. Article 43 then made it incumbent upon the UK 'to take all the measures in [its] power to restore, and ensure, *as far as possible*, public order and safety, while respecting, *unless absolutely prevented*, the laws in force in the country'. (I will return to the words I have italicised.) These obligations are predicated not on effective control but on 'the authority of the legitimate power having in fact passed into the hands of the occupant'. Geneva IV, Article 27, adds to them an obligation to respect 'in all circumstances' the persons of civilians and to protect them from acts of violence.

333 (2001) 11 BHRC 435.
334 [2005] EWCA Civ 1609, paras 80–81.
335 Preliminary objections, 23 March 1995, EHRR Series A No 210.
336 App No 48789/99, 8 July 2004.
337 [2005] EWCA Civ 1609, paras 81–82.
338 App No 31821/96, 16 November 2004.
339 App No 46221/99, 12 May 2005.
340 [2005] EWCA Civ 1609, esp paras 97 and 108.
341 [2005] EWCA Civ 1609, paras 125 and 111 respectively.
342 [2005] EWCA Civ 1609, para 109.
343 [2005] EWCA Civ 1609, paras 128–129.
344 [2005] EWCA Civ 1609, para 196.

197 No doubt it is absurd to expect occupying forces in the near-chaos of Iraq to enforce the right to marry vouchsafed by Art. 12 or the equality guarantees vouchsafed by Art. 14. But I do not think effective control involves this. If effective control in the jurisprudence of the ECtHR marches with international humanitarian law and the law of armed conflict, as it clearly seeks to do, it involves two key things: the *de facto* assumption of civil power by an occupying state and a concomitant obligation to do all that is possible to keep order and protect essential civil rights. It does not make the occupying power the guarantor of rights; nor therefore does it demand sufficient control for all such purposes. What it does is place an obligation on the occupier to do all it can.

198 If this is right, it is not an answer to say that the UK, because it is unable to guarantee everything, is required to guarantee nothing. The question is whether our armed forces' effectiveness on the streets in 2003–4 was so exiguous that despite their assumption of power as an occupying force they lacked any real control of what happened from hour to hour in the Basra region. My own answer would be that the one thing British troops did have control over, even in the labile situation described in the evidence, was their own use of lethal force. Whether they were justified in using it in the situations they encountered, of which at least four of the cases before us are examples, is precisely the subject of the inquiry which the appellants seek. It is in such an inquiry that the low ratio of troops to civilians, the widespread availability of weapons and the prevalence of insurgency would fall to be evaluated....

But his Lordship came to the conclusion that he was prevented from relying on this analysis by the ECtHR's decision in *Banković*.[345]

On the question of the extraterritorial application of the HRA, as distinct from that of the ECHR, Brooke LJ stated:

145 I am not disposed to accept the whole of the reasoning of the Divisional Court. For instance, this country was not obliged to incorporate the ECHR into its national law, either in whole or in part. The HRA would still be compatible with (or consonant with) the UK's international obligations under the ECHR even if it were not co-extensive with the ECHR in its territorial scope. Furthermore, the House of Lords has recently made it clear that a person may have rights enforceable in Strasbourg and not in the UK if those rights accrued before the HRA came into force (see *In re McKerr* [2004] UKHL 12; [2004] 1 WLR 807 at [25] and [68]: the extent of the rights under national law depends on the language of the national statute (see *McKerr* at [63]).

146 I am also willing to accept that the decision of this court in *R (B) v Foreign Secretary* ... is not strictly binding on us. In *B* this court held that even if it was assumed in favour of the claimants that they were within the jurisdiction of the UK for the purposes of the ECHR (see para. 66 of the judgment), there had in fact been no breach of their Convention rights (see para. 97). It was therefore not necessary for the court to hold that the territorial ambit of the HRA was co-extensive with that of Article 1 of the ECHR: it could have reached its decision without including this stage of its reasoning in its judgment at all. The *ratio decidendi* of a case has been defined as any rule of law expressly or impliedly treated by the judge as a necessary step in reaching his conclusion, having regard to the reasoning adopted by him (Cross & Harris, *Precedent in*

345 [2005] EWCA Civ 1609, para 203.

English Law, 4th Edition (1991), p. 72; and see *Dunnachie* v. *Kingston upon Hull Council* [2004] EWCA Civ 84 at [82]; [2004] ICR 482). For these reasons I accept that we are not strictly bound by the judgment in *B*.

147 On the other hand it constitutes strong persuasive authority, as does the dictum of Lord Nicholls in *Quark* ... [The Secretary of State]'s submissions include the unnatural substitution of the word 'in' for the words 'in relation to' in ss. 1(4), 1(6) and 21(1) of the HRA ... , and carry the unhappy consequence that a victim offended by a decision of an instrument of the UK government would have to take a complaint all the way to Strasbourg, as opposed to the British courts, if the relevant decision was taken within a consulate or embassy abroad and not in a Whitehall department. Given the purpose of the HRA, as explained by Lord Nicholls, it can be naturally interpreted as impliedly having extra-territorial effect in the very limited number of cases in which the state has exercised extra-territorial jurisdiction on SAA ['state agent authority'] principles. I am not persuaded that the very general statements in a Government White Paper or in Hansard ... , on which the Secretary of State relied, should dissuade us from being willing to follow the dicta in *B* and *Quark*. There is no doubt that jurisdiction is essentially territorial: the question is whether any very limited exceptions exist, and broad statements of policy do not usually concern themselves with detail of this kind.

148 In any event I consider on general grounds that it should be for the House of Lords, and not for this court, to say whether these dicta are wrong. [Counsel for the Secretary of State] told us that he had deployed much fuller argument than had been advanced on behalf of the Foreign Secretary in *B*, but it would be very much more satisfactory if these arguments were authoritatively considered at a higher level than the Court of Appeal rather than that different divisions of this court should express perhaps conflicting opinions upon them. Accordingly I would hold that the HRA has extra-territorial effect in those cases where a public authority is found to have exercised extra-territorial jurisdiction on the application of SAA principles.

It followed 'that when s 6(1) of the HRA prescribes that it is unlawful for a public authority to act in a way which is incompatible with a Convention right, this may include a right arising from some extra-territorial jurisdiction that the public authority in question (the Secretary of State in the present case) has elected to exercise, since the phrase "Convention right" is defined as one of the rights and fundamental freedoms set out in the ECHR as it has effect for the time being in relation to this country'.[346] Sedley LJ came to the same conclusion:

186 [The Secretary of State argues for] the domesticity of the Human Rights Act: nothing in the Act or its genesis indicates any intention that it is to apply to events occurring beyond the shores of the United Kingdom. Absent any such indication, he submits, it is a primary rule of construction that the Act is to be taken not to have any extra-territorial reach. Although I am unpersuaded that there are any positive indicators of this in the Act, I accept that there is nothing in it to contra-indicate the presumption on which [the Secretary of State] relies.

[346] [2005] EWCA Civ 1609, para 149.

187 But [the sixth claimant] relies on an equal and opposite principle of construction: that, absent some clear indication to the contrary, domestic legislation is to be taken to have been intended to cohere with the state's international obligations. If so, there is a presumption at the very least that, if the Convention reaches the military prison in Basra, so does the Act.

188 The second presumption is not always easy to apply, but it fits the Human Rights Act well. Its avowed purpose was to make accessible in the courts of this country all the scheduled rights—including those contained in Article 2—which the United Kingdom had since 1950 undertaken by treaty to vouchsafe to individuals within its jurisdiction. The reason why the Act did not reproduce Article 1, with its reference to the state's jurisdiction, is that the enactment itself was intended to implement Article 1. The same was true of Article 13.

His Lordship therefore held, 'in agreement with the Divisional Court and with Brooke and Richards LJJ', that the sixth claimant's case '[was] justiciable in the courts of this country'.[347] But Richards LJ was more ambivalent than Sedley LJ portrayed him as being:

The issue that has caused me a degree of hesitation is the territorial scope of the HRA. When first faced with that issue, at first instance in *R (Abbasi)* v. *Secretary of State for Foreign and Commonwealth Affairs* [2002] EWHC 651 (Admin), I accepted the case for the Secretary of State that, in accordance with the normal legislative presumption, the HRA extended, with limited exceptions, only to the territory of the United Kingdom. Since then the competing arguments have become much more sophisticated, the Court of Appeal in *R (B)* v. *Secretary of State for Foreign and Commonwealth Affairs* [2005] QB 643 has reached a different conclusion, albeit strictly *obiter*, and the observations of Lord Nicholls in *R (Quark Fishing Ltd)* v. *Secretary of State for Foreign and Commonwealth Affairs* [2005] UKHL 57 have provided support for the conclusion in *B*. In my view there is still considerable force in the Secretary of State's case, but the matter is more finely balanced than it first appeared ... [348]

'[I]n the circumstances', his Lordship agreed with Brooke LJ 'that the right course [was] to follow the dicta in *B* and *Quark* and leave it to the House of Lords to decide whether those dicta are wrong'.[349]

As for the merits of the various claims, Brooke LJ outlined the content, in the specific situation before the court, of the procedural obligation under articles 2 and 3 of the ECHR to inquire into the circumstances of a death and alleged severe ill-treatment respectively at the hands of State forces:

[I]f international standards are to be observed, the task of investigating incidents in which a human life is taken by British forces must be completely taken away from the military chain of command and vested in the RMP [Royal Military Police]. It contains the requisite independence so long as it is free to decide for itself when to start and when to cease an investigation, and so long as it reports in the first instance to the APA [Army Prosecuting Authority] and not to the military chain of command. It must then conduct an effective investigation, and

347 [2005] EWCA Civ 1609, para 189.
348 [2005] EWCA Civ 1609, para 211.
349 [2005] EWCA Civ 1609, para 211.

it will be helped in this regard by the passages from ECHR case-law I have quoted. Many of the deficiencies highlighted by the evidence in this case will be remedied if the RMP perform this role, and if they are also properly trained and properly resourced to conduct their investigations with the requisite degree of thoroughness.[350]

In the first five cases, the question was rendered moot by the court's finding that the ECHR did not, in fact, apply. In the sixth case, in the light of up-to-date evidence not available to the Divisional Court, including notification of court-martial proceedings, Brooke LJ considered it premature to rule on the matter and remitted it to the Administrative Court, 'with the recommendation that all further proceedings on that issue be stayed until after the conclusion or other disposal of the pending court-martial proceedings'.[351]

The Court of Appeal's decision is not implausible. Brooke LJ's contention that, even after *Banković*, the application of the ECHR is not restricted to the Convention's *espace juridique* would seem to find support in the ECtHR's subsequent decisions in *Issa* and *Öçalan*, the first of which was decided after the main hearing before the Divisional Court, necessitating further written submissions and an additional oral hearing, the second after the Divisional Court's decision. For his part, Sedley LJ had the good grace to acknowledge that the other members of the court did not concur in his idiosyncratic analysis and the good sense to realize that it was flatly contradicted by *Banković*. His Lordship's preferred reasoning boils down to the proposition that the mere fact that organs of a Contracting State are in a position to violate what would be Convention rights brings the situation within the jurisdiction of that State for the purposes of article 1 of the ECHR. But if the Grand Chamber's judgment in *Banković* makes one thing clear, it is that a putative breach of the Convention attributable to a Contracting State does not of itself render the Convention applicable. As for his Lordship's favoured argument, this is strained and implausible. Sedley LJ prefaces a crucial passage with the words '[i]f effective control in the jurisprudence of the ECtHR marches with international humanitarian law and the law of armed conflict, as it clearly seeks to do . . .'. It seems the European Court could have spared itself the trouble of *Loizidou*, *Banković*, and *Issa*. And it could have spared us all its judgment in the second: since the law of armed conflict applied to NATO's bombing of Yugoslavia by virtue of the existence of an international armed conflict, the ECHR must 'clearly' have applied as well.

On the question of the extraterritorial application of the HRA, in relation to which the Court of Appeal placed weight on the dicta of Lord Nicholls in *Quark*, what is remarkable is that their Lordships were seemingly not

[350] [2005] EWCA Civ 1609, para 141.

[351] [2005] EWCA Civ 1609, para 179. Sedley and Richards LJJ agreed: [2005] EWCA Civ 1609, paras 208 and 210 respectively.

directed towards the equally relevant dicta of both Lord Nicholls and Lord Hoffman in the same case, which, while directed towards the immediate question of the Convention's application to territories for whose international relations the UK is responsible, surely have a wider import. Lord Nicholls himself stated elsewhere in *Quark*: 'The Human Rights Act is a United Kingdom statute .... It is not expressed to apply elsewhere in any relevant respect'.[352] Lord Hoffman emphasized that the HRA 'is concerned only with the Convention as it applies to the United Kingdom and not by extension to other territories'.[353] More fundamentally, however, although the Court of Appeal was probably right to leave the matter to the House of Lords, the scepticism evidenced by Brooke and Richardson LJJ towards the extraterritorial application of the HRA deserves support. The argument that a construction of the HRA which restricts its application to the UK places the UK in breach of its obligations under the Convention is simply not right. If the UK breaches the Convention, it does so when it violates the substantive right in question. The availability of recourse to the UK courts by way of the HRA does not alter this. Conversely, the non-applicability of the HRA to foreign territory does not breach the UK's obligations but merely prevents the victims or their next-of-kin from enforcing their Convention rights in the UK courts. In the words of Brooke LJ, '[t]he HRA would still be compatible with (or consonant with) the UK's international obligations under the ECHR even if it were not co-extensive with the ECHR in its territorial scope'.[354]

The case has gone on appeal to the House of Lords, with judgment expected in late 2006.

352 [2005] 3 WLR 837, 850, para 36.

353 [2005] 3 WLR 837, 855, para 62. Baroness Hale expressly left the question undecided: [2005] 3 WLR 837, 866, para 98.

354 [2005] EWCA Civ 1609, para 145.

B. PRIVATE INTERNATIONAL LAW*

1. Jurisdiction, discretion, and the Judgments Regulation: *Konkola Copper Mines plc v Coromin;*[1] *Grovit v De Nederlandsche Bank;*[2] *Viking Line ABP v International Transport Workers' Federation;*[3] *Through Transport Mutual Insurance Association (Eurasia) Ltd v New India Assurance Association Ltd;*[4] *West Tankers Inc v Ras Riunione Adriatica di Securita;*[5] *JP Morgan Europe Ltd v Primacom AG.*[6]

In March 2005, in *Owusu v Jackson*,[7] the European Court delivered itself of a judgment in which it held that a holidaymaker, injured on vacation in Jamaica and having a claim for damages for personal injury against one English and five Jamaican defendants, was entitled to proceed against the English defendant in England, and that the fact that Jamaica was or may have been the *forum conveniens* was irrelevant to the matter of whether the claimant could insist that the English court adjudicate his claim against the English defendant. So ended the period of uncertainty during which we had been unsure whether *Re Harrods (Buenos Aires) Ltd*[8] had been rightly decided. Of course, 'rightly decided' bears a very specialized meaning in this context, for rightness is only what the judges of the European Court say is right. And as to that, no common lawyer judge sat on the decision in *Owusu*, and what fell from the Court is so embarrassingly conclusory that that it barely counts as reasoning at all. For all that, it is now the law of the land that where jurisdiction over the defendant to a claim in a civil or commercial matter is founded on Article 2 of the Judgments Regulation, a court has no power to order a stay of proceedings in favour of the courts of a non-Member State on the ground that England is a *forum non conveniens*: it must adjudicate, and that is all there is to be said about it. Taken together with the earlier decisions that an English court denominated with exclusive jurisdiction by a valid and binding contractual agreement may not be asked to hear the case if the other party has launched the Italian torpedo,[9] and that anti-suit injunctions

1 [2005] EWHC 898 (Comm), [2005] 2 Lloyd's Rep 555, Colman J. An appeal to the Court of Appeal on the case management component of the decision was dismissed: [2006] EWCA Civ 5, [2006] 1 Lloyd's Rep 410, but there was no appeal against the decision of the judge on the point examined here.

2 [2005] EWHC 2944 (QB), [2006] 1 Lloyd's Rep 636, Tugendhat J.

3 [2005] EWHC 1222 (Comm), Gloster J. On appeal, [2005] EWCA Civ 1299, [2006] 1 Lloyd's Rep 303, the Court of Appeal stayed the proceedings and referred several questions of European law to the European Court, but at para 2, did not take issue with the judge's conclusion that she should hear and determine the case.

4 [2005] EWHC 455 (Comm), [2005] 2 Lloyd's Rep 378, Moore-Bick J.

5 [2005] EWHC 454 (Comm), [2005] 2 Lloyd's Rep 257, Colman J. A leapfrog appeal to the House of Lords is pending.

6 [2005] EWHC 508 (Comm), [2005] 2 Lloyd's Rep 665, Cooke J.

7 Case C-281/02, [2005] ECR I-1383.

8 [1992] Ch 72 (CA).

9 For the genesis of this expression, see (2004) 75 BYIL, 537, 560 n 87.

are proscribed by the Regulation,[10] the result is that the goals—surely they still are goals?—of commercial morality and adjudicatory efficiency have been gravely damaged.[11] The air has since been filled with the sound of chickens coming home to roost, though it is improbable that anyone in Luxembourg cares very much.

So far as *Owusu* is concerned, if the decision is regrettable, the Court of Appeal must shoulder the greater part of the blame. Given the fact that there was an order of reference, it must be taken that the court believed that a stay of proceedings was possible in a case in which a claimant, rendered quadriplegic in an accident which he blamed on the defendants, would be told *eight years after the accident* that he was required to instruct lawyers in Jamaica and start again from square one. The most cursory of reality checks would surely have revealed that this was one of those cases in which, whatever were and wherever lay the objective points of contact between case, law, and courts, there were exceptional reasons which made it impossible to order a stay. No thought of reference to the European Court should ever have crossed the court's mind. If the judges on the European Court had thought about this aspect of the matter, they would certainly have been troubled; though it has to be admitted that no trace of such concern comes through in the judgment. It is also apparent that in Australia, the one common law jurisdiction to have turned its face against staying local proceedings by reference to the principle in *Spiliada Maritime Corp v Cansulex Ltd*,[12] the leading cases have tended to be cases of personal injury brought by local claimants against large foreign corporations, and in which the natural forum was even further away from the claimant's Australian home than was Jamaica from England. On such facts, the real attractions of a stay of Australian proceedings were close to nil. But *Owusu v Jackson* was a case which should never have been allowed anywhere near the European Court.

The Court of Appeal, though, had asked a second question. This sought to identify any cases in which a court was still entitled to apply its own sense of what jurisdictional justice required in ordering a stay of proceedings which had been founded on Article 2. The obvious candidates for attention were cases where the claim concerned title to land or the validity of intellectual property rights in a non-Member State; the case where the parties to a contract had conferred exclusive jurisdiction on the courts of a non-Member State; cases in which there was a *lis alibi pendens* in a non-Member State; and cases in which the proceedings were part of, or inseparably connected to, a matter excluded from the material scope of the Regulation. The Court, displaying little respect for the Court of Appeal's assessment of what it needed to know, disdained to answer. But the questions are still questions, and they need an answer. It

[10] C-159/02 *Turner v Grovit* [2004] ECR I-3565.
[11] See, for further analysis, Briggs, *Zeitschrift für Schweizerisches Recht* (2005) 124 II 231.
[12] [1987] AC 460.

has therefore fallen to the Commercial Court to discern what *Owusu* really means, and to fill in the gaps accordingly. In the nine months since *Owusu* it has had to consider whether an English court has to exercise jurisdiction over an English defendant when the parties have agreed that the courts of a non-Member State have exclusive jurisdiction. It has had to decide whether the Regulation encroaches on the principle of sovereign immunity. It has had to decide whether it has to exercise jurisdiction to determine a question of interpretation of rights conferred by the Constitution of the Finnish Republic. It has had to consider how to proceed when the narrow issue before it is one of arbitration but judicial proceedings are pending in respect of the same broad claim before the Finnish courts. And it has had to consider how to proceed when, as the court nominated with exclusive jurisdiction, a party in open breach of contract brings torpedo proceedings before the courts of another Member State. It has been quite a year.

The facts of *Konkola Copper Mines plc v Coromin* were complex in ways which render them unsuitable for re-telling.[13] But in the course of his judgment, Colman J had to consider how he would have proceeded if he had found that the parties had made an agreement to confer exclusive jurisdiction on the courts of Zambia in relation to the claim before him. The defendant was domiciled in England. The conclusion of the judge, who was surely correct, was that nothing in *Owusu* stood in the way of a stay of proceedings, even though the claim was made against a defendant domiciled in England. He identified two good reasons why this was so. First, the European Court had previously indicated that the validity of a jurisdiction agreement for a non-Member State was to be determined by a court applying its rules of national law, including the conflict of laws.[14] The judge observed that it was hardly to be supposed that the national court should so proceed but then have no power to grant the relief which its national law would have allowed on a finding that the agreement was valid and binding. Secondly, he noted that the criticism which had been voiced in the course of *Owusu*—ignorant[15] criticism, to be sure—was that the doctrine of *forum non conveniens* led to uncertainty in the allocation and exercise of jurisdiction. But for a court to ignore the provisions of a jurisdiction agreement for a non-Member State was more likely to contribute to uncertainty than to prevent it, and therefore a jurisdiction agreement for a non-Member State was to be given effect. He was quite right.

The judge did not have to consider whether the jurisdiction agreement was required to conform to the formal requirements set out in Article 23 for those agreements for the courts of a Member State to have jurisdiction.

[13] For confirmation of this, see the introduction to the judgment of Rix LJ in the Court of Appeal (n 1 above).

[14] Case C-387/98 *Coreck Maritime GmbH v Handelsveem BV* [2000] ECR I-9337.

[15] See para 42 of the judgment for a dumbfounding error on the part of the Court, which reveals it simply has no idea how *forum non conveniens* works in an English court.

The clause, if it had been agreed to at all, was in writing; and as he found on the facts that there had been no such agreement between the parties, the judge was not required to ask whether he would have been obliged[16] or only permitted[17] to stay the proceedings. The answer to these questions should have been that there was no need for the agreement, if found to exist as a matter of fact and law, to comply with the formalities set out in Article 23; and the response of the court would properly have been to exercise a discretion to stay, as opposed to its being required to stay, English proceedings brought in breach of such a contractual promise. The formalities in Article 23 make sense when answering the question whether a court in a Member State has jurisdiction by virtue of an agreement, but if the question is posed in relation to a non-Member State, there is no particular reason why the underlying rules ought to be the same. As to the nature of the relief, a discretion to stay proceedings is appropriate. The mandatory dismissal of the English proceedings, which may make some sense within the framework of the Regulation, would be too draconian in relation to the rest of world from China to Peru: account must be taken of the court in question, the nature of the proceedings brought, the impact of the jurisdiction agreement on the court's duty to manage complex litigation in an orderly way, and so forth.

As to the legal foundation for these conclusions, the answer has to be that the application of Articles 22, 23, 27, and 28 by analogy is what allows an English court to give effect to its domestic rules within the territory defined by reference to these rules. Others prefer to say that certain Articles of the Regulation are to be given a 'reflexive effect', which is to say much the same thing.[18] The question is, of course, one of how close the analogy needs to be to justify the outcome. The view preferred here is that it means 'jurisdiction agreements' rather than 'jurisdiction agreements which comply with the formal requirements of Article 23'; 'cases which require a court to determine title to foreign land' rather than 'proceedings which have as their object rights in rem in foreign land'; 'lis alibi pendens in a non-Member State which was seised first' rather than 'proceedings between the same parties and in respect of the same cause of action in respect of which the foreign court was seised first'. Also preferred is the view that when an English court considers that the question before it falls within the territory defined by analogy or by reflexive effect, the relief should take the form of the procedural or equitable discretion found in *Spiliada* and in *Donohue v Armco Inc*,[19] rather than its being a Chinese copy of the mandatory declining of jurisdiction provided for by Articles 22, 23, and 27. Once again, the fact that the jurisdictional connection lies with a non-Member State should suffice to

[16] As Art 23 says for cases to which it applies.

[17] As the common law provides for cases to which it applies.

[18] See Briggs [2005] LMCLQ 378 and the writings there cited.

[19] [2002] 1 Lloyd's Rep 425.

explain why an unthinking jurisdictional reflex to dismiss the proceedings is not attractive. Such a view is consistent with the major French writings, and seems to be closer in spirit to *Coreck Maritime GmbH v Handelsveem BV*.[20] Though it is understood that there are some who prefer the view that jurisdictional relief should be mandatory, not yielding to the usual discretionary elements, as it is under Articles 22 and 23, the pragmatic arguments against it are overwhelming, and the doctrinal ones given in its support unconvincing.

Konkola Copper Mines is, one has to say, the easy case: holding adults to their agreements, in circumstances where the consent of neither may be said to be impaired, is wholly rational. Just as easy, though for different reasons, was the issue before the judge in *Grovit v De Nederlandsche Bank*, who confirmed the existence of another jurisdictional defence to a claim over which the English court appeared to have jurisdiction on the basis of the Judgments Regulation. The ever-litigious Mr Grovit fancied that he had a claim for defamation against certain officers of the Dutch central bank who, as he alleged, had libelled him by sending certain comments to recipients in England. Invoking Article 5(3) of the Judgments Regulation, he brought proceedings for libel on the unchallengeable footing that the damage he alleged had occurred in England. The bank and its officers claimed sovereign immunity as a complete answer to the jurisdiction of the English court in respect of wrongs said to result from their activity and Tugendhat J, finding the claim to sovereign immunity to be well founded in law, dismissed the claim. He recognized that the consequence was that Grovit would have to raise his claim before the Dutch courts instead, but denied that this meant that the inadmissible principle of *forum non conveniens* had been at work. He too was, of course, quite right.

The case therefore lends its modest weight to support the sensible proposition that where there is a jurisdictional defence whose application lies outside the material scope of the Judgments Regulation, the defence cannot be considered to conflict with the Regulation and will still be applied. The judge did not found his decision upon a separate point which he mentioned, that sovereign immunity is in part a matter of international convention, and that Article 71 of the Regulation makes an express saving for pre-existing international conventions which deal with jurisdiction and the recognition of judgments. That argument seems reasonably well founded, but the judge was unwilling to take a step which may have had the effect of relegating the *common law* of sovereign immunity to a lower level of significance, as well he might. There are limits to what effect can be attributed to the Judgments Regulation or its predecessor, all instruments concerned to establish jurisdictional rules for civil and commercial matters before the courts of Member or Contracting States. It has been held, in England, astonishingly enough, that it precludes

[20] Case C-387/98, [2000] ECR I-9337.

the operation of a rule of the common law that an English court has no jurisdiction to rule on the validity of foreign patents or other intellectual property rights;[21] and it had even been held that it overrode the common law choice of law rule for foreign torts.[22] Both these conclusions seemed wrong at the time, and seem just as hard to defend now. It is true that a literal reading of the judgment in *Owusu* lent some support to the construction advanced by Mr Grovit, but to adopt such an approach requires a suspension of critical intelligence at which even the judges of the European Court may baulk.

Customary or treaty-based sovereign immunity exists because of a fundamental view that there are some issues which simply cannot be properly litigated before the courts of a foreign country; and sovereign liability is one of these. A question in some ways similar, but more problematic, came before Gloster J when she was called upon to deal with the umpteenth stage of the endless campaign of the International Transport Workers' Federation for the defence of the rights of seamen. The ITWF takes industrial action against the owners of sea-going vessels who propose to de-register in countries where seamen have wages and workplace rights and to re-register them in countries where local crews will work for peanuts and without the standards of social protection which the country of original registration insists on. In *Viking Line ABP v ITWF and the Finnish Seamen's Union*, the Finnish Seamen's Union, and through them the ITWF, got wind of the owners' intention to re-flag a vessel from Finland to Estonia. Viking Line sought to take advantage of the free movement[23] provisions of EU law in relation to one of the states which acceded to membership in 2004; and to recruit a local crew which would undercut the existing Finnish crew. The ITWF and the Union fought for their rights and brought their muscle to bear on the owners. Viking Line sought relief from the English courts against what they claimed was unlawful industrial action. As the ITWF was based in London, the English courts had jurisdiction over it under Article 2 of the Judgments Regulation. Article 6(1) jurisdiction was therefore available against the Union. But the defendants argued that this was not a matter fit to be tried in the English courts. The principal defence to the claim for a final injunction to restrain the unions was going to be that the Finnish Constitution gave workers a guarantee of the right to take industrial action; and that the compatibility of the constitution of a sovereign state with the law of the EU was a matter which was more appropriately decided in Finland than in London.[24] Gloster J was having none of it. She denied that, as she saw the matter, the Finnish Constitution gave the seamen any such right to strike as would be incompatible with EU law,

[21] *Pearce v Ove Arup Partnership Ltd* [2000] Ch 433 (CA).

[22] *Pearce v Ove Arup Partnership Ltd* [1997] Ch 293 (Lloyd J).

[23] Though the free movement of jobs is an indirect, rather than a direct, freedom.

[24] It was not, apparently, contended that the subject matter of the proceedings was other than a civil or commercial one.

not least because the EU and its laws was also part of the Finnish legal order, and the Constitution had to be read with that in mind. She denied that there was any problem in her adjudicating on a matter of Finnish constitutional law, and if the Finnish courts were later to find or think otherwise, they were free to use Article 34(1) to withhold recognition from her judgment. But in large part this was the bolstering of a decision which was forced on the judge by *Owusu v Jackson*: the only basis on which an English court could decline jurisdiction would be on the basis of *forum non conveniens*, and that was no longer admissible as a jurisdictional plea. So the question whether the Constitution of Finland gave and still gives workers a right to take industrial action against an employer seeking to take advantage of the free movement provisions of the EU treaty will be decided by an English judge. This is heady stuff.

It is a curiosity of the Regulation that though public policy may be deployed to deny recognition to a judgment, there is no general[25] equivalent which allows it to deny or relinquish jurisdiction to adjudicate. It is worth asking why this is, for public policy appears to be as engaged by adjudication as it is with recognition of foreign judgments. It cannot be that the specific grounds of jurisdiction which make up Chapter II of the Regulation are drafted in such a way as to exclude the possibility that it could ever challenge the public policy of an English court for it to be asked to adjudicate. If an English court is to be asked to adjudicate on an act of state, or on an act which triggers the 'political question' basis on which a matter may be found to be non-justiciable, or which requires it to investigate whether a foreign government has acted with bad faith in promoting legislation, it should surely be open to it to decline jurisdiction over the matter before it, as distinct from striking out a particular plea. Perhaps such a question would be regarded as outside the scope of the 'civil and commercial matters' which define the material scope of the Regulation. But such limited authority as exists in England suggests that the jurisdictional exclusionary rule of the common law is inapplicable where the matter is otherwise within the material scope of the Regulation, and that as long as the claim is within the Regulation, a defence does not take it outside it again.[26] It is hard to see the sense of this, unless it is motivated by a simple fear that if a court is allowed to find that its public policy risks being offended by adjudication, it should simply be entitled to decline to accept the case. Gloster J, to be sure, seemed perfectly happy to rule on the inter-relationship between the law of the EU and the Finnish Constitution. It is not clear that she should have been.

The exercise of discretion in jurisdiction is permitted, though, in cases which fall outside the material scope of the Regulation. Last year we

[25] Though Art 22 contains rules of exclusive jurisdiction which are founded on some sense of what public policy will and will not tolerate in the exercise of civil jurisdiction.

[26] See Briggs and Rees, *Civil Jurisdiction and Judgments* (4th edn, 2005) para 2.25.

observed how, in a most challenging decision, the Court of Appeal accepted that it had not lost its power to restrain by injunction a respondent who, in breach of what was found to be an obligation to arbitrate a dispute with an insurer, brought proceedings in the Finnish courts in respect of the same claim. In *Through Transport Mutual Insurance Association (Eurasia) Ltd v New India Assurance Association Ltd*,[27] the Court of Appeal pulled its punches at the end, declining to issue the injunction it concluded it had power to issue. We noted this with concern, as the predictable result was that the claim would proceed in Finland notwithstanding the contractual promise to arbitrate it in London. The applicant duly returned to the Commercial Court seeking an order against the respondent that an arbitrator be appointed 'for' the unwilling respondent. The judge concluded that he was bound to make the appointment, as the arbitration had its seat in England and there was nothing in the decision of the Court of Appeal to suggest that the English arbitration should give way to the Finnish judicial resolution of the claim. It was apparent that each side was pressing on with its strategy which was to obtain a ruling (adjudication in Finland; award in London) before its opponent succeeded in the same-but-contradictory aim, and to try and use this ruling to put a spoke in the wheels of the procedure in the other country. In this context, a less dignified procedure would be hard to imagine; but the lack of an anti-suit injunction was the culprit. Nor is there much doubt that an anti-suit injunction would have been granted in support of the arbitration agreement if the judicial proceedings had been in a non-Member State. Indeed, in *West Tankers Inc v Ras Riunione Adriatica di Securita*,[28] the Commercial judge ordered an injunction against the respondent who, in breach of an arbitration agreement, had seised the Italian courts. The decision is much to be preferred to the pulling of punches by the Court of Appeal the year before. The judge observed that the Italian courts had no cause to be offended by the grant of the injunction, because they could ignore it if that was what Italian law required, and something which was to be ignored gave no cause to take offence. Even so, some will see in it the conclusion that the Italian court was wrong to believe that it had jurisdiction to adjudicate a civil or commercial matter, and that any relief which is predicated on that initial finding is objectionable.

The last of the year's chickens flew home in *JP Morgan Europe Ltd v Primacom AG*. Despite the fact that the parties had agreed to the exclusive jurisdiction of the English courts, the German borrower brought proceedings against the English bank in Germany. There was, so far as Cooke J could tell, no remotely plausible legal basis on which this could properly have been done, but *Erich Gasser GmbH v MISAT srl*[29] required the English courts to regard themselves as the second-seised courts

[27] [2004] EWCA Civ 1598, [2005] 1 Lloyd's Rep 67, noted (2004) 75 BYIL 549.
[28] [2005] 2 Lloyd's Rep 257. [29] Case C-116/02, [2004] ECR I-14693.

which, as a matter of simple chronology, they were. It was not clear whether the German torpedo would be as dilatory as its Italian counterpart had been; but the effect of seising the German court was to impede the exercise of jurisdiction by the English courts.

But Cooke J considered that he had noticed a significant palliative. Though Article 27 applied to prevent the English court proceeding to exercise jurisdiction to try the case on its merits, this did not mean that the English court *had* no jurisdiction, or that it was not seised. All Article 27 required was that it stay the proceedings *pro tem*. It followed from that that the English court was entitled to grant interlocutory relief, this not restricted to those measures which were permitted to be granted by a court which had no, and knew it had no, jurisdiction over the merits of the dispute. In *Van Uden Maritime v Deco-Line*,[30] the European Court had drawn a clear distinction. A court with jurisdiction over the merits of the case was entitled to grant any such relief as was available under its procedural law; but a court with no jurisdiction over the merits, as was the case in *Van Uden*, where a valid and binding agreement on arbitration meant that no court had jurisdiction over the merits, its powers were confined to the types of relief available under what is now Article 31 of the Regulation. But the clarity of this binary distinction is illusory in a case like *Primacom*, where the court neither had nor did not have jurisdiction. Cooke J considered that the English court, validly nominated but temporarily subject to torpedo attack, was a court with jurisdiction rather than a court without it. He therefore concluded that he could make a substantial order for interlocutory relief which could go far to secure the rights of the bank against the borrower.

Two arguments stand in the way of simply accepting the attractive conclusion of the judge. As Article 27 has no obvious application to provisional or protective measures,[31] it may be thought that the seisin of the German courts left untouched the power of the English courts to grant provisional measures. But the only application for relief which is protected by Article 31 from the jurisdictional rules of Chapter II is one for those measures which fall within Article 31. If the interlocutory measure sought could only be granted by a court with jurisdiction to adjudicate, and as Chapter II seeks to ensure that only one court will have jurisdiction to adjudicate, it does not seem open to the court seised second to grant it. Moreover, although Cooke J considered that the English court was seised, perhaps the real question was to ask what it had been seised *with*. It is not at all clear that it had been seised with jurisdiction to adjudicate, as distinct from the question of whether it had jurisdiction to adjudicate, and that it was precluded from answering that question until the German procedure had run its course. For Cooke J to

[30] Case C-391/95, [1998] ECR I-7091.

[31] Case C-88/00 *Italian Leather SpA v WECO Polstermöbel GmbH* [2002] ECR I-4995 holds that what is now Art 34(3) does apply to such cases, but does not suggest that Art 27 does.

consider that he was seised, if precariously, with jurisdiction to adjudicate was, perhaps, to take a step too far.

It will take a little while for the dust to settle after the devastation wrought by the European Court, and the judges of the Commercial Court are certainly not to be criticized for the occasional slip. When parties to commercial contracts behave disreputably, as MISAT srl and Primacom AG did, using sneaky applications to their own courts to rub salt in the wounds of the victim of their contractual breaches, a decent judge is likely to be receptive to a submission that he can, in fact and in law, do something about it. MISAT srl and Primacom AG added insult to injury: quickly after defaulting on their commercial contracts they followed it up with a breach of the dispute-resolution one. No doubt wronged commercial parties in the position of Erich Gasser GmbH and JP Morgan Europe Ltd will look for new territory on which to fight for the vindication of their contractual rights; and if the European Court seriously believes that it has put an end to such shenanigans, it may yet discover that it has only succeeded in breathing new life into them.

2. English jurisdiction clauses and foreign statutes: *OT Africa Line Ltd v Magic Sportswear Corp.*[32]

A small consignment of goods was to be carried by sea from New York to Monrovia. The carrier, OTAL, was an English company with an office in Toronto, and it was from that office that it issued a bill of lading which provided for the exclusive jurisdiction of the English courts. Alleging short delivery, the cargo interests sought damages from the carrier. But rather than sue in London they did so in Canada. Their justification for doing so was that Canadian legislation[33] permitted the jurisdiction agreement to be overridden and proceedings to be brought in Canada if the bill of lading was issued in Canada. The carrier retaliated with proceedings for a declaration of non-liability to the cargo owners, bringing the proceedings in London, and applying for an anti-suit injunction to reinforce the agreement on English jurisdiction. By judgment in November 2004, Langley J[34] declined to stay the proceedings and granted the injunction, taking the view that Canadian legislation overriding the jurisdiction agreement furnished no sufficient reason to overcome the basic rule that exclusive jurisdiction agreements should be enforced by specific order. The appeal was heard in May 2005, and the Court of Appeal dismissed the appeal, largely confirming the reasoning of the judge below. Though this was an unimpeachable exercise of common law reasoning, it is less clear why the Court of Appeal paid no attention to the Judgments Regulation.

[32] [2005] EWCA Civ 710, [2005] 2 Lloyd's Rep 170: Laws, Rix, and Longmore LJJ.

[33] Marine Liability Act 2001, s 46(1).

[34] [2004] EWHC 2441 (Comm), [2005] 1 Lloyd's Rep 252.

All legal systems place limits on the effect they will give to exclusive jurisdiction clauses. As a matter of English law, the Carriage of Goods by Sea Act 1971 prevented an English court giving effect to a jurisdiction clause for a foreign court which would have applied the old Hague Rules to limit the sum recoverable on the claim.[35] Various consumer and worker protection statutes have, from time to time, restricted the ability of suppliers and employers to impose jurisdiction or arbitration provisions on weaker parties who may be disadvantaged by them. Australian law famously did so in relation to certain contracts of insurance;[36] and for the Canadian parliament to legislate in this vein in relation to sea carriage was unremarkable. The question for the court was to decide whether this had any impact upon its basic view that contractual agreements on jurisdiction are meant to be kept, and will be enforced unless strong reason exists for not doing so. After all, it was not unlawful for the cargo interests to sue in London: Canadian law did not forbid the bringing of the action outside Canada. The cargo interests had a choice, and they exercised it by breaking their contractual agreement on jurisdiction. Faced with this, the English courts will restrain the breach unless there is shown to be a strong reason not to do so. Such a strong reason tends to require that there be complex and multi-partite litigation, which would be complicated by the enforcement of the jurisdiction as between the parties to it, or which would impose burdens on non-parties to the agreement if it were enforced. No such facts were present in this case.

Moreover, the facts fell into the pattern[37] previously established in the litigation between Akai Pty Ltd and the People's Insurance Co. An insurance policy issued in Australia, but governed by English law, had provided for English exclusive jurisdiction; the High Court of Australia[38] had ruled that the jurisdiction agreement was rendered ineffective by Australian legislation of mandatory effect, and had refused to stay proceedings brought in New South Wales. Soon after that decision, the Commercial Court[39] granted an anti-suit injunction to restrain Akai from suing in Australia in breach of its contractual agreement to submit to the exclusive jurisdiction of the English courts. The fact that the contractual agreement was, and had been shown to be, unenforceable in an Australian court was not significant, never mind decisive,[40] when a claim was made in the court which had been agreed upon. So here: the fact that the Canadian Federal Court was, as it was obliged to do, allowing the action to proceed in Toronto did not alter the conclusion that there was a breach of contract voluntarily being committed by a party who was, or who could be made to be, subject to the personal jurisdiction of the English court. An anti-suit injunction was almost inevitable. The justification is that the parties had not made a

[35] *The Hollandia* [1983] 1 AC 565.
[36] *Akai Pty Ltd v People's Insurance Co* (1997) 188 CLR 418.
[37] Described by Longmore LJ at para 26 as a 'moderately close parallel'. But it is surely much closer than that.
[38] *Akai Pty Ltd v People's Insurance Co* (1997) 188 CLR 418
[39] *Akai Pty Ltd v People's Insurance Co* [1998] 1 Lloyd's Rep 90.
[40] Given the finding of Thomas J that there had been no submission to the Australian court.

Canadian contract, but had made an English contract. It is a common, and dangerous, misconception to analyse a contract as having an existence detached from its governing law: Lord Diplock famously warned against it,[41] and the lesson needs periodic repetition if it is not to be forgotten.[42] If these parties had made 'a contract', there would be no real reason to prefer an English court's analysis of its content and enforceability and governing law over that of a Canadian court. Certainly the jurisdiction agreement would furnish no such ground for, unless and until the governing law issue has been answered, there is no certainty that the contract contains a valid jurisdiction agreement. But the parties made an *English* contract; and by doing so made an agreement on jurisdiction which was valid and binding according to its terms. What was going on in Canada may have been relevant to any discretionary or procedural remedy available in respect of the breach, but the proposition that a party may point to his own breach as a reason why he should not be held to the letter of the contract would be a terrible heresy. An unrepentant contract-breaker needs to be ordered to obey; and that is, more or less, how the Court of Appeal saw it. What a Canadian court may have been told to think by its legislator was without legal relevance in an English court. The injunction followed as a matter of course.

But the court had first to reject the submission that it should stay the English proceedings. Longmore LJ upheld the judge's conclusion. That was really not good enough. For though Langley J had given his judgment four months before the decision in *Owusu v Jackson*, the hearing in the Court of Appeal came eight weeks after that decision of the European Court. In it, the European Court ruled that if an English court had jurisdiction under Article 2 of what is now the Judgments Regulation, it had no power to decline to exercise that jurisdiction, even in favour of the courts of a non-Member State, on the ground of *forum non conveniens*. A fair reading of the judgment is that when the English court has jurisdiction on the basis of other provisions of Chapter II of the Regulation, it is equally prevented from staying proceedings in favour of the Canadian courts. As the jurisdiction clause in question was one to which Article 23 of the Regulation applied, being for the courts of a Member State in which one of the parties was[43] domiciled, Article 23 served to give the English court jurisdiction under Chapter II of the Regulation. As the only conceivable ground for a stay was that it made sense for the claim to be heard in Canada, where it appeared to be proceeding in any event, the application for a stay was manifestly inadmissible, at least after 1 March 2005. On this view, the Court of Appeal should simply have dismissed the appeal, though on grounds which were not those of the judge who was bound by *Re Harrods (Buenos Aires) Ltd*[44] to accept that he had a

[41] *Amin Rasheed Shipping Corp v Kuwait Insurance Co* [1984] AC 50.

[42] See in particular (2003) 74 BYIL 520, noting *Wight v Eckhardt Marine GmbH* [2004] 1 AC 147 (PC).

[43] The carrier was described by Longmore LJ as an English company: at para 3.

[44] [1992] Ch 72 (CA).

discretion to stay the proceedings. Why this point was not taken in the Court of Appeal, by the parties or by the court of its own motion, is not clear, but the judgments make no reference to it. Presumably it was overlooked.

If there were to be a discretion to decline to exercise jurisdiction conferred by the Regulation, it would have to be consistent with the Regulation. It is well known that this instrument, like the Brussels Convention before it, made no reference to points of contact outside the community of Member States in the allocation of jurisdiction. But as discussed in the previous Note,[45] it was arguable that Article 27 of the Regulation may have been applicable by analogy, to allow an English court to decline to exercise jurisdiction on the ground that the Canadian courts were seised first, and given that they were, to exercise a *forum non conveniens* discretion over whether to proceed with the claim in England. If that were permissible, it would doubtless have been right to refuse to stay the English proceedings, notwithstanding the prior Canadian proceedings, for the reasons the court actually gave;[46] and in this respect the case is a good illustration of why an argument made by analogy with Article 27 of the Regulation should result in a discretion, and not an obligation, on the English court to cede jurisdiction to the court seised first. But the opportunity to confirm this in the Court of Appeal went begging.

It has been observed before that the scheme of the Regulation is characterized by some rigidity in jurisdiction. In those cases where it applies, the existence of an agreement on jurisdiction may prevent a court from managing complex litigation in a manner which secures a single trial by which all are bound: sometimes it is necessary for a court to override the parties' agreement on jurisdiction[47] to coordinate the overall adjudication. The Regulation does not allow for this, instead applying a rigid enforcement of the agreement, and in this respect, mimicking the law on arbitration.[48] The common law, through its use of discretionary remedies to enforce a contract, has the capacity to accept that a jurisdiction agreement is valid, has been breached, and will not be enforced by specific remedy. The result is that the court can properly manage litigation, while leaving the parties, if so advised, to pursue by a claim in damages any loss which results from the undeniable breach of contract. The result is a subtle and responsive approach to international commercial litigation. It is, perhaps, understandable that the Court of Appeal should have felt more at home with a set of rules which allowed the judges to reach the best solution, and did not instinctively grasp that the ground rules had changed, and that all such judicial balancing and evaluation had been

[45] See text accompanying nn 18–20 above.

[46] As one may say, even if a judge may not: *ex turpi causa non oritur exceptio*.

[47] Maybe leaving them to an alternative remedy in damages if loss can be proved to have resulted from the breach by one of the parties.

[48] Arbitration Act 1996, s 9.

consigned to history. But the decision in *Owusu* had done just that; and in this respect the judgment must be taken to have proceeded on a false premise.

3. Lis alibi pendens and uncertainty as to dates: *Chorley v Chorley;*[49] *Tavoulareas v Tsavliris;*[50] *Advent Capital plc v GN Ellinas Imports-Exports Ltd.*[51]

Though the Judgments Regulation has attended to the vexing question of how to decide which of two Member State courts was seised first, there is still a chance that difficulties can arise. This year saw three, which is something of a record.[52]

In *Chorley v Chorley*, the marriage of the parties had broken down. In January 2003 the husband, a British citizen, invoked the procedures of French law for the dissolution of marriage on the ground of fault committed by his French wife. This involved submitting a *requête* to the French courts, which led in turn to an automatic reference to conciliation proceedings, which themselves generated a number of applications to the French courts. But the eventual ruling that conciliation had failed cleared the way for the husband to file an *assignation* for divorce, which he did in May 2004. But in January 2004 the wife had petitioned the High Court for a divorce. The husband considered that he had seised the French courts before the wife had seised the English courts, and that therefore Article 11 of Council Regulation 1347/2000[53] required the English courts to declare that they had no jurisdiction. He proposed that the English proceedings be stayed to allow him to obtain a ruling from the French court which would determine the date of its seisin. But the Family Division decided to rule for itself, and Roderic Wood J reached the conclusion that the English court was seised first. By the time an application to the Court of Appeal for permission to appeal was heard, a French

[49] [2005] EWCA Civ 68, [2005] 1 WLR 1469: Thorpe, Tuckey, and Dyson LJJ, reversing [2004] EWHC 1959 (Fam).

[50] [2005] EWHC 2140 (Comm), [2006] 1 AUER (Comm) 109, [2005] EWHC 2643 (Comm), [2006] 1 AUER (Comm) 130: Andrew Smith J.

[51] [2005] EWHC 1242 (Comm), [2005] 2 Lloyd's Rep 607: Colman J.

[52] There was a fourth, in *Phillips v Symes* [2005] EWHC 1880 (Ch): Peter Smith J. The case was one part of a complex and quite extraordinarily acrimonious commercial dispute. The case concerned, among other things, the effect of irregular service of English proceedings in Switzerland, and the effect of the jurisdiction to cure irregularity in the context of the question of the date on which the English court was seised of the proceedings. In the light of the decision of the court of Appeal, [2006] EWCA Civ 654, [2006] 1 WLR 2598, which will be noted next year, there is no need, alas, for the decision of the judge to be noted in any detail. But his observation at para 45 deserves to be known by a wider audience. The learned judge introduced it this way: 'I now set out the nub of the present dispute which has given rise to the present proceedings. It has led to a detailed and complicated argument based on facts which are so bizarre as to defy belief. The resultant difficulties based on those bizarre facts have led to a problem which a Professor of International Law would be proud of if he were setting a conflicts law question based on service'. As well he might.

[53] And referred to by the shorthand of 'Brussels II'. It has been superseded by Reg 2201/2003, known in its turn as Brussels 'II*bis*'.

appellate court had ruled that it had been seised from the date of the *requête*. Though this ruling was in principle subject to review by an appeal *en cassation*, the Court of Appeal has held that the sensible path was to allow the French judicial process to deliver a final ruling upon when the French courts were seised with the cause of action for divorce: at the date of the *requête*, or on the date of the *assignation*. As a matter of common sense the Court of Appeal was right, and it is a mystery how the High Court had allowed itself to come to a different decision.

The question of when proceedings are definitively pending will often depend on a proper understanding of legal procedure in the various Member States. Article 11 of the Brussels II Regulation echoed Article 30 of the Judgments Regulation, and directs attention to whether France was a file-and-serve, or serve-and-file state. But the problem in *Chorley* lay not in deciding whether French divorce proceedings conformed to one pattern or the other, but whether the *requête* or the assignation was to be seen as 'the document instituting the proceedings'. This begged the question of whether 'the proceedings' meant what was instituted in January 2003, or May 2004. It was, for sure, arguable that the French courts were not seised of the claim for a divorce until the conciliation had failed and the husband had chosen—and he had a choice; nothing was automatic—to file the *assignation*. But this was never terribly convincing. After all, in England, parties who institute proceedings may be directed to mediation or ADR; and even if not, a claimant may never get round to serving particulars of a claim, or to applying for a date for the hearing. Steps in the process of civil litigation are rarely automatic, but depend on the will of the parties to make progress. The fact that a document needed to be served to continue a judicial process that began in January 2003 was unremarkable, and it came as little surprise to an outsider that the French courts should consider that they had been seised since January 2003. As a more general issue of legal policy, the contrary conclusion would be inane: it would mean that a claimant who started in a system which required mediation before trial could never be sure of having started first, as his opponent would have a window of opportunity to start proceedings in another Member State, just as Mrs Chorley did. No rational person could see sense in that, which is what made the decision of the High Court appear so strange. It was essential that the Court of Appeal put it right.

The decision of the English court to allow a foreign court to rule on the date on which it was seised had a forerunner in *Polly Peck International v Citibank NA*.[54] The only argument against such a procedure is the suspicion that the foreign court is not to be trusted, which is plainly inadmissible within the context of the community of Member States. It is fair to say that the question of when a court is seised remains one of considerable complexity, even after Article 30 of the Judgments

[54] [1994] ILPr 71 (not cited in the Court of Appeal).

Regulation, as litigation in the courts becomes increasingly encrusted with modish and conciliatory alternatives to litigation. Unless and until there is an autonomous definition of what constitutes the document instituting the proceedings, which is broad and detailed enough to answer all questions, the approach of the Court of Appeal has much to commend it, at least in cases in which one may be confident that the foreign court will deliver a ruling within a reasonable timeframe.

Less tractable difficulties were encountered as judges grappled with cases which had been commenced before the coming into force of one of the jurisdictional instruments generated by the EU but whose parties were still slogging it out on the battleground of jurisdiction after a new jurisdictional regime came into force. The results were most unattractive. In *Tavoulareas v Tsavliris* it was the effect of the Judgments Regulation coming into force in two states[55] which had hitherto been bound by the Brussels Convention; and in *Advent Capital plc v Ellinas Imports-Exports Ltd*, it was the coming into force of the Act of Accession which turned Cyprus from a non-Member State into a Member State.[56] In *Tavoulareas* the dispute was over a contract of loan made between two teams of Greeks who were evidently determined to litigate each other and their families into the ground. In one corner stood Tavoulareas, who was resident at all material times in Florida. In the other were the Tsavliris brothers, resident in London, and their family company, established under Greek law. In 2004 the Court of Appeal had to decide whether the English or the Greek courts were seised first in the context of a case in which there had been deficiencies in the process of service of the documents which instituted the Greek proceedings.[57] The relevant jurisdictional text was the Brussels Convention, with its unreconstructed 'first seised' rule. That is where the simplicity ends.

At the end of 2001, an English clam form was issued on behalf of Tavoulareas, and was served on the two Tsavliris defendants[58] in London within the month; no one sought to contend that service was irregular or ineffective. But the day after the claim form was issued in this first English action, and weeks before it was served, the Tsavliris parties retaliated by instituting proceedings against Tavoulareas, in Pireaus, alleging duress and claiming a declaration of non-liability. The Greek writ was delivered to the local public prosecutor, in purported accordance with

[55] The UK, Greece.

[56] A similar issue concerned the jurisdiction of the English courts in matters of parental responsibility, as the Brussels II Regulation was superseded on 1 March 2005 by the Brussels II*bis* Regulation. The proceedings in *M v H* [2005] EWHC 1186 (Fam) had been commenced under the jurisdictional regime of Brussels II, but judicial orders continued to be applied for and made after that date. Charles J faced an unenviable task, not least because the parties appeared in person. His decision is not examined here.

[57] [2004] EWCA Civ 48, [2004] 1 Lloyd's Rep 445. The case was not noted in 2004, on the assumption, plainly wrong, that there was little more to be said about it than was apparent on the face of the court's judgment.

[58] The family company was not a defendant to the first English action.

domestic Greek law for service on defendants out of the jurisdiction. Whether the document ever arrived in Florida is unclear, but attempts made to serve it in London were hampered by the fact that Tavoulareas had given up his former London address many a year long since.[59] The question asked by Article 21 of the Brussels Convention, namely when the Greek courts were seised, would determine whether the English court had jurisdiction. This had to be answered by reference to Greek law as only it could specify the moment at which the Greek proceedings were definitively pending. The Court of Appeal, in reversing Tomlinson J and wrestling, as the judge did, with contradictory and 'partisan' Greek expert evidence, reached the conclusion that the Greek proceedings were not pending until process had been served on Tavoulareas in a manner which met the requirements of the Service Regulation.[60] In other words, having found as a fact that Greek law required service to be made before the proceedings could be said to be definitively pending, and noting that Greece was bound by the Service Regulation, the conclusion followed that proceedings were not pending before the Greek court until service on Tavoulareas had been made in accordance with that Regulation. As this instrument did not allow for the service of Greek proceedings by delivery to the Greek public prosecutor, the Greek court was not seised on the date on which such pretend service was made in Greece. As by the time of service of the English process there had been no such service as met the requirements of the Service Regulation, the Court concluded that the English court was seised first in respect of the first[61] English action. It therefore restored the English proceedings. It deferred consideration of an application for an anti-suit injunction to restrain the Greek proceedings; and when *Turner v Grovit* was decided, it became clear that no such injunction could be granted. Tavoulareas then brought a second action in England, this time against the Tsavliris family company.[62]

Meanwhile in Greece, the local action was still pending. So far as one can tell, the Greek court was apparently informed that Tomlinson J had stayed the first English action but, scarcely credibly, was not told of the Court of Appeal's reversal of that judgment, or of the steps which Tsavliris had been taking to defend it. The Greek court therefore concluded, on woefully incomplete information, that there was no English impediment to its hearing the claim, and rejected the challenge to its jurisdiction. Tsavliris, even less credibly, claimed not to have been informed of the outcome of the jurisdictional challenge in Greece when various applications caused both sets of English proceedings to come back before David Steel J. The judge took the view that the heart of the problem lay in the fact that the Greek court had been kept in the dark about the proceedings in the Court of Appeal. He therefore ordered that

59 It was not denied that he came to have knowledge of it, though.

60 Regulation 1348/2000.

61 And at that date, the only.

62 It appears to have been a serious tactical error not to have done this to begin with.

the Greek court be informed by Tsavliris of the full history of the English proceedings. After some prevarication the letter was sent to the Greek court, which replied in terms which, unless they have gained something in translation, are not inaccurately described as bristling with offended indignation. In due course Andrew Smith J concluded that the first set of English proceedings should indeed still go ahead, as the English court had been seised before the Greek one was; and as to the second English proceedings, concluded that the English court had special jurisdiction over the family company.

This last point was problematic, though. For the Greek courts had been seised of a claim involving the family company, and were therefore arguably seised[63] of a claim founded on this cause of action sooner than was the English court. But the second English action had been commenced after the coming into force of the Judgments Regulation. This, in Article 30, contained its own rule about the date of seisin, which superseded the previous requirement of Greek and of English law that the process be served before the court could be regarded as seised. Andrew Smith J therefore concluded that he had to apply Article 30 of the Regulation, rather than Article 21 of the Brussels Convention, and that according to that, the Greek court was seised first.[64] But he was further troubled by the argument that even though the Greek court was seised first, and was still seised on the date on which the second English action had been commenced, it had since given judgment. He sent the parties away to prepare further submissions; and on receiving these, concluded that once the Greek court had given judgment, its proceedings ceased to be an obstacle in the sense of Article 27. Though the second English proceedings had had to be stayed under Article 27 to begin with, the stay had simply remained in place. As there was no longer an impediment to the English court proceeding to determine the issues raised in the second English proceedings, and though there was an obligation under the Regulation on the English court to consider the recognition of the Greek judgment, there was no impediment to proceeding with the action. It is not clear that the judge was right, though, for Article 27 does not allow a court to stay its proceedings for any longer than is necessary to allow the foreign court to rule on its jurisdiction: once that is done it is required to declare that it has no jurisdiction. But it is hardly his fault that he took a decision which was designed to try and bring the miserable battle to a conclusion.

Also taking no prisoners were the parties in *Advent Capital plc v Ellinas Imports-Exports Ltd*. A contract of insurance provided for the exclusive jurisdiction of the English courts, but the insured, Cypriot entities, brought proceedings against the English insurer in Cyprus, obtaining permission to serve out of Cyprus in open and astonishing breach of the agreement on jurisdiction. The insurers challenged the

[63] Though subject to service.

[64] The failures to complete service in accordance with the Service Regulation not being sufficient to trigger the condition in Art 30, as Tavoulareas had plainly had notice of the Greek proceedings and had appeared in them.

jurisdiction of the Cypriot court;[65] but also brought proceedings in London for an anti-suit injunction. The Cypriot insured disputed the jurisdiction of the English courts to try the claim for an injunction, and contended that the insured had in any event submitted to the jurisdiction of the Cypriot court. Morison J found that the English court did have jurisdiction and that it should be exercised, and granted the injunction. In February 2004 an application was made to the Cypriot courts for the registration and enforcement of the injunction ordered by Morison J.[66] And then on 1 May 2004, Cyprus became a Member State of the EU.

This only breathed new life into the dispute. In May 2004 the Cypriot court dismissed the jurisdictional challenge. In July 2004 the insurers brought separate proceedings in London for a declaration that they had avoided the insurance. The insured challenged the jurisdiction of the English courts, but also applied for the setting aside of the injunction ordered by Morison J on the footing that it was, insofar as it continued to bind the insured after Cyprus became a Member State, inconsistent with the decision of the European Court in *Turner v Grovit*.[67] Colman J stayed the declaratory proceedings by reference to the *lis alibi pendens* provisions in Article 27 of the Judgments Regulation, but rejected the argument that the injunction fell to be set aside once Cyprus became a Member State. There seems little likelihood that this will have brought the parties to their senses, or the proceedings to a close.

The application to set aside the injunction seemed speculative. A final judgment entered at a time when Cyprus was a non-Member State is manifestly immune from the jurisdictional rules of Chapter II of the Judgments Regulation. Nor would an application to enforce it in another Member State be governed by the transitional provisions set out in Chapter VI, which do not extend to judgments given before the Regulation came into effect. Quite apart from that, there is not a shred of authority for the view that judgments, indisputably valid when made, are all liable to be unpicked at the behest of a judgment debtor and required to be re-justified by reference to jurisdictional rules which never applied to them. Colman J was quite right to dismiss such preposterous submissions.

But on the application to stay the second English action, Colman J applied Article 66 of the Regulation. He concluded that as the Cypriot court was in fact seised first, it was required to decide whether it had jurisdiction; and if it did, that the English court was bound to defer to the court first seised. As to this, it is surprising to think that his reasoning may have been correct. Article 66 provides for the recognition or not of judgments given in proceedings instituted before the Regulation came into effect. It imposes a rule to the effect that if the Cypriot court had assumed jurisdiction on the basis of a rule which accorded with the provisions in Chapter II of the Regulation, its judgment is liable to be

[65] Perhaps rather ineptly, for the Cypriot judge took the view that they had actually submitted to the jurisdiction of the Cypriot courts.

[66] It is hard to see how this could have been done.

[67] Case C-159/02, [2004] ECR I-3565.

treated as though Chapter III of the Regulation applied to it. But Article 66 does not provide a rule to deal with *lis alibi pendens*. It does not provide that a court is bound to defer to proceedings which were commenced in a non-Member State if the jurisdiction of that foreign court accords with the provisions of the Regulation. Such a rule may have been a rational one to enact, but it was not enacted. However, that did not stop the European Court, in *Von Horn v Cinnamond*,[68] from reading the predecessor to Article 66 as though it contained a rule on *lis alibi pendens*: that if the jurisdiction of the first court had been taken on the basis of a rule which corresponded to that established in Chapter II of the Regulation, a court seised second was obliged to apply what is now Article 27 and stay or decline jurisdiction. The plain fact that Article 66 does not say this is, in the scheme of the Regulation, irrelevant. A purposive interpretation apparently produces that result.

Colman J should then have asked whether the jurisdiction asserted by the Cypriot court was in accordance with the Regulation. He should surely have said that proceedings brought in a court in open defiance of a written agreement on jurisdiction are not brought on the basis of a rule which accorded with Chapter II of the Regulation, and should have deduced from this that *Von Horn* did not require the English court to give way to the Cypriot proceedings. Instead, he took the view that it was for the Cypriot court to decide whether it had a jurisdiction which was in accord with the Regulation; and if it gave an affirmative answer, that was conclusive. This is terribly wrong. Such reasoning appears to be infected by a virus which prevents a court enquiring into the jurisdiction of another court even when it is required to, and which prevents an English court observing that a foreign court has disregarded an agreement on jurisdiction. But Article 66 is not so limited. Even the European Court in *Von Horn* allowed that, in order to apply Article 66 properly, a court seised second must enquire for itself whether the court seised first took jurisdiction on the basis of a rule which accorded with Chapter II. The text of Article 66 dictates an answer 'if jurisdiction was founded on . . .', which imposes on the second court the right and the obligation to decide whether that condition is satisfied. It does not say 'if the foreign court says that jurisdiction was founded on . . .'; and still less does it say 'if the foreign court had jurisdiction in the same way that the Italian court did in *Erich Gasser GmbH v MISAT srl* . . .'. Colman J was being *plus communautaire que la cour*, and there is no warrant for that.

4. Choice and proof of foreign law in insurance placed on the London market: *King v Brandywine Reinsurance Co*.[69]

The financial aftermath of the Exxon Valdez oil spillage in Alaskan waters in 1989 continues to generate litigation. Exxon was insured under

[68] Case C-163/95, [1997] ECR I-5451.

[69] [2005] EWCA Civ 235, [2005] 1 Lloyd's Rep 655.

a policy which contained a service of suit clause for New York and for all matters to be decided by the law and practice of the court seised; and a provision for arbitration in New York, which was to be effective only if invoked by both sides, and which made no reference to choice of law. Reinsurance was arranged on the London market. A dispute arose in relation to the extent of the cover provided by the reinsurance. To resolve it, the court had first to decide what law governed the insurance in order to determine what Exxon had been entitled to recover from the insurers under it. The contenders were New York law, by making reference to the provision for service of suit; and English law, because the insurance had been placed on the London market. Colman J decided that the insurance was governed by New York law;[70] the Court of Appeal agreed with him. The court further considered that it was entitled to review Colman J's findings on the law of New York, but went on to conclude that he had made no mistake in relation to it.

Insurance placed before it came into effect lies outside the temporal scope of the Rome Convention; choice of law was therefore assessed by reference to the common law rules. The contract of insurance did not choose its own law by express words; and it called into question the weight of two traditional presumptions as to proper law. On the one hand, as the insurance was for all practical purposes negotiated and placed on the London market, and as a long line of authority held that the market in which insurance is placed is a powerful indicator of the governing law, at least where that market is London, there was a strong argument that the proper law was English. But on the other, the provisions for dispute resolution, while not cast in the form of an obligation on all parties to accept arbitration or litigation in New York, came fairly close to being such an obligation; and that supported a strong argument that the proper law was that of New York. As between the two presumptions, the court could not see the general inference derived from the placing of insurance on the London market as being powerful enough to overcome the contrary indications derived from arrangements for dispute resolution. It is hard to say that they were wrong, though as the insurance contained an unusual number of dispute-resolution provisions, all tending to indicate New York if they indicated anything at all, it is unlikely that the decision will be one of general significance, even in the context of insurance. It is unclear whether the answer would have been any different if the question of interpretation on which the case depended were to have been one on which English law diverged from the other potential law. The truth of the case is probably a little different from the analysis offered by the court. The significance of the identity of the market in which insurance is placed is frequently jurisdictional rather than simply a matter of choice of law: if the insurance is governed by English law, England will tend to be the most appropriate forum for the resolution of disputes. In *King* the alternative to England was New York. Though the question of jurisdiction

[70] [2004] Lloyd's Rep IR 554.

did not arise, the case was not one in which there would have been any disadvantage in trying the case in New York, and the difference between New York and English law on a question of construction was not likely to be great. As the court was content that the case was one which belonged in New York, the claim of English as governing law was weakened by the very fact that England was not the proper jurisdiction. The strands in the jurisdictional argument which would have underpinned the case if there had been a jurisdictional dispute appeared to determine the choice of law.

It is sometimes asked whether a choice of dispute resolution should be seen as giving some indication of choice of law, and if so, what sort of indication. English tradition has it that a choice for dispute resolution in a particular place brings with it a clear indication of choice of law; and even in the context of the Rome Convention there is a general perception that this rule of English private international law has survived. Despite this venerable heritage, it has always been a slightly odd piece of reasoning. Agreements on jurisdiction or for arbitration are in several ways ancillary to the performance obligations put in place by the contract. They provide for a solution when what has been agreed to has broken down and the parties move from being insurer and insured and enter into a new form of relationship of litigant and litigant. It is a strange thing to say that because parties made provision for that relationship, it is to be inferred that they intended that tribunal's law to apply to govern all the obligations which were due to be performed to ensure that everything went right and that the question of their becoming litigants would never arise. One could see a respectable argument to the effect that provision for what is to happen when it all goes wrong is not a window into the minds of the parties revealing what they supposed was to happen if it all went right. This is not to say that the proper law should change: that the law of X, but if the parties move to litigate, then the law of Y will be applied. Even if a *lex arbitri* allows a law to be applied in arbitration which was not that which a judge would say governed the contract if he had been asked the question,[71] the law as applied in the courts cannot permit this. But one may question whether the deduction of choice of law from choice of forum should not now be reconsidered, and much less made of it than was once the case. It is now accepted,[72] for example, that a dispute resolution clause is severable from the contract of which it forms a part, for the pragmatic reason that rational parties presumably intended the nominated court or tribunal to have power to adjudicate even if there were a serious question about the main contract. All very sensible; but a clause which is semi-detached from the primary obligations of the

[71] See, eg Arbitration Act 1996, s 46(3).

[72] By statute in the case of arbitration: Arbitration Act 1996, s 7; by the European Court in case C-269/95 *Benincasa v Dentalkit srl* [1997] ECR I-3767. The position in respect of jurisdiction clauses at common law awaits final confirmation, but it is practically certain that the answer will be the same.

contract is rather less obviously a powerful indirect indication of a choice of law. Secondly, it has been accepted in the past that the fact that parties expressed a choice for English law but did not choose English dispute resolution should make a judge hesitate before concluding that the parties wanted English dispute resolution. The reverse is also attractive: if the parties chose English adjudication, one may wonder why they failed to make an express selection of English law: if choice was so in their minds, why should it be nearly supposed that they chose English law? They could have done if they had wanted to; and they did not. That speaks volumes. In this regard, it is surprising to find that Article 3.1 of the Draft Regulation on the law applicable to contractual obligations,[73] contains a presumption that where parties to a contract have made provision for dispute resolution in a particular state, the law of that state shall be presumed to govern the performance obligations of the contract. The explanatory report suggests that one of the changes to be brought about on the conversion of the Rome Convention to a Regulation is that the search for governing law will be for the 'true tacit will' of the parties. If this is so, deduction of this law from the location of the dispute resolution tribunal may be a funny way to go about it.

However, this meant that the question of the extent of Exxon's entitlement under its policy of insurance fell to be decided as a matter of New York law. Colman J made the appropriate finding of fact, and when this was challenged, it was submitted that a finding of fact was not a matter on which the Court of Appeal was entitled to substitute a view of its own. But the Court of Appeal had previously decided that findings of foreign law made for a rather special kind of fact and that the usual view of such matters as something for the primary judge did not apply in the same way. Plenty of cases exist in which an appellate tribunal has re-examined the evidence given below on the content of foreign law. It is far too late, and far too doctrinaire, to argue that this power should be closed to it.

5. Obtaining an anti-suit injunction: *Seismic Shipping Inc v Total E & P UK plc*,[74] *CNA Insurance Co Ltd v Office Depot International*,[75] *Tonicstar Ltd v American Home Assurance Co*.[76]

If the right to obtain an anti-suit injunction is dependent on something other than a legal right not to be sued in the foreign court, it has to be on the basis that the acts which the respondent is carrying out, or threatening to carry out, are wrongful in some other sense of wrongful. That wrongfulness may be found in vexation or oppression of the applicant, or

[73] COM (2005) 650.
[74] [2005] EWCA Civ 985, [2005] 2 Lloyd's Rep 359: Clarke, Rix LJJ; Sir Martin Nourse.
[75] [2005] EWHC 456 (Comm): [2005] Lloyd's Rep IR 658: Langley J.
[76] [2004] EWHC 1234 (Comm), [2005] Lloyd's Rep IR 32: Morison J.

in other forms of unconscionable dealing aimed at the applicant. It may also be found in activity which undermines the jurisdiction of the English court over a matter before it.[77] There are no neat lines of division separating these grounds for relief, which avoids much anxious classification, but the overlapping of these species of wrongdoing does sometimes make for a lack of clarity of view. *Seismic Shipping Inc v Total E & P UK plc* is a good illustration of the problems this can cause; but the three cases noted for this year show that some underpinnings of principle are in place and are discernible.

In *Seismic Shipping* the owners' vessel negligently collided with an oil drilling rig in the North Sea, doing considerable damage. The owners brought proceedings in England for a decree of limitation against all interested parties (which meant only Total), and this was granted by the judge.[78] But he refused an application by the owners for an injunction to restrain Total, the only party with a claim for damages against the owners, from bringing proceedings for damages in Texas. Total appealed on the ground that there was, as they said, no jurisdiction to make a decree of limitation where the substantive claim for damages to be limited was not brought in England. On this point the Court of Appeal, having construed the Convention on Limitation of Liability for Maritime Claims 1976,[79] agreed with the judge that there was no such restriction as that argued for by Total. But the owners, having held onto their decree, wanted more. They appealed against the refusal to order an injunction, contending that though there was no breach of contract in the owners proceeding before the Texan courts, it was otherwise wrongful for Total to take proceedings after the English courts had issued a decree of limitation.

The approach of the court was interesting. Clarke LJ, with whom Rix LJ and Sir Martin Nourse agreed, took the view that the owners needed to show that the conduct of Total was vexatious or oppressive, and that they could not do so. He rejected[80] a submission that the Texas proceedings could be seen as an attempt to subvert the judgment of the English court, as the owners had no inherent right to have the English decree recognized by a foreign court. It was, he thought, up to the Texas courts to decide for themselves what effect, if any, to give to the English limitation decree, and it was wrong to suppose that the English limitation decree attached to and restricted the right of Total to recover damages. The English court's judgment decreeing limitation did not have international legs, or if it did, it was for the Texas court to say so. Motivated by a concern, increasingly frequently heard, that the court should exercise self-restraint, observe comity, and so forth, especially in a case in which there had been no promise by Total to do otherwise than it was proposing to do, the judge's refusal to order an injunction was approved.

[77] *Turner v Grovit* [2002] 1 WLR 107 (HL).
[78] [2005] EWHC 460 (Comm), [2005] 2 All ER (Comm) 51.
[79] Merchant Shipping Act 1995, Sch 7. [80] At para 47.

In practical terms, the judgment is probably right. To begin with, nothing on foot in Texas was designed to prevent proceedings before the English courts from running their natural course; indeed, they had run that course. The notion of 'undermining' the jurisdiction of the court could not easily be stretched to mean that once an English court had ruled on the issues before it, the parties to that litigation and judgment, wherever in the world they were, were under some form of obligation to act only in accordance with that judgment. Something similar had been raised in *ED & F Man (Sugar) Ltd v Haryanto (No 2)*[81] where breach of contract proceedings involving Haryanto, an Indonesian, had been settled. Some time thereafter, Haryanto had brought a fresh claim before his home court, obtaining a judgment annulling the underlying contract and the settlement. An attempt to obtain an injunction to restrain Haryanto from making an attempt to enforce his Indonesian judgment was advanced on the footing that it was, in effect, an attempt to subvert the earlier English decision; the Court of Appeal did not accede to the argument. It concluded that it was up to any foreign court before which Man and Haryanto joined issue to work out for itself what to make of the conflicting judgments, and it was not for the English court to pre-empt their decision. The principle in *Haryanto* would have sufficed to justify the English court in refusing to intervene: the English courts were not in a position to lay down the law for the rest of the world.

It would have been different if the English proceedings had been in a court whose jurisdiction had been agreed to by contract. It could then have been fairly said that an attempt by Total then to bring proceedings elsewhere should be restrained as a breach of contract. That would be orthodox, even though it raises the question of whether the promise made by a party to contracts for the jurisdiction of a court also contains a promise to obey the judgment and not to take steps to resist its enforcement. That question has been raised elsewhere,[82] but receives no illumination from *Seismic Shipping*. In the case itself, the jurisdiction of the English court over Total was based on their being present within the jurisdiction; their objection to the proceedings in England was jurisdictional only in the sense that they contested the proper interpretation of the 1976 Convention. Otherwise they were subject to the court's personal jurisdiction by reason of presence, and participated before the court only to object to the limitation proceedings and to oppose the application for an injunction. It is important that the English proceedings were simply for a decree of limitation, not for a determination of liability; and they were brought against,[83] and not by, Total.

[81] [1991] 1 Lloyd's Rep 429 (CA), rather unexpectedly not referred to in the proceedings.

[82] (2004) 8 *Singapore Year Book of International Law* 1.

[83] In some sense, they are not brought against any individual potential claimant, but as against them all. But as Total was the only potential claimant, it is not unrealistic to regard the proceedings for a decree as brought 'against' Total.

In *CNA Insurance Co Ltd v Office Depot International* the court took the view that if the defendant had submitted by appearance in the English proceedings, any subsequent attempt by it to act on a change of mind and start proceedings elsewhere was to be regarded as 'unprecedented'[84] and as liable to restraint. An insurance dispute had been brought before the English courts and, after some considerable jurisdictional skirmishing, had resulted in the English proceedings making their slow way toward trial. After a period of two years or so, however, the insureds changed tack and decided to launch proceedings of their own in Florida, apparently because of a change in perception of where their interests would be best served. They abandoned part of the allegations they had made in the English proceedings against them, seeking to put some distance between their Floridan and the English proceedings; and applied very late indeed for a stay of the English proceedings. The insurers contended that the stay application was made far too late; and applied for an anti-suit injunction. All commercial tactical considerations aside, the behaviour of the insureds was pretty brazen; and Langley J was having none of it. He observed that the insureds had submitted by participation in the English proceedings, and that the application for a stay was made far too late in the day. He considered the behaviour as oppressive or vexatious, and ordered an anti-suit injunction. It was, one notes, of no apparent concern to him to wonder how this would strike the Florida judge.

The point on which the decision turned was that the insured had, in some decisive way, consented to the jurisdiction of the English courts, and having consented, could not rescind or resile from that consent. The case is therefore crucially different from *Seismic Shipping* in that Total had participated in England only in relation to the claim for a limitation decree, and then to oppose the very idea of it: there had never been proceedings in England to ascertain the existence or non-existence of liability, still less any proceedings brought by Total. It could not be said that Total had opted to claim damages in England. The fact that the amount of the limitation fund had been ordered by the judge to be paid to Total, and had been paid to them, did not cross a line: Total had not asked for it,[85] though they had not apparently sent the cheque back, which must have brought them a little close to the edge. In the end the two cases illuminate the broad proposition that where the respondent has opted into or otherwise consented to proceedings to determine liability before the English courts, there will be a clear basis for a judge to take the view that the decision is irreversible, and that the defendant is in much the same position as if he had contracted for the jurisdiction of the English courts all along. Consent and the absence of consent are the touchstone for relief.

We need to say a little about *Tonicstar Ltd v American Home Assurance Co*. Reinsurance was arranged on the London market and though it did

[84] At para 1. Unprecedented it may be, but it has certainly been seen before.

[85] *Seismic Shipping* (n 74 above) at para 53.

not provide for dispute resolution in London, or provide that English was the applicable law, Morison J had little doubt that the latter was well-established, with the result that England would be the natural forum for the litigation. A significant degree of manoeuvring took place, with proceedings being commenced and then abandoned in the United States. The position in England was that proceedings were then begun by the reinsurers, and an application was made for a stay for arbitration by the reinsured. But some considerable time later, the reinsured also brought proceedings in New York for an order that there be arbitration, believing that the New York court would determine the seat of the arbitration in a fashion more agreeable to them. It was supposed by Morison J that the strategy was then to ask the New York court to restrain the reinsurers from their proceedings in London. According to the judge, the effect of the New York proceedings was 'to seek to pre-empt this court from reaching its own decisions',[86] which was so intolerable that it should be labelled as vexatious and restrained by injunction. Again, the irony of the fact that involved dishing out to the New York court the very same treatment as that apprehended by Morison J went unmentioned; the indignant decision of Langley J in *General Star International Indemnity Ltd v Sterling Cooke Brown Reinsurance Brokers Ltd*[87] was cited and applied without significant pause for thought.

How very odd this is. What the judge should have done was to ask whether the insured had, by their previous conduct before the English court, consented to the jurisdiction of the English court. If they had, it was certainly vexatious for them to try and start all over again somewhere else; but if they had not, and had simply participated in England to object to the jurisdiction of the English court, it is very much harder to see how fault could have been found in their behaviour. Instead, to focus on the impact of the insurers' behaviour on the English court's sense of *amour propre* shows the hollowness of the truth—even if it is a truth—that injunctions are aimed at wrongdoers only, and not at courts: the English courts appear to be willing to issue an injunction on the very ground (that their jurisdiction is being interfered with) which they deny is a reason for not ordering one (that is, that their order does not interfere with the jurisdiction of the foreign court). Hypocrisy is an unattractive characteristic, even when pressed into service to try and make litigants behave properly. Morison J was on slightly safer ground when he declined to find that the reinsurers put themselves out of court by suing in England without a letter before action, or by bringing a claim for declaratory relief. He knew perfectly well that the reinsured were kicking themselves for having taken their eye off the ball, and that if the boot had been on the other foot the arguments would have been just the same.

[86] At para 13.

[87] [2003] EWHC 3 (Comm); noted (2003) 74 BYIL 528. It is, of course, also to be noted that Langley J expressed no concern for the view of the Florida judge when ordering an injunction in *Tonicstar Ltd*.

The judge's instinct was that there should be an orderly resolution of the question of whether there was a binding agreement to arbitrate, and if so where its seat should be, and that he should decide it and no one else should be asked to. He was not, unlike the Court of Appeal in *Seismic Shipping*, prepared to decide the question of jurisdiction over his own action and then leave it to the court in New York to work out what to do next. But he did not appear to analyse the case in terms of whether the respondents had made an election to which they should be held. His concern was instead for an orderly resolution of proceedings.

If a party has appeared before an English court for something other than a challenge to the jurisdiction, it is perfectly sensible that he has, by his conduct, opted to litigate in England; and that for him to try and undermine that election, and to try and do better elsewhere, is wrongful and liable to restraint. It cannot be the law that when a litigant sees the way the tide is running, he can dash off to another court and try again for a better result. That was the perception which triggered the avalanche in *The Atlantic Star*,[88] and it still makes admirable sense. It memorably motivated the court to grant an anti-suit injunction in *Glencore International AG v Exter Shipping Ltd*,[89] and the same principle was used to doubt the availability of an anti-suit injunction in a case in which there had been submission to a foreign court, in *Advent Capital plc v GN Ellinas Importers-Exporters Ltd*.[90] It goes to show why there is, and why there should be, a world of difference between the jurisdictionally-consenting and the jurisdictionally-unconsenting litigant;[91] and why a conscious decision to fight in a particular court should be a strong reason for holding the litigant to his choice. *Seismic Shipping* and *CNA Insurance* stand for that proposition. For that the decisions are welcome. It is rather harder to applaud the decision in *Tonicstar*, which seems to find its justification in more immediately orthodox, but much less compelling, material.

6. Jurisdiction over cross-border defamation: *Jameel v Dow Jones & Co Inc*.[92]

Sanity may be slowly returning to the private international law of defamation. For the last five years we have noted[93] how savvy claimants who considered themselves to have been injured by words uttered overseas, but who saw with perfect clarity the further humiliation which would have resulted from unsuccessful litigation there, made common cause with the

[88] [1974] AC 436.

[89] [2002] EWCA Civ 528, [2002] 2 All ER (Comm) 1.

[90] [2003] EWHC 3330 (Comm), [2004] ILPr 377 (though holding that there had, in fact, been no deliberate submission to the Cypriot court).

[91] In a close context, see also Briggs, (2004) 8 *Singapore Year Book Of International Law* 1.

[92] [2005] EWCA Civ 75, [2005] QB 946: Lord Phillips of Worth Matravers MR; Sedley, Jonathan Parker LJJ.

[93] Most recently in (2004) 75 BYIL 565.

defamation bar to bring their claims in London. All they needed to aver was a reader in England who could be presumed to hold the claimant in hatred, ridicule, and contempt, and the result was a completed English tort. All English defamations are governed by English domestic law,[94] and the only appropriate place to litigate a tort committed in England and governed by English law was England. This development would have been bad enough, but it came at the same time as[95] the development of the world wide web, so making it almost inconceivable that a story of any interest should find no readership in England. These two elements then combined to make a hybrid of peculiar virulence, which exploded into a pandemic of defamation litigation. This time last year, no cure was in sight, and claims displaying the most egregious opportunism continued to be launched in the Queen's Bench Division. But 2005 began and ended with signs that the development of an antidote was not as far away as we had feared. If it arrives it will be not a moment too soon.

The objection to these claims is three-fold. First, they clutter up the English courts with claims which should never be there in the first place; indeed, many of them should never be anywhere in the first place, but the proposition that they have anything proper to do with England is risible. Secondly, the impact of the English law of defamation, one of the common law's more primitive torts, on free speech and honest debate is bad enough when it stifles comment in England. But project it into an overseas environment and it is utterly malign. Thirdly, it proceeds on the basis of a terribly artificial analysis. It is supposed that each time a reader reads there is a new tort, separate and distinct from those involving every other reader. Each time in a particular country a reader reads, the claimant sustains a new wound, and the damage done is to his English, Russian, or Victorian reputation, as the case may be. If the claim is restricted to the damage done to his 'English reputation', this represents damage done to a peculiarly English thing or a uniquely English interest. To put it another way, the claimant has as many reputations as there are countries in which a single person may recognize his or her name. It is absurd.

The progenitor of this madness was Friedrich Herzog von Braunschweig-Wolfenbüttel, a German aristocrat then exiled in London, who sent a manservant to buy a seventeen-year-old copy of an English newspaper in which an apparent libel was written. Despite the fact that only the servant, if literate at all, read the story, the Duke managed to obtain damages from the publisher for a sum, measured in today's money, in excess of a quarter of a million pounds.[96] The internet breathed life

[94] As the Private International Law (Miscellaneous Provisions) Act 1995, s 13 exempts defamation from the choice of law rules otherwise established by the Act.

[95] Or just prior to: though the claim in *Berezovsky v Michaels* [2000] 1 WLR 1004 concerned the print media, the House of Lords noted that the application of the material principles to such statements uttered on the world wide web had not arisen for analysis or decision.

[96] He was awarded damages of £500. For the equivalent purchasing power of the pound, see <http://web.ukonline.co.uk/thursday.handleigh/demography/occupations-wages-money/purchase-power/purchase-power-2.htm>.

into this horrible precedent, and led to some truly grotesque awards of damages. So when Jameel, a Saudi Arabian businessman, was libelled in the e-pages of the *Wall Street Journal*, he too sued in London. He claimed that there were records which showed seven readers to have accessed the story online from computers in England, and that this allowed him to claim relief in respect of seven English torts. That he chose not to raise a claim in respect of publication elsewhere was *nihil ad rem*. Dow Jones, publisher of the offending article, applied to have the claim struck out. They must have been rather surprised to succeed. For though the Court of Appeal was clearly constrained by authority to allow the claim to be advanced as an English tort it accepted a submission that the proceedings were an abuse of the process of the court, and disposed of them on that basis.[97]

It is not the first time that perceived deficiencies in the rules of the conflict of laws have been supplemented by a court finding an argument, technically unimpeachable, to be an abuse of the process of the court. In the context of judgment debtors, whose complaint against the recognition of a foreign judgment was that it had been procured by fraud, some judges have reacted against the right to ventilate an issue[98] as one of fraud by branding it an abuse of process.[99] It is still a worry that this reaction, understandable as it is, runs the risk of flattening the clear and careful rules on foreign judgments with the juggernaut, impatiently driven by judges, of procedural control. So here: the proposition that Jameel was abusing the process of the court simply allowed the Court of Appeal to side-step the work of its own hand. It acknowledged that other cases, starting with *Duke of Brunswick v Harmer*, would have been decided differently if this principle had been applied to them, but simply observed that such a submission had not been made in those cases, and that precedent therefore furnished no insuperable objection.

So what made it an abuse of process for Jameel to complain in England of what was read in England? The court said that the test to be applied would be the one which would have arisen had Dow Jones chosen to challenge the jurisdiction:[100] that there was a real and substantial tort committed within the jurisdiction. It is not clear what answer it gave, because it was bound to accept that the tort, such as it was, was committed within the jurisdiction. But it appears that it was not considered to be real and substantial, this finding resting on the proposition that if Jameel wanted vindication of his reputation by decision of an English court, this was incapable of achievement. The court would not declare the statement to

[97] One may have supposed that the proper order was that the proceedings be struck out. But the court ordered a stay, presumably on the footing that another judgment in the same matter, reported as [2005] EWCA Civ 74, [2005] QB 904, is under appeal to the House of Lords, and that a stay was therefore more appropriate.

[98] Or to litigate an issue which should properly have been raised elsewhere and previously.

[99] *Owens Bank Ltd v Etoile Commerciale SA* [1995] 1 WLR 44 (PC).

[100] Which presumably means on an application under CPR Part 11 to challenge the jurisdiction of the court invoked by an application for permission to serve process out of the jurisdiction.

have been libellously false; any damages would be modest and far less than the costs incurred in litigating the claim; and judges have better things to do with their time. The aim of Jameel could not be accomplished by the proceedings he brought; they were therefore abusive.

The proposition that the proceedings were an abuse because even if they were successful, they could not accomplish what Jameel hoped to achieve is an extraordinary one. Many litigants hope that the decision of a court will bring about a state of affairs which is simply incapable of being achieved; and to accuse each of them of abusing the process of the court would be a very strong thing. It cannot be enough that Jameel would not have his reputation restored by the verdict of the English court. Indeed, most libel claimants will accept that mud sticks, even after a verdict in their favour, and that after the publication of a libel they remain damaged. But they will not be accused of abusing the process of the court. Jameel seems to have attracted such opprobrium for reasons which are peculiar to himself, and into these it is not wise to trespass. So does this represent the right way to turn the tide, and to prevent libel tourists filling up the courts?

The Department of Constitutional Affairs seems to think not. According to a news story published at the end of the year in the *Guardian* newspaper,[101] it was reported that the government was to initiate a project to reverse the tide of libel tourism by legislation. One has to say that, the judges having led themselves first into a cul-de-sac, and then us all into dangerously uncharted territory, this may well be the best solution. Though the House of Lords is free to reverse its decision in *Berezovsky v Michaels*, and accept that publication in England of a tiny fraction of a print run does not give rise to a tort committed in England and actionable as such, there is no good reason to allow claimants in the meantime to enjoy the sport of persecuting foreign news agencies or newspapers. Swift and effective legislation should establish that such artfully-contrived fragments of claims should be brought where the whole of the claim belongs, whether this is England or elsewhere, and whether or not the claimant will win there, and that should be that. It may not be the most elegant of solutions, but given the mess which the judges have contrived to make of the law, it is by far the best one.

7. Choice of law in restitution and the role of renvoi: *Barros Mattos Jr v MacDaniels*.[102]

A Brazilian bank was defrauded of gigantic sums by a group of Nigerian criminals, some of whom were of Indian origin. The money, in the form of notional US dollars, sped through a series of bank accounts, but a

[101] <http://technology.guardian.co.uk/news/story/0,16559,1674047,00.html>.
[102] [2005] EWHC 1323 (Ch), [2005] ILPr 630; Lawrence Collins J.

significant slice of it arrived in Swiss bank accounts held in the name of one Asnani. He was duly tried and convicted of money laundering by a criminal court in Geneva. Proceedings were brought by the bank[103] in relation to sums paid by Asnani from his Swiss account to another Swiss bank account in the name of Vaswani, another Indian carrying on business in Nigeria under conditions of tight exchange control. Proceedings of elaborate complexity were begun against Vaswani who, after failing in a challenge to the jurisdiction of the court, admitted the underlying fraud of Asnani but pleaded that the purchase of dollars by him was an ordinary incident of commerce in Nigeria. In due course the claimants applied for summary judgment against Vaswani on the footing that even if he were innocent and ignorant of the fraud of Asnani, the money in his bank account could be traced and recovered from him, as the circumstances of its receipt made it unconscionable for him to retain it. But as the process of pleading progressed, Vaswani asserted that the claim against him was governed by Swiss law, under which the claim to trace the money would fail. By way of answer it was pleaded by the bank that Nigerian, rather than Swiss law, should govern, as the transaction was really a Nigerian operation simply being processed through Switzerland; and that if this submission failed, and Swiss law were to be applied, this should be taken to mean Swiss law including its conflicts rules,[104] which would point in turn to the application of Nigerian domestic[105] law. But matters were not helped by the nature of the written expert evidence on foreign law which was voluminous but not obviously responsive in nature: each side said what it wanted to say, as if it were the only evidence to be given to the court. By the time the case came before the judge, the application for summary judgment had been withdrawn, but an application for permission to amend required the judge to examine whether the proposed amendments ought to be allowed. This required him to grapple with choice of law as it applied to the issues presented by the claim.

He had therefore to deal with the peculiar state of English private international law on restitutionary claims. The law is in a state of complex contradiction. Dicey and Morris state a Rule which selects the proper law of the obligation to make restitution, and a sub-Rule which favours the law of the place of the enrichment,[106] but the editors also comment that though this formulation has been judicially approved, there will be many cases in which it does not identify the law which has

[103] In fact, the shareholders of the bank: the bank had been sold by its shareholders, who had reimbursed the bank for the losses it had sustained and had taken an assignment of the claims which the bank had against the fraudsters.

[104] Private International Law Act, Art 133 dealing with tort claims in which there is no choice of law by the parties.

[105] It appears to have been accepted that Swiss private international law would have made the limitation to Nigerian domestic law clear: Swiss Private International Law Act, Arts 128, 129; judgment at paras 106–108.

[106] *The Conflict of Laws* (13th edn, 2000), Rule 200; Rule 200(2)(c). In the 14th edn (2006) it is Rule 230.

the closest connection to the obligation to make restitution, and it is to be inferred from this that they would not die in a ditch to defend the sub-Rule. The case law on restitutionary claims comprises some which approve the rule but then fail to apply it on the ground that the claim is not really restitutionary, and some which express no view about the rule but still reach conclusions consistent with it. The judge's summary[107] of the state of the law is helpful in demonstrating the lack of clear guidance; it is also clear that no authoritative solution has yet been developed. The narrow problem is that 'receipt-based' claims for restitution may make sense as a category in the domestic law of restitution, but such a term of art still has to justify its utility as an organizing principle in the conflict of laws.[108] The broader problem is that restitutionary claims may arise in connection with wrongs, for which a statutory choice of law rule now exists,[109] or in connection with relationships which are, or are akin to, contracts, for which a separate choice of law rule exists. Domestic English law on recovery of the proceeds of fraud is in part a creature of the common law, but in greater part an area of equitable doctrine and remedy; and there is within equity a degree of resistance to being governed by rules on choice of law at all.[110] Leaven that with the observation that, in the opinion of most, the common law method allows claimants to pick and choose choice of law rules[111] and one can only observe that until the House of Lords is presented with a case in which it can lay down the law once and for all,[112] the result will never be one of clear and satisfying precedent.

The judge was therefore faced with a case in which the choice of law rules were mired in uncertainty and in which the evidence of foreign law called to mind the image of ships which pass in the night. He therefore declined to decide the question of choice of law, preferring instead to allow it to go off to trial. But he noted that the mechanical application of the law of the place of enrichment was unsupported by any authority worthy of the name, and that the present case—a scam in which Nigerians bought and sold dollars for Nigerian currency, but where the dollars were to be delivered in Switzerland—was perhaps one where the application of the law of the place of enrichment was not obviously appropriate. He did not say, though perhaps he might have, that the place of enrichment is itself a rather tricky one to pin down when cases involve the electronic transfer of funds, and that in the end the result may not justify the effort involved in reaching it. Maybe in a couple of years' time, if the claim ever comes to be tried and the decision appealed, we will know better than we currently do.

107 At paras 84–105.

108 See *Macmillan v Bishopsgate Investment Trust plc (No 3)* [1996] 1 WLR 387.

109 Private International Law (Miscellaneous Provisions) Act 1995, Part III.

110 For a superlative analysis, Yeo, *Equity in the Conflict of Laws* (2004).

111 See in particular, *Base Metal Trading Ltd v Shamurin* [2005] 1 WLR 1157 (noted (2004) 75 BYIL 572).

112 Even then, legislation from the organs of the EU is to be anticipated.

The judge was equally non-committal on the question of whether any application of Swiss law would have involved a choice of its domestic or its private international law. Again, the expert evidence on Swiss law lacked the clarity needed to show the judge that he had a choice to make: it was not clear that a Swiss judge, dealing with the claim in Geneva, would apply the law of Nigeria to it. He referred[113] to the hostility to renvoi exhibited by its treatment in Dicey and Morris, but without specifically associating himself with it. This may have been wise, for later in the year, the High Court of Australia decided that renvoi was an integral part of Australian choice of law rules for overseas tort.[114] In *Neilson v Overseas Projects Corp of Victoria Ltd*[115] a majority[116] of the High Court accepted that where a tort had taken place in China, and the evidence showed that a Chinese judge dealing with the claim would have applied Australian law as the law of the common nationality, an Australian court should do likewise. Renvoi was seen as contributing to the broad and dominant aim of applying to a claim in tort the law which would be applied by a court at the place of the tort. The court declined to take a doctrinaire view for or against renvoi in all cases, and declined to be hypnotized by prospect of being trapped inside a 'hall of mirrors'[117] which the doctrine of total renvoi may appear to generate when both legal systems implicated in a given case would apply that same principle: the majority preferred to take the view that if the Chinese judge would have tried to apply the law which the Australian judge would have, the Australian court will simply apply its own domestic law.[118] Its decision is a wonderful example of common law pragmatism, of incorporating renvoi where it will do more perfect justice, and eschewing any grander ambitions. Were such an approach to be taken to the claim in *Barros Mattos*, it is hard to see why one would rationally object to the application of Swiss law including any applicable rule of Swiss private international law. If the choice of law rules for restitution lead to the conclusion that the law of Switzerland is to be applied, and there is nothing in the analysis which suggests that this should be interpreted as limited to Swiss domestic law—there was no express choice[119] of Swiss law by the

[113] At para 108.

[114] As a matter of English common law, renvoi had never been clearly adopted as part as the choice of law for claims in tort.

[115] [2005] HCA 54, (2005) 79 ALJR 1736. For comment, see Briggs, [2006] LMCLQ 1.

[116] By 6 to 1. The majority was 5 to 2 on the question of whether the rules of Chinese law had been sufficiently established by evidence for an Australian judge to apply them.

[117] The image is that of McHugh J, who dissented.

[118] Adopting the solution proposed by Scrutton LJ in *Casdagli v Casdagli* [1918] P 89.

[119] If parties have expressed a choice of law to govern a contract, for example, there is every reason to interpret that as a choice of the domestic law of the country concerned. But where the applicable law is identified on the basis of closeness of connection, the parties not having turned their minds to it in advance of the dispute arising, the incentive to limit the choice of law to the domestic law of the country concerned is much reduced, and competing concerns, such as the need to discourage forum shopping, may then be taken into account.

parties, for example—it may be appropriate to read this as the law which a Swiss court would have applied if it had been hearing the case. The use of renvoi will tend to discourage forum shopping, which is a sufficient justification for it. If the court trying *Barros Mattos* comes to the conclusion, first, that the connection with Switzerland outweighs the connection with Nigeria, so that the choice of law will be for Swiss law, but second, that the evidence is that a Swiss court would have applied Nigerian law, it is not irrational for English law to do likewise and apply Nigerian law. Whether this is attributed to the doctrine of renvoi, or to the refinement of rules for choice of law, or to some form of governmental interest analysis of choice of law rules, which leads to the conclusion that there is a false conflict of choice of law, may not matter as much as the need to secure the most rational outcome to the claim to establish liability.

8. Acquisition of domicile by unlawful means: *Mark v Mark*.[120]

Can an illegal overstayer acquire a domicile of choice in England sufficient to allow her to petition for divorce ? Section 5 of the Domicile and Matrimonial Proceedings Act 1973 gave the English court jurisdiction to dissolve the marriage if (among other things) either party was domiciled in England, or had been habitually resident for a year prior to the institution of proceedings. Mrs Mark, who had overstayed her permission to remain in the United Kingdom, had brought proceedings to divorce her husband who had returned to Nigeria from where both hailed. Hughes J held that the wife had established a domicile of choice; the Court of Appeal[121] went further and added that she had also shown a year's habitual residence in England, all notwithstanding the illegality of her presence in the country. The House of Lords dismissed the husband's further appeal, and accepted that the wife satisfied each of the jurisdictional grounds set out in section 5. That she was present in the United Kingdom illegally was not decisive against her, and may not even have been relevant.

The sources of the submission that illegal presence in the United Kingdom was incompatible with the acquisition of an English domicile were two in number. As a matter of judicial authority, the Court of Appeal had said as much in *Puttick v AG*, when a member of a German terrorist organization, the Baader–Meinhof Group, sought a declaration that she was married to an English husband, the better to resist her deportation to Germany. The court, in a judgment dripping with

[120] [2005] UKHL 42, [2006] 1 AC 98: Lord Nicholls of Birkenhead, Lord Hoffmann, Lord Hope of Craighead, Lord Phillips of Worth Matravers, and Baroness Hale of Richmond.

[121] [2004] EWCA Civ 168, [2005] Fam 267.

distaste, declined to make the declaration, on grounds which included the proposition that as the applicant, Proll, had entered the United Kingdom fraudulently and illegally, she could not acquire the English domicile which was a necessary ground for the declaratory jurisdiction of the court. Dicey and Morris observed, in editions which pre-dated *Puttick*, the observation being approved in that case, that 'it has been held' that illegal residence in the United Kingdom prevented the acquisition of a domicile of choice in England, also noting that it was unclear whether this would also apply to those who took up residence in other countries illegally. The significance of this formulation, understood by those on the inside to convey that 'it has been, but should not have been, held' was missed by the court in *Puttick*, and by Baroness Hale who simply expressed disagreement with the Dicey formulation.[122]

It is now clear that illegality in the satisfaction of the requirements for a domicile of choice is irrelevant: bogus asylum seekers, those entering with fraudulent documents, those coming to the country to traffic young girls for the sex trade, none will necessarily be found to lack what it takes to establish a domicile of choice in England. All that is required, in addition to residence, is an intention to remain indefinitely. This intention is not affected by the fact, if it is a fact, that the propositus will be required to apply for permission to act on his or her intention: an intention is an intention is an intention. It follows that domicile at common law may overlap with, but is certainly not dependent upon, the propositus' having a right to reside in the country. If this leads to results which are just too unpalatable, a rule of public policy may save the court from having to draw a conclusion which just sticks in the judicial throat, though Baroness Hale[123] may be read as casting doubt on the possibility of making any recourse to public policy at all. Domicile stands for the existence of a connection between the individual and a legal system by reference to which certain rights and liabilities are defined. The connection is neither a privilege nor a liability, but a legal fact.

The analysis of the court, which led it to the conclusion that the wife had established a domicile of choice in England was, however, misleading. The wife had not entered the country illegally, but had done so pursuant to limited permission granted by the immigration authorities. It was open to her to establish a domicile of choice in England at that stage, or when later she decided (as was apparently[124] the case) to remain in England. When she failed to leave the country her residence became illegal but she had not entered the country illegally. She was not, therefore, in the same position as the petitioner in *Puttick*, who had

[122] Which only goes to show that the editors of Dicey and Morris rather brought it on themselves.
[123] At para 47.
[124] Baroness Hale said so at para 48, without seeming to attach significance to the point.

used false papers to deceive the immigration officer in the first place. Had the decision in *Mark* been that the wife had no English domicile of choice because of her change of status from legal resident to illegal overstayer, it would have opened the way to the argument that the domicile of choice had been lost. But it is hornbook law that one can lose a domicile of choice, otherwise than by supplanting it with another, only by abandoning residence and abandoning the intention to reside indefinitely. To hold that the wife had forfeited the right to claim that she was resident in England would not have sufficed to deprive her of a domicile of choice which she was, like countless refugees from oppression before her, perfectly entitled to establish the moment she set foot on English soil. It was therefore very hard to see how she could be found to lack a domicile of choice unless there were to be a rule that as soon as someone with an English domicile of choice commits a crime, he or she loses that domicile, by operation of law. Such a rule could not possibly be supported. If, as may have been the case, the wife had not established the intention to remain indefinitely[125] until she was an overstayer, any conclusion that she failed to establish a domicile of choice would have to be rested on the proposition that she did not intend to remain, or was not present as a resident. Neither would be remotely defensible, because neither would be remotely true. The intention would not be contradicted by the fact that the propositus knew of his or her vulnerability to deportation, for the same has long been true for all refugees, who still obtain domiciles of choice in England. The presence-as-resident would not be contradicted, and this for precisely the same reason.

It was a shame that Baroness Hale passed up the opportunity to examine one objectionable element of the common law of domicile. Ever since Cook's great essay on the topic,[126] there has been a basis for challenging the view that domicile in its common law sense means the same thing in every context in which it serves as the connecting factor: liability to taxes, capacity to marry, ability to dispose of property by will, and so forth. Cook submitted that if domicile meant no more than a sufficient connection for the purposes of the legal rule in question, it was at least arguable that the common law should be flexible enough to define domicile according to its context. But Baroness Hale dismissed this argument without mentioning the existence of the debate.[127] Given that the Law Commission and the government have, in effect, given up on the statutory reform of domicile, the way was open for the House of Lords to re-examine some of the fundamentals of the law. But this one went untouched.

[125] At para 48 Baroness Hale speaks of the intention to remain *permanently* rather than *indefinitely*, which must be understood as a statement of fact rather than a requirement of the law of domicile.

[126] Cook, *The Logical & Legal Base of the Conflict of Laws* (1942) 194.

[127] At para 37.

9. Co-operation between courts in international insolvency: *Re T & N Ltd*,[128] *Re HIH Casualty and General Insurance Ltd, McMahon v McGrath*,[129] *Al Sabah v Grupo Torras SA*,[130] *Re Cambridge Gas Transport Corp.*[131]

Ten years ago, in *Re Bank of Credit and Commerce International SA (No 10)*,[132] Scott V-C noticed something strange. In that case, a Luxembourg-based bank had collapsed in fraud and insolvency, and proceedings were under way in Luxembourg to wind it up and sort out the mess. An insolvent liquidation was under way in England, in relation to assets and creditors within the jurisdiction of the English court. Taking the rational view that sorting out the wreckage of the affairs of the bank was better served by a coordinated approach to the liquidation, the English liquidators sought directions as to whether they should remit the English assets to the Luxembourg liquidator, so as to be part of a single distribution. The objection to this, raised on behalf of some creditors, was that English insolvency law allowed creditors to set off in full amounts owed by them to the insolvent, and to prove only for the balance. Luxembourg law did not allow this; and therefore those creditors who sought to prove in the English insolvency were at risk of disadvantage if they were left to the similar-but-different insolvency regime of Luxembourg law.

Scott V-C observed that the idea had got about that, in circumstances such as the present, the English insolvency was to be regarded as ancillary to the insolvency in the centre of the bank's operations, and that a consequence of this was that certain provisions of English insolvency law would be overlooked or set aside, in the interests of a single and coordinated administration. For example, earlier in the BCCI litigation, Dillon LJ had said:[133] 'As I see it, in a liquidation there can be a departure from the *pari passu* rule by a scheme of arrangement under section 425 [of the Companies Act 1985]; but, equally, there can be a departure from the *pari passu* rule if it is merely ancillary to an exercise of any of the powers which are exercisable with the sanction of the court under Part I of Schedule 4 to the Insolvency Act 1986'. The trouble was that there was no explicit statutory basis for this. When legislating the rules to govern an English insolvency, Parliament had not provided that in certain cases, certain provisions should be inapplicable; and therefore the identification of English insolvency laws as susceptible to such an overlooking was fraught with difficulty. Scott V-C decided, however, that whatever the

128 [2005] EWHC 2990 (Ch), [2006] 1 WLR 1728; David Richards J.

129 [2005] EWHC 2125 (Ch): David Richards J.

130 [2005] UKPC 1, [2005] 2 AC 333: Lord Scott of Foscote, Lord Rodger of Earlsferry, Lord Walker of Gestingthorpe, Lord Brown of Eaton-under-Heywood. On appeal from the Court of Appeal of the Cayman Islands.

131 The decision of the Staff of Government Division (ie the Appellate Division) of the Isle of Man High Court is undated and unreported, but was affirmed by the Privy Council: [2006] UKPC 26 (IOM). The decision of the Privy Council will be noted next year.

132 [1997] Ch 213.

133 *Re Bank of Credit and Commerce International SA (No 3)* [1993] BCLC 1490.

principle was, the set-off provisions of the Insolvency Rules were of mandatory effect, and it was not therefore open to the English liquidators to remit the moneys to Luxembourg to the general disadvantage of the creditors entitled to prove in England.

This left the scope of the principle almost wholly unclarified. But the clear trend of cases in 2005 was to restrict it, and to reassert the rule that insolvency is governed in its entirety by local law, and that there is no power in a judge to remit proceeds to another court in which the substantive rights of creditors will be impaired: as one may say, salt is not to be rubbed into the creditors' wounds. Two decisions of David Richards J serve to make the point; and to much the same effect, the scope of a common law power of a local court to 'assist' a foreign court administering an insolvency has been rather chilled by a judgment of the Privy Council. The result is that there is now rather little room for the view that any provision of English insolvency law will be set aside in order to give preferential effect to the insolvency law of another country in which insolvency proceedings are also being taken.

The *Re BCCI (No 10)* point, and the general retreat from it, is significant. There is a very great deal to be said for the proposition that no deserving person benefits from competing or parallel liquidations of companies with international business. Sometimes there is legislative organization;[134] in others a statutory power to seek and to give assistance to courts in other jurisdictions.[135] But this leaves a lot of the world on the outside, and the incentive to improve on the written law as otherwise governs in such cases is not a fanciful one. But the proposition that the written rules of English insolvency law may be set aside in actual cases with real creditors appears to attract little more than lip-service. David Richards J has declined to find anything of substance in the principle. In *Re T & N Ltd* he was asked to give directions in relation to a Plan, propounded by American administrators to sort out and organize the problems of debt which threatened to overwhelm a group of companies with liability for injuries caused by asbestos. In passing, he cited *Re BCCI*, but only to observe that while comity and cooperation were in general terms most desirable, the principles of comity '[do] not, however, enable the court to alter or dispense with mandatory provisions of the law which it administers'. On the application before him, though, it was not necessary for the judge to refine or apply the principle, whatever it was. But in *Re HIH Casualty and General Insurance Ltd* the issue could not be ducked. An Australian insurer with international business had become insolvent. It was again common ground that the sensible solution to the problem was to proceed by schemes of arrangement in Australia and England. The provisional liquidators considered that they needed to

134 Most significantly, Council Regulation (EC) 1346/2000, [2000] OJ L160/1; and the UNCITRAL model law on cross-border insolvency, to which Insolvency Act 2000, s 14 applies.

135 Insolvency Act 1986, s 426.

know whether an English court, regarding its insolvency proceedings as ancillary to the Australian ones, would allow certain reinsurance funds, located in England, to be remitted to Australia, where the principal insolvency was taking place. Again, the objection to doing so was that in this particular context, Australian insolvency law diverges from the corresponding rules of English law. In an exception to the general principle of distribution *pari passu*, an Australian liquidator would be required instead to ring-fence and allocate the particular reinsurance money for the primary benefit of the insurance claimants whose risks had been reinsured: it was as though these particular creditors enjoyed a limited form of priority not corresponding to the position in English law. The judge held that the English liquidators would be authorized to remit the English assets to Australia only if those assets would there be distributed as in an English insolvency. If that were not the case, there would be no remission. The English insolvency may have been ancillary, but it was still an English insolvency; the *pari passu* provision of English insolvency law was not susceptible to being got round or down under. The conclusion that the same would have been true of almost all provisions of the Insolvency Act is hard to avoid. The apparent inconsistency with what Dillon LJ had said was explained by interpreting Dillon LJ's observation as confined to instances within Schedule 4 or the approval of a scheme of arrangement, which may read it down more than his Lordship intended.

No one seems to challenge the principle that an English insolvency may be ancillary, and that consequences flow from this. But its content is vanishing before our eyes, so that it really only applies to rules of law which are properly seen as procedural, such as whether the English liquidator or the foreign administrator actually makes the payment to a creditor. If one asks where there is authority for the proposition that there may be an insolvency proceeding in England to which a substantive rule of English insolvency law does not apply, the answer is that there really is none. One may put it this way. Parliament has enacted insolvency law in express terms. Where has it enacted the provision which says, in effect 'but these written laws shall not apply if . . .'? If the answer is that it has not, it is hard to see any proper basis for disregarding the clear terms of the legislation. That seemed to be the instinct of David Richards J, and when confronted by real creditors who have sustained real losses, one can see a lot to be said for it.

A different kind of cooperation was in issue before the Privy Council, in a case on appeal from the Cayman Islands. In *Al Sabah v Grupo Torras SA*, a Bahamian trustee in bankruptcy obtained a letter of request that the Cayman Islands court assist the Bahamian court in setting aside two Caymanian trusts established by the debtor as settlor. It came to the conclusion that United Kingdom legislation, section 122 of the Bankruptcy Act 1914, still in force in the Cayman Islands, did give the Cayman Islands court a statutory power to assist the Bahamian court. But it dealt in passing with what the result would have been had it reached the opposite conclusion on the statute law, observing[136] that the 'non-statutory' principles, whatever they were, which allowed a court to act to assist a court in another jurisdiction, were much more limited in scope than the statute law of the Cayman Islands, and though it did not question their existence, it did nothing to support the argument that their scope was wide or widening.

In this respect, the broad approach of the Privy Council stands in sharp contrast with the decision of the Staff of Government Division[137] of the Manx High Court, in *Re Cambridge Gas Transport Corp.*[138] The court claimed to find that it had a general discretion to respond favourably to a Letter of Request from a US court, which asked that the Manx court direct the Registrar of Companies to delete X and inscribe Y as proprietor of shares in a Manx company. As X had not been party to the proceedings in the United States, there was no basis on which the judgment or order of the US court was binding on X as a matter of common law;[139] and for the Manx court to strip a person of his shareholding in a Manx company, for no reason other than that it had been asserted by the US court that this would assist an orderly American reconstruction of an insolvent company, was hopelessly wrong. That it should have been seen differently by the Staff of Government Division is incomprehensible; the decision is under appeal to the Privy Council where, one trusts, it will be reversed in a manner which justifies a Note next year.

By contrast, in *Re Impex Services Worldwide Ltd*,[140] the Chancery Division of the Manx High Court saw the cooperation and support offered by Manx common law as leading to the recognition of an English provisional liquidator, and preparedness to order the examination of a witness to alleged fraud, pursuant to an English Letter of Request. No substantive Manx law rights were sacrificed by acceding to the Request. The same was true in *Al Sabah v Grupo Torras SA* where the bankrupt was subject to the international jurisdiction of the Bahamian court by reason of his residence in the Bahamas. It was therefore justifiable[141] for the Cayman court to recognize the Bahamian judgment and to give effect to the Letter of Request which was predicated upon it, and it was a little surprising that the Privy Council was so cautious about the common law of international cooperation. In sum, it follows that a court asked to assist another court in the administration of an insolvency will recognize a foreign liquidator, and may[142] accede to a Letter of Request that

[136] At para 35. [137] The appellate Division. [138] See n 131 above.

[139] Manx law is on this point identical with English law.

[140] [2003–5] Manx LR 115, Deemster Doyle.

[141] There is or will be room for debate about this, as there were beneficiaries of the trust who had not been subject to the personal jurisdiction of the Bahamian court, and who were not party to the bankruptcy proceedings, and who stood to be prejudiced by the Request. But at para 47 the Privy Council suggested that such objections were not likely to be substantial.

[142] But has no obligation to: *England v Smith* [2001] Ch 419 (where the request was acceded to even though an English court could not have made it); *Re Duke Group Ltd* [2001] BCC 144 (to the same effect); *Re JN Taylor Finance Pty Ltd* [1999] 2 BLC 256 (where the request was not acceded to).

evidence be taken. But it will not make an order which has the effect of setting aside substantive provisions of insolvency law, and it must follow that it will not make orders which override other substantive legal rules either, such as those on the recognition of foreign judgments. From this, it must follow that *Re Cambridge Gas Transport Corp* is wrong; and that the principle discussed in *Re BCCI (No 10)* is more apparent than real. In the end, any judicial discretion to assist a foreign court in cases such as these has to be limited by principles of law. The right and duty of a court to assist in these cases is based on a discretion which has a will-o'-the-wisp quality to it. Perhaps more legislation is the only solution.

UNITED KINGDOM MATERIALS ON INTERNATIONAL LAW 2005

Compiled by Kaiyan Kaikobad,[1] Jacques Hartmann,[2] Sangeeta Shah,[3] and Colin Warbrick[4]

1. This selection of UK materials on international law is made from published sources. It does not purport to include everything which could be of interest to an international lawyer but it is not wholly restricted to materials which could be called "state practice" in the strictest sense: some context is provided.

We have had to make substantial exclusions of material which we know would be of interest to some international lawyers. We bear in mind the need, first, to avoid the purely ephemeral and second, to exclude materials which are concerned mainly with the UK's implementation of the international law of cooperation, particularly at the general level. We are very sparing with matters of EU law, though we report some EU positions on questions of international law with which the UK is associated.

There is only limited material on UK treaties because the texts and explanatory memoranda are readily available on the Web: **<www.fco.gov.uk/treaties>.**

We have inserted a small amount of editorial material in the form "[. . .Ed.]" where it appears helpful to do so. Extracts are generally reproduced in their original form, which leads to inconsistencies, eg in spelling ("judgement"/"judgment") or capitalization "UN charter" or designation ("Chapter Seven"/"Chapter VII"/"Chapter 7").

2. Hansard references are to the Web version. There may be minor discrepancies between the column references in the Web edition and the bound volumes.

References to Hansard are given in the following forms:

Commons—HC Deb 13 November 2001 Vol. 374 c345 or c134W or c101 WH or c1WS, where W, WH, and WS stand for Written Answers, Westminster Hall, and Written Statements;

Lords—HL Deb 8 October 2002 Vol. 639 c222 or 16 October 2003 Vol. 653 cWA125, where WA stands for Written Answer or HL Deb 29 January 2003 Vol. 643 cGC170, where GC stands for Grand Committee.

[1] Law Department, Durham University. [2] Jesus College, Cambridge.
[3] Human Rights Centre, Nottingham University.
[4] School of Law, University of Birmingham.

3. Some sources are given as **<www.fco.gov.uk>.** These are references to Press Releases or Speeches on the FCO website. The appropriate link should be followed to the date for the item given in the text.

4. From its start in 1978 and up to and including 1996, the materials in UKMIL were classified on the basis of the *Model Plan for the Classification of Documents concerning State Practice in the Field of Public International Law* adopted by the Committee of Ministers of the Council of Europe in its Resolution (68) 17 of 28 June 1968. The Committee of Ministers considered that developments in public international law since 1968 made it necessary to amend the Model Plan. Accordingly, by Recommendation (97) 11 of 12 June 1997, it adopted an Amended Model Plan as a contribution by the Council of Europe towards implementing General Assembly Resolution 2099 (XX) on technical assistance to promote the teaching, study, dissemination, and wider understanding of international law. The present issue of UKMIL is based on the 1997 Amended Model Plan.

5. We are glad to acknowledge the assistance of Chanaka Wickremasinghe, Sarah Williams and their colleagues in the Legal Adviser's Department of the Foreign & Commonwealth Office.

6. We are grateful for financial assistance in the preparation of UKMIL to the Whittuck Trust.

Index

Part One: International Law in General

Part One: I. A. *International Law in General—Nature, basis, purpose—In general*

1/1

The following statement was made on behalf of the European Union at the Informal Thematic consultations of the General Assembly:

The rule of law is the underlying principle at the basis of the UN. It is the indispensable basis of our interaction at the international level.

The rule of law forms the bedrock for peace, security and development, both at national and international levels. For instance, the rule of law will contribute to an environment of trust, predictability and security in which economic development can thrive and will function as an incentive for foreign direct investment. Equally, through transparent and just procedures and institutions, the rule of law will provide ways and means to address injustice before it risks developing into a situation of tension and conflict. But institutions and procedures, however important, are not enough by themselves. A just legal system must build upon international human rights, norms and standards. The rule of law and human rights are interdependent and mutually supporting.

The EU also welcomes the trend of an increased number of cases being brought before the International Court of Justice with a view to settling issues peacefully. We share the Secretary-General's view that means should be considered to strengthen the work of the ICJ, including through streamlining and simplifying of its working methods to facilitate expeditious adjudicating of cases.

All these are reasons why the EU stresses the importance of the rule of law in terms of adherence to international law, its translation into domestic legislation and strengthening of national capacities in the legal field. We emphasize the need to continue, where necessary, to strengthen the existing body of international norms and rules. To this end, Member States could solemnly reaffirm at the Summit their commitment to an international order based on rules, including their commitment to the UN Charter and other international instruments, norms and principles, that form the legal foundation of the international system. Member States which have not yet done so, should become parties to these international instruments as a matter of priority. In this context, the EU welcomes the Secretary-General's intention to hold a treaty event with a focus on "Responding to Global Challenges" in the margins of the Summit. In particular, the EU calls upon all Member States to sign and ratify the convention for the Suppression of Acts of Nuclear Terrorism, which was adopted last week by the General Assembly, and will be open for signature at the beginning of the treaty event on 14 September 2005.

Human rights, civil and political, as well as economic, social and cultural rights, are one of the fundamental pillars of the UN system which the UN has a mission to promote and to protect. In this regard, the EU stresses the need to strengthen the overall human rights system, most notably by mainstreaming human rights throughout the UN system, including in the deliberations of the Security Council.

...

Institutional reform in the field of human rights must strengthen the United Nations' human rights machinery as a whole. In that regard, we welcome the proposal for the creation of a standing Human Rights Council, reflecting the centrality of human rights in the UN system. We emphasize again that human rights are universal in nature and that all countries have a responsibility to respect, implement and promote human rights without any exception.

...

The EU endorses the concept of "Responsibility to protect". Grave and massive violations of human rights and acts of genocide call for strong response and action on the part of the international community.

The EU endorses the Secretary-General's important proposal concerning the "Responsibility to protect". In our view, this proposal should be considered from a broad perspective. The basic principle of state sovereignty is and should remain undisputed. It should also be recognized that state sovereignty implies not only rights, but also responsibilities. One of these responsibilities is the responsibility of each state to protect its own citizens—that comes first. However, if a state is unable or unwilling to do so, and if a situation of genocide, war crimes and crimes against humanity or massive human rights violations occurs or threatens to occur, the international community will have a responsibility to help protect these civilians and thereby also help to maintain international peace and security; first and foremost through diplomatic, humanitarian and other measures, such as support to capacity building and other development activities. But if such measures would have no immediate effect or would come too late, enforcement measures through the Security Council or approved by the Security Council should be possible, if needed and as a measure of last resort.

The responsibility to protect encompasses a responsibility to prevent. In the Secretary-General's words: "an ounce of prevention is worth significantly more than a pound of cure".

(19 April 2005, text supplied by FCO)

Part Two: I. B. *Sources and Codification of International Law—Sources of international law—Custom*

1/2

In a statement at the Meeting Of National Committees on International Humanitarian Law of Commonwealth States, Nairobi, 20 July 2005, an FCO Legal Adviser said:

ICRC Customary International Humanitarian Law Study

I have to express some reservations about the Study.

The Study is a formidable piece of research, but overall one is left with the impression that it shows how difficult it is to isolate rules of customary international law in any area.

The first question is what is customary international law and how is it formed. What is required is a "general practice accepted as law by States". What is needed? As regards practice, the practice must be a practice of States which is "dense" and uniform enough. Also, one has to take account of the position of "specially affected" States. Finally, one needs an "opinio juris", ie a belief that action is required by law. Overall, identifying a rule of customary international law is a rigorous process.

In the field of international humanitarian law, almost the whole field is covered by treaty provisions. Therefore States act as they do because of their treaty obligations, not because of any customary international law rule. In other words, their actions are referable to the treaty, not to any customary international law rule. In my view, it is difficult in those circumstances to say that States which are parties to the treaties believe their actions are required by customary international law, as opposed to being required by the treaty.

One also needs a rigorous evaluation of State practice. Sometimes in the Study, practice is not so uniform amongst specially affected States that it can be said to generate a customary international law rule. A particular example is one of the rules on the environment (Rule 45), where the practice of a number of important military States is discounted; also, the State practice referred to in the Commentary is not uniform, and does not justify the conclusions in the Rule.

Sometimes the practice relied upon is not State practice. For example there are a number of references to documents which are described as guidance or guidelines. Also, some practice is not that of States; for example the practice of the ICRC: its function, and that of other NGOs, is to ensure that States are aware of their obligations and comply with them. In other words, the ICRC's function is to get States to act better; it does not help to regard its practice as State practice: on the contrary.

I am also troubled by cases where the Rules in the Study misstate or incompletely state treaty provisions; often treaty provisions contain a delicate balance, and one cannot take away part and treat the remainder as reflecting customary international law. There are many examples of this, but I will only mention here Rule 4: this,—defines what is an armed force, but omits the requirement in Article 43(1) of Additional Protocol 1 that there is a need for an internal disciplinary system enforcing compliance with IHL, which seems a rather crucial requirement.

Of course, treaties only apply as between the parties. In my view, one must not try to force States into accepting obligations which they have chosen not to participate in; the better course is to use pressure to persuade States to ratify and implement treaties.

My conclusion is that the Study is an impressive piece of research, and will be a very useful quarry for the future. But we at least will treat the Rules with some degree of reservation. Overall, we feel that they represent too much of what States should do, rather than what they actually do, ie they state not what the law is but what it should be.

(Text provided by FCO)

Part Two: I. D. *Sources and Codification of International Law—Sources of international law—Unilateral acts, including acts and decisions of international organizations and conferences*

(See also **Part Nineteen: VI**)

2/1

The representative of the United Kingdom made a statement at the Inter-sessional Open-Ended Working Group Mandated to Elaborate a Draft Legally Binding Normative Instrument for the Protection of All Persons from Enforced Disappearances 12–23 September 2005. He said:

National Interpretative Statement on Article 25(4)

The UK fully appreciates the importance of this Article for many delegations and does not propose any further amendments to Article 25(4) to those already raised in consultations. However, we would wish to note our understanding of the obligations contained in this paragraph. The paragraph requires states to have legal procedures in place to review and, where appropriate, to annul adoptions or placements of children that resulted from an enforced disappearance.

We understand that this Article does not entail an obligation to provide a legal procedure which would lead to an automatic review or consideration as to whether to annul the adoption. We also understand that the Article does not require the automatic annulment of an adoption which stems from an enforced disappearance. We interpret the Article to require States Parties to have a procedure or procedures providing a possibility to apply for review of an adoption covered by this Article. Whether a review or annulment is in fact ordered will be an issue to be determined according to the applicable legal procedures in the state concerned.

20 September 2005

(Text supplied by FCO)

[Article 25 deals with the wrongful removal of children subject to "disappearance" or whose parent(s) or guardians are subject to "disappearance". Article 25(4) requires states to have in place procedures to review the adoption or replacement of such children and, where appropriate, to annul any adoption or placement, Ed.]

2/2

The representative of the United Kingdom made a statement at the Inter-sessional Open-Ended Working Group Mandated to Elaborate a Draft Legally Binding Normative Instrument for the Protection of All Persons from Enforced Disappearances 12–23 September 2005.

He said:

... we wish to place the following understandings on the record...

In relation to Article 2, the UK notes, as it has in previous sessions, that the placing of a person outside the protection of the law is an important element of the definition of an enforced disappearance, additional to its other elements. As such, the UK considers that the definition of an enforced disappearance in Article 2 comprises the following elements:

First, an arrest, detention, abduction or any other form of deprivation of liberty;

Second, that such acts are committed by agents of the State or by persons or groups acting with the authorisation, support or acquiescence of the State;

Third, that the act is followed by a refusal to acknowledge the deprivation of liberty or by concealment of the fate or whereabouts of the disappeared person;

And fourth, that the disappeared person is placed outside the protection of the law.

The UK understands the term "outside the protection of the law" to mean that the person's deprivation of liberty or detention is not regarded by the State as being within the scope of its legal rules governing deprivations of liberty or detention, or that those rules are not compatible with applicable international law.

The UK also wishes to place on record its understanding of Article 43 of the draft Convention.

The UK understands this provision to confirm that a State Party's obligations under international humanitarian law, including its obligations and rights under the Geneva Conventions of 1949 and their Additional Protocols of 1977, remain the lex specialis in situations of armed conflict and other situations to which international humanitarian law applies. The UK understands this Article to operate as a "savings clause" in order to ensure that, where applicable, the relevant provisions of international humanitarian law take precedence over any other provisions contained in this Convention.

23 September 2005

(Text supplied by FCO)

2/3

The representative of the UK made the following general statement on the draft resolution on the Principles and Guidelines on the right to a remedy and reparations for victims of gross violations of international human rights law and serious violations of international humanitarian law [A/C.3/60/L.24] in the Third Committee of the General Assembly at its Sixtieth Session:

The UK has been pleased to cosponsor this resolution adopting, in the General Assembly, the Basic Principles and Guidelines on the right to a remedy and reparation for victims of gross violations of international human rights law and serious violations of international humanitarian law. I would like to make the following statement on the United Kingdom's understanding of this resolution.

The Basic Principles and Guidelines are the result of over 15 years of work by independent experts, during which 3 consultative meetings were held for input by States, international organisations and NGOs. . .

The United Kingdom notes that the Chairperson-Rapporteur, in his report of the third consultative meeting, has made it clear that the revised Principles and Guidelines do not introduce new principles in international law. This is clearly right: the Principles and Guidelines are non-legally binding, and do not create any new obligations on States in international law.

Nevertheless, the United Kingdom is convinced that the Basic Principles and Guidelines will serve as an extremely valuable tool for States to take into account in considering relevant policies on remedies and reparation and we welcome their adoption in this resolution. In other words, without being prescriptive, the Basic Principles and Guidelines will be of great assistance in enabling States to decide how to pursue their own national policies in this field.

(Text supplied by FCO)

[The Resoultion was approved without a vote by the General Assembly as Res 60/147, Ed.]

Part Two: II. *Sources and Codification of International Law—Codification and progressive development of international law*

(See also **Part Two: I. D**)

2/4

The representative of the United Kingdom made the following statement at the Conference on Disarmament, Plenary meeting on the Prevention of an Arms Race in Outer Space, 30 June 2005:

Since the launch of the first man-made satellite, Sputnik, into outer space in 1957, mankind has achieved major advances in space exploration and use. Atmospheric observation, lunar and interplanetary exploration have become the basis for environmental sciences. There have also been significant advances in communications, navigation, meteorology and sensing. All states have the right to explore outer space and make the most of opportunities for scientific, economic, environmental and communications advances.

As well as these civil and scientific uses, the scope of national security activities in outer space has also grown. Although the focus of our governments' policies on space is on civil and scientific uses, the security benefits we derive from its use are important: satellite communications, surveillance, reconnaissance, mapping, early warning, navigation and sensing are all integral to our national security responsibilities.

But as more and more countries become involved in space activities, it is essential that we avoid misperceptions and mistrust by promoting clarity and co-operation. This is particularly important given the unique characteristics of the space environment and space technology. Although space is relatively difficult to access, it lies not far above every nation. Operating equipment in space can be hazardous: risks are posed by radiation, by natural meteoroids and debris from human space activities. And yet once in orbit, a satellite can move at more than 25,000 kilometres each hour, circling the globe up to 16 times a day and providing a unique vehicle for observations of earth.

The right of all states to explore and use this unique shared environment for the benefit and in the interest of all humankind is a universally accepted legal principle. It is the concern and responsibility of all states to ensure that these rights are realised in the interest of maintaining international peace and security. The cornerstone of international space law is the 1967 Outer Space Treaty, to which the United Kingdom is a Depository. This treaty places important constraints on military activity in space: it bans the deployment of WMD in space and military activity on the moon and other celestial bodies. The United Kingdom continues to be a firm supporter. Our commitment to efforts to prevent an arms race in outer space was also demonstrated through our support for the First Committee resolution on this subject last October.

But as national security activities in space have grown, so have concerns by some states about the risk of an arms race in outer space. Some states would wish to see additional and more extensive arms control measures. We acknowledge colleagues' concerns, but there is no international consensus on the need for further treaties and further legal codification of the use of space would be difficult both to agree and verify. But, that said, we recognise that many states and CD partners, would wish to discuss this subject as part of what they would regard as a balanced programme of work in this forum.

However, even agreeing the terms of such a discussion would not be easy and would require debate in itself. The Chinese and Russian delegations have set out some interesting thoughts on definitions in a non-paper issued earlier this month. It is not a simple task to find a widely acceptable definition of what constitutes either "militarisation" or "weaponisation" of space. Views also differ on whether weapons used for the defensive or peaceful use of space would be classified in the same way as offensive space or anti-space capabilities. It would seem sensible to distinguish between offensive and defensive weapon capabilities, but again this is not an issue on which all nations agree. Without agreeing the terms of the debate, it is difficult to discuss these important issues.

Also space presents both challenges and opportunities for verification of any arms control agreements. The vast distances of space, the sophisticated technologies of space systems and the difficulty of differentiating between systems used for both civilian and military purposes can make verification complex. At the same time, space is the most transparent of environments, open in all directions.

Given the difficulty of verifying or agreeing further legal treaties, we suggested last year in an informal setting, that it might be a useful idea to think about adopting "rules of the road" in space, similar to those that already exist at sea. These would not be easy to reach agreement upon, but they might have immediate benefits such as reducing the risk of accidental collisions, preventing incidents, and promoting "safe passage" for satellites. We would welcome CD partners' views on this informal suggestion.

(Text supplied by FCO)

Part Three: The Law of Treaties

Part Three: I. C. *The Law of Treaties—Definition, conclusion, and entry into force of treaties—Reservations, declarations, and objections*

(See also **Part Six: VIII (CRC)**)

3/1

The Government sent the following communication to the Depositary (the UN Secretary-General):

The Government of the United Kingdom of Great Britain and Northern Ireland have examined the reservation relating to Article 14, of the International Convention for the Suppression of the Financing of Terrorism made by the Government of Belgium at the time of its ratification of the Convention.

The Government of the United Kingdom note that the effect of the said reservation is to disapply the provisions of Article 14, in "exceptional circumstances" Article 14, provides that:

> "None of the offences set forth in Article 2, shall be regarded for the purposes of extradition or mutual legal assistance as a political offence or as an offence connected with a political offence or as an offence inspired by political motives. Accordingly, a request for extradition or for mutual legal assistance based on such an offence may not be refused on the sole ground that it concerns a political offence or an offence inspired by political motives."

The Government of the United Kingdom note that the provisions of Article 14, reflect in part the principle that claims of political motivation must not be recognised as grounds for refusing requests for the extradition of alleged terrorists. The Government of the United Kingdom consider this principle to be an important measure in the fight against terrorism and the provisions of Article 14, of the Convention in particular to be an essential measure in States' efforts to suppress the financing of terrorist acts.

The Government of the United Kingdom note that paragraph 1, of the reservation made by the Government of Belgium is expressed to apply only "in exceptional circumstances" and that, notwithstanding the application of the reservation, Belgium continues to be bound by the principle of aut dedere aut judicare as set out in Article 10, of the Convention. The Government of the United Kingdom note further, however, that the exceptional circumstances that are envisaged are not specified in the reservation.

In light of the grave nature of the offences set forth in Article 2, of the Convention, the Government of the United Kingdom consider that the provisions of Article 14, should apply in all circumstances. A reservation that seeks to disapply Article 14, even while reaffirming the application of the principle of aut dedere aut judicare, undermines the effectiveness of the provisions of Article 14, of the Convention as a measure in States' efforts to suppress the financing of terrorist acts.

The Government of the United Kingdom therefore objects to the aforesaid reservation made by the Government of Belgium to the International Convention for the Suppression of the Financing of Terrorism. However, this objection shall not preclude the entry into force of the Convention between the United Kingdom and Belgium.

(Treaty Series No. 37 (2005), Cm 6676)

Part Three: I. D. *The Law of Treaties—Definition, conclusion, and entry into force of treaties—Provisional application, and entry into force*

3/2

The Government was asked:

Whether the following provisions are still in force, and binding upon the high contracting parties:

(a) the 1960 Treaty Concerning the Establishment of the Republic of Cyprus (Cmnd. 1252); and

(b) the 1960 Cyprus: Treaty of Guarantee (Cmnd. 1253), and the Basic Articles of the Constitution of Cyprus guaranteed therein;

and, if not, on what date they ceased to be in force.

An FCO Minister wrote:

The 1960 Treaty Concerning the Establishment of the Republic of Cyprus and the Cyprus Treaty of Guarantee were both signed in Nicosia on 16 August 1960. They remain in force, and are binding upon the high contracting parties.

(HL Deb 11 January 2005 Vol. 668 c30WA)

Part Three: II. B. *The Law of Treaties—observance, application, and interpretation of treaties—Application of treaties*

3/3

European Convention on Human Rights—Sovereign Base Areas

The Government was asked why the Human Rights Ordinance (9 of 2004) made by the administrator of the sovereign base areas of Akrotiri and Dhekelia in Cyprus excludes the protection of the convention rights contained in Protocol 1 to the European Convention on Human Rights. A Minister wrote:

The Human Rights Ordinance does not include the convention rights contained in the First Protocol to the convention because that protocol was not extended to the sovereign base areas by the United Kingdom. This is because the requirement to hold free elections under Article 3 of that protocol could not be given full effect to in the sovereign base areas as a result of the constitutional arrangements in place for the areas whereby the administrator is not an elected post. However, two ordinances have been enacted by the administrator to provide domestic rights based on those contained in Articles 1 and 2 of the First Protocol—the Protection of Property Ordinance 2004 (Ordinance 35 of 2004) and the Right to Education Ordinance 2005 (Ordinance 8 of 2005).

(HL Deb 6 April 2005 Vol. 671 cWA118)

Part Three: II. C. *The Law of Treaties—Observance, application, and interpretation of treaties—Interpretation of treaties*

3/4

Her Majesty's Government was asked to list the occasions since 1997 where the Government have formally challenged the legal treaty basis for legislative activity at European Community level. In reply, an FCO Minister wrote:

The UK Government have formally challenged the legal treaty basis for legislative activity on two occasions. They are as follows:

C-66/04 UK *v*. Parliament and Council (ongoing)

C-217/04 UK *v*. Parliament and Council (ongoing).

(HC Deb 5 July 2005 Vol. 436 c332W)

Part Three: IV. C. *The Law of Treaties—Invalidity, termination and suspension of the operation of treaties—Termination and suspension of operation, denunciation, and withdrawal*

3/5

The Government sent the following communication to the Government of Ethiopia:

NOTE NO: 44/2005

UK/ETHIOPIA DEBT AGREEMENTS

Her Britannic Majesty's Embassy present their compliments to the Ministry of Finance of the Federal Democratic Republic of Ethiopia and have the honour to refer to the Agreed Minute on the Reduction and Reorganisation of the Debt of the Federal Democratic Republic of Ethiopia which was signed in Paris on 13 May 2004 and to confirm that, in accordance with that Agreed Minute, the Government or the United Kingdom has cancelled certain sums due under the United Kingdom/Ethiopia Debt Agreement No.1 (1992), the United

Kingdom/Ethiopia Debt Agreement No.2 (1997), and the United Kingdom/ Ethiopia Debt Agreement No.3 (2001), and that the Government of the United Kingdom will shortly settle with the Export Credits Guarantee Department on behalf of your Government all the other sums that remain outstanding under the United Kingdom/Ethiopia Debt Agreement No.3 (2001).

Please note that no further action is required on your side. As no obligations remain outstanding under the United Kingdom/Ethiopia Debt Agreement No.1 (1992), and the United Kingdom/Ethiopia Debt Agreement No.2 (1997), the Government of the United Kingdom considers these agreements terminated. You will be notified once all remaining sums due under the United Kingdom/ Ethiopia Debt Agreement No.3 (2001), have been settled, at which point the Government of the United Kingdom will deem that no obligations remain outstanding under the said agreement and therefore will consider it terminated.

British Embassy Addis Ababa

17 February 2005

[This is one of a number of similar notes sent to other States about the effects of debt relief, Ed.]

(Treaty Series No. 37 (2005), Cm 6676)

Part Three: VII. *The Law of Treaties—Consensual arrangements other than treaties*

3/6

The FCO published the following document:

TREATIES AND MOUs

GUIDANCE ON PRACTICE AND PROCEDURES
Second Edition. April 2000 Revised May 2004

TREATY SECTION

INFORMATION MANAGEMENT DEPARTMENT
FOREIGN & COMMONWEALTH OFFICE

1. TREATIES AND MOUs

RESPONSIBILITY FOR CONCLUDING TREATIES

The responsibility for concluding treaties involving the United Kingdom lies with the Secretary of State for Foreign and Commonwealth Affairs. The FCO is responsible for Foreign and Commonwealth policy aspects of all treaties, as well as for dealing with questions of form and procedure. It must also consider points of international law. This remains the case even when the negotiation of the treaty is led by another Government Department, i.e. the Department which will carry out the treaty's provisions. FCO Legal Advisers and FCO Treaty Section must be given the opportunity to comment on the drafts of all treaties under negotiation to ensure that they are drafted in accordance with correct international practice. The same applies to MoUs (see below).

WHAT IS A TREATY?

The term treaty describes an international agreement concluded in writing between States which is intended to create rights and obligations in international law. Treaties are known by a variety of names, for example Agreement, Convention, Protocol, Treaty etc. They may be in the form of a single instrument with numbered articles or in the form of an Exchange of Notes. There can also be treaties between a State and an international organisation.

WHAT IS AN MOU?

An MOU records international "commitments", but in a form and with wording which expresses an intention that it is not to be legally binding. An MOU is used where it is considered preferable to avoid the formalities of a treaty—for example, where there are detailed provisions which change frequently or the matters dealt with are essentially of a technical or administrative character; in matters of defence or technology where there is a need for such documents to be classified; or where a treaty requires subsidiary documents to fill out the details. Like a treaty, an MOU can have a variety of names and can also be either in the form of an Exchange of Notes or a single document. However, the formalities which surround treaty-making do not apply to it and it is not usually published. The term "MOU" is short for Memorandum of Understanding, which is the most common name for non-legally binding instruments. (NB: Confusingly some treaties also have that name.)

2. HOW DO YOU DISTINGUISH AN MOU FROM A TREATY?

Basically, by the terms in which they are written. It is becoming generally accepted international practice to show clearly by the form of the document and its terminology the intention either to create legally binding obligations, or not, i.e. either a treaty or an MOU. Thus, in order to ensure that MOUs are not worded in such a way as to amount to treaties care should be taken to avoid the use of "treaty language". Guidance on the terminology to be used (and to be avoided) as well as on the form is given on pages 15–18.

Although an MOU is not legally binding it should be no less carefully drafted than if it were a treaty, given that it is always the intention to perform all HMG's commitments, whether legally binding or not. As with treaties, ***all*** draft MOUs should be sent to the relevant FCO department for clearance by their Legal Adviser, and foreign language versions should be checked. Moreover, there should be the same level of inter Departmental consultation as for treaties (see page 3).

DOCUMENTS REQUIRED BY FCO TREATY SECTION

Original treaty documents should always be sent to FCO Treaty Section, which arranges for their publication as Command Papers and laying before Parliament. It also arranges for their transfer to the National Archives for permanent preservation upon entry into force for the UK and for their registration with the United Nations in accordance with Article 102 of the UN Charter.

In addition, all notifications about treaties (i.e. notifications about the signature or ratification of treaties by the UK and by other states, about declarations, reservations and objections made by other states, and about the entry into force of treaties), which are received by other Government Departments directly from a depositary should be forwarded to FCO Treaty Section.

MOUs, as opposed to treaties, are entered on Departmental files. However, a photocopy of the final (and preferably signed) text of an MOU should be sent to FCO Treaty Section for its collection of MOUs.

(Text supplied by FCO)

Part Four: Relationship between International Law and Internal Law

Part Four: II. *Relationship between International Law and Internal Law—Application and implementation of international law in internal law*

(See also **Part Five: II. A.1.(b)**)

4/1

At the Report stage of the International Organisations Bill, an FCO Minister said:

When we enter into international treaties and international bodies are set up under those treaties, all those who sign up to the treaties become, if you like, members of a club obligated by the terms of the relevant treaty. They are obligated to ensure that the organisations set up under the terms of that treaty are dealt with in an even-handed way in every country that is a party to that treaty.

Some of the organisations that are set up will take residence in the United Kingdom. In fact, we have been extremely successful as a nation ... in that we have attracted a number of those organisations which believe that it is beneficial to be based in the United Kingdom and to conduct their international work from here. Others, by definition, will be set up elsewhere. However, they will all be treated the same way by the nature of the international obligation which all signatories to the treaty, in joining the club that that treaty represents, have given their undertakings toward ... That is why, even if the relevant people do not come here other than for occasional visits, I should have thought that our obligations are wholly and manifestly clear.

(HL Deb 11 January 2005 Vol. 668 c27GC)

4/2

At the Report stage of the International Organisation Bill, an FCO Minister said:

... the importance of conferring privileges and immunities on family members of officials of international organisations should not be underestimated. It is important to ensure that the work of officials cannot be undermined by threats against close family members. The proposed amendment [sc to the Bill] would make it impossible for the UK to confer privileges and immunities on family members of judges of the European Court of Human Rights.

As a result, the United Kingdom would not be able to withdraw the reservation it made when it ratified the Sixth Protocol to the General Agreement on Privileges and Immunities of the Council of Europe of 1949. This reservation provides that,

> "until such time as the necessary legislation is enacted, the UK reserves the right not to apply Article 1 of the Sixth Protocol in respect of the spouses and minor children of judges".

The reasoning behind the reservation was that at the time of ratification the UK legislation was not in place to enable us to implement Article 1 of the Sixth Protocol. Clause 7 fills the gap historically left there and allows us to give full effect to the Sixth Protocol. Conferring privileges and immunities on family members of senior staff of an international organisation is nothing new ... It reflects, under the current conventions of international law, most of the ways in which these matters are conducted.

(HL Deb 11 January 2005 Vol. 668 c53GC)

4/3

During a debate in the House of Commons on the Terrorism Bill, the Secretary of State for the Home Department said:

The [Terrorism] Bill extends the provisions to those who disseminate terrorist material, including on the internet, but makes clear that those who simply transmit material that does not reflect their views will not be caught. That will, among other things, enable the United Kingdom to ratify the Council of Europe's convention on the prevention of terrorism, which I think is an important step.

...

Some concern has been expressed about the appropriate definition of terrorism, particularly by the Chairman of the Home Affairs Committee ... The definition that will apply to the new offences in the Bill is the one that was agreed by Parliament for the Terrorism Act 2000, with the addition of a small change which will bring threats against international bodies, such as the United Nations, within the scope of the definition. Beyond that, the Bill uses the definition of terrorism that has become established in our law.

The definitions used internationally, such as that used in the recent European Union Council framework decision of 13 June 2000, do not appear to be substantially different, and we do not consider them to have advantages over the definition used in the UK legislation. Following the Security Council resolution [1624, 14 September 2005] from which I quoted earlier, the UN is still seeking agreement—which I think will be difficult to achieve—on an appropriate definition of terrorism.

(HC Deb 26 October 2005 Vol. 438 c334–335)

Part Five: Subjects of International law

Part Five: I. A.1. *Subjects of International Law—States—Status and powers—Personality*

5/1

In a written Ministerial Statement, the Foreign Secretary wrote:

On 26 October, President Mahmud Ahmadinejad of Iran addressed a conference in Tehran on "A World Without Zionism". In his speech, he is reported to have called for "Israel to be wiped from the map", and said that "the Islamic world will not let its historic enemy live in its heartland", "the new wave of (attacks) in Palestine ... will erase this stigma from the Islamic world" and that "anybody who recognises Israel will burn in the fire of the Islamic nation's fury".

As my right hon. Friend the Prime Minister said in his press conference at the European Council at Hampton Court on 27 October, these sentiments are completely unacceptable. I welcome the clear condemnation by the United Nations Security Council on 28 October and the statement by the UN Secretary-General, Kofi Annan, expressing his dismay. They have spoken for the world. Israel is a long-standing member of the United Nations with the same rights and obligations as every other. Under the United Nations Charter, Iran, like other members of the organisation, has undertaken to refrain from the threat or use of force against the territorial integrity or political independence of any state.

Mr Annan has also said he intends to place at the top of his agenda when he visits Iran in the next few weeks the Middle East Peace Process and the right of all states in the area to live in peace within secure and recognised boundaries free from threats or acts offered. I welcome that.

At the informal summit of European Union Heads of Government at Hampton Court on 27 October, the Presidency issued the following statement:

> "EU leaders meeting at Hampton Court today condemned in the strongest terms the comments in respect of the State of Israel attributed to President Ahmedinejad of Iran. Calls for violence, and for the destruction of any state, are manifestly inconsistent with any claim to be a mature and responsible member of the international community.
>
> Such comments will cause concern about Iran's role in the region, and its future intentions. The fact that these comments were made on the same day as a horrific attack on Israeli civilians should reinforce the lesson that incitement to violence, and the terrorism that it breeds, are despicable and unacceptable acts. For its part, the EU remains committed to a solution to the Arab-Israeli dispute based on the principle of two states living side-by-side in peace and security. It urges all parties in the region to do their utmost to bring that vision to fulfilment".

In addition, on 27 October, the Foreign Office summoned the Iranian Chargé d'Affaires in London on behalf of the European Union to protest at the remarks. Many of our European partners and other countries have done likewise.

We welcome too the international community's forthright condemnation, and their reaffirmation of the right of Israel to exist. We welcome particularly the statements by officials of the Palestinian Authority and other governments in the region.

(HC Deb 31 October 2005 Vol. 438 c24WS–25WS)

Part Five: I. A.2. *Subjects of International Law—States—Status and powers—Sovereignty and independence*

(See also **Part Six: VIII (Iraq)**)

5/2

Economic Community of West African States

During a Security Council Meeting the representative of the United Kingdom stated:

... picking up on what the Secretary-General said earlier. ECOWAS and the African Union have had the courage to take a stance on Togo. The Secretary-General has done so on several occasions. Yet the Council has been silent. We have said nothing on Togo. The question the Council must ask itself—this year, of all years, as we approach a summit—is, when do the situation and the developments in a country actually justify the involvement of the Security Council? Is the failure of a Government to protect its citizens a grossly unconstitutional act? Whatever the circumstances, is such failure a basis for the Council to say, "We ought to stand up and be counted"? Or is the traditional view of national sovereignty and non-interference to be exercised without qualification, without regard to developments in the real world? Does that mean that the Council then must stand silent on these issues, or do we have an obligation in terms of international peace and security actually to stand up? I am quite clear for myself what the answer is.

(UN Doc. S/PV.5131, 25 February 2005)

5/3

European Union

In a written answer, an FCO Minister wrote:

... The EU's Hague Programme refers to a feasibility study into a "European system of Border Guards" but makes no commitment to establishing one ...

Like many EU member states, the Government remain unconvinced of the need for a European Border force ...

But we fully support the Border Agency, which will play a key role in co-ordinating joint operations between EU member states to strengthen the EU's external border. The UK supports the increased number of joint activities and co-operation between member states at the EU external borders where that activity is conducted on an operationally focused, intelligence-led basis. Such action has the potential to enhance the security of the EU's external borders to the benefit of all member states. It should complement, not replace, the work of national border services.

We also welcome the statement in the Programme that the control and surveillance of external borders falls within the sphere of national border authorities—this is a matter of sovereignty.

(HC Deb 4 July 2005 Vol. 436 c128W)

5/4

Kaliningrad

The Government was asked if it will make a statement on its policy towards the future status of Kaliningrad. An FCO Minister wrote:

The UK supports the EU's policy of pursuing constructive discussion with Russia on issues relating to Kaliningrad. The EU and Russia agreed joint statements on the Kaliningrad region on 11 November 2002 and 27 April 2004. Copies can be found at the following links:

> http://europa.eu.int/comm/external_relations/russia/summit_11_02/js_kalin.htm
> http://europa.eu.int/comm/external_relations/russia/russia_docs/js_elarg_270404.htm

The joint statements acknowledge the unique situation of the Kaliningrad region as part of the Russian Federation, but separated from the rest of the federation by other states, and agree to make a special effort to accommodate the concerns of both sides relating to the transit of persons and goods between the Kaliningrad region and other parts of Russia, and to intensify their co-operation to promote the social and economic development of the region as a whole. The UK supports the implementation of the commitments in the two joint statements.

(HC Deb 13 January 2005 Vol. 429 c640W)

5/5

Papua/Indonesia

The Government was asked, pursuant to the answer of 21 December 2004, *Official Report*, column 1626W, on West Papua, what format it expects a review of the Act of Free Choice for Papua to take; whether there is a timetable for the review. An FCO Minister wrote:

The report of the special representative who oversaw the implementation of the UN backed 1969 Act of Free Choice resulting in West Papua becoming a province of Indonesia was accepted by a majority vote of the UN in November 1969. Any review of it is a matter between the UN and the Indonesian Government.

The British Government, together with other members of the international community, has continued to stress to the Indonesian Government at the highest level the need to fully implement the 2001 special autonomy law for Papua.

This law allows for the establishment of a Truth and Reconciliation Committee to look at the incorporation of Papua into Indonesia in the 1960s.

(HC Deb 25 February 2005 Vol. 431 c861W)

5/6

Rwanda

In a debate an FCO Minister said:

Since Rwanda, the United Kingdom has taken the lead in pushing for guidelines which would recognise that the Security Council and the UN have a responsibility to protect people subjected to this sort of violence. The Prime Minister suggested some in 1999, and we strongly endorse the [UN Secretary-General's High Level] Panel's decision to address this controversial issue.

Member states of the United Nations are, of course, rightly protective of their own sovereignty. But Her Majesty's Government believe that there is a limit to that independence when a state begins to persecute its own people or when a state stands by to see one part of its population persecute and slaughter another part of its population . . .

Frankly, I believe that a prime example of this was the action that we, the United States and our allies in NATO took over Kosovo in 1999 . . . two things were clear in Kosovo. First, the humanitarian situation in Kosovo was something that none of us could ignore. Secondly, action through the Security Council was not possible. The United Kingdom Government realised that they could not stand by and do nothing. The action we took was decisive, and eventually it was successful. We acted to prevent an immediate and overwhelming humanitarian catastrophe. I believe that we should be ready to act similarly, should similar circumstances ever arise in the future . . . it was not the lack of a clear definition of overwhelming humanitarian catastrophe that frustrated action in Kosovo; it was the lack of political will to act.

[It was] argued that a United Nations properly reformed, properly revitalised and properly resourced would be a far better means of dealing with the international responsibility to deal with humanitarian catastrophe. But to do that, the Security Council has to overcome the reluctance that it has shown not only over Kosovo and Rwanda but that it is now showing over Darfur, and to act in cases where human life is lost or where thousands of lives are threatened on an unimaginable scale.

(HL Deb 2 February 2005 Vol. 669 c300–301)

5/7

Zimbabwe

During a Security Council Meeting the representative of the United Kingdom stated:

It is right that members of the Council should express concern about the impact that food security has on conflict, on peace and on wider security. But we must highlight, too, that bad governance and a failure to work with the international community to prevent food insecurity, as in Zimbabwe, is a legitimate concern for the international community.

(UN Doc. S/PV.5220, 30 June 2005)

Part Five: I. A.3. *Subjects of International Law—States—Status and powers—Non-intervention*

5/8

The Government was asked what position it took at the recent Organisation for Security and Co-operation in Europe ministerial meeting in Sofia, concerning the withdrawal of Russian forces and military material from Moldova, which is some two years overdue; and what prospects it foresees for the implementation of the relevant agreement. An FCO Minister wrote:

Our position is set out in the UK's statement at the Organisation for Security and Cooperation in Europe (OSCE) ministerial meeting in Sofia. We want Russia to fulfil commitments made when signing the Adapted Conventional Forces in Europe (CFE) Treaty at the OSCE summit in Istanbul in 1999. These commitments include the full withdrawal of arms and ammunition from Transdnistria, or their destruction in situ, and the withdrawal of Russian forces.

Together with NATO allies we have stated that

> "we can envisage ratification of the Adapted CFE Treaty only in the context of full compliance by all State Parties with agreed treaty limits and consistent with the commitments contained in the CFE Final Act".

The final communiqué of the NATO ministerial meeting on 9 December 2004 underlines this position: "We recall that fulfilment of the remaining Istanbul commitments on the Republic of Georgia and the Republic of Moldova will create the conditions for Allies and other States Parties to move forward on ratification of the Adapted CFE Treaty. Given the lack of progress in 2004 on withdrawal of Russian military forces from the Republic of Moldova it is essential that efforts be intensified to complete the withdrawal as soon as possible".

The full text of the UK's statement is available on the OSCE website at http://www.osce.org/events/mc/bulgaria2004/documents/files/mc_1102435776_e.pdf.

The full text of the final communiqué is available on the NATO website at http://www.nato.int/docu/pr/2004/p04–170e.htm.

(HL Deb 10 January 2005 Vol. 668 c4WA)

Part Five: I. A.4. *Subjects of International Law—States—Status and powers—Domestic jurisdiction*

5/9

Nepal

The Government was asked what assessment it has made of the political situation in Nepal and its development since January 2004. An FCO Minister wrote:

We are deeply concerned by the current political situation in Nepal. The King's recent move to assume direct control of the country is a backward step for democracy. Following the royal takeover I summoned the Nepalese ambassador to express our grave concern and released a public statement in which I said that his action would increase the risk of instability in Nepal and undermine the institutions of democracy and constitutional monarchy in the country. I also called for the immediate restitution of multi-party democracy. A copy of my statement is available on the Foreign and Commonwealth Office website www.fco.gov.uk/policy/news/press-releases.

Immediately after the takeover of power by the King the EU presidency issued a statement on behalf of the EU which expressed our concerns about restrictions on liberty and calling for human rights to be respected. Our ambassador in Kathmandu raised these issues directly with the King in an audience on 8 February. With other EU member states' ambassadors he also raised them with the new Nepalese Foreign Minister on 7 February.

On 14 February ... the Foreign Secretary recalled our ambassador in Nepal to London for consultations. Following those consultations with our ambassador and other key international partners we decided to withdraw the proposal, laid before Parliament in a minute of 20 January 2005, for a further tranche of military assistance to Nepal.

(HC Deb 2 March 2005 Vol. 431 c1253W)

5/10

Taiwan/China

The Government was asked what recent assessment it has made of the relationship between Taiwan and China. An FCO Minister wrote:

In recent months there have been a few signs suggesting an improvement in the political relationship between China and Taiwan. For example, over the Chinese new year there were direct flights across the Strait for Taiwanese businessmen, the first time for over 50 years that mainland commercial aircraft have landed in Taiwan. Moreover, cross-Strait trade increased by a third last year.

We welcome these developments and believe that such practical measures build confidence and promote dialogue. We believe that through such pragmatism, real progress can be made. We continue to oppose the use of force and to take the view that the Taiwan question should be settled peacefully through negotiation between the people on both sides of the Taiwan Strait.

We are paying close attention to the development of China's proposed anti-secession legislation, the background to which I discussed recently with the Vice Minister of China's Taiwan Affairs Office. We continue to urge both sides to avoid unilateral measures.

(HC Deb 15 March 2005 Vol. 432 c215W)

5/11

The Government was asked what assessment it has made of the Chinese Anti-secession Bill; what discussions he has had with his *(a)* Chinese, *(b)* Taiwanese, *(c)* European, and *(d)* US counterparts regarding the Bill and its implications for the region. An FCO Minister wrote:

... Ministers have taken a close interest in the development of China's Anti-Secession legislation. We have discussed it at both ministerial and official level with the Chinese, the US and other EU member states and institutions. Officials have discussed the issue through informal channels with the Taiwanese authorities.

The legislation enacted on 14 March is largely a codification of China's long-held position regarding Taiwan. The impact of the legislation will depend on the reaction of others and how China seeks to apply it.

Although the legislation refers to China's desire to resolve the issue peacefully, we are concerned that it makes reference to the possibility of the use of "non-peaceful means". We remain strongly opposed to the use of force.

The EU issued a Statement on 14 March appealing to both sides to avoid unilateral measures which might heighten tensions.

(HC Deb 16 March 2005 Vol. 432 c338W)

Part Five: I. A.5. *Subjects of International Law—States—Status and powers—Equality of States*

5/12

The Secretary of State for International Development made the following written Ministerial Statement:

I have placed in the Libraries of both Houses copies of a new paper entitled "Why we Need to Work More Effectively in Fragile States" published by the Department for International Development (DFID).

Fragile states—where Governments cannot or will not deliver security or basic services to the majority of its people—are one of the biggest challenges to the achievement of the millennium development goals and to global stability and security. Fragile states include countries with weak governance, those affected by conflict and those on the brink of conflict. It is often difficult to ensure that aid is delivered effectively in these countries, and there is a pressing need for the international community to reach agreement on new policies and ways of working to tackle these challenges.

The policy paper sets out how the Government will work in fragile states, by:

reviewing the way we allocate aid;
having more long-term planning and more realistic expectations;
developing better early warning systems;
bringing together the policies of UK Government Departments;
using more regional programming to address the causes of weakness;
increasing aid and making more use of civil society organisations to deliver it;
and making more effort to coordinate with other donors.

The implementation of these approaches will need collaboration across UK Government Departments, and internationally, a partnership with developing country Governments (wherever we can), international agencies and donors, civil society, the private sector and the research community. As a first step, DFID will this week host a senior level forum on development effectiveness in fragile states to secure agreement between major bilateral and multilateral donors on how to provide better aid to fragile states.

(HC Deb 12 January 2005 Vol. 668 WS17–WS18)

Part Five: I. B.1. *Subjects of International Law—States—Recognition—Recognition of States*

5/13

Cyprus

During a debate in the House of Commons, the Foreign Secretary said:

We must not see just one side of the issue. It is two-sided. The history of the conflict on the island of Cyprus is very complicated. We need each side to recognise the other with dignity and within a unified single Government.

I have already made it clear that in the European Union it would not be possible for us to operate if members did not recognise, de jure, the states around the table. That does not mean, however, that the obligations to achieve that position rest entirely on Turkey or on the Turkish Cypriot community. They rest equally on Turkey, the Turkish Cypriot community and the Government of Cyprus, as well as on the international community. That is made absolutely clear in a number of Security Council resolutions, including resolution 1250.

(HC Deb 11 October 2005 Vol. 437 c163)

5/14

Republic of Macedonia

During a debate in the House of Commons, the Foreign Secretary said:

In our bilateral relations, the name that we recognise is the Republic of Macedonia. The difficulty in international forums is that because of a long-standing historical dispute between Macedonia and Greece the name that is recognised is that of the former Yugoslav Republic of Macedonia. Discussions are taking place between Macedonia and Greece, and once those are resolved, the name issue will be resolved. This is a further indication of the tortured past that haunts the present in the Balkans.

(HC Deb 19 July 2005 Vol. 436 c1094)

5/15

Somalia

In a written answer, an FCO Minister wrote:

The international community does not recognise Somaliland as an independent state. We have urged the Somaliland authorities to agree a mutually acceptable solution on their future status with any eventual government in Somalia. We believe that African countries should take a lead in any eventual recognition process.

(HC Deb 13 December 2005 Vol. 440 c1956W)

5/16

Taiwan/China

The Government was asked about the effect of the UK's relations with Taiwan on any lifting of the arms embargo against China. An FCO Minister wrote:

We do not recognise Taiwan as a State. Despite having no diplomatic ties we enjoy good relations in areas such as trade, investment, culture and education.

We take every appropriate opportunity to convey to the Taiwanese authorities, through informal channels, and to the Chinese Government our strong opposition to the use of force or to any action that raises cross-straits tensions.

(HC Deb 20 January 2005 Vol. 429 c1055W)

Part Five: I. B.2. *Subjects of International Law—States—Recognition—Recognition of governments*

5/17

In a written answer, an FCO Minister wrote:

The Government's position continues to be that, where a new regime comes to power unconstitutionally, our attitude on the question of whether it qualifies to be treated as a government will be left to be inferred from the nature of the dealings, if any, that we may have with it, and in particular whether we are dealing with it on a normal government-to-government basis.

(HL Deb 14 November 2005 Vol. 675 cWA121)

5/18

Haiti

During a Security Council Meeting the representative of the United Kingdom stated:

The United Kingdom fully supports the Transitional Government [sc of Haiti]. It is important that all necessary effort be made to move towards a lasting, secure and stable environment in Haiti. In order to achieve that, it is essential that all democratic elements in the country have the opportunity to participate in the transitional process and the elections, including those members of the Lavalas party who have renounced violence.

The United Kingdom Government remains concerned by the human rights situation in Haiti. It is essential that those individuals who are and have been involved in human rights violations not have any place within the Government or associated bodies. Establishing an effective and respected Haitian National Police force, the officers of which are subject to thorough vetting, will be an important step towards improving that human rights record.

(UN Doc, S/PV.5110, 12 January 2005)

Part Five: I. B.6 *Subjects of International Law—States—Recognition—Non-recognition and its effects*

5/19

The Government was asked why, after rejecting the Annan plan, Greek Southern Cyprus was admitted as a constituent member of the European Union; and what benefits now enjoyed by Greek Southern Cyprus are still withheld from the Turkish Republic of Northern Cyprus, particularly in relation to trade, travel and education. An FCO Minister wrote:

The European Council decided at Helsinki in 1999 that a Cyprus settlement was not a precondition for the accession of Cyprus to the European Union (EU). On this basis, Cyprus signed the Treaty of Accession to the EU on 16 April 2003.

The Republic of Cyprus, including the northern part of the island, is an EU member state, but the acquis remains suspended in the north. Therefore in practice, Turkish Cypriots living north of the green line are unable to enjoy most of the benefits of EU membership.

With regard to travel, under UK Immigration Rules, Turkish Cypriots travelling on passports issued by the Republic of Cyprus have the same right of freedom and freedom to work in the UK as any other EU national. However, as the UK does not recognise the "Turkish Republic of Northern Cyprus", those travelling on documents issued by the authorities in the north are subject to immigration control. In the field of education, only Turkish Cypriots with Republic of Cyprus passports are eligible for EU fees at UK universities.

The Government are committed to ending the isolation of the Turkish Cypriots. Although Turkish Cypriots are currently unable to trade directly with the EU, a Commission proposal to that end is under discussion, as is a proposal to disburse 259 million euros of aid in the north. We fully support both proposals. The Green Line Regulation (GLR), agreed in August 2004, allows for limited trade across the green line. We support the Commission's proposals to amend the GLR to increase intra-island trade.

(HL Deb 1 February 2005 Vol. 669 c42WA)

5/20

The Government was asked what progress has been made during the nine months since the Turkish Cypriots voted to accept the Annan plan to end the Turkish Republic of Northern Cyprus's international isolation in respect of (a) direct flights, and (b) direct exporting facilities; and what progress they have made to meet any undertakings given at the time of the referendum. An FCO Minister wrote:

Following the referendum on both sides of the island on 24 April 2004, European Union Foreign Ministers expressed their determination to end the isolation of the Turkish Cypriots at the General Affairs and External Relations Council on 26 April 2004. In July, the European Commission drew up proposals for two regulations on financial aid and direct trade to help achieve this. The Government support these proposals. It has not been possible to agree these regulations as yet, but we support the presidency in its efforts to obtain agreement on this package as soon as possible.

Direct flights to the north of Cyprus would of course contribute to ending this isolation. This is an immensely complex area and we are examining the issue with our lawyers.

(HL Deb 1 February 2005 Vol. 669 c29WA)

5/21

The Government was asked whether (a) United Kingdom; (b) European Union; and (c) United States official trade delegations now fly into Ercan airport in Turkish Northern Cyprus; and whether the isolation of Northern Cyprus is likely to decrease following the general election there on 20 February. A Minister wrote:

I am unable to comment on whether official trade delegations from the EU or the US now fly into Ercan Airport in the north of Cyprus, but I can confirm that no official UK trade delegations have done so.

The EU has already made clear its determination to end the isolation of the Turkish Cypriots. We support this and believe that it will make a Cyprus settlement more likely, less costly and easier to consolidate—something that is undoubtedly in the interests of all Cypriots.

The Government's objective remains the reunification of Cyprus, and we continue to support all efforts to achieve this aim in a manner that is fair, viable and lasting for the benefit of all Cypriots. We therefore welcome the continued strong support for settlement and re-unification among Turkish Cypriots as reflected in the outcome of their elections on 20 February.

(HL Deb 7 March 2005 Vol. 670 cWA71)

5/22

The Government was asked which Member States of the EU were blocking the Commission proposal to allow direct trade between EU States and Northern Cyprus. An FCO Minister wrote:

The European Commission's proposed regulation on direct trade uses a legal base which would be subject to qualified majority voting. There has been no vote on this regulation, but some member states have expressed reservations about aspects of the regulation, including the legal base itself, and the Republic of Cyprus has expressed firm opposition. The Government support the proposal and are working to reassure those partners who have doubts that this regulation would be an effective way to fulfil the European Union's commitment to end the isolation of the Turkish Cypriots.

(HL Deb 4 April 2005 Vol. 671 cWA72)

5/23

An FCO Minister told the House of Lords:

We do not and will not recognise the self-styled "Turkish Republic of Northern Cyprus". In any case, the terms of the treaty of Cyprus's accession to the EU make it legally impossible. In addition, UN resolutions, some sponsored by the UK, prohibit this. And yet . . . the EU and the international community at large needs to embrace the Turkish Cypriots. This is not just a UK position.

The British Government maintain a dialogue with the Turkish Cypriots on all Cyprus settlement issues, including property, but we are not able to prevent property development. It is a matter of great regret that the island did not reunite on the basis of the UN Secretary-General's proposals last year, with its system of property restitution and compensation. Naturally, however, we do not encourage British citizens to buy property in northern Cyprus and through our travel advice website and response to queries we explain the unique circumstances in Cyprus.

Regarding direct flights to northern Cyprus, as reflected in the Foreign Secretary's response to the Foreign Affairs Committee, we continue to support in principle the commencement of direct flights to Northern Cyprus. We continue to believe that direct flights between the UK and the north would contribute significantly to the prospects for reunification through reducing economic disparities between the north and the south. This is an immensely complex legal area. As yet, no decision has been reached on the basis of legal considerations. The UK Government have no intention of pursuing a policy that is in contravention of international law . . . extradition is complicated by the non-recognition of the north.

(HL Deb 5 July 2005 Vol. 673 c591–593)

Part Five: I. E. *Subjects of International Law—States—Self-determination*

5/24

Iraq

In a debate in the House of Commons, referring to the position of the Kurds in Iraq, the Foreign Secretary said:

[This is] the way in which we are dealing with those secessionist tendencies. Like every previous relevant Security Council resolution, resolution 1546 reaffirms the territorial integrity of Iraq—its existing borders. Democracy is about giving people freedom—freedom to argue for any cause that they wish to support—and that is what these people have done. International borders, however, cannot be rewritten by any political party of any one country, and they will not be in this case. The future of Iraq's constitution must lie within the existing international borders.

(HC Deb 31 January 2005 Vol. 430 c586)

5/25

Kashmir

The Government was asked about the future of Kashmir—"Does the Minister agree that the wishes of the Kashmiri people must be paramount as this process moves forward?" The Minister replied:

Of course their views need to be taken into account, but since that discussion, civil society has come together in Kathmandu, and these issues and what is happening have been discussed among the Kashmiris.

(HL Deb 2 February 2005 Vol. 669 c226–227)

5/26

Non-self-governing Territories

The representative of the United Kingdom explained why the UK had abstained in the vote on "Information from Non-self-governing

Territories transmitted under Article 73e of the Charter of the United Nations". He said:

As in previous years, the UK abstained on this draft resolution. We do not take issue with the main objective of the resolution, which is to seek compliance with Article 73e of the Charter of the United Nations. We continue to meet our obligations fully in this regard, in respect of the United Kingdom Overseas Territories.

However, we believe that the decision as to whether a Non-Self-Governing Territory has reached a level of self-government sufficient to relieve the Administering Power of the obligation to submit information under Article 73e of the Charter is ultimately for the government of the territory and the Administering Power concerned and not the General Assembly.

(Text provided by FCO)

5/27

Papua/Indonesia

The Government was asked what steps it is taking to seek to facilitate dialogue between the Indonesian Government and the Papuan people to find a peaceful resolution to the West Papua conflict.

An FCO Minister wrote:

We have consistently made clear to the Indonesian Government our support for full implementation of the 2001 Special Autonomy Law. We believe this takes into account the aspirations of the Papuan people and respects Indonesia's territorial integrity. The new Government of President Yudhoyono has publicly committed itself to taking steps to implement this Law. We welcome this.

...

We are not aware of any discussions held with the UN to send Human Rights observers to Papua. We have followed the situation in Papua closely, and continue to make clear to the Indonesian Government our support for full implementation of the 2001 Special Autonomy Law.

(HC Deb 25 January 2005 Vol. 430 c240W)

5/28

Western Sahara

The Government was asked several questions about Western Sahara. An FCO Minister wrote:

The Government regard the sovereignty of Western Sahara as undetermined pending United Nations efforts to find a solution to the dispute over the territory. The UN legal counsel gave an opinion on the signing of contracts for exploration of mineral resources in Western Sahara in 2002 (S/2002/161 of 12 February 2002). We fully support this advice.

... The United Kingdom fully supports the efforts of the UN Secretary-General and his special representative Alvaro de Soto to find a just, lasting and mutually acceptable solution to the Western Sahara dispute which provides the people of the Western Sahara with an opportunity to exercise their right to self-determination.

We believe UN efforts to find a solution to the dispute should be maintained and continue to urge all parties to the dispute to engage constructively with the UN.

... The UK Government have had no recent discussions regarding fishing lands off Western Sahara. However the EU has, on several occasions held discussions with Morocco on fishing since the expiry of the EU Morocco fisheries agreement on 30 November 1999 ...

(HC Deb 24 February 2005 Vol. 431 c816–817W)

Part Five: II. A.1.(b). *Subjects of International Law—International organizations—In general—Status and powers—Privileges and immunities of the organization*

5/29

International Organisations Bill

At the Report stage of the International Organisations Bill, an FCO Minister explained why the legislation would not be retrospective. She said:

... the Government's firm view is that as a matter of legal policy it would not be appropriate for the new extended immunity to apply retrospectively ... to disputes in relation to contracts agreed before this new legislation comes into force. Why have we come to that conclusion? Because individuals or entities entering into contracts with the [Commonwealth] Secretariat—for example, into employment or commercial contracts—may be taken to have done so on the basis that their consent to be bound by that contract is predicated on the assumption that their contractual relations will be governed by the law regulating the legal position of the secretariat at the time on the contract. Therefore, the Secretariat should not have complete immunity from the jurisdiction of the courts in the UK in relation to claims under such contracts.

In those circumstances, I believe that it would be unfair to change the legal position in respect of existing contracts by taking away the right to challenge certain decisions of CSAT through the UK courts ... the general presumption of governments historically is that legislation should not make retrospective provision. There are exceptions to that—for example, when a retrospective provision can be justified on the basis that it would be of overriding public benefit. But conferring immunity from jurisdiction on the Secretariat so that it applies to contracts agreed before this legislation comes into force cannot be justified, in the Government's legal view. It would not be fair to those who entered into those contracts on an understanding that they would have recourse to the UK courts if necessary.

(HL Deb 11 January 2005 Vol. 668 cGC2)

5/30

In refusing to accept an amendment which would have limited the immunity of the Commonwealth Secretariat, the Minister said:

... we cannot agree to any limitation to the extended immunity conferred on the secretariat under the Act. The Bill simply brings the immunity conferred on the secretariat into line with that conferred on many other international organisations based in the United Kingdom.

Neither can we accept the amendment if its intention is to ensure the fairness of the CSAT dispute settlement procedure by requiring the tribunal to refer to the Human Rights Act 1998 and the Arbitration Act 1996 ... The important point is that the statute of the tribunal already takes into account the need for it to provide a fair and independent procedure. For example, Article 6, paragraph 2, of the statute reads,

> "The rules of the Tribunal shall ensure that applications are dealt with in a manner that is independent and impartial and consistent with the Commonwealth Harare Principles relating to fundamental human rights and the independence of the judiciary".

...

[I was] also asked about the independence of CSAT in relation to other governments. Although [it] is correct to say that the Secretary General formally appoints the members of the tribunal under Article 4 of the CSAT statute, those members must first have been selected by the Commonwealth governments on a regionally representative basis. The members ... are appointed for four-year terms, which also assists in ensuring their independence. All members of the tribunal are required by the statute to be of high moral character and to have appropriate experience.

The United Kingdom confers immunity from jurisdiction on many international organisations based in the UK and abroad. We are not aware that in those cases any such provision referring to the Human Rights Act and the Arbitration Act is in place and has been included in the relevant legislation. The amendment would therefore undermine that aim of bringing the treatment accorded to the secretariat by the UK into line with that accorded to many international organisations. We want to treat the secretariat as we treat other international organisations—no more, no less.

The amendment appears to concern the applicability of certain legislation to the Secretariat, which is a different and separate issue to that of immunity from jurisdiction of the courts. In referring to two particular Acts of Parliament, the amendment seems to suggest that CSAT need not have any regard to UK legislation—which it ought to have. Also, the fact that it refers only to disputes that affect the Secretariat staff suggests that the two Acts referred to would have no relevance to the context of disputes with, for example, external contractors, such as companies supplying goods to the Secretariat. The amendment refers only to staff. Those points are additional to the reasons that I have already given Committee members about why the amendment is not appropriate.

(HL Deb 11 January 2005 Vol. 668 cGC9–10)

5/31

The Minister went on:

... the Bill, in according immunity on the presidents and members of CSAT in respect of acts in the course of their official functions for the tribunal and providing an enabling provision to confer the same immunity on members of any successor body, implements a commitment in the agreed memorandum of the Commonwealth Secretariat, revised in 2002 ...

We do not consider that the immunity to be conferred, which relates to only the official functions of the members of the arbitral tribunal, is out of line with the immunity conferred by the UK on other international organisations and individuals connected with them, based in the UK or abroad. It assists in enabling the members of the tribunal to carry out their official functions independently—which comes to the heart of why we want to bring about these immunities and privileges—without fear of legal action against them as individuals as a result of their work for the tribunal.

(HL Deb 11 January 2005 Vol. 668 cGC11)

5/32

The Minister continued:

... the issue of the compatibility of the immunity provision with the European Convention on Human Rights [was raised] ... The issue of the compatibility of the conferral of immunity on international organisations with the European Convention on Human Rights has been considered in the past by the European Court of Human Rights in Strasbourg. The court has held, in a number of cases, that the right of access to a court under Article 6 of the convention is not absolute and may be subject to limitations, providing that they pursue a legitimate aim and are proportionate.

The Court in Strasbourg has accepted that conferring immunity from jurisdiction on international organisations is a legitimate aim, as it is an important means of ensuring that the proper functioning of such organisations continues free from unilateral interference by individual governments. It is also relevant to consider whether there is a reasonable alternative means by which individuals may pursue claims against the organisation ... would say that with the Commonwealth Secretariat, as is the case with many international organisations, there is an internal dispute resolution mechanism in place to hear such claims.

Since the creation of CSAT in 1995, a number of changes have been made to its statute. It is proposed that the revised version of the CSAT statute will be attached to the revised agreed memorandum of the Commonwealth Secretariat. Any further changes to the statute in future will be subject to the agreement of Commonwealth governments.

(HL Deb 11 January 2005 Vol. 668 cGC17)

5/33

The Minister concluded:

Finally, why do we need to confer privileges and immunities on any of these organisations and bodies, which is the underlying thrust of some of the arguments ... ? Privileges and immunities are conferred on organisations and bodies to ensure that they are able to carry out their functions without being impeded. That is the simple basis of this Bill. The general policy of Her Majesty's Government, which goes back to the 1980s, is that privileges and immunities should be granted primarily on the basis of functional need.

The scope of the privileges and immunities conferred and the organisations and bodies on which they are conferred are determined by the UK's international obligations ... As regards the organisations and bodies covered by the Bill, as I have said already we have signed international agreements committing us to confer privileges and immunities on them. A number of those agreements are long-standing, for example, those relating to the OSCE, ECHR and ITLOS were signed in 1993, 1996 and 1997 respectively. Further delay in fully implementing those agreements could be interpreted as a lack of commitment by the UK to those organisations. We would certainly not want that impression to go abroad.

(HL Deb 11 January 2005 Vol. 668 cGC18)

5/34

Another FCO Minister addressed the question of a proposed amendment affecting the privileges and immunities of the OSCE. He said:

The intention of the [amendment] appears to be to prevent the conferral of the privileges and immunities on the OSCE ... The reality is that this clause is needed to enable the UK to implement its political commitments in the Rome Council decision of 1993 by conferring legal capacity and privileges and immunities on the OSCE.

Deletion of the clause, as proposed, would make it impossible for the UK to comply with that undertaking.

The OSCE is an important instrument for the attainment of the Government's foreign policy priorities in international security. The Government do not want to see any weakening of our relationship with the OSCE. A failure to take this opportunity to implement the political commitments in the Rome Council decision must call into question our commitment to the OSCE altogether, whereas to include the OSCE in the Bill would be of little practical cost. It is unlikely that the OSCE will open a mission or an office in any part of the UK.

The privileges and immunities conferred by the Bill would have an effect only on the occasional visits of OSCE officials—we believe that there are about 10 overnight stays by those officials per year—such as the Secretary-General and the High Commissioner on National Minorities.

. . .

Apart from wanting to fulfil our international obligations properly, the UK remains committed to the OSCE's comprehensive and co-operative approach to security and our reasons are strong. The OSCE is the only security organisation in Europe considered a regional arrangement under Chapter VIII of the United Nations Charter. That is itself a distinction. In its region, it is the primary instrument for early warning and conflict prevention, crisis management and post-conflict rehabilitation. Its membership, which brings together the Euro-Atlantic and Euro-Asian communities, provides a unique forum for development and implementation of common values and democratic standards which we regard as essential to our security in the UK. A large number of activities have given practical expression to those objectives.

[The unamended clause was agreed to, Ed.]

(HL Deb 11 January 2005 Vol. 668 c25–26GC)

5/35

An FCO Minister said:

It is important to confer privileges and immunities on family members of officials of international organisations to ensure that the work of officials is not undermined by threats against close family members. That is why we want to cover family members . . . .

The proposed amendment would make it impossible for the UK to confer privileges and immunities on family members of senior staff of the International Criminal Court. The consequence would be that the UK would not be able fully to implement its obligations under the agreement on privileges and immunities of the International Criminal Court of 2002, which it signed on 10 September 2002.

Conferral of immunities and privileges on family members of senior staff of an international organisation is nothing new. Privileges and immunities have been conferred, for example, on family members and officials of the following organisations: the World Trade Organisation; the International Maritime Organisation; the International Seabed Authority; the Comprehensive Nuclear Test Ban Treaty Organisation.

Similarly, family members of diplomats enjoy privileges and immunities by virtue of the 1961 Vienna Convention on Diplomatic Relations. Furthermore, by conferring privileges and immunities on family members of senior staff of the ICC, the UK will be doing nothing more than has been agreed by the other 62 states which have signed the ICC agreement, including nearly all of the European member states . . .

[I was asked] whether, if an elderly relatives resides for half a year with the judge and half a year somewhere else, how the relative would benefit from privileges and immunities. The elderly relative will enjoy privileges and immunities only when residing with the judge. Once she stops residing, she will not enjoy privileges and immunities.

[I was] asked about refunds of VAT to officials of the International Criminal Court. Refunds of VAT will be made only to the organisation—to the ICC itself—for official activities and not to individual officials.

(HL Deb 11 January 2005 Vol. 668 c49GC)

5/36

The Joint Committee on Human Rights reported on the International Organisations Bill:

The Human Rights Implications of the Bill

3.3 Immunity from suit in UK courts engages the right to a fair hearing under Article 6 ECHR. Immunity from suit as provided for in the Bill might mean that, for example, employees of the organisations dealt with in the Bill would be unable to bring employment disputes before the UK courts.

3.4 Article 6 of the European Convention on Human Rights (ECHR) protects the right to have disputes concerning civil rights and obligations determined by a competent tribunal. Article 6 therefore guarantees a right of access to court in relation to such disputes. This right includes not only the right to institute proceedings before the court, but the right to a determination of the merits of the claim. This right is not however, an absolute one, since the right of access to court by its nature requires regulation by the state.

3.5 Therefore, procedural bars which prevent the full consideration of disputes are in certain circumstances permissible, where they pursue a legitimate aim and are proportionate to that aim. In order for such limitations to be permissible, they must not impair the very essence of the right of access to court.

3.6 In particular, the ECtHR accepts the need for immunity from suit of international organisations as a legitimate aim which may justify interference with Article 6 rights of access to court. Where an immunity from suit is based on clear rules of international law, its application in national law in a way that interferes with Article 6 rights cannot be regarded as arbitrary but the existence of such international rules does not of itself absolve the state of its obligations to comply with rights under Article 6. Any restriction of Article 6 rights arising from immunities from suit requires justification on the basis that it pursues a legitimate aim and is proportionate, and must be assessed in light of the particular circumstances of the case.

3.7 In the case of *Waite and Kennedy v Germany*, the ECtHR found that an immunity from suit of the European Space Agency in an employment dispute before the German courts constituted a proportionate interference with Article 6 rights. In that case, the finding that the interference was not arbitrary and pursued a legitimate aim was based in part on the existence of clear international rules making provision for the immunity, which had been implemented by the German national courts. The finding that the interference was proportionate was based on the existence of reasonable alternative means to protect effectively the applicant's rights under the Convention, through an independent appeals board. The existence of this mechanism meant that the very essence of the right of access to court had not been impaired.

3.8 In relation to a number of the organisations provided for in the Bill, immunity from suit is required by international agreements to which the UK is party, or to which it intends to become a party. This is the case in relation to EU bodies established under Title V and Title VI of the TEU.

3.9 The conferring of immunities on certain persons connected with the ICC implements an obligation under the Agreement on the Privileges and Immunities of the International Criminal Court 2002. The conferring of immunities on family members of the European Court of Human Rights in clause 7 of the Bill enables the UK to withdraw its current reservation to the Sixth Protocol to the General Agreement on the Privileges and Immunities of the Council of Europe. The provisions in relation to ITLOS permit the UK to ratify the Agreement on the Privileges and Immunities of the International Tribunal of the Law of the Sea.

3.10 A number of the immunities conferred do not appear to be required by international legal obligations, however. This appears to be the case in relation to the Commonwealth Secretariat and the Commonwealth Secretariat Arbitral Tribunal. Although the Explanatory Notes observe that conferring more extensive immunities on these bodies and persons connected with them would "bring the Secretariat into line with a number of other international organisations based in the UK", it is not clear that there is any international legal obligation in this regard, or in regard to the immunity from suit of CSAT and its members.

3.11 In relation to the OSCE, although the explanatory notes point out that the conferring of immunity follows the recommendations of the OSCE Ad Hoc Group of Legal and Other Experts, it is similarly unclear that there is any legal requirement to confer such immunity.

3.12 **We have written to the Foreign and Commonwealth Office asking for confirmation of whether it is considered that each of the immunities conferred by the Bill is required by a rule of international law; and in any cases where there is no such requirement, the reasons why the department considers that the interference with Article 6 rights pursues a legitimate aim.**

3.13 **We have also asked the Minister for clarification as to whether sufficient alternative avenues of redress are available to satisfy Article 6 rights of effective access to court in respect of each of the organisations dealt with in the Bill, and how these alternative mechanisms ensure that the very essence of the right of access to court is not impaired.**

[Footnotes omitted, Ed.]

(Fourth Report, 24 January 2005, HL26/HC224 (2005))

5/37

The Chair of the JCHR wrote to the FCO:

The Joint Committee on Human Rights is considering how to report on the International Organisations Bill. The Committee has conducted an initial examination of the Bill, and would be grateful for further information to assist in its scrutiny of the human rights compatibility of the Bill.

The immunities conferred by the Bill engage the right of access to court, protected by Article 6 ECHR. ECtHR jurisprudence accepts that immunities from suit of international organisations may amount to justifiable interferences with Article 6 rights, given the importance of international co-operation through such organisations. However, it requires that such immunities should have a basis in international law, and that they should be proportionate to their aim.

The European Court of Human Rights, in *Waite and Kennedy v Germany*, found the immunity from suit of an international organisation to be compliant with Article 6. Significant factors in the case were the basis of the immunity in clear rules of international law and the existence of reasonable alternative means to protect the applicant's Convention rights, through an independent appeals board.

We would be grateful for further information on two points.

1. **Can you confirm whether it is considered that each of the immunities conferred by the Bill is required by a rule of international law? In any cases where there is no such requirement, please provide reasons why the department considers that the interference with Article 6 rights pursues a legitimate aim.**
2. **Please clarify what alternative avenues of redress are available to satisfy Article 6 rights of effective access to court in respect of each of the organisations dealt with in the Bill, and how these alternative mechanisms ensure that the very essence of the right of access to court is not impaired.**

[Footnotes omitted, Ed.]

(Fourth Report, 24 January 2005, HL26/HC224 (2005)), Appendix 3)

5/38

The FCO replied:

As you rightly point out the European Court of Human Rights, in *Waite and Kennedy v Germany*, found immunity from suit of an international organisation to be compliant with Article 6 of the ECHR. The Court also noted in that case that the attribution of privileges and immunities to international organisations is an essential means of ensuring the proper functioning of such organisations free from unilateral interference by individual governments, and that the immunity from jurisdiction commonly accorded by States to international organisations is a long-standing practice established in the interests of the good working of the organisations.

I will respond to the two points set out in your letter on which the Committee requires further information below.

1. BASIS IN INTERNATIONAL LAW

The Bill confers jurisdictional immunities on the Commonwealth Secretariat and the President and members of the Commonwealth Secretariat Arbitral Tribunal (CSAT). The Commonwealth Secretariat was established by a Memorandum on the Commonwealth Secretariat (the 1965 Agreed Memorandum), which was agreed at a Commonwealth Heads of Government meeting in 1965. Annex A of that Memorandum sets out the privileges and immunities that the UK is required to accord; this includes immunity from jurisdiction currently enjoyed by the Secretariat. The 1965 Agreement is implemented in the UK by the Commonwealth Secretariat Act 1966. In 2002, at the Meeting of Commonwealth Heads of Government in Australia, a revised text of the 1965 Memorandum was agreed (the Revised Agreed Memorandum). The Revised Agreed Memorandum adds a new paragraph to Annex A conferring official act immunity on the President and members of CSAT. The purpose of clause 2 of the Bill is to implement this change.

CSAT was established by the Commonwealth Secretariat in 1995 as an internal arbitral body to deal with contractual disputes between the Commonwealth Secretariat on the one hand, and its staff and any other person who enters into a written contract with the Commonwealth Secretariat on the other. However, the exclusive nature of the jurisdiction of CSAT to determine employment and contractual disputes was limited by the 2002 High Court decision *Selina Mohsin v Commonwealth Secretariat* when the court found that Part I of the Arbitration Act 1966 was applicable to the decisions and procedures of CSAT, and therefore the UK courts retained some jurisdiction. In light of this decision the Commonwealth Secretariat and a number of Commonwealth Governments have raised concerns about the level of immunity from the jurisdiction of the UK courts conferred on the Commonwealth Secretariat. The UK accepts, in principle, that the Commonwealth Secretariat's jurisdictional immunity should be on the same level as that enjoyed by other international organisations based in the UK. Amendments to Annex A of the Revised Agreed Memorandum to reflect the extended immunity are expected to be acceptable to the Commonwealth Governments and will be formally agreed once the Bill receives Royal Assent. Clause 11(4) of the Bill provides that clauses 1 to 3 of the Bill will come into force on such day as the Secretary of State appoints. We will ensure that clause 1 of the Bill, which will confer the extended immunity on the Commonwealth Secretariat, enters into force at the same time as the agreed changes to Annex A. To agree changes to Annex A before the Bill enters into force could result in the UK not being able to fulfil its commitments in the Revised Agreed Memorandum as HMG could not be sure that clause 1 of the Bill will proceed through both Houses without any amendments.

Clauses 4 to 8 of the Bill concern the Organization for Security and Co-operation in Europe (the OSCE), bodies established under the Treaty on European Union (EU bodies), the International Criminal Court (the ICC), the European Court of Human Rights (the ECHR) and International Tribunal for the Law of the Sea (ITLOS). These are enabling clauses which do not confer any privileges or immunities but will enable the conferral of privileges and immunities by Orders in Council. I have, however, set out below the bases of the Orders in Council which will be made pursuant to clauses 4 to 8 of the Bill—

(a) OSCE: The OSCE was previously known as the Conference on Security and Co-operation in Europe (the CSCE). Clause 5 of the Bill will enable the United Kingdom to implement the provisions regarding legal capacity and privileges and immunities on the OSCE and certain categories of persons connected with it, as set out in a report of the CSCE Ad Hoc Group of Legal and Other Experts annexed to the decision of the CSCE Council of Ministers of 1 December 1993 held in Rome (the 1993 Rome Council Decision). The OSCE is based upon political commitments rather than any binding international agreement. However, the OSCE has been established by agreement between States and the various Documents and Charters of the OSCE, including the 1993 Rome Council Decision, evidence a commitment amongst participating States that the Organisation should be constituted and administered according to the terms of those instruments.

The OSCE is an important instrument for the attainment of HMG's foreign policy priorities for international security. The UK is committed to the OSCE's comprehensive and co-operative approach to security and values the unique contribution it makes in support of conflict prevention and nation building including in the Balkans, the Caucasus and Central Asia. Its membership, which brings together Euro-Atlantic and Euro-Asian communities, provides a unique forum for development and implementation of common values and democratic standards we regard as essential to our security. HMG does not want to see any weakening of the UK's relationship with the OSCE. A failure to take this opportunity to implement the political commitments in the Rome Council Decision could call into question our commitment to the OSCE.

(b) EU bodies: Clause 5 of the Bill will enable the conferral of legal capacity and privileges and immunities on bodies established under the Treaty on European Union, and certain categories of individuals connected with those bodies. There are currently three EU bodies on which privileges and immunities will be conferred pursuant to this clause, and in all three cases, the basis of the privileges and immunities are EU Council Decisions—

(i) ATHENA: Decision of the Representatives of the Governments of the Member States meeting within the Council of 28 April 2004 concerning privileges and immunities granted to ATHENA.

(ii) Institute for Security Studies and the EU Satellite Centre: Decision of the Representatives of the Governments of the Member States of the European Union, meeting within the Council on the privileges and immunities granted to the European Union Institute for Security Studies and the European Union Satellite Centre, and to their bodies and staff members.

(c) ICC: The international law basis of the privileges and immunities conferred pursuant to the entry into force of clause 6 of the Bill is the Agreement on the Privileges and Immunities of the International Criminal Court of 10 September 2002 which obliges States Parties to confer legal capacity and privileges and immunities on the ICC and specified categories of individuals connected with the ICC.

(d) ECHR: The international law basis for the conferral of privileges and immunities on the family members of the judges of the Court is article 1 of the Sixth Protocol to the General Agreement on the Privileges and Immunities of the Council of Europe of 1949.

(e) ITLOS: The international law basis for the conferral of privileges and immunities on ITLOS and various categories of individuals connected with it is the Agreement on the Privileges and Immunities of the International Tribunal of the Law of the Sea done at New York on 23 May 1997.

2. ALTERNATIVE AVENUES OF REDRESS

The alternative avenues of redress available in respect of each organisation covered by the Bill are set out below—

(a) Commonwealth Secretariat: There is an internal dispute resolution mechanism in place, the Commonwealth Secretariat Arbitral Tribunal, in which individuals may pursue claims against the organisation. CSAT was established in 1995 by the Commonwealth Secretariat. A number of changes were made to the Statute of the CSAT in 2002 to ensure that it is an independent and impartial mechanism for settlement of disputes.

(b) OSCE: In 2003 the OSCE adopted Staff rules and regulations which made provision for an appeals procedure for staff or mission members against administrative decisions concerning alleged non-observance of their letters of appointment or terms of assignment, or of any provisions governing their working conditions, as well as in relation to disciplinary measures taken against them. In the event of an appeal, an Internal Review Board is established.

Staff or mission members also have a right of final appeal to a Panel of Adjudicators against an administrative decision directly affecting them in accordance with the Terms of Reference of employment. The Panel of Adjudicators is appointed from a roster to which all participating States are invited to nominate candidates.

(c) EU bodies: The ATHENA financing mechanism has no permanent staff. Staff from the Commission or Council Secretariat seconded to ATHENA will be subject to the rules and regulations for employees of the Institutions. Secondees from Member States are subject to the rules on "Seconded National Experts".

The EU Satellite Centre and the Institute for Security Studies have both agreed separate staff regulations for employees. There is an appeals procedure which includes mediation by a qualified, independent legal expert and an independent Appeals Board made up of staff from outside the agencies. Temporary staff also have access to this appeals procedure. In addition the staff regulations state that disputes not relating to the rights and remuneration of temporary staff come under the jurisdiction of the courts of the host State.

(d) ICC: The ICC is at a formative stage in its development. It is currently working to develop its internal procedures. Article 11.2 of the ICC Staff Regulations states that "The Administrative Tribunal of the International Labour Organisation shall, under conditions prescribed in its statute, hear and pass judgement upon applications from staff members alleging non-observance of their terms of appointment, including all pertinent regulations and rules."

Article 31 of the Agreement on Privileges and Immunities obliges the Court to make provision for various types of dispute with third parties, including where these relate to an ICC official with immunity. In addition, States parties are currently reviewing a Code of conduct for counsel before the ICC which will have a disciplinary procedure.

(e) ECHR: While the Bill only concerns family members of judges of the Court, staff of the ECHR have access to the Council of Europe's Administrative Tribunal, which is made up of three judges. One is appointed by the European Court of Human Rights and should hold, or have held, judicial office in one of the Member States of the Council of Europe or with another international judicial body, other than present judges of the European Court of Human Rights. The other two judges are selected by the Council of Europe's Committee of Ministers from among jurists or other persons of high standing. The judges of the Administrative Tribunal are appointed for a term of three years.

(f) ITLOS: Staff are employed by the UN and have access to the UN Administrative Tribunal.

(Seventh Report, 9 February 2005, HL47/HC333 (2005), Appendix 1)

5/39

Having had this reply, the JCHR said:

Proportionality of the interference

1.6 In our first report on the Bill, we raised two queries: first the degree to which the immunities conferred by the Bill were necessary to fulfil international legal obligations, and secondly the extent to which the organisations affected by the Bill had in place alternative dispute resolution procedures sufficient to ensure that the very essence of the right to a fair hearing under Article 6 ECHR would not be impaired by the conferral of immunity from suit. Both of these matters are relevant to the justification for an immunity from suit as in pursuit of a legitimate aim, and to the proportionality of the immunity to that aim. We are grateful for the comprehensive information provided by the FCO in response to these queries.

1.7 We retain some concerns regarding the extended immunities conferred on the Commonwealth Secretariat by clause 1 of the Bill. As Mr Rammell notes in his letter to us, privileges and immunities accorded to the Commonwealth Secretariat have their basis in Annex A to the 1965 Agreed Memorandum agreed at a Commonwealth Heads of Government meeting in 1965, implemented in the UK by the Commonwealth Secretariat Act 1966. The FCO explains that, in response to the High Court decision in *Selina Mohsin v Commonwealth Secretariat*, where it was held that Part I of the Arbitration Act 1996 was applicable to the Commonwealth Secretariat Arbitral Tribunal (CSAT), the Bill intends to clarify that there is no recourse to the courts under the Arbitration Act, from decisions of CSAT.

1.8 Currently, the Commonwealth Secretariat Act 1966 allows an exception to the Commonwealth Secretariat's immunity from suit in respect of arbitration proceedings. Therefore, under Part I of the Arbitration Act, there is some judicial supervision of arbitration proceedings, including the power to enforce an award, power to challenge the jurisdiction of the arbitral tribunal, power to challenge a serious irregularity in the arbitral proceedings, and power to appeal to the courts on a point of law (unless otherwise agreed by the parties to the arbitration). The nature of the courts' jurisdiction under Part 1 of the Arbitration Act is therefore limited, and provides minimum protections against procedural unfairness.

1.9 The Government does not suggest that the exclusion of CSAT proceedings from judicial supervision under Part I of the Arbitration Act 1996 is required by the current terms of the Agreed Memorandum. However, it points out that "both the Commonwealth Secretariat and a number of Commonwealth Governments have raised concerns about the level of immunity from the jurisdiction of the UK courts conferred on the Commonwealth Secretariat" and states that therefore "amendments to Annex A of the Revised Agreed Memorandum to reflect the extended immunity are expected to be acceptable to the Commonwealth Governments and will be formally agreed once the Bill receives Royal Assent". **In our view, the extension of the Commonwealth Secretariat's immunity under clause 1 of the Bill, beyond that required by existing international obligations, to exclude the limited judicial oversight currently available under Part I of the Arbitration Act 1996, may risk disproportionate interference with the Article 6 right of access to court.**

1.10 We also asked the FCO for further information on the alternative recourse available to employees of the Commonwealth Secretariat, and other international organisations affected by the Bill. We note that concerns have been expressed in debates on the Bill as to the independence of CSAT from the Commonwealth Secretariat, in particular as regards appointment and remuneration. In its letter to us, the FCO characterised CSAT as "an internal dispute resolution mechanism" but stated that "changes were made to the Statute of the CSAT in 2002 to ensure that it is an independent and impartial mechanism for settlement of disputes."

1.11 We emphasise that, for an immunity from suit to be Article 6 compliant, alternative mechanisms must be in place to provide recourse to a tribunal which is fully independent, both institutionally and in practice, of the international organisation involved in the dispute. An internal dispute resolution mechanism is unlikely to satisfy this requirement. Where recourse to an independent tribunal is not provided, the very essence of the right of access to court under Article 6 ECHR may be impaired.

(Seventh Report, 9 February 2005, HL47/HC33 (2005))

5/40

An FCO Minister wrote to the JCHR:

I refer to the Seventh Report of the Joint Committee on Human Rights in which the Committee expresses some concerns about clause 1 of the International Organisations Bill.

The Committee considers that extending the Commonwealth Secretariat's immunity under Clause 1 of the Bill in the absence of an international obligation to do so risks disproportionate interference with the Article 6 right of access to court.

It would be improper and a breach of the UK's duties under international law for the Government to undertake to be bound by an international obligation before the legislation necessary to implement that obligation was in place. To do otherwise would mean that the UK would not be in a position to fulfil its obligation and this could result in a breach by the UK of its international obligation. If Parliament decided not to pass relevant legislation, the UK would continue to be in breach of the obligation. That is why the invariable practice with any treaty is that the Government does not ratify the treaty until legislation has been passed enabling the UK to fulfil the obligations it contains. For example, the UK has not undertaken an international obligation to confer privileges and immunities on the International Tribunal for the Law of the Sea (ITLOS) because it has not ratified the Agreement on the Privileges and Immunities of the International Tribunal of the Law of the Sea. It will only ratify the Agreement and become bound by the obligations contained in the Agreement once this Bill has received Royal Assent. In the same way, therefore, although the Government has agreed to revisions to Annex A of the Revised Agreed Memorandum on the Commonwealth Secretariat in principle, these revisions will only be formalised once the UK is able to implement the commitments in the Annex by means of the International Organisations Act. This is the proper and normal process.

It is also important to note the entry into force provisions of the Bill. Clause 11(4) provides that clauses 1 to 3 of the Bill will come into force on such day as the Secretary of State appoints. We will ensure that clause 1 of the Bill, which will confer the extended immunity on the Commonwealth Secretariat, enters into force at the same time as the agreed changes to the Revised Agreed Memorandum. Clause 1 will not therefore be in force unless and until there is an obligation in the Memorandum.

The Committee also questioned whether the Commonwealth Secretariat Arbitral Tribunal is fully independent from the Commonwealth Secretariat. Although it is correct that the Secretary-General formally appoints the members of the Tribunal, under Article IV of the CSAT Statute those members must first have been selected by the Commonwealth Governments on a regionally representative basis. The Members are appointed for 4-year terms, which also assists in ensuring their independence. All members of the Tribunal are required by the Statute to be of high moral character and to have appropriate experience. Of the five current members, four are former Chief justices of Commonwealth countries, and the other a practising QC. The members are selected on a geographically representative basis as well as on gender basis. Significantly, the Statute also requires that the Rules of the Tribunal, which are drawn up by the members and the President of the Tribunal, must ensure that applications before the Tribunal are dealt with in a manner that is independent and impartial and consistent with the Commonwealth Harare principles relating to fundamental human rights and independence of the judiciary.

The UK Government would obviously be very concerned if the CSAT failed to provide for an independent and impartial mechanism for the settlement of disputes and it would be something that should be raised with the Secretariat and Commonwealth Governments for discussion, and revision of the Statute as appropriate. But we do not believe this is the case.

25 February 2005

(JCHR, Fifteenth Report, Scrutiny: Seventh Progress Report, HL97/HC496 (2005), Appendix 4))

5/41

The Joint Committee on Human Rights reported on the International Organisations Bill:

Introduction

1.1 The International Organisations Bill was introduced in the House of Lords on 24 November 2004.[3] A statement has been made by Baroness Symons of Vernham Dean under section 19 (1)(a) of the Human Rights Act 1998 that, in her view, the provisions of the Bill are compatible with Convention rights. The Bill completed its committee stage in the House of Lords on 11 January 2005. We reported our preliminary views on the human rights compatibility of the Bill in our Fourth Report of this Session.[4] We also wrote to the Foreign and Commonwealth Office requesting clarification on two points. We have now received a reply to that letter from Bill Rammell MP, Minister of State at the FCO,[5] and in light of this we set out our conclusions on the human rights compatibility of the Bill.

The purpose of the Bill

1.2 The International Organisations Bill is intended to allow privileges and immunities from suit to be conferred on a number of international organisations and bodies which operate in the UK, and on certain individuals connected to those organisations and bodies.[6]

The right of access to court

1.3 The conferring of immunities from suit engages the right to a fair hearing in the determination of civil rights and obligations, protected by Article 6 ECHR. Where civil rights and obligations are in dispute, Article 6 requires a right of access to an independent and impartial tribunal, with competence to hear and determine the dispute.[7]

1.4 It is important to emphasise that neither the European Convention of Human Rights, nor the Human Rights Act 1998 are in any way disapplied in respect of international organisations operating in the UK.[8] In particular, proceedings relating to international organisations are not exempt from fair hearing obligations under Article 6 ECHR. Rather, Convention law recognises that the right of access to court under Article 6 may be legitimately qualified in the interests of the immunity of such organisations. Thus the European Court of Human Rights has stated that—

where States establish international organisations in order to pursue or strengthen their cooperation in certain fields of activities, and where they attribute to these organisations certain competences and accord them immunities, there may be implications as to the protection of fundamental rights. It would be incompatible with the purpose and object of the Convention, however, if the Contracting States were thereby absolved from their responsibility under the Convention in relation to the field of activity covered by such attribution.[9]

1.5 Since the right of access to court is not absolute, limitations on access to court, including procedural bars to access such as immunity from suit, may be justified where they are in accordance with law, pursue a legitimate aim and are proportionate to that aim. However, the European Court of Human Rights has stressed that restrictions on access to court such as immunity from suit must not impair the very essence of the right to a fair hearing under Article 6.[10] A key factor in determining whether the very essence of the right has been impaired, is whether those affected by the immunity have recourse to alternative and adequate avenues of dispute resolution.[11]

Proportionality of the interference

1.6 In our first report on the Bill, we raised two queries: first the degree to which the immunities conferred by the Bill were necessary to fulfil international legal obligations, and secondly the extent to which the organisations affected by the Bill had in place alternative dispute resolution procedures sufficient to ensure that the very essence of the right to a fair hearing under Article 6 ECHR would not be impaired by the conferral of immunity from suit. Both of these matters are relevant to the justification for an immunity from suit as in pursuit of a legitimate aim, and to the proportionality of the immunity to that aim. We are grateful for the comprehensive information provided by the FCO in response to these queries.

1.7 We retain some concerns regarding the extended immunities conferred on the Commonwealth Secretariat by clause 1 of the Bill. As Mr Rammell notes in his letter to us, privileges and immunities accorded to the Commonwealth Secretariat have their basis in Annex A to the 1965 Agreed Memorandum agreed at a Commonwealth Heads of Government meeting in 1965, implemented in the UK by the Commonwealth Secretariat Act 1966. The FCO explains that, in response to the High Court decision in *Selina Mohsin v Commonwealth Secretariat*,[12] where it was held that Part I of the Arbitration Act 1996 was applicable to the Commonwealth Secretariat Arbitral Tribunal (CSAT), the Bill intends to clarify that there is no recourse to the courts under the Arbitration Act, from decisions of CSAT.

1.8 Currently, the Commonwealth Secretariat Act 1966 allows an exception to the Commonwealth Secretariat's immunity from suit in respect of arbitration proceedings. Therefore, under Part I of the Arbitration Act, there is some judicial supervision of arbitration proceedings, including the power to enforce an award, power to challenge the jurisdiction of the arbitral tribunal, power to challenge a serious irregularity in the arbitral proceedings, and power to appeal to the courts on a point of law (unless otherwise agreed by the parties to the arbitration).[13] The nature of the courts' jurisdiction under Part 1 of the Arbitration Act is therefore limited, and provides minimum protections against procedural unfairness.

1.9 The Government does not suggest that the exclusion of CSAT proceedings from judicial supervision under Part I of the Arbitration Act 1996 is required by the current terms of the Agreed Memorandum. However, it points out that "both the Commonwealth Secretariat and a number of Commonwealth Governments have raised concerns about the level of immunity from the jurisdiction of the UK courts conferred on the Commonwealth Secretariat" and states that therefore "amendments to Annex A of the Revised Agreed Memorandum to reflect the extended immunity are expected to be acceptable to the Commonwealth Governments and will be formally agreed once the Bill receives Royal Assent".[14] **In our view, the extension of the Commonwealth Secretariat's immunity under clause 1 of the Bill, beyond that required by existing international obligations, to exclude the limited judicial oversight currently available under Part I of the Arbitration Act 1996, may risk disproportionate interference with the Article 6 right of access to court.**

1.10 We also asked the FCO for further information on the alternative recourse available to employees of the Commonwealth Secretariat, and other international organisations affected by the Bill. We note that concerns have been expressed in debates on the Bill as to the independence of CSAT from the Commonwealth Secretariat, in particular as regards appointment and remuneration.[15] In its letter to us, the FCO characterised CSAT as "an internal dispute resolution mechanism" but stated that "changes were made to the Statute of the CSAT in 2002 to ensure that it is an independent and impartial mechanism for settlement of disputes."

1.11 We emphasise that, for an immunity from suit to be Article 6 compliant, alternative mechanisms must be in place to provide recourse to a tribunal which is fully independent, both institutionally and in practice, of the international organisation involved in the dispute. An internal dispute resolution mechanism is unlikely to satisfy this requirement. Where recourse to an independent tribunal is not provided, the very essence of the right of access to court under Article 6 ECHR may be impaired. **We draw this matter to the attention of both Houses.**

Footnotes

3 HL Bill 2

4 Fourth Report of Session 2004–05, Scrutiny: First Progress Report, HL Paper 26, HC 224

5 Appendix 1

6 The relevant organisations are: the Commonwealth Secretariat (clause 1); the Commonwealth Secretariat Arbitral Tribunal (CSAT) (clause 2); the Organisation for Security and Co-operation in Europe (OSCE) (clause 4); certain EU bodies (clause 5); the International Criminal Court (ICC) (clause 6); the European Court of Human Rights (ECtHR) (clause 7); and the International Tribunal for the Law of the Sea (ITCLOS) (clause 8).

7 Golder v UK (1979–80) 1 EHRR 524
8 Article 1 ECHR requires States Party to the Convention to secure the Convention rights to everyone in the jurisdiction. Matthews v United Kingdom (1999) 28 EHRR 361 paras. 29–35
9 Waite and Kennedy v Germany, App. No. 26083/94, para. 67
10 ibid., para. 59
11 ibid., para. 73
12 [2002] EHC 377 (Comm)
13 Sections 66–69, Arbitration Act 1996
14 Appendix 1
15 HL Deb, 11 January 2005, Cols. GC5-GC10

(JCHR, Seventh Report, Scrutiny: Third Progress Report, HL47/HC333 (2005))

5/42

At the Report stage of the International Organisations Bill, an FCO Minister referred to the observations of the JCHR and the FCO reply to them [see **5/40** and **5/41**, Ed.]. She said:

The noble Baroness also raised her concerns about human rights issues. She referred to correspondence between the Joint Committee and the Minister. She spoke of concerns to do with an adequate alternative remedy to CSAT applicants. I would say in reply that the important point is that the statute of CSAT already makes provision for a fair and independent procedure which is consistent with fundamental human rights. Article 6.2 of the statute reads:

> "The rules of the tribunal shall ensure that applicants are dealt with in a manner that is independent, impartial and consistent with the Commonwealth Harare principles relating to fundamental human rights and the independence of the judiciary".

(HL Deb 7 February 2005 Vol. 669 c549)

5/43

At the Report stage of the International Organisations Bill, an FCO Minister said:

In the modern world, [privileges and immunities] are still considered by the international community to be essential to ensure that relations between states, bilateral or multilateral, through the medium of an international organisation, can be conducted without fear of intimidation or harassment of their representatives. It follows that international organisations and their staff—if they find themselves benefiting from those immunities to enable them to fulfil their roles effectively and independently and without fear of undue pressure from any quarter—will do those jobs properly, in a way that is of benefit to the international community.

The Government's approach to questions of privileges and immunities for international organisations and their staff is long established. It is based on the fundamental principle that privileges and immunities are not for the benefit of individuals, and should be granted only where they are necessary to ensure that the organisation and its staff can perform their legitimate functions effectively. On the question of fiscal privileges, our policy adheres to the internationally accepted principles that one state should not tax another through the medium of an international organisation, and that states should not benefit financially from the presence of an organisation which happens to be located on their soil. The agreements setting up international organisations establish the level of privileges and immunities necessary for their efficient operation, and all are subject to separate negotiation.

When the Government consider their position on the level of privileges and immunities appropriate to each organisation, some factors are relevant ... The first factor is the area of activity—whether the organisation is of a political, commercial, social, cultural, technical, scientific or some other nature. Then there is the geographical scope—whether the organisations cover a wide area or are limited to a particular region, and whether they operate in the UK. For example, if an organisation has its headquarters in the UK, it may well be appropriate to confer a wider range of privileges and immunities on it.

The third factor is the power of decisions—whether an organisation's decisions are binding on member states and on individuals within them, or are recommendatory or only advisory. The fourth point is the role and purpose of the organisation—whether it serves limited interests, such as those of a few producers, or has wider aims, such as serving both producers and consumers; whether it is of a financial nature, aimed at the development and improvement of social conditions; or whether it is of considerable political or economic importance.

The fifth factor is financial considerations about functions—whether the organisation is non-profit-making and funded entirely by member states or has any commercial activities. The sixth is membership—whether it is composed entirely of sovereign states or extends to non-governmental entities, and which states are members. The final factor is size. A large multinational organisation will normally require more extensive privileges and immunities than a small one.

The Government believe that to test against that template is the right practical and flexible approach. We will therefore continue to look closely at privileges and immunities proposed for international organisations on an individual basis, judged against those criteria. It is important to note that the immunities granted to the staff of international organisations are in general very restricted. Of the 3,000 staff of international organisations based or with offices in the United Kingdom, only 20 high officers enjoy the equivalent of full diplomatic immunity. The remainder have no immunity entitlement beyond immunity for acts performed in the course of their official duties.

There have been very few cases where staff of international organisations in the UK have abused their privileges or immunities.

(HL Deb 7 February 2005 Vol. 669 c567–569)

5/44

An FCO Minister introduced the second reading of the International Organisations Bill in the House of Commons. He said:

The International Organisations Bill is designed to ensure the effective functioning of international organisations and bodies. The measures are required to enable Her Majesty's Government to meet outstanding international commitments to confer legal capacity and privileges and immunities on a number of international organisations and bodies and certain categories of individuals connected to them, or to ensure parity of treatment between organisations where appropriate.

Under existing legislation, we are unable to confer privileges and immunities on these organisations, even though we have signed international agreements committing us to do so. Some of the agreements are of long standing, dating back more than a decade.

For most of the organisations concerned, the privileges and immunities will be conferred by Orders in Council, which will be subject to the affirmative procedure. Consequently, Parliament will have ample opportunity to scrutinise and debate the specific privileges and immunities that will be conferred on these organisations.

Let me now turn to why we grant privileges and immunities to international organisations and bodies. Privileges and immunities are conferred on organisations and bodies so that they can carry out their functions without being impeded. The long-standing policy of HMG is that privileges and immunities should be granted primarily on the basis of functional need, to ensure that only those privileges and immunities necessary for the organisation to function effectively are granted. All cases are separately negotiated and it is rare that two organisations benefit from identical privileges and immunities.

Immunities granted to the staff of international organisations are generally very restricted. Of the 3,000 staff of international organisations based, or with offices, in the UK, only 80 senior officers enjoy the equivalent of full diplomatic privileges and immunities. The remainder have no entitlement beyond immunity for acts performed in the course of their official duties.

As regards privileges, the Government's policy adheres to the internationally accepted principle that states should not financially benefit from the presence of an organisation on their soil, and that one member state should not tax another through the medium of an international organisation. Immunity from the jurisdiction of the courts of the host state is justified by the need for independence of the international organisation and the necessity of precluding any undue interference by the host state with the activities of the international organisation. That ensures that the organisation can then work in an environment of independence and security without fear of legal reprisals. That is an established principle of international relations.

I turn to the details of the Bill. Clauses 1 to 3 concern the Commonwealth Secretariat and the Commonwealth Secretariat Arbitral Tribunal. The Commonwealth Secretariat is the primary intergovernmental organisation of the

Commonwealth. The CSAT is an internal arbitral body established to resolve contractual disputes between the Secretariat and its staff, or any other person who enters into a written contract with it.

The Bill will change the following three aspects of the privileges and immunities enjoyed by the Commonwealth Secretariat. At present, the Secretariat has immunity from the jurisdiction of the courts in the UK, except in cases where the immunity is waived by the Secretary-General, in cases concerning motor accidents or motor traffic offences, and where arbitration proceedings are undertaken in respect of a written contract with the Secretariat.

That last exception, concerning arbitration proceedings, has been interpreted by the courts in the UK as allowing the courts to exercise supervisory jurisdiction over CSAT arbitration proceedings under the Arbitration Act 1996. That particular exception to immunity will be removed by clause 1 of the Bill, which will bring the Secretariat's immunity provisions into line with those enjoyed by many other international organisations based in the UK.

The extended immunity will not apply to written contracts entered into by, or on behalf of, the Secretariat before clause 1 enters into force. For those contracts courts will continue to have supervisory jurisdiction under the Arbitration Act 1996.

The Bill will also change the privileges and immunities of the Commonwealth Secretariat staff. Clause 2 will accord the president and members of CSAT the same immunity from legal process in relation to their official acts that is conferred on the Commonwealth Secretariat staff under the Commonwealth Secretariat Act 1966. The Bill provides that if the CSAT is replaced by an equivalent successor body, an order may be made by the Secretary of State to amend the 1966 Act for the purposes of conferring privileges and immunities on the successor body equivalent to those enjoyed by the CSAT.

Clause 3 confers exemption from UK income tax on all staff of the Secretariat in respect of salaries and emoluments that they receive as its staff. That new exemption will not apply to pensions, annuities payments or to income received by staff from other sources. It is conditional on the Secretariat establishing an internal tax system for its own benefit, as is currently the case with a number of other international organisations.

I turn to the other organisations affected. Clause 4 concerns the Organisation for Security and Co-operation in Europe. The Bill will bring it within the scope of the International Organisations Act 1968, enabling the United Kingdom to implement the political commitments it made when it endorsed the 1993 Rome Council decision to confer on the OSCE domestic legal capacity and privileges and immunities. That will confirm our support for its work.

Clause 5 deals with EU bodies established under title V—Provisions on a Common Foreign and Security Policy—or title VI—Provisions on Police and Judicial Cooperation in Criminal Matters—of the treaty on the European Union. To ensure there is no misunderstanding, I should emphasise here that we are not talking about bodies or institutions set up under the treaty establishing the European Community.

Under existing obligations, the Government are committed to conferring legal capacity and privileges and immunities on title V and title VI bodies of the treaty on the EU, and certain categories of individuals connected to them. At present there is no legislation which allows us to do this. The Bill will add a further section to the International Organisations Act 1968 to enable the UK to confer the necessary legal capacity and privileges and immunities, by Order in Council, on those bodies and individuals.

At present there are three EU bodies on which privileges and immunities will be conferred under this Bill. They are: ATHENA, the EU Satellite Centre and the Institute for Security Studies. ATHENA is a financing mechanism set up to enable member states to contribute towards the financing of EU military peace-keeping missions, as the EU budget cannot be used for military operations. The satellite centre provides valuable satellite imagery analysis which helps the EU monitor crises across the world, and the Institute for Security Studies adds academic analysis and strategic thinking to the development of common foreign and security policy as a whole.

Clause 6 concerns the International Criminal Court. The ICC is a permanent court, based in The Hague, established by the Rome statute of the ICC. The purpose of the ICC is to try individuals for some of the most serious crimes known to mankind: genocide, crimes against humanity and war crimes.

The court is now taking its first operational steps. It has opened two investigations, in northern Uganda and in the Democratic Republic of Congo. Most recently, on 31 March, the Security Council passed a UK-sponsored resolution to refer the situation in Darfur to the court. The court will have to operate in some of the world's most difficult environments, so safety is paramount. In order to ensure its staff can work effectively, they need to be granted the added security provided by the ICC privileges and immunities agreement, which the United Kingdom signed in 2002. The Bill will amend the International Criminal Court Act 2001 to allow the UK to confer all the privileges and immunities necessary to fulfil its obligations under the ICC privileges and immunities agreement.

Clause 7 applies to the European Court of Human Rights. The court forms part of the Council of Europe. It enforces the Council of Europe's convention for the protection of human rights and fundamental freedoms, also known as the European convention on human rights.

The sixth protocol to the general agreement on the privileges and immunities of the Council of Europe confers privileges and immunities on members of the court. The UK has signed and ratified the sixth protocol subject to a reservation on article 1, which requires the conferral of privileges and immunities on family members of judges. The Bill will amend the International Organisations Act 1968 to allow the UK to implement article 1 of the sixth protocol fully and withdraw its reservation.

Clause 8 concerns the International Tribunal for the Law of the Sea, ITLOS, which was established by the UN Convention on the Law of the Sea, to which the UK is a state party. The agreement on the privileges and immunities of ITLOS provides that the tribunal, and various categories of individuals connected with it, shall enjoy privileges and immunities. The UK signed the agreement but cannot ratify it as existing legislation does not permit its implementation. The Bill will bring ITLOS within the scope of the 1968 Act, enabling the UK to confer privileges and immunities on the tribunal and so ratify the agreement. The financial implications of the Bill are minimal. The only loss of revenue that might occur would be by way of refunds of VAT on travel and incidental costs for visiting officials. We estimate that this would be under £1,000 per annum. The Bill will not impose any additional regulation on the business, charities or voluntary sectors. By enabling us to confer privileges and immunities on them, the Bill will confirm our support for the work of these organisations and will be a clear demonstration that the UK is meeting its international commitments.

...

The points raised by hon. Members have been thoroughly discussed in the other place. In its 15th report of the current Session [the JCHR] ... concluded that the Bill did not need to be brought to the attention of either House on human rights grounds [the Report did not say this, see **5/40** and **5/41**, Ed.].

Hon. Members have expressed concern about the general principle of conferring immunities and privileges, but it is simply the old injunction, "Do unto others as you would have done unto yourself." If we want British officials serving in international organisations in many different parts of the world to have appropriate immunities and privileges, it is rather arrogant of us not to be willing to find a small amount of parliamentary time—this Bill has been waiting for some years to be brought before Parliament—to put our own house in order in this regard.

Let me stress that privileges and immunities are there to protect officials, not Governments. I completely agree with the points raised about Belarus and other dictatorial countries, but citizens of any of those countries can serve honestly and openly on international bodies, and those gentlemen and, where appropriate, their families, should be thus protected.

Let me stress again that the House is not conferring such immunities and privileges on any single individual in any single organisation. They will all have to be brought before the House by way of affirmative motion under the Order-in-Council procedure. That will allow genuine concerns, which I fully accept, to be raised and debated.

I am not entirely surprised that the European Union was brought up. However, this is about existing treaty agreements—we are not talking about the constitutional treaty in any way. Some EU bodies need legal capacity and privileges and immunities to operate. Once one has agreed to European Council decisions—that is where Ministers of national Governments decide, not the Commission or a bureaucracy—or to other measures to establish them, the UK is under an obligation to confer them under international law. The fact that the EU does not have a legal personality except to the extent that it concludes agreements pursuant to articles 24 or 38 of the treaty on the European Union is immaterial.

(HC Deb 7 April 2005 Vol. 432 c1632–1639)

5/45

The FCO wrote again to the JCHR:

I refer to the Seventh Report of the Joint Committee on Human Rights in which the Committee expresses some concerns about clause 1 of the International Organisations Bill.

The Committee considers that extending the Commonwealth Secretariat's immunity under Clause 1 of the Bill in the absence of an international obligation to do so risks disproportionate interference with the Article 6 right of access to court.

It would be improper and a breach of the UK's duties under international law for the Government to undertake to be bound by an international obligation before the legislation necessary to implement that obligation was in place. To do otherwise would mean that the UK would not be in a position to fulfil its obligation and this could result in a breach by the UK of its international obligation. If Parliament decided not to pass relevant legislation, the UK would continue to be in breach of the obligation. That is why the invariable practice with any treaty is that the Government does not ratify the treaty until legislation has been passed enabling the UK to fulfil the obligations it contains. For example, the UK has not undertaken an international obligation to confer privileges and immunities on the International Tribunal for the Law of the Sea (ITLOS) because it has not ratified the Agreement on the Privileges and Immunities of the International Tribunal of the Law of the Sea. It will only ratify the Agreement and become bound by the obligations contained in the Agreement once this Bill has received Royal Assent. In the same way, therefore, although the Government has agreed to revisions to Annex A of the Revised Agreed Memorandum on the Commonwealth Secretariat in principle, these revisions will only be formalised once the UK is able to implement the commitments in the Annex by means of the International Organisations Act. This is the proper and normal process.

It is also important to note the entry into force provisions of the Bill. Clause 11(4) provides that clauses 1 to 3 of the Bill will come into force on such day as the Secretary of State appoints. We will ensure that clause 1 of the Bill, which will confer the extended immunity on the Commonwealth Secretariat, enters into force at the same time as the agreed changes to the Revised Agreed Memorandum. Clause I will not therefore be in force unless and until there is an obligation in the Memorandum.

The Committee also questioned whether the Commonwealth Secretariat Arbitral Tribunal is fully independent from the Commonwealth Secretariat. Although it is correct that the Secretary-General formally appoints the members of the Tribunal, under Article IV of the CSAT Statute those members must first have been selected by the Commonwealth Governments on a regionally representative basis. The Members are appointed for 4-year terms, which also assists in ensuring their independence. All members of the Tribunal are required by the Statute to be of high moral character and to have appropriate experience. Of the five current members, four are former Chief justices of Commonwealth countries, and the other a practising QC. The members are selected on a geographically representative basis as well as on gender basis.

Significantly, the Statute also requires that the Rules of the Tribunal, which are drawn up by the members and the President of the Tribunal, must ensure that applications before the Tribunal are dealt with in a manner that is independent and impartial and consistent with the Commonwealth Harare principles relating to fundamental human rights and independence of the judiciary.

The UK Government would obviously be very concerned if the CSAT failed to provide for an independent and impartial mechanism for the settlement of disputes and it would be something that should be raised with the Secretariat and Commonwealth Governments for discussion, and revision of the Statute as appropriate. But we do not believe this is the case.

(Fifteenth Report, 23 March 2005, HL97/HC496 (2005), Appendix 4)

[The Bill became law as the International Organisations Act 2005, Ed.]

5/46

International Tribunal for the Law of the Sea

An FCO Minister moved the approval of the International Tribunal for the Law of the Sea (Immunities and Privileges) Order 2005. She said:

The order was laid before the House on 30 June 2005, together with an explanatory memorandum now required for all affirmative statutory instruments. It is required to enable the Government to ratify the Agreement on the Privileges and Immunities of the International Tribunal for the Law of the Sea, which was opened for signature in New York on 1 July 1997 and signed by the United Kingdom on 24 August that same year.

The International Organisations Act 2005 allowed for the International Tribunal for the Law of the Sea—the tribunal—to be treated for the purposes of Section 1 of the International Organisations Act 1968 as an organisation of which the UK and other sovereign governments are members. Prior to that it had only been possible to confer privileges and immunities on the members of the tribunal and limited privileges and immunities on the registrar of the tribunal under Section 5 of the International Organisations Act 1968. That was done by the first International Tribunal for the Law of the Sea (Immunities and Privileges) Order 1996. This second order confers legal capacity on the organisation itself as well as extending immunities and privileges to various other categories of persons employed by, and connected with it. It revokes the 1996 order.

The tribunal was established by the 1982 United Nations Convention on the Law of the Sea—UNCLOS—but it did not come into existence until the entry into force of UNCLOS on 16 October 1994. After the election of the first judges, the tribunal took its seat in Hamburg on 1 October 1996. It is an international court and has jurisdiction to hear disputes submitted to it in accordance with UNCLOS and all matters specifically provided for in any other agreement which confers jurisdiction on it. Funding is through a budget adopted annually by the Meeting of States Parties to UNCLOS, on the basis of budget proposals submitted by the tribunal. The states parties to the tribunal pay contributions based on the scale of assessments of the budget of the UN adjusted to take into account participation in UNCLOS. The 2004 budget was set at $8,039,000 with the UK contributing £373,320.

[The motion was approved, Ed.]

(HL Deb 7 July 2005 Vol. 676 cGC80–GC81)

Part Five: II. A.1.(c). *Subjects of International Law—International organizations—In general—Status and powers—Powers, including treaty-making power*

5/47

Economic Community of West African States

During a Security Council Meeting the representative of the European Union stated:

The European Union is following with great concern the recent developments in the political situation in Togo. We call for full respect for civil liberties and demand an immediate return to constitutional and legal order to open the way for free and transparent presidential elections. In that context, we fully support the actions by the African Union and the Economic Community of West African States (ECOWAS) with a view to re-establishing constitutional order and the democratic process.

...

The proliferation of small arms remains a significant factor of instability and conflict in the region. Resolute and coordinated action is needed. During the open debate on small arms that was held last week (see S/PV.5127), the European Union had the opportunity to express its willingness to help put an end to the scourge of the uncontrolled accumulation of small arms. While the European Union welcomes the recent three-year renewal of the moratorium on the importation, exportation and manufacture of small arms in West Africa, we also encourage efforts in the framework of the ECOWAS Small Arms Control Programme to transform the moratorium into a legally binding instrument.

In addition, the European Union supports the Secretary-General's recommendation that the Security Council consider giving peacekeeping missions the authority and the resources needed to monitor and enforce arms embargoes, as well as the idea of marking and tracing small arms used in peacekeeping missions. We should consider publishing a "naming and shaming" list of individuals and entities violating arms embargoes and the ECOWAS moratorium, and bringing before the International Criminal Court those responsible for criminal activities related to the trafficking of persons and of natural resources.

(UN Doc. S/PV.5131, 25 February 2005)

5/48

The Government was asked if it would list the proposals from the European Commission put into effect since 1 June [2005] that have Articles 94, 95 or 308 as their base. An FCO Minister wrote:

In general, the legal basis of Community legislation is determined on the basis of objective factors that are amenable to judicial review, in particular with regard to the aim and content of the measure. The Government are committed to ensuring that the correct legal base is used in European legislation. There may be occasions when the Government disagree with the Commission and other member states over the use of a particular legal base. In these circumstances a number of options remain open to the Government, including either to vote against or abstain from supporting the proposal. We also have the option of recording our disagreement with the legal base in a minutes statement.

Two pieces of legislation falling directly within the departmental responsibilities of the Foreign and Commonwealth Office fall under the category the hon. Member set out. A Council Regulation imposing certain restrictive measures directed against persons acting in violation of the arms embargo with regard to the Democratic Republic of the Congo was adopted at the General Affairs and External Relations Council on 18 July. This used Article 308 as one of three legal bases. A Council Regulation imposing specific restrictive measures directed against certain persons impeding the peace process and breaking international law in the conflict in the Darfur region in Sudan was adopted at the same Council. This also used Article 308 as one of three legal bases. The Government did not challenge the legal base of these regulations. In so far as the question relates to the business of other Government Departments, it would be most appropriately be directed to their Secretaries of State.

(HC Deb 18 October 2005 Vol. 437 c904W–905W)

5/49

Security Council

During a Security Council Meeting the representative of the United Kingdom stated:

The Security Council is of course only one actor in the international response to humanitarian crises, so I would like to begin with some reflections on what contribution it can make.

First, the Council should have an important political role in conflict prevention and in dealing with the early stages of an emerging humanitarian crisis. The United Nations as a whole, and the Security Council in particular, should therefore be alert to signs of an imminent breakdown in international peace and security, in particular those situations that threaten widespread humanitarian consequences. The Council should be prepared from the earliest stage to make a leading contribution to international efforts to avert a descent into conflict and humanitarian suffering. That means being prepared to give attention to new and neglected crises without waiting for the level of humanitarian suffering to rise to unacceptable levels. It means reminding Governments of their primary responsibility to assure the security, safety and humanitarian needs of their own people, and reminding them too that the international community has a legitimate interest if they are unable or unwilling to do that. In that regard, the European Union welcomes the debate on the important concept of the responsibility to protect.

Prevention is obviously better than having to pick up the pieces of broken lives and humanitarian suffering after conflict has broken out. We need to ensure that the Security Council is properly informed of possible threats, including through early warnings by the Secretary-General. One positive development in that regard has been the introduction of regular briefings of the Council by Jan Egeland, the Humanitarian Coordinator. We should continue and extend that practice, including with the Office of the High Commissioner for Human Rights. The second key role for the Council is its primary responsibility to take action where international peace and security have broken down, where we must take full account of the humanitarian requirements of a crisis. It is not, of course, the Council's role to coordinate or direct humanitarian action, but it can do more to galvanize international humanitarian efforts and to lend political weight to them. In considering our political response to a crisis, we should always give due priority to humanitarian considerations. The Council and its individual members should lend weight to efforts to ensure that political leaders on both sides of a conflict ensure access by humanitarian agencies to affected populations.

A major Security Council responsibility will be to establish multidimensional United Nations peace support operations that ensure that humanitarian considerations and activities are fully taken into account. In accordance with relevant Council resolutions, we also need to promote the role that peacekeepers play in protecting civilians, particularly with regard to vulnerable groups such as internally displaced persons, women and children. The Council also has a role in ensuring that where humanitarian suffering is a result of deliberate human rights abuses or war crimes, those responsible are brought to justice. The European Union therefore strongly supports efforts to end impunity for such crimes, in particular through the effective functioning of the International Criminal Court.

But equally important is a third area of the Council's activity, namely, building the conditions for lasting peace and stability in order to prevent the recurrence of conflict and humanitarian suffering.

I would like to summarize three key areas of peacebuilding, namely, the rule of law, disarmament, demobilization and reintegration (DDR) and security-sector reform.

First, strengthening the rule of law and good governance is essential to building societies that protect and improve the lives of all their citizens. The Secretary-General's excellent report on the subject last August (S/2004/616) and the subsequent Security Council discussion in October showed consensus on the need to treat the justice sector as a key element in building sustainable peace. An independent judiciary, humane and secure prisons and an effective and accountable police force are necessities. Without them, we risk anarchy and impunity; we undermine not only stability and security, but also democracy, the return of refugees and economic recovery.

But we have not yet done enough. The United Nations is still a long way from being able to effectively promote the rule of law and an end to impunity in the post-conflict situations in which it is engaged. For that reason, we welcome the Secretary-General's decision contained in his report entitled "In larger freedom" (A/59/2005) to create a Rule of Law Assistance Unit to deal specifically with post-conflict situations.

The second important area of peacebuilding that we need to improve is our approach to disarmament, demobilization and reintegration—DDR. We need to draw together past experience, both good and bad, and ensure that we understand what works and why it works. We therefore welcome the United Nations interagency process to develop guidelines on DDR. The challenge will be to implement those guidelines in a practical way that lifts our collective performance.

The third priority area, which is closely linked to the other two, is security-sector reform. Democratically controlled security services can be developed only in the context of establishing effective governance structures and the rule of law. DDR programmes can succeed only as part of a broader reform effort to deliver security services that guarantee, rather than threaten, the people they are meant to serve.

In all the three areas that I have described, the Security Council and the missions that it mandates are usually only one of a number of international players. Within the United Nations system, we must make sure that even as we create new capacities, we do not create new divisions. We must therefore ensure that we develop a coherent, overarching vision in the wider justice and security field, and that that is matched organizationally both at Headquarters and in the field.

That is why the European Union strongly supports the proposed establishment of a Peacebuilding Commission that would oversee the provisions of coherent security, political, economic and other assistance to countries emerging from conflict, and advise on and promote comprehensive strategies for peacebuilding.

(UN Doc. S/PV.5225, 12 July 2005)

Part Five: II. A.2.(a) *Subjects of International Law—International organizations—In general—Participation of States in international organizations and in their activities—Admission*

5/50

European Union—Croatia

During a debate in the House of Commons, Her Majesty's Government was to confirm that no progress will be made on Croatia's application to join the European Union until Croatia makes progress on indicted war criminals in former Yugoslavia. In reply, the Foreign Secretary said:

We all want to see negotiations with Croatia that lead to full membership of the European Union, beginning as soon as possible. As the European Council has clearly stated, however, that process must take place on the basis of full co-operation with the International Criminal Tribunal in The Hague. So far, sadly, such co-operation has not been adequate.

...

The same point applies to Serbia and Montenegro, and to all the territories that were formerly part of the Republic of Yugoslavia. We see their future inside the European Union, but that must be on the basis of full co-operation with the tribunal in The Hague and on other matters. Serbia and Montenegro is at an earlier stage than Croatia. It is looking forward to agreeing a stabilisation and assistance arrangement with the EU, but that, too, depends on full co-operation and, in particular, on the delivery of Mladic and Karadzic.

(HC Deb 19 July 2005 Vol. 436 c1092)

5/51

World Health Organisation

In a written answer, an FCO Minister wrote:

There are difficulties over Taiwanese involvement in a UN forum where statehood is a prerequisite for full membership. We hope that the World Health Organisation (WHO) secretariat, and others organising meetings and working groups under WHO auspices, will show flexibility in finding mechanisms to allow Taiwanese medical and public health officials to participate in these activities.

The WHO secretariat and China recently signed a memorandum of understanding on technical exchanges with Taiwan. We understand that the WHO and Taiwan already share information on an informal basis.

(HC Deb 7 December 2005 Vol. 440 c1398W)

Part Five: II. A.2.(b) *Subjects of International Law—International organizations—In general—Participation of States in international organizations and in their activities—Suspension, withdrawal, expulsion, and deportation*

5/52

During a debate in the House of Lords, an FCO Minister said:

As regards the issue of expelling UN members, [it is suggested] that the UN excludes members who are in clear breach of the charter. It is a superficially attractive argument, and it is allowed for under the current UN Charter. However, it is both difficult to enforce in practice, requiring votes in both the

Security Council and the General Assembly and arguably counter-productive as one of the great strengths of the UN is universal membership, in clear contrast with the failed League of Nations. Suspension has been used, for instance, in the case of South Africa. [Suspension, that is, from participation in the General Assembly, Ed.]

(HL Deb 18 January 2005 Vol. 668 c739)

Part Five: II. A.2.(c) *Subjects of International Law—International organizations—In general—Participation of States in international organizations and in their activities—Obligations of membership*

5/53

The Foreign Secretary was asked by the FAC about the finding of the Mehlis Inquiry (into the responsibility for the death of ex-Prime Minister [Rafik Hariri] of Lebanon). He said:

You cannot have a member of the United Nations (viz Syria) that has subscribed to the Charter of Human Rights, and much else besides, deciding that the way it resolves its problems is having people, at least at a pretty senior level, complicit in the murder of political opponents in a country that is regarded by every other member of the United Nations as independent; this is simply intolerable. [Q.99]

(FAC, Foreign Policy Aspects of the War against Terrorism, HC 573-ii (2005), Qu.110)

5/54

During a General Assembly meeting, the Foreign Secretary made the following statement:

I also think that the United Nations has learned the lessons of the past decade. At the summit this week, we agreed on the further steps that we need to take for the Organization to be even more effective. Of all that was agreed at the summit, I believe it will be the agreement on our "responsibility to protect" that will be seen in the future as having the greatest significance of all. If we follow through on the responsibility to protect, then never again will genocide, ethnic cleansing and crimes against humanity be allowed to take place under our noses with nothing done.

The responsibility to protect is, of course, a reflection of our common morality. But it is also a recognition that the world in which we now live is too small for us to be unaffected by, or indifferent to, the innocent victims of murder and oppression. This shrinking of the world has been as sudden as it has been profound. When the Berlin wall fell, a generation of ideological certainties was swept away. People could suddenly see partners where before they had only glimpsed adversaries. And as that very visible barrier was noisily being breached, a revolution in information technology was quietly erasing the barriers of distance and time. Continents and cultures are now cabled together and bound by trade and services in a way that was unimaginable even a decade ago.

In this new world, we can no longer safely tolerate the general threat that can come from a particular human tragedy, wherever it takes place. To a greater extent than ever before, we share the same world: the same threats and responsibilities, the same opportunities and interests. And precisely because the boundaries of our world have contracted, the horizons—the ambitions—of many people around the globe have infinitely expanded. For the first time in our history, mankind has the ability to realize the potential of individuals in societies of all kinds and in every region through an open exchange of goods, investment, technology and, above all, ideas.

...

The fundamental purpose of the United Nations remains today what it was at its foundation: to remove the scourge of war, to reaffirm the worth of the human person and to promote social progress and better standards of life. In this changed and changing world, it is the responsibility of us all to ensure that this Organization has the powers and the resources to achieve all these aims.

(UN Doc. A/60/PV.9, 17 September 2005)

Part Five: II. A.2.(d) *Subjects of International Law—International organizations—In general—Participation of States in international organizations and in their activities—Representation of States and international organizations, including privileges and immunities (see also Part Five: II. A.1.(b)., above and II. A.4., below)*

5/55

During a General Assembly meeting, the representative for the European Union said:

The European Union fully supports the renewal of the mandate of the United Nations Informal Consultative Process on Oceans and the Law of the Sea (ICP). The Consultative Process has contributed positively, inter alia, and by facilitating the annual review of the Secretary-General's report on oceans and the law of the sea. At the same time, we recognize that some improvement in the workings and contents of the Consultative Process need to be made. We look forward to the early appointment of the two co-chairpersons for the next meeting of the Consultative Process, so that they can begin effective preparations in conjunction with States and relevant bodies.

In that connection, we would note, however, that the European Union attaches great importance to resolving the discrepancy that currently exists between the observer status of the European Community and its competencies—whether exclusive or mixed—with respect to many issues that have been discussed in previous ICP meetings. The European Community is a contracting party to the United Nations Convention on the Law of the Sea and the United Nations 1995 Fish Stocks Agreement in its own right, and has thus accepted legal obligations with respect to oceans and law of the sea that are particularly relevant to the Consultative Process. Although no solution could be found this year, we welcome the commitment of delegations to continue negotiations bilaterally with a view to resolving the problem in the near future.

(UN Doc. A/60/PV.54, 28 November 2005)

Part Five: II. B.1. *Subjects of International Law—International organizations—Particular types of organization—Universal organizations*

5/56

The Government was asked what its response was to the proposal for the future of the United Nations Commission on Human Rights, put forward by the [UN] High Level Panel on Threats, Challenges and Change. An FCO Minister wrote:

We support the work of the high level panel, and welcome the emphasis given to human rights issues. In particular, we welcome the proposals to improve links between the High Commissioner for Human Rights and the Security Council/ Peacebuilding Commission, and to increase the Office of the High Commissioner of Human Rights' funding from the regular budget. On the other recommendations, our position is as follows:

Universalising membership of the Commission on Human Rights (CHR): this could potentially remove accusations of lack of representation, and the need for divisive elections. But we are not convinced it would address issues of legitimacy. And we would need to consider how this would work in practice, to ensure it would not have a counter-productive effect on the overall handling of human rights in the UN system.

Human rights figures to head CHR delegations: we agree with the principle that there should be human rights expertise throughout CHR delegations. However, it is for governments to send who they wish—many governments will wish to keep their head of delegation as a government representative.

Advisory council or panel to advise the CHR on country-specific issues and thematic mandates: the UK would like to see more detail on this. It would be important that this does not duplicate the current CHR sub-commission.

The Office of the High Commissioner of Human Rights' annual report on the situation of human rights worldwide: we welcome the aim of providing a neutral and objective basis for discussion at the CHR. However, this should not be seen as a substitute for country action, but an objective basis on which the UN can choose to take action.

(HL Deb 7 March 2005 Vol. 670 cWA59)

Part Five: II. B.2. *Subjects of International Law—International organizations—Particular types of organization—Regional organizations*

(See also **Part Five: II. A.1.(b)**)

Part Five: II. B.3. *Subjects of International Law—International organizations—Particular types of organization—Organizations constituting integrated (eg economic) communities*

5/57

The Government was asked what the total fines that have been imposed by the European Court of Justice on each member state are since 1974. A Minister wrote:

The power to fine member states was given to the European Court of Justice when the Treaty on European Union came into force (on 1 November 1993). Fines can either be in the form of a lump sum or a penalty payment (Article 228(2) EC).

The ECJ has only imposed fines on two occasions under Article 228(2) EC:

(i) Greece was ordered to pay a penalty payment of EUR 20,000 for each day of delay (from the date of service of the judgment), in implementing the measures necessary to ensure that waste was disposed of without endangering human health and without harming the environment (Case C-387/97, Commission *v.* Greece).

(ii) The ECJ considered that Spain had not taken the measures necessary to ensure that the quality of inshore bathing water conformed to the Community's standards. It ordered Spain to pay to the Commission a penalty payment of EUR 624,150 per year and per 1 per cent. of bathing areas in Spanish inshore waters which had been found not to conform to the limit values laid down for the year in question (Case C-278/01, Commission *v.* Spain).

(HC Deb 11 January 2005 Vol. 429 c442W)

5/58

The Government was asked what sanctions would be available under the proposed EU Constitution against member states in breach of their duty under Article I-16 *(a)* actively and unreservedly to support the Union's common foreign and security policy and *(b)* to refrain from action contrary to the Union's interests or likely to impair its effectiveness. An FCO Minister wrote:

The Article I-16 obligations referred to in the question are in substance the same as those first set out in Article J.1 (4) of the Maastricht treaty (currently Article 11(2) TEU). As under the Maastricht treaty and the treaty on European Union, member states are under the constitutional treaty required to comply in good faith with their treaty obligations, including those relating to the common foreign and security policy mentioned in Article I-16. Any consequences which might follow if a member state failed to fulfil its obligations would depend on the circumstances. But the jurisdiction of the European Court of Justice is excluded from common foreign and security policy issues by Article III-376.

(HC Deb 20 January 2005 Vol. 429 c1058W)

Part Five: IV. B. *Subjects of International Law—Other subjects of international law and other entities or groups—Dependent territories*

5/59

Diego Garcia

The Government was asked what arrangements US military forces have for access to the British territory of Diego Garcia; and for how long these arrangements are programmed to continue. A Minister wrote:

Under the Exchange of Notes between the United Kingdom and United States concerning the Availability for Defence Purposes of the British Indian Ocean Territory of 30 December 1966 (Cmnd. 3231), the whole territory is to remain available to meet the possible defence needs of the two countries for an initial period of 50 years from 1966, and thereafter for a further period of 20 years unless either party has given prior notice to terminate it. A further Exchange of Notes concluded in 1976 (Cmnd. 6413) regulates the establishment and functioning of the facilities of the United States in Diego Garcia and related matters.

(HC Deb 18 January 2005 Vol. 430 c917W)

5/60

Her Majesty's Government was asked what the UK's military commitment is to Diego Garcia; what other overseas forces are stationed there. In reply, the Minister of State for Armed Forces wrote:

The United Kingdom's military commitment to Diego Garcia, in the British Indian Ocean Territory, is to maintain and exercise UK sovereignty over the territory, including its territorial waters and airspace. In total, 41 UK military personnel are based there. United States forces are also stationed on the island.

(HC Deb 22 November 2005 Vol. 439 c1881W)

5/61

The Government was asked what permission is required from (a) [the FCO] Department and (b) the UK diplomatic representative of the British Indian Ocean Territory for (i) US military missions and

(ii) landing of US military or civilian aircraft on the island of Diego Garcia. In reply, an FCO Minister wrote:

The 1976 Exchange of Notes, the Diego Garcia Agreement, between the Government and the Government of the United States of America concerning a United States Navy Support Facility on Diego Garcia, British Indian Ocean Territory, states in paragraph 3 that:

> "Both Governments shall consult periodically on joint objectives, policies and activities in the area. As regards the use of the facility in normal circumstances, the US Commanding Officer and the Officer in Charge of the United Kingdom Service element shall inform each other of intended movements of ships and aircraft. In other circumstances the use of the facility shall be a matter for the joint decision of the two Governments."

The Diego Garcia Agreement is published by Her Majesty's Stationery Office in the United Kingdom Treaty Series, No. 19 (1976).

(HC Deb 1 December 2005 Vol. 440 c734W–735W)

5/62

Falkland Islands

The Government was asked (1) what the situation is regarding air links between the Falkland Islands and the South American mainland ... and (2) how many charter flights operate to the Falkland Islands using Argentine airspace, for the purposes of cruise ship passenger exchange. The Foreign Secretary wrote:

No charter flights currently operate between the Falkland Islands and the South American mainland. Charter flights between the Falkland Islands and the South American mainland have been halted since the end of 2003, when the Argentine Government stopped granting permission for charter flights to the Falkland Islands to use Argentine airspace. The scheduled LAN Chile flight is not affected by discussions over charter flights and continues to operate on a weekly basis between Southern Chile and the Falkland Islands.

(HC Deb 7 March 2005 Vol. 431 c1577W)

5/63

During a General Assembly meeting the representative of the United Kingdom, Mr. Williams, took the floor to reply to remarks made by His Excellency Mr. Rafael Bielsa, Minister for Foreign Relations, International Trade and Worship of the Argentine Republic, on the sovereignty of the Falkland Islands. The representative stated:

The United Kingdom has no doubts about its sovereignty over the Falkland Islands. There can be no negotiations on the sovereignty of the Falkland Islands unless and until such time as the islanders so wish.

(UN Doc. A/60/PV.14, 19 September 2005)

5/64

The FCO drew up this report of an exchange which took place in the General Assembly on 18/19 September 2005:

2. During his address to UNGA 60 on 18 September, Argentine Foreign Minister, Rafael Bielsa, reiterated Argentina's claim to sovereignty over the Falkland Islands. Bielsa said that "the recovery of the full exercise of sovereignty over the Malvinas Islands, South Georgia and South Sandwich Islands and the surrounding maritime areas" was one of the "national interests" that was an "essential component of" Argentina's identity as a democratic nation.

3. Bielsa said that "all Argentines" were "strongly committed" to a "peaceful solution", and this was a priority of the Argentine government. Bielsa restated Argentine readiness to resume negotiations over sovereignty.

4. Due to a procedural error on 18 September, [the UK] were not offered the opportunity at the end of that session to reply to Bielsa's remarks. [The UK] therefore did so on 19 September. The UK representative said:

> "I am taking the floor in Right of Reply to the remarks just made by His Excellency Rafael Bielsa, Minister of Foreign Relations, International Trade and Worship of the Argentine Republic on the sovereignty of the Falkland Islands.
>
> The UK's position on this issue is well known, and was last set out in detail by the UK's Permanent Representative to the United Nations, Sir Emyr Jones Parry, in a written right of reply to the statement by His Excellency President Nestor Carlos Kirchner of the Republic of Argentina in the High-Level Plenary session of the General Assembly on 14 September 2005.
>
> The United Kingdom has no doubts about its sovereignty over the Falkland Islands. There can be no negotiations on the sovereignty of the Falkland Islands unless and until such time as the Islanders so wish".

(Text supplied by FCO) (UN Doc. A/60/PV.14, 19 September 2005)

5/65

Gibraltar

The Government was asked what steps [it] is taking to ensure that the legal system in Gibraltar prevents discrimination on the grounds of sexual orientation. An FCO Minister wrote:

Under the constitutional reform proposals, an assessment of the powers required by the UK Government will take full account of the fact that the UK is responsible for Gibraltar's compliance with EU law, including ultimately before the European Court of Justice. We wish to ensure that Gibraltar's constitution is in line with its international obligations, including the European Convention on Human Rights.

We have previously told the Gibraltar Government that we believe the age of consent should be equalised for homosexual and heterosexual couples to avoid a potential breach of Articles 8 and 14 of the European Convention on Human Rights.

(HC Deb 23 February 2005 Vol. 431 c658W)

5/66

This is a report drawn up by the FCO of an exchange which took place in the General Assembly on 20 September 2005:

2. During his address to UNGA 60 on 20 September, Spanish Foreign Minister Moratinos raised the issue of Gibraltar.

3. Moratinos said that there was a need to "put an end to this dispute" through the implementation of "repeated mandates of the General Assembly" which had urged "Spain and the United Kingdom to continue their negotiations with a view to completing the decolonisation process in accordance with the pertinent UN resolutions".

4. Moratinos said that Spain was willing to work in a "constructive spirit". This spirit was reflected in the creation of a "Trilateral Dialogue Forum" the aim of which was to produce an atmosphere of mutual trust and co-operation for the "benefit and prosperity of Gibraltar and the surrounding area."

5. [The UK] exercised [its] Right of Reply at the end of the session. The UK representative said:

> "I would like to respond to the remarks made today by the distinguished Minister of Foreign Affairs of Spain about Gibraltar.
>
> The British Government welcomes and shares Spain's willingness to work in a constructive spirit. We agree that issues relating to Gibraltar can only be resolved through dialogue, and therefore welcome the newly established Trilateral Forum on Gibraltar, through which all parties, including Gibraltar, can express their views. Our aim remains to build a better future for the people of Gibraltar. And in doing that the UK Government stands by its long-term commitment to the people of Gibraltar to respect their wishes."

(Text supplied by FCO)

[The Trilateral Forum on Gibraltar consists of representatives of the governments of the UK, Spain, and Gibraltar, Ed.]

5/67

Mauritius/Diego Garcia

The representative of the UK made the following statement in exercise of the right of reply to the remarks made by the Prime Minister of Mauritius in the general debate on 19 September 2005:

The British Government maintains that the British Indian Ocean Territory is British and has been since 1814. It does not recognise the sovereignty claim of the Mauritian Government.

However, the British Government has recognised Mauritius as the only State which has a right to assert a claim of sovereignty when the United Kingdom relinquishes its own sovereignty.

Successive British Governments have given undertakings to the Government of Mauritius that the Territory will be ceded when no longer required for defence purposes.

The British Government remains open to discussions regarding arrangements governing the British Indian Ocean Territory or the future of the Territory. The British Government has stated that when the time comes for the Territory to be ceded it will liaise closely with the Government of Mauritius.

(Text supplied by FCO)

Part Five: IV. C. *Subjects of International Law—Other subjects of international law and other entities or groups—Special regimes*

5/68

The Government was asked what [its] policy is on China's occupation of Tibet. An FCO Minister wrote:

Successive British Governments have regarded Tibet as autonomous while recognising the special position of the Chinese authorities there.

We monitor Tibet-related developments closely ... the Foreign Secretary raised the case of a Tibetan prisoner during his visit in January 2005. I personally raised the issue of Tibet with Assistant Foreign Minister Li Hui during my visit to China in October 2004. We also discuss Tibet at our biannual UK/China Human Rights Dialogue, the last round of which was held in Beijing on 22 November 2004.

We have welcomed visits to China by representatives of the Dalai Lama. We have made clear to the Chinese authorities our view that a long-term, peaceful solution to the Tibet issue can be found only through substantial dialogue without pre-conditions.

(HC Deb 15 March 2005 Vol. 432 c214W)

Part Five: IV. D. *Subjects of International Law—Other subjects of international law and other entities or groups—Insurgents*

5/69

The Government was asked what steps [it] is taking to persuade the Government of Sudan to allow access to conflict-affected populations in

Darfur by non-governmental organisations and human rights organisations. A Minister wrote:

We regularly discuss with both the Government of Sudan and the rebels the importance of access for all non-governmental organisations throughout Darfur. Our Ambassador raised this matter with the Government on 21 March and I discussed this with the Secretary General of the Sudanese Liberation Movement on 22 March ... the Foreign Secretary secured access for human rights groups, including Amnesty International and Human Rights Watch, in August 2004. Lack of security is the key factor hampering access throughout Darfur. We have made it clear to the Government and the rebels that they must abide by their commitments under the Abuja humanitarian and security protocols and improve the situation in Darfur.

(HC Deb 5 April 2005 Vol. 432 c1318W)

Part Five: IV. F. *Subjects of International Law—Other subjects of international law and other entities or groups—Others (indigenous peoples, minorities, national liberation movements, etc)*

5/70

Civil Society

During a General Assembly meeting, the representative for the European Union said:

The European Union also welcomes the decision to open the [September] summit to representatives of non-governmental organizations, civil society organizations and the private sector, as was done in 2000 during the Millennium Summit. During consultations on the draft resolution, we took the opportunity to express emphatically, on several occasions, our preference for the greatest possible participation of such actors in the various segments of the September summit. In this respect, we would like to reaffirm the principle of the participation of non-governmental organizations, civil society organizations and the private sector in the summit's plenary meetings.

(UN Doc. A/59/PV.92, 15 April 2005)

5/71

During a Security Council Meeting the representative of the United Kingdom stated:

Let us be frank: there are different views among members of the Council on the legitimacy of some civil society organizations and on the role that such organizations should be allowed to play in comparison with that played by Governments. The European Union believes that all United Nations Member States should accept the legitimate right of civil society to express views, make recommendations and express concerns and disagreements with Governments, even though at times that may be a difficult process. It is through such genuine dialogue that democracy is strengthened and that Governments are better able to meet the needs of their people.

(UN Doc. S/PV.5264, 20 September 2005)

5/72

India

The Government was asked what discussions [the FCO] has had with the Government of India regarding Sikh separatism in the Punjab. An FCO Minister wrote:

The Government have not raised the issue of Sikh separatism in the Punjab with the Government of India. We continue regularly to raise the issue of religious minorities, at official level, with the Indian authorities.

(HC Deb 28 June 2005 Vol. 435 c1478W)

5/73

Israel/Palestine

In response to a question, the Foreign Secretary said:

Hezbollah's stated aim of the elimination of the state of Israel is totally unacceptable, as are Hezbollah's military and terrorist activities, particularly along the blue line, in the occupied territories and in Iraq. We call on Hezbollah to contribute to peace and security in the middle east by renouncing violence, disarming in compliance with UN Security Council resolution 1559, and entering into the democratic process on an exclusively non-violent basis.

(HC Deb 29 November 2005 Vol. 440 c126–127)

5/74

In a written answer, an FCO, wrote:

We do not have contact with the Hamas leadership. We will have no dialogue with them so long as they advocate violence and do not accept Israel's right to exist.

(HL Deb 12 December 2005 Vol. 676 cWA140)

5/75

Turkey

The Government was asked whether [it] will raise with the European Union Commission in connection with the accession negotiations with Turkey:

(a) the constitutional limitation on the recognition of minority religions, such as the Greek Orthodox and Armenian Churches; and

(b) the case for defining and protecting ethnic and cultural minorities, such as Kurds and Circassians.

An FCO Minister wrote:

Although three non-Muslim minorities (Armenians, Greeks and Jews) are recognised in the 1923 Treaty of Lausanne, Turkey does not formally recognise its minority communities under its constitution. Rather, the constitution is designed to afford the same protection, in terms of civil and political rights, to all its citizens—as citizens of Turkey.

There is no single European model to guarantee the protection of minority rights in a member state. Some of our European partners, including Greece and France, adopt a similar approach—of non-recognition of minorities—as does Turkey.

The UK will not, therefore, raise the need for recognition under the Turkish constitution of specific minority groups. Representatives of the Kurdish community in Turkey, including Leyla Zana, have made clear that they do not want to be recognised as a minority. We will, however, continue to urge the Turkish Government further to strengthen and protect the rights of all citizens of Turkey, including the three Lausanne minorities. We believe that any remaining concerns will be resolved during the accession negotiation process.

(HL Deb 7 February 2005 Vol. 669 c79WA)

Part Six: The Position of the Individual (including the Corporation) in International Law

Part Six: I. *The Position of the Individual (including the Corporation) in International Law—Nationality*

6/1

In a written answer, an FCO Minister wrote:

All British citizens have the right of abode in the United Kingdom, and all are deemed to be "nationals of the United Kingdom" for the purposes of the Treaty Establishing the European Community. Most British subjects do not have the right of abode in the United Kingdom, but some do on the basis of a pre-1983 marital or ancestral connection with this country. British subjects who do have the right of abode here are deemed to be "nationals of the United Kingdom" for European Community purposes. Other distinctions may stem from statutory or non-statutory rules for which the Home Office is not responsible, or from the laws of other countries.

(HC Deb 5 July 2005 Vol. 436 c376W–377W)

Part Six: II. *The Position of the Individual (including the Corporation) in International Law—Diplomatic and consular protection (see also Part Thirteen II. A.1.(c), below)*

(See **Part Six: VIII. (Guantanamo Bay, 6/71, 72; Protection of Human Rights of Nationals, 6/89)**)

6/2

The Foreign Secretary in a written statement told the House of Commons:

During the course of my statement of 11 January to the House, Official Report, columns 173–186 [HC Deb Vol. 429], on the release of British detainees held at Guantanamo Bay, I said that there were no other British citizens detained in Guantanamo Bay. I also stated that I knew of no other citizens detained in similar circumstances elsewhere. That statement in the House was clear and remains accurate.

I would however like to bring to the attention of the House the cases of two British nationals being held as security internees by the coalition forces in Iraq; one is a British national being held by US forces at Camp Bucca, the other is a dual British/Iraqi national and is being held at Shaibah by UK forces.

Both men are being held as security internees in accordance with United Nations Security Council Resolution 1546 (2004). The International Committee of the Red Cross has access to both detention facilities and family visits are also permitted. Both internees' cases are reviewed regularly by the appropriate authorities.

(HC Deb 22 February 2005 Vol. 431 c13WS)

6/3

The Government was asked how many UK nationals are under sentence of death in China; and what steps the Government [is] taking to assist in these cases. An FCO Minister wrote:

In February 2003, two British nationals (Overseas) were sentenced to death in China. We have not been granted consular access to these British nationals, nor have we received any information about them from the Chinese authorities.

In March 2003 ... the Minister responsible for consular matters, wrote to the Vice Minister of the Chinese Ministry for Foreign Affairs (MFA) and requested that the sentences be commuted to terms of imprisonment. We did not receive a response. In February 2005, the British Embassy in Beijing wrote to the MFA requesting an update on these two cases. We are awaiting a response.

We are resolutely opposed to the death penalty in all circumstances. We will continue our enquiries about these British nationals and will make representations on their behalf at every appropriate opportunity.

(HC Deb 6 April 2005 Vol. 432 c1485W)

6/4

The Government was asked what representations [it has] made to the United States regarding its decision to withdraw from the Optional Protocol to the Vienna Convention on Consular Relations. An FCO Minister wrote:

The UK Government have not made representations to the United States following its decision to withdraw from the Optional Protocol to the Vienna Convention on Consular Relations. We note that the US Government has stated that it will continue to fulfil its obligations under the Convention and that it remains committed to its principles and provisions.

Consular relations between the UK and the United States are principally governed by the 1951 UK-US Bilateral Consular Convention.

(HC Deb 6 April 2005 Vol. 432 c1497W)

6/5

The Government was asked what provision [it] makes for assistance to UK citizens encountering long delays in legal actions in other EU countries. An FCO Minister wrote:

Under international law we cannot interfere in on-going legal proceedings in another country. Our own proceedings are similarly protected.

However, where there are unreasonable delays in criminal proceedings overseas in a case involving a UK national, we may consider, on a case by case basis, whether it would be appropriate to raise the issue with the state concerned. We would take into account any relevant information from the individual's lawyer before doing so.

(HC Deb 7 April 2005 Vol. 432 c1776W)

6/6

The Government was asked if the Foreign Secretary would take steps through (a) the UN, (b) the EU, and (c) diplomatic channels to ensure the December 2000 killings in which British national Charlotte Wilson was killed in Burundi is fully pursued and its perpetrators are brought to justice and are not given any amnesty; and if he will make a statement.

An FCO Minister wrote:

We will continue to press the Burundian authorities for progress in bringing Charlotte Wilson's killers to justice. Our ambassador to Burundi raised this most recently with the Burundian Interior Minister on 17 June.

We have made clear in recent UN Security Council and European Union statements that the climate of impunity in the Great Lakes region must end. We will continue to push for those that have committed serious human rights abuses to be brought to trial.

We have expressed support for the UN Secretary-General's proposal for a mixed UN and Burundian special chamber to investigate and prosecute those most responsible for such crimes.

(HC Deb 30 June 2005 Vol. 435 c1734W)

Part Six: IV. *The Position of the Individual (including the Corporation) in International Law—Members of minorities*

6/7

Introducing an Order under s.94 Nationality, Immigration and Asylum Act 2002 [which provides for non-suspensive appeals against refusal of refugee status, ie appeals which may be exercised after removal from the UK, Ed.], to extend non-suspensive appeals to applicants who would be returned to India, a Minister said:

The designation of India for non-suspensive asylum appeals is solely related to the handling of asylum and human rights claims. India is generally a safe country where people are not routinely fleeing from human rights abuses, and very few people need our protection under the refugee convention.

... it [may be] helpful if I briefly recall the main elements of the non-suspensive appeals process. Those countries that are designated for non-suspensive asylum appeals are considered to be generally safe in the context of asylum and human rights claims. An unsuccessful asylum or human rights claim made by a person entitled to reside in a designated state will be certified as clearly unfounded unless the Secretary of State deems that the claim is not clearly unfounded. The effect of a clearly unfounded certificate is that there will be no in-country right of appeal against the refusal of their claim. The right of appeal will be exercisable only from outside the United Kingdom.

Section 94 of the 2002 Act contains a provision to add countries to the list by affirmative order, but only when the Secretary of State is satisfied that there is in general in that state no serious risk of persecution of persons entitled to reside in that state or part, and that removal to that state or part of it of persons entitled to reside there will not in general contravene the United Kingdom's obligations under the Convention on Human Rights.

In considering the addition of India to the list of designated countries, we have taken this legal test as the starting point. We have, as before, taken full account of the available current country information we publish. We have also taken account of other factors such as the number of asylum applications made, the grant rates and the outcome of appeals. I should like to comment on each of the three elements in turn.

The first element is the legal test. We are satisfied that there is in general no serious risk of persecution in India and that it is a country to which removal of an individual would not in general breach the United Kingdom's ECHR obligations. We are not saying that India—or any of the other 14 countries currently on the list—is entirely safe for everyone. No country would meet that test. What we are saying is that these countries are safe for most people.

India has signed and ratified all six of the core UN human rights treaties except the Convention Against Torture, which has been signed but not ratified. India has a democratic, parliamentary system of government with representatives elected in multi-party elections. The constitution provides citizens with the right to change their government peacefully, and citizens exercise this right in practice through periodic, free and fair elections held on the basis of universal suffrage. The constitution provides for an independent judiciary. We have considered particularly the situation of women in India and made the decision to designate the country only following a fact-finding mission to India which found that options for redress were generally available for women in India.

As I said, inclusion on the list reflects a general level of safety, not a total absence of any mistreatment. It is for this reason that we continue to give every asylum or human rights claim from a resident of a designated country full consideration on its individual merits. The claim would not be refused or certified as clearly unfounded unless we were satisfied, after individual consideration, that the claim fell to be refused and certified.

Particular care is taken to ensure that initial decisions from the designated states are correct. All decisions are undertaken by caseworkers who have undergone specific additional training and have been accredited to make such decisions. Each and every decision is approved by a trained senior caseworker before being served. These are additional safeguards over and above what is in place for those claims that are not from the designated countries. Although cases which are certified do not give rise to an in-country right of appeal, as a further failsafe to this process, individuals whose claims are certified have the opportunity to seek judicial review of the certification of their claim as clearly unfounded if they consider it has been incorrectly certified. Such individuals will not be removed while their judicial review applications are pending.

The second element that we took into account in considering the addition of India to the list of designated countries is our published country information material. Noble Lords will recall that we had previously given a commitment to consult the independent Advisory Panel on Country Information on the country information being used by the Government before making an order to add a country to the list.

The panel has been established since September 2003. Its remit is to provide rigorous external scrutiny of country information material produced by the Home Office and make recommendations to help ensure that it is of the highest quality. The panel has shown itself to be working very effectively and its work has resulted in the introduction of a range of measures to improve the way the material is produced and assure quality. That has led to a widely acknowledged improvement in the quality and presentation of Home Office country information material.

The panel's role in non-suspensive appeals is to provide advice regarding the accuracy and objectivity of the country information produced on the countries proposed for designation. It is not expected to comment on the proposal to designate a particular country.

In that context, the panel held an extraordinary meeting on 7 December 2004 to consider the country information on India. The October 2004 Country Report and the report of a fact-finding mission to India were also considered in regard to the position of women ...

On the Country Report, the panel had a few concerns about the way the material was organised, but generally found it a fair reflection of the position in India. On the report of the fact-finding mission, it said that relevant information was included in the report, but there were some comments suggesting that it could be presented in a more accessible way. We will ensure that those comments are taken on board as we review the methodology.

I should like finally to turn to the third element that we took into account before deciding to designate India—the statistical evidence.

The number of asylum and human rights applications made by Indians in the United Kingdom is at a high level and not consistent with what is known about conditions in the country. Very few claims are granted. In 2003, excluding dependants, there were 2,290 asylum claims from Indians, 2,335 decisions were taken and only 10 grants of asylum were made. In the first nine months of 2004, there were 1,095 claims, 1,220 initial decisions, but only one or two grants of asylum. In both years less than 5 per cent of appeals have been successful ...

Designating a country for non-suspensive appeals provides a disincentive for people with no genuine protection needs misusing the asylum process. That leads to enhanced public confidence in the overall asylum system, a reduction in intake, a speeding up of the process and a consequent releasing of resources which can be used to improve performance in other areas. This order adding India to the list of designated countries is a sensible and measured step towards the increased use of non-suspensive appeals.

(HL Deb 4 February 2005 Vol. 669 c502–506)

Part Six: VI. *The Position of the Individual (including the Corporation) in International Law—Refugees*

6/8

The Government was asked what are the benefits to the United Kingdom of membership of the 1951 United Nations Convention relating to the status of refugees. A Minister wrote:

We are proud of the UK's record in providing a safe haven for refugees, many of whom are fleeing in fear of their lives from the most desperate human cruelty and we remain committed to the 1951 convention relating to the status of refugees.

The Government strongly believe in engaging with other states to address refugee and asylum issues. Membership of the UN Convention is vital to this objective. Membership also allows us to participate in UN led initiatives such as "Convention Plus" that build on the principles of the convention by addressing the challenges posed by refugee situations today.

(HL Deb 8 February 2005 Vol. 669 c101WA)

6/9

During a debate in the House of Commons, a Minister said:

The Government remain committed to the 1951 Refugee Convention, which is part of a legal and ethical framework that enshrines basic principles of human decency—a civilised society may be judged on how it treats desperate people who are fleeing persecution. I do not accept that the new policy of granting refugees five years' limited leave to remain in the first instance rather than immediate settlement represents an erosion of the Government's commitment to refugees or to the international protection system in general. Hon. Members are understandably concerned about how the new policy will operate, which is why I want to take this opportunity clearly to set out why we are introducing it, how we envisage that it will work in practice and what its consequences will be for refugees and their families.

... the Government's five-year strategy on asylum and immigration, which was published in February, set out our intention to introduce a policy of limited leave rather than immediate settlement for refugees, which was also a manifesto commitment. My hon. Friend the Minister for Immigration, Citizenship and Nationality announced the new policy to both Houses in a written ministerial statement on 19 July, and it was implemented on 30 August. From that date onwards, all refugees, other than those arriving in the UK under resettlement programmes, have been granted five years' limited leave to remain rather than immediate indefinite leave to remain.

We made that change for two main reasons: first, there should be a clear and consistent approach to those obtaining leave under the immigration rules on how long they have to be here before they become eligible for settlement, and we have decided to set that period at 5 years for most categories; secondly, we should provide refuge to people for as long as they need it, but if conditions in their country improve significantly, it is reasonable to expect them to return, particularly where they have spent only a relatively short period in the UK.

Some have argued that the new policy is not within the spirit of the Refugee Convention ... while others have suggested that it flies in the face of the Government's decision in 1998 to give recognised refugees immediate indefinite leave to remain. Those considerations are important, and I shall address each of them in turn.

The Refugee Convention states that it shall cease to apply to someone who

> "can no longer, because of the circumstances in connection with which he has been recognised as a refugee have ceased to exist, continue to refuse to avail himself of the protection of his country of nationality."

In other words, an individual is only a refugee for as long as he needs the protection of the refugee convention and for no longer. Our new policy is therefore within the spirit of the Refugee Convention, but there should be no doubt that where the conditions that gave rise to a refugee's fear of persecution continue to exist after five years, we will allow them to seek permanent settlement in the UK. However, where there has been a significant and non-temporary change in conditions in their country sufficient to suggest that they could return in safety, they will be expected to return there—indeed, I am sure that many refugees would wish to go home in such circumstances.

. . .

We believe that that process of reform should continue, and we are rolling out what we call the new asylum model that will result in tighter case management of asylum claims through to the final outcome, whether that be integration or removal. The new policy of limited leave for refugees is a return to one of the basic principles of the Geneva Convention—that generally someone is a refugee only for as long as the conditions that mean that they will be at risk of persecution continue to exist. It brings the UK into line with most other European countries—that is an important point to stress. France, Germany, Spain, the Netherlands and Denmark, for example, all require a refugee to complete a period of temporary leave before applying for permanent residence. Refugees are now granted five years' limited leave from day one, which may—I stress that word—be subject to review if they bring themselves within the scope of the Refugee Convention's exclusion or cessation clauses through their own actions: for example, where a person commits a terrorist act or re-establishes himself in his country of origin.

Those triggers for review are not new. The new element is that refugee status and limited leave may—again, I stress that word—also be reviewed where there is a significant and non-temporary change in conditions in a country or part of a country that places in doubt the continuing need for protection in the UK of all or certain groups of refugees from that country or part of it. We would determine that such changes had taken place on the basis of objective country information. When we determine on the basis of that information, and other sources such as case law, that certain categories of claim are likely to be clearly unfounded and that the change is of a durable nature, we will consider whether to instigate a review of previous grants of refugee status and limited leave to those falling within the scope of those categories.

However, I can give my hon. Friend assurances on a number of points, and I hope that they will go some way towards reassuring him. First, any review will be conducted on a case-by-case basis, and the burden of proof will be on the immigration and nationality directorate—

. . .

The second assurance is that any decision to trigger a review on the basis of a change in country conditions will be made only following consultation with the United Nations High Commissioner for Refugees.

The quality of the country reports is obviously crucial in reaching a reasoned and fair judgment on the conditions and circumstances that exist in a country. The reports originate in the Foreign Office. The hon. Gentleman will have seen some of them. The material is drawn from many different sources; the documents are well grounded. If he considers the recent process that we went through on Zimbabwe, great effort was made and care taken to establish the conditions in that country. I can give him the assurance that he wants. We will continue to take great care in establishing facts on the ground before taking further action. We do not want to act on wrong or misleading information.

We are ensuring through the Immigration, Asylum and Nationality Bill that refugees will have an in-country right of appeal against a decision to take away their leave and that the decision will not take effect until that appeal has been heard. I can further assure my hon. Friend the Member for Walthamstow that when an individual no longer qualifies for leave as a refugee, we would always consider whether a grant of leave on another basis was appropriate, for example, on European Convention on human rights grounds. Although it is possible that some refugees will be allowed to remain because they have established a private and/or family life in the UK, we need to get the balance right between offering a family a permanent life in the UK and expecting them to return to their country of origin if conditions improve there.

(HC Deb 10 October 2005 Vol. 437 c130–133)

Part Six: VII. B. *The Position of the Individual (including the Corporation) in International Law—Immigration and emigration, extradition, expulsion, asylum—Extradition*

(See also **Part Nineteen: VIII**)

6/10

In a written answer, a Minister wrote:

The US-UK Extradition Treaty 2003 is not yet in force, although certain provisions in it have been given effect in the 2003 Extradition Act which came into force on 1 January 2004. Part 2 of that Act provides the framework for the scrutiny of requests from countries outside the EU. Requests which are certified by the Home Office as valid are submitted to the court, whose role includes establishing that the request is for conduct which is extraditable in UK law, and that extradition would not breach the person's human rights. Unless discharged by the court, they are then passed to Ministers for consideration of issues relating to the death penalty, speciality and earlier extradition if applicable, and for final decision. There is an avenue of appeal against the decisions of both Ministers and the courts. These procedures apply regardless of the person's nationality.

(HC Deb 14 July 2005 Vol. 436 c1219W)

6/11

In a written answer, a Minister wrote:

There are full and adequate safeguards in the Extradition Act 2003 to ensure that extraditions approved under its procedures are fair, and these apply regardless of the requested person's nationality. The 2003 [US-UK Extradition] treaty has not yet been ratified by the USA, and until its ratification the 1972 US-UK Extradition Treaty remains in force.

(HC Deb 14 July 2005 Vol. 436 c1219W)

6/12

In a written answer, a Minister wrote:

Farj Hassan Faraj was first informed that he was the subject of an extradition request from Italy on 24 July 2003, when he was arrested on a warrant issued pursuant to that request.

In 2004 the Italian constitutional court ruled that domestic time limits on pre-trial custody applied to people in custody outside Italy for whom a request for extradition had been made. This time limit would not however have applied in Faraj's case had he been notified by the relevant UK authorities of the completion of a pre-trial investigation on him in Italy. The Italian authorities requested on eighth April 2003 that such notification be given urgently.

They did not specify a deadline. Unfortunately, although an earlier request for the transmission of evidence was acted on immediately, the notification was, by oversight, not made to Faraj. The fact, and significance, of this omission were not appreciated at the time.

The UK authorities were first alerted by the Italian authorities to the implications of the constitutional court's ruling on custody time limits for the Faraj case in October 2005, and notification was then immediately given. On 10 October the Italian authorities withdrew their extradition request, stating that the order for pre-trial custody in prison had been revoked following the dismissal of proceedings. Faraj remains in immigration detention in the UK, pending further consideration of his immigration position.

(HC Deb 16 November 2005 Vol. 439 c1259W–1260W)

6/13

In a written answer, a Minister wrote:

As we have made clear on a number of occasions deportations will only take place if the removal is consistent with our international obligations.

(HC Deb 29 November 2005 Vol. 440 c593W)

6/14

In a written answer, a Minister wrote:

The United Kingdom is a signatory to two multi-party prisoner transfer agreements; the Council of Europe Convention on the Transfer of Sentenced Persons, and the Commonwealth Scheme for the Transfer of Convicted Offenders. In addition, the Government have concluded bilateral prisoner transfer agreements with 18 countries. The UK has prisoner transfer agreements with a total of 97 countries and territories and is in regular contact with the Governments concerned about the transfer of individual prisoners.

Prisoner transfer under these agreements is voluntary; the consent of both states involved, and of the prisoner concerned, is required before repatriation can take place. In 2004, 107 prisoners were transferred from prisons in England and Wales to other countries to continue serving their sentences.

(HC Deb 19 December 2005 Vol. 440 c2365W)

6/15

Extraordinary Rendition

(See also **Part Twelve: I. A.**)

The Foreign Secretary was asked by the FAC about "extraordinary rendition". He said:

We are not aware of the use of our territory or air space for the purpose of extraordinary rendition. We have not received any requests or granted any permissions for use of UK territory or air space for such purposes. It is perfectly possible that there have been two hundred movements of United States aircraft in and out of the United Kingdom and I would have thought it was many more; but that is because we have a number of US air force bases here, which, under the Visiting Forces Act and other arrangements they are entitled to use under certain conditions. I do not see for a second how the conclusion could be drawn from the fact that there have been some scores of movements of US military aircraft—well, so what—that that therefore means they have been used for rendition. That is a very long chain! [Q.105]

He was asked if the Government was co-operating with the UN Commission on Human Rights Inquiry into "extraordinary rendition". He said:

I assume we are co-operating with it. I am not aware of any requests, but we always co-operate with such requests. [Q.106]

The Foreign Secretary was asked further about flights by non-military aircraft to civilian airports. He said:

If there is evidence [that the planes were being used for extraordinary rendition], we will look at it, but a suggestion in a newspaper that there have been flights by unspecified foreign aircraft in and out of the United Kingdom cannot possibly add up to evidence that our air space or our facilities have been used for the purpose of unlawful rendition. [Q.107]

And the Foreign Secretary went on:

... there are no circumstances in which British officials use torture, nor any question of the British Government seeking to justify the use of torture. Again, the British Government, including the terrorist and security agencies, has never used torture for any purpose including for information, nor would we instigate or connive with others in doing so. [Q.109]

He added:

I ought to say that whether rendition is contrary to international law depends on the particular circumstances of the case; it depends on each case, but we do not practise it. [Q.110]

(FAC Report, Foreign Policy Aspects of the War Against Terrorism, HC573-ii (2005))

6/16

In a written answer, an FCO Minister wrote:

The Government's policy is not to deport or extradite any person to another State where there are substantial grounds to believe that the person will be subject to torture or where there is a real risk that the death penalty will be applied.

(HC Deb 19 October 2005 Vol. 437 c1093W–1094W)

6/17

In a written answer, the Foreign Secretary wrote:

The term "rendition" is currently being used to describe informal transfers of individuals in a wide range of circumstances. Whether any particular "rendition" is lawful depends on the facts of each individual case. Where we are requested to assist another State and our assistance would be lawful, we will decide whether or not to assist taking into account all the circumstances. We would not assist in any case if to do so would put us in breach of UK law or our international obligations. In particular, we would not facilitate the transfer of an individual from or through the UK to another State where there were grounds to believe that the person would face a real risk of torture.

Careful research by officials has been unable to identify any occasion since 11 September 2001, or earlier in the Bush administration, when we received a request for permission by the United States (US) for a rendition through UK territory or airspace, nor are we otherwise aware of such a case.

Additional research covering the remainder of the period of office of this Government (i.e. back to May 1997) has been undertaken. This shows there were some renditions via the UK during that period. Specifically, we have identified two definite occasions in 1998 when requests were made by the US. These occasions, for which records have been identified, were for transfer to the US for the person concerned to stand trial there. As the then Home Secretary I agreed these requests.

Although confirmatory records have yet to be identified, we believe that there may have been one or two other possible cases, also in 1998, which concerned requests by the US but for transfer to a third country. We have information on one such case which is incomplete and does not tell us whether the request was refused. We also have information on a case based on the recollection of officials involved in such matters, without any confirmatory records. The officials' recollection is that the case was refused. It is likely, but not certain, that the two cases are in fact one and the same. I have some recollection of such a case, but, given the passage of time, I cannot be certain. The search for records continues.

(HC Deb 12 December 2005 Vol. 440 c1652W–1653W)

Part Six: VII. C. *The Position of the Individual (including the Corporation) in International Law—Immigration and emigration, extradition, expulsion, asylum—Expulsion*

(See also **Six: VIII. (Algeria)**)

6/18

The Government was asked its policy is on where responsibility should lie for Chinese nationals in the UK who have not been granted asylum in the UK and who are not accepted back by the Chinese authorities. A Minister wrote:

Chinese nationals whose applications for asylum have been unsuccessful are expected to leave the UK, and their removal may be enforced.

The Chinese authorities will accept the return of Chinese nationals whose nationality and identity has been verified. In cases where travel documents have been lost or destroyed, an Emergency Travel Document must be obtained from the Chinese Embassy. We are working closely with the Chinese Government to improve the effectiveness of the redocumentation process.

(HC Deb 20 January 2005 Vol. 429 c1082W)

6/19

In a written Ministerial Statement, the Secretary of State for the Home Office wrote:

The Government have been actively seeking the agreement of Memoranda of Understanding on human rights assurances with key foreign Governments to enable deportations to proceed. The first such Memorandum was signed with Jordan in August and a copy has been placed in the Library. We are pursuing similar agreements with a number of other countries. These negotiations are ongoing.

The Government have debated with European partners how caselaw around the application of the European Convention on Human Rights (ECHR) has developed, particularly in respect of how national security considerations are taken into account in deportation cases involving Article 3. Using normal practice, and with the support of the Netherlands, the UK has been granted leave from the

European Court of Human Rights to intervene as a third party in a case which the Netherlands currently has before the Court, which turns on Article 3. We will ask the Court to revisit the issues surrounding national security expulsions in light of current circumstances.

(HC Deb 12 October 2005 Vol. 437 c33WS)

6/20

During a debate in the House of Lords, an FCO Minister said:

... the Prime Minister announced on 5 August that the United Kingdom was seeking to negotiate memoranda of understanding with a number of countries in the Middle East and North Africa, containing assurances against torture or ill treatment of those being returned. We have subsequently signed two such MOUs with Jordan and Libya; the MOUs and the assurances contained within them are subject to a monitoring regime conducted by an independent and capable body. The texts are in the Library. A body has agreed to carry out that important role in Jordan; we have agreed in principle with a body in Libya to do the same, and we are now tying down the details with that body.

...

My Lords, the necessity for the memoranda is to ensure that standards that we would regard as acceptable are sustained. The methodology described in them is sufficiently robust and contains all the essential elements that we need. The monitors will be chosen on a basis such that we are confident of their efficacy. When individuals fearing any return go to the British courts, I have no doubt that the courts will protect them from any threat of the death penalty or torture. Those are real-world commitments, made on a bilateral arrangement, and commitments that we are confident will be sustained because they have been made in serious negotiation in good faith.

...

My Lords, I am confident that we will be in full compliance with Article 3 [of the ECHR]. The proposition is specific in the memoranda; the intention is that these are specific agreements about specific people on a case-by-case basis, who are returned to countries because they pose a terrorism threat to the people of the United Kingdom. We are not asking people to monitor every prison; we are ensuring that the people covered by the specific arrangements meet the full criteria in the memoranda.

(HL Deb 15 November 2005 Vol. 675 c950–951)

6/21

In a written answer, a Minister wrote:

We have signed Memoranda of Understanding with Jordan and with Libya regulating the provision of assurances in respect of people who are being deported. We have said that we are in negotiations with the governments of Algeria and the Lebanon. Those negotiations are continuing, and we hope to conclude them shortly . . .

The power to exclude relates solely to cases where the person concerned is outside the United Kingdom. It is a unilateral decision, and we have not had any negotiations with other countries regarding the use of this power.

(HC Deb 29 November 2005 Vol. 440 c602W–603W)

6/22

Diplomatic Assurances—Jordan

During a debate in the House of Commons, the Secretary of State for the Home Department said:

The power of exclusion is necessarily targeted at those outside the UK. When people who are already in the UK engage in the kind of behaviour that I have identified and described, it may well be appropriate to deport them under statutory powers. I will ensure that a consistent stance is taken in relation to both deportation and exclusions. In the past, there have been some successful challenges to proposed deportations under article 3 of the European Convention on Human Rights. For that reason, we have actively been seeking memorandums of understanding with a number of Governments to address those legal concerns.

(HC Deb 20 July 2005 Vol. 436 c1256)

6/23

Memorandum of Understanding Between the Government of the United Kingdom of Great Britain and Northern Ireland and the Government of the Hashemite Kingdom of Jordan Regulating the Provision of Undertakings in Respect of Specified Persons Prior to Deportation

Application and Scope

This arrangement will apply to any person accepted by the receiving state for admission to its territory following a written request by the sending state under the terms of this arrangement. Such a request may be made in respect of any citizen of the receiving state who is to be returned to that country by the sending state on the grounds that he is not entitled, or is no longer entitled, to remain in the sending state according to the immigration laws of that state.

Requests under this arrangement will be submitted in writing either by the British Embassy in Amman to the Ministry of the Interior or by the Jordanian Embassy in London to the Home Office. Where a request is made under the terms of this arrangement, the department to which it is made will acknowledge receipt of the request within 5 working days.

A response to a request under the terms of this arrangement may be given verbally, but must be confirmed in writing within 14 days by the Home Secretary, in the case of a request made to the United Kingdom, or by the Minister of

Interior in the case of a request made to the Hashemite Kingdom of Jordan before any return can take place.

To enable a decision to be made on whether or not to return a person under this arrangement, the receiving state will inform the sending state of any penalties outstanding against the subject of a request, and of any outstanding convictions or criminal charges pending against him and the penalties which could be imposed.

Requests under this arrangement may include requests for further specific assurances by the receiving state if appropriate in an individual case.

Understandings

It is understood that the authorities of the United Kingdom and of Jordan will comply with their human rights obligations under international law regarding a person returned under this arrangement. Where someone has been accepted under the terms of this arrangement, the conditions set out in the following paragraphs (numbered 1–8) will apply, together with any further specific assurances provided by the receiving state.

1. If arrested, detained or imprisoned following his return, a returned person will be afforded adequate accommodation, nourishment, and medical treatment, and will be treated in a humane and proper manner, in accordance with internationally accepted standards.

2. A returned person who is arrested or detained will be brought promptly before a judge or other officer authorised by law to exercise judicial power in order that the lawfulness of his detention may be decided.

3. A returned person who is arrested or detained will be informed promptly by the authorities of the receiving state of the reasons for his arrest or detention, and of any charge against him.

4. If the returned person is arrested, detained or imprisoned within 3 years of the date of his return, he will be entitled to contact, and then have prompt and regular visits from the representative of an independent body nominated jointly by the UK and Jordanian authorities. Such visits will be permitted at least once a fortnight, and whether or not the returned person has been convicted, and will include the opportunity for private interviews with the returned person. The nominated body will give a report of its visits to the authorities of the sending state.

5. Except where the returned person is arrested, detained or imprisoned, the receiving state will not impede, limit, restrict or otherwise prevent access by a returned person to the consular posts of the sending state during normal working hours. However, the receiving state is not obliged to facilitate such access by providing transport free of charge or at discounted rates.

6. A returned person will be allowed to follow his religious observance following his return, including while under arrest, or while detained or imprisoned.

7. A returned person who is charged with an offence following his return will receive a fair and public hearing without undue delay by a competent, independent and impartial tribunal established by law. Judgment will be pronounced publicly,

but the press and public may be excluded from all or part of the trial in the interests of morals, public order or national security in a democratic society, where the interests of juveniles or the protection of the private life of the parties so require, or to the extent strictly necessary in the opinion of the court in special circumstances where publicity would prejudice the interests of justice.

8. A returned person who is charged with an offence following his return will be allowed adequate time and facilities to prepare his defence, and will be permitted to examine or have examined the witnesses against him and to call and have examined witnesses on his behalf. He will be allowed to defend himself in person or through legal assistance of his own choosing, or, if he has not sufficient means to pay for legal assistance, to be given it free when the interests of justice so require.

Withdrawal

Either government may withdraw from this arrangement by giving 6 months notice in writing to the Embassy of the other government.

Where one or other government withdraws from the arrangement, the terms of this arrangement will continue to apply to anyone who has been returned in accordance with its provisions.

Signature

This Memorandum of Understanding represents the understandings reached between the Government of the United Kingdom of Great Britain and Northern Ireland and the Government of the Hashemite Kingdom of Jordan upon the matters referred to therein.

Signed in duplicate at Amman on 10 August 2005 in the English and Arabic languages, both texts having equal validity.

For the Government of the United Kingdom of Great Britain and Northern Ireland

For the Government of the Hashemite Kingdom of Jordan

The following letter was attached to the agreement.

British Embassy Amman
Abdoun PO Box 87 Amman 11118 Jordan
10 August 2005
HE Mr Awni Yervas Minister of Interior
Amman

Today we have signed a Memorandum of Understanding (MOU) on behalf of our two Governments regulating the provision of undertakings in respect of persons prior to deportation. Signature of the MOU reflects the British Government's strong wish to strengthen co-operation with the Government of Jordan to counter the threat of international terrorism. The content of the MOU also reflects the British Government's intention to respect its international and domestic human rights obligations and responsibilities and Jordanian law and sovereignty.

During our discussions on the MOU we agreed that it would be right to exchange letters on the use of the death penalty on which, for constitutional reasons, the Government of Jordan has been unable to give an undertaking in the MOU itself. This letter, and the Government of Jordan's formal response to it, set out the joint understanding of our two Governments on this issue.

The British Government is opposed to the use of the death penalty in all circumstances. We would not return a person to Jordan if that person faced significant risk of the death penalty on return. If a person returned to Jordan is, at any time after his return, subsequently sentenced to death, the British Government would consider asking the Jordanian Government to commute the sentence.

The Government of Jordan has indicated that it would be open to the Government of Jordan to give a specific assurance in relation to a particular case. Such specific assurances being sought by either Government is recognised in the MOU itself (7th paragraph under application and scope). The British Government records here that it may well seek a specific assurance on this issue in relation to particular cases.

In our discussions, both Governments have recognised the vital importance of appointing independent bodies capable of monitoring the execution of the undertakings given under the MOU, including any specific assurances given in particular cases. Our discussions continue on the identity and specific terms of reference of these bodies.

The MOU requires the two Governments to consult closely on the circumstances and identity of those who might be subject to its provisions. The British Government attaches considerable importance to maximum transparency and timely consultation. The MOU also provides for the two Governments to seek assurances specific to individual cases, in addition to the issue of the death penalty described in this letter. The British Government considers this provision an important means of meeting the counter-terrorism and human rights objectives which underpin the MOU.

Pat Phillips
Charge d'Affaires a.i.

(Text provided by FCO)

6/24

Diplomatic Assurances—Libya

Memorandum of Understanding Between the General People's Committee for Foreign Liaison and International Co-Operation of the Great Socialist People's Libyan Arab Jamahiriya and the Foreign and Commonwealth Office of the United Kingdom of Great Britain and Northern Ireland Concerning the Provision of Assurances in Respect of Persons Subject to Deportation

Application and Scope
A request for assurances under this Memorandum may be made by the sending state in respect of any citizen of the receiving state, any stateless person who was habitually resident in the receiving state, or any third-country national whom the receiving state is prepared to admit.

Such requests will be submitted in writing either by the British Embassy in Tripoli to the General People's Committee for Foreign Liaison and International Co-operation or by the People's Bureau of the Great Socialist People's Libyan Arab Jamahiriya in London to the Foreign and Commonwealth Office. The state to which the request is made will acknowledge receipt of the request within 5 working days.

A final response to such a request will be given promptly in writing by the Foreign Secretary in the case of a request made to the United Kingdom, or by the Secretary of the General People's Committee for Foreign Liaison and International Co-operation in the case of a request made to Libya.

To assist a decision on whether to request assurances under this Memorandum, the receiving state will inform the sending state of any penalties outstanding against a person to be deported, and of any outstanding convictions or criminal charges pending against him and the penalties which could be imposed.

Requests under this Memorandum may include requests to the receiving state for further specific assurances. It will be for the receiving state to decide whether to give such further assurances.

The United Kingdom and the Great Socialist People's Libyan Arab Jamahiriya will comply with their human rights obligations under international law regarding a person in respect of whom assurances are given under this Memorandum. The assurances set out in the following paragraphs (numbered 1–9) will apply to such a person, together with any further specific assurances provided by the receiving state.

An independent body ("the monitoring body") will be nominated by both sides to monitor the implementation of the assurances given under this Memorandum, including any specific assurances, by the receiving state. The responsibilities of the monitoring body will include monitoring the return of, and any detention, trial or imprisonment of, the person. The monitoring body will report to both sides.

Assurances
1. Where, before his deportation, a person has been tried and convicted of an offence in the receiving state in absentia, he will be entitled to a re-trial for that offence on his return.

2. In cases where the person may face the death penalty in the receiving state, the receiving state will, if its laws allow, provide a specific assurance that the death penalty will not be carried out. In any case, where there are outstanding charges, or where charges are subsequently brought, against the person in respect of an offence allegedly committed before his deportation, the authorities of the receiving state will utilise all the powers available to them under their

system for the administration of justice to ensure that, if the death penalty is imposed, the sentence will not be carried out.

3. If arrested, detained or imprisoned following his deportation, the deported person will be afforded adequate accommodation, nourishment, and medical treatment, and will be treated in a humane and proper manner, in accordance with internationally accepted standards.

4. If the deported person is arrested or detained, he will be informed promptly by the authorities of the receiving state of the reasons for his arrest or detention, and of any charge against him. The person will be entitled to consult a lawyer promptly.

5. If the deported person is arrested or detained, he will be brought promptly before a civilian judge or other civilian official authorised by law to exercise judicial power in order that the lawfulness of his detention may be decided.

6. The deported person will have unimpeded access to the monitoring body unless they are arrested, detained or imprisoned. If the person is arrested, detained or imprisoned, he will be entitled to contact promptly a representative of the monitoring body and to meet a representative of the monitoring body within one week of his arrest, detention or imprisonment. Thereafter he will be entitled to regular visits from a representative of the monitoring body in co-ordination with the competent legal authorities. Such visits will include the opportunity for private interviews with the person and, during any period before trial, will be permitted at least once every three weeks. If the representative of the monitoring body considers a medical examination of the person is necessary, he will be entitled to arrange for one or to ask the authorities of the receiving state to do so.

7. The deported person will be allowed to follow his religious observance following his return, including while under arrest, or while detained or imprisoned.

8. If the deported person is charged with an offence he will receive a fair and public hearing without undue delay by a competent, independent and impartial civilian court established by law. The person will be allowed adequate time and facilities to prepare his defence, and will be permitted to examine or have examined the witnesses against him and to call and have examined witnesses on his behalf. He will be allowed to defend himself in person or through legal assistance of his own choosing, or, if he has not sufficient means to pay for legal assistance, to be given it free when the interests of justice so require.

9. Any judgment against the deported person will be pronounced publicly, but the press and public may be excluded from all or part of the trial in the interests of morals, public order or national security in a democratic society, where the interests of juveniles or the protection of the private life of the parties so require, or to the extent strictly necessary in the opinion of the court in special circumstances where publicity would prejudice the interests of justice.

Withdrawal
Either participant may withdraw from this Memorandum by giving 6 months notice in writing to the diplomatic mission of the other.

Where one or other participant withdraws from the Memorandum any assurances given under it in respect of a person will continue to apply in accordance with its provisions.

Signature
This Memorandum of Understanding represents the understandings reached upon the matters referred to therein between the Great Socialist People's Libyan Arab Jamahiriya and the United Kingdom of Great Britain and Northern Ireland.

Signed in duplicate at Tripoli on 18 October 2005 in the English and Arabic languages, both texts having equal validity.

Abdulati Ibrahim Obeidi,
Acting Secretary for European Affairs,
Secretariat for Foreign Liaison and International Co-operation, Tripoli
For the Great Socialist People's Libyan Arab Jamahiriya

Anthony Layden HM Ambassador
British Embassy, Tripoli
For the United Kingdom of Great Britain and Northern Ireland

The following letter was attached to the agreement

From the Ambassador
British Embassy Tripoli
PO Box 4206
18 October 2005

Ambassador Abdulati Ibrahim al-Obidi Acting Secretary for European Affairs Secretariat for Foreign Liaison and International Co-operation Tripoli

[Your Excellency]

Today we have signed a Memorandum of Understanding (MOU) on behalf of our two Governments regulating the provision of undertakings in respect of persons prior to deportation. Signature of the MOU reflects the British Government's strong wish to strengthen co-operation with the Great Socialist People's Libyan Arab Jamahiriya to counter the threat of international terrorism. The content of the MOU also reflects the British Government's intention to respect its international and domestic human rights obligations and responsibilities and Libyan law and sovereignty.

The MOU and this letter set out the joint understanding of our two Governments on the death penalty. The MOU specifies that in cases where the deported person may face the death penalty in the receiving state, the receiving state will, if its laws allow, provide a specific assurance that the death penalty will not be carried out. In any case, where there are outstanding charges or charges are subsequently brought, against the deported person in respect of an offence allegedly committed before his deportation, the authorities of the receiving state will utilise all the powers available to them under their system for the administration of justice to ensure that, if the death penalty is imposed, the sentence will not be carried out.

During our discussions on the MOU we explained the British Government's policy on the death penalty. This letter re-affirms that position. The British Government is opposed to the use of the death penalty in all circumstances. We would not return a person to the Great Socialist People's Libyan Arab Jamahiriya if that person faced significant risk of the death penalty on return. If a person returned to the Great Socialist People's Libyan Arab Jamahiriya is, at any time after his return, subsequently sentenced to death, the British Government would consider asking the Great Socialist People's Libyan Arab Jamahiriya to commute the sentence.

In our discussions, both Governments have recognised the vital importance of appointing independent bodies capable of monitoring the execution of the undertakings given under the MOU, including any specific assurances given in particular cases. Our discussions continue on the identity and specific terms of reference of these bodies.

The MOU requires the two Governments to consult closely on the circumstances and identity of those who might be subject to its provisions. The British Government attaches considerable importance to maximum transparency and timely consultation. The MOU also provides for the two Governments to seek assurances specific to individual cases, in addition to the issue of the death penalty described in this letter. The British Government considers this provision an important means of meeting the counter-terrorism and human rights objectives that underpin the MOU.

[Yours sincerely,
Anthony Layden]

(Text provided by FCO)

6/25

Diplomatic Assurances—Lebanon

Memorandum of Understanding Between the Government of the United Kingdom of Great Britain and Northern Ireland and the Government of the Lebanese Republic concerning the provision of Assurances in respect of Persons Subject to Deportation

Application and Scope

A request for assurances under this Memorandum may be made by the sending state in respect of any citizen of the receiving state, any stateless person who was habitually resident in the receiving state, or any third-country national whom the receiving state is prepared to admit.

Such requests will be submitted in writing either by the British Embassy in Beirut to the Ministry of the Interior or by the Lebanese Embassy in London to the Home Office. The Government to which the request is made will acknowledge receipt of the request within 5 working days.

A final response to a such a request will be given promptly in writing by the Home Secretary in the case of a request made to the United Kingdom, or by the Minister of Justice in the case of a request made to Lebanon.

To assist a decision on whether to request assurances under this Memorandum, the receiving state will inform the sending state of any penalties outstanding against a person, and of any outstanding convictions or criminal charges pending against him and the penalties which could be imposed.

Requests under this Memorandum may include requests to the receiving state for further specific assurances.

The Governments of the United Kingdom and of the Lebanese Republic will comply with their human rights obligations under international law regarding a person in respect of whom assurances are given under this Memorandum. The assurances set out in the following paragraphs (numbered 1–7) will apply to such a person, together with any further specific assurances provided by the receiving state.

An independent body will be nominated by both Governments to monitor the implementation of the assurances given under this Memorandum, including any specific assurances, by the receiving state ("the monitoring body"). The responsibilities of the monitoring body will include, but are not limited to, monitoring the return of, and any detention, trial or imprisonment of, the person. The monitoring body will report to both Governments.

Assurances

1. If arrested, detained or imprisoned following his deportation, the person will be afforded adequate accommodation, nourishment, and medical treatment, and will be treated in a humane and proper manner, in accordance with internationally accepted standards.

2. If the person is arrested or detained, he will be informed promptly by the authorities of the receiving state of the reasons for his arrest or detention, and of any charge against him. The person will be entitled to consult a lawyer promptly.

3. If the person is arrested or detained, he will be brought promptly before a judge or other official authorised by law to exercise judicial power in order that the lawfulness of his detention may be decided.

4. The person will have unimpeded access to the monitoring body for three years after his return except at any time when he is arrested, detained or imprisoned. If the person is arrested, detained or imprisoned in respect of matters occurring before or within three years after the date of his return, he will be entitled to contact promptly, and in any event within 48 hours, a representative of the monitoring body. Thereafter he will be entitled to regular visits from a representative of the monitoring body. Such visits will include the opportunity for private interviews with the person and, during any period before trial, will be permitted at least once a week. If the representative of the monitoring body considers a medical examination of the person is necessary, he will be entitled to arrange for one or to ask the authorities of the receiving state to do so.

5. The person will be allowed to follow his religious observance following his return, including while under arrest, or while detained or imprisoned.

6. If the person is charged with an offence he will receive a fair and public hearing without undue delay by a competent, independent and impartial tribunal, properly constituted by law. The person will be allowed adequate time and facilities to prepare his defence, and will be permitted to examine or have examined the witnesses against him and to call and have examined witnesses on his behalf. He will be allowed to defend himself in person or through legal assistance of his own choosing, or, if he has not sufficient means to pay for legal assistance, to be given it free when the interests of justice so require.

7. Any judgment against the person will be pronounced publicly, but the press and public may be excluded from all or part of the trial in the interests of morals, public order or national security in a democratic society, where the interests of juveniles or the protection of the private life of the parties so require, or to the extent strictly necessary in the opinion of the court in special circumstances where publicity would prejudice the interests of justice.

Withdrawal
Either Government may withdraw from this Memorandum by giving 6 months notice in writing to the Embassy of the other government.

Where one or other Government withdraws from the Memorandum any assurances given under it in respect of a person will continue to apply in accordance with its provisions.

Signature
This Memorandum of Understanding represents the understandings reached between the Government of the United Kingdom of Great Britain and Northern Ireland and the Government of the Lebanese Republic upon the matters referred to therein.

Signed in duplicate at Beirut on 23 December 2005 in the English and Arabic languages, both texts having equal validity.

For the Government of the United Kingdom of Great Britain and Northern Ireland

For the Government of the Lebanese Republic

The following letter was attached to the agreement:

British Embassy Beirut
23 December 2005

His Excellency Mr. Charles Rizk Minister of Justice Ministry of Justice

Today we have signed a Memorandum of Understanding (MOU) on behalf of our two Governments regulating the provision of undertakings in respect of persons prior to deportation. Signature of the MOD reflects the British Government's strong wish to strengthen co-operation with the Lebanese Government to counter the threat of international terrorism. The content of the MOU also reflects the British Government's intention to respect its international and domestic human rights obligations and responsibilities and Lebanese law and sovereignty.

During our discussions on the MOD we agreed that it would be right to exchange letters on the use of the death penalty on which, for constitutional reasons, the Lebanese Government has been unable to give an undertaking in the MOD itself. The MOD and this letter set out the joint understanding of our two Governments on this issue.

The British Government is opposed to the use of the death penalty in all circumstances. We would not return a person to Lebanon if that person faced significant risk of the death penalty on return. If a person returned to Lebanon is, at any time after his return, subsequently sentenced to death, the British Government would consider asking the Lebanese Government to commute the sentence.

The Lebanese Government has indicated that it would be open to the Lebanese Government to give a specific assurance in relation to a particular case within the limits of the Lebanese Constitution. Such specific assurances being sought by either Government is recognised in the MOD itself (5th paragraph under application and scope). The British Government records here that it may well seek a specific assurance on this issue in relation to particular cases.

In our discussions, both Governments have recognised the vital importance of appointing independent bodies capable of monitoring the execution of the undertakings given under the MOU, including any specific assurances given in particular cases. Our discussions continue on the identity and specific terms of reference of these bodies.

The MOU requires the two Governments to consult closely on the circumstances and identity of those who might be subject to its provisions. The British Government attaches considerable importance to maximum transparency and timely consultation. The MOU also provides for the two Governments to seek assurances specific to individual cases, in addition to the issue of the death penalty described in this letter. The British Government considers this provision an important means of meeting the counter-terrorism and human rights objectives which underpin the MOU.

James Watt

HM Ambassador

(Text provided by FCO)

[The full texts of the MOUs and supporting letters are printed because of the difficulties of otherwise gaining access to them, Ed.]

6/26

Zimbabwe

A Minister made the following statement in the House of Lords:

Like all issues of removals, policy in this area [removal to Zimbabwe] is inevitably difficult and sensitive. On 16 November last year, the [Government] announced the lifting of the temporary suspension of enforced removals of failed asylum seekers to Zimbabwe. The effect of this announcement was to make the process of removals to Zimbabwe the same as for every other country in the world. In short, the Home Office assesses cases on their individual merits, providing protection to those who need it and seeking to remove those who do not.

This means that Zimbabweans who meet the definition of a refugee in the 1951 Geneva Convention are granted asylum. If they do not qualify for asylum, but there are other circumstances that make them particularly vulnerable and engage our obligations under the European Convention on Human Rights, they are granted humanitarian protection or discretionary leave. If their application is refused, they have a right of appeal to the independent asylum and immigration tribunal. If the appeal is unsuccessful, that means that it has been judged safe for that particular individual to return to Zimbabwe.

I have considered, with the Foreign Secretary, whether, in the light of recent events in Zimbabwe, we should reverse last November's decision. We have agreed that recent events do not materially change our earlier decision, but that we will keep the situation, together with any new information, under constant review. As before, it is clear that there are Zimbabweans in need of international protection. In particular, members of the Opposition in Zimbabwe or others who establish that they have engaged in activities that will cause them to be persecuted by the Zimbabwean Government will continue to be granted asylum. In the 15 months to March this year, we granted asylum or discretionary leave at initial decision to 270 Zimbabweans with no substantiated reports of mistreatment on return.

But not all Zimbabweans who claim asylum here genuinely face persecution. It is an important part of ensuring an effective and fair asylum system that those found not to be in need of international protection are removed from the UK. The blanket suspension of all removals to any country can only encourage those seeking to get round our controls for reasons nothing to do with their political activity or fear of persecution. Having a moratorium on returns to one country means that failed asylum seekers from other countries will mount legal challenges to get their country treated in the same way.

That is why we are right to look at each case on its merits. We will examine with great care each individual case before removal and we will not remove anyone who we believe is at risk on their return. As part of this, we will remain in close contact with civil society and opposition parties in Zimbabwe.

Our policy on returns does not in any way change our categorical opposition to human rights abuses in Zimbabwe. There is no doubt that political persecution, abuses of human rights and denial of basic freedom persist in Zimbabwe, and we will continue to provide asylum to those Zimbabweans who need our protection. We will also continue, bilaterally and with our international partners, to push the Government of Zimbabwe to end human rights abuses there and restore democracy so that all Zimbabweans can, in time, return safely to help build a prosperous and stable country.

(HL Deb 27 June Vol. 673 c21–22)

Part Six: VII. D. *The Position of the Individual (including the Corporation) in International Law—Immigration and emigration, extradition, expulsion, asylum—Asylum*

6/27

The FCO wrote to the JCHR about its Report on the Nationality, Immigration and Asylum Act 2002 (Specification of Particularly Serious Crimes Order) 2004 (see UKMIL 2004 p.687). It said:

The Refugee Convention is framed in a way which reflects not only the need to protect individuals fearing persecution in their country of origin or habitual residence but also the needs of States to protect themselves from persons who pose a threat to their national security or a danger to their communities. In enacting section 72 of the Nationality, Immigration and Asylum Act 2002 and in laying the Order made under powers in that section we have been aware of both of these aspects of the Convention. We consider that section 72 and the Order provide for a proper application and construction of that part of Article 33(2) of the Refugee Convention to which they relate.

Turning to your specific questions.

1. In relation to each of the offences specified in the Order, which of the factors in para 14 of the UNHCR's guidelines and para 39 of the Background Note are relied on as indicating that the offence in question amounts to a "serious crime"?

2. What additional criteria have been relied on by the Government to determine that specified offences are not only "serious crimes" within the meaning of the Refugee Convention, but *particularly* serious crimes within the meaning of Article 33(2)?

The UNHCR papers referred to relate to Article 1F of the Refugee Convention. The Order is concerned with Article 33(2) of the Convention and does not provide any interpretation of Article 1F.

In considering whether an offence was a "particularly serious crime" suitable for inclusion in the Order we paid regard to the seriousness of the offence (for which the maximum imposable sentence normally provides a good guide) and the extent to which the nature of the offence was such as to indicate that a person committing it was likely to be a danger to the community (see also the answer to Question 9).

...

5. How will the particular circumstances of an offence committed by an individual be taken into account in deciding under the Order whether a "particularly serious crime" has been committed for the purposes of deciding whether Article 33(2) applies?

For the second part of Article 33(2) to apply a person must have committed a particularly serious crime <u>and</u> be a danger to the community. Where a person is convicted of an offence specified in the Order there is an unrebuttable presumption that a particularly serious crime has been committed so no special circumstances relating to the offence will alter the fact that a particularly serious crime has been committed for the purposes of section 72 (and hence Article 33(2)).

A person convicted of such an offence will also be presumed to be a danger to the community but that presumption is rebuttable. In assessing whether the person is a danger to the community we will consider any relevant information which may have a bearing on the person's current and future risk to the community. That information might include, for example, the judge's comments at the trial, police reports, prison reports, probation reports and comments from the Parole Board.

If the person rebuts the presumption that they are a danger to the community then, even though they will still have committed a particularly serious crime, section 72 will not apply. If the person does not rebut the presumption then section 72 will apply.

6. Who will bear the burden of proof on the issue of whether an individual is a danger to the community?

The burden will lie on the individual. Section 72 creates the presumption that a person who has committed an offence listed under the Order is a danger to the community so it will be for an individual to show that is not the case. However, as stated in the previous answer, a range of factors will be taken into account in assessing this matter so if there is evidence that a person does not present a danger to their community despite their commission of a listed offence they will be able successfully to rebut the presumption.

7. How will the gravity of the fear or risk of persecution be taken into account in deciding whether Article 33(2) applies?

Subsection (8) of section 72 makes it clear that in considering whether Article 33(2) applies no account is to be taken of the gravity of the fear or risk of persecution a person may face if returned to their country. This reflects the wording of Article 33(2) which does not make any provision for balancing the severity of the crime against the gravity of risk a person may face. We—and Parliament in passing section 72—do not agree with UNHCR that any balancing act of this kind is to be carried out.

Section 72 and the Order are concerned only with the United Kingdom's obligations under the Refugee Convention. Obligations under the European Convention on Human Rights (ECHR) will of course be fully addressed in any cases to which section 72 applies (see answer below to Question 10).

8. In light of the clear distinction between Article 1F(b) of the Refugee Convention, which deals with serious crimes committed outside the country of refuge, and Article 33(2) which deals with particularly serious crimes committed within the country of refuge, does the Secretary of State intend to exercise his power under s72(4)(b) of the 2002 Act to certify that in his opinion an offence committed outside the UK is similar to an offence specified by the Order?

Any case that arose to which section 72(4)(b) might be relevant would be assessed on an individual basis but in making that individual assessment the offence committed abroad would be compared with offences listed in the Order, so in effect the answer is "yes".

I should add that it is only in very rare circumstances that the provision under section 72(4)(b) may be needed. As you say, crimes committed abroad would normally be covered by Article 1F of the Refugee Convention rather that Article 33(2) and section 72 is not concerned with Article 1F. A rare situation in which 72(4)(b) could be relevant is where a person arrives in the United Kingdom, is recognised as a refugee, leaves the United Kingdom, commits a crime and then returns. In such a case it would be Article 33(2) rather than Article 1F(b) which would be potentially relevant and thus where section 72(4)(b) may come into play. Such cases are, as I have said, unlikely to arise often.

9. In light of the above, how does the Government consider the Order to be compatible with the UK's obligations under the Refugee Convention, interpreted in accordance with its object and purpose, and under Article 26 of the Vienna Convention on the Law of Treaties, to perform binding treaty obligations in good faith?

As noted in response to Question 2, in considering whether an offence was a "particularly serious crime" we had regard to the seriousness of the offence, for which the maximum imposable sentence normally provides a good guide. As noted in response to Question 4, about 85% of the offences in the Schedules relating to England and Wales have a maximum sentence of ten or more years. These high sentences indicate a high degree of seriousness. For those offences on the list with shorter maximum sentences we nevertheless considered the offence in question to be very serious and to meet the "particularly serious crime" threshold—for example, several of the firearms offences in the Offences under the Aviation Security Act 1982 carry five year maximum sentences yet are clearly very serious. Our approach is narrower than, for example, Australia where any violent, drug or property crime carrying a maximum sentence of three years or more is considered to be a particularly serious crime.

We also had regard to the nature of the offence and whether its commission indicated the perpetrator was likely to be a danger to the community. The Order lists crimes of violence, sexual offences, crimes against children, drugs offences and terrorism offences and other offences which in our view do indicate a danger to the community. Many of these offences clearly show a direct physical threat to the community, others pose a danger to the community in ways not confined to the narrow context of physical danger by creating significant anxieties within communities and breaking down cohesion.

The terms of section 72 recognise that while those committing certain particularly serious crimes are likely to be a danger to the community that cannot be a hard and fast rule—a person may show that despite committing an offence contained in the Order (or being convicted for two years or more imprisonment for any offence not contained in the Order) they do not pose a danger to the community. So the scope for individual consideration is maintained. Where we take the view that a person has failed to rebut the presumption of being a danger to the community the decision that their asylum claim should be refused on the basis that Article 33(2) applies will be appealable if and when removal action is taken or they are granted more than one years' aggregate leave, ensuring our decisions are subject to the usual independent oversight.

As for the object and purpose of the Refugee Convention, as stated in my introductory comments, the Refugee Convention clearly recognises that communities have rights as well as individuals. The inclusion of Articles 1F and 33(2) make this clear. It is important that States take the needs of the community as well as the needs of individuals into account and that Article 33(2) is interpreted in that light.

For the above reasons we are satisfied that Section 72 and the Order are a proper interpretation of Article 33(2).

(JCHR HL 35/HC 283, 24 January 2005, Appendix 4)

6/28

The Government was asked what training is provided to officials dealing with asylum applications regarding the grounds for granting refugee status to applicants who have fled persecution because of their homosexuality. A Minister wrote:

Training is given to asylum caseworkers on making decisions based upon the criteria set out in the 1951 UN Convention relating to the Status of Refugees. Homosexuality is not specifically mentioned under the 1951 Convention, but in the training of asylum caseworkers it is advised that homosexuality in certain limited circumstances may constitute a significant factor in the recognition of a particular social group under the terms of the Convention.

Under the terms of the Convention a refugee is a person who can demonstrate a well-founded fear of persecution in his country of origin for reasons of race, religion, nationality, membership of a particular social group or political opinion.

Asked further about the circumstances in which homosexual people from Jamaica applying for asylum in the UK would be returned to their country of origin, the Minister wrote:

Asylum and human rights claims by Jamaican homosexuals are, like those of all claimants, from all countries, considered on their individual merits in accordance with our obligations under the 1951 UN Refugee Convention and the European Convention on Human Rights (ECHR). If the claimant meets the definition of a refugee in the 1951 Refugee Convention, they are granted asylum. If they do not qualify for asylum, but there are other circumstances that make them particularly vulnerable and engage our obligations under the ECHR, they are granted humanitarian protection or discretionary leave. If an application is refused, and any appeal is unsuccessful, then we expect the individual concerned to leave the UK voluntarily. If they do not, we consider that it is entirely reasonable for us to enforce the return of that individual.

(HC Deb 17 March 2005 Vol. 432 c383–384W)

6/29

The Government was asked what criteria are applied in granting humanitarian protection to individuals refused asylum; and by what means applications for such grant may be made. A Minister wrote:

Humanitarian Protection (HP) is granted to individuals who would, if removed, face in the country of return a serious risk to life or person arising from:

the death penalty
unlawful killing
torture or inhuman or degrading treatment or punishment.

Asylum claimants are automatically considered for HP if they fail to qualify for refugee status. They will be granted leave under the HP policy if they meet the criteria set out above and are not excluded on the basis that there are serious reasons for considering that they:

fall within Articles 1 F*(a)* or 1 F*(c)* of the Refugee Convention
have committed a serious crime in the UK or overseas
are a danger to national security.

Individuals may also be excluded from HP where this is considered appropriate in light of their character, conduct or associations.

There is further information on the HP policy and detailed guidance on its application in the Asylum Policy Instruction on Humanitarian Protection which is published on the Immigration and Nationality Directorate website.

(HC Deb 17 March 2005 Vol. 432 c384W)

6/30

The Government was asked whether it is the Government's policy to consider claims for asylum from member states of the Council of Europe; and if it will make a statement on the claims of [three named individuals] from Russia. A Minister wrote:

As a signatory to the 1951 United Nations Convention relating to the Status of Refugees, we consider each claim for asylum on its individual merits to determine whether the claimant can demonstrate a well-founded fear of persecution for reasons of race, religion, nationality, membership of a particular social group or political opinion. An asylum claim made by a national of one of the member states of the Council of Europe would be given individual consideration.

Nationals of EU member states are subject to separate immigration arrangements. Very few EU nationals claim asylum, and claims that are received are likely to be certified as clearly unfounded with the result that there is no right of appeal against refusal.

We do not discuss or disclose the immigration status of any individual, other than matters already in the public domain, without the written consent of that person.

(HC Deb 4 April 2005 Vol. 432 c1119W)

6/31

The Government was asked what the UK policy is on granting (a) residence permits, (b) asylum, and (c) citizenship to alleged war criminals. A Minister wrote:

The Government's policy that the UK should not provide a safe haven for alleged war criminals was set out in the 2002 White Paper, Secure Borders, Safe Haven. The Government are committed to making wider use of existing immigration and nationality powers to prevent suspected war criminals and those who may have committed crimes against humanity from entering the UK or from establishing themselves here. These powers include the ability to refuse leave to enter or remain on the grounds that the person's presence in the UK is not conducive to the public good, to refuse or deprive an individual of British citizenship and to exclude individuals from refugee protection if there are serious reasons for considering that they have committed war crimes or crimes against humanity.

(HC Deb 4 April 2005 Vol. 432 c1286W)

6/32

In a written answer, a Minister wrote:

If a claimant has a well founded fear of persecution in their home area we will consider whether there is another part of their country in which they would be safe from persecution and to which it would be reasonable to expect the claimant to move. If there is, the claimant would not qualify for asylum. However, if there is no other part of the country that is safe from persecution or it would be unduly harsh to expect a claimant to relocate to a safe part of the country, then their fear of persecution in relation to the country as a whole would be well-founded. Instructions to caseworkers on the question of internal relocation are published on the Immigration and Nationality Directorate's website.

(HC Deb 11 July 2005 Vol. 436 c757W)

6/33

In a written answer, a Minister wrote:

Each asylum and human rights claim is considered on its individual merits in accordance with our obligations under the 1951 UN Refugee Convention and the European Convention on Human Rights (ECHR). Claimants who meet the definition of a refugee in the 1951 convention are granted asylum. If they do not qualify for asylum, but there are other circumstances that make them particularly vulnerable and engage our obligations under the ECHR, they are granted humanitarian protection or discretionary leave. If their application is refused, they have a right of appeal to the independent Asylum and Immigration Tribunal. In this way we ensure that we provide protection to those who need it. Conditions in the countries of origin of asylum applicants are continuously monitored.

Each application is considered against the background of the latest available country of origin information from a wide range of reliable sources including intergovernmental organisations (such as the UN), governmental sources (including the Foreign and Commonwealth Office) and human rights organisations (for example Amnesty International and Human Rights Watch). We fully recognise that the precarious conditions in Sudan for those of non-Arab ethnicity originating from Darfur are such that there are individuals who are able to demonstrate a need for international protection. In particular leading members of non-Arab ethnic Darfuri tribes, those classed as "intellectuals" or who are prominent human rights activists from non-Arab ethnic groups. We do not however consider that each and every Sudanese national from Darfur who applies for asylum is in need of international protection. In a recent country guidance appeal determination (AE (Sudan) CG [2005] UKAIT 00101, promulgated 3 May 2005), the independent tribunal considered the most recent situation reports by a range of key sources including UNHCR, Amnesty International and Global IDP Project and ruled that ordinary non-Arab ethnic Darfuris may relocate internally to the capital Khartoum where they are safe from persecution. In accordance with these tribunal findings, we consider that, depending on the individual circumstances of the case, internal relocation for ordinary non-Arab ethnic Darfuris is a safe and viable option. In such cases, Khartoum is the most practical location in terms of safety and viability and we specifically advise that this profile of Darfuri is safe from persecution in the capital. We do not routinely monitor the treatment of individuals once removed from the UK. However, any specific allegations of ill-treatment of returned failed asylum seekers would be followed up through the Foreign and Commonwealth Office and with those NGOs operating within the country concerned.

(HC Deb 11 July 2005 Vol. 436 c757W–758W)

6/34

In a written answer, a Minister wrote:

Returns of applicants [for asylum] to other European states, including France, are governed by the provisions of the Dublin II and Eurodac regulations. Where there is evidence that France is the responsible state, then the appropriate procedures will be initiated by the Immigration Service to secure the transfer of the applicant to France.

If the evidence and application of the Dublin arrangements establishes that responsibility lies with any other participating state then the appropriate transfer would be sought to that state rather than to France.

If no other participating state (including France) has responsibility in accordance with the Dublin II criteria then the application for asylum is considered by the United Kingdom.

(HC Deb 4 July 2005 Vol. 436 c112W–113W)

6/35

In a written answer, a Minister wrote:

The European Commission has recently launched a comprehensive evaluation process to cover all aspects of the Dublin arrangements, including the operation of the secure electronic communications network for Dublin II requests ("DubliNet") and the supporting Eurodac fingerprint database. The resulting report, expected in 2006, will analyse the impact of the Dublin arrangements to draw conclusions on the added value of Dublin II and the Eurodac Regulation EC No. 2725/2000.

The second Annual Report to the Council and the European Parliament on the activities of the Eurodac Central Unit concluded that Eurodac represents an extremely important tool for a faster and more efficient application of the Dublin arrangements. The report also notes that Eurodac data provide a sound indicator of the phenomenon of "asylum shopping" in member states. Copies of the report can be found in the Libraries. The Home Office's assessment of the report is set out in Explanatory Memorandum 10464/05 sent to the Parliamentary Scrutiny Committees on 14 September 2005.

Our own assessment of the new Dublin arrangements, supported by Eurodac is favourable. Dublin II and Eurodac enabled us to return 1,982 applicants in 2004 to other European countries without considering their claims ourselves. This is far more effective than the gentleman's agreement which applied until 1997, under which fewer people were removed in a year than the Dublin arrangements have enabled us to remove in a month. While it is not possible to prove to what extent asylum shopping that would otherwise have happened is not happening as a result of the new arrangements, asylum intake across the EU15 has fallen by 21 per cent. between 2003 and 2004 (source IRSS).

On the question of refugees in orbit, the Dublin II Regulation is based on a mechanism to identify the member state responsible for determining an asylum claim and provides guarantees that the identified state will take charge of or take back an asylum seeker within prescribed time limits. In addition, unlike the old Dublin Convention, the regulation reflects the agreement that member states fully accept to take responsibility for an asylum applicant where a procedural time limit is breached. This ensures that asylum applicants do not face prolonged periods of uncertainty.

(HC Deb 8 November 2005 Vol. 439 c334W)

6/36

During a debate in the House of Lords, a Minister said:

Asylum claims where female genital mutilation is raised are, like all others, carefully considered on their individual merits by caseworkers in the Home Office's Immigration and Nationality Directorate. Caseworkers assess each claim under the terms of the 1951 UN Convention relating to the Status of Refugees. Under the terms of that convention, a refugee is a person who,

> "owing to a well founded fear of being persecuted for reasons of race, religion, nationality, membership of a particular social group or political opinion, is outside the country of his [or her] nationality and is unable or, owing to such fear, is unwilling to avail himself of the protection of that country".

Unsurprisingly, the Government readily accept that female genital mutilation is a practice serious enough to constitute persecution. Where there is a reasonable likelihood that the applicant will be subjected to female genital mutilation for one of the grounds set out in the convention—race, religion, nationality, membership of a particular social group or political opinion—she will be granted asylum. The noble Baroness, Lady Rendell, made particular reference to the significance of being a member of a particular social group. That plays a very important part in these considerations.

In theory, FGM could occur for any one of the reasons set out in the convention. However, generally caseworkers see very few applicants who fear being subjected to FGM because of their religious or political beliefs or for reasons of their nationality or race. In reality, most claims involving female genital mutilation will be based on the applicant's alleged membership of a particular social group.

Case law has established that women are most likely to be recognised as members of a particular social group if they come from countries where they face widespread societal discrimination. This could occur in societies where traditional, patriarchal or cultural attitudes towards women create a general perception that women have fewer rights than men. This, in turn, may lead to reluctance on behalf of the state authorities to protect women from harm or to interfere in what are termed family matters.

I am aware that not all applicants who are at risk of female genital mutilation are able to show that their fear of being subjected to the practice is for a convention reason. In these cases, caseworkers cannot grant asylum under the terms of the Refugee Convention, but they can grant leave to remain in accordance with our policies on humanitarian protection.

(HL Deb 8 December 2005 Vol. 676 c863–864)

6/37

In a written answer, a Minister wrote:

The immigration rules require a person to be in the United Kingdom or at a port of entry in order to claim asylum here. Under our published asylum policy instruction on Applications from Abroad, [the Immigration and Nationality Directorate] may consider exceptionally outside the rules a claim for asylum made abroad if certain strict criteria are met.

A person cannot be a refugee for the purposes of the 1951 Refugee Convention while in their country of origin, so it would only be in truly exceptional circumstances that the UK would consider an asylum claim from a person within their own country.

The policy applies to Zimbabwean nationals on the same basis as it applies to others.

(HC Deb 8 November 2005 Vol. 439 c355W)

6/38

Somalia

In a written answer, a Minister wrote:

The safety or otherwise of a particular part of Somalia for a particular claimant will depend on the individual circumstances of that claimant. We do not make a generalised assessment of safety irrespective of the individual circumstances.

All Somali asylum and human rights applications are considered by the Home Office on their individual merits, in accordance with our obligations under the 1951 UN Refugee Convention and the European Convention on Human Rights (ECHR). Each application is considered against the background of the latest available information about the situation in the country of origin. These sources include intergovernmental organisations, governmental sources and human rights organisations. Full account is taken of the ability of the individual concerned to safely reside in other parts of Somalia. Caseworkers have access to the Somalia Country report produced by the Immigration and Nationality Directorate's (IND) Country of Origin Information Service as well as the Somalia Operational Guidance Note which assesses the most common types of asylum claims received and the circumstances in which they are likely to prove well founded or unfounded. Both documents are published on the IND website.

The Government firmly believe that the right approach is to continue to carefully assess the protection needs of individuals on an individual basis. Returns are similarly taken forward on a case by case basis and we only enforce the return of an individual where we are satisfied that the person concerned will not be at risk and has been unsuccessful in any appeals against the decision in their particular case.

(HC Deb 9 November 2005 Vol. 439 c537–538W)

6/39

Uzbekistan

In a written answer, an FCO Minister wrote:

Our Ambassador, James Sharp, who is accredited to Kyrgyzstan, has visited the country twice since early June 2005. On the first occasion, he publicly emphasised the importance of the Kyrgyz Government's honouring its international commitments on refugees. Both the Kyrgyz Foreign Minister and National Security Council Chairman assured him that the Government would do so. Mr. Sharp also met the local United Nations High Commission for Refugees (UNHCR) and United Nations Development Programme (UNDP) representatives to review the refugee situation.

The handing of four Uzbek refugees to the Andizhan Prosecutor on 9 June appears to have been a clear breach of the Kyrgyz Government's obligations. As a result, on 21 June we, acting with our EU partners, delivered a demarche to the Kyrgyz Government over its treatment of refugees, insisting that it abided by its commitments to the 1951 UN Convention on Refugees.

(HC Deb 12 July 2005 Vol. 436 c871W)

6/40

Zimbabwe

In a written answer, a Minister wrote:

Asylum and human rights claims by Zimbabwean nationals, like those from nationals of every other country, are considered on their individual merits in accordance with our obligations under the 1951 UN refugee convention and the European convention on human rights (ECHR). We do not consider it appropriate to grant indefinite leave to remain purely on the basis of a person's nationality.

As with any other nationality, Zimbabweans who meet the definition of a refugee in the 1951 convention are granted asylum. If they do not qualify for asylum, but there are other circumstances that make them particularly vulnerable and engage our obligations under the ECHR, they are granted humanitarian protection or discretionary leave. If their application is refused, they have a right of appeal to the independent asylum and immigration tribunal. If an asylum and human rights claim is refused, and any appeal to the independent asylum and immigration tribunal is unsuccessful, that means that it would be safe for that particular individual to return to Zimbabwe. It is in this way we ensure that we provide protection to those Zimbabweans who need it.

(HC Deb 4 July 2005 Vol. 436 c116W–117W)

Part Six: VIII. *The Position of the Individual (including the Corporation) in International Law—Human rights and fundamental freedoms*

(See also **Part Two: I. B., Part Two: I. D., Part Two: II. B., Part Three: II. B., Part Five: II. B.1.**)

6/41

The Government was asked what plans [it] has made to "assist those seeking to liberate themselves from tyranny and to build democracy" as requested by the US Secretary of State on 8 February 2005. An FCO Minister wrote:

The promotion of democracy, alongside human rights, the rule of law and good governance is a thread which runs through all of the Government's foreign policy. These issues are mainstreamed throughout everything the Foreign and Commonwealth Office (FCO) does. At the strategic level, this is highlighted by two of the FCO's eight strategic priorities aiming to support the development of democracy and the rule of law (Strategic Priority 3: An international system based on the rule of law, which is better able to resolve disputes and prevent conflicts; and Strategic Priority 6: Sustainable Development, underpinned by democracy, good governance and human rights).

At an operational level we adapt our approach on these issues to reflect the situation in the countries in which we work. This might range from; what might be considered traditional diplomatic measures (e.g. advocacy; resolutions in international fora; or sanctions); it may mean technical capacity building to support an emerging democratic culture in a country with no history of participatory government; or it may mean working in partnership with more established democracies to reinforce democracy in third countries, or to improve transparency and accountability throughout the international system. We also promote democracy, human rights, the rule of law and good governance in international fora, and press countries to adhere to the commitments they've signed up to in these bodies.

(HC Deb 22 February 2005 Vol. 669 c591W)

6/42

Commenting on the Report of the UN Secretary-General on the work of the Organization (A/60/1), the representative for the European Union, Sir Emyr Jones Parry (United Kingdom), said:

... with respect to the international legal order and human rights, over 50 years the United Nations has had remarkable success. It has built a framework of international human rights law and set clear standards by which all States are to be judged. But in setting standards, we have neglected for too long their implementation. When standards have been breached, we have not always done enough. The Union therefore welcomes the unprecedented recognition of the international community's responsibility to protect populations from the threat of genocide, war crimes, ethnic cleansing or crimes against humanity.

The summit took two other important steps towards creating more effective human rights machinery within the United Nations: the decision to establish a Human Rights Council and the commitment to reinforce the role of, and double the resources available to, the Office of the High Commissioner on Human Rights. Protection and promotion of human rights has been reinforced as the third pillar of the work of the United Nations, alongside development and peace and security. The EU will work to complete as soon as possible, during this sixtieth session, negotiations on the mandate, modalities, functions, size, composition, membership, and working methods of the new Council.

(UN Doc. A/60/PV.24, 29 September 2005)

6/43

During a UN General Assembly meeting, the representative for the European Union said:

Full respect for all human rights and fundamental freedoms, for democracy and for the rule of law, as set out in the Universal Declaration of Human Rights, is essential if we are to promote and protect those values common to humanity. And whilst working to promote those aims, we must also defend against those who seek to undermine those values. We must act against those that incite and promote extremism. It is our duty to do so.

(UN Doc. A/60/PV.35, 20 October 2005)

6/44

Algeria

The Government was asked about the return of terrorist suspects to Algeria and whether any assurances would be sought from the Government that the persons returned would not be tortured. A Minister wrote:

We will not remove anyone to a country where there is a real risk he or she will be tortured or subjected to inhuman or degrading treatment. Each case is assessed individually, and whether or not assurances should be sought is decided on a case-by-case basis. Where assurances have been obtained they, and any monitoring arrangements, are liable to scrutiny in the course of any appeal against, or other judicial challenge to, the removal decision.

(HL Deb 7 June 2005 Vol. 672 cWA50)

6/45

Bangladesh

The Government was asked what assessment it has made of human rights in Bangladesh; what recent research it has evaluated on the situation; and what representations it has made to the Bangladeshi authorities on action to prevent human rights abuses. An FCO Minister wrote:

We will continue to raise our concerns with the Government of Bangladesh about the human rights situation and the need to strengthen the rule of law both bilaterally and with our EU partners. We look to the Government of Bangladesh to uphold its international human rights obligations, such as those contained in the International Covenant on Civil and Political Rights, of which Bangladesh is a signatory [party, Ed].

(HC Deb 30 June 2005 Vol. 435 c1733W)

6/46

Botswana

The Government was asked:

Whether the United Nations' continuing role in promoting and protecting the rights of indigenous people is part of customary international law; and whether they will ask the Secretary-General to discuss with the government of Botswana the proposed removal of references to the Bushmen from their constitution. An FCO Minister wrote:

By Article 55 of its Charter, the United Nations has a mandate to promote universal respect for, and observance of, human rights and fundamental freedoms for all without distinction as to race, sex, language or religion. This includes people belonging to indigenous groups.

The British High Commission in Botswana regularly discusses the Basarwa issue with the government and other interested parties. High Commission staff have visited the Central Kalahari Game Reserve (CKGR) on three occasions over the past two years. [An FCO Minister] also discussed the issue with interested parties, including President Mogae, when they met in Abuja in December 2003. We believe that the Botswana Government's removal of all references to ethnicity in the constitution has been handled through parliamentary procedures in line with constitutional proprieties and as such does not need to be taken forward by the Secretary-General.

(HL Deb 8 June 2005 Vol. 672 cWA68)

6/47

Burma/Myanmar

The Government was asked a number of questions about the human rights situation in Burma, including specific allegations of the use of forced labour. An FCO Minister wrote:

We have not made representations to the State Peace and Development Council about these specific cases.

The Burmese Government have still to address the international community's concerns over the use of forced labour in Burma. We fully support the efforts of the International Labour Organisation (ILO) and other agencies to end permanently the use of forced labour. Our embassy is in close touch with the ILO office in Rangoon.

Burma's General System of Preferences trade privileges were suspended by the EC in 1997 in response to our concerns over forced labour in the country. Targeted restrictive measures against Burma have been steadily strengthened through the EU's Common Position, most recently in October 2004, to reflect the lack of progress on this and other issues.

...

We have highlighted our concerns over freedom of expression and assembly in Burma in successive UK and EU co-sponsored UN resolutions, most recently at the UN General Assembly on 23 December. These resolutions emphasise that the Burmese regime should fully respect all human rights and fundamental freedoms, including the freedom of expression and association.

...

We remain concerned about reported prison conditions in Burma and call on the Burmese regime to implement fully its international human rights obligations, including the humane treatment of prisoners.

We maintain that all prisoners should be held in accordance with international standards. There can be no excuse for the deliberate mistreatment or neglect of prisoners. Our embassy in Rangoon keeps in close contact with the International Committee of the Red Cross and Amnesty International, which have been able to visit prisons in Burma, in order to monitor conditions in which prisoners are kept. We are fully supportive of their efforts to improve such conditions.

...

We believe that the Burmese justice system continues to fall short of international fair trial standards. Our concerns over human rights and the rule of law in Burma are well known and have regularly been made clear to the Burmese authorities, most recently when I met the Burmese ambassador on 29 November.

We maintain that all prisoners should be tried fairly in accordance with international standards.

We fully support the efforts of the UN special rapporteur for human rights in Burma, Professor Sergio Pinheiro and urge the regime to co-operate fully with him and allow him to visit Burma.

(HC Deb 27 January 2005 Vol. 430 c519–522W) (See also HC Deb 31 October 2005 Vol. 438 c750W–751W)

6/48

Chechnya

In a written answer, an FCO Minister wrote:

We remain concerned about the human rights situation in Chechnya. We are especially concerned about the culture of impunity, with continuing reports of extra-judicial killings, arbitrary detention and torture. We frequently raise our concerns with the Russian Government, both bilaterally and in multilateral fora. These include concerns about the military component of Russia's response to the problems in Chechnya. Bilaterally, we most recently discussed Chechnya in depth during the UK-Russia Human Rights dialogue on 23 May, when we expressed our belief that effective maintenance of security and actions to counter terrorism should be pursued within a framework that respects human rights and international humanitarian law. We also discussed Chechnya during the EU-Russia human rights consultations held in March 2005.

(HC Deb 12 July 2005 Vol. 436 c870W)

6/49

China

In a written answer, an FCO Minister wrote:

We and our European Union (EU) partners have raised in a series of démarches with the Chinese authorities our serious concerns about the way in which the trial of Tenzin Deleg Rinpoche was conducted and the death sentence. The most recent EU démarche took place on 25 November 2004. The Dutch presidency, on behalf of the EU, wrote to the Chinese Ministry of Foreign Affairs about the case on 22 December 2004. The case was also included on our list of individual cases of concern at the UK-China human rights dialogue round which took place on 22 November in Beijing. [An FCO Minister] raised this case with Assistant Foreign Minister Zhang Yesui in December 2003.

(HL Deb 17 January 2005 Vol. 668 c87WA)

6/50

The Government was asked what recent discussions on human rights [it] has had with the Government of China. An FCO Minister wrote:

... the Foreign Secretary raised human rights issues in his meetings with Chinese Premier Wen Jiabao and Foreign Minister Li Zhaoxing in Beijing on 21 January. He encouraged China to ratify the International Covenant on Civil and Political Rights (ICCPR), called for progress in the reform of China's re-education through Labour system and lobbied on behalf of several individual cases of concern.

(HC Deb 1 March 2005 Vol. 431 c1047W)

6/51

The Government was asked what representations it had made about the treatment of asylum-seeking North Koreans in China. An FCO Minister wrote:

We have concerns about the situation of North Korean asylum seekers in China. We have raised the matter on a number of occasions with the Chinese Government, most recently during the UK/China Human Rights Dialogue in Beijing on 22 November 2004. We continue to urge China to observe its obligations under the 1951 UN Convention on Refugees and allow the United Nations High Commissioner for Refugees (UNHCR) access to the China/North Korea border region.

(HL Deb 8 June 2005 Vol. 672 cWA76)

6/52

The FAC asked if the Government's policy about human rights violations in China (which were described as a "disgrace") was sufficiently robust. An FCO Minister said:

I think we have a disagreement on this. I genuinely do not think it is a disgrace. It has not achieved all that we would have wished from it. I think there have been some examples of progress. The fact that the Chinese are prepared to sit down with us, and they have not yet agreed it, and discuss how they can move forward on a timetable for ratification of the ICCPR is a positive development; the fact that they are prepared to engage with us on re-education through labour is a positive development; the fact that there have been a number of changes within Chinese society that are positive, and I referred to it earlier; the fact that now you can go and live and work wherever you want within China. Ten years ago that would have been completely unthinkable. I think those are positive steps in the right direction. Nevertheless, there are a number of remaining significant concerns. You are right about the death penalty; you are right about the situation in Tibet where we certainly regard the recent visit of representatives of the Dalai Lama to Beijing as being a positive development and want to see an engagement on that issue, but we have to make a judgment about what is the most effective way to continue to get change in China, and I am genuinely not convinced. What is the logical implication of your suggestion? It is that actually we go back to just tabling resolutions of the Commission on Human Rights, an imperfect body for all the reasons that we have already outlined, where you would probably get a blocking position on the resolution coming forward and we really cannot engage with the Chinese. I am genuinely not convinced that is the best way to go forward. [Q.144]

The Minister added that there was engagement by the Chinese government in the dialogue on human rights. [Q.145]

(FAC Fourth Report, Human Rights Annual Report 2004, HC 109 (2005), Minutes of Evidence 11 January 2005)

6/53

In a written answer, an FCO Minister wrote:

The Government have never questioned China's right or need to implement family planning policies but has [*sic*] made it clear that we believe they should be based on the principles of the International Conference on Population and Development; that is on consent not coercion. We have raised concerns about this policy, including reports of enforced sterilisation and abortion. We have also raised the case of the lawyer Chen Guancheng who is being held under house arrest after he highlighted abuses in the implementation of the one child policy in Shandong. The Chinese Government have admitted there have been occasional problems with maladministration of the policy, but insists that this is down to individuals rather than overall malign intent.

(HC Deb 7 December 2005 Vol. 440 c1387W)

6/54

Christians in south-east Asia and China

During a debate in the House of Commons, a Minister said:

I welcome the opportunity to set out the Government's position and to respond to the points of concern that were expressed by hon. Members in the debate. I share hon. Members' deep concern about the persecution of Christians in south-east Asia and China. I recognise that it is an issue that hon. Members and many people in the United Kingdom feel deeply about. I have been a Foreign Office Minister for about two months and from my mailbag I already know about the strong interest that hon. Members have in the subject. First I will set out some general observations.

Promotion of human rights, including freedom of thought, conscience and religion, lies at the heart of our foreign policy. We condemn cases where individuals are persecuted because of their faith or belief, wherever it happens and whatever the religion of the individual or group concerned. Persecution is frequently counter-productive. Rather than crushing religious belief, it often has the opposite effect and inspires people. For example, the Chinese Christian Brother Yun, while suffering in prison in Burma in 2001, saw himself as a seed

> "ready to spring to life and to produce a harvest that will feed many."

It is, in my view, important not only to condemn persecution but to take action on a case-by-case basis. A large number of cases have been raised and I will refer to some of them. I will ask for further information on the others so that we can take them up. We raise our concerns in relevant international forums such as the United Nations Commission on Human Rights. We raise specific cases of religious persecution both bilaterally and with our EU partners. We take every opportunity to urge states to promote tolerance and mutual respect and to protect religious minorities against discrimination, intimidation and attacks.

In general, we believe that dialogue with individual countries, wherever possible, is the best way to achieve our goals. Foreign and Commonwealth Office officials, both here and overseas, work closely with representatives of religious groups and non-governmental organisations, such as Christian Solidarity Worldwide. I pay tribute to them and acknowledge the work that they do in this field.

...

I assure hon. Members that human rights, including freedom of religion, is firmly on the agenda in our relations with the Government of Vietnam. We have an open and frank dialogue with Vietnam over human rights, including freedom of religion, both bilaterally and with our EU partners. For example, on 22 March [a Minister] raised the issue in this very House with the President of the Vietnamese National Assembly.

As part of our regular EU-Vietnam human rights dialogue, on 7 June the EU, including the UK, pressed the Vietnamese Government on freedom of religion, restrictions on religious organisations and the situation of Protestant groups. We have urged Vietnam to guarantee in practice the right of all religious groups to practise their faith freely in a community.

I believe that international pressure, including by the UK and the EU, is having some positive effect. Vietnam is now moving in the right direction on religious freedom. The US ambassador for international religious freedom, Ambassador Hanford, has recently recognised that and there is now positive engagement between the US and Vietnam on the issue of religious freedom. The Vietnamese authorities have recently eased restrictions on officially recognised Protestant groups and granted recognition to a number of new congregations.

Relations between Protestant groups and the authorities have shown a modest improvement. For example, the new ordinance on belief and religion published last November, and the prime ministerial instruction on Protestantism in

February, are steps forward. We hope that they will lead to the recognition of more Protestant groups, so that those groups can worship free from official harassment . . .

The EU list of prisoners and detainees of concern enables us to raise specific cases with the Vietnamese authorities. Seven of the 17 cases on the list are religious figures. So far in 2005, nine persons on the list have been released. We welcome that, but we will continue to press the Vietnamese Government for progress on the remaining cases on the EU list, as we did most recently on 7 June. Pastor Truong's case, which we are well aware of, was raised. We share the concerns that have been expressed in the debate over his treatment and we are particularly concerned at reports that he has been given drugs. At our suggestion, he has recently been added to the EU list of prisoners and detainees of concern. His case was raised on 7 June. We have also asked to meet him and are awaiting a response . . .

I shall now turn to the case of Christians in China . . . The UK Government are concerned about the freedom to practise religion in China and follow developments in this area carefully. We raise our concerns at every appropriate opportunity.

As hon. Members will know, the Chinese state constitution permits freedom of religious belief and we acknowledge that the number of people practising religion in China, including Christianity, has increased greatly in recent years. Reports suggest that there are over 140 million official religious believers in China and that some 21 million people practise through official Protestant and Catholic churches. However, it is very clear to us that the Chinese Government and the Communist party want to strictly control religion in China. That is done through a number of mechanisms: state registration of all churches; state approval and vetting of all religious personnel; and strict controls on the publication of religious materials. In our view those and other sorts of controls seriously undermine, and in some cases effectively deny, the freedom to practise religious belief in China today.

We receive regular reports about the harassment of unofficial Christian groups in China—many such cases have been mentioned today—that cause us grave concern. In September 2004, Foreign and Commonwealth Office officials raised concerns with Chinese Government officials about the mass arrests of unofficial Protestant church leaders in Xinjiang, Kaifeng, and Wuhan and about the detention of several members of the Baoding diocese clergy.

Of course, sometimes people who are detained by the Chinese authorities are released quickly, but others are held for long periods and are sentenced to terms of re-education through labour or sent to prison. We have received credible reports of torture and abuse of such people in detention. Chinese officials tell us that people are never arrested for being religious believers and that a person must always have done something else to warrant punishment, but in our view there are people in prison in China for doing things that we consider to be the peaceful and legitimate expression of their religious beliefs. Chinese Catholics who, for example, recognise the authority of Rome rather than the Chinese Communist party should not, in our opinion, be harassed or imprisoned.

We have raised, over the years, a number of religious cases of concern with the Chinese authorities, including most recently that of Pastor Zhang Rongliang. Foreign Minister Li and my right hon. Friend the Foreign Secretary spoke about this case during his visit to China in January. We continue to urge that Pastor Zhang has access to a legal adviser of his choice and, if he has to stand trial, that the trial should be open.

The hon. Member ... referred to the new regulations on religion that China introduced in March 2005. The regulations reaffirm restrictions on religious practice and maintain the requirement for all religious groups to register. Penalties are set out for non-compliance. There is an appeals mechanism that may allow local authorities that take a particularly hard line on unofficial believers to be challenged. However, our assessment is that those regulations are aimed primarily at limiting and controlling the development of religion. We do not expect that the situation of unofficial religious believers will improve ...

We monitor the situation in China carefully, and we raise incidents and cases with the Chinese authorities, through the human rights dialogue, through ministerial activity and through our support for EU activity. We are always willing to consider action when we have specific information. My officials have heard his speech and the particular cases that he raised. We shall require further information, and I am sure that they will approach either him or Christian Solidarity Worldwide about these matters.

He went on:

Our contacts with the authorities in Laos are limited; relations are covered by our embassy in Bangkok. However, we regularly raise with the Laos authorities our concerns about the persecution of Christians. Only last month a representative of the British embassy in Bangkok raised the issue with the Ministry of Foreign Affairs in Vientiane.

We also regularly raise the situation of the Hmong people with the Laos Government; most recently, that was done by an official from our embassy in Bangkok. Like the UN Secretary-General, we welcome reports that those Hmong people recently coming out of remote areas have been treated humanely and we call on the Laos Government to continue to provide the necessary humanitarian assistance to them.

A number of hon. Members raised the situation in Burma. I agree that there remain instances of restriction on the right to exercise freedom of religion in Burma and we have condemned that in successive, highly critical UK and EU-sponsored UN resolutions—most recently in April's United Nations Commission on Human Rights resolution on Burma, which expressed grave concern at discrimination and persecution on the basis of religious or ethnic background.

We are very concerned that offensives continue in Karen state, despite ongoing ceasefire talks with the Karen National Union. The Burmese Government are well aware of our concerns about human rights abuses in the ethnic minority areas. Most Burmese Christians are able to follow their religion relatively freely, but their freedom of assembly and expression are severely curtailed, as is that of other groups in Burma.

Our views on the human rights situation in the country are extremely well known and we will continue to press the Burmese Government to improve human rights. However, our simple trouble is that the Burmese authorities show no great willingness at all to listen to the representations that we and others make. We will continue to work with our EU partners and throughout the international community to promote national reconciliation in Burma so that all faiths there can live freely. We shall continue to put what pressure we can on the Burmese authorities to ensure that they address the issue of human rights, as they are clearly not doing at the moment.

The hon. Member ... raised the issue of religious freedom in Indonesia and the case of three women recently arrested there. Members of the British embassy in Jakarta are looking into those reports. We have not been able to verify them so far, but will continue to look into the case. Together with our European partners, we are in regular dialogue with the Indonesian Government and we encourage them to ensure religious freedom, to maintain law and order and promote reconciliation in areas of conflict ...

The hon. Member ... raised the question of what auditing we do and gave the example of what is done in the States. We produce an annual human rights report, which is an extremely well researched and thorough document, drawing on a wide range of reliable sources, not just the Foreign and Commonwealth Office and our embassies and consulates. Last year it ran to more than 400 pages. This year's human rights report is due to be published this month. I can assure hon. Members that it covers religious persecution in south-east Asia and China, as well as human rights abuses in all other parts of the world.

(HC Deb 13 July 2005 Vol. 436 c303W–308WH)

6/55

Colombia

The Government was asked what recent representations it has made to President Uribe of Colombia on *(a)* human rights issues and *(b)* the conduct of the Colombian Army.

An FCO Minister wrote:

Human rights lie at the heart of our policy towards Colombia. We regularly raise with the Colombian Government specific human rights cases. Through our Embassy in Bogotá, we monitor the human rights situation in Colombia, keeping in close contact with the Colombian authorities. I have highlighted the importance we attach to human rights with President Uribe and other senior Colombian officials during my visits to Colombia in 2003, 2004 and during my most recent visit last month. I reinforced this again when I met Defence Minister Uribe here in London on 11 February. We continue to urge the Colombian Government to implement all outstanding recommendations by the UN High Commissioner for Human Rights. We have also made it plain that the armed forces must act in accordance with human rights and international humanitarian law, and have provided funding for training in these areas. Where members of the armed forces are proven to have committed human rights abuses they must be punished in accordance with the law. Impunity must not be allowed, a message we have also reiterated to the Colombians.

(HC Deb 16 March 2005 Vol. 432 c339W)

6/56

In a written answer, an FCO Minister wrote:

Human rights lie at the heart of our policy towards Colombia. We regularly urge the Colombian Government to implement all outstanding UN human rights recommendations arising from successive annual reports of the Colombia office of the UN High Commissioner for Human Rights (UNHCHR), and have offered our assistance to achieve this goal. When Vice-President Francisco Santos called on Foreign and Commonwealth Office (FCO) officials in August 2005, we made clear, as Presidency, the importance the EU attaches to active progress by the Colombian Government in implementing the UNHCHR recommendations. We regularly reinforce this message in our contacts with the Colombian Government.

In addition, the EU Ministerial Council conclusions, which were agreed on 3 October 2005, state the willingness of the EU to discuss a mid-year progress on the implementation of the UNHCHR recommendations within the framework of the G24, the group drawn from participants in the 2003 London meeting of international support for Colombia, in Bogotá. We will continue to look for ways to encourage and assist the Colombian Government to improve the human rights situation in Colombia. [An FCO Minister] discussed human rights issues with Vice-President Santos on 28 November 2005.

(HC Deb 2 December 2005 Vol. 440 c873W)

6/57

Convention on the Elimination of All Forms of Racial Discrimination

During a debate in the House of Commons, an FCO Minister said:

The Government firmly believe that everyone is entitled to all the rights and freedoms set out in the universal declaration of human rights, without discrimination of any kind. Discrimination based on descent, to give it the title used by the UN convention on the elimination of all forms of racial discrimination, encapsulates discrimination based on forms of social stratification—caste or similar systems of inherited status—that impair a person's equal enjoyment of their human rights. Caste discrimination of the type found in India, which has featured prominently in this debate, is the most well-known example of discrimination based on descent. In that system, in which social mobility is severely limited and status is completely ascribed, the Dalits, or untouchables, about whose plight we have heard so much this morning, suffer multiple forms of discrimination and are typically assigned tasks or occupations that are considered filthy or polluting.

However, it is not only in south or south-east Asia that caste-like practices, including discrimination based on occupation and descent from slaves, are found. As we have heard today, they are also found in other parts of the world such as Africa. The discrimination suffered by such communities takes the form of a variety of human rights violations, including the lack of ability to alter inherited status; restrictions on marriage outside the community; private and public segregation in housing, health and education, and in access to public spaces, places of worship and even sources of food and water; inability to renounce inherited occupations or degrading or hazardous work; subjection to debt bondage; subjection to dehumanising references such as "polluting" or "untouchable"; and a general lack of respect for their human dignity and equality.

Discrimination based on caste or descent determines an individual's position in the social and economic hierarchy, not on the basis of merit but of heritage. It perpetuates social exclusion and reduces the rate at which poverty reduction can be achieved, as the hon. Member for South-West Bedfordshire said. The framework of international covenants and national legislation outlawing discrimination based on descent is an important step towards its elimination, but it has not been enough . . .

As we all know, such practices remain all too entrenched despite the many international commitments made by the countries in question. It is therefore important that the international community engages at a more practical level to help to implement such commitments. One example of engagement is the child health programme: the Department for International Development has worked with the Indian Ministry of Health to develop targets for including Dalit and Adivasi women and children in the programme. It has worked hard with other donors to develop a monitoring system and incentives to ensure that such women are included. DFID supports similar initiatives in education and other areas.

It is clear that deep-rooted social attitudes and customs must also change. Of course, that is a much more difficult task, as was recognised by some of the speakers this morning. We welcome the fact that that is beginning to happen through natural social change. Migration, urbanisation, greater contact with other societies and new forms of employment all have an effect, but we can and must do more. We must encourage states, for example, to be proactive in tackling prejudice and changing behaviour to ensure that socially excluded groups benefit from public expenditure and have access to services such as health care and education.

(HC Deb 22 November 2005 Vol. 439 c385WH–386WH)

6/58

Convention on the Elimination of All Forms of Discrimination against Women

During a Security Council Meeting the representative of the United Kingdom stated:

Article 8 of the United Nations Charter and the Convention on the Elimination of All Forms of Discrimination against Women (CEDAW) both commit us to ensuring the equal participation of women in international relations. That commitment is crucial to the successful implementation of resolution 1325 (2000). But we must also apply that commitment to all levels of decision-making—international, regional and national. One can look around the Council table and draw some conclusions from that statement.

(UN Doc. S/PV.5294, 27 October 2005)

Convention on the Rights of the Child

(See also **Part Six: VIII. (Pakistan)**)

6/59

In a written answer, a Minister wrote:

The Government are satisfied that the United Kingdom (UK) is fully compliant with Articles 37(a), (b) and (d) of the United Nations Convention on the Rights of the Child. When ratifying the convention in 1991, the UK entered a reservation against Article 37(c). The reservation concerns the separation of under- and over 18 year-olds and states: "Where at any time there is a lack of suitable accommodation or adequate facilities for a particular individual in any institution in which young offenders are detained, or where the mixing of adults and children is deemed to be mutually beneficial, the United Kingdom reserves the right not to apply Article 37(c) in so far as those provisions require children who are detained to be accommodated separately from adults". In recent years, a series of measures have been taken to make the secure estate for under 18s completely separate from that for older offenders. A separate estate for boys was established in 2000. Since the end of 2003, girls under 17 who are sentenced to custody have routinely been placed in secure training centres or secure children's homes. Two special units for 17 year-old girls have been opened and two more are due to open shortly. This will enable all girls under 18 to be held completely apart from over 18 year-olds. There may continue to be particular circumstances where an under 18 year-old may need to be placed in the young adult estate, but we believe the above measures not only meet our obligations under the convention, but accord with the intention underlying Article 37(c). We are also satisfied that we are meeting our obligations under the other provisions of Article 37(c).

(HL Deb 25 October 2005 Vol. 674 cWA181–WA182)

6/60

In a written answer, a Minister wrote:

... The United Kingdom treats children according to the standards laid down in the United Nations Convention on the Rights of the Child (UNCRC). However, upon signing up to the UNCRC, the United Kingdom entered a reservation that made it clear that nothing in the UNCRC was to be interpreted as affecting the operation of UK immigration and nationality law. This reservation for immigration purposes under the UNCRC in no way inhibits the discharge of our obligations under Article 22 of the UNCRC.

(HL Deb 1 November 2005 Vol. 675 cWA11)

6/61

In a written answer, a Government representative wrote:

The United Kingdom ratified the United Nations Convention on the Rights of the Child on 16 December 1991. It came into force in the UK on 15 January 1992.

This Answer covers the UK's two reservations on immigration and the separation of young offenders as well as under-eighteens serving in the Armed Forces, which were the subject of discussion on 19 October.

With regard to immigration, the Government have carefully reviewed the reservation in light of recent requests that it should be withdrawn. We believe that it is necessary to retain this reservation which makes it clear that nothing in the convention is to be interpreted as affecting the operation of UK immigration and nationality legislation. The UK has entered other, similar reservations in respect of other human rights instruments.

However, no child will be denied their human rights as guaranteed by the Human Rights Act when in the UK. We have also worked hard on proposing new measures to address some specific and practical issues relating to children. For example, a White Paper in 2002 proposed that specially trained immigration staff will be able to interview children about their asylum claims in a wider set of circumstances than at present. This will give officials a greater understanding of children's background and circumstances and help them better determine appropriate levels of care.

In addition, as I explained in the House of Lords on 19 October, the level of support for children here as part of an asylum seeking family is equivalent to that provided for children in families on income support. The full support package includes fully furnished accommodation, associated utility bills and council tax is paid for centrally. The total support package is roughly equivalent to income support levels.

The dispersal of unaccompanied asylum seeking children is not automatic. The Government will not generally seek to disperse those who have been in care and for whom a decision on their asylum claim has not been made. The cases of other unaccompanied young asylum seekers are judged on merit—they may not, for example, be dispersed if they are already in full-time education or if they have younger siblings in care.

With regard to detaining under-eighteens in the same accommodation with adults, I should like to stress that we are doing all that we can to be in a position to be able to withdraw the reservation about custody and accommodation, if following review, we decide that this is desirable. We have made good progress in this field. We are building four new separate facilities for 17 year-old girls; one opened in December 2004 and a second in September 2005. The other two are due to open shortly.

In terms of under-eighteens serving in the Armed Forces, we have made excellent progress since ratification of the UNCRC. The UK ratified the optional protocol (OP) to the UNCRC on the involvement of children in armed conflict on 24 June 2003, subject to a declaration. The declaration states that the UK will take all feasible measures to ensure that members of its Armed Forces who are under 18 do not take a direct part in hostilities. However, the UK understands that the OP does not exclude the deployment of under-eighteens where there is a genuine military need to deploy a unit or ship to an area where hostilities are taking place or the urgency and nature of the situation merits their involvement.

Work has focused on reviewing the Armed Forces' policies and practice for the recruitment, employment and deployment of under-eighteens to ensure that they accord with the requirements of the OP. In addition, all possible steps are taken to ensure that no serviceman or servicewoman under 18 is deployed on operations unless it is purely for humanitarian reasons. No applicant under 18 years of age may join the Armed Forces unless the application is accompanied by the formal written consent of his/her parent or guardian.

Commanding Officers take their responsibilities towards all their people extremely seriously. They are well aware of the particular welfare needs of younger recruits and trainees, even if they are not formally in loco parentis. The Ministry of Defence (MoD) recognises the vital role parents play in support of their children both before and after they have joined the Armed Forces. The MoD makes continual efforts to engage with parents and encourage trainees to keep in touch with home.

(HL Deb 8 November 2005 Vol. 675 cWA71–WA74)

6/62

Counter-terrorism

The Government was asked by the FAC:

Amnesty and Human Rights Watch have criticised human rights abuses at Abu Ghraib, in Afghanistan, in Guantanamo, not as isolated incidents but as part of a pattern of behaviour. How can we prosecute the war on terror, which in part must be a campaign to promote human rights, whilst at the same time being a party to the deprivation of human rights to our opponents?

The Foreign Secretary said:

I do not think any country or any Government anywhere in the world can say that there will never under its remit be abuses of human rights. I cannot think of any country anywhere in the world where that has been the case. What divides the civilised world and those countries that respect human rights from others is what you do about it when you have allegations of human rights abuses. Let me take first of all our actions. We have very clear procedures. As soon as there is any allegation of abuse there is a thorough investigation, for example, in respect of what happened in Iraq, and I am speaking from memory. Among 65,000 troops that have been engaged in Iraq there were ultimately about seven cases that have gone through to prosecution. I do not think anybody has made the argument that we have not dealt with that seriously. Similarly, the United States has now held three inquiries into the allegations. People will have seen the evidence that the new Attorney General going before the Senate has undertaken in the last couple of weeks where on the record he has confirmed what President Bush said last June in terms of the US opposition to the use of torture. Undoubtedly, I have to say, not just as a politician but also as an ordinary human being, some of what we saw at Abu Ghraib and elsewhere was absolutely disgusting and shameful. At one level we are not directly responsible for that but the fact that it happened as part of a coalition that we were involved with does cause us concern. What divides us is, are these individual incidents that we take action about or is this something that we are institutionally urging to happen? It most emphatically is not. [Q.84]

(FAC Fourth Report, Human Rights Annual Report 2004, HC 109 (2005), Minutes of Evidence 11 January 2005)

6/63

Commenting on the Report of the Secretary-General on the work of the Organization (A/60/1), the representative for the European Union said:

... Not only are development, security and human rights each imperative in their own right; they are mutually reinforcing. We have seen time and time again how conflict and instability in developing countries have destroyed fragile social, environmental and economic progress. The threats of terrorism and proliferation endanger the stable global environment within which trade flourishes and economies grow. The summit agreement to establish a peacebuilding commission will make a major contribution to a better coordinated international response to the needs of countries emerging from conflict. It will help prevent conflicts from restarting and encourage countries to make the transition from violent instability to peaceful, sustained development.

The European Union is committed to seeing the Commission established by the end of this year. Increasingly, conflict and violence take place beyond the boundaries of conventional war. No continent is safe from the threat of terror. International terrorism requires an international response. We pay the price for each others' vulnerabilities. The United Nations has already done much to set international standards against terrorism and to encourage and help States to meet them. The European Union welcomes the summit outcome's clear condemnation of terrorism and the undertaking to conclude a comprehensive convention on international terrorism during this sixtieth session. The European Union firmly believes that the targeting and deliberate killing of civilians and non-combatants cannot be justified or legitimized by any cause or grievance.

(UN Doc. A/60/PV.24, 29 September 2005)

6/64

During a debate in the House of Lords, a Minister said:

It is vital that we act against those who threaten our national security. The Home Secretary—as the noble Lord, Lord Avebury, said—has decided to deport 23 detainees on grounds of national security. Each is being detained pending the making of a deportation order and the outcome of any appeal. The detainees have a right of appeal to the Special Immigration Appeals Commission. We will not deport people unless we are in a position to satisfy the courts that their removal would be consistent with the United Kingdom's international obligations. The Government would not extradite a person where there is a real risk of the death penalty being imposed. Similarly, we would not remove a person under immigration powers in the knowledge that this would lead to treatment contrary to Article 3.

We are determined, however, to pursue deportation action against those who have no right to remain in the United Kingdom, while ensuring full compliance with our international obligations. Where necessary, our approach includes entering into discussions with foreign governments in order to ensure the proper treatment of those who are deported. Noble Lords have rightly referred—including the noble Lord, Lord Judd, the right reverend Prelate the Bishop of Oxford and the noble Lords, Lord Avebury and Lord Lester of Herne Hill—to the fact that memorandums of understanding are being sought with certain countries to which deportations are contemplated. It will be for the Special Immigration Appeals Commission to determine whether those memorandums of understanding give sufficient protection to the relevant deportees. We should trust our courts to address these issues in a sensible way in accordance with the terms of Article 3.

I also submit that noble Lords should not deprecate seeking these memorandums of understanding, because they could provide protection and improve the human rights conduct of those countries with which they are made. We should not be in any way embarrassed in seeking those memorandums of understanding, and people should not say that they are ineffective until they have seen what they say.

On the interpretation of Article 3 of the European Convention on Human Rights, prior to the judgment of *Chahal* v *United Kingdom*, to which the noble Lord, Lord Lester, referred, the European Court of Human Rights had already established that Article 3 prevented extradition or removal where there were substantial grounds for believing that the person would face a real risk of being subjected to torture or inhuman or degrading treatment or punishment in the receiving state.

However, passages in the court's earlier judgment in *Soering* v *United Kingdom* referred to the "fair balance" to be struck between individual rights and the interests of the wider community. *Soering* was decided seven years earlier in 1989. *Soering* was not itself concerned with national security. However, these passages were relied on by the United Kingdom in *Chahal* to argue that Article 3 did not prevent expulsion where this was required on national security grounds. This argument was also supported by the exceptions in Articles 32 and 33 of the refugee convention.

The court in *Chahal* rejected this argument by a majority of 12 to 7. The dissenting judges held that the removing state was entitled to strike a fair balance between the nature of the threat to national security and the potential risk of ill-treatment in the receiving state. We think that the view of the minority was the right one, but I make it clear that we accept whatever conclusion is reached in relation to Article 3.

The second issue rightly identified by the noble Lord, Lord Kingsland, is the use of torture evidence in relation to court proceedings in this country. I make it clear that we would never use torture evidence in relation to criminal proceedings. As noble Lords have rightly identified, the problem arises in respect of SIAC. The dilemma that faces countries is what happens when intelligence is received on which they act, and that act could then be subject to judicial review. Are they entitled to put before the court all the material they have relied on? In many cases, although my noble friend Lady Kennedy of The Shaws says that the ticking time bomb never arises, there will be occasions when there is a legitimate threat identified by a foreign intelligence where the precise source is not known. Should the country act in relation to it? In many circumstances I think they must.

I make it clear that in the case of *A.* which is going to the House of Lords next week, the Court of Appeal found that there was no evidence that the material relied on had been obtained as a result of torture, but it addressed the issue. The difficulty for any state is whether it should sit by and ignore the evidence it has. That is the dilemma, and that is the dilemma which the House of Lords will address next week. It is the dilemma which the Court of Appeal decided by a majority of two to one that it could understand; that, given material where there was a threat that people might be killed or maimed, they would have to act in relation to it.

It is an incredibly difficult dilemma. Noble Lords should be sympathetic to the problems of a government who are not remotely involved in torture itself but feel an obligation to protect people from being tortured.

(HL Deb 12 October 2005 Vol. 674 c374–375)

6/65

Cuba

In the course of a debate on Latin America, an FCO Minister said:

There has been a good deal of attention on Cuba in the past few days. I am glad to say that there is some sign of movement. The Cuban Government have allowed a meeting of 150 members of a peaceful organisation in Havana to go ahead—an event unprecedented since the revolution in 1959. However, several MEPs and journalists who attempted to attend the event were expelled from Cuba. That is unacceptable.

In January the EU agreed temporarily to suspend measures that it had introduced in response to a crackdown on dissidents by the Cuban Government in 2003. That policy is due for review in June.

We shall seek an outcome in the review which allows us to maintain a firm stance on human rights, and our embassy's active programme of contact with the peaceful opposition will continue. We also want to be in a position to have meaningful dialogue with the Cuban Government, not least because we want to raise human rights concerns. However, we also want to co-operate on matters of mutual interest such as child protection, drugs trafficking and money laundering.

(HL Deb 26 May 2006 Vol. 672 c644)

6/66

During a General Assembly meeting, the representative for the European Union said:

The European Union believes that critical engagement with the Cuban Government, along with dialogue with wider Cuban civil society, is the most effective way to promote peaceful change in Cuba. However, the European Union considers that full cooperation with Cuba will depend upon improvements in human rights and political freedom in that country. The European Union remains deeply concerned about the human rights situation in Cuba. Following the arrests and sentencing of 75 members of the peaceful opposition in spring 2003, the situation has not improved, and in the past few months, has deteriorated. In July, the Presidency of the European Union issued statements condemning the suppression of peaceful demonstrations by the State and the arrests of a number of people connected with peaceful demonstrations. In September, the European Union issued a declaration about the situation of three political prisoners who were on hunger strike in protest against harsh treatment, all of whom were suffering severe health problems. The European Union urges the Cuban Government unconditionally to release all political prisoners and appeals to the Cuban authorities to cooperate fully with international human rights bodies and mechanisms.

(UN Doc. A/60/PV.45, 8 November 2005)

6/67

Death Penalty

The Government was asked what representations [it] has made to the Indian Government concerning their decision to end the UN moratorium on the death penalty. An FCO Minister wrote:

The UK initiated a demarche with EU partners to the Government of India in June 2004 in relation to the death sentence passed on Mr. Dhananjoy Chatterjee. The UK supported a further EU demarche in August 2004 in relation to the same case. On each occasion the EU urged the Indian Government to maintain their de facto moratorium on the death penalty.

[Chatterjee was hanged on 14 August 2005, India's first execution since 1995. He had been convicted of the rape and murder of a 14-year-old girl, Ed.]

(HC Deb 21 March 2005 Vol. 432 c593W)

6/68

The Government was asked what assessment [it] has made of the implications of the European Convention on Human Rights for the Government's policy on the provision of information to overseas prosecuting authorities in cases which would lead to the imposition of the death penalty. An FCO Minister wrote:

The opposition of the Government to the death penalty is well known. When deciding whether to provide information to prosecuting authorities abroad the Government takes all relevant factors into account, including the possibility of the death penalty being imposed and our international obligations. Our view is that this policy is in line with the obligations of the UK under the European Convention on Human Rights.

(HC Deb 30 June 2005 Vol. 435 c1736W)

6/69

Eritrea

In a written answer, an FCO Minister wrote:

The Foreign and Commonwealth Office (FCO) make representations to the Eritrean Government on human rights issues at every suitable opportunity. The Government expressed our concern on the issue of arrests and detention without trial to the Eritrean ambassador on 28 July and we have since pressed him at senior official level. Our ambassador in Asmara also regularly raises these issues with the Eritrean Government, both bilaterally and with our EU colleagues. The Government will continue to press the Eritreans to improve human rights, including in its role of EU presidency.

(HC Deb 14 October 2005 Vol. 437 c640W)

6/70

France

In a written answer, an FCO Minister wrote:

. . . the Foreign Secretary has not made representations to the French Government on this issue but officials remain in regular contact on the full range of social and human rights issues. The human rights of members of the Roma community are protected by the core international human rights instruments, to which France is a party.

(HC Deb 12 July 2005 Vol. 436 c871W)

6/71

Guantanamo Bay

(See also **Part Seventeen: I. B.6.**)

The Foreign Secretary made the following statement to the House of Commons:

I should like to make a statement concerning the return to the United Kingdom of the four British citizens detained at Guantanamo Bay.

Let me first recall the context. The attacks of 11 September 2001 were the worst terrorist atrocity that the United States, the United Kingdom and the whole world have ever suffered. In response to those attacks, a coalition of countries came together to launch a military campaign against al-Qaeda and its Taliban supporters, to remove them from their strongholds in Afghanistan and elsewhere.

In those operations, thousands of individuals believed to be al-Qaeda or Taliban fighters or their supporters were detained by coalition forces. The vast majority of those individuals were released, but those who were deemed to pose a substantial risk of returning to the conflict were sent by the United States to detention facilities at its naval base at Guantanamo Bay, there to be detained and questioned about their knowledge of al-Qaeda's activities. As a result, valuable information has been gained, which has helped to protect the international community from further al-Qaeda and related terrorist attacks.

Approximately 200 individuals have been released from Guantanamo Bay since their original detention. However, the United States Government believe that a number of detainees so released have returned to terrorism, demonstrating the dilemma faced by the United States in considering such releases.

Nine British citizens were among those originally detained at Guantanamo Bay. I and the Government as a whole have taken our consular responsibilities to those detained very seriously. British officials have visited them regularly, delivered messages and mail from their families and secured improvements in the physical conditions of their detention. I have made a written ministerial statement to the House following each of those visits.

I have also set out to the House on many occasions the British Government's consistent position in relation to these detainees and their detention. As the House will recall, discussions took place in 2003, led by my noble and learned Friend the Attorney-General on the UK side. The Government then requested the return of all of the British detainees held at Guantanamo Bay.

Five of the nine detainees were returned to the United Kingdom last March. In announcing their return to the House on 24 February last year, I said that the Government would continue to work to resolve the position of the remaining four British detainees: Feroz Abbasi, Moazzam Begg, Jamaal Belmar and Martin Mubanga. Since last March, the Government have been in regular discussion with the United States authorities about this. Foreign Office Ministers and I have also held a number of meetings with the families and lawyers of the four men and with their Members of Parliament, and officials have been in regular contact with them.

Following contact between the United Kingdom and the United States—involving, in particular . . . the Prime Minister and his office—and between United States Secretary of State Colin Powell and myself, the United States Government have now agreed to the return of all four men to the United Kingdom. That decision follows intensive and complex discussions to address United States security concerns. All the families have been informed of that decision this morning, as have their Members of Parliament.

The four men will be returned in the next few weeks. Once they are back in the United Kingdom, the police will consider whether to arrest them under the

Terrorism Act 2000 for questioning in connection with possible terrorist activity. Any subsequent action will be a matter for the police and the Crown Prosecution Service. The House will understand that it would therefore not be right for me to comment further on that aspect of the matter.

I should like to assure the House that every practical step will be taken by the relevant United Kingdom authorities to maintain national security and to protect public safety. Throughout the period of detention of British nationals in Guantanamo Bay, the Government have sought to balance the need to safeguard the interests of Britons detained overseas with our duty to meet the threat from international terrorism.

Terrorism is opposed to the values of every faith and religion, and seeks to deny the most basic of human rights—the right to life, to security and to go about our daily business free from harm. Working with our allies, we will continue resolutely to defend those rights through a robust and determined approach to combating terrorism and its networks of support wherever these are found.

(HC Deb 11 January 2005 Vol. 429 c173–175)

6/72

In answer to questions following his statement, the Foreign Secretary said:

We have an immediate locus in so far as our consular duties are concerned in respect of British citizens. With their return to the United Kingdom, representations about the specific conditions at Guantanamo Bay in respect of the British citizens will obviously come to an end. However, as members of the international community and signatories to various international conventions, we remain concerned about the conditions in which individuals have been, and continue to be, held there, and within that context, we will continue to make representations about them.

(HC Deb 11 January 2005 Vol. 429 c 176)

6/73

In answer to a question about Jamil el-Banna, a Jordanian refugee . . . a long-time British resident and the efforts being made to secure his release, the Foreign Secretary said:

As for Mr. el-Banna, the House will be aware that in international law we only have the standing to take up consular matters in respect of British citizens. That is a fact of international law, and it applies to citizens and nationals of all third countries. It means that we cannot make representations on behalf of people, however long they have been resident in the UK, who are not our nationals. More to the point, the US Government, consistent with their obligations under international law, would not accept such representations. I know that that is frustrating, and I have seen the families of a number of people in that position, but that is the situation.

(HC Deb 11 January 2005 Vol. 429 c180)

6/74

The Foreign Secretary said in the House of Commons:

[I am asked] about the allegations of mistreatment made by Moazzam Begg in particular. I am aware of those allegations, and I have already received oral representations about them by his family and his lawyers. We are pursuing those allegations with the United States authorities, and we will continue to do so. British consular officials visited the detainees on nine separate occasions in very difficult circumstances. It is fair to say that our officials, on my behalf, gave the British detainees a higher level of consular representation than did the foreign Governments of any other nationals who were held at Guantanamo Bay.

. . .

[I am asked] whether I can be satisfied that no British citizen is held in any similar circumstance. The answer is that it is almost impossible to prove a negative, but I know of no other British citizen held at Guantanamo Bay in those circumstances; neither do I expect that any will be dispatched there.

(HC Deb 11 January 2005 Vol. 429 c175)

6/75

The Government was asked by the FAC whether or not its response to the detentions in Guantanamo had been too slow and too narrow, being confined to representations about British nationals detained there, particularly given the Government's concerns for human rights violations on a world-wide basis. An FCO Minister said:

Because primarily, although not exclusively, we have a responsibility for UK citizens and I think that the biggest locus that we have in intervening on Guantanamo Bay is first and foremost in respect of our own nationals. We have concentrated on those to maximise our leverage with the US Government but at the same time we have always made clear that the concerns we have been expressing on behalf of the UK nationals have wider import and, for Members who were in the chamber this afternoon, the Foreign Secretary was making clear that just because we have now secured the release of the nine UK nationals that does not mean that we do not continue to have concerns about the process. Let us put this into context: 9/11 and what followed was the worst terrorist attack in history. I think in those circumstances the United States has been absolutely right to take the greatest of care with terrorist suspects and it is a fact as well that information that has been obtained through that process has helped to protect all of us from potential further terrorist attack. From the beginning of this process, and I have sat through numerous statements from the Foreign Secretary and others in the Chamber and elsewhere, we have consistently said that our position with regard to the US is that you either try these people in accordance with fair international standards or you release them. That has been the focus of our activity and I think the results, and it is arguable and we would say it has taken longer than ideally we would have wished, justify that approach. Throughout that as well I think we have done more for our own nationals than any other government in terms of the regularity of visits and the improvements to conditions of detention that we have secured. This has been a very complex and complicated situation but we have always said that it is not one that can continue indefinitely. [Q.76]

He was then asked about compensation for British nationals who had been held for a long time and then released without charge. He said:

If individual citizens choose to take that path they can make representations to us and we will look at it. [Q.77]

Asked again about non-British nationals, he said:

... our first priority and our major locus has been in respect of our own UK nationals but we are also members of the international community. We are also bound by numerous international treaties and covenants and within that context we will continue to raise our concerns about the process. As I said, it is complicated, it is a difficult situation. I understand the fears and concerns of the United States but I do think you cannot indefinitely go through with this kind of process. [Q.78]

and

what I would say is that the concern about Guantanamo, both in terms of the way the detainees are held and the legal procedures and the lack of consistency with fair standards of international law, are concerns we have for however long people are held in detention. [Q.79]

(FAC Fourth Report, Human Rights Annual Report 2004, HC 109 (2005), Minutes of Evidence 11 January 2005)

6/76

Human Rights Conditionality

In a written answer, a Minister wrote:

DFID has recently launched a new policy on conditionality. Our policy makes it clear that we do not believe that conditionality can "buy" reform. Our aid programmes are based on partner commitment to reducing poverty, respect for human rights and international obligations and the strengthening of financial systems. Should a partner country move substantially away from these commitments, then we will consider revoking our aid commitments.

Within this framework of partner commitments, 'political policies' per se are not specifically identified. But political actions which relate to rights and international obligations, for example with respect to good governance, the rule of law and conduct of elections, will be considered in respect of whether a country is substantially undermining the basis of our partnership.

(HC Deb 20 July 2005 Vol. 436 c1839W)

6/77

Human Trafficking

The government was asked whether any of the provisions in the Council of Europe Convention on Action against Trafficking in Human Beings currently concern them; if so, which provisions; and what are those concerns. A Minister wrote:

There are aspects of the Council of Europe Convention on Action against Trafficking in Human Beings that are currently of concern. The particular areas of concern relate to issues surrounding the provision of recovery and reflection periods (Article 13) and residence permits (Article 14). The mandatory nature of these provisions when coupled with the scope of the convention has led to concerns that the provisions will act as an immigration pull factor, encourage spurious claims, and be used by those who have no right to remain in an effort to frustrate removal. Abuse of the provisions would ultimately impact on those in genuine need of assistance. Provision already exists for my right honourable friend the Home Secretary to exercise his discretion where it is clear that it is not appropriate to remove an individual or where it is appropriate to allow them time to recover before any decision is made in respect of their immigration status.

(HL Deb 5 July 2005 Vol. 673 cWA77)

6/78

Indigenous Peoples

The Government was asked whether it would publish the legal advice on which it based its decision not to sign [sic support] the Draft Declaration on the Rights of Indigenous Peoples. An FCO Minister wrote:

The Draft Declaration on the Rights of Indigenous Peoples is still under negotiation. Like most other members of the working group, the UK has a number of concerns with the original text. Only two out of 64 articles of the original text have been agreed, and there are alternative proposals on the table for much of the remaining text. The issue has therefore been one of discussion and negotiation, not signature.

(HL Deb 7 March 2005 Vol. 670 cWA61)

6/79

Indonesia

In a written answer, an FCO Minister wrote:

We are concerned about reports of human rights abuses in Papua, and we raise these regularly with the Government of Indonesia, We also encourage the Indonesian Government to engage in dialogue with Papuan representatives and to proceed with full implementation of the Special Autonomy legislation.

We are encouraged by President Yudhoyono's recent statements that his Government wishes to solve the issue in Papua through dialogue,

> "in a peaceful, just and dignified manner".

(HC Deb 17 October 2005 Vol. 437 c733W)

6/80

Iran

The Government was asked to make a statement on the Bahá'í community in Iran. An FCO Minister wrote:

The Bahá'ís are the largest non-Muslim religious group in Iran yet, unlike Christians, Jews and Zoroastrians, are not recognised in Iran's constitution. Members of the Bahá'í community have suffered intimidation and harassment, had property confiscated and been denied access to education and employment, apparently on account of their faith. A number of Bahá'í sites have been demolished, organisers of Bahá'í community activities have reportedly been harassed and the Bahá'í faith has been denigrated in the state-owned media. Many of these acts appear to have been carried out by, or with the support or acquiescence of, the Iranian authorities. We have raised our concerns about the situation of the Bahá'ís in Iran with the Iranian authorities on many occasions, and will continue to do so, bilaterally and with our European Union partners.

(HC Deb 28 June 2005 Vol. 435 c1478W)

6/81

In a written answer, an FCO Minister wrote:

Senior members of the Iranian Government and election officials, as well as several of the candidates, have complained of widespread interference, including by the security forces. We have made clear our concern, which is widely shared in the EU and elsewhere. The EU has also expressed regret that a large majority of candidates, including many reformists and all the women, were excluded from the elections, making a genuine democratic choice difficult. We continue to urge the Iranian Government to allow its citizens to benefit from the full range of democratic freedoms and human rights.

(HC Deb 6 July 2005 Vol. 436 c484W)

6/82

During a debate in the House of Lords, an FCO Minister said:

... we are making representations on those subjects. There is a dispute about how many are involved but a number of young people—not only women but also people under the age of 18—who were alleged to have committed crimes have been executed. The European Council has been engaged and has agreed a statement, which the United Kingdom with the presidency of the EU has also backed directly, expressing the EU's deep concern. We have called on Iran to clarify the position immediately. It is a contravention of Article 37 of the Convention on the Rights of the Child and Article 6 of the International Covenant on Civil and Political Rights, and we are pursuing those with great vigour.

(HL Deb 16 November 2005 Vol. 675 c1069)

6/83

Iraq

The Government was asked how many persons arrested by British service personnel in Iraq have been in custody for over a year without charges having been brought against them. A Minister wrote:

Two internees originally taken into custody by the United Kingdom have been held for more than a year. Both are held at the Divisional Temporary Detention Facility in Basrah Province. They were interned on the basis that they represented an imperative threat to security and not on the basis that they were suspected of any specific criminal offence.

(HC Deb 4 April 2005 Vol. 432 c1211W)

6/84

In a written answer, the Minister of State for Defence wrote:

I have received no reports to indicate that any persons taken into custody by UK forces in Iraq, and subsequently transferred to US custody, have been subject to the unlawful use of sensory deprivation techniques during interrogation.

(HC Deb 5 July 2005 Vol. 436 c259W)

6/85

In a written answer, a Minister wrote:

We are helping the Iraqis restore stability and build a democratic state. A strong, functioning, legal system is central to this project.

We take all practicable steps to ensure that any prisoners handed over to the Iraqi criminal justice system are not mistreated. We have agreed a memorandum of understanding (MoU) with the Iraqis governing prisoner transfer. Under the terms of the MoU, we seek written guarantees for each prisoner transferred to the Iraqis ensuring that they will not be mistreated. And once transferred, court liaison teams from the Royal Military Police monitor their cases to ensure no abuse is occurring.

However, once transferred their treatment is ultimately a matter for a sovereign Iraqi government.

(HL Deb 14 November 2005 Vol. 675 cWA123)

6/86

Israel

The Government was asked what assessment [it] has made of whether Israel is fulfilling human rights commitments made to the EU. An FCO Minister wrote:

Along with our EU partners, we have followed a policy of constructive engagement with Israel on humanitarian and human rights issues. We have raised our concerns on human rights violations both bilaterally and through the institutions established by the EU/Israel Association Agreement. This happened most recently at the EU/Israel Association Committee on 14 April in Jerusalem. Our primary concerns are the impact on human rights of barrier construction, restrictions imposed on the freedom of movement and settlement expansion.

(HC Deb 28 June 2005 Vol. 435 c1480)

6/87

Kashmir

The Government was asked about the situation in Kashmir. An FCO Minister wrote:

We remain concerned by continued credible reports of human rights abuses in Kashmir, including acts reportedly perpetrated by members of the Indian security forces . . . the Foreign Secretary raised this with the Indian Minister of Home Affairs during his visit to India in February 2005. The UK condemns all acts of violence that bring suffering to the people of Kashmir, and believes that only through dialogue between India and Pakistan will a durable solution to the Kashmir issue be reached. We welcome the Indian Chief of Army Staffs public commitment to "reach out to the Kashmiri People", and the UK will continue to encourage the Indian Government to implement such pledges to improve the human rights situation in Kashmir.

. . .

It is important that Pakistan does all it can to fulfil President Musharraf's commitment, made at the South Asian Association for Regional Co-operation (SAARC) Summit in Islamabad in January 2004, not to permit any Pakistani territory to be used to support terrorism ... the Foreign Secretary raised the need for Pakistan to fulfil this commitment during his visit to Islamabad in February 2005, and the UK continues to make this point clearly to senior Pakistani interlocutors.

(HC Deb 28 June 2005 Vol. 435 c1479W)

6/88

Pakistan—Death Penalty

The Government was asked what representations the Government have made to authorities in Pakistan regarding their decision to re-instate the death penalty for child offenders. An FCO Minister wrote:

In December 2004 the Lahore High Court annulled the Juvenile Justice System Ordinance 2000 which, if implemented, would effectively reinstate the possibility of the death sentence for juvenile offenders in Punjab province of Pakistan. On 17 December 2004 the EU made a demarche to the Pakistan authorities to raise their concerns on this and other human rights concerns. Officials from our high commission in Islamabad have also raised this bilaterally with Pakistani officials. The UK is entirely opposed to the death penalty, which it considers to be a cruel and inhuman punishment, and notes that the imposition of the death penalty on those under 18 at the time of the crime is contrary to the Convention on the Rights of the Child to which Pakistan is a signatory. We hope that steps can be taken by the relevant Pakistani authorities to ensure that the death penalty for juvenile offenders is not reinstated as a result of this recent annulment by the Lahore High Court.

(HC Deb 31 January 2005 Vol. 430 c716W)

6/89

Protection of the human rights of nationals

The FAC asked the Government whether it treated abuse of the human rights of UK nationals "slightly differently" from the way it treated abuse by States of the human rights of their own nationals. An FCO Minister said:

I am not saying we are not concerned about abuse of human rights of foreign nationals, but our first responsibility is obviously to British citizens. [Q.121]

And asked further if it were not "quite so easy" to take up with another Government the treatment of its nationals in "strong terms", he said:

It does not mean we do not do it in respect of other countries' nationals; certainly we do do it. I think if you look at our track record, we do it effectively on behalf of our own nationals in a number of different countries in very difficult circumstances. [Q.122]

With respect to the ill-treatment of British nationals, the Minister was asked if he could give any examples of where the Government has requested not necessarily prompt but an impartial investigation of allegations?

The Minister said:

Certainly in the case of Egypt with the detainees there we have requested a full investigation into the men's allegations. [Q.125]

but that no inquiry had been held.

Another example was Guantanamo where the Government had requested an inquiry ... [s]pecifically in respect of Mr Begg, who has made allegations about his ill-treatment, we asked for an investigation by the US government. They came back. We have now asked for further clarification and a further investigation. [Q.129]

When asked about British nationals held in Saudi Arabia, the Minister said:

The difference, of course, with both Egypt and Guantanamo is that in respect of Saudi Arabia the detainees have now been released ... The focus of our efforts was to secure the release of the detainees within Saudi Arabia, and I think it is no exaggeration to say that we expended enormous diplomatic efforts in that regard at the highest level within government to the lowest level within government and, had it not been for that diplomatic effort, I am not sure that the men would have been released today as they are. [Q.130]

(FAC Fourth Report, Human Rights Annual Report 2004, HC 109 (2005), Minutes of Evidence 11 January 2005)

6/90

Slavery

During a debate in the House of Lords, a Minister said:

One of the key forms of contemporary slavery is bonded labour, where a person is required to give his labour as security for a loan.

...

The Government strongly condemn forced labour in all its forms. We fully support the work of the ILO and work closely with the organisation to ensure that the international framework to combat abuses of workers' rights throughout the world is in place and effective. We also provide substantial financial support.

The UK has ratified the ILO's "core labour standards", including those covering the abolition of forced labour. We have also taken specific actions to tackle forced labour within the United Kingdom.

(HL Deb 7 July 2005 Vol. 673 c773)

6/91

An FCO Minister told the House of Lords:

I trust ... I will be able to demonstrate that this Government are firmly taking action to tackle the abhorrent forms of modern slavery.

... contemporary slavery covers a wide variety of human rights violations, from debt-bondage and forced labour to people trafficking and child labour. Slavery affects the poorest and most vulnerable groups in society. It is difficult to uncover and to resolve since fear and the need for survival deter its victims from coming forward. Solutions require governments, international organisations, civil society and the private sector to work together to break the cycle of poverty and social exclusion that are at the root of most forms of slavery today.

Since contemporary forms of slavery persist where poverty denies people their rights, we also support country-led development agendas and poverty-reduction strategies ...

One of the key forms of contemporary slavery is bonded labour, where a person is required to give his labour as security for a loan. The DfID programme in Nepal assisted former bonded labourers through the freed Kamaiya food security programme. It supported a number of activities, including income generation, scholarships and access to drinking water and sanitation, in partnership with international, national and local NGOs. This work continues through a number of smaller-scale projects under the community support programme.

... a striking feature of debt bondage is its inextricable link with caste discrimination and social exclusion. DfID is preparing a policy paper on social exclusion. That will outline how DfID intends to step up its work with its partners to ensure that the needs of all groups in society are included in country-assistance plans.

...

The Government strongly condemn forced labour in all its forms. We fully support the work of the ILO and work closely with the organisation to ensure that the international framework to combat abuses of workers' rights throughout the world is in place and effective. We also provide substantial financial support.

The UK has ratified the ILO's "core labour standards", including those covering the abolition of forced labour. We have also taken specific actions to tackle forced labour within the United Kingdom .... those include the establishment of the Gangmasters Licensing Authority. Over the coming months, the authority will consult on the conditions that should be attached to the issue of a licence. It is anticipated that some of those will be based on tackling aspects of forced labour.

...

Next week, officials from across Whitehall will meet government officials from a number of "source" and "destination" countries, together with colleagues from the ILO special action programme, to combat forced labour as part of a project aimed at raising awareness and capacity of those responsible for implementing policies to combat the forced labour dimensions of human trafficking....

... in 1999–2000 the UK supported a proposal from Anti-Slavery International for the creation of a UN special rapporteur on contemporary forms of slavery. Sadly, it did not receive sufficient support and the idea died. However, we would in theory support a special rapporteur on contemporary forms of slavery to replace the working group of the same name, provided that it had a robust mandate.

The UK has also enacted legislation to criminalise trafficking. The Sexual Offences Act 2003 and the Asylum and Immigration (Treatment of Claimants, etc.) Act 2004 both include tough maximum penalties of 14 years for new offences covering trafficking into, out of, or within the United Kingdom. Overseas the UK works to build capacity in source countries so that they can fight trafficking themselves. The Home Office is leading an EC-funded project with the Czech Ministry of the Interior to strengthen its capacity to combat trafficking.

... the UK chose not to opt in [to the EU directive on short-term permits], owing to the potential adverse implications in respect of immigration controls. It was considered that the introduction of a specific immigration provision for victims of trafficking would encourage abusive claims, and that this would impact on the very people whom the measures were designed to help. This does not mean, however, that the UK is unsympathetic to the spirit of the directive or that we are unconcerned about the plight of the victims of this abuse.

...

The UK supports the ILO's International Programme for the Elimination of Child Labour, which provides technical support to countries combating child labour and trafficking. We support initiatives through the World Bank, UNICEF and NGOs which are working to demobilise and rehabilitate these children.

Vulnerable children are a high priority for the Government. We have endorsed the UNICEF Strategic Framework for the Protection, Care and Support of Orphans and Vulnerable Children living in a world with HIV/AIDS. This provides guidance for countries on developing national policies and programmes to respond to the needs of vulnerable children, including orphans, street children and those at risk from drugs, prostitution, trafficking, HIV and AIDS.

...

We are greatly concerned by the human rights violations in Sudan, and strongly condemn the slave-like practices of abduction, trafficking and forced labour. Slavery is explicitly prohibited by both the outgoing 1998 constitution, the comprehensive peace agreement and the current draft of the interim constitution. But we continue to be gravely concerned by the ongoing human rights abuses.

(HL Deb 17 July Vol. 673 c771–776)

6/92

Sudan

In a written answer, an FCO Minister wrote:

Our embassy in Khartoum made representations, both bilaterally and through the EU, to the Government of Sudan on this case on 27 June. Following these interventions the Sudanese authorities postponed the execution.

We are resolutely opposed to the death penalty in all circumstances, and raise these concerns with the Government of Sudan on a regular basis. The case also goes against the provisions of the N'djamena Cease-Fire Agreement of 2004 in which the parties agreed to release all prisoners of war and those detained in relation to the conflict. We will continue to follow this case closely.

(HC Deb 4 July 2005 Vol. 436 c180W)

6/93

In a written answer, an FCO Minister wrote:

We make regular representations to the Government of Sudan regarding the treatment of prisoners and the release of political detainees. We welcome the release on 30 June of 29 political prisoners, among them the leader of the Popular Congress Party Dr. Hassan al-Turabi and General Secretary of the Beja Congress Abdulla Musa. We continue to press the Government of Sudan to release those political detainees still held.

Under the terms of the Interim National Constitution, signed on 6 June 2005, and the Comprehensive Peace Agreement (CPA), signed on 9 January 2005, the rights to freedom of thought, conscience, expression and association are guaranteed to all. They also guarantee freedom from discrimination on any grounds, including for political or other opinions. We continue to urge the parties to implement fully the CPA and to ensure that swift progress is made on the provisions on human rights.

(HC Deb 12 July 2005 Vol. 436 c879W)

6/94

In a written answer, an FCO Minister wrote:

We regularly raise with the Government of Sudan the need to respect human rights and abide by international human rights treaties such as the International Covenant on Civil and Political Rights. We hold these discussions both bilaterally and through multilateral forums such as the EU-Sudan Human Rights dialogue.

We continue to stress to the Government of Sudan the importance of fully implementing the Comprehensive Peace Agreement and the new Interim National Constitution, which make explicit provisions for the protection of human rights.

(HC Deb 18 October 2005 Vol. 437 c908W)

6/95

Torture

(See also **Part Six: VII. B.**)

The Government was asked by the FAC about the use of information extracted under torture in another country. An FCO Minister said:

. . . let me start by saying that we emphatically and vehemently oppose torture as a matter of fundamental principle. I think you would find it very difficult to find a country that has got as strong a track record as we have. For example, we were the third country in the world to ratify the optional protocol to the Convention against Torture. We oppose the use of torture ourselves. We would never advocate anybody else using torture and to my knowledge we have not knowingly received intelligence that we have known has been gained under torture ... As far as I am aware ... we have not received such information ... I am not saying that because I am unsure. Certainly it is not a practice that we endorse and we have no knowledge of such information coming into our hands. It is not because I am not aware of the circumstances. I am simply saying that as far as we are aware that is the case. (Qs 80–82)

(FAC Fourth Report, Human Rights Annual Report 2004, HC 109 (2005), Minutes of Evidence 11 January 2005)

6/96

The Government was asked if it will make it its policy to regard as not valid information which it believes to have been obtained by torture. The Foreign Secretary said:

The UK vehemently opposes torture as a matter of fundamental principle. The UK intelligence and security agencies carefully evaluate the intelligence they receive against a range of factors; any concerns about the source of the intelligence or the means by which it may have been obtained would be taken into account. Where we are helping other countries to develop their own counter-terrorism capability, we ensure that our training or other assistance promotes human rights compliance.

(HC Deb 11 January 2005 Vol. 429 c413W)

6/97

In a written answer, an FCO Minister wrote:

The UK unreservedly condemns the use of torture as a matter of fundamental principle. We have worked hard with our international partners to eradicate this abhorrent practice. The UK abides by its commitments under international law including the UN Convention against Torture and the European Convention on Human Rights, and expects all countries to comply with their international legal obligations. We are active in pressing other countries to live up to their human rights obligations and to deliver on human rights commitments they have made.

International action against torture has been a priority for the Government since they launched an initiative to tackle torture throughout the world in 1998. We pursue the worldwide abolition of torture through diplomatic activity, practical projects and funding for research, This has included worldwide lobbying campaigns for the universal ratification of the UN Convention Against Torture and its Optional Protocol, This year the Foreign and Commonwealth Office has committed over £400,000 in our efforts to combat torture through concrete project work, which includes the production and dissemination of a new manual aimed at guiding police forces on alternative and more humane investigative techniques and a project to increase police professionalism in China.

(HC Deb 28 October 2005 Vol. 438 c636W–637W)

6/98

In a written answer, the Foreign Secretary wrote:

The Government, including the intelligence and security agencies, never uses torture for any purposes, including to obtain information. Nor would we instigate others to do so. Where we are helping other countries to develop their own counter-terrorism capability, we ensure that our training or other assistance promotes human rights compliance. Our rejection of the use of torture is well known by our liaison partners.

I am unaware of any adverse impact on the UK's international standing and reputation and the success of British foreign policy from this approach.

(HC Deb 30 November 2005 Vol. 440 c674W)

6/99

The Government was asked what assessment [it] has made of the implications of the United States (a) reservations and (b) derogations from the UN Convention Against Torture for UK policy on the rendition of detainees to third countries. In reply, an FCO Minister wrote:

The UK policy on rendition of detainees to third countries is very clear. Where we are requested to assist another State and our assistance would be lawful, we will decide whether or not to assist taking into account all the circumstances. We would not assist in any case if to do so would put us in breach of UK law or our international obligations, including the UN Convention Against Torture. In particular, we would not facilitate the transfer of an individual from or through the UK to another State where there were grounds to believe that the person would face a real risk of torture. This is not affected by the position of other States on the Convention.

(HC Deb 20 December 2005 Vol. 440 c2840W)

6/100

Transnational Corporations

The Government was asked what role the UN Norms on Business and Human Rights play in the setting of governance standards for UK and EU companies in domestic and global markets; and if it will make a statement on *(a)* the UK and *(b)* the EU position regarding the UN Norms. An FCO Minister wrote:

The recent report from the Office of the High Commissioner on Human Rights (OHCHR) on business and human rights notes that the UN Norms have the status of a "draft proposal". Therefore, the draft Norms have no formal or legal role in setting governance standards for business. However, through the Business Leaders' Initiative on Human Rights (BLIHR), a number of multinational-companies have been "road-testing" the draft Norms, using the content to inform their codes of practice. This process will continue until December 2006. In addition, the FTSE4Good benchmark takes the draft Norms into account in its assessment of companies' performance. And some potential investors consider the draft Norms in their requirement for "human rights impact assessments".

The UK continues to play a constructive role in the debate on corporate responsibility and human rights. While we see merit in clarifying minimum standards for business in relation to human rights, we believe, as does the OHCHR, that future action on this agenda should take into account the many codes and initiatives which exist in this field, rather than focussing exclusively on the draft Norms. These include the Organisation for Economic Cooperation and Development Guidelines on Multinational Enterprises, the International Labour Organisation Tripartite Declaration of Principles concerning Multinational Enterprises and Social Policy and the UN Global Compact.

The UK will be active at the forthcoming Commission on Human Rights in seeking to ensure proper follow-up to the OHCHR's report. We firmly believe that this exercise should listen to the views of all stakeholders.

(HC Deb 16 March 2005 Vol. 432 c340W)

6/101

In a written answer, an FCO Minister wrote:

We actively encourage UK-based international companies which operate in other countries, to apply high standards of corporate behaviour, including adhering to relevant internationally agreed standards which respect human rights and the environment.

In April 2005 the UN High Commission on Human Rights requested the UN Secretary-General to appoint a special representative to take forward work on the area of business and human rights. The two year mandate of the special representative includes identification and clarification of standards of corporate responsibility and accountability for business with regard to human rights.

The UK plays a leading role in ensuring that the international framework to promote and to tackle abuses of workers rights throughout the world is in place, particularly through its work with the International Labour Organisation (ILO). We play an active role in the ILO Committee on Multinational Enterprises and support the promotion and follow-up of the ILO Declaration of Principles Concerning Multinational Enterprises and Social Policy which seeks to enhance the positive social and labour effects of multinational corporations' operations throughout the world.

We actively support the UN Global Compact, launched by Kofi Anann in July 2000. The Compact is an agreement between the UN and business to uphold and promulgate 10 principles covering human rights, labour, the environment and corruption. We also promote the OECD Guidelines for Multinational Enterprises which recommend standards of responsible business conduct for businesses operating in or from the 37 adhering countries and we have written to the FTSE 100 companies to raise awareness of these expectations.

We have set out our approach to encouraging environmentally and socially responsible practice internationally in our International Strategic Framework on Corporate Social Responsibility published in March this year.

The Government are building Sustainable Development Dialogues with China, India, Brazil and other emerging economies. These dialogues seek to engage companies and civil society in both countries in the move towards sustainable development. The UK-India Dialogue was launched on 11 October.

(HC Deb 24 October 2005 Vol. 438 c289W–290W)

6/102

Uzbekistan

In a written answer, the Minister of State for Europe wrote:

We remain deeply concerned by the reports of ongoing human rights abuses in Uzbekistan, including the mistreatment of human rights defenders and others, and take every opportunity to raise this issue with the Uzbek Government.

We made our most recent representation on 14 October. In a diplomatic note, passed by our Embassy in Tashkent to the Uzbek Ministry of Foreign Affairs, we expressed our alarm at the reported treatment of three human rights defenders. One of these was the recently arrested Mukhtabar Tojibaeva; we have requested clarification of the charges brought against her. The Other two were Elena Urlaeva and Shavkat Madumarov. We have asked the Uzbek Government to confirm that all three are being treated in a manner compliant with international standards.

We will continue, both bilaterally and through international institutions such as the EU and The Organisation for Security and Co-operation in Europe, to encourage Uzbekistan to take greater steps towards full respect for human rights, and stand ready to provide any necessary assistance.

(HC Deb 20 October 2005 Vol. 437 c1206W–1207W)

Part Six: IX. *The Position of the Individual (including the Corporation) in International Law—Crimes under international law*

6/103

The Government was asked whether officials of the UK Government have visited Saddam Hussein since he has been in custody; what reports it has received on (a) Saddam Hussein's health and (b) the prison conditions in which Saddam Hussein is being held. An FCO Minister wrote:

Saddam Hussein was transferred into the Iraqi criminal justice system on 1 July 2004, and is currently awaiting trial. At the request of Prime Minster Allawi, the US will maintain physical custody of Saddam Hussein until such time as the Iraqi Correctional Service is able to provide for his safe and secure detention.

UK Government officials have not visited Saddam Hussein but the International Committee of the Red Cross (ICRC) has regular access to him. The ICRC would raise any concerns it has about Saddam Hussein's health and conditions of detention in confidential reports to the US and Iraqi authorities.

(HC Deb 8 February 2005, Vol. 430 c1464W)

6/104

The Government was asked whether the court to be constructed to try Saddam Hussein will be capable of trying other persons. An FCO Minister wrote:

We expect that Saddam Hussein will be tried before the Iraqi Special Tribunal, which is part of the Iraqi criminal justice system and is composed of senior Iraqi judges. The tribunal was established to try members of the former regime accused of genocide, crimes against humanity, war crimes and certain other serious crimes under existing Iraqi law including the manipulation of the judiciary, squandering public resources and the threat or use of force against other Arab states. It is a matter for the Iraqi judiciary to decide precisely who should be brought before which court.

(HL Deb 10 February 2005 Vol. 669 c128WA)

6/105

The Government was asked how many times lawyers representing Saddam Hussein have met their client since 16 December 2004. An FCO Minister wrote:

Saddam Hussein is a criminal detainee and is liable to prosecution under the Iraqi criminal justice system. He was transferred into the Iraqi criminal justice system on 1 July 2004, and is currently awaiting trial. At the request of Prime Minster Allawi, the US will maintain physical custody of Saddam Hussein until such time as the Iraqi Correctional Service is able to provide for his safe and secure detention. The US authorities have told us that Saddam Hussein has seen his lawyer once since 16 December 2004. He has not requested to see his lawyer since that meeting.

(HC Deb 4 April 2005 Vol. 432 c1090W)

6/106

The Government was asked what account was taken of Article 64 of the Fourth Geneva Convention in the appointment of the Iraqi Special Tribunal. A Minister wrote:

Article 64 of the Fourth Geneva Convention would not apply to the establishment of the Iraq Special Tribunal (IST) or any appointment of the IST because it was established by the Iraqi Governing Council and not by an Occupying Power. It is part of the Iraqi criminal justice system and comprises of Iraqi judges.

(HC Deb 5 April 2005 Vol. 432 c1326W)

6/107

In a speech, "How far can laws reach? The problem of extraterritoriality" given by the Attorney-General at the IBA Annual Conference, Prague 28 September 2005, he said:

. . . there is an additional reason for extraterritorial jurisdiction in the field of certain serious crime. That is to avoid impunity for those who are powerful in their own countries and able therefore to avoid the due process of law. This is part of the change since the Second World War which has led to the creation of international human rights standards. It counters the old Austinian version of sovereignty which enabled despots and tyrants to commit atrocities in their own countries without being held to account by others on the grounds that for another country to bring them to account would constitute an unwarranted interference in a country's domestic affairs and in its sovereignty. That has changed.

Part of the way that this has changed is through the creation of international tribunals able to bring people to justice: Nuremberg, the International Criminal Tribunals for Yugoslavia and Rwanda, the Special Court for Sierra Leone and now the International Criminal Court. Iraq has adopted a different model so that the trial of those accused of crimes under the regime of Saddam Hussein will be tried locally before the Iraqi Higher Criminal Court. That is on the basis that where national justice is available it is to be preferred.

Setting up ad hoc international tribunals is not without difficulty. The negotiations at the international level can be lengthy and getting funding can prove difficult. Now that we have the ICC there may be less need for that to happen in the future. However, the ICC itself took a number of years to set up and its jurisdictional base is far from universal in that whether it can exercise jurisdiction will depend on where the crime was committed or the nationality of the accused i.e. only states parties are bound by the Rome Statute. Further the principle of complementarity is such that it will only act where the state of nationality will not.

The other way is by giving other states the ability to bring proceedings and indeed [sometimes] the obligation to do so. Thus, for example, the Geneva Conventions have created an obligation for states parties to prosecute war crimes and grave breaches of the Conventions. A number of treaties provide similarly for the prosecution of torture, genocide, hostage-taking and so on.

Being able to prosecute elsewhere than the home country where, for a variety of reasons, prosecution may not be possible, is an important way to avoid impunity and to discourage any would be despot from wrongdoing thinking that he will be able to escape justice . . .

I can illustrate this principle with a concrete example. Torture and hostage-taking were of relevance in a recent case in the UK. On 18 July this year, a jury at the Old Bailey convicted Faryadi Zardad of offences of conspiracy to torture and conspiracy to take hostages, offences committed during the Afghan civil war between 1991 and 1996. Zardad had been a commander in the Heb-e-Islami (Islamic Party) run by the notorious warlord, Gulbuddin Hikmatyar. During the war that group controlled large tracts of Afghanistan, and in particular the trade road from Kabul to Peshawar. Zardad was the commander who controlled that road at a key choke-point, and a nearby hydro-electric dam and prison.

Over the course of this trial, this British jury heard from 16 of his victims, who told of: the slaughter of 10 or 11 men in a minibus, separated from their wives and children left screaming at the roadside; an old man imprisoned in a metal cupboard and whipped with bicycle cables; a father having his ear cut off in front of his seven year-old son; petrol being poured over a man as Zardad's men joked about matches; and of Zardad's systematic hostage taking for ransom. One of his victims told this British jury of how he was held hostage for four months and beaten so frequently that his family failed to recognise him when he was eventually released.

So far as we were able to establish, this was the first time ever that a case of this type had been prosecuted anywhere. There were a number of important features to this groundbreaking case:

- Firstly that the trial happened at all. I believe it sent a very clear message that those who commit such grave crimes will find no hiding place. The UK in particular will not be a safe haven for despots
- Secondly, it showed that an English jury would convict if the evidence was there, even though neither the offender nor his victims were British and the offences had been committed overseas. I put it this way when opening the case in our Central Criminal Court, the Old Bailey;

  > " . . . It is unusual to try cases in our criminal courts, when the matters concerned did not occur in the United Kingdom. It is more unusual still to try matters when the defendant is not a British subject nor the victims British. Crimes which occur in foreign countries, with foreign defendants and foreign victims are often best left to be tried where they happened. . . . However, there are some crimes which are so heinous, such an affront to justice that not only can they be tried in any country, but there is a positive duty on any country where such an alleged offender is found to try that person and bring him to justice."

- Thirdly, it showed that whilst it is possible to bring such proceedings it is also difficult to do so. The English police needed to be able to trace witnesses in Afghanistan, and needed armed escorts to be able to do so. Not all the witnesses were able to travel to London for the trial, and so some had to give their evidence from the British embassy in Kabul by video link to a courtroom in the Old Bailey. A team from the Metropolitan Police Service were stationed in the embassy in order to make the necessary arrangements. And the impact of the evidence given in this way—with time lags on top of the need to interpret everything that was said—could render it perhaps less immediate, and therefore have less impact, than evidence given directly to the jury within the courtroom.

- And finally, the case also showed the gaps in the jurisdiction. The prosecution was for torture and hostage taking. As I have already mentioned, the jury also heard evidence of killings for which Zardad was responsible, but for which he could not be convicted. As a consequence, these killings could not be reflected in his sentence. Zardad got 20 years imprisonment.

It was plain that it was in the interests of justice that Zardad should be prosecuted: he had settled down in England ... and the Afghan authorities did not seek his extradition.

But the question arises—should there be limits to when such a prosecution is possible and by whom it can be brought? For example Belgium's law on universal jurisdiction was previously very wide but in recent years has been amended to add in a filter to prevent its misuse.

These problems may be especially acute where another state could assume jurisdiction. Yet there are no sophisticated rules on the criminal side to mirror the concepts of forum non conveniens or lis pendens on the civil side. There are no conventions or treaties (which can be used to help determine which jurisdiction should be exercised) like there are on the civil side such as the Brussels Convention on Jurisdiction and the Enforcement of Judgments (now echoed in an EC Regulation) or the Lugano Convention. If we were to attempt to set out such principles we would have to take account of a large number of factors such as: the location of the accused; availability of extradition; the attendance and protection of witnesses; interests of victims; evidential problems; sentencing powers. It is not obvious what weight those factors should take. I am glad to say that some useful work has already been done on this by EUROJUST.

(www.lslo.gov.uk/speeches.htm)

6/108

The Government was asked what [its] position is on (a) Belgium's decision to charge Hissene Habre with crimes against humanity and torture and (b) the extradition of Hissene Habre to Belgium. In reply, an FCO Minister wrote:

It is a matter for the Belgian authorities to decide whether to bring charges against Hissene Habre in accordance with Belgian law, and whether to request his extradition from Senegal. However, I can confirm that Mr. Habre was detained in Dakar on 15 November pending a Court of Appeal judgment on the merits of the Belgian extradition request. While the request is still under consideration, it is our policy not to pre-judge the outcome of the judicial deliberations.

(HC Deb 22 November 2005 Vol. 439 c1990W)

6/109

In a written answer, a Minister wrote:

The Government takes all allegations of war crimes and crimes against humanity very seriously and is fully committed to its obligations under international law, which it has implemented through the Geneva Conventions Act 1957, the International Criminal Court Act 2001 and section 134 of the Criminal Justice Act 1988.

The prosecution of particular cases in England and Wales is a matter for the police and the Crown Prosecution Service. The recent successful trial of Faryadi Zardad, found guilty in July 2005 of torture and hostage taking in Afghanistan, demonstrated the commitment on the part of the police and CPS to pursue major war crimes cases.

(HC Deb 28 November 2005 Vol. 440 c49W–50W)

6/110

Armenian Massacre

During a debate in the House of Lords, an FCO Minister said:

I say unequivocally that what took place [the massacre of Armenians at the hands of the Turkish authorities in 1915, Ed.] was by any standards an atrocity of the first order. The judgment required under the United Nations Convention [against Genocide] is that it can be demonstrated that a state had intent. That is the element that the lawyers have concluded is not shown in this case. That is why the difference is made. However, that does not alter the fact that every nation responsible for atrocities on such a scale needs to face them, think about them and consider what can be done or said to help to heal some of the wound that was caused, even if some time ago.

(HL Deb 14 July 2005 Vol. 673 c1212)

6/111

In a written answer, an FCO Minister wrote:

There is no consensus among EU member states that the [Armenian] massacres of 1915–16 should be categorised as genocide as defined by the 1948 UN Convention on Genocide and there is no reference to the issue in the Negotiating Framework agreed by EU member states that will guide Turkey's accession negotiations. The Turkish government does not accept that there was any intention or act that constituted genocide.

We welcomed open discussion of this and related matters at a recent conference in Istanbul, and the Turkish Foreign Minister's statement to that conference expressing hope that research into the era could improve relations between Turkey and Armenia. It was also welcome that, on 9 March, the Turkish Prime Minister and the leader of the main opposition party called for an impartial investigation into the 'genocide' allegations by Turkish and Armenian historians under the supervision of an international organisation such as the United Nations Educational Scientific and Cultural Organisation. The Armenian President, however, rejected the proposal on the grounds that establishing diplomatic relations was a necessary prior step.

(HC Deb 17 October 2005 Vol. 437 c733W)

6/112

In a written answer, an FCO Minister wrote:

The long-standing position of the Government is well known. The Government acknowledge the strength of feeling about this terrible episode of history and recognise the [Armenian] massacres of 1915–16 as a tragedy. However, neither this Government nor previous governments have judged that the evidence is sufficiently unequivocal to persuade us that these events should be categorised as genocide as defined by the 1948 UN Convention on Genocide.

(HC Deb 28 October 2005 Vol. 438 c624W)

6/113

Darfur

The Government was asked if the International Commission of Inquiry into the situation in Darfur had uncovered any evidence which would allow trials to proceed in the UK or in other States giving effect to the UN Convention against Torture. An FCO Minister wrote:

It is for the national prosecution services of the United Kingdom to decide whether there is sufficient evidence to prosecute here those referred to in the International Commission of Inquiry's report under the convention against torture. The situation in Darfur was referred to the International Criminal Court (ICC) by a United Nations Security Council Resolution on 31 March. The UK sponsored this resolution, and we believe that the ICC is the best judicial mechanism to deal with the perpetrators of the crimes in Darfur.

(HL Deb 6 April 2005 Vol. 671 cWA114)

6/114

The Government was asked what progress has been made towards encouraging an end to impunity for those committing attacks against humanitarian workers in Darfur. An FCO Minister wrote:

We condemn the recent attacks against humanitarian workers in Darfur. Many of these attacks appear to be the result of opportunistic banditry and general lawlessness. The African Union mission in Darfur has made a positive impact on security in the areas in which it has deployed and we fully support its expansion as the best way of addressing the security situation in Darfur. We continue to make clear to the Government of Sudan that it is their responsibility to provide security for all their people, and to actively pursue those who breach the law. We have made clear to all parties that attacks against humanitarian workers are in violation of international humanitarian law and it is imperative that those responsible are brought to justice. UN Security Council Resolution 1591, adopted on 29 March, allows for sanctions to be brought against those who commit violations of international humanitarian or human rights law or other atrocities. And Resolution 1593, which we sponsored on 31 March, referred the situation in Darfur to the International Criminal Court. Both these Resolutions provide a means towards addressing the impunity which has been prevalent in Darfur to date; we will follow their impact closely.

The government was asked further what assessment it has made of reports that the Government of Sudan continues to arm and supply the Janjaweed forces in Darfur.

The Minister wrote also:

The report of the International Commission of Inquiry stated that, in the past, the Government of Sudan has armed and operated in close co-ordination with a number of militias in Darfur. The latest report by the UN Secretary-General states that the Government of Sudan has made some progress in reining in its allied militias, but has failed to prevent continuing acts of banditry and attacks on civilians by other armed groups. We continue to make clear to the Government of Sudan that it bears the primary responsibility for security in Darfur, and that it must rein in and neutralise these armed militias, as it committed to doing in the Abuja Security Protocol.

The government was asked further what assessment it has made of the impact of the UN Security Council's referral of the situation in Darfur to the International Criminal Court upon the behaviour of the Government of Sudan.

The Minister wrote also:

The Government of Sudan appear to be taking the referral of the situation in Darfur to the International Criminal Court (ICC) seriously. Since UN Security Council Resolution 1593 referred the situation in Darfur to the International Criminal Court on 31 March, the UN Secretary-General has concluded, in his monthly report on the situation in Darfur in April, that there were no incidents of regular Government forces attacking either rebel groups or civilians, and that they had made no hostile use of aircraft. We understand that the Government have established a legal committee to study how it [*sic*] can co-operate with the ICC. We continue to press the Government, and all parties in Sudan, to address the problems within their own judicial system; to co-operate fully with the ICC; and to ensure that those responsible for crimes in Darfur are brought to justice.

(HC Deb 25 May 2005 Vol. 434 c134–136W)

6/115

The Government was asked:
what criteria it used to establish that what has taken place in Darfur is not genocide; and in what ways such criteria differed from those used by the United States State Department, and the governments of Canada and Germany. An FCO Minister wrote:

There is no doubt that violations of international humanitarian and human rights law have been committed in Darfur. We have consistently made clear that the perpetrators of these terrible crimes must be brought to justice.

The UK applies the definition of genocide given in the International Criminal Court Act 2001. Under the Act, "genocide" is defined by reference to Article 6 of the Rome Statute of the International Criminal Court, as certain acts "committed with intent to destroy, in whole or in part, a national, ethnical, racial or religious group". This mirrors the language contained in the 1948 United Nations Convention on the Prevention and Punishment of the Crime of Genocide, particularly Article 2. The UK, Canada and Germany are party to the Rome Statute and, together with the US, to the Genocide Convention. It is up to individual countries to choose how to interpret and apply these definitions.

The UK did not have sufficient evidence to judge whether the crimes perpetrated in Sudan were undertaken with the intent necessary to constitute genocide.

For this reason, we pressed for the Secretary-General of the United Nations to establish an expert international commission of inquiry (ICI) to investigate reports, of violations of international humanitarian and human rights law in Darfur in 2004, and to determine whether genocide had occurred. The ICI's report, issued to the Security Council on 31 January 2005, concluded that the government of Sudan (GoS) did not appear to have pursued a policy of genocide in Darfur and that, while individuals may have done so, this was a determination which only a competent court could make. The conclusion that no genocidal policy had been pursued by the GoS in no way detracted from the gravity of the crimes committed, including crimes against humanity and/or war crimes. The UK played a leading role in sponsoring UN Security Council Resolution 1593 (2005) of 31 March, in which the Security Council referred the situation in Darfur to the International Criminal Court (ICC)—as recommended by the ICCI. The prosecutor of the ICC announced a formal investigation on 6 June.

(HL Deb 27 June 2005 Vol. 673 cWA9)

Part Six: X. *The Position of the Individual (including the Corporation) in International Law—Responsibility of the Individual*

(See also **Part Thirteen**)

6/116

The following statement was made on behalf of the European Union at the Informal meeting of the plenary to discuss the revised text of the Draft

Outcome Document of the High-level Plenary Meeting of the General Assembly, 28 July–2 August, 2005, General Assembly (New York):

The EU strongly endorses the statement made by the Secretary-General in Madrid in March this year that terrorism is unacceptable under any circumstances and in any culture. The Summit must send a forceful message on terrorism and initiate more concerted action to combat it. It has been five months since the Secretary-General launched a UN counter-terrorism strategy: how can our leaders say only that they are ready to "consider" it? We must explicitly endorse the strategy and its five basic pillars and agree that we will implement it. And we must agree to conclude a comprehensive convention on international terrorism, at the latest during the sixtieth session of the General Assembly, including a legal definition of terrorist acts.

Our efforts to combat terrorism must be carried out in full conformity with international law and should always adhere to the fundamental principle of respect for human rights. In addition, more emphasis should be given to protection for victims and the need to strengthen the verification, monitoring and enforcement capacities of the Security Council in its role on Counter-Terrorism.

...

We must reaffirm that proliferation of weapons of mass destruction and their means of delivery is a threat to international peace and security. We must reaffirm our support to the Treaty and its centrality to our policy, drawing attention to the potential implications for international peace and security of withdrawal from the NPT and we should urge the adoption of measures to discourage withdrawal from the Treaty. Given the importance of the Treaty on the Non-Proliferation of Nuclear Weapons for international peace and security, a withdrawal notification under article X, paragraph 1, should be qualified as being of immediate relevance to the Security Council. In addition, we should adopt the IAEA Model Additional Protocol as the standard for verification; negotiations on a Fissile Material Cut-Off Treaty should begin in the Conference on Disarmament; and we must commit to real and early implementation of Security Council Resolution 1540. We further believe that those States that forgo the nuclear fuel cycle, and meet all nuclear non-proliferation obligations, should enjoy assured access to the market for nuclear fuel and related services. In the conventional field we must commit to strong steps against the spread of Small Arms and strengthen verification and implementation, including for the BTWC.

...

Responsibility to protect
... the EU believes that international agreement on the concept of the responsibility to protect is long overdue. We cannot stand by as genocide, war crimes, ethnic cleansing or other gross violations of international humanitarian law and human rights are committed. The primary responsibility for the protection of civilian populations lies first and foremost with each individual state. That flows from the Universal Declaration of Human Rights. However, where the state in question is unable or unwilling to do so, the principle of non-interference cannot be an absolute block on action, the international community should help, and if necessary, should be able to take action where such help is refused. So let us send a clear message that the international community has the responsibility to decide

and to act through a comprehensive range of measures, including collective action through the Security Council, and in extreme cases, and out of necessity, by use of force, authorised by the Security Council. We should agree and endorse this concept in September.

(28 July 2005, text supplied by FCO)

Part Seven: Organs of the State and their Status

Part Seven: I. *Organs of the State and their Status—Heads of State*

(See also **Part Six: IX.**)

Part Seven: IV. *Organs of the State and their Status—Diplomatic missions and their members*

7/1

In answer to a question, an FCO Minister wrote:

Records held by the Foreign and Commonwealth Office indicate that there are currently 22,851 persons entitled to some degree of privilege and immunity under international agreements. Of these, 7,405 are members of diplomatic missions and 2,952 are officials of international organisations. The remainder are dependants ... it is estimated that fewer than 10 members of diplomatic missions and around 500 officials of international organisations hold British citizenship. Most have no entitlement to privileges and immunities other than immunity for official acts.

(HL Deb 10 January 2005 Vol. 668 c3WA)

7/2

In reply to a question about the diplomatic bag, an FCO Minister wrote:

Our diplomatic bag and its transit complies with Article 27 of the Vienna Convention. We have diplomatic service procedures in place to ensure compliance of the convention. These procedures are regularly reviewed in consultation with our legal, protocol and security advisers.

(HC Deb 27 January 2005 Vol. 430 c523W)

7/3

An FCO Minister made a written statement to the House of Lords. She wrote:

In light of the continuing instability in the Democratic Republic of Congo (DRC) and the fragile security situation in Kinshasa, the Government have authorised the deployment of armed guards to our British Embassy in Kinshasa in order to safeguard embassy staff and ensure the mission can continue to operate.

The Government take seriously their obligations to contribute to peace and security in the DRC. We have a development programme for the DRC worth £34 million for the financial year 2004–05. Upgrading the security of our embassy will enable staff to continue to contribute to the peace process in the DRC. The DRC Government have been informed of our intention and are content with the arrangements we propose to protect our staff.

A UN arms embargo targeting rebel groups operating in the east of the country has been in place on the DRC since 28 July 2003. An EU embargo has been in place on the country since 7 April 1993. We fully support these measures and have informed the UN DRC Sanctions Committee and EU partners of the deployment.

(HL Deb 2 February 2005 Vol. 669 c11WS)

7/4

The Government was asked on how many occasions since 1 May 1997 it has waived the immunity of British diplomats or members of their families; what the circumstances of the waiver were in each case; how many requests from foreign Governments for waivers were turned down in the same period; and what the circumstances of each refusal were. An FCO Minister wrote:

We regularly waive the immunity of British diplomats to enable them to give evidence in civil or criminal matters. Details are not held centrally . . .

We have no record of any requests from foreign Governments for the waiver of diplomatic immunity from criminal jurisdiction of British diplomats or their families during the period in question.

(HC Deb 9 February 2005 Vol. 430 c1549W)

7/5

The Government was asked what progress has been made to establish an embassy in Astana, Kazakhstan; whether sites for this embassy have been identified; whether the authorities in Astana have extended support for such an embassy; and whether the decision is dependent upon co-operation from other European Union member states. An FCO Minister wrote:

A suitable location in Astana has been identified for the move of the British Embassy in Kazakhstan during the next financial year.

The Kazakh authorities have been very helpful in identifying possible sites for a British long-term presence in Astana.

We continue to discuss the matter closely with other European Union members, but the decision to establish an embassy in Astana is not dependent upon their co-operation.

(HL Deb 21 February 2005 Vol. 669 c156WA)

7/6

The Government was asked whether it was content for a person accredited to a national diplomatic mission in the United Kingdom to hold the citizenship of a country other than that of the mission concerned; if so, whether such persons are also required to hold the citizenship of the country from which they are accredited; and whether they will list those national diplomatic missions where they believe any of those accredited hold citizenship of countries other than that of the mission. An FCO Minister wrote:

The Vienna Convention on Diplomatic Relations 1961 provides that a country may freely appoint its own nationals as members of the diplomatic staff of its diplomatic mission. However, the consent of the receiving state is required where a person is a national of the country he is appointed to represent and also a national of the receiving country or is a national only of the receiving state. Whether or not a person holds the citizenship of a third country is not relevant to his or her acceptance as a member of a mission. The Foreign and Commonwealth Office would not consider British nationality a bar to the appointment of a person to the diplomatic mission of a country of which they are also nationals ... we estimate that fewer than 10 members of diplomatic missions in London hold British citizenship ...

The Vienna Convention on Diplomatic Relations 1961 also provides that receiving states may reserve the right to consent to the appointment of a third country national, who is not also a national of the sending country, to the diplomatic staff of a mission. Any such request would be considered on its merits. The Foreign and Commonwealth Office is not aware of any current appointments that would fall into this category.

The appointment of other categories of staff (administrative and technical and service) at diplomatic missions is not subject to any nationality considerations.

(HL Deb 21 March 2005 Vol. 671 cWA6)

7/7

In a written answer, an FCO Minister wrote:

We are not aware of any offences committed overseas in 2004 by UK nationals holding diplomatic immunity.

(HC Deb 11 October 2005 Vol. 437 c460W)

7/8

The Government was asked what steps it has taken to advise diplomatic missions to the UK that the congestion charge does not constitute a form of direct taxation under the Vienna Convention. In reply, the Foreign Secretary wrote:

We informed all missions by Note Verbale in March 2002 of our sustained view that there were no legal grounds to exempt diplomatic missions from payment of the congestion charge. Since then, in formal and informal exchanges, we have informed missions of our view that the congestion charge does not constitute a form of direct taxation under the Vienna Convention, but is a charge analogous to a motorway toll, and that they are expected to pay.

(HC Deb 10 November 2005 Vol. 439 c745W)

7/9

In a written answer, an FCO Minister wrote:

British diplomatic and consular staff working in Iraq are required under the Vienna conventions on diplomatic and consular relations to respect the laws of the host state, but in most cases they are immune from its jurisdiction, although such immunity can be waived by the sending state.

All non-Iraqi contractors working in Iraq for the US and UK Governments are required to respect the laws of Iraq, except that by virtue of Coalition Provisional Authority (CPA) Order No 17 (Revised) they are not subject to Iraqi laws or regulations in matters relating to the terms and conditions of their contracts. Such contractors are immune from the jurisdiction of the Iraqi courts with respect to acts performed pursuant to the terms and conditions of their contract, but this immunity may be waived by the state which has employed the contractor.

CPA Order 17 also confers immunity from Iraqi jurisdiction on non-Iraqi nationals employed by the US and UK Governments as consultants to the Government of Iraq and on military personnel forming part of the Multi-National Force in Iraq. Such persons are, however, required to respect the laws of Iraq and their immunity may be waived by the sending state.

If a contractor of British nationality, or a British diplomat or consultant, were to commit a criminal offence in Iraq, it is possible that in some circumstances he could be prosecuted in this country. This will depend on whether extra-territorial jurisdiction exists for the offence under English law. Members of the British armed forces remain subject to military law and the criminal law of England and Wales at all times.

(HC Deb 7 December 2005 Vol. 440 c1396W)

7/10

In a written answer, an FCO Minister wrote:

The Government cannot introduce a policy of wheel clamping of diplomatic vehicles as this would be in breach of International Law. Article 31.1 of the Vienna Convention on Diplomatic Relations 1961 states that

> "A diplomatic agent shall enjoy immunity from the criminal jurisdiction of the receiving State."

Provision for exemption from wheel clamping is also made for owners of vehicles with "D" plates under Section 70 of the Road Traffic Act 1991.

(HC Deb 19 December 2005 Vol. 440 c2478W)

Part Seven: VIII. *Organs of the State and their Status—Armed forces*

7/11

In response to a written question, a Minister wrote:

The UK military police have lawful authority to arrest an individual suspected of a criminal offence if that person is subject to UK military law. The power is set out in the Service Discipline Acts. The United States visiting force is not subject to the Service Discipline Acts.

Under Article VII of the Agreement regarding the Status of Forces of the parties to the North Atlantic Treaty (SOFA), the United States visiting force stationed in the United Kingdom have the right to police the premises which they occupy and may take all appropriate measures to ensure the maintenance of order and security on such premises. Where there are no United States policing and security forces present, or a significant threat exists from demonstrator activity, the United States forces have agreed that the Ministry of Defence Police (MDP) can undertake the policing task on their behalf.

The MDP is a statutory British police force with constabulary powers as defined in the MDP Act 1987, as amended by the Anti-Terrorism, Crime and Security Act 2001. Although the MDP can exercise these constabulary powers, incidents solely involving United States visiting force personnel and associated civilians will normally be handled by the United States authorities in accordance with SOFA.

(HC Deb 14 December 2005 Vol. 440 c2043W–2044W)

Part Eight: Jurisdiction of the State

Part Eight: I. B. *Jurisdiction of the State—Bases of jurisdiction—Personal principle*

8/1

In a written answer, a Minister wrote:

The Foreign and Commonwealth Office (FCO) leads on engaging with British companies overseas. It has developed guidance explaining the effect of part 12 of the Anti-Terrorism, Crime and Security (ATCS) Act 2001. This Act gives UK courts jurisdiction over certain offences of bribery and corruption committed overseas by UK companies or nationals and gives UK companies a strong defence against attempts to extort bribes from them. DFID works closely with other UK Government departments, (including the FCO, the Home Office, HM Treasury, the Department for Trade and Industry and the Attorney General's Office) on anti-corruption activities, including raising awareness of the provisions of the ATCS act. We have a productive relationship with the Infrastructure sector Anti-Corruption Forum and the British Consultants and Construction Bureau.

(HC Deb 28 October 2005 Vol. 438 c624W)

Part Eight: II. B. *Jurisdiction of the State—Types of jurisdiction—Jurisdiction to adjudicate*

8/2

In a written answer, an FCO Minister wrote:

The case [C-105/3 *Mario Pupino*] concerned a request for a preliminary ruling from an Italian criminal court, in which the Court of Justice was asked to rule on the scope of the framework decision on the standing of victims in criminal proceedings. The court had jurisdiction to give such a ruling because Italy had accepted the jurisdiction of the court by a declaration under Article 35 (2) of the Treaty of European Union.

The UK has not made a declaration giving the court jurisdiction in such cases so there could not be a similar reference from a UK court.

(HL Deb 6 July 2005 Vol. 673 cWA110)

Part Eight: III. A. *Jurisdiction of the State—Extra-territorial exercise of jurisdiction—General*

8/3

In a written answer, a Minister wrote:

The UK Government oppose all assertions of extraterritorial jurisdiction by other states on UK individuals and/or companies.

The European Commission has competence for dealing with extraterritorial measures taken by third countries against EU member states. Council Regulation EC 2271/96 was introduced by the EU in 1996 to offer protection to EU individuals and companies against extraterritorial legislation including the Helms-Burton Act and the Iran/Libya Sanctions Act, both of which are explicitly extraterritorial in content and whose adoption in the US prompted the introduction of the above so-called blocking legislation.

In the same year, the UK ratified the EU regulation by means of an amendment to the UK Protection of Trading Interests Act 1980. Both pieces of legislation are designed to protect Community interests by making it illegal for its individuals and companies to comply with US extraterritorial demands. Further, under the terms of the legislation, UK companies are obliged to inform HMG and the European Commission of any extraterritorial action taken against them in order that appropriate protective measures can be taken.

In May 1998, following lengthy negotiations between the EU and the US in which the UK played a prominent part, an understanding was reached. The EU agreed to suspend action in the World Trade Organisation against the extraterritorial aspects of Helms-Burton in exchange for an EU-wide exemption by the US from the extraterritorial elements of the Act.

The US continues to introduce new legislation with extraterritorial effect and to apply extraterritorial provisions to certain of its exports. The Government will continue to place pressure on the US to adhere to multilateral trade rules, which assert that the prevailing precepts for deciding the limits of a sovereign state's jurisdiction are the territorial and nationality principles.

UK trade officials are in close contact with Commission officials with responsibility for the dossier and meet them when cases of extraterritoriality against UK individuals or companies are reported, in order that appropriate, protective steps can be taken.

(HL Deb 21 July 2005 Vol. 673 cWA277–WA278)

8/4

In a speech, "How far can laws reach? The problem of extraterritoriality" given by the Attorney General at the IBA Annual Conference, Prague 28 September 2005, he said:

... this programme on extra-territoriality is very timely as this is a topic of increasing importance and topicality in the criminal sphere as well as in the civil sphere. The cross border enforcement of the law is an increasingly important issue. I want to look at this from my perspective as Attorney General in the UK.

We must start by recognising that extra-territoriality is not, and should not be, a free-for-all. Whether a State can take extra-territorial jurisdiction over a matter is not a mere question of choice. Jurisdictional competence is a matter regulated by international law. The general rule is that states do not seek to exercise jurisdiction over foreign nationals in foreign states. Of course, like all general rules there are exceptions, some of which are generally accepted and others which are more controversial. But although jurisdiction is based on state sovereignty it is not co-extensive with it. As that seminal international law text book "Oppenheim's International Law" says: the fact that "jurisdiction is based on sovereignty does not mean that each state has in international law a sovereign right to exercise jurisdiction in whatever circumstances it chooses. . . . What one State may see as the exercise of its sovereign right of jurisdiction another state may see as an infringement of its own sovereign rights of territorial or personal authority". [p. 457]

Nevertheless it is important that we recognise the need for extra-territorial jurisdiction in some cases. In an increasingly globalised world where it is easy for the effects of wrong conduct done in one country to reach and to be felt in different countries there may be a need for extra-territorial jurisdiction so that we can tackle effectively international wrongdoing. This can apply both to the civil and criminal fields.

Let me turn firstly, but very briefly, to the issue of the civil law. There are a number of areas where the issue arises. For example, laws that effectively deter and penalise anti-competitive collusion between businesses and abuses of market power play an important part in developing efficient and competitive open market economies. It goes without saying that as a result, States have a strong mutuality of interest in the development and enforcement of effective competition laws. Nevertheless, it is important that Governments and the Courts develop arrangements for effective cooperation in enforcing our respective competition laws and minimise conflicts in their application. There are a number of things that can help in that respect:

1) Bringing our laws closer together—the trend in recent years has been for laws in this area to draw on other states' experience in operating their laws. The closer our laws get the less likelihood there is of conflict.

2) Having due regard to the accepted principles of international law, both private and public, including the principle that some connection (views differ as to how much) between the state and the purported defendant is necessary.

3) Developing arrangements for mutual cooperation in the enforcement of law e.g. the EC/US Cooperation Agreements of 1991 and 1998. Continued dialogue and cooperation is the best way of encouraging a degree of self restraint and consideration of the position in other states.

4) Having regard to the principles of comity when developing, interpreting and applying legislation.

The question arises as to what can be done in those circumstances where extra-territorial jurisdiction is asserted in circumstances which we would not consider to be appropriate or consistent with international law. We have not been slow as a Government in objecting to some exercises by the USA of extra-territorial jurisdiction. We have protested even in the Supreme Court and so we have submitted Amicus briefs in appropriate cases. We welcome the approach that those courts have taken in reining back those cases.

In the criminal sphere different considerations apply, terrorism, money laundering, trafficking of drugs and people, internet fraud are all examples of the truly global nature of crime today. Increased mutual legal assistance and improved extradition procedures are essential in order effectively to combat organised and serious crime by helping to avoid a situation where it is possible to evade justice by fleeing the state with territorial jurisdiction over an offence. But they do not offer a complete solution. The ability to prosecute in relation to certain conduct which has taken place outside one's borders is now an essential element in the pursuit of justice and the rule of law.

This does give rise to acute problems of dealing with competing claims to jurisdiction. Offences committed in more than one jurisdiction provide particular challenges for the prosecutor. At present we have a case in the UK where three British defendants whose extradition has been requested by the US in a cross border fraud are judicially reviewing the decision of the UK investigator not to prosecute them in the UK. In particular they claim that there is a prima facie right to be tried in one's own country where the offence is justiciable there. They also claim that the UK prosecutor has a duty to consider whether their rights under Article 8 of the ECHR (the right to private and family life) would be breached by their extradition. Such arguments, if accepted, would undermine the principles of national comity and international extradition arrangements. The prosecutor will argue that it is a proper exercise of discretion for a prosecutor to decide that it is more appropriate for the prosecution to take place elsewhere. He will also argue that a decision not to investigate an individual here does not involve a violation of Article 8. Where extradition is justified in the prevention of crime, the fact that the defendant's family life will be interfered with will never amount to a violation of his rights. We believe this argument will succeed, but this case is a good illustration of the satellite litigation that can result where defendants fight to avoid facing trial abroad for offences allegedly committed in more than one jurisdiction.

(www.lslo.gov.uk/speeches.htm) (See also **6/107**)

8/5

During a General Assembly meeting, the representative for the European Union said:

The European Union believes that the United States trade policy towards Cuba is fundamentally a bilateral issue. Notwithstanding this, the European Union and its member States have been clearly expressing their opposition to the extraterritorial extension of the United States embargo, such as that contained in the Cuban Democracy Act of 1992 and the Helms-Burton Act of 1996.

In November 1996, the Council of Ministers of the European Union adopted a regulation and a joint action to protect the interests of natural or legal persons resident in the European Union against the extraterritorial effects of the Helms-Burton legislation, which prohibits compliance with that legislation. Moreover, on 18 May 1998, at the European Union/United States summit held in London, a package was agreed covering waivers to titles III and IV of the Helms-Burton Act, a commitment by the United States administration to resist future extraterritorial legislation of that kind and an understanding with respect to disciplines for the strengthening of investment protection. The European Union continues to urge the United States to implement its side of the 18 May 1998 understanding.

(UN Doc. A/60/PV.45, 8 November 2005)

8/6

In a written answer, an FCO Minister wrote:

The Export Control Act (2002) introduced comprehensive controls on the brokering of all equipment on the UK's Military List where any part of the activity takes place in the UK. In addition, where a UN or full-scope EU, Organisation for Security and Co-operation in Europe or UK national arms embargo is in place, these controls extend extra-territorially to UK nationals wherever they are.

The Government continues to believe that, given the very real concerns about conflict of jurisdiction, and over administration and enforcement, extra-territorial controls should only be applied to the most sensitive transfers. The Government believes that, in most cases, multilateral action remains the most effective way to combat the illicit and irresponsible trade in small arms and light weapons. This approach is at the heart of our support for the UN Programme of Action on small arms and light weapons, and for a treaty on the international arms trade.

(HC Deb 21 November 2005 Vol. 439 c1582W)

Part Nine: State Territory

Part Nine: II. A. *State Territory—Boundaries and frontiers—Delimitation*

9/1

The Government was asked if [it] will list those areas of *(a)* current and *(b)* prospective EU member states where border definition is in dispute. A Minister wrote:

Border definition (ie the demarcation of borders between two internationally recognised sovereign states with an adjoining territorial or maritime border) is politically disputed as follows:

(a) Current EU states:
Greece—Turkey (eastern Aegean)
Ireland—UK (Lough Foyle, Carlingford Lough—quiescent)
Portugal—Spain (Olivenza)
Slovenia—Croatia (Piran Bay/Dragonja River and Sveta Gera/Trvdin Vrh)
Spain—UK (Isthmus Gibraltar)
Spain—Morocco (Ceuta, Melilla)

(b) Prospective EU states (in addition to those listed above):
Macedonia—Serbia and Montenegro (Kosovo: north west Shara Mountain region and Kudra Fura elevation)
Romania—Ukraine (Serpent's Island)*
Turkey—Armenia

In addition, Cyprus joined the EU as a divided island on 1 May 2004. The EU acquis is suspended in northern Cyprus which Turkey recognises as the so-called "Turkish Republic of Northern Cyprus".

(HC Deb 13 January 2005 Vol. 429 c637W)

[* In fact, Romania recognised Ukraine's claim to Serpent Island in 1997. There is a continuing dispute about maritime boundaries which is presently before the ICJ, See www.icj-cij.org (Press release 2004/31), Ed.]

9/2

The Secretary of State for International Development told the House of Commons:

The UK's position on the border question between Ethiopia and Eritrea remains that the boundary commission decision is final and binding, and that both parties should discuss the issues that separate them.

(HC Deb 29 June 2005 Vol. 435 c1279)

Part Nine: II. B. *State Territory—Boundaries and frontiers—Demarcation*

(See also **Part Fourteen: II.G.1.**)

Part Nine: II. C. *State Territory—Boundaries and frontiers—Stability*

9/3

The Government was asked about its position on the Eritrea/Ethiopia boundary dispute. An FCO Minister wrote:

Our assessment is that neither side wants a return to war, but it is correct to say that there is always a danger that a small spark on the border will reignite the conflict. Our approach is based on three principles: no return to war; that the findings of the boundary commission are binding; and that dialogue between the two parties must take place.

Professor Lauterpacht, who was the chairman of the Eritrea-Ethiopia boundary commission, has said that any issue can be discussed, provided that both parties agree. We think that that should happen, and that is the view that we are making clear to all parties, including the Eritreans.

. . .

A settlement of this dispute will require both sides to move. We welcome the recent movement by the Ethiopians, which we had been urging upon them. In due course they may have to make some further concessions. At the moment it would be welcome to have some sign from Eritrea that it is willing to engage in discussions. So far there have been no such signs from Eritrea.

(HC Deb 25 January 2005 Vol. 430 c146–147)

Part Nine: III. A. *State Territory—Acquisition and transfer of territory—Acquisition*

9/4

The Government was asked if [it] will make a statement on *(a)* the circumstances in which the Government of Mauritius told his Department that the Mauritius Shipping Company cancelled a visit to Diego Garcia for Chagossians and *(b)* the implementation of his undertaking to Chagossians that they be allowed to visit ancestral graves in the British Indian Ocean Territory. An FCO Minister replied:

The British High Commission in Mauritius was informed in November 2004 by the Mauritius Shipping Corporation (MSC), a parastatal company, that the M/V Trochetia would be available for a visit to the British Indian Ocean Territory to take place in April. A provisional booking of the vessel was made on 29 December. In the meantime, I had written to the Mauritian Foreign Minister on 13 December to inform him of the visit and that we were entering into negotiation with the MSC. On 7 January the MSC informed the British High Commission that the M/V Trochetia could not be made available, and the Prime Minister of Mauritius told me on 13 January that it was he who had personally intervened to prevent its use because he felt it would undermine Mauritius' claim to sovereignty.

My officials are seeking to make alternative arrangements to enable the visit to go ahead.

(HC Deb 26 January 2005 Vol. 430 c427W)

Part Nine: III. B. *State Territory—Acquisition and transfer of territory—Transfer*

Part Eleven: Seas and Vessels

Part Eleven: II. *Seas and Vessels—Territorial sea*

11/1

Opposing a motion to annul the South-west Territorial Waters (Prohibition of Pair Trawling) Order 2004, a Minister said:

Let me point out two or three things about the debate. First, everybody recognised that there is a problem with dolphin, cetacean, by-catch. We should do something about that. Secondly, everybody recognised that although it would be better to do something on a Community basis, the UK Government have some responsibility. Thirdly, everybody recognised that pair trawling is not a desirable practice in these fisheries. There is rather more common ground in this debate than might have been assumed at the beginning.

Perhaps I may explain the Government's position—which ends up looking bizarre because we are planning the introduction of statutory instruments to ban UK vessels from participating in a fishery while other member states are allowed to continue.

Our research first identified a problem in the pair trawl fishery in 2001. We have been trying to make progress in reducing the by-catch. . . . we have invested a fair amount of research money in trying to find a system of separation, a grid that would limit that by-catch. It appeared that that device might have the potential to reduce significantly the number of dolphins caught by the fishery. Regrettably, those experiments were disappointing. They showed clearly that the exclusion grid would not present an early or immediate solution to the problem.

There is long-term potential for a solution, as Community legislation now requires observer schemes to be set up, particularly for pelagic fisheries. The data collected from those, once undisputed, could lead to Community action. However, that review will not take place until 2007–08. On the basis of the data we have available, and certainly with the assumptions on the French catch as well, there is a significant threat to dolphin stocks and numbers.

... the RIA made it clear that as this is a fishery where the majority of vessels are from other member states, if we take the total fishery, Community action would be desirable. We applied to the Commission in July 2004 to use those provisions for an emergency closure of pelagic pair trawl fishing for bass in the English Channel. We felt that we had presented the Commission with a substantial case, given all the scientific information that had been assembled by the UK.

But, as has been said, regrettably the Commission did not accept our case or regard it as sufficient for an immediate closure. It acknowledged that considerable efforts were being made to try to find a solution and we are continuing to pursue these options with the Commission.

However ... there is a considerable and wide concern, not least in the south-west, about the effects of such fishing on the dolphin. It was necessary, therefore, in default of a Community approach, for the UK to consider what we could do ourselves at least to limit the damage that was being caused. To demonstrate that, we decided to use what are, effectively, the only powers available to us in the CFP, and to take action within the 12 nautical mile zone of the south-west coast of England, in our own territorial waters, to ban the practice for this year's fishing season ...

At the same time, we had applied to the Commission to have the UK ban extended—which the Commission would have powers to do—to all pair trawlers in that 12-mile zone. Under long-established arrangements, France and Belgium have historic rights of access to this zone and, although there are only a limited number of French vessels making use of those rights, there remained the potential for them to make greater use of the zone. They form a larger element than the UK vessels.

We made it clear that this would be an interim step in moving towards a co-ordinated Community-level project but, even on that limited basis, the Commission was not prepared to accept the extension to non-British trawlers. We were disappointed that it was not prepared to do so but we still considered that we would do what was within our powers—and for which the Commission's permission was not required—and that was to limit fishing in that form in the fishery for UK vessels.

Obviously this is not a particularly satisfactory position. It is not one which endangers the south-west fisheries or the Scottish fisheries, which are also involved in this—Scottish boats fish in that area—to the extent that some people are claiming. Nevertheless, it is, in one sense, discriminatory and aimed at UK vessels. But the UK vessels are the only ones which, under the rules of the CFP, we can limit within this area.

It is important to recognise that although the Commission has rejected immediate action in this area it recognises the problem. It is therefore legitimate for us to say . . . that this is the first step in establishing, first within the British control zone and then within the whole of the fishery, a move to limit all boats from trawling in this way, with its knock-on effect on dolphins and other species.

If there is a step that we can take, we should take it. We have taken a step. It is a very limited step but we believe it demonstrates our determination to do something. It is one which, for all the criticism from all sides, it is essential for us to take if we are to convince others to take it.

. . . [There had not been a satisfactory response from France to an offer of bilateral negotiations.] If we are not going to reach a bilateral arrangement with the French our best bet is, therefore, to go through the Commission, which is more sympathetic. Yet the Commission is not prepared to take immediate action until it has more evidence. We are working on establishing the further evidence we need.

(HL Deb 2 March 2005 Vol. 670 c338–340)

11/2

The Government was asked what action it is taking to protect coral reefs and sea-mounts in UK territorial waters. A Minister wrote:

Reefs are included in annex I of the EC Habitats Directive and the UK has designated 33 Natura sites in territorial waters under article 4 of the directive which have reefs listed as a feature of interest. These are biogenic and rocky reefs rather than coral reefs given available data on the nature and distribution of reefs in UK territorial waters. However, the UK's statutory nature advisers will be investigating whether there are further occurrences of marine habitats listed in annex I that meet the criteria in annex III of the directive as part of a wider exercise in which EC member states are working with the European Commission to extend the Habitats Directive into the marine environment.

In 1999 a habitat action plan for *Lophelia pertusa* reefs was published as part of the UK Biodiversity Action Plan (*UKBAP*). The objectives of the action plan are to protect the distribution and status of the *Lophelia pertusa* reefs to enhance their density and community richness.

The UK is also working through OSPAR's Biodiversity Committee to identify species (and habitats) in need of protection. *Lophelia pertusa* reefs have been classified as a priority habitat, OSPAR is currently investigating possible management measures. There are no known occurrences of seamounts in UK territorial waters.

(HC Deb 3 March 2005 Vol. 431 c1299W)

11/3

In a written answer, a Minister wrote:

The taking of whales, dolphins and porpoises is prohibited in EU and UK waters. In addition to EU measures adopted in 2004 to tackle the threat to small cetaceans from incidental capture in fisheries operating in Community waters, the UK has also put in place measures to protect common dolphins through a prohibition on pelagic pair trawl fishing for bass within 12 nautical miles of the south-west coast

(HC Deb 11 July 2005 Vol. 436 c645W)

Part Eleven: VI. *Seas and Vessels—Exclusive economic zone, exclusive or preferential fisheries zones*

11/4

A Minister made the following statement to the House of Lords:

[The Government are] inviting applications for petroleum licences for unlicensed seaward blocks which will form the 23rd round of offshore petroleum licensing. These blocks are located in the strategic environmental assessment (SEA) areas 1–5 ... Strategic Environmental Assessment (SEA)—Post Adoption Procedures

The DTI's draft plan to offer licences for offshore oil and gas exploration and production through a 23rd licensing round was the subject of a strategic environmental assessment (SEA) initiated in 2003. The SEA is documented on a dedicated website (www.offshore-sea.org.uk) and includes commissioned reports on various components of the natural environment, cultural features and socio-economic considerations. In addition, as part of the SEA new information was collected, for example, on selected seabed features through sea-floor mapping, sampling and photography, and on the offshore behaviour of seals by means of satellite tagging. The draft plan for the 23rd licensing round included offering blocks within the area to the east of Scotland, and also in those areas that had been subject to earlier DTI SEAs (SEAs 1, 2, 3, and 4) which covered the remaining parts of the UK North Sea exclusive economic zone and the UK EEZ to the north and west of Orkney and Shetland.

The potential implications of the exploration and production activities which could follow if the draft plan was adopted were considered at an expert assessment workshop and a stakeholder workshop. The results of these workshops were assessed further and documented in an environmental report which then formed the basis for consultation with the consultation bodies and the public. The initiation of a three month consultation period on the DTI's draft plan and environmental report was advertised in a number of local and national newspapers and by e-mail notification to a wide range of individuals and organisations.

All responses received from statutory and other consultees on the draft plan and the environmental report have been considered by the DTI and a post-consultation report for SEA 5 has been prepared and placed on the SEA website. This summarises consultee comments and DTI responses to them. The full texts of consultee comments have also been placed on the SEA website.

In deciding to proceed with a 23rd offshore licensing round the DTI has considered the conclusions and recommendations of the SEA 5 environmental report together with feedback received from consultees. As a result of the SEA process, a number of blocks are being withheld from licensing for the present on environmental grounds . . .

Licensing of these blocks may be revisited in the future; for example, as more information on the features of interest becomes available. In addition, a number of blocks may be licensed but with conditions attached restricting or prohibiting marine activities. It should be noted that the Offshore Petroleum Production and Pipe-lines (Assessment of Environmental Effects) Regulations 1999 and the Offshore Petroleum Activities (Conservation of Habitats) Regulations 2001 variously require that all major activities undertaken in connection with UK offshore hydrocarbon exploration and production include environmental assessment as part of consenting.

In addition, 34 blocks will not be offered for licensing in these SEA areas at the request of the Ministry of Defence

The DTI has established an offshore oil and gas environmental monitoring committee which is charged with co-ordinating the monitoring of significant environmental effects of the industry, including those that could arise from the implementation of the plan to hold a 23rd round of offshore licensing. The results of this monitoring will be made publicly available, including through the SEA website.

(HL Deb 10 March 2005 Vol. 670 cWS42)

Part Eleven: VIII. A. *Seas and Vessels—High Seas—Freedoms of the high seas, including overflight*

11/5

During a General Assembly meeting, the representative for the European Union said:

The European Union (EU) would like to stress the importance of the principle of freedom of navigation, including the rights of innocent passage and transit passage through straits used for international navigation. In addition, port States should exercise their right with regard to access to their ports in a manner that is non-discriminatory and consistent with the United Nations Convention on the Law of the Sea and international law.

(UN Doc, A/60/PV.54, 28 November 2005)

Part Eleven: VIII. D. *Seas and Vessels—High Seas—Piracy*

11/6

The Government was asked what action it was taking to assist in the control of piracy, both within Asian international waters and in the territorial waters of Malaysia and Indonesia. An FCO Minister wrote:

The UK Government recognise the continuing threat posed by piracy attacks across the world today. The Indonesian and Malaysian archipelagos, centring in particular on the Straits of Malacca, are acknowledged as piracy hotspots.

With this in mind, the Foreign and Commonwealth Office and the Department for Transport (DfT) have a co-ordinated counter-piracy strategy and action plan designed to protect seafarers and ships from piracy attack. This includes a proactive outreach programme to assist those countries in which piracy is prevalent.

As a first step the Government, using the Foreign and Commonwealth Office global opportunities fund, recently gave a substantial contribution to the International Maritime Organisation (IMO) to help fund a Middle East regional security seminar in Yemen specifically addressing the issue of piracy. We hope to do the same for future seminars in South-East Asia.

In addition, we plan to use senior official and ministerial visits to the region to raise the issue, and to work with the IMO and other international organisations and states to encourage a more co-ordinated effort to combat the problem. The DfT is also in discussions with the IMO regarding the provision of a substantial donation of funds over the coming year to combat piracy and other related security issues in a number of countries, which include countries of concern in South-East Asia.

(HL Deb 8 June 2005 Vol. 672 cWA80)

11/7

In a written answer, an FCO Minister wrote:

We are aware of the hijacking of the merchant vessels "Semlow", "Ibn Batuta" and "MV Torgelow" in Somali waters. After being detained for some time, the "Semlow" has been released and her crew freed. The International Maritime Bureau has logged some 20 attacks on ships in Somali waters since March.

We take a very serious view of piracy along the Somali coast, but we do not believe that a UN mandate to use force would address the root causes of this problem or the wider problems of lawlessness within Somalia. We are working closely with the international community to promote the establishment of an effective government in Somalia. We believe that only by assisting the return of Somalia to stability, good governance and the rule of law can piracy, terrorism and other forms of criminal activity be brought under control.

(HL Deb 19 October 2005 Vol. 674 cWA133)

Part Eleven: XIII. *Seas and Vessels—Protection of the marine environment*

11/8

The Government was asked if [it] will make a statement on the state of the UK's coral reefs; and what future changes [are expected] due to climate change. A Minister wrote:

The UK has a small number of known cold-water coral reefs. The best studied of these is the Darwin Mounds some 150 km off the north-west coast of Scotland. When last surveyed in 2000, there was evidence of damage from bottom trawling. The UK sought, and was granted in 2003, emergency European Commission measures to restrict this type of fishing and so avoid further damage to the reef. The emergency measures were made permanent in 2004. It is hoped that surveys in 2005 will enable the condition of other possible reefs to be checked.

It is not certain what the full effects of global warming will be on the seas of the UK although it seems unlikely that warming of the seas will be great enough to affect cold-water corals in the short to medium future. Deep-water reefs are less likely to be affected.

The rise in CO_2 in the atmosphere is likely to cause a rise in acidity of surface waters, and affect the amount of calcium carbonate used by coral reefs for growth in shallow waters. How these predicted effects in shallower waters will affect deeper waters is not known, but any decreases in amounts of available calcium carbonate will not be beneficial to coral reefs.

(HC Deb 25 January 2005 Vol. 430 c209W)

11/9

In an answer to a question, a Minister said:

Carbon dioxide capture and storage technologies can play a very important role in tackling climate change but not by themselves. Those technologies will be extensively covered in the carbon abatement technology strategy, which the DTI will publish shortly. We also support work by the IPCC and international experts who are working with the EU on the basis of including those technologies under the European Emissions Trading Scheme. They are also working to resolve outstanding legal issues under the Ospar and London Conventions.

He was then asked:

... the Minister referred to the Ospar Convention ... Is it the case that it is illegal under that convention to pump sequestered carbon dioxide back into sources under the sea? Presumably, that is why the Minister said that the convention would have to be renegotiated. Why have the Norwegians therefore been allowed to do that without any renegotiation of the Ospar Convention? Why does it loom so large in the eyes of present Ministers when other countries do not seem to face the same difficulty?

The Minister replied:

[It] is right to suggest that under-ocean storage is in general illegal in most cases under the Ospar Convention. However, in relation to the enhanced oil recovery aspects—in other words, if it is part of the management of an oil or gas field—it is not illegal. The Ospar Convention is referred to in order to establish whether it could be extended to other potential sites.

(HL Deb 23 February 2005 Vol. 669 c1214–1215)

11/10

In a written answer, a Minister wrote:

The placement of materials in the maritime area (which includes geological structures under the seabed) is regulated internationally by the London Convention and the 1996 protocol to the Convention, and by the OSPAR Convention for the protection of the marine environment of the north-east Atlantic. The 1996 protocol to the London Convention is not yet in force, but has been ratified by the United Kingdom and we would expect to abide by its provisions.

The question of the compatibility of carbon dioxide placement in geological structures, including depleted or partly depleted oil and gas fields, has been discussed in both conventions. Under both conventions, there is no bar on the use of carbon dioxide for operational purposes. This implies that carbon sequestration in association with enhanced oil recovery would be permitted.

The contracting parties to the OSPAR convention agreed a position statement on carbon sequestration in 2004. This established that in other certain circumstances carbon sequestration is compatible with the convention. The position is set out in full in Annex 12 to the summary record of the 2004 meeting of the OSPAR Commission. A copy will be placed in the Library of the House, and it is also available on the OSPAR web site, www.ospar.org.

The United Kingdom raised the issue of the carbon sequestration during the 2004 consultative meeting of the parties to the London Convention. The legal position has not yet been established. It was agreed to set up an inter-sessional correspondence group to consider the legal issues raised under both the convention and the 1996 protocol. The UK is coordinating the work of this group. The issue will be discussed again at the 2005 consultative meeting in October, when results of the inter-sessional work will be considered. Any proposed project for carbon sequestration would also need to comply with relevant European directives and domestic legislation, for example in relation to the assessment of environmental impacts and to the protection of the environment.

(HC Deb 4 July 2005 Vol. 436 c3W–4W)

11/11

In a written answer, a Minister wrote:

The UK is a signatory to ASCOBANS (Agreement on the Conservation of Small Cetaceans of the Baltic, North East Atlantic, Irish and North Seas). At the 4th Meeting of Parties in 2003, Resolution 4.5 invited Parties and Range States to conduct research into the effects on small cetaceans of acoustic disturbances.

In October 2004, the Department let a contract to the Zoological Society of London to assess the feasibility of researching induced anthropogenic acoustic damage to cetaceans in British waters through the detailed examination of the auditory apparatus of stranded or by-caught animals.

As well as furthering the objectives of ASCOBANS, the work will also form a valuable contribution towards the UK's cetacean biodiversity action plans which call for studies into the effects of underwater sounds on cetacean species.

The Department also contributes to the Inter Agency Committee for Marine Science and Technology and a Crown Estate initiative which includes sound research and development in relation to piling noise for wind farms.

The Joint Nature Conservation Committee has produced guidelines for minimising acoustic disturbance to marine mammals for seismic surveys (available from www.jncc.gov.uk). It is a legal binding condition of the consent issued for seismic surveys under regulation 4 of the Petroleum Activities (Conservation of Habitats) Regulations 2001 by the Department of Trade and Industry that the JNCC guidelines must be followed at all times for all seismic surveys.

(HC Deb 5 July 2005 Vol. 436 c246W)

Part Eleven: XVIII. A.3. *Seas and Vessels—Vessels—Legal regimes—Merchant ships*

11/12

During a debate in the House of Commons, a Minister said:

Ships entered on the UK registry must demonstrate compliance with international conventions and standards, and meet all the provisions of the Merchant Shipping Act 1995 and the Merchant Shipping (Registration of Ships) Regulations 1993. A United Kingdom-registered ship is entitled to fly the red ensign, and to operate anywhere in the world. Wherever they sail, UK ships are subject to applicable domestic laws and international conventions to which the UK is a state party.

(HC Deb 11 October 2005 Vol. 437 c139)

11/13

In a written answer, a Minister wrote:

The UK's approach to the regulation of shipping is to apply international standards to ships flying its flag and to ships entering its ports or operating in UK waters. Work on reducing maritime emissions goes through the International

Maritime Organisation (IMO). At the last Maritime Environment Protection Committee (MEPC) meeting in July 2005, the United Kingdom contributed significantly to difficult negotiations on the adoption of Interim Guidelines for Voluntary Ship CO_2 Emission Indexing for Use in Trials (as well as Guidelines for On-board Exhaust Gas SOx Cleaning Systems).

Ships under the United Kingdom flag are being encouraged to participate in these trials, which will help identify a ship's greenhouse gas index where the information obtained may be used in the context of reducing CO_2 emissions.

(HC Deb 18 October 2005 Vol. 437 c855W)

Part Eleven: XVIII. C.1. *Seas and Vessels—Vessels—Jurisdiction over vessels—Flag State*

11/14

The Government was asked what plans [it] has to ban single-hulled tankers from operating in UK coastal waters. A Minister wrote:

The UK has played a key role in both the International Maritime Organisation (IMO) and the EU in negotiating an acceleration of a programme to phase out single hull tankers from world trade, while ensuring continuity of energy supply. The IMO has recently agreed to an accelerated programme, under which the large majority of single hull tankers will have been phased out by the end of 2010. Single hull tankers which will be under 25 years of age at the end of 2010 will be allowed to continue in service until the end of 2015, or on reaching age 25 if earlier, but only if they first pass a rigorous assessment of their condition. Based on the IMO agreement, there is a EU Regulation, now in force, which prohibits single hull tankers entering or leaving EU ports and anchorages when carrying heavy grades of oil as cargo.

The United Nations Convention of the Law of the Sea, to which the UK acceded in 1997, gives rights of innocent passage through territorial waters for ships which comply with internationally agreed standards governing their construction and use, which includes single hull tankers which have yet to reach their phase out date. The Secretary of State has no powers to curtail such rights, which benefit UK ships when participating in world trade.

(HC Deb 26 January 2005 Vol. 430 c350W)

11/15

The Government was asked how many wrecks of Royal Navy vessels lie in UK waters that have (a) not been legally explored, (b) been illegally explored, and (c) been legally explored. A Defence Minister wrote:

Unless a RN wreck is specifically designated under the appropriate legislation (e.g. Protection of Military Remains Act 1986, Protection of Wrecks Act 1973), no licence is needed to dive on it.

To date, a total of seventeen RN wrecks have been designated under the Protection of Military Remains Act 1986, of which twelve lie within UK waters. No licences to carry out activities on the designated wrecks have yet been issued.

Asked further what steps [were being taken] to prevent historic wrecks of Royal Navy vessels being looted by treasure hunters, he said,

Under both United Kingdom and international law wrecked military aircraft and vessels remain the property of the state, regardless of their location and condition. Such ships have sovereign immunity from interference and the state may seek enforcement of this in an appropriate court.

The Ministry of Defence uses the Protection of Military Remains Act 1986 to afford protection from unwanted interference to RN vessels wrecked after 4 August 1914, where this is considered necessary and appropriate . . .

Historic wrecks, including those of RN vessels, may also be designated under the Protection of Wrecks Act 1973. Such designations are however the responsibility of the Secretary of State for Culture, Media and Sport and the Devolved Administrations, depending on the individual wreck's location.

Asked specifically about the archaeological examination and records of any finds from HMS Sussex, he said,

All items recovered from the site, including those coins that may later be sold, will be fully recorded to appropriate professional standards. Post-fieldwork assessment and analysis will result in the creation of a post-excavation assessment report. The archaeological team may then elect to undertake specific analysis or invite or permit other scholars to do so.

It is too early to speculate on the timing of disposals. Such decisions will eventually be informed by what is recovered. Under the Licence Agreement, the Government, as owner of the wreck and artefacts, retains complete discretion to retain any artefact. A decision on the sale or retention of assets can only be taken with the benefit of far more information on the wreck, its state and contents.

(HC Deb 31 January 2005 Vol. 430 c735W)

11/16

During a General Assembly meeting, the representative for the European Union said:

The European Union attaches the highest priority to improving oceans and fisheries governance, including in areas beyond national jurisdiction.

. . .

Most importantly, we need to address the crucial issue of the genuine link between States and their flagged vessels—an issue that is much broader than IUU fishing alone. The key in that regard is that flag States must exercise effective control over ships flying their flags, taking all necessary measures to establish effective maritime administrations to ensure compliance. In that connection, the European Union looks forward to the introduction later this year, at the International Maritime Organization, of the Member State Audit Scheme.

(UN Doc, A/60/PV.54, 28 November 2005)

Part Eleven XVIII. C.2. *Seas and Vessels—Vessels—Jurisdiction over vessels—Coastal State*

11/17

The Government was asked what powers exist to regulate shipping movements within UK territorial waters; and who may exercise these powers. A Minister wrote:

The Secretary of State's statutory powers of intervention to regulate shipping in UK territorial waters can be found in Schedule 3A of the Merchant Shipping Act 1995, the Marine Safety Act 2003 which amends the 1995 Act and extends his powers, and the Dangerous Vessels Act 1985.

This gives the Secretary of State for Transport the function of giving direction for, or co-ordinating, measures to reduce risks to life or safety of a ship or ships or prevent, reduce and minimise the effects of marine pollution. The Secretary of State's Representative (SOSREP), or an officer of the Department's Maritime and Coastguard Agency acting on SOSREP's behalf, may exercise these functions, including the Secretary of State's intervention powers.

The UK implements the Convention on the International Regulations for Preventing Collisions at Sea, which, among other things, obliges ships to comply with Traffic Separation Schemes, as exists in the English Channel, which have been adopted by the International Maritime Organisation (IMO). Enforcement of these requirements is carried out by the Maritime and Coastguard Agency. Other recommendatory routeing measures, for example Areas to be Avoided and Precautionary Areas, are in place to assist safe navigation around the shores of the UK.

Any action taken by the UK to regulate shipping movements must necessarily be consistent with international law, most particularly the United Nations Convention on the Law of the Sea (UNCLOS).

(HC Deb 17 January 2005 Vol. 429 c678W)

Part Eleven XVIII. C.3. *Seas and Vessels—Vessels—Jurisdiction over vessels—Port State*

11/18

The Government was asked if it will make a statement on the latest position in respect of the ghost ships at Hartlepool, indicating what action it plans to take. A Minister wrote:

The future of the four US ships at Teesside is primarily a matter for the US Marine Administration, as owners of the vessels, and Able UK, who are intending to seek the necessary permissions for dismantling the vessels at their Teesside facility.

The four US ships are currently docked in Able UK's Graythorp dock on Teesside. Able UK submitted applications for planning permission on 18 January 2005. These applications, which include proposals for the construction and refurbishment of quays, the construction of a cofferdam and new dock gates, will be determined by the relevant planning authority, Hartlepool borough council. An application for a waste management licence is expected in the next few weeks. Any such application would be determined by the Environment Agency.

In the meantime dismantling work is prevented by a waste management licence condition. The dock facility itself is subject, as necessary, to regular inspection by the Environment Agency in liaison with the Health and Safety Executive.

(HC Deb 31 January 2005 Vol. 430 c578W)

11/19

In a written answer, a Minister wrote:

Any vessel involved in a pollution event within UK controlled waters as defined by the Merchant Shipping (Prevention of Pollution) (Limits) Regulations 1996 must immediately contact Her Majesty's coastguard and report the identity and position of the ship; the port of departure and next port of call; the number of people onboard; the date, time and details of the incident; and a contact point for further information about the cargo.

UK ships involved in an incident outside UK controlled waters but within Europe must report to the appropriate state responsible for the geographical area.

Data on reported discharges of dangerous or harmful cargoes (including oil) as defined by the internationally agreed Marine Pollution (MARPOL) Convention is collated by the Advisory Committee on Protection of the Sea (ACOPS) on behalf of the Maritime and Coastguard Agency (MCA). ACOPS collects data in addition to that reported to the coastguard.

(HC Deb 8 March 2005 Vol. 431 c1629W)

Part Twelve: Airspace, Outer Space, and Antarctica

Part Twelve: I. A. *Airspace, Outer Space, and Antarctica—Airspace—Status*

12/1

In a written answer, a Minister wrote:

UK law on civil air operations is governed by the UK's obligations under the Chicago Convention on Civil Aviation 1944. These obligations are translated into UK law principally through the Civil Aviation Act 1982 and the Air Navigation Order 2005 (S.I. 2005/1970).

Under the Convention, contracting States may for reason of emergency, military necessity or public safety, restrict or prohibit uniformly the aircraft of other States from flying over the whole or part of its territory (Article 9).

The Convention also provides that scheduled international air services and State aircraft of another contracting State may only fly over or land in UK territory with the permission or authorisation of the UK (Articles 3 and 6), and this can be denied. The UK also requires non-scheduled services where payment is made for carriage, and passengers and cargo are embarked or disembarked, to seek prior permission.

All other aircraft have the right to land in or to fly across UK territory without the need to obtain prior permission from the UK (Article 5). However, the commander of each aircraft operating in controlled airspace in Europe is required to file a flight plan with Eurocontrol, the European Organisation for the Safety of Air Navigation. The flight plan is passed to each air navigation service provider along the route.

(HC Deb 13 December 2005 Vol. 440 c1856W)

12/2

In a written answer, a Minister wrote:

The Chicago Convention on International Civil Aviation sets out the international rights and obligations of the airlines of contracting states, including when it is necessary to seek prior permission to operate flights over or into another state. This is implemented by Article 138 of the Air Navigation Order 2005. Permission from the Secretary of State for Transport is only required by foreign aircraft operating civil flights into the UK where they land and take on board or discharge passengers or cargo, and where valuable consideration is given or promised in respect of that carriage. The Department for Transport has no records of aircraft operated by Stevens Express Leasing landing in the UK.

(HC Deb 14 December 2005 Vol. 440 c2027W)

Part Twelve: I. B. *Airspace, Outer Space, and Antarctica—Airspace—Uses*

12/3

The Government was asked what its policy is on the transportation by air of nuclear materials related to the United Kingdom nuclear weapons programme. The Minister of Defence wrote:

Within the United Kingdom, our policy is to use surface transportation for all movements of nuclear material related to the UK nuclear weapons programme. Any necessary movement by air of nuclear material outside of the UK is undertaken in compliance with the UK's International Treaty obligations and in accordance with International Air Transport Association regulations, MOD Health and Safety requirements and all statutory legislative requirements. All Ministry of Defence movements of nuclear materials are conducted only by suitably qualified and experienced personnel under procedures designed to reduce foreseeable risk in accordance with the As Low As Reasonably Practicable principle.

(HC Deb 21 March 2005 Vol. 432 c571W)

12/4

Extraordinary Rendition

The Foreign Secretary was asked by the FAC about the awareness of the Government about British airspace for "extraordinary rendition" and what permissions were required by foreign aircraft entering British airspace. He said:

Official permission (ie Diplomatic clearance) is not needed for non-scheduled, non-commercial civil aircraft, including VIP flights over-flying or landing at civilian airports in the UK. In such cases the flight operator simply files the aircraft flight plan to the central Integrated Flight Plans Systems (IFPS).

In the case of military or State aircraft landing at military airfields, clearance is sought from the MOD. Certain countries have a block clearance on a yearly renewable basis in a quid pro quo agreement (US, Germany, Italy and many others). Otherwise all nations must formally request permission to land or transit. However, neither international nor national aviation regulations require the provision of passenger information when transiting UK territory or airspace. [Q.110]

(FAC, Foreign Policy Aspects of the War against Terrorism, HC 573–ii (2005))

12/5

The Government was asked whether UK Government policy permits the *(a)* touching down and *(b)* refuelling in the UK of US aircraft, where such aircraft are carrying individuals destined for interrogation in countries that routinely use torture in their prisons. A Minister wrote:

The Chicago Convention on International Civil Aviation entitles foreign civil aircraft to make technical stops, for example for refuelling, without requiring the permission of the state it stops in. As such the Department is not notified if technical stops of this nature are made.

(HC Deb 18 January 2005 Vol. 430 c834W)

12/6

Her Majesty's Government was asked to make a list the dates when UK *(a)* territory and *(b)* airspace has been used for the transport of persons held as prisoners by US civilian or military authorities in the past 12 months. In reply, a Minister wrote:

International and national aviation regulations do not require the provision of passenger information when transiting UK territory or airspace. The UK

Government have not received any requests, nor granted any permissions, for the use of UK territory or airspace for the purpose raised in the hon. Member's question.

(HC Deb 10 October 2005 Vol. 437 c109W)

12/7

In a written answer, an FCO Minister wrote:

The Government are not aware of the use of their territory or airspace for the purposes of "extraordinary rendition". The Government have not received any requests, nor granted any permissions, for the use of UK territory or airspace for such purposes.

Under UK and international law, carriers on technical stopovers are not obliged to provide a passenger list, or even, under the Chicago Convention and the US/UK bilateral Air Services Agreement, to obtain permission from the Government to refuel.

(HC Deb 19 October 2005 Vol. 437 c1093W–1094W)

12/8

In a written answer, a Minister wrote:

Under the UK/USA Air Services Agreement and the Chicago Convention, the permission of the United Kingdom is required to operate scheduled and non-scheduled services between the United States and the United Kingdom or United Kingdom Overseas Territories. Under the Chicago Convention, permission is not needed for non-scheduled, non-commercial civil aircraft overflying or landing at civilian airports in the UK or its Overseas Territories.

(HC Deb 5 December 2005 Vol. 440 c1023W)

Part Twelve: I. C. *Airspace, Outer Space, and Antarctica—Airspace—Legal regime of aircraft*

12/9

In a written answer, a Minister wrote:

International aviation is already subject to a well-developed and closely monitored regulatory regime established by the Convention on International Civil Aviation (the Chicago Convention). Under the Convention the International Civil Aviation Organisation (ICAO) establishes detailed standards and recommended practices for the airworthiness of aircraft, the operational standards of airlines, and many other aspects of aviation. These standards and recommended practices relate primarily to safety and security issues, and cover safety issues relating to the carriage of munitions and other dangerous goods. In addition the

Convention itself provides that weapons and munitions of war may only be carried through the airspace of a state with the permission of that state.

To ensure that these standards are properly implemented, ICAO has established the Universal Safety Oversight Audit Programme under which the regulatory regime of each Contracting State is audited at regular intervals, and the results made available to all other States. Where deficiencies are identified, the State concerned is required to draw up an Action Plan agreed with ICAO, and ICAO subsequently assesses the implementation of the Plan. Within Europe there is already a regulatory regime on aviation insurance, with the relevant national authority required to ensure that airlines/carriers have sufficient insurance cover, and in line with EU law and our bilateral agreements with third countries we require foreign aircraft visiting the UK to demonstrate evidence of adequate cover. Further rules on insurance would impose an additional regulatory burden in already well-regulated States but might not be adequately implemented or enforced in countries with less stringent governance.

(HC Deb 12 July 2005 Vol. 436 c993W–994W)

12/10

In a written answer, a Minister wrote:

We have been in discussion with the Isle of Man Government regarding the establishment of an aircraft register. An Isle of Man aircraft register would, for the purposes of the Convention on International Civil Aviation, be a sub-part of the UK aircraft register. As such it could operate internationally only with the approval of Her Majesty's Government. We would not object to the establishment of such a register provided that appropriate regulatory arrangements are put in place to ensure that the register would be operated in accordance with UK's obligations under the convention.

(HL Deb 19 October 2005 Vol. 674 cWA123)

12/11

In a written answer, a Minister wrote:

There are no aircraft types currently banned from UK airspace.

Any airline from outside the EU, Iceland, Norway or Switzerland which wishes to pick up or put down passengers or cargo in the UK requires a permit from the Secretary of State for Transport. It is a condition of the permit that the airline's aircraft should be operated in accordance with international safety standards. Any individual aircraft that does not meet those standards would be refused a permit.

In addition, it is a condition of the permit that aircraft meet the environmental standards in Annex 16 to the Chicago Convention. Aircraft unable to meet the current ICAO noise certification requirements (Chapter 3 of Annex 16, Volume 1 or better) are not permitted unless there are exceptional circumstances.

(HC Deb 11 November 2005 Vol. 439 c779W)

Part Twelve: II. B. *Airspace, Outer Space, and Antarctica—Outer space and celestial bodies—Uses*

(See also **Part Two: II.**)

12/12

The Government was asked if it had made any representations to the United States over proposals to deploy weapons in outer space. An FCO Minister said:

... the White House issued a statement explicitly on the matter. I shall quote it because it is important to understand intentions:

> "We believe in the peaceful exploration of space, and there are treaties in place and we continue to abide by those treaties".

So do we in this country. We are completely committed to the 1967 Outer Space Treaty, which makes it clear that there can be no arms race in space. Each year, there is a resolution on the prevention of an arms race in outer space—the PAROS resolution—at the United Nations. We have supported it each year. The Government remain wholly committed to the proposition that no steps should be taken that create an arms race in outer space.

...

[It] is plainly right that we all wish to see the peaceful use of space rather than the militarised use. We ought to acknowledge that there is a degree of military use of space to which we are also committed. Satellite communications, surveillance, mapping, reconnaissance, early warning, the monitoring of arms control agreements, navigation, sensing and meteorology are all vital to our security and our defence. They are also a resource for research, which we do not always acknowledge in the same way. Those are the legitimate uses, and they seem to me, along with the general scientific thrust, to be the way that we should obey the international treaties to which we are signatories.

(HL Deb 25 May 2005 Vol. 672 c461)

Part Twelve: III. A. *Airspace, Outer Space, and Antarctica—Antarctica—Status*

12/13

The Government was asked what action is being taken to conserve the historic huts used by the British explorers Scott and Shackleton in Antarctica. An FCO Minister wrote:

... as the Minister of State at the Foreign and Commonwealth Office ... on 11 October 2004, *Official Report*, column 6, in [the House of Lords],

New Zealand has territorial responsibility for the Scott and Shackleton huts located in the Ross Dependency in Antarctica. The British Government, through the British Antarctic Territory, provide an annual donation of £12,500 to the UK Antarctic Heritage Trust, which in turn supports the conservation of the Ross Island huts. In 2002, the Foreign and Commonwealth Office, again through the British Antarctic Territory, donated £70,000 to support the proposed Ross Sea heritage restoration project to undertake major preservation work on the huts in question.

(HC Deb 21 March 2005 Vol. 432 c589W)

Part Twelve: III. C. *Airspace, Outer Space, and Antarctica—Antarctica—Protection of the environment*

12/14

In a written answer, an FCO Minister wrote:

The Government of South Georgia and South Sandwich Islands (GSGSSI) encourages visits by tourist cruise vessels to South Georgia by attending the annual meeting of the International Association of Antarctica Tour Operators (IAATO), by providing services to shipping, by supporting the South Georgia Museum Trust and by preserving the wildlife and environment that attracts tourists. There are no facilities for tourists in the South Sandwich Islands.

The Antarctic Treaty, to which the UK is a Consultative Party, designates Antarctica as a continent for peace and science. While the Government considers sustainable tourism a legitimate activity in Antarctica, they do not promote tourism to the British Antarctic Territory.

The GSGSSI takes very seriously its responsibilities in restricting the impact of tourism on wildlife in South Georgia and the South Sandwich Islands (SGSSI). A strict permitting process is in place, and visits to the Islands require the permission of the Commissioner for SGSSI. No cruise ship may land passengers other than at Grytviken/King Edward Point without being a member of IAATO. All IAATO vessels follow the Antarctic Treaty Environmental Protocol guidelines while at SGSSI. Expeditions to SGSSI are vetted by an independent panel of experts, which considers the potential impact on wildlife and the environment. The GSGSSI has banned the use of helicopters for the purpose of tourism, and any other flying is strictly regulated. The GSGSSI has closed many areas of South Georgia to tourists in order that wildlife should remain undisturbed.

The UK has actively promoted measures to restrict the impact of tourism on Antarctic flora and fauna through the Antarctic Treaty System. These have included, for example, the development of Site Guidelines for visitors to key Antarctic tourism sites, and new requirements to ensure adequate insurance and search and rescue provision for Antarctic expeditions.

(HC Deb 19 December 2005 Vol. 440 c2472W–2473W)

12/15

In a written answer, an FCO Minister wrote:

The territorial waters around the British Antarctic Territory fall under the remit of the Antarctic Treaty and the Commission for the Conservation of Antarctic Marine Living Resources. Fishing in these waters is confined to Krill. No illegal fishing has been reported. No prosecutions have taken place.

(HC Deb 19 December 2005 Vol. 440 c2484W)

Part Thirteen: International Responsibility

Part Thirteen: II. C.2. *International Responsibility—General issues of international responsibility—Procedure—Consular protection*

13/1

In a written answer, an FCO Minister wrote:

Mr. Maharaj's case is currently before the US Federal Court of Appeals. In January 2005, the Government submitted an amicus curiae brief to the Court of Appeals in relation to lack of consular notification. We continue to monitor the case in consultation with Mr. Maharaj's legal representatives in the US and UK.

(HC Deb 17 October 2005 Vol. 437 c731W–732W)

Part Thirteen: III. A. *International Responsibility—Responsible entities—States*

13/2

In a written answer, the Minister of State for Armed Forces wrote:

Operation Spear was a combined US-Iraqi security force anti-terrorist operation co-ordinated by US forces and the Iraqi Ministry of Defence [in Western Iraq in June 2005, Ed]. Detailed operational information is therefore a matter for the US or Iraqi authorities.

Although there were no specific British plans to support the operation, three RAF Tornado GR4s on routine patrols in Iraq were tasked to respond to calls for close air support assistance from US forces during the course of the operation. Those UK aircraft did not expend any weapons in support of the operation.

It is UK government policy on legal liability on combined operations in Iraq, that each nation would be directly liable for the consequences of actions taken by its own forces

(HC Deb 12 July 2005 Vol. 436 c862W)

13/3

In a written answer, an FCO Minister wrote:

We have been informed that the Telstar 12 satellite has experienced some technical interference and note it has been alleged that the interference has originated from Libya. Our understanding is that, if true, the alleged action might be a breach of the International Telecommunications Regulations of the United Nations International Telecommunications Union.

Government communications may have been disrupted and we are investigating the matter further. Following discussions with the United States authorities, the Office of Communications and Loral Skynet, the British ambassador in Tripoli raised the issue with the Libyan authorities at senior level.

The Government continues to work to eliminate barriers to freedom of expression and information and to create an environment in which free speech and free media flourish.

(HC Deb 8 December 2005 Vol. 440 c1554W)

Part Thirteen: III. D. *International Responsibility—Individuals and groups of individuals (including Corporations)*

13/4

In a written answer, the Minister of State for Trade wrote:

The UK Government believe that Charles Taylor should face justice at the Special Court for Sierra Leone. We have made this clear to the Nigerian Government and will continue to do so. We remain in discussion with Nigeria and our international partners over the next steps.

(HC Deb 7 July 2005 Vol. 436 c569W)

Part Fourteen: Peaceful Settlement of Disputes

Part Fourteen: II. A. *Peaceful Settlement of Disputes—Means of settlement—Negotiations and Consultations*

14/1

The Government was asked what action [it is] taking to encourage greater consultation by United Nations personnel with national mediators, regional organisations, non-governmental organisations and civil society as a whole, not least women, in conflict resolution and other peace processes. An FCO Minister wrote:

The Government give firm support to United Nations (UN) conflict resolution and peacebuilding. In doing so, we encourage the UN to engage with a broad range of actors.

We have prompted and supported UN co-operation with regional organisations, particularly in Africa. In Liberia and Cote d'Ivoire, Economic Community of West African States peacekeeping troops have deployed in support of UN efforts. The UN and the Intergovernmental Authority on Development worked closely together in the Naivasha peace process which culminated in the Comprehensive Peace Agreement in Sudan on 9 January 2005. We are supporting the UN in the development of its relations with the African Union (AU) and welcome the latter's co-operation with the UN's special political mission in Darfur.

We have used the joint Foreign and Commonwealth Office/Department for International Development (DfID)/Ministry of Defence Global Conflict Prevention Pool to support a range of projects that strengthen the UN's capacity to anticipate, analyse and address the causes of conflict. Many of these projects have been taken forward in collaboration with non-governmental organisations (NGOs) such as the International Centre for Transitional Justice, the International Peace Academy and the Conflict Prevention and Peace Forum.

We have been active in encouraging the UN to ensure that it takes account of gender and other human rights aspects in its conflict work. The UK has promoted the expansion of mandates for all current UN peace support operations to authorise the deployment of specialist staff or advisers to deal with all issues of conflict resolution including gender, the special needs of children and human rights. DfID has provided £96,000 to the UN Department of Peacekeeping Operations to develop a training manual on gender related issues in most aspects of peacekeeping, such as political and civil affairs and strategies in effective gender mainstreaming.

The Global Conflict Prevention Pool has financed several initiatives in support of implementation of UN Security Council Resolution 1325 on women, peace and security. These include, for example, supporting the UN's Development Fund for Women in its efforts to gather information on women's peace-building and gender justice initiatives, and also work with the Urgent Action Fund for Women's Human Rights, an NGO that supports grass-roots activities in countries where there are multinational peacekeeping operations. More detail of how the UK has supported implementation of UN Security Council Resolution 1325 is contained in our response to the UN Security Council in May 2004, which can be found on the following website:

www.un.org/womenwatch/osagi/responsesl1325/UK–E.pdf

Looking forward . . . the Prime Minister has welcomed the report of the UN Secretary-General's high-level panel, published on 2 December 2004, which makes a wide range of recommendations aimed at improving the international response to threats to global peace and security. The Government will be giving the UN Secretary-General firm support in taking this agenda forward, in particular the establishment of a UN Peacebuilding Commission to ensure proper co-ordination and sequencing of peacebuilding activities, including issues of local consultation.

(HL Deb 21 February 2005 Vol. 669 c154WA)

14/2

In a written answer, an FCO Minister wrote:

The UK supports the territorial integrity of Indonesia. We believe the best solution to the internal differences in Papua is to be found through peaceful dialogue between the Government of Indonesia and representatives of the Papuan people, and the implementation of the Special Autonomy Law of 2001. We welcome President Yudhoyono's recent statement that he is committed to a "just, comprehensive and dignified solution", including through "consistent implementation" of Special Autonomy.

(HC Deb 10 November 2005 Vol. 439 c750W)

14/3

During a General Assembly meeting, the representative for the European Union said:

I would like to explain the vote by the countries of the European Union on the resolution on the Syrian Golan. [This was Res 60/108, for which the EU states voted, calling, inter alia, for the rescission of Israeli law which applied to Golan, Ed.]

The European Union remains concerned about the situation in the Middle East. It reiterates to all parties the importance of maintaining forward momentum towards full implementation of the road map. There can be no military solution to the Middle East conflict.

A just, lasting and comprehensive settlement of the situation in the Middle East, including on the Syrian and Lebanese tracks, must be based on Security Council resolution 242 (1967), which emphasizes the inadmissibility of the acquisition of territory by force and the need to work for a just and lasting peace in which every State in the region can live in security, and on subsequent Security Council resolutions 338 (1973), 1397 (2002) and 1515 (2003). It must be based on the terms of reference of the Madrid Conference, in particular the principle of land for peace, as well as on the implementation of the road map and all existing agreements between the parties. We will continue to work relentlessly with the regional parties, as part of the Middle East Quartet, towards that goal.

The European Union wishes to reiterate that a final peace settlement will not be complete without taking account of the Israel-Syria and Israel-Lebanon aspects. Negotiations should resume as soon as possible with the aim of reaching an agreement. It should be recalled that, earlier this month, the European Union voted in favour of the resolution on the Syrian Golan in the Fourth Committee, which called upon Israel to desist from changing the demographic composition of the occupied Syrian Golan and, in particular, to desist from the establishment of settlements. We believe that the resolution on the Syrian Golan under today's agenda item contains references that could undermine the process of bilateral negotiations. For that reason, as in previous years, the European Union abstained in the voting on that resolution.

Finally, in the spirit of rationalizing the work of the General Assembly, the European Union would prefer to have only one resolution dealing with this issue before this body.

(UN Doc. A/60/PV.60, 1 December 2005)

14/4

In a written answer, an FCO Minister wrote:

The UK, in line with the EU, considers that the only viable solution to the armed conflict in Colombia is through a negotiated settlement. We have made it plain to the Colombian Government that the rights of the victims of the armed conflict to truth, justice and reparation must be taken into account in the paramilitary demobilisation process. These issues were raised directly with President Uribe during his visit to London on 14 July. The EU expressed its willingness, in the EU Ministerial Council conclusions of October 2005, to work with the Government, institutions and civil society of Colombia, as well as with the UN High Commissioner for Human Rights (UNHCHR), Michael Fruhling, the Inter-American Commission on Human Rights, and others who may be involved in monitoring the implementation of the judicial process of the demobilisation of the paramilitary groups. The EU also welcomes the continued engagement of the Organisation of American States in accompanying the demobilisation process. The Conclusions also spelled out specific areas of intervention where the EU is willing to assist Colombia in support of the search for peace. While we do have some concerns over the pace of paramilitary demobilisation, we acknowledge that effective and transparent implementation of the recently agreed Colombian Justice and Peace Law would make a positive contribution to the search for peace in Colombia.

(HC Deb 2 December 2005 Vol. 440 c873W–874W)

Part Fourteen: II. D. *Peaceful Settlement of Disputes—Means of settlement—Mediation*

14/5

In a written answer, an FCO Minister wrote:

We welcome the signature on 5 July in Abuja, of the Declaration of Principles for the resolution of the conflict in Darfur. We congratulate the parties on this achievement, and commend the African Union (AU)-led mediation team for its efforts. This is an important step. It is the first document agreed by the parties to the Darfur conflict that deals with political, rather than humanitarian and security, issues. Although not a peace deal in itself, it sets the framework within which the negotiations towards such a deal should proceed. We are pressing the parties to return to Abuja on 24 August, the date set for resumption of talks by the AU Special Envoy Salim Salim, and to negotiate in good faith, towards a full political agreement, necessary to achieve peace in Darfur. Such an agreement will need to be complementary to the Comprehensive Peace Agreement, signed in Nairobi on 9 January. We also continue to insist that the parties abide by the commitments they have already made to improve the security situation in Darfur, notably the Humanitarian Ceasefire Agreement and the Abuja Humanitarian and Security Protocols.

(HC Deb 12 July 2005 Vol. 436 c880W)

Part Fourteen: II. G.1. *Peaceful Settlement of Disputes—Means of settlement—Judicial settlement—International Court of Justice*

14/6

In a written answer, an FCO Minister wrote:

We have made representations to the Nigerian authorities about upholding the International Court of Justice ruling on Bakassi. We maintain a close dialogue with both Nigeria and Cameroon on the completion of the demarcation exercise, and have urged both sides to continue to cooperate closely with the UN Mixed Commission to this end.

(HC Deb 4 July 2005 Vol. 436 c185W)

14/7

In a written answer, an FCO Minister wrote:

As provided for in Article 9 of the Convention on the Prevention and Punishment of the Crime of Genocide, it is open to contracting parties to submit cases relating to the responsibility of a state for genocide to the International Court of Justice. It will be for the court to make a judgment on the case.

We look to all countries with International Criminal Tribunal for the former Yugoslavia indictees on their territory, notably Karadzic and Mladic, indicted for genocide at Srebrenica, together with Gotovina, indicted for Operation Storm, to transfer them without delay to The Hague Tribunal.

We have made no representations regarding the application of the Convention on the Prevention and Punishment of the Crime of Genocide. We have had informal discussions with Bosnian, Croatian and Serbia and Montenegro representatives, as well as certain NATO allies and EU partners, about the joint declaration issued by the Presidents of Croatia, Serbia and Montenegro and Bosnia and Herzegovina in Belgrade on 27 June.

(HL Deb 13 July 2005 Vol. 673 cWA146)

Part Fourteen: II. G.2. *Peaceful Settlement of Disputes—Means of settlement—Judicial settlement—Other courts of tribunals*

14/8

International Criminal Court

The Government was asked by the FAC about the attitude of the US to the ICC. An FCO Minister said:

The United States has concerns about the ICC and fears malicious prosecution and unjustified prosecution of its citizens through the ICC—and there is a debate to be had about whether this is seeking to undermine the court or seeking to see a way through it—and actively supports what are called the bilateral non-surrender agreements. We have taken the view that those bilateral non-surrender agreements are consistent with the ICC statute, as long as they meet a number of key criteria that we have set out within the European Union common position. Principally those are that if you are not going to go through the ICC, there are, nevertheless, provisions to ensure that people who have committed crimes falling within the jurisdiction of the court would not enjoy immunity, and, secondly, in terms of the exemption, that you should only consider those sent on government business and not all citizens. That is the principal vehicle through which the United States is seeking to engage on this issue. We believe there is a way through that, but it has to be in accordance with the EU common position. The US came to us back in 2002 putting forward a draft bilateral non-surrender agreement. We said we were not prepared to accept it because it did not conform to those criteria, and the US has not come back to us. [Q.102]

14/9

The Minister was then asked about the possibility of an SC reference to the ICC of the situation in Darfur. He said:

On the issue of genocide within Sudan we do not have the evidence as to whether or not genocide has been committed, which is why we have been one of the strongest supporters of the establishment of a Commission of Inquiry. That is due to report very shortly. If that does conclude that there has been genocide and urges a reference to the ICC, we would strongly support that and would urge other states to do so as well ... All other states ... we strongly supported the Commission. If it concludes genocide and urges reference to the ICC, firstly and most importantly, we would support that ourselves, but we would urge all other states to follow that path as well. Throughout this process we have made clear our view that we do understand the concerns of the United States. Their troops are probably more exposed, because of their global position, than any other country. I understand those concerns, but I do not share them, and I hope over time, as the ICC beds down and it becomes clear ... Apart from anything else, under the ICC statute, as long as you are taking action against these crimes yourself as an individual country, it does not of necessity have to involve the ICC. I would hope over time that the United

States becomes convinced that its fears are unfounded and it can support the ICC. [Qs 103–105]

14/10

During a debate in the House of Lords, a Minister said:

It has been suggested there is a real possibility that our forces will find themselves standing in the dock on trial in The Hague, whether the UK likes it or not. That is wrong, and I shall explain why. The court's jurisdiction is carefully set out in the ICC statute. The entire premise of the court is based on the principle that it can only—I repeat, only—exercise its jurisdiction when a state is unable or unwilling genuinely to investigate or prosecute itself. Surely we do not envisage that the United Kingdom will ever be in that position.

I am happy to reassure noble Lords . . . that it is unthinkable for British forces personnel to be sent to the ICC. At Second Reading of the International Criminal Court Bill in the other place in 2001, the Foreign Secretary told the House that,

> "British service personnel will never be prosecuted by the International Criminal Court because any bona fide allegation will be pursued by the British authorities".—[*Official Report*, Commons, 3/4/2001; col. 222.]

We remain confident that UK authorities will always act properly. As long as they do, there will never be any basis for the ICC to exercise jurisdiction.

Some have also suggested that the ICC will be politically driven and cannot be trusted to act properly. The Government have complete confidence in the independence and integrity of the court and the prosecutor. We are in good company in that judgment; 99 countries have so far ratified the statute, including 22 of our 25 NATO partners and 22 Commonwealth countries. We have nothing to fear from the ICC.

Another myth is that, by ratifying the statute and enacting the International Criminal Court Act 2001, the Government have exposed our forces to a risk of prosecution that they did not previously face. That is not the case. Those who oppose the ICC often overlook the fact that, before we ratified the ICC statute, the UK had already fought one conflict while subject to the jurisdiction of an international criminal tribunal.

(HL Deb 14 July 2005 Vol. 673 c1262–1263)

14/11

In a written answer about Sudan, an FCO Minister wrote:

Under the Interim National Constitution (INC), which came into force on 9 July 2005, the president and first vice-president shall be immune from any legal proceedings during their tenure of office, except in cases of high treason, gross violation of the constitution or gross misconduct in relation to state affairs, where they may be charged if three quarters of the National Assembly agree.

In line with the Comprehensive Peace Agreement (CPA), which we strongly support, the INC was drawn up by the National Constitutional Review Commission, which included representatives of the parties to the agreement and other political forces in Sudan.

We have made no representations on this issue. However, we regularly press the Government of Sudan on the need to establish an open, transparent and fair judicial system; and we plan to support the comprehensive review of the judiciary provided for by the C[omprehensive] P[eace] A[greement].

The International Criminal Court is currently conducting investigations into allegations of crimes in Darfur. Though Sudan is not a state party to the ICC statute, it was referred to the court by the UN Security Council Resolution 1593 (2005) which was made pursuant to Chapter VII of the United Nations Charter. Sudan is therefore legally obliged to co-operate with the ICC including by surrendering any Sudanese nationals indicted by the ICC, irrespective of the individual's position under Sudanese domestic law.

(HC Deb 21 July 2005 Vol. 436 c2106W)

14/12

In a written answer about Sudan and the ICC, an FCO Minister wrote:

The UK has concluded a generic witness relocation agreement with the Court and is negotiating agreements on sentence enforcement and information-sharing. The Court will carry out its investigations in Darfur and elsewhere in an entirely independent capacity. Because of the need to respect this independence, and to protect the integrity of the Court's operations, it would not be appropriate to comment on the operational aspects of specific ICC investigations, nor to reveal what support the UK is providing in that regard. The UK remains ready to consider any specific request put forward by the Court.

(HC Deb 21 July 2005 Vol. 436 c2107W)

14/13

In a written answer, an FCO Minister wrote:

Under the principle of "complementarity", the International Criminal Court (ICC) is only able to exercise jurisdiction in a situation when the state, of which the alleged perpetrator of the crime is a national, is unwilling or genuinely unable to carry out its own investigation or prosecution.

The International Criminal Court Act 2001 consolidated various existing legislative instruments, using the precise legal definitions provided for under the statute of the ICC. This enables the United Kingdom to prosecute for all such crimes, as stipulated by the Rome statute. This legislative approach was adopted in order to ensure that any necessary investigations or prosecutions could take place under UK law. Any allegations that crimes under this Act have been committed by British citizens would be considered and investigated by the relevant British authorities. As such, we believe that ICC involvement would not be required.

(HL Deb 21 July 2005 Vol. 673 cWA286)

14/14

In a written answer, an FCO Minister wrote:

Under the Rome statute of the International Criminal Court, situations may be referred to the court by a state party, as has been the case in Uganda and the Democratic Republic of Congo, or by the Security Council, as was most recently the case with Darfur.

In addition, the prosecutor may begin an investigation on his own initiative, based on any information received by his office. Although it is open to any individual to communicate information relating to allegations of ICC crimes to the Office of the Prosecutor, the prosecutor is required to examine all allegations received rigorously and independently. Any decision that he might take to proceed with an investigation in such circumstances would first be reviewed again by an ICC pre-trial chamber composed of three judges. We understand that the prosecutor has received a large number of such communications.

The ICC would have jurisdiction to investigate and, if necessary, prosecute any particular case only where the state of nationality of the suspect or the state where the crimes took place is unable or willing to act.

(HL Deb 21 July 2005 Vol. 673 cWA286)

14/15

International Criminal Tribunal for Yugoslavia

Responding to an adjournment motion calling for the winding up of the ICTY, an FCO Minister said:

This year marks the 10th anniversary of the Dayton accords and the end of the bloodiest conflict in the former Yugoslav Federation. We should remember that in the past 10 years so much has changed for the better. Free and fair elections have been held throughout the region, large-scale conflict no longer threatens and the European Union and other international partners are united in working with the region to maintain stability and create prosperity. The dark days of the early 1990s thankfully now seem a distant memory.

However, a shadow remains and will do so as long as the truth is suppressed and denied. It is cast by the war crimes committed during the bloody conflicts in the early 1990s and it will not be removed until those responsible for the appalling atrocities committed during the conflict are held to account. That is why the United Kingdom remains a firm supporter of the International Criminal Tribunal for the Former Yugoslavia. We will continue to lend our political, financial and practical support for an efficient tribunal that can deliver effective justice for the thousands of victims who suffered so much during the conflict.

At the same time, we recognise concerns about the operation of the tribunal, in particular its cost, slowness and geographical distance from the victims. Others have alleged, as we have heard today, that it is biased against Serbs. I will seek to address those questions. The tribunal has so far cost United Nations member states some $860 million since its inception in 1993, of which the UK's share is some $54 million. We have taken a close interest in the efficient management of the tribunal and will continue our policy of bearing down on its costs.

However, we must recognise that international justice is an expensive process. The complexity and nature of the cases before the tribunal make them inherently expensive. Cases arising from three separate conflicts are being prosecuted and indictees often face multiple counts. The Lockerbie trial, by way of comparison, cost UK taxpayers some £60 million.

The Minister was asked if he would explain why a similar tribunal has not been set up for Iraq. Why is Saddam Hussein to be tried by his own people? He said:

It is fair to say that the basis on which the actions were taken, the nature of the conflicts and the circumstances of the conflicts in the former Yugoslavia and Iraq are fundamentally different. The consequences for the judicial processes that follow on from that conflict reflect the fact that there are very different circumstances in Iraq and Yugoslavia.

. . .

assistance is being rendered to the Iraqi authorities in bringing forward a proper system of judicial authority, which will allow in turn for prosecutions to take place, not least in relation to Saddam Hussein. I return to the substantive point that I am conscious that the issue of Iraq has divided both this Chamber and some within our party. However, it is only common sense to recognise that there are distinctive circumstances at work in the former Yugoslavia and in Iraq, which gave rise to the action that was taken.

Continuing about the ICTY, the Minister said:

On fugitives from justice, we have made clear our belief that the ICTY should plan its work within the deadlines that it has set out. However, its progress is also clearly subject to factors outside its control, the most important of which is co-operation from states in the region in apprehending fugitive indictees, and providing access to documents and witnesses. The president and prosecutor have both made it clear that lack of such co-operation will affect the tribunal's final closure date. We take that lack of co-operation extremely seriously and will take action to support the tribunal. There can be no closure until all the accused have been brought to The Hague to face trial.

Many of the accused have voluntarily surrendered and pleaded guilty; others have been tried and sentenced. Three individuals stand accused of ordering and orchestrating the most serious crimes: Ratko Mladic, Radovan Karadzic and Ante Gotovina. They remain fugitives from justice. The charges against Mladic and Karadzic include the massacre at Srebrenica where more than 7,000 Muslim men and boys were killed in cold blood because in the views of those who perpetrated the action they held the wrong religious beliefs. Their refusal to surrender, while others face trial, is shameful.

Even worse is the refusal of the relevant authorities in Bosnia and Herzegovina and Serbia and Montenegro to take all possible steps to secure their arrest. We have welcomed recent transfers of lower-level indictees and provided co-operation at a bureaucratic level, but there remains in the Serb body politic a refusal to face up to the past. That has tragic consequences for the people of Serbia and Montenegro and Bosnia. Their future prosperity is held hostage by a few fugitives and by their elected representatives' refusal to grasp the nettle and accept their international legal and moral obligations.

The authorities in Belgrade and Banja Luka are not alone. Croatia is on the cusp of an historic step: opening accession negotiations with the European Union. As a champion of enlargement, the United Kingdom is committed to helping all the countries of the western Balkans to take their rightful place within Europe, but that can not be at the expense of political conditionality. All countries, including our own, are under an obligation to co-operate fully with the tribunal.

Since gaining candidate status last June, the Croatian authorities have failed to satisfy the chief prosecutor that they are doing everything they possibly can to locate and apprehend the fugitive general, Ante Gotovina. The European Council conclusions in December 2004 made it clear that accession negotiations could begin only when the authorities were co-operating fully with The Hague. However, the Croatian Government seem unwilling to meet their obligations. Instead they indulge in cosmetic measures and public relations campaigns in the hope that negotiations will begin anyway. We continue to make it clear that they need to take action now to enable negotiations to begin in March. The importance of conditionality policy and the tribunal is not just about Gotovina, Karadzic or Mladic; it is about the rule of law, about European norms of behaviour and about these countries' willingness to confront the past in order to be able to face the future.

The tribunal has brought a sense of justice to many thousands of victims across the region, guaranteeing that their suffering is acknowledged and not ignored. More than 3,500 witnesses have had the chance to tell their stories while testifying in court. For many, though not all, that has helped the process of personal closure.

As we heard in the debate, the tribunal has been criticised by some for concentrating more on one ethnic group—the Bosnian Serbs—than any other. However, it is important to remember that the indictments are against individuals, not groups. The emphasis on individual responsibility dispels any notion of collective punishment of the Serbs as a group, as has been suggested.

The tribunal's influence will continue after its closure. It will have left an historic record of the atrocities and of jurisprudence. It is not possible for the tribunal to hear every case against every individual, but its experience will be an invaluable resource for the regional courts, such as the special war crimes chamber of the Bosnian state court, which will continue to prosecute suspected war criminals. Together with its sister tribunal, the International Criminal Tribunal for Rwanda, it will leave a legacy of ground-breaking case law, which is already proving an important resource for the newly established International Criminal Court.

The international community has learned valuable lessons from the International Criminal Tribunal for Yugoslavia and the International Criminal

Tribunal for Rwanda. They are likely to be the last tribunals of their kind. More recent tribunals such as the special court for Sierra Leone are smaller and more tightly focused in terms of the number of indictees and counts, which makes for a much shorter lifespan and much lower costs.

For the future, the United Kingdom will work together with like-minded partners for the widest possible jurisdiction of the International Criminal Court so that we can ensure that there is no impunity for those who commit the most serious violations of international humanitarian law and crimes against humanity. The court, which the UK regards as a milestone in the development of international justice, was founded in part to avoid the need to set up such ad hoc tribunals as that in Yugoslavia. We believe that over time the permanent court will develop into a powerful deterrent against would-be perpetrators of the most heinous crimes, which it is the shared responsibility of the international community to punish.

(HC Deb 23 February 2005 Vol. 431 c140–144WH)

14/16

The Government was asked whether the mandate for the EUFOR force in Bosnia-Herzegovina should be expanded to include the apprehension of war criminals. An FCO Minister said:

The British force commander for EUFOR, who took over at the beginning of this year—Major General Leakey—has underlined in his public statements that EUFOR would lead efforts to tackle networks that sheltered and financed war criminals. In the first month of its mission, EUFOR, under the British general, mounted an operation to secure bunker complexes that were believed to have been used to shelter the fugitive, Ratko Mladic.

... I can reassure him that EUFOR has full authority to monitor the military aspects of the general framework agreement for peace in Bosnia and Herzegovina. Both EUFOR and NATO have the authority to apprehend persons indicted for war crimes. Their mandate explicitly states that.

(HL Deb 3 March 2005 Vol. 670 c350)

14/17

International Labour Organisation Administrative Tribunal

The Government was asked the following written question:

... pursuant to the answer of 22 June 2005, *Official Report*, column 1081W, what assessment he has made of the reasons that damages were awarded to the former Director General of the Organisation for the Prevention of Chemical Weapons, other than for loss of earnings.

In reply, an FCO Minister wrote:

Following the original judgment of the International Labour Organisation Administrative Tribunal (ILOAT) and the subsequent review of the level of damages awarded, requested by the Organisation for the Prohibition of

Chemical Weapons (OPCW) with the support of States Party, which resulted in a reduced award to Mr. Bustani for material damages, the UK and other States Party accepted the judgment and supported OPCW's payment of the award, since ILOAT judgments are final.

(HC Deb 6 July 2005 Vol. 436 c486W–487W)

14/18

Khmer Rouge Tribunal

In a written answer, an FCO Minister wrote:

The UK supports the efforts of the United Nations and the Government of Cambodia to bring to justice some of those who bear the greatest responsibility for crimes against humanity carried out by the Khmer Rouge. A successful outcome to the Khmer Rouge Tribunal (KRT) will help strengthen accountability, the rule of law and judicial reform in Cambodia and will send a strong international signal that war crimes, crimes against humanity and genocide will not be treated with impunity.

Progress in achieving a KRT has been slow to date for many reasons and significant hurdles still need to be overcome. The Government of Cambodia has encountered major difficulties in raising the $13.8 million contribution it is expected to deliver. Less than $2 million has been made available to date. Other factors include finding, selecting and training suitably qualified, experienced and politically independent national judicial staff including judges, prosecutors, investigators etc. who can meet international standards. In that context, we welcome the recent appointments of a director and a deputy director by the Government of Cambodia and the UN respectively. Addressing gaps in Cambodia's national legislation to ensure it is compatible with international criminal law has also proved problematic.

The UK has been one of the leading financial contributors to the KRT to date. We provided £500,000 in 2004–05 and expect to do so again for 2005–06 and 2006–07. Bilaterally, EU members have pledged a total of $8.5 million approximately and the European Commission has additionally pledged a further €1 million. We continue to underline the importance we attach to a credible Tribunal starting work as soon as possible with the Cambodian authorities at official and ministerial level and have offered our support.

(HC Deb 2 December 2005 Vol. 440 c872W–873W)

Part Fourteen: II. H.1. *Peaceful Settlement of Disputes—Means of settlement—Settlement within international organizations—United Nations*

14/19

In a written answer, an FCO Minister wrote:

We agree that the UN has a vital role to play in Burma. We strongly support the UN Secretary-General's efforts to promote national reconciliation and democratisation in Burma, and agree with his most recent 'good offices' report of 10 October. We also support the work of the UN Special Rapporteur for Human Rights in Burma, Professor Sergio Pinheiro, and the UN Secretary-General's Special Envoy to Burma, Tan Sri Razali, who have not been allowed to visit Burma since November 2003 and March 2004 respectively. We also support the efforts of Ali Alatas, who visited Burma on behalf of the UN Secretary-General earlier this year. We urge the State Peace and Development Council to allow free access for the UN Secretary-General's representatives, and to work closely with the UN and its agencies in the interests of lasting peace and inclusive democratic reform in Burma.

(HC Deb 2 December 2005 Vol. 440 c872W)

Part Fourteen: II. H.2. *Peaceful Settlement of Disputes—Means of settlement—Settlement within international organizations—Other organizations*

Part Fourteen: II. I. *Peaceful Settlement of Disputes—Means of settlement—Other means of settlement*

14/20

The Government was asked a series of questions about its acceptance of the right of individual petition under the CEDAW, including its estimate of the public expenditure that is likely to be incurred during the next two years as a result of its acceptance of the right of petition.

A Minister wrote:

The UK Government are confident that their legislation on sex discrimination and wider provisions on gender equality broadly cover the rights and freedoms within the United Nations Convention for the Elimination of All Forms of Discrimination Against Women (CEDAW). The UK's fifth periodic CEDAW report (June 2003) illustrates the various measures the UK Government have taken to implement CEDAW. Following this, the UK Government do not expect a significant amount of public expenditure to be incurred during the next two years as a result of their acceptance of the individual right of petition under the United Nations Convention for the Elimination of Discrimination Against Women.

What is its estimate of the total number of complaints that are likely to be incurred during the next two years as a result of its acceptance of the individual right of petition under the United Nations Convention for the Elimination of Discrimination Against Women?

The Minister wrote:

The UK Government are confident that their legislation on sex discrimination and wider provisions on gender equality broadly cover the rights and freedoms within the United Nations Convention for the Elimination of All Forms of Discrimination Against Women (CEDAW). Following this, and from the experience of other countries (during the period 2000–02 no cases were brought in New Zealand), the Government do not expect a significant number of complaints to be incurred during the next two years as a result of accepting the individual right of petition under the United Nations Convention for the Elimination of Discrimination Against Women.

What are the likely practical benefits for women in the United Kingdom resulting from the acceptance of the individual right of petition under the United Nations Convention for the Elimination of Discrimination Against Women?

The Minister wrote:

Following the Government's decision to sign the optional protocol to the Convention on the Elimination of All Forms of Discrimination Against Women (CEDAW), women in the UK may now petition the UN committee on issues either not covered by domestic legislation or when they have no other international right of appeal available. The practical benefits resulting from the acceptance of the individual right of petition will be monitored on a case by case basis.

(HL Deb 21 February 2005 Vol. 669 c176–177WA)

Part Fifteen: Coercive Measures Short of the Use of Force

Part Fifteen: I. A. *Coercive Measures Short of the Use of Force—Unilateral measures—Retorsion*

15/1

China

In his reply in an adjournment debate on the Government's refusal to grant an export licence for a night vision monocular and a night intensification module to China, a Trade and Industry Minister said:

Our export licensing commitments are clear. We assess each export licence application on a case-by-case basis against the consolidated EU export licensing criteria and our own national arms export licensing criteria. We take fully into consideration the circumstances prevailing at the time. In addition, we reserve the right to impose our own stricter criteria in line with Government policy. If it is judged that an export is inconsistent with any of the criteria, the application is refused.

We take the criteria very seriously. The case was refused under criterion 1, which covers international embargos and, on appeal, also under criterion 2, which refers to the possibility of internal repression. There is an EU embargo on arms to China, which we in the UK interpret as including the export of any goods that might be used for internal repression.

The manufacturer made the following statement in its letter of 13 September:

> "we ... are wholly and totally unable to fathom how it might be in any way conceivable, practical or technically possible to make use of either of these items of equipment for 'internal repression' purposes".

Let me explain why that is, in fact, possible. The night vision monocular can be strapped to a helmet to free hands for other tasks, and the night intensification module can be fitted to a camera to provide night vision capabilities. Of course ... the items can be used legitimately, but they can also be used to enhance significantly the capabilities of internal security forces to conduct repressive night raids on civilians. It is frankly disingenuous for anyone in the business to claim otherwise.

...

Let me be clear: although the case was refused initially only under criterion 1, had the embargo not been in place the clear risk that the goods would be used for internal repression would have led me to refuse the export under criterion 2 of the consolidated criteria, which also relates to internal repression.

... every EU member state is committed to considering export licence applications against the binding EU code of conduct on arms exports or against any EU or UN embargoes. To ensure that no country grants a licence without realising that such a licence might have been refused by another member state, we have an EU-wide denial notification system, which ensures that refusal in one state is noted in every state.

(HC Deb 3 February 2005 Vol. 430 c1072–1074)

15/2

Ethiopia

The Secretary of State for International Development told the House of Commons:

On the Ethiopian elections, we have made clear our view that the complaints investigation process should be completed as soon as possible, that the deaths resulting from civil disturbances should be investigated, and that those detained should either be released or charged. Until the situation is clearer, I am putting on hold plans to increase budget support this year by £20 million.

(HC Deb 29 June 2005 Vol. 435 c1279)

15/3

Iran

An FCO Minister made the following statement to the House of Commons:

In March 2005, after consultation with the Ministry of Defence and the export control organisations, DTI, the Foreign and Commonwealth Office donated armoured vests and body armour plates to the Iranian Anti-Narcotics Police (ANP). This gift was to provide an element of protection for the ANP in their work of countering drugs smuggling from Afghanistan. We are satisfied that these goods would only be used for anti-narcotics operations and are therefore prepared to make an exception to the UK national embargo announced in 1993, as amended in 1998.

We are fully committed to implementing the UK embargo on Iran. However, we are, in limited circumstances, prepared to make exceptions where denying an export or a gift would be contrary to the intention of the embargo. As the UK has been active in encouraging and assisting Iran with combating the smuggling of drugs from Afghanistan, I am confident that granting this exception is fully consistent with this responsible approach of supporting the ANP whilst respecting the aims of the embargo.

...

All export licences, F680s and Crown immunity gifts are considered on a case by case basis judged against the consolidated and national arms export licensing criteria.

(HC Deb 15 March 2005 Vol. 432 c14WS)

15/4

Nepal

(See also **Part Five: I. A.4.**)

The Government was asked what steps it was taking to restore constitutional power in Nepal following the assumption of power by the King. An FCO Minister said:

... the United Kingdom is working with European Union partners to seek the return of constitutional government in Nepal. We have raised our concerns over the King's takeover of power, both publicly and privately, as we believe it will increase the risk of instability, undermine democracy and cause the already poor human rights situation to deteriorate further. As a result of the King's actions we temporarily recalled our ambassador, and we have withdrawn plans to gift a further tranche of military equipment to Nepal.

(HL Deb 23 March 2005 Vol. 671 c243)

15/5

Zimbabwe

The Government was asked several questions about the elections in Zimbabwe. The Foreign Secretary said:

As the House is aware, elections were held in Zimbabwe last Thursday, 31 March. The declared results give ZANU-PF 78 seats, the Movement for Democratic Change 41, and Independent one. With 30 further seats being by appointment, the gift of the president, the declared result will give ZANU-PF the two-thirds majority required for amending the Zimbabwe constitution.

Those are the official published results, but there is strong evidence that they do not reflect the free democratic will of the Zimbabwean people. There was, it is true, less violence than in 2000 and 2002 but, overall, the election process was seriously flawed. Thousands were turned away from the polling booths. There are serious unexplained discrepancies between the votes tallied and the official number announced, and other abuse was rife. That included the misuse of food aid, ghost voters, a lack of equal access to the media, the use of draconian security legislation, and an election commission packed with ZANU-PF supporters.

If Mr. Mugabe had had nothing to hide over the conduct of these elections, he would have allowed full access by the international media and experienced external election observers. Yet the BBC and others were banned, Commonwealth and EU monitors were refused access and, most revealing of all, even observers from the experienced and respected Southern African Development Community Parliamentary Forum were banned—presumably to punish them for their critical report in 2002.

The recent official report by the Commission for Africa rightly set out the need for stronger action by the international community to address Africa's problems. However, the commission also made it crystal clear how much bad governance has "blighted"—its word, not mine—parts of Africa, and frustrated people's hopes of building for themselves a better and more prosperous future. There is, tragically, no more powerful example of that than the situation in Zimbabwe.

Given all of that, I am surprised and saddened that Zimbabwe's neighbours have chosen to ignore the obvious and serious flaws in these elections, and have declared them fair. However, many in southern Africa have spoken out about the reality of the situation in Zimbabwe. Just two months ago, Archbishop Desmond Tutu said that Zimbabwe was a

"huge blot on the record"

of the world's poorest continent. Moreover, the deputy president of the Confederation of South African Trades Unions. Mr. Joe Nkosi, complained that free and fair elections could not occur "under current legislation". Confederation delegations have been banned from Zimbabwe for their stand.

The UK will continue to work with its international partners for a return to accountable, democratic government that respects the rule of law and the human rights of Zimbabweans.

The EU's common position on Zimbabwe is the strongest on any country in Africa, and includes targeted sanctions against the Government of Zimbabwe and an arms embargo. Meanwhile, the UK is committed to doing all that it can to help to meet the humanitarian needs of the Zimbabwean population. The UK has made a major contribution to ensuring that Zimbabwe's food shortages do not lead to a famine by donating over £71 million in food aid since September 2001. We have also contributed £26.5 million to efforts by non-governmental organisations to tackle the AIDS epidemic now affecting one in four Zimbabweans.

A strong statement about the elections was issued last night by the EU presidency. That statement concluded that the elections could not be judged free or fair, and called on Zimbabwe to restore democracy. International measures taken show the widespread condemnation of President Mugabe's ruinous policies. Until Mr. Mugabe and his regime respond, that regime will continue to be isolated internationally.

...

I understand the frustration felt by everyone in the House and around the world about President Mugabe, but in the absence of military action—neither we nor the Conservatives have ever countenanced that and it has never been on the agenda—there are understandable limits to the action that can be taken.

(HC Deb 5 April 2005 Vol. 432 c1261–1262)

Part Fifteen: I. E. *Coercive Measures Short of the Use of Force—Unilateral measures—Other unilateral measures*

15/6

In a written answer, an FCO Minister wrote:

The issue was discussed by Sir Brian Fall, the UK Special Representative for the South Caucasus, during his visit to Ankara in April. The Turkish Government explained that the closed border is linked to the conflict between Armenia and Azerbaijan over Nagorno-Karabakh ...

The UK Government do not take the view that the closed border with Turkey constitutes an economic blockade on Armenia. There are regular direct flights between Armenia and Istanbul and bilateral trade between the two countries.

(HL Deb 21 July 2005 Vol. 673 cWA263)

Part Fifteen: II. A. *Coercive Measures Short of the Use of Force—Collective measures—United Nations*

15/7

The following statement was made on behalf of the European Union at the Informal Thematic Consultations of the General Assembly:

The EU would like to confirm its commitment to the universalization of the Treaty on the Non-Proliferation of Nuclear Weapons, and to work toward preservation of the integrity of the Treaty and the strengthening of its implementation, including during the upcoming Review Conference. The EU underlines the need to strengthen the role of the Security Council as a final arbitrator when obligations under the Treaty are violated, in order to take appropriate action.

. . .

The EU expresses its support for the recommendations aiming at an effective implementation and enforcement of sanctions. According to our overall concern for the rule of law, the Human Rights/terrorism relationships should be given adequate consideration. The role of the Security Council to mitigate the humanitarian consequences of sanctions is to be particularly underlined. Assistance to third states affected by the application of sanctions—such as the ones foreseen in Article 50 of the Charter—could contribute to strengthening an effective and comprehensive approach by the international community to sanctions imposed by the Security Council.

The EU underlines the importance of establishing procedures to review the cases of those claiming to have been incorrectly placed or retained on sanction lists of individuals or entities involving the application of sanctions. Due process and respect for human rights, accountability and regular and reasonable review will make UN sanctions mechanisms more effective and more credible.

(21 April 2005, text supplied by FCO)

15/8

In a written Ministerial Statement, an FCO Minister wrote:

The Government have committed themselves to informing Parliament on an annual basis of the sanctions regimes being implemented by the United Kingdom. Currently the United Kingdom implements mandatory United Nations sanctions, imposed by the UN Security Council acting under Chapter VII of the Charter of the United Nations, in relation to Al-Qaeda and the Taliban, Côte d'Ivoire, the Democratic Republic of the Congo, Iraq, Liberia, Rwanda, Sierra Leone, Sudan and Somalia. The UK also implements sanctions regimes imposed autonomously by the EU in relation to Belarus, Bosnia and Herzegovina, Burma, China, the former Federal Republic of Yugoslavia (in connection with individuals indicted by the International Criminal Tribunal for the former Yugoslavia), Moldova, Sudan and Zimbabwe. In accordance with a decision of the Organisation for Security and Co-operation in Europe (OSCE), the United Kingdom implements arms embargoes on Armenia and Azerbaijan. The Government also take full account of the Economic Community of West African States moratorium on certain exports of small arms and light weapons to the Economic Community of West African States members. A full list of sanctions regimes and restrictive measures implemented by the UK has been published on the Foreign and Commonwealth Office website at: www.fco.gov.uk/sanctions.

(HC Deb 8 November 2005 Vol. 439 c9WS)

15/9

Côte d'Ivoire

In a written answer, an FCO Minister wrote:

The situation in Côte d'Ivoire remains fragile and the Government are concerned at any report of activities by either the Côte d'Ivoire Government or rebels which could re-ignite conflict. United Nations Security Council resolutions 1572 and 1584 imposed an arms embargo on all parties involved in the conflict, to be closely monitored by the UN. A group of experts has recently submitted a report to the Security Council on the present state of the embargo. We and other Security Council members are now carefully considering this report. We would view with the utmost concern evidence of the Government of Côte d'Ivoire rebuilding their airforce, which would clearly contravene the embargo and threaten the fragile ceasefire. We also strongly support recent efforts by the UN, African Union and the Economic Community of West African States to move the peace process forward following the postponed elections of 30 October.

(HC Deb 15 November 2005 Vol. 439 c1185W)

15/10

Democratic Republic of Congo

In a written answer, an FCO Minister wrote:

Despite recent international efforts to strengthen and enforce the UN and EU arms embargoes, and the creation in 2004 of a UN group of experts to monitor implementation and examine reported breaches, there is some evidence that rebel groups in the Democratic Republic of Congo continue to receive supplies of arms and ammunition.

The UK takes the enforcement of these embargoes very seriously and will examine carefully the latest reports of breaches of the arms embargo before assessing what further action might be appropriate. Any information we receive relating to the potential involvement of UK entities in alleged sanctions-breaches is reported promptly to the relevant UK authorities for their investigation.

(HC Deb 14 July 2005 Vol. 436 c1177W)

15/11

During a debate in the House of Lords, an FCO Minister said:

... the United Kingdom continues to observe and to support strongly the UN and EU arms embargoes on the Democratic Republic of Congo. We take seriously any allegations that UK entities may have been involved in the illicit supply of arms to embargoed destinations. Any evidence that we receive is passed promptly to the relevant United Kingdom authorities for their investigations. Her Majesty's Revenue and Customs, the appropriate investigating body, made full inquiries into these allegations in 2003, but found no evidence of offences.

(HL Deb 13 July 2005 Vol. 673 c1100)

15/12

In a written answer, an FCO Minister wrote:

The UK continues to observe and support strongly the UN and EU arms embargoes on the Democratic Republic of Congo (DRC). Despite international efforts to enforce the embargoes, and the monitoring of the embargo by UN peacekeepers and by the UN Group of Experts, there is some evidence that rebel groups operating in eastern DRC continue to use illegally supplied arms and ammunition.

We continue to work to strengthen enforcement of the embargoes. We are close to securing agreement in the UN Security Council on identifying a list of arms embargo violators to be subject to assets freezes and travel bans.

(HC Deb 3 November 2005 Vol. 438 c1361W)

15/13

Peacekeeping

The Government was asked what action it was taking to strengthen the part played by civilian policing in UN peacekeeping operations. An FCO Minister wrote:

Working through its mission to the UN in New York, the Foreign and Commonwealth Office (FCO) co-operates closely with the Department of Peacekeeping Operations (DPKO) on the role civilian policing plays in UN peace support operations (PSOs). Already a key element of PSOs, we are working proactively to ensure civilian policing needs are considered at all stages of the establishment of a mission, including pre-mission needs assessment, definition and development of mandates, intelligence gathering, rapid deployment—on which we await further information on the DPKO's proposal to establish a standing civilian policing capability and pre-deployment training. In particular, we strongly support the DPKO's efforts to develop integrated mission planning, combining three closely interconnected pillars of the criminal justice system—police, judiciary and penal institutions. To that end, a UK secondee to the DPKO helped in the development of a handbook on integrated planning last year.

At an operational level, the UK contributes police officers to two UN missions, with 93 officers currently deployed to UNMIK (Kosovo) and six to UNAMSIL (Sierra Leone). Building on our commitment to the 2000 Brahimi Report on Peacekeeping Operations, we support the development of other member states' international civilian policing capability, and have to date delivered 11 "Train the Trainer" courses around the world. We are also in the process of developing a G8 initiative to help build African civilian policing capability. In addition, we continue to play an active role in the development and delivery of civilian police standardised training module workshops to assist in the training of military and police officers who are likely to serve in specialised functions in PSOs.

As far as the UK's own civilian policing contribution is concerned, the FCO is leading cross-Whitehall and Police Service consultation aimed at improving the UK's approach to international policing, and better prioritising and strengthening our response to calls for contributions from the UN and other international organisations. A strategic task force is expected to submit recommendations to Ministers in July 2005.

(HL Deb 7 March 2005 Vol. 670 cWA56)

15/14

Sudan

In a written answer, an FCO Minister wrote:

We have received unconfirmed reports that the Government of Sudan airforce have been used in recent operations in Darfur. The African Union is currently investigating and we await their report. Offensive military overflights by the Government of Sudan would constitute a breach of their obligations under the Abuja Security Protocol and, under United Nations Security Council Resolution 1591, those responsible are liable to targeted sanctions.

(HC Deb 3 November 2005 Vol. 438 c1363W–1364W)

Part Fifteen: II. B. *Coercive Measures Short of the Use of Force—Collective measures—Collective measures outside the United Nations*

15/15

In a written Ministerial Statement, an FCO Minister wrote:

The Government remain committed to the Organisation for Security and Co-operation in Europe arms embargo against both Azerbaijan and Armenia, which we interpret as covering all goods and technology controlled under entries in part III of schedule 1 to the Export of Goods (Control) Order 1994 (commonly known as the military list).

In November 2005, the Government approved an export licence application for bomb disposal clothing and equipment for the special state protection service in Azerbaijan.

The decision was made in accordance with our practice occasionally to make an exemption to our interpretation of the embargo by approving exports of non-lethal military goods where it is clear that the embargo was not intended to prevent those exports. The Government believe that this export is justifiable on humanitarian grounds.

(HC Deb 29 November 2005 Vol. 440 c7WS–8WS)

15/16

China

In a written answer, an FCO Minister wrote:

The Government do not believe that the EU arms embargo is an entirely effective way to control the EU's strategic exports to China. Member states do not share a common interpretation of the scope of the embargo.

In practice, the EU code of conduct, rather than the embargo, is the primary instrument with which the possible export to China of military listed goods and technology is considered. The code has either been integrated directly into member states' national law, or they consider it binding guidance on the implementation of national law. The code effectively controls the EU's exports for countries like North Korea, Iran, Syria and Libya, where no EU or UN embargoes are in place.

In the UK, the code is considered binding guidance under the Export Control Act, and we accordingly treat it as seriously as the rest of the Act. The code is used in more than 80 per cent. of all our decisions to refuse export licences for China.

(HL Deb 21 November 2005 Vol. 675 cWA200)

15/17

Democratic Republic of Congo

Her Majesty's Government was asked whether it would seek to revise the legislative position on controls on arms brokering to ensure that UK citizens are unable to exploit a legal loophole in order to profit from the sales of arms to the Democratic Republic of the Congo. In reply, a Minister from the Department of Trade and Industry wrote:

The Government do not accept that any such loophole exists. The Democratic Republic of the Congo (DRC) is subject to an EU arms embargo and as such the UK's controls on overseas trade in military equipment to the DRC are fully extraterritorial, applying to persons in the UK and UK persons anywhere in the world, including those whose sole involvement in the transaction is, for example, advertising, transport, or finance.

(HC Deb 20 July 2005 Vol. 436 c1736W)

15/18

In a written answer, an FCO Minister wrote:

The established policy of the EU is not to supply arms to Iran. We assess export licence applications on a case-by-case basis against the consolidated EU and national arms export licensing criteria and other policies taking into account the prevailing circumstances at the time. We will not issue an export licence if approval would be inconsistent with national embargoes observed by the UK. I refer my hon. Friend to the parliamentary statements made by Douglas Hurd, the then Foreign Secretary, on 1 March 1993 and my hon. Friend Tony Lloyd, the then Minister of State, on 28 September 1998, which set out our approach in respect of Iran. We will not issue licences for the export to Iran of goods or technology on the military or nuclear list, except for goods essential for the safety of civil aircraft and air traffic control systems and certain radioactive substances for medical use. No licences will be approved for any equipment where there is knowledge or reason to suspect that it will go to a military end-user or be used for military purposes. On very rare occasions, and with parliamentary agreement, exceptions are made where denying an export or gift would be against the spirit of the embargo. For example, we did so earlier this year with a small donation of body armour for the anti-narcotics police, who work closely with the UK and United Nations Office on Drugs and Crime to prevent drugs trafficking.

(HC Deb 18 October 2005 Vol. 437 c905W)

15/19

Iran

In respect of allegations about Iran's programme for developing nuclear weapons, the Government was asked, bearing in mind the Government's use of intelligence over Iraq, how we can trust their assessment of Iran's weapons of mass destruction. The Foreign Secretary said:

We have made no published assessment based on intelligence about Iran and we have no plans to do so. The international community is concerned about Iran not because we have seen incontrovertible evidence that it has a nuclear weapons programme, but because of what is plainly on the record in the reports of the director general and the board of the International Atomic Energy Agency—namely, that Iran, over a period that goes back 20 years, has failed to comply with its safeguard agreements to give notice to the IAEA of all areas in which it was pursuing dual-use nuclear programmes. That is the basis on which we, in the so-called E3, have been taking forward the negotiations. I hope and believe that they are tough and will produce an acceptable solution.

On military action, I have made it clear beyond peradventure that we can conceive of no circumstances in which military action against Iran would be justified. I cannot be clearer than that . . .

(HC Deb 5 April 2005 Vol. 432 c1252)

15/20

Kurdistan

The was to make a statement on the (a) nature and (b) policy underlying UK involvement in ECJ case C0229/05, on certain Kurdistan political groups. In reply, an FCO Minister wrote:

European Court of Justice (ECJ) case C0229/05 involves a freeze on assets imposed by the European Community pursuant to United Nations Security

Council Resolution (UNSCR) 1373 (2001). Effective implementation of UNSCR 1373 (2001) is a priority for the UK as a central component of the international community's efforts against terrorism. The UK fully supported the decision by the European Council to impose an asset freeze on certain Kurdish political groups and intervened in support of the European Council before the Court of First Instance. The action against the European Council was dismissed by that court. Although the UK has not intervened again in the appeal of the case to the ECJ, it continues to support fully the case put forward by the European Council.

(HC Deb 16 November 2005 Vol. 439 c1267W)

15/21

Organisation for Security and Co-operation in Europe

In a written Ministerial Statement, an FCO Minister wrote:

The Government remain committed to the Organisation for Security and Co-operation in Europe arms embargo against both Azerbaijan and Armenia, which we interpret as covering all goods and technology controlled under entries in Part III of Schedule 1 to the Export of Goods (Control) Order 1994 (commonly known as the military list).

In November 2005, the Government approved an export licence application for bomb disposal clothing and equipment for the Special State Protection Service in Azerbaijan.

The decision was made in accordance with our practice occasionally to make an exemption to our interpretation of the embargo by approving exports of non-lethal military goods where it is clear that the embargo was not intended to prevent those exports. The Government believe that this export is justifiable on humanitarian grounds.

(HL Deb 29 November 2005 Vol. 676 cWS5)

Part Sixteen: Use of Force

Part Sixteen: I. *Use of Force—Prohibition of the use of force*

16/1

During a Security Council Meeting the representative of the United Kingdom stated:

While having repeatedly condemned terrorist atrocities against Israelis, and recognizing Israel's right to protect its citizens against terrorist attacks, the European Union has consistently opposed extrajudicial killings, which are contrary to international law. The European Union emphasizes that Palestinians and Israelis must not return to the cycle of violence that has been characteristic of recent years. We urge Israel to exercise maximum self-restraint and the

Palestinian Authority to take immediate and effective action against those involved in attacks.

(UN Doc. S/PV.5230, 21 July 2005)

Part Sixteen: II. A. *Use of Force—Legitimate use of force—Self-defence*

16/2

Anticipatory Self-defence

The Government was asked whether it supported the doctrine of anticipatory self-defence. An FCO Minister wrote:

Th[e] right of self-defence is not limited to a response to an actual armed attack. It has been the consistent position of successive United Kingdom Governments over many years that the right of self-defence under international law includes the right to use force where an armed attack is imminent.

(HC Deb 31 January 2005 Vol. 430 c712W)

16/3

Israel

In a written answer, an FCO Minister wrote:

We recognise Israel's right to defend itself against terrorism but it must act in accordance with international law. In this context we have made representations at every level to the Israeli authorities raising our concerns regarding the disproportionate use of force by the Israeli defence forces in Gaza, and the number of civilian casualties, particularly children, which have resulted from their actions.

(HC Deb 7 March 2005 Vol. 431 c1578W)

16/4

The Government was asked about the construction of a sea barrier by Israel. An FCO Minister wrote:

We are seeking clarification from the Government of Israel on its reported plans to build a sea barrier. We fully support Israel's right to defend itself against terrorism, which the UK condemns absolutely. But we would expect the construction of any such sea barrier to comply with international law.

(HC Deb 28 June 2005 Vol. 435 c1480W)

16/5

In a written answer, an FCO Minister wrote:

The Government's consistent policy is that as long as it acts within international law, Israel has the right to protect its citizens from terrorist attacks which we condemn absolutely. Targeted killings are contrary to international law.

(HC Deb 17 October 2005 Vol. 437 c731W)

Part Sixteen: II. B.1. *Use of Force—Legitimate use of force—Collective measures—United Nations*

16/6

The Government was asked what assessment its Department has made of the impact on the peace process in Côte d'Ivoire of General Henri Poncet's announcement on 18 January on the willingness of the French force in Côte d'Ivoire to use force if asked to do so by the UN mission. An FCO Minister wrote:

We welcome General Poncet's expressed willingness for French forces in Côte d'lvoire to use necessary force when requested to do so by the UN Operation (UNOCI). This is provided for in UN Security Council resolution 1528 (2004). With UNOCI, French forces have helped preserve the peace by maintaining the zone of confidence separating the two sides, and have helped restore order after the recent violence; we value their continued support of UNOCI.

...

On 18 November my right hon. Friend the Foreign Secretary thanked Foreign Minister Barnier for French military assistance in the evacuation of British citizens.

(HC Deb 26 January 2005 Vol. 430 c425W)

16/7

The Government was asked:
Which of the following five basic criteria of legitimacy for the authorisation by the United Nations Security Council of the use of military force, as spelt out in detail by the [UN] High Level Panel on Threats, Challenges and Change, [it endorsed]:

(a) seriousness of threat;
(b) proper purpose;
(c) last resort;
(d) proportional means; and
(e) balance of consequences.

An FCO Minister wrote:

These criteria are similar to those set out by my right honourable friend the Prime Minister in his speech in Chicago in 1999. We support the development of such principles as a tool to assist the Security Council in deciding when to authorise the use of force. We also note that the high level panel identifies that the Security Council needs to be more proactive in dealing with threats and that in certain circumstances force may be justified not just reactively, but preventively.

(HL Deb 7 March 2005 Vol. 670 cWA61)

16/8

In a written answer, the Minister for Defence wrote:

The Government declare forces to NATO and the EU through the Defence Planning Questionnaire and Force Catalogue respectively. The declarations entail that those forces are earmarked as available in principle for potential deployment on NATO or EU operations. Any actual decision to deploy is taken by the Government, voluntarily and on a case-by-case basis. However the Government are committed under article V of the North Atlantic Treaty to deployment in collective defence as required.

(HC Deb 10 October 2005 Vol. 437 c7W)

16/9

Humanitarian Intervention

The Government was asked whether it will commit itself to the emerging norm, as set out by the UN High Level Panel on Threats, Challenges and Change, that "there is a collective responsibility to protect, exercisable by the United Nations Security Council authorising military interventions as a last resort, in the event of genocide and other large-scale killing, ethnic cleansing or serious violations of humanitarian law which sovereign governments have proved powerless or unwilling to prevent"; and, if so, by what action.

An FCO Minister wrote:

The Government welcome this recommendation of the high level panel. The proposals are similar to those outlined by my right honourable friend the Prime Minister in his speech in Chicago in 1999 and the report of the International Commission on Intervention and State Sovereignty in 2001. The UK will work with like minded countries to take forward this recommendation at the Millennium Review Summit in September 2005.

(HL Deb 7 March 2005 Vol. 670 c.WA56)

16/10

During a Security Council Meeting the representative of the European Union stated:

While we renew our commitment to those principles [in SC Res 1296 on the protection of civilian populations, Ed.], we cannot forget that the primary responsibility to protect lies with individual sovereign States. However, when a State is unable or unwilling to protect its civilians, or when crimes such as genocide, ethnic cleansing, crimes against humanity, war crimes or massive and grave human rights violations occur or threaten to occur, the international community must respond.

. . .

I mentioned briefly the situation of refugees and internally displaced persons. As they seek protection abroad or in their own country, fleeing armed conflict or specific threats, they sometimes remain in danger even in their place of refuge. Men are killed, and women and girls are raped and sometimes killed. Sometimes camps are targeted; they are often inadequately protected. There is therefore a clear need for increased physical protection. Where States will not or cannot provide such protection, the international community must do so. In that context, I would like to repeat our call for improved humanitarian access in all areas where aid is so desperately needed.

(UN Doc. S/PV.5209, 21 June 2005)

16/11

Iraq

An FCO Minister wrote:

Under United Nations Security Council Resolution 1483 of 22 May 2003, the occupying powers shared joint responsibility for the actions of the CPA, including management of the DFI. The UK supported the establishment of the IAMB, an independent international board to oversee the auditing of Iraq's oil revenues and their management, so that the coalition was seen to discharge its financial responsibilities as occupying power properly.

(HL Deb 24 January 2005 Vol. 668 c131WA)

16/12

The Foreign Secretary said in a debate in the House of Commons:

The mandate for the multinational force—it of course includes the British force—was established in resolution 1546, which states that the mandate will be reviewed in June this year and will terminate, unless extended by a further Security Council resolution, this December. Meanwhile, as the Iraqi Interior Minister implied, the question of whether foreign forces should be on Iraqi soil is entirely a matter for the Iraqis themselves. I heard Dr. Shaikhly, the Iraqi ambassador to the United Kingdom, say yesterday on the BBC that this election could not have taken place but for the presence of the multinational force of the United States, the United Kingdom and other contributor forces to the coalition. We proved yesterday that it is there not as an army of occupation, but as a force for democracy by, for and of the Iraqis. We will only stay there as long as we are needed, but how long that is depends almost entirely on how quickly the Iraqis' own forces can be built up. However, yesterday's experience was a good one in terms of their ability to deal with such matters.

... we have an obligation not only to listen to the elected representatives of the new Transitional Government, but to do what they say in respect of the future of the multinational force. Frankly, an issue about ending the occupation does not arise. In terms of its legal and practical effect, the occupation ended with the passage of resolution 1546. Since then, the multinational force has been there at the invitation, and only at the invitation, of the Interim Iraqi Government, who are now to be the Transitional Government. Of course, one item on that Government's agenda will be when they want us to go, but we have had no indication that any serious and responsible Iraqi politicians want us to go before our job is done. The moment they do so—it is their judgment, not ours—we will go.

(HC Deb 31 January 2005 Vol. 430 c578, 582)

16/13

The Prime Minister told the House of Commons:

... as a result of evidence that has emerged subsequent to the Iraq war, it is perfectly obvious that there were indeed multiple breaches of UN resolutions—and it was on the basis of breaches of UN resolutions that we went to war.

(HC Deb 9 March 2005 Vol. 431 c1516)

16/14

The Government was asked if it will list the individuals detained in Iraq by coalition forces because of alleged connection with weapons of mass destruction programmes; how long each has been detained; when they are expected to be released. An FCO Minister wrote:

The Multi-National Force (MNF) has the power to intern individuals for imperative reasons of security in accordance with UN Security Council Resolution 1546 and the annexed exchange of letters between Prime Minister Allawi and the then US Secretary of State Colin Powell.

Each case of detention is regularly reviewed by the detaining power and a decision taken on whether continued detention is necessary. While the reasons for these decisions are recorded, they have not been collated in a form that would enable us to answer this question on behalf of all multi-national forces. We would not, as a matter of policy, in any case release the names of those who had been detained so as to respect their privacy and to ensure there were no security repercussions for them.

We can, however, confirm that the United Kingdom is not detaining any individuals in Iraq on the basis of alleged connection with weapons of mass destruction programmes.

(HC Deb 14 March 2005 Vol. 431 c91W)

16/15

The Government was asked if it will make representations to the Iraqi administration that it makes it a condition sine qua non that there be a determination by the UN about the legality of the use of force against Iraq before any person is accused of having committed crimes in Iraq. An FCO Minister wrote:

As the Solicitor-General made clear in his written answer of 17 March 2003, *Official Report*, column 515W, authority to use force against Iraq derived from the combined effect of UNSCRs 678, 687 and 1441; and all of these resolutions were adopted under Chapter VII of the UN Charter, which allows the use of force for the express purpose of restoring international peace and security. We would therefore have no reason to make representations to the Iraqi Government about the legality of the use of force in Iraq.

(HC Deb 15 March 2005 Vol. 432 c221W)

16/16

In a debate about the circumstances surrounding the resignation of an FCO legal adviser immediately before the attack against Iraq in March 2003, the Foreign Secretary said:

Let me take the two parts of the question in turn: first, the circumstances surrounding Ms Wilmshurst's letter to the Foreign and Commonwealth Office's legal adviser of 18 March 2003.

Elizabeth Wilmshurst was one of the deputy legal advisers at the Foreign and Commonwealth Office. As is now well known, she submitted her resignation on 18 March 2003 because she disagreed—I quote from her minute of that date—that it was

> "lawful to use force against Iraq without a second Security Council resolution to revive the authorisation given in SCR 678".

Given that difference of views, her resignation was an honourable course to take and in accordance with the civil service code.

The Foreign and Commonwealth Office has received a number of requests for the text of Ms Wilmshurst's letter under the Freedom of Information Act, which came into force on 1 January this year. These requests were initially refused, mainly because much of the content of Ms Wilmshurst's letter contained personal data, the disclosure of which would have contravened the first data protection principle under section 40 of the Act.

Following the publication in *The Guardian* on 23 February of a number of quotations from the letter, however, we took the view that disclosure of this information would no longer contravene the first data protection principle. We therefore disclosed the letter yesterday. Two sentences were however omitted by the Foreign and Commonwealth Office from the document because their content concerned the provision of legal advice in relation to the use of force against Iraq. Regardless of whether these references were accurate, this information was covered by exemptions in the Act that apply to confidential legal advice and the formulation or development of Government policy. Some were also covered by exemptions for ministerial communications and for Law Officers' advice.

It was entirely proper for the Government to withhold information under the provisions of this Act. Indeed, as the Minister who was responsible for taking what was then the Freedom of Information Bill through Parliament, I can recall no suggestion from any party in the House that the Government's legal advice should not be exempt from such disclosure.

Let me now turn to the second aspect of the question: the Attorney-General's opinion on the legality of military action in Iraq. This whole question is covered extensively in Lord Butler's report on intelligence on weapons of mass destruction at paragraphs 366 to 387, and I commend those paragraphs to the House. Ms Wilmshurst gave evidence to the Butler inquiry, and the substance of her position, then as now, is covered in paragraph 376 of the report.

In the light of Saddam's failure to comply with his very clear obligations, set out in United Nations Security Council resolution 1441 of November 2002, the United Kingdom, United States and Spain tabled in February 2003 a further draft resolution in the Security Council, posing tough but attainable tests for Iraq. That gave Saddam Hussein the final opportunity to comply, which was offered by resolution 1441.

I attended a series of ministerial Security Council meetings in the early months of 2003, the last of which was on 7 March 2003. As I said in my speech to the Security Council on that day, not a single member of the Security Council disputed that Saddam was in material breach of his obligations under resolution 1441 and preceding resolutions. He had not fully complied with the clear obligations set out in 1441 and the preceding resolutions.

The Attorney-General, in his written answer of 17 March 2003, gave what he has described as his genuinely and independently held view that military action in Iraq was lawful on the basis of Saddam's breach of the then existing UN resolutions. As he then said, authority to use force against Iraq derived from the combined effect of resolutions 678, 687 and 1441. A large majority of the House supported on 18 March 2003 the Government's motion before the House to take military action in respect of Iraq, in view of Saddam Hussein's continued failure to comply with his clear obligations, imposed by the Security Council.

...

First, on why we refused to publish those two sentences, I have set out the reasons. The issue for the whole House, and not least the shadow Attorney-General, is whether he and his party are now moving from a clear position that Law Officers' advice should not be published to proposing that Law Officers' advice, and that which contributes to it, should be published.

I draw the House's attention to the fact that when a similar issue arose, albeit in respect of a different subject—legal advice in respect of the ratification of the

Maastricht treaty—the then Attorney-General set out clearly that he could not recall any occasion when the Law Officers' advice had been disclosed, and would not break precedent.

When we discussed the issue of the Freedom of Information Bill in the House, the House as a whole was absolutely clear that legal advice, and the background to that legal advice, should not be disclosed for very good reasons. If the hon. Gentleman is now saying, on behalf of his party, that that should change, he had better say so; but the implications for good government are very grave indeed.

The hon. Gentleman then made a wholly tendentious claim based on his reading of Ms Wilmshurst's letter. He said that it showed clearly that the Attorney-General had one view on 7 March and a different view later. He asked what change of law or fact had taken place. The letter showed nothing of the kind—but yes, there was a change of fact, which was before the House on 18 March. I am astonished that the hon. Gentleman, who voted for the resolution in favour of military action on 18 March, seems to have forgotten that.

Throughout the period following the passage of resolution 1441, my right hon. Friend the Prime Minister and I, every other member of this Government and, indeed, all the Governments who later formed the coalition were seeking to ensure that there was clear compliance by Saddam with the obligations imposed on him by resolution 1441 and the resolutions that preceded it. When it became clear that that was not the case, we worked night and day for a second resolution. We did not work night and day for a second resolution because it was required by the terms of resolution 1441: it was not. I can go into the negotiating history of resolution 1441 in very great detail. I can point out to the House that France proposed at one stage that there should indeed be a lock requiring a second resolution in resolution 1441, but backed off from that proposal. Everyone who knows the text of resolution 1441, and that of operative paragraphs 4, 12 and 13 in particular, will know that there was no requirement whatever for a second resolution. We sought a second resolution because we sought a consensus in the Security Council, and what changed between 7 and 17 March was this: it became very clear that that consensus was not possible.

The hon. Gentleman's last point concerned the effect of refusing to disclose the Attorney-General's advice. The Attorney-General's advice was before the Butler inquiry. The Attorney-General gave advice to the Butler inquiry, and so, as I have said, did Ms Wilmshurst. That was the appropriate setting in which to examine the advice in detail. Lord Butler concluded that the Attorney-General had given clear and categorical advice to the Cabinet, and that in his judgment it was lawful under resolution 1441 to use force without a further United Nations Security Council resolution. That was the position after full examination, and that is the position now.

...

We are all aware of what the Secretary-General of the United Nations said. It emphasises the fact that on this issue there were disagreements about the legal position. That is well known—but the truth is that there are often disagreements about legal positions and legal advice. There are disagreements in respect of matters of domestic law, on which the law is always more certain; still more are there disagreements in respect of matters of international law. These judgments were held independently, they were held honourably, and they were well known in advance of the debate on 18 March and the House's decision to take military action. With great respect to Ms Wilmshurst, what she has said in the letter and in the evidence that she gave to Lord Butler does not change that position one iota. It was a matter of debate. But, while I respect those people who took a different view, the truth is that the view of the British Attorney-General was widely shared across the world—not just by the Law Officers' equivalent in the United States, but by many other Governments. There was just a genuine difference of opinion.

In response to a claim that there was no material change in the facts, the Foreign Secretary said:

I am sorry, but he was not at the Security Council five times between January and March 2003, and I was. There was a significant change in the facts. We had hoped in early January was that there was going to be full compliance by Saddam with the terms of the resolution. He was given a very clear obligation to do so. It became clear, however, not least on 7 March in the 173-page document submitted to the Security Council at the end of that meeting by Dr. Hans Blix, with 29 separate respects, talking about unanswered disarmament issues. I put this before the House on 18 March. It spelled out in detail, if any were needed, why Saddam was failing to comply with his clear obligations. Those facts were on the record and they have never been contradicted since. That was the judgment of UNMOVIC, the United Nations Monitoring, Verification and Inspection Commission. We did not need intelligence to make our judgment before the House on 18 March; we could see for ourselves that Saddam was in further material breach, and, as I pointed out to the Security Council on 7 March, there was not a single Minister around the table at the Security Council at that stage—even on 7 March—who was denying that Saddam was not fully in compliance with his obligations.

What also changed between 7 and 17 March . . . was that we were hoping against hope for a second resolution and we did not get one. We still judged that Saddam was in material breach, and that was the basis on which the House came to its view on 18 March.

The Attorney-General's legal advice was clear. It was known. It was reflected in the view of his advice, which he put before the House of Lords on 17 March, and which I repeated in this House, along with a longer explanation of the basis of his view in respect of the legality. His view was that it was lawful for us to take military action in respect of Iraq. That was the view that he came to at that stage. He was examined in very great detail by Lord Butler, and Lord Butler confirms his view. There is a very much wider issue about whether the House should go down the road of requiring the advice of Attorneys-General to be made public. As I have said, when the matter was debated by the House, and for very, very good reasons, not one Member of this House ever suggested that the exemption for legal advice proposed in the Freedom of Information Act 2000 should be removed. It is there for very good reasons and nothing material has changed. Indeed, just to underline the paucity of the view taken by the shadow Attorney-General, in this particular case, unusually, what was made known to the House was the view of the Attorney-General set out in that written answer of 17 March. When Lord Butler examined the Attorney-General in detail, he also confirmed that that was his view.

. . .

[It] is also right to draw attention to the fact that the requirement to protect the confidentiality of legal advice has been supported not only by successive Governments . . . but by the Law Lords in a series of judgments, as well as by working barristers represented by the Bar Council. There is every reason for it, and it is good government that would suffer were we to remove that requirement.

Asked whether the Government would waive its privilege in the confidentiality of the Attorney's advice, the Foreign Secretary said:

I do not accept that, and the Butler inquiry set out in some detail the very rare circumstances in which, in the last 100 years, the advice of Attorneys-General has been released. I think that it pointed out that it has happened on only three occasions: two in respect of legal action and one, as it happened, in respect of the Westland affair where the whole of the advice was leaked by a divided Cabinet and it was made public in any case.

Asked further about Ms Wilmshurst's position, the Foreign Secretary said:

Elizabeth Wilmshurst was a very fine legal adviser in the Foreign Office, she has acted honourably throughout, and it is certainly the case that her view about the potential legality of any military action without a second resolution after 1441 was well known to me, and I think to others within the Government. But as I have said, that was her view, and I think she accepted—certainly it has to be accepted that the final arbiter of the Government's legal position is the Attorney-General and not any individual legal adviser, however distinguished.

On the second point that [I am invited] to discuss, what is the case is that before the passage of resolution 1441, there was a widespread view that military action would at the very best be wholly ill-advised without what became the first UN resolution in 2002, and could be unlawful, but that was changed by the passage of resolution 1441. I simply invite my right hon. Friend to refresh his memory about the terms of resolution 1441, which set out clear obligations on Saddam Hussein. Operative paragraph 4 set out the terms of a further material breach; operative paragraphs 11 and 12 set out how any further material breach should be reported and considered by the Security Council; and operative paragraph 13 made it very clear to Saddam Hussein that "serious consequences" would follow in respect of a further material breach. It was the judgment of the Attorney-General—and I may say, although I am not the Government legal adviser, it was my judgment based on my intense knowledge of the negotiating history of resolution 1441—that the effect of 1441 was to revive the authority of resolutions 678 and 687 . . . Well, we did not get a second resolution because it was not possible, but it was never needed legally, and I made that very clear to the House—crystal clear, on the record—when I reported the passage of 1441 to the House on 24 November 2002 . . . the resolution is worthy of re-reading. It sets out clearly the position. The Attorney-General was in no doubt by the middle of March that Saddam, on the basis of evidence that we provided, was in clear further material breach, and that military action was justified.

It was put to the Foreign Secretary that [he had] been reminded that the Secretary-General of the United Nations said that the war was unlawful. Would [he] not ... accept that the Secretary-General is singularly well placed to advise as to the legal impact of Security Council resolutions? Is not the truth this: the Attorney-General, as a good House lawyer, came to give the best argument that he could in order to provide legal cover for a decision already taken when war was then inevitable and in order to provide the best justification that he could for a war that was being prosecuted for reasons outside those publicly stated by the Prime Minister?

The Foreign Secretary replied:

That allegation is completely untrue ... I made it clear, and so did the Prime Minister, repeatedly, that we wanted to see the issue of Saddam Hussein's clear breach of United Nations Security Council resolutions resolved peacefully. The phrase that I used repeatedly, in the Security Council and outside, was that we would of course take yes for an answer. Had there been any evidence of compliance with resolution 1441 in those Security Council resolutions, it would not have lain in my mouth to say to my colleagues, without demur from any of them, in the Security Council on 7 March, that not one had claimed that Saddam was in compliance with the Security Council, nor would it have been remotely possible to have come before this House on 17 and 18 March and make the case for military action. The case for military action, I remind the House, was on the basis of a breach of Security Council resolutions rather than on any matter of intelligence. The evidence was put before the House in two successive Command Papers and, I add, the Iraq Survey Group has confirmed that it ascertained a clear and continuing breach by Saddam of those disarmament obligations.

A further question was asked:

The Foreign Secretary will know that the Attorney-General has a duty to provide legal advice to Parliament in addition to his duties in relation to the Executive. Was not his written answer of 17 March 2003 effectively the provision of such advice to Parliament? In that case, should not Members of Parliament be entitled to see the background papers, setting out the detailed considerations relating to the legal issues on which the Attorney-General's published view was based?

The Foreign Secretary replied:

... the requirement on the Attorney-General to provide legal advice to Parliament is very limited indeed and it is a wholly separate duty from the clear and continuing requirement to provide legal advice to the Government internally. Such advice is very clearly protected by the long-standing principle of legal professional privilege, confirmed by the Law Lords and many other courts. It is protected by the ministerial code. As recently as four years ago, the House had every opportunity during the passage of the Freedom of Information Bill to disagree with that. As I have already said, not a single Member on either side of the House ever proposed that the advice of the Attorney-General should be made public in the way that is now being suggested ...

... There has been not the slightest evidence of providing anything other than the straightforward facts of the matter both to this House and to the other place. There is no secret about the fact that the Attorney-General sought the view of the Prime Minister as to whether Iraq was in further material breach. That was set out clearly in the Butler inquiry's report ...

As to the matter of the ministerial code, that charge, which my right hon. Friend has made in the past, was fully dealt with by Sir Andrew Turnbull, the Cabinet Secretary. Paragraph 23 of the code, which I happen to have in front of me, is much more narrowly drawn than she suggests. The Attorney-General was actually present in the Cabinet—I re-examined the minutes this morning—and offered the clear view that military action in respect of Iraq, as of 17 March, was lawful. I recall that my right hon. Friend was there and voted in favour of military action—and I am glad that she did. The Attorney-General was there to take questions.

(HC Deb 24 March 2005 Vol. 432 c1003–1012)

16/17

An FCO Minister told the House of Commons:

... the multinational force is in Iraq with the agreement of the Iraqi Government, who may terminate their presence at any time or request their continued presence. The UK therefore will continue to provide troops for as long as the Iraqi Government want us to remain. We have no desire to stay a moment longer than necessary, but we will not leave the job before it is done.

(HC Deb 18 May 2005 Vol. 434 c162)

16/18

The Minister of Defence told the House of Commons:

Resolution 1441 was the last resolution demanding immediate, unconditional and full disclosure and acceptance of all the UN resolutions thus far, and its purpose was not regime change, but to respond to the breach of the UN resolutions, so the substance of the legal basis for the 1998 intervention and the latest intervention [viz in 2003] is exactly the same.

(HC Deb 18 May 2005 Vol. 434 c245)

16/19

During a press conference on 7 June 2005 in the White House the Prime Minister was asked whether the the so-called Downing Street Memo from July, 2002, which says, "Intelligence and facts remain fixed around the policy of removing Saddam through military actions,'' is an accurate reflection of what happened. In reply the Prime Minister said:

No, the facts were not being fixed in any shape or form at all. And let me remind you that that memorandum was written before we then went to the United Nations.

Now, no one knows more intimately the discussions that we were conducting as two countries at the time than me.

And the fact is, we decided to go to the United Nations and went through that process, which resulted in the November, 2002, United Nations resolution to give a final chance to Saddam Hussein to comply with international law.

He didn't do so. And that was the reason why we had to take military action. But, all the way through that period of time, we were trying to look for a way of managing to resolve this without conflict.

As it happened, we weren't able to do that because, as I think was very clear, there was no way that Saddam Hussein was ever going to change the way that he worked or the way that he acted.

(www.pm.gov.uk/output/Page7600.asp)

16/20

During a press conference on 27 June 2005 with the Iraqi Prime Minister, Ibrahim Al-Jaafari, the UK Prime Minister was asked the following question:

There is interference from the neighbouring countries of Iraq, and as the observers see, this interference is probably supported by the governments of these countries. Will you take part, involve yourself to prevent such interference, or will you leave this to the Iraqis to solve it?

In reply the Prime Minister said:

... it is important that we emphasise this is now a United Nations backed process. It is the duty of every country in the international community to cooperate and work with the new Iraqi government, and we make it very clear to the neighbouring countries of Iraq that it is important that they work with the democratic Iraqi government and do not try to undermine it. And that is a message reinforced constantly by us, and I am sure by the Iraqi government itself ... Now sometimes I worry that there are others within the Middle East who are frightened of this example coming to pass, who will see Iraq as a sovereign democratic country, making progress, people investing in the country, the people with the same rights that we take for granted in countries like this, they will look at Iraq developing like that and they will worry. But we are determined to give every support to the Iraqi government in making that journey of progress because it is vitally important. And sometimes people say, and this is implicit in the first question I got asked, it is a very tough security situation in Iraq at the moment, but why is it tough—it is tough because people are trying to stop the democratic will of the Iraqi people. Well our response has got to be to defeat that obstruction, not to give in to it. That is why it is important that the will of the Iraqi people remains firm, as I am sure it will, and I can tell you our will will remain firm too, because this is in our joint interest, in the interests of people in Iraq, but also in the interests of a country like Britain. If we defeat this terrorism in Iraq, we will defeat it everywhere, that is why it is important and that is why we will stay and see it through. And those countries who neighbour Iraq should understand they have a responsibility too to make this work.

(www.pm.gov.uk/output/Page7745.asp)

16/21

The Government was asked what account it took of United Nations Security Council Resolution 949 concerning Iraq and Kuwait in determining the legality of air strikes carried out by Coalition aircraft in Iraq in 2002. In reply, a Minister wrote:

UN Security Council Resolution 688 of April 1991 condemned the repression of the Iraqi population in many parts of Iraq, and demanded an immediate end to that repression. The No-fly zones were established in 1991 and 1992 as necessary and proportionate steps to prevent a humanitarian crisis, and enabled monitoring of Iraqi compliance with SCR 688. UK aircraft patrolling the Iraqi no-fly zones were entitled to use force in self-defence.

UN Security Council Resolution 949 had no bearing on the entitlement to use force in self defence in monitoring the No-fly zones.

(HC Deb 12 September 2005 Vol. 436 c2281–2282W)

16/22

The Secretary of State for Defence made the following statement in the House of Commons:

... Let us remind ourselves of our objective in Iraq. It is to work, along with the rest of the international community, and now the United Nations under United Nations Security Council resolution 1546, to assist the Iraqi people and their elected representatives: first, to establish their own democratic Government and institutions; secondly, to build their own security forces to safeguard that democracy; and thirdly, to develop their economy and civil society. We are helping the Iraqis to build all three of them; the terrorists want to impede and destroy all three of them. That is the battleground. I can put it no better than President Talibani did in *The Times* this morning:

> "The battle of Iraq cannot be won by retreat or compromise, but by the vision and determination for which Britain is renowned."

And that means, as Prime Minister Jafaari said when I met him recently:

> "The presence of multinational forces in Iraq for us is based on need, security need for those forces to support our forces."

The United Kingdom is in Iraq for as long as we are needed, and as long as we need to be there, and no longer than either.

The political process, despite the worst intentions of the terrorists, continues to be on track. Following the elections in January of this year and the establishment of the constitutional commission, the Iraqis have now produced a draft constitution that will be the subject of an historic national referendum later this week. Few people thought that we would get to this point. Preparations are also under way for full, democratic, national elections in December. These are, in any context, enormous strides forward, and, in the context of the continual terrorist activity, hugely significant strides forward which have been made in spite of the terrorist attempts to derail Iraq's progress towards a peaceful and democratic future.

Against this political backdrop, the coalition's top priority is working with the Iraqis to improve the security environment and to build the capability of the Iraqi security forces so that they themselves are increasingly able to take responsibility for delivering law and order. In this we are working not alone, but with 27 other nations under the United Nations Security Council resolution. Despite, again, all the efforts of the terrorists, I can report to the House that we are beginning to see real progress in building up the Iraqi security forces. There are now more than 190,000 Iraqi security force personnel who have been trained and are capable thus far, and the number of Iraqi units capable of conducting effective counter-insurgency operations is increasing steadily. That means that there are now, for the first time, more trained and capable Iraqi security forces than there are multinational forces in Iraq.

But as everyone involved in this process recognises, there are no quick fixes, and building the Iraqi leadership, command and control, logistics and support structures will take more time. We have always said that our handover to the Iraqis themselves will be conditional upon their developing their own security capabilities, and that we will see the job through until those conditions have been met.

The House may wish to be reminded of the criteria and the terms on which those conditions might be fulfilled, since there has been some demand outside this House for clarification on what is sometimes called the exit strategy. The conditions that will permit the transfer of security responsibility to the Iraqi security forces have been defined by the joint committee to transfer security responsibility, which, as the House may recall, was formed by the Iraqi Prime Minister over the summer.

The basic principles for transfer of security to the Iraqi authorities are based on four broad categories: an assessment of the insurgents' threat level; Iraqi security forces' ability to take on the security task themselves; the capacity of provincial bodies to cope with the changed security environment; and the posture and support available from coalition forces. Those are the criteria; we expect the Committee's criteria to be confirmed soon. Thereafter, assessments will be made by the Iraqis to determine which areas of Iraq are ready to transfer to Iraqi control.

I emphasise that we therefore stand by the strategy that we have maintained up to now, which sets out the conditions under which we will hand security to the Iraqis themselves and begin to draw down our forces. I want to emphasise again that we will stay in Iraq until the job is done and that we will not make significant changes to the United Kingdom's force posture in Iraq until we, the coalition partners and, in particular, the Iraqis themselves, are confident that the conditions are right. That was, is and remains our position and any speculation to the contrary is simply wrong. Indeed, I would go further and say that the biggest obstacle now to our leaving Iraq in view of the build-up of the Iraqi forces' capability is the actions of the terrorists themselves. Terrorist activity only delays our leaving Iraq; it does not hasten it.

(HC Deb 10 October 2005 Vol. 437 c24–25)

16/23

During a debate in the House of Commons, a Minister said:

The British Government will always have the sovereign right to make that decision [withdraw troops from Iraq], and we will do so, but we have entered into obligations, and no British Government lightly abandons obligations seriously entered into. Those obligations, which we entered into with the democratically elected transitional Government in Iraq, and which we will discuss with them in December, mean that we will stay there until the conditions are right, first, for us to hand over the lead to the Iraqi security forces and then eventually to withdraw. Those conditions are plain. The criteria on which our judgment will be based include the Iraqi security forces' ability gradually to take the lead; the control of central and local government in order to compete with the threat against them; and the level of the threat. Ultimately, the choice will be for the British people and the British Government, but we will act in consultation with the Iraqis, as we agreed.

(HC Deb 17 October 2005 Vol. 437 c615–616)

16/24

The Government was asked whether the present rules of engagement of UK forces and special forces in Iraq permit forces to operate over the border with Iran. In reply, the Secretary of State for Defence said:

No

(HC Deb 31 October 2005 Vol. 438 c723W)

16/25

During a Security Council Meeting the representative of the United Kingdom stated:

Most important of all, the resolution [1637 (2005)] we have unanimously adopted today responds to a request from the Government of Iraq, as set out by Prime Minister al-Jaafari in his letter of 27 October. The resolution extends for 12 months the mandate of the Multinational Force (MNF) on the terms set out in resolution 1546 (2004), including the letters annexed to that resolution, as well as the arrangements for the Development Fund for Iraq and the International Advisory and Monitoring Board.

But as also set out by Prime Minister al-Jaafari, the resolution comes with important guarantees. The Iraqi Government will at any time be able to seek a review of the arrangements or the termination of the MNF mandate. The fact that we have been addressing Iraqi needs through this negotiation has, in the view of the United Kingdom, been quite crucial.

(UN Doc. S/PV.5300, 8 November 2005)

16/26

In a written answer, a Minister wrote:

The United Kingdom's armed forces continue to assist the Iraqi Government in providing security and building the capability and capacity of the Iraqi Security Forces so that they may take responsibility for their own security. UK forces remain in Iraq under the UN mandate set out in United Nations Security Council Resolution (UNSCR) 1546. Following a written request by the Iraqi Government, on 8 November the United Nations Security Council unanimously adopted resolution 1637, which comes into effect on 31 December 2005. This extends the mandate of the Multi-National Force in Iraq (MNF-I), if required, until 31 December 2006. UNSCR 1637 includes the same guarantees as UNSCR 1546, including a commitment on the part of the UN Security Council to review these provisions no later 15 June 2006 and to terminate the mandate of the MNF-I if requested by the new Iraqi Government.

(HC Deb 22 November 2005 Vol. 439 c1881W–1882W)

16/27

In a written answer, the Secretary of State for Defence wrote:

The Ministry of Defence does not contract any private military companies or private security companies in Iraq, and we hold neither employment records nor company policy documents for those which do operate there. Contractors working for Coalition nations are immune from Iraqi legal process only with respect to acts performed by them pursuant to the terms and conditions of a contract or subcontract. Otherwise, they must respect all relevant Iraqi laws, including Coalition Provisional Authority order regulations, orders, memoranda and public notices.

(HC Deb 24 November 2005 Vol. 439 c2205W)

16/28

Regime change

During a debate in the House of Commons, Her Majesty's Government was asked what its policy is on regime change in respect of Governments whose policies it considers unacceptable. In reply, the Foreign Secretary said:

Without context, regime change is an abstraction. Our focus is on ensuring that all other states live up to their international obligations. Where they fail to do so we seek to change their behaviour. We actively encourage and support the development of democracy across the world, as that is the best way by far to secure change in regimes by peaceful means.

(HC Deb 19 July 2005 Vol. 436 c1102)

16/29

In the continued debate, the Foreign Secretary was asked:

... Will the Foreign Secretary accept that there is inconsistency in a policy that takes us to war against a country that has no weapons of mass destruction, yet chooses to ignore countries such as North Korea, which is developing nuclear weapons programmes, or, even worse, Burma, which is using chemical weapons against neighbouring countries? I anticipate that in his reply the Foreign Secretary will fall back on the United Nations, in which case will he explain why there is no UN resolution condemning either country?

In reply, the Foreign Secretary said:

I am indeed going to rely on the UN Charter, as it is one of the fundamental foundations of international law. It is not a question of falling back on it; it happens to be the whole of the explanation. In the case of Iraq, there were 12 years of mandatory chapter VII resolutions that authorised the use of force—all necessary means—in 687, 678 and subsequently 1441. In the case of the Democratic People's Republic of Korea and Burma there are no such resolutions. Why? Because of the difficulty of securing international consensus.

(HC Deb 19 July 2005 Vol. 436 c1102)

16/30

In the continued debate, the Foreign Secretary was asked:

The Foreign Secretary will be aware that paragraph 36 of the Attorney-General's opinion of 7 March 2003, which was published during the general election, stated that

> "regime change cannot be the objective of military action"—

no doubt in recognition of article 2, paragraph 4, of the United Nations Charter to which the Foreign Secretary has just referred. Perhaps today the right hon. Gentleman could take the House into his confidence. Was there ever any doubt that once military action was commenced against Iraq it would be pursued to the point of the removal of Saddam Hussein? Indeed, was there ever any doubt that regime change was the objective of that military action?

In reply, the Foreign Secretary said:

It is a matter of record that we gave Saddam an ultimatum in the second week of March 2003, which was for him to leave the country and so not face the prospect of military action. He failed to meet it. I accept that the matter has been the subject of controversy and will remain so, but the position of the British, American and many other Governments around the world is that under the UN Charter, in principle, if there is an appropriate chapter VII resolution, regime change can be a legitimate consequence of military action so authorised. In the case of Iraq it was our judgment, and the Attorney-General's advice, that such military action was indeed justified.

(HC Deb 19 July 2005 Vol. 436 c1103)

16/31

The Foreign Secretary told the FAC about the decision to use force against Iraq in March 2003. He said:

... we only came to the decision about military action very late and very reluctantly. It was after the failure of the Security Council on 7 March 2003 to agree a Second Resolution, albeit the modified one which I put forward, and then the announcement by the French President on the tenth that whatever the circumstances he would vote no, that we were then into a situation when seven days later after the Cabinet's decision and then Parliament's decision the next day to take military action. I believed, and I still believe, that the military action that we took in Iraq was justified on the basis that was set out: non-compliance by Saddam of about a dozen Chapter 7 Resolutions. [Q.62]

(FAC Report, Foreign Policy Aspects of the War Against Terrorism, HC573-iii (2005))

16/32

In a written answer, an FCO Minister wrote:

We continue to press Iran to take effective action against members of al-Qaeda and other terrorist groups using Iran as a base, transit route or refuge. We have also sought information about members of al-Qaeda that Iran is reportedly detaining. We want to see Iran co-operate actively with the rest of the international community against these groups. It is vital for all states to work closely together to defeat terrorism.

(HC Deb 22 November 2005 Vol. 439 c1899W)

Part Sixteen: II. B.2. *Use of Force—Legitimate use of force—Collective Measures—Outside the United Nations*

16/33

The Government was asked what the relationship is between the new European peacekeeping force in Bosnia and the European Union; what command and control structures operate; what the relationship is between the new force and NATO. The Defence Secretary wrote:

The European Union peacekeeping force in Bosnia and Herzegovina, Operation ALTHEA, operates under the political control and strategic direction of the

European Union. This is implemented through the Political and Security Committee and the EU Military Committee to the EU Operation Commander, General Sir John Reith, who also holds the NATO position of Deputy Supreme Allied Commander Europe.

The EU is able to draw on many NATO assets and capabilities in support of Operation ALTHEA in accordance with the Berlin Plus arrangements. There is a close working relationship between the EU and NATO in relation to operations in Bosnia and Herzegovina, supported by the collocation of personnel at all levels of command. In Bosnia, there is a very close working relationship between the Commander of the EU Force and the Senior Military Representative in NATO HQ Sarajevo.

(HC Deb 12 January 2005 Vol. 429 c573W)

16/34

In a written answer, a Minister wrote:

The majority of UK forces in Afghanistan are deployed with the International Security Assistance Force under NATO leadership. NATO's operational plan enables forces to support Afghan-led operations, but not to lead on targeted counter-narcotics operations such as eradication of poppy fields or heroin production factories. These general constraints are reflected in UK forces rules of engagement. The objective of ISAF and the UK is to help the Afghans create a secure environment in their country which is an essential contribution to the eventual elimination of the Afghan opium industry.

(HL Deb 19 October 2005 Vol. 674 cWA123)

Part Sixteen: II. C. *Use of Force—Legitimate use of force—Others*

(See also **Part Five: I. D.2., Part Five: II. A.2.**)

Part Sixteen: III. *Use of Force—Disarmament and arms control*

16/35

An FCO Minister said in the House of Commons in a debate on weapons of mass destruction:

Given such clear threats [from terrorists, North Korea, Iran, Ed], we must strengthen international co-operation against the proliferation and the use of WMD. We must at all costs maintain an effective multilateral regime . . . the nuclear non-proliferation treaty remains the cornerstone of nuclear non-proliferation. It is a strong treaty, with the widest membership of any arms control treaty, and it retains the wholehearted support of the UK and the vast majority of the international community.

However, recent events have shown that a number of states continue to pursue clandestine nuclear weapons programmes and that there are individuals willing to assist them by providing sensitive materials and technology. The treaty must, therefore, be strengthened.

. . .

We have no wish to reopen the treaty, but we need stronger measures to address non-compliance. We also want to build support for new measures to combat the spread of sensitive technology. We want to ensure that sensitive nuclear items are not exported to states that may use them for weapons purposes or allow them to fall into terrorist hands.

We are working with partners to make the necessary amendments to the Nuclear Suppliers Group guidelines. We are also working to put into effect the principles set out in the written statement to the House of 25 February 2004 from . . . the Foreign Secretary, which said that states that fail to comply with their IAEA safeguards obligations should forfeit access to enrichment and reprocessing equipment and technology.

As regards biological and chemical weapons, we continue to work towards universal adherence to the chemical weapons convention and the biological and toxin weapons convention, in particular to include states such as Egypt, Syria and Israel. This year marks the 80th anniversary of the Geneva protocol against the use of chemical and biological warfare and the 30th anniversary of the biological and toxin weapons convention. The UK will chair this year's annual meetings, where we will be discussing such issues as codes of conduct for scientists. As president of the G8, we will follow up on a range of earlier suggestions on tackling biological threats.

A stronger international framework is essential, but not sufficient in itself . . . to meet the proliferation threat. We want greater practical engagement in counter-proliferation by other states and regional groups. We played a major role in the formulation and unanimous adoption of UN Security Council resolution 1540, adopted on 28 April 2004, which was the first to address the threat posed by WMD proliferation. It obliges all countries to introduce robust legislation to tackle the threat. We welcome work done by the UN Secretary-General's high-level panel.

We are also committed to supporting the G8's global partnership and the proliferation security initiative. We contribute £36.5 million to the global partnership, which deals with dismantling nuclear submarines; safe and secure storage of over 20,000 spent nuclear fuel assemblies; the safe destruction of Russia's chemical weapons stocks; and new employment opportunities for former nuclear scientists and engineers in the former Soviet Union. Over a 10-year period, we expect to invest about $750 million.

The UK strongly supports the May 2003 proliferation security initiative to prevent trafficking in weapons of mass destruction and related technology by states and terrorist groups or criminal networks. Export control is only as strong as its weakest link. We must ensure that multilateral export control regimes are effective and that progressive proposals are not unreasonably held back by one or two states. We must also keep such controls proportionate and simple to administer. In addition to those international efforts, we must act effectively at home.

The first line of defence is an effective outreach programme to alert industry and academic institutions to the possibility that UK technology could help proliferators and to raise awareness of export legislation. The Export Control Act 2002 includes a range of measures aimed at preventing WMD technology from falling into the wrong hands. We should never underestimate the potential threat posed by WMD, but the Government believe that such threats can be minimised through effective multilateralism and concerted domestic efforts. Counter-proliferation will remain a key priority for us and we shall continue to take the lead in promoting a strong international response.

(HC Deb 22 March 2005 Vol. 432 c246WH)

16/36

In a written answer, a Minister wrote:

In the Treaty on Conventional Armed Forces in Europe (CFE) the term "reduction" refers to the method used to bring Treaty Limited Equipment below agreed ceilings. Disposal of redundant weapons is the permanent removal from service of Treaty Limited Equipment that is already below treaty ceilings. All former Soviet Union countries that are CFE signatories are below their ceilings. The disposal of surplus equipment within the ceilings stipulated in the CFE Treaty is a national responsibility.

(HL Deb 20 October 2005 Vol. 674 cWA141)

16/37

Non-Proliferation Treaty

The Foreign Secretary was asked by the FAC about Iran's obligations under the NPT.

He said:

The argument over the Non-Proliferation Treaty is complicated. The Iranians say: "Article 4 of the Non-Proliferation Treaty entitles us to the full panoply that is necessary to generate electricity by nuclear power." On the face of it, that is correct. However, there is an obligation under Article 2 not to do anything towards developing nuclear weapons capability. The intersection of these two comes at the point of the fuel cycle, and that is why there is such anxiety about the use to which the Iranians are intending to put the fuel that they would generate. [Q.93]

(FAC, Foreign Policy Aspects of the War against Terrorism, HC 573–ii (2005))

16/38

Asked about compliance with the UK's obligation under Article VI of the Nuclear Non-Proliferation Treaty, the Minister of Defence wrote:

The United Kingdom is committed to all its obligations under the Nuclear Non-Proliferation Treaty (NPT), including under Article VI, and has a good record on disarmament. For example, we have reduced the total explosive power of our nuclear forces by over 70 per cent. since the end of the Cold War and in the 1998 Strategic Defence Review we announced that only one Trident submarine would be on deterrent patrol at any one time. That submarine would normally be on several days notice to fire with its missiles de-targeted.

(HC Deb 2 February 2005 Vol. 430 c900W)

16/39

During a debate in the House of Commons, an FCO Minister said:

My hon. Friend asked about our plans for replacing Trident. As I am sure he knows, no decision has yet been taken, but we are keeping our options open. A decision will need to be taken during the next Parliament. He asked what is going on at Aldermaston and whether it is consistent with the NPT. My advice is that what is happening is consistent with the treaty and that the modernisation of facilities at Aldermaston and the decommissioning of those no longer required, of which we have made no secret, is an ongoing programme of work to meet safety, regulatory and operational requirements. Were there to be significant developments, we would, of course, inform Parliament.

(HC Deb 8 March 2005 Vol. 431 c420WH)

16/40

Later, there was the following exchange between the questioner:

In the advice that the Minister has been given, what is the legal position of Britain in developing a new generation of nuclear weapons within the terms of the NPT of 1970?

and the Minister:

My advice is that it is permitted.

(HC Deb 8 March 2005 Vol. 431 c423WH)

16/41

In other parts of his reply, the Minister said:

[I was] asked about the comprehensive test ban treaty and the position of the United States and China. I do not speak for the Governments of the US or China, but I am not aware of any change in their position. We believe that they should both ratify.

The nuclear non-proliferation treaty is the cornerstone of the non-proliferation regime. We remain fully committed to the treaty and we participate actively in the review process. The treaty is strong; it has the widest membership of any arms control treaty and retains the wholehearted support of the United Kingdom and the majority of the international community. We want universal membership, although that may not be achievable in the current circumstances. We are also committed to strengthening the treaty to face new challenges.

Several hon. Members have asked what we want out of the review conference that will take place soon. The UK's main goal will be to emphasise the need for greater efforts in the non-proliferation and compliance parts of the treaty. Recent events have shown that a number of states continue to seek clandestine nuclear weapons programmes and also that individuals are willing to assist them in the proliferation of sensitive materials and technology. The treaty must therefore be strengthened and the political will generated to prevent such action.

The treaty remains at the core of our nuclear counter-proliferation policy. It has proved successful in limiting the number of countries deciding to develop nuclear weapons. It provides the essential underpinning to maintain international cohesion when addressing the challenges posed by Iran and North Korea, as it did recently in respect of Libya's nuclear programmes. It also serves to strengthen the controls on the transfer of sensitive technology, without which progress in the International Atomic Energy Agency and other forums would become more difficult.

During the review conference, we will outline the considerable progress that we had made on nuclear disarmament ... The United Kingdom has made considerable progress on the 13 practical steps towards nuclear disarmament that were agreed at the previous review conference five years ago. For example, we are working on a programme to develop UK expertise in verifying the reduction and elimination of nuclear weapons internationally. It is a three-part exercise, which sets out the methodologies for the verification of nuclear disarmament.

We will focus at the review conference on monitoring the nuclear warhead complex. We shall also summarise the range of technologies and approaches that have been researched during the five-year programme. The work will provide the basis for methodologies that could be used in a verification regime for a future disarmament treaty. We will publish a consolidated paper on that work at the conference. The United Kingdom remains fully committed to all aspects of the nuclear non-proliferation treaty, including global and verifiable nuclear disarmament. We have a good record of fulfilling our NPT obligations on nuclear disarmament ... We have withdrawn and dismantled the RAF's freefall bomb, so Trident is now our only nuclear weapons system. We dismantled the last Chevaline warhead in 2002. We have reduced our operationally available stockpile to fewer than 200 warheads, which is a reduction of more than 70 per cent. in the potential explosive power of our nuclear forces since the end of the cold war. We have reduced the readiness of our nuclear forces: only one Trident submarine is now on deterrent patrol; it carries 48 warheads. The submarine on patrol is usually on several days' notice to fire and its missiles are detargeted.

We have signed and ratified the comprehensive nuclear test ban treaty and continue to promote its early entry into force. We have placed fissile material no longer required for defence purposes under international safeguards. All enrichment and reprocessing facilities in the United Kingdom are now liable to international inspection. We have continued to press for negotiations on a fissile material cut-off treaty. Indeed, we announced in 1995 that we had stopped the production of fissile material for nuclear weapons and other nuclear explosive devices.

We have been more transparent about our stockpiles of nuclear and fissile materials, and have begun a national historical accounting study for fissile material produced. We have signed and ratified the relevant protocols of both the treaty of Rarotonga, which is the south Pacific nuclear weapons-free zone, and the treaty of Pelindaba, the African nuclear weapon-free zone. We are also engaged in negotiations on nuclear weapon-free zones in central Asia and south-east Asia.

The Government's policy on nuclear weapons remains as set out in the 1998 strategic defence review and the 2003 defence White Paper. We are committed to working towards a safer world in which there is no requirement for nuclear weapons. We continue to play a full role in international efforts to strengthen arms control and prevent proliferation of chemical, biological and nuclear weapons. However, the continuing risk from the proliferation of nuclear weapons and the certainty that a number of other countries will retain substantial nuclear arsenals means that our minimum nuclear deterrent capability, currently represented by Trident, is likely to remain a necessary element of our security for the foreseeable future. We continue to support multilateral negotiations towards mutual balanced and verifiable reductions in nuclear weapons worldwide. When we are satisfied that sufficient progress has been made to allow us to include British nuclear weapons in any negotiations without endangering our security interests, we shall do so.

It has been suggested that the non-signatory status of India, Pakistan and Israel fundamentally undermines the non-proliferation treaty. Those countries are not subject to all international non-proliferation norms. As has already been suggested, such a lack of control might, in the case of Pakistan, have contributed to the serious case of proliferation of nuclear technology through the A. Q. Khan network.

The UK continues to call on all non-signatory states to become signatories to the NPT, as non-nuclear weapon states. We are additionally pressing them to sign up to other agreements that control nuclear proliferation. We want them to join early negotiations on a fissile material cut-off treaty; we would like India and Pakistan to become party to the comprehensive nuclear test ban treaty, and Israel to ratify its accession to that treaty. We have been encouraging negotiations on a weapons of mass destruction-free zone in the middle east and look forward to the proposed conference on the issue in the near future.

We live in an uncertain world. The non-proliferation treaty faces challenges from states such as Iran and North Korea. We believe that the global community needs to strengthen the treaty by ensuring full compliance by such states. For our part, the UK is continuing to work in collaboration with the international community to ensure that Iran operates within its obligations under the treaty. We have also worked with the United States to secure Libya's agreement to renounce its clandestine nuclear weapons programme. Both of those efforts demonstrate our clear commitment to strengthening the non-proliferation regime. As part of the work, we also want to see a strengthened International Atomic Energy Agency. We are committed to spending up to £400 million over 10 years through the global partnership to help tackle the weapons legacy of the former Soviet Union. It is also intended that the work should be expanded to cover states such as Libya and Iraq.

I hope that those efforts, and others that time does not permit me to enumerate, demonstrate our commitment to building a secure and peaceful world, free from nuclear weapons. We are working towards creating a future in which the UK is secure enough to be able to disarm completely.

(HC Deb 8 March 2005 Vol. 431 c420–423WH)

16/42

In a written answer, the Foreign Secretary wrote:

My assessment is that no African country possesses nuclear weapons or is currently developing them.

However . . . the former South African President, FW De Klerk, announced in March 1993 that South Africa had decided in 1974 to develop a limited nuclear deterrent capability, and that six of seven projected nuclear fission devices had been completed by the time it decided in 1990 to dismantle and destroy all the nuclear devices and accede to the Nuclear Non-Proliferation Treaty (NPT). South Africa duly acceded to the NPT in July 1991, and its consequent comprehensive safeguards agreement with the International Atomic Energy Agency (IAEA) came into force in September 1991. The IAEA subsequently conducted a number of inspections to verify the completeness and correctness of South Africa's initial report of its inventory of nuclear material. In 1993 South Africa also asked the IAEA to conduct visits to confirm the abandoned status of its former nuclear weapon programme. As a result of these activities, the IAEA concluded that it had found nothing inconsistent with the South African account of the programme.

. . . on 19 December 2003 Libya announced that it had shown US and UK experts "the materials, equipments and programmes which lead to the production of internationally proscribed weapons", including centrifuge machines, and that it had decided "to eliminate these materials, equipments and programmes". Libya has since acknowledged to the IAEA that it received documentation related to nuclear weapon design and fabrication from a foreign source as well as some pre-assembled centrifuge machines and many components for other such machines. The United Kingdom has strongly welcomed Libya's renunciation of these activities, as well as its conclusion of an Additional Protocol in March 2004 to its existing Comprehensive Safeguards Agreement with the IAEA, and strongly supports its continued co-operation with the IAEA.

The United Kingdom is a strong supporter of the Treaty of Pelindaba, which seeks to establish a nuclear weapon free zone in Africa. We have ratified the relevant Protocols to the Treaty, and continue to call on enough states to ratify the Treaty for it to enter into force.

(HC Deb 4 July 2005 Vol. 436 c185–186W)

16/43

The representative of the United Kingdom made the following statement at the Conference on Disarmament, Plenary Meeting on Security Assurances, 7 July 2005:

Since the United Kingdom ratified the Nuclear Non-Proliferation Treaty and formally recognised its responsibilities as one of the Nuclear Weapon States, we have set about meeting our disarmament obligations under Article VI of the Treaty. We are fully committed to those obligations. They contribute to the ultimate objective of the Treaty: a safer world free from the dangers of nuclear weapons.

The United Kingdom gave Negative and Positive Security Assurances to Non-Nuclear Weapon States in our letter to the UN Secretary General in 1995, subsequently noted in the United Nations Security Council Resolution 984. We remain committed to those Security Assurances.

In addition we have given legally binding NSAs in Treaty form through the Protocols we have signed to the Nuclear Weapon Free Zone Treaties. The United Kingdom fully supports the principle of Nuclear Weapon Free Zones and plays an active and constructive role as a Nuclear Weapon State in their development. We believe they can make a valuable contribution to nuclear non-proliferation and global and regional peace and security, as long as they are based on arrangements freely arrived at by all the States in the region concerned. And for that reason the United Kingdom has signed and ratified protocols to the zones which cover Latin America and the Caribbean—the Tlatelolco Treaty; Africa—the Pelindaba Treaty; and the South Pacific—the Raratonga Treaty. We continue to work with the ASEAN States to produce an agreed protocol to the treaty of Bangkok, and hope ASEAN will continue consultations with the Nuclear Weapon States so that the Protocol can be concluded. We continue to support the principle of a Central Asia Nuclear Weapon Free Zone and look to the 5 Central Asian States to resume and conclude their consultations with the Nuclear Weapon States, in accordance with UNDC guidelines, before signing the Treaty establishing the Zone.

We believe that our 1995 NSA and the Protocols we have signed offer Non-Nuclear Weapon States the assurance they seek regarding nuclear use. Furthermore we consider that the way forward is to make further progress with the Nuclear Weapon Free Zone Treaties and Protocols, which will provide, on a credible, regional basis, the internationally binding legal instruments on NSAs that many are looking for.

(Text supplied by FCO available at www.fco.gov.uk/Files/kfile/paterson7july05.pdf)

16/44

In a written answer, an FCO Minister wrote:

The United Kingdom strongly supports the establishment of a zone free from all Weapons of Mass Destruction in the Middle East. The UK, together with the Russian Federation and United States, sponsored the Resolution on the Middle East agreed at the 1995 Nuclear Non-Proliferation Treaty Review and Extension Conference which included a call for the establishment of a such a zone.

(HC Deb 12 July 2005 Vol. 436 c878W)

16/45

In a written answer, an FCO Minister wrote:

We are aware of the widespread assumption that Israel possesses nuclear weapons, but note that the Israeli Government had refused to confirm it. The British Government have, on a number of occasions, called on Israel to accede to the Nuclear Non-Proliferation Treaty as a non-nuclear weapon state, and to conclude a full scope safeguards agreement and Additional Protocol with the International Atomic Energy Agency. We take appropriate opportunities to discuss all aspects of non-proliferation with representatives of the Israeli Government.

(HC Deb 21 July 2005 Vol. 436 c2102W)

16/46

In a written answer, an FCO Minister wrote:

For the purposes of this answer 'nuclear capable' is taken to refer to countries capable of producing fissile material for nuclear weapons, other than the five nuclear weapons states recognised by the nuclear non-proliferation treaty (NPT) and the other states which have carried out nuclear test explosions (India and Pakistan).

To produce fissile material, a state must master enrichment or reprocessing technology. The International Atomic Energy Agency (IAEA) has listed the following non-nuclear weapons states (NNWS) as having enrichment plants, including pilot plants: Argentina, Brazil, Germany, Iran, Japan, and the Netherlands. It has also listed the following NNWS as possessing chemical reprocessing plants, including pilot plants: the [DPRK], Germany, Italy and Japan. Israel is also widely assumed to possess reprocessing facilities.

Possession of enrichment or reprocessing facilities does not imply an intention to produce fissile material for nuclear weapons. But nor does the lack of such facilities mean that a country could not acquire them in the future. A number of other states would be capable of constructing enrichment or reprocessing facilities if they chose to do so.

This is why the NPT remains such an important instrument. It enshrines the principle that, with the exception of the nuclear weapon states, who are bound by the disarmament principles of Article VI, States Party to the Treaty will not manufacture or otherwise acquire nuclear weapons and will allow any nuclear material that they do possess to be subject to IAEA safeguards.

The hon. Member may find further information on IAEA assessments at http://www.iaea.org/OurWork/SV/Safeguards/sv.html.

(HC Deb 13 October 2005 Vol. 437 c569–570W)

16/47

In a written answer, an FCO Minister wrote:

The UK continues to regard the Nuclear Non-Proliferation Treaty as the cornerstone of the nuclear non-proliferation regime and has played an active role over the past five years of the treaty review cycle. We have promoted strengthening of the treaty and have addressed the challenges it faces, by implementing the decisions of past review conferences, and taking forward work in the International Atomic Energy Agency and the Nuclear Suppliers' Group. We played an active role in the adoption of UN Security Council Resolution (UNSCR) 1540 and continue to do so in the 1540 Committee.

The UK takes part in the Proliferation Security Initiative (PSI), which contributes to fulfilling the requirement of UNSCR 1540 to take co-operative action to prevent illicit trafficking in nuclear, chemical or biological weapons, their means of delivery and related materials. The UK secured important counter-proliferation amendments to the Convention on the Suppression of Unlawful Acts at Sea. The UK has been active on specific country issues. Working with the US, the UK was able to convince Libya in December 2003 to abandon its weapons of mass destruction programmes, which led to the uncovering and dismantlement of the international proliferation network run by AQ Khan and his associates. With France and Germany, supported by the office of the EU high representative, we have been working for two years to reach a long term arrangement which will give the international community objective guarantees regarding the exclusively peaceful nature of Iran's nuclear programme. While not directly involved in the 6 Party Talks on North Korea's nuclear programme, the UK has regularly expressed its support for the process as the best available means to reach a solution based on negotiation.

(HC Deb 1 December 2005 Vol. 440 c738W–739W)

16/48

In a written answer, an FCO Minister wrote:

The recent statement by President Mugabe is not the first announcement of uranium discoveries in Zimbabwe. It is not yet clear if the uranium is viable for extraction, or if Zimbabwe intends to invest the considerable time and money required to develop this resource. Zimbabwe is a signatory to the Non Proliferation Treaty (NPT) and a member of the International Atomic Energy Agency (IAEA). In accordance with its NPT obligations, Zimbabwe has signed a nuclear safeguards agreement with the IAEA. Any proliferation in this area would, therefore, be subject to international oversight, in accordance with their safeguards agreement. We will continue to monitor the situation.

(HC Deb 12 December 2005 Vol. 440 c1654W)

Part Seventeen: The Law of Armed Conflict and International Humanitarian Law

Part Seventeen: I. B.6. *The Law of Armed Conflict and International Humanitarian Law—The Law of International Armed Conflict—Distinction between combatants and non-combatants*

17/1

It was put to the Foreign Secretary that he had drawn "a distinction between two of the four detainees to be returned from Guantanamo Bay. Were some of the detainees engaged in activities that would have led to their being taken prisoner of war in a declared state of war?" He said:

On the last point, the answer is for some, yes, and for some, no. The international conventions on the treatment of prisoners of war—the Geneva conventions—were designed before we faced the threat of international terrorism and failing states, so the instruments have not quite caught up with the new reality.

(HC Deb 11 January 2005 Vol. 429 c184)

Part Seventeen: I. B.7. *The Law of Armed Conflict and International Humanitarian Law—The Law of International Armed Conflict—International humanitarian law*

17/2

(See also Part Two: I. D., Part Six: VIII. (Guantanamo Bay))

A Defence Minister made the following statement in the House of Lords:

Since May 2004 Ministers have made Statements in both Houses of Parliament and in Written Answers to the effect that the use of hooding in Iraq by the British Armed Forces ceased at the end of September 2003. These Answers referred to conventional forces and remain true with respect to them. It has been drawn to Ministers' attention, however, that UK Special Forces from time to time used hooding as a temporary measure for the safe arrest and transit of detained persons until May 2004. For the sake of completeness the parliamentary record should be corrected to reflect this.

Most of the criticism about the use of hooding has related to the obscuring of vision during interrogation. This practice is contrary to the instructions given by the then Prime Minister in 1972 and was ceased by UK military interrogators thereafter. UK military interrogators are made fully aware of this as part of their training and there have been no reported incidents where UK military interrogators have interrogated individuals while they have been hooded.

Our legal advice remains that the practice of temporarily obscuring the vision of a detained person, for the purposes of initial detention and transit, by the use of a hood is not contrary to the law. In Iraq, the initial circumstances on the ground were such that it was judged by certain military commanders that its use was appropriate given the numbers of detainees and in some cases the need to obscure the identities of particular detainees for their own protection.

I can, however, confirm that no UK forces are currently authorised to use hooding in any circumstances.

(HL Deb 10 March 2005 Vol. 670 cWS39)

17/3

The Government was asked:

What training, guidance and instructions have been given to members of Her Majesty's armed services during the past four years regarding compliance with the obligations imposed upon the United Kingdom by international humanitarian law and international human rights law.

A Defence Minister said:

Obligations imposed upon the United Kingdom by international humanitarian law are covered within Her Majesty's Armed Forces through instruction and training in the Law of Armed Conflict (LoAC). All new entrants to the Armed Forces, of all ranks, receive training on LoAC during initial training and specialist training courses. Such training has been delivered throughout the past four years. On entry into productive service Army and Royal Marines personnel renew this training annually as part of their individual training directives.

Prior to deployment to an operational theatre, all personnel receive pre-deployment training (PDT), either collectively or as individuals. Royal Navy and Royal Air Force personnel receive specific training on LoAC during PDT as, unlike their Army and Royal Marine counterparts, they do not receive such training on an annual basis. All personnel receive an additional theatre-specific operational law brief and cultural awareness training as part of PDT.

In addition, officers receive enhanced packages during their career development and through attendance at the Joint Services Command and Staff College, where they receive education on the analysis of international law, the role of ethics and their impact on military operations.

International human rights law is not taught as a subject in its own right to service personnel. However, all service personnel are subject to their respective service disciplinary codes and will be dealt with by their commanding officers or (depending on the gravity of the offences) by courts martial for breaches overseas of service discipline or the commission of criminal law offences contrary to the law of England and Wales. The object of service disciplinary law has always been to maintain discipline within the Armed Forces and thereby both to guarantee respect from the local population overseas for the behaviour of service personnel and to help maintain operational effectiveness.

Service personnel receive annual common core skills training, part of which relates to live armed guarding duties in peacetime within the United Kingdom. The law of self-defence is an essential part of that training and seeks to impart the basic principle that only reasonable and proportionate force may be used where a necessity of defence arises. The teaching, which is given partly by video and partly by instructors, is in line with Section 3 of the Criminal Law Act 1967 and supporting case law. Section 3 comprises the basis for the use of force in most peace-keeping operations conducted by HM forces overseas.

(HL Deb 22 March 2005 Vol. 671 cWA22)

17/4

In a written answer, an FCO Minister wrote:

Article VI of the Biological and Toxin Weapons Convention (BTWC) permits any State Party to the convention to lodge a complaint with the Security Council of the United Nations if they find that any other State Party is in breach of obligations deriving from the provisions of the convention. To date no complaints of breaches of the obligations of the convention have been submitted to the United Nations. As one of the Depositary Governments of the BTWC, the UK views the issue of compliance with the convention as being of central importance and routinely monitors the compliance of all States Parties to the convention.

(HC Deb 14 July 2005 Vol. 436 c1176W)

17/5

In a written answer, an FCO Minister wrote:

The Government take very seriously the need to respect Iraq's cultural heritage. As United Nations Security Council Resolution 1546 of June 2004 stressed, all parties need to respect and protect Iraq's archaeological, historical, cultural and religious heritage. The Iraqi Ministry of Culture has begun implementation of an Archaeological Site Protection Plan and the Iraq State Board of Antiquities and Heritage is working to build an archaeological site patrol force to provide a guard force for cultural heritage sites.

The 1954 Hague Convention for the Protection of Cultural Property in the Event of Armed Conflict directs that combatants must avoid directing attacks against protected sites, unless there is a military imperative to do so. The UK is in the process of ratifying the convention and its two protocols. This process is still at an early stage and there have been no discussions with the Iraqi authorities relating to the convention. However, UK troops are already acting in accordance with the spirit of the convention.

The UK is a signatory to the 1977 Additional Protocol (AP 1) of the 1949 Geneva Conventions, which requires that civilian objects are to be protected from attack, unless that object is being used for military purposes; in which case it may lose its special protected status. UK forces in Iraq have strict instructions not to fire on cultural sites such as mosques and heritage sites, as well as important economic and social infrastructure properties, unless these sites are being used for militarily offensive purposes.

(HL Deb 25 October 2005 Vol. 674 cWA178–WA179)

17/6

During a Security Council Meeting the representative of the United Kingdom stated:

As regards protection [of civilians in armed conflicts], parties to conflict must comply fully with the requirements of international humanitarian, human rights and refugee law, especially concerning the prohibitions on physical attack, sexual violence, the use of child soldiers and forced displacement. They must also ensure that specific measures for the protection of civilians are included in peace agreements. The United Nations must give peacekeeping missions the mandates and the resources to protect civilians, in particular those under imminent threat of physical attack.

Humanitarian access is a crucial part of protection. The right to food and the right to health are fundamental human rights, but the denial of humanitarian access is increasingly used as a political tool, and even as a weapon of war. All parties to conflict—as well as neighbouring States—must, as our draft resolution proposes, provide unimpeded access to humanitarian assistance and take all necessary measures to guarantee the safety, security and freedom of movement of humanitarian personnel. United Nations peace support operations must have the mandates and resources to ensure the provision of humanitarian assistance.

...

At the world summit [High-level Plenary Meeting of the 60th Session of the General Assembly, 14–16 September 2005] three months ago, our heads of State and Government reached a historic agreement on the responsibility to protect populations from genocide, war crimes, ethnic cleansing and crimes against humanity. My Government and the European Union regarded this outcome, embracing the concept at the highest level, as one of the most important of the summit. The responsibility to protect is a distinct concept, carefully set out in the World Summit Outcome. But it is clearly relevant to the issue of the protection of civilians in armed conflict, and it is only appropriate that it should be recalled in the draft resolution on which we are working.

Protection of civilians also includes the special protection needs of displaced persons, women and children. The draft resolution calls on parties to conflict to take concrete measures for the safe and sustainable return of displaced persons and calls for peacekeeping missions to have the mandates and the resources to guarantee this by, for example, providing security for and around displaced-persons camps.

Given the increasing incidence of sexual violence, child abduction and the use of child soldiers, it is more important than ever to have a strong message, as in the draft resolution, to all parties to a conflict to refrain from such actions. Peace support operations should be mandated to employ all feasible measures to prevent such crimes and to address their effects where they take place.

(UN Doc. S/PV.5319 (Resumption 1), 9 December 2005)

Part Seventeen: I. B.8. *The Law of Armed Conflict and International Humanitarian Law—The Law of International Armed Conflict—Belligerent occupation*

17/7

Iraq

The Government was asked what mechanisms [it is] using to assess [its] responsibility towards Iraqi civilians under the Geneva conventions in the absence of a reliable estimate of Iraqi casualties. A Minister wrote:

The United Kingdom takes seriously its responsibilities and obligations under Geneva Conventions which identify civilians as "protected persons". The Ministry of Defence has not previously published estimates of civilian casualties because there are no reliable means of producing such estimates. There is no specific requirement under the Geneva Conventions to produce estimates of civilian casualties.

We take great care to ensure that civilians are protected and that our obligations under the Geneva Conventions are met. All personnel serving in Iraq are fully briefed on the Law of Armed Conflict and appropriate measures are taken to avoid loss of civilian life or property. We always evaluate planned operations to ensure that they do not carry an unacceptable risk of causing unintended civilian casualties.

(HC Deb 27 January 2005 Vol. 430 c542W)

17/8

The Government was asked how many explosive remnants of war have been cleared in Iraq to date; at what cost; how many casualties have resulted; what assessment has been made of the amount remaining; how much longer the clearance is expected to take; at what cost. A Defence Minister wrote:

Significant quantities of munitions exist in Iraq as a result of the most recent period of hostilities, as well as the 1990–91 Gulf Conflict and Iraq's conflict with Iran. These consist of large stockpiles of Captured Enemy Ammunition (CEA) as well as explosive remnants of war, and the United Kingdom is not responsible for clearing these munitions, but any details of sites we hold are passed onto the relevant organisations.

The clearance of CEA is organised across Iraq by the Multi-National Corps-Iraq, and is done by civilian contractors, non-governmental organisations and military Explosive Ordnance Disposal teams. Over 850,000 individual munitions have been cleared from MND(SE). We do not have details of progress made by other coalition partners. Neither the total cost of the clearance of CEA nor the number of casualties from unexploded ordnance is available.

(HC Deb 21 February 2005 Vol. 431 c128W)

17/9

In a written answer about Iraq, an FCO Minister wrote:

Coalition Provisional Authority (CPA) Orders remain in effect until they are properly amended or rescinded by the Iraqi Government. CPA orders can all be found on the CPA website at www.cpa-iraq.org. A link to this can be found on the Foreign and Commonwealth Office website at www.fco.gov.uk.

(HC Deb 27 October 2005 Vol. 438 c509W–510W)

17/10

Israel

In answer to a question about Israel's security barrier, an FCO Minister wrote:

The Israeli government has said it will revise the route of the barrier. This follows a decision by the Israeli High Court on 30 June 2004 and considerable international concern about the impact of the barrier on the Palestinians in the Occupied Territories. The new route has yet to be published. In the meantime, we continue to express our view that the barrier construction in the Occupied Territories is illegal and damages the prospects of a peaceful settlement based on a two-state solution.

(HC Deb 1 February 2005 Vol. 430 c864W)

17/11

The Government was asked what assessment [it] has made of Israel's opening of the Erez crossing between Israel and Gaza; what assessment [it] has made of the *(a)* social and *(b)* economic impact this will have on (i) the Palestinian workers, (ii) the local community and (iii) the community in the Gaza strip as a whole. An FCO Minister wrote:

We welcome the announcement by Israeli Defence Minister Shaul Mofaz on 10 February that 1,000 Palestinian workers will be permitted to go through the Erez crossing from Gaza into the Erez industrial zone and Israel.

We have not made a detailed assessment of the impact of Israel's opening of the Erez crossing. We are, however, concerned about the humanitarian and economic consequences of closures and curfews, which restrict the free movement of people and essential supplies between the Occupied Territories and Israel and other countries, as well as within the Occupied Territories themselves. We would like to see the easing of these restrictions continue, notwithstanding further terrorist or suicide attacks at or near the crossing.

(HC Deb 24 February 2005 Vol. 431 c812W)

17/12

The Government was asked what estimate it has made of the amount of Palestinian *(a)* arable land and *(b)* water resources which are now on the Israeli side of the separation barrier. In reply, a Minister wrote;

UN reports last year estimated that around 157,000 acres of land, some 11.5 per cent. of the West Bank and home to over 93,000 Palestinians would lie between the completed separation barrier and the 1949 Armistice Line (excluding East Jerusalem). This land includes some of the West Bank's richest agricultural land and covers part of the aquifer system which is a major source of water resources for the West Bank. The barrier also affects Palestinian access to groundwater wells in the West Bank which had previously supplied water for both drinking and agriculture. Precise figures on this are not available. The proposed route of the barrier has recently been altered by the Israeli Cabinet in response to calls from the international community and the Israeli judicial system to minimise the impact on Palestinian livelihoods. There has been no authoritative analysis yet of the impact of the changes. While some improvement is expected there will continue to be inevitable and significant disruption to the lives of Palestinians living near the route of the barrier.

(HC Deb 4 March 2005 Vol. 431 c1448W)

17/13

In reply to several questions, an FCO Minister wrote:

We have made frequent representations to the Israeli Government expressing our concern over continued settlement activity and the routing of the separation barrier. While Israel has a legitimate right to defend itself against terrorist attacks, we consider construction of the barrier on occupied land to be unlawful and we note that this was also the conclusion of the International Court of Justice in its Advisory Opinion. We have also made clear our view that settlements are illegal under international law. The Roadmap requires that Israel freeze all settlement expansion and dismantle outposts erected since March 2001.

The barrier and settlements were raised most recently by [an FCO Minister] with the Israeli ambassador on 22 February. The British embassy in Tel Aviv has also made representations to the Israeli Government on construction in Jayyous . . .

. . .

We believe that settlement expansion is a major obstacle to the peace process. We welcome Prime Minister Sharon's commitment in the Roadmap to freeze construction in settlements and to dismantle settlement outposts that are illegal even under Israeli law. We expect to see these commitments met. The Israeli

Government are currently working on both mapping the outposts and investigating the legal framework for evacuating them. We are monitoring their work closely.

(HC Deb 7 March 2005 Vol. 431 c1579W)

17/14

The Government was asked what discussions it had at the recent London meeting to support the Palestinian Authority on the impact of the separation barrier on water supplies and arable land. An FCO Minister wrote:

The focus of the London Meeting was to help the Palestinian leadership strengthen the institutions of the Palestinian Authority. The meeting saw the Palestinian Authority put forward detailed plans for institutional renewal in the fields of security, governance and economic development. The participants agreed that achievement of the objectives set out in the London Meeting would constitute a major step towards the Palestinian Authority achieving its Roadmap commitments. Participants also urged and expected Israel to deliver on its Roadmap commitments.

While we understand that Israel has a legitimate right to defend itself against terrorist attacks, construction of the barrier on Palestinian land is unlawful, creates a physical obstacle to the two-state solution, and causes unacceptable humanitarian hardship for many Palestinians ... [An FCO Minister] raised our continuing concerns over the barrier's route with the Israeli Foreign Minister Silvan Shalom on 3 March during her visit to Israel.

(HC Deb 16 March 2005 Vol. 432 c342W)

17/15

The Government was asked if it will commission research on the impact of the separation barrier in Palestine on availability of *(a)* water and *(b)* arable land to Palestinians. A Minister wrote:

DFID does not plan to commission research on the impact of the separation barrier. Other donors are already active. A preliminary analysis of the barrier's revised route published by the UN's Office for the Co-ordination of Humanitarian Affairs (OCHA) in March 2005 identified that some 142,640 acres (10 per cent.) of West Bank land will lie between the completed barrier and the Green Line. This is some of the most fertile land in the West Bank and currently home to 49,400 Palestinians. Thousands more Palestinians living to the east of the barrier will be separated from their land on the west. The OCHA plans to publish a more extensive technical analysis towards the end of this month. Other bodies researching this issue include the DFID-funded Palestinian Negotiations Support Unit (NSU). The NSU's work indicates that the barrier will deny Palestinian access to 25 per cent. of the 20 million cubic metres of groundwater currently abstracted annually from the Western Aquifer Basin, and that in the Eastern Aquifer Basin estimated losses will be in the order of 3 to 5 million cubic metres per year.

(HC Deb 16 March 2005 Vol. 432 c261W)

17/16

In answer to a question about the Middle East "road map", an FCO Minister said:

Where it is helpful, we have made it clear bilaterally and through the quartet that the issues around the barrier, which could now take in two major settlement blocks, are a problem in producing a contiguous state for the Palestinians. Israel has a right to self-defence, but the barrier certainly should be on or behind the green line, if that how it is dealt with. The issue of the settlements is also very important.

I made the point ... just last week that we regard as illegal a good deal of the buildings. We have also made that point to the Israeli Government. Both sides have obligations that they have to meet, and the Israelis will be sensitive to those.

(HL Deb 26 May 2005 Vol. 672 c570)

17/17

The Government was asked about the annexation of certain land near Bethlehem. An FCO Minister wrote:

According to UNOCHA (United Nations Office for the Co-ordination of Humanitarian Affairs), a number of land requisition orders have been issued for an area between the Palestinian village of Walaja and the Israeli settlement of Gilo, near Bethlehem, for the construction of the barrier.

We are extremely concerned at the route for the barrier approved by the Israeli Cabinet on 20 February. The approved route takes in the two Israeli settlements of Ma'ale Adumim, east of Jerusalem, and Gush Etzion to the west of Bethlehem. These settlements are illegal under international law. The barrier's route also threatens to divide the West Bank in two, which in turn undermines the prospects for a two-state solution.

We deplore the destruction of Palestinian homes and the confiscation of land associated with the barrier's construction. We have made our concerns extremely clear to the Israeli Government and will continue to do so.

(HL Deb 8 June 2005 Vol. 672 cWA75)

17/18

In a written answer, an FCO Minister wrote:

Prime Minister Sharon's stated position is that the barrier and restrictions on freedom of movement are defensive measures necessary to protect Israel against terrorism. On settlements, Prime Minister Sharon has stated that no new settlements are being built and has said that following the completion of disengagement, the Israeli Government will dismantle outposts built since March 2001.

The UK Government's consistent view is that, while Israel has the right to protect its citizens from terrorist attacks such as suicide bombings, which we condemn absolutely, Israel must act within international law. Settlement construction and the building of the barrier on occupied land are contrary to international law.

(HC Deb 5 July 2005 Vol. 436 c330W)

17/19

In a written answer, an FCO Minister wrote:

We fully recognise Israel's right to self-defence. A barrier is a reasonable way to achieve this. But the barrier's route should be on or behind the Green Line, and not on occupied territory. Construction of the barrier on Palestinian land is illegal.

On 15 September the Israeli High Court ordered the re-routing of the barrier around Alfei Menashe, a West Bank settlement near the Green Line, because of its damaging impact on Palestinian villagers in the area. This ruling will reduce the humanitarian impact of the barrier in that area. However, we continue to be concerned at the route of the barrier on occupied territory. The route is particularly damaging around Jerusalem, as this risks cutting the city off from the West Bank and dividing the West Bank in two. We continue to raise our concerns over the barrier with the Israeli Government at all levels. Most recently I discussed this with Israeli Foreign Minister Silvan Shalom and Housing Minister Isaac Herzog during my visit to Israel on the 28–29 September.

(HC Deb 10 October 2005 Vol. 437 c122W–123W)

17/20

The Government was asked what assessment [it] has made of *(a)* the legality of Israel's E1 plan outside Jerusalem and *(b)* its implications for progress with the Road Map. In reply, an FCO Minister wrote:

The plan to expand the Israeli settlement of Ma'aleh Adumim into the so-called "E1" area east of Jerusalem, combined with the proposed route of the barrier, threatens to complete the encircling of the city by settlements and cut off Palestinian East Jerusalem from the rest of the West Bank. This would have serious economic, social and humanitarian consequences for Palestinians who live in these areas.

These Israeli actions are in violation of Israel's Roadmap obligations and international law. If they continue, they will make it harder to reach a final status agreement on Jerusalem. We and others in the international community have made our concerns on this clear to the Government of Israel.

(HC Deb 17 October 2005 Vol. 437 c731W)

17/21

The Government was asked what measures [it has] taken as a state party to the fourth Geneva Convention to fulfil its obligation to take measures to ensure compliance with the convention under the ruling of the International Court of Justice ruling of 9 July 2004, no. 131, legal consequences of the construction of a wall in the occupied Palestinian territory. In reply, an FCO Minister wrote:

We supported United Nations General Assembly Resolution ES (Emergency Session) 10/15 which acknowledged the International Court of Justice (ICJ) Advisory Opinion of 9 July 2004 on the legal consequences of the construction of the barrier in the occupied Palestinian territory. We agree with the broad conclusion of the ICJ, that building a barrier on parts of the current route is unlawful. We have discussed the way forward with EU partners and others, and we continue to urge Israel to comply with international law.

(HC Deb 24 October 2005 Vol. 438 c77W)

Part Seventeen: I. B.9. *The Law of Armed Conflict and International Humanitarian Law—The Law of International Armed Conflict—Conventional, nuclear, bacteriological, and chemical weapons*

17/22

The Government was asked whether substances similar to napalm have been used by the Coalition *(a)* during and *(b)* since the recent war in Iraq. A Minister wrote:

The UK has not used napalm (or similar substances) during or since the end of decisive combat operations in Iraq. Furthermore, the US has confirmed that they also have not used napalm (or similar substances) during or since the end of decisive combat operations in Iraq.

(HC Deb 10 January 2005 Vol. 429 c78W)

17/23

The Government was asked whether Mark 77 firebombs have been used by Coalition forces *(a)* in Iraq and *(b)* in or near areas in Iraq where civilians lived; whether this weapon is equivalent to napalm; whether (i) the UK and (ii) the US has signed the UN convention banning the use of napalm against civilian targets. A Minister wrote:

The United States have confirmed to us that they have not used Mark 77 firebombs, which are essentially napalm canisters, in Iraq at any time. No other Coalition member has Mark 77 firebombs in their inventory.

The United Kingdom is bound under Protocol III to the 1980 Convention on Certain Conventional Weapons (CCW) not to use incendiary weapons (which would include napalm) against military targets located within concentrations of civilians.

US policy in relation to international conventions is a matter for the US Government, but all of our allies are aware of their obligations under international humanitarian law.

(HC Deb 11 January 2005 Vol. 429 c374W)

17/24

The Government was asked what recent research it has (a) commissioned and (b) evaluated on (i) improving the reliability of cluster munitions and (ii) finding militarily-adequate alternatives to cluster munitions. A Minister wrote:

No research has been commissioned in respect of air launched cluster munitions as they are gradually being withdrawn from service over the next five years. Recent statistics show an overall failure rate which is in line with expectations. For Ground Launched systems, the Multiple Launch Rocket System (MLRS) is due to be replaced by the future GMLRS Area Effects Munition (AEM) with a planned in service date of early 2007. The new system has bomblets fitted with a self destruct faze giving a failure rate of less than 1 per cent. Whilst the Shell 155mm HE L20A1 Extended Range Bomblet Shell (ERBS) has a maximum failure rate of 2 per cent. at the 95 per cent. Confidence Level. The bomblet fuze has a self destruct mechanism. Analysis shows that for a significant percentage of likely targets the bomblet remains the most effective munition.

(HC Deb 26 January 2005 Vol. 430 c332W)

17/25

The Government was asked a number of questions about nuclear weapons.

What arrangements [is it] making to reaffirm their previous commitments not to use nuclear weapons against non-nuclear weapon states[?].

An FCO Minister wrote:

The United Kingdom stands by the security assurances given to non-nuclear weapon states in our letter of 6 April 1995 to the Secretary-General of the United Nations and noted in Security Council Resolution 984 of that year. We reaffirmed these commitments at the Review Conference of the Nuclear Non-Proliferation Treaty in 2000 and intend to do so again at the review conference to be held in May 2005. The UK also stands by the security assurances we have given in the protocols we have ratified to nuclear weapon-free zone treaties.

What action [is it] taking together with the United States, the Russian Federation, and other states to ensure that practical arrangements are in place to reduce the risk of accidental war, including a schedule for de-alerting their strategic nuclear weapons [?].

An FCO Minister wrote:

The UK has implemented a range of significant de-alerting measures. As announced in the 1998 Strategic Defence Review only one Trident submarine is on patrol at any one time, carrying a reduced load of 48 warheads and with a reduced state of alert. The submarine's missiles are not targeted and it will normally be at several days "notice to fire". A variety of procedural and technical means ensure that it is impossible for a single person to initiate the launch sequence for a UK nuclear weapon.

In their joint statement at the 2000 Review Conference of the Nuclear Non-Proliferation Treaty, the five recognised nuclear weapon states declared that none of their nuclear weapons is targeted at any state.

What action [is it] taking to promote a pledge by the United Nations Security Council to take collective action in response to a nuclear attack or threat of nuclear attack on a non-nuclear weapon state [?].

An FCO Minister wrote:

The United Kingdom stands by the security assurances in our letter of 6 April 1995 to the Secretary-General of the United Nations and noted in Security Council Resolution 984 of that year. This reaffirmed the UK's intention, as a permanent member of the United Nations Security Council, to seek immediate Security Council action to provide assistance to non-nuclear weapon states party to the Nuclear Non-Proliferation Treaty that are victims of an act of aggression or an object of a threat of aggression in which nuclear weapons are used. The United Kingdom would also be prepared to take appropriate measures in response to a request from the victim for technical, medical, scientific or humanitarian assistance. We reaffirmed these commitments at the Review Conference of the Nuclear Non-Proliferation Treaty in 2000 and intend to do so again at the review conference to be held in May 2005.

(HL Deb 21 February 2005 Vol. 669 c157–158WA)

17/26

The Government was asked what action [it is] taking to ensure that all chemical weapon states expedite the destruction of all existing chemical weapons stockpiles by the agreed target date of 2012. An FCO Minister wrote:

The Government support this recommendation from the recent United Nations high-level panel report and regularly urge all chemical weapons possessor states to meet their chemical weapons convention obligations. We are committed to providing practical assistance to help states meet and better the 2012 deadline. For example, we continue to provide assistance towards Russia's destruction programme, in particular at the Shchuch'ye chemical weapon destruction facility.

(HL Deb 21 February 2005 Vol. 669 c159WA)

17/27

The Government was asked what recent progress [it] has been made in fulfilling the UK's obligations under the Ottawa Convention on landmines. In reply, a Minister wrote:

The United Kingdom completed its destruction of its stockpiles of anti-personnel mines in October 1999 and only retains a number of anti-personnel mines under Article 3 of the Ottawa Convention for the development of, and training in, mine detection, mine clearance, or mine destruction techniques. Under the Ottawa

Convention, the UK is also required to clear all anti-personnel mines from its territory by March 2009. The only UK territory affected is in the Falkland Islands. Discussions have taken place with the Government of Argentina to agree a joint feasibility study, including a field survey of the Islands. A decision on how to proceed will be made once the results of the feasibility study are known.

(HC Deb 10 November 2005 Vol. 439 c708W)

17/28

The Government was asked what definition [it] uses of the special nuclear materials referred to in the 1958 Mutual Defence Agreement [with the US].

In reply, the Secretary of State for Defence wrote:

The definition of special nuclear material referred to in the 1958 Mutual Defence Agreement is that recognised by the International Atomic Energy Agency (IAEA) and is as detailed in article 1 of the IAEA's 1959 co-operation agreement with the United States of America.

(HC Deb 1 December 2005 Vol. 440 c678W)

17/29

In a written answer, a Minister wrote:

Cluster bombs are lawful weapons and are always used by United Kingdom forces in a manner consistent with our obligations under international law.

(HL Deb 5 December 2005 Vol. 676 cWA79)

Part Seventeen: II. *The Law of Armed Conflict and International Humanitarian Law—Non-international armed conflict*

(See also **Part Five: IV. D.**)

Part Nineteen: Legal Aspects of International Relations and Co-operation in Particular Matters

Part Nineteen: I. A. *Legal Aspects of International Relations and Co-operation in Particular Matters—General economic and financial Matters—Trade*

19/1

A Minister said:

Given the title of the Unstarred Question—to ask HMG what action they plan to take to safeguard the interests of Caribbean banana growers—I start by stating the obvious: there is little, unilaterally, that we can do to help. The responsibilities towards ACP banana exporters expressed in the Lomé convention are a collective EU responsibility and not specifically that of the UK. The UK can only assist the other 24 member states in ensuring that the EU meets those responsibilities. It would also be unlawful for the UK unilaterally to use tariffs to ensure that the Caribbean banana growers continued to export their bananas to Europe.

...

We have to accept that changes to the regime are inevitable. As we heard, the banana regime was challenged in the World Trade Organisation in the 1990s by Ecuador and the United States, among others. The resulting "banana war" was ended in 2001 only by the EU reaching understanding in the World Trade Organisation to replace the quota system with a tariff-only regime. It was agreed that the regime should be in place by 1 January 2006 and that the waiver allowing ACP bananas to enter the EU duty-free would expire at the end of 2007. Failure to act on the 2001 understandings could lead to retaliatory action by countries such as the United States with potentially damaging consequences.

In parallel, preferential trading relations between the EU and the ACP are being renegotiated in economic partnership agreements to start in 2008. One objective of EPAs will be to continue to allow duty-free access for ACP bananas. EPAs will provide the framework to improve and build on the region's trade and aid relationship with the EU, helping the Caribbean to respond to the challenges of preference erosion and fulfil the potential for economic development.

(HL Deb 14 January 2005 Vol. 668 c524–526)

19/2

The Government was asked what representations it has received since May 2003 in response to the challenge by the US in the World Trade Organization to the EU's precautionary approach to GM food and farming and what steps the Government is taking in response to the challenge. A Minister wrote:

In May 2003, the USA, Argentina and Canada filed a complaint with the World Trade Organisation against the procedures regulating the import and marketing of GMOs in the European Union. The focus of the complaints is that the EU has allegedly not been operating its own approvals system for GM products since 1998. It is alleged that this is more trade restrictive than is required to achieve the desired level of public health protection, that it is not based on proper scientific criteria, and that it unfairly discriminates between GMO and non-GMO products. The case is made against the European Commission, not individual member states, but it specifically cites Austria, France, Luxembourg, Germany, Italy and Greece.

The Department has received correspondence from stakeholders and the public in relation to this WTO case, in the main supporting the EU regulatory position. The UK Government has also raised this issue in meetings with the US administration.

The UK Government has expressed its disappointment that this action has been taken by the USA and we are working with our EU partners to defend the case and find a solution. As with any WTO dispute we will be bound by the ruling, which will be reached after due consideration of the evidence. The UK agrees with the European Commission that existing EU legislation on GMOs is compatible with trade rules and that significant progress has recently been made in dealing with applications under the legislation for placing GM products on the market.

(HC Deb 9 March 2005 Vol. 431 c1813W)

19/3

The Government was asked about progress with the EU framework for export licences for conventional weapons. A Minister wrote:

Since its adoption during the UK presidency of the European Union in 1998, the EU Code of Conduct on Arms Exports has provided the framework for the case-by-case control of arms exports from EU countries to the rest of the world. A revised version of the code is currently under discussion, which would include new provisions covering licensed production overseas, brokering and intangible technology transfers. The revised code would also introduce a new obligation on member states to refuse exports licences if they consider that there is a clear risk that the items covered by the licence would be used to commit serious violations of international humanitarian law. This amendment was suggested by the International Committee of the Red Cross. The Government are committed to enhance further the transparency of application of the code of conduct, and we will be pursuing this objective during our forthcoming presidency of the EU.

(HL Deb 8 June 2005 Vol. 672 cWA72)

19/4

Commenting on the Report of the Secretary-General on the work of the World Trade Organization (A/60/1), the representative for the European Union, Sir Emyr Jones Parry (United Kingdom), said:

... the EU believes that, through the Doha round, the international community must deliver real gains. With a comprehensive, pro-development agenda combining trade liberalization with rulemaking and complementary aid for both trade and trade-related assistance, the Doha round can bring benefits to all trading partners and in particular, and crucially, to developing countries. We therefore need to make all the efforts necessary to produce a successful conclusion to the Doha round, and in particular to ensure that the opportunity of the Hong Kong Ministerial Meeting is not missed.

We need to ensure that development, in rich and poor countries alike, is sustainable. The Union therefore welcomes the summit's recognition of the need to meet the commitments and obligations undertaken in the Framework Convention on Climate Change, which we consider to be the appropriate forum for negotiating future action on climate change. The Union is firmly committed to urgent global action to mitigate climate change—a serious, long-term challenge for every part of the world. The EU welcomes the summit's decision to explore the possibility of a more coherent framework and more efficient environmental activities in the United Nations system, including through a more integrated structure. Thirdly, improving international architecture for humanitarian response and operational activities is long overdue. The response to the appalling tsunami in the Indian Ocean in December demonstrated the willingness of Governments, civil society and the private sector to respond rapidly and generously to an unprecedented crisis. But the Sudan, northern Uganda and the Democratic Republic of the Congo continue to illustrate the fact that we must do better. At an operational level, the Union is determined to see improvements in the predictability of humanitarian funding and capacity and standby arrangements, inter alia through the modernization of the Central Emergency Revolving Fund.

(UN Doc. A/60/PV.24, 29 September 2005)

Part Nineteen: I. B. *Legal Aspects of International Relations and Co-operation in Particular Matters—General economic and financial Matters—Loans*

(See also **Part Three: IV. C.**)

19/5

During a debate in the House of Commons, the Financial Secretary to the Treasury said:

The Government accept that we have a special responsibility to Iraq ... In part, that is a product of our historical relationship with that country; in part, it is in recognition of the special circumstances of Iraq's economy at present. My hon. Friend completely dismisses the value of the Paris club agreement, with the 80 per cent. debt write-off at its heart, but that view is not shared by elected representatives in Iraq. That is particularly true of the new Minister of Finance, who has been to the Treasury in the past month to meet my right hon. Friend the Chief Secretary to the Treasury. In that discussion, Mr. Ali Alawi made it clear that he and the Iraqi Government appreciate the UK's help in putting the Iraqi economy on a sensible footing and the work that we have done on the Paris club agreement. They also recognise that the aid that the UK is putting directly into Iraq is being put to good use. On our part, we welcome our close, continuing dialogue with the Iraqi Government. As my right hon. Friend made clear, we are ready to consider further requests from the Iraqi Government as part of our contribution to their country's reconstruction and economic rehabilitation.

I promised to pick up several of my hon. Friend's points that I felt were not strictly correct. First, no UK export credit guarantees were granted for weapons—there were no credit guarantees for the sale of guns, as he put it. Some guarantees were related to defence expenditure, but not to the purpose that he suggested. Secondly, as a result of the Paris club deal, debt is set to be restructured over 23 years, not 50, and no payments at all will fall due until 2008. Thirdly, as I am sure my hon. Friend appreciates although it did not come through clearly in his remarks, the International Monetary Fund programme to which he referred critically was negotiated with Iraq, not imposed on it. The stand-by agreement, to which he also referred, is in the process of being negotiated. Like other Governments, we must await the outcome of the IMF's negotiations with Iraq to see the SBA's precise content. My hon. Friend raised a couple of points about that, but, in all honesty, I would expect certain conditions and a reduction in fuel subsidies to be part of the stand-by agreement once it is settled with Iraq, for the simple reason that a system of subsidies such as the one for fuel in Iraq creates strong economic incentives for smuggling and corruption. I think that he, like me, would want that to be stamped out.

...

Iraq is not considered to be one of the world's poorest countries. Nevertheless, as my hon. Friend pointed out, it faces immense social and economic challenges and hardships. Although Iraq's first democratic elections were an historic occasion, with 58 per cent. turnout and almost 8.5 million people voting, the upsurge of violence since the formation of the new Iraqi Government only adds to the challenges. Not only does Iraq face the challenge of establishing a truly inclusive political process, drafting a constitution that reflects its diversity and building security, but it faces a significant reconstruction challenge. Iraq has one of the largest estimated petroleum reserves in the world, but years of economic mismanagement, international sanctions and the recent conflict have hit economic activity hard. My hon. Friend vividly described the impact on Iraq's people. Social development that was once well ahead of the regional average has now fallen well behind to be one of the lowest.

Neither my hon. Friend nor the Government underestimate the challenges that Iraq faces in rebuilding the economy or the challenge that we face in trying to assist. Under Saddam Hussein, mismanagement and embezzlement of Iraq's resources was rife. The oil sector was starved of investment and the regime built up huge debts. Infrastructure, public services and industry were left in a poor state, unemployment was high and 60 per cent. of the population were dependent on food rations. Overall, GDP per capita is estimated to have fallen from more than $3,000 in the early 1980s to about $500 by 2003. It was then, through analysis by the IMF and World Bank, that Iraq's external debt—approximately $120 billion at that time—was judged to be unsustainable. The UK Government have therefore worked hard with the Americans and others to devise what we regard as a fair and sustainable solution to Iraq's debt problems.

We have also been at the forefront of international efforts to rebuild Iraq's economic institutions. In passing, I pay tribute to a number of officials from the Treasury and from HM Revenue and Customs who served for periods in Iraq to help with that rebuilding effort, in some cases putting themselves in danger in the process. Specific economic achievements have included some recovery in oil production, the stabilisation of inflation and the exchange rate, a financial management law, a new currency and an IMF emergency post-conflict assistance package of $436 million. However, by far the most important achievement with the most significant long-term gain was the negotiation of a debt relief deal with the new Iraqi Government. That is the view of the Iraqi Government, albeit not that of my hon. Friend.

The Paris club deal in November 2004 was an agreement to give to Iraq 80 per cent. debt relief, to be delivered in three tranches, linked to Iraq's economic reform. The first 30 per cent. tranche of relief was delivered on 31 December 2004. More than £340 million of Iraq's debt to the UK has already been written off. Part of the Paris club agreement was a moratorium on debt repayments until 2008, and part was a rescheduling of debt over 23 years. The latest reports from Iraq indicate that good progress is being made with other creditors, and even though a number of technical issues have to be resolved we feel that the risk of Iraq's not achieving comparable treatment with its other creditors, which was one of the conditions of the deal, is low.

Once the agreement is fully implemented, Iraq is expected to receive almost $100 billion of debt relief. The US and a few other creditors have offered to give 100 per cent. debt relief; we welcome that generosity, but we have taken a different view. The UK intends to focus its resources on maximising the immediate benefits to the Iraqi people through aid, and we have pledged $544 million in direct aid over three years to March 2006. That money is being put to good use now, as the Iraqi Finance Minister made clear to my right hon. Friend the Chief Secretary when they met last month. It is being used to rebuild facilities and to set up new infrastructure and new institutions, particularly in southern Iraq, as well as to provide support to key ministries of the new Government. If the UK offered 100 per cent. bilateral debt relief, some of that aid money would have to be diverted, Iraq would not feel the benefit of further debt relief until 2008 because of the moratorium on payments, and the benefits would be spread over 23 years, rather than concentrated now, when the need is greatest. However, as I said to my hon. Friend, we have an historical relationship with Iraq and therefore stand ready to consider any request for aid or debt relief that the Iraqi Government might make of us.

Despite the difficulties, there is real hope of progress and hope for the future of Iraq. It is not merely a country beset by severe economic difficulties but one with the prospect of and potential for a sound economic future. However, my hon. Friend will recognise that the deep damage done by decades of a repressive regime cannot be rectified in one, two or three years. It will take time to build Iraqi institutions and to improve infrastructure, and for the private sector to flourish. We hope that by 2008, Iraq will be in a position not only to start repaying the remaining debt, but to become the major economy in the region that it once was.

(HC Deb 5 July 2005 Vol. 436 c50WH–53WH)

19/6

In a written answer, a Minister wrote:

Debt relief is provided to enable countries to make faster progress towards the Millennium Development Goals. It is essential therefore that the resources made available by the relief are used for poverty reduction. In providing debt relief under the Heavily Indebted Poor Countries Initiative, the UK abides by the standards agreed internationally. Under these standards, countries must demonstrate a sustained commitment to poverty reduction and macroeconomic stability as part of an International Monetary Fund programme, Macroeconomic stability is critical to provide a foundation for growth, avoid adverse effects of inflation on the poor and to protect Government expenditure that benefits the poor. The debt stock cancellation recently proposed by the G8 would also use these standards.

(HC Deb 12 July 2005 Vol. 436 c2226W)(see also HC Deb 10 October 2005 V.l. 437 c55W)

19/7

In a written answer, a Minister said:

Under a 1945 agreement, the United States Government lent the United Kingdom a total of $4,336 million (around £1,075 million at 1945 exchange rates) in war loans. Repayment of the war loans to the United States Government should be completed on 31 December 2006, subject to the United Kingdom not choosing to exercise its option to defer repayment.

Currently principal of $84 million is outstanding on the loans provided by the United States Government in 1945. The most recent repayments were made on 31 December 2004. There remain two more scheduled repayments of interest and principal sums of $142 million in December 2005 and $83 million in December 2006 that relate to previously deferred interest and principal payments.

Successive governments have undertaken, as with all external debt, to meet their obligations under the terms of the Second World War loan agreement with the US. The Government intend to meet their obligations under the 1945 agreement by repaying the United States Government in full the amounts lent in 1945.

(HL Deb 13 July 2005 Vol. 673 cWA160)

19/8

In a written answer, the Secretary of State for International Development wrote:

Countries will qualify for debt stock cancellation under the proposals by completing the Heavily Indebted Poor Countries (HIPC) Initiative. By definition, Completion Point HIPCs have demonstrated a sustained commitment to poverty reduction and sound macroeconomic management that provides confidence that the savings from debt relief will be used for poverty reduction. Good governance is part of this, with standards drawn from national strategies. Once countries have qualified for debt stock cancellation, they will get 100 per cent. irrevocable relief. There will be no ongoing conditionality.

Countries that have already completed the HIPC Initiative must demonstrate that they have maintained their commitment to poverty reduction and good macro-economic management in order to qualify for relief. They must therefore have remained current with their repayment obligations to the International Financial Institutions, and not have experienced serious lapses, including in governance, such that their International Monetary Fund (IMF) programmes would be at risk.

In addition, extra donor resources will be provided to the World Bank and African Development Bank to compensate for the costs of the debt stock cancellation. These resources will be allocated to all poor countries through the Institutions' existing Performance Based Allocation System, thereby providing a strong incentive for good policy (including governance) and performance. The World Bank and IMF staff will also continue to monitor and report on the overall efficiency of public expenditure as well as on progress in reducing corruption and enhancing transparency in recipient countries.

(HC Deb 24 October 2005 Vol. 438 c28–29W)

Part Nineteen: I. F. *Legal Aspects of International Relations and Co-operation in Particular Matters—General economic and financial Matters—Development*

19/9

During a General Assembly meeting, the representative for the European Union said:

The European Union recognizes the importance of non-development-related policies for assisting developing countries in achieving the Millennium Development Goals. Building on the Community's existing treaty obligation, the European Union will take account of development-cooperation objectives in all policies that it implements which are likely to affect developing countries.

The European Union also remains committed to finding solutions, in cooperation with international financial institutions, to unsustainable debt burdens, and it is committed to full implementation of the enhanced Heavily Indebted Poor Countries (HIPC) Debt Initiative. In that context, we welcome the progress made by the International Monetary Fund (IMF) and the World Bank in preparing their debt sustainability framework and the proposal made by the Group of Eight (G-8) at its meeting held on 10 and 11 June 2005 to cancel the debt stock of HIPC countries which have reached the completion point. It will be vital to agree on the details of such further multilateral debt relief and to successfully implement it. It is crucial that donors fulfil their commitment under the G-8 proposal to compensate the institutions for the costs of debt stock cancellation in order not to compromise the financial integrity of those institutions.

(UN Doc. A/59/PV.106, 27 June 2005)

Part Nineteen: III. *Legal Aspects of International Relations and Co-operation in Particular Matters—Environment*

19/10

In a written answer, a Minister wrote:

The UK Government and the EU remain committed to the framework set out by the Kyoto protocol. It remains crucially important, as the first ever legally binding framework, to set quantified emissions reductions for developed countries. The UK Government and the EU want to build on the Kyoto protocol and its key elements such as targets and timetables, monitoring and reporting, compliance and the flexibility mechanisms for the period after 2012.

In addition, on the basis of the European Commission's communication "Winning the battle against global climate change" (February 2005) the European Council of Ministers concluded that the EU's future climate change strategy should:

(*a*) Strive at the widest possible cooperation by all countries;
(*b*) Include all important greenhouse gases, sectors and mitigation options;
(*c*) Drive technological innovation, employing an optimal mix of "push" and "pull" policies, in particular in the transport and energy sector;
(*d*) Promote the transfer of technologies to appropriate markets;
(*e*) Provide for the continued use of market-based and flexible instruments, and;
(*f*) Support the adaptation to unavoidable climate change in all countries, particularly in the most vulnerable developing countries.

However, the UNFCCC remains the place to agree on future frameworks.

(HC Deb 27 October 2005 Vol. 438 c473W)

19/11

In a written answer a Minister wrote:

The UK has been closely engaged with Indonesia concerning illegal logging since preparing for the Ministerial Forest Law Enforcement and Governance (FLEG) Ministerial Conference in Bali in September 2002. The resulting declaration led to the UK-Indonesia Memorandum of Understanding (MoU) which aims to tackle illegal logging in Indonesia and ultimately eliminate trade in illegally harvested timber between the two countries.

Our ambassador in Jakarta and DFID officials have maintained frequent and direct contact with the Indonesian Minister of Forestry and his officials concerning implementing the MoU and we are making steady progress.

. . .

Since the trade issues must be dealt with at the EU level, these cannot be tackled under the MoU and DFID, together with the Department for the Environment, Food and Rural Affairs (DEFRA) and the Foreign and Commonwealth Office, have been working to put in place the EU forest law enforcement, governance and trade (FLEGT) action plan. These will provide for voluntary partnership agreements between the EU and timber producing countries with a licensing scheme to control illegal trade as their focus. The European Commission is leading on preparations for such an agreement with Indonesia, which we hope will supersede and strengthen our MoU. Our ambassador underlined the importance of such an agreement in a meeting with the Indonesian Minister of Forestry last July and DFID officials, through the commission in Brussels and its delegation in Jakarta, are lending practical support to the current preparations.

The UK has been working closely with the Government of Cameroon over a number of years to tackle illegal logging and forest governance problems. We have supported the Government to develop a comprehensive national programme to address illegal logging and improve forest management and have also supported an independent monitor in Cameroon to help the Government combat forest crime. We worked closely with the Minister of Forests and Prime Minister to support Cameroon hosting the Pan African Ministerial Conference on Forest Law Enforcement and Governance in 2003. Most recently DFID officials met the Minister responsible for Forestry and Ministry of Finance in October to finalise plans for our support to the national programme and to further understanding about the opportunities afforded by the voluntary partnership agreement with Europe for the timber trade.

The UK has been supporting the Cameroon Government in preparing for negotiations with the European Commission for such an agreement alongside Germany, who co-ordinates this work for the member states. The Forest Minister recently indicated to us that they would like to negotiate a partnership agreement in July 2006 when work reviewing the legal code is completed.

(HC Deb 14 November 2005 Vol. 439 c867W–868W)

19/12

In a written Ministerial Statement, a Minister wrote:

The 1999 Protocol to abate acidification, eutrophication and ground-level ozone—known as the Gothenburg Protocol—was adopted under the United Nations Economic Commission for Europe (UNECE) Convention on Long-Range Transboundary Air Pollution. The UK signed the Protocol in 1999. The Protocol came into effect in May 2005 and has now been ratified by 18 Parties.

The Government placed an Explanatory Memorandum on the Protocol before both Houses of Parliament in September 2002. At that time it was thought that additional legislation would be required to allow the UK to ratify the Protocol.

However, further analysis of the provisions of the Protocol has allowed us to establish that further legislation will not be required. I have tabled a revised Explanatory Memorandum indicating that we propose to ratify the Protocol forthwith. I intend that the instrument of ratification will be deposited with the United Nations in the course of December 2005.

The UK will ratify the Protocol subject to a reservation. The new Explanatory Memorandum sets out the reservation that the UK will make. It relates to a provision on a type of gas engine where the UK considers that it is not technically feasible to meet the limit values required by the Protocol. As the Government take these urgent steps to ratify, we are conscious that Parliament will have less time than convention normally allows to consider the revised Memorandum. However, we believe this to be a special case on the ground that the earlier Memorandum on the Protocol has been available to both Houses since 2002. In these circumstances, the Government consider that a shortening of the normal scrutiny period is reasonable.

(HC Deb 7 December 2005 Vol. 440 c1094W)

19/13

In a written answer, a Minister wrote:

The latest meeting of the International Whaling Commission (IWC) was a successful meeting for the UK. All key UK objectives were achieved, most notably: retention of the moratorium on commercial whaling and the Southern Ocean Sanctuary; rejection of secret ballots; adoption of a Resolution, criticising Japan's plans to significantly increase its scientific whaling programme; and agreement by consensus to hold a Workshop on Whale Killing Methods and Associated Issues.

The UK is opposed to whaling and strongly supports the current IWC moratorium on commercial whaling. We do not believe there is any justification for whaling apart from some limited subsistence whaling by indigenous people. We believe that whaling does not serve any genuine need and involves unacceptable cruelty.

(HC Deb 5 July 2005 Vol. 436 c253W)

19/14

In a written answer, a Minister wrote:

We will continue to press Norway to desist from commercial whaling, which we believe contrary to the spirit of the International Whaling Commission moratorium. We made our objections very clear with regard to Norwegian whaling at the recent annual International Whaling Commission meeting in Korea. I also raised the matter with the Norwegian Fisheries Minister during a visit to Norway in November 2004.

(HC Deb 6 July 2005 Vol. 436 c430W)

19/15

In a written answer, a Minister wrote:

Seven countries are currently involved in whaling operations. Of these Norway carries out commercial whaling under objection to the International Whaling Commission Moratorium. Japan and Iceland take whales under special permit (so called "scientific" whaling) and the remaining four countries are involved in aboriginal subsistence whaling.

Aboriginal whaling is not affected by the moratorium on commercial whaling and is permitted under IWC rules from Denmark (Greenland, fin and minke whales), the Russian Federation (Siberia, gray whales), St. Vincent and the Grenadines (humpback whales), and the USA (Alaska, bowhead and occasionally off Washington State, gray whales).

In 2004–05 13 fin, one humpback, 1,368 minke, three sperm, 44 bowhead, 11 gray, 100 sei and 51 brydes were killed, as reported to the International Whaling Commission.

(HC Deb 12 October 2005 Vol. 437 c474W)

19/16

In a written answer, an FCO Minister wrote:

We are not aware of any countries which currently undertake (or intend to undertake) illegal whaling. All those members of the International Whaling Commission which conduct whaling operations do so legally. We continue to protest at the highest diplomatic level against those countries' activities; together with other like-minded countries, we made known our opposition to Japanese "scientific" whaling in a recent joint demarche; in addition, together with colleagues from the French and German embassies, HM ambassador in Reykjavik issued a statement on 24 May repeating our strong opposition to Iceland's continuing "scientific whaling" programme.

(HC Deb 13 July 2005 Vol. 436 c1041W)

19/17

In a written answer, a Minister wrote:

Under Article VIII of the International Convention for the Regulation of Whaling any whales taken under special permits shall so far as practicable be processed and the proceeds shall be dealt with in accordance with directions issued by the Government by which the permit was granted.

It is therefore a matter for those countries who conduct whaling operations under special permit to decide how they dispose of the meat of the whales taken. Only Japan and Iceland conduct such operations and we understand that the vast majority of the whale meat derived there from is sold on their domestic markets.

(HC Deb 31 October 2005 Vol. 438 c695W)

19/18

In a written answer, an FCO Minister wrote:

All great whale species are included in the moratorium on commercial whaling introduced by the International Whaling Commission (IWC) in 1985–86. The Government strongly support the retention of the IWC moratorium. Scientific research whaling, which is permitted under the 1946 International Convention for the Regulation of Whaling, is not covered by the moratorium. The Southern Ocean Sanctuary was established by the IWC in 1994 as a protected area for whales.

Commercial whaling in the waters of the 200-nautical mile Maritime Zone of South Georgia and the South Sandwich Islands is prohibited by the Fisheries (Conservation and Management) Ordinance 2000, as amended.

(HC Deb 19 December 2005 Vol. 440 c2484W)

Part Nineteen: V. *Legal Aspects of International Relations and Co-operation in Particular Matters—Technology*

19/19

Iran—Peaceful uses of nuclear power

The Government was asked what [its] assessment is of the production of enriched uranium by the government of Iran; whether [it] has assessed Iran as being in breach of the non-proliferation treaty as a result of such production. An FCO Minister wrote:

The International Atomic Energy Agency (IAEA) has reported extensively on Iran's past nuclear activities, including on some enrichment of uranium to low levels. Iran agreed to suspend all its enrichment-related activities under the so-called "Paris Agreement" of 15 November 2004. This suspension has been verified by the IAEA.

Iran's past enrichment activities were not declared to the IAEA at the time, as Iran was obliged to do under its Comprehensive Safeguards Agreement with the IAEA, pursuant to its obligations under the nuclear non-proliferation treaty.

Our policy towards Iran is one of constructive, but critical, engagement. We maintain a robust dialogue on issues of concern, such as Iran's nuclear programme; human rights record; approach to the fight against terrorism; and attitude to the middle east peace process.

(HC Deb 6 April 2005 Vol. 432 c1491W)

19/20

The Government was asked what its response was to reports that Iran was to resume uranium enrichment, which could be weapons-related. An FCO Minister said:

... representatives of the Government of Iran have made a number of statements indicating a wish to resume the conversion of uranium at its facility at Esfahan. We have made it clear to Iran that such action would breach the November 2004 Paris agreement. In this case, the United Kingdom, along with France and Germany, shall have no choice but to support referring Iran's nuclear programme to the UN Security Council. We remain committed to seeking mutually acceptable long-term arrangements with Iran, but that must be within the context of the Paris agreement.

... the efforts that we are all taking must be to try to ensure that a nuclear-weapons capability does not develop in Iran. That must be our first and foremost objective. In that light, I can report to the House that the Foreign Secretary will meet with the E3 and the Iranian counterparts in Geneva on 24 May to emphasise that a resumption of conversion activities would breach the Paris agreement and inevitably lead to the E3 proposing to the IAEA that it reports Iran to the UN Security Council. It is essential to give the meeting on 24 May every chance of success. That must be our priority . . . .

. . .

The first priority must be to ensure that the fuel cycle arguments are either verified or not verified. That requires detailed work in the meeting that is to come and in other meetings. The E3 group meets regularly on this. That must be the first and fundamental point.

. . .

One of the activities involved in all non-proliferation work is to make an assessment of whether the fuel cycle is being used to branch out in the direction of weapons of mass destruction and in particular the manufacture of nuclear weapons. That is the discussion that has to take place around Iran, and 24 May is a staging post in that.

If the Iranians are convincing that they are trying to generate power of a peaceful kind rather than power of a disastrous kind, no doubt the international community will be mightily relieved. Otherwise the international community will have to face the responsibilities that fall upon it.

(HL Deb 23 May 2005 Vol. 672 c235–238)

19/21

In a written answer, the Prime Minister wrote:

Ministers and officials are in frequent contact with their French, German and US counterparts about Iran's nuclear programme. We share deep concern at Iran's decision to resume uranium conversion activities, contrary to successive International Atomic Energy Agency (IAEA) Board resolutions and in violation of the framework agreed by Iran for negotiations on long-term arrangements. The E3/EU have urged Iran to honour its obligations and comply fully with the requests of the IAEA Board of Governors. I hope Iran will reinstate its suspension of fuel cycle activities and return to talks with the E3/EU on the basis of the Paris Agreement.

(HC Deb 26 October 2005 Vol. 438 c407–408W)

19/22

During a debate in the House of Commons, the Prime Minister said:

I am very happy to say that, first, I did not talk either explicitly or implicitly about a military threat to Iran, but what I did say was this. Iran has to realise that the international community cannot tolerate continuing conduct that, frankly, is supporting terrorism around the world; that is supporting terrorism not just in the middle east, but elsewhere; and that is in breach of its nuclear weapons responsibilities and obligations under the International Atomic Energy Agency. I did want to make it clear, and I do so again now, that the statements by the Iranian President in respect of Israel are completely and totally unacceptable. Obviously, as I made clear at the press conference, we want to discuss this with other allies and with other members of the Security Council. Nobody is talking about military threats, invasion of Iran or any of the rest of it. What we are saying, however, is that the Iranian Government have got to understand that the international community simply will not put up with their continued breach of the proper and normal standards of behaviour that we expect from a member of the United Nations. The most important thing at the moment is that that is a unified message, and that it goes out not just from this House and this country, but right across the world.

(HC Deb 2 November 2005 Vol. 438 c819)

19/23

Nuclear Non-Proliferation Treaty

The Government was asked whether the United Kingdom has made representations to any non-nuclear weapons states in respect of the development or operation of *(a)* spent nuclear fuel reprocessing plants, *(b)* uranium enrichment plants and *(c)* separated plutonium stores. A Minister wrote:

The UK, as a State Party to the Nuclear Non-Proliferation Treaty (NPT), upholds the inalienable right of non-nuclear weapon states to the peaceful use of nuclear energy under Article IV of the Treaty, in conformity with Articles I and II of the Treaty. The UK also seeks to uphold, and is committed to, all other Articles of the Treaty. It actively participates in and promotes, in the International Atomic Energy Agency, the Nuclear Suppliers Group and other relevant fora such as the G8, compliance with the international nuclear non-proliferation obligations set out in the NPT and other international instruments.

(HC Deb 5 April 2005 Vol. 432 c1329W)

19/24

The Government was asked what assessment [it] has made of the possibility of limiting uranium enrichment and reprocessing plants to countries that already have the facilities. A Minister wrote:

The Government is committed to ensuring that sensitive nuclear items, such as enrichment and reprocessing plants, which have clear proliferation potential, are not exported to states that may seek to use them for weapons purposes.

Recognising this, the UK is committed to strengthening the Nuclear Suppliers Group Guidelines, which control the export of such equipment, with a series of tough criteria that a recipient state must adhere to in order to receive such transfers. This will provide suppliers of nuclear items with adequate assurances that transferred items will not be used for non-peaceful purposes. The criteria are relevant whether or not the recipient state is in possession of equipment and reprocessing facilities.

(HC Deb 5 April 2005 Vol. 432 c1330W)

Part Nineteen: VI. *Legal Aspects of International Relations and Co-operation in Particular Matters—Social and health matters*

19/25

During a General Assembly meeting, the representative for the United Kingdom said:

The United Kingdom voted against the draft Declaration on Human Cloning because of the reference to human life, which we consider can be interpreted as a call for a total ban on all forms of human cloning. We cannot accept such an ambiguous declaration, which may sow confusion about the acceptability of that important field of research.

The General Assembly has missed another opportunity to adopt a convention prohibiting reproductive cloning. Why is that so? It is because of the intransigence of those that were not prepared to recognize that other sovereign States, after extensive dialogue and due democratic process, may decide to permit strictly controlled applications of therapeutic cloning.

The United Kingdom is a strong supporter of therapeutic cloning research because it has the potential to revolutionize medicine in this century in the way that antibiotics did in the last. The United Kingdom Government announced this week more than $2 billion in funding over the next three years for biotechnology research, including stem cell research.

The Declaration voted upon today is a weak, nonbinding political statement that does not reflect anything approaching consensus within the General Assembly. Nor will it affect the United Kingdom's strong support of stem cell research.

(UN Doc A/59/PV.82, 8 March 2005)

Part Nineteen: VIII. *Legal Aspects of International Relations and Co-operation in Particular Matters—Legal matters (eg judicial assistance, crime control, etc.)*

UK-US Extradition

19/26

The Government was asked a number of questions about extradition to and from the US. A Minister said:

... I do not agree that the arrangement is unfair ... prior to the introduction of the 2003 Act we were not obliged to produce prima facie evidence in support of our applications to the United States, whereas we demanded prima facie from it. The new position is, we believe, an appropriate one ... we believe that this is a proportionate and proper response to one of our oldest and most trusted partners.

...

The new arrangements regarding the evidential requirement are not precisely reciprocal, but they are comparable. The Americans have demanded for some time that we provide probable cause. That was the position under the old Act when we demanded of them a prima facie case. Their probable cause is very similar to the information base that we now demand. For the many who say that it was unfair to the Americans in the past, it is more proportionate now. The provisions in our Act are robust ... There are appropriate safeguards to make sure that extradition takes place only when it is merited and in accordance with our law.

...

We do not extradite unless there is an undertaking from the United States that the death penalty will not be applied to any person so extradited. We have no intention whatever of changing that position.

... the 2003 Act is not retrospective. It will operate in relation to all the applications received after the Act came into operation. There is no element of retrospection.

(HL Deb 12 January 2005 Vol. 668 c252–254)

19/27

The Government was asked what steps it is taking to ensure reciprocity of extradition arrangements with the United States, following the recent agreement allowing British nationals to be handed over to the US authorities to face charges for any criminal offence. A Minister wrote:

Her Majesty's Government are satisfied that the extradition treaty concluded with the USA on 31 March 2003 is broadly reciprocal, and that there are sufficient safeguards in the treaty and in the Extradition Act 2003, which governs extradition requirements in the UK, to prevent unfairness.

The arrangements apply only to serious criminal charges, as defined in the Treaty and the Extradition Act 2003, these being punishable under the laws of both States by deprivation of liberty for a period of one year or more. This modernises the definition of an extradition offence in line with international practice. Both nations have been prepared to extradite their own citizens to each other, and to other states with whom they have had arrangements, since the 19th century.

The Government was asked what the URL is for the internet text of the US/UK extradition treaty as amended in 2003. A Minister wrote:

The link for the US/UK bilateral extradition treaty can be found on the Foreign and Commonwealth Office website, at www.fco.gov.uk. The document is available in pdf format under the "Command Papers" section on the FCO site. [There was an usually long delay between the presentation of the Command Paper containing the Extradition Treaty and its appearance on the FCO website, Ed.]

(HC Deb 1 March 2005 Vol. 431 c1108W)

19/28

The Government was asked when it expects that the US Congress will ratify the amendment to the extradition treaty between the US and the United Kingdom; on what basis the United Kingdom has agreed to fulfil its obligations under the amended treaty prior to ratification by the US. A Minister wrote:

The extradition treaty signed between the US and the UK in 2003 is a completely new treaty, and requires the advice and consent of the US Senate Foreign Relations Committee before it can be ratified by the US Government. We have been advised by the US State Department that, although the Committee has a heavy schedule, the US State Department has asked it to consider the treaty at the earliest possible time.

Some of the important, modernising provisions of the new treaty were given effect in the Extradition Act 2003 (and are therefore available generally in extradition, and are not linked solely to the US-UK treaty.) Secondary legislation was required under the new Act to designate all our extradition partners for the purposes of extradition to those states. The United States was, of course, included in that legislation.

(HC Deb 4 March 2005 Vol. 431 c1476W)

19/29

The Government was asked about UK-US extradition arrangements. A Minister told the House of Lords:

We do not intend to renegotiate the treaty with the United States, and I must disappoint noble Lords by saying that nor do we intend to revoke the designation of the United States as one of our partners.

I hope that we made it plain when we were going through the Bill that our intention was to include the USA in the schedule and to allow that matter to be debated when it came before the House. We did debate it before the order applied. Noble Lords discussed that issue and the order was made.

... the Extradition Act 2003 effectively implemented the provisions of the new UK/US extradition treaty. Our experiences ... of the new regime have been extremely positive. For example, the average time it took for the United Kingdom to process an extradition request from America, under the old arrangements, was 30 months. In stark contrast, the average time it takes the US to process requests from the United Kingdom is five months. I am sure that noble Lords will agree that our prosecuting authorities, pursuing fugitives from our justice system, must have cause to be grateful to the United States authorities for that level of service.

Under the new arrangements we have improved our turnaround times to an average of seven months. That is much closer to the US level, though not equal to it. In any event, to those who are concerned that we have made extradition to the United States too easy and have had nothing in return ... I simply invite them to look at the evidence. I hope that noble Lords will also agree that the considerable reduction in the time period for completing extradition requests is not only in the interests of government, but also in those of victims, witnesses, our courts and fugitives themselves.

Indeed, I cannot see how improving our extradition arrangements by updating our domestic extradition legislation, which included implementing provisions in the new US/UK extradition treaty, can be seen as anything other than in the interests of justice. The Government have ensured that the very important safeguards remain in place for individuals who may find themselves the subjects of extradition requests.

(HL Deb 30 June 2005 Vol. 673 c406–408)

19/30

In a written answer, a Minister wrote:

The UK-US Extradition Treaty 2003 has not yet been brought into force but some of its provisions have been given effect by the Extradition Act 2003, which came into force on [1] January 2004. Eight British citizens, and three US citizens, have been extradited to the US under the Extradition Act 2003. The Act and the Treaty have not changed the position whereby both the UK and the US are prepared to consider the extradition of their own citizens.

(HC Deb 12 July 2005 Vol. 436 c906W)

19/31

Trafficking

In a written answer, a Minister wrote:

There are aspects of the Council of Europe Convention on Action against Trafficking in Human Beings that are currently of concern. The particular areas of concern relate to issues surrounding the provision of recovery and reflection periods (Article 13) and residence permits (Article 14). The mandatory nature of these provisions when coupled with the scope of the convention has led to concerns that the provisions will act as an immigration pull factor, encourage spurious claims, and be used by those who have no right to remain in an effort to frustrate removal. Abuse of the provisions would ultimately impact on those in genuine need of assistance. Provision already exists for my right honourable friend the Home Secretary to exercise his discretion where it is clear that it is not appropriate to remove an individual or where it is appropriate to allow them time to recover before any decision is made in respect of their immigration status.

(HL Deb 5 July 2005 Vol. 673 cWA77)

19/32

In a written answer, a Minister wrote:

The UK has not yet taken the decision on whether or not to sign the Council of Europe Convention on Action against Trafficking in Human Beings and has no timetable for adoption at present. There are certain provisions in the Convention which present concerns for the UK and which remain under active consideration. We want to resolve these issues before taking a decision on signature. We support fully all of the aims of the Convention and we too want to see widespread action to tackle this abhorrent trade at source, to protect and support the victims and bring those responsible to justice.

We will be gathering evidence about how the Convention measures are operating in other European transit or destination countries where they have been introduced. We also want to work with non-Government organisations (NGOs) and others working in the field of human trafficking to ensure that we explore thoroughly with them the potential benefits and disadvantages of the approach set out in the Convention.

During the UK's Presidency of the EU the Government intends to treat combating trafficking in human beings as one of its Justice and Home Affairs priorities. We are committed to agreeing a wide-ranging EU action plan before the end of 2005 and will jointly host with Eurojust a conference focusing on investigating and prosecuting traffickers. We are considering other ways of highlighting this issue during our Presidencies of the G8 and EU, both at Ministerial and official levels.

The Government is committed to tackling trafficking in human beings, domestically and internationally, and is determined that the measures we take bring the criminals responsible for it to justice, protect the victims of trafficking, but do not undermine our ability to control our borders.

(HC Deb 6 July 2005 Vol. 436 c515W)

19/33

In a written answer, a Minister wrote:

We consider that, taken together with existing United Kingdom law, the introduction of the trafficking offences contained in section four of the Asylum and Immigration (Treatment of Claimants, etc.) Act 2004 which came into force on 1 December 2004, mean that we fully comply with our legislative obligations under the Palermo Protocol.

To enable us to ratify the protocol we must first ratify the UN convention against transnational organised crime. The legislative measures required to comply with the Convention have now been introduced and the Home Office and Foreign and Commonwealth Office are taking forward the necessary steps to ratify the Convention and Protocol

(HC Deb 29 November 2005 Vol. 440 c466W–467W)

19/34

Transfer of Offenders

In a written answer, a Minister wrote:

The Council of Europe Convention on the Transfer of Sentenced Persons, the Commonwealth Scheme for the Transfer of Convicted Offenders, and bilateral prisoner transfer agreements to which the UK is a party, enables a contracting party to transit through UK airports to another contracting party, or to a third party, where transfer has been agreed in accordance with the relevant international agreement.

One or two requests for transit are received each year. Transit enables a prisoner and escort to transfer from one commercial flight to another at Heathrow or Gatwick airport. The prisoner and foreign escort remain in UK territory for a matter of hours and overnight transit is not allowed. Records of transit applications are not kept once the transit has been completed.

(HC Deb 13 July 2005 Vol. 436 c1094W)

19/35

In a written answer, a Minister wrote:

As of 1 January 2005 the UK participates in the judicial cooperation, drugs cooperation, obligations on carriers, measures to combat trafficking of human beings and police cooperation parts of the Schengen acquis. The relevant Schengen articles and implementing conventions are listed in articles 1*(a)*(i), *(b)*, *(c)*(i) and *(d)*(i) of Council Decision 2000/365/EC, and the relevant Schengen building measures adopted since Decision 2000/365/EC are listed in the annexes to Council Decision 2004/926/EC.

(HC Deb 10 October 2005 Vol. 437 c179W)

Part Nineteen: IX. *Legal Aspects of International Relations and Co-operation in Particular Matters—Military and security matters*

19/36

Arms Exports

An FCO Minister wrote:

The global control of small arms and light weapons (SALW) is one of the highest priorities of the Government's global conflict prevention strategy. Internationally, the United Kingdom fully supports the United Nations programme of action (POA) on SALW. The UK is one of the largest and most influential donors on small arms issues. Under the Global Conflict Prevention Pool, the UK has allocated £13.25 million (2004–07) to control and reduce the supply, demand and availability of SALW. The funding supports projects that assist UN agencies, regional organisations, governments and non-governmental organisations to combat the proliferation and misuse of small arms. One of our key priorities is promoting the transfer control initiative, which aims to secure agreement on common international standards governing small arms transfers at the UN POA review conference on small arms in 2006.

(HL Deb 10 January 2005 Vol. 668 c6WA)

19/37

In reply to a question, an FCO Minister said:

... we want the treaty [on the Arms Trade, Ed.] to be as comprehensive as possible ... We want the treaty to be a legally binding set of rules on arms exports, with the objective of reducing, and ultimately eradicating, the irresponsible arms exports which fuel conflict and human rights abuses.

... the EU code of conduct is being revised at this moment. The state of play so far is that we would increase the scope of the code—which, as I have said, has been in place since 1989—to cover applications for brokering, transhipment and electronic technology transfer licences. It would also oblige member states to refuse export licences if they consider that there is a clear risk that the items covered by the licence could be used to commit serious violations of international human rights law.

(HL Deb 18 January 2005 Vol. 668 c643–644)

19/38

During a Security Council Meeting the representative of the United Kingdom stated:

The United Kingdom supports the full implementation at national, regional and international levels of the United Nations Programme of Action ... The availability of small arms and light weapons is so widespread that restraint by traditional suppliers, although absolutely necessary, is not sufficient. We think that a broader international approach is needed. The United Nations Programme of Action contains important guidance on controlling transfers, and we need to build on that. For example, we need to identify common factors for consideration before issuing a licence for an international transfer of small arms and light weapons. We also need to support regions and countries concerned with their capacity building.

Our objective is to introduce minimum common international controls on small arms and light weapons transfers within the United Nations Programme of Action at the United Nations review meeting on small arms in 2006. We think that there are signs that an increasing number of countries support the need for improved transfer controls. Certainly, an agreement on reducing illicit transfers would be a major achievement. In the longer term, we are also working with partner Governments in support of an international arms trade treaty. That would be a vital tool, extending the international rule of law on conventional arms.

(UN Doc. S/PV.5127, 17 February 2005)

19/39

The Government was asked what action [it is] taking to ensure that member states of the United Nations expedite and conclude negotiations on legally binding agreements covering the marking, tracing, brokering and transfer of small arms and light weapons. An FCO Minister wrote:

Working with other United Nations (UN) member states to reduce illicit movements of small arms and light weapons (SALW) is a high priority for the Government. We have allocated £13.25 million between 2004–07 to support programmes aimed at achieving this. The UK is an active participant in the open-ended working group on marking and tracing of SALW, and, along with European Union member states, we continue to push for a legally binding instrument that includes SALW ammunition. We recognise that brokering is another area where tighter controls are needed and fully support the establishment, no later than 2007, of a UN group of government experts to consider this important issue in depth.

One of our SALW priorities is promoting the Transfer Control Initiative, which aims at agreement on common international standards governing small arms transfers at the UN Programme of Action Review Conference on Small Arms in 2006. The UK is supporting this initiative by organising sub-regional workshops and bilateral meetings, which we hope will lead to common agreement on responsibility in SALW transfers.

The Government was asked further what action [it is] taking to ensure that all member states of the United Nations report fully and accurately on all matters covered by the United Nations Register of Conventional Arms, and that the Secretary-General reports annually to the General Assembly and the Security Council on any inadequacies in such reporting. The Minister wrote:

The United Kingdom has supported the operation and development of the United Nations Register on Conventional Arms since its establishment in 1992. The Government have reported every year on all seven categories of major equipment covered by the register and have provided additional background information.

The UK encourages member states to participate in the register. We have supported the work of the United Nations Department for Disarmament Affairs (UN DDA) by participating and funding regional workshops which explain the register's operation. Through the formal periodic reviews of the register, we have been at the forefront of efforts to expand the register's scope, and have proposed recommendations to encourage reporting and participation.

Member states are themselves responsible for the accuracy and timeliness of their reports. We have supported the UN DDA in its ability to verify the accuracy of information provided, but we recognise that participation in the register is voluntary and the scope of information provided is a national prerogative.

The UK also co-sponsors the annual UN General Assembly resolution that underpins the register's operation by inviting all states to participate.

(HL Deb 21 February 2005 Vol. 669 c152WA)

19/40

The Government was asked, pursuant to the written ministerial statement of 21 December 2004, *Official Report*, column 171WS [UKMIL (2004) **16/75**, Ed.], on EU Code of Conduct on Arms Exports, what legal remedy through *(a)* national courts and *(b)* the European Court of Justice exists if an EU member state breaches the Code of Conduct. The Foreign Secretary wrote:

The domestic consequences of a member state breaching its obligations under the EU Code of Conduct on Arms Exports will depend upon its national laws. For the UK, I refer the right hon. Gentleman to the written statement of 21 December 2004, *Official Report*, column 171WS. The EU Code of Conduct on Arms Exports is not justiciable in the European Court of Justice.

He wrote further:

The EU embargo on the sale of arms to China reflects a political commitment by member states. It sets a high common standard for all member states' assessment of applications to export all items on the EU Common Military List. All EU member states have incorporated the Code of Conduct into their export licensing procedures, according to their national laws. There is no common interpretation of this commitment among member states. In the UK, exporters are required to seek a licence before exporting controlled goods or technology. A licence will not be issued if approval would be inconsistent with, inter alia, the UK's interpretation of the China embargo. The UK's interpretation of the embargo was set out by the then Minister of State at the Foreign and Commonwealth Office, the late Derek Fatchett, in a reply on 3 June 1998, *Official Report*, columns 240–41 ... The legal penalty under the Export Control Act 2002 for exporting controlled goods or technology without a licence may be imprisonment for up to 10 years.

And:

The EU Code of Conduct sets a high standard for all member states' assessment of applications to export all items on the EU Common Military List. All EU member states have incorporated the Code of Conduct into their export licensing procedures, according to their national laws ... To ask what specific equipment the code 'forbids' is to misunderstand the way it functions. The code obliges member states to refuse to license the export of any item on the list if, inter alia, there is a clear risk that it might be used for internal repression, aggressively against another country, or to assert by force a territorial claim. There is also a provision in the code which provides for denial of export licences for equipment which may affect "the national security of the UK, of territories whose external relations are the UK's responsibility, and of allies, EU member states and other friendly countries". The code applies to exports to China and all other countries, and has proved effective since its inception in 1998. It is the criteria in the Code of Conduct, rather than the Arms Embargo on China, which have formed the basis for the clear majority of the licence refusals made by EU member states in respect of China.

(HC Deb 7 March 2005 Vol. 431 c1574W)

19/41

In a written Ministerial Statement, an FCO Minister wrote:

On 11 October 2004, ... the Secretary of State for Foreign and Commonwealth Affairs (Mr. Jack Straw) announced in a written ministerial statement, *Official Report*, column 3WS, that, upon receipt of an application to export arms or related material to an end user not explicitly exempt from the embargo, the Government will seek certification on a case-by-case basis from the Government of Iraq or the multinational force. The certification is to ensure that the proposed export is required by the Government of Iraq or the multinational force to serve the purposes of Resolution 1546 and is therefore exempted from the embargo. A certification process has been established with the Government of Iraq.

Following consultation with the Foreign and Commonwealth Office and the Ministry of Defence, the Department of Trade and Industry recently made four exceptions to this procedure and issued licences in advance of receipt of certification from the Government of Iraq. All licences were for equipment to be used by a private security company to protect election monitors and ballot boxes for the Iraqi referendum. Equipment concerned included: armoured vehicles, body armour, military helmets, smoke grenades, mini signal flares, stun grenades and six machine guns. The Government received certification for the licences after they were issued.

(HC Deb 10 November 2005 Vol. 439 c23WS–24W)

19/42

Chile

The Government was asked what assessment it has made of the Government of Chile's adherence to end user certificates in respect of arms exports from the UK. An FCO Minister wrote:

We believe that the Government of Chile issues end user certificates in respect of arms exports in good faith and that they take appropriate steps to safeguard UK-origin defence equipment. The UK Government undertake monitoring in the recipient country of arms supplied by UK manufacturers when we believe that this would genuinely help to minimise the risk of diversion and where such monitoring is practical. In addition, UK overseas Posts have standing instructions to report any misuse of UK-origin defence equipment. Evidence of misuse would be taken into account when the Government assess any subsequent licence applications for the end-user and we may also, if appropriate, revoke related licences.

(HC Deb 4 April 2005 Vol. 432 c1228W)

19/43

Nepal

In a written answer, an FCO Minister wrote:

All of the military equipment the UK has gifted to Nepal since 2001 as part of our conflict prevention strategy has been non-lethal and cannot easily be adapted for offensive purposes. The main items of hardware have been two transport helicopters and two unarmed Short Take-Off and Landing (STOL) surveillance aircraft. We have also provided land rovers, bomb disposal equipment and basic individual equipment.

Both the helicopters and the STOL aircraft were provided on the basis of a Memorandum of Understanding between the UK and the Government of Nepal, under which the Nepalese have committed themselves not to use or adapt the aircraft for attack purposes. The Defence Attaché at the British Embassy in Kathmandu and his staff make regular random visits to inspect the helicopters, only one of which survives owing to accident, and the STOL aircraft to ensure that they have not been fitted with offensive capabilities. In the case of the STOL aircraft such fixtures would involve considerable structural alteration. We have seen no evidence to suggest that these aircraft have been armed or used improperly. Periodically we remind the Nepalese of their obligations as set out in the Memorandum of Understanding governing the use of this equipment.

(HC Deb 5 July 2005 Vol. 436 c331W)

19/44

Pakistan

The Government was asked what assessment [it] has made of the request by the chairman of Pakistan's Atomic Energy Commission to the nuclear security conference in London that the nuclear suppliers group lift controls on the export of dual-use nuclear technology to Pakistan. An FCO Minister wrote:

Countering the proliferation of nuclear weapons technology is a key priority of the Government.

Given that Pakistan remains outside the Non Proliferation Treaty, and has placed very few nuclear facilities under International Atomic Energy Agency safeguards, it is difficult for suppliers to be confident that transfers of dual-use nuclear technology will not contribute to a nuclear explosive activity. Any lifting of these controls would require amending the Nuclear Suppliers Group Guidelines, which would need the unanimous agreement of all 44 Participating Governments.

The UK's position on the export of Nuclear Dual Use items remains as set out . . . on 15 March 2002, *Official Report*, columns 1298–1300W. It states, inter alia, that:

> "We will continue to deny all export licence applications (ELAs) for items listed on the Nuclear Suppliers Group (NSG) Dual use list to nuclear and nuclear related end users in India and Pakistan".

(HC Deb 4 April 2005 Vol. 432 c1091W)

19/45

Venezuela/Russia

The Government was asked what recent assessment [it] has made of the relationship between Venezuela and the United States of America, with particular reference to the effects of arms purchases by Venezuela from Russia.

An FCO Minister wrote:

Bilateral relations between Venezuela and the US are a matter for the two countries concerned.

Venezuela has stated its intention to purchase a number of assault rifles from Russia for use by army reservists. Venezuela is committed to the politically binding United Nations Programme of Action to Prevent, Combat and Eradicate the Illicit Trade in Small Arms and Light Weapons adopted in July 2001. Under this Programme of Action Venezuela has a right to import weapons for its self-defence and security. It is also required to ensure that these weapons are properly stored and managed and that proper records are kept.

(HC Deb 7 March 2005 Vol. 431 c1582W)

TABLE OF CASES

INDEX

Page references to footnotes are followed by the letter 'n'.